MEASURING the Real Size of the WORLD ECONOMY

The Framework, Methodology, and Results of the International Comparison Program—ICP

MEASURING the Real Size of the WORLD ECONOMY

The Framework, Methodology, and Results of the International Comparison Program—ICP

THE WORLD BANK

1818 H Street NW, Washington DC 20433
Telephone: 202-473-1000; Internet: www.worldbank.org

1 2 3 4 16 15 14 13

ISBN (paper): 978-0-8213-9728-2
ISBN (electronic): 978-0-8213-9731-2
doi: 10.1596/978-0-8213-9728-2

Cover design: Jomo Tariku, The World Bank.

Contents

Preface

The International Comparison Program (ICP) has become not only the largest international statistical program in the world, but also the most complex. The first coordinated attempt to produce purchasing power parities was carried out from 1967 to 1970; it was based on 10 countries. In the years leading up to 2005, six rounds of the ICP were conducted, each with more countries and each with improved methodology. The 2005 ICP included 100 countries from Africa, the Asia-Pacific, the Commonwealth of Independent States, South America, and Western Asia, plus 46 countries from the comparison conducted by Eurostat (the statistical office of the European Union) and the Organisation for Economic Co-operation and Development. The 2005 ICP stands on the shoulders of those who developed the theory and methodology used in previous rounds.

The lessons learned from previous ICP rounds led to the development of several significantly new and improved methods for the 2005 ICP. The subsequent analysis of the 2005 data set the stage for additional improvements to the 2011 ICP.

This volume is a comprehensive review of the statistical theory and methods underlying the estimation of PPPs and real expenditures, the choices made for the 2005 ICP round, and the lessons learned that led to improvements in the 2011 ICP. Disclosing the theory, concepts, and methods underlying estimates enhances the transparency of the 2011 ICP process. This allows interested stakeholders and users to fully understand the strengths, limitations, and assumptions underlying the estimates. This volume also contains several chapters about uses of the data from the 2005 ICP. These uses are significant because they expand the boundaries of the needs served by the ICP to encompass poverty estimation and analysis of the global economic situation.

Worldwide, no other statistical program requires so much cooperation among national, regional, and international organizations. The ICP greatly depends on the overwhelming support received from national statistical offices. They assume the effort of and responsibility for providing the prices and other measures underlying all components of the gross domestic product and breaking it down into subaggregates.

On behalf of the World Bank and the ICP Executive Board, I thank all who have contributed to this volume. It is not possible to give credit in this limited space to all of the individuals responsible for its successful completion. Many are listed in the acknowledgments section that follows. Here I highlight the contributions of two special groups. Much of the material presented is based on the wholehearted discussions of the ICP's Technical Advisory Group, which included many of the authors. The Global Office team, which is located in the World Bank, provided the means for the expert data analysis underlying many of the chapters and championed completion of the book.

Finally, to everyone involved in producing this book, thanks very much for a job well done.

Shaida Badiee, Director
Development Data Group, World Bank

Acknowledgments

This report by the International Comparison Program (ICP), *Measuring the Real Size of the World Economy*, was prepared by the World Bank, with contributions from the leading international experts in the fields of economics and statistics on international comparisons. The contributors and their affiliations are listed separately.

This volume was prepared under the aegis of the Bank's Development Data Group, which is led by Shaida Badiee, director, and Grant Cameron, manager. The global manager of the International Comparison Program is Michel Mouyelo-Katoula. The effort to prepare the ICP book was guided and overseen by Frederic A. Vogel. The book was edited by Sabra Ledent. Virginia Romand assisted with the coordination effort. Jomo Tariku and Virginia Romand steered the book through production.

The World Bank is grateful for the efforts of the authors, who contributed ground-breaking analysis and results describing complicated methodology in a transparent fashion. Members of the ICP Global Office provided valuable input about the scope and content of the book, and special mention is made of Nada Hamadeh, who helped manage the overall project. Other members of the ICP Global Office are recognized in the chapters in which they provided the computations and other input. Individual mention is also made of D. S. Prasada Rao at the University of Queensland, Australia, for his suggestion that the World Bank publish a book about the ICP and for his early input into the development of the scope and content of many of the chapters.

Contributing Authors

Derek Blades, World Bank consultant and former staff member, Organisation for Economic Co-operation and Development, Paris

Shaohua Chen, Senior Statistician, Development Research Group, World Bank

James Coonan, U.S. Federal Reserve Board

Angus S. Deaton, Dwight D. Eisenhower Professor of International Affairs and Professor of Economics and International Affairs, Woodrow Wilson School of Public and International Affairs, Princeton University

W. Erwin Diewert, Professor, Department of Economics, University of British Columbia

Yuri Dikhanov, Senior Economist/Statistician, Development Data Group, World Bank

Olivier Dupriez, Lead Statistician, Development Data Group, World Bank

Sean Fahle, University of California, Los Angeles

Alan Heston, Professor Emeritus, Department of Economics, University of Pennsylvania

Robert Inklaar, Groningen Growth and Development Centre, Faculty of Economics and Business, University of Groningen

Jaime Marquez, U.S. Federal Reserve Board

Paul McCarthy, consultant, International Comparison Program, World Bank

D. S. Prasada Rao, Professor and ARC Professorial Fellow, School of Economics, University of Queensland, Australia

Martin Ravallion, Director, Development Research Group, World Bank

David Roberts, World Bank consultant and former staff member, Statistics Directorate, Organisation for Economic Co-operation and Development, Paris

Mick Silver, Statistics Department, International Monetary Fund

Charles Thomas, U.S. Federal Reserve Board

Marcel P. Timmer, Groningen Growth and Development Centre, Faculty of Economics and Business, University of Groningen

Frederic A. Vogel, International Comparison Program, World Bank, and former Global Manager, ICP

Executive Summary

Frederic A. Vogel

In its 2005 round, the International Comparison Program (ICP) became the largest and most complex international statistical program in the world. One hundred and forty-six countries and economies provided the thousands of prices and related measures used to estimate purchasing power parities (PPPs) in order to deflate national gross domestic product (GDP) expenditures into a common global currency. The resulting PPPs and volume indexes make possible sound comparisons between countries that are based on economic and statistical theory. Each successive round of the ICP since its launch in the 1960s has involved more countries and more innovations in methodology. The results of each round provided the building blocks for the new theory and methods introduced in the next rounds.

This book describes the challenges faced by the 2005 round of the ICP, the new theories and methods developed to address those problems, and the lessons learned that can be applied to future rounds of the ICP. This book has been prepared to ensure complete transparency in the theory and methods used and the problems encountered. Much of the analysis presented by the authors of the chapters was made possible by giving them access to a data file containing the basic heading PPPs and expenditures for the 146 participating countries.

The book refers to six geographic regions of the world. The five geographic ICP regions in 2005 were Africa, Asia-Pacific, Commonwealth of Independent States (CIS), South America, and Western Asia. Although Eurostat (the statistical office of the European Union) and the Organisation for Economic Co-operation and Development (OECD) jointly conduct their own PPP program, the Eurostat-OECD and ICP programs are coordinated so that all are included in the global results. For the purposes of this book, the Eurostat-OECD comparison is considered as the sixth region. In a similar fashion, the ICP includes both countries and economies. The term *countries* as used throughout this book refers to both.

What Is a Purchasing Power Parity?

In its simplest form, a PPP is a price ratio. PPPs for the total consumption aggregate of the GDP, for example, are built up from comparisons of the prices of products purchased by households. To ensure that comparable products are being priced, the characteristics of each product must be carefully defined.

This summary relies on the data example in table 1 to explain the concepts and methods used in the ICP. The table shows examples[1] of prices for three products and four countries for the rice basic heading. The PPP between the Arab Republic of Egypt and the United Kingdom for prepacked long grain rice is the average price in Egypt in its national currency (Egyptian pound or LE) divided by the average price in U.K. pounds sterling (£). The price ratio 7.54 means that LE 7.54 is the cost of an amount of long grain rice in Egypt that would cost £1.0 in the United Kingdom. Likewise, LE 3.30 is the cost of the same quantity of long grain rice sold loose that would cost £1.0 in the United Kingdom.

As table 1 illustrates, the relative prices (product PPPs) differ by product. Therefore, the product PPPs are averaged to arrive at a PPP for the rice basic heading. The simple geometric mean is the bilateral PPP. In practice, multilateral PPPs are computed, and this computation takes into account the relative prices between all of the countries as a group. More will be said about this in the sections that follow.

Because there are no weights reflecting the quantities of each product purchased, the basic heading PPPs are computed with products and countries treated equally. However, expenditures are available for each basic heading, and thus they are used as weights when averaging basic heading PPPs to major aggregates such as food. The PPPs for the major aggregates are then averaged to the GDP, again using weights. Table 2 shows PPPs for selected basic headings in the food aggregate and the average PPP for food. The food PPP means that LE 4.22 is the cost of an amount of food in Egypt that would cost £1.0 in the United Kingdom. More important, the expenditures in Egyptian pounds for the food aggregate of the GDP in Egypt can be converted to the U.K. currency by dividing it by the PPP, or 4.22. The food expenditures in the other countries can also be converted to the U.K. pound by dividing them by their respective PPPs.

Table 1 Prices of Products in Rice Basic Heading and Their Ratios to U.K. Prices for Selected Countries

	Egypt, Arab Rep./ United Kingdom		Estonia/ United Kingdom		Philippines/ United Kingdom		United Kingdom	
Rice basic heading	National price	PPP to U.K.	National price	PPP to U.K.	National price	PPP to U.K.	National price	PPP
Long grain, prepacked	5.51	7.54	11.59	15.87	32.73	44.83	.73	1.00
Long grain, loose	3.47	3.30			23.35	22.23	1.05	1.00
Basmati	5.69	5.69	45.68	20.48			2.23	1.00
Geometric mean—bilateral PPP		5.22		18.02		31.56		1.00
Multilateral PPP		4.80		19.98		33.36		1.00
Exchange rate	10.12		22.78		90.87			

Source: ICP 2005.

Table 2 PPPs for Selected Basic Headings and Countries (UK = 1.00)

	Basic heading PPPs (UK = 1.00)			
Basic heading	**Egypt, Arab Rep./ United Kingdom**	**Estonia/ United Kingdom**	**Philippines/ United Kingdom**	**United Kingdom**
Rice	4.80	19.98	33.36	1.00
Other cereals	7.12	18.46	95.28	1.00
Bread	6.80	15.98	60.73	1.00
Beef and veal	4.60	10.60	31.22	1.00
... 29 basic headings				
Food aggregate PPP	4.22	14.67	47.32	1.00
Exchange rate	10.12	22.78	90.87	1.00
Price level index	0.42	0.64	0.52	

Source: ICP 2005.

Another important measure is the price level index (PLI), which is simply the PPP divided by the exchange rate. PLIs that are less than 1.0 mean the products or aggregates are relatively cheap. The PLI is also a measure of the ratio of nominal expenditures (based on the exchange rate) to real expenditures based on PPPs. The price level indexes for food shown in table 2 indicate that food is relatively cheap in Egypt, Estonia, and the Philippines, and also that the nominal expenditures for food in those countries would be 0.42, 0.64, and 0.52 of the real expenditures, respectively.

The PPP for the GDP is based on the prices collected for about 1,000 products plus measurements for other aggregates such as housing, government, and construction that are used to first estimate basic heading PPPs and then average them to the GDP. The PPPs at each level of aggregation and for the GDP are simply a form of exchange rate to calibrate expenditures in national currencies to a common currency. While simple to say, the resulting PPPs are based on the very complex statistical and economic theories presented in detail in chapters 4, 5, and 6 and summarized here in a later section.

Uses of PPPs

The PPP-based expenditures allow direct comparisons of indicators of well-being, such as expenditures per capita, because they are now in a common currency. Similar comparisons can be made for other aggregates such as health, education, housing, government, and GDP. The PPPs for household consumption are the main input for estimation of the international poverty line, which is a main driver of international development efforts. Countries with different rates of economic growth can compare their price levels and per capita expenditures to guide their development policies. PPP-based expenditures allow comparisons across countries for different sectors. For example, the 2005 ICP showed that China accounted for 29 percent of global real expenditures on construction.

A major use of PPPs is for poverty assessments (see chapters 20 and 21). National poverty assessments differ by country because purchasing power differs. Therefore, an international poverty line is established using PPPs to hold the real value constant across countries. The international poverty line of $1.25 in international dollars is translated to the national level using PPPs. Household survey data are then used to determine the number of people living with per capita consumption below the poverty line.

The U.S. Federal Reserve Board uses PPP-based data on the GDP and aggregates to undertake an empirical analysis of international price levels (see chapter 22).

The International Monetary Fund (IMF) uses PPP-based GDP to determine the quota subscriptions of member countries (see chapter 23). The quota not only determines the financing each country must provide to the IMF, but also determines the amount of financing a country can obtain from the IMF and largely determines its voting power in IMF decisions. The IMF also uses PPP-based GDP numbers in its *World Economic Outlook,* which provides estimates of regional and world output and growth.

Other organizations and researchers use PPPs for international comparisons of output and productivity at the sector level (agriculture, manufacturing, and services). These comparisons produce useful complements to comparisons of GDP or expenditure categories (see chapter 24).

Why Not Use Exchange Rates?

This question arises often. First, exchange rates do not reflect the different price levels across components of the GDP—for example, table 2 shows the variability of selected basic headings in the food aggregate. Table 3 shows the PLIs for the GDP and major aggregates for Brazil and India. If exchange rates were used to deflate GDP expenditures by aggregate, the same value would be used regardless of the difference in price levels. The comparisons of per capita expenditures across countries would then not reflect the relative price differences. Second, the use of PPPs allows direct comparisons. Again using table 3, the PLI for health in both countries is considerably less than the food price level. The PLI also reveals the difference in health expenditures if they are deflated using the exchange rate instead of PPPs. In other words, the nominal expenditures for health in Brazil and India based on the exchange rate would be 55 and 13 percent, respectively, of the real expenditures based on PPPs.

Steps to Estimating PPPs

The ICP has three major components. The first component is the conceptual framework, which is determined by the set of national accounts making up the GDP. The second component is the national annual average prices or quantity or value data for a basket of goods and services that are comparable across countries and are representative of purchasing patterns within each country. The third component is the methodology used to compute the PPPs at the following levels: product, basic heading, aggregates of GDP, and GDP.

Table 3 Price Level Indexes for Major Aggregates, Brazil and India

	Price level indexes (world = 100 for major aggregates)					
	GDP	Food	Health	Education	Collective government	Gross fixed capital formation
Brazil	69	77	55	78	62	76
India	41	53	13	16	35	48

Source: ICP 2005.

These three components are carried out under a governance structure whereby countries are grouped into regions with a regional coordinator. The ICP Global Office in the World Bank provides the overall coordination of the program across the regions and also the coordination with the Eurostat-OECD comparison (see chapter 2).

Figure 1 is an overview of the different steps required to produce estimates of PPPs. The starting point is the GDP. The best practice in the measurement of economic activities is the *System of National Accounts 1993*, which forms the basis of the ICP (see chapter 3). The breakdown of the GDP expenditures into 155 basic headings forms the building blocks to estimate PPPs. The basic

Figure 1 Main Components of the International Comparison Program

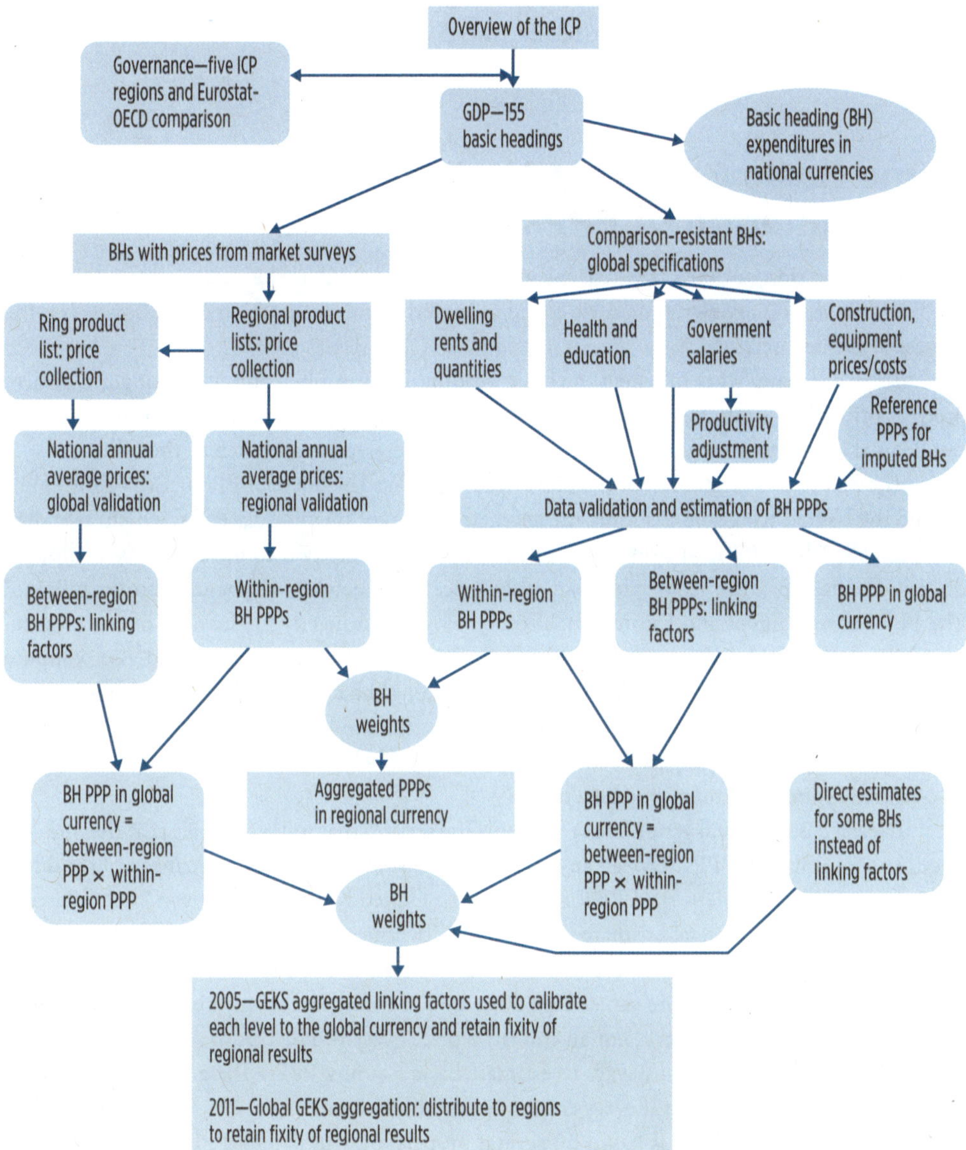

Source: ICP.
Note: GEKS = Gini-Éltetö-Köves-Szulc.

heading represents the categories into which individual products are grouped for pricing purposes; it is the lowest level for which expenditure estimates (breakdown of the GDP) are required. Use of the GDP as the main element of the conceptual framework of the ICP means that the prices to be collected must be consistent with the underlying values in the national accounts. The prices must be national annual averages and basically represent purchaser prices that include taxes and other costs.

Basic headings fall into three main categories. The first category is those basic headings containing products consumers purchase in various markets. Prices for these basic headings are obtained by means of market surveys. The second category is made up of the basic headings that are "comparison-resistant" because of the difficulties encountered in collecting data to estimate PPPs. These include the basic headings grouped into dwelling rents, health, education, government, construction, and equipment. The third category is those basic headings in which the prices either are not available or are too expensive to obtain. Therefore, their PPPs are imputed using PPPs from other basic headings (reference PPPs).

Some Basic Concepts Underlying the Estimation of PPPs

The previous section outlined the steps taken to collect and validate the data used for estimation of PPPs. This section reviews some basic concepts underlying the estimation of PPPs, which is the subject of the next section.

There are many ways in which the basic heading PPPs can be computed using the relative product prices or simply the product PPPs—each has strengths and weaknesses. Many methods can be used as well to average the basic heading PPPs to aggregates and then to the GDP.

The first step is estimation of the basic heading PPPs. The bilateral PPP between any country and the United Kingdom is simply the geometric mean of the product PPPs, which, as shown in table 1, equals 18.02 for Estonia. Also, the PPP between any two countries can be computed directly. For example, the geometric mean of the price ratios between Egypt and Estonia is 0.243. The PPP between Egypt and Estonia can also be measured indirectly by the ratio of their respective PPPs to the United Kingdom as the base, or 5.22/18.02 = 0.289. One could also compute the PPP between Egypt and Estonia indirectly by dividing the PPP for Egypt and the Philippines by the PPP for Estonia and the Philippines. If n countries are in the comparison, a PPP can be obtained directly between any two countries, and $n - 1$ PPPs between the same two countries can be obtained indirectly through the base country.

In each case, one will get different answers. The section that follows reveals that the one way to estimate multilateral PPPs between any two countries is to take the geometric mean of the direct and indirect PPPs. In table 1, the PPP for Egypt to the United Kingdom goes from 5.22 (bilateral) to 4.80 when the multilateral estimate is computed. This means that the PPPs between any two countries are affected by their respective PPPs with each other country. This also means that the PPPs between any two countries can change if the mix of countries included in the computations changes. As illustrated in table 1, not all countries price every product. And as shown in the sections that follow, there are many ways to estimate basic heading PPPs. These methods would all provide about the same answer if every country priced every item.

The choice of methods is based on several properties. Multilateral PPPs are computed so that the results satisfy two basic properties—transitivity and base country invariance. *Transitivity* simply means that the PPP between any two countries should be the same whether it is computed directly or indirectly through a third country. The second requirement is that the PPPs be *base country–invariant,* which means that the PPPs between any two countries should be the same regardless of the choice of base country. A simple solution is to use the geometric mean of the direct and indirect PPPs.

The basic heading PPPs shown in table 1 are essentially averages of the relative prices with no weights taken into account, which means that every product is treated equally. However, in reality expenditure shares for each would not be equal. For example, the prices for long grain rice sold loose are cheaper than the prices for Basmati. It is likely that in Egypt and the Philippines long grain rice sold loose is purchased in much greater quantities than long grain prepacked and Basmati, and that in Estonia and the United Kingdom prepacked long grain is the most popular of the two kinds. Because products with the greatest expenditures are likely to have the lowest prices, it would improve the quality of the estimates if some form of weighting could be introduced. This brings in the concept of representativity used by the Eurostat-OECD and CIS regions in the 2005 ICP and attempted in the other regions.

A *representative product* is one that is purchased frequently by households and has a price level consistent with all products in the basic heading. This classification can be used in applying a form of weighting in the estimation of basic heading PPPs, as shown in chapter 4. Most countries in the ICP regions had difficulty applying the concept, especially the meaning of price level. To simplify the classification of products for its 2011 round, the ICP adopted a simpler concept, *importance*. Each country is asked to use expert judgment to determine which product(s) would have the largest expenditure shares. This will allow the introduction of simple weights for the products deemed important and used to estimate basic heading PPPs.

Weights based on basic heading expenditures are used in the methodology to average a group of basic headings to an aggregate level. The food aggregate, for example, contains 29 basic headings. In table 2, for the column of basic heading PPPs between, say, Egypt and the United Kingdom, there are two sets of weights: the expenditure shares for Egypt and those for the United Kingdom. Another basic concept that determines the choice of index method is that countries be treated equally. Therefore, the basic heading PPPs are first averaged using Egypt's weights (Laspeyres index), and are then averaged using the United Kingdom's weights (Paasche index). Each index provides a PPP between Egypt and the United Kingdom, and therefore the geometric mean is taken. The result is a Fisher index. As discussed in chapter 5, this is a superlative multilateral index that is consistent with economic comparisons of utility across countries. For each pair of countries, the multilateral PPP is the geometric mean of the direct and indirect Fisher indexes. This method was used for the 2005 ICP even though it does not satisfy the additivity requirement.

Additivity means that, for example, the expenditures for each food basic heading (in national currency) divided by the respective PPPs should add to the sum of food expenditures (in national currency) divided by the aggregated food PPP. The addition of major aggregate expenditures in PPP terms to the GDP should equal the real expenditures obtained by dividing GDP expenditures (in national currency) by the aggregated PPP for the GDP. However, the requirement that countries be treated symmetrically produces results that are not additive. Because the nonadditive method was used for the 2005 ICP, the real world GDP was about 2 percent smaller than the GDP obtained by the summation of the aggregate real expenditures. These differences were many times larger at the national level. However, at each level of aggregation the results were consistent with economic comparisons of utility and also minimized the differences between the bilateral and multilateral PPPs.

Additive methods can be used, but they have the disadvantage of giving more weight to the relative prices of the larger, more developed countries. As a result, the real expenditures for poor countries become larger and move further away from the bilateral PPPs.

Fixity is another concept that determines the methodology used. This means that the relative volume (ratio of real expenditures) between any pair of countries in a region remains the same after the region has been combined with other countries or regions. This concept is critical when a region prepares its results, which are then later converted from a regional currency to the global currency.

Estimating PPPs—Within Regions

As depicted in figure 1, the PPPs between countries within a region are estimated in two steps. The first step is to estimate the basic heading PPPs. The next step is to average or, using ICP jargon, to aggregate the basic heading PPPs for each country to higher aggregates and the GDP using expenditure weights. The basic requirement for each stage of aggregation is that the resulting PPPs are transitive and base country–invariant, as defined earlier.

From Product PPPs to the Basic Heading

This section provides a brief overview of the material presented in chapter 4 and builds off table 1 in this executive summary. The bilateral PPPs for each country shown in table 1 are a form of a Jevons index. If the table is full—that is, if every country priced every item—then the bilateral PPPs would be transitive and base country–invariant.

In practice, not every country can price every item. Two basic methods are used in the ICP to calculate basic heading PPPs. The first approach is based on the Jevons index and the Gini-Éltetö-Köves-Szulc (GEKS) method, which turns the bilateral PPPs into multilateral PPPs to make them transitive and base country–invariant. The GEKS method is based on averaging the direct PPPs between any two countries with the $n - 1$ PPPs that can be obtained indirectly. The other method uses a regression model known as the Country Product Dummy (CPD), which directly estimates PPPs that are transitive and base country–invariant in one step.

As noted earlier, both methods treat every product equally regardless of their relative expenditures. For that reason, the concepts of representativity and importance were introduced.

Table 4 repeats the data shown in table 1 for Egypt and the United Kingdom with representative products indicated. Long grain rice, prepacked, is representative of the basic heading in the United Kingdom, whereas long grain rice sold loose is representative in Egypt. There are two ways to compute basic heading PPPs using this information. The PPP between Egypt and the United Kingdom is computed first using only products representative of Egypt, and then again using only products representative of the United Kingdom. The bilateral PPP between Egypt and the United Kingdom is then the geometric mean of these two PPPs. Basmati is not considered representative in either country, even though prices were provided. Thus those prices are not used in the price comparison for either country. These bilateral PPPs are made transitive and base country–invariant using the GEKS* method. This method is used by the Eurostat-OECD comparison and the CIS region. The GEKS method becomes the GEKS* method when the representativity variable is introduced.

The other regions in the 2005 ICP attempted to use the Country Product Representative Dummy (CPRD) method, with representativity included as another variable in the regression. However, the countries were not able to consistently provide the representativity coding because the concept required judgment about both price levels and relative expenditures. Therefore, the

Table 4 Estimating PPPs When Products Are Classified as Representative or Nonrepresentative

Rice basic heading	Egypt, Arab Rep., national price	United Kingdom national price	Egypt, Arab Rep.*/ United Kingdom	Egypt, Arab Rep./ United Kingdom*
Long grain, prepacked	5.51	0.73*		7.54
Long grain, loose	3.47*	1.05	3.30	
Basmati	5.69	2.23		
Geometric mean			3.30	7.54
Bilateral PPP			4.98	

Source: ICP 2005.
Note: The asterisk (*) indicates products representative of the basic heading price structure and frequently purchased.

concept was not used in the remaining four regions. The concept has been simplified for the 2011 ICP, and the importance classification is being used only to indicate those products with the greatest expected expenditures. Because the importance classification is based on assumptions about expenditures, the Country Product Dummy-Weighted (CPD-W) method is being used in the 2011 ICP, with important products receiving weights greater than 2.

Table 5 shows the methods that can be used to estimate basic heading PPPs. The Jevons, Jevons-GEKS, and CPD methods provide the same results if every country prices every product and the representative or importance classifications are not used. However, the results produced by the GEKS* method and either the CPRD or CPD-W method will differ for one basic reason illustrated in table 4. In that table, Basmati rice was not representative for any country, and thus it would not enter into the estimation of PPPs for the group of countries using the Jevons-GEKS method. However, the CPRD and CPD-W regressions include all data, thereby becoming more robust when the price matrix is incomplete.

The main outcome of the analysis of the 2005 ICP data is the realization that some classification process must be used to ensure that the products purchased most widely receive more weight than the other products being priced. The classification of "importance" discussed earlier is being used in the ICP regions for the 2011 ICP round, and basic heading PPPs are being estimated using the CPD-W method.

Table 5 Methods for Estimating Basic Heading PPPs

	Methods for estimating basic heading PPPs					
	Jevons	Jevons-GEKS	CPD	Jevons-GEKS*	CPRD	CPD-W
Properties	Transitive and base-invariant with full matrix	Multilateral procedure to ensure transitivity and base invariance with less than full price table	Multilateral procedure to ensure transitivity and base invariance with less than full price table	Implied weights used for representative products. Results are transitive and base-invariant.	Implied weights used for representative products. Results are transitive and base-invariant.	Specific weights used for "important" products. Results are transitive and base-invariant.

Source: ICP.
Note: GEKS = Gini-Éltető-Köves-Szulc; CPD = Country Product Dummy; CPRD = Country Product Representative Dummy; CPD-W = Country Product Dummy-Weighted.

From Basic Headings to Major Aggregates to the GDP

Chapter 5 is an extensive review of the different methods used to aggregate basic heading PPPs to the GDP and their properties. Because expenditure weights are available for each country, the input to the estimation process is a matrix of 155 basic heading PPPs by country in the region and another matrix of basic heading expenditures in national currencies.

Chapter 5 examines three methods. The method used in five of the six regions was the GEKS. The basic heading PPP between any two countries has two weights, one for each country. Therefore, two weighted averages of basic heading PPPs are computed to estimate the GDP basic heading, using the weights for each country in turn. The Fisher indexes, the geometric mean of these weighted averages, are then made transitive and base country–invariant using the GEKS process described earlier. The GEKS method has the property that each country is treated in a symmetric way. One disadvantage is that the results are not additive.

The ICP has used two additive methods—Geary-Khamis (GK) and Iklé-Dikhanov-Balk (IDB)—but the results are not consistent with economic comparisons of utility across countries. In addition, large countries have a greater impact on the final results. If large countries have higher prices, then the impact is to raise the price levels of the poorer, smaller countries. The IDB method, however, has a smaller large-country effect. In the 2005 ICP, the GEKS method was used in every region except Africa. There, the IDB method was used because it was important that results be additive (see chapter 5 for an extensive review of its properties).

A problem with the GEKS method is that countries at very different stages of development with very different relative prices are given the same weight as countries with similar stages of development and relative prices. Therefore, chapter 5 examines the minimum spanning tree approach, which builds up the multilateral set of comparisons starting with bilateral comparisons with countries very similar in structure. This method offers considerable promise for the future, but still contains some arbitrary aspects, suggesting that further analysis and research are needed. The 2011 round of the ICP is thus mainly using the GEKS method to aggregate basic heading PPPs to the GDP.

From Within-Region to Global Basic Heading PPPs

As indicated in figure 1, at this stage there is a set of PPPs and related indexes for each of the six regions, each in the currency of one of the countries in the region. The PPPs for each level of aggregation and the GDP in each region are transitive and base country–invariant. However, at this stage it is not possible to compute the PPPs between two countries in different regions. Therefore, the final step is to convert the within-region PPPs to a common global currency. The requirements remain the same, which means that the concepts of transitivity and base country invariance apply to the global results. In addition, there must be adherence to the principle of fixity. This simply means that the relative volumes between any two countries shown in the regional comparison remain the same after they are converted to a common global currency. This concept applies at every level of aggregation from the basic heading to the GDP.

A new method introduced for the 2005 ICP meets all of these requirements and is described in chapters 6 and 8. Two sets of PPPs are required for each basic heading to convert regional PPPs to a common global currency. The first set is the within-region PPPs by country for each region. The second set is six between-region PPPs or linking factors for each basic heading, with one region serving as the base and with the between-region PPP equal to 1.0.

In the 2005 ICP, the between-region PPPs for household consumption were based on separate prices (the Ring list, which is described shortly) collected by 18 countries: six African countries, four countries in the Asia-Pacific region, four Eurostat-OECD countries, and two countries each from the Western Asia and South America regions. For each of these there was a set of Ring product prices for each basic heading and its within-region PPP in a regional currency. These Ring prices for each country were converted to the currency of the regional base country by dividing each country's basic heading Ring prices by its within-region PPP from the regional comparison. For each basic heading, there was a set of five[2] prices, each in the currency of a regional base country. A CPD model that treated each set of regional prices as a country provided a set of PPPs for each region that reflected the relative prices (between-region PPPs or linking factors) for each basic heading. These linking factors were transitive and base country–invariant.

Chapters 11–16 describe the process undertaken to link the health, education, government, construction, and machinery and equipment basic headings. Because the same set of specifications was used for every region, the between-region PPPs were computed from the same data used for the regional comparisons for all basic headings except dwelling rents. The between-region PPPs for dwelling rents were computed using quantities of housing for a large number of countries within each region. Even though each region used different methods to estimate within-region housing PPPs, they were linked using the quantity method.

The basic heading linking factors for each region were scalars used to convert the within-region basic heading PPPs to the global currency. Because the within-region basic heading PPP for each country was multiplied by the same between-region basic heading scalar, the fixity principle was met. The outcome was a matrix of 146 countries and 155 basic heading PPPs that satisfied the transitivity and base country requirements, all relating to the same base country.

The 2011 ICP methodology is similar, but improvements are being made to the linking and aggregation. Instead of only selected countries pricing a large Ring list, all countries will price a smaller set of global core products. Analysis of the 2005 results revealed that the between-country variability was greater than the variability in product level prices. In other words, the optimum design calls for more countries to price fewer products for linking purposes. Therefore, a set of global core products was defined and will be part of the regional price comparisons as well. The prices for these core products from all countries are being used in the same two-step process described earlier: first estimate between-region basic heading PPPs and then use those as scalars to convert the within-region PPPs to the global currency.

In the 2005 ICP, the representativity concept was not used for the Ring prices. However, because of the diversity of economies across the world, it will be essential that the importance classification be applied to all of the prices in the set of global core products. Although countries will be able to price a large number of the core items, it is very unlikely that all countries will have the same price levels or the same relative expenditures. Products that are common in some countries may be found only in boutiques with higher prices in other countries; the importance classification is needed to prevent an upward bias in the price levels used to estimate the between-region PPPs. The importance classified will be used on both the regional and core prices. The between-region PPPs will be computed using the CPD-W method.

Aggregating (Averaging) Global PPPs to Higher Aggregates and the GDP

At this stage in the 2005 ICP, there was a matrix of five regional linking factors for each of the 155 basic headings and the summation of national expenditures to a total for each region in the currency of the regional base country. In the 2005 ICP, the between-region basic heading PPPs or linking factors were aggregated to the GDP and other aggregates using the GEKS method. Just as at the basic heading level, the aggregated linking factors at each level times the within-region PPP for each country at the same aggregated level converted the regional PPP to the global currency. This step preserved fixity at all levels of aggregation. Later analysis, however, showed that the linking factors at the aggregated level were not base country–invariant—that is, they were dependent on the choice of regional base country.

For this reason, a global aggregation is being used for the 2011 ICP. The input will be the outcome of the linking at the basic heading level, which will provide a matrix of 155 basic heading PPPs for 180-plus countries and another for expenditures. A global GEKS aggregation of the entire matrix will directly estimate a set of PPPs to a global base country at every level of the GDP breakdown and the GDP. The resulting expenditures for each country in the global currency will be summed to regional totals. These regional totals can be distributed to each country within a region to ensure that fixity is maintained with the within-region results.

Basic Headings with Prices Collected from Market Surveys

These basic headings account for about 100 out of the total of 155 basic headings and for about 60 percent of the world GDP (see chapters 7 and 8). Each region determines the products to be priced in these basic headings and prepares their specifications using structured product definitions—a new method introduced for the 2005 ICP that provides a systematic and consistent way to describe products. Under the regional concept, the goods and services to be priced can be chosen as those the most representative of a region's countries. Although this approach provides the best comparison between countries in the same region, say India and Indonesia, it is not possible to compare either with Brazil or the United States. For that reason, a method coined the "Ring" was adopted for the 2005 ICP.

The Ring concept involved creating a list of products that represented a composite of what was priced in each region. Eighteen countries representing the geographic ICP regions and the Eurostat-OECD program (this group included one economy, Hong Kong SAR, China) priced the set of Ring products in addition to the products in their regional list. National annual average prices were provided by all countries for their regional products, and the Ring countries also provided prices for the Ring products. The prices from the regional lists were used by each region to compute *within-region* basic heading PPPs for its countries. These within-region basic heading PPPs were used to deflate the Ring prices into five sets of *regional prices* that were then used to estimate between-region PPPs. These between-region PPPs were in effect scalars that calibrated each country's within-region basic heading PPPs to a common global currency.

Data Validation

Prices and other measurements are first validated at the national level (see chapters 9 and 10). This review ensures that the same products were priced across the different outlets over the country. The validation then moves to the regional and global levels where the main goal is to ensure the same products were priced across countries. In the 2005 ICP, the validation at these levels was carried out by first putting the prices in each basic heading into a common currency using PPPs. Two methods were used: the Quaranta tables from the Eurostat-OECD comparison and the Dikhanov tables derived by the World Bank. The Quaranta tables incorporate both exchange rates and PPPs in the identification of outliers. The Dikhanov tables allow the validation to be across basic headings in addition to the within–basic heading review. Both methods involve an iterative process because the basic heading PPPs will change as prices that are outliers are checked by the respective countries and are either revised or removed. For the 2005 ICP, the data validation of the regional prices was conducted region by region, whereas the Global Office validated the prices from the Ring price survey.

Because the regions published their results first, the *within-region* basic headings had to be taken "as is" for the estimation of linking factors and the global aggregation. Analysis since then indicates that the regional basic heading PPPs should be subjected to additional review when the global linking factors are being validated and estimated (see chapters 9 and 10). A major outcome is that the regional results will remain open for review until the global results have been finalized.

Comparison-Resistant Basic Headings

A common feature of the comparison-resistant basic headings is that *global* specifications for pricing or data collection are defined, whereas each region prepares its own lists of products for which prices are collected in market surveys.

Health and Education

The difficulty with comparing health and education across countries is that countries have different arrangements for providing their citizens with health and education goods and services (see chapter 11). In the majority of countries, health and education are provided by a mix of government-run and private services. PPPs for the health aggregate therefore include seven basic headings in household consumption and 12 basic headings in individual consumption by government aggregate. For education, there is one basic heading in household consumption, but six basic headings in individual consumption expenditures by government. Prices are collected for pharmaceutical products, therapeutic appliances and equipment, outpatient and hospital services, and other medical products for household consumption health basic headings. The same prices are used for the basic headings under government health benefits. For the government basic headings for the production of health and education services, it has been assumed that the comparative value of the government output is equal to input costs as measured by employee compensation. The problem with the traditional method of using government compensation to estimate PPPs is exacerbated by developments in the use of technologies; that method ignores the productivity gains from the use of technology.

For the 2005 ICP, prices were collected for products and services purchased by consumers for health and private education, and average salaries were obtained for a selection of occupations for certain health and education basic headings. For the first time, productivity adjustments were used in three ICP regions to adjust the compensation PPPs for differences in productivity across countries.

Dwelling Rents for Owner-Occupied Households

Household dwelling expenditures consist of market-rented housing and imputations for non-market rents and owner-occupied housing (see chapter 12). The imputations complicate both the preparation of the national accounts and the estimation of PPPs for housing. Therefore, it is difficult to compare housing across countries because of the varying mix of rental versus owner-occupied dwellings. In the 2005 ICP, PPPs for dwellings were computed three different ways. Where there was a large rental market, rental surveys provided average rental rates by size and type of housing—these were also used to estimate PPPs for owner-occupied dwellings. However, in many countries the rental market is not sufficient to provide data to impute PPPs for owner-occupied housing. The preferred method in this case is to derive PPPs based on the relationship provided by expenditures = prices × quantities. Here prices = expenditures/quantities. Therefore, an indirect PPP is the ratio of the derived prices between countries. This is called the quantity approach because total housing quantities such as number of structures, rooms, and square footage from housing surveys and censuses are used as the quantity measure after the quantities are adjusted for quality. This method was used in some of the Eurostat-OECD countries and in the CIS and South America regions because the rental market was too small to provide rents to impute for owner-occupied housing. Because there was a similar lack of a rental market in Africa and Asia, the quantity method was also attempted in the Africa and Asia-Pacific regions, but it produced implausible results. Therefore, PPPs were imputed for countries in the Africa and Asia-Pacific regions using the PPP for individual consumption expenditures by households (excluding housing), which means that the housing PPP probably does not reflect the true volume of housing services in those countries.

Data users, especially those undertaking poverty analysis, were very critical of the method used in the Africa and Asia-Pacific regions. Therefore, in the 2011 ICP round efforts are being redoubled to enable all countries to base dwelling PPPs on a combination of dwelling rents and quantities. Chapter 12 explains in detail how the within-region dwelling PPPs were linked in the 2005 ICP using a set of quantity data representing each region.

Construction

The comparison of construction across countries depends on the concept of comparability, just as for any other component of the ICP (see chapter 13). Construction poses special problems because most construction outputs are unique. No two office buildings in different countries are identical, nor are the bridges, highways, and dams. One method of making comparisons is based on comparing input prices. Inputs are materials, labor, and equipment hire, each of which can be described so that the resulting costs are comparable between countries. The main problem with using input costs is that productivity, profits, and overhead costs are assumed to be the same relative size in each country.

Output pricing involves creating a model building or civil engineering project with detailed specifications describing the final product. Construction professionals in each country are asked to quote a price for the construction output. This output price takes into account differences in productivity and other components such as profits and overhead. The disadvantage is that it is very costly to create the model projects and then to have them priced in each country. This method was used in the Eurostat-OECD comparison, but it was considered too costly to use in the ICP regions.

In the 2005 ICP, construction was compared using an approach called the basket of construction components. It involved collecting prices for a range of major construction components and basic inputs that were common across countries. Detailed specifications were prepared for components such as a column footing and the cost of labor, materials, and equipment. Basic input costs such as a fixed quantity of cement or an amount of reinforcing steel were also obtained. Because the component prices included labor, materials, and equipment, they met the requirement for output prices (still excluding profits and overhead). The problem was that a complex set of weights was required to combine the construction components, and most countries had difficulty providing them.

For the 2011 ICP, 38 different kinds of materials, 7 types of labor, and 5 types of equipment will be priced based on detailed specifications. PPPs will be computed for each of these three components within each of the three basic headings. Each country will furnish weights indicating the relative shares of materials, labor, and equipment for the residential buildings, nonresidential buildings, and civil engineering basic headings to aggregate the three component PPPs to the respective basic heading PPPs.

Machinery and Equipment

The procedure used for pricing machinery and equipment in the 2005 ICP was similar to that used for household goods and services (see chapter 14). Structured product descriptions were developed for different kinds of equipment and then used as the basis for product specifications, so that comparable products could be priced across countries. The major difference was that the product specifications were very technical and dealt with combinations of characteristics such as torque, power, and lifting capacity. As a result, outside experts had to be brought in to assist countries with price collection to ensure that the products purchased were comparable across countries.

In addition, a set of 108 products was defined at the global level because of the difficulty in describing the price-determining characteristics. These products were used in the price collection for the ICP regions. Some equipment goods are unique because they are designed for a specific location or purpose. Examples are sea vessels, oil platforms, and power plants. No attempt was made to price these items; pricing was confined to the standard, generally mass-produced items. The set of global specifications prepared for 2005 has been updated for use in the 2011 ICP.

Government Services

As described earlier, in the 2005 ICP government services were compared by using government compensation as a measure of the value of output (see chapter 15). Detailed specifications were prepared describing 50 different government occupations in terms of the work done. For each, annual salaries were obtained that reflected gross salaries and wages that included payments for benefits and employee contributions for insurance and pensions. These salaries for each occupation and country were treated as national annual average prices, and PPPs were computed accordingly. Also as described earlier, the average salaries were adjusted for productivity in the Africa, Asia-Pacific, and Western Asia regions. Because this was the first time productivity adjustments were made, chapter 16 is devoted to this issue. The adjustments were needed because the very low salaries in some countries would have resulted in implausible levels of real expenditures. The assumption underlying the productivity adjustments was that the output per worker was likely to increase with more capital per worker.

The issue for the 2011 round is whether to make adjustments for productivity or to find output measures such as numbers of health care workers or other health outputs and numbers of students and test scores for education that are comparable across countries for the estimation of PPPs. The situation becomes even more complex if different methods are used across regions, because the PPPs will have to be linked. One of the outcomes of the debate is that all countries will furnish compensation data for the same set of occupations. These will be used in a global aggregation to the basic heading and aggregates that in one run will provide regional and global PPPs and real expenditures. If a region prefers to use a different method to estimate within-region PPPs, it can do so, and the regional share of the world expenditures from the global aggregation will be distributed to its countries to maintain within-region fixity.

Basic Headings for Which PPPs Were Imputed

PPPs were imputed for different reasons (see chapter 17). One was that no good measures were available for comparing government basic headings such as intermediate services, gross operating surplus, net taxes on production, and receipts from sales. Household consumption also contained basic headings for narcotics, prostitution, games of chance, and animal-drawn vehicles, which would be difficult to price. Moreover, some regions had found it difficult to define price-determining characteristics for basic headings such as repair of furniture and appliances and maintenance of major durables and household services.

The basic heading PPPs used to impute for those that were missing were called "reference" PPPs. For example, the reference PPPs for intermediate consumption for government health services were PPPs for individual consumption expenditures by households (excluding health, education, and other basic headings imputed using reference PPPs). At the global level, the imputed PPPs accounted for 14 percent of the global real expenditures. Countries with low government expenditures had smaller amounts from imputation; those with high government expenditures had much larger amounts. The Africa and Asia regions had higher levels because they imputed PPPs for owner-occupied housing. One outcome of this review was to set stricter standards on when PPPs would be imputed and to increase efforts to directly estimate PPPs for dwellings.

Imputing PPPs for Missing Countries and Extrapolating PPPs between Benchmarks

The 2005 ICP covered 146 countries, and therefore PPPs were not available for about 65 other economies for a variety of reasons, ranging from resources to country interest (see chapter 18). Data users, however, requested a complete database, and so PPPs were imputed for the missing economies. For these economies, PPPs were imputed using a model based on benchmark data. The model imputed PLIs based on GDP per capita in U.S. dollars, imports and exports as shares of GDP, and an age dependency ratio as explanatory variables.

This process provided a database of PPPs to the U.S. dollar for 180-plus countries for 2005. However, many data users want PPPs for succeeding years. Therefore, PPPs are extrapolated forward and published each year in the World Bank's *World Development Indicators*. These extrapolations are based on GDP deflators. The problem is that the extrapolated PPPs will differ from the new benchmark PPPs. The challenge is explaining to data users why consumer price index price changes and GDP growth rates are not consistent with the changes in PPPs between benchmarks. Chapter 18 provides an in-depth look at the reasons the two data series will not always be consistent.

Chapter 19 is an overview of the main results from ICP 2005 plus an empirical analysis to show how results would differ using different indexing methods. Specifically, additive results from the GK and IDB methods are compared with the nonadditive GEKS results. This comparison confirms that the additive methods increase the real size of poor countries' GDPs relative to those of richer countries.

Chapters 20 and 21 reflect the work of poverty experts who use PPPs to construct internationally comparable poverty lines. Chapter 20 presents the methods used by the World Bank to determine the international poverty line ($1.25 international dollars per day) and the number of people living below those levels. Chapter 21 explores how the recalculation of PPPs using the expenditure patterns of those at the poverty line compares with those based on the entire population. The underlying theory of poverty-weighted PPPs is presented, along with the methodology developed for the analysis.

Chapter 22 provides an analysis of international price levels, especially the relationship between the cross-country price levels and income levels. It shows that this relationship is sensitive to whether products are tradable.

The International Monetary Fund is a major user of PPPs. Chapter 23 describes in detail how the IMF uses PPPs to determine membership quotas and in the analysis it publishes in its *World Economic Outlook* report. Chapter 24 concludes this volume by further expanding on the use of PPPs; it describes the adjustments needed to convert expenditure-based PPPs into output PPPs by sector such as agriculture, manufacturing, and services.

Conclusion

Although the 2005 round of the ICP was a vast improvement over previous rounds because of the significant effort made to improve methodologies, much was also learned that has been taken forward to the 2011 round. A brief review of lessons learned and improvements being made follows:

- *National accounts.* More attention is being paid to the national accounts, starting with the national estimates of GDP and then the breakdown to the 155 basic headings. The comparisons between countries are based on volume indexes and per capita measures—a perfectly good PPP is of no use if the GDP it converts is of weak quality. Therefore, a concerted effort is being made from the beginning to improve national accounts and make them more consistent between countries.
- *From Ring list to global core products.* The most significant change is moving from the use of a Ring list priced by a few countries for linking to the development of a set of global core products that will be priced by all countries. This change will greatly improve estimation of the between-region linking factors used as scalars to convert within-region PPPs to the global currency. It also carries with it adoption of the principle of "importance" to classify products in order to give more weight to those most widely consumed in each country.
- *Difficult-to-compare basic headings.* Considerable effort is going into improving the estimates of PPPs for the difficult-to-compare basic headings.
- *Dwelling rent PPPs.* Because of the criticism from data users that dwelling rent PPPs were imputed in Africa and Asia, efforts are being redoubled to ensure that direct PPPs are provided for both regional and global comparisons. The use of output measures for health and education are also being explored.
- *Productivity adjustments.* The issue of productivity adjustments for government services is being addressed. In the 2005 ICP, productivity adjustments were not used in every region, making it difficult to compare results between countries in different regions. A significant improvement for the 2011 ICP is using a global aggregation of government compensation across all countries that is adjusted for productivity differences.
- *Construction.* The methodology for construction is being simplified so that countries can carry out data collection without having to engage expert consultants.
- *Data validation.* Greater attention is being given to data validation at the basic heading level and above for both the regional and core comparisons. A major change is that regional PPPs will be open for review while the core prices and PPPs are being validated, because the within-region PPPs are an input in the estimation of linking factors.

NOTES

1. The prices used here were taken from various sources for illustrative purposes.
2. The linking factors for the CIS region were based on the PPPs for the Russian Federation from the Eurostat-OECD comparison. Russia also priced the CIS products and was the base country for the region.

Introduction: Reshaping the World

Angus S. Deaton

The rounds of the International Comparison Program (ICP) are like successive Olympic Games. Similar to the Olympics, they do not happen every year, and in the first modern games only a few countries sent competitors, there were only a few events, and the standards of competition were relatively low. The participants were amateurs with day jobs, and, although they were great natural athletes, they did not take their training very seriously. Yet the first modern Olympics was a watershed, which eventually grew into the record-breaking professional event it is today in which almost all nations of the world come together in a truly global competition.

The ICP began in the late 1960s and early 1970s, led by Irving Kravis, Alan Heston, and Robert Summers from the University of Pennsylvania and Zoltan Kennessy from the United Nations. Like the Olympics, only a few countries (six) took part in the first round in 1967—four more were added in 1970—and prices were collected for only a small range of goods and services. Since then, each round has become bigger and better (and more expensive), with more countries represented, with more and more professional statisticians and economists involved, and with lots of preparatory training in the form of expert workshops, theoretical papers, and figuring out how to deal with problems that could not be solved in the previous round. The 2005 round of the ICP was by far the most professional, the biggest, the most thoroughly researched, and the most international—with 146 countries. It was the first round to be organized by a Global Office housed in the World Bank. Its findings changed the economic map of the world.

The 2005 ICP revealed a world that was much more unequal than we economists and others had thought. It was not quite like discovering water on the moon perhaps, but it was like discovering that the craters were deeper or that the planets were farther from the sun than we had always thought. And when the World Bank reworked the global poverty counts using the new data, it also found a world that was much poorer than it had previously thought.

The gaps between rich countries and poor countries—which we long knew were enormous—were even larger than previously measured. The average gap in the per capita gross domestic product

(GDP) in 2005 between two randomly selected countries in the world was about 5 percent larger as a result of the new data. For some individual pairs of countries, particularly a pair in which one was rich and the other was poor, the reshaping was much larger. The ratio of China's per capita income to U.S. per capita income was 40 percent smaller than it was based on earlier data. Much the same was true for India. And for many of the countries in Sub-Saharan Africa the widening of the gap was larger still. Meanwhile, what was true for countries was also true of individuals, and the average difference between the rich and the poor of the world was newly enlarged. As a consequence, the world had many more poor people below any global poverty line fixed in rich country currency, although, as will be seen, this is not the only way of setting the line.

Comparing Countries

What is the ICP good for? Why do we need it? And how did the world manage before it began? When it works well and the ideas match the measures, the ICP allows us to make sound comparisons of living standards between countries and between widely separated periods of time. The ICP collects the prices of thousands of items in each country and averages them to calculate price indexes for GDP, for consumption, and for its components. These indexes allow us to make international comparisons of the price of rice, or the price of food, or the price of all consumption items. The national accounts of each country reveal how much its citizens spend on rice, on food, or on all consumption, so that the price indexes from the ICP allow us to convert these money amounts, measured in local currency units, to "real" amounts expressed in a common unit, which is nearly always the U.S. dollar. The dollar amounts, such as Kenya's per capita GDP in U.S. dollars, is per capita GDP in Kenyan shillings (calculated by Kenya's statistical office) divided by the price index of Kenya's GDP in shillings per dollar.

These comparisons in common units reveal the relative sizes of different economies. They indicate not just that one country is richer than another, but by how much. Without the price indexes, it is impossible to calculate differences in living standards between countries or people's well-being in different countries, or to measure global inequality. Without them, it is also impossible to convert a global poverty line into its local equivalent, which is the number needed to calculate the number of globally poor in each country and therefore in the world. The World Bank's global poverty line is constructed from an average of the poverty lines of the world's poorest countries, and these local lines must be converted into international dollars before they can be compared and averaged.

Since World War II, a uniform set of principles for measuring national income has been in place. The principles evolved by Richard Stone, James Meade, and Maynard Keynes in wartime Britain were codified under UN auspices after the war under the guidance of Stone. These principles have since evolved into successive versions of the UN's *System of National Accounts*, or SNA, the latest in 2008 (Commission of the European Communities et al. 2008). In following this system, each country provides estimates of national income in its local currency, and this process, at least in principle, is carried out in the same way everywhere.

When trying to compare economic characteristics across countries, the obvious method is to use market exchange rates to convert everything into a common currency—such as the U.S. dollar—but conversion using exchange rates does not do a very good job. Many factors—such as movements of speculative capital—affect the exchange rate in the short run, so that the rupee-to-dollar exchange rate may fluctuate from day to day, even though neither India's nor the United States' living standards are changing. Expectations about the future can affect current exchange rates—for example, between the euro and the dollar—even though there is no change in the current levels of income in Europe or the United States.

If all goods and services were freely traded between countries, traders would iron out these fluctuations, at least in the long run. But many goods and services are not traded at all—such as housing, many government and private services, the law courts, police services, haircutting, waiting tables, or babysitting—and there is no way in which to bring the prices of these items into line. In poorer countries, where labor is cheap, these nonexportable goods and services tend to be relatively cheaper than traded goods (such as wheat, gasoline, cameras, or machine tools), so that if common international units are used to value these nontraded goods, poor countries look less poor relative to rich countries than if domestic prices converted at market exchange rates are used.

All of this is just what every traveler knows. If an American gets off a plane in Delhi or an Italian disembarks in Addis Ababa and changes dollars into rupees or euros into birr, the amount of local currency received will go much further than the original dollar in Washington or the euro in Rome. In effect, the price level in poorer countries is lower than in richer countries. People in Delhi and Addis Ababa are indeed poorer than Americans, but because of the lower price levels they face, the difference is not nearly as large as it appears to be at market exchange rates. The alternative exchange rate that converts dollars and euros into rupees and birr in a way that preserves comparable purchasing power is called the purchasing power parity (PPP) exchange rate, and it is these PPPs that are measured by the ICP. In essence, PPPs are the price indexes computed from the hundreds of thousands of prices collected by the ICP.

The differences between market and PPP exchange rates are large and important. For poor countries, GDP per capita at international prices can be three (India) or four (Ethiopia) times larger than GDP per capita in domestic prices converted at exchange rates. But the ratio of market exchange rates to purchasing power parity exchange rates is not constant over time, nor is it the same for all countries with the same level of per capita income. So there is no choice but to actually collect the prices, and to do so, if not every year, at least on a regular basis.

Key Findings: Inequality

How did the 2005 ICP reshape the view of the world? The headline numbers came from India and China, whose economies "shrank" under the new estimates. The international dollar value of China's per capita GDP in 2005 fell from $6,757 in the 2007 *World Development Indicators* (WDI) to $4,088 in the 2008 WDI (World Bank 2007, 2008). For India, the same comparison shows a reduction from $3,453 to $2,222. All of these numbers are for a single year, 2005, and because they come from converting the same local currency values but at different PPPs, another way of stating the change is that the PPP for China rose by a factor of 1.65, while the PPP for India rose by a factor of 1.55. Recall that GDP in international dollars is obtained by dividing a country's own GDP by the PPP measured by the ICP, so that higher PPPs translate into lower estimates of GDP. The reduction in China's and India's GDP stems from the fact that the price index for China relative to that of the United States was 1.65 times higher than previously estimated, and that for India relative to that for the United States was 1.55 times higher.

Because international comparisons are carried out in international dollars, and because everyone is familiar with U.S. dollars, the obvious first interpretation of these data is that China's and India's economies are smaller than previously thought. But if the ICP had used not the U.S. dollar but, say, the Indian rupee as its unit of account, the change would have been that the U.S. economy was *much larger* than previously thought and China's economy *slightly smaller* than previously thought. All of these international comparisons are essentially relative; the ICP does not measure quantities, so it cannot say whether the absolute values of China's or India's per capita incomes were previously overestimated.

All of this may seem like hairsplitting, but it points to an important fact: the ICP widened the gaps between both India and China and the United States. Neither India nor China is any smaller or poorer (or indeed richer) than it was, although both are estimated to be smaller and poorer relative to the United States. In the 2007 *World Development Indicators*, the per capita income in the United States in 2005 was more than six times the per capita income in China, and more than 10 times the per capita income in India (World Bank 2007). In light of the 2005 ICP as reported in the 2008 *World Development Indicators*, these ratios increased to 12 times and nearly 19 times.

India and China are only two of the countries that moved farther apart from the United States in the 2005 ICP. Indeed, the effect was quite widespread, with many of the world's poorest countries shrinking relative to the United States. There was relatively little change among the world's richest countries (because many of them calculate PPPs every year, there is little opportunity for revision), so that the 2005 ICP caused a general widening of the dispersion of per capita incomes around the world.

Figure 1 plots the ratios of the "old" PPPs to the "new" PPPs against the logarithm of per capita GDP. Each point is a country, and the ratio is the ratio of the PPP reported in the 2007 *World Development Indicators* to the PPP reported in the 2008 WDI (World Bank 2007, 2008). If the ratio is greater than 1, measured per capita income has decreased relative to that of the United States; if it is less than 1, per capita income has increased relative to that of the United States.

Figure 1 shows a strong downward slope, which means that the revisions of the 2005 PPPs were generally larger for poorer countries. As a consequence, many of the poorer countries are poorer relative to the United States, while the richer countries stay about where they were. Inequality between countries is therefore larger under the 2005 ICP. The upward revaluation of the PPPs for India and China turns out to be quite common, with many other countries in Africa and some in Asia experiencing similar or larger upward revisions. Indeed, the top left of the figure shows that some African countries had much larger upward revisions than India and China. A number of these had never been benchmarked in an ICP, and so the previous PPPs were little more than imputations or educated guesses.

Branko Milanović (2009) has calculated the Gini coefficient for income inequality among all the citizens of the world. This number is much bigger than the Gini coefficients for even the most unequal of individual countries because world inequality is dominated by differences *between* countries rather than by differences *within* them. According to Milanović's calculations, the world Gini coefficient in 2002 rose about 5 percentage points because of the revisions in the 2005 ICP, from 66 percent to 71 percent. Even if we ignore inequality within countries and compute the world Gini coefficient on the (counterfactual) assumption that everyone in each country has the same income, there is a similar increase of 5 to 6 percentage points just from the ICP revision.

Key Findings: Poverty

If the ICP made the poor world poorer relative to the United States, did it increase global poverty? Not necessarily, because the outcome depends on whether poverty is viewed from a rich country perspective or from a poor country perspective.

From a rich country perspective, the global poverty line is taken to be a dollar a day and is held fixed in real dollars. The global line in use before the 2005 revision was not precisely a dollar,

FIGURE 1 Ratios of Old to New PPPs in Relation to Income

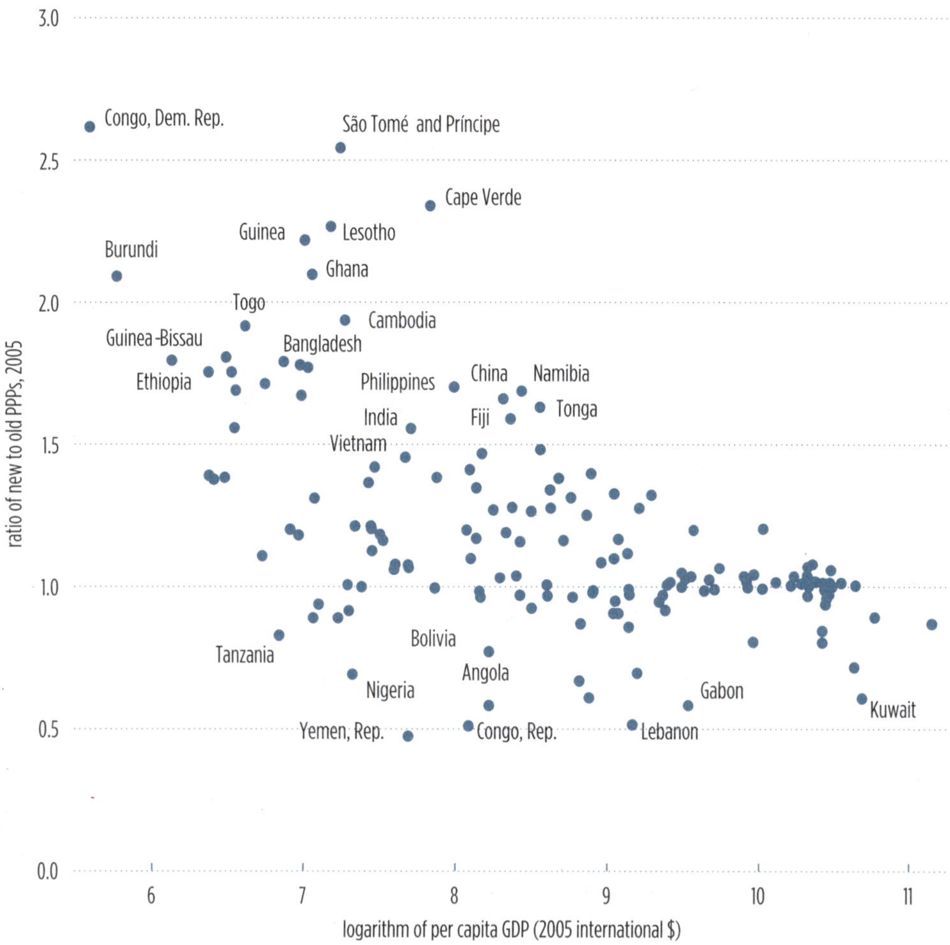

Source: ICP 2005.

but $1.08 in 1993 prices. By 2005 consumer prices in the United States had risen by 35 percent, and so the dollar-a-day line was actually $1.46 in 2005 prices. When that global line was used *with the old PPPs* to calculate global poverty, the global poverty count was 931 million people. If the same global line, $1.46 at 2005 prices, is used *with the new PPPs*, the global poverty count increases to 1.76 billion people, almost twice as many as before. Because the global poverty line is fixed in U.S. dollars and because the PPPs of poor countries have increased, the local equivalents of the global line have increased, and many more poor people are beneath them. Relative to the United States, then, the poor world is poorer than was thought, and there are many more poor people.

But use of this rich country perspective is not the only way to make the calculation. In 2005, at the old PPP of 11.3 rupees to the dollar, $1.46 was worth 16.5 rupees in India (this figure lies between India's two domestic poverty lines of 17.7 rupees for urban India and 12.0 rupees for rural India). Thus using the old PPPs, at a global poverty line of 16.5 rupees per person per day, there were 931 million poor people in the world, which is just a restatement of the old dollar calculation. However, if the global poverty line is fixed not in dollars at $1.46 but in rupees at 16.5, and if the new PPP exchange rates are used, the new global poverty estimate is 943 million people, which is close to the original number. Relative to India, then, the world is neither poorer nor richer than first thought; the ICP revision has had very little effect.

One feature of this second calculation is worth noting. At the new, higher PPP for India, the global poverty line of 16.5 rupees is now worth only $1.04 in 2005 U.S. dollars. This number is not only lower than the global poverty line in 2005 dollars (which it must be because of the increase in the PPP), but also actually lower than the global poverty line in 1993 dollars! However, this is just a consequence of the happenstance that the proportional increase in India's PPP was larger than the U.S. rate of inflation from 1993 to 2005.

Which of these two approaches is right, and why did the World Bank arrive at yet a third answer? Taking the second question first, the World Bank uses (a version of) the poor country perspective and calculates its global poverty line not as India's line but as the average of the poverty lines of the world's poorest countries. In principle, this approach should yield something like the just-described India-based calculation. And yet the Bank's calculations using the new PPPs show that 1.37 billion people are living in poverty, a substantial increase over the original estimate. The Bank arrived at this figure because it made other changes while implementing the ICP revision. In particular, it took the opportunity to update the group of countries whose poverty lines were used to calculate the global poverty line, and it turned out that, on average, the new reference group had higher poverty lines than the old reference group. Much of this was attributable to one country alone. India, which has one of the lowest poverty lines in the world but is no longer one of the poorest countries in the world, was dropped from the group, so the global poverty line went up. As the India example shows, it was this change in the global poverty line, not the ICP revision, that was responsible for increasing the global poverty count.

Of course, there is no *right* answer here. A good case could be made for holding the line fixed in dollars: the international community understands rich world currencies, is justifiably appalled by the number of people living on an unimaginably small but comprehensible amount, and is confused by a standard that appears to be denominated in dollars but is actually denominated in poor country currencies. The case in favor of the poor country standard is based on the reasonable belief that the poverty lines of the world's poorest countries are likely to be a good indication of the absolute minimal standard of living anywhere in the world. (But note that the Bank's new poverty line of $1.25 at 2005 prices is substantially *above* India's rural poverty line, beneath which live nearly a quarter of a billion people.) Likewise, there is certainly a case for revising the line from time to time, and there is no compelling reason to always use the poverty lines of the same set of countries. Even so, the combination of a revision of the line and a revision of the PPPs at the same time is certainly confusing, and has made the whole process—which has always been hard to explain—even less transparent than usual.

More Countries in 2005, Fewer Imputations

What did the 2005 round of the ICP do differently? Do these changes make the new results more or less credible than the earlier numbers?

The most obvious improvement in 2005 was the increase in the number of participating countries. The 2005 ICP collected prices for 146 countries in all regions of the world, including 48 countries in Africa, a continent that is often underrepresented in international statistical compilations. Meanwhile, China was a full participant for the first time, and India participated for the first time since 1985. The only major gaps in 2005 were in Central America, the Caribbean, and a number of small island economies.

The very first ICP, run jointly by the University of Pennsylvania and the United Nations Statistical Office, collected prices in only six economies: Hungary, India, Japan, Kenya, the United Kingdom, and the United States. Four other countries—Colombia, France, Germany, and Italy—collected data for 1970, and were included in the first ICP set of PPPs published in 1975. With successive rounds, the number of countries gradually increased, reaching 60 in the 1980 round, 64 in the 1985 round, and 118 in the 1993 round, the last before the 2005 round.

For most academic economists who use them, the results of the ICP are accessed through the Penn World Table (PWT), Mark 1 of which appeared in 1980. Mark 5 (Summers and Heston 1991), based on the 1985 round, contained results for 139 countries and covered the period from 1950 through 1988, though not with all years for all countries. Mark 5, described by Robert Summers and Alan Heston in an important article in the *Quarterly Journal of Economics* in 1991, was responsible for reigniting an academic interest in the empirical study of economic growth, and there is now a huge literature using these data as well as the later versions of PWT Mark 6 based on the 1993 round. Mark 7, using the 2005 ICP, is currently in preparation.

For countries not covered by the ICP, PPP exchange rates are "filled in" by estimating the price level based on each country's level of development. For example, in the examples just cited, the price level for India is 0.33 and for Ethiopia 0.25, so that for a country with per capita incomes between the two the price level would be somewhere around 0.30, and the PPP would be 30 percent of the market exchange rate. In practice, prediction of the price level can be improved by taking into account factors in addition to per capita GDP. However, each country is special in some way, and the predictions of a regression are never as good as using actual data.

In past rounds, when a country missed an ICP round, such as India in 1993, a guess could also be made by taking a previous PPP exchange rate, from the 1985 benchmark, and "updating" it from the relative rates of inflation in the United States and India. But the basket of goods in each country's consumer price index (CPI) is not the same as the international baskets used in the ICP. Nor are domestic CPIs always constructed to the same principles. So this, too, is only a rough and ready substitute for collecting the data.

In summary, one of the great strengths of the 2005 ICP was that very few imputations and updates were required because it covered all major countries together for the first time.

Better Linking of the World in 2005

An important improvement in the 2005 ICP was the way in which the price collection was organized. In the early days when only a few countries were participating, the ICP was carried out centrally—for example, at the University of Pennsylvania—but as the number of countries grew over time, price collection was regionally dispersed. Each region calculated its own set of regional PPPs relative to a regional base country, with PPPs for the world calculated at a final "linking" stage.

By the 1993 ICP, the dispersal had reached the point at which the central organization had become very weak. This situation caused many problems, and one of the main aims of the 2005 round was to develop a coherent global structure for the ICP. It was at this point, too, that the World Bank was brought into the ICP and became not only a major funder but also the home of the Global Office, which was responsible for the overall design of the project and for combining the regional estimates into a set of global PPPs. Each of the five regions had its own office, each maintained its own data collection machinery, and each calculated its own set of PPPs for the region. Meanwhile, Eurostat and the Organisation for Economic Co-operation and Development (OECD) were jointly conducting their own regular process of calculating PPP exchange rates for their countries, but in coordination with the ICP regions. For other regions, such as Africa, the 2005 ICP was a new regional effort with an emphasis on statistical capacity building that would not have taken place otherwise. At the center of the regions was the Global Office in the World Bank, which was responsible for coordination and for the final linking stage in which a global set of purchasing power parity exchange rates was calculated from the information submitted by the regions. The Global Office worked under the auspices of an executive board formed by the UN Statistical Commission and was provided with technical advice by the panel of experts who formed the Technical Advisory Group. Overall, the World Bank furnished the organizational and technical skills to make this enormous operation work.

What were the payoffs from this reorganization? What had gone wrong in the 1993 round, and how did the new structure help to remedy it?

The 1993 round was neither centrally coordinated nor controlled, and in the face of underfunding at the center it became a set of regional exercises carried out at different times, each of which collected data and calculated regional PPPs. A United Nations report circulated in 1998, commissioned jointly by the UN, the World Bank, and the International Monetary Fund, and commonly referred to (after its chairman) as the Ryten report, argued that the estimates from the 1993 ICP were not credible. It concluded, with faint praise, that the "ICP is a programme worth keeping but that its current condition, if little is done about it in terms of credibility, quality of output, and survival prospects, is poor" (United Nations 1998).

One credibility problem came from the way the global PPPs were constructed. Without adequate central coordination, not all of the planned links could be carried out, so that the global PPPs were calculated by linking the regions ex post. The linking was accomplished by using countries included in more than one region as bridges. This approach is conceptually similar to linking an old and a new time series from a price index through its value in a bridge year for which both price indexes are available. But spatial price indexes cover many countries simultaneously and do not have the natural ordering that comes in time series. This difference means that the results of linking two regions through a common country will depend on which country is used, a choice that needs to be made on principle and not by happenstance, as was the case in 1993. One particular concern is whether the linking country is special in some way—for example, whether it has patterns of consumption and relative prices that are somehow unusual, something that is often thought to be the case for Japan, which was one of the linking countries in 1993.

The results also depend on just how the linking is done. For example, one possibility is to use the PPP exchange rates between Japan and India, both in the Asia-Pacific region, and Japan and the United States, both in the OECD region, to derive a PPP exchange rate between the United States and India. A more detailed exercise can be done to convert the price of individual goods and services in India—rice, clothing, automobiles—from rupees into dollars using the price of each good in Japan as a bridge. As with the choice of bridge countries, the level of disaggregation will affect the final answer. The spirit of the ICP dictates that the linking be done at the finest level possible, but without central coordination this, too, was dictated by happenstance, and from the uncoordinated choices of each region.

China actively participated in 1993, at least to the extent of making a number of comparisons between cities in China and elsewhere, but those were never fully incorporated into the 1993 ICP. As a result, the PPPs for China in 1993 were based on data collected in 1986 to make a bilateral comparison with the United States, and then extrapolated forward to 1993.

In the 2005 ICP, the linking of the regions was centrally planned and implemented. Instead of relying on a few countries that happened to be in more than one region, a group of 18 "Ring" countries[1] was selected in advance, with two or more countries in each region. Each Ring country carried out a second round of price collection, relying on a common special list of more than 1,000 items. The Ring can be thought of as a separate, self-contained mini-ICP, although "mini" is relative, because the number of countries in the Ring was larger than the number of countries in the first round of the ICP. It generated a set of Ring PPPs, and beyond that a set of Ring prices—in common Ring currency—for each of the goods and services in the ICP. These prices, appropriately averaged, were then used to "glue" the regions together into a global set of accounts in which there was a purchasing power parity exchange rate for each country (relative to the U.S. dollar, which was the numeraire), but also a set of prices—in U.S. dollars—for each of the 155 goods and services ("basic headings") covered by the ICP.

The linking of the regions in the ICP 2005 was not without its problems. The most serious of these were not failings of the ICP itself, but came from the conceptual difficulties associated with all exercises of this kind, particularly when comparing countries whose patterns of consumption and relative prices are radically different. It is one thing to make PPP comparisons of France and Germany, or of Kenya and Tanzania, but it is on altogether shakier ground to compare Canada with Cameroon, Japan with Senegal, or Bolivia with Tajikistan. Such comparisons are difficult in theory and subject to a wide margin of uncertainty in practice. Indeed, this is something that anyone using the results of the ICP should always keep in mind.

That the linking procedures in the 2005 ICP were well documented and well thought out, even if not unchallengeable and certainly not the final word, made the 2005 round much more credible, more reliable, and safer than any of its predecessors.

More Precise Definitions of Goods and Services in 2005

With its better coordination, the Global Office was able in the 2005 ICP to provide the technical support needed to help each country collect prices in a coherent way and to check and edit the results for credibility and correctness. Such advances attract little attention from the outside, and any description is soporific both to write and to read, but their importance is hard to exaggerate. One of the criticisms in the 1998 UN report was that the ICP was very strong on the theory of the index numbers underlying the PPPs, but much weaker on giving statistical offices precise instructions on how to collect prices. That weakness was remedied in 2005.

In the 2005 ICP, each region developed its own list of prices—something that makes sense when countries are more similar within regions than across them. The Ring list was put together centrally by the Global Office, based on inputs from each region. This list is crucial in linking the world and plays a central role in determining the distance between poor and rich countries, and the extent of world inequality. The 2005 Ring included countries as disparate as Senegal and Cameroon in Africa, Japan and Estonia in the OECD, Jordan and Oman in Western Asia, and Malaysia and the Philippines in the Asia-Pacific.

Any list that runs across such countries has to satisfy two criteria that are often at odds. One criterion, in order to validate the international comparisons, is that the goods being priced are the same in all countries. This criterion calls for precise definitions of the goods in the list. If the definitions are too vague—for example, a "shirt" or a "family car"—the ICP runs the risk of pricing lower-quality items in the poorer countries, so that it is not comparing like with like and is underestimating (overestimating) price levels in poorer (richer) places.

The second criterion is that the goods in the list be widely consumed in each country, so that the goods are genuinely representative of what people buy.

The 1998 UN report noted the difficulty of satisfying both of these criteria at the same time, as well as the consequences for the credibility of the ICP, but it did not propose any solution. In any event, the 2005 ICP dealt with the issue by developing very precise lists, especially for the Ring list. For example, instead of wine, or even red wine, the item was "Bordeaux *supérieur*, with state certification of origin and quality, alcohol content 11–13 percent, vintage 2003 or 2004, with region and wine farmer listed." This level of detail clearly does very well according to the first criterion of pricing the same item everywhere. The second criterion was dealt with by asking enumerators to report whether the item was representative of local consumption, with the aim of down-weighting non-representative products. For a number of reasons, including the difficulty of defining *representative*, the reporting did not work in some regions. Nevertheless, it was clear that the 2005 ICP was a huge improvement on one of the two criteria, if not on both. Making both criteria work remains an active research area, and there will undoubtedly be further refinements in the 2011 ICP.

Continuing Progress on Other Issues

The ICP has long had a list of problem children known as "comparison-resistant" goods and services. Many of these are services for which it is traditionally difficult to define quantities—for example, how does one compare a hip replacement or brain surgery in Nairobi, Tokyo, and Buenos Aires?—and many relate to government activities—that is, the provision of education, defense, or administrative services by civil servants. These are all areas in which there are long-standing problems of measurement, even for domestic national accounts, and these problems tend to be even more difficult in cross-country comparisons. The handling of these issues occupies a large portion of the time of the technical committees that support the ICP. None of them is definitively solved, and none of the current solutions is above criticism. But there is also no doubt that progress is being made, and that better methods and better data collection are constantly being brought on line.

The ICP relies heavily on data it does *not* collect—the national accounts of the participating countries. Because the ICP collects data on *prices,* not on expenditures or quantities, when it reports levels of real income in international dollars in different countries, it is relying on local estimates of income in local currency and then converting them to international dollars by dividing by the price indexes from the ICP. Indeed, even the construction of the price indexes from the prices of individual goods and services relies on the local national accounts to provide the weights that indicate the relative importance of each category. Thus the ICP comparisons are only as good as the national accounts that go into them, over which the ICP has no direct control.

Put more positively, the ICP itself is an opportunity for the Global Office to help countries improve their national accounts. A good deal of this was done in 2005, and more is being done now in preparation for the 2011 ICP. Thus the ICP, like the Olympic Games, can leave a lasting legacy of better local infrastructure.

Credibility of the ICP Revisions

According to figure 1, the 2005 ICP made few revisions among the richer countries, and there were essentially no revisions among the Eurostat-OECD countries. These countries have their own PPP program, run by the European Union and OECD statistical offices, which calculates PPPs on an annual basis, and which was incorporated into the 2005 ICP. For those countries with annual monitoring, there is no possibility of the large revisions that can happen when a country has not been benchmarked for a dozen years or more. The large number of rich countries without revision illustrates the benefits of calculating PPPs at a higher frequency than is the case for much of the rest of the world.

Are the revisions elsewhere credible? Are the new PPPs more reliable than the old ones? Are the higher inequality measures better than the old ones?

The answer to all of these questions is certainly affirmative. As documented in the UN report, the 1993 ICP was in some disarray and had lost much of its credibility. This disarray was particularly evident in the way the regions were linked, and it is the linking that is responsible for establishing the PPPs in Africa and Asia relative to the United States and the other OECD countries. The linking in the 2005 ICP through the Ring countries was well thought out in advance and centrally and systematically implemented.

In addition to the improvements in the linking itself, there were many more countries to be linked. Most of the African countries had never been benchmarked, nor had China, and the Indian benchmark was more than 20 years out of date. Even if there had been no linking and the 2005 ICP had produced only a set of unconnected regional accounts, it would have been a huge advance in the supply of credible price information from all countries.

Of course, it is always good to keep in mind that international comparisons are difficult, especially between countries that are very different in their consumption patterns and in the structure of relative prices. No matter how accurate, detailed, and careful is the price collection by the ICP, comparisons of, say, Senegal and Japan, Brazil and Bangladesh, or the United States and Tajikistan are going to be rough at best. Indeed, a good starting point for anyone using the ICP results is to take such comparisons with a large grain of salt.

One central issue also identified in the UN report was how to resolve the conflict between, on the one hand, wanting to measure the same goods in different places and, on the other, ensuring that the goods whose prices were being measured were representative of consumption in each country. In the 2005 ICP, this conflict was resolved in favor of ensuring that the items were closely comparable. If the list of such items contains many items that are common in rich countries but rare and expensive in poor countries, it is possible that linking through the Ring would exaggerate the difference in prices between poor and rich countries, and this exaggeration would contribute to an overstatement of global inequality.

However, work by this author (Deaton 2010) failed to yield much evidence of this effect in the details of the Ring comparison in the 2005 ICP, or at least that the effect contributed very much to the widening of the gap between rich and poor countries. Instead, the main source of uncertainty is a more fundamental one—because of the different relative prices and different weights, there is a wide range of reasonable ways of calculating PPPs. This issue cannot be resolved by better measurement, although research can certainly build on what has been done so far in order to suggest new measurement. In the meantime, transparency about methods and about data is of the greatest importance. To aid this, the Global Office has provided data sets to researchers that allow methodologies to be compared, and this analysis will surely guide further improvements in the 2011 ICP and beyond.

NOTE

1. This group included the economy of Hong Kong SAR, China.

REFERENCES

Commission of the European Communities, International Monetary Fund, Organisation for Economic Co-operation and Development, United Nations, and World Bank. 2008. *System of National Accounts 2008*. http://unstats.un.org/unsd/nationalaccount/SNA2008.pdf.

Deaton, Angus. 2010. "Price Indexes, Inequality, and the Measurement of World Poverty." *American Economic Review* 100 (1): 5–34.

Milanović, Branko. 2009. "Global Inequality Recalculated: The Effect of New PPP Estimates on Global Inequality." Policy Research Paper 5061, World Bank, Washington, DC, September.

Summers, Robert, and Alan Heston. 1991. "The Penn World Table (Mark 5): An Expanded Set of International Comparisons, 1950–1988." *Quarterly Journal of Economics* 106 (2): 327–68.

United Nations. 1998. "Evaluation of the International Comparison Program." UN Economic and Social Council, E/CN.3/1999/8. http://unstats.un.org/unsd/methods/icp/8-e.pdf.

World Bank. 2007. *World Development Indicators 2007*. Washington, DC: World Bank. http://data.worldbank.org/data-catalog/world-development-indicators.

———. 2008. *World Development Indicators 2008*. Washington, DC: World Bank. http://data.worldbank.org/data-catalog/world-development-indicators.

CHAPTER 1

The Framework of the International Comparison Program

D. S. Prasada Rao

A global statistical initiative, the International Comparison Program (ICP) collects comparative price data and then estimates the purchasing power parities (PPPs) of the currencies of the world's economies.[1] Conducted under the auspices of the United Nations Statistical Commission (UNSC), the program is designed to meet the data needs of the international community of government policy makers, international organizations, multinational enterprises, and researchers.[2] Worldwide, there is considerable demand for data on internationally comparable national income aggregates, including gross domestic product (GDP), per capita income, and government expenditures on health, education, defense, and investment. In a world that is increasingly integrated economically, interest is high in the relative size, structure, and performance of nations based on a comparative analysis of real incomes and growth performance. Meanwhile, serious debates are under way on the effects of globalization on the welfare of the global society as reflected in real incomes and global inequality. The evidence on global inequality is patchy at best. The current research in the area relies heavily on the availability of reliable real income measures, together with information on the distribution of income at the national level.

Country-specific data are regularly produced and disseminated by the national statistical offices. However, the direct comparability of national data is limited because such data are usually expressed in the respective national currency units. The incomparability of published data on national aggregates also stems from differences in price levels, which imply the differential purchasing powers of currencies. For example, all countries in the Euro Area produce their national accounts aggregates in euros, but such figures are not directly comparable because there are marked differences in price levels. For several decades, it was standard practice to use market exchange rates in converting national aggregates, and this practice was adopted by major international organizations as well. However, since the seminal work of Gilbert and Kravis (1954) the reliance on market exchange rates for converting national aggregates has lessened, and exchange rates are gradually being replaced by the purchasing power parities of currencies.

The International Comparison Program[3] began in 1968 as a small research project conducted by Prof. Irving Kravis at the University of Pennsylvania under the auspices of the UNSC. Gradually, the project, which covered 10 countries in its first phase, grew to its most recent exercise, the 2005 ICP, which covered 146 countries, accounting for 95 percent of the world's population and 98 percent of the world's gross domestic product in nominal terms. Thus the general framework for undertaking these cross-country comparisons has been evolving over 40 years, and the methods for compilation of PPPs are being continually refined.

A brief review of the principal finding of the 2005 round of the ICP confirms the significance of the project.[4] In PPP terms, the size of the world economy in 2005, as measured by the world GDP, was US$55 trillion, which was 24 percent larger than GDP converted to U.S. dollars using market exchange rates. According to the ICP estimates of PPPs for 2005, the United States is the largest economy in the world with a world share of 22.5 percent. It is followed by China with 9.7 percent and Japan with 7.0 percent. When these shares are computed using exchange rates, they are 27.9 percent for the United States, followed by 10.3 percent for Japan, 6.3 percent for Germany, and 5.1 percent for both China and the United Kingdom. It is obvious that the sizes of the economies do not necessarily correspond with the living standards enjoyed in different countries.

In 2005 the economies with the highest per capita incomes (per capita GDP) were Luxembourg at 780 percent of the world average, followed by Qatar at 765 percent, Norway at 530 percent, Brunei Darussalam at 529 percent, and Kuwait at 501 percent. The per capita income of the United States was only 465 percent of the world average. By contrast, the poorest country was the Democratic Republic of Congo with a per capita GDP of US$264 (in PPP terms), which was 6.6 percent of the world average. However, the *per capita actual individual consumption*[5] used in the ICP provides a more accurate measure of the current welfare enjoyed by people in different countries. Indeed, the ICP revealed some interesting results. Luxembourg was still ranked first in terms of actual individual consumption (553 percent of the world average). However, on the basis of this measure the United States was a close second with 525 percent of the world average. Even more interesting was Qatar, where the level of actual consumption was only 207 percent compared with 765 percent in per capita GDP terms. Similar sizes of actual consumption were revealed for Kuwait and Brunei Darussalam. A more complete overview of the results is presented in chapter 19 of this volume.

On the flip side of income comparisons data was the information on the relative price levels in different countries. Inferences on price levels were drawn through a comparison of the PPPs from the ICP and the corresponding exchange rates of currencies. Price level indexes[6] (PLIs) were generally low for the poorer countries, and they were around and above unity for high-income countries. For example, at the GDP level the PLI for India was 41 percent of the world level compared with Luxembourg, which had a PLI of 142 percent. These PLIs varied across countries belonging to different income groups and also across different aggregates. For example, for the machinery and equipment aggregate the PLI for India was 75 percent of the world level, whereas it was about 102 percent for Luxembourg.

Measures of real income are a useful source of data for the study of inequality in the distribution of income worldwide. Recent work by Milanović (2009) has shown that world inequality as measured by the Gini coefficient was 0.71[7] in 2005 compared with 0.66 in 2002. This level of inequality is far greater than that observed in countries with the most inequality. Results reported by Chen and Ravallion (2010) based on the 2005 ICP results indicate that the world is poorer than was previously thought. The number of poor under an international poverty line approximately equal to US$1 per day in 1993 terms is now considered to be about 1.5 billion compared with the 1 billion estimated by relying on previous data on real incomes based in turn on extrapolations from the 1996 round of the ICP.[8]

The results from the 2005 ICP just discussed reinforce the significant role of the ICP in providing internationally comparable economic aggregates. There is little doubt about the significance of and the importance attached to the findings of the 2005 ICP. But to use these results effectively, one must understand the process and methods employed in the compilation of the ICP results. The main objective of this chapter is to provide an overview of the framework of the ICP and briefly describe the concepts and methods employed. The chapters that follow are designed to provide the reader with details of the actual procedures used in implementation of the ICP at the regional and global levels.

This chapter is organized as follows. Section 1.1 describes the national accounts concepts that underpin the ICP, and it highlights the decomposition of value aggregates into price and volume/quantity components. The pivotal concept of purchasing power parities and related measures such as price level indexes and real expenditures are discussed in section 1.2. Because the ICP strives to provide measures of PPPs of currencies, section 1.3 presents the framework used for price comparisons across countries. Various aspects of price surveys, data validation, and the methods used in the process of aggregating the price data are the main elements of this section. Section 1.4 then focuses on the regionalization of the ICP and the approach used in deriving global comparisons by linking regional comparisons. The chapter ends with concluding comments.

1.1 National Accounts as a Basis for the ICP

The principal objective of the ICP is to provide internationally comparable data on suitable measures of economic activity and incomes in different countries. The United Nations and other international organizations such as the Organisation for Economic Co-operation and Development (OECD) and Eurostat, the statistical office of the European Union, have been actively engaged in setting up a framework to measure economic activity. The current best practice in economic measurement is the *System of National Accounts 1993* (SNA93)[9] published by the Commission of the European Communities et al. (1993). It forms the basis for the ICP.

The gross domestic product is the most commonly used measure of economic activity.[10] Within the framework of national accounts, GDP can be measured using three different methods: the production measure, the income measure, and the expenditure measure. For the purpose of international comparisons, the focus has always been on the production and expenditure measures. The reason for this focus is mainly operational: it is difficult to gather the data needed to compare income measures across countries.

On the expenditure side, GDP is expressed as the sum of (1) final consumption by households; (2) government expenditure; (3) gross fixed capital formation; and (4) exports net of imports. Because the basic building blocks are expenditures within different categories, it is feasible to collect data on the prices paid by the purchasers associated with different transactions, which can then be used in making price comparisons across countries. Since its inception, the ICP has based all of its comparisons on data from the expenditure side.

GDP can equivalently be derived from the production side of the national accounts—that is, as the value of gross output less intermediate consumption plus taxes less subsidies. The production approach provides the most direct measure of GDP, and it is the main approach used by many countries because output measures are available through enterprise surveys and so forth. International comparisons on the production side are often referred to as the industry-of-origin approach to international comparisons.[11]

In obtaining measures of economic activity and well-being, it is more appropriate to focus on the expenditure approach to the measurement of GDP. Using this approach, one could examine the role of government expenditures, and in particular the level of government expenditures in the areas of health and education. By contrast, the production side of GDP and the industry-of-origin approaches are useful in comparing economic performance in different countries and by different industries. Using sectoral data, one would find it possible to measure and compare productivity by different industries and sectors of the economy. Operationally, though, it is more difficult to collect the data necessary for undertaking international comparisons on the production side.[12]

Structure and Components of GDP from the Expenditure Side

GDP consists of the following main components. In particular, GDP is equal to

individual consumption expenditure by households +
individual consumption expenditure by nonprofit institutions serving households (NPISH) +
government expenditure (consisting of individual consumption expenditure by government) +
collective consumption expenditure by government +
gross fixed capital formation +
changes in inventories and net acquisitions of valuables +
balance of exports and imports.

For the purpose of the ICP, GDP is then divided into 13 major *categories*, which are further subdivided into 43 *groups*. An example of a category is "food and nonalcoholic beverages," which is divided further into two groups: "food" and "nonalcoholic beverages." The category "clothing and footwear" is similarly split into two groups. Groups are then broken into classes—for example, the food group contains nine classes that include bread and cereals, meat, fish, and so forth. Each of these classes is then divided into basic headings—for example, rice is a basic heading in the bread and cereals class.

Basic Headings

The basic heading (BH) is a pivotal concept used in the ICP. It is the lowest level of aggregation within the national accounts at which expenditure and expenditure share data are available. For example, if *rice* is a basic heading, then national accounts data would show the total expenditure on the rice basic heading. However, if different kinds of rice (such as long grain rice and short grain rice with a percentage of broken rice) belong to the rice basic heading, then no expenditure or quantity data are available at the item level, although price data can be collected for each of the rice items in countries in which they are sold. Therefore, basic headings are important from the perspective of the aggregation of price data (this aspect of aggregation is discussed further in section 1.3).

In the 2005 ICP, a total of 155 basic headings were placed in categories. Of the total, 110 basic headings fell into the aggregate "individual consumption expenditure by households." By contrast, only 12 basic headings fell into the "gross fixed capital formation" aggregate. The ICP essentially uses a pyramid approach, as illustrated in figure 1.1. Price data for different items are aggregated to yield price comparisons at the BH level, which are then aggregated upward to yield price comparisons for different commodity groups, for broad categories, for the main components of GDP, and, at the end, for GDP as a whole. Aggregation above the BH level makes use of the weights data available from the national accounts.

FIGURE 1.1 Hierarchical Approach to ICP 2005

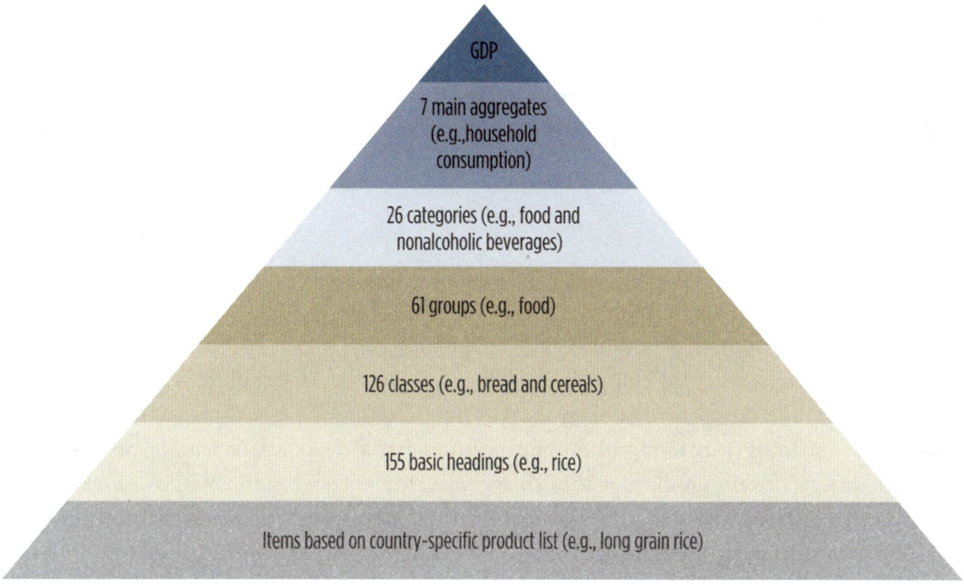

Source: ICP 2005.

The Basic Index Number Problem: Decomposition of Value Aggregates

The main objective of the ICP is to compile national income aggregates from the expenditure side in an internationally comparable form expressed in the same currency unit and also adjusted for price level differences. For example, consider the aggregate "food consumption." Let the aggregate be based on the consumption of a range of food items. Let N be the number of commodities within the food category, and let p_{ij} and q_{ij}, respectively, denote the price and quantity of the i-th commodity in j-th country.[13] Then the food consumption expenditure aggregate for country j, E_j, is given by

$$E_j = \sum_{i=1}^{N} p_{ij} q_{ij}. \tag{1.1}$$

Typically, the price data are expressed in the currency unit of country j, and price levels vary across counties. The main problem is to decompose the value or expenditure aggregate in (1.1) into a price level component P_j and a quantity or volume component Q_j so that

$$E_j = P_j \cdot Q_j. \tag{1.2}$$

The price level component, P_j, may be interpreted as a PPP[14] of currency j expressed in terms of the currency of a reference or numeraire country. Suppose country 1 is selected as numeraire, and so $P_1 = 1$. Then Q_j can be interpreted as the real expenditure or the volume of food consumption in country j. From equation (1.2) it can be seen that

$$\frac{E_j}{P_j} = \text{expenditure expressed in reference currency units} = Q_j.$$

Once the volumes or real expenditures are obtained, then the relative expenditure comparisons may be made either through the ratio Q_j/Q_k comparing the real expenditure on food in countries j and k or through country shares, computed as

$$\frac{Q_j}{\sum_{k=1}^{C} Q_k} \tag{1.3}$$

where C is the total number of countries in the comparison.

The steps involved in the compilation of P_j and Q_j are the subject of this chapter and chapters 4, 5, and 6. The survey methodology used in the collection of price data and the aggregation methods for obtaining price level and volume measures vary a great deal, depending on the type of aggregate used. If certain products within an aggregate are not sold in the market—for example, hospital services in a country may be provided by the government—it is difficult to observe the price and quantities of the various types of hospital services provided. This situation calls for a different approach, which is discussed in chapter 16.

Sources of Price and Expenditure Data

Although the conceptual framework of the ICP is provided by the SNA and national accounts aggregates from the expenditure side, the sources of data for the decomposition discussed in the previous section and shown in equations (1.2) and (1.3) are quite different. The national accounts, which are published on an annual and quarterly basis in almost all countries, provide data only on the expenditure values, E_j, for different aggregates. These are typically expressed in current prices or prices in the year of the publication or in constant prices where the aggregates are expressed using prices in a fixed base year. Expenditure aggregates at current prices are available from the national accounts publications. By contrast, national accounts do not contain any price data. Therefore, the data needed for price comparisons within the ICP must be compiled from a completely different source, and usually these are through carefully planned and executed price surveys in different countries.

The main conclusion to be drawn from this discussion is that the quality of international comparisons depends on the quality of price data as well as that of the published national accounts data. In assessing the plausibility of the international comparison results, it is important that one examine both of these sources carefully in order to identify the main source of any problem.

1.2 Conceptual Framework of the ICP

The ICP focuses mainly on providing estimates of the three core measures—PPPs, price level indexes, and measures of real and nominal expenditures—needed to conduct international comparisons of real incomes and standards of living. The first and foremost is the PPPs of the currencies of different countries. These PPPs are used in turn to derive measures of price levels in different countries. As explained earlier, PPPs are used in converting expenditure data from national accounts expressed in respective country currency units into real expenditures or volumes of expenditures that are directly comparable across countries. These three measures are elaborated further in the sections that follow.

Purchasing Power Parities

The main step involved in international comparisons is the conversion of national income aggregates expressed in national currency units into a common currency unit. Such a conversion makes it possible to compare the aggregates across countries, and one should also be able to sum them across countries or regions and examine the country shares within the global economy. The simplest method and one that was followed for a long time was the use of market exchange rates to convert national aggregates. Conversion using exchange rates makes it possible to compare and aggregate across countries, but the resulting aggregates are not very meaningful because exchange rate conversion does not necessarily account for price level differences. It is now well recognized that exchange rates are volatile, reflecting sizable movements of capital across countries. The exchange rates are less likely to refer to the actual price levels in different countries and the purchasing power of the currencies.[15] Therefore, PPPs are used in the place of exchange rates.

A working definition of a PPP is that it represents *the number of currency units required to purchase the amounts of goods and services equivalent to what can be bought with one unit of the currency unit of the base or reference or numeraire country*. This simple but effective definition of a PPP has several key elements. The first element is to determine the number of currency units of a given country that have the same purchasing power as one unit of the currency of another country. Index number methods in conjunction with data on prices paid by consumers in different countries are used in determining the purchasing power. For example, a PPP of 13.5 Indian rupees (Rs) per U.S. dollar for the basic heading rice means that the quantity of a basket of different varieties of rice that can be bought for one U.S. dollar costs 13.5 Indian rupees at the prices prevailing in India.[16] Thus Rs 13.5 represents the PPP for the commodity rice. An implication is that the PPP can vary, depending on the commodity or commodity group being considered.

The second element is that PPPs are measured relative to a numeraire or reference currency unit. In the example just given, the U.S. dollar is used as the *numeraire currency*—that is, the currency in which PPPs and real expenditures in different countries are expressed. The numeraire is usually an actual currency such as the U.S. dollar, but it can also be a world average currency or regional average currency. A commonsense requirement would be that international comparisons and relative levels of income or GDP not be affected by the choice of the reference currency.

A simple and celebrated example of a PPP is the Big Mac index (published in *The Economist* since 1986). It measures PPPs based on just a single item, McDonald's Big Mac, and its prices in different countries. According to the index,[17] the price of a Big Mac in the United States is US$3.73, in Australia $A 4.35, and in Japan ¥320. These prices imply PPPs of $A 1.17 and ¥85.79 per U.S. dollar. An interesting feature is that the PPP for Japanese yen per Australian dollar can be either directly computed as the ratio of ¥320 to $A4.35, which is equal to ¥73.56, or indirectly obtained as the ratio of the PPPs of the Japanese yen (JY) and the Australian dollar (AUD), both expressed with respect to the U.S. dollar as

$$PPP_{JY,AUD} = \frac{PPP_{JY,USD}}{PPP_{AUD,USD}} = \frac{85.79}{1.17} = ¥73.56.$$

This *transitivity property* of PPPs is automatically satisfied when only one commodity is included in the basket of goods and services used for the PPP computation. However, more complex methods are required when more goods and services are included. Chapters 4, 5, and 6 of this volume describe the index number methods used in the computation of PPPs. The property of transitivity is more formally defined in section 1.3.

It is important to note that PPPs are similar to the price index numbers computed over space—that is, across countries or regions within a country—and very similar to the price index numbers over time. But there are two important differences. First, the magnitude of a PPP has the currency dimension, and therefore it cannot be readily interpreted as a price index. Reverting to the example of PPPs based on the Big Mac index, a PPP of ¥85.79 per U.S. dollar simply says that what a consumer can buy for one U.S. dollar requires 85.79 Japanese yen. Can one infer the price level from this? It would be possible only if the currency unit were the same in both countries (the problem of measuring price level is considered shortly). The second difference is that price comparisons over time are undertaken in a sequence determined by chronological order. However, such sequencing is not possible where cross-country comparisons are concerned. For this reason, it is necessary to ensure that the PPPs satisfy the transitivity property.

What are the uses of PPPs? Purchasing power parities are gradually replacing market exchange rates as the conversion factors used to make international comparisons of the real incomes, price levels, and economic performances of countries. The use of PPPs is in fact essential to make real GDP comparisons—that is, comparisons of the underlying volume of goods and services in different countries. There is an exact parallel here between the use of PPP exchange rates for GDP comparisons between countries at a given point in time and the use of constant prices in comparisons of GDP for a given country over time. In both cases, comparisons are impossible to interpret unless differences in the underlying volumes are separated from differences in prices. The spectacular growth in the use of PPPs for international economic analysis largely stems from the increased availability of PPP data from the World Bank through its International Comparison Program and also from the extrapolated series made available through the Penn World Table (PWT). The 2005 ICP covered 146 countries, including most of Africa, China for the first time, and India for the first time since its last participation in 1985. The PWT, constructed and made popular by Summers and Heston (1991) and Heston, Summers, and Aten (2009), provides extrapolated PPPs for over 170 countries covering the period 1970–2005.[18]

The World Bank's flagship publication *World Development Indicators* makes use of extrapolated PPPs and presents cross-country real income data (World Bank 2011).[19] The Bank has also been using PPPs from the ICP to measure regional and global poverty; it provides estimates of the number of people whose income/expenditure is below US$1 a day or $2 a day. Chen and Ravallion (2010) provide estimates of global poverty based on the recent 2005 ICP PPP data. They find that poverty is much worse than what was thought before release of the latest PPP data. Chapters 20 and 21 of this volume describe how PPPs from the ICP are used in the measurement of regional and global inequality and poverty.[20]

The ICP's PPPs have gained prominence from their use in the Human Development Index (HDI) by the United Nations Development Programme (UNDP). The HDI uses PPPs in the measurement of real per capita GDP, which is one of the three components of the HDI. In recent years, large countries such as India have begun to measure the HDI at the state and district levels. Thus PPPs are also being used for interregional price comparisons within a country.

The most important use of PPPs is in measuring the real GDP of countries, thereby making it possible to rank countries by their relative size as well as by their real per capita GDP. Total and per capita GDP converted to a common currency using PPP exchange rates also provide the basis for a range of key analytic statistics such as CO^2 emissions or energy consumption per unit of GDP. The ICP produces PPPs not only at the GDP level but also for lower-level aggregates such as private consumption, government consumption, and investment. For example, government expenditures on health and education expressed in a common currency unit using PPPs are often used by institutions such as the World Health Organization (WHO) and the United Nations

Educational, Scientific and Cultural Organization (UNESCO). Per capita gross fixed investment, per capita government collective expenditures, and per capita actual individual consumption of households are widely used in analyzing economic growth, the role of government, and living standards, respectively.

Given the long list of uses of PPPs, one might wonder whether there is a role for exchange rates in international economic analysis. Market exchange rates are useful in determining whether a country's exports can meet the costs of imports, in calculating the value of the current account balance in the balance of payments, and in comparing share prices. In addition, the traditional analysis of growth in GDP at constant prices, productivity growth, domestic inflation, and the structure of GDP within a country are best based on domestic data in which the value aggregates are all expressed in domestic currency units. For these purposes, it is not necessary to convert the value aggregates using PPPs.

Finally, it is also useful to note the purchasing power parity theory put forth by Gustav Cassel (1918), which states that if all goods and services were traded freely without barriers, then the purchasing power of currencies would coincide with the market exchange rates. This theory assumes that exchange rates are determined only by the demand for currencies to finance trade in goods and services. But this is clearly not the case; foreign currencies are also purchased for tourism, for folio and direct investment, and in expectation of speculative gains from movements in exchange rates. Purchases of currencies in order to finance trade may often be a relatively small part of the total volume of currency transactions. Market exchange rates do not tend to converge toward PPPs nor PPPs toward exchange rates, and the purchasing power parity theory of equilibrium exchange rates has long been discarded. As a result, there is a definite need for reliable PPPs for converting aggregates into common currency units.

Measuring Price Level

An ICP concept that matches PPPs in importance is the price level in a country, which is commonly measured by the price level index or PLI. As noted earlier, a PPP indicates the number of currency units that have the same purchasing power as one unit of a reference currency. It is not possible to make any inferences about the price level in the country concerned, but people do like to know which countries have lower prices and for what commodity categories. The general perception is that developing countries are relatively cheaper than more developed countries.

A measure of price level in a given country for a basket of goods and services is the ratio of the PPP for a particular basket to the market exchange rate for the currency. Thus the price level index for country j with respect to a commodity group is given by

$$PLI_j = \frac{PPP_j}{XR_j} \cdot 100 \tag{1.4}$$

where XR_j is the exchange rate of the currency of country j. For example, the 2005 ICP found that the PPP for the British pound[21] was US$1.00 = £0.65, where the exchange rate, XR, was US$1.00 = £0.55. Thus if a tourist from the United States exchanges $10 for £5.5 at a bank, he or she would have to spend £6.5 to buy what could be bought using $10.[22] This means that the price level index using equation (1.4) is equal to 118, which indicates that prices in the United Kingdom are 18 percent higher than those in the United States. Table 1.1 shows the PPPs, exchange rates, and price levels at the GDP level, which means that all the goods and services in all categories form the basket.

TABLE 1.1 PPPs, Exchange Rates, and Price Level Indexes: Selected Countries, ICP 2005

Country	*PPPs* (US$ = 1.00)	XR_j (US$ = 1.00)	PLI_j (US = 100)	PLI_j (world = 100)
Australia	1.39	1.31	106	132
Germany	0.89	0.80	111	138
Switzerland	9.24	7.46	140	174
India	14.67	44.10	33	41
China	3.45	8.18	42	52
Vietnam	4,712.69	15,858.90	30	37
Egypt, Arab. Rep.	1.62	5.78	28	35
Kenya	9.52	75.55	39	48
Ethiopia	2.25	8.67	26	32
South Africa	3.87	6.36	61	76
United States	1.00	1.00	100	124

Source: World Bank 2008, summary table and table 2.

Several features of table 1.1 are worth noting. The first feature is that the PLI for the United States defined when the U.S. dollar is the numeraire currency is equal to 100. Relative to that, countries in Europe appear to have higher PLIs, with Switzerland 40 percent above the price level of the United States. By contrast, all the developing countries have PLIs of less than 50 percent, except for South Africa, which has a PLI of 61. From the table, a negative relationship between income level and the PLI may be postulated. There is a lot of research explaining why the national price levels exhibit this type of relationship. Of particular importance is the work of Kravis and Lipsey (1983), Clague (1988), and Bergstrand (1996). The main conclusion is that price level differences are induced by differences in the prices for tradable and nontradable goods, as well as the productivity level differences between developed and developing countries.

The second feature of table 1.1 worth noting is that when the PLI for India is 33 with the United States set at 100, it is difficult to know whether prices in India are low or prices in the United States are high. Column 3 of table 1.1 provides no answer. And it is for this reason that the ICP often reports PLIs relative to a world average level of 100.[23] From the last column, it is clear that the U.S. prices are themselves above the world average by 24 percent and that the Indian price level is now 41 percent of the world average.

In conclusion, the PLI is an important concept that has significant practical relevance. Obviously, PLIs for the same country vary across different commodity groups. It is usually true that consumption goods are cheaper in developing countries, which is what the average tourist experiences during visits to Africa or South Asia. However, investment goods such as machinery and equipment are usually a lot more expensive than consumption goods or the whole of the GDP. For example, Bhutan has a PLI of 114 for machinery and equipment compared with a PLI of 44 for GDP. The respective figures for Vietnam are 86 and 37 and for the Democratic Republic of Congo 153 and 63. These PLIs illustrate the importance of PLI data for different commodity groups because policy makers need to ensure that investment goods are more cheaply available.

Real and Nominal Expenditures

The main focus of the ICP is on the expenditure side of GDP. Therefore, all the aggregates of interest relate to expenditures associated with certain commodity groups. The data available from the national accounts of countries are in the form of expenditures expressed in national currency units. These are denoted by E_j as defined in equation (1.1). Obviously, these E_j's are not comparable across countries. In this case, it is necessary to convert them into common currency units. The nominal expenditure aggregates are obtained by converting the value aggregates in national currency units using exchange rates. Let NE_j represent nominal expenditures, and then

$$(1.5) \qquad NE_j = \frac{E_j}{XR_j} = \frac{\sum_{i=1}^{N} p_{ij} q_{ij}}{XR_j}.$$

The term *nominal* is used in describing this aggregate because NE_j does not account for price level differences.

The real expenditures, which are also referred to as *volumes* for any expenditure category, are simply the expenditures for the category in national currency units converted using the PPPs for the category. Therefore, the volumes denoted by Q_j are given by

$$(1.6) \qquad Q_j = \text{real expenditure} = \frac{E_j}{PPP_j} = \frac{\sum_{i=1}^{N} p_{ij} q_{ij}}{PPP_j}.$$

The real value aggregate in (1.6) converts the national currency value aggregate into a reference or numeraire currency after adjusting price level differences using the PPPs.

1.3 Methodological Framework for Price Comparisons

The ICP is designed to yield reliable global comparisons of prices and real expenditures. As it has evolved over the last four decades, the ICP has become increasingly regionalized for reasons that will become clearer in this section. The 2005 ICP covered 146 countries from different regions of the world and at different levels of development. The ICP has devised an approach in which PPP computations and real expenditure comparisons are first undertaken at the regional level, where the items used in consumption are likely to have significant overlaps and the price structures in these countries are likely to be similar. The regional comparisons are then linked through the additional data collected for a set of countries selected from different regions—the so-called Ring countries—and for a single list of items. The additional price data are then used to link regional comparisons to yield global comparisons.

The general architecture of global comparisons is discussed in section 1.4. This section provides a brief description of the ICP methodology for compiling PPPs and real expenditures at the regional level. As mentioned in section 1.1, price data and national incomes data are the two key inputs for this process. The national accounts framework and the nature of data from national agencies are discussed further in chapter 3. The methods and procedures employed in the collection of suitable price data and some basic principles that underpin the choice of the methods used in aggregating the price data are the main elements of this section. It begins by explaining the structure of the ICP at the regional level. It then turns to identification of the product lists and important considerations such as the *comparability*, *representativeness*, and *importance* of the products and the need to maintain consistency between national accounts. Price surveys for *comparison-resistant services* and special product categories such as machinery and equipment are also briefly described. The section concludes with an overview of the methodological considerations for the compilation of PPPs, including the *transitivity*, *base invariance*, *characteristicity*, and *additivity* properties of multilateral comparisons.

Structure of ICP Comparisons

The ICP has adopted a pyramid approach (see figure 1.1) to building up PPPs at various levels. Following on from the definition of a PPP and given that a PPP based on a single item of consumption is simply the ratio of prices,[24] the ICP starts with the price data at the item level. These price data are combined to yield PPPs at the basic heading level, where a basic heading is identified as the lowest-level aggregate for which information on expenditure is available from the national accounts. The ICP has 155 basic headings. Some examples of basic headings are rice; lamb, mutton, and goat; eggs and egg-based products; coffee, tea, and cocoa; small electric household appliances; motor cars; passenger transport by railway; newspapers, books, and stationery; pharmaceutical products; compensation of employees in the health sector; general-purpose machinery; and residential buildings.[25] At the first stage, the ICP compiles PPPs for each of the 155 basic headings.[26] The index number methods used in deriving basic heading PPPs are discussed in chapter 4.

The 155 basic headings are combined to form 126 classes. The main aggregation is in the food and nonalcoholic beverages area where 29 basic headings are grouped to form 11 classes. For example, the basic headings fresh milk, preserved milk and other milk products, cheese, and eggs and egg-based products are combined to form the class milk, cheese, and eggs. These classes are designed to provide PPPs useful for researchers who may wish to reweight them to derive PPPs for specific applications.[27] For example, the BH-level PPPs are combined with expenditure patterns of the poor in deriving poverty PPPs. The methodology used for this purpose is elaborated in chapter 21.

The 126 classes are then combined to form 61 broad commodity groups such as food, clothing and footwear, health, transport, construction, and machinery and equipment. For example, the group food is made up of nine classes, which include bread and cereals; meat; fish and seafood; milk, cheese, and eggs; oils and fats; fruit; vegetables; sugar, jam, honey, chocolate, and confectionery; and food products not elsewhere classified.

Finally, the 61 groups are aggregated into 26 categories, which are listed in table 1.2. This list is indeed important because it represents the level of aggregation at which the PPP results from the ICP are actually published.[28]

The methods used to compute PPPs at the BH level and at higher levels of aggregation differ because of the nature of the data available at those levels. These are discussed further in section 1.3.

Collection of Price Data

Price data are the crucial input for PPP compilation within the ICP. The meaningfulness of the final PPPs from the ICP critically depends on the accuracy, reliability, and representativeness of the price data collected. A few of the important considerations involved in the collection of price data are discussed in this section.

TABLE 1.2 Main Aggregates Used in the ICP

Main aggregates	No. of basic headings
Individual consumption expenditure by households	*110*
01 Food and nonalcoholic beverages	29
02 Alcoholic beverages, tobacco, and narcotics	5
03 Clothing and footwear	5
04 Housing, water, electricity, gas, and other fuels	7
05 Furnishings, household equipment, and maintenance	13
06 Health	7
07 Transport	13
08 Communication	3
09 Recreation and culture	13
10 Education	1
11 Restaurants and hotels	2
12 Miscellaneous goods and services	10
13 Net purchases abroad	2
Individual consumption expenditure by NPISH	*1*
Individual consumption expenditure by government	*21*
01 Housing	1
02 Health	12
03 Recreation and culture	1
04 Education	6
05 Social protection	1
Collective consumption expenditure by government	*5*
Gross fixed capital formation	*12*
01 Machinery and equipment	8
02 Construction	3
03 Other products	1
Change in inventories and acquisitions less disposals of valuables	*4*
01 Change in inventories	2
02 Acquisitions less disposals of valuables	2
Balance of exports and imports	*2*
GDP	*155*

Source: World Bank 2008, appendix C.
Note: NPISH = nonprofit institutions serving households.

Consistency with National Accounts Data

Because PPPs are price level measures that are in turn used in deriving estimates of real expenditures and volumes, it is important that the price data used in the ICP are consistent with the national accounts notion of the aggregates under consideration. Equations (1.1) and (1.2) applied to a commodity aggregate such as food would be

$$E_j^{food} = \sum_{i \in food} p_{ij} q_{ij} = P_j^{food} \cdot Q_j^{food}. \tag{1.7}$$

Equation (1.7) implies that the food value aggregate in country *j* is determined by the prices and quantities of items that belong to the food group in country *j*. However, international comparisons are made using a common list of items priced in different countries within a region. If the product list in the ICP is significantly different from the product list of the country, then there is a serious mismatch between the ICP and the national accounts data that underpin the expenditure data. Therefore, a degree of consistency must be maintained between the product list of the ICP and the items used in arriving at the national income aggregates at the country level. The consistency requirement has implications for the process involved in identifying and preparing the product list used in the price surveys. In deciding on the product list for a particular aggregate, one must examine the coverage of the particular aggregate in national accounts and then identify the products for inclusion in the list. For example, if the aggregate concerned is equipment, the products identified must relate to the types of equipment used in deriving the expenditure aggregates.

Unless a reasonable degree of consistency between the national accounts coverage and the ICP item lists is maintained, the PPPs and real expenditures from the ICP will be less meaningful for comparative purposes.

Product Lists for Price Surveys

A critical first step in the ICP that has far-reaching implications for deriving PPPs is the preparation of the item or product list for use with the price surveys. Within the ICP, these lists are prepared separately for the individual consumption expenditure by households, individual consumption expenditure by government, and gross fixed capital formation components of GDP. No price data are collected for imports and exports because exchange rates are used as PPPs for the balance of trade component of GDP.[29]

The regionalized approach, which is discussed further in section 1.4, has reduced the need to prepare a global list of products to be priced by all participating countries.[30] Because the regions are more homogeneous and are more likely to have similar tastes and preferences, it is easier to identify consumption items that are *comparable* across countries and at the same time *representative*. The process is much simpler in some regions such as the Eurostat-OECD—countries in this group are at a similar level of development. Furthermore, most of the countries in this group are in Europe, making it possible to identify products for price surveys. However, the process is more complex when diverse regions such as the Asia-Pacific are considered. In the 2005 ICP, the process of determining the product lists for the Asia-Pacific region was conducted through a series of workshops in which representative experts from all the participating countries discussed and identified a product list for the price surveys. For example, 656 goods and services were in the list for the individual consumption aggregate. Despite the elaborate process followed, there was a feeling that the region has identifiable subregions such as South Asia and East Asia with fairly different consumption baskets.[31]

Because the prices collected will be used in the PPP computations, several considerations arise. First, from the national accounts perspective discussed earlier, the products included must be *representative* and also consistent with the national accounts. Another consideration is the *comparability* of products in the list for the price surveys. To derive meaningful PPPs based on comparisons of prices at the item level, one must ensure that the products priced in different countries are comparable. Indeed, it is important to compare like with like in the process of deriving PPPs.

The PPP based on the price of a Big Mac is a good example. Because the Big Mac is comparable across countries, it meets the comparability requirement. However, the Big Mac is only one consumption item, and it may not be representative of consumption patterns in different countries. In some developing countries, the Big Mac is an item consumed by high-income individuals. Thus it may not be typical of consumption, and reliance only on the Big Mac would tend to distort the price levels in the countries being compared.

In general, there is a tension between the two criteria, *representativity* and *comparability*, and so the ICP strives to strike a balance between these two requirements, as discussed in the sections that follow. The *ICP 2005 Methodological Handbook* (World Bank 2007) is an excellent source of discussion of the concepts of representativity and comparability, and this discussion draws on this major source.

Representativity

An important requirement of the product list for the ICP is that the products selected be representative of the products purchased in each country in the region. In practice, it is inevitable that differences will arise in the types of products purchased in the same basic heading in different economies, particularly in view of the cultural and economic diversity in the Africa and Asia-Pacific regions. The *ICP 2005 Methodological Handbook*[32] defines *representativity* as follows: "Representative products [are those that] figure prominently in the expenditures within a basic heading within a country. They are therefore products that are frequently purchased by resident households and are likely to be widely available throughout the country" (World Bank 2007).

The representativity of an item within a basic heading is also related to the general price level of the basic heading. The price levels of nonrepresentative products are generally higher[33] than those of representative products. Therefore, if in the same basic heading one country prices representative products while another prices nonrepresentative products, the price comparisons can be distorted. Because of these issues, price collectors or statisticians must exercise a fair degree of judgment in identifying products considered representative for a given basic heading. In this process, items in the consumer price index (CPI) of a given country may be considered representative for that country.

At the stage at which the product list is being prepared, it is important to ensure that countries would find it feasible to identify representative products to price. Each country is not expected to price all the products in the list for a given basic heading. All the countries are expected to price both representative and unrepresentative products. In the 2005 ICP, countries were asked to identify the *representativeness status* of each item they priced, but the responses were mixed, and it was evident that the concept of representativeness was difficult to implement. Thus the information collected on representativity was simply ignored.[34]

The criterion of representativity was used in the 2005 ICP only for items in basic headings that belonged to individual consumption expenditure by households. The government expenditure comparisons were based on wages and salaries data and therefore did not require any product list. The ICP's Global Office (located at the World Bank) prepared a list of items in order to compute PPPs for gross fixed capital formation and endeavored to make the list as representative as possible for all ICP countries.

Comparability

Comparability is an important requirement that has implications for meaningful interpretation of the PPPs derived. The *ICP 2005 Methodological Handbook* defines *comparability* as follows: "Two or more products are said to be comparable either if their physical and economic characteristics are identical, or if they are sufficiently similar that consumers are indifferent between them. Alternatively, two similar products may be said to be comparable if consumers are indifferent to which of the two they consume. This implies that consumers are not prepared to pay more for one than the other" (World Bank 2007).

Identifying comparable products is difficult when undertaking comparisons in regions with diverse cultures and standards of living. In such cases, a useful starting point is to define detailed specifications for each product to be priced. When there are subregional variations such as in the Asia-Pacific region, it may be necessary to have products that are comparable across countries in the subregion. This means that some products that can be priced in one subregion cannot be priced in another.

Usually, it is difficult to decide on the level of comparability to be achieved. A product selected for pricing is more likely to be comparable between economies if the specifications are tightly defined. This is the approach followed in the Eurostat-OECD region. But the more tightly defined the product, the more difficult it becomes to find products meeting the specifications. Similarly, two products that differ in some price-determining characteristics will generally not be comparable. In such cases, it may be necessary to define products more loosely to enable countries to find products that meet the specifications. A disadvantage of this approach is that in such cases it becomes difficult to determine whether countries priced the same item.

Within the ICP, comparability is closely related to the price-determining characteristics. For example, rice sold loosely in small quantities may be considered different from rice sold in packets of 5 kilograms. Here the size of the purchase is one of the price-determining characteristics because the price per kilogram could be higher when rice is purchased in small quantities. Similarly, an item, say potatoes, bought from an open market may be considered different from potatoes bought from a supermarket even if the quality characteristics are the same. Potatoes sold in a supermarket may have other service components, such as an air-conditioned store and help with packing the purchases made. It is recommended that these price-determining characteristics become part of the specifications and are used in pricing the products.

In the preparation of product lists, it is important to strike a balance between *comparability* and *representativity*. On the one hand, comparability is clearly important because it is difficult to make sense of price comparisons unless the products have similar characteristics, including quality. On the other hand, representativity is also important because the prices of nonrepresentative products are usually higher than those of representative ones. If a good balance is not struck, the resulting comparisons are likely to be distorted.

The actual aggregation methodology used in computing PPPs from the price data is designed to make use of information on representativity, as well as on the price-determining characteristics of the product. Chapter 4 of this volume looks at the aggregation of item-level prices and describes procedures that can incorporate representativity. In particular, the Country Product Representativity Dummy (CPRD) and GEKS (Gini-Éltető-Köves-Szulc) methods are used in handling the additional information on representativity.

Importance

The practical use of the concept of *representativity* proved difficult in the Asia-Pacific and Africa regions. Considerable confusion arose as to whether a particular product was representative. In many instances, products considered representative were not actually priced in the surveys. Meanwhile, a large proportion of nonrepresentative products were actually priced. Such imbalances in the surveys can lead to highly distorted estimates of PPPs. As a result, it was decided not to use the representativity information provided by the countries; it was used only for post-ICP research into this concept.

Consequently, for the 2011 round of the ICP it was recommended that the notion of the *importance* of a product be used in dealing with the price data provided by the countries. Because price surveys are usually based on a self-weighted design in which the weights represent the volume shares of the products in a particular basic heading, any notion based on either volume of the product sold or share of total sales could be used as an indicator of importance.

Basically, then, product lists should be prepared with the main focus on comparability. Once all the product characteristics are specified, then the price statisticians in each country provide an indication, in the first instance, as to whether the product is important or not. "Importance" refers to expenditure shares within the basic heading. Although statisticians will not usually know expenditure weights within basic headings, they are asked to use their expert judgment as to whether, if such weights were available, they would be relatively large. If so, the product concerned is to be regarded as "important." As a working rule, it has been agreed that any products also priced for a country's consumer price index would automatically be defined as "important."

Structured Product Descriptions

Once the product lists are finalized and their price-determining characteristics are identified, they are recorded in the form of *structured product descriptions* (SPDs). In the 2005 ICP, the product characteristics were identified using the checklist of the consumer price index of the U.S. Bureau of Labor Statistics as a starting point. The SPD of a product defines those characteristics that are price-determining. Once the SPD is set for a product cluster, products within the cluster are identified by selecting the specific characteristic of each product included in the pricing list. The SPDs, which were developed by the Global Office, were used as a basis for preparing product lists at the regional level.

National Annual Average Prices

Once the product list is finalized and price surveys are conducted in the participating countries, these prices are reported back to the regional office for further processing. In the 2005 ICP, there was considerable discussion about the merits of using individual price quotations, but it was decided for operational reasons to use *national annual average prices* as price data in the computation of PPPs. In concept, the national annual average price of a commodity would be obtained for each product as its average unit value for 2005 (defined as the value of the total quantity of the item sold during the year divided by the number of units of the item sold across the whole country). In practice, however, it was impossible to obtain the detailed data required to calculate unit values, and so the process adopted for the ICP was similar to that used within the CPI.

In the 2005 round, a sample of products was selected for pricing, and their characteristics were defined in detail using the SPDs. Prices were collected for these products in each quarter of 2005 from a range of outlets, including supermarkets, local stores, and markets, and from various regions (rural and urban and provinces) within each country. Basically, this was a self-weighting design in which collections were spread across outlets and regions broadly in proportion to their importance (sales or quantities) in the economy.[35] If sufficient information was available to enable the application of explicit weighting, especially to the urban and rural components to ensure they reflected the relative importance of each, such information was used in computing a weighted national average price.[36] Weighting the rural and urban prices was considered important. In cases in which no weights were available, simple arithmetic averages of the prices were used. If the product under consideration was not a seasonal product, the annual average was calculated as a simple arithmetic average of the quarterly prices. If the products were seasonal, the weighted averages of quarterly averages were used.

Participating countries reported to the regional coordinators the national annual average prices of selected items in the product list. Along with the averages, countries supplied detailed data on the number of quotations used in the computation of the averages, as well as the standard deviations of the price quotations used in the averages. The standard deviations could serve as measures of reliability of the price data used as input for the PPP computations in future rounds of the ICP.

Price Surveys for Comparison-Resistant Areas

The preceding discussion focused mainly on the product lists used in comparisons of individual consumption by households. Individual consumption consists of 110 basic headings, and international comparisons of consumption are intrinsically important. However, the real problems encountered within the ICP are with the *comparison-resistant areas*. These are the components of GDP that are not easily amenable to international price comparisons. The difficulty stems in part from the fact that these components largely consist of nonmarketed services provided by the government either for individual consumption, such as health and education, or for collective consumption in the form of police and defense services and in the form of parks and the like for the enjoyment and benefit of the general population.

In the 2005 ICP, the government expenditure was classified by function, such as health and education, and then by type of expenditure, including compensation of employees, intermediate consumption, gross operating surplus, and net taxes on production and receipts from sales. Essentially, government expenditure PPPs were computed by means of the *input* approach and used prices for various inputs, including the wages and salaries of employees. Because the *input* approach does not explicitly account for productivity differences, a direct comparison of salaries could lead to misleading PPPs and inflated real expenditures or volumes for countries with low productivity. The Asia-Pacific, Africa, and Western Asia regions implemented a productivity adjustment, but it was not applied in other regions or when regions were linked to yield global comparisons.[37] Because of the difficulties associated with comparisons in the government sector, two chapters of this volume are devoted to this topic—chapter 15 to comparisons of government compensation and chapter 16 to the methodology for productivity adjustments.

Health goods and services were considered under several basic headings covering health products and health services. Because health services could be provided by both the government and private providers on a fee-for-service basis, the 2005 ICP relied on the basic principle that price should reflect the full price irrespective of who paid for the services. Similarly, detailed guidelines were established for pricing private education services to ensure that the prices collected for education were comparable. Education was divided into primary, secondary, and tertiary levels, and tutoring-type services were also included. Chapter 11 on health and education details the procedures used in the 2005 ICP, and refinements are being considered for the 2011 round of the ICP.

Price comparisons for construction and equipment are difficult when the countries involved range from low to high income and the technology used in such a diverse range of countries could be quite different. In the 2005 ICP, a new approach known as the *basket of construction components* (BOCC) was employed. The PPPs for construction were based on the prices of the major installed components of major construction projects, which were then built up from the costs of the more basic building materials (e.g., sand, cement, steel) and labor. Chapter 13 of this volume on construction provides an overview of the issues and also explains the differences in the methodologies employed in different regions. Moreover, the chapter describes in detail a new approach under consideration for use in the 2011 ICP. PPPs for equipment were based on price surveys for equipment goods using specifications for equipment developed by the Global Office. Because comparison of the prices of equipment goods is a complex task, experts from different regions provided advice on product characteristics and their representativity in different countries. Chapter 14 on machinery and equipment provides further details on the procedures used in compiling PPPs for this aggregate.

Finally, one of the most difficult areas for international comparisons is dwelling services. Comparisons of rents even within a country present many difficulties, which are greatly compounded when it comes to international comparisons. Even using a regionalized approach, it is difficult to compile PPPs for dwelling services in regions such as the Asia-Pacific where the countries range from developed ones such as Singapore to lower-income countries such as Cambodia and Vietnam. A simple approach known as the *quantity ratio method* was used by the Eurostat-OECD region for some countries and for all in the Commonwealth of Independent States (CIS) region. Basically, the national accounts data could be used in measuring value ratios in countries. If a quality-adjusted quantity ratio could be computed, then an indirect PPP could be derived. Although the approach is simple and well founded, actual implementation was not easy because it was difficult to compile reliable and meaningful quality-adjusted quantity ratios. Therefore, in the 2005 ICP the *reference volume method* was employed[38] in the Africa and Asia-Pacific regions. Other regions used price ratios or quantity ratios or both. Basically, then, the treatment of dwelling services was less than satisfactory in the last round of the ICP. This is an area in which major improvements are expected for the 2011 ICP. Details of the procedure used in compiling PPPs for dwelling services are presented in chapter 12.

Data Editing and Validation

Once the price data are collected from the price surveys conducted in different countries, an important next step is to ensure the quality of the price data. Data editing and validation were undertaken at various steps during implementation of the 2005 ICP. At the first step, the national ICP coordinators were expected to check the data for outliers. Then the price data were transmitted to the regional office where they were checked using data submitted by all the participating countries. The regional price data were validated through a series of workshops attended by the national statisticians in charge of price surveys for the ICP. Outliers in the price data were identified using the Quaranta tables developed and employed in the Eurostat-OECD regional comparisons. In the 2005 ICP, specially developed Dikhanov tables were employed to detect outliers in the price observations. More details on data validation, along with illustrations drawn from 2005 ICP, are provided in chapters 9 and 10.

Aggregation of Price Data and Computation of PPPs

The price data collected through price surveys in participating countries within a region are subsequently edited, validated, and prepared for use in the computation of PPPs. PPPs are computed using a hierarchical approach (see figure 1.1). The lowest level at which PPPs are computed is at the basic heading level.[39] PPPs at this level are computed without any quantity or expenditure share weights because such information is not available at the product level.[40] These PPPs then form the building blocks for the computation of PPPs at higher levels of aggregation, leading to PPPs for different classes, commodity groups, categories, and finally major aggregates of the GDP. Chapters 4, 5, and 6 are devoted to a detailed description of the various methods used for the computation of PPPs at various levels. The main purpose of this section is to provide an overview of the index number issues confronted in the context of international price and volume comparisons.

Bilateral versus Multilateral Comparisons

Bilateral comparisons are comparisons that involve two periods or two countries. By contrast, multilateral comparisons are comparisons made between all pairs of countries belonging to a set of countries. Typical examples of bilateral comparisons are temporal comparisons in which the prices in period t are compared with the prices in period $t - 1$, or in some cases the prices in period t

(current) with the prices in period 0 (base period). Furthermore, time periods appear in a chronological sequence that facilitates easy chaining of comparisons over time. In the ICP, comparisons are sought between all pairs of countries within a region or between all the participating countries. The countries are not ordered in any systematic way.

When the notion of PPPs was introduced in section 1.2, the purchasing power parity of the currency of country j with respect to a numeraire country was denoted by PPP_j. Although this notation was adequate for expositional purposes, it is incomplete because it does not show the numeraire country used in computing the PPP. The more general notation introduced here will facilitate discussion of the various properties expected of PPPs in the context of the ICP. Let PPP_{jk} represent the purchasing power parity for the currency of country k with the currency of country j as the numeraire. Thus

$$PPP_{USA,India} = 14.67$$

which implies that 14.67 Indian rupees have the same purchasing power as one U.S. dollar with respect to a specific basket of goods and services.

If bilateral comparisons between two countries, denoted by 1 and 2, are the focus, then only the price and quantity data from these two countries are used in deriving a PPP or price comparison between these two countries. Let p_{i1}, p_{i2}, and q_{i1}, q_{i2} ($I = 1, 2, \ldots, N$) represent, respectively, the price and quantity of the i-th commodity in countries 1 and 2. In this case, PPP_{12} is simply the price index computed using these price and quantity data. The recommended formulas for this purpose are the Fisher ideal index and the Tornqvist index. These indexes possess impressive axiomatic and economic theoretic properties. Balk (1996) provides a detailed exposition of the axiomatic theory, and Diewert (1976, 1992) discusses the economic theoretical approach to the construction of consumer price index numbers. The Fisher and Tornqvist indexes are known to be *exact* and *superlative*, two concepts developed by Diewert (1976). The Fisher index is given by

$$(1.8) \qquad PPP_{12}^{Fisher} = \left[\frac{\sum_{i=1}^{N} p_{i2} q_{i1}}{\sum_{i=1}^{N} p_{i1} q_{i1}} \cdot \frac{\sum_{i=1}^{N} p_{i2} q_{i2}}{\sum_{i=1}^{N} p_{i1} q_{i2}} \right]^{\frac{1}{2}}.$$

This index is the geometric average of the Laspeyres and Paasche indexes in the brackets of (1.8). The Tornqvist index is given by

$$(1.9) \qquad PPP_{12}^{Tornqvist} = \prod_{i=1}^{N} \left[\frac{p_{i2}}{p_{i1}} \right]^{\frac{w_{i1}+w_{i2}}{2}} \quad \text{where } w_{ij} = \frac{p_{ij} q_{ij}}{\sum_{i=1}^{N} p_{ij} q_{ij}}, j = 1, 2.$$

The Tornqvist index is the weighted geometric average of the price relatives computed for each of the commodities.

Equations (1.8) and (1.9) are typical examples of bilateral price index numbers in which only price data from countries 1 and 2 are used in computing the PPPs. By contrast, if multilateral comparisons between all pairs from a set of M countries are of interest, then comparisons between all possible pairs of countries are necessary. In the 2005 ICP, the total number of participating countries was $M = 146$. All these pair-wise comparisons can be represented in the form of a matrix as

$$(1.10) \qquad \mathbf{PPP} = \begin{bmatrix} PPP_{11} & PPP_{12} & PPP_{13} & PPP_{1M} \\ PPP_{21} & PPP_{22} & PPP_{23} & PPP_{2M} \\ PPP_{31} & PPP_{32} & PPP_{33} & PPP_{3M} \\ PPP_{M1} & PPP_{M2} & PPP_{M3} & PPP_{MM} \end{bmatrix}.$$

For example, these PPPs could be between pairs of countries such as (United States, Japan), (United States, China), and (China, India). A simple approach to the computation of elements of the matrix **PPP** in (1.10) is to use the Fisher or Tornqvist index number formula in (1.8) and (1.9). However, such a simplistic approach is not adequate because the elements of **PPP** need to be internally consistent and also to satisfy a number of useful properties. These are discussed in the subsections that follow.

Transitivity

The first and the most important property in the context of international price comparisons is *transitivity*. Transitivity stipulates that the PPP computed between two countries, j and k, should be the same whether it is computed directly or computed indirectly through a third country, ℓ. Stated formally, the matrix **PPP** in (1.10) is said to be transitive if for any three countries, j, k, and ℓ, the PPPs satisfy

$$(1.11) \qquad PPP_{jk} = PPP_{j\ell} \cdot PPP_{\ell k}.$$

For example, this requirement guarantees that for any set of three selected countries—say, India, Germany, and South Africa—the computed and published PPPs from the ICP should satisfy

$$PPP_{Germany,India} = PPP_{Germany,South\ Africa} \cdot PPP_{South\ Africa,\ India}.$$

These numbers from table 1 in the World Bank's 2008 report on the 2005 ICP are

$$PPP_{Germany,India} = 16.48;\ PPP_{Germany,South\ Africa} = 4.35;\ \text{and}\ PPP_{South\ Africa,\ India} = 3.79.$$

It is useful to note here that when transitivity is satisfied by a matrix of PPPs, then a binary comparison between two countries, j and k, is influenced by the price and quantity data for all other countries in the global comparisons. In the illustrative example just presented, it is clear that the comparison between Germany and India is influenced by the data for South Africa and all other countries. However, compensating for this factor is the internal consistency of all the PPPs for all the countries in the ICP.

Which formula should one use in this context? It is easy to see that neither the Fisher index nor the Tornqvist index satisfies the transitivity property, but many index number methods could be used for this purpose. Balk (2009) reviews all these methods, and chapter 5 in this volume canvasses the core methods currently being used in international comparisons.

Base Invariance or Country Symmetry

Because the ICP is a global comparison exercise with participating countries from all regions of the world, it is important that all countries be treated equally in deriving the matrix of PPPs that satisfy transitivity. It is possible to derive transitive multilateral comparisons by picking a country to serve as the star country through which all other countries are compared. For example, in the two sets of comparisons shown in figure 1.2 the United States and the United Kingdom serve as the star countries.

In Figure 1.2a, all the comparisons are made through the United States, the star country. For example, India and China are compared in this case by comparing India first with the United States and then the United States with China. The star country approach does not allow for a direct comparison between India and China. Either the Fisher index in equation (1.8) or the Tornqvist index in equation (1.9) could be used in making comparisons between pairs of countries. It is easy to show that the comparisons made using this approach satisfy transitivity. Similarly, one could generate another set of transitive PPPs using the United Kingdom as the star country. Unfortunately, these two sets would not give the same numerical answers. This means that the choice of the star country is crucial, and that the star country is treated asymmetrically within the international comparisons. Thus figures 1.2a and 1.2b show that *transitivity* does not necessarily imply *country symmetry*, and so the PPPs between any two countries should be the same regardless of the choice of base country.

A simple solution to this problem is to generate star country comparisons using each and every country as a star country in turn in the comparisons. Therefore, when there are 146 participating countries, as for the 2005 ICP, 146 different sets of star country comparisons could be derived, and each of them would give a different answer. Because all countries should be treated symmetrically, a geometric average of the 146 star country comparisons could be obtained using a simple geometric mean. The results become base country–invariant. The resulting set of comparisons is exactly the same as that derived using the GEKS method, which is discussed in detail in chapters 4 and 5 of this volume.

Characteristicity

Drechsler (1973) was the first to note that *characteristicity* is an important requirement for international comparisons. When transitivity as defined in (1.11) is imposed, binary comparisons between pairs of countries are influenced by data on prices and quantities from other participating countries. The binary comparisons are then distorted as a result of the imposition of transitivity as an internal consistency requirement. The characteristicity property stipulates that distortions arising out of the use of transitive methods should be kept to a minimum. The GEKS method mentioned earlier is specially designed to maintain the characteristicity of binary comparisons. This is one of the main reasons why the GEKS method was selected as the main aggregation method for the 2005 ICP comparisons at the regional and global levels.

FIGURE 1.2A Comparisons Using United States as Star Country

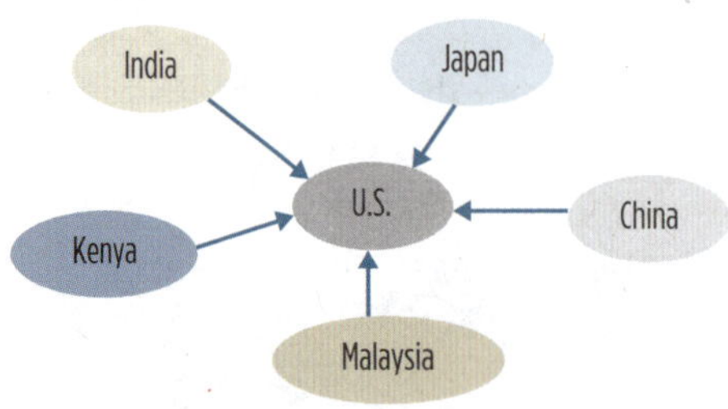

FIGURE 1.2B Comparisons Using United Kingdom as Star Country

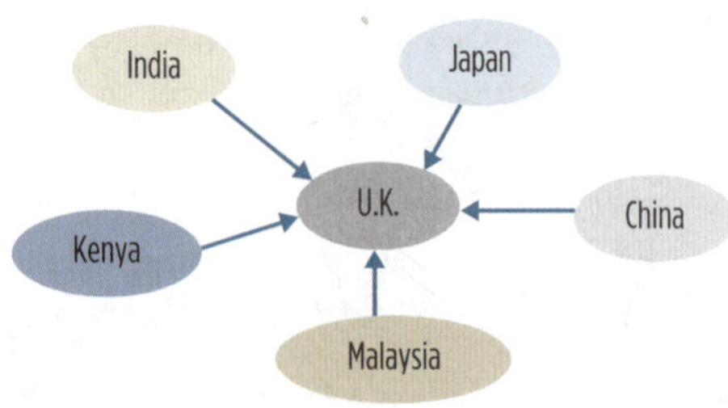

Source: ICP.

Additivity

Another desirable property for international comparisons is *additivity*. This property ensures that the additive nature of the national accounts within a country, expressed in national currency units, is also maintained when international comparisons are made. Basically, additivity means that the real expenditure aggregates derived by converting the aggregates in national currency units into a common currency unit using PPPs should add up to the real GDP, which is obtained by converting GDP using PPPs derived at the aggregate level. Additivity would enable researchers to examine the structure of the components of GDP in real terms after conversion using PPPs. However, additivity imposes certain theoretical restrictions and thus is not always preferred as a property to be maintained in international comparisons (see chapter 5 for more discussion of these theoretical restrictions). In temporal comparisons, additivity is not guaranteed when national accounts are constructed at constant prices.[41] Nevertheless, several aggregation procedures such as the Geary-Khamis (GK) and Iklé-Dikhanov-Balk (IDB) methods possess the additivity property. Until the 2005 ICP round, Geary-Khamis was the main aggregation procedure used in the ICP, even though the GEKS method had been used in the Eurostat-OECD region since 1985.

In addition to these four important properties expected of PPPs in the context of international comparisons, several other properties are discussed in the literature. For example, Balk (1996, 2009) and Diewert (1988) discuss a range of other properties used in evaluating the relative merits of various aggregation methods.

Aggregation of Price Data at the Basic Heading Level

Each of the 155 basic headings used in the ICP covers a list of products or items used in price surveys by the participating countries in each region. A distinguishing feature of the BH level is that only data on the prices of items in the basic heading are available. The quantities purchased at the observed prices are not known. Hence the aggregation at this level must be essentially unweighted. A complication to be handled at the BH level is that not all items in the basic heading are priced in all countries. Thus PPPs have to be compiled in the presence of large gaps in the price data. The aggregation methods used at the BH level are designed to make efficient use of all the available price data.

As discussed earlier, the prices collected by a given country within the basic heading are not all equally important. For example, a number of unrepresentative items may have been priced by countries within the region. Because unrepresentative items are likely to exhibit higher prices compared with representative items, the aggregation methods used at this level must take adequate account of the representativity of the products priced.[42]

The aggregation methods used in deriving PPPs at the BH level must satisfy transitivity and base invariance. A range of aggregation methods including the CPD, CPRD, Country Product Dummy-Weighted (CPDW), GEKS, and GEKS* methods, are commonly used for the computation of PPPs at the BH level. These methods are discussed in detail in chapter 4 of this volume.

PPPs above the Basic Heading Level

Once parities are computed for each of the 155 basic headings for all the participating countries, they are used as inputs for the higher levels of aggregation. Let PPP_{ij} represent the PPP for the i-th basic heading in the j-th country using one of the countries as a numeraire. Because the numeraire is the same for all countries, it is not explicitly mentioned in this notation. Typically, expenditure data are available for each of the basic headings. Let e_{ij} represent the expenditure on basic heading i in country j expressed in the currency unit of country j. Because expenditures are expressed in national currency units, it is not possible to sum these expenditures across different countries.

An implicit quantity associated with a given basic heading can be derived simply by converting the national currency into common currency units using the BH PPPs. For example, the implicit quantity of the i-th basic heading (which itself is made up of a number of items and hence can be considered a composite commodity) is measured by

$$Q_{ij} = \frac{e_{ij}}{PPP_{ij}}. \tag{1.12}$$

These Q_{ij}'s are in fact *real expenditures* obtained by converting nominal expenditures in national currency units by PPPs and thus adjusting for price level differences across countries at the BH level. These real expenditures are also referred to as *volumes*. Just as quantities of a single item can be added across countries, the real expenditures/volumes can be added and used in comparing the relative shares of countries for a given basic heading. These shares are given by

$$s_{ij} = \frac{Q_{ij}}{\sum_{j=1}^{C} Q_{ij}} = \frac{e_{ij}/PP_{ij}}{\sum_{j=1}^{C} e_{ij}/PPP_{ij}}.$$

The shares are used in the ICP for comparing the relative sizes of countries with respect to a specific basic heading i, with $i = 1, 2, \dots, 155$ and countries $j = 1, 2, \dots, C$.

The price and quantity data used in deriving PPPs at higher levels of aggregation are given by the PPPs at the BH level and the implicit quantities defined in (1.12). These can be represented by PPP_{ij}, Q_{ij} for $i = 1, 2, \dots, 155$, and $j = 1, 2, \dots, C$.

The aggregation methods used in computing PPPs at higher levels of aggregation are also expected to satisfy the basic properties of transitivity, base invariance, characteristicity, and, if desired, additivity. The main procedures currently used in international comparisons are the GEKS, Geary-Khamis, and IDB methods for aggregation. These methods and their properties are discussed in detail in chapter 5 of this volume.[43]

In summary, this section has provided a detailed account of the methodological framework that underpins the collection of price data and the aggregation methods used in deriving PPPs at the BH level and at higher levels of aggregation. These procedures are applicable when international comparisons of a group of countries, such as the ICP regions, are considered. These methods were used by the Asia-Pacific, South America, Eurostat-OECD, Africa, and Western Asia regions within the 2005 ICP. The global comparisons reported in World Bank (2008) were obtained by linking the regional comparisons using a set of Ring countries. The process of linking is the topic for the next section.

1.4 Regional and Global Comparisons

The 2005 ICP embraced a totally regionalized approach to global comparisons. The global comparison benefited from the participation of 146 countries from all the regions of the world. Based on the analytical considerations that underpin the preparation of the product lists for price surveys where *representativity* and *comparability* are important, it is indeed difficult to construct product lists that truly represent the whole world. Recognizing this need, the ICP classified the 146 participating countries by geographic region with the exception of the Eurostat-OECD countries, which included countries from several continents. The distribution of the countries by region is presented in table 1.3.

Even though table 1.3 lists 148 participating countries, the actual number was 146, with the Arab Republic of Egypt participating in both the Africa and Western Asia regions and the Russian Federation participating in both the CIS and Eurostat-OECD regions. Of the 23 participating countries in the Asia-Pacific region, three were economies: Hong Kong SAR, China; Macao SAR, China; and Taiwan, China.[44]

The regional ICP comparisons were undertaken under the auspices of the regional coordinating bodies: African Development Bank, Asian Development Bank, Statistics Canada, Economic Commission for Latin America and the Caribbean (ECLAC), Economic and Social Commission for Western Asia (ESCWA), Interstate Statistical Committee of the Commonwealth of Independent States (CISSTAT), Federal State Statistics Service (Rosstat) of the Russian Federation, and Eurostat-OECD. The procedures discussed in section 1.3 were generally followed by the regions in compiling region-specific PPPs at the BH level, as well as at the higher levels of aggregation listed in table 1.2. Thus within each region, the relativities of countries with respect to real GDP and to other aggregates such as consumption were determined by the results of the regional comparisons. The Global Office of the ICP coordinated compilation of the global comparisons using a linking methodology developed specifically for the 2005 ICP.

Linking Regional Comparisons and Fixity

The compilation of global comparisons, obtained through linking the regional comparisons, was undertaken with strict adherence to the principle of *fixity*. The fixity principle stipulates that the relative volumes in the global comparisons between any pair of countries belonging to a given region should be identical to the relative volumes of the two countries established in the regional comparisons to which they belong. For example, consider Malaysia and Singapore in the Asia-Pacific region. The real GDPs of these two countries in the regional comparison were HK$1,703,958 million and HK$1,024,330 million, respectively.[45] The implied relative GDP level is that Malaysia's GDP is 1.663 times Singapore's GDP. The corresponding real GDP figures from the global comparisons[46] are US$299,582 and US$180,093, respectively. These figures also show the same relative GDP level at which Malaysia's level is once again 1.663 times that of Singapore.

TABLE 1.3 Participating Countries by Region, ICP 2005

Region	No. of countries
Africa	48
Asia-Pacific	23
CIS	10
Eurostat-OECD	46
South America	10
Western Asia	11
Total	148

Source: World Bank 2008.

The principle of fixity is applied at all levels of comparisons, starting at the BH level. The methodology for generating global comparisons respecting fixity was developed during the 2005 ICP round and can be found in Diewert (2004).[47] Because of their adherence to the fixity principle, the regions were able to publish their regional comparison results, expressed in their own numeraire currencies, as the results became available. The global comparison results, which were the last to be published, were consistent with the previously published regional results.

Use of Ring Countries for Linking

In contrast to some past comparisons in which regions were linked essentially through price data collected by one or two bridge countries, the 2005 ICP followed a more robust approach. Eighteen countries—the Ring countries—were selected to provide links between regions. The selection of the Ring countries was based on a set of criteria designed to ensure that prices in those countries were not distorted in any way and that a wide range of goods and services were likely to be found and priced in those countries. A fuller description of the criteria appears in chapter 8 of this volume.

Six Ring countries were selected from Africa (reflecting the size of the continent and diverse nature of the subregions), four from the Asia-Pacific region, and two each from the Eurostat-OECD and Western Asia regions. The CIS region was linked using Russia as the bridge country. Russia priced both the OECD and CIS product lists. Overall, the strategy of using a large group of Ring countries appeared to have worked well in the 2005 ICP.

Ring Product Lists and Surveys

The product list for the Ring country surveys was developed by the Global Office. The product list of household consumption items for those surveys was constructed after a careful examination of the product lists used in different regions. Out of the combined product lists from all the regions, any product that was not priced by a Ring country was discarded, and the remaining products were considered to be potential candidates for inclusion in the Ring product list. The regional SPDs for these products were examined in order to establish their comparability across regions. The list for the price surveys was finalized after a series of consultations with the Ring countries.

This process was not needed for the categories of housing, government consumption, health, construction, and machinery and equipment; global specifications were used in the regional surveys and comparisons. These categories were priced by all countries, including the Ring countries. As a result, the same data were used for both the regional and Ring comparisons for the Africa, Asia-Pacific, South America, and Western Asia regions. Ring countries in the Eurostat-OECD region priced the global specification for the Ring comparison.[48]

Methodology for Linking Regional Comparisons

The basic process of linking regional comparisons is depicted in the flow chart in figure 1.3. The panel on the left-hand side represents the comparisons undertaken in the six regions. These comparisons essentially follow the procedures described in section 1.3. At the conclusion of the regional comparisons, a set of PPPs for all the basic headings expressed relative to the regional numeraire, and PPPs and volumes at higher levels of aggregation, are available from all the regions. These results represent one component of the inputs into the linking process.

The panel on the right-hand side represents the process of linking through the Ring countries. Price data are collected through surveys in the 18 Ring countries based on the Ring product

FIGURE 1.3 Methodology for Linking Regional Comparisons

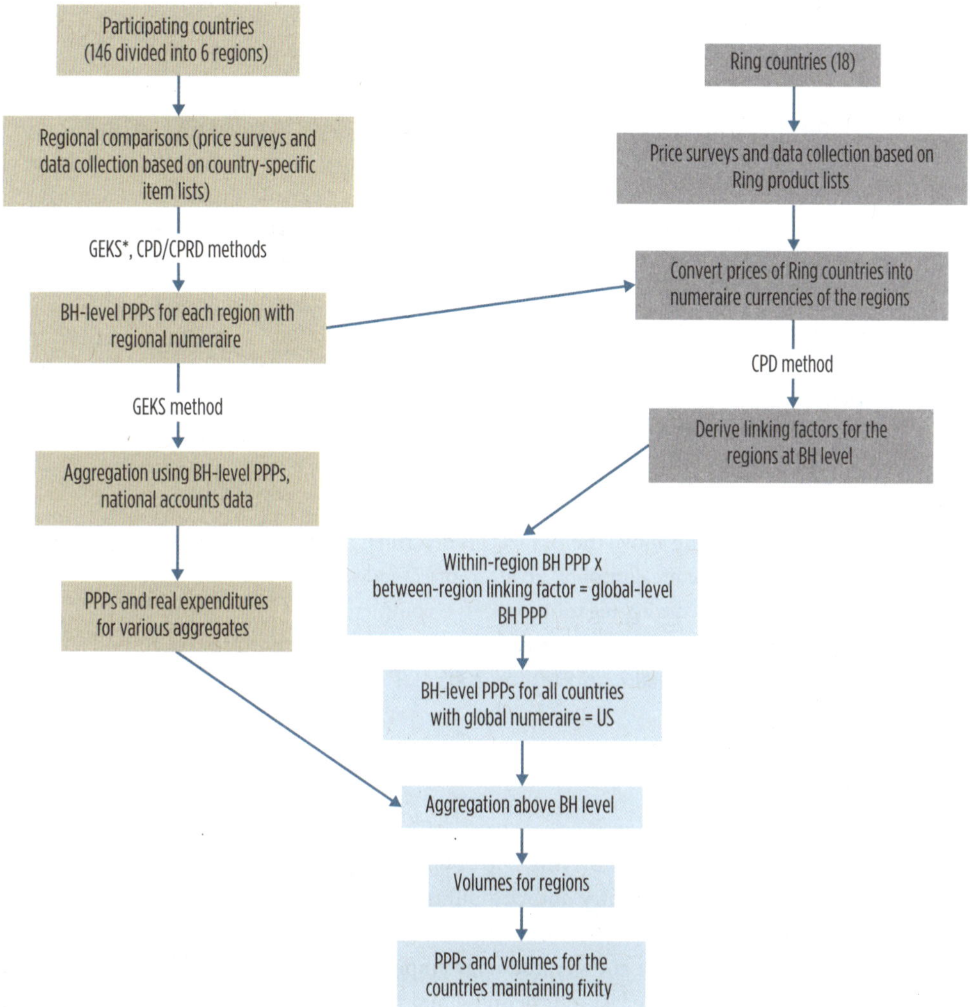

Note: GEKS = Gini-Éltetö-Köves-Szulc; CPD = Country Product Dummy; CPRD = Country Product Representative Dummy.

lists prepared by the Global Office. For each BH level, prices collected by the Ring countries are converted into their respective numeraire currencies using the BH parities from the regional comparisons available from the left-hand panel. Once this process is completed, 18 vectors of prices for items in the basic heading are under consideration, and the prices are expressed in the six numeraire currency units of the six regions. For example, in the 2005 ICP the four vectors of prices from the Asia-Pacific Ring countries were all converted to Hong Kong dollars using the PPPs available from the region. Similarly, the Eurostat-OECD Ring prices were converted into British pounds. The Ring price data in the form of 18 price vectors were then aggregated using the CPD method (discussed in chapter 4), resulting in a single set of between-region parities for a given basic heading, which provide PPPs for each of the regional numeraire currencies expressed in terms of U.S. dollars. These are called the *linking factors*.

Once the linking factors are obtained for each of the 155 basic headings, the regional basic heading PPPs are converted into PPPs relative to the U.S. dollar using the linking factors. At the end of this process, as shown in the top step in the middle panel of figure 1.3, a matrix of BH-level PPPs for 146 countries and 155 basic headings are available. In addition, the expenditure data from all 146 countries are available in national currency units from the respective national accounts. Implicit quantity data could be computed along the lines suggested in equation (1.12).

The next step in the left-hand panel for global comparisons is to combine the BH-level PPPs and expenditure data to derive global comparisons for selected higher-level aggregates. If the principle of fixity were not applied, the next step would be quite simple. Any of the aggregation methods (GEKS, Iklé, or GK) could be employed directly for the full data set in one step, thereby providing an *unrestricted set of global comparisons*. Because of the fixity requirement, in the 2005 ICP the linking factors were aggregated for each level to calibrate the regional volumes to the global level. The unrestricted results were not published as a part of the 2005 ICP.

The application of the *fixity* principle in the derivation of PPPs and volumes or real expenditures at a higher level of aggregation is a complicated process. Following a method proposed by Diewert (2004), the linked global comparisons satisfying the fixity principle were derived. The methodology used for linking above the BH level is described in chapter 6 of this volume. Because the methods discussed there are complex, no attempt is made here to describe them.

Finally, at the end of the aggregation process a complete set of PPPs at the BH level and at higher levels of aggregation and the associated volumes and real expenditures are compiled. These results were presented in the final report for the 2005 ICP (World Bank 2008).

1.5 Conclusion

The 2005 ICP was a major project covering 146 countries in all regions of the world. If comparing prices over time within a country and compiling the consumer price index are considered difficult tasks, comparing price levels across countries is a Herculean one. Reflecting the complex nature of the ICP, the framework and methodology employed by the ICP are also complex. These procedures have evolved over the last four decades, and the methods continue to be refined. The aim of this chapter is to provide an overview of and create an appreciation for the approaches used in the 2005 ICP. The most innovative aspect of the 2005 ICP was the complete regionalization of international comparisons, thereby improving the comparability and representativity of products priced for the purpose of PPP computations. The development of a methodology for linking comparisons to derive global comparisons satisfying *fixity* was a major achievement as well. The new methodology, along with the significant step of using a large number of Ring countries to strengthen the linking process, has helped to improve the quality and reliability of global PPPs. Armed with a working knowledge of the framework of the ICP provided by this chapter, it is hoped that readers will be encouraged to delve into the detailed descriptions provided in the chapters that follow.

NOTES

1. The 2005 ICP comprised five geographic regions: Africa, Asia-Pacific, Commonwealth of Independent States (CIS), South America, and Western Asia. It was conducted in parallel

with the Eurostat-OECD comparison for their member countries. Chapter 2 provides more details about the coordination between the two programs. For the purposes of this chapter, the methodology applies to the ICP regions and the Eurostat-OECD as another region.

2. The revised version of this chapter has benefited at various stages in its preparation from the comments of Frederic A. Vogel, Derek Blades, Michel Mouyelo-Katoula, and Erwin Diewert.
3. The ICP was initially known as the International Comparisons Project, but over time it evolved into the International Comparison Program, reflecting its transformation from a small research project to a global statistical exercise.
4. See the full report on the 2005 ICP, *Global Purchasing Power Parities and Real Expenditures: 2005 International Comparison Program*, which was published by the World Bank (2008).
5. Actual individual consumption includes individual consumption by the household, as well as consumption by the government on behalf of the household. Government consumption in the areas of education and health are important contributors. This concept is further elaborated in chapter 3 on national accounts.
6. A formal definition of price level indexes and further explanations are provided in section 1.2 of this chapter.
7. The Gini coefficient is a commonly used measure of inequality. It takes values of between 0 and 1: a value of 0 means perfect equality in the distribution of income, and a value of 1 represents perfect inequality in which one individual receives all the income and the rest of the population receives no income. For most countries, the Gini coefficient is in the range of 0.3–0.4.
8. See Deaton's introduction to this volume.
9. The 2005 ICP was based entirely on the SNA93, and the 2011 round of the ICP also makes use of the SNA93, even though it was recently revised.
10. These concepts are covered in detail in chapter 3, which focuses on the national accounts framework of the ICP.
11. More details about this approach and the interrelationships between the expenditure and production side approaches to international comparisons appear in chapter 24 of this volume.
12. The literature on international comparisons on the production side is large. Interested readers could refer to van Ark and Maddison (1994), Maddison and van Ark (2002), Feenstra et al. (2009), van Ark and Timmer (2009), and chapter 24 of this volume for more details.
13. It is quite possible that not all the items listed under this category are consumed in all countries. In such cases, the corresponding quantities are equal to zero and prices are unobserved. These possibilities are taken into consideration when the price data are aggregated (see chapter 4 on aggregation at the basic heading level).
14. This concept is the most important one within the ICP. It is further elaborated later in this chapter.
15. See Kravis, Heston, and Summers (1982) and chapter 1 of the *ICP 2005 Methodological Handbook* (World Bank 2007) for more detailed discussions of the suitability (or lack of it) of the exchange rates for the conversion of national income aggregates.
16. In this example, the PPP of the U.S. dollar using the Indian rupee as the numeraire currency would be the reciprocal of 13.5, which is equal to 7.4 U.S. cents to one Indian rupee. The relative expenditures in India and the United States would not be influenced by the choice of either currency for conversion.
17. See http://www.onada.com/currency/big-mac-index for details. The figures in the text were retrieved on February 20, 2011.
18. The most recent version, PWT 7, provides PPPs and real expenditures in current and constant 2005 prices.

19. The World Bank makes its own extrapolations, which are published in *World Development Indicators* (WDI). These differ from those published in the Penn World Table. The WDI extrapolations are based on the relative GDP growth rate of each country to that of the United States.
20. Chapter 21 also discusses the derivation of PPPs that are conceptually more suitable for poverty measurement than what is available from the ICP.
21. This figure is drawn from the summary table in the 2005 ICP final report (World Bank 2008, 23–27).
22. Strictly speaking, this interpretation holds if the tourist spends money on the items that make up the whole GDP. In practice, tourist expenditure patterns differ significantly from the composition of the GDP. See Dwyer, Forsyth, and Rao (2009) for an example of PPPs relevant for tourists.
23. In this case, it can be shown that the numeraire currency is no longer the U.S. dollar but a basket of all the world's currencies.
24. See the example of the PPP associated with the Big Mac and its prices in different countries.
25. A complete list of basic headings and various aggregates used in the ICP are available in appendix C of *Global Purchasing Power Parities and Real Expenditures: 2005 International Comparison Program* (World Bank 2008).
26. In practice, it is not always possible to compile PPPs for all the basic headings. In such cases, *reference PPPs* are used. The concept and the rationale for using reference PPPs are fully discussed in chapter 17.
27. See Dwyer, Forsyth, and Rao (2009) for an application in which PPPs at the BH level are combined to derive PPPs for making comparisons of price competitiveness of various destinations for tourists from different origin countries.
28. The PPP results for groups, classes, and basic headings are available from the World Bank upon request. Dissemination of the PPP results is guided by the dissemination policy determined by the Executive Board set up to oversee the ICP.
29. Recently, Feenstra et al. (2009) extended this approach by using export and import unit values as price data in the derivation of PPPs for exports and imports. This approach has not yet been adopted by the ICP because the procedure is data-intensive and further research is needed to develop implementable procedures.
30. However, in the 2005 ICP a global product list was used in the process of linking regions by means of a set of Ring countries. These Ring countries priced a common list of products irrespective of their region. In the next ICP round in 2011, the linking of regional PPPs will be facilitated by the use of a list of *core products* that will be priced by all the countries in all the regions.
31. The possibility of subregionalization is currently being researched by the Asian Development Bank, the regional coordinator for the Asia-Pacific region. Such regionalization may be relevant to the Africa region as well.
32. See chapter 4 of the handbook for a discussion of these concepts (World Bank 2007).
33. This need not be universally true for all nonrepresentative products. For example, an item such as beef is not representative of meat consumption of the predominantly Hindu population in India. However, the relative price of beef tends to be lower than the price of other meats consumed in the country. The same is likely to hold for pork in countries such as Pakistan and Bangladesh.
34. See chapter 4 of this volume for a discussion of aggregation methods that are designed to take into account additional information on the representativity of a given price quotation from a country in the computation of the PPP for a given basic heading.

35. For more details, see chapter 7 of this volume on the survey framework for household consumption.
36. See chapter 4 of the *ICP 2005 Methodological Handbook* (World Bank 2007) for more details on this process.
37. Details of the methodology for productivity adjustments used in the 2005 ICP can be found in appendix D of *Global Purchasing Power Parities and Real Expenditures: 2005 International Comparison Program* (World Bank 2008).
38. Because it was not possible to use reference PPPs, a reference volume relative was used in the place of a reference PPP. The volume relative selected was based on the individual consumption expenditure by households, excluding housing rentals. This approach ensured that the volume relatives for the household consumption expenditure aggregate remained unchanged.
39. Strictly speaking, PPPs can be computed at the item level where the PPP is simply given by the price relative or the ratio of the price of the product in the two countries under comparison.
40. However, it is possible to attach weights to products based on the importance classification.
41. See Balk and Reich (2008) for a discussion of the problems arising out of the additivity property in the context of national accounts at constant prices.
42. See chapter 4 for further details on how information on representativity could be used in aggregating item-level price data leading to PPPs at the BH level.
43. The global comparisons for the 2005 ICP were all derived using the GEKS method. The Asia-Pacific region published results based on the GK method in the appendix of its report (Asian Development Bank 2007).
44. This is the main reason why the 2005 ICP final report on the Asia-Pacific region refers to participating economies rather than countries (ADB 2007). In this chapter, all the economies are simply referred to as countries.
45. These figures are taken from table 4 in *Purchasing Power Parities and Real Expenditures: 2005 International Comparison Program in Asia and the Pacific* (ADB 2007, 27). The numeraire currency for the Asia-Pacific region was the Hong Kong dollar.
46. These figures are drawn from table 4 in *Global Purchasing Power Parities and Real Expenditures: 2005 International Comparison Program* (World Bank 2008, 60).
47. Chapters 4 and 6 provide further details on this methodology.
48. See table 5 in *Global Purchasing Power Parities and Real Expenditures: 2005 International Comparison Program* (World Bank 2008) for more details on the exact number of products priced by region and for the Ring comparison.

REFERENCES

ADB (Asian Development Bank). 2007. *Purchasing Power Parities and Real Expenditures: 2005 International Comparison Program in Asia and the Pacific*. Manila: Asian Development Bank. http://www.adb.org/Documents/Reports/ICP-Purchasing-Power-Expenditures/PPP-Real-Expenditures.pdf.

Balk, B. M. 1996. "A Comparison of Ten Methods for Multilateral International Price and Volume Comparisons." *Journal of Official Statistics* 12: 199–222.

———. 2009. "Aggregation Methods in International Comparisons: An Evaluation." In *Purchasing Power Parities of Currencies: Recent Advances in Methods and Applications*, ed. D. S. Prasada Rao, 59–85. Cheltenham, U.K.: Edward Elgar.

Balk, B., and U.-P. Reich. 2008. "Additivity of National Accounts Reconsidered." *Journal of Economic and Social Measurement* 33: 165–78.

Bergstrand, J. 1996. "Productivity, Factor Endowments, Military Expenditures, and National Price Levels." In *International Comparisons Prices, Output and Productivity*, ed. D. S. Prasada Rao and Salazar-Carrillo, 297–317. Amsterdam: North-Holland.

Cassel, Gustav. 1918. "Abnormal Deviations in International Exchanges." *Economic Journal* 28 (December): 413–15.

Chen, S., and Martin Ravallion. 2010. "The Developing World Is Poorer than We Thought, but No Less Successful in the Fight against Poverty." *Quarterly Journal of Economics* 125 (4): 1577–1625.

Clague, C. 1988. "Explanations of National Price Levels." In *World Comparisons of Incomes, Prices and Product*, ed. Salazar-Carrillo and D. S. Prasada Rao, 237–62. Amsterdam: North-Holland.

Commission of the European Communities, International Monetary Fund, Organisation for Economic Co-operation and Development, United Nations, and World Bank. 1993. *System of National Accounts 1993*. http://unstats.un.org/unsd/sna1993/toctop.asp?L1=5.

Diewert, W. E. 1976. "Exact and Superlative Index Numbers." *Journal of Econometrics* 4: 114–45.

———. 1988. "Test Approaches to International Comparisons." In *Measurement in Economics: Theory and Applications of Economic Indices*, ed. W. Eichhorn, 6786. Heidelberg: Physica-Verlag.

———. 1992. "Fisher Ideal Output, Input and Productivity Indexes Revisited." *Journal of Productivity Analysis* 3: 211–48.

———. 2004. "On the Stochastic Approach to Linking the Regions in the ICP." Discussion Paper 04-16, Department of Economics, University of British Columbia, Vancouver.

Drechsler, L. 1973. "Weighting of Index Numbers in Multilateral Comparisons." *Review of Income and Wealth* (March).

Dwyer, L. P. Forsyth, and D. S. Prasada Rao. 2009. "PPPs and the Price Competitiveness of International Tourism Destinations." In *Purchasing Power Parities of Currencies: Recent Advances in Methods and Applications*, ed. D. S. Prasada Rao, 367–88. Cheltenham, U.K.: Edward Elgar.

Feenstra, Robert C., Alan Heston, Marcel P. Timmer, and Haiyan Deng. 2009. "Estimating Real Production and Expenditures across Countries: A Proposal for Improving the Penn World Tables." *Review of Economics and Statistics* 91 (1): 201–12.

Gilbert, M., and I. B. Kravis. 1954. *An International Comparison of National Products and the Purchasing Power Parities of Currencies*. Paris: Organisation for European Economic Co-operation.

Heston, A., R. Summers, and B. Aten. 2009. "Penn World Table Version 6.3." Center for International Comparisons of Production, Income and Prices, University of Pennsylvania, August.

Kravis, I. B., A. Heston, and R. Summers. 1982. *World Product and Income: International Comparisons of Real Gross Product*. Statistical Office of the United Nations and the World Bank. Baltimore: Johns Hopkins University Press.

Kravis, I. B., and R. Lipsey. 1983. "Towards an Explanation of National Price Levels." *Princeton Studies in International Finance*, no. 52.

Maddison, A., and B. van Ark. 2002, "The International Comparison of Real Product and Productivity." In *The Asian Economies in the Twentieth Century*, ed. A. Maddison, D. S. Prasada Rao, and W. F. Shepherd, 5–26. Cheltenham, U.K.: Edward Elgar.

Milanović, B. 2009. "Global Inequality Recalculated: The Effect of New 2005 PPP Estimates on Global Inequality." MPRA Working Paper No. 16535, University of Munich.

Summers, R., and A. H. Heston. 1991. "The Penn World Table (Mark 5): An Expanded Set of International Comparisons, 1950–1988." *Quarterly Journal of Economics* (106): 327–68.

van Ark, B., and A. Maddison. 1994. "The International Comparison of Real Product and Productivity." Research Memorandum No. 567 (GD-6), Groningen Growth and Development Centre, University of Groningen, Groningen, The Netherlands.

van Ark, B., and M. P. Timmer. 2009. "Purchasing Power Parity Adjustments for Productivity Level Comparisons." In *Purchasing Power Parities of Currencies: Recent Advances in Methods and Applications*, ed. D. S. Prasada Rao, 59–85. Cheltenham, U.K.: Edward Elgar.

World Bank. 2007. *ICP 2005 Methodological Handbook*. http://web.worldbank.org/WBSITE/EXTERNAL/DATASTATISTICS/ICPEXT/0,,contentMDK:20126612~pagePK:60002244~piPK:62002388~theSitePK:270065,00.html.

———. 2008. *Global Purchasing Power Parities and Real Expenditures: 2005 International Comparison Program*. http://siteresources.worldbank.org/ICPINT/Resources/icp-final.pdf.

———. 2011. *World Development Indicators 2011*. http://data.worldbank.org/data-catalog/world-development-indicators.

CHAPTER 2

Governance Structure of ICP 2005

PAUL MCCARTHY

The 2005 round of the International Comparison Program (ICP) was the first since 1993. The main reasons for the long gap between rounds were the problems encountered in finalizing the 1993 data, in particular insufficient resources (both financial and staff) for the program and the inability to properly link the regional results because the processes were not standardized across regions. A perceived shortcoming in the process was the inadequate coordination, mainly between regions but also within some regions, which was attributed in turn to the lack of a formal governance structure. As a result, planning for the next ICP round was delayed pending the outcome of a wide-ranging review of the 1993 process.

At its 29th session, held in 1997, the United Nations Statistical Commission (UNSC) agreed both on the need to conduct an evaluation of the global International Comparison Program to address the reservations by certain member states about ICP implementation and the uses of ICP results, and on the need to seek ways to improve the credibility of ICP data.

On the basis of that evaluation, a report was prepared and presented to the UNSC during its 30th session, held in March 1999 (UNSC 1999). One of the recommendations was that the program have "a global or world coordinator." The UNSC also noted other problems identified by the report and appointed a group, coordinated by the World Bank, to advise on steps to overcome these shortcomings and to report back to the UNSC at its 31st session at the end of February 2000. At that meeting, the UNSC considered the World Bank's report and recommended (among several other recommendations) that the start of the next ICP round be postponed by one year while an adequate management structure was designed and instituted at both the global and regional levels. It also empowered the chair of the UNSC to appoint a group of "Friends of the Chair" to review the World Bank's implementation plan.

The World Bank presented a detailed implementation plan to the 33rd session of the UNSC in March 2002. The plan provided details about a proposed research and development program, financing arrangements, country participation, and governance arrangements, including regional management. Under the governance arrangements proposed, the ICP secretariat (better known as the ICP Global Office) would be based within an existing international organization, an international governing body would be responsible for the overall strategic management, an advisory group would provide technical advice, and regional organizations would manage the ICP in countries other than those coordinated by Eurostat (the European Union's statistical office) and the Organisation for Economic Co-operation and Development (OECD) as part of their ongoing purchasing power parity (PPP) program. The UNSC accepted the recommendations of the report and endorsed the World Bank as the most appropriate location for the international secretariat for the global coordination and management of the ICP. The secretariat was duly established within the Development Data Group (DECDG) of the World Bank. As a result, the staff of the Global Office were subject to the World Bank's rules and procedures on working conditions, travel, managing ICP databases, and data confidentiality.

The Friends of the Chair participated in the formulation of the final plan and the selection of the ICP global manager. The Friends of the Chair, in conjunction with the World Bank, also established the ICP Executive Board.

Figure 2.1 is an overview of the governance structure of the 2005 ICP, which essentially will be replicated for the 2011 ICP. The next section provides detail about the different levels of the governance structure and the roles and responsibilities of each.

Governance Structure of ICP 2005

A governance structure was implemented to ensure that consistent results would be produced in each region. This outcome would be achieved by coordinating the work globally, establishing a single set of standards, providing centralized technical and practical guidance, and ruling on issues that had the potential to be interpreted in different ways in the regions. Several tiers of governance were needed, ranging from worldwide coordinating groups to regional bodies. However, the basic level of governance comprised the national coordinators in each economy to ensure that the relevant agencies in their economies approached the ICP with a consistent view of what was required and how to achieve it. An important element of the governance arrangements was to ensure that sufficient financial resources were made available to implement them fully. In addition, each region required sufficient finances to employ the skilled personnel needed to successfully complete the 2005 ICP round. The nature of the ICP and its global reach meant that the UNSC should be the apex governing body. Because the membership of the UNSC includes national statistical offices and other international organizations, it was well suited to provide the overall oversight of the functioning of the ICP. To provide a more hands-on overview, an Executive Board was formed. The director of the United Nations Statistics Division (UNSD) was a member of that board to facilitate communications among the UNSC, the Executive Board, and the Global Office at the World Bank.[1]

Executive Board

The Executive Board was established to provide strategic leadership and to make decisions about the ICP's priorities, standards, overall work program, and budget (see annex A for a list of members). It also was given a key role in overseeing the activities of the ICP Global Office. Representation on the Executive Board was agency-based (either an international organization or a national statistics office), with the specific requirement that representatives be very senior staff. Thus those

FIGURE 2.1 ICP 2005 Governance Arrangements

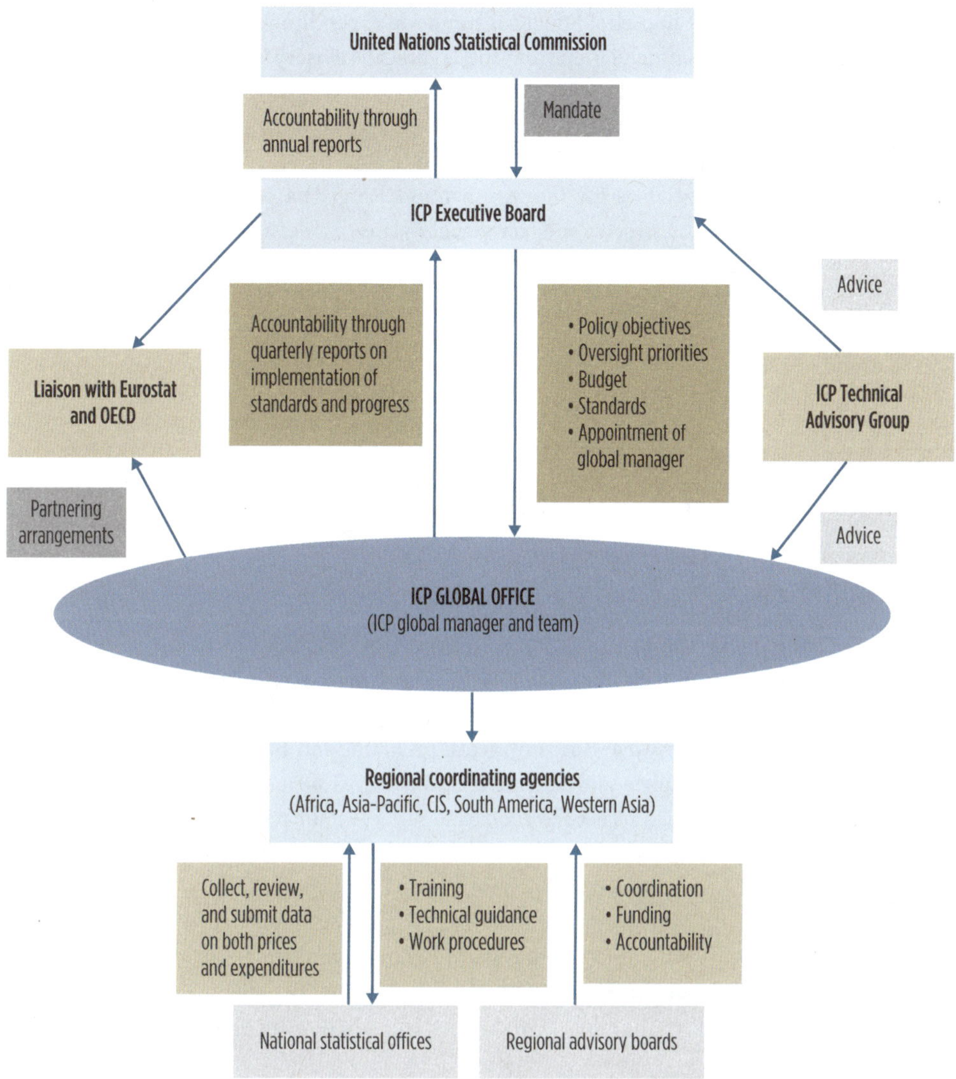

Source: ICP.

attending board meetings were eminent economists or statisticians and experienced statistical managers. Many were heads of national statistical offices or of statistics departments in international organizations, and others were managers of economic statistics divisions, with skills and experience in national accounts or price statistics.

The Executive Board met at least twice a year; once in conjunction with the meetings of the UNSC and once again about halfway between the annual UNSC meetings. Examples of actions taken by the board are the following:

- Reviewed nominations for the membership of the Technical Advisory Group (TAG—described later in this chapter) and approved the final selection.

- After a review of the funding situation, directed the ICP Global Office to produce purchasing power parities for all major components of the gross domestic product (GDP) rather than for the household final consumption expenditure only.
- Approved the recommendation from the Technical Advisory Group that the ICP regions and the Eurostat-OECD PPP Programme be linked using the Ring methodology (described in chapters 4 and 6). Later, the board approved the selection of countries that would participate in the Ring price collection.
- Approved the timetables for the regional and Ring data collections. The board also approved the risk assessments and contingency plans that determined a country's readiness to begin data collection, along with the requirements to be included in the global report.
- Approved the data access policy established by the Global Office.
- Approved the level of detail to be published in the global report. Later, it delegated the responsibility for the final decision on the data to be published in the global report to the chair of the Executive Board and the global manager.

Annual reports on the status and progress of the ICP were prepared by the Global Office and submitted to the UNSC through the Executive Board.

Global Office

The Global Office was established in 2002 within the World Bank to carry out the day-to-day work required to implement the ICP worldwide. The global manager was responsible for its operations, supported by a team of professional statisticians and administrative staff. The Global Office reported regularly to the Executive Board on work programs and budgets. Important activities carried out by the Global Office and its external consultants were developing ICP standards, preparing the framework to determine the goods and services to be priced in the ICP round, preparing the *ICP 2005 Methodological Handbook* and the "ICP Operational Manual" (World Bank 2005, 2007), producing the software for countries to input and edit price data, analyzing the data collected for the ICP, and aggregating the price and national accounts data within and between regions. The Global Office was subject to the World Bank's administrative and fiduciary rules and regulations, including all requirements related to the confidentiality of data.

On day-to-day activities, the Global Office reported to the director of the World Bank's Development Data Group. The ICP was not only a global program under the auspices of the UNSC, but also a World Bank program and initiative in which the DECDG director was accountable to the World Bank management for the program. DECDG established the ICP database and managed access to the ICP data. The group's director was responsible for ensuring that data confidentiality was maintained according to World Bank rules and procedures. On matters related to the execution and implementation of the ICP mission, policy, programs, priorities, and standards, the global manager acted within Executive Board directives and within the framework of board-approved work programs and budgets. Other key responsibilities of the Global Office were the following:

- Organized meetings of the Technical Advisory Group, kept it apprised of methodological issues requiring input, and guided the research required to develop the new methodologies.
- Developed new methodologies, including the use of structured product definitions to describe the price-determining characteristics of the products to be priced; methods to price construction goods and services; and methods to link the regions. Improvements

were also made in the procedures to compare expenditures for housing, government, and equipment by preparing global specifications for the price data collection for these items.
- Prepared global specifications for the Ring list for which selected countries provided prices in addition to those they provided for their regional list. The office also coordinated the data collection for the Ring price survey and, with the regional coordinators, carried out the data validation.
- Worked closely with the regional coordinating agencies to ensure that timetables, work plans, and methodologies were consistently followed.
- Organized the meetings of the regional coordinating agencies at which they were apprised of the new methodologies. At these meetings, regional coordinators presented the validation tables showing the diagnostics for the prices submitted by the countries in their regions. This approach allowed regions to assess jointly whether they were following the methods consistently.
- Prepared software for data validation and estimation of the PPPs and related indexes. This software included new validation methods known as the Dikhanov tables.
- Provided technical assistance to the regions in the estimation of the regional PPPs.
- Computed the global PPPs and related indexes and published the final global results.
- Worked with the Executive Board to develop data access policies.

The Global Office also worked with other stakeholders within the World Bank and in outside organizations on the use of PPPs, on understanding the quality of the results because it affected the decisions to be made, and on answering questions raised by the press and other data users.

Technical Advisory Group

The Technical Advisory Group (TAG) was responsible for providing advice on technical issues related to the ICP; it resolved conceptual and methodological matters (see annex B for the 2005 membership list). TAG's members, appointed by the Executive Board, were all internationally known experts in the fields of prices or national accounts. To overcome the shortcomings of previous rounds, several major methodological improvements were implemented in the ICP program, with TAG providing technical advice. The main innovations and methodological enhancements provided by TAG included the following:

- Analyzed and reviewed the methods used to compute basic heading PPPs and average them to the global level. Upon TAG's recommendation, the Country Product Dummy (CPD) method was used to compute basic heading PPPs and the traditional Gini-Éltetö-Köves-Szulc (GEKS) method was used to aggregate those to the higher-level aggregates, including GDP.
- With misgivings, endorsed implementation of a new methodology to estimate construction PPPs.
- Proposed a new methodology for linking the regional PPPs into a global set in a way that maintained the consistency of the regional results.
- Recommended to the Global Office and the Executive Board those countries that should represent their regions in the Ring price data collection.
- Provided the Global Office and the World Bank with guidance on what data needed to be collected in the ICP to enhance poverty analysis. A significant recommendation was that there be no specific price collection of a poverty basket. Instead, separate weights

reflecting the spending patterns of the poor would be used for aggregating basic heading PPPs to higher levels of the household final consumption expenditure, including its total.

- Provided the Global Office with advice on other technical matters such as how to weight PPPs for basic headings that can have negative values (e.g., net exports), how to improve the data collection for owner-occupied housing, and how to impute equipment PPPs.

Several important papers were authored by TAG members on the many methodological issues faced by the ICP. These papers and minutes of the technical discussions are on the ICP website (http://siteresources.worldbank.org/ICPEXT/Resources/ICP_2011.html) for use by other researchers.

Regional Coordinating Organizations

Regional offices coordinated ICP activities in each of the five geographic regions—Africa, Asia-Pacific, Commonwealth of Independent States (CIS), South America, and Western Asia—through the African Development Bank (AfDB); Asian Development Bank (ADB); Interstate Statistical Committee of the Commonwealth of Independent States (CISSTAT), in partnership with the Federal State Statistics Service (Rosstat) of the Russian Federation and the Bureau of Economic Analysis (Moscow); Statistics Canada, in cooperation with the Economic Commission for Latin America and the Caribbean (ECLAC); and the Economic and Social Commission for Western Asia (ESCWA). In addition, the economies included in the regular PPP program run by Eurostat and OECD were treated as though they were in an autonomous region for the purposes of incorporating their estimates into the worldwide estimates.

Some regions also had advisory boards responsible for establishing the governance structure of the regional program, making decisions on technical aspects relevant to the region, and monitoring the work program and financial and staff resource requirements. The boards also were expected to promote flows of information, disseminate the PPP results, and promote their use in the region. The regional coordinating agencies set up agreements with each of their participating countries outlining the respective roles and responsibilities of the regional coordinator and the country. These agreements provided a formal basis for mutual cooperation.

The main functions of the five regional coordinating organizations acting under the auspices of the Global Office were to liaise with the national agencies responsible for providing data in their region, to develop the regional product pricing lists, to train the staff involved in collecting prices and estimating the basic heading expenditures, to validate the data received, and to produce and publish the regional results. The regional coordinators and the Global Office maintained close ties to ensure the highest degree of consistency across regions.

A very important role of the regional coordinator was preparation of the regional list of products to be priced by the countries. This task required extensive consultations with the countries so that they were able to participate in the selection of products and then understand the nature of the product descriptions for their own data collection. The consultation process continued through the data validation stage when countries in each region were brought together to review jointly the national prices.

The regional coordinators took part in meetings organized by the Global Office, and at those meetings worked together to review the regional results, decide on best practices, and agree on work plans and timetables.

National Coordinating Agencies

In most economies, several different agencies provided the national accounts and price data for the ICP. In such cases, one agency was nominated as the national coordinating office, and within that agency a national ICP coordinator was appointed. The main role of the national coordinator was to ensure that the economy's ICP data (national accounts, prices, and wages) were estimated correctly, that statistical and field staff (involved in collecting prices) were trained in the concepts underlying the ICP and the practical implications for collecting prices, that data were edited and entered into the ICP database, and that editing queries from the regional coordinator were handled promptly. The national coordinators also attended the data validation workshops held in each region to check the consistency of the data supplied by those regions.

As stated earlier, the national coordinators participated fully in specifying the list of products to be priced. A major responsibility was to determine the framework for the price surveys. This task included selecting outlets to ensure their cooperation in the price collection and training the price collectors in the ICP methodology on product specifications.

Coordination with the Eurostat-OECD PPP Programme

The World Bank, Eurostat, and OECD maintained close communications during both the planning and operational phases of the 2005 ICP. The aim was to incorporate the Eurostat-OECD results directly into the ICP by treating the Eurostat-OECD program as a sixth "region" of the world for ICP purposes. The techniques used by Eurostat and OECD differed in some respects from those used in the other regions because the Eurostat-OECD program had developed certain methods over the years that could not always be replicated in other regions. However, the close relationships among the coordinating organizations meant that the results could be satisfactorily integrated despite the different procedures used.

Summary

An important part of the governance structure of the 2005 ICP was the division of the world into five geographical regions; a sixth "region" was devoted to the countries in the Eurostat-OECD PPP Programme. Regionalizing the ICP meant adding to it an extra layer of governance to cater to each of the regions. However, the extra complexity was more than offset by the benefits: the products specified for pricing were more homogeneous within regions, the expenditure patterns were generally more similar among countries in each region, and the language differences were reduced. Also important, dividing the ICP organization among regional offices in closer proximity to the countries they were coordinating produced some operational benefits, particularly the regular personal contact with (and among) the countries.

The Global Office managed and coordinated the program across the regions, disseminated details of the statistical methodology to be employed, and either provided direct financial support or assisted with regional fund-raising activities. The Global Office's activities were supported by the ICP Trust Fund, which was in turn supported financially by several national and international organizations and the World Bank. The regional coordinators met several times in Washington,

DC, and all regional coordinating agencies were represented on the Executive Board to ensure consistency across the regions in all aspects of the ICP.

The regionalization worked very well, although its downside was the need to link together the regional results to obtain a set of worldwide real expenditures and price level indexes. A completely new process, the Ring country method, was developed to link together the regional results, but problems arose in implementing the approach (see chapter 8 for details). As a result, a new methodology has been proposed to link the regions in the 2011 ICP. It is based on all countries collecting, in addition to prices for their region-specific products, prices for a range of products on a worldwide product list.

Although it was not part of the original governance strategy, several partnering arrangements established between some national statistics offices and the regional and global coordinators proved to be very effective. The Federal State Statistics Service of the Russian Federation and Statistics Canada were the respective coordinators of the CIS and South America regions. Using funding made available by the Australian Agency for International Development (AusAID), the Australian Bureau of Statistics led the development of the product specifications for consumption in the Asia-Pacific region and also provided technical support for the overall program. The U.K. Office for National Statistics supplied not only the Africa region with technical support but also the Global Office in coordinating the Ring program. France's statistical office, Institut national de la statistique et des études économiques (INSEE), gave the Africa region technical support as well. As a result of the success of the partnering arrangements in the 2005 round, a similar process is being adopted for the 2011 ICP.

Overall for the 2005 ICP, the ICP Executive Board proved to be an effective policy-making body, ensuring support from all stakeholders. The Technical Advisory Group also provided valuable methodological support for several complex problems. Meanwhile, the regional and national coordinators effectively organized and executed their respective programs. However, problems did arise on several occasions, and, as a result, questions were raised about the legal status of the Executive Board, its authority, and whether members served in their own right or as representatives of their organizations. Questions were also raised about the authority of the Global Office as it extended to implementing the methodology in the regions.

Because the requirements for data access and sharing were not clearly defined at the start of the 2005 ICP, some countries were reluctant to furnish data at the desired level of detail and to have their data reviewed by the Global Office and other regions. Fairly late in the process, the Global Office had to prepare some detailed policies dealing with access to microdata and the conditions under which data could be shared between the regional coordinator responsible for a country, other regions, and the Global Office. The policies also covered issues related to access to unpublished data sets after the final global results were published. These policies provide a firm basis for the 2011 ICP and so are unlikely to be modified significantly.

Overall, the governance arrangements worked very well, with only relatively minor fine-tuning required over the duration of the 2005 ICP. Their effectiveness has resulted in similar governance arrangements being put in place for the 2011 ICP round, albeit with some more fine-tuning, including enlarging the Executive Board and the Technical Advisory Group to enable more broadly based representation on those bodies.

Full details of the governance arrangements for the 2011 ICP round are available in a paper presented to the Executive Board at its meeting on February 21, 2010 (World Bank 2009).[1]

ANNEX A

ICP Executive Board—ICP 2005

For the 2005 ICP, the membership of the Executive Board was based on institutions and agencies rather than on individuals. Dennis Trewin, Australian Bureau of Statistics, was appointed chair. Senior members of the ICP Global Office, including the global manager, were *ex officio* members. The following agencies were represented on the Executive Board:

African Development Bank (AfDB)
Asian Development Bank (ADB)
Australian Bureau of Statistics (ABS)
Ecole Nationale Supérieure de Statistique et d'Economie Appliquée (ENSEA)
Economic and Social Commission for Western Asia (ESCWA)
Economic Commission for Latin America and the Caribbean (ECLAC)
Eurostat (European Commission)
Federal State Statistics Service (Rosstat), Russian Federation
International Monetary Fund (IMF)
Interstate Statistical Committee of the Commonwealth of Independent States (CISSTAT)
Ministry of Statistics and Programme Implementation, India
National Bureau of Statistics of China (NBS)
Office for National Statistics (ONS), United Kingdom
Organisation for Economic Co-operation and Development (OECD)
Statistics Canada
Uganda Bureau of Statistics (UBOS)
United Nations Statistics Division (UNSD)
World Bank

ANNEX B

ICP Technical Advisory Group (TAG)—ICP 2005

Unlike the Executive Board, the membership of TAG was largely based on the selection of individuals rather than on the agency to which they belonged. The exceptions were Eurostat and the Organisation for Economic Co-operation and Development (OECD), which were represented at all TAG meetings on an agency basis. At times, experts in a particular field were invited to attend a meeting to discuss specific issues.

The following were ongoing members of TAG:

Alan Heston, University of Pennsylvania, United States, *Chair*
Frederic A. Vogel, ICP Global Manager, World Bank, *Ex officio*
Angus S. Deaton, Princeton University, United States
W. Erwin Diewert, University of British Columbia, Canada
Francette Koechlin, OECD
Paulus Konijn, Eurostat, Luxembourg
Paul McCarthy, Australian Bureau of Statistics
D. S. Prasada Rao, University of Queensland, Australia
David Roberts, OECD
Sergey Sergeev, Statistics Austria
Silke Stapel, Eurostat, Luxembourg
Kimberly D. Zieschang, International Monetary Fund

NOTE

1. The United Nations Statistical Commission oversees the work of the United Nations Statistics Division.

REFERENCES

UNSC (United Nations Statistical Commission). 1999. *Evaluation of the International Comparison Programme* (1–5 March 1999). Document for Item 3 (e) of the provisional agenda of the 30th session of the UNSC, Document E/CN.3/1999/8. http://unstats.un.org/unsd/statcom/doc99/report-e.pdf.

World Bank. 2005. "ICP Operational Manual." http://siteresources.worldbank.org/ICPINT/Resources/ICPOperationalManual2005.pdf.

———. 2007. *ICP 2005 Methodological Handbook*. http://web.worldbank.org/WBSITE/EXTERNAL/DATASTATISTICS/ICPEXT/0,,contentMDK:20126612~pagePK:60002244~piPK:62002388~theSitePK:270065,00.html.

———. 2009. "Governance Framework for the Management and Implementation of the 2011 Round of the International Comparison Program." http://siteresources.worldbank.org/ICPINT/Resources/270056-1255977007108/6483550-1255989768843/6484877-1263333952121/01.02_ICP-EB02_GovernanceFrameworkforICP2011.pdf.

CHAPTER 3

National Accounts Framework for International Comparisons: GDP Compilation and Breakdown Process

Paul McCarthy

The primary purpose of the International Comparison Program (ICP) is to provide the purchasing power parities (PPPs) used to convert national estimates of the gross domestic product (GDP) into a common currency.[1] GDP is a measure of a country's economic production, computed without double counting by calculating the value of gross output and then deducting the value of the goods and services used up as intermediate inputs (or intermediate consumption). GDP can also be measured as the market value of all final goods and services produced within a country in a year. The purpose of this chapter is to explain how the concepts underlying GDP must be considered in collecting prices and estimating PPPs. These concepts include defining the final expenditure components of GDP, explaining the prices used to value them, introducing the classifications to be used for the different expenditure components, and describing the data sources commonly used to break down the expenditures into the necessary detail.

The ICP is designed to compare levels of economic activities between countries by estimating PPPs to convert values in national currencies into a common currency in order to provide estimates of "volumes" or "real expenditures" of activity. The real expenditures are commonly based on data from the national accounts, but in practice PPPs can be used to convert any values into a common currency. One of the major uses of PPPs is for poverty analysis. Determining a country's poverty line expressed in both national currency units and an international poverty line of one or two U.S. dollars per day is an important use of PPPs.

Over time, changes in the current values of GDP are a combination of changes in prices and changes in the underlying volume of output. For many purposes, analysts are interested in abstracting from changes in prices to enable them to better assess changes in actual levels of activity, or volumes. Various techniques are used to estimate changes in volumes, and their common element is that the effects of price changes are removed from the changes in the current values. Spatial comparisons also have an equivalent of these times series volumes. It is the outcome of dividing current values of GDP (and its major aggregates) by a PPP. The resulting values can be compared directly between countries, with the values expressed in terms of a common currency and adjusted for differences in price levels between the countries.

The ICP, as a major statistical exercise, requires a great deal of cooperation and coordination between price statisticians and national accountants. A large part of the overall work program is directed at identifying the products to be priced and then collecting and checking the prices required to produce PPPs. Both the selection of the products (the basis of the prices to be collected) and the survey framework for data collection must be consistent with the underlying estimates of expenditures making up GDP. Because of these links between PPPs and national accounts, it is clear that the prices collected in the ICP have to be consistent with the basis on which the national accounting values were recorded.

It is also important that national accounts estimates are consistent between countries. The international framework for national accounts for the 2005 ICP was the *System of National Accounts 1993* (SNA93) and will be again for the 2011 ICP (Commission of the European Communities et al. 1993).

In 2005 the majority of countries worldwide were compiling their national accounts according to SNA93. However, some were still using the version from 1968 or an even earlier one. Countries' national accounts also tend to vary to some extent from the ideal because of the limitations imposed by the statistical data sources available for compiling the accounts. In particular, the extent to which countries adjust their estimates of GDP to ensure they completely cover all economic activities tends to vary significantly. Such an adjustment is relatively more important in developing countries than in developed countries because of activities such as subsistence production.

So that the national accounts data were as consistent as possible, during the preparations for the 2005 ICP country statisticians were brought together to review their estimates of GDP and the breakdowns to the basic headings to make sure they were following the SNA requirements. Some countries had to revise their data so they were more comparable with those of other countries. Considerable effort also went into ensuring that the prices provided for the ICP were consistent with the national accounts expenditures.

One of the main requirements for each country participating in the ICP is to provide national accounts estimates of expenditure on GDP, expressed in terms of its national currency and broken down into 155 detailed expenditure subclasses of GDP known as basic headings. This breakdown of the national accounts aggregates into basic headings provided the values that were converted into real expenditures at detailed levels and also were used as weights when averaging PPPs to more aggregated levels, up to the level of GDP. Because the basic heading values were used as weights, the PPPs of goods and services that accounted for large shares of the final expenditure were given a larger weight in calculating the PPPs for higher-level aggregates than the PPPs of goods and services that had relatively small shares (see chapters 5 and 6 for details on aggregation methods).

In explaining how the concepts underlying GDP must be considered in collecting prices and estimating PPPs, this chapter is organized as follows. The first section describes the three different methods of measuring GDP and those expenditures that have to be imputed to ensure that GDP completely covers all relevant economic activity. The second section explains the components of the expenditure approach to measuring GDP and the specific ICP requirements that result in some modifications in the breakdown of the national accounts expenditure classification into categories such as health and education. The third section goes into detail about the breakdown of GDP into basic headings. The section that follows then describes the basis on which product prices are collected for the ICP to ensure they are consistent with the national accounts values. The final section provides a brief summary and outlines the process proposed for collecting national accounts expenditures in the 2011 ICP. This chapter also contains an annex that lists the 155 basic headings specified for the 2005 ICP.

Concept and Measurement of GDP

GDP measures a country's economic output as the market value of all final goods and services produced within an accounting period (generally a year or a quarter) by enterprises resident in the country. The market value is expressed in terms of "purchasers' prices."[2] The value of GDP measured at purchasers' prices is often referred to as "GDP at current prices" or "current values of GDP" or "nominal GDP." It includes the out-of-country production of a resident producer and excludes in-country production by nonresident producers. For example, a resident producer may have employees working abroad temporarily (less than one year) installing equipment in an oil field. Such output is recorded as part of the GDP of the country in which the producing unit resides (as an export of that producer and the country) rather than as part of the GDP of the country in which the activity is undertaken. In practice, the bulk of a country's output is attributable to business units resident in the country.

Three Methods of Estimating GDP

In concept, GDP is a measure of value added (i.e., gross output less intermediate consumption[3]) from all economic activity within an economy. The three approaches to measuring GDP are as follows, all of which should give the same result:

1. The *production measure* of GDP is derived as the value of gross output (minus intermediate consumption) plus any taxes (minus subsidies[4]) on products not already included in the value of output. The most direct measure of GDP, it is the sum of the value added of every class of enterprise. Many countries use only the production method to estimate their GDP. However, these countries are required to provide the expenditure breakdowns for the ICP. The production approach to measuring GDP is not used to estimate PPPs because prices would be needed for both final output and intermediate consumption, broken down into detailed aggregates, and these would be difficult to collect. Also, a major use of PPPs is to estimate poverty lines, which rely on PPPs for household consumption expenditures.
2. The *income measure* of GDP is derived as the value of compensation of employees added to gross operating surplus, gross mixed incomes,[5] and taxes (minus subsidies) on both production and imports. This approach works off the principle that the incomes of producers and their employees are equal to the value of their products. Therefore, GDP is the sum of all producers' incomes and those of their employees. Income-based estimates of GDP cannot be used by the ICP because no prices are available for gross operating surplus, which is a major component.
3. The *expenditure measure* of GDP is derived as the sum of expenditures on final consumption by households and by government added to gross fixed capital formation[6] and exports (minus imports). This measure is based on the principle that all of the final products are either purchased by someone or put into inventories. The breakdown of GDP into aggregates and basic headings for the ICP is based on the expenditure method

because it is easier to obtain the underlying prices for these components. The values of final expenditures recorded in the national accounts are closely associated with the data and prices used for the national consumer and producer price indexes for household consumption and equipment purchases by businesses, respectively.

Conceptually, each of these methods results in the same estimate of GDP, but, in practice, data deficiencies can lead to differences between them.

The difference between the production-based measure of GDP and each of the income- and expenditure-based estimates of GDP may be shown explicitly as a "statistical discrepancy" for each of those accounts. In some countries, the three approaches are balanced using supply-use tables, which provide a framework for systematically removing any discrepancies between these three conceptually identical estimates of GDP.

Expenditure-based estimates of GDP comprise (1) final consumption expenditure by households and by government, (2) gross fixed capital formation by businesses and government, and (3) net exports (exports minus imports) of goods and services. Gross capital formation by businesses consists of the buildings or equipment acquired (such as a factory or industrial machinery) and civil engineering works (such as a port acquired or built by a coal exporter) and changes in inventories. Examples of gross capital formation by government would be the construction of government schools or the purchase of equipment for a government hospital. Imports of goods and services have to be deducted in calculating GDP because, although they are included in the final expenditures, they are part of the production of the countries from which they have been imported rather than part of domestic production (i.e., GDP). The expenditure for an import appears in the basic heading in which the purchase takes place—for example, the expenditures for an automobile imported and purchased by a consumer are recorded in "household final consumption expenditure on motor car purchases."

GDP Compared with Gross National Income

GDP measures the production by producers who reside within a country's territory. The income generated from such production is distributed mainly to residents of the country, but some of the income may accrue to nonresidents (such as the interest or dividends that have to be paid abroad or the cost of servicing foreign debt). Similarly, some residents may receive income from nonresidents (such as interest or dividends paid to residents from abroad). For some types of analysis, these income flows can be of interest, which leads to the concept of gross national income (GNI). GNI measures the value of the incomes received by residents. It differs from GDP by the net amount of the income flows between a country's residents and the residents of other countries.

National Accounts Production Boundary

The production boundary of GDP defines the activities to be included or excluded from the measure of economic output. In theory, all output for market is included in the production boundary of GDP, which has implications for the data required for the ICP. Some nonmarket production is also included in the production boundary.

Market output is output that is sold at economically significant prices or is otherwise disposed of on the market. Prices are said to be economically significant when they have a significant influence on the amounts that producers are willing to supply and on the amounts purchasers wish to buy. Apart from certain service industries that have adopted special conventions, the value of the market output of a producer is obtained as follows for an accounting period (year or quarter):

Market output of a producer
equals the total value of goods and services sold
plus the total value of goods and services bartered
plus the total value of goods and services used for payments in kind, including employees' compensation in kind
plus the total value of goods and services supplied by one establishment to another belonging to the same market enterprise to be used as intermediate inputs
plus the total value of changes in inventories of finished goods and work in progress intended for one or other of the above uses.

The goods and services sold should be valued at the prices received for their sale—that is, at purchasers' prices, taking into account any own-account consumption that has no taxes or margins included in the price. These same prices provide a means to impute values for goods and services bartered, for those provided as payments in kind, and for any goods and services transferred within the enterprise. Income in kind should be valued at purchasers' prices if the employer has purchased the goods and services being provided to the employees. It should be valued at producers' prices if the goods and services were produced by the enterprise itself. Valuing inventories for national accounting purposes is a complicated process; SNA93 states that goods entering inventories should be valued at the prices at which they could have been sold when first produced, and goods withdrawn from inventories should be valued at the prices at which they could be sold at a later time.

The production boundary requires that values be imputed for some of the expenditure components of GDP. Some goods and services are acquired without any payment. For national accounting purposes, values must be imputed for these types of transactions to ensure that GDP measures the value of all the production in an economy and that countries are comparable. The main imputations are income in kind, the rents of owner-occupiers, financial intermediation services indirectly measured (FISIM), barter transactions, and consumption of goods produced for one's own final use. Values are imputed for these goods and services based on the prices of similar goods and services sold on the market, or based on the costs of production when suitable prices are not available.

In theory, the three different measures of GDP (expenditure, income, and production) are identical, although data deficiencies can in practice result in differences. Any imputations have to be recorded for each of these three approaches to measuring GDP to maintain the conceptual identity between them. For example, the value of the personal use of a business vehicle by an employee would be included as part of the "transport" component of the household final consumption expenditure in the expenditure measure of GDP, thereby increasing both that component and GDP itself. On the production side of the accounts, the value of the personal use of the vehicle would be deducted from intermediate consumption and shifted into "income in kind" within compensation of employees, thereby increasing value added for the industry concerned and thus production-based GDP. This increase in the compensation of employees (recorded as "income in kind" within that aggregate) would also flow through directly to the income-based measure of GDP. The imputation and methods used are important to the ICP because they not only affect the value of the real expenditures in the basic headings involved, but also the expenditure weights used to aggregate basic heading PPPs. There are implications as well for the underlying prices to be collected, which is especially important for housing and own consumption.

Imputed Expenditures

This section describes briefly the issues underlying the imputations required.

Income in Kind

Employees sometimes receive goods and services free or at very low prices as part of their compensation. For example, railway workers may have the right to free train travel, coal miners may receive a regular ration of coal, and members of the armed forces may be provided with meals. In the national accounts, goods and services provided as income in kind that is recorded as part of employee compensation should be matched by a corresponding amount in the household final consumption expenditure to ensure that the expenditure-based and income-based estimates of GDP are identical. The category in which such expenditures are recorded depends on the nature of the good or service provided—that is, free railway travel provided to railway employees would be recorded as part of the "transport" component of the household final consumption expenditure, and a coal ration provided to coal miners would be allocated to the "housing, water, electricity, gas, and other fuels" component of this aggregate. For pricing purposes, the income in kind is priced at producers' prices if produced by the employer or at the full price paid by consumers (purchasers' prices) if purchased by the employer for the employee.

Rents of Owner-Occupiers

Under the SNA, people who live in their own dwellings are selling dwelling services to themselves. Therefore, expenditures on rents are estimated both for those who really do pay rents to the owners of their dwellings and for those who own their own houses or apartments.

Expenditures on housing make up a significant part of household consumption. It is difficult to compare housing across countries because residents of some countries live mostly in rental units, while in other countries most persons live in housing they own. Although rental surveys can provide the basis to estimate expenditures for rental properties, it is more difficult to estimate comparable expenditures for those who occupy a dwelling they own.

The general rule is that the rents of owner-occupied dwellings are imputed by reference to rents actually paid for similar dwellings. "Similarity" in the case of dwellings is usually judged by the type of dwelling (single-family or multifamily), location (city center, suburban, or rural), and facilities (such as floor space, running water, indoor toilet, electricity, and central heating). The recommended approach is to complete a matrix of prices showing the average rents actually paid for different types of dwellings. The number of owner-occupied dwellings of each type is then distributed over the same matrix to obtain, by multiplication, the imputed rents of owner-occupiers for each type of dwelling, which are then aggregated to a national total. Problems arise in countries that do not have a well-developed and broadly based rental sector—for example, the rental sector might be mainly confined to the higher-priced part of the rental market such as for expatriates working in the country for a relatively short time. For the 2005 ICP, when countries did not have an adequate rental market to impute housing rentals, they were advised to estimate the expenditures based on the user cost method. The same concept will apply to the 2011 ICP with enhancements made based on the 2005 experience.

The user cost method consists of estimating each cost that the owners of dwellings would have to take into account in fixing a market rent if they decided to rent their dwellings to other people. These costs are intermediate consumption, other taxes (minus subsidies) on production, consumption of fixed capital, and real net operating surplus—that is, nominal operating surplus *minus* nominal holding gain (see table 3.1 for a description of these costs).

The nominal operating surplus is calculated as the value of the dwelling multiplied by the nominal rate of interest. The nominal holding gain is calculated as the value of the dwelling multiplied by the overall rate of inflation.

The main difficulties in applying the user cost method are (1) estimating the stock of owner-occupied dwellings, which is required to calculate both consumption of fixed capital and the net operating surplus; (2) calculating the consumption of fixed capital once the stock has been estimated; and (3) choosing the real rate of return to be applied to the current value of the stock of owner-occupied dwellings to calculate the net operating surplus.

Estimating the expenditure on the services provided by owner-occupied dwellings via the user cost method requires a range of data, but at a fairly aggregated level. The data are generally available in countries that produce estimates of capital stock as part of their national accounts. The basic source for much of the data is a census of population and housing. Table 3.1 shows the data items required and the ways in which they are aggregated.

In many developing countries, particularly in Africa, people build their own houses from locally gathered materials. This so-called traditional housing is almost always occupied by its owners, and so there are no market rentals for equivalent types of dwellings to use in imputing the values of the services of owner-occupied dwellings. As a result, in many countries no values are imputed for these

TABLE 3.1 Estimating the Expenditure on Owner-Occupied Dwelling Services: User Cost (UC) Method

Item no.	Item description
	Intermediate consumption
UC01	Expenditure on maintenance and repair of owner-occupied dwellings
UC02	Gross insurance premiums paid on owner-occupied dwellings
UC03	Insurance claims paid to owners
UC04	Net insurance premiums paid by owners (UC02) – (UC03)
UC05	Total intermediate consumption (UC01) + (UC04)
	Other taxes on production
UC06	Taxes paid by owners on dwelling services
UC07	Taxes paid by owners on the value of owner-occupied dwellings and their associated land
UC08	Total taxes paid by owners (UC06) + (UC07)
	Consumption of fixed capital
UC09	Consumption of fixed capital on owner-occupied dwellings at current prices (excluding land)
	Net operating surplus
UC10	Current market value of stock of owner-occupied dwellings at beginning of year (including land)
UC11	Current market value of stock of owner-occupied dwellings at end of year (including land)
UC12	Current market value of stock of owner-occupied dwellings at midyear (including land) ((UC10) + (UC11))/2)
UC13	Real rate of return on owner-occupied dwellings (including land) expressed as percent per annum
UC14	Real net operating surplus (UC13) x (UC12)/100
	Expenditure on owner-occupied dwelling services
UC15	Expenditure on owner-occupied dwelling services (UC05) + (UC08) + (UC09) + (UC14)

Source: ICP.

services, while in others the imputations appear to be based on actual rents paid for dwellings that may be quite unlike most of the owner-occupied dwellings. Generally, these dwellings would be of higher quality than traditional housing, and therefore the outcome would be an overstatement of the services provided by such dwellings. The approach preferred for the ICP is to impute a value for the services provided by traditional housing by adopting the user cost approach. The estimates can be amalgamated if necessary with those from the rental-equivalence approach for other types of dwellings.

Financial Intermediation Services Indirectly Measured

Financial institutions accept deposits from units (such as households) that want to receive interest on spare funds and then lend these funds to units (such as businesses or households) that wish to borrow funds. The money involved is not matched directly between a depositor and a borrower. Instead, a pool of funds is provided collectively by depositors, and funds are loaned to borrowers from this pool. Unlike most businesses that charge directly for the goods they sell or the services they provide, financial institutions, because of the different nature of financial services, charge for their services in a variety of ways. Examples are a flat fee to provide a particular type of account, a certain price for each transaction on an account, or a fee for every transaction above a specified number in a month. Various combinations of such charges may apply in different countries or even between different financial institutions within a country. Most institutions, however, do have one means of charging in common: they pay lower rates of interest to those who lend them money and charge higher rates of interest to those who borrow from them. This margin between the interest rates on loans and deposits provides financial institutions with the bulk of their funds. In national accounts, the value of production by financial institutions is measured as the sum of their receipts from direct charges plus their receipts from the margins between the interest rates they charge for loans and those they pay for deposits. The indirect charges levied via the differentials in interest rate margins are known as financial intermediation services indirectly measured, or FISIM.

FISIM is paid by everyone (households, unincorporated enterprises, corporations, and government) who use the services of banks and other types of financial institutions. FISIM can also be exported (i.e., paid by nonresidents to resident financial institutions) or imported (i.e., paid by resident businesses or households to nonresident financial institutions). If FISIM is paid by corporations or unincorporated enterprises, it is part of their intermediate consumption. But if it is paid by households as consumers, it is included in their final consumption expenditures and so is part of expenditures on GDP. The situation is slightly more complicated, however, for government and nonprofit institutions serving households (NPISH) because FISIM is part of their intermediate consumption. Because the national accounting convention values the output of general government and NPISH as the sum of their costs of production, FISIM directly affects their final consumption expenditure, and so it also becomes part of the expenditure on GDP. Typically, the GDP level in developed countries is increased by about 2 percent by allocating FISIM across the final expenditures, although it can be higher in countries with large financial sectors. In developing countries, GDP is likely to be increased by about 1 percent by allocating FISIM, although it is also affected by the size of a country's financial sector.

Barter Transactions

Barter is the exchange of goods or services for other goods or services without money changing hands. In principle, the final consumption expenditure by households should include barter transactions, which should be valued at the market worth (purchasers' prices) of the goods or services exchanged. In practice, neither taxes on products nor transportation costs may apply, in which case the purchasers' prices will be the same as the basic prices ("farm gate" prices) of the products involved. If the goods or services exchanged are not of equal value, the average market value of the goods or services involved should be used.

Output Produced for Own Final Use

Goods consumed by the households that produce them (in many countries the largest item will be the crops and livestock produced by small farmers) should be included as part of the output produced for own final use and as part of the household final consumption expenditure. The value imputed for goods arising from subsistence production should be based on the prices that could be obtained by farmers if they had sold the goods rather than consumed them—that is, based on the farm gate prices, which are formally described in the national accounts as being expressed in basic prices. In the ICP, it is important that the prices used to compare such production are recorded consistently in each country. Output produced for own final use also refers to goods or services retained for final use by the owners of the businesses in which the goods and services were produced. Examples are those used for own gross fixed capital formation such as special machine tools produced by engineering businesses and a wide range of construction activities, particularly in rural areas, including the individual or communal construction activities undertaken by households (or groups of households) to build dwellings or add extensions to dwellings. The services produced by employing paid domestic staff also are included as output for own final use. However, the output of domestic and personal *services* produced for own consumption within households is not included. Examples of this type of output are cooking and washing clothes, which are often called "unpaid household services." However, the materials used in producing these outputs, such as food and washing powder, are included in the household final consumption expenditure.

In this area, two issues arise for the ICP. The first is that the value of output produced for own final use cannot be directly valued because it is not sold on the market. As a result, that part relating to businesses must be estimated by applying the basic prices for similar products sold on the market (if such prices are available) to estimates of the quantities of output produced on own account; the sum of the costs of production would be an alternative. Any goods consumed by the households that produce them are best valued using the basic prices (excluding taxes and margins) of similar goods in local markets. The second issue is ensuring that the prices used in the ICP are consistent with the valuation methods used in each country's national accounts.

The importance of the activities discussed in this section varies significantly from one country to the next. For example, surveys conducted by some national statistical offices may be adjusted to take into account informal producers, whereas in other countries no corresponding adjustment is made. Some countries do not include any illegal activities in their data, while others either include some explicit estimates, such as for smuggling, or use a source such as income tax data, which contains the income from illegal activities to the extent they are reported for tax purposes. The expenditure classification of the ICP includes basic headings for narcotics and prostitution, which can account for sizable expenditures, but are also illegal in many countries. In the 2005 ICP, countries were encouraged to account for these expenditures; however, reference PPPs were used for these basic headings. Overall, in the 2005 ICP the Global Office encouraged countries to ensure to the best of their abilities that their national accounts were "exhaustive"—that is, they included the value of all productive activities within the SNA's production boundary.

Expenditure Aggregates of GDP

National accounts estimates based on the expenditure approach and expressed in national currency units are required for the ICP because the prices most readily observed are those related to final expenditures. For example, the consumer price index (CPI) collects prices directly related to many components of the household final consumption expenditure, and producer price indexes (PPIs) include prices for the types of equipment purchased by businesses and included in gross fixed capital formation on machinery and equipment. However, it is important to ensure that PPIs used for the ICP are recorded on (or adjusted to) the basis of purchasers' prices.

The main expenditure aggregates are the following:

- Household final consumption expenditure
- Final consumption expenditure by NPISH
- Government final consumption expenditure
  - Individual consumption expenditure by government
  - Collective consumption expenditure by government
- Final consumption expenditures on health and education
- Actual final consumption
- Gross fixed capital formation
- Change in inventories
- Net acquisitions of valuables
- Balance of exports and imports of goods and services.

Final Consumption Expenditures

The household final consumption expenditure consists of the expenditure (including that whose value must be estimated indirectly) incurred by resident households for individual consumption goods and services, including those sold at prices not economically significant and consumption goods and services acquired abroad.

NPISH consist of nonmarket nonprofit institutions that are not controlled by government. They provide goods and services to households free or at prices that are not economically significant. Examples are social and sports clubs, trade unions, charities, and some types of research bodies and environmental groups.

Market goods and services are recorded in the national accounts on the basis of the values in the accounts of the businesses concerned such as the value of sales by retailers. However, measuring the values of nonmarket services (principally those provided by government bodies and by NPISH) is not a straightforward exercise because the services are provided free or at prices not economically significant, and therefore no prices underlie the output. The convention adopted in the SNA is that the output of nonmarket services is valued at the cost of producing them. The value required for ICP purposes is their final consumption expenditure, which is calculated as the value of the inputs minus the value of any receipts from sales of the services provided. The input components summed to obtain the value of "output" are compensation of employees, intermediate consumption, gross operating surplus (equal to consumption of fixed capital because net operating surplus should be zero), and net taxes on products.

The government final consumption expenditure consists of the expenditure (including that whose value must be estimated indirectly) incurred by general government on both individual consumption goods and services and collective consumption services. Such expenditures can be incurred by the central (or national), state (or provincial), or local levels of government. In some countries, social security funds also constitute government units.

An important distinction is made within the government final consumption expenditure between an individual consumption good or service—that is, one acquired by a household and used by members of that household—and a collective consumption service—that is, a service provided simultaneously to all members of the community or to all members of a particular section of the community such as all households living in a particular region. Collective services are financed by general government units out of tax revenues or other incomes. Examples are public administration and police services.

Government expenditures defined as individual fall into two categories:

1. Services produced by the government for the benefit of individual households such as running schools and hospitals. The government organizes and finances the production of these services for consumption by individual households.
2. Goods and services purchased by government from other producers that are then passed on to households, either free or at prices below the costs of production, without any further processing by government. Examples are medicines and medical services for outpatients. In some cases, households obtain these goods and services free or at very low prices at the point of sale, while in others households pay the full price at the point of sale and are later reimbursed in part or in full by the government.

All expenditures within the household final consumption expenditure are considered to be individual. Similarly, most goods and services produced by NPISH represent individual consumption, but it is possible for NPISH to provide collective services—for example, research institutes that make their research freely available. However, for practical purposes all expenditures by NPISH can be considered individual, which was the procedure adopted for the 2005 ICP.

Final Consumption Expenditures on Health and Education

Health and education expenditures make up over 20 percent of the world's expenditures on GDP expressed in international dollars. Because health and education services are provided by both private and government sources, the estimation of expenditures and PPPs requires steps not needed for other consumption items. The methods used to estimate the expenditure breakdowns to the basic headings, the prices required, and the estimation of PPPs are described in chapter 11. The purpose of this section is to provide an overview of how health and education expenditures are to be recorded and the prices used in the estimation of PPPs.

Health products and education services can be obtained in three different ways: (1) they are paid for in full by the purchaser; (2) they are paid for in full by the government and provided free to households; or (3) they are paid for in part by households and in part by the government.

Countries differ in how they provide and charge for health and education goods and services. They may be supplied to varying degrees by the private sector or by the government. Even if they are provided by the private sector, government subsidies can affect the prices charged. The subsidies may be applied directly to the service charge to reduce it, such as providing a certain amount for a patient to consult a doctor, or they may be provided at a broader level, such as an annual subsidy to individual schools. In addition, in many countries households can purchase insurance cover for many health goods and services. The outcome is that the extent of charging, the prices charged, and the types of subsidies provided can vary significantly from one country to another, which makes it difficult to directly compare prices for health and education services. For this reason, the concept of actual final consumption is used for the ICP. To compare health and education expenditures (real expenditures or per capita real expenditures), it is necessary to combine the respective expenditures made by households, NPISH, and the government.

The prices required for the 2005 ICP for health and education had to reflect the full price, no matter who was paying for the goods or services—that is, the purchasers' prices. In the 2005 ICP, the actual price paid was required for products purchased and paid for in full by consumers.

In many cases, it was not possible to identify a price for products paid for in full by the government and provided free to households because the products may have been produced by the government and not sold on the market. In such cases, the full cost of each product to the government was the "price" required. The price required for the 2005 ICP for products paid for in part by households and in part by the government was the total of any amounts paid for each product by the consumer plus any contribution to the unit cost made by the government. However, the different combinations of payment methods adopted by countries made it very difficult to collect consistent prices from country to country. As a result, investigations are under way of alternative methods of deriving real expenditures for health and education for the 2011 ICP.

Actual Final Consumption

The total value of goods and services acquired by households for final consumption includes the individual goods and services used by but not directly purchased by the final user. The distinction between who consumes (individuals or the community) and who pays (households, NPISH, or government) is used in SNA93 to derive a new aggregate called "actual final consumption," which is an important measure for the ICP, especially for health and education. The actual individual consumption of households is obtained by adding individual consumption expenditures by NPISH and by government to the final consumption expenditure by households. Collective consumption is entirely attributable to government. The ICP uses the concept of actual final consumption rather than that of final consumption expenditure when presenting the results for consumption expenditures.

The relationships between the components of final consumption expenditure and actual final consumption are shown in table 3.2.

When actual final consumption is used as the basis for the ICP, the comparisons of services such as health and education provided in part by government and in part by private suppliers are consistent across countries because the total of these services is being compared no matter who provides them.

Table 3.3 shows for selected countries the potential size of the differences that can arise between the household final consumption expenditure and actual final consumption expenditure when countries have very different institutional arrangements for providing individual services such as health and education. In this comparison of the individual consumption expenditure by households, individual consumption expenditure by government, and actual individual consumption, it is not possible to show the first two data columns as a share of the third because the estimation methods used in the 2005 ICP resulted in nonadditive real expenditures within a country. However, it is legitimate to directly compare countries' real expenditures per capita for each expenditure category. The table reveals that the United States has a level of individual

TABLE 3.2 Relationship between Final Consumption Expenditure and Actual Final Consumption

Final consumption expenditure	Actual final consumption
Households Individual consumption expenditure by households *NPISH* Individual consumption expenditure by NPISH	*Actual individual consumption* Individual consumption expenditure by households + individual consumption expenditure by NPISH + individual consumption expenditure by government
Government Collective consumption expenditure by government + individual consumption expenditure by government	*Actual collective consumption* Collective consumption expenditure by government

Source: ICP.

TABLE 3.3 Comparison of Per Capita Individual Consumption Expenditure by Households and by Government and Actual Individual Consumption: Selected Countries

international dollars

Country	Individual consumption expenditure by households	Individual consumption expenditure by government	Actual individual consumption[a]
Brazil	4,480	1,648	5,720
India	1,176	319	1,455
Norway	17,362	7,793	24,610
Russian Federation	5,546	2,837	7,918
Sweden	14,372	8,712	21,818
United States	29,332	2,673	31,995

Source: ICP.

a. Actual individual consumption in international dollars is not the sum of the individual consumption expenditure by households and the individual consumption expenditure by government because real expenditures are not additive within a country under the method used to compute PPPs. See chapters 5 and 6 for descriptions of these methods.

consumption expenditure by households that is more than double that of Sweden and about two-thirds greater than that of Norway, but its individual consumption by government is well under half that of Sweden and Norway. These per capita values reflect the more important role of the government sector in providing health and education in Sweden and Norway. The values shown in table 3.3 are real expenditures per capita, expressed in international dollars.

Gross Fixed Capital Formation

This category includes the total value of the gross fixed capital formation, changes in inventories, and acquisitions (minus disposal of valuables). Gross fixed capital formation includes construction of residential and nonresidential buildings, construction of civil engineering works such as roads, and purchases of machinery and equipment. Because these items are difficult to both measure and compare, separate chapters in this volume describe the methodology used to estimate PPPs for construction (chapter 13) and equipment (chapter 14). Gross fixed capital formation is measured by the total value of a producer's acquisitions (minus disposals) of fixed assets during the accounting period plus a certain specified expenditure on services that adds to the value of nonproduced assets (fixed assets are defined as those used in production for more than one year). Changes in inventories are measured by the value of the entries into inventories minus the value of withdrawals and the value of any recurrent losses of goods held in inventories during an accounting period. Valuables are produced goods of considerable worth that are not used primarily for production or consumption but are held as stores of value over time.

Changes in Inventories, Net Acquisition of Valuables, and Balance of Exports and Imports

Exports are goods and services produced within the domestic economy but used by other economies. Imports are goods and services supplied from outside the domestic economy. For the ICP, the aggregate required is the net balance of exports and imports of goods and services, which, of course, could be positive or negative.

Three aggregates of GDP could have negative values: changes in inventories, net acquisition of valuables, and balance of exports and imports. In an annual set of estimates such as those for the 2005 ICP, the one most likely to be significant is the balance of exports and imports. The major implication of having negative values is that they complicate the process of aggregating basic heading PPPs to obtain the PPP for GDP because the weight has a negative value.

Another potentially negative component is the net expenditures of residents abroad. The value can be positive or negative, depending on whether the expenditures of visitors to the country outweigh those of the country's residents who go abroad or vice versa. It can also be zero in countries that use data from household expenditure surveys of their residents to compile estimates of the household final consumption expenditure. SNA93 does not include net expenditures of residents abroad as a specific category within GDP, but it is a required basic heading for the ICP.

In the 2005 ICP, the net expenditures of residents abroad were not reported consistently by participating countries. Many countries reported zero expenditure for this item, indicating that either it had been allocated across relevant components of the household final consumption expenditure or it had not been estimated. A zero value may be recorded in a country's accounts because the item is considered insignificant or because the data sources, such as a household expenditure survey, used to calculate the household final consumption expenditure did not require this balancing adjustment.

Breakdown of GDP Expenditures into Basic Headings

This section explains the concepts that determine the classification of the components of GDP into expenditure aggregates, and from there the breakdown into basic headings. The level at which the most detailed national accounts data for the ICP are provided is known as the "basic heading." Ideally, both values and prices would be available for all major individual products so that PPPs and real expenditures could be estimated at the product level. In practice, however, it is not possible to obtain values in such fine detail. The compromise, then, is to determine the lowest level for which expenditures can be supplied and to which products can be uniquely assigned. The basic heading expenditures are also used as weights in the aggregation to higher levels of expenditures on GDP. Therefore, the importance of the basic heading extends beyond its role as simply a means of classifying the most detailed value component within the ICP. In fact, it is no exaggeration to describe the basic headings as the backbone of the ICP.

The Eurostat–Organisation for Economic Co-operation and Development (OECD) PPP Programme uses 225 basic headings. These basic headings are compatible with the 155 used in the 2005 ICP; some of them are, however, broken down into more levels than those specified for the ICP. The importance of the basic heading as the most detailed building block of the ICP is embodied in its definition:

> The basic heading is the lowest level of aggregation of items in the GDP breakdown for which parities are calculated. In theory, a basic heading is defined as a group of similar well-defined goods or services. In practice, it is defined by the lowest level of final expenditure for which explicit expenditure weights can be estimated. Thus, an actual basic heading can cover a broader range of products than is theoretically desirable. Basic headings are the building blocks of a comparison. It is at the level of the basic heading that expenditures are defined, products selected, prices collected, prices edited, and PPPs first calculated and averaged. (World Bank 2007)

The use of basic headings as "building blocks" for the broader national accounts aggregates is obvious in the following structure of gross fixed capital formation for machinery and equipment. The structure consists of two product groups: metal products and equipment, which contains five basic headings, and transport equipment, which consists of three basic headings.

150000	**EXPENDITURE ON GROSS FIXED CAPITAL FORMATION**
150100	**MACHINERY AND EQUIPMENT**
150110	**Metal products and equipment**
150111.1	Fabricated metal products, except machinery and equipment
150112.1	General-purpose machinery
150113.1	Special-purpose machinery
150114.1	Electrical and optical equipment
150115.1	Other manufactured goods n.e.c. (not elsewhere classified)
150120	**Transport equipment**
150121.1	Motor vehicles, trailers, and semitrailers
150121.2	Other road transport
150122.1	Other transport equipment

Several aspects of the role of the basic heading as a building block affect both the values and the prices collected for the ICP. The basic headings are the starting point for identifying the products to be priced for the ICP, and so each one is defined in terms of a set of like products. For example, "rice" is a basic heading, but many different types of rice can be priced in different countries. In the 2005 ICP, the number of specifications for individual types of rice varied by the region. In Asia, where rice is an important staple food, 19 different types of rice were specified, whereas in the Eurostat-OECD PPP Programme only eight rice specifications were used. A basic heading can also be very broad in its coverage. For example, gross fixed capital formation on nonresidential building construction includes the full range of structures. Examples are farm buildings such as stables and machinery sheds, industrial buildings such as factories and warehouses, commercial buildings such as offices and shops, and other nonresidential buildings such as hospitals, schools, hotels, and cinemas.

SNA Classifications

International classifications provide a coherent and consistent means of defining the structure of the economic activities within their scope based on a set of internationally agreed concepts, definitions, principles, and rules. Their importance is that they provide a comprehensive framework within which data can be collected, reported, and analyzed. The most important aspect of any classification is that the categories defined by the classification are both complete (have no gaps) and consistent (have no overlaps). The 2005 ICP was no exception; the expenditure classification was designed to ensure full coverage of all components of GDP.

Classification systems are required to ensure that every possible product with expenditures going into GDP is uniquely assigned to a basic heading. For example, fresh meat is in a different basic heading than sausage because the latter involves additional processing and storage requirements. Although the basic heading is the lowest level at which expenditures are needed, the classification is important so that products included in each heading are as homogeneous as possible. The starting point for the detailed classifications used in the 2005 ICP was those defined in SNA93. The SNA classifications for consumption expenditures are Classification of Individual Consumption by Purpose (COICOP) and Classification of the Functions of Government (COFOG).

COICOP is designed to provide estimates of the individual consumption expenditure based on the purpose of the expenditure being incurred. In the 2005 ICP, the individual consumption expenditure by household was divided into 110 basic headings. The starting point identified aggregates such as food, clothing and footwear, transport, and communication. More detailed data breakdowns were defined within each of these aggregates at the next level of the classification. For example, food was divided into nine classes as shown in the annex to this chapter. Table 3.4 lists the basic headings assigned to the bread and cereals and meat classes.

The individual consumption expenditure by NPISH was treated as a single basic heading. Because many countries were not able to separate NPISH expenditures from those by households, for publication purposes the Global Office distributed NPISH expenditures where provided back into the individual consumption expenditure by households. The Global Office is examining the usefulness of including NPISH as a separate basic heading before deciding how to handle this component in the 2011 ICP round.

The Classification of the Functions of Government is designed to classify general government transactions at all levels of government by function or purpose such as health and education. COFOG can be applied to various types of transactions, including the final consumption expenditure, subsidies and current transfers, capital formation and capital transfers, and acquisition of financial assets by general government. For the 2005 ICP, COFOG played an important role in identifying the final expenditure categories by function for which the basic headings were defined.

The individual consumption expenditures by government were classified into 21 basic headings, each linked to a five-digit code in COFOG. The government expenditures were first distributed according to purpose (such as housing, health, recreation and culture, education, and social protection) and then, in the case of health and education, by whether the expenditure was for the purchase of health or education services from other producers or whether it was for the production of health or education services by government itself (see chapter 11 for additional details about the linkage between government and household expenditures for health and education).

The basic headings for government individual consumption that included the production of health and education services consisted of the following cost components: compensation of employees, which is the largest component of government expenditures; intermediate consumption;

TABLE 3.4 Example of Basic Headings Assigned to Bread and Cereals and Meat Aggregates

ICP group	Basic heading
Bread and cereals	Rice Other cereals, flour, and other cereal products Bread Other bakery products Pasta products
Meat	Beef and veal Pork Lamb, mutton, and goat Poultry Other meat and meat preparations

Source: ICP.

gross operating surplus (equal to consumption of fixed capital because net operating surplus should be zero for government); net taxes on production; and receipts from sales.

Collective consumption expenditures by government were classified by cost component in a way similar to that for individual consumption by government.

To define the basic headings, gross fixed capital formation was classified in the 2005 ICP by type of product according to the Statistical Classification of Products by Activity (CPA). Twelve basic headings were identified: eight for machinery and equipment, three for construction, and one for "other products," which included those of agriculture, forestry, fisheries and aquaculture; computer software; expenditures on land improvement such as fencing, leveling, irrigation, and drainage; mineral exploration; and creation of entertainment, literary, and artistic originals.

Two basic headings were used for inventories: opening value of inventories and closing value of inventories. Similarly, acquisitions of valuables and disposals of valuables were identified separately.

A detailed breakdown of expenditures on exports and imports of goods and services was not required because the balance of exports and imports was classified into only two basic headings: exports of goods and services and imports of goods and services.

In the 2005 ICP, considerable effort went into reviewing each country's basic heading expenditures to ensure that consistent approaches were followed. As might be expected, this exercise was difficult for countries that lacked good statistical capabilities, but they received assistance; data from similar countries were used to break down data to the basic heading. A basic heading is also a form of stratification, and it is the first stage at which PPPs are computed. These first-stage PPPs are then averaged to higher aggregates using the basic heading expenditures as weights. From a sampling point of view, statistical variability is greatest at this level and precludes publishing data for most basic headings. However, as the accounts are aggregated the degree of confidence in the estimates grows.

Table 3.5 presents details on the distribution of the basic headings used in the 2005 ICP for the major expenditure aggregates of GDP.

Data Sources and Methods

An essential requirement for participating in the ICP was that a country provide details of its expenditure on GDP, including expenditures for the 155 basic headings. The Global Office encouraged countries to use a commodity flow approach (preferably going the extra step of producing supply-use tables) to help in breaking down the expenditure aggregates into basic headings. For example, import data could be used to estimate the basic heading breakdown of gross fixed capital formation on machinery and equipment in countries that had little domestic production of capital equipment. However, even countries that had detailed supply-use tables had to take some special steps to estimate the details for every basic heading. For example, food balances compiled by the UN Food and Agriculture Organization could be used as a data source to break down food expenditures to the basic heading. In some countries, the national statisticians had to use expert judgment to break down the data to basic headings. The regional coordinators also reviewed the national breakdowns and advised countries to follow the allocations of similar economies in their region if they had no other data. The exercise was most difficult in countries that did not systematically estimate all expenditure components in their annual accounts.

Other sources of information for the breakdown into basic headings were production statistics from industrial and agricultural censuses and surveys to provide estimates of expenditures on food, surveys of restaurants and hotels to obtain sales volumes, records of motor vehicle registrations to make the distinction between freight and passenger vehicles, reports on sales to

TABLE 3.5 Number of Categories, Groups, Classes, and Basic Headings, ICP 2005

Main aggregates	Categories	Groups	Classes	Basic headings
Individual consumption expenditure by households	**13**	**43**	**90**	**110**
01 Food and nonalcoholic beverages		2	11	29
02 Alcoholic beverages, tobacco, and narcotics		3	5	5
03 Clothing and footwear		2	5	5
04 Housing, water, electricity, gas, and other fuels		4	7	7
05 Furnishings, household equipment, and maintenance		6	12	13
06 Health		3	7	7
07 Transport		3	13	13
08 Communication		3	3	3
09 Recreation and culture		6	13	13
10 Education		1	1	1
11 Restaurants and hotels		2	2	2
12 Miscellaneous goods and services		7	10	10
13 Net purchases abroad		1	1	2
Individual consumption expenditure by NPISH	**1**	**1**	**1**	**1**
Individual consumption expenditure by government	**5**	**7**	**16**	**21**
01 Housing		1	1	1
02 Health		2	7	12
03 Recreation and culture		1	1	1
04 Education		2	6	6
05 Social protection		1	1	1
Collective consumption expenditure by government	**1**	**1**	**5**	**5**
Gross fixed capital formation	**3**	**6**	**11**	**12**
01 Machinery and equipment		2	7	8
02 Construction		3	3	3
03 Other products		1	1	1
Change in inventories and acquisitions minus disposals of valuables	**2**	**2**	**2**	**4**
01 Change in inventories		1	1	2
02 Acquisitions minus disposals of valuables		1	1	2
Balance of exports and imports	**1**	**1**	**1**	**2**
GDP	**26**	**61**	**126**	**155**

Source: ICP.

households by utility companies and state monopolies to obtain expenditure data, and statistics on the value added tax (VAT) or other sales taxes classified according to the goods and services taxed.

The problems most commonly encountered in estimating basic heading values were the final consumption expenditure by NPISH and gross capital formation, especially on software, inventories, valuables, and relevant parts of defense expenditures. Government accounts and annual reports were the most important sources of data on public investment, and the two main sources for private capital expenditure were investment surveys of enterprises and the commodity flow method. The latter involves estimating the total supply—domestic production plus imports, both at basic prices—of goods used for capital formation. Margins for any wholesaling and retailing involved separately invoiced transport charges, and net product taxes were then added to obtain the estimated value of gross fixed capital formation at purchasers' prices.

Price Concepts

Two key characteristics of the prices collected for the ICP are that they must be comparable between countries and representative of the expenditures in each. It is very important that the prices underlying the national accounts values and the prices collected for the ICP are consistent with each other—that is, they are representative of the products underlying the corresponding value. But in practice that meant for the 2005 ICP that the annual national average prices had to be collected to ensure consistency with the national accounts values. In large countries, it was necessary to collect prices across a number of regions or to adjust the prices collected in a smaller number of regions to national average prices. For the 2005 ICP, prices were collected in most regions across the four quarters of 2005 to provide an estimate of annual average prices that took into account prices that varied on a seasonal basis.

SNA Concepts

The *System of National Accounts* identifies three different bases for measuring prices: basic prices, producers' prices, and purchasers' prices. The differences between these prices depend on how taxes and subsidies on products, transport charges, and trade margins are recorded. Deductible taxes, such as value added taxes and similar deductible taxes, may also affect the prices recorded. It is important to correctly identify the pricing basis for each type of transaction because the differences can be significant.

The values recorded for the components of expenditure on GDP are expressed in purchasers' prices because the transactions are based on the prices paid by the final users of the goods and services, such as households for consumption goods and businesses for capital goods. It is important to ensure consistency between the prices underlying the national accounts values and the prices collected for the ICP. In practice, it means the pricing basis required for the ICP is purchasers' prices (except for any imputed expenditures valued on a basis other than purchasers' prices such as some own-account production). The relationships between basic prices, producers' prices, and purchasers' prices are as follows:

Basic prices
plus taxes on products excluding invoiced VAT
less subsidies on products
equal **producers' prices**
plus VAT not deductible by the purchaser
plus separately invoiced transport charges
plus wholesalers' and retailers' margins
equal **purchasers' prices.**

Valuing Own-Account Production and Consumption

As indicated earlier in this chapter, any goods consumed by the households that produce them should be valued at basic prices. In developing countries, the values of own-account consumption can be a significant proportion of overall consumption of some products, particularly foodstuffs such as meat, milk, eggs, vegetables, potatoes, fruits, and even wine and spirits. The value of each of these types of products purchased from shops, markets, or elsewhere is recorded in the national accounts at purchasers' prices, which is consistent with the prices collected for the consumer price index. Unlike basic prices, purchasers' prices include taxes, as well as trade and transport margins, and so they are higher than basic prices. It is important that the prices collected for the ICP are appropriately adjusted to take into account the two different price bases underlying the valuation of such products. The preferred method is to obtain details of the basic prices used to value each of these products in the national accounts and weight them together with the purchasers' prices that are obtained from the CPI or other similar sources to obtain the prices required for the ICP. (The basic prices should be farm gate prices, usually obtained by a special survey such as a household budget survey.) The level of (product) detail at which the prices can be weighted together will vary from one country to another. Ideally, the prices and weights would be available for every individual product, but realistically it is more likely that all the data required for these calculations will not be available below the basic heading level. At that level, some assumptions will be required to obtain an average unit price underlying all the products within a basic heading. The weights should be estimated using the expenditures recorded in the national accounts for each of the shares of own-account consumption and purchased components of each product. Table 3.6 provides an example of the calculations required.

In the table the first set of columns shows the expenditure values, the basic price, and the implied quantities of each good produced for own-account consumption. The next set of columns provides the same breakdown for purchased products. Note that the prices for own-account consumption and purchased quantities differ. The implied quantities are used to compute a weighted average.

The ratio in column (10) is divided into the purchasers' prices for each product within the relevant basic heading to obtain the average prices to use for that product in the ICP. For example, if the country represented by the table collected prices for rump steak, beef for a stew or curry, minced beef, and veal chops under the "beef and veal" heading, then each unit price would be adjusted for the ICP by dividing it by 1.231 (see table 3.7 for an example).

Similarly, the purchaser's price for each of the products this country priced under the "poultry" heading would be adjusted by dividing each price by the factor calculated for poultry products, 1.267.

Pricing Market Output

The SNA points out that different households may pay different prices for identical products because of the costs of identifying the retail outlets selling at the lowest prices, or households may find it be too inconvenient or costly to visit the outlets selling at the lowest prices. However, household expenditures are recorded at the prices actually paid, even though identical goods or services may not be valued uniformly.

Prices and Nonmarket Output

Nonmarket output should be valued using the prices of equivalent market output (if these are available). Otherwise, it should be valued at the cost of production. The prices required for ICP purposes are those that correspond to those underlying the values recorded in the national accounts. For example, the government final consumption expenditure is valued at the cost of production, which largely consists of the wages paid to the government employees involved in the production of government services. As a result, the ICP collects details of the wages of a range of government employees to calculate the PPPs required to estimate the real expenditures for the government final consumption expenditure.

TABLE 3.6 Estimating Adjustment Factor Price for Products with Significant Amounts of Own-Account Production

national currency

Product	Own-account consumption			Purchased products			Total			
	Value	Average underlying price	Implied quantity	Value	Average underlying price	Implied quantity	Value	Quantity	Average price	Ratio to divide into purchasers' prices to obtain average prices for ICP
	(1)	(2)	(3) = (1)/(2)	(4)	(5)	(6) = (4)/(5)	(7) = (1) + (4)	(8) = (3) + (6)	(9) = (7)/(8)	(10) = (9)/(2)
Meat										
Beef and veal	2,000	9	222.2	6,000	12	500.0	8,000	722.2	11.1	1.231
Pork	500	12	41.7	1,800	14	128.6	2,300	170.2	13.5	1.126
Lamb and mutton	4,500	8	562.5	7,000	11	636.4	11,500	1,198.9	9.6	1.199
Poultry	7,000	6	1,166.7	12,000	9	1,333.3	19,000	2,500.0	7.6	1.267

Source: ICP.

TABLE 3.7 Obtaining Adjusted Price to Use in ICP

national currency

Basic heading	Product	Purchaser's price	Adjustment factor	Adjusted price for ICP
Beef and veal			**1.231**	
	Rump steak	17.0		13.8
	Beef for a stew or curry	8.1		6.6
	Minced beef	6.5		5.3
	Veal chops	12.7		10.3

Source: ICP.

Prices for Gross Fixed Capital Formation

In many developing countries, almost all investment machinery and equipment are imported. Because most countries have detailed import statistics through their customs systems, estimates of gross fixed capital formation on machinery and equipment can be obtained through commodity flow techniques. In such cases, though, the valuation basis of the imports will not correspond to that required for national accounts expenditures on GDP. The differences stem from the transport and trade margins that will increase the landed price (the basic price) of each item of machinery and equipment. Any taxes levied will also have to be added to the landed price to estimate the purchaser's price, which can then be used in the commodity flow approach to estimate a value for each group of like items of machinery and equipment. The prices required for the ICP are these estimated purchasers' prices for those investment items specified in the ICP product list.

Reference PPPs

Several PPPs are not directly estimated. Instead, these PPPs are imputed using PPPs from other basic headings that reflect the price levels of each country. For example, the earlier discussion of FISIM clearly demonstrated the difficulty of estimating those expenditures. Therefore, the PPP for FISIM is imputed using the average of PPPs for household final consumption (excluding the health and education basic headings) and other basic headings where PPPs were imputed. The PPPs used for the imputation are known as reference PPPs. Chapter 17 provides a summary of the reference PPPs used in the different regions and their impact on the PPPs at the GDP level.

Summary

The national accounts are an integral component of the ICP. The statistical framework used in the 2005 ICP was the 1993 *System of National Accounts*. Even though the 2008 SNA is now available, the 1993 SNA will be used as the basis for compiling national accounts estimates for the 2011 ICP because most countries will still be using this version in 2012 when the national accounts data have to be supplied.

The 2005 ICP's main requirements for the national accounts were estimates based on the expenditure approach to measuring GDP, divided into 155 basic headings. A similar set of basic headings will be used in the 2011 ICP to facilitate comparisons between the two benchmark years.

The national accounts also provide the basis for the prices to be collected, because it is critical that the prices be consistent with the values recorded in the national accounts so that the real expenditures obtained by dividing national accounts values by PPPs are not distorted.

The national accounts are thus clearly an integral component of the ICP. In the 2005 ICP, the collection of prices received the most emphasis because so much intensive work was required to draw up the product lists in each region and to prepare the Ring list—that is, the prices needed to link together the regions (see chapter 8 for details). As a result, the national accounts data were collected relatively late in the process and several problems were encountered. For example, the national accounts estimates were not always consistent with those given to the various international organizations in the annual national accounts questionnaire; some countries' estimates of GDP were not exhaustive; and several countries were unable to supply values for all the basic headings. Resolving these problems proved to be difficult because of the relatively short time available.

The ICP's special focus on the real expenditure estimates of GDP gives countries an opportunity to improve their national accounts. The ICP also gives countries that do not have national accounts (or whose national accounts may be lagging by several years) an incentive to produce a set of accounts or to update them to 2011. Therefore, the national accounts will be placed at the center of the 2011 ICP framework.

In the 2005 ICP, no earlier benchmark was available to check the reliability of the detailed national accounts data. However, in the 2011 ICP it will be possible to compare the structure of the expenditures on GDP with those reported in the 2005 round and follow up any major inconsistencies. To help in this process, preliminary national accounts data for the years 2005–09 were collected in late 2010. The goal is to identify any problems that countries are facing with their data and resolve them before the 2011 national accounts data are collected during the second half of 2012.

Meanwhile, a training program will be provided to help countries produce the detailed accounts for 2011 required for the ICP. Because some countries have only production-based estimates of GDP, they will receive assistance in identifying the potential data sources that may be available to help them produce expenditure-based GDP.

The national accounts will be reviewed at an earlier stage than was possible in the 2005 ICP. The preliminary data for the latest year available (i.e., earlier than 2011) will also be used in editing the price data, which may indicate potential problem areas in the national accounts data themselves.

ANNEX

ICP Classification

Code	Description
100000	**GROSS DOMESTIC PRODUCT**
110000	**FINAL CONSUMPTION EXPENDITURE BY HOUSEHOLDS**
110100	**FOOD AND NONALCOHOLIC BEVERAGES**
110110	**Food**
110111	*Bread and cereals*
110111.1	Rice
110111.2	Other cereals, flour, and other cereal products
110111.3	Bread
110111.4	Other bakery products
110111.5	Pasta products
110112	*Meat*
110112.1	Beef and veal
110112.2	Pork
110112.3	Lamb, mutton, and goat
110112.4	Poultry
110112.5	Other meats and meat preparations
110113	*Fish*
110113.1	Fresh, chilled, or frozen fish and seafood
110113.2	Preserved or processed fish and seafood
110114	*Milk, cheese, and eggs*
110114.1	Fresh milk
110114.2	Preserved milk and other milk products
110114.3	Cheese
110114.4	Eggs and egg-based products
110115	*Oils and fats*
110115.1	Butter and margarine
110115.3	Other edible oils and fats
110116	*Fruit*
110116.1	Fresh or chilled fruit
110116.2	Frozen, preserved, or processed fruit and fruit-based products
110117	*Vegetables*
110117.1	Fresh or chilled vegetables other than potatoes
110117.2	Fresh or chilled potatoes
110117.3	Frozen, preserved, or processed vegetables and vegetable-based products

Code	Description
110118	*Sugar, jam, honey, chocolate, and confectionery*
110118.1	Sugar
110118.2	Jams, marmalades, and honey
110118.3	Confectionery, chocolate, and ice cream
110119	*Food products n.e.c.*
110119.1	Food products n.e.c.
110120	**Nonalcoholic beverages**
110121	*Coffee, tea, and cocoa*
110121.1	Coffee, tea, and cocoa
110122	*Mineral waters, soft drinks, fruit and vegetable juices*
110122.1	Mineral waters, soft drinks, fruit and vegetable juices
110200	**ALCOHOLIC BEVERAGES, TOBACCO, AND NARCOTICS**
110210	**Alcoholic beverages**
110211	*Spirits*
110211.1	Spirits
110212	*Wine*
110212.1	Wine
110213	*Beer*
110213.1	Beer
110220	**Tobacco**
110221	*Tobacco*
110221.1	Tobacco
110230	**Narcotics**
110231	*Narcotics*
110231.1	Narcotics
110300	**CLOTHING AND FOOTWEAR**
110310	**Clothing**
110311	*Clothing materials, other articles of clothing, and clothing accessories*
110311.1	Clothing materials, other articles of clothing, and clothing accessories
110312	*Garments*
110312.1	Garments
110314	*Cleaning, repair, and hire of clothing*
110314.1	Cleaning, repair, and hire of clothing
110320	**Footwear**
110321	*Shoes and other footwear*
110321.1	Shoes and other footwear
110322	*Repair and hire of footwear*
110322.1	Repair and hire of footwear
110400	**HOUSING, WATER, ELECTRICITY, GAS, AND OTHER FUELS**
110410	**Actual and imputed rentals for housing**

(continued)

Code	Description
110411	*Actual and imputed rentals for housing*
110411.1	Actual and imputed rentals for housing
110430	**Maintenance and repair of the dwelling**
110431	*Maintenance and repair of the dwelling*
110431.1	Maintenance and repair of the dwelling
110440	**Water supply and miscellaneous services relating to the dwelling**
110441	*Water supply*
110441.1	Water supply
110442	*Miscellaneous services relating to the dwelling*
110442.1	Miscellaneous services relating to the dwelling
110450	**Electricity, gas, and other fuels**
110451	*Electricity*
110451.1	Electricity
110452	*Gas*
110452.1	Gas
110453	*Other fuels*
110453.1	Other fuels
110500	**FURNISHINGS, HOUSEHOLD EQUIPMENT, AND ROUTINE MAINTENANCE OF THE HOUSE**
110510	**Furniture and furnishings, carpets, and other floor coverings**
110511	*Furniture and furnishings*
110511.1	Furniture and furnishings
110512	*Carpets and other floor coverings*
110512.1	Carpets and other floor coverings
110513	*Repair of furniture, furnishings, and floor coverings*
110513.1	Repair of furniture, furnishings, and floor coverings
110520	**Household textiles**
110521	*Household textiles*
110521.1	Household textiles
110530	**Household appliances**
110531	*Major household appliances whether electric or not*
110531.1	Major household appliances whether electric or not
110532	*Small electric household appliances*
110532.1	Small electric household appliances
110533	*Repair of household appliances*
110533.1	Repair of household appliances
110540	**Glassware, tableware, and household utensils**
110541	*Glassware, tableware, and household utensils*
110541.1	Glassware, tableware, and household utensils
110550	**Tools and equipment for house and garden**
110551	*Major tools and equipment*
110551.1	Major tools and equipment

Code	Description
110552	*Small tools and miscellaneous accessories*
110552.1	Small tools and miscellaneous accessories
110560	**Goods and services for routine household maintenance**
110561	*Nondurable household goods*
110561.1	Nondurable household goods
110562	*Domestic services and household services*
1105 62.1	Domestic services
110562.2	Household services
110600	**HEALTH**
110610	**Medical products, appliances, and equipment**
110611	*Pharmaceutical products*
110611.1	Pharmaceutical products
110612	*Other medical products*
110612.1	Other medical products
110613	*Therapeutic appliances and equipment*
110613.1	Therapeutic appliances and equipment
110620	**Outpatient services**
110621	*Medical services*
110621.1	Medical services
110622	*Dental services*
110622.1	Services of dentists
110623	*Paramedical services*
110623.1	Paramedical services
110630	**Hospital services**
110631	*Hospital services*
110631.1	Hospital services
110700	**TRANSPORT**
110710	**Purchase of vehicles**
110711	*Motor cars*
110711.1	Motor cars
110712	*Motorcycles*
110712.1	Motorcycles
110713	*Bicycles*
110713.1	Bicycles
110714	*Animal-drawn vehicles*
110714.1	Animal-drawn vehicles
110720	**Operation of personal transport equipment**
110722	*Fuels and lubricants for personal transport equipment*
110722.1	Fuels and lubricants for personal transport equipment
110723	*Maintenance and repair of personal transport equipment*

(*continued*)

Code	Description
110723.1	Maintenance and repair of personal transport equipment
110724	*Other services in respect of personal transport equipment*
110724.1	Other services in respect of personal transport equipment
110730	**Transport services**
110731	*Passenger transport by railway*
110731.1	Passenger transport by railway
110732	*Passenger transport by road*
110732.1	Passenger transport by road
110733	*Passenger transport by air*
110733.1	Passenger transport by air
110734	*Passenger transport by sea and inland waterway*
110734.1	Passenger transport by sea and inland waterway
110735	*Combined passenger transport*
110735.1	Combined passenger transport
110736	*Other purchased transport services*
110736.1	Other purchased transport services
110800	**COMMUNICATION**
110810	**Postal services**
110811	*Postal services*
110811.1	Postal services
110820	**Telephone and telefax equipment**
110821	*Telephone and telefax equipment*
110821.1	Telephone and telefax equipment
110830	**Telephone and telefax services**
110831	*Telephone and telefax services*
110831.1	Telephone and telefax services
110900	**RECREATION AND CULTURE**
110910	**Audiovisual, photographic, and information processing equipment**
110911	*Audiovisual, photographic, and information processing equipment*
110911.1	Audiovisual, photographic, and information processing equipment
110914	*Recording media*
110914.1	Recording media
110915	*Repair of audiovisual, photographic, and information processing equipment*
110915.1	Repair of audiovisual, photographic, and information processing equipment
110920	**Other major durables for recreation and culture**
110921	*Major durables for outdoor and indoor recreation*
110921.1	Major durables for outdoor and indoor recreation
110923	*Maintenance and repair of other major durables for recreation and culture*
110923.1	Maintenance and repair of other major durables for recreation and culture
110930	**Other recreational items and equipment, gardens, and pets**

Code	Description
110931	*Other recreational items and equipment*
110931.1	Other recreational items and equipment
110933	*Gardens and pets*
110933.1	Gardens and pets
110935	*Veterinary and other services for pets*
110935.1	Veterinary and other services for pets
110940	**Recreational and cultural services**
110941	*Recreational and sporting services*
110941.1	Recreational and sporting services
110942	*Cultural services*
110942.1	Cultural services
110943	*Games of chance*
110943.1	Games of chance
110950	**Newspapers, books, and stationery**
110951	*Newspapers, books, and stationery*
110951.1	Newspapers, books, and stationery
110960	**Package holidays**
110961	*Package holidays*
110961.1	Package holidays
111000	**EDUCATION**
111010	**Education**
111011	*Education*
111011.1	Education
111100	**RESTAURANTS AND HOTELS**
111110	**Catering services**
111111	*Catering services*
111111.1	Catering services
111120	**Accommodation services**
111121	*Accommodation services*
111121.1	Accommodation services
111200	**MISCELLANEOUS GOODS AND SERVICES**
111210	**Personal care**
111211	*Hairdressing salons and personal grooming establishments*
111211.1	Hairdressing salons and personal grooming establishments
111212	*Appliances, articles, and products for personal care*
111212.1	Appliances, articles, and products for personal care
111220	**Prostitution**
111221	*Prostitution*
111221.1	Prostitution
111230	**Personal effects n.e.c.**

(*continued*)

Code	Description
111231	*Jewelry, clocks, and watches*
111231.1	Jewelry, clocks, and watches
111232	*Other personal effects*
111232.1	Other personal effects
111240	**Social protection**
111241	*Social protection*
111241.1	Social protection
111250	**Insurance**
111251	*Insurance*
111251.1	Insurance
111260	**Financial services n.e.c.**
111261	*Financial intermediation services indirectly measured (FISIM)*
111261.1	Financial intermediation services indirectly measured (FISIM)
111262	*Other financial services n.e.c.*
111262.1	Other financial services n.e.c.
111270	**Other services n.e.c.**
111271	*Other services n.e.c.*
111271.1	Other services n.e.c.
111300	**BALANCE OF EXPENDITURES OF RESIDENTS ABROAD AND EXPENDITURES OF NONRESIDENTS ON THE ECONOMIC TERRITORY**
111310	**BALANCE OF EXPENDITURES OF RESIDENTS ABROAD AND EXPENDITURES OF NONRESIDENTS ON THE ECONOMIC TERRITORY**
111311	*BALANCE OF EXPENDITURES OF RESIDENTS ABROAD AND EXPENDITURES OF NONRESIDENTS ON THE ECONOMIC TERRITORY*
111311.1	Final consumption expenditure of resident households in the rest of the world
111311.2	Final consumption expenditure of nonresident households on the economic territory
120000	**INDIVIDUAL CONSUMPTION EXPENDITURE BY NPISH**
120100	**INDIVIDUAL CONSUMPTION EXPENDITURE BY NPISH**
120110	**Individual consumption expenditure by NPISH**
120111	*Individual consumption expenditure by NPISH*
120111.1	Individual consumption expenditure by NPISH
130000	**INDIVIDUAL CONSUMPTION EXPENDITURE BY GOVERNMENT**
130100	**HOUSING**
130110	**Housing**
130111	*Housing*
130111.1	Housing
130200	**HEALTH**
130210	**Health benefits and reimbursements**
130211	*Medical products, appliances, and equipment*
130211.1	Pharmaceutical products
130211.2	Other medical products
130211.3	Therapeutic appliances and equipment

Code	Description
130212	*Health services*
130212.1	Outpatient medical services
130212.2	Outpatient dental services
130212.3	Outpatient paramedical services
130212.4	Hospital services
130220	**PRODUCTION OF HEALTH SERVICES**
130221	*Compensation of employees*
130221.1	Compensation of employees
130222	*Intermediate consumption*
130222.1	Intermediate consumption
130223	*Gross operating surplus*
130223.1	Gross operating surplus
130224	*Net taxes on production*
130224.1	Net taxes on production
130225	*Receipts from sales*
130225.1	Receipts from sales
130300	**RECREATION AND CULTURE**
130310	**Recreation and culture**
130311	*Recreation and culture*
130311.1	Recreation and culture
130400	**EDUCATION**
130410	**Education benefits and reimbursements**
130411	*Education benefits and reimbursements*
130411.1	Education benefits and reimbursements
130420	**Production of education services**
130421	*Compensation of employees*
130421.1	Compensation of employees
130422	*Intermediate consumption*
130422.1	Intermediate consumption
130423	*Gross operating surplus*
130423.1	Gross operating surplus
130424	*Net taxes on production*
130424.1	Net taxes on production
130425	*Receipts from sales*
130425.1	Receipts from sales
130500	**SOCIAL PROTECTION**
130510	**Social protection**
130511	*Social protection*
130511.1	Social protection
140000	**COLLECTIVE CONSUMPTION EXPENDITURE BY GOVERNMENT**

(continued)

Code	Description
140100	**COLLECTIVE SERVICES**
140110	**Collective services**
140111	*Compensation of employees*
140111.1	Compensation of employees
140112	*Intermediate consumption*
140112.1	Intermediate consumption
140113	*Gross operating surplus*
140113.1	Gross operating surplus
140114	*Net taxes on production*
140114.1	Net taxes on production
140115	*Receipts from sales*
140115.1	Receipts from sales
150000	**EXPENDITURE ON GROSS FIXED CAPITAL FORMATION**
150100	**MACHINERY AND EQUIPMENT**
150110	**Metal products and equipment**
150111	*Fabricated metal products, except machinery and equipment [CPA 28.11 to 28.75]*
150111.1	Fabricated metal products, except machinery and equipment
150112	*General-purpose machinery [CPA 29.11 to 29.24]*
150112.1	General-purpose machinery
150113	*Special-purpose machinery [CPA 29.31 to 29.72]*
150113.1	Special-purpose machinery
150114	*Electrical and optical equipment [CPA 30.01 to 33.50]*
150114.1	Electrical and optical equipment
150115	*Other manufactured goods n.e.c. [CPA 36.11 to 36.63]*
150115.1	Other manufactured goods n.e.c.
150120	**Transport equipment**
150121	*Road transport equipment [CPA 34.10 to 34.30 and 35.41 to 35.50]*
150121.1	Motor vehicles, trailers, and semitrailers
150121.2	Other road transport
150122	*Other transport equipment [CPA 35.11 to 35.30]*
150122.1	Other transport equipment
150200	**CONSTRUCTION**
150210	**Residential buildings**
150211	*Residential buildings*
150211.1	Residential buildings
150220	**Nonresidential buildings**
150221	*Nonresidential buildings*
150221.1	Nonresidential buildings
150230	**Civil engineering works**
150231	*Civil engineering works*

Code	Description
150231.1	Civil engineering works
150300	**OTHER PRODUCTS**
150310	**Other products**
150311	*Other products*
150311.1	Other products
160000	**CHANGES IN INVENTORIES AND ACQUISITIONS LESS DISPOSALS OF VALUABLES**
160100	**CHANGES IN INVENTORIES**
160110	**Changes in inventories**
160110.1	Opening value of inventories
160110.2	Closing value of inventories
160200	**ACQUISITIONS LESS DISPOSALS OF VALUABLES**
160210	**Acquisitions less disposals of valuables**
160211	*Acquisitions less disposals of valuables*
160211.1	Acquisitions of valuables
160211.2	Disposals of valuables
170000	**BALANCE OF EXPORTS AND IMPORTS**
170100	**BALANCE OF EXPORTS AND IMPORTS**
170110	**BALANCE OF EXPORTS AND IMPORTS**
170111	*BALANCE OF EXPORTS AND IMPORTS*
170111.1	Exports of goods and services
170111.2	Imports of goods and services

Source: ICP.
Note: Basic headings are shaded gray. NPISH = nonprofit institutions serving households; CPA = Statistical Classification of Products by Activity; n.e.c. = not elsewhere classified.

NOTES

1. For more on the subject of this chapter, see World Bank (2008).
2. *Purchaser's price* is the amount paid by the purchaser, excluding any value added tax (VAT) or similar tax deductible by the purchaser, in order to take delivery of a unit of a good or service at the time and place required by the purchaser. The purchaser's price of a good includes any transport charges paid separately by the purchaser to take delivery at the required time and place, as well as the wholesale and retail trade margins and any taxes on products (excluding the VAT deductible by the purchaser) minus the subsidies on products.
3. *Intermediate consumption* is the value of the goods and services consumed as inputs by a process of production, excluding fixed assets whose consumption is recorded as consumption of fixed capital.
4. *Subsidies* are current unrequited payments that government units, including nonresident government units, make to enterprises on the basis of the levels of their production activities or the quantities or values of the goods or services that they produce, sell, or import. A subsidy on a product is a subsidy payable per unit of a good or service.
5. *Operating surplus* is a measure of the surplus accruing from production processes before deducting any explicit or implicit interest charges, rent, or other property incomes payable on the financial assets, land, or other natural resources required to carry on the production. Business profits are a large part of the gross operating surplus. *Mixed income* is the term used to describe the operating surplus of unincorporated enterprises because it implicitly contains an element of remuneration for work done by the owner (or other members of the household to which the unincorporated enterprise belongs) that cannot be separately identified from the return to the owner as an entrepreneur.
6. Gross capital formation shows the acquisition, minus disposal, of produced assets for purposes of fixed capital formation, inventories, or valuables. Gross fixed capital formation is measured by the total value of a producer's acquisition (minus disposal) of fixed assets during the accounting period plus certain specified expenditures on services that adds to the value of nonproduced assets.

REFERENCES

Commission of the European Communities, International Monetary Fund, Organisation for Economic Co-operation and Development, United Nations, and World Bank. 1993. *System of National Accounts 1993.* http://unstats.un.org/unsd/sna1993/toctop.asp?L1=5.

———. 2008. *System of National Accounts 2008.* http://unstats.un.org/unsd/nationalaccount/SNA2008.pdf.

World Bank. 2007. *ICP 2005 Methodological Handbook.* http://web.worldbank.org/WBSITE/EXTERNAL/DATASTATISTICS/ICPEXT/0,,contentMDK:20962711~menuPK:2666036~pagePK:60002244~piPK:62002388~theSitePK:270065,00.html.

———. 2008. *Global Purchasing Power Parities and Real Expenditures: 2005 International Comparison Program.* http://siteresources.worldbank.org/ICPINT/Resources/icp-final.pdf.

CHAPTER 4

Computation of Basic Heading PPPs for Comparisons within and between Regions

D. S. Prasada Rao

This chapter is the first in a set of three devoted to describing the aggregation methods used at various stages of the International Comparison Program (ICP) in compiling the purchasing power parities (PPPs) of currencies of countries within regions and for comparisons between regions.[1] A schematic diagram showing the various stages in the computation of PPPs appears in figure 1.3 in chapter 1. The main objectives of this chapter are to provide a detailed description of the methods used in the computation of PPPs at the basic heading (BH) level at the regional level[2] and to describe how BH-level PPPs are compiled for the purpose of making global comparisons of prices. Chapter 5 by W. Erwin Diewert focuses on the methods for aggregating price and quantity data in the computation of PPPs for higher-level aggregates such as consumption, investment, and, finally, the gross domestic product (GDP) at the regional level. Chapter 6, also by Diewert, examines the problem of linking regional comparisons above the basic heading level to make global comparisons.

The literature on aggregation methods for international comparisons has traditionally focused on aggregation at levels above the basic heading level—see Balk (2008) and Rao (2009) for excellent reviews of such methods—and relatively little weight is placed on the problem of constructing PPPs at the basic heading level. In a recent paper, Hill and Hill stress the importance of PPPs at the basic heading level:

> Perhaps the most pressing concern in the international comparisons literature is the problem of obtaining unbiased price indexes at the basic heading level (the lowest level of aggregation at which expenditure weights are available). The basic heading price indexes provide building blocks from which the overall comparison is constructed. If these building blocks are biased or otherwise flawed, then everything that builds on them will be likewise tainted. (Hill and Hill 2009, 192–93)

The importance of reliable PPPs at the basic heading level was reiterated after the release of the 2005 ICP results (World Bank 2008), which showed substantial revisions to the global GDP and to the real incomes of major economies such as China and India. Deaton and Heston (2008) examined possible reasons for such revisions and concluded that one of the underlying factors is the price data used for compilation of PPPs at the basic heading level.

Reflecting concerns about improving the quality and reliability of PPPs at the basic heading level, this chapter is designed to provide an appreciation of the core issues surrounding the compilation of PPPs at the basic heading level, including a description of the characteristics of the price data, as well as the characteristics of the products priced in different countries. The chapter seeks to illustrate how the aggregation methods used in the ICP are designed to take full account of the information on such characteristics. Reflecting the forward-looking nature of this ICP volume, this chapter not only reviews the methods used in the 2005 ICP, but also describes the new approaches and methods being considered for the 2011 ICP. A significant new approach in the 2011 ICP is the use of a *list of core products* for the purpose of linking regions. Although there is an ongoing discussion on how to calibrate the aggregation methods to best utilize prices on core products, a consensus has emerged on the method to be used for linking PPPs at the basic heading level.[3]

This chapter draws on material from a number of sources, including (1) the extensive discussion of the issues surrounding aggregation at the basic heading level in the *ICP 2005 Methodological Handbook* (World Bank 2007); (2) the final report of the 2005 ICP issued by the Global Office (World Bank 2008); and (3) various published and unpublished papers and reports on the subject.

The chapter is organized as follows. Section 4.1 focuses on features and aspects specific to comparisons at the basic heading level. It discusses in detail the nature of price data, product characteristics, and the features of price quotations that have a direct bearing on the aggregation methods used. Section 4.2 discusses briefly the analytical requirements for the aggregation methods used at the basic heading level. Sections 4.3 and 4.4 are devoted to a description of the aggregation methods used in the compilation of PPPs at the regional level. The Jevons binary price indexes and the Gini-Éltetö-Köves-Szulc (GEKS) method of constructing transitive parities are the subject of section 4.3. Variants of the Jevons-GEKS indexes designed to use information on the *representativity* and *importance* of products[4] are also discussed in this section. Section 4.4 is devoted to a description of the Country Product Dummy (CPD) method and its variants used in the computation of basic heading PPPs.[5] Section 4.5 focuses on the problem of linking the regional basic heading PPPs and describes the methodology used in the 2005 ICP based on *Ring countries* and a *Ring product list,* as well as the new approach based on the use of *core products* proposed for the 2011 ICP. Section 4.6 presents some concluding remarks.

4.1 Features of Data for Computing PPPs at the Basic Heading Level

As a starting point, it is useful to note the main features of the BH-level data and what distinguishes the basic heading level from higher levels of aggregation. The features discussed in this section have a direct bearing on the methodology used in aggregating data. The number of products priced in the basic heading and the relative overlap across countries can lead to differences in results from different methods. If all products are priced in all countries and if all products are treated as equally important, then the two major approaches used within the ICP—the Jevons index with GEKS and the CPD methods—will lead to identical PPPs, thereby eliminating the need to choose between methods. In addition, it is important to understand the concept of the basic heading and the concepts of representativity and importance before identifying an appropriate index number method.

Basic Headings

Within the pyramid approach to price comparisons, as illustrated in figure 1.1 in chapter 1, price comparisons begin with the identification of products in the regional list of items for which price data are collected through price surveys.[6] These products are grouped into different basic headings. As a working definition, the *basic heading* is the lowest level of aggregation for which expenditure share weight information is available. An immediate implication is that in the ICP no quantity data are available for the products priced in the surveys.[7] Thus price comparisons at the basic heading level are derived as aggregates of item-level price ratios, and the basic heading PPPs are similar to the *elementary indexes* gathered as part of the compilation of the consumer price index (CPI).[8] An additional consideration is that basic headings consist of groups of similar products defined within a general product classification. Similarity of products within the basic heading is supposed to ensure the similarity in the magnitudes of price relatives for products included in the basic heading.[9] However, in the ICP the composition of basic headings is necessarily dictated by the detailed classification used in the national accounts and the availability of national account expenditure share weights for a desired grouping of products. Therefore, it is possible that basic headings used in ICP price comparisons may not always include products that exhibit similar price movements. For example, the clothing and footwear aggregate consists of the following five basic headings: (1) clothing materials; (2) garments (men's, women's, and children's); (3) cleaning, repair, and hire of clothing; (4) shoes and other footwear; and (5) repair and hire of footwear. In this example, it is clear that similar products are grouped together. However, there is considerable heterogeneity within groups. The garments group includes men's, women's, and children's clothing, and, moreover, there would be heterogeneity within men's garments, which include shirts, trousers, and suits, as well as undergarments. It is difficult to determine whether all the products within the garments group are likely to exhibit similar price relatives or price movements.

From the perspective of computing a PPP for a given basic heading, the most ideal situation is one in which item-specific weights in the form of quantities or expenditure share weights are available. In the absence of such information, several characteristics of the products included in the basic heading are taken into account in computing basic heading PPPs. It is useful to review these characteristics because they play a critical role in the choice of an appropriate formula for the computation of basic heading PPPs.

Product Characteristics

In the 2005 ICP, a new approach based on *structured product descriptions* (SPDs) was introduced. The SPDs provide a structured, systematic way in which to describe the price-determining characteristics for products that households purchase. In that way, the prices collected in different countries refer to the same products, ensuring *comparability*. The SPDs were used to prepare the product specifications given to the price collectors. For example, in the Asia-Pacific region 20 different varieties of rice were defined by the rice SPD for pricing purposes (ADB 2007). However, it is widely recognized that a product comparable in its characteristics across countries may not be *representative* of consumption in all countries in which the product is priced. In general, there is a trade-off between comparability and representativity in identifying products for inclusion in the basic headings and price surveys.

Representativity

The concept of *representativity* was developed as part of the Eurostat–Organisation for Economic Co-operation and Development (OECD) PPP Programme as way of accounting for the possibility that some of the items in the product lists may not be representative of consumption in some of the participating countries.[10] It makes intuitive sense that the prices of representative products should have a greater influence on the PPPs for the basic heading and that the converse should be true for unrepresentative products. The actual implementation requires a formal process for identifying representative products.

The representativity of a product is determined on the basis of two main considerations:

1. A particular item is representative in a country for a particular basic heading if the item has a significant market share as reflected by the expenditure share or by the volume of sales associated with the item. This notion of representativity is consistent with the approach one would take if quantity or expenditure data were available at the item level. In the presence of such information, the aggregation of price ratios would be weighted proportional to the expenditure shares. However, because expenditure share data are not available at the item level, labeling a product as representative has to be left to the price statistician or local experts.
2. Representative products have lower price levels than unrepresentative products, and not accounting for such differences in aggregating price data could result in biased PPPs.[11] If products could be labeled as representative or unrepresentative in each of the countries, such information could be incorporated into the aggregation process. However, it is difficult to decide a priori whether a particular product is representative on the basis of whether the price relative of the product in two countries is typical of the products in the basic heading. A possible approach could be based on the fact that a cheap product would be purchased in large quantities and therefore would be popular.[12]

An important reason for distinguishing between representative and unrepresentative products is that the relative prices of these products would be different. Products purchased in large quantities are associated with lower prices relative to other products in the basic heading, and unrepresentative products may have higher relative prices. On the basis of this finding, a product may be considered unrepresentative if its relative price is high and therefore may not be representative of the relative prices of products that are representative and included in the basic heading. This notion of a representative commodity underpins the use of the Country Product Representative Dummy (CPRD) model and the starred-GEKS (Gini-Éltető-Köves-Szulc) methods used in international comparisons.

Although the conceptual basis for identifying representative products within a basic heading is sound and appealing, in practice the national and regional ICP coordinators have no real objective measures to use in deciding whether a particular product is representative. In particular, the notion of whether it is representative on the basis of relative prices is a difficult concept to implement. These issues underscored the failure of the national and regional coordinators to meaningfully identify representative products in the 2005 ICP. In the Asia and Africa regions, much confusion surrounded the identification of representative products, to the extent that including such information induced biases in the estimated PPPs at the basic heading level. Thus the information collected on the representativeness of products within basic headings was discarded at the stage of computing PPPs for basic headings. The Eurostat-OECD and Commonwealth of Independent States (CIS) regions are the only ICP regions that used the information on representativeness.

Importance of Products

In view of the difficulties encountered during the 2005 ICP, it was decided that the concept of representativeness would be replaced by an indication of whether a product is important among the list of products within a basic heading. Aggregation methods leading to basic heading PPPs should explicitly account for the importance of a particular item in a particular country, with unimportant products accorded a smaller weight. The notion of importance is supposed to reflect whether either the sales or the expenditure share is significant enough to warrant the label that the product is important. National statisticians have a reasonable understanding of importance as reflected by sales or shares. The notion of importance of the product is not related in any way to the relative price of the product, and therefore it is a weak alternative to the use of actual quantity data along with price data in the computation of PPPs at the basic heading level. It was generally agreed that in the 2011 ICP an important product will be accorded a weight of 3, or three times the weight attached to the remaining products, which are considered unimportant.[13]

Price Data: National Average Prices

The price concept relevant for the ICP is the national annual average price of the items priced in each of the countries. In the 2005 ICP, national annual average prices were computed as the arithmetic averages of a large number of price quotations for each of the items in the product lists.[14] The average price should ideally cover the whole country, representing the rural and urban regions, as well as different geographic regions for larger countries. The countries supply the regional coordinator of the ICP with the following data:

- National annual average price
- Number of price quotations used in computation of the average price
- Standard deviation of the price quotations used in computing the national annual average price.

The reliability of a given national annual average price can be computed as the standard error associated with that price.[15]

The PPPs computed at the basic heading level must make use of all the information available associated with the price data (national annual average prices) from the countries participating in the comparisons. In particular, it is statistically desirable to accord lower weights to prices that have higher standard errors. Though this is a desirable approach, the standard errors of the national annual average prices have not so far been incorporated into the PPP computations.

Basic Data for Computing Basic Heading PPPs

This section establishes the notation used throughout this chapter and describes the nature of price data used in the compilation of PPPs at the basic heading level. For the purpose of this exposition, without loss of generality, the focus is on a single region and a selected basic heading. Let N represent the number of commodities included in a given basic heading and C represent the number of countries included in a given region.[16] Let p_i^c denote the price of the i-th commodity in country c ($i = 1, 2, \ldots, N$; $c = 1, 2, \ldots, C$) where the price is assumed to be strictly positive. The problem of determining the number of items and the actual items for inclusion in the basic heading is dealt with in chapter 7 in this volume on the survey framework for the ICP. In practice, the following three scenarios are possible:

1. All the items are priced in all countries, leading to a complete tableau or matrix of prices.[17]
2. Not all items are priced in all the countries, leading to an incomplete tableau of prices.
3. Some items may be priced in only one of the countries in the region.

Table 4.1 presents two examples of incomplete tableau.

TABLE 4.1 Two Examples of an Incomplete Tableau for the Basic Heading Rice

national currency units

	Prices							
	Tableau I				Tableau II			
	Country				Country			
Items in basic heading	A	B	C	D	A	B	C	D
Long grain	10	40	50	100	10	40	—	—
Medium grain	12	16	—	—	—	—	25	55
Short grain	—	15	30	—	—	—	15	40
Low quality	4	—	—	—	4	—	—	—
Imported	25	—	—	100	25	80	—	—

In tableau I, price data are missing in some cells, but it would be possible to compute PPPs for the four countries in the comparison because the data exhibit overlaps between countries. Note that the fourth item, low-quality rice, is priced only in country A and therefore cannot be used in the PPP computation. Thus at the basic heading level, in order to influence the PPP computations, an item must be priced in at least two countries. Tableau II is an interesting case in which the long grain and imported rice items are priced only in countries A and B. By contrast, the medium grain and short grain items are priced only in countries C and D. Although it is possible to compare prices across A and B and between C and D, it is not possible make price comparisons between countries A and C or A and D. Similarly, B cannot be compared with either C or D. In this case, the price tableau can be reduced to two blocks, one for countries A and B and another for countries C and D, with nothing in common between the blocks.

Three important conclusions can be drawn from the examples in table 4.1:

1. When the price tableau is incomplete, it is important that the price data collected be connected and price comparisons between all the countries involved be made if and only if the price tableau is connected or irreducible. The price tableau is said to be *connected* if the price data are such that it is not possible to place the countries in two groups in which no item priced by any country in one group is priced by any other country in the second group. In tableau II, it is possible to place countries into two groups (A and B, C and D) in which no rice item priced in the first group is priced by any country in the second group and vice versa. In such cases, the process of price comparisons breaks down.[18]
2. If a product is priced in only one country, its price will have no influence on the PPPs computed.
3. When a price tableau is incomplete, the quality of price comparisons depends on the strength of interconnections and overlaps in the priced items across different countries. If the overlaps are strong, then one can make reliable price comparisons across different countries. A corollary of this observation is that countries within a particular region should strive to price as many items in the basic heading as possible.[19] (Chapter 7 on the survey framework for the ICP provides guidelines on the minimum numbers of items to be priced within each basic heading.)

4.2 Aggregation Methods for Computing PPPs at the Basic Heading Level: Analytical Requirements

To identify the properties expected of aggregation methods for computing PPPs at the basic heading level, it is useful to recall a working definition of the PPP and then apply it to the special case of a single product. The purchasing power parity between the currencies of countries A and B may be defined as the number of currency units of country A that have the same purchasing power as one unit of the currency of country B, defined with respect to a designated product or set of products such as a basic heading.

PPPs for Individual Products

Suppose p_i^j and p_i^k are, respectively, the prices of product i in countries j and k. The PPP for country k with respect to country j is then given by

$$PPP_{jk} = \frac{p_i^k}{p_i^j}. \tag{4.1}$$

Obviously, the PPP defined in (4.1) depends on the particular product selected. For a selected commodity i, the following transitivity property can be observed. For any three countries j, k, and m, it is easy to see that

$$PPP_{jk} = \frac{p_i^k}{p_i^j} = \frac{p_i^k}{p_i^m} \cdot \frac{p_i^m}{p_i^j} = PPP_{jm} \cdot PPP_{mk}. \tag{4.2}$$

Equation (4.2) shows that the PPP between countries j and k is equal to the indirect PPP comparison derived through a third country, m. The equation guarantees the level of internal consistency required for international comparisons. This property is known as transitivity, and equation (4.2) shows that when PPPs are based on the prices of a single product, transitivity is automatically satisfied.

Transitivity for PPPs in Multilateral and Multiproduct Comparisons

Multilateral PPPs, represented by the matrix of PPP comparisons between all pairs of countries based on price data on more than one item (i.e., in the presence of multiple products), is said to be transitive if for any three countries in the group, such as j, k, and m, *the direct* PPP for country k with respect to country j is equal to the *indirect* PPP derived through the use of the third country, m:

$$PPP_{jk} = PPP_{jm} \cdot PPP_{mk} = \frac{PPP_{mk}}{PPP_{mj}}. \tag{4.3}$$

The last part of equation (4.3) requires the assumption that PPP_{jm} is the reciprocal of PPP_{mj}.

Because the PPPs based on a single product defined in (4.1) are automatically transitive and because the PPPs based on price data for multiple items in a basic heading would require some sort of averaging of item-level PPPs, it is necessary to consider only those methods that retain the property of transitivity, as displayed in (4.3). Unless stated otherwise, all the procedures considered in the reminder of this section satisfy transitivity.

Base Invariance of PPPs for Multilateral Comparisons

In addition to the transitivity requirement stated in (4.3), it is important that all countries participating in the price comparisons are treated symmetrically and that no country is accorded a special status. This condition is particularly relevant because it is possible to generate transitive PPPs using a "star" method, in which a single country such as the United States is at the center and all countries are compared only through the star country (see figure 1.2 in chapter 1 for an illustration). Even though comparisons based on a selected star are transitive, the comparisons are sensitive to the star country selected. For example, the relative comparisons and PPPs between two countries, say j and k, would be different when two different countries, say the United States and Germany, are used as the star countries. Again, unless stated otherwise, all the methods discussed in the ensuing sections produce PPPs that are base-invariant.

Traditionally, there have been two main approaches to aggregation at the basic heading level. The first approach is based on the Jevons index, which is used in the computation of elementary price index numbers, and the GEKS method (Gini 1924, 1931; Éltetö-Köves 1964; Szulc 1964). An alternative approach, developed originally by Summers (1973), makes use of a regression model known as the Country Product Dummy as a way of filling or imputing missing price data. However, it was also used as a method of aggregation below the basic heading level in the earlier rounds of the ICP conducted by Kravis and his associates (Kravis, Heston, and Summers 1982). In recent years, the model has received attention through the work of Rao (1990, 2004, 2005, 2009), Sergeev (2002, 2003), Diewert (2004b, 2005, 2010b), Rao and Timmer (2003), and Hill and Timmer (2006). Although no specific references are given, the following material draws heavily on chapter 11 in the *ICP 2005 Methodological Handbook* (World Bank 2007) and on Diewert (2010b). The next two sections of this chapter describe the two major approaches to the compilation of PPPs at the basic heading level.

4.3 Jevons Index and GEKS Method for PPPs at the Basic Heading Level

This section describes the methodology used by Eurostat since the 1980s, as well as the current Eurostat-OECD methodology adopted for aggregating item-level price data to compute BH-level PPPs (see Roberts 2009 for a detailed description of the Eurostat-OECD PPP Programme). The basic element of the Eurostat approach is the Jevons index, which is the main index number formula used in the computation of elementary price indexes in the compilation of the consumer price index.[20] The Jevons index by itself does not yield transitive comparisons except in the special case in which all countries price all products in the basic heading. This index is suitably transformed using the GEKS approach and so is employed in the computation of basic heading PPPs. As the Eurostat-OECD program collects reliable information on the representativity of different items in the basic heading in different countries, the Jevons-GEKS method is further modified to account for the additional information on representativity. A variation of the Eurostat-OECD approach has been proposed by Sergeev (2003). Thus the following scenarios are considered here:

- All items are priced in all the countries (a complete tableau) with no weights attached to the items reflecting representativity or importance. Under this scenario, the standard Jevons index is used.

- Scenario refers to an incomplete price tableau in which not all items are priced in all countries, but all items are treated with equal weight. Here the Jevons-GEKS index is used in deriving transitive comparisons.
- Scenario refers to the most general case in which the price tableau is incomplete. At the same time, a distinction is made between representative and unrepresentative commodities. Because representative products are marked with an asterisk (*), the method used is denoted as the Jevons-GEKS* index. A variation of this method proposed by Sergeev (2003) is referred to as the Jevons-GEKS*(S) index.

Jevons Index: Complete Price Tableau without Weights

In the simplest case in which all N items are priced in all countries and are treated as equally important in the absence of any implicit weights, the PPPs at a given basic heading level can be computed using

$$(4.4) \qquad PPP_{jk}^{Jevons} = \prod_{i=1}^{N} \left[\frac{p_i^k}{p_i^j} \right]^{\frac{1}{N}} \quad \text{for all } j,\ k = 1, 2, \ldots, C.$$

The index in (4.4) is a simple geometric mean of all the price relatives for countries j and k for all the commodities in the basic heading. This formula is referred to as the Jevons index in the index number literature (see Diewert 2004a for more details).

It is easy to check that the Jevons index in (4.4) results in PPPs that are transitive and base-invariant. It is also useful to note here that in this case in which all N items are priced in all countries, the CPD method discussed in the next section produced PPPs identical to those based on the Jevons index.

Jevons-GEKS Index: Incomplete Tableau without Weights

Consider the case in which not all commodities are priced in all countries. Let N_j be the number of commodities, out of N, priced in country j. In addition, suppose that all the price data are connected so that price comparisons are feasible. Note that any binary comparison between countries j and k can be made on the basis of overlapping price data consisting of the items that are commonly priced. If a commodity is not priced in one of the two countries, that commodity cannot be included in the PPP computation. Let N_{jk} represent the set and number of commodities in the basic heading that are commonly priced in countries j and k. Then the PPP for a binary comparison between j and k is given by

$$(4.5) \qquad PPP_{jk}^{Jevons} = \prod_{i \in N_{jk}} \left[\frac{p_i^k}{p_i^j} \right]^{\frac{1}{N_{jk}}}.$$

The binary PPP for countries j and k based on the commonly priced items given in (4.5) does not satisfy the transitivity property. The GEKS procedure is a technique that generates transitive multilateral indexes (PPPs), which may be denoted by PPP_{jk}^{EKS}. Details of the GEKS procedure can be found in Balk (2009) and Rao (2009). The GEKS-based PPPs are given by

$$(4.6) \qquad PPP_{jk}^{Jevons-GEKS} = \prod_{\ell=1}^{C} \left[PPP_{j\ell}^{Jevons} \cdot PPP_{\ell k}^{Jevons} \right]^{\frac{1}{C}} = \prod_{\ell=1}^{C} \left[\prod_{i \in N_{j\ell}} \left(\frac{p_i^\ell}{p_i^j} \right)^{\frac{1}{N_{j\ell}}} \cdot \prod_{i \in N_{\ell k}} \left(\frac{p_i^k}{p_i^\ell} \right)^{\frac{1}{N_{\ell k}}} \right]^{\frac{1}{C}}.$$

It is easy to check that the Jevons-GEKS PPPs in (4.6) satisfy transitivity. Rao, Maddison, and Lee (2002) provide an intuitive interpretation of the PPPs based on the GEKS method, which also establishes its base–invariant property. If the price tableau is complete, then it is possible to show that the use of Jevons-GEKS indexes in equation (4.6) will lead to PPPs identical to those in equation (4.4).

Jevons-GEKS* Index: Incomplete Tableau with Asterisks for Representative Items

Consider the case in which products are labeled as "representative" or "unrepresentative" in different countries. Representative commodities are marked with an asterisk (*). In this case, the Eurostat-OECD comparisons are based on a modified Jevons-GEKS method, which is also known as the Jevons-GEKS* method. The modification is driven by the fact that for any given pair of countries *j* and *k* there may be (1) a set of products that is priced in both countries and is considered representative; (2) a set of products priced that is representative in country *j* but not in country *k;* (3) a set of products priced that is representative in country *k* but not in country *j;* or (4) a set of products priced that is not representative in either country. This approach can also be used when "representativeness' is replaced by the "importance" of commodities. The following notation is used in the equations that follow:

Let N_{jk} represent the number of products that are representative in either country *j* or country *k* and for which price data are reported in both countries *j* and *k*. N_{jk} will generally be smaller than the total number of commodities *N* in the basic heading.
Let N_{jk}^R represent the set and number of products that are representative in country *j* and that are also priced in country *k*. They may not all be representative in country *k*.
Let N_{kj}^R represent the set and number of products that are representative in country *k* and that are also priced in country *j*. They may not all be representative in country *j*.[21]

The PPP for a binary comparison between *j* and *k* based only on representative or starred commodities in country *j*, denoted by $PPP_{jk}^{Jevons(j-*)}$, is then given by

$$PPP_{jk}^{Jevons(j-*)} = \prod_{i \in N_{jk}^R} \left[\frac{p_i^k}{p_i^j} \right]^{\frac{1}{N_{jk}^R}}. \tag{4.7}$$

However, an equally meaningful PPP measure can be defined using commodities that are representative in country *k* and are also priced in *j*, which is denoted by $PPP_{jk}^{Jevons(k-*)}$ and given by

$$PPP_{jk}^{Jevons(k-*)} = \prod_{i \in N_{kj}^R} \left[\frac{p_i^k}{p_i^j} \right]^{\frac{1}{N_{kj}^R}}. \tag{4.8}$$

From a statistical or analytical perspective, the two PPP measures given in equations (4.7) and (4.8) are equally desirable because each makes use of the representative products priced in the country that are also priced in the other country. Therefore, an asterisk (*)-based Jevons index of PPP between *j* and *k* could be defined using a geometric average of the two PPPs in (4.7) and (4.8). The "representative" or (*)-based Jevons index is denoted by $PPP_{jk}^{Jevons(*)}$, which is given by

$$PPP_{jk}^{Jevons(*)} = \left[PPP_{jk}^{Jevons(j-*)} \cdot PPP_{jk}^{Jevons(k-*)} \right]^{\frac{1}{2}} = \left[\prod_{i \in N_{jk}^R} \left[\frac{p_i^k}{p_i^j} \right]^{\frac{1}{N_{jk}^R}} \cdot \prod_{i \in N_{jk}^R} \left[\frac{p_i^k}{p_i^j} \right]^{\frac{1}{N_{kj}^R}} \right]^{\frac{1}{2}}. \tag{4.9}$$

The new index in (4.9) is the geometric mean of the indexes in (4.7) and (4.8).[22]

Because $PPP_{jk}^{Jevons(*)}$ makes use of only information on countries j and k from the price tableau, the resulting indexes are not transitive even when the price tableau is complete. Therefore, it is necessary to use the GEKS procedure, which results in a transitive PPPs incorporating "representativity" information at the same time. This is the Jevons-GEKS* index. Basically, the $PPP_{jk}^{Jevons(*)}$'s are used along with the GEKS approach, leading to $PPP_{jk}^{Jevons-GEKS(*)}$ for all j and k. These are given by

$$(4.10) \qquad PPP_{jk}^{Jevons-GEKS(*)} = \prod_{\ell=1}^{C} \left[PPP_{j\ell}^{Jevons(*)} \cdot PPP_{\ell k}^{Jevons(*)} \right]^{\frac{1}{C}}.$$

The $PPP_{jk}^{GEKS(*)}$'s given in (4.10) are transitive and base-invariant.

These were used by the Eurostat-OECD program until the recently proposed modification of the Jevons-GEKS* method stemming from the work of Sergeev (2003). As noted earlier, this modification is known as the Jevons-GEKS*(S) method. The Sergeev (2003) approach explicitly recognizes and provides additional weights to those items that are representative in both countries and also priced in both countries.

Jevons-GEKS*(S) Index: Incomplete Tableau with Asterisks for Representative Items with Differential Weights

The Jevons-GEKS*(S) method is similar to the GEKS* method and so a similar notation may be used:

Let N_{jk}^{R} represent the set and number of products that are representative in country j and that are also priced in country k but are not representative in k.

Let N_{kj}^{R} represent the set and number of products that are representative in country k and that are also priced in country j but are not representative in country j.

Let N_{jk}^{**} be the number of commodities that are priced in both countries and are also representative in both countries.

Then the PPP for a binary comparison between j and k based only on representative commodities in country j that are not representative in k is denoted by $PPP_{jk}^{Jevons(j-*)}$ and given by

$$(4.11) \qquad PPP_{jk}^{Jevons(j-*)} = \prod_{i \in N_{jk}^{R}} \left[\frac{p_i^k}{p_i^j} \right]^{\frac{1}{N_{jk}^{R}}}.$$

However, an equally meaningful PPP measure can be defined using commodities that are representative in country k and that are also priced in j but are not representative in j, which is denoted by $PPP_{jk}^{Jevons(j-*)}$ and given by

$$(4.12) \qquad PPP_{jk}^{Jevons(k-*)} = \prod_{i \in N_{kj}^{R}} \left[\frac{p_i^k}{p_i^j} \right]^{\frac{1}{N_{kj}^{R}}}.$$

The Sergeev (2003) method uses a third index that is based purely on those commodities priced in both countries and representative in both countries. The third index is given by

$$(4.13) \qquad PPP_{jk}^{Jevons(**)} = \prod_{i \in N_{kj}^{**}} \left[\frac{p_i^k}{p_i^j} \right]^{\frac{1}{N_{kj}^{**}}}.$$

From a statistical or analytical perspective, there is no way of choosing between the three PPP measures given in equations (4.11), (4.12), and (4.13) because each, respectively, makes use of the representative products priced in the country that are also priced in the other country. Therefore, an asterisk (*)–based index of PPP between *j* and *k* may be defined using a weighted geometric average of the three PPPs in (4.11), (4.12), and (4.13), in which the weights are proportional to the number of products in different groups. In particular, the Sergeev (2003) method gives double the weight for the index based on representative products in both countries. The resulting modified "representative" product–based PPP, denoted by $PPP_{jk}^{Jevons^*(S)}$, is given by

$$(4.14) \qquad PPP_{jk}^{Jevons^*(S)} = \left[PPP_{jk}^{Jevons(**)}\right]^{w_1}\left[PPP_{jk}^{Jevons(j-*)}\right]^{w_2}\left[PPP_{jk}^{Jevons^*(k-*)}\right]^{w_3}$$

where

$$w_1 = \frac{2 \cdot N_{jk}^{**}}{2 \cdot N_{jk}^{**} + N_{jk}^{R} + N_{kj}^{*}} \text{ and } w_2 = w_3 = 0.5 \cdot \frac{N_{jk}^{R} + N_{kj}^{*}}{2 \cdot N_{jk}^{**} + N_{jk}^{R} + N_{kj}^{*}}.$$

A simple example may be useful in understanding the weighting scheme used here. Suppose that 12 items are commonly priced in countries *j* and *k*. Let items 1–7 be the products that are representative in *j* but not in *k;* let products 8–10 be representative in both countries; and let products 11 and 12 be representative in *k* but not in *j*. Then $N_{jk}^{R} = 7$; $N_{jk}^{**} = 3$; $N_{kj}^{R} = 2$; and, in this case, $w_1 = \frac{2 \cdot 3}{2 \cdot 3 + 7 + 2} = \frac{6}{15} = 0.4$; $w_2 = w_3 = 0.3$. Now to complete the procedure by generating transitive indexes, it is necessary to use the GEKS procedure on all bilateral comparisons of the form, leading to

$$(4.15) \qquad PPP_{jk}^{Jevons-GEKS^*(S)} = \prod_{\ell=1}^{C}\left[PPP_{j\ell}^{Jevons^*(S)} \cdot PPP_{\ell k}^{Jevons^*(S)}\right]^{\frac{1}{C}}.$$

The resulting indexes are transitive and based on the binary indexes that take into account the representativity of the items priced in different countries.

The Eurostat-OECD method represents a viable approach that makes use of the representativity status of products priced in different countries. A few points of interest are noted here. First, in a given binary comparison the procedures described in section 4.4 use data corresponding to those items that are representative in one country and also priced in the other country. In this process, information can be lost. For example, data on representative price items in country *j* that are not priced in country *k* do not enter the computation. Similarly, the prices of products that are considered unrepresentative products in both countries do not influence the binary comparison. Second, a more important point is that the Jevons-GEKS* and Jevons-GEKS*(S) indexes do rely heavily on price comparisons for commodities that are representative in one country but not in the other. Intuitively, such comparisons tend to be distorted because the commodity is representative in one country but not representative in the other. There is no guarantee that these distortions cancel each other.[23] In that case, it is likely that these distortions are in fact accumulating, and that the resulting basic heading parities may be highly distorted. This may not be a major problem when comparisons are made in a region in which all the countries are fairly similar and there is a significant overlap of products. The Eurostat-OECD approach addresses this issue through the use of equi-representativity, which endeavors to equalize the number of representative products in each country. Third, it is difficult to generalize the Jevons-GEKS* index to attach different weights to the representative and unrepresentative items in the basic heading.[24] And, fourth, the Eurostat-OECD approach, which uses the Jevons index, requires one single price observation for each item from each country. This is not a major restriction because it is common practice to use the national annual average price of the item as input into the basic heading PPP computations. However, when each country provides all the price quotations, the Eurostat-OECD approach cannot make direct use of the price quotations, and these detailed data need to be aggregated into an average before they can be used. The regression-based approach that underpins the Country Product Dummy method solves this problem to a certain degree.

4.4 The Country Product Dummy Method for the Computation of Basic Heading PPPs

The Country Product Dummy method was first introduced by Summers (1973). He proposed a simple regression-based method to fill missing price data in an incomplete tableau of prices at the basic heading level. The method was later used in various phases of the ICP conducted by the research team at the University of Pennsylvania. The report by Kravis, Heston, and Summers (1982) on the third phase of the ICP is a detailed account of how the CPD method provided an aggregation method at the basic heading level. However, the Eurostat-OECD program has continued to use the GEKS methods and its variants over the last three decades. And yet it has shown renewed interest in the CPD method because of the recent work of Rao (2004, 2005, 2009) and Diewert (2004b, 2005) and also because of the recent use of the method in PPP computations for poverty (Deaton and Dupriez 2009).

This section describes the CPD method and shows how it can be used in the computation of basic heading PPPs, especially when information is available on the representativity status of items in different countries.

The Basic CPD Model

Following the notation used in section 4.1, let p_i^j represent the price of item i in country j ($i = 1, 2, \ldots, N; j = 1, 2, \ldots, C$). It is useful to state the CPD model in a form that is directly relevant for international comparisons. Thus the basic statistical model underlying the CPD method can be stated as

$$(4.16) \qquad p_i^j = PPP_j \, P_i \, u_{ij}; \quad j = 1, 2, \ldots, C; \, i = 1, 2, \ldots, N$$

where PPP_j is the purchasing power parity of the currency of the j-th country; P_i is the international average price of the i-th commodity; and u_{ij}'s are independently and identically distributed random variables. In this chapter, these disturbances are assumed to be lognormally distributed, or that ln u_{ij}'s are normally distributed with a zero mean and a constant variance σ^2. Several features of the CPD model are noteworthy.

First, prices used in the CPD model may be considered a single price observation for each item in each country in which it is priced. The CPD model is general enough to accommodate the case in which several price quotations are available for each commodity in each country—a case considered in Diewert (2004b). When individual price quotations are used, it would be possible to extend the CPD model to incorporate additional characteristics associated with each quotation, including information on the type of outlet and on the rural/urban location for the transaction.

Second, in the ICP only single price observations representing the annual average prices of items in the basic heading are used. If information is available on the standard error associated with the average price, then this information can be incorporated into the model using different variances for different products.

Third, the CPD model in (4.16) is usually referred to as the *law of one price*, reflected by a single average price for a commodity across all the countries and a single measure of price level for each country represented by PPP_j.

Finally, the CPD model can be best described as a hedonic regression model in which the characteristics used are the country and the commodity specifications. The CPD model can be written as a standard hedonic model by using logarithmic prices. Taking natural logs on both sides, the model can be written as

$$\text{(4.17)} \qquad \begin{aligned} \ln p_{ij} &= \ln PPP_j + \ln p_i + \ln u_{ij} \\ &= \alpha_j + \gamma_i + \nu_{ij} \end{aligned}$$

where ν_{ij} are random disturbance terms that are independently and identically (normally) distributed with a zero mean and variance σ^2.[25] The CPD model can be seen as a simple fixed-effects model in which country effects provide estimates of purchasing power parities and commodity-specific effects provide estimates of international prices.

The parameter α_j is interpreted as the general price level in country j relative to prices in other countries included in the comparison. It is possible to express α_j relative to a reference country (say country 1). Then α_j represents the purchasing power parity of country j, showing the number of country j currency units that have the same purchasing power as one unit of currency of country 1 or the reference country.

Then the PPP for country j is given by

$$\text{(4.18)} \qquad PPP_j = \exp(\hat{\alpha}_j).$$

Because the estimated PPP depends on the estimated parameter values, it is possible to derive the standard errors associated with PPP_j, which is not possible when the Jevons method discussed in section 4.3 is used.

The CPD Regression Model

The simple model in (4.17) is called the Country Product Dummy method because it can be expressed as a regression equation in which all the explanatory/regressor variables are essentially dummy variables (one for each country and one for each commodity). The basic model $\ln p_{ij} = \alpha_j + \gamma_i + \nu_{ij}$ can be written as

$$\text{(4.19)} \qquad y_{ij} = \ln p_{ij} = \alpha_1 D_1 + \alpha_2 D_2 + \cdots + \alpha_C D_C + \eta_1 D_1^* + \eta_2 D_2^* + \cdots + \eta_N D_N^* + \nu_{ij}$$

where D_j ($j = 1, 2, \ldots, C$) and D_i^* ($i = 1, 2, \ldots, N$) are, respectively, country and commodity dummy variables. Equation (4.19) can be written as

$$y_{ij} = x_{ij}\beta + \nu_{ij}$$

where $x_{ij} = [D_1\ D_2 \ldots D_C\ D_1^*\ D_2^* \ldots D_N^*]$ and $\beta = [\alpha_1\ \alpha_2\ \alpha_C\ \gamma_1\ \gamma_2\ \gamma_N]'$ and where the values of the dummy variables are determined at the ij-th observation.

The main advantage of the CPD model in (4.19) is that it is possible to use very sophisticated econometric tools to derive interesting results—see Rao (2004) for more details on how the CPD model can be used in dealing with some of the data-related issues to be discussed shortly.[26] In their recent work, Hajargasht and Rao (2010) derive the Iklé-Dikhanov-Balk (IDB), Rao, and Geary-Khamis methods by using different distributional assumptions and thus are able to compute standard errors or measures of reliability associated with PPPs from these methods.

CPD Method: Complete Price Tableau and Item-Specific Weights

Now consider the case in which all items in the basic heading are priced in all countries. Here the Jevons index is used—when all countries price the same set of products.

In this case, for the aggregation at the basic heading level where there no weights, the parameters α_j and η_i can be estimated using simple unweighted or ordinary least squares by minimizing

$$\sum_{i=1}^{N}\sum_{j=1}^{C}(\ln p_{ij} - \alpha_j - \gamma_i)^2. \tag{4.20}$$

The first-order conditions for optimization with respect to α_j and η_i lead to the following system of $C + N$ equations in as many unknowns:

$$\alpha_j = \frac{1}{N}\sum_{i=1}^{N}\ln p_{nc} - \sum_{i=1}^{N}\gamma_i \; \textit{for } j = 1, 2, \ldots, C \textit{ and}$$

$$\gamma_i = \frac{1}{C}\sum_{j=1}^{C}\ln p_{nc} - \sum_{j=1}^{C}\alpha_c \; \textit{for } n = 1, 2, \ldots, N.$$

This system can be solved by imposing a linear restriction on the unknown parameters. For example, if $\alpha_1 = 0$ is the restriction imposed, it can be easily shown that, for each $j = 2, \ldots,$ C,

$$\hat{\alpha}_j = \frac{1}{N}\sum_{i=1}^{N}\left[\ln p_{nj} - \ln p_{n1}\right] \quad or \quad PPP_j = \exp(\hat{\alpha}_j) = \prod_{i=1}^{N}\left[\frac{p_{ij}}{p_{i1}}\right]^{\frac{1}{N}}. \tag{4.21}$$

Using the solution in (4.20), comparisons of price levels between countries j and k, represented by PPP_{jk}, can be derived as

$$PPP_{jk} = \frac{\exp(\hat{\alpha}_k)}{\exp(\hat{\alpha}_j)} = \prod_{i=1}^{N}\left[\frac{p_{ik}}{p_{ij}}\right]^{\frac{1}{N}}. \tag{4.22}$$

The PPP_{jk} obtained using the CPD model in (4.22) is identical to the Jevons index presented in equation (4.4) in section 4.3. As in the case of the Jevons index, the index in (4.22) is obviously transitive and base-invariant. The only difference is that because the CPD method uses a regression model, it is possible to derive the standard error associated with each PPP_{jk}. It was shown in Rao (2004) that the estimated variance of PPP_{jk} is given by

$$EstVar\,(\hat{\alpha}_j) = \frac{2}{N}\hat{\sigma}^2$$

where $\hat{\sigma}^2$ is an unbiased estimator of σ^2, which is given by

$$(4.23) \qquad \hat{\sigma}^2 = \frac{\sum_{j=1}^{C}\sum_{i=1}^{N} e_{ij}^2}{CN - (C + N - 1)}$$

where $e_{ij} = \ln p_{ij} - \hat{\alpha}_j - \hat{\gamma}_j$ is the least squares residual. Using (4.23), the estimated variance of PPP_j with a numeraire country—say country 1—is given by

$$(4.24) \qquad EstVar\,(\hat{PPP}_j) \approx EstVar\,(\hat{\alpha}_j) \cdot (\hat{\alpha}_j)^2 .$$

Equation (4.24) can then be used in deriving the estimated variance for PPPs with any other countries as the reference country.

CPD Method: Incomplete Price Tableau

In practice, rarely are all items priced in all countries. In fact, the general experience in international comparison exercises is that only a few items are priced in each of the participating countries, resulting in a rather sparse price tableau. This section examines the nature and role of the CPD method in this context, and it is contrasted with the alternative aggregation method based on variants of the Jevons method used by the Eurostat-OECD program.

The CPD model described in equations (4.17) and (4.19) can be used in conjunction with incomplete data if the price data set is connected as illustrated in table 4.2, which appears later in this chapter.[27] The CPD model and the least squares estimation shown in equations (4.20) and (4.21) can be used with appropriate modifications. Rao (2004) provides algebraic expressions and the necessary proofs to support the following properties of the CPD method relative to the Jevons-GEKS approach described in section 4.3:

- The CPD and the GEKS methods provide identical estimates of PPPs when the price tableau is complete, or equivalently when all countries price the same set of products. There is no real problem of choice. However, the GEKS method, which expresses the PPP_{jk} as a geometric mean of the price relatives for all the items, provides no measure of reliability as in the case of the CPD approach.
- When the price tableau is incomplete, the CPD and the Jevons-GEKS methods provide different numerical values. The CPD method makes use of all the price information in a single step, whereas the Jevons-GEKS method uses the information in two stages. At the first stage, binary comparisons are made using only the prices of items that are priced in a given pair of countries. Obviously, data on the prices of items that are priced in one country but not the other are ignored. Indirect use is made of the price data for the other items through the GEKS extension of the binary Jevons indexes. Once again, no standard errors are available for the PPPs derived using the Jevons-GEKS method.
- When the price tableau is incomplete, one can estimate the CPD model and fill in the missing price data to complete the tableau of prices. The CPD-based PPPs remain unchanged if the CPD model is applied a second time after filling in the missing prices. This is an indication that the price data were fully used under the CPD method. However, the Jevons-GEKS method applied to the incomplete tableau differs from the Jevons method applied to the tableau after the missing price data are imputed using the CPD model. This means that the Jevons-GEKS method can be improved through the use of

CPD fillers, which in turn implies that the GEKS method does not make full use of the price data in the incomplete tableau.

CPD Method: Information on Representativity and Importance

This section discusses two possible modifications of the simple CPD model depicted in (4.17) and (4.19). The first modification refers to the case in which additional information on the representativity of each item priced in each of the countries is available. In this case, it is possible to extend the CPD regression model to directly account for the possible upward (or downward) bias caused by the prices of *unrepresentative items*. The representativeness concept was used in the 2005 ICP. The second modification concerns the notion of *importance*, whereby each item is classified as important or unimportant in each of the countries. The notion of importance has been adopted for the 2011 round of the ICP. A discussion of extensions of the CPD model in these two cases follows.

Country Product Representative Dummy Model

Recalling the discussion of *representativity* in section 4.2 of this chapter as well as in chapter 1, the basic idea is that representative products tend to be cheaper than unrepresentative products within a basic heading.[28] This means that in addition to the country and product dimensions used in the CPD model, another dimension of representativity is considered critical and is therefore included.

Accommodating representativity information is quite straightforward through the introduction of another dummy variable representing the additional dimension. In this case, for each price observation a representativeness dummy variable, R, is defined so that the value of R equals 0 if the price observation corresponds to a representative item and equals 1 if the particular item is not representative. The basic CPD model in equation (4.19) may be extended to include the representativeness dummy as follows:[29]

$$\begin{aligned} y_{ij} = \ln p_{ij} &= \alpha_1 D_1 + \alpha_2 D_2 + \cdots + \alpha_C D_C + \eta_1 D_1^* + \eta_2 D_2^* + \cdots + \eta_N D_N^* + \delta R + \nu_{ij} \\ &= \sum_{j=1}^{C} \alpha_j D_j + \sum_{i=1}^{N} \eta_i D_i^* + \delta R + \nu_{ij}. \end{aligned} \tag{4.25}$$

The parameters in the model can be estimated using the standard least squares method after imposing the numeraire restriction setting one of the α_j's equal to unity. The resulting estimates of PPPs are essentially adjusted for the upward bias caused by those price observations that are not representative. It is expected that in the general case in which unrepresentative items are more expensive the estimate of δ will be positive.[30]

Using the CPRD model, it is much easier to handle the bias induced by the prices of unrepresentative items through the magnitude of δ. Such an adjustment is not possible in the case of the Jevons-GEKS procedure. In addition, it is clear that considerable price information is lost in the general architecture of the Jevons-GEKS* and Jevons-GEKS*(S) methods described in section 4.3.

Based on the advantages of the CPRD model and because it uses all the information contained in the data set, the CPRD model was recommended for use in the 2005 ICP round for aggregation at the basic heading level. However, the CPRD model could not be used in the Africa and Asia-Pacific regions because of the problems associated with the determination of representative and unrepresentative products. The CPRD method was used in the South America region comparisons. The Eurostat-OECD program used the Jevons-GEKS*(S) method described in section 4.3.

CPD Model with Importance Weights Attached to Price Observations

Because of the practical problems associated with identifying the representativeness of items priced in different countries, the 2011 ICP will use the notion of *importance* of the product priced. In particular, each item priced will be identified as either *important or unimportant*. The *importance* information will be used by means of attaching weights to price observations. In its meeting in April 2011, the Technical Advisory Group (TAG) of the ICP recommended that a weight of 3 be attached to products identified as important and a weight of 1 be attached to items deemed unimportant.[31]

It is fairly simple to attach weights in the estimation of the parameters of the CPD model. It is equivalent to running *weighted least squares* in the place of simple unweighted least squares. Suppose w_{ij} is the weight attached to the price quotation for the i-th commodity in the j-th country. Then the weighted least squares simply minimizes

$$(4.26) \qquad \sum_{i=1}^{N}\sum_{j=1}^{C} w_{ij}(\ln p_{ij} - \alpha_j - \gamma_i)^2 =$$

$$\sum_{i=1}^{N}\sum_{j=1}^{C}\left[w_{ij}(\ln p_{ij} - \alpha_1 D_1 - \alpha_2 D_2 - \cdots - \alpha_C D_C - \eta_1 D_1^* - \eta_2 D_2^* - \cdots - \eta_N D_N^*)^2\right]$$

with respect to the unknown parameters, which in turn results in estimates of PPPs. The TAG recommendation is to use $w_{ij} = 3$ if the commodity is important or representative and $w_{ij} = 1$ if it is unimportant.

As an extension of this procedure, it may be possible to include information on approximate expenditure or sales shares in the place of arbitrarily stated weights. The main feature of the model in (4.26) is that it is exactly the model one would use if expenditure share weights were available. Rao (2009) discusses the expenditure share–weighted CPD model.

The extensions and variations of the CPD model discussed in this section are limited to the cases applicable to the estimation of basic heading PPPs. It is clear that the CPD method offers major advantages over the alternative based on the Jevons index and variations of the Jevons-GEKS index. Because of the noise in the price data arising from the fact that the data are collected through price surveys, methods such as the CPD based on statistical models are best suited to account for noise and also to provide estimates of reliability in the form of standard errors associated with the PPPs at the basic heading level.

A Numerical Example

A numerical example designed to illustrate the various methods of aggregation used in deriving PPPs at the basic heading level is presented in table 4.2. In particular, the properties of the Jevons-GEKS, Jevons-GEKS*, Jevons-GEKS*(S), and CPD, CPRD, and weighted CPD methods are illustrated using a simple example.[32]

The example refers to the basic heading materials for maintenance and repair of the dwelling. Four items are listed under this basic heading, and four countries are used in this example. All the items are priced in all the countries, which is useful in illustrating the equivalence of the CPD and Jevons-GEKS methods in special cases. The representativity of different products is indicated by an asterisk (*), shown in the adjacent column, attached to the price quotation.

In this example, all four commodities are priced in all four countries. Therefore, the GEKS parities should be identical to those derived using the CPD model. Only one item is considered representative in country 1, whereas in countries 2 and 3 three products are representative. By contrast, only one item is representative in country 4.

TABLE 4.2 Price Data for Aggregation at the Basic Heading Level (Materials for Maintenance and Repair of the Dwelling)

Description	Qty.	Unit	Country 1	Rep.	Country 2	Rep.	Country 3	Rep.	Country 4	Rep.
Paint, indoor use	10	l	33.88		34.90	*	753.36	*	89.45	*
Paint, outdoor use	10	l	49.19		71.34		1317.93	*	149.05	
Silicone	300	g	4.54	*	5.29	*	84.74		7.54	
Cement	25	kg	4.57		6.30	*	60.07	*	5.55	

The following aggregation methods are considered in the example:

- Simple unweighted CPD model
- CPRD model with a representativeness dummy
- CPD model with weights for representative items equal to 3 and equal to 1 for unrepresentative items similar to the TAG recommendation
- Jevons-GEKS(*) method in which representativeness is taken into account
- Jevons-GEKS*(S) method, which gives additional weight to commodities representative in both countries.

The computed PPPs using different methods are presented in table 4.3.

Several features of table 4.3 are worth noting. First, the PPPs derived by the GEKS method without (*) are identical to the values obtained using the unweighted CPD. This result is consistent with the analytical result that shows the equivalence of these two methods when the price tableau is complete. However, when the representativity information is incorporated, the methods lead to different results. Otherwise, there are no obvious trends. The weighted CPD method with the 3:1 weighting scheme seems to perform quite well. The CPRD method appears to produce the lowest PPP values, followed by the GEKS* method.

Because the CPD method makes it possible to employ a range of econometric techniques on the price data used and also produces standard errors for the estimated PPPs, the use of the weighted CPD appears to be a particularly good choice.

4.5 Linking Regions at the Basic Heading Level in ICP 2005 and Looking Forward to ICP 2011

The main objective of this section to outline the methodology used in linking PPPs at the basic heading level in the 2005 ICP and provide a brief overview of the methodology being considered for the 2011 ICP. The problem of linking PPPs above the basic heading level is considered in depth in chapter 6 by Diewert. In essence, that chapter uses the linked PPPs at the basic heading level as inputs into the aggregation process.

Linking BH-Level PPPs in ICP 2005

The 2005 ICP embraced a fully regionalized approach to the compilation of PPPs and international comparisons of real gross domestic product and its components. As a part of the regionalized

TABLE 4.3 Multilateral PPPs for Basic Heading (Materials for Maintenance and Repair of the Dwelling, Four Items) by Different Methods

Method of calculation	Purchasing power parities			
	Country 1	Country 2	Country 3	Country 4
Jevons-GEKS*	1.000	1.170	18.722	2.160
Jevons-GEKS without *	1.000	1.245	19.548	2.004
Jevons-GEKS*(S)	1.000	1.088	18.456	2.339
CPRD	1.000	1.164	18.280	2.004
CPD unweighted (weights 1:1)	1.000	1.245	19.548	2.004
CPD weighted (weights 3:1)	1.000	1.232	18.917	2.115
Exchange rate	1.000	2.150	8.664	1.000

Note: GEKS*(S) = Gini-Éltetö-Köves-Szulc (Sergeev); CPRD = Country Product Representative Dummy; CPD = Country Product Dummy.

approach, all the participating countries were classified into six regions: Africa, Asia-Pacific, CIS, Eurostat-OECD, South America, and Western Asia. In the 2005 ICP, the Arab Republic of Egypt and the Russian Federation belonged to two different regions at the same time. Egypt participated in the Africa and Western Asia regional comparisons, whereas Russia participated in the Eurostat-OECD and CIS regions. Two major steps were involved in compiling the BH-level PPPs for the 146 participating countries in the global comparison. First, price comparisons were undertaken in each of the regions, coordinated by a regional agency that worked under the guidance of the ICP Global Office.[33] At the conclusion of the activities at the regional level, PPPs at the basic heading level were compiled in each region for the 155 basic headings in the GDP comparisons. Also in each region, one country was selected as the numeraire or reference country, so that the PPPs were expressed in the currency units of the reference country. In order to use these regional sets of PPPs within a global comparison, it was necessary to express the regional basic heading PPPs in the currency units of a global numeraire. A major requirement in this process was *fixity*, which stipulates that the relativities between purchasing powers of currencies of countries within a region must remain unaltered in the process of conversion to a global numeraire. For a more complete description of the general approach used in making global comparisons, see chapter 1 of this volume.

The methodology used in the 2005 ICP to convert the regional BH-level PPPs maintaining fixity is described in this section. The essential steps involved in the process are as follows:

- PPPs were compiled for the currencies of countries within each region using a regional numeraire currency for all 155 basic headings in the GDP.
- A set of 18 Ring countries[34] was identified: six countries from Africa, four from the Asia-Pacific, and two each from the Eurostat-OECD and Western Asia regions. The CIS region was linked using Russia as the bridge country.
- All the Ring countries conducted additional surveys to collect prices of items in the *Ring product list*. The Ring list was developed by the Global Office after examining the regional product lists. This process was used only for household consumption. For all the other aggregates, regional comparisons were based on a global list of items.

- The price data collected by the 18 Ring countries were used in compiling *linking factors*, which were in turn used to convert the regional numeraire currency units into the global numeraire currency. The U.S. dollar was used as the global numeraire.

The methodology used for linking both at the basic heading level and at higher levels of aggregation was developed by Diewert and is described in detail in Diewert (2008, 2010a). The aggregation methodology used in the computation of linking factors is described in the rest of this section.

Notation

Suppose there are R regions in the comparison, with C(r), for $r = 1, 2, \ldots, R$, countries in region r. In the 2005 ICP, R equaled 6, and table 1.3 of chapter 1 in this volume shows the distribution of countries by region. Let L(r) ($r = 1, 2, \ldots, R$) be the number of linking countries for a total of $L = \sum_{r=1}^{R} L(r)$. In the 2005 ICP, L equaled 18.

The Method

Let PPP_{rcn} represent the PPP for the n-th basic heading in country c belonging to region r. Without loss of generality, let the first country in each region be the numeraire country. The following steps are used in the computation of linking factors for the n-th basic heading:

Step 1. Consider all the Ring countries in region r. Let p_{ircn}^{L} represent the price of the i-th item priced in linking country c in region r. These are expressed in the national currency units of country c.

Step 2. Convert all the prices of Ring list items in the n-th basic heading in linking country c in region r into the numeraire or reference country currency units using

$$p_{ircn}^{L*} = \frac{p_{ircn}^{L}}{PPP_{rcn}}. \tag{4.27}$$

This means that the price in the linking country is converted using PPP_{rcn}. For example, if the PPP for the rice basic heading in Sri Lanka in the Asia-Pacific region is 5.85 to the Hong Kong dollar, which was the numeraire currency in the Asia-Pacific region, then the prices of Ring products belonging in the rice basic heading collected from Sri Lanka are all divided by 5.85, thereby expressing Ring product prices in Hong Kong dollars. At the end of this step, the prices of all the Ring list items priced by Ring countries in the Asia-Pacific region are expressed in Hong Kong dollars.

Step 3. Use the converted Ring list prices for all the Ring countries in a CPD regression model to derive PPPs for the numeraire currencies in different regions. The CPD model used can be written as

$$\ln p_{ircn}^{L*} = \alpha_{rn} + \beta_{n} + u_{ircn} \tag{4.28}$$

where $\exp(\alpha_{rn})$ represents the purchasing power parity of the currency of region r in terms of currency units of the global numeraire or reference currency (say the U.S. dollar) for the n-th basic heading.

Step 4. Apply the CPD regression in (4.28) in step 3 for all 155 basic headings.

Step 5. Convert the basic heading PPPs within each region expressed in the reference currency of the region (e.g., Hong Kong dollars in the Asia-Pacific) into the global numeraire using the PPPs derived in step 4. At the end of this step, the linked PPPs at the basic heading level are given by

$$PPP^{*}_{rcn} = PPP_{rcn} \cdot \exp(\alpha_{rcn}). \tag{4.29}$$

For example, if the basic heading PPP for rice in Sri Lanka in the Asia-Pacific comparison is 5.85 Sri Lankan rupees per HK\$1 and if the linking factor computed using Ring prices leads to, say, HK\$6 per US\$1, then the PPP for the rice basic heading for Sri Lanka in the global reference currency, the U.S. dollar, is SL Rs 35.10 per U.S. dollar.[35]

Sergeev (2009) raises an interesting issue that grows out of the different number of Ring or linking countries from different regions—that is, $L(r)$ varies with r. In the 2005 ICP, six countries from Africa and four countries from Asia were compared with four countries from the OECD.[36] The main point is that within the CPD framework it can be shown that the international average prices are averages of prices from the linking countries. Therefore, regions with a greater number of linking countries may appear to exert a larger influence.[37] However, the rationale for including more than one country in a region in the Ring list is that for those regions that are large and those that exhibit a large variation in prices it is necessary to use more price data drawn from a diverse set of countries representing the region. There are, then, two possible solutions to the issue raised by Sergeev (2009):

1. Express the uncertainty attached to prices from a region through a larger variance for the corresponding disturbance term in the CPD model and then apply the generalized least squares method, which accords less weight to those observations with larger variance. This eliminates the problem discussed by Sergeev. However, it is difficult to know the extent of variability in prices across countries within a region.
2. Alternatively, a suggestion made by Sergeev in his paper may be implemented. Instead of using country-specific prices for each of the linking countries in a region, simply take the geometric mean of the prices after converting them into the currency of the numeraire country. In this case, one can simply use

$$p^{L^*}_{irn} = \prod_{c=1}^{C} \left[\frac{p^{L^*}_{ircn}}{\alpha_{r1n}} \right]^{\frac{1}{L(r)}}. \tag{4.30}$$

In the next step, use these geometric means as inputs into the CPD model to generate the regional linking factors described in equation (4.28). Use of the geometric mean ensures that each region is represented by a single vector of prices in the CPD regression model, thereby guaranteeing that no region exerts more than a proportionate influence on the BH-level parities that are used in deriving linking factors at higher levels of aggregation.

Because the different regions exhibit different levels of variability and because the use of geometric average prices from Ring countries entails a loss of information on prices, it is appropriate to continue with the current practice of using different numbers of Ring countries in the basic heading computations.

Finally, an additional comment is in order here on the possible use of representativity and importance information in the derivation of the linking factors. Because the CPD regression in equation (4.28) uses price observations from a number of countries within each region and because each country may have a different representativity status for a product in the Ring list, it would be possible to make use of such information in deriving the regional linking factors for different basic headings. However, use of representativity information would not be possible if Sergeev's suggestion for using the regional average price in (4.30) is implemented (Sergeev 2009). It is difficult to attach any meaning for representativity for a price that is the average over a number of different countries.

A New Approach Based on Core Products in ICP 2011

An evaluation of the Ring country approach used in the 2005 ICP raised some issues: the choice of Ring countries from each of the regions and the likely influence of a less than ideal choice of reference countries on the linking factors that have a direct impact on the global PPPs at the GDP level and the resulting real income comparisons. Construction of the Ring product lists and the pricing of these products in a limited set of Ring countries from each region were also considered to be less than satisfactory.

In an effort to improve the 2005 methodology, it was decided to link the 2011 regional comparisons through price data collected for *core products*. The core product list is supposed to represent the products used in both developed and developing countries. A list of more than 600 core products was prepared by the Global Office. The core products are expected to strengthen the link between regional and global comparisons through the following steps:

- Include the core products in the product lists of all the regions.
- Encourage the regions to price as many core products as possible in their regional price surveys.
- Have regions use the price data on core products, as well as the region-specific product lists in the computation of PPPs for different basic headings.
- Ensure that linking factors to link regional basic heading PPPs use the prices of core products collected by all the participating countries in all the regions and not just the prices collected for a selected set of Ring countries.
- Base the CPD regression in (4.28) on prices of all the core products in all the countries participating in the 2011 round of the ICP. The number of countries is expected to be about 180. Use of price data from all countries will conceivably produce a more robust and reliable set of linking factors that are likely to improve the quality of the global comparisons.

Exploratory empirical analyses using core product prices collected in the first two quarters of the 2011 ICP will be conducted to examine the nature and reliability of the linking factors resulting from the new approach. Meanwhile, research is continuing into alternative ways of using core product prices. Hill (2011) is proposing methods to use the core product prices in computing PPPs at and above the basic heading levels, imposing within-region fixity in the ICP.

4.6 Conclusion

The Jevons-GEKS and the CPD are the two main aggregation methods used to compile PPPs at the basic heading level. When all items are priced in all countries and if all items are considered to be equally important, then these two methods lead to the same numerical values for the estimated

PPPs. However, the CPD method has the advantage of providing standard errors that can be used as measures of reliability. In the case in which some products are representative or important, then three variants of the GEKS method and two variants of the CPD method are available. On a conceptual level, the CPD with weights reflecting the importance of the product is superior to the use of the CPRD, which relies on a systematic bias induced by unrepresentative products. As for the Jevons-GEKS and its variants, in general methods based on Jevons-GEKS appear to discard some price data, which is not the case when the CPD-based methods are used. The Jevons-GEKS*(S) method, thanks to Sergeev (2003), appears to perform well among the GEKS-based methods.

Looking forward to the 2011 ICP, the Jevons-GEKS and the CPD-based methods should be reexamined in light of the decision to use a list of "core products" that will be priced in all countries in all regions. The use of core products is designed to eliminate the reliance on a few selected Ring countries for the purpose of linking regions. A number of methods are currently being developed and discussed at various meetings of the Technical Advisory Group. The CPD method is ideally placed for the current approach of using core product prices collected from all the countries in the global comparisons. The Jevons-GEKS method would be of limited applicability in this case because the method can be used only if average prices representing each of the regions are available. However, use of average prices implies a loss of information. Although the search is continuing to identify suitable aggregation methods to link regional basic heading PPPs using the core product price data, in the interim the CPD method is currently best suited to make use of all the core product prices collected from all countries.

NOTES

1. The author wishes to acknowledge comments from W. Erwin Diewert, Robert Hill, Sergey Sergeev, and Frederic A. Vogel on the material covered in this chapter. Additional thanks are due to Sergeev for providing data and results for the numerical example included in this chapter.
2. PPPs compiled at the regional level are based exclusively on data for countries in the region. The PPPs are expected to satisfy the usual properties of transitivity and base invariance only for those countries. By contrast, global comparisons make use of data from all the countries included in the global comparison, and PPPs at that level satisfy transitivity across countries from different regions.
3. At its meeting in April 2011, the ICP's Technical Advisory Group recommended procedures for linking PPPs across regions at the basic heading level.
4. Representativeness of products is discussed briefly in chapter 1, and it is further elaborated in this chapter.
5. The CPD and the CPRD (Country Product Representative Dummy) methods were recommended for use in the 2005 ICP at the basic heading level.
6. The survey framework for the collection of price data is described in chapter 7 by Frederic A. Vogel.
7. Lack of quantity or expenditure share data makes it impossible to use standard index number formulas such as the Laspeyres, Paasche, Fisher, and Tornqvist.
8. For a description of elementary indexes and the methods used, see the manual for the compilation of the CPI issued by the International Labour Organization et al. (2004).
9. In the case of temporal movements in prices, products within a basic heading are expected to show similar price changes over time.

10. For more details on the Eurostat-OECD treatment of representativity, see the paper by Roberts (2009), which provides a comprehensive account of the methodology used by Eurostat and the OECD.
11. Consider a hypothetical example in which country A prices only representative products and country B prices only unrepresentative products. In this case, the PPP for country B relative to country A would overstate the price level in country B.
12. This may not hold for all products. For example, beef is not representative of meat consumption in India, but it is not relatively more expensive than other meats such as lamb or chicken. In fact, beef and pork are generally cheaper because they are not commonly consumed.
13. This is the recommendation made at the April 2011 meeting of the Technical Advisory Group. These weights will be used in conjunction with the CPD method. Details of the procedure are given in section 4.3.
14. For a discussion of determining the number of quotations and related issues, see chapter 7 on the survey framework for the ICP.
15. If σ is the standard deviation associated with a given price (average) and if n is the number of price quotations used, then $\sigma/\sqrt{n}$ is the standard error associated with the given average price.
16. Generally, N (number of items) would vary with the basic heading, and therefore ideally a subscript needs to be added. Similarly, the number of countries varies across different regions, and therefore C needs to have a regional descriptor. Because the focus is on a single region and on a single basic heading, for expositional purposes subscripts for the basic heading and the regions are dropped.
17. This case is the same as the one in which all the countries in the region price the same subset of items, which implies that the remaining items are not priced in any of the countries and can therefore be dropped from the computations.
18. In the case in which the price data are not connected, then even the idea of using a spatial chain of countries will fail because there is no way to connect countries A and B with countries C and D in the second block.
19. Because price data collection is resource-intensive, a balance should be struck between the cost of collection and the need to price as many items as possible to strengthen the price comparisons.
20. A comprehensive discussion of elementary price indexes and the properties of the Jevons index can be found in Diewert (2004a). The publication *Consumer Price Index Manual: Theory and Practice* is an excellent source of material on methods used in the compilation of the consumer price index (International Labour Organization et al. 2004). Chapter 20 of that publication is based on Diewert (2004a).
21. Hill and Hill (2009) use a more complex notation in presenting these methods.
22. Hill and Hill (2009) interpret this formula as a variant of the standard Tornqvist index, which uses the geometric mean of price relatives, with the average budget shares in two periods as the weight.
23. This is easily true in the hypothetical case in which no items are priced that are considered representative in both countries.
24. For example, it would be difficult to accord a weight of 3 to a price observation for a representative or important product and a weight of 1 to unrepresentative products. This difficulty will require a further modification of the Sergeev (2003) suggestion.
25. The model in (4.16) is not identified, and it requires normalization before the parameters of the model can be estimated.

26. Hill and Syed (2010) demonstrate how the CPD model can be used along with individual price quotations from different countries to obtain estimates of rural-urban price differentials and the outlet effects.
27. This is the case where not all items in the basic heading are priced in all countries.
28. The CPD model can equally incorporate the opposite case in which unrepresentative products are cheaper.
29. The model presented here is in a format slightly different from that used in the *ICP 2005 Methodological Handbook* (World Bank 2007).
30. In a recent study, Hill and Syed (2010) present estimates of the representativity coefficients computed using data from a selected set of countries in the 2005 ICP Asia-Pacific region. They found that the coefficients could be negative for some basic headings and positive for others and that no definite conclusions could be drawn. Their findings may reflect in part the difficulties the national price statisticians had in determining whether a particular product was representative in their countries.
31. It was noted that the unweighted use of price observations amounts to giving equal weight to products that are important and that are unimportant.
32. The author is greatly indebted to Sergey Sergeev for providing the data and the computations required for the numerical example.
33. See chapter 2 of the *ICP 2005 Methodological Handbook* for more details on the organizational structure of the ICP (World Bank 2007).
34. This group included one economy, Hong Kong SAR, China.
35. A numerical example of the computation of the linking factors using illustrative data can be found in appendix H of World Bank (2008).
36. Ring countries for the 2005 ICP round were Brazil; Cameroon; Chile; Arab Republic of Egypt; Estonia; Hong Kong SAR, China; Japan; Jordan; Kenya; Malaysia; Oman; the Philippines; Senegal; Slovenia; South Africa; Sri Lanka; the United Kingdom; and Zambia.
37. Equations (4.26)–(4.28) in Sergeev (2009) can be derived from the normal equations associated with the ordinary least squares method.

REFERENCES

ADB (Asian Development Bank). 2007. *Purchasing Power Parities and Real Expenditures: 2005 International Comparison Program in Asia and the Pacific*. Manila: ADB.

Balk, B. M. 2008. *Price and Quantity Index Numbers: Models for Measuring Aggregate Change and Difference*. New York: Cambridge University Press.

———. 2009. "Aggregation Methods in International Comparisons: An Evaluation." In *Purchasing Power Parities of Currencies: Recent Advances in Methods and Applications*, ed. D. S. Prasada Rao, 59–85. Cheltenham, U.K.: Edward Elgar.

Deaton, A., and O. Dupriez. 2009. "Global Poverty and Global Price Indexes." http://www.Princeton.edu/~deaton/downloads/Global_Poverty_and_Global_Price_Indexes.pdf.

Deaton, A., and A. H. Heston. 2008. "Understanding PPPs and PPP-based National Accounts." NBER Working Paper No. 14499, National Bureau of Economic Research, Cambridge, MA.

Diewert, W. E. 2004a. "Elementary Indices." In *Consumer Price Index Manual: Theory and Practice*, chap. 20. Geneva: International Labour Organization.

———. 2004b. "On the Stochastic Approach to Linking Regions in the ICP." Paper prepared for Development Economics Data Group (DECDG), World Bank, Washington, DC.

———. 2005. "Weighted Country Product Dummy Variable Regressions and Index Number Formulae." *Review of Income and Wealth* 51: 561–70.

———. 2008. "New Methodological Developments for the International Comparison Program." Joint UNECE/ILO Meeting on Consumer Price Indices, Geneva, May 8–9. http://www.econ.ubc.ca/diewert/dp0808.pdf.

———. 2010ba. "Approaches to Linking the Regions." Paper prepared for meeting of the Technical Advisory Group of the International Comparison Program, World Bank, Washington, DC, February 17–19.

———. 2010b. "New Methodological Developments for the International Comparison Program." *Review of Income and Wealth*, series 56, special issue 1 (June): S11–31.

Éltetö, O., and P. Köves. 1964. "On a Problem of Index Number Computation Relating to International Comparison." *Statisztikai Szemle* (42): 507–18.

Gini, C. 1924. "Quelques considérations au sujet de la construction des nombres indices des prix et des questions analogues." *Metron* 4 (1): 3–162.

———. 1931. "On the Circular Test of Index Numbers." *Metron* 9 (9): 3–24.

Hajargasht, G., and D. S. Prasada Rao. 2010. "Stochastic Approach to Index Numbers for Multilateral Price Comparisons and Their Standard Errors." *Review of Income and Wealth*, series 56, special issue 1 (June): S32–S58.

Hill, R. J. 2011. "The Imposition of Within-Region Fixity in the International Comparison Program." Unpublished paper, Department of Economics, University of Graz, Graz, Austria.

Hill, R. J., and T. P. Hill. 2009. "Recent Developments in the International Comparison of Prices and Real Output." *Macroeconomic Dynamics* (13, supplement): 194–217.

Hill, R. J., and I. Syed. 2010. "Improving International Comparisons of Real Output: The ICP 2005 Benchmark and Its Implications for China." Discussion Paper 2010-25, School of Economics, University of New South Wales.

Hill, R. J., and M. P. Timmer. 2006. "Standard Errors and Weights in Multilateral Price Indexes." *Journal of Business and Economic Statistics* 24 (3): 366–77.

International Labour Organization, International Monetary Fund, Organisation for Economic Co-operation and Development, United Nations Economic Commission for Europe, Eurostat, and World Bank. 2004. *Consumer Price Index Manual: Theory and Practice,* ed. Peter Hill. Geneva: International Labour Office.

Kravis, I. B., A. W. Heston, and R. Summers. 1982. *World Product and Income: International Comparisons of Real Gross Domestic Product.* Baltimore: Johns Hopkins University Press.

Rao, D. S. Prasada. 1990. "A System of Log-Change Index Numbers for Multilateral Comparisons." In *Comparisons of Prices and Real Products in Latin America,* ed. J. Salazar-Carillo and D. S. Prasada Rao, 127–39. New York: Elsevier.

———. 2004. "The Country-Product-Dummy Method: A Stochastic Approach to the Computation of Purchasing Power Parities in the ICP." Paper presented at SSHRC Conference on Index Numbers and Productivity Measurement, Vancouver, British Columbia, June 30–July 3.

———. 2005. "On the Equivalence of Weighted Country-Product-Dummy (CPD) Method and the Rao-System for Multilateral Price Comparisons." *Review of Income and Wealth* (51): 571–80.

———. 2009. "Generalised Eltetö-Köves-Szulc (EKS) and Country-Product-Dummy (CPD) Methods for International Comparisons." *In Purchasing Power Parities of Currencies: Recent Advances in Methods and Applications,* ed. D. S. Prasada Rao, 86–120. Cheltenham, U.K.: Edward Elgar.

Rao, D. S. Prasada, A. Maddison, and B. Lee. 2002. "International Comparison of Farm Sector Performance: Methodological Options and Empirical Findings for Asia-Pacific Economies, 1900–94." In *The Asian Economies in the Twentieth Century,* ed. A. Maddison et al., 27–52. Cheltenham, U.K.: Edward Elgar.

Rao, D. S. Prasada, and M. P. Timmer 2003. "Purchasing Power Parity Comparisons Using Weighted Elteto-Koves-Szulc (EKS) Methods." *Review of Income and Wealth* 49 (4): 491–511.

Roberts, D. 2009. "The Compilation of Purchasing Power Parities: The Eurostat-OECD Purchasing Power Parity Programme." In *Purchasing Power Parities of Currencies: Recent Advances in Methods and Applications,* ed. D. S. Prasada Rao, 7–56. Cheltenham, U.K.: Edward Elgar.

Sergeev, S. 2002. "Calculation of Equi-characteristic PPPs at the Basic Heading Level (Modification of the Method of 'Asterisks')." Paper prepared for meeting of Working Part on PPP, Item 6.3 of the Agenda, Doc. PPP02/P2/7, Eurostat, June 12–13.

———. 2003. "Equirepresentativity and Some Modifications of the EKS Method at the Basic Heading Level." ECE-UN Consultation on the European Comparison Programme, Geneva, March 31–April 2, 2003.

———. 2009. "The Evaluation of the Approaches Used for the Linking of the Regions in the ICP 2005." Unpublished paper, Statistics Austria, Vienna, December.

Summers, R. 1973. "International Price Comparisons Using Incomplete Data." *Review of Income and Wealth* (19): 1–6.

Szulc, B. 1964. "Indices for Multiregional Comparisons." *Przeglad Statystyczny* (3): 239–54.

World Bank. 2007. *ICP 2005 Methodological Handbook.* http://web.worldbank.org/WBSITE/EXTERNAL/DATASTATISTICS/ICPEXT/0,,contentMDK:20126612~pagePK:60002244~piPK:62002388~theSitePK:270065,00.html.

———. 2008. *Global Purchasing Power Parities and Real Expenditures: 2005 International Comparison Program.* http://siteresources.worldbank.org/ICPINT/Resources/icp-final.pdf.

CHAPTER 5

Methods of Aggregation above the Basic Heading Level within Regions

W. Erwin Diewert

Chapter 4 describes how the 155 basic heading price parities for each of the *K* countries in a region were constructed for 2005 round of the International Comparison Program (ICP).[1] Once these purchasing power parities (PPPs) have been constructed, aggregate measures of country prices and relative volumes between countries can be constructed using the wide variety of multilateral comparison methods suggested over the years. These aggregate comparisons assume that, in addition to basic heading price parities for each country, national statisticians have provided country expenditures (in their home currencies) for each of the 155 basic heading categories for the reference year 2005. Then the 155 × *K* matrices of basic heading price parities and country expenditures are used to form average price levels across all commodities and relative volume shares for each country.

Many different methods can be used to construct these aggregate purchasing power parities and relative country volumes. P. Hill (2007a, 2007b) surveyed the main methods used in previous rounds of the ICP, as well as other methods that could be used.[2] Only two multilateral methods have been used in previous ICP rounds: (1) the Gini-Éltetö-Köves-Szulc (GEKS) method based on Fisher's bilateral indexes (Fisher 1922), and (2) the Geary-Khamis (GK) method, which is an additive method (Geary 1953; Khamis 1972).

In the 2005 ICP round, aggregate PPPs and relative volumes for countries within each region were constructed for four of the five geographic ICP regions using the GEKS method.[3] However, the Africa region wanted to use an additive method, and so it relied on the relatively new Iklé-Dikhanov-Balk (IDB) additive method for constructing PPPs and relative volumes within the region.[4] The purpose of this chapter is to describe the properties of these three methods—GEKS, GK, and IDB—for making multilateral comparisons between countries in a region.[5] These methods are discussed in sections 5.1, 5.2, and 5.3 of this chapter. The extensive annex to the chapter discusses the properties of the IDB method in more detail because this method is relatively unknown. It may not be of interest, however, to the casual reader.

To discriminate between the various multilateral index number methods suggested for the ICP, it is useful to look at the axiomatic properties of the various methods. Thus section 5.4 lists various axioms or properties or tests that have been suggested for multilateral indexes to see which tests are satisfied by the GEKS, GK, and IDB methods.

Now, a brief comment on the relative merits of the GEKS, GK, and IDB methods is warranted. The GK and IDB methods are *additive methods*—that is, the real final demand of each country can be expressed as the sum of the country's individual basic heading final expenditures. Each real final demand component is weighted by an international price, which is constant across countries. This feature of an additive method is tremendously convenient for users, because the components of final demand can be aggregated consistently across both countries and commodity groups, and so for many purposes it is useful to have available a set of additive international comparisons. However, additive methods are not consistent with the *economic approach* to index number theory (which allows for substitution effects), whereas the GEKS method is consistent. Section 5.5 explains the economic approach and why additive methods are not fully consistent with that approach.

The GEKS multilateral method is fully consistent with the economic approach to making multilateral comparisons. The GEKS approach also has the property that each country in the comparison is treated in a fully symmetric manner—that is, the method is a democratic one. This aspect of GEKS can be considered an advantage of the method. However, from a technical point of view there are some disadvantages to the method in that countries that are at very different stages of development and that face very different relative prices are given the same weight in the method as countries that are at very similar stages of development and face the same structure of relative prices. Bilateral comparisons of countries similar in structure are likely to be much more accurate than comparisons of countries that are very dissimilar. Thus section 5.6 of this chapter introduces an economic approach that builds up a complete multilateral set of comparisons that rests on making bilateral comparisons of countries very similar in structure. Called the minimum spanning tree (MST) method and introduced by R. J. Hill (1999a, 1999b, 2001, 2004, 2009),[6] this method has some advantages over GEKS, and thus it could be considered for use in the next ICP round.

Section 5.7 of this chapter uses the artificial data example in Diewert (1999) to illustrate how the four methods (GEKS, GK, IDB, and MST) differ in a rather extreme numerical example. Two less extreme numerical examples are presented in chapter 6.

5.1 GEKS Method

The GEKS method originated with Gini (1924, 1931), and was independently rediscovered by Éltetö and Köves (1964) and Szulc (1964).

This method is more easily explained by introducing some notation. Let N equal 155 and K be the number of countries in the regional comparison for the reference year. The basic heading PPP for final demand commodity category n and for country k in the region is denoted by $p_n^k > 0$ and the corresponding expenditure (in local currency units) on commodity class n by country k in the reference year by e_n^k for $n = 1, \ldots, N$ and $k = 1, \ldots, K$.[7] Using this information, it is possible to define volumes[8] or implicit quantity levels q_n^k for each basic heading category n and for each country k as the category expenditure deflated by the corresponding basic heading commodity PPP for that country:

$$(5.1) \qquad q_n^k \equiv \frac{e_n^k}{p_n^k}; \quad n = 1, \ldots, N; k = 1, \ldots, K.$$

It is useful to define country commodity expenditure shares s_n^k for basic heading class n and country k as

$$(5.2) \qquad s_n^k \equiv \frac{e_n^k}{\sum_{i=1}^{N} e_i^k}; \quad n = 1, \ldots, N; k = 1, \ldots, K.$$

Now define country vectors of basic heading PPPs as $p^k \equiv \left[p_1^k, \ldots, p_N^k\right]^T$,[9] country vectors of basic heading volumes as $q^k \equiv \left[q_1^k, \ldots, q_N^k\right]^T$, country expenditure vectors as $e^k \equiv \left[e_1^k, \ldots, e_N^k\right]$, and country expenditure share vectors as $s^k \equiv \left[s_1^k, \ldots, s_N^k\right]^T$ for $k = 1, \ldots, K$.

To define the GEKS parities $P^1, P^2, \ldots, P^K$ between the K countries in the comparison, first define the Fisher (1922) ideal bilateral price index P_F between country j relative to k:[10]

$$(5.3) \qquad P_F(p^k, p^j, q^k, q^j) \equiv \left[\frac{p^j \cdot q^j \, p^j \cdot q^k}{p^k \cdot q^j \, p^k \cdot q^k}\right]^{\frac{1}{2}}; \quad j = 1, \ldots, K; k = 1, \ldots, K.$$

Note that the Fisher ideal price index is the geometric mean of the Laspeyres price index between countries j and k, $P_L(p^k, p^j, q^k, q^j) \equiv \frac{p^j q^k}{p^k q^k}$,[11] and the Paasche price index, $P_P(p^k, p^j, q^k, q^j) \equiv \frac{p^j q^j}{p^k q^j}$.[12] Various justifications for the use of the Fisher ideal index in the bilateral context have been made by Diewert (1976; 1992; 2002, 569) and others.[13] The Fisher index can be justified from the point of view of finding the "best" symmetric average of the Paasche and Laspeyres indexes, or from the point of view of the axiomatic or test approach to index number theory, or from the viewpoint of the economic approach to index number theory.[14]

The aggregate PPP for country j, P^j, is defined as

$$(5.4) \qquad P^j \equiv \prod_{k=1}^{K} \left[P_F(p^k, p^j, q^k, q^j)\right]^{\frac{1}{K}}; \quad j = 1, \ldots, K.$$

Once the GEKS P^j's have been defined by (5.4), the corresponding GEKS country real expenditures or volumes Q^j can be defined as the country expenditures $p^j q^j$ in the reference year divided by the corresponding GEKS purchasing power parity P^j:

$$(5.5) \qquad Q^j \equiv \frac{p^j q^j}{P^j}; \quad j = 1, \ldots, K.$$

If all of the P^j defined by (5.4) are divided by a positive number, say α, then all of the Q^j defined by (5.5) can be multiplied by this same α without materially changing the GEKS multilateral method. If country 1 is chosen as the numeraire country in the region, then set α equal to P^1 defined by (5.4) for $j = 1$, and the resulting price level P^j is interpreted as the number of units of country j's currency required to purchase one unit of country 1's currency and receive an equivalent amount of utility. The rescaled Q^j is interpreted as the volume of final demand of country j in the currency units of country 1.

It is also possible to normalize the aggregate real expenditure of each country in common units (Q^k) by dividing each Q^k by the sum $\sum_{j=1}^{K} Q^j$ in order to express each country's real expenditure or real final demand as a fraction or share of total regional real expenditure—that is, define country k's share of regional real expenditures, S^k, as follows:[15]

$$(5.6) \qquad S^k \equiv \frac{Q^k}{\sum_{j=1}^{K} Q^j}; \quad k = 1, \ldots, K.$$

The country shares of regional real final demand, S^k, remain unchanged after rescaling the PPPs by the scalar α.[16]

5.2 Geary-Khamis Method

The method was suggested by Geary (1958), and Khamis (1972) showed that the equations that define the method have a positive solution under certain conditions.

The GK system of equations involves K country price levels or PPPs, $P^1, \ldots, P^K$, and N international basic heading commodity reference prices, $\pi_1, \ldots, \pi_N$. The equations that determine these unknowns (up to a scalar multiple) are

$$(5.7) \qquad \pi_n = \sum_{k=1}^{K} \left[\frac{q_n^k}{\sum_{j=1}^{K} q_n^j} \right] \left[\frac{p_n^k}{P^k} \right]; \quad n = 1, \ldots, N$$

and

$$(5.8) \qquad P^k = \frac{p^k q^k}{\pi q^k}; \quad k = 1, \ldots, K$$

where $\pi \equiv [\pi_1, \ldots, \pi_N]$ is the vector of GK regional average reference prices. If a solution to equations (5.7) and (5.8) exists, then if all of the country parities P^k are multiplied by a positive scalar, say λ, and all of the reference prices π_n are divided by the same λ, another solution to (5.7) and (5.8) is obtained. Thus π_n and P^k are determined only up to a scalar multiple and an additional normalization is required such as

$$(5.9) \qquad P^1 = 1$$

in order to uniquely determine the parities. It can also be shown that only $N + K - 1$ of the N equations in (5.7) and (5.8) are independent. Once the parities P^k have been determined, the real expenditure or volume for country k, Q^k, can be defined as country k's nominal value of final demand in domestic currency units, $p^k q^k$, divided by its PPP, P^k:

$$(5.10) \qquad Q^k = \frac{p^k q^k}{P^k}; \quad k = 1, \ldots, K,$$

which equals πq^k using (5.8).

The second set of equations in (5.10) characterizes an additive method[17]—that is, the real final demand of each country can be expressed as a sum of the country's individual basic heading final demand volume components, where each real final demand component is weighted by an *international price* that is constant across countries.

Finally, if equations (5.10) are substituted into the regional share equations, (5.6), then country k's share of regional real expenditures is

$$S^k = \frac{\pi q^k}{\pi q}; \quad k = 1, \ldots, K \tag{5.11}$$

where the region's total volume vector q is defined as the sum of the country volume vectors:

$$q \equiv \sum_{j=1}^{K} q^j \tag{5.12}$$

Equations (5.10) show the convenience of having an additive multilateral comparison method: when country outputs are valued at the international reference prices, values are additive across both countries and commodities. However, additive multilateral methods are not consistent with economic comparisons of utility across countries if the number of countries in the comparison is greater than two; see section 5.5. In addition, equations (5.7) reveal that large countries will have a larger contribution to determination of the international prices π_n, and thus these international prices will be much more representative for the largest countries in the comparison than for the smaller ones.[18] This observation leads to the next method for making multilateral comparisons: an additive method that does not suffer from this problem of big countries having an undue influence on the comparison.

5.3 Iklé-Dikhanov-Balk Method

Iklé (1972, 202–4) proposed this method in a very indirect way; Dikhanov (1994, 1997) suggested the much clearer system described here—see equations (5.13) and (5.14); and Balk (1996, 207–8) provided the first existence proof. The equations produced by Dikhanov (1994, 9–12) that are the counterparts to the GK equations (5.7) and (5.8) are

$$\pi_n = \left[\frac{\sum_{k=1}^{K} s_n^k \left[\frac{p_n^k}{P^k} \right]^{-1}}{\sum_{j=1}^{K} s_n^j} \right]^{-1}; \quad n = 1, \ldots, N \tag{5.13}$$

and

$$P^k = \left[\sum_{n=1}^{N} s_n^k \left[\frac{p_n^k}{\pi_n} \right]^{-1} \right]^{-1}; \quad k = 1, \ldots, K \tag{5.14}$$

where the country expenditure shares s_n^k are defined by (5.2).

As in the GK method, equations (5.13) and (5.14) involve the K country price levels or PPPs, $P^1, \ldots, P^K$, and N international commodity reference prices, $\pi_1, \ldots, \pi_N$. Equations (5.13) indicate that the n-th international price, π_n, is a share-weighted harmonic mean of the country k basic heading PPPs for commodity n, p_n^k, deflated by country k's overall PPP, P^k. The country k share weights for commodity n, s_n^k, do not sum (over countries k) to unity, but when s_n^k is divided by $\sum_{j=1}^{K} s_n^j$, the resulting normalized shares do sum (over countries k) to unity. Thus equations (5.13) are similar to the GK equations (5.7), except that now a harmonic mean of the deflated basic heading commodity n "prices," $\frac{p_n^k}{P^k}$, is used in place of the old arithmetic mean. Also, in the GK equations country k's volume share of commodity group n in the region, $\frac{q_n^k}{\sum_{j=1}^{K} q_n^j}$, was used as a weighting factor (and thus large countries had a large influence in forming these weights), but now the weights involve country *expenditure* shares, and so each country in the region has a more equal influence in forming the weighted average. Equations (5.14) indicate that P^k, the PPP for country k, is equal to a weighted harmonic mean of the country k basic heading PPPs, p_n^k, deflated by the international price for commodity group n, π_n, where the summation is over commodities n instead of over countries k as in equations (5.13). The share weights in the harmonic means defined by (5.14), s_n^k, sum to one when the summation is over n, and so there is no need to normalize these weights as was the case for equations (5.13).

If a solution to equations (5.13) and (5.14) exists, then multiplication of all of the country parities P^k by a positive scalar λ and division all of the reference prices π_n by the same λ will lead to another solution to (5.13) and (5.14). Thus π_n and P^k are determined only up to a scalar multiple, and an additional normalization is required such as (5.9), $P^1 = 1$.

Although the IDB equations (5.14) do not appear to be related very closely to the corresponding GK equations (5.8), these two sets of equations are actually the same system. To see this, note that the country k expenditure share for commodity group n, s_n^k, is represented by

$$(5.15) \qquad s_n^k = \frac{p_n^k q_n^k}{p^k q^k}; \quad n = 1, \ldots, N; k = 1, \ldots, K.$$

Now substitute equations (5.15) into equations (5.14) to obtain

$$(5.16) \qquad \begin{aligned} P^k &= \frac{1}{\sum_{n=1}^{N} s_n^k \left[\frac{P_n^k}{\pi_n}\right]^{-1}}; \quad k = 1, \ldots, K \\ &= \frac{1}{\sum_{n=1}^{N} \left[\frac{p_n^k q_n^k}{p^k q^k}\right]\left[\frac{\pi_n}{p_n^k}\right]} \\ &= \frac{p^k q^k}{\sum_{n=1}^{N} \pi_n q_n^k} \\ &= \frac{p^k q^k}{\pi q^k}. \end{aligned}$$

Thus equations (5.14) are equivalent to equations (5.8), and the IDB system is an additive system—that is, equations (5.10)–(5.12) can be applied to the present method just as they were applied to the GK method for making international comparisons.[19]

The annex to this chapter demonstrates several different ways of representing the IDB system of parities, and provides proofs of the existence and uniqueness of the IDB parities. Effective methods for obtaining solutions to the system of equations (5.13) and (5.14) (with a normalization) are presented as well.

As noted at the outset of this chapter, the IDB method was used by the Africa region to construct regional aggregates. This method appears to be an "improvement" over the GK method in that large countries no longer have a dominant influence on the determination of the international reference prices π_n, and so if an additive method that has more democratic reference prices is required, IDB appears to be "better" than GK. In addition, Deaton and Heston (2010) have shown empirically that the IDB method generates aggregate PPPs that are much closer to the GEKS PPPs than are the GK PPPs, using the 2005 ICP data. However, in section 5.5 it is shown that if one takes the economic approach to index number comparisons, then any additive multilateral method will be subject to some substitution bias.

For many users, however, possible substitution bias in the multilateral method is not an important issue: these users want an additive multilateral method so they can aggregate in a consistent fashion across countries and commodity groups. For these users, it may be useful to look at the axiomatic properties of the GK and IDB multilateral methods in order to determine a preference for one or the other of these additive methods. Thus in the next section, various multilateral axioms or tests are listed, and the consistency of GK, IDB, and GEKS with these axioms is determined.

5.4 Test or Axiomatic Approach to Making Multilateral Comparisons

Balk (1996) proposed a system of nine axioms for multilateral methods based on the earlier work of Diewert (1988).[20] Diewert (1999, 16–20) further refined his set of axioms, and this section lists 11 of the 13 "reasonable" axioms he proposed for a multilateral system. The notation used here is $P \equiv [p^1, \ldots, p^K]$ signifies an $N \times K$ matrix for which domestic basic heading parities (or "price" vectors) $p^1, \ldots, p^K$ serve as its K columns, and $Q \equiv [q^1, \ldots, q^K]$ signifies an $N \times K$ matrix for which country basic heading volumes (or "quantity" vectors) $q^1, \ldots, q^K$ serve as its K columns.

Any multilateral method applied to K countries in the comparison determines the country aggregate volumes, $Q^1, \ldots, Q^K$, along with the corresponding country PPPs, $P^1, \ldots, P^K$. The country volumes Q^k can be regarded as functions of the data matrices P and Q so that the country volumes can be written as functions of the two data matrices P and Q—that is, the functions $Q^k(P, Q)$ for $k = 1, \ldots, K$. Once the functions $Q^k(P,Q)$ have been determined by the multilateral method, then country k's share of total regional real expenditures, $S^k(P, Q)$, can be defined as

$$(5.17) \qquad S^k(P, Q) \equiv \frac{Q^k(P, Q)}{[Q^1(P, Q) + \cdots + Q^K(P, Q)]}; \quad k = 1, \ldots, K.$$

Both Balk (1996, 2008) and Diewert (1988, 1999) used the system of regional share equations $S^k(P,Q)$ as the basis for their axioms.

What follows are 11 of Diewert's 13 tests or axioms for a multilateral share system, $S^1(P, Q)$, $\ldots$, $S^K(P, Q)$ (Diewert 1999, 16–20).[21] It is assumed that the two data matrices, P and Q, satisfy some mild regularity conditions, which are listed in section 5A.1.1 in the annex to this chapter. In keeping with the literature on test approaches to index number theory, components of the data matrix Q will be referred to as "quantities" (when they are actually basic heading volumes by commodity group and country) and the components of data matrix P will be referred to as "prices" (when they are actually basic heading PPPs by commodity group and by country).

T1: *Share Test:* There exist K continuous, positive functions, $S^k(P, Q)$, $k = 1, \ldots, K$, such that $\sum_{k=1}^{K} S^k(P, Q) = 1$ for all P, Q in the appropriate domain of definition.

This is a very mild test of consistency for the multilateral system.

T2: *Proportional Quantities Test:* Suppose that $q^k = \beta_k q$ for some $q >> 0_N$ and $\beta_k > 0$ for $k = 1, \ldots, K$, with $\sum_{k=1}^{K} \beta_k = 1$. Then $S^k(P, Q) = \beta_k$ for $k = 1, \ldots, K$.

This test says that if the quantity vector for country k, q^k, is equal to the positive fraction β_k times the total regional quantity vector q, then that country's share of regional real expenditures, $S^k(P, Q)$, should equal that same fraction β_k. Note that this condition is to hold no matter what P is.

T3: *Proportional Prices Test:* Suppose that $p^k = \alpha_k p$ for $p >> 0_N$ and $\alpha_k > 0$ for $k = 1, \ldots, K$. Then $S^k(P, Q) = \dfrac{pq^k}{\left[p\sum_{i=1}^{K} q^i\right]}$ for $k = 1, \ldots, K$.

This test says the following: suppose that all of the country price vectors p^k are proportional to a common "price"vector p. Then the country k share of regional real expenditure, $S^k(P, Q)$, is equal to the value of its quantity vector, valued at the common prices p, $pq^k \equiv \sum_{n=1}^{N} p_n q_n^k$, divided by the regional value of real expenditures, also valued at the common prices p, $p\sum_{i=1}^{K} q^i$. Thus if prices are proportional to a common set of prices p across all countries, then these prices p can act as a set of reference international prices and the real expenditure volume of country k, Q^k, should equal pq^k up to a normalizing factor.

T4: *Commensurability Test:* Let $\delta_n > 0$ for $n = 1, \ldots, N$, and let Δ denote the $N \times N$ diagonal matrix with the δ_n on the main diagonal. Then $S^k(\Delta P, \Delta^{-1}Q) = S^k(P, Q)$ for $k = 1, \ldots, K$.

This test implies that the country shares $S^k(P, Q)$ are invariant to changes in the units of measurement. This is a standard (but important) test in the axiomatic approach to index number theory that dates back to Fisher (1922, 420).

T5: *Commodity Reversal Test:* Let Π denote an $N \times N$ permutation matrix. Then $S^k(\Pi P, \Pi Q) = S^k(P, Q)$ for $k = 1, \ldots, K$.

This test says that the ordering of the N commodity groups should not affect each country's share of regional real expenditure. This test also dates back to Fisher (1922, 63) in the context of bilateral index number formulas.

T6: *Multilateral Country Reversal Test:* Let $S(P, Q)$ denote a K dimensional column vector that has the country shares $S^1(P, Q), \ldots, S^K(P, Q)$ as components, and let Π^* be a $K \times K$ permutation matrix. Then $S(P\Pi^*, Q\Pi^*) = S(P, Q)\Pi^*$.

This test implies that countries are treated in a symmetric manner—that is, the country shares of world output are not affected by a reordering of the countries. The next two tests are homogeneity tests.

T7: *Monetary Units Test:* Let $\alpha_k > 0$ for $k = 1, \ldots, K$. Then $S^k(\alpha_1 p^1, \ldots, \alpha_K p^K, Q) = S^k(p^1, \ldots, p^K, Q) = S^k(P, Q)$ for $k = 1, \ldots, K$.

This test implies that the absolute scale of domestic prices in each country does not affect each country's share of world output—that is, only relative prices within each country affect the multilateral volume parities.

T8: *Homogeneity in Quantities Test:* For $i = 1, \ldots, K$, let $\lambda_i > 0$ and let j denote another country not equal to country i. Then $\frac{S^i(P, q^1, \ldots, \lambda_i q^i, \ldots, q^K)}{S^j(P, q^1, \ldots, \lambda_i q^i, \ldots, q^K)} = \frac{\lambda_i S^i(P, q^1, \ldots, q^i, \ldots, q^K)}{S^j(P, q^1, \ldots, q^i, \ldots, q^K)} = \frac{\lambda_i S^i(P, Q)}{S^j(P, Q)}$.

This test is equivalent to saying that the volume share of country i relative to country j is linearly homogeneous in the components of the country i quantity vector q^i.

T9: *Monotonicity in Quantities Test:* For each k, $S^k(P, q^1, \ldots, q^{k-1}, q^k, q^{k+1}, \ldots, q^K) = S^k(P, Q)$ increasing in the components of q^k.

This test says that country k's share of world output increases as any component of the country k quantity vector q^k increases.

T10: *Country Partitioning Test:* Let A be a strict subset of the indexes $(1, 2, \ldots, K)$ with at least two members. Suppose that for each $i \in A$, $p^i = \alpha_i p^a$ for $\alpha_i > 0$, $p^a >> 0_N$, and $q^i = \beta_i q^a$ for $\beta_i > 0$, $q^a >> 0_N$ with $\sum_{i \in A} \beta_i = 1$. Denote the subset of $\{1, 2, \ldots, K\}$ that does not belong to $A \times B$, and denote the matrices of country price and quantity vectors that belong to $B \times P^b$ and Q^b, respectively. Then, (i) for $i \in A, j \in A$, $\frac{S^i(P, Q)}{S^j(P, Q)} = \frac{\beta_i}{\beta_j}$, and (ii) for $i \in B$, $S^i(P, Q) = S^{i*}(p^a, P^b, q^a, Q^b)$, where $S^{k*}(p^a, P^b, q^a, Q^b)$ is the system of share functions that is obtained by adding the group A aggregate price and quantity vectors, p^a and q^a respectively, to the group B price and quantity data, P^b, Q^b.

Thus if the aggregate quantity vector for the countries in group A were distributed proportionally among its members (using the weights β_i) and each group A country faced prices that were proportional to p^a, then part (i) of T10 requires that the group A share functions reflect this proportional allocation. Part (ii) of T10 requires that the group B share functions are equal to the same values no matter whether one uses the original share system or a new share system where all of the group A countries have been aggregated up into the single country that has the price vector p^a and the group A aggregate quantity vector q^a. Conversely, this test can be viewed as a consistency in aggregation test if a single group A country is partitioned into a group of smaller countries.

T11: *Additivity Test:* For each set of price and quantity data, P, Q, belonging to the appropriate domain of definition, there exists a set of positive world reference prices $\pi >> 0_N$ such that

$$S^k(P, Q) = \frac{\pi q^k}{\left[\pi \sum_{i=1}^{K} q^i\right]} \quad \text{for } k = 1, \ldots, K.$$

Thus if the multilateral system satisfies test T11, then it is an additive method because the real expenditure Q^k of each country k is proportional to the inner product of the vector of international prices π with the country k vector of commodity volumes (or "quantities"), q^k.

It is useful to contrast the axiomatic properties of the IDB method with the other additive method that has been used in the ICP, the GK system. Based on the results in Diewert (1999) on the GK system and the results in the annex to this chapter on the IDB system, it can be seen that both methods satisfy tests T1–T7 and T11 and that both methods fail T9, the monotonicity in quantities test. Thus the tests that discriminate between the two methods are T8 and T10: the IDB multilateral system passes T8, the homogeneity test, and fails T10, the country partitioning test, and vice versa for the GK system.[22] There has been more discussion of test T10 than test T8. On the one hand, proponents of the GK system like its good aggregation (across countries) properties, and the fact that big countries have more influence on the determination of the world reference price vector π is regarded as a reasonable price to pay for these "good" aggregation properties.[23] On the other hand, proponents of the IDB method like the fact that the world reference prices are more democratically determined (large countries play a smaller role in determination of the vector of international prices π), and they place less weight on good aggregation properties. Also, from evidence presented by Deaton and Heston (2010) using the 2005 ICP database, it appears that the IDB parities are closer to the GEKS parities than the GK parities. Thus the IDB method has the advantage that it is an additive method that does not depart too far from the parities generated by the GEKS method.

Diewert (1999, 18) showed that the GEKS system (using the Fisher ideal index as the basic building block) passed tests T1–T9 but failed T10, the country partitioning test, and T11, the additivity test. Thus all three of the multilateral methods considered thus far fail 2 out of the 11 tests.

At this point, it is difficult to unambiguously recommend any one of the three multilateral methods over the other two. The following section considers an economic approach to making multilateral comparisons that may help in evaluating the three methods.

5.5 Additive Multilateral Methods and the Economic Approach to Making Index Number Comparisons

It is useful to begin this section by reviewing the essential assumptions for the economic approach to index number theory:

- Purchasers have preferences over alternative bundles of the goods and services they purchase.
- As a result, they buy more of the things that have gone down in relative price and fewer of the things that have gone up in relative price.

This kind of substitution behavior is well documented, and therefore it is useful to attempt to take it into account when doing international comparisons.

The economic approach to index number theory does take substitution behavior into account. This approach was developed by Diewert in both the bilateral context (1976)[24] and the multilateral context (1999). This theory works as follows:

- Assume that all purchasers have the same preferences over commodities and that these preferences can be represented by a homogeneous utility function.
- Find a functional form that can approximate preferences to the second order[25] and has an exact index number formula associated with it. The resulting index number formula is called a *superlative index number formula*.[26]
- Use the superlative index number formula in a bilateral context so that the real output of every country in the region can be compared with the real output of a numeraire country using this formula. The resulting relative volumes are dependent on the choice of the numeraire country.
- Take the geometric average of all K sets of relative volumes using each country in the region as the numeraire country. This set of average relative volumes can then be converted into regional shares as in section 5.1. The resulting method is called a *superlative multilateral method* (see Diewert 1999, 22).

It turns out that the GEKS method discussed earlier in section 5.1 is a superlative multilateral method (see Diewert 1999, 36). The GEKS method also has quite good axiomatic properties as was shown in section 5.4.

In view of the importance of the GEKS multilateral method, it is worth explaining that the GEKS volume parities can be obtained by alternative methods.

In the first method, described by Deaton and Heston (2010), the GEKS parities can be obtained by using a least squares minimization problem (Gini 1924) that will essentially make an $K \times K$ matrix of bilateral Fisher volume parities that are not transitive into a best-fitting set of transitive parities. In the second method for deriving the GEKS parities, implicitly explained earlier, the parities are obtained by picking any country as the base country and then using the Fisher bilateral quantity index to form the real final demand volume of every country relative to the chosen base country. This process gives estimated volumes for all countries in the comparison relative to the chosen base country. Then this process is repeated, choosing each country in turn as the base country, which leads to K sets of relative volume estimates. The final step for obtaining the GEKS relative volumes is to take the geometric mean of all of the K base country dependent sets of parities.

The problem with an additive multilateral method (from the perspective of the economic approach) if the number of countries in the region is greater than two can now be explained with the help of a diagram (figure 5.1).

The solid curved line in figure 5.1 represents an indifference curve for purchasers of the two goods under consideration. The consumption vectors of countries A, B, and C are all on the same indifference curve, and thus the multilateral method should show the same volume for the three countries. If one uses the relative prices that country B faces as "world" reference prices in an additive method, then country B has the lowest volume or real consumption, followed by country A; country C has the highest volume. But they all have equal volumes! It is possible to devise an additive method that will make the volumes of any two countries equal, but it is not possible to devise an additive method that will equalize the volumes for all three countries. On the other hand, the common indifference curve in figure 5.1 can be approximated reasonably well by a flexible functional form that has a corresponding exact index number formula (such as the Fisher index), and thus a GEKS method that used the Fisher bilateral index as a basic building block would give the right answer to a reasonable degree of approximation. The bottom line is that an additive multilateral method is not really consistent with economic comparisons of utility across countries if the number of countries in the comparison is greater than two.[27]

FIGURE 5.1 Indifference Curve for Two Products, Three Countries

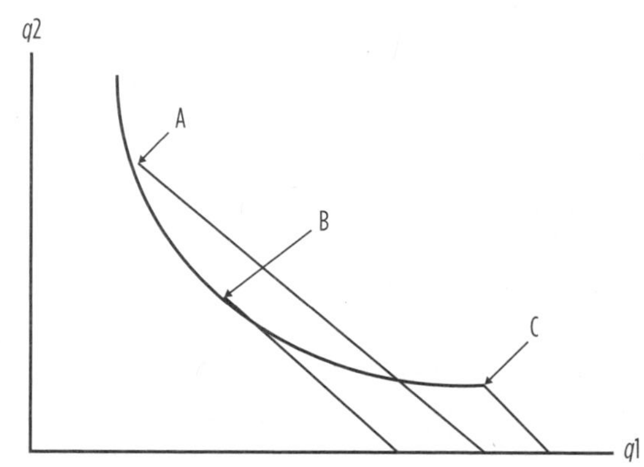

Source: Based on Marris 1984, 52, and Diewert 1999, 48–50.

Although additive multilateral methods have their problems in that they are not consistent with substitution in the face of changing relative prices, the economic approach as explained earlier is not without its problems. Two important criticisms of the economic approach are (1) the assumption that all final purchasers have the same preferences over different baskets of final demand purchases is suspect, and (2) the assumption that preferences are homothetic—that is, can be represented by a linearly homogeneous utility function—is also suspect.

The second criticism of the economic approach to multilateral comparisons based on superlative bilateral index number formulas has been discussed in the recent literature on international comparisons, and some brief comments on this literature are in order here.

An important recent development is Neary's GAIA multilateral system. It can be described as a consumer theory–consistent version of the GK system, which allows for nonhomothetic preferences on the part of final demanders (Neary 2004). Deaton and Heston (2010) point out that a weakness of the Neary multilateral system is that it uses a single set of relative prices to value consumption or the gross domestic product (GDP) in all countries, no matter how different are the actual relative prices in each country. This problem was also noted by Feenstra, Ma, and Rao (2009), who generalized Neary's framework to work with two sets of cross-sectional data in order to estimate preferences.[28] They also experimented with alternative sets of reference prices. In their discussion of Feenstra, Mao, and Rao, Barnett, Diewert, and Zellner (2009) noted that a natural generalization of their model would be use of a set of reference prices that would be representative for each country in the comparison. Using representative prices for each country would lead to K sets of relative volumes, and in the end these country-specific parities could be averaged, just as the GEKS method averages country-specific parities. Barnett, Diewert, and Zellner conjectured that this geometric average of the country estimates would probably be close to GEKS estimates based on traditional multilateral index number theory, which, of course, does not use econometrics. It remains to be seen if econometric approaches to the multilateral index number problem can be reconciled with superlative multilateral methods.[29]

The next section describes another economic approach to constructing multilateral comparisons—a method that is based on linking countries that have similar economic structures.

5.6 Minimum Spanning Tree Method for Making Multilateral Comparisons

Recall that the Fisher ideal quantity index can be used to construct real volumes for all K countries in the comparison, using one country as the base country. Thus as each country is used as the base country, K sets of relative volumes are obtained. The GEKS multilateral method treats each country's set of relative volumes as being equally valid, and thus an averaging of the parities is appropriate under this hypothesis. The method is therefore "democratic" in that each bilateral index number comparison between any two countries receives the same weight in the overall method. However, not all bilateral comparisons of volume between two countries are equally accurate. On the one hand, if the relative prices in countries A and B are very similar, then the Paasche and Laspeyres volume or quantity indexes will be very close, and so it is likely that the "true" volume comparison between these two countries (using the economic approach to index number theory) will be very close to the Fisher volume comparison. On the other hand, if the structure of relative prices in the two countries is very different, then it is likely that the structure of relative quantities in the two countries will also be different. Therefore, the Paasche and Laspeyres quantity indexes will likely differ considerably, and it is no longer so certain that the Fisher quantity index will be close to the "true" volume comparison. These considerations suggest that a more accurate set of world product shares could be constructed if initially a bilateral comparison was made between the two countries that had the most similar relative price structures.[30] At the next stage of the comparison, one could look for a third country that has a relative price structure most similar to the those of the first two countries and link in this third country to the comparisons of volume between the first two countries, and so on. At the end of this procedure, a minimum spanning tree would be constructed, which is a path between all countries that minimizes the sum of the relative price dissimilarity measures.[31] The conclusion is that similarity linking[32] using Fisher ideal quantity indexes as the bilateral links is an alternative to the GEKS method, which has some advantages over it.[33] Both methods are consistent with the economic approach to index number theory.

A key aspect of this methodology is the choice of the measure of similarity (or dissimilarity) of the relative price structures of two countries. Various measures of the similarity or dissimilarity of relative price structures have been proposed by Allen and Diewert (1981); Kravis, Heston, and Summers (1982, 104–6); Aten and Heston (2009); Diewert (2009); R. J. Hill (1997, 2009); and Sergeev (2001, 2009). A few of these suggested measures of dissimilarity will now be discussed.

Suppose one wishes to compare the similarities in the structure of relative prices for two countries, 1 and 2. They have the strictly positive basic heading PPP vectors p^k and the basic heading volume vectors q^k for $k = 1, 2$. For convenience of exposition, in remainder of this section the PPP vector p^k is referred to as a "price" vector and the volume vector q^k as a "quantity" vector. A *dissimilarity index*, $\Delta(p^1, p^2, q^1, q^2)$, is a function defined over the "price" and "quantity" data pertaining to the two countries, p^1, p^2, q^1, q^2, which indicates how similar or dissimilar the structure of relative prices is in the two countries being considered. If the two price vectors are proportional so that the relative prices in the two countries are equal, then one wants the dissimilarity index to equal its minimum possible value, zero—that is, one wants $\Delta(p^1, p^2, q^1, q^2)$ to equal zero if $p^2 = \lambda p^1$ for any positive scalar λ. If the price vectors are not proportional, then one wants the dissimilarity measure to be positive.[34] Thus the larger is $\Delta(p^1, p^2, q^1, q^2)$, the more dissimilar is the structure of relative prices between the two countries.

The first measure of dissimilarity in relative price structures was suggested by Kravis, Heston, and Summers (1982, 105)[35] and R. J. Hill (1999a, 1999b, 2001, 2004). It is essentially a normalization of the relative spread between the Paasche and Laspeyres price indexes, and so it is known as the Paasche-Laspeyres spread (PLS) relative price dissimilarity measure, $\Delta_{\text{PLS}}(p^1, p^2, q^1, q^2)$, for which

$$(5.18) \qquad \Delta_{\text{PLS}}(p^1, p^2, q^1, q^2) \equiv \max\left[\frac{P_L}{P_P}, \frac{P_P}{P_L}\right] - 1 \geq 0$$

where $P_L \equiv \dfrac{p^2 q^1}{p^1 q^1}$ and $\dfrac{p^2 q^2}{p^1 q^2}$. Thus if $P_L = P_P$, the dissimilarity measure defined by (5.18) takes on its minimum value of zero. Because P_L differs more markedly from P_P, the dissimilarity measure increases and the relative price structures are regarded as being increasingly dissimilar. Diewert (2009, 184) pointed out a major problem with this measure of relative price dissimilarity; it is possible for P_L to equal P_P, and yet p^2 could be very far from being proportional to p^1. The following two measures of dissimilarity do not suffer from this problem.

Diewert (2009, 207) suggested the following measure of relative price similarity, the weighted log quadratic (WLQ) measure of relative price dissimilarity, $\Delta_{\text{WLQ}}(p^1, p^2, q^1, q^2)$, for which

$$(5.19) \quad \Delta_{\text{WLQ}}(p^1, p^2, q^1, q^2) \equiv \sum_{n=1}^{N}\left(\frac{1}{2}\right)\left(s_n^1 + s_n^2\right)\left[\ln\left(\frac{p_n^2}{p_n^2\, P_F(p^1, p^2, q^1, q^2)}\right)\right]$$

where $P_F(p^1, p^2, q^1, q^2) \equiv \left[\frac{p^2 \cdot q^1 p^2 \cdot q^2}{p^1 \cdot q^1 p^1 \cdot q^2}\right]^{\frac{1}{2}}$ is the Fisher ideal price index between countries 2 and 1, and $s_n^c \equiv \frac{p_n^c q_n^c}{p^c q^c}$ is the country c expenditure share on commodity n for $c = 1, 2$ and $n = 1, \ldots, N$.

There is a problem with the dissimilarity measure defined by (5.19) if for some commodity group n either p_n^1 or p_n^2 equals zero (or both prices equal zero), because in these cases the measure can become infinite.[36] If both prices are zero, then commodity group n is irrelevant for both countries and the n-th term in the summation in (5.19) can be dropped. In the case in which one of the prices, say p_n^1, equals zero but the other price p_n^2 is positive, then it would be useful to have an imputed PPP or "price" for commodity group n in country 1 that will make the final demand volume for that commodity group equal to zero. This reservation price, say p_n^{1*}, could be approximated by simply setting p_n^{1*} equal to $\frac{p_n^2}{P_F(p^1, p^2, q^1, q^2)}$. If p_n^1 equal to zero in (5.19) is replaced by this imputed price p_n^{1*}, then $\frac{p_n^2}{p_n^{1*} P_F(p^1, p^2, q^1, q^2)}$ is equal to one, and the n-th term on the right-hand side of (5.19) vanishes. Similarly, in the case in which p_n^2 equals zero but the other price p_n^1 is positive, then set the reservation price for the n-th commodity group in country 2, say p_n^{2*}, equal to $p_n^1 P_F(p^1, p^2, q^1, q^2)$. If the zero price p_n^2 in (5.19) is replaced by the imputed price p_n^{2*}, then $\frac{p_n^{2*}}{p_n^1 P_F(p^1, p^2, q^1, q^2)}$ is equal to one, and the n-th term on the right-hand side of (5.19) also vanishes in this case. Thus if there is a zero "price" for either country for commodity group n, then the earlier convention for constructing an imputed price for the zero price leads to dropping the n-th term on the right-hand side of (5.19).[37]

If prices are proportional for the two countries so that $p^2 = \lambda p^1$ for some positive scalar λ, then $P_F(p^1, p^2, q^1, q^2) = \lambda$, and the measure of relative price dissimilarity $\Delta_{PLQ}(p^1, p^2, q^1, q^2)$ defined by (5.19) will equal its minimum of zero. Thus the smaller is $\Delta_{PLQ}(p^1, p^2, q^1, q^2)$, the more similar is the structure of relative prices in the two countries.

The method of spatial linking using the relative price dissimilarity measure defined by (5.19) is illustrated in the next section.[38] The shares generated by the minimum spanning tree—not the GEKS country shares defined by (5.6) in section 5.1—are used to link all of the countries in the comparison.

Diewert (2009, 208) also suggested the following measure of relative price similarity, the weighted asymptotically quadratic (WAQ) measure of relative price dissimilarity, $\Delta_{WAQ}(p^1, p^2, q^1, q^2)$, for which

$$(5.20) \qquad \Delta_{WAQ}(p^1, p^2, q^1, q^2) \equiv \sum_{n=1}^{N} \left(\frac{1}{2}\right)\left(s_n^1 + s_n^2\right)\left\{\left[\frac{p_n^2}{p_n^1 P_F(p^1, p^2, q^1, q^2)} - 1\right]^2 + \left[\left(\frac{P_F(p^1, p^2, q^1, q^2) p_n^1}{p_n^2}\right) - 1\right]^2\right\}$$

As was the case with the dissimilarity index defined by (5.19), the index defined by (5.20) will equal plus infinity if one of the prices for commodity group n, p_n^1 or p_n^2, equals zero.[39] Again, it is useful to define an imputed price for the zero price to insert into the formula, and a reasonable convention is to use the same imputed prices that were suggested for (5.19)—that is, if $p_n^1 = 0$, then define $p_n^{1*} \equiv \frac{p_n^2}{P_F(p^1, p^2, q^1, q^2)}$, and if $p_n^2 = 0$, then define $p_n^{2*} \equiv p_n^1 P_F(p^1, p^2, q^1, q^2)$.

Recently, Rao, Shankar, and Hajarghasht (2010) used the MST method for constructing PPPs across the member countries of the Organisation for Economic Co-operation and Development (OECD) based on data for 1996. Relying on the PLS and WAQ dissimilarity measures defined by (5.18) and (5.20), they compared the resulting spatial chains with the standard GEKS method. They found some fairly significant differences among the three sets of parities for the 24 countries in the comparison, with differences in the PPP for a single country of up to 10 percent. Thus the choice of method does matter, even if the methods of comparison are restricted to multilateral methods that allow for substitution effects. An interesting aspect of their study is that they found that when the WAQ was used as the dissimilarity measure as opposed to the PLS, the linking of the countries was much more intuitive:

> As is generally the case with MSTs, there are a number of counter intuitive paths. For example, Spain and Greece are connected through Portugal, Denmark, USA, UK, Germany, Switzerland, Austria, Sweden, Italy. Similarly Australia and New Zealand are connected through the UK, Germany, Switzerland and Austria. Now we turn to Figure 2 where MST based on relative price distance measure is provided. The links in WRPD based MST are a lot more intuitive and are consistent with the notion of price similarity of the countries. For example, Spain, Italy, Portugal, Greece and Turkey are all connected directly, USA-Canada has a direct link so is the pair Ireland-United Kingdom. Countries like Sweden, Finland, Iceland, Norway and Denmark are all connected together. The main conclusion emerging from Figure 2 is that the WRPD [WAQ] is a better measure of price similarity than the PLS used in the standard MST applications. (Rao, Shankar, and Hajarghasht 2010)

Thus it appears that the pattern of bilateral links that emerges when using the MST method is much more "sensible" when a more discriminating measure of dissimilarity is used in the linking algorithm, as compared with use of the Paasche-Laspeyres spread measure defined by (5.18). Thus in future applications of the MST method it is recommended that (5.18) not be used as the dissimilarity measure that is a key input for the MST method.

The narrowing of Paasche-Laspeyres spreads by the use of a spatial chaining method is not the only advantage of this method of linking countries; there are also advantages at lower levels of aggregation. If countries similar in structure are compared, generally it will be found that product overlaps are maximized, and therefore the basic heading PPPs will be more accurately determined for countries similar in structure:

> Many differences in quality and proportion of high tech items ... are likely to be more pronounced between countries with very different economic structures. If criteria can be developed to identify countries with similar economic structure and they are compared only with each other, then it may overcome many of the issues of quality and lowest common denominator item comparisons. Economically similar countries are likely to have outlet types in similar proportions carrying the same types of goods and services. So direct comparisons between such countries will do a better job of holding constant the quality of the items than comparisons across more diverse countries. (Aten and Heston 2009, 251)
>
> Using the same spanning tree for a number of years would dramatically simplify multilateral international comparisons. Each country would only have to compare itself with its immediate neighbors in the spanning tree, thus reducing the cost and increasing the

> timeliness of international comparisons. Furthermore, by construction, each country's immediate neighbors in the minimum spanning tree will tend to have similar consumption patterns. This may substantially increase the characteristicity of the comparisons. Geary-Khamis, by contrast, compares all countries using a single average price vector. In a comparison over rich and poor countries the average price vector may bear little resemblance to the actual price vectors of many of the countries in the comparison. Conversely, EKS uses all possible combinations of bilateral comparisons. This also requires all countries to provide price and expenditure data on the same set of basic headings, thus reducing the characteristicity of each comparison. (R. J. Hill 2009, 236–37)

Thus the method of spatial linking, if adopted, would involve some changes to country commodity lists. Each country in the minimum spanning tree would be linked to at least one other country, and so for each bilateral link a list of representative commodities pertaining to that link would have to be priced by the two countries in the link. If a country was a local "star" country and linked to several other countries, then the local star country would have to price out a commodity list that pertained to each pair of bilateral links.

Hill has also pointed out that the basic MST methodology could be adapted to impose a priori restrictions on possible links between certain countries: "Suppose for example ... we do not want India to be linked directly with Hong Kong [SAR, China]. This *exclusion* restriction can be imposed by replacing the PLS between India and Hong Kong [SAR, China], in the K × K PLS matrix, by a large dummy value.... Similarly, suppose we want Korea to be linked directly with Japan. This *inclusion* restriction can be imposed by replacing the PLS measure between Korea and Japan with a small dummy value.... This ensures that the corresponding edge is selected" (R. J. Hill 2009, 237).

Finally, Hill has noted that not all statistical agencies produce data of the same quality, and that the MST method can be adapted to take this fact into account: "In particular, some countries have better resourced national statistical offices than others. It would make little sense to put a country with an under resourced national statistical office at the center of a regional star even if so specified by the minimum spanning tree" (R. J. Hill 2009, 237).

The MST algorithm can be modified to ensure that countries with under-resourced statistical offices enter the spanning tree with only one bilateral link to the other countries in the comparison.

To sum up, the *advantages* of the MST method for making multilateral comparisons are as follows:

- The MST method, using a superlative index number formula for forming bilateral links, is, like GEKS, consistent with the economic approach to making multilateral comparisons—that is, it takes into account substitution effects.
- The MST method is likely to lead to a more accurate set of parities than those generated by the GEKS method, because the bilateral links between pairs of countries are based on comparisons between countries with the most similar structures of relative prices—that is, the MST method is the spatial counterpart to chained annual indexes in the time series context.
- The influence of countries with under-resourced statistical agencies can be minimized in a simple modification of the basic MST method.

There are also some *disadvantages* to the spatial linking method:

- The method is not as familiar as GEKS and GK, and hence it will be more difficult to build up a constituency for its use.

- When compared with GEKS, the method does have some arbitrary aspects in that (1) different measures of dissimilarity could be used, and there is no universal agreement at this stage as to which measure is the most appropriate one to use; (2) the treatment of zero "prices" and "quantities" in the measures of dissimilarity is not completely straightforward; and (3) the treatment of countries with under-resourced statistical agencies is also not completely straightforward, and, moreover, it may prove difficult to decide exactly which countries are under-resourced.
- The path of bilateral links between countries generated by the method could be unstable—that is, the minimum spanning tree linking the countries could change when moving from one cross-sectional comparison between countries to another cross-sectional comparison.[40]

As of this writing, spatial linking will not be used in the 2011 ICP. Before the MST method is widely adopted, it will be necessary to do more experimentation and trial runs using the method.

5.7 An Artificial Data Set Numerical Example

Diewert (1999, 79–84) illustrated the differences between various multilateral methods by constructing country PPPs and shares of "world" final demand volumes for a three-country, two-commodity example. The GEKS, GK, IDB, and MST parities are calculated in this section using his numerical example.

The price and quantity vectors for the three countries are

$$p^1 \equiv [1, 1]; \quad p^2 \equiv \left[10, \frac{1}{10}\right]; \quad p^3 \equiv \left[\frac{1}{10}, 10\right]; \tag{5.21}$$

$$q^1 \equiv [1, 2]; \quad q^2 \equiv [1, 100]; \quad q^3 \equiv [1000, 10].$$

Note that the geometric average of the prices in each country is one, so that average price levels are roughly comparable across countries, except that in country 2 the price of commodity 1 is very high and the price of commodity 2 is very low, and vice versa for country 3. As a result of these price differences, in country 2 consumption of commodity 1 is relatively low and consumption of commodity 2 is relatively high, and vice versa in country 3. Country 1 can be regarded as a tiny country, with total expenditure (in national currency units) equal to three; country 2 is a medium country with total expenditure equal to 20; and country 3 is a large country with expenditure equal to 200.

The Fisher (1922) quantity index Q_F can be used to calculate the volume Q^k of each country k relative to country 1—that is, calculate $\frac{Q^k}{Q^1}$ as $Q_F(p^1, p^k, q^1, q^k) \equiv \left[\frac{p^1 \cdot q^k p^k \cdot q^k}{p^1 \cdot q^1 p^k \cdot q^1}\right]^{\frac{1}{2}}$ for $k = 2, 3$. Set Q^1 equal to 1.0, thereby determining Q^2 and Q^3. These volumes using country 1 as the base or star country are reported in the Fisher 1 column of table 5.1. In a similar manner, taking country 2 as the base, use the Fisher formula to calculate Q^1, $Q^2 = 1$, and Q^3. Then divide these numbers by Q^1, thereby obtaining the numbers listed in the Fisher 2 column of table 5.1. Finally, taking country 3 as the base, use the Fisher formula to calculate Q^1, Q^2, and $Q^3 = 1$. Then divide these numbers by Q^1 and obtain the numbers listed in the Fisher 3 column of table 5.1. Ideally, these

TABLE 5.1 Fisher Star, GEKS, GK, and IDB Relative Volumes for Three Countries

	Fisher 1	Fisher 2	Fisher 3	GEKS	GK	IDB
Q^1	1.00	1.00	1.00	1.00	1.00	1.00
Q^2	8.12	8.12	5.79	7.26	47.42	33.67
Q^3	57.88	81.25	57.88	64.81	57.35	336.67

Note: GEKS = Gini-Éltetö-Köves-Szulc; GK = Geary-Khamis; IDB = Iklé-Dikhanov-Balk.

Fisher star parities would all coincide, but because they do not, take their geometric mean and obtain the GEKS parities listed in the fourth column of table 5.1. Thus for this example, the GEKS economic approach to forming multilateral quantity indexes leads to the volumes of countries 2 and 3 being equal to 7.26 and 64.81 times the volume of country 1.[41]

Turning to the spatial linking method, one can see that country 1 has the price structure most similar to those of both countries 2 and 3—that is, countries 2 and 3 have the most dissimilar structure of relative prices.[42] Thus in this case, the spatial linking method leads to the Fisher star parities for country 1—that is, the spatial linking relative outputs are given by the Fisher 1 column in table 5.1. Note that these parities are reasonably close to the GEKS parities.

The GK parities for P^k and π_n can be obtained by iterating between equations (5.7) and (5.8) until convergence has been achieved.[43] Once these parities have been determined, Q^k can be determined using equations (5.10). These country volumes are then normalized so that $Q^1 = 1$. The resulting parities are listed in the GK column in table 5.1. The GK parity for $\frac{Q^3}{Q^1}$, 57.35, is reasonable, but the parity for $\frac{Q^2}{Q^1}$, 47.42, is much too large to be reasonable from an economic perspective. The cause of this unreasonable estimate for Q^2 is the fact that the GK international price vector, $[\pi_1, \pi_2]$, is equal to [1, 9.00] so that these relative prices are closest to the structure of relative prices in country 3, the large country. Thus the relatively large consumption of commodity 2 in country 2 receives an unduly high price weight using the GK vector of international reference prices, leading to an exaggerated estimate for its volume, Q^2. This illustrates a frequent criticism of the GK method: the structure of international prices to which it gives rise is "biased" toward the price structure of the biggest countries.

The IDB parities for this numerical example are now calculated to determine whether the method can avoid the unreasonable results generated by the GK method. The parities for P^k and π_n can be obtained by iterating between equations (5.13) and (5.14) until convergence has been achieved.[44] Once these parities have been determined, the Q^k can be determined using equations (5.10). These country volumes are then normalized so that $Q^1 = 1$. The resulting parities are listed in the IBD column in table 5.1. The GK parity for $\frac{Q^2}{Q^1}$ is 33.67, which is well outside the suggested reasonable range (from the viewpoint of the economic approach) of 5–9, and the GK parity for $\frac{Q^3}{Q^1}$ is 336.7, which is well outside the suggested reasonable range of 50–90. What is the cause of these problematic parities?

The problematic IDB volume estimates are not caused by an unrepresentative vector of international prices, because the IBD international price vector, $[\pi_1, \pi_2]$, is equal to [1, 1], which in turn is equal to the vector of (equally weighted) geometric mean commodity prices across countries. The problem is that no additive method can take into account the problem of declining marginal utility as consumption increases if three or more countries are in the comparison. Thus the IBD vector of international prices $\pi = [1, 1]$ is exactly equal to the country 1 price vector $p^1 = [1, 1]$, and so the use of these international prices results in an accurate volume measure for country 1. But the structure of the IBD international prices is far different from the prices facing consumers in country 2, where the price vector is $p^2 \equiv \left[10, \frac{1}{10}\right]$. The very low relative price for commodity 2 leads consumers to demand a relatively large amount of this commodity (100 units), and the relatively high price for commodity 1 leads to a relatively low demand for this commodity (1 unit). Thus at international prices, the output of country 2 is πq^2, which is equal to 101, as compared with its nominal output $p^2 q^2$, which is equal to 20. The use of international prices therefore overvalues the output of country 2 relative to country 1 because the international price of commodity 2 is equal to 1, which is very much larger than the actual price of commodity 2 in country 2 (which is $\frac{1}{10}$). Note that $\frac{Q^2}{Q^1}$ is equal to $\frac{\pi q^2}{\pi q^1} = \frac{101}{3} = 33.67$, an estimate that fails to take into account the declining marginal utility of the relatively large consumption of commodity 2 in country 1. A similar problem occurs when the outputs of countries 1 and 3 are compared using international prices, except in this case the use of international prices tremendously overvalues country 3's consumption of commodity 1. The problem of finding international reference prices that are "fair" for two country comparisons can be solved,[45] but the problem cannot be solved in general if three or more countries are being compared, as was seen in section 5.5.

The tentative conclusion at this point is that additive methods for making international price and quantity comparisons in which there are tremendous differences in the structure of prices and quantities across countries are likely to give rather different answers than methods based on economic approaches. For this reason, it is important that the International Comparison Program provide two sets of results—one set based on a multilateral method such as GEKS or MST that allows for substitution effects and another set based on an additive method such as GK or IDB. Users then can decide which set of estimates to use in their empirical work based on whether they need an additive method (with all of its desirable consistency in aggregation properties) or whether they need a method that allows for substitution effects.

5.8 Conclusion

This chapter discusses four multilateral methods for constructing PPPs and relative volumes for countries in a region. Two of the methods are additive: the Geary-Khamis method and the Iklé-Dikhanov-Balk method. Additive methods are preferred by many users because the components of real GDP add up across countries and across commodities when an additive multilateral method is used.

Which additive method is "best"? The axiomatic properties of the IDB and GK systems are very similar, and so it is difficult to discriminate between the two methods based on their axiomatic properties. The main *advantages of the IDB method* are as follows:

- The IDB international prices are not as influenced as the GK international prices by the structure of relative prices in the biggest countries in the region—that is, the IDB method is more "democratic" than the GK method in its choice of international prices.
- From evidence presented by Deaton and Heston (2010) using the 2005 ICP database, it appears that the IDB parities are closer to the GEKS parities than the GK parities. Thus the IDB method may have the advantage that it is an additive method that does not

depart too far from the parities generated by the GEKS method.[46]

The main *advantages of the GK system* are as follows:

- The GK system has been used widely in previous ICP rounds, and so users are familiar with the method and may want to continue to use the results of this method.
- The GK system is similar in some ways to the construction of national accounts data when quantities are aggregated over regions, and thus GK estimates may be regarded as a reasonable extension of countrywide national accounts to the world.

The other two methods discussed in this chapter are the GEKS method and the minimum spanning tree method of similarity or spatial linking developed by R. J. Hill using Fisher ideal indexes as basic bilateral building blocks. These two methods can be regarded as being consistent with an economic approach to a multilateral method—that is, these methods deal adequately with substitution behavior on the part of the purchasers of a country's outputs. The spatial linking method was not used in the 2005 ICP, but it has some attractive features, which were discussed in section 5.6.

ANNEX

The Properties of the Iklé-Dikhanov-Balk Multilateral System

Multilateral index number theory is much more complicated than bilateral index number theory. Thus a rather long annex is required to investigate the axiomatic and economic properties of the IDB multilateral system, particularly when some prices and quantities are allowed to be zero.[47]

There are many equivalent ways of expressing the equations that define the IDB parities. Section 5A.1 lists the alternative systems of equations that can be used to define the method. Section 5A.2 provides proofs of the existence and uniqueness of solutions to the IDB equations. Section 5A.3 considers various special cases of the IDB equations. When there are only two countries so that $K = 2$, a bilateral index number formula is obtained, and this case is considered along with the case in which $N = 2$, so that there are only two commodities. These special cases cast some light on the structure of the general indexes. Finally, section 5A.4 explores the axiomatic properties of the IDB method, and section 5A.5 looks at the system's economic properties.

Throughout this annex it is assumed that the number of countries K and the number of commodities N is equal to or greater than two.

5A.1 Alternative Representations

5A.1.1 The P^k, π_n Representation

The basic data for the multilateral system are the prices and quantities for commodity n in country k at the basic heading levels p_n^k and q_n^k, respectively, for $n = 1, \ldots, N$ and $k = 1, \ldots, K$, where the number of basic heading categories N is greater than or equal to two and the number of countries K is greater than or equal to two. The $N \times 1$ vectors of prices and quantities for country k are denoted by p^k and q^k, and their inner product is $p^k q^k$ for $k = 1, \ldots, K$. The share of country k expenditure on commodity n is denoted by $s_n^k \equiv \dfrac{p_n^k q_n^k}{p^k q^k}$ for $k = 1, \ldots, K$ and $n = 1, \ldots, N$.

It is assumed that for each n and k, either p_n^k, q_n^k, and s_n^k are all zero or p_n^k, q_n^k, and s_n^k are all positive. Thus the possibility that some countries do not consume all of the basic heading commodities is taken into account. This factor complicates the representations of the equations because division by zero prices, quantities, or shares leads to difficulties and complicates proofs of existence.[48] For now, the following assumptions are made:

Assumption 1: For every basic heading commodity n, there exists a country k such that p_n^k, q_n^k, and s_n^k are all positive so that each commodity is demanded by some country.

Assumption 2: For every country k, there exists a commodity n such that p_n^k, q_n^k, and s_n^k are all positive so that each country demands at least one basic heading commodity.

In section 5A.1, these assumptions will be strengthened to ensure that the IDB equations have unique, positive solutions.

Recall that the IDB multilateral system was defined by the Dikhanov equations (5.13) and (5.14), plus one normalization such as (5.9). Taking into account the division-by-zero problem, these equations can be rewritten as[49]

(5A.1) $$\pi_n = \frac{\left[\sum_{j=1}^{K} s_n^j\right]}{\left[\sum_{k=1}^{K}\left(\frac{q_n^k P^k}{p^k q^k}\right)\right]}; \quad n = 1, \ldots, N$$

and

(5A.2) $$P^k = \frac{p^k q^k}{\pi q^k}; \quad k = 1, \ldots, K$$

where π is a vector whose components are $\pi_1, \ldots, \pi_N$.

Under assumptions 1 and 2, equations (5A.1) and (5A.2) will be well behaved even if some p_n^k and q_n^k are zero. Equations (5A.1) and (5A.2) (plus a normalization on the P^k or π_n such as $P^1 = 1$ or $\pi_1 = 1$) provide the second representation of the IDB multilateral equations.[50]

To find a solution to equations (5A.1) and (5A.2), one can start by assuming that $\pi = 1_N$, a vector of ones, and then use equations (5A.2) to determine a set of P^k. These P^k can then be inserted into equations (5A.1) to determine a new π vector. This new π vector can in turn be inserted into equations (5A.2) to determine a new set of P^k, and so on. The process can be continued until convergence is achieved.

5A.1.2 An Alternative P^k, π_n Representation using Biproportional Matrices

Equations (5A.1) and (5A.2) can be rewritten as

(5A.3) $$\sum_{k=1}^{K} q_n^k \left[p^k q^k\right]^{-1} \pi_n P^k = \sum_{j=1}^{K} s_n^j; \quad n = 1, \ldots, N$$

and

(5A.4) $$\sum_{n=1}^{N} q_n^k \left[p^k q^k\right]^{-1} \pi_n P^k = \sum_{n=1}^{N} s_n^j = 1; \quad k = 1, \ldots, K.$$

Define the $N \times K$ normalized quantity matrix A, which has element a_{nk} in row n and column k where

(5A.5) $$a_{nk} \equiv \frac{q_n^k}{p^k q^k}; \quad n = 1, \ldots, N; \ k = 1, \ldots, K.$$

Define the $N \times K$ expenditure share matrix S, which has the country k expenditure share for commodity n, s_n^k in row n and column k. Let 1_N and 1_K be vectors of ones of dimension N and K, respectively. Then equations (5A.3) and (5A.4) can be written in matrix form as[51]

(5A.6) $$\hat{\pi} AP = S1_K$$

and

(5A.7) $$\pi^T A\hat{P} = 1_N^T S$$

where $\pi \equiv [\pi_1, \ldots, \pi_N]$ is the vector of IDB international prices, $P \equiv [P^1, \ldots, P^K]$ is the vector of IDB country PPPs, $\hat{\pi}$ denotes an $N \times N$ diagonal matrix with the elements of the vector π along the main diagonal, and $\hat{P}$ denotes an $K \times K$ diagonal matrix with the elements of the vector P along the main diagonal. There are N equations in (5A.6), and K equations in (5A.7). However, examination of (5A.6) and (5A.7) reveals that if $N + K - 1$ of these equations is satisfied, then the remaining equation is also satisfied. Equations (5A.6) and (5A.7) are a special case of the biproportional matrix fitting model from Deming and Stephan (1940) in the statistics context and from Stone (1962) in the economics context (the RAS method). Bacharach (1970, 45) studied this model in great detail and provided rigorous conditions for the existence of a unique positive π, P solution set to (5A.6), (5A.7), and a normalization such as $P^1 = 1$ or $\pi_1 = 1$.[52] In section 5A.1, Bacharach's analysis is used to provide simple sufficient conditions for the existence and uniqueness of a solution to equations (5A.6) and (5A.7) (plus a normalization).

To find a solution to (5A.6) and (5A.7), one can use the procedure suggested at the end of section 5A.1.1, because equations (5A.1) and (5A.2) are equivalent to (5A.3) and (5A.4).[53] Experience with the RAS method has shown that this procedure tends to converge quite rapidly.

5A.1.3 The Q^k, π_n Representation

The previous representations of the IDB system are in terms of a system of equations involving the N international reference prices, π_n, and the K country PPPs, P^k. It is useful to substitute equations (5.8) in the main text. In those equations, $Q^k = \frac{p^k q^k}{P^k}$ defines the country volumes or aggregate quantities Q^k in terms of the country k price and quantity vectors (p^k and q^k) and the country k aggregate PPP, (P^k) into equations (5A.1) and (5A.2) in order to obtain the following representation of the IDB multilateral system in terms of the Q^k and the π_n:

(5A.8) $$\pi_n = \frac{\left[\sum_{j=1}^{K} s_n^j\right]}{\left[\sum_{k=1}^{K}\left(\frac{q_n^k}{Q^k}\right)\right]}; \quad n = 1, \ldots, N$$

and

(5A.9) $$Q^k = \pi q^k; \quad k = 1, \ldots, K.$$

A normalization such as $Q^1 = 1$ or $\pi_1 = 1$ needs to be added to obtain a unique positive solution to (5A.8) and (5A.9).[54] A biproportional iteration process could be set up to find a solution to equations (5A.8) and (5A.9) along the lines suggested at the end of section 5A.1.1, except that now the Q^k are determined rather than the P^k.

5A.1.4 The Q^k Representation

If equations (5A.8) are substituted into equations (5A.9), the following K equations are obtained, involving only the country volumes, $Q^1, \ldots, Q^K$:

(5A.10) $$Q^k = \sum_{n=1}^{N}\left\{\frac{\left[s_n^1 + \cdots + s_n^K\right] q_n^k}{\left[\left(\frac{q_n^1}{Q^1}\right) + \cdots + \left(\frac{q_n^K}{Q^K}\right)\right]}\right\}; \quad k = 1, \ldots, K.$$

A normalization such as $Q^1 = 1$ on the Q^k is required to obtain a unique solution. It also can be seen that the K equations (5A.10) are not independent—that is, if both sides of equation k in (5A.10) are divided by Q^k for each k and then the resulting equations are summed, the identity K equals K is obtained, using the fact that $\sum_{n=1}^{N} s_n^k = 1$ for each k. Thus once any $K - 1$ of the K equations in (5A.10) is satisfied, the remaining equation is also satisfied.

Equations (5A.10) can be used in an iterative fashion to obtain a $Q^1, \ldots, Q^K$ solution—that is, make an initial guess at these volume parities and calculate the right-hand side of each equation in (5A.10). This will generate a new set of volume parities that can then be normalized to satisfy, say, $\sum_{k=1}^{K} Q^k = 1$. Then these new volume parities can again be inserted into the right-hand side of equations (5A.10), and so on.[55]

5A.1.5 The P^k Representation

If equation $Q^k = \dfrac{p^k q^k}{P^k}$ is substituted into equations (5A.10), the following K equations involving only the country PPPs, $P^1, \ldots, P^K$, are obtained:

$$(5A.11) \qquad (P^k)^{-1} = \sum_{n=1}^{N} \left\{ \frac{\left[s_n^1 + \cdots + s_n^K\right]\left[\dfrac{q_n^k}{p^k q^k}\right]}{\left[\left(\dfrac{P^1 q_n^1}{p^1 q^1}\right) + \cdots + \left(\dfrac{P^K q_n^K}{p^K q^K}\right)\right]} \right\}; \quad k = 1, \ldots, K.$$

As usual, a normalization such as $P^1 = 1$ on the P^k is needed to obtain a unique solution. The K equations (5A.11) are not independent—that is, if both sides of equation k in (5A.11) are multiplied by P^k for each k and then the resulting equations are summed, the identity K equals K is obtained, using the fact that $\sum_{n=1}^{N} s_n^k = 1$ for each k. Thus once any $K - 1$ of the K equations in (5A.11) are satisfied, the remaining equation is also satisfied.

Equations (5A.11) can be used iteratively to find a solution in a manner similar to the method described at the end of section 5A.1.4.

Equations (5A.10) and (5A.11) are difficult to interpret at this level of generality, but when the axiomatic properties of the method are studied, it will be seen that the IDB parities have good axiomatic properties.

5A.1.6 The π_n Representation

Finally, substitute equations (5A.2) into equations (5A.1) to obtain the following system of N equations that characterize the IDB international prices π_n:

$$(5A.12) \qquad \sum_{k=1}^{K} \left[\frac{\pi_n q_n^k}{\pi q^k}\right] = \sum_{k=1}^{K} s_n^k; \quad n = 1, \ldots, N.$$

Equations (5A.12) are homogeneous of degree zero in the components of the π vector, and so a normalization such as $\pi_1 = 1$ is required to obtain a unique positive solution. If the N equations in (5A.12) are summed, the identity K equals K is obtained, and so if any $N - 1$ of the N equations in (5A.12) are satisfied, then so is the remaining equation.

Equations (5A.12) can be rewritten as

$$\text{(5A.13)} \qquad \pi_n = \frac{\left[\sum_{k=1}^{K} s_n^k\right]}{\left[\dfrac{\sum_{k=1}^{K} q_n^k}{\pi q^k}\right]}; \quad n = 1; \ldots, N.$$

Equations (5A.13) can be used iteratively in the usual manner to obtain a solution to equations (5A.12).

Equations (5A.12) have an interesting interpretation. Using the international reference prices π_n, define country k's expenditure share for commodity n using these international prices as

$$\text{(5A.14)} \qquad \sigma_n^k \equiv \frac{\pi_n q_n^k}{\pi q^k}; \quad k = 1, \ldots, K; n = 1, \ldots, N.$$

Substituting (5A.14) into (5A.12) leads to

$$\text{(5A.15)} \qquad \sum_{k=1}^{K} \sigma_n^k = \sum_{k=1}^{K} s_n^k; \quad n = 1, \ldots, N.$$

Thus for each basic heading commodity group n, the international prices π_n are chosen by the IDB method to be such that the sum over countries' expenditure shares for commodity n using the international reference prices $\sum_{k=1}^{K} \sigma_n^k$ is equal to the corresponding sum over countries' expenditure shares using domestic prices in each country, $\sum_{k=1}^{K} s_n^k$, and this equality holds for all commodity groups n.[56]

5A.2 Conditions for the Existence and Uniqueness of Solutions to the IDB Equations

The biproportional matrix representation explained in section 5A.1.2 is used to find conditions for positive solutions to any set of the IDB equations.[57]

Bacharach (1970, 43–59) provided very weak sufficient conditions for the existence of a strictly positive solution $\pi_1, \ldots, \pi_N, P^1, \ldots, P^K$ to equations (5A.3) and (5A.4), assuming that assumptions 1 and 2 also hold. His conditions involve the concept of matrix connectedness. Let A be an $N \times K$ matrix. Then Bacharach (1970, 44) defines A to be disconnected if after a possible reordering of its rows and columns it can be written in block rectangular form as

$$\text{(5A.16)} \qquad A = \begin{bmatrix} A_{n \times k} & 0_{n \times (K-k)} \\ 0_{(N-n) \times k} & A_{(N-n) \times (K-k)} \end{bmatrix}$$

where $1 \le n < N$, $1 \le k < K$, $A_{n \times k}$, and $A_{(N-n)\times(K-k)}$ are submatrices of A of dimension $n \times k$ and $N - n \times K - k$, respectively, and $0_{n\times(K-k)}$ and $0_{(N-n)\times(K-k)}$ are $n \times K - k$ and $N - n \times K - k$ matrices of zeros. As Bacharach (1970, 47) noted, the concept of disconnectedness is a generalization to rectangular matrices of the concept of decomposability, which applies to square matrices. Bacharach (1970, 47) defined A to be connected if it is not disconnected (this is a generalization of the concept of indecomposibility, which applies to square matrices). Bacharach (1970, 47–55) went on to show that if the matrix A defined by (5A.5) is connected, assumptions 1 and 2 hold, and if a normalization such as $\pi_1 = 1$ or $P^1 = 1$ is added to equations (5A.3) and (5A.4), then these equations provide a unique positive solution that can be obtained by using the biproportional procedure suggested at the end of section 5A.1.1, which will converge.

It is useful to have somewhat simpler conditions on the matrix A defined by (5A.5), which will imply that it is connected. Either of the following two simple conditions will imply that A is connected (and thus these are sufficient conditions for the existence of unique positive solutions to any representation of the IDB equations):

Condition 1: There exists a commodity n that is demanded by all countries—that is, there exists an n such that $y_n^k > 0$ for $k = 1, \ldots, K$.

Condition 2: There exists a country k that demands all commodities—that is, there exists a k such that $y_n^k > 0$ for $n = 1, \ldots, N$.

Conditions 1 and 2 are easy to check. They will be used in the following section.

5A.3 Special Cases

In this section, some of the general N and K representations of the IDB equations are specialized to cases in which the number of commodities N or the number of countries K is equal to two.

5A.3.1 The Two-Country, Many-Commodity Quantity Index Case

Suppose that the number of countries K is equal to two. Set the country 1 volume equal to one so that Q^1 equals one and the first equation in (5A.10) becomes

$$\text{(5A.17)} \qquad \sum_{n=1}^{N} \left\{ \frac{\left[s_n^1 + s_n^2\right] q_n^1}{\left[q_n^1 + \left(\frac{q_n^2}{Q^2}\right)\right]} \right\} = 1.$$

Equation (5A.17) is one equation in the one unknown Q^2, and it implicitly determines Q^2. Q^2 can be interpreted as a Fisher-type bilateral quantity index, $Q_{\text{IDB}}(p^1, p^2, q^1, q^2)$, in which p^k and q^k are the price and quantity (or more accurately, volume) vectors for country k. Thus in what follows in the remainder of this section, Q^2 is replaced by Q.

At this point, assume that the data for country 1 satisfy condition 2 (so that q^1, p^1, and s^1 are all strictly positive vectors), which guarantees a unique positive solution to (5A.17). With this condition, the quantity relatives r_n are well defined as

$$\text{(5A.18)} \qquad r_n \equiv \frac{q_n^2}{q_n^1} \geq 0; \quad n = 1, \ldots, N.$$

Assumption 2 implies that at least one quantity relative r_n is positive. Because each q_n^1 is positive and letting Q equal Q^2, (5A.17) can be rewritten using definitions (5A.18) as[58]

$$\text{(5A.19)} \qquad \sum_{n=1}^{N} \left\{ \frac{\left[s_n^1 + s_n^2\right]}{\left[1 + \left(\frac{r_n}{Q}\right)\right]} \right\} = 1.$$

Now define the vector of quantity relatives r as $[r_1, \ldots, r_N]$. Then the function on the left-hand side of (5A.19) can be defined as $F(Q, r, s^1, s^2)$, where s^k is the expenditure share vector for country k for $k = 1, 2$. Note that $F(Q, r, s^1, s^2)$ is a continuous, monotonically increasing function of Q for Q positive. It is assumed that the components of q^1 and thus s^1 are all positive. Now compute the limits of $F(Q, r, s^1, s^2)$ as Q tends to plus infinity:

$$\text{(5A.20)} \qquad \lim_{Q \to +\infty} F(Q, r, s^1, s^2) = \sum_{n=1}^{N} \left[s_n^1 + s_n^2 \right] = 2.$$

To compute the limit of $F(Q, r, s^1, s^2)$ as Q tends to zero, two cases must be considered. For the first case, assume that both countries consume all commodities so that $q^2 >> 0_N$ (this is in addition to the earlier assumption that $q^1 >> 0_N$). In this case, it is easy to verify that

$$\text{(5A.21)} \qquad \lim_{Q \to 0} F(Q, r, s^1, s^2) = 0.$$

For the second case, assume that one or more components of q^2 are zero, and let N^* be the set of indexes n such that q_n^2 equals zero. In this case,

$$\text{(5A.22)} \qquad \lim_{Q \to 0} F(Q, r, s^1, s^2) = \sum_{n \in N^*} s_n^1 < 1$$

where the inequality in (5A.22) follows from the fact that it is assumed that all s_n^1 are positive and the sum of all s_n^1 is one.

The fact that $F(Q, r, s^1, s^2)$ is a continuous, monotonically increasing function of Q along with (5A.20)–(5A.22) implies that a finite positive Q solution to the equation $F(Q, r, s^1, s^2) = 1$ exists and is unique. Denote this solution as

$$\text{(5A.23)} \qquad Q = G(r, s^1, s^2).$$

Now use the implicit function theorem to show that $G(r, s^1, s^2)$ is a continuously differentiable function that is increasing in the components of r. Thus

$$\text{(5A.24)} \qquad \frac{\partial G(r, s^1, s^2)}{\partial r_n} = \frac{\left[s_n^1 + s_n^2 \right] \left[1 + \left(\frac{r_n}{Q} \right) \right]^{-2} Q}{\left\{ \sum_{i=1}^{N} \left[s_i^1 + s_i^2 \right] \left[1 + \left(\frac{r_i}{Q} \right) \right]^{-2} r_i \right\}} > 0; \quad n = 1, \ldots, N$$

where Q satisfies (5A.23). However, the inequalities in (5A.24) do not imply that the IDB bilateral index number formula $Q_{IDB}(p^1, p^2, q^1, q^2)$ is increasing in the components of q^2 and decreasing in the components of q^1. The derivatives in (5A.24) were calculated under the hypothesis that r_n equal to $\frac{q_n^2}{q_n^1}$ increased, but the share vectors s^1 and s^2 were held constant as r_n was increased. In fact, it is not the case that $Q_{IDB}(p^1, p^2, q^1, q^2)$ is globally increasing in the components of q^2 and globally decreasing in the components of q^1.[59]

It is clear that $Q_{IDB}(p^1, p^2, q^1, q^2)$ satisfies the identity test—that is, if $q^1 = q^2$ so that all quantity relatives r_n equal one, then the only Q that satisfies (5A.19) is $Q = 1$. It is also clear that if $q^2 = \lambda q^1$ for $\lambda > 0$, then $Q_{IDB}(p^1, p^2, q^1, \lambda q^1) = \lambda$.[60]

Define $\alpha \geq 0$ as the minimum over n of the quantity relatives $r_n = \frac{q_n^2}{q_n^1}$ and define $\beta > 0$ as the maximum of these quantity relatives. Then using the monotonicity properties of the function $F(Q, r, s^1, s^2)$ defined by the left-hand side of (5A.19), it can be shown that

$$\alpha \leq Q_{\text{IDB}}(p^1, p^2, q^1, q^2) \leq \beta \tag{5A.25}$$

with strict inequalities in (5A.25) if the r_n are not all equal. Thus the IDB bilateral quantity index satisfies the usual mean value test for bilateral quantity indexes.[61]

It is possible to develop various approximations of $Q_{\text{IDB}}(p^1, p^2, q^1, q^2)$ that cast some light on the structure of the index. Recall that (5A.19) defined Q_{IDB} in implicit form. This equation can be rewritten as a weighted harmonic mean equal to two:

$$\left\{\sum_{n=1}^{N} w_n \left[1 + \left(\frac{r_n}{Q}\right)\right]^{-1}\right\}^{-1} = 2 \tag{5A.26}$$

where the weights w_n in (5A.26) are defined as

$$w_n \equiv \left(\frac{1}{2}\right)\left(s_n^1 + s_n^2\right); \quad n = 1, \ldots, N \tag{5A.27}$$

Now approximate the weighted harmonic mean on the left-hand side of (5A.26) by the corresponding weighted arithmetic mean to obtain the following approximate version of equation (5A.26):

$$\sum_{n=1}^{N} w_n \left[1 + \left(\frac{r_n}{Q}\right)\right] \approx 2 \tag{5A.28}$$

Using the fact that the weights w_n sum up to one, (5A.28) implies that $Q = Q_{\text{IDB}}$ is approximately equal to the following expression:

$$Q_{\text{IDB}}(r, w) \approx \sum_{n=1}^{N} w_n r_n = \sum_{n=1}^{N} \left(\frac{1}{2}\right)\left[\left(\frac{p_n^1 q_n^1}{p^1 q^1}\right) + \left(\frac{p_n^2 q_n^2}{p^2 q^2}\right)\right]\left[\frac{q_n^2}{q_n^1}\right]. \tag{5A.29}$$

If the weighted arithmetic mean on the right-hand side of (5A.29) is further approximated by the corresponding weighted geometric mean, then $Q_{\text{IDB}}(r, w)$ is approximately equal to

$$Q_{\text{IDB}}(r, w) \approx \prod_{n=1}^{N} r_n^{w_n} \equiv Q_T(r, w) \tag{5A.30}$$

where Q_T is the logarithm of the Törnqvist Theil quantity index defined as $\ln Q_T = \sum_{n=1}^{N} w_n \ln r_n$. If all of the quantity relatives r_n are equal to the same positive number, say λ, then the approximations in (5A.28)–(5A.30) will be exact, and under these conditions, where q^2 is equal to λq^1, then the following equalities will hold:

$$Q_{\text{IDB}}(\lambda 1_N, w) = Q_T(\lambda 1_N, w) = \lambda. \tag{5A.31}$$

In the more general case, where the quantity relatives r_n are about equal to the same positive number so that q^2 is approximately proportional to q^1, then the Törnqvist Theil quantity index

$Q_T(r, w)$ will provide a good approximation of the implicitly defined IDB quantity index, $Q_{\mathrm{IDB}}(r, w)$.[62] However, in the international comparison context it is frequently the case that quantity vectors are far from proportional, and in this nonproportional case Q_{IDB} can be rather far from Q_T and other superlative indexes such as Q_F as was seen earlier in section 5.7 of the main text.

5A.3.2 The Two-Country, Many-Commodity Price Index Case

Again, suppose that the number of countries K is equal to two. Set the country 1 PPP, P^1, equal to one and the first equation in (5A.11) becomes

$$\text{(5A.32)} \qquad \sum_{n=1}^{N} \left\{ \frac{(s_n^1 + s_n^2)\left(\dfrac{q_n^1}{p^1q^1}\right)}{\left[\left(\dfrac{q_n^1}{p^1q^1}\right) + \left(\dfrac{P^2q_n^2}{p^2q^2}\right)\right]} \right\} = 1.$$

Equation (5A.32) is one equation in the one unknown P^2 (the country 2 PPP), and it implicitly determines P^2. P^2 can be interpreted as a Fisher-type bilateral price index, $P_{\mathrm{IDB}}(p^1, p^2, q^1, q^2)$, where p^k and q^k are the price and quantity vectors for country k. Thus in what follows, P^2 will be replaced by P.

Again, it is assumed that the data for country 1 satisfy condition 2 (so that p^1, q^1, and s^1 are all strictly positive vectors), which guarantees a unique positive solution to (5A.32). It is convenient to define the country k normalized quantity vector u^k as the country k quantity vector divided by the value of its output in domestic currency, p^kq^k:

$$\text{(5A.33)} \qquad u^k \equiv \frac{q^k}{p^kq^k}; \quad k = 1, 2.$$

Because q^1 is strictly positive, so is u^1. Hence definitions (5A.33) can be substituted into (5A.32) to obtain the following equation, which implicitly determines $P^2 = P = P_{\mathrm{IDB}}$:

$$\text{(5A.34)} \qquad \sum_{n=1}^{N} \left\{ \frac{[s_n^1 + s_n^2]}{\left[1 + P\left(\dfrac{q_n^2}{q_n^1}\right)\left(\dfrac{p^1q^1}{p^2q^2}\right)\right]} \right\} = \sum_{n=1}^{N} \left\{ \frac{[s_n^1 + s_n^2]}{\left[1 + P\left(\dfrac{u_n^2}{u_n^1}\right)\right]} \right\}.$$

Define $r_n \equiv \dfrac{u_n^2}{u_n^1}$ for $n = 1, \ldots, N$ and rewrite P as $\dfrac{1}{Q}$. Equation (5A.34) then becomes equation (5A.19) in the previous section, and so the analysis surrounding equations (5A.19)–(5A.25) can be repeated to give the existence of a positive solution $P(r, s^1, s^2)$ to (5A.34), along with some of the properties of the solution.

Equation (5A.34) can be used to show that the IDB bilateral price index P, which is the solution to (5A.34), regarded as a function of the price and quantity data pertaining to the two countries, $P_{\mathrm{IDB}}(p^1, p^2, q^1, q^2)$, satisfies the first 11 of the 13 bilateral tests listed in Diewert (1999, 36).[63] It fails only the monotonicity in the components of p^1 and p^2 tests—that is, it is not necessarily the case that $P_{\mathrm{IDB}}(p^1, p^2, q^1, q^2)$ is decreasing in the components of p^1 and increasing in the components of p^2. Thus the axiomatic properties of the IDB bilateral price index are rather good.

The bounds on the IDB bilateral quantity index given by (5A.25) do not have exactly analogous price counterparts. To develop counterparts to the bounds (5A.25), it is convenient to assume that all of the price and quantity data pertaining to both countries are positive. Under these conditions, the N implicit partial price indexes ρ_n can be defined as

$$\rho_n \equiv \frac{\left[\frac{p^2q^2}{q_n^2}\right]}{\left[\frac{p^1q^1}{q_n^1}\right]} = \frac{\left[\frac{p^2q^2}{p^1q^1}\right]}{\left[\frac{q_n^2}{q_n^1}\right]}; \quad n = 1, \ldots, N. \tag{5A.35}$$

An implicit bilateral price index is defined as the value ratio, $\frac{p^2q^2}{p^1q^1}$, divided by a quantity index, say $Q(p^1, p^2, q^1, q^2)$, where Q is generally some type of weighted average of the individual quantity relatives, $\frac{q_n^2}{q_n^1}$. Thus each quantity relative, $\frac{q_n^2}{q_n^1}$, can be regarded as a partial quantity index, and hence the corresponding implicit quantity index, which is the value ratio divided by the quantity relative, can be regarded as an implicit partial price index. Substitution of definitions (5A.35) into (5A.34) leads to the following equation, which implicitly determines P equal to $P_{\text{IDB}}(p^1, p^2, q^1, q^2)$:

$$\sum_{n=1}^{N} \left\{ \frac{\left[s_n^1 + s_n^2\right]}{\left[1 + \left(\frac{P}{\rho_n}\right)\right]} \right\} = 1. \tag{5A.36}$$

Define α as the minimum over n of the partial price indexes ρ_n, and define β as the maximum of these partial price indexes. The monotonicity properties of the function defined by the left-hand side of (5A.36) can then be used to establish the following inequalities:

$$\alpha \le P_{\text{IDB}}(p^1, p^2, q^1, q^2) \le \beta \tag{5A.37}$$

with strict inequalities in (5A.37) if the ρ_n are not all equal.

An approximate explicit formula for P_{IDB} can be readily developed. Recall that (5A.36) defined P_{IDB} in implicit form. This equation can be rewritten as a weighted harmonic mean equal to two:

$$\left\{ \sum_{n=1}^{N} w_n \left[1 + \left(\frac{P}{\rho_n}\right)\right]^{-1} \right\}^{-1} = 2 \tag{5A.38}$$

where the weights w_n in (5A.37) are the average expenditure shares, $\left(\frac{1}{2}\right)[s_n^1 + s_n^2]$ for $n = 1, \ldots, N$. Now approximate the weighted harmonic mean on the left-hand side of (5A.37) by the corresponding weighted arithmetic mean to obtain the approximate version of equation (5A.26):

$$\sum_{n=1}^{N} w_n \left[1 + \left(\frac{P}{\rho_n}\right)\right] \approx 2. \tag{5A.39}$$

In view of the fact that the weights w_n sum up to one, (5A.39) implies that $P = P_{IDB}$ is approximately equal to

$$(5A.40)\qquad P_{IDB}(\rho, w) \approx \left[\sum_{n=1}^{N} w_n(\rho_n)^{-1}\right]^{-1} = \left\{\sum_{n=1}^{N}\left(\frac{1}{2}\right)\left[\left(\frac{p_n^1 q_n^1}{p^1 q^1}\right)+\left(\frac{p_n^2 q_n^2}{p^2 q^2}\right)\right]\left[\frac{q_n^2}{q_n^1}\right]\left[\frac{p^1 q^1}{p^2 q^2}\right]\right\}^{-1}$$

where $\rho \equiv [\rho_1, \ldots, \rho_N]$ and $w \equiv [w_1, \ldots, w_N]$. Thus the IDB bilateral price index P_{IDB} is approximately equal to a weighted harmonic mean of the N partial price indexes ρ_n defined earlier by (5A.35).[64]

5A.3.3 The Many-Country, Two-Commodity Case

Consider the case in which there are K countries but only two commodities so that $N = 2$. Recall that equations (5A.2) and (5A.9) determine the IDB country PPPs, P^k, and the country volumes, Q^k, in terms of the country price and quantity vectors, p^k and q^k, and a vector of international reference prices, $\pi \equiv [\pi_1, \ldots, \pi_N]$. Thus once π is determined, P^k and Q^k can be readily determined. In this section, it is assumed that $N = 2$ so that there are only two commodities and K countries. To ensure the existence of a solution to the IDB equations, it is assumed that commodity 1 is consumed by all countries:

$$(5A.41)\qquad q_1^k > 0; \quad k = 1, \ldots, K.$$

The first international prices will be set equal to one:

$$(5A.42)\qquad \pi_1 = 1.$$

Equations (5A.12) determine π_n, but because N equals two, the second equation in (5A.12) can be dropped. Using the normalization (5A.42), the first equation in (5A.12) becomes

$$(5A.43)\qquad \sum_{k=1}^{K} \frac{q_1^k}{\left[q_1^k + \pi_2 q_2^k\right]} = \sum_{k=1}^{K} s_1^k,$$

which determines the international price for commodity 2, π_2.

Using assumptions (5A.41), the country k commodity relatives R^k (the quantities of commodity 2 relative to 1 in country k) are well defined as

$$(5A.44)\qquad R^k \equiv \frac{q_2^k}{q_1^k} \geq 0; \quad k = 1, \ldots, K.$$

Assumption 1 implies that at least one quantity relative R^k is positive. Because each q_1^k is positive, (5A.43) can be rewritten using definitions (5A.44) as[65]

$$(5A.45)\qquad F(\pi_2, R, s_1) \equiv \sum_{k=1}^{K} \frac{1}{\left[1 + \pi_2 R^k\right]} = \sum_{k=1}^{K} s_1^k \equiv s_1$$

where s_1 is defined to be the sum over countries k of the expenditure share of commodity 1 in country k, s_1^k.[66] Define the vector of country quantity relatives R as $[R^1, \ldots, R^K]$. Then the function on the left-hand side of (5A.45) can be defined as $F(\pi_2, R, s_1)$.[67] Note that $F(\pi_2, R, s_1)$ is a continuous, monotonically decreasing function of π_2 for π_2 positive, because the R^k are nonnegative with at least one R^k positive. Now compute the limits of $F(\pi_2, R, s_1)$ as π_2 tends to zero:

$$\text{(5A.46)} \qquad \lim_{\pi_2 \to 0} F(\pi_2, R, s_1) = K > \sum_{k=1}^{K} s_1^k = s_1.$$

To compute the limit of $F(\pi_2, R, s_1)$ as π_2 tends to plus infinity, consider two cases. For the first case, assume that all countries consume both commodities so that $R >> 0_K$. Using the definition in (5A.45), the following inequality is obtained:

$$\text{(5A.47)} \qquad \lim_{\pi_2 \to +\infty} F(\pi_2, R, s_1) = 0 < \sum_{k=1}^{K} s_1^k = s_1.$$

For the second case, assume that one or more components of R are zero, and let K^* be the set of indexes k such that R^k equals zero. In this case, the following limit is obtained:

$$\text{(5A.48)} \qquad \lim_{\pi_2 \to +\infty} F(\pi_2, R, s_1) = \sum_{k \in K^*} s_n^1 < \sum_{k=1}^{K} s_1^k = s_1.$$

The fact that $F(\pi_2, R, s_1)$ is a continuous, monotonically decreasing function of π_2 along with (5A.46)–(5A.48) implies that a finite positive π_2 solution to equation (5A.45) exists and is unique. Denote this solution as $\pi_2 = G(R, s_1)$. It is straightforward to verify that G is decreasing in the components of R and decreasing in s_1.

Suppose that all country quantity relatives R^k are positive, and define α and β to be the minimum and maximum over k, respectively, of these quantity relatives. Then it is also straightforward to verify that π_2 satisfies the following bounds:[68]

$$\text{(5A.49)} \qquad \frac{\left[\left(\frac{s_1}{K}\right)^{-1} - 1\right]}{\beta} \le \pi_2 \le \frac{\left[\left(\frac{s_1}{K}\right)^{-1} - 1\right]}{\alpha}.$$

Thus if all of country quantity relatives $R^k = \dfrac{q_2^k}{q_1^k}$ are equal to the same positive number λ, then the bounds in (5A.49) collapse to the common value $\dfrac{\left[\left(\frac{s_1}{K}\right)^{-1} - 1\right]}{\lambda}$.

In the case in which prices and quantities are positive across all countries (so that all R^k are positive), it is possible to rewrite the basic equation (5A.45) in a more illuminating form as

$$\text{(5A.50)} \qquad \sum_{k=1}^{K} s_1^k = \sum_{k=1}^{K} \frac{1}{\left[1 + \pi_2 R^k\right]}$$

$$= \sum_{k=1}^{K} \left\{ \frac{s_1^k}{\left[s_1^k + \pi_2 s_1^k \left(\frac{y_2^k}{y_1^k}\right)\right]} \right\}$$

$$= \sum_{k=1}^{K} \left\{ \frac{s_1^k}{\left[s_1^k + \pi_2 s_2^k \left(\frac{p_2^k}{p_1^k}\right)^{-1}\right]} \right\}.$$

Equation (5A.50) shows that the π_2 that solves the equation is a function of the K country share vectors, $s^1, \ldots, s^K$ (each of which is of dimension 2), and the vector of K country price relatives, $\left[\frac{p_1^2}{p_1^1}, \ldots, \frac{p_K^2}{p_k^1}\right]$. If all of these country price relatives are equal to a common ratio, say $\lambda > 0$, then the solution to (5A.53) is $\pi_2 = \lambda$. In the case in which all of these country price relatives are positive, let α^* and β^* be the minimum and maximum over k, respectively, of these price relatives. Then it is straightforward to verify that π_2 satisfies the following bounds:

$$\alpha^* \leq \pi_2 \leq \beta^*. \tag{5A.51}$$

5A.3.4 The Two-Country, Two-Commodity Case

In this section, it is assumed that $K = 2$ (two countries) and that $N = 2$ (two commodities). In this case, it is possible to obtain an explicit formula for the country 2 volume Q^2 relative to the country 1 volume Q^1, which is set equal to one—that is, it is possible to obtain an explicit formula for the IDB bilateral quantity index, $Q^2 = Q = Q_{\text{IDB}}(p^1, p^2, q^1, q^2)$. The starting point for this case is equation (5A.17), which determines Q implicitly. In the case in which N equals two, this equation becomes

$$\left\{\frac{\left[s_1^1 + s_1^2\right]q_1^1}{\left[q_1^1 + \left(\frac{q_1^2}{Q}\right)\right]}\right\} + \left\{\frac{\left[\left(1-s_1^1\right) + \left(1-s_1^2\right)\right]q_2^1}{\left[q_2^1 + \left(\frac{q_2^2}{Q}\right)\right]}\right\} = 1. \tag{5A.52}$$

As usual, it is assumed that the data for country 1 are positive so that $q_1^1 > 0$ and $q_2^1 > 0$. Thus the two quantity relatives, $r_n \equiv \frac{q_2^n}{q_1^n}$ for $n = 1, 2$, are well-defined nonnegative numbers. It is assumed that at least one of the relatives r_1 and r_2 are strictly positive. Substitution of these quantity relatives into (5A.52) leads to the following equation for Q:

$$\left\{\frac{\left[s_1^1 + s_1^2\right]Q}{\left[Q + r_1\right]}\right\} + \left\{\frac{\left[\left(1-s_1^1\right) + \left(1-s_1^2\right)\right]Q}{\left[Q + r_2\right]}\right\} = 1. \tag{5A.53}$$

This equation simplifies into the following quadratic equation:[69]

$$Q^2 + \left[s_1^1 + s_1^2 - 1\right]\left[r_2 - r_1\right]Q - r_1 r_2 = 0. \tag{5A.54}$$

In the case in which both r_1 and r_2 are positive, there is a negative and a positive root for (5A.54). The positive root is the desired bilateral quantity index, and it is equal to

$$\begin{aligned} Q_{\text{IDB}}(p^1, p^2, q^1, q^2) = &-\left(\frac{1}{2}\right)(s_1^1 + s_1^2 - 1)(r_2 - r_1) \\ &+ \left(\frac{1}{2}\right)\left[(s_1^1 + s_1^2 - 1)^2 (r_2 - r_1)^2 + 4r_1 r_2\right]^{\frac{1}{2}}. \end{aligned} \tag{5A.55}$$

Now suppose that $r_1 = \frac{q_1^2}{q_1^1} = 0$ so that $q_1^1 > 0$ and $q_1^2 = 0$. Then $s_1^2 = 0$ as well. Using (5A.54),

$$Q = \left[1 - s_1^1\right]r_2 = \left[1 - s_1^1\right]\left[\frac{q_2^2}{q_2^1}\right]. \tag{5A.56}$$

Equation (5A.56) makes sense in the present context. Recall that Q is supposed to reflect the country 2 volume or average quantity relative to country 1. If, as a preliminary estimate of this relative volume, Q is set equal to the single nonzero quantity relative r_2, then this would overestimate the average volume of country 2 relative to 1 because country 2 has a zero amount of commodity 1 while country 1 has the positive amount q_1^1. Thus r_2 is scaled down by multiplying it by one minus country 1's share of commodity 1, s_1^1. The bigger this share, the more the preliminary volume ratio r_2 is downsized.

Now suppose that $r_2 = \frac{y_2^2}{y_2^1} = 0$ so that $q_2^1 > 0$ and $q_2^2 = 0$. Then if $s_1^2 = 1$, and using (5A.54),

$$Q = s_1^1 r_1 = \left[1 - s_2^1\right]\left[\frac{q_1^2}{q_1^1}\right]. \tag{5A.57}$$

Again, equation (5A.57) makes sense in the present context. If Q is set equal to the single nonzero quantity relative r_1, then this would overestimate the average volume of country 2 relative to 1 because country 2 has a zero amount of commodity 2 while country 1 has the positive amount q_2^1. Thus scale down r_1 by multiplying it by one minus country 1's share of commodity 2, s_2^1. The bigger this share, the more the preliminary volume ratio r_1 is downsized.

Two other special cases of (5A.54) are of interest. Consider the cases in which the following conditions hold:

$$r_1 = r_2 \tag{5A.58}$$

and

$$s_1^1 + s_1^2 = 1. \tag{5A.59}$$

If either of these two special cases holds, then Q equals $(r_1 r_2)^{\frac{1}{2}}$, the geometric mean of the two quantity relatives. This first result is not surprising because this result is implied by the earlier N commodity results for two countries—see (5A.25). The second result is more interesting. If (5A.59) holds so that the sum of the two country expenditure shares on commodity 1 is equal to one, then the sum of the two country expenditure shares on commodity 2 is also equal to one—that is, it is also the case that $s_2^1 + s_2^2 = 1$ and the IDB quantity index is equal to the geometric mean of the two quantity relatives, $(r_1 r_2)^{\frac{1}{2}}$.[70]

The next section provides a discussion of the axiomatic or test properties of the IDB multilateral system.

5A.4 Axiomatic Properties of the IDB Multilateral System

Recall section 5.4 in the main text of this chapter where 11 tests or axioms for multilateral systems are listed. The axiomatic properties of the IDB system are summarized in the following result.

PROPOSITION 1: Assume that the country price and quantity data P, Q satisfy assumptions 1 and 2 and at least one of the conditions 1 and 2. Then the IDB multilateral system fails only tests 9 and 10 for the 11 tests listed in section 5.4 of the main text.

Proof: The existence and uniqueness of a solution to any one of the representations of the IDB equations are discussed in section 5A.2. The continuity (and once continuous differentiability) of the IDB share functions $S^k(P, Q)$ in the data follow using the Implicit Function Theorem on the system of equations (5A.6) and (5A.7) (plus a normalization) by adapting the arguments in Bacharach (1970, 67–68). This establishes T1.

The proofs of tests T2 and T4–T8 follow by straightforward substitution into equations (5A.10).

The proof of T3 follows by setting π equal to p and then showing that this choice of π satisfies equations (5A.12). Once π has been determined as p, then the Q^k are determined as πq^k for $k = 1, \ldots, K$, and finally the share functions are determined using (5A.15).

The results in section 5A.3.4 can be used to show that T9, the monotonicity test, fails.

The "democratic" nature of the IDB system (each country's shares are treated equally in forming the reference prices π) leads to a failure of test T10.[71]

The main text showed that the IDB method satisfied T11, the additivity test.
Q.E.D.

5A.5 Economic Properties of the IDB Multilateral System

An economic approach to bilateral index number theory was initiated by Diewert (1976) and generalized to multilateral indexes in Diewert (1999, 20–23). The properties of the IDB system in this economic framework are examined in this section.

The basic assumption in the economic approach to multilateral indexes is that the country k quantity vector q^k is a solution to the following country k utility maximization problem:

$$\text{(5A.60)} \qquad \max_q \left\{f(q) : p^k q = p^k q^k\right\} = u_k = Q^k$$

where $u^k \equiv f(q^k)$ is the utility level for country k, which can also be interpreted as the country's volume Q^k; $p^k >> 0_N$ is the vector of positive prices for outputs that prevail in country k for $k = 1, \ldots, K$;[72] and f is a linearly homogeneous, increasing concave aggregator function that is assumed to be the same across countries. This aggregator function has a dual unit cost or expenditure function $c(p)$, which is defined as the minimum cost or expenditure required to achieve the unit volume level if purchasers face the positive commodity price vector p.[73] Because purchasers in country k are assumed to face the prices $p^k >> 0_N$, the following equalities hold:

$$\text{(5A.61)} \qquad c(p^k) \equiv \min_q \left\{p^k q : f(q) \geq 1\right\} \equiv P^k; \quad k = 1, \ldots, K$$

where P^k is the (unobserved) minimum expenditure required for country k purchasers to achieve unit utility or volume level when the purchasers face prices p^k. P^k can also be interpreted as country k's aggregate PPP. Under assumptions (5A.60) it can be shown[74] that the country k price and quantity vectors, p^k and q^k, satisfy

$$\text{(5A.62)} \qquad p^k q = c(p^k) f(q^k) = P^k u_k = P^k Q^k; \quad k = 1, \ldots, K.$$

To make further progress, it is assumed that either the utility function $f(q)$ is once continuously differentiable with respect to the components of q, or the unit cost function $c(p)$ is once continuously differentiable with respect to the components of p (or both).

In the case in which f is assumed to be differentiable, the first-order necessary conditions for the utility maximization problems in (5A.60), along with the linear homogeneity of f, imply the following relationships between the country k price and quantity vectors, p^k and q^k, respectively, and the country unit expenditures e_k, defined in (5A.64):[75]

$$p^k = \nabla f(q^k)P^k; \quad k = 1, \ldots, K \tag{5A.63}$$

where $\nabla f(q^k)$ denotes the vector of first-order partial derivatives of f with respect to the components of q evaluated at the country k quantity vector, q^k.

In the case in which $c(p)$ is assumed to be differentiable, then Shephard's Lemma implies the following equations:

$$q^k = \nabla c(p^k)u_k = \nabla c(p^k)Q^k; \quad k = 1, \ldots, K \tag{5A.64}$$

where $u_k = f(q^k) = Q^k$ denotes the utility level for country k, and $\nabla c(p^k)$ denotes the vector of first-order partial derivatives of the unit cost function c with respect to the components of p evaluated at the country k price vector p^k.

If $f(q)$ or $c(p)$ are differentiable, then because both of these functions are assumed to be linearly homogeneous, Euler's Theorem on homogeneous functions implies the following relationships:

$$f(q^k) = \nabla f(q^k)q^k = \sum_{n=1}^{N} \left[\frac{\partial f(q^k)}{\partial q_n}\right] q_n^k; \quad k = 1, \ldots, K \tag{5A.65}$$

and

$$c(p^k) = \nabla c(p^k)p^k = \sum_{n=1}^{N} \left[\frac{\partial c(p^k)}{\partial p_n}\right] p_n^k; \quad k = 1, \ldots, K. \tag{5A.66}$$

Recall that the expenditure share on commodity n for country k was defined as $s_k^n \equiv \dfrac{p_n^k q_n^k}{p^k q^k}$. In the case in which $f(q)$ is differentiable, substitution of (5A.63) and (5A.65) into these shares leads to

$$s_n^k = \frac{q_n^k f_n(q^k)}{f(q^k)}; \quad n = 1, \ldots, N; \; k = 1, \ldots, K \tag{5A.67}$$

where $f_n(q^k) \equiv \dfrac{\partial f(q^k)}{\partial q_n}$. In the case in which $c(p)$ is differentiable, substitution of (5A.64) and (5A.66) into the expenditure shares s_n^k leads to

$$s_n^k = \frac{p_n^k c_n(p^k)}{c(p^k)}; \quad n = 1, \ldots, N; \; k = 1, \ldots, K \tag{5A.68}$$

where $c_n(p^k) \equiv \dfrac{\partial c(p^k)}{\partial p_n}$. Now that the preliminaries have been laid out, it is time to attempt to determine what classes of preferences (i.e., differentiable functional forms for f or c) are consistent with the IDB system of equations (5A.10).

Begin by considering the case of a differentiable utility function $f(q)$, which is positive, increasing, linearly homogeneous, and concave for $q >> 0_N$.[76] Let $q^k >> 0_N$, $Q^k = f(q^k)$, for $k = 1, \ldots, K$, and substitute these equations and (5A.67) into equations (5A.10). Then f must satisfy the following system of K functional equations:

$$\text{(5A.69)} \quad \sum_{n=1}^{N} \frac{\left\{\left[\frac{q_n^1 f_n(q^1)}{f(q^1)}\right] + \cdots + \left[\frac{q_n^K f_n(q^K)}{f(q^K)}\right]\right\}\left[\frac{q_n^k}{f(q^k)}\right]}{\left\{\left[\frac{q_n^1}{f(q^1)}\right] + \cdots + \left[\frac{q_n^k}{f(q^k)}\right]\right\}} = 1; \quad k = 1, \ldots, K.$$

Note that all of the terms in this system of K equations are the same in each equation except the terms $\frac{q_k^n}{f(q^k)}$ in the middle of equation k. Suppose that $f(q)$ is a linear function of q so that

$$\text{(5A.70)} \quad f(q) = f(q_1, \ldots, q_N) = a_1 q_1 + \cdots + a_N q_N; \quad a_1 > 0, \ldots, a_N > 0.$$

It is straightforward to verify that the linear function $f(q)$ defined by (5A.70) satisfies the maintained hypotheses on f, and it also satisfies the system of functional equations (5A.69). Thus the IDB multilateral system is consistent with linear preferences.

Now consider the case of a differentiable unit cost function $c(p)$, which is positive, increasing, linearly homogeneous, and concave for $p >> 0_N$. Let $p^k >> 0_N$, $P^k = c(p^k)$ for $k = 1, \ldots, K$, and substitute these equations and (5A.64) into equations (5A.10). Then c must satisfy the following system of K functional equations:

$$\text{(5A.71)} \quad \sum_{n=1}^{N} \frac{\left\{\left[\frac{p_n^1 c_n(p^1)}{c(p^1)}\right] + \cdots + \left[\frac{p_n^K c_n(p^K)}{c(p^K)}\right]\right\} c_n(p^k)}{\{c_n(p^1) + \cdots + c_n(p^K)\}} = 1; \quad k = 1, \ldots, K.$$

Note that all of the terms in the previous system of K equations are the same in each equation except the partial derivative terms $c_n(p^K)$ in the middle of equation k. Now suppose that $c(p)$ is a linear function of p so that

$$\text{(5A.72)} \quad c(p) = c(p_1, \ldots, p_N) = b_1 y_1 + \cdots + b_N y_N; \quad b_1 > 0, \ldots, b_N > 0.$$

It is straightforward to verify that the linear function $c(p)$ defined by (5A.72) satisfies the maintained hypotheses on c, and it also satisfies the system of functional equations (5A.71). Thus the IDB multilateral system is consistent with Leontief (no substitution) preferences.

These computations show that the IDB multilateral system is consistent with preferences that exhibit perfect substitutability between commodities (the linear utility function case) and with preferences that exhibit no substitution behavior as prices change (the case of Leontief preferences where the unit cost function is linear). It turns out that if the number of countries is three or more, then these are the only (differentiable) preferences that are consistent with the IDB system as is shown by the following result.

Proposition 2: If the number of countries is greater than two, then the linear utility function defined by (5A.73) is the only regular differentiable utility function that is consistent with the IDB equations (5A.69), and the preferences that are dual to the linear unit cost function defined by (5A.72) are the only differentiable dual preferences that are consistent with the IDB equations (5A.71).

PROOF: Let $K \geq 3$ and let $q^k >> 0_N$ for $k = 1, \ldots, K$. Then the first two equations in (5A.69) can be rearranged as

$$(5A.73) \quad f(q^2) - f(q^1) = \sum_{n=1}^{N} \left\{ \left[\frac{q_n^1 f_n(q^1)}{f(q^1)}\right] + \cdots + \left[\frac{q_n^K f_n(q^K)}{f(q^K)}\right] \right\} \left\{ \frac{\left[q_n^2 - q_n^1\right]}{\left[\frac{q_n^1}{f(q^1)} + \cdots + \frac{q_n^K}{f(q^K)}\right]} \right\}.$$

Fix n and let the components of q^1 and q^2 satisfy the following assumptions:

$$(5A.74) \quad q_n^2 \neq q_n^1; \quad q_i^2 = q_i^1 \text{ for I} \neq n.$$

Now look at equation (5A.73) when assumptions (5A.74) hold. The left-hand side is independent of the components of q^3, and thus the right-hand side of (5A.73) must also be independent of q^3. Using the linear homogeneity of f, this is sufficient to show that $f_n(q^3)$ must be a constant for any $q^3 >> 0_N$—that is, for all $q >> 0_N$, $f_n(q)$ is equal to a constant a_n, which must be positive under our regularity conditions on f. This proof works for $n = 1, \ldots, N$, which completes the proof of the first part of the proposition.

Let $K \geq 3$ and let $p^k >> 0_N$ for $k = 1, \ldots, K$. Then equations (5A.71) can be rewritten as

$$(5A.75) \quad \sum_{n=1}^{N} \rho_n(p^1, \ldots, p^K) c_n(p^K) = 1; \quad k = 1, \ldots, K$$

where the coefficients $\rho_n(p^1, \ldots, p^K)$ in (5A.75) are defined for $n = 1, \ldots, N$ as

$$(5A.76) \quad \rho_n(p^1, \ldots, p^K) \equiv \frac{\left\{\left[\frac{p_n^1 c_n(y^1)}{c(p^1)}\right] + \cdots + \left[\frac{p_n^K c_n(p^K)}{c(p^K)}\right]\right\}}{\left\{c_n(p^1) + \cdots + c_n(p^K)\right\}}.$$

The first two equations in (5A.75) can be subtracted from each other to give

$$(5A.77) \quad \sum_{n=1}^{N} \rho_n(p^1, \ldots, p^K)\left[c_n(p^2) - c_n(p^1)\right] = 0.$$

Then define the vector $\rho(p^1, \ldots, p^K) \equiv [\rho_1(p^1, \ldots, p^K), \ldots, \rho_N(p^1, \ldots, p^K)]$. Because $K \geq 3$, the definitions (5A.76) show that the components of p^3 can be varied (holding the remaining price vectors constant) so that N is found to be linearly independent $\rho(p^1, \ldots, p^K)$ vectors. Substitution of these linearly independent vectors into equation (5A.77) implies that

$$(5A.78) \quad \nabla c(p^2) = \nabla c(p^1).$$

Because equations (5A.78) hold for all positive p^1 and p^2, the partial derivatives of $c(p)$ are constant, which completes the proof of the proposition.
Q.E.D.

Thus the IDB multilateral system suffers from the same defect as the GK system.[77] Neither of these additive systems is consistent with an economic approach that allows consumer preferences to be represented by flexible functional forms, whereas the GEKS system is consistent with preferences that are representable by flexible functional forms.[78]

NOTES

1. The author is indebted to Yuri Dikhanov, D. S. Prasada Rao, Sergey Sergeev, and Frederic A. Vogel for their helpful comments.
2. For additional methods, see Rao (1990), Balk (1996; 2009, 232–60), R. J. Hill (1997, 1999a, 1999b, 2001, 2004, 2009), and Diewert (1999).
3. The five geographic ICP regions in 2005 were Africa, Asia-Pacific, Commonwealth of Independent States (CIS), South America, and Western Asia. The Eurostat-OECD members constituted a sixth region.
4. Iklé (1972, 203) proposed the equations for the method in a rather difficult-to-interpret manner and provided a proof for the existence of a solution for the case of two countries. Dikhanov (1994, 6–9) used the much more transparent equations (5.13) and (5.14) that appear later in this chapter. He also explained the advantages of the method over the GK method and illustrated the method with an extensive set of computations. Balk (1996, 207–8) used the Dikhanov equations and provided a proof of the existence of a solution to the system for an arbitrary number of countries. Van Ijzeren (1983, 42) also used Iklé's equations and provided an existence proof for the case of two countries.
5. These methods can also be used to make comparisons between regions, as will be seen in chapter 6.
6. Fisher (1922, 272–74), in his discussion on comparing the price levels of Norway, Arab Republic of Egypt, and Georgia, came close to introducing this method. Kravis, Heston, and Summers (1982, 104–11) used similarity measures to cluster countries into groups and also came close to introducing Hill's spatial linking method.
7. Note that the expenditures e_n^k are drawn from the national accounts of country k in the reference year and refer to total expenditures on commodity category n—that is, these expenditures are not in per capita terms.
8. National income accountants distinguish between a "quantity" and a "volume." A *volume* is an aggregate of a group of actual quantities. Because country expenditures in each of the basic heading categories are aggregates over many commodities, it is appropriate to refer to q_n^k as volumes rather than quantities. The price levels p_n^k that correspond to q_n^k are called basic heading PPPs.
9. Notation: if $x = [x_1, \ldots, x_N]$, an N dimensional row vector, then x^T denotes the transpose of x and is an N dimensional column vector with the same components. Thus p^k is an N dimensional column vector.
10. Notation: $pq \equiv \sum_{n=1}^{N} p_n q_n$ denotes the inner product between the vectors p and q.
11. Define the country k expenditure share on commodity group n as $s_n^k \equiv \dfrac{p_n^k q_n^k}{p^k q^k}$ for $n = 1, \ldots, N$.

    Then the Laspeyres price index between countries j and k can be written in the following expenditure share form: $P_L(p^k, p^j, q^k, q^j) \equiv \dfrac{p^j q^k}{p^k q^k} = \sum_{n=1}^{N} \left(\dfrac{p_n^j q_n^k}{p^k q^k}\right) = \sum_{n=1}^{N} \left(\dfrac{p_n^j}{p_n^k}\right) \dfrac{p_n^k q_n^k}{p^k q^k} =$ $\sum_{n=1}^{N} \left(\dfrac{p_n^j}{p_n^k}\right) s_n^k$, which is a country k share weighted *arithmetic* mean of the price relatives $\dfrac{p_n^j}{p_n^k}$.
12. Define the country j expenditure share on commodity group n as $s_n^j \equiv \dfrac{p_n^j q_n^j}{p^j q^j}$ for $n = 1, \ldots, N$.

    Then the Paasche price index between countries j and k can be written in the following expenditure share form: $P_P(p^k, p^j, q^k, q^j) \equiv \dfrac{p^j q^j}{p^k q^j} = \left[\sum_{n=1}^{N} \left(\dfrac{p_n^k q_n^j}{p^j q^j}\right)\right]^{-1} = \left[\sum_{n=1}^{N} \left(\dfrac{p_n^j}{p_n^k}\right)^{-1} \left(\dfrac{p_n^j q_n^j}{p^j q^j}\right)\right]^{-1} =$

$\left[\sum_{n=1}^{N}\left(\frac{p_n^j}{p_n^k}\right)^{-1} s_n^j\right]^{-1}$, which is a country j share weighted *harmonic* mean of the price relatives $\frac{p_n^j}{p_n^k}$. Using these formulas for the Laspeyres and Paasche price indexes, it can be seen that the Fisher price index can also be written in terms of expenditure shares and price relatives.

13. See Balk (2008, 91–97) for a review of the literature on axiomatic justifications for the Fisher index.
14. See chapters 15, 16, and 17 in the *Consumer Price Index Manual* (International Labour Organization et al. 2004).
15. For several additional ways of expressing the GEKS PPPs and relative volumes, see Balk (1996), Diewert (1999, 34–37) and section 5.5 of this chapter.
16. All of the multilateral methods described in this section can be applied to subaggregates of the 155 basic heading categories—that is, instead of working out aggregate price and volume comparisons across all 155 commodity classifications, one could just choose to include the food categories in the list of N categories and use the multilateral method to compare aggregate food consumption across countries in the region.
17. An additive multilateral system is sometimes said to have the property of matrix consistency.
18. Hill (1997) and Dikhanov (1994, 5) made this point.
19. What makes the IDB system special is the fact that equations (5.16) are equivalent to equations (5.14). Instead of using harmonic means in equations (5.13) and (5.14), one could use more general means, such as means of order r—that is, equations (5.13) could be replaced by $\pi_n = \left[\frac{\sum_{k=1}^{K} s_n^k \left[\frac{p_n^k}{P^k}\right]^r}{\sum_{j=1}^{K} s_n^j}\right]^{\frac{1}{r}}$ and equations (5.14) by $P^k = \left[\sum_{n=1}^{N} s_n^k \left[\frac{p_n^k}{\pi_n}\right]^r\right]^{\frac{1}{r}}$, where $r \neq 0$. But it is only when $r = -1$ that the second set of equations simplifies to equations (5.16), which implies the additivity of the method.
20. Balk's axioms were somewhat different from those proposed by Diewert because Balk also introduced an extra set of country weights into Diewert's axioms. Balk's example will not be followed here because it is difficult to determine precisely what these country weights should be. For the most up-to-date review of the axiomatic approach to multilateral indexes, see Balk (2008, 232–60).
21. Diewert's test for bilateral consistency in aggregation is omitted, because this test depends on choosing a "best" bilateral quantity index, and there may be no consensus on what this "best" functional form is (Diewert 1999, 18). His final axiom involving the consistency of the multilateral system with the economic approach to index number theory is discussed in section 5.5 of this chapter.
22. Balk (1996, 212) also compares the performance of the two methods (along with other multilateral methods) using his axiomatic system.
23. The fact that big countries play a more important role in determining the international prices when test T10 is satisfied is analogous to a property that national prices have to regional prices when a country's national accounts by product are constructed: the national price for a commodity is taken to be the unit value price for that commodity over regions within the country. Thus large regions with large final demands will have a more important role in determining the national price vector than the smaller regions.
24. The pioneers in this approach were Konüs and Byushgens (1926).
25. Diewert (1974, 113) termed such functional forms *flexible.*

26. Diewert (1976, 117) introduced this concept and terminology.
27. According to Diewert (1999, 50), figure 5.1

> illustrates the Gerschenkron effect: in the consumer theory context, countries whose price vectors are far from the 'international' or world average prices used in an additive method will have quantity shares that are biased upward.... It can be seen that these biases are simply quantity index counterparts to the usual substitution biases encountered in the theory of the consumer price index. However, the biases will usually be much larger in the multilateral context than in the intertemporal context since relative prices and quantities will be much more variable in the former context.... The bottom line... is that the quest for an additive multilateral method with good economic properties (i.e., a lack of substitution bias) is a doomed venture: nonlinear preferences and production functions cannot be adequately approximated by linear functions. Put another way, if technology and preferences were always linear, there would be no index number problem and hundreds of papers and monographs on the subject would be superfluous!

28. Methods that rely on the econometric estimation of preferences across countries are probably not suitable for the ICP, because it becomes very difficult to estimate flexible preferences for 155 commodity categories.
29. One limitation of econometric approaches is that they cannot be used (it is not impossible, but it would be very difficult because there would be 12,000 parameters to estimate in this case).
30. Note that if all countries in the multilateral comparison have proportional "price" vectors, then the GEKS relative volume for any two countries j relative to i, $\frac{S^j}{S^i}$, is simply the Fisher ideal quantity index between the two countries, which in turn is equal to $\frac{p^iq^j}{p^iq^i}$ and to $\frac{p^jq^j}{p^jq^i}$, the Paasche and Laspeyres quantity indexes between the two countries. If a vector of international prices π is chosen to be any one of the country price vectors, then $\frac{S^j}{S^i} = \frac{\pi q^j}{\pi q^i} = \frac{Q^j}{Q^i}$. Thus under the hypothesis of price proportionality across countries, the country real expenditure levels, Q^k, are proportional to πq^k, and the GEKS multilateral method can be regarded as an additive method.
31. This linking methodology was developed by R. J. Hill (1999a, 1999b, 2004, 2009).
32. Perhaps more descriptive labels for the MST method for making international comparisons are the *similarity linking method* or the *spatial chaining method.*
33. Deaton (2010, 33–34) noticed the following problem with the GEKS method. Suppose there are two countries, A and B. The expenditure share on commodity 1 is tiny for country A and very big for country B. Also suppose that the price of commodity 1 in country A is very large relative to the price in country B. Then look at the Törnqvist price index between A and B. The overall price level for country A will be blown up by the relatively high price for good 1 in country A relative to country B and by the big expenditure share in country B on commodity 1. Because the Törnqvist price index will generally closely approximate the corresponding Fisher index, one has ended up exaggerating the price level of country A relative to B. This problem can be mitigated by spatial linking of countries that have similar price and quantity structures.

34. For a more complete discussion of dissimilarity indexes and their properties, see Diewert (2009).
35. Kravis, Heston, and Summers (1982, 105) proposed another similarity measure that is related to a weighted correlation coefficient between two country price or PPP vectors. However, their measure is not a "pure" bilateral similarity measure because their weights depend on the data of all countries in the comparison.
36. If a price p_n^k equals zero, then it is assumed that the corresponding quantity is also zero.
37. Diewert (2009) did not deal with the zero price problem, but it is a real problem that needs to be addressed in order to implement his suggested dissimilarity measures for relative price structures using real data. For additional discussion of the difficulties associated with making comparisons across countries in which different commodities are being consumed, see Deaton and Heston (2010) and Diewert (2010).
38. Some additional examples are presented in chapter 6.
39. If both prices are zero, then simply drop the n-th term in the summation on the right-hand side of (5.20).
40. However, this evidence of unstable links comes from the results of the MST method using the Paasche and Laspeyres spread measure of dissimilarity. Based on the recent research of Rao, Shankar, and Hajarghasht (2010), it is likely that this instability will be reduced if a better measure of dissimilarity is used in the MST algorithm, like those defined by (5.19) and (5.20), as opposed to the use of the PLS measure defined by (5.18).
41. Because the Fisher star parities are not all equal, it must be recognized that the GEKS parities are only an approximation of the "truth." Thus it could be expected that an economic approach would lead to a $\frac{Q^2}{Q^1}$ parity in the 5–9 range and to a $\frac{Q^3}{Q^1}$ parity in the 50–90 range. Note, however, that the IDB parities are well outside these ranges, and the GK parity for $\frac{Q^2}{QY^1}$ is also well outside this suggested range.
42. This MTS result is obtained for all three measures of dissimilarity considered in the previous section—see equations (5.18), (5.19), and (5.20).
43. Only five iterations were required for convergence.
44. Because all of the prices and quantities are positive in this example, equations (5.13) and (5.14) in the main text can be used instead of the more robust (to zero entries) equations (5A.3) and (5A.4) in the annex. Eighteen iterations were required for convergence.
45. See Diewert (1996, 246) for examples of superlative indexes that are additive if there are only two countries or observations.
46. However, the second example in chapter 6 indicates that the IDB parities may not always be closer to the GEKS parities than the GK parities.
47. Balk (1996, 207–8) has written the most extensive published discussion of the properties of the IDB system, but he considers only the case of positive prices and quantities for all commodities across all countries. He does not discuss the economic properties of the method.
48. Balk's existence proof assumed that all prices and quantities were strictly positive (Balk 1996, 208).
49. Equations (5A.1) are equivalent to Balk's equations (38a) in the case in which all price p_n^k are positive, and equations (5A.2) are Balk's equations (38b) (Balk 1996, 207).
50. Equations (5.13) and (5.14) provide a first representation in the case in which all prices and quantities are positive.

51. Notation: when examining matrix equations, vectors such as π and P are to be regarded as column vectors, and π^T and P^T denote their row vector transposes.
52. It is obvious that if the positive vectors π and P satisfy (5A.6) and (5A.7), then $\lambda\pi$ and $\lambda^{-1}P$ also satisfy these equations where λ is any positive scalar. Dikhanov (1997, 12–13) also derived conditions for the existence and uniqueness of the solution set using a different approach.
53. Bacharach (1970, 46) calls this method of solution the biproportional process. He establishes conditions for the existence and uniqueness of a solution to the biproportional process—that is, for the convergence of the process (Bacharach 1970, 46–59). The normalization—say $P^1 = 1$ or $\pi_1 = 1$—can be imposed at each iteration of the biproportional process, or it can be imposed at the end of the process when convergence has been achieved.
54. It can be verified that if $N + K - 1$ of equations (5A.8) and (5A.9) are satisfied, then the remaining equation is also satisfied. Equations (5A.10) may be used to establish this result.
55. When this method was tried on the data for the numerical example in Diewert (1999, 79)—see section 7—it was found that convergence was very slow. The iterative methods described in section A.1.1 converged much more quickly.
56. Dividing both sides of (5A.15) by K means that for each commodity group the average (over countries) expenditure share using the IDB international prices is equal to the corresponding average expenditure share using the domestic prices prevailing in each country.
57. Once the existence and uniqueness of a positive solution to any one of the representations of the IDB equations have been established, using assumptions 1 and 2 it is straightforward to show that a unique positive solution to the other representations is also implied.
58. Equation (5A.19) shows that Q depends only on the components of two N dimensional vectors, r and $s^1 + s^2$.
59. This negative monotonicity result also applies to the Törnqvist Theil bilateral index number formula, Q_T—see Diewert (1992, 221). The logarithm of Q_T is defined as $\ln Q_T = \sum_{n=1}^{N} (\frac{1}{2}) \left[s_n^1 + s_n^2\right] \ln r_n$.
60. It is also clear from (5A.19) that $Q_{\text{IDB}}(p^1, p^2, q^1, q^2)$ satisfies the following four homogeneity tests: $Q_{\text{IDB}}(p^1, p^2, q^1, \lambda q^2) = \lambda Q_{\text{IDB}}(p^1, p^2, q^1, q^2)$, $Q_{\text{IDB}}(p^1, p^2, \lambda q^1, q^2) = \lambda^{-1} Q_{\text{IDB}}(p^1, p^2, q^1, q^2)$, $Q_{\text{IDB}}(\lambda p^1, p^2, q^1, q^2) = Q_{\text{IDB}}(p^1, p^2, q^1, q^2)$, and $Q_{\text{IDB}}(p^1, \lambda p^2, q^1, q^2) = Q_{\text{IDB}}(p^1, p^2, q^1, q^2)$ for all $\lambda > 0$. Equations (5A.17) or (5A.19) can be used to show that $Q_{\text{IDB}}(p^1, p^2, q^1, q^2)$ satisfies the first 11 of Diewert's 13 tests for a bilateral quantity index, failing only the monotonicity in the components of the q^1 and q^2 tests (Diewert 1999, 36). Thus the axiomatic properties of the IDB bilateral quantity index are rather good.
61. See Diewert (1992) for the history of these bilateral tests.
62. If $Q_{\text{IDB}}(r)$ and $Q_T(r)$ are regarded as functions of the vector of quantity relatives, then it can be shown directly that $Q_{\text{IDB}}(r)$ approximates $Q_T(r)$ to the second order around the point $r = 1_N$.
63. The role of prices and quantities must be interchanged—that is, Diewert tests referred to quantity indexes (Diewert 1999, 36), whereas price indexes are now being considered.
64. The expressions involving the reciprocals of ρ_n require that q^2 be strictly positive (in addition to the maintained assumption that y^1 be strictly positive). Equations (5A.32) and (5A.34) require only that y^1 be strictly positive.
65. Equation (5A.19) shows that Q depends only on the components of two N dimensional vectors, r and $s^1 + s^2$.
66. Note that s_1 satisfies the inequalities $0 < s_1 < K$.

67. Thus the π_2 solution to (5A.45) depends only on the vector of country quantity relatives, R, and the sum across countries k of the expenditure shares on commodity 1, s_1^k. Alternatively, π_2 depends on the K dimensional vector R and the sum across countries commodity share vector, $s^1 + \ldots + s^K$, which is a two-dimensional vector in the present context where $N = 2$.
68. It can be verified that $0 < s_1 < K$ so that $\left(\frac{s_1}{K}\right)^{-1} > 1$. The bounds in (5A.49) are positive when $R >> 0_K$. In the case in which $R > 0_K$, the lower bound is still valid, but the upper bound becomes plus infinity.
69. This equation can be utilized to show that $Q_{IDB}(p^1, p^2, q^1, q^2)$ is not necessarily monotonically increasing in the components of q^1 or monotonically decreasing in the components of q^1.
70. Under these conditions, it is also the case that all prices and quantities are positive in the two countries, because it was assumed that y^1 is strictly positive and y^2 is nonnegative and nonzero—that is, $q^1 >> 0_2$ and $q^2 > 0_2$.
71. Diewert (1999, 27) showed that the GK system satisfied all 11 tests except the homogeneity test, T8, and the monotonicity test, T9. The GK system is a "plutocratic" method in which the bigger countries have a greater influence in determining the international price vector π.
72. In this section, it will be assumed that all country prices and quantities are positive, so that $p^k >> 0_N$ and $q^k >> 0_N$ for $k = 1, \ldots, K$.
73. The unit cost function $c(p)$ is an increasing, linearly homogeneous concave function in p for $p >> 0_N$.
74. See Diewert (1974) for material on duality theory and unit cost functions.
75. See Diewert (1999, 21) for more details on the derivation of these equations.
76. The functions f or c are defined to be regular if they satisfy these regularity conditions.
77. Diewert (1999, 27) showed that when K is greater than or equal to three, the GK system is only consistent with a linear or Leontief aggregator function.
78. See Diewert (1999, 46) for descriptions of multilateral methods that have good economic properties—that is, methods that are consistent with maximizing behavior on the part of consumers with preferences represented by flexible functional forms. See Diewert (1976) for the concept of a flexible functional form and the economic approach to index number theory. In addition to the GEKS system, the weighted and unweighted balanced methods of Own Share, MTS, and van Ijzeren (1983) have good economic properties.

REFERENCES

Allen, R. C., and W. E. Diewert. 1981. "Direct versus Implicit Superlative Index Number Formulae." *Review of Economics and Statistics* 63: 430–35.

Aten, B., and A. Heston. 2009. "Chaining Methods for International Real Product and Purchasing Power Comparisons: Issues and Alternatives." In *Purchasing Power Parities of Currencies: Recent Advances in Methods and Applications,* ed. D. S. Prasada Rao, 245–73. Cheltenham, U.K.: Edward Elgar.

Bacharach, M. 1970. *Biproportional Matrices and Input-Output Change.* London: Cambridge University Press.

Balk, B. M. 1996. "A Comparison of Ten Methods for Multilateral International Price and Volume Comparisons." *Journal of Official Statistics* 12: 199–222.

———. 2008. *Price and Quantity Index Numbers: Models for Measuring Aggregate Change and Difference.* New York: Cambridge University Press.

———. 2009. "Aggregation Methods in International Comparisons: An Evaluation." In *Purchasing Power Parities of Currencies: Recent Advances in Methods and Applications,* ed. D. S. Prasada Rao, 59–85. Cheltenham, U.K.: Edward Elgar.

Barnett, W. A., W. E. Diewert, and A. Zellner. 2009. "Introduction to Measurement with Theory." *Macroeconomic Dynamics* 13 (Supplement 2): 151–68.

Deaton, A. 2010. "Price Indexes, Inequality and the Measurement of World Poverty." Presidential Address, American Economic Association, Atlanta, January.

Deaton, A., and A. Heston. 2010. "Understanding PPPs and PPP-Based National Accounts." *American Economics Journal: Macroeconomics* 2 (October).

Deming, W. E., and F. F. Stephan. 1940. "On a Least Squares Adjustment of a Sampled Frequency Table When the Expected Marginal Totals Are Known." *Annals of Mathematical Statistics* 1: 427–44.

Diewert, W. E. 1974. "Applications of Duality Theory." In *Frontiers of Quantitative Economics,* Vol. 2, ed. M. D. Intriligator and D. A. Kendrick, 106–71. Amsterdam: North-Holland.

———. 1976. "Exact and Superlative Index Numbers." *Journal of Econometrics* 4: 114–45.

———. 1988. "Test Approaches to International Comparisons." In *Measurement in Economics: Theory and Applications of Economic Indices,* ed. W. Eichhorn, 6786. Heidelberg: Physica-Verlag.

———. 1992. "Fisher Ideal Output, Input and Productivity Indexes Revisited." *Journal of Productivity Analysis* 3: 211–48.

———. 1996. "Price and Volume Measures in the System of National Accounts." In *The New System of National Accounts,* ed. J. W. Kendrick, 237–85. Boston: Kluwer Academic Publishers.

———. 1999. "Axiomatic and Economic Approaches to International Comparisons." In *International and Interarea Comparisons of Income, Output and Prices,* Studies in Income and Wealth, Vol. 61, ed. A. Heston and R. E. Lipsey, 13–87. Chicago: University of Chicago Press.

———. 2002. "Harmonized Indexes of Consumer Prices: Their Conceptual Foundations." *Swiss Journal of Economics and Statistics* 138: 547–637.

———. 2009. "Similarity Indexes and Criteria for Spatial Linking." In *Purchasing Power Parities of Currencies: Recent Advances in Methods and Applications,* ed. D. S. Prasada Rao, 183–216. Cheltenham, U.K.: Edward Elgar.

———. 2010. "Understanding PPPs and PPP-Based National Accounts: Comment." *American Economic Journal: Macroeconomics* 2: 1–12.

Dikhanov, Y. 1994. "Sensitivity of PPP-Based Income Estimates to Choice of Aggregation Procedures." Paper presented at 23rd General Conference of the International Association for Research in Income and Wealth, St. Andrews, Canada, August 21–27. World Bank, Washington, DC, June 10.

———. 1997. "Sensitivity of PPP-Based Income Estimates to Choice of Aggregation Procedures." Development Data Group, International Economics Department, World Bank, Washington, DC, January. http://siteresources.worldbank.org/ICPINT/Resources/icppapertotal.pdf.

Éltetö, O., and P. Köves. 1964. "On a Problem of Index Number Computation Relating to International Comparison." *Statisztikai Szemle* 42: 507–18.

Feenstra, R. C., H. Ma, and D. S. Prasada Rao. 2009. "Consistent Comparisons of Real Incomes across Time and Space." *Macroeconomic Dynamics* 13 (Supplement 2): 169–93.

Fisher, I. 1922. *The Making of Index Numbers.* Boston: Houghton Mifflin.

Geary, R. G. 1958. "A Note on Comparisons of Exchange Rates and Purchasing Power between Countries." *Journal of the Royal Statistical Society Series A* 121: 97–99.

Gini, C. 1924. "Quelques considérations au sujet de la construction des nombres indices des prix et des questions analogues." *Metron* 4 (1): 3–162.

———. 1931. "On the Circular Test of Index Numbers." *Metron* 9 (9): 3–24.

Hill, P. 2007a. "Aggregation Methods." In *ICP 2005 Methodological Handbook*. Washington, DC: World Bank. http://siteresources.worldbank.org/ICPINT/Resources/ch12.doc.

———. 2007b. "Estimation of PPPs for Basic Headings within Regions." In *ICP 2005 Methodological Handbook*. Washington, DC: World Bank. http://siteresources.worldbank.org/ICPINT/Resources/Ch11.doc.

Hill, R. J. 1997. "A Taxonomy of Multilateral Methods for Making International Comparisons of Prices and Quantities." *Review of Income and Wealth* 43 (1): 49–69.

———. 1999a. "Comparing Price Levels across Countries Using Minimum Spanning Trees." *Review of Economics and Statistics* 81: 135–42.

———. 1999b. "International Comparisons Using Spanning Trees." In *International and Interarea Comparisons of Income, Output and Prices,* Studies in Income and Wealth, Vol. 61, ed. A. Heston and R. E. Lipsey, 109–20. Chicago: University of Chicago Press.

———. 2001. "Measuring Inflation and Growth Using Spanning Trees." *International Economic Review* 42: 167–85.

———. 2004. "Constructing Price Indexes across Space and Time: The Case of the European Union." *American Economic Review* 94: 1379–1410.

———. 2009. "Comparing Per Capita Income Levels across Countries Using Spanning Trees: Robustness, Prior Restrictions, Hybrids and Hierarchies." In *Purchasing Power Parities of Currencies: Recent Advances in Methods and Applications,* ed. D. S. Prasada Rao, 217–44. Cheltenham, U.K.: Edward Elgar.

Iklé, D. M. 1972. "A New Approach to the Index Number Problem." *Quarterly Journal of Economics* 86 (2): 188–211.

International Labour Organization, International Monetary Fund, Organisation for Economic Co-operation and Development, UN Economic Commission for Europe, Eurostat, and World Bank. 2004. *Consumer Price Index Manual: Theory and Practice,* ed. Peter Hill. Geneva: ILO.

Khamis, S. H. 1972. "A New System of Index Numbers for National and International Purposes." *Journal of the Royal Statistical Society Series A* 135: 96–121.

Konüs, A. A., and S. S. Byushgens. 1926. "K probleme pokupatelnoi cili deneg." *Voprosi Konyunkturi* 2: 151–72.

Kravis, I. B., A. Heston, and R. Summers. 1982. *World Product and Income: International Comparisons of Real Gross Product.* Statistical Office of the United Nations and the World Bank. Baltimore: Johns Hopkins University Press.

Marris, R. 1984. "Comparing the Incomes of Nations: A Critique of the International Comparison Project." *Journal of Economic Literature* 22: 1, 40–57.

Neary, J. P. 2004. "Rationalizing the Penn World Tables: True Multilateral Indices for International Comparisons of Real Income." *American Economic Review* 94: 1411–428.

Rao, D. S. Prasada. 1990. "A System of Log-Change Index Numbers for Multilateral Comparisons." In *Comparisons of Prices and Real Products in Latin America,* ed. J. Salazar-Carillo and D. S. Prasada Rao, 127–39. New York: Elsevier Science Publishers.

———. 2009. "Generalised Éltetö-Köves-Szulc (EKS) and Country-Product-Dummy (CPD) Methods for International Comparisons." In *Purchasing Power Parities of Currencies: Recent Advances in Methods and Applications,* ed. D. S. Prasada Rao, 86–120. Cheltenham, U.K.: Edward Elgar.

Rao, D. S. Prasada, S. Shankar, and G. Hajarghasht. 2010. "A Minimum Distance and the Generalized EKS Approaches to Multilateral Comparisons of Prices and Real Incomes." Unpublished paper, University of Queensland, Australia, May 7.

Sergeev, S. 2001. "Measures of the Similarity of the Country's Price Structures and Their Practical Application." Conference on the European Comparison Program, UN Statistical Commission, Economic Commission for Europe, Geneva, November 12–14.

———. 2009. "Aggregation Methods Based on Structural International Prices." In *Purchasing Power Parities of Currencies: Recent Advances in Methods and Applications,* ed. D. S. Prasada Rao, 274–97. Cheltenham, U.K.: Edward Elgar.

Stone, R. 1962. "Multiple Classifications in Social Accounting." *Bulletin de l'Institut International de Statistique* 39: 215–33.

Szulc, B. 1964. "Indices for Multiregional Comparisons." *Przeglad Statystyczny* 3: 239–54.

van Ijzeren, J. 1983. *Index Numbers for Binary and Multilateral Comparison.* Statistical Studies 34. The Hague: Central Bureau of Statistics.

CHAPTER 6

Methods of Aggregation above the Basic Heading Level: Linking the Regions

W. Erwin Diewert

This chapter discusses the various methods for linking the five regions[1] of the International Comparison Program (ICP) and those countries in the Eurostat-OECD PPP Programme in such a way that the relative country volumes within each region are preserved.[2]

The 2005 ICP round of international comparisons was quite different from earlier ICP rounds for a number of reasons:

- Each of the six regions prepared its own list of representative (for its region) products. These products were priced by each country in the region over the reference year, whereas in previous ICP comparisons there was a single product list for all countries over all regions.
- Each region was allowed to use its preferred multilateral method to make comparisons within the region. Five of the six regions chose to use the Gini-Éltetö-Köves-Szulc (GEKS) method, and the Africa region used the additive Iklé-Dikhanov-Balk (IDB) method.[3]
- Each region was also allowed to use slightly different methods for constructing basic heading purchasing power parities (BH PPPs) across countries in the region.[4]
- To link the regions, another separate product list was developed, and these products were priced by *18 Ring countries* of which two or more were in each region.[5] This additional set of prices across regions allowed the 155 BH PPPs to be linked across regions.
- At the final stage of aggregation of the 2005 ICP (the subject of this chapter), the within-region aggregate volumes for each country in a region were linked across the six regions, giving rise to a complete set of 146 aggregate PPPs and relative volumes for each country.

The final stage in the process, which involved linking the regions, proved to be the most challenging. The various regions involved in the 2005 ICP wanted the final linking procedure to leave unchanged the relative volumes for the countries in their region—that is, they sought a so-called *fixity constraint* on the final step, which links the regional parities into a set of global parities. The problem associated with linking the regions in a way that would preserve the within-region parities was not new to the 2005 ICP; Kravis, Heston, and Summers (1982, 117–23) and Heston (1986) discussed this problem many years ago.

Diewert (2004, 46–47) suggested a class of methods for linking the regions in the 2005 ICP round that would preserve relative volumes for country aggregates within a region, but would at the same time link the various regions so that volumes could be compared across all countries in the ICP comparison in a consistent manner—that is, his suggested interregional linking method would satisfy the fixity constraint. The basic idea behind the method is as follows. Once information on country expenditures for each basic heading (BH) category in each country in a region is determined, along with the 155 corresponding BH PPPs, then the BH expenditures in the local currencies can be divided by the corresponding PPPs to obtain country volumes in consistent comparable units by basic heading category. These volumes (or loosely speaking, quantities) can then be added across countries within the region in order to obtain *total regional volumes* or "quantities" by basic heading category. Then, with an appropriate choice of BH prices for each region, these BH regional "prices" and "quantities" can be linked using any multilateral method such as the GEKS method (see chapter 5).[6] Once the regional real expenditure shares have been determined by the chosen multilateral method, they can be combined with each region's country shares of regional real expenditures to give each country's share of world real expenditures. Note that this method will not affect the country shares of regional expenditures that are determined independently by each region. Note also that this method is very similar to the methods used by national income accountants to determine the annual real output of a nation by aggregating over quarterly data.

The problem with this class of methods for linking the regions is determining exactly how the *regional* basic heading "prices" should be chosen. These regional "price" or PPP vectors should be chosen so that the overall method leads to country (and regional) relative volumes that are independent of the choice of both the numeraire region and the numeraire countries within each region. Section 6.1 of this chapter explores several options for the regional BH prices. Option 1 does lead to relative volumes that are independent of the choice of numeraire regions and numeraire countries within each region, but the resulting method involves the use of country exchange rates, which is not a desirable feature. Option 2 does not involve the use of exchange rates, but the resulting method is dependent on the choice of the regional numeraire countries, which again is not a desirable feature.[7] Finally, option 3, which was suggested by Sergeev (2009b), does lead to relative volumes that are independent of the choice of numeraire regions and numeraire countries within each region, and this method for linking the regions does not involve the use of exchange rates.

All of the variants of the method just described for linking the regions are based on two important properties within each region: (1) volumes are added up across countries in the region to obtain total regional volumes by BH category of expenditure; and (2) a single set of BH reference PPPs or "prices" is applied to those regional volumes for each region.

As mentioned earlier, the first property is analogous to practices in the *System of National Accounts* in which annual quantities by expenditure category are obtained by adding up quarterly or monthly quantities. Therefore, this aspect of the linking method is not necessarily problematic. However, in the national accounting context the structure of prices tends to be very similar from quarter to quarter within a year. Thus in the national accounts, the annual price for a commodity is usually taken to be an annual unit value—that is, the total expenditure or revenue for the commodity is summed up over, say, quarters and divided by the total quantity used or produced during the year, and this unit value is used as the annual price of the commodity.[8] Using an annual unit value price in the context of aggregating over time is generally not a problem, because the price of a commodity usually does not vary too much within a year. However, when one is aggregating quantities across countries within a region, the variations in commodity prices can be very large, and, generally speaking, no single vector of commodity prices will be representative of the structure of commodity prices for every country in the region. Thus the property of these methods in which a regional quantity vector is calculated by addition over country quantity vectors means that all of these methods are essentially *additive methods* (within each region) and hence subject to *substitution bias.*[9] For the 2011 ICP, then, other methods for linking the region should be considered, but while respecting within-region parities.

Sections 6.2, 6.3, and 6.4 of this chapter consider alternative linking methods. Section 6.2 describes the first alternative method for constructing interregional parities while respecting within-region parities—see Heston (1986, 3) and Dikhanov (2007). Heston suggested using the Geary-Khamis (GK) method, whereas Dikhanov suggested that the GEKS method be used in a single comparison over all countries in the comparison. It will generate shares of world real expenditures for each country. One can then simply add up the shares of world real expenditures of the countries in each region in order to obtain the regional shares. These between-region shares plus the within-region shares (determined independently by the regions) will generate an overall set of shares that respect the within-region parities.

Section 6.3 discusses a variant of the method used in section 6.2. Instead of relying on the GEKS method to generate individual country shares for each country in the comparison, one could use Robert J. Hill's minimum spanning tree (MST) or similarity or spatial linking method to form the shares of each country's output in the world aggregate.[10] As noted in chapter 5, the basic idea behind this method is to link countries through a series of bilateral comparisons in which the overall comparison rests on a chain of bilateral comparisons between countries that are most similar in their (relative) price structures.

Section 6.4 of this chapter discusses a "new" method for linking the regions while respecting the within-region parities.[11] In section 6.5, regional parities are computed for a small artificial data set using the methods suggested in sections 6.1–6.4. In section 6.6, another numerical example based on a subset of the 1985 ICP data is computed to again illustrate the fact that different methods can give quite different results.

The methods suggested in this chapter that could be used to form aggregate PPPs for the 146 countries in the comparisons (over the entire set of 155 basic heading product groups) while respecting the fixity constraint within regions could also be used to form PPPs for *subsets* of the 155 BH product groups—for example, the same techniques could be used to form a set of consumption PPPs for the 146 countries.

6.1 Variants of Diewert's Suggested Method for Linking the Regions

This section begins by defining what basic data are needed to link the ICP regions in a fashion that will respect the parities and relative volumes determined within each region. It is assumed that R regions are in the comparison, and region r is made up of $C(r)$ countries for $r = 1, 2, \ldots, R$. In the 2005 ICP, R was equal to 6, with varying numbers of countries in each region. Assume there are N basic heading commodity groups and each country in the comparison has collected expenditure data on these N commodity groups in its own currency. In the 2005 ICP, N was equal to 155. Let E_{rcn} be the expenditure (in the currency of country c in region r) on commodity class n for the reference year for $r = 1, \ldots, R$; $c = 1, \ldots, C(r)$; $n = 1, \ldots, N$. Assume that these country expenditure data have been collected.

Also assume that each region r has constructed a purchasing power parity for each BH commodity group n and each country c in region r, α_{rcn} say, for $r = 1, \ldots, R$; $c = 1, \ldots, C(r)$, and $n = 1, \ldots, N$. Assume that country $c = 1$ is the numeraire country in each region, and so the PPP for this numeraire country is set equal to unity so that

$$\alpha_{r1n} = 1; \quad r = 1, \ldots, R; n = 1, \ldots, N. \tag{6.1}$$

Thus for $c \neq 1$, α_{rcn} is the price in the currency of country c in region r of a bundle of the products in BH commodity group n, which costs one currency unit in the currency of the numeraire country (country 1) for region r.

The next assumption is that the central office has constructed a set of *interregional linking PPPs*, β_{rn}, that link the PPPs of the numeraire country in each region with the numeraire country in the numeraire region, which is assumed to be region 1. Thus assume that

$$\beta_{1n} = 1; \quad n = 1, \ldots, N. \tag{6.2}$$

For $r \neq 1$, β_{rn} is the price in the currency of country 1 in region r of a bundle of commodity n, which costs one currency unit in the currency of the numeraire country (country 1) in region 1, the numeraire region.

Now the two sets of PPPs can be multiplied to form a consistent set of *world basic heading PPPs*, γ_{rcn}, defined as

$$\gamma_{rcn} \equiv \beta_{rn}\alpha_{rcn}; \quad r = 1, \ldots, R; c = 1, \ldots, C(r); n = 1, \ldots, N. \tag{6.3}$$

Thus γ_{rcn} is the price in the currency of country c in region r of a bundle of BH commodity group n, which costs one currency unit in the currency of the numeraire country (country 1) in the numeraire region (region 1).

If the numeraire region is changed, what happens to the world BH PPPs, γ_{rcn}, defined by (6.3)? Suppose region 2 replaces region 1 as the numeraire region. In this case, the original linking BH PPPs, β_{rn}, should be replaced by the new linking PPPs, defined as

$$\beta^*_{rn} \equiv \frac{\beta_{rn}}{\beta_{2n}}; \quad r = 1, \ldots, R; n = 1, \ldots, N \tag{6.4}$$

and the original set of world BH PPPs, γ_{rcn}, defined by (6.3) should be replaced by the following new set of world BH PPPs:

$$\gamma^*_{rcn} \equiv \beta^*_{rn}\alpha_{rcn} = \frac{\gamma_{rcn}}{\beta_{2n}}; \quad r = 1, \ldots, R; c = 1, \ldots, C(r); n = 1, \ldots, N. \tag{6.5}$$

Thus the new set of world BH PPPs is equal to the old set of world BH PPPs except for a divisor that depends on the BH commodity n under consideration. Hence the net effect of switching the numeraire region is to leave the PPPs unchanged except that the new set of PPPs is measured in a *new system of units*. Instead of measuring commodity units in terms of a dollar's worth of purchases of BH commodity n in the numeraire country of region 1, commodity units are now measured in terms of a peso's worth of purchases of BH commodity n in the numeraire country of region 2.

Now suppose that the numeraire country in a region is changed. If the change of numeraire country is outside region 1 (say, in region 2 where there is a switch from country 1 to country 2 as the numeraire country), then nothing will happen to the world BH PPPs, γ_{rcn}. The old $\gamma_{rcn} = \beta_{rn}\alpha_{rcn}$ will remain the same for all regions r except for $r = 2$, and for the second region α_{2cn} will be replaced by $\frac{\alpha_{2cn}}{\alpha_{22n}}$ for $n = 1, \ldots, N$ and $c = 1, \ldots, C(2)$, and β_{2n} will be replaced by $\beta_{2n}\alpha_{22n}$ for $n = 1, \ldots, N$. Thus the new γ^*_{rcn} will still equal the old γ_{rcn} for all r, including $r = 2$.

If the change of numeraire country is within region 1 so that the new numeraire country in region 1 is country 2 in place of country 1, then the within-region parities for region 1 become $\frac{\alpha_{1cn}}{\alpha_{12n}}$ for $n = 1, \ldots, N$, and the new set of interregional linking BH PPPs becomes $\frac{\beta_{2n}}{\alpha_{12n}}$ for $n = 1, \ldots, N$. Thus in this case, the new set of world BH PPPs becomes

(6.6) $$\gamma^*_{rcn} = \frac{\gamma_{rcn}}{\alpha_{12n}}; \quad r = 1, \ldots, R; c = 1, \ldots, C(r); n = 1, \ldots, N.$$

Thus in this change of the numeraire country within the numeraire region, the new set of world BH PPPs is equal to the old set of world BH PPPs except for a divisor that depends on the BH commodity n under consideration. Hence as it is for the change in the numeraire region, the net effect of switching the numeraire country within the numeraire region is to leave the BH PPPs unchanged except that the new set of BH PPPs is measured using a *new system of units.*

Recall that a knowledge of the expenditures (in the local currencies) of country c in region r by BH commodity class n, E_{rcn}, is assumed for $r = 1, \ldots, R$; $c = 1, \ldots, C(r)$; $n = 1, \ldots, N$. This expenditure information is used, along with the consistent set of world BH PPPs, γ_{rcn} as defined by (6.3), to define consistent (across countries) *volumes* or *imputed quantities*, Q_{rcn}, for each BH commodity group n and each country c in each region r as

(6.7) $$Q_{rcn} \equiv \frac{E_{rcn}}{\gamma_{rcn}}; \quad r = 1, \ldots, R; c = 1, \ldots, C(r); n = 1, \ldots, N.$$

These imputed quantities or volumes are measured in units that are comparable across countries and regions. Thus these "quantities" can be added across countries within a region. The resulting regional totals, Q_{rn}, are also comparable across regions—that is, they define *regional total volumes by commodity class* as

(6.8) $$Q_{rcn} \equiv \sum_{c=1}^{C(r)} Q_{rcn}; \quad r = 1, \ldots, R; n = 1, \ldots, N.$$

Now form *regional volume* or *imputed quantity* vectors from Q_{rn}:

(6.9) $$Q^r \equiv [Q_{r1}, \ldots, Q_{rN}]; \quad r = 1, \ldots, R.$$

Note that if the numeraire region or the numeraire countries within a region are changed, then, if the world BH PPPs are changed in a consistent manner, the regional volume vectors will be identical to the initial regional volume vectors defined by (6.7)–(6.9), except that the units of measurement for these vectors may have been changed by the change in numeraires. In other words, a change in the numeraire region or numeraire country within a region will lead to identical regional quantity vectors Q^r or to a new set of Q^{r*} that is equal to $\hat{\delta}Q^r$ where $\hat{\delta}$ is a diagonal matrix in which the diagonal elements reflect changes in the units of measurement of the N commodity groups.

Regional BH PPP or "price" vectors P^r are now needed to match up with the regional volume vectors Q^r defined by (6.9). At this point, there are at least three possible strategies, and each is discussed in turn in the sections that follow.

Option 1: Conversion to Regional Currency Unit Values

The strategy using this option would be to first convert country expenditures in each BH commodity classification category into common regional expenditures (in a numeraire country's currency) using market exchange rates for the reference year. Then, deflate these regional commodity expenditures by the corresponding regional quantities defined by (6.8) in order to form regional unit value prices, which will be used as the regional prices. As noted at the outset of this chapter, this is the same type of strategy used by national income accountants in forming annual price and quantity vectors from subannual information.

Suppose the *reference year exchange rate* for country c in region r is ε_{rc} for $r = 1, \ldots, R$ and $c = 1, \ldots, C(r)$. Assume that country 1 in each region is the numeraire region as usual so that

$$(6.10) \qquad \varepsilon_{r1} = 1; \quad r = 1, \ldots, R.$$

Thus ε_{rc} for $c \neq 1$ indicates how many units of the currency of the numeraire country (country 1) in region r is equal to one unit of the currency unit of country c in region r. These market exchange rates can be used to convert country expenditures (in the country's currency) on commodity class n within region r into region r numeraire currency units $V_{rcn} \equiv \varepsilon_{rc} E_{rcn}$, and then these country expenditures on BH commodity class n in a common regional currency can be summed to regional totals V_{rn} defined as

$$(6.11) \qquad V_{rn} \equiv \sum_{c=1}^{C(r)} \varepsilon_{rc} E_{rcn}; \quad r = 1, \ldots, R; n = 1 \ldots, N.$$

Now *regional PPPs* or *unit value prices* P_{rn} can be formed by taking the regional values defined by (6.11) and dividing them by the corresponding regional volume or quantity totals Q_{rn} defined by (6.8) so that

$$(6.12) \qquad P_{rn} \equiv \frac{V_{rn}}{Q_{rn}}; \quad r = 1, \ldots, R; n = 1, \ldots, N.$$

Finally, form *regional unit value price vectors* from the components P_{rn} so that

$$(6.13) \qquad P^r \equiv [P_{r1}, \ldots, P_{rN}]; \quad r = 1, \ldots, R.$$

Now consider what happens to the regional total expenditures on commodity class n, V_{rn}, if a numeraire country within a region is changed or there is a change in the numeraire region. If the numeraire region is changed, nothing happens to regional expenditures defined by (6.11) because it is not necessary to relate the regional exchange rates across regions. However, if the numeraire country within region r is changed, then it can be seen that all the regional values for this region will change by a scalar factor—that is, if in region r the numeraire country is changed from country 1 to country 2, then the new market exchange rates will be $\frac{\varepsilon_{rc}}{\varepsilon_{r2}}$ for $c = 1, \ldots, C(r)$, and hence the new regional totals for region r will be

$$(6.14) \qquad V^*_{rn} \equiv \sum_{c=1}^{C(r)} \left[\frac{\varepsilon_{rc}}{\varepsilon_{r2}}\right] E_{rcn} = \frac{V_{rn}}{\varepsilon_{r2}}; \quad n = 1, \ldots, N.$$

Thus the new regional expenditure totals on the N commodity groups in region r, V^*_{rcn}, will be equal to a scalar multiple $\left(\frac{1}{\varepsilon_{r2}}\right)$ times the old regional expenditure totals in region r, V_{rn}.

This is a careful exposition of the regional unit value method for forming regional price and quantity vectors that could be used to link the regions by relying on a multilateral index number method with the regional price and quantity vectors as the input vectors to the method.

Now consider linking the R regions using a *multilateral index number method* (see chapter 5). Diewert (1999) defined such methods in terms of share functions for the R regions—that is, he looked at a system of *shares of world output or real expenditures*, $s_1(P^1, \ldots, P^R; Q^1, \ldots, Q^R), \ldots, s_R(P^1, \ldots, P^R; Q^1, \ldots, Q^R)$, where $s_r(P^1, \ldots, P^R; Q^1, \ldots, Q^R)$ is region r's share of world output and considered the axiomatic properties of such multilateral systems. The next question to be addressed: what properties does the multilateral method have to satisfy to ensure that the regional shares are independent of the choice of the numeraire region and the numeraire countries within the regions?

From the previous discussion, it is clear that the multilateral method must satisfy the following two properties:

Property 1: Invariance to changes in the units of measurement.
Thus let $\delta_n > 0$ for $n = 1, \ldots, N$ and define δ as the $N \times N$ matrix with the elements δ_n running down the main diagonal. Then this property requires that the multilateral share system satisfy the following equations:

$$(6.15) \qquad s_r(\hat{\delta}P^1, \ldots, \hat{\delta}P^R; \hat{\delta}^{-1}Q^1, \ldots, \hat{\delta}^{-1}Q^R) = s_r(P^1, \ldots, P^R; Q^1, \ldots, Q^R); \quad r = 1, \ldots, R.$$

Property 2: Homogeneity of degree zero in the regional price vectors.
Let $\lambda_1 > 0, \ldots, \lambda_R > 0$. Then this property requires that the multilateral share system satisfy the following equations:

$$(6.16) \qquad s_r(\lambda_1 P^1, \ldots, \lambda_R P^R; Q^1, \ldots, Q^R) = s_r(P^1, \ldots, P^R; Q^1, \ldots, Q^R); \quad r = 1, \ldots, R.$$

This homogeneity property means that it is the relative regional prices that affect the interregional volume comparisons and not the absolute level of regional prices.

These two properties are also sufficient to imply that a multilateral method using the unit value regional price and quantity vectors defined earlier will generate regional shares that are independent of the choice of the numeraire region and the numeraire countries within the regions. The GEKS multilateral method satisfies these two properties (see Diewert 1999, 33).

A drawback of this method for linking the regions is that it brings market exchange rates into the picture. Because these rates are often far removed from their corresponding PPPs, it is desirable to avoid their use in constructing the interregional PPPs and relative volumes. The following two methods make use of the regional "quantity" vectors Q^r defined by (6.8), but the corresponding regional "price" vectors P^r do not use exchange rates.

Option 2: Use of Regional Numeraires as Regional Price Weights

It is not necessary to bring in market exchange rates to convert regional expenditures into a common currency. Instead, one can simply use the PPPs for each numeraire country 1 in each region r

(relative to the numeraire country in the numeraire region, β_{rn}, as described earlier) as the price for commodity n in region r—that is, one can define the regional price for commodity n in region r as

$$(6.17) \qquad P_{rn} \equiv \beta_{rn}; \quad r = 1, \ldots, R; n = 1, \ldots, N.$$

Then use (6.13) to form the *regional price* or *PPP vectors* P^r in the usual way. The regional *total volume* or *quantity vectors,* Q^r, are defined as before by (6.7)–(6.9), and these equations do not involve exchange rates. Finally, use these regional price and quantity vectors, P^r and Q^r, to calculate the share functions for the R regions using a favored multilateral method, $s_1(P^1, \ldots, P^R; Q^1, \ldots, Q^R), \ldots, s_R(P^1, \ldots, P^R; Q^1, \ldots, Q^R)$, where $s_r(P^1, \ldots, P^R; Q^1, \ldots, Q^R)$ is region r's share of world output.

Unfortunately, as Sergeev (2009b) points out, this method is not invariant to the choice of the numeraire countries within the regions. Thus this method should not be used in the 2011 ICP.

Option 3: Use of the Geometric Average of the Regional Numeraires as Regional Price Weights

Sergeev (2009b) suggested a way to avoid the lack of numeraire invariance in option 2: within each region take the *geometric mean of the country parities* over all countries in the region. Thus (6.17) is replaced by[12]

$$(6.18) \qquad P_{rn} \equiv \prod_{c=1}^{C(r)} \gamma_{rcn}^{\frac{1}{C(r)}}; \quad r = 1, \ldots, R; n = 1, \ldots, N.$$

Then use (6.13) to form the *regional price vectors,* P^r, in the usual way. Finally, use the regional "price" and "quantity" vectors defined by (6.9), P^r and Q^r, to calculate the share functions for the R regions using a favored multilateral method, $s_1(P^1, \ldots, P^R; Q^1, \ldots, Q^R), \ldots, s_R(P^1, \ldots, P^R; Q^1, \ldots, Q^R)$, where $s_r(P^1, \ldots, P^R; Q^1, \ldots, Q^R)$ is region r's share of world output. If the multilateral method satisfies property 1 (invariance to changes in the units of measurement), then the resulting regional shares will be invariant to the choices of both numeraire countries and the numeraire region.

As noted earlier, option 2 can be ruled out as a method for linking the regions for the 2011 ICP because of its lack of country numeraire invariance within the regions. However, there is a good case for ruling out options 1 and 3 as well because all the methods in this section *impose a set of common prices to add up the volumes or quantities within a region*—that is, the methods impose a form of *additivity.* Additive multilateral methods are subject to *substitution bias* if three or more countries are in the comparison.[13]

Thus the two sections that follow discuss *nonadditive methods* for linking the regions that avoid the substitution bias inherent in the methods discussed in this section.

6.2 The Global Comparison GEKS Method

Recall the definitions in (6.7) that defined the volume or "quantity" of commodity n, Q_{rcn}, that was finally demanded by purchasers in country c in region r. Define country c in the region r volume vector, Q^{rc}, in the usual way, using the definitions in (6.7) to define the components Q_{rcn}:

$$(6.19) \qquad Q^{rc} \equiv [Q_{rc1}, \ldots, Q_{rcN}]; \quad r = 1, \ldots, R; c = 1, \ldots, C(r).$$

The country "price" vectors P^{rc} that correspond to the country "quantity" vectors Q^{rc} defined by (6.19) are in turn defined using the global set of PPPs, γ_{rcn}, defined by (6.3). Recall that γ_{rcn} is the price in the currency of country c in region r of a bundle of commodity n, which costs one currency unit in the currency of the numeraire country (country 1) in the numeraire region (region 1). The basic heading price vector for country c in region r, P^{rc}, is defined as

$$(6.20) \qquad P^{rc} \equiv [\gamma_{rc1}, \ldots, \gamma_{rcN}]; \quad r = 1, \ldots, R; c = 1, \ldots, C(r).$$

Thus there are country "price" and "quantity" vectors (P^{rc}, Q^{rc}) for all $C(1) + C(2) + \cdots + C(R)$ countries in the ICP.

At this stage, any multilateral method could be used to form price comparisons between each individual country participating in the ICP. One such multilateral method with good axiomatic and economic properties is the GEKS.[14] The algebra for this method works as follows. First, define the *Fisher quantity index* (Fisher 1922) for country c in region r relative to country d in region s as[15]

$$(6.21) \qquad Q_F\left(\frac{rc}{sd}\right) \equiv \left[\frac{P^{rc} \cdot Q^{rc} P^{sd} \cdot Q^{rc}}{P^{rc} \cdot Q^{sd} P^{sd} \cdot Q^{sd}}\right]^{\frac{1}{2}}; \quad \begin{array}{l} r = 1, \ldots, R; c = 1, \ldots, C(r); \\ s = 1, \ldots, R; d = 1, \ldots, C(s) \end{array}$$

where $P^{rc} \cdot Q^{rc} \equiv \sum_{n=1}^{N} P_{rcn} Q_{rcn}$ denotes the inner product between the vectors P^{rc} and Q^{rc}. If the base country is fixed (i.e., fix region s and country d in region s) and if $r = 1, \ldots, R$ and $c = 1, \ldots, C(r)$, then the Fisher indexes defined by (6.21) can be interpreted as the volume of each country rc in the comparison relative to the base country sd, and then these relative volumes can be normalized into a set of shares of world product using country sd as the base country—that is, a set of country "star" shares are obtained for each rc with country sd as the "star" country.[16] The GEKS method is then used to take the geometric mean of all of these country parities over all possible "star" bases. Thus define these geometric mean relative parities as

$$(6.22) \quad Q(rc) \equiv \left[\prod_{s=1}^{R} \prod_{d=1}^{C(s)} Q_F\left(\frac{rc}{sd}\right)\right]^{\frac{1}{[C(1)+\cdots+C(R)]}}; \quad r = 1, \ldots, R; c = 1, \ldots, C(r).$$

Now normalize the relative parities given by (6.22) into country shares of world product. Thus define the sum of the parities defined by (6.22) as σ:

$$(6.23) \qquad \sigma \equiv \sum_{r=1}^{R} \sum_{c=1}^{C(r)} Q(rc).$$

The GEKS share of world real final expenditure for country c in region r can now be defined as $Q(rc)$ divided by σ:

$$(6.24) \qquad s_{rc} \equiv \frac{Q(rc)}{\sigma}; \quad r = 1, \ldots, R; c = 1, \ldots, C(r).$$

Following Heston (1986) and Dikhanov (2007),[17] one can aggregate over the individual country shares of world product defined by (6.24) within each region to obtain the following *GEKS regional shares of world output:*

$$(6.25) \qquad S_r \equiv \sum_{c=1}^{C(r)} s_{rc}; \quad r = 1, \ldots, R.$$

The between-region shares $S_1, S_2, \ldots, S_R$ defined by (6.25) can be used in conjunction with the within-region shares in each region to obtain a system of world product shares for each country. The resulting parities will respect the regional parities that are independently determined by the regions.

Why should the GEKS regional shares defined by (6.25) be preferred over the various regional shares defined in the previous section? The GEKS shares are consistent with broader patterns of substitutability between commodities—that is, if the preferences of each country can be represented by certain homothetic preferences (that can approximate arbitrary homothetic preferences to the second order), then the GEKS country shares will give exactly the "right" relative volumes across countries.[18]

The following section describes a variant of the method used in this section.

6.3 Spatial Comparisons Based on Similar Price Structures

The GEKS multilateral method treats each country "star" parity as equally valid, and hence an averaging of the parities is appropriate under this hypothesis. However, are all bilateral comparisons of volume between two countries equally accurate? One could argue that the answer to this question is yes if the relative prices in countries A and B are very similar. Then the Paasche and Laspeyres quantity indexes will be very close, and therefore it is likely that the "true" volume comparison between these two countries (using the economic approach to index number theory) will be very close to the Fisher volume comparison. On the other hand, if the structure of relative prices in the two countries is very different, it is likely that the structure of relative quantities in the two countries will also be different. Then the Paasche and Laspeyres quantity indexes will likely differ considerably, and one can no longer be certain that the Fisher quantity index will be close to the "true" volume comparison. These considerations suggest that a more accurate set of world product shares could be constructed if an initial bilateral comparison were made between the two countries that have the most similar relative price structures. Then look for a third country that has the price structure most similar to those of the first two countries and link this third country to the comparisons of volume between the first two countries and so on. At the end of this procedure, Hill's *minimum spanning tree* would be constructed: a path between all countries that minimizes the sum of the relative price similarity measures. A key aspect of this methodology is the choice of the measure of similarity (or dissimilarity) of the relative price structures of two countries. Various measures of the similarity or dissimilarity of relative price structures have been proposed by Aten and Heston (2009), Diewert (2009), Hill (2009), and Sergeev (2001, 2009a). Diewert (2009, 207) suggested the following *weighted log quadratic (WLQ) measure of relative price dissimilarity*, $\Delta_{WLQ}(p^1, p^2, q^1, q^2)$ (the smaller the measure, the more similar is the structure of relative prices between the two countries):

$$\Delta_{WLQ}(p^1, p^2, q^1, q^2) \equiv \sum_{n=1}^{N} \left(\frac{1}{2}\right)\left(s_n^1 + s_n^2\right)\left[\ln\left(\frac{p_n^2}{p_n^1 P_F(p^1, p^2, q^1, q^2)}\right)\right]^2 \quad (6.26)$$

where $P_F(p^1, p^2, q^1, q^2) \equiv \left[\frac{(p^2 \cdot q^1 p^2 \cdot q^2)}{(p^1 \cdot q^1 p^1 \cdot q^2)}\right]^{\frac{1}{2}}$ is the Fisher ideal price index between countries 2 and 1,

and $s_n^c \equiv \frac{p_c^n \cdot q_c^n}{p^c \cdot q^c}$ is the country c expenditure share on basic heading category n for $c = 1, 2$ and $n = 1, \ldots, N$.

Diewert (2009, 208) also suggested the *weighted asymptotically quadratic (WAQ) measure of relative price dissimilarity,* $\Delta_{\text{WAQ}}(p^1, p^2, q^1, q^2)$:[19]

$$\text{(6.27)} \quad \Delta_{\text{WAQ}}(p^1, p^2, q^1, q^2) \equiv \sum_{n=1}^{N} \left(\frac{1}{2}\right)(s_n^1 + s_n^2)\left\{\left[\frac{p_n^2}{p_n^1 P_F(p^1, p^2, q^1, q^2)} - 1\right]^2 + \left[\frac{P_F(p^1, p^2, q^1, q^2)\, p_n^1}{p_n^2} - 1\right]^2\right\}.$$

If prices are proportional for the two countries so that $p^2 = \lambda p^1$ for some positive scalar λ, then $P_F(p^1, p^2, q^1, q^2) = \lambda$, and the measures of relative price dissimilarity defined by (6.26) and (6.27) will equal its minimum of 0. Thus the smaller is $\Delta_{\text{WLQ}}(p^1, p^2, q^1, q^2)$ or $\Delta_{\text{WAQ}}(p^1, p^2, q^1, q^2)$, the more similar is the structure of relative prices in the two countries. These two measures of price dissimilarity were the measures of relative price dissimilarity preferred by Diewert (2009), and they will be used in sections 6.5 and 6.6 in numerical examples to illustrate the MST method for making multilateral comparisons. The following measure of relative price dissimilarity is used in the numerical examples as well; it was also used by Kravis, Heston, and Summers (1982, 105) and Hill (1999a, 1999b, 2001, 2004). It is essentially a normalization of the relative spread between the Paasche and Laspeyres price indexes, and so it is known as the *Paasche-Laspeyres spread (PLS) relative price dissimilarity measure:*

$$\text{(6.28)} \quad \Delta_{\text{PLS}}(p^1, p^2, q^1, q^2) \equiv \max\left\{\frac{P_L}{P_P}, \frac{P_P}{P_L}\right\} - 1$$

where $P_L \equiv \dfrac{p^2 \cdot q^1}{p^1 \cdot q^1}$ and $\equiv \dfrac{p^2 \cdot q^2}{p^1 \cdot q^2}$. As noted in chapter 5, a major problem with this measure of relative price dissimilarity is that it is possible for P_L to equal P_P, and yet p^2 could be very far from being proportional to p^1.

As noted, Hill's MST method of similarity or spatial linking using the three measures of relative price dissimilarity just described will be illustrated in the sections 6.5 and 6.6. using small numerical examples. Basically, instead of using the GEKS country shares s_{rc} defined by (6.24) in the previous section, the shares generated by the minimum spanning tree (relying on the three dissimilarity measures) are used to link all of the countries in the ICP. Once these country shares s_{rc} have been defined, again use equations (6.25) in order to form the regional shares S_r.

The next section describes yet another method proposed for linking the regions.

6.4 A Least Squares Method for Linking the Regions

Recently, another method for linking the regions while respecting regional parities was proposed by Robert J. Hill (2010). In order to explain how this method works, it is useful to define some new notation that is related to the notation used at the beginning of this chapter. As in section 6.1, it is assumed that there are R regions, and that region r is made up of $C(r)$ countries for $r = 1, 2, \ldots, R$. It is also assumed that each region r has constructed a purchasing power parity for a national accounts aggregate such as consumption or aggregate final demand. Within each region r, the country c aggregate PPP is denoted by $\alpha_{rc} > 0$, say, for $r = 1, \ldots, R$ and $c = 1, \ldots, C(r)$. Assume that country $c = 1$ is the numeraire country in each region, and so the PPP for this numeraire country is set equal to unity so that $\alpha_{r1} = 1$ for $r = 1, \ldots, R$. As usual, each region would like these relative PPPs to be respected in a world comparison of the same national accounts aggregate.

In addition to the regional PPPs α_{rc}, Hill (2010) assumes that a global or worldwide comparison has been undertaken for the same aggregate using some method such as GEKS. The world PPP for country c in region r is denoted by $\gamma_{rc} > 0$ for $r = 1, \ldots, R$, and $c = 1, \ldots, C(r)$. It is assumed that country 1 in region 1 is the numeraire country in the global comparison so that $\gamma_{11} = 1$.

It would be ideal if the global parities (the γ_{rc}) were completely consistent with the regional parities, the α_{rc}. This will be the case if there exists a set of *interregional parities,* $\beta_r > 0$ for $r = 1, \ldots, R$ such that the following equations hold:

$$(6.29) \qquad \gamma_{rc} = \beta_r \alpha_{rc}; \quad r = 1, \ldots, R; c = 1, \ldots, C(r).$$

In general, it would not be possible to find $\beta_1, \ldots, \beta_R$ so that equations (6.29) hold. Thus Hill follows the example of Gini (1924) and the other founders of the GEKS method and chooses β_r in order to solve the following *least squares minimization problem:*

$$(6.30) \qquad \min_{\beta_1, \ldots, \beta_R} \sum_{r=1}^{R} \sum_{c=1}^{C(r)} \left[\ln \gamma_{rc} - \ln \beta_r - \ln \alpha_{rc}\right]^2 .$$

The first-order conditions for the minimization problem (6.30) lead to the following solution for the interregional PPPs:

$$(6.31) \qquad \beta_r^* = \prod_{c=1}^{C(r)} \left[\frac{\gamma_{rc}}{\alpha_{rc}}\right]^{\frac{1}{C(r)}}; \quad r = 1, \ldots, R.$$

Thus the interregional parity for region r, β_r^*, is equal to the geometric mean of all the ratios $\frac{\gamma_{rc}}{\alpha_{rc}}$ (the global PPP for country c in region r, γ_{rc}, to the corresponding regional PPP for country c in region r, α_{rc}) over all countries c in the r-th region. Looking at the minimization problem, one can see that each ratio $\frac{\gamma_{rc}}{\alpha_{rc}}$ can be regarded as an estimate for β_r, and the overall estimator is the geometric mean of these country-specific estimators. Note the similarity between this method for linking the regions and Diewert's variant of the Country Product Dummy method for linking basic heading PPPs across regions while respecting regional BH parities.

Once the regional parities β_r^* have been determined by equations (6.31), the global PPPs that respect the within-region relative parities can be given by $\beta_r^* \alpha_{rc}$ for $r = 1, \ldots, R$ and $c = 1, \ldots, C(r)$.

What are the advantages and disadvantages of this method for linking the regions as opposed to the Heston-Dikhanov method? The Hill method has two advantages:

- It is a democratic method: each country c in region r contributes equally to the formation of the regional parity β_r^*.
- It is possible to work out standard errors for the regional parities β_r^*, treating each ratio $\frac{\gamma_{rc}}{\alpha_{rc}}$ for $c = 1, \ldots, C(r)$ as an equal contributor to the overall geometric average that is equal to β_r^*.

However, the democratic nature of the Hill method could be regarded as a disadvantage as well: why should a tiny country in region r have the same weight as a very large country in the region in determining the regional parity β_r? The Heston-Dikhanov method does not suffer from this problem: a large country in a region will contribute a large country share to the overall region's share of world product, whereas a small country will contribute only a small country share to the regional share.

The two small numerical examples that follow in sections 6.5 and 6.6 demonstrate how the different methods suggested in this and the previous three sections perform in practice. The first example uses an artificial data set, and the second example uses a small subset of the 1985 ICP data.

6.5 A Numerical Example Based on an Artificial Data Set

In this example, there are only four countries and two commodities. There are also two regions: region 1 consists of the first two countries, and region 2 consists of the second two countries (see table 6.1). The basic data for the countries are the within-region r basic heading PPP for commodity n for country c in region r, α_{rcn}; the expenditure on commodity class n for country c in region r in domestic currency, E_{rcn}; and the market exchange rate for country c in region r, ε_{rc} (which does not depend on commodity n), for $r = 1, 2$; $c = 1, 2$; and $n = 1, 2$. The basic heading interregional PPPs for the numeraire countries in each region, β_{rn}, are the parities for commodity n for region r relative to region 1.

Eight world basic heading PPPs are obtained using equations (6.3), $\gamma_{rcn} \equiv \beta_{rn}\alpha_{rcn}$. Thus for commodity class 1, the following world BH PPPs are obtained: $\gamma_{111} = 1$; $\gamma_{121} = 20$; $\gamma_{211} = 2$; $\gamma_{221} = 20$. For commodity class 2, the following world BH PPPs are obtained: $\gamma_{112} = 1$; $\gamma_{122} = 4$; $\gamma_{212} = 4$; $\gamma_{222} = 16$.

Working through the algebra in section 6.1, the option 1 shares of world output for regions 1 and 2 turn out to equal 0.45134 for region 1 and 0.54866 for region 2. As expected, the same regional shares are obtained no matter which region is chosen as the numeraire region and no matter which country is chosen as the numeraire country within a region.

The option 2 regional shares turn out to depend on the choice of the regional numeraire countries as expected. Letting country 1 in each region be the numeraire country, 0.45676 and 0.54324 are obtained as the two regional shares of the world product. Letting country 2 in region 1 be the numeraire country and maintaining country 1 in region 2 as the numeraire country results in 0.46287 and 0.53713 as the new regional shares of the world product. Letting country 1 in region 1 be the numeraire country and letting country 2 in region 2 be the numeraire country results in 0.46041 and 0.53959 as the new regional shares of the world product. The bottom line is that the option 2 regional shares are not invariant to the choice of the numeraire countries in the regions.[20]

The option 3 regional shares[21] (Sergeev option) turn out to be $S_1 = 0.46186$ and $S_2 = 0.53814$. Recall that the option 1 regional shares were 0.45134 for region 1 and 0.54866 for region 2. Thus the option 1 and 3 regional shares differ by about 2.3 percent.

TABLE 6.1 Numerical Example: Four Countries in Two Regions

	Region 1						Region 2						Regional basic heading parities	
	Country 1			Country 2			Country 1			Country 2				
n	α_{11n}	E_{11n}	ε_{11}	α_{12n}	E_{12n}	ε_{12}	α_{21n}	E_{21n}	ε_{21}	α_{22n}	E_{22n}	ε_{22}	β_{1n}	β_{2n}
1	1	10	1	20	2	5	1	20	3	10	20	18	1	2
2	1	10	1	4	8	5	1	20	3	4	160	18	1	4

TABLE 6.2 Star and GEKS Country Shares of World Product

	Region 1		Region 2	
	Country 1	Country 2	Country 1	Country 2
Region 1, country 1 star	0.43523	0.02879	0.30775	0.22823
Region 1, country 2 star	0.47078	0.03114	0.32258	0.17550
Region 2, country 1 star	0.42439	0.02897	0.30009	0.24655
Region 2, country 2 star	0.44331	0.04125	0.28296	0.23248
GEKS	0.44436	0.03226	0.30387	0.21951

Note: GEKS = Gini-Éltetö-Köves-Szulc.

The regional shares for the methods explained in section 6.3 will now be calculated. The individual country shares of world output using each of the four countries as the "star" in the bilateral Fisher index number comparisons are listed in the first four rows of table 6.2. The table reveals some relatively large differences between these world shares, particularly for the small country 2 in region 1. The GEKS country shares of world product are listed in the last line of table 6.2.

The GEKS volume shares in the last row of table 6.2 are defined by equations (6.24)—that is, the entries for the last row of the table are the GEKS shares s_{11}, s_{12}, s_{21}, and s_{22}, respectively. Using these country shares, one can define the *regional GEKS shares* S_r by (6.25) so that, by using the entries in the last line of table 6.2, S_1 and S_2 are defined as

$$S_1 = s_{11} + s_{12} = 0.47662; S_2 = s_{21} + s_{22} = 0.52338. \tag{6.32}$$

Thus the GEKS share of world output for region 1 is 0.47662, which is higher than the corresponding region 1 shares for the option 1 method (0.45134) and for the option 3 method (0.46479).

Finally, the MST or similarity or spatial linking method regional shares are calculated using the three dissimilarity measures defined by (6.26) (WLQ), (6.27) (WAQ), and (6.28) (PLS).

The first measure of relative price dissimilarity is the weighted log quadratic measure of relative price dissimilarity between countries 1 and 2, $\Delta_{WLQ}(p^1, p^2, q^1, q^2)$, as defined by (6.26). The 4 × 4 matrix of relative price dissimilarity measures appears in table 6.3. For convenience in labeling the countries, set country 1 equal to country 1 in region 1, country 2 equal to country

TABLE 6.3 Weighted Log Quadratic Relative Price Dissimilarities between Countries *i* and *j*

	Country 1	Country 2	Country 3	Country 4
Country 1	0.00000	0.59465	0.12011	0.01057
Country 2	0.59465	0.00000	1.22741	0.25253
Country 3	0.12011	1.22741	0.00000	0.17933
Country 4	0.01057	0.25253	0.17933	0.00000

2 in region 1, country 3 equal to country 1 in region 2, and country 4 equal to country 2 in region 2.

Table 6.3 reveals that countries 1 and 4 have the most similar structures of relative prices, with a dissimilarity measure equal to 0.01057. The next pair of countries with the most similar structures of relative prices is 1 and 3; they have a dissimilarity measure equal to 0.12011. Thus countries 3 and 4 can be linked to country 1 using the bilateral Fisher quantity index between 4 and 1 and between 3 and 1. The next pair of countries most similar in structure is 3 and 4, with a dissimilarity measure equal to 0.17933. But these two countries are already linked, and so the next lowest measure of relative price dissimilarity is considered. The next most similar pair of countries is 2 and 4, with a dissimilarity measure equal to 0.25253. The bilateral Fisher quantity index is used to link country 2 to country 4, and so now all countries in the "world" have been linked using bilateral links. The volumes of all four countries relative to country 1 turn out to be 1.00000, 0.09305, 0.70711, and 0.52440. This result leads to the following vector of country shares of world output: 0.43019, 0.04003, 0.30419, and 0.22559. Adding up the shares of the countries in each region produces the following *spatially or similarity linked regional shares of world output:*

$$S_1 = s_{11} + s_{12} = 0.47022; S_2 = s_{21} + s_{22} = 0.52978. \tag{6.33}$$

Thus under the spatial linking method, 0.47022 is region 1's estimated share of world output, compared with the Heston-Dikhanov-GEKS estimate of 0.47662 and the Sergeev option 3 estimate of 0.46479.

The second measure of relative price dissimilarity is the weighted asymptotically quadratic measure of relative price dissimilarity, $\Delta_{WAQ}(p^1, p^2, q^1, q^2)$, defined by (6.27). The corresponding 4 × 4 matrix of relative price dissimilarity measures appears in table 6.4. The labeling of countries is the same as in table 6.3.

Table 6.4 shows that countries 1 and 4 have the most similar structures of relative prices, with a dissimilarity measure equal to 0.02135. The next pair of countries with the most similar structures of relative prices is 1 and 3 with a dissimilarity measure equal to 0.25736. The next pair of countries most similar in structure is 3 and 4, with a dissimilarity measure equal to 0.41607. But these two countries are already linked, so the next lowest measure of relative price dissimilarity is for countries 2 and 4, with a dissimilarity measure equal to 0.91013. The bilateral Fisher quantity index is used to link country 2 to country 4, and so now all countries in the "world" have been linked using bilateral links. One ends up with exactly the same minimum spanning tree produced using the weighted log quadratic measure of dissimilarity, and

TABLE 6.4 Weighted Asymptotically Quadratic Relative Price Dissimilarities between Countries *i* and *j*

	Country 1	Country 2	Country 3	Country 4
Country 1	0.00000	1.74216	0.25736	0.02135
Country 2	1.74216	0.00000	4.94541	0.91013
Country 3	0.25736	4.94541	0.00000	0.41607
Country 4	0.02135	0.91013	0.41607	0.00000

TABLE 6.5 Paasche-Laspeyres Spread Relative Price Dissimilarities between Countries *i* and *j*

	Country 1	Country 2	Country 3	Country 4
Country 1	0.00000	1.52000	0.12500	0.10000
Country 2	1.52000	0.00000	3.51000	0.13333
Country 3	0.12500	3.51000	0.00000	0.63333
Country 4	0.10000	0.13333	0.63333	0.00000

so all further analysis of this case is the same as that in the previous case. It is encouraging that Diewert's two most preferred measures of relative price dissimilarity give rise to exactly the same set of links.

The third measure of relative price dissimilarity is the Paasche-Laspeyres spread, $\Delta_{PLS}(p^1, p^2, q^1, q^2)$, defined by (6.28). The 4 × 4 matrix of relative price dissimilarity measures generated by this measure appears in table 6.5. The countries are labeled in the same fashion as in table 6.3.

Working through the information in table 6.5, one can see that the minimum spanning tree using the Paasche-Laspeyres spread measure of dissimilarity is exactly the same as the MST using the previous two dissimilarity measures. Thus for this example all three dissimilarity measures generate the same set of bilateral linkages and hence the same estimates of country and region relative volumes.

A summary of the region 1 share of world output using the various methods appears in table 6.6.

The differences between the various methods are fairly substantial: a 4.2 percent difference in the share of region 1 for the highest share method (spatial linking with any of the three dissimilarity measures) compared with the lowest share method (regional unit values method).

The following section considers another numerical example based on actual ICP 1985 data that leads to even bigger numerical differences between the various methods.

TABLE 6.6 Share of World Output for Region 1 Using Various Methods

	Region 1 share of world output
Option 1 (regional unit values method)	0.45134
Option 2: base countries: 1 in region 1; 1 in region 2	0.45676
Option 2: base countries: 2 in region 1; 1 in region 2	0.46287
Option 2: base countries: 1 in region 1; 2 in region 2	0.46041
Option 3: geometric mean average prices in each region	0.46186
Heston-Dikhanov-GEKS	0.47662
Spatial linking (weighted log quadratic dissimilarity)	0.47022
Spatial linking (weighted asymptotic quadratic dissimilarity)	0.47022
Spatial linking (Paasche-Laspeyres spread dissimilarity)	0.47022

Note: GEKS = Gini-Éltetö-Köves-Szulc.

6.6 A Numerical Example Based on 1985 ICP Data

Yuri Dikhanov (1994 and 1997) generated some highly aggregated data (across basic heading groups) from the 1985 ICP on five consumption components for eight countries/economies:

1 = Hong Kong SAR, China
2 = Bangladesh
3 = India
4 = Indonesia
5 = Brazil
6 = Japan
7 = Canada
8 = United States.

Hong Kong SAR, China; Japan; Canada; and the United States can be considered to be "rich," while Bangladesh, India, Indonesia, and Brazil can be considered to be "less rich."

The five consumption categories are as follows:

1 = durables
2 = food, alcohol, and tobacco
3 = other nondurables, excluding food, alcohol, tobacco, and energy
4 = energy
5 = services.

The expenditure data (converted to U.S. dollars) and the volume or "quantity" data for the eight countries are listed in tables 6.7 and 6.8, respectively.

If the entries in table 6.7 (expenditures converted to U.S. dollars at market exchange rates) are divided by the entries in table 6.8 (quantities in comparable units), the basic heading prices (converted into U.S. dollars at market exchange rates) for each commodity class for each country are obtained. These prices are listed in table 6.9.

Thus the U.S. price level for each commodity group is set equal to 1, and the other prices are the average domestic prices for the commodity group converted into U.S. dollars at the 2005

TABLE 6.7 Expenditures for Eight Countries/Economy and Five Consumption Categories

US$ millions

Category	HK	BGD	IND	INDO	BRA	JPN	CAN	US
1	4,320	1,963	23,207	8,234	52,722	307,547	94,121	967,374
2	10,562	24,835	176,782	83,882	105,527	448,995	82,056	778,665
3	14,951	5,100	60,748	15,158	60,798	272,875	69,461	992,761
4	2,619	3,094	42,126	17,573	39,933	125,835	43,342	524,288
5	62,124	11,627	166,826	61,248	273,669	1,736,977	379,629	5,559,458

Source: Yuri Dikhanov, tabulations of 1985 ICP results.
Note: 1 = durables; 2 = food, alcohol, and tobacco; 3 = other nondurables, excluding food, alcohol, tobacco, and energy; 4 = energy; 5 = services. HK = Hong Kong SAR, China; BGD = Bangladesh; IND = India; INDO = Indonesia; BRA = Brazil; JPN = Japan; CAN = Canada; US = United States.

TABLE 6.8 Quantities (Volumes) in Comparable Units for Eight Countries/Economy and Five Consumption Categories

Category	HK	BGD	IND	INDO	BRA	JPN	CAN	US
1	15,523	2,312	30,189	9,781	46,146	280,001	81,021	967,374
2	9,164	47,509	356,756	138,273	163,868	251,846	63,689	778,665
3	317,564	10,588	180,964	29,879	65,274	200,614	58,261	992,761
4	1,095	3,033	38,377	22,084	23,963	59,439	35,714	524,288
5	81,148	47,611	786,182	223,588	541,236	1,695,136	417,210	5,559,458

Note: See table 6.7 for consumption categories and country/economy abbreviations.

market exchange rates. For durables, India has the lowest price level at 0.77, and Canada has the highest at 1.16. For food, India has the lowest prices at 0.50, and Japan has the highest at 1.78. For other nondurables, India has the lowest price level at 0.33, and Japan has the highest level at 1.36. For energy, Indonesia has the lowest price level at 0.79, and Japan has the highest at 2.12. Finally, for services India has the lowest price level at 0.21, and Japan has the highest at 1.02. Thus the amount of price level variation across countries ranges from 38 percent for durables to 500 percent for services.

These data are used to compute relative consumption volumes for the eight countries using various multilateral methods. Instead of normalizing the relative volumes into shares of "world" consumption, the consumption of each country relative to the consumption of the United States is calculated. This is simply an alternative normalization of the country relative volumes.

The star method of constructing relative volumes for the eight countries is explained briefly in section 6.2. Basically, one country is chosen as the "star" country, and the Fisher quantity index of all other countries is calculated relative to the star country. Thus the volumes of all eight countries are given relative to that of the star country. Table 6.10 lists these star relative volumes, but they have been normalized so that the volume of country 8 (the United States) has been set equal to unity, thereby giving some indication of the variability in the data.

The Fisher star parities for the seven countries relative to the United States have the following relative volume ranges: Hong Kong SAR, China: 0.01257–0.01355 (7.7 percent variation); Bangladesh, 0.01277–0.01437 (12.5 percent); India, 0.14351–0.16439 (14.5 percent);

TABLE 6.9 Prices or PPPs of Consumption Components for Eight Countries/Economy and Five Consumption Categories

U.S. dollars

Category	HK	BGD	IND	INDO	BRA	JPN	CAN	US
1	0.92250	0.84905	0.76872	0.84184	1.14250	1.09838	1.16169	1.0
2	1.15255	0.52274	0.49553	0.60664	0.64398	1.78282	1.28839	1.0
3	0.85123	0.48168	0.33569	0.50731	0.93143	1.36020	1.19224	1.0
4	2.39178	1.02011	1.09769	0.79573	1.66644	2.11704	1.21359	1.0
5	0.76556	0.24421	0.21220	0.27393	0.50564	1.02468	0.90992	1.0

Note: See table 6.7 for consumption categories and country/economy abbreviations.

TABLE 6.10 Fisher Star Volumes Relative to That of United States

Category	HK	BGD	IND	INDO	BRA	JPN	CAN	US
Star 1	0.01346	0.01367	0.16021	0.05158	0.09192	0.27530	0.07444	1.00000
Star 2	0.01257	0.01277	0.14351	0.04660	0.08984	0.24629	0.07129	1.00000
Star 3	0.01275	0.01350	0.15178	0.04984	0.09040	0.25596	0.07328	1.00000
Star 4	0.01277	0.01341	0.14902	0.04894	0.09141	0.25496	0.07262	1.00000
Star 5	0.01323	0.01284	0.15169	0.04837	0.09035	0.26357	0.07372	1.00000
Star 6	0.01355	0.01437	0.16439	0.05322	0.09504	0.27724	0.07464	1.00000
Star 7	0.01343	0.01331	0.15387	0.05007	0.09105	0.27596	0.07429	1.00000
Star 8	0.01346	0.01277	0.15178	0.04894	0.09035	0.27724	0.07429	1.00000

Note: See table 6.7 for country/economy abbreviations.

Indonesia, 0.04660–0.05322 (14.2 percent); Brazil, 0.08984–0.09504 (5.8 percent); Japan, 0.24629–0.27724 (12.6 percent); and Canada, 0.07129–0.07464 (4.7 percent). Thus the variation in relative volumes is quite large, depending on which country is used as the base country in a comparison based on the use of Fisher star parities.

The GEKS, GK, and IDB methods[22] for comparing relative volumes were explained in previous sections and in chapter 5. Consumption volumes (relative to the United States) for the eight countries were computed using these methods, and they are listed in table 6.14, which appears later in this chapter.

Hill's MST spatial linking method was used as well. The relative volumes were computed using the three dissimilarity measures in equations (6.26)–(6.28). The first measure of relative price dissimilarity is the weighted log quadratic measure of relative price dissimilarity as defined by (6.26). The 8 × 8 matrix of relative price dissimilarity measures appears in table 6.11.

Table 6.11 reveals that the eight countries plus one economy fall into two groups that have similar price structures: the rich countries—Hong Kong SAR, China; Japan; Canada; and the United States (countries 1, 6, 7, and 8)—form one group, and the less rich countries—Bangladesh, India, Indonesia, and Brazil (2, 3, 4, and 5)—form the other group. The linking between the two

TABLE 6.11 Weighted Log Quadratic Relative Price Dissimilarities between Eight Countries/Economy

	HK	BGD	IND	INDO	BRA	JPN	CAN	US
HK	0.00000	0.10056	0.11017	0.09067	0.07011	0.01381	0.03660	0.06143
BGD	0.10056	0.00000	0.01188	0.01165	0.05632	0.10506	0.13237	0.23223
IND	0.11017	0.01188	0.00000	0.03133	0.08980	0.13429	0.18955	0.29841
INDO	0.09067	0.01165	0.03133	0.00000	0.07084	0.07726	0.09610	0.19600
BRA	0.07011	0.05632	0.08980	0.07084	0.00000	0.09146	0.08770	0.14328
JPN	0.01381	0.10506	0.13429	0.07726	0.09146	0.00000	0.01904	0.05322
CAN	0.03660	0.13237	0.18955	0.09610	0.08770	0.01904	0.00000	0.02020
US	0.06143	0.23223	0.29841	0.19600	0.14328	0.05322	0.02020	0.00000

Note: See table 6.7 for country/economy abbreviations.

TABLE 6.12 Weighted Asymptotic Quadratic Relative Price Dissimilarities between Eight Countries/Economy

	HK	BGD	IND	INDO	BRA	JPN	CAN	US
HK	0.00000	0.24097	0.27260	0.20885	0.15436	0.02914	0.10005	0.18062
BGD	0.24097	0.00000	0.02444	0.02455	0.11694	0.28243	0.32119	0.58729
IND	0.27260	0.02444	0.00000	0.07050	0.19169	0.36590	0.50994	0.85586
INDO	0.20885	0.02455	0.07050	0.00000	0.15038	0.20144	0.21328	0.45346
BRA	0.15436	0.11694	0.19169	0.15038	0.00000	0.21447	0.20876	0.36462
JPN	0.02914	0.28243	0.36590	0.20144	0.21447	0.00000	0.04023	0.11820
CAN	0.10005	0.32119	0.50994	0.21328	0.20876	0.04023	0.00000	0.04106
US	0.18062	0.58729	0.85586	0.45346	0.36462	0.11820	0.04106	0.00000

Note: See table 6.7 for country/economy abbreviations.

groups took place via Hong Kong SAR, China and Brazil.[23] The details of the spatial linking process are as follows. Country 7, Canada, is linked to country 8, the United States (the WLQ dissimilarity measure, Δ_{WLQ}, equals 0.0202), and also to country 6, Japan (Δ = 0.019). Then country 6, Japan, is linked to country 1, Hong Kong SAR, China (Δ = 0.0138), which completes the linking of the rich countries. Country 2 acts as a star country for the poorer countries: country 2, Bangladesh, is linked to country 4, Indonesia (Δ = 0.0116), to country 3, India (Δ = 0.0118), and to country 5, Brazil (Δ = 0.056). Finally, the two groups of countries are linked via countries 1, Hong Kong SAR, China, and 5, Brazil (Δ = 0.070). The resulting MST volumes relative to the United States are listed in table 6.14.

The second measure of relative price dissimilarity is the weighted asymptotic quadratic measure of relative price dissimilarity, as defined by (6.27). The 8 × 8 matrix of relative price dissimilarity measures appears in table 6.12.

The WAQ dissimilarity measures listed in table 6.12 are roughly two to three times the size of the WLQ measures listed in table 6.11. The lowest measure of dissimilarity is between Bangladesh and India (Δ_{WAQ} = 0.02444) and between Bangladesh and Indonesia (Δ = 0.02444). Then there is a shift to the rich countries, where the next lowest measure of dissimilarity is between Hong Kong SAR, China and Japan (Δ = 0.02914). The next lowest measure is between Japan and Canada (Δ = 0.04023) and then between Canada and the United States (Δ = 0.04106). Thus the rich countries are linked: Hong Kong SAR, China to Japan, then Japan to Canada, and then Canada to the United States. The next lowest measure of dissimilarity is between India and Indonesia, but Bangladesh has already been linked to both India and Indonesia, and so one must move to the next lowest measure of dissimilarity, which is between Bangladesh and Brazil (Δ = 0.11694). Thus all of the poor countries are now linked: Bangladesh is a poor country star, directly linked to India, Indonesia, and Brazil. Now to link the rich and poor countries, and the lowest dissimilarity measure between these two groups is again between Hong Kong SAR, China and Brazil. Thus the MST generated by the weighted asymptotic quadratic measure of relative price dissimilarity is exactly the same as the tree generated by the weighted log quadratic measure. Thus the MST (WLQ) relative volume parities will be exactly the same as the MST (WAQ) parities (see table 6.14).

The third measure of relative price dissimilarity is the Paasche-Laspeyres spread measure of relative price dissimilarity defined by (6.28). The 8 × 8 matrix of relative price dissimilarity mea-

TABLE 6.13 Paasche-Laspeyres Spread Relative Price Dissimilarities between Eight Countries/Economy

	HK	BGD	IND	INDO	BRA	JPN	CAN	US
HK	0.00000	0.06486	0.06860	0.08716	0.12845	0.01907	0.08539	0.09904
BGD	0.06486	0.00000	0.02484	0.02354	0.09876	0.09420	0.06389	0.02905
IND	0.06860	0.02484	0.00000	0.04596	0.00007	0.10421	0.13058	0.08134
INDO	0.08716	0.02354	0.04596	0.00000	0.05308	0.06806	0.02150	0.03897
BRA	0.12845	0.09876	0.00007	0.05308	0.00000	0.09387	0.11206	0.11177
JPN	0.01907	0.09420	0.10421	0.06806	0.09387	0.00000	0.01615	0.03390
CAN	0.08539	0.06389	0.13058	0.02150	0.11206	0.01615	0.00000	0.00133
US	0.09904	0.02905	0.08134	0.03897	0.11177	0.03390	0.00133	0.00000

Note: See table 6.7 for country/economy abbreviations.

sures appears in table 6.13.

The lowest measure of dissimilarity is between India and Brazil (Δ_{PLS} = 0.00007) and then between Canada and the United States (Δ = 0.00133). The next lowest measure of dissimilarity is between Japan and Canada (Δ = 0.01615) and then between Japan and Hong Kong SAR, China (Δ = 0.01907). Thus the rich countries are linked: Hong Kong SAR, China to Japan, then Japan to Canada, and then Canada to the United States, which is exactly the same set of linkages generated by the WLQ and WAQ measures of dissimilarity. The next lowest measure of dissimilarity is between Indonesia and Canada (Δ = 0.02150), and so the rich and poor countries are now linked by Indonesia and Canada! Recall that in the previous two spanning trees, the rich and poor countries were linked by Hong Kong SAR, China and Brazil. The next lowest measure of dissimilarity is between Bangladesh and Indonesia (Δ = 0.02354) and then between Bangladesh and India (Δ = 0.02484). Thus now all of the poor countries are linked: Indonesia to Bangladesh, Bangladesh to India, and India to Brazil. As mentioned earlier, rich and poor countries are linked via Indonesia and Canada. Thus the MST generated by the Paasche-Laspeyres spread measure of relative price dissimilarity is quite different from the trees generated by the WLQ and WAQ measures. The MST (PLS) relative volume parities are reported in table 6.14. It lists the country consumption volumes relative to those of the United States

TABLE 6.14 Country/Economy Consumption Volumes Relative to the Those of the United States Using Six Multilateral Methods

Method	HK	BGD	INDIA	INDO	BRA	JPN	CAN	US
GEKS	0.01315	0.01332	0.15317	0.04966	0.09128	0.26556	0.07357	1.0
MST (WLQ)	0.01349	0.01310	0.14720	0.04779	0.09214	0.27596	0.07429	1.0
MST (WAQ)	0.01349	0.01310	0.14720	0.04779	0.09214	0.27596	0.07429	1.0
MST (PLS)	0.01349	0.01372	0.15420	0.05007	0.09184	0.27596	0.07429	1.0
GK	0.01386	0.01357	0.16258	0.05057	0.09613	0.27814	0.07431	1.0
IDB	0.01346	0.01392	0.16187	0.05143	0.09441	0.27076	0.07417	1.0

Note: GEKS = Gini-Éltető-Köves-Szulc; MST = minimum spanning tree; WLQ = weighted log quadratic; WAQ = weighted asymptotically quadratic; PLS = Paasche-Laspeyres spread; GK = Geary-Khamis; IDB = Iklé-Dikhanov-Balk. See table 6.7 for country/economy abbreviations.

for the six multilateral methods.

In table 6.14, the volume parities for the seven countries relative to the United States have the following ranges: Hong Kong SAR, China, 0.01315–0.01386 (5.4 percent variation); Bangladesh, 0.01310–0.01392 (6.3 percent); India, 0.14720–0.16258 (10.4 percent); Indonesia, 0.04779–0.05143 (7.6 percent); Brazil, 0.09128–0.09613 (5.3 percent); Japan, 0.26556–0.27814 (4.7 percent); and Canada 0.07357 to 0.07429 (1.1 percent). Thus the variation in relative volumes is quite large, depending on which multilateral method is used.

The relative consumption volumes generated by the four methods based on the use of a bilateral superlative index (the GEKS and the MST or similarity linking methods) are fairly close to each other, and the relative consumption volumes generated by the two additive methods (GK and IDB) are also fairly close to each other. However, the additive methods tend to overstate the consumption levels of the poorer countries (Bangladesh, India, Indonesia, and Brazil) relative to that of the United States.[24]

Based on table 6.14, it is difficult to choose between GK and IDB if an additive method is required: both methods tend to overstate the volumes of poor countries relative to those of rich countries, but the degree of overstatement seems to vary between poor countries.

Turning to methods based on the economic approach to multilateral comparisons, the MST method based on the Paasche-Laspeyres spread is not recommended because this measure of dissimilarity does not adequately distinguish dissimilar price vectors. In the empirical example just given, the WLQ and WAQ measures of dissimilarity gave rise to the same set of comparisons, and so for this example these two variants of the MST method cannot be distinguished from one another. The differences between the GEKS volume estimates and the MST (WLQ) estimates are smaller than the differences between the GEKS estimates and the two additive methods, but there are some significant differences.[25]

What are the advantages and disadvantages of using the GEKS method versus the MST (WLQ) or MST (WAQ) method? The GEKS method has the advantage of using all possible bilateral comparisons between each pair of countries in the comparison, and thus it is more robust to data problems in any one country. On the other hand, the MST method is very dependent on each set of bilateral comparisons in the final tree of comparisons, and so poor-quality data for any single country could adversely affect the overall quality of the comparison. But if the quality of the data is roughly the same across countries, the MST method is the spatial counterpart to the use of the chain principle in annual intertemporal comparisons—that is, using the MST method, the countries that have the most similar structures of relative prices are compared, and bilateral comparisons are generally regarded as being more accurate if the structure of relative prices is similar. Thus in the empirical example just presented, the United States and Canada (which have very similar structures of relative prices) are linked directly via the Fisher index between these two countries using the MST method, whereas under GEKS, links involving all other countries enter the comparison. Thus if data quality were uniformly high across countries, the MST method would seem to be preferred over the GEKS method.[26]

Now consider the problems associated with forming regional shares of "world" consumption, where the "world" is simply the eight countries listed earlier. Suppose the first four countries form an "Asian" region, region 1, and the remaining four countries form a "rest of the world" region, region 2. Obviously, the Heston-Dikhanov method for forming regional shares can be applied to the data in table 6.14. The consumption volumes (relative to that of the United States) listed there for the GEKS method, the three MST methods, the GK method, and the IDB method can be converted into shares of "world" consumption, and then the first four country shares can be summed to form the region 1 shares, $S1$ and $S2$. The resulting region 1 shares for the six methods

TABLE 6.15 Regional Consumption Quantities or Volumes Q_{rn} by Consumption Category

	Consumption category				
	1	2	3	4	5
Region 1	57,805	551,702	238,995	64,589	1,138,529
Region 2	1,374,542	1,258,068	1,316,910	643,404	8,213,040

Note: See table 6.7 for consumption categories.

are listed in table 6.18.

It is also useful to calculate the region 1 shares of "world" consumption for the option 1 (Diewert) and option 3 (Sergeev) methods. Equations (6.7) and (6.8) are first used to calculate the country and regional quantity vectors; the country expenditures E_{rcn} are listed in table 6.7, and the country basic heading PPPs (which can be set equal to γ_{rcn}) are listed in table 6.9. The resulting matrix of regional consumption volumes or "quantities" defined by (6.8), Q_{rn}, are listed in table 6.15.

The regional unit value commodity prices n for each region r, P_{rn}, defined by (6.12) are listed in table 6.16.

As could be expected, the region 2 unit value commodity prices are all relatively close to the U.S. prices (which are all equal to unity) because three out of four of the region 2 countries are "rich" and hence have price structures similar to the U.S. structure. The region 1 unit value prices are all lower than the corresponding region 2 prices, and for commodity group 5, services, the region 1 unit value price is considerably lower. Now the Fisher quantity index for region 2 relative to region 1 can be calculated using the regional price and quantity data listed in tables 6.15 and 6.16. The resulting index is equal to 6.26177. Thus the relative regional consumption volumes are 1 and 6.17739, and when these volumes are converted into shares, the region 1 share of world consumption is 0.13771 and the region 2 share is 0.86229.

Finally, the option 3 additive method suggested by Sergeev (2009) is evaluated. To implement this method, it is necessary to compute the geometric mean of the regional basic heading prices listed in table 6.8. Recall equations (6.18). These regional geometric mean prices P_{rn}^* are listed in table 6.17.[27]

The pattern of regional commodity prices is fairly similar in tables 6.16 and 6.17. To complete the analysis for this case, the Fisher quantity index for region 2 relative to region 1 is calculated using the regional quantity and price data listed in tables 6.15 and 6.17, respectively, and the resulting index is equal to 6.17739, which is very similar to the corresponding option 1

TABLE 6.16 Regional Unit Value Consumption Prices or PPPs P_{rn} by Consumption Category

	Consumption category				
	1	2	3	4	5
Region 1	0.82560	0.53663	0.40150	1.01274	0.26510
Region 2	1.03435	1.12493	1.05998	1.13987	0.96794

Note: See table 6.7 for consumption categories.

TABLE 6.17 Regional Geometric Mean Prices or PPPs P_{rn}^* by Consumption Category

	Consumption category				
	1	2	3	4	5
Region 1	0.84377	0.65236	0.51405	1.20824	0.32287
Region 2	1.09882	1.10282	1.10861	1.43846	0.82863

Note: See table 6.7 for consumption categories.

Fisher index, which was equal to 6.26177. Thus the relative regional consumption volumes for the Sergeev method are 1 and 6.17739, and when these volumes are converted into shares, then the region 1 share of world consumption is 0.13933 and the region 2 share is 0.86067.

The resulting region 1 shares of "world" consumption generated by the various methods discussed earlier are summarized in table 6.18.

Although the variations in the region 1 shares that the various methods generate are not huge, they certainly are not negligible. The percentage differences between the various estimated shares and the preferred MST (WLQ) and MST (WAQ) shares are listed parenthetically in table 6.18. The preferred MST measure of the region 1 "world" share of real consumption is 3.7–7.6 percent below the region 1 shares generated by the other methods for linking the regions. More experimentation using data from the 2005 round of the ICP should be carried out before a definitive decision can be made on which method should be used to link the regions in the 2011 ICP.

6.7 Conclusion

Some tentative conclusions can be drawn from the analysis and examples presented in this chapter:

- The option 2 method should be ruled out for the 2011 ICP because, as Sergeev has pointed out, it is not invariant to the choice of the numeraire countries in the regions.
- The option 1 method should also be ruled out for the 2011 ICP because it depends on market exchange rates, which are not reliable and hence their use should be avoided

TABLE 6.18 Share of World Output for Region 1 Using Various Methods

	Region 1 share of consumption
Option 1 (regional unit values method)	0.13771 (3.4 %)
Option 3: geometric mean average prices in each region	0.13933 (4.6 %)
GEKS	0.13815 (3.7 %)
GK	0.14243 (7.0 %)
IDB	0.14326 (7.6 %)
MST (PLS)	0.13831 (3.9%)
MST (WLQ) and MST (WAQ)	0.13316

Note: See table 6.14 for methodology abbreviations.

if possible.

- The option 3 method is not fully consistent with the economic approach to index number theory because the method is inherently an additive one (when constructing regional volume aggregates), and additive methods are subject to substitution bias.
- The use of the GK or IDB method should perhaps be ruled out for "headline" estimates for country and interregional parities for major aggregates because of their inherent substitution biases. These methods could be used, however, to provide users with analytical tables when they demand an additive method.[28]
- GEKS remains a viable method for constructing regional shares in a consistent manner.
- Various forms of spatial linking should also be considered for the 2011 ICP, but the use of this method should await more experimental results using the 2005 ICP database.

NOTES

1. The five geographic ICP regions in 2005 were Africa, Asia-Pacific, Commonwealth of Independent States (CIS), South America, and Western Asia. The Eurostat–Organisation for Economic Co-operation and Development (OECD) members constituted a sixth region.
2. The author is indebted to Yuri Dikhanov, D. S. Prasada Rao, Sergey Sergeev, and Frederic A. Vogel for their helpful comments.
3. These multilateral methods are described in chapter 5.
4. The Country Product Dummy (CPD) method was used by the Africa, Asia-Pacific, and Western Asia regions; the Country Product Representative Dummy (CPRD) method was used by the South America region; and the Gini-Éltetö-Köves-Szulc (GEKS*) method was used by the Eurostat-OECD and CIS regions. See chapter 4 for a review of these methods. For details on how the commodity lists were chosen and how the basic heading PPPs were linked across regions, see chapters 4 and 5. For a summary of the new methodologies used in the 2005 ICP, see Diewert (2010).
5. The 18 Ring countries were the Arab Republic of Egypt; Brazil; Cameroon; Chile; Estonia; Hong Kong SAR, China; Japan; Jordan; Kenya; Malaysia; Oman; the Philippines; Senegal; Slovenia; South Africa; Sri Lanka; United Kingdom; and Zambia.
6. This method flows from the work of Gini (1924, 1931), Éltetö and Köves (1964), and Szulc (1964).
7. Sergeev (2009b) first noticed this problem with this method, which was used to link the regions in the 2005 ICP.
8. If the country experiences high inflation within the year, finding an appropriate annual price is more complicated—see Hill (1996).
9. See the discussion in chapter 5 on additive methods and substitution bias.
10. See Hill (1999a, 1999b, 2001, 2004). The work by Fisher (1922, 271–274) was a precursor to the work by Hill.
11. The method was recently suggested by Robert J. Hill (2010), but it is possible that Eurostat and OECD have been using variants of this method for some time.
12. This method of aggregation within a region is related to the geometric average price multilateral method originally suggested by Walsh (1901, 381,398). It was noted by Gini (1924, 106) and implemented by Gerardi (1982, 387). These authors used reference world prices that were the geometric mean over all countries in the world. They were applied to all countries, so that the resulting volume estimates were additive over all countries and all regions. In section 6.5

of this chapter, the Sergeev method parities are computed using a subset of the 1985 ICP data. The regional parities and price parities P_{rn} are equal to a regional constant times the parities defined by (6.18). This will retain the fixity of the final regional parities.

13. For an explanation of the problem, see Marris (1984, 52), Diewert (1999, 48–50), or chapter 5.
14. See Gini (1924, 1931), Éltetö and Köves (1964), Szulc (1964), and Diewert (1999, 31–37) for the properties of this method.
15. Instead of using the Fisher ideal quantity index as the basic building block for this method, any other superlative quantity index could be used in this multilateral method. However, the Fisher index is generally preferred because of its strong axiomatic and economic properties; see Diewert (1976, 1992).
16. Kravis (1984, 10) introduced this "star" terminology.
17. Heston (1986, 3) suggested essentially the same methodology except that he suggested the world comparison be made using the GK multilateral method.
18. On the other hand, the additive methods discussed in the previous section are consistent with homothetic preferences that can provide only a first-order approximation to arbitrary homothetic preferences. For further explanation of this point, see Diewert (1999, 31), who introduced the concept of a superlative multilateral system. The GEKS system is a superlative method, whereas the additive methods are not. Balk (2009, 82) recently provided an overview of various multilateral methods and endorsed the GEKS-Fisher method as a center stage method, particularly from the economic approach to international comparisons.
19. For a discussion of how to deal with the problems with (6.26) and (6.27) that arise if any of the PPPs p_n^r are zero, see chapter 5.
20. See table 6.6 for a summary of the differences due to the choice of different numeraires.
21. The Sergeev regional price and quantity vectors P^r and Q^r for $r = 1, 2$ turn out to be $P^1 = [4.472, 2.000]$, $P^2 = [6.325, 8.000]$, $Q^1 = [10.1, 12.0]$, and $Q^2 = [11.0, 15.0]$.
22. See Geary (1958), Khamis (1972), and Iklé (1972).
23. Another possible bilateral link between the two regions would be via Indonesia and Japan. They have a dissimilarity measure equal to 0.07726, which is a bit higher than the Hong Kong SAR, China and Brazil dissimilarity measure, which is equal to 0.07011.
24. The GK volumes relative to the GEKS volumes (with U.S. volumes normalized to equal 1) were all higher for the seven non-U.S. countries by the following percentages: 5.4 percent, Hong Kong SAR, China; 1.9 percent, Bangladesh; 6.1 percent, India; 1.8 percent, Indonesia; 5.3 percent, Brazil; 4.7 percent, Japan; and 1.0 percent, Canada. The IDB volumes relative to the GEKS volumes (with U.S. volumes normalized to equal 1) were also all higher for the seven non-U.S. countries by the following percentages: 2.3 percent, Hong Kong SAR, China; 4.5 percent, Bangladesh; 5.7 percent, India; 3.6 percent, Indonesia; 3.4 percent, Brazil; 2.0 percent, Japan; and 0.8 percent, Canada.
25. The MST (WLQ) volumes relative to the GEKS volumes (with U.S. volumes normalized to equal 1) differed by the following percentages: 2.6 percent, Hong Kong SAR, China; −1.7 percent, Bangladesh; −3.9 percent, India; −3.8 percent, Indonesia; 0.9 percent, Brazil; 3.9 percent, Japan; and 1.0 percent, Canada.
26. However, data quality is not uniformly high across countries, and so this argument for the use of the MST method is not decisive.
27. For comparison purposes, the vector of international prices generated by the GK method (with the price of commodity group 1 normalized to equal 1) is [1.00000, 1.16099, 0.99626, 1.22554, 0.86834] and the vector of international prices generated by the IDB method is [1.00000, 1.10438, 0.92265, 1.53623, 0.66525]. The U.S. prices are all equal to 1. Thus

when the price of durables is set equal to unity for all three price vectors, the GK and IDB price levels for food and for energy are above the corresponding U.S. price levels, while the GK and IDB price levels for other nondurables and services are below the U.S. levels. As expected, the GK prices are closer to the structure of U.S. prices, whereas the IDB prices are a more "democratic" average of U.S. and poorer country prices.

28. Based on some empirical evidence developed by Deaton and Heston (2010) using the entire set of 2005 ICP data, if it is desired to have the additive method parities approximate the GEKS parities, then IDB appears to be better than GK (the axiomatic properties of IDB may be more attractive to users than the axiomatic properties of GK). See chapter 5 for a discussion of the axiomatic properties of the GK and IDB methods.

REFERENCES

Aten, B., and A. Heston. 2009. "Chaining Methods for International Real Product and Purchasing Power Comparisons: Issues and Alternatives." In *Purchasing Power Parities of Currencies: Recent Advances in Methods and Applications,* ed. D. S. Prasada Rao, 245–73. Cheltenham, U.K.: Edward Elgar.

Balk, B. M. 2009. "Aggregation Methods in International Comparisons: An Evaluation." In *Purchasing Power Parities of Currencies: Recent Advances in Methods and Applications,* ed. D. S. Prasada Rao, 59–85. Cheltenham, U.K.: Edward Elgar.

Deaton, A., and A. Heston. 2010. "Understanding PPPs and PPP-Based National Accounts." *American Economics Journal: Macroeconomics* 2 (4): 1–35.

Diewert, W. E. 1976. "Exact and Superlative Index Numbers." *Journal of Econometrics* 4: 114–45.

———. 1999. "Axiomatic and Economic Approaches to International Comparisons." In *International and Interarea Comparisons of Income, Output and Prices,* Studies in Income and Wealth, Vol. 61, ed. A. Heston and R. E. Lipsey, 13–87. Chicago: University of Chicago Press.

———. 2004. "On the Stochastic Approach to Linking the Regions in the ICP." Discussion Paper 04-16, Department of Economics, University of British Columbia, Vancouver.

———. 2009. "Similarity Indexes and Criteria for Spatial Linking." In *Purchasing Power Parities of Currencies: Recent Advances in Methods and Applications,* ed. D. S. Prasada Rao, 183–216. Cheltenham, U.K.: Edward Elgar.

———. 2010. "New Methodological Developments for the International Comparison Program." *Review of Income and Wealth,* series 56, special issue 1 (June): S11–S31.

Dikhanov, Y. 1994. "Sensitivity of PPP-Based Income Estimates to Choice of Aggregation Procedures." Paper presented at 23rd General Conference of the International Association for Research in Income and Wealth, St. Andrews, Canada. World Bank, Washington, DC, June 10.

———. 1997. "Sensitivity of PPP-Based Income Estimates to Choice of Aggregation Procedures." Development Data Group, International Economics Department, World Bank, Washington, DC, January.

———. 2007. "Two Stage Global Linking with Fixity: Method 1 (EKS)." Unpublished paper, World Bank, Washington, DC.

Éltetö, O., and P. Köves. 1964. "On a Problem of Index Number Computation Relating to International Comparison." *Statisztikai Szemle* 42: 507–18. http://siteresources.worldbank.org/ICPINT/Resources/icppapertotal.pdf.

Fisher, I. 1922. *The Making of Index Numbers.* Boston: Houghton Mifflin.

Geary, R. G. 1958. "A Note on Comparisons of Exchange Rates and Purchasing Power between Countries." *Journal of the Royal Statistical Society Series A* 121: 97–99.

Gerardi, D. 1982. "Selected Problems of Intercountry Comparisons on the Basis of the Experience of the EEC." *Review of Income and Wealth* 28: 381–405.

Gini, C. 1924. "Quelques considérations au sujet de la construction des nombres indices des prix et des questions analogues." *Metron* 4 (1): 3–162.

———. 1931. "On the Circular Test of Index Numbers." *Metron* 9 (9): 3–24.

Heston, A. 1986. *World Comparisons of Purchasing Power and Real Product for 1980.* New York: United Nations and Eurostat.

Hill, P. 1996. *Inflation Accounting: A Manual on National Accounting under Conditions of High Inflation.* Paris: Organisation for Economic Co-operation and Development.

Hill, R. J. 1999a. "Comparing Price Levels across Countries Using Minimum Spanning Trees." *Review of Economics and Statistics* 81: 135–42.

———. 1999b. "International Comparisons Using Spanning Trees." In *International and Interarea Comparisons of Income, Output and Prices,* Studies in Income and Wealth, Vol. 61, ed. A. Heston and R. E. Lipsey, 109–20. Chicago: University of Chicago Press.

———. 2001. "Measuring Inflation and Growth Using Spanning Trees." *International Economic Review* 42: 167–85.

———. 2004. "Constructing Price Indexes across Space and Time: The Case of the European Union." *American Economic Review* 94: 1379–410.

———. 2009. "Comparing Per Capita Income Levels across Countries Using Spanning Trees: Robustness, Prior Restrictions, Hybrids and Hierarchies." In *Purchasing Power Parities of Currencies: Recent Advances in Methods and Applications,* ed. D. S. Prasada Rao, 217–44. Cheltenham, U.K.: Edward Elgar.

———. 2010. "Linking the Regions in the International Comparison Program at the Basic Heading Level and at Higher Levels of Aggregation." Unpublished paper, Department of Economics, University of Graz, Austria, November 23.

Iklé, D. M. 1972. "A New Approach to the Index Number Problem." *Quarterly Journal of Economics* 86 (2): 188–211.

Khamis, S. H. 1972. "A New System of Index Numbers for National and International Purposes." *Journal of the Royal Statistical Society Series A* 135: 96–121.

Kravis, I. B. 1984. "Comparative Studies of National Income and Prices." *Journal of Economic Literature* 22: 1–39.

Kravis, I. B., A. Heston, and R. Summers. 1982. *World Product and Income: International Comparisons of Real Gross Product.* Statistical Office of the United Nations and World Bank. Baltimore: Johns Hopkins University Press.

Marris, R. 1984. "Comparing the Incomes of Nations: A Critique of the International Comparison Project." *Journal of Economic Literature* 22: 1, 40–57.

Sergeev, S. 2001. "Measures of the Similarity of the Country's Price Structures and Their Practical Application." Conference on the European Comparison Program, United Nations Statistical Commission. Economic Commission for Europe, Geneva, November 12–14.

———. 2009a. "Aggregation Methods Based on Structural International Prices." In *Purchasing Power Parities of Currencies: Recent Advances in Methods and Applications,* ed. D. S. Prasada Rao, 274–97. Cheltenham, U.K.: Edward Elgar.

———. 2009b. "The Evaluation of the Approaches Used for the Linking of the Regions in the ICP 2005." Unpublished paper, Statistics Austria, December.

Szulc, B. 1964. "Indices for Multiregional Comparisons." *Przeglad Statystyczny* 3: 239–54.

Walsh, C. M. 1901. *The Measurement of General Exchange Value.* New York: Macmillan.

CHAPTER 7

The ICP Survey Framework

Frederic A. Vogel

The primary purpose of the International Comparison Program (ICP) is to provide the means for converting national estimates of the gross domestic product (GDP) to a common currency. The foundation of the ICP is a system in which GDP is measured strictly according to the *System of National Accounts* and in which purchasing power parities (PPPs) based on a comparison of national prices for a selected basket of goods and services are used as the currency converters.

Chapter 3 presents the scope of the GDP expenditures and their breakdown into the major aggregates and basic headings required by the ICP. It is followed by the overview in chapter 4 of the basic concepts underlying the prices to be collected and the calculation of PPPs.

The PPPs for the more than 100 basic headings included in the final consumption expenditures by household aggregate of GDP are based on a comparison of the national annual average prices for a set of goods and services purchased by households. The goods and services must be precisely defined so that comparable products are priced across countries. The national annual average prices required are obtained from data collected from a sample of sales outlets. This chapter, devoted to the survey framework, describes the process used to select the products and the outlets.

Not all basic heading PPPs are based on direct price comparisons. For example, indirect methods are used to estimate PPPs for owner-occupied housing and government services, as described in chapters 12 and 16.

Within the survey framework presented in this chapter are the processes used (1) to describe the price-determining characteristics of each product to ensure that like products are priced across countries, (2) to determine the number of products to be priced, (3) to select the products to be priced, and (4) to select the sample of outlets where the prices will be obtained. These steps take into account the fact that basic heading PPPs are essentially an average of the individual product PPPs within the basic heading. The goal when defining the products is to select those with relative prices, so that either the Country Product Dummy (CPD) or the Gini-Éltetö-Köves-Szulc (GEKS) method described in chapter 4 provides the basic heading PPP that would be an unbiased estimate of the target population's PPP. The overall reliability of the PPPs at the level of the basic heading is dependent on the product specifications, the number of products priced, where they are priced, and the number of countries that provide the prices. As this chapter reveals, the development of the survey framework is an iterative process that continues through data validation. However, for discussion purposes these topics will be presented as follows.

The first section describes the process that uses structured product descriptions (SPDs) to depict the price-determining characteristics of all possible products within the basic heading that could be selected for price collection.

The second section provides guidelines, using data from the 2005 ICP, for determining the number of products that should be included within each basic heading and the number that each country should try to price. This is a crucial step because the PPPs for individual products vary considerably, even within the same basic heading. When the basic heading product PPPs vary widely by country, more products must be selected for price collection. Smaller numbers of products can be selected for pricing in basic headings in which only small differences appear in the product PPPs.

The actual selection of the products each country would price in each basic heading is covered in the third section of this chapter. Each country would want to include products widely consumed and considered to be representative of its price and consumption patterns. However, what is important in one country may not be so in another. Therefore, each country would have to agree to price products that may be comparable with those in other countries, even though those products may not be important in its own economy. This section provides the guidelines needed by countries to label each product as "important" or "less important." As described in chapter 4, this form of stratification is used in estimating the basic heading PPPs.

The fourth section describes how the sampling frame is determined and how the outlets for price collection are selected. The number of outlets, the type of outlet, and their location and distribution across the country all need to be considered. Guidelines are provided for each of these steps.

The concluding section reviews how the different aspects of the survey framework should be considered in the data validation step of the ICP.

Determining Product Specifications

A new approach to product classification and identification was developed for the 2005 ICP. This approach was based on a new international product coding system and a process to describe price-determining characteristics using structured product descriptions. SPDs provided a standardized process for creating the detailed specifications for the products to be priced.

Structured Product Descriptions

The first step in devising the SPDs for the 2005 ICP was to harmonize existing classifications for household consumption items. These classifications included the Eurostat–Organisation for Economic Co-operation and Development (OECD) classification of expenditure on GDP (described in chapter 3) and the Classification of Individual Consumption by Purpose (COICOP) established for household budget surveys. The Eurostat-OECD classification served as the base classification structure for the 2005 ICP when assigning products to basic headings. But the Eurostat-OECD classification had 222 basic headings, which for ICP purposes was too detailed, especially for developing countries. Thus the 222 basic headings were combined into 155. The

COICOP classification structure was then mapped to the Eurostat-OECD structure of 155 basic headings so that countries using the COICOP classification structure could be integrated into the ICP process.

After the Eurostat-OECD and COICOP classifications were harmonized, detail was added about the price-determining characteristics for products within each basic heading. The starting point was the coding system established by the U.S. Bureau of Labor Statistics (BLS) for the price surveys for the consumer price index (CPI). Commonly known as the BLS checklist, it is used during the price collection stage to identify the specifications of the products being priced. The BLS checklist is designed to describe products in a consistent way. Each checklist contains a list of characteristics describing a cluster of similar products in a basic heading. In some cases, the product cluster was the same as the basic heading. For example, there was only one BLS product cluster each for the rice and fresh milk basic headings. However, in the garment basic heading there were separate product clusters for men, women's, and children's clothing.

The characteristics related to each BLS product cluster were used to form the SPDs—one SPD for each product cluster within a basic heading. Annex A shows two examples of SPDs: the first for the fresh milk basic heading, which is represented by one SPD, and the second for women's clothing, which is one of several product clusters in the garment basic heading (men's and children's clothing have separate SPDs for the garment basic heading). A review of these two examples illustrates the different number of combinations of price-determining characteristics that can be used to define individual products.

The initial SPDs for each BLS product cluster were prepared by the Global Office and then reviewed by the ICP regional coordinators to ensure that the product characteristics reflected the realities of the countries in their regions. For example, in one update to reflect the regional input, type of milk—cow or buffalo—was added to the milk SPD.

SPDs can be used to define a large number of different products, even for a basic heading as homogeneous as rice. Rice comes in various forms: white and brown rice; long, medium, and short grain; and varieties such as basmati, which are sometimes sold under a brand name in many different package types and sizes. Quality can enter into the definition as well—for example, the various percentages of broken rice.

SPDs contain the following classification variables:

- *Quantity and packaging.* Indicates the units in which the product is sold. The specification should provide the range of the number of units, or size or weight, that determine the price of the product—for example, for a liter of milk versus 250 milliliters of milk.
- *Source.* Usually identifies whether the product is produced domestically or imported.
- *Seasonal availability.* Important for fruits and vegetables, indicates whether the product is available year-round or only seasonally.
- *Product characteristics.* The SPDs shown in annex A provide the product characteristics for milk and women's clothing. These illustrate that the number of characteristics depends on the heterogeneity of the products being specified.
- *Brand/label name.* Brands play an important role in the specification of products. International brands and model numbers may by themselves completely define a product. However, the characteristics of even branded products should be defined because these products can be sold in different sizes or models. The brand identifier should be viewed as an additional characteristic that is superimposed on an otherwise complete product specification. Table 7.1 from the *ICP 2005 Methodological Handbook* (World Bank 2007) defines the role of brands in product specifications.

TABLE 7.1 Role of Brands in Product Specifications

	Single international brand or cluster of international brands named in specification		Branded product, but brand not named in specification	Product without any brand
Brand value	**Some brand value exists**			**No brand value**
Product searched for by price collectors	Actual brand(s) and model(s) as specified; should be found in most or all countries in the region		National or local brands that have a reputation only within a country or locality	Products without a brand name
	One single brand	One out of a cluster of named brands	One out of a set of unnamed brands widely known within the country or locality	An unbranded product whose name or label, if any, has no significance to the buyer
Typical selling point	Reputation of the producer and assumed quality of the product		Reputation of the producer, shop, or other outlet and assumed quality of the product	Low price

Source: World Bank 2007.

Brands can have a significant price effect because of perceived or real quality differences. A general guideline is that price comparisons should be made only between products within the brand stratum. In other words, if a product with the same specifications has an international brand name in one country and is brandless in another country, it becomes, in effect, two different products and should not be directly compared. Another guideline when including international brands is to ensure they are consumed widely by the consumers. Some branded products may be comparable between countries, but are consumed by only a small number of consumers because they are luxury items.

Using SPDs to Define Product Specifications

To determine the product specifications (PSs) using the SPDs, each country first mapped its consumer price index products to the SPDs. Each mapping determined a product specification. Each country then submitted this initial set of product specifications to its regional coordinator. The regional coordinator reviewed the PSs to identify overlaps, or where a change or additional price-determining characteristics would result in a product described in such a way that several countries could provide prices. This iterative process was repeated several times and culminated in a meeting of the national coordinators at which they agreed on the final specifications of the products to be priced.

This iterative process is based on some complex concepts underlying the preparation of the product specifications. Products can be very tightly specified, with absolute characteristics to be met for matching. An alternative is to tightly specify some characteristics, but leave some latitude to the price collectors for others. For example, the rice specification may call for long grain rice, but leave it to the price collector to determine the type and size of container and record those values along with the price. This approach provides the opportunity for the country to provide more prices. However, it can introduce more variability into the matching exercise unless prices are adjusted—for example, to standard quantities or package weights.

A presurvey is an important part of the process to define product specifications. The final test of a product specification is to determine whether price collectors in each country can actually find and price the same product. The 2005 ICP revealed that many products had to be redefined after the first data collection because the review of the prices showed that products were not tightly specified, leading to different products being priced. In some cases, problems occurred when translating the product specifications into the local language.

Closely linked to the process to define the product specifications is determining the number of products to price within a basic heading. This step is explained in the following section and is part of the iterative process to determine the final set of products to be priced.

Determining the Number of Products to Price

The overall reliability of the PPPs at the level of the basic heading and higher levels of aggregation depends on the interaction of several factors:

- The specificity of the price-determining characteristics—that is, rice as a product versus long grain rice parboiled and packaged as a product.
- The number of products to be priced in each basic heading, which will depend on the heterogeneity of the basic heading, the degree of overlap of products across countries, and the overlap of products each country labels as important to its economy as described in the following section.
- The importance of the basic heading as measured by its expenditure shares of consumption. Basic heading PPPs should be measured with precision for those with larger expenditure shares, because those shares receive more weight in the aggregation process.
- The sample design for the price survey, which provides the number and types of outlets to be included.

This section illustrates the sources of variability inherent in the estimation of PPPs and how to use the relative amount of variability to set targets for the number of products each country should try to price within a basic heading.

Table 7.2 is based on data from the 2005 Ring survey for the rice basic heading for six countries. The Ring survey was based on a global set of products priced by a subset of countries in each region; the purpose was to compute interregional PPPs (see chapter 8 for more details about the Ring price surveys). The basic heading PPPs for each country were used to convert the national price for each product into the currency of the base country, effectively becoming a PPP price. The geometric mean of the PPP prices for each product becomes its international price. In country B, the deviation of the PPP price for brown rice from the international price for brown rice is 0.80. The variation in the PPP product prices in country B ranges from 1.32 to 0.80. Medium grain rice in country B is relatively expensive compared with brown rice. The relative standard deviation of the residuals in country B is 0.17. The variability shown by the standard deviations in countries E and F were both around 0.30. The standard deviations, as well as the number of products within the basic heading and the number each country priced, provide guidelines for the survey framework. Note that the countries were not able to price every product; the number of products priced is a determining factor in the estimates of the sampling error.

Even though the sample of products is not from a random selection, the principles of sampling theory can be used to determine the number of products to price (see annex B for a useful

TABLE 7.2 Variability of PPP Prices by Product and Relative Sampling Errors

	CPD residuals[a]					
	Country A	Country B	Country C	Country D	Country E	Country F
Rice (basic heading)						
Long grain, prepacked	0.95			1.31	0.66	0.69
Long grain, loose		0.88		1.00		
Basmati		1.02		1.34	1.16	
Medium grain		1.32		0.22		1.45
Short grain	1.05	1.05	1.27	0.39		
Brown		0.80	0.55	1.22	1.31	1.00
Basic heading PPP	1.795	853.1	1,047.0	4.801	19.98	319.6
Standard deviation of residuals[b]	0.05	0.172	0.236	0.285	0.298	0.303
Relative sampling error[c]	0.035	0.077	0.169	0.117	0.172	0.175
90 percent confidence interval	±0.058	±0.128	±0.282	±0.195	±0.288	±0.292

Source: ICP.
Note: CPD = Country Product Dummy.
a. Shown as the ratio of each product price converted to the currency of the base country (PPP price) to the geometric mean of the PPP prices across countries for each product. The geometric mean is the "international price" of each product.
b. Expressed as ratios, the standard deviation of the residuals provides an estimate of the variability of the relative product prices in each country.
c. Standard deviation divided by the square root of the number of products priced.

overview). Table 7B.1 in annex B shows suggested sample sizes by the desired precision, given the standard deviations of the relative prices in the basic headings. The goal is to price enough products that the sampling error of the basic heading PPP based on the product PPPs is within a target level of precision.

The standard deviation of the residuals for each country can be used as a measure of the variability stemming from the differences in product PPPs. If one assumes random sampling, inferences can be made about the precision of the estimated basic heading PPP for each country using the relative sampling error. The relative sampling error is a function of the variability of the relative product prices and the number of products priced—that is, the standard deviation divided by the square root of number of products priced. Although in table 7.2 the standard deviation for country D was only slightly less than that for country E, country D priced twice as many products, resulting in a sampling error for its PPP of 11.7 percent, compared with over 17 percent for country E. The estimated PPP for country D was thus more precise.

The relative sampling error can be used to make probability statements about the precision of the estimates of the basic heading PPPs. The last row in table 7.2 shows the confidence interval or the range within which the basic heading PPP should fall 90 percent of the time if the sampling process was repeated. The confidence interval ranges from 0.058 for country A to 0.292 for country F. The value for country F implies that the PPP for the rice basic heading could vary as much as ±30 percent with repeated sampling. If country F had priced all of the products resulting in the same standard deviation, the confidence interval would have fallen to ±20 percent. Instead, just three products were priced. Only country D priced all six products, but because of the variability of the relative prices, it has a PPP with about a 20 percent confidence band.

This discussion and review of the rice basic heading indicate the following:

- Two of the six countries priced only two products, and another two priced only three products. This finding implies that either more products should have been included, or that the product descriptions should be reviewed to make them more comparable across countries.
- Medium grain rice was priced only by three countries, but shows extreme variability—the ratios of the PPP prices to the international prices range from 0.22 to 1.45 and contribute considerably to the relative sampling errors in the countries pricing this kind of rice. This finding suggests that the product description be reviewed with each country to determine whether they were pricing the same item.
- Countries A and C, especially, should be queried to determine whether they priced only products important to their own economies rather than all available and comparable products.

Table 7B.1 in annex B is based on sampling theory and shows the relationships between the number of products, the relative standard deviations, and the target levels of precision. These relationships are used to evaluate the number of products priced for the Ring price survey for several basic headings using data in table 7B.2 in annex B. This evaluation can be used as guidelines for the number of products to be priced in the 2011 ICP round.

The fresh or chilled fruit basic heading contains 12 products, with countries pricing between 6 and 11 of them. Even though the standard deviations of the residual ratios are about as large as they are for rice, the sampling errors are considerably less because more products were priced.

The garment basic heading contains 68 products with large standard deviations. However, the sampling errors are small because of the large numbers priced by each country. The garment basic heading is very heterogeneous because it includes clothing for women, men, and children. It also has a relatively large share of the expenditures, and so it is important that the PPPs be precise.

In the electricity basic heading are only five products, which were priced by all countries except the one that priced three. All have homogeneous relative prices. Therefore, the sampling variability is very small. Products such as milk and eggs show similar patterns, suggesting that only a small number of products be selected for those basic headings.

The pharmaceutical products basic heading contains 43 products, but the countries priced only 8–19 of them. Because of these sample sizes and the variability in the relative prices, the sampling variability could be considered reasonable. In view of the importance of the basic heading and the difficulty encountered by the countries in pricing all products, the large number of products is warranted, but the specifications should be reviewed.

Table 7.3 presents the ranges of the basic heading standard deviations across countries for rice and the four basic headings just described and the suggested number of products to be priced

TABLE 7.3 Examples of Target Numbers of Products to Price

Product	Standard deviation of relative prices	Target number of products to price	Number in 2005 Ring survey
Rice	0.05–0.30	10–15	6
Fresh or chilled fruit	0.19–0.37	10–15	12
Garments	0.24–0.30	70–100	68
Electricity	0.03–0.17	3–5	5
Pharmaceuticals	0.26–0.38	50+	43

Source: ICP.

as compared with the number included in the 2005 Ring survey. The target sample sizes are shown in ranges, using the guidelines in table 7B.1 in annex B. The larger number should be used when the basic heading has above-average expenditure shares.

The relative price levels for rice are more variable across countries, ranging from 0.05 to 0.30. This finding suggests that more than 10 products be priced unless the country or region is willing to accept a level of precision at the 15 percent rather than the 10 percent level.

Because electricity is usually furnished by a very small number of providers, there is very little variability in the rates, as evidenced by the relative standard deviations, ranging from 0.03 to 0.17 across countries (the 0.17 deviation suggests an additional review of country D's prices). With these small deviations, a country may need to price only three to five items to be 90 percent confident that the resulting PPP is within 5 percent of the target. As noted, products such as milk and eggs also exhibit very little price variability.

Another point to be considered is the relative importance of the basic heading. If the basic heading is an important part of the consumption basket, then a country would want a precise measure of the relative prices. Therefore, the country or region would target a number of products to achieve a 5–10 percent level of precision. However, if the basic heading has a very small weight, then the target level of precision could be increased to 10–15 percent so that resources can be directed toward the more important basic headings. The garment basic heading requires a large number of products because it is both heterogeneous and accounts for a significant part of household consumption expenditures.

A final point is that not every country will be able to price every product. For that reason, the target number of products will have to be increased so that each country can price the minimum number. In other words, as the number of products that overlap across countries decreases, more products will have to be defined so that each country can submit prices for a minimum number. A relevant point is that the number of products priced should be similar across countries. Because expenditure weights are not available for individual products, the only weighting is provided by the importance classification, described in the next section, and the number of products each country prices.

These guidelines to the number of products to price will now serve as the basis for the next step, which is to select the set of products to be in the regional basket for the price surveys.

Selecting the Products to Be Priced and Classifying Them as Important or Less Important

As described in the first section of this chapter, each country begins the estimation process by submitting product specifications to its regional coordinator for those products important to its economy. Development of the regional set of products is an iterative process during which the countries and the regional coordinator reach agreement on the final list. The resulting regional set of specifications will contain products submitted by some countries that, while available in other countries, are not important to those countries.

Background

It should be clear by now that comparability of the products being priced is an essential principle underlying the estimation of PPPs. A dilemma facing the ICP since its inception has been that even though a product may be available in several countries, it may be important or a significant part of consumption in only a few countries. Should the product PPP for a type of rice consumed widely in country A but not in country B be assigned the same weight as the type more important in country B? To overcome this dilemma, the Eurostat-OECD in its PPP program has adopted the practice of having each country place every product being considered for inclusion in the price collection into one of two categories: (1) representative or (2) not representative but still comparable. A representative or important product is one that accounts for a significant share of a country's expenditures within a basic heading. The representative or nonrepresentative classification is determined for products within the basic heading and is country-specific.

Each country will want to price products that are purchased by a large proportion of its population and account for a significant part of the total expenditures of the basic heading. Although some of these products may be available in other countries, those countries may have other products more important to their economies. For this reason, the GEKS method was developed for the Eurostat-OECD PPP Programme. Using this method, countries classify each product as representative or nonrepresentative, which provides a form of weighting.

In the 2005 ICP, countries in the ICP regions also used the representative or nonrepresentative classification. A "representative" product was defined as one whose expenditure share was important and whose price was representative of the price level of the products in the basic heading. The countries participating in the Eurostat-OECD program and also the Commonwealth of Independent States (CIS) region have been identifying representative products for the last several years, but countries in other regions had difficulty making the distinction as it related to price levels. All countries tried to do so, but it was apparent they were using different criteria. As a result, "representativity" was not taken into account in calculating PPPs in other regions for the 2005 ICP. However, for the reasons spelled out in chapter 4, some method is still needed to give more weight to products more important to a given country.

Classifying Products as Important or Less Important

For the 2011 ICP, countries in regions other than Eurostat-OECD and CIS will be asked to classify all goods and services in the household final consumption expenditures that are available as either important or less important. If a good or service is not available in the country, the notion of important or less important is not applicable to that good or service. Importance is defined by reference to the expenditure share of the item within a basic heading. Products that are identified as important by a country will then be given more weight in calculating its PPPs.

Defining importance by reference to expenditure shares raises an obvious problem in that countries are never asked to provide expenditure weights below the basic heading level. The basic headings are in fact defined as the most detailed level of expenditures for which countries can reasonably be asked to supply expenditure shares. Countries cannot therefore be expected to classify goods and services according to their known expenditure shares. Instead, they are asked to say whether, if expenditure shares were available at the product level, the expenditure shares for each product would be large or small within the basic heading. If it is thought that the expenditure share, if known, would probably be large, the item is classified as important; if small, it is classified as less important.

Three basic rules determine whether a product is important or less important:

1. *Is it in the consumer price index?* If an item is the same as, or very similar to, one in the country's consumer or retail price index, the country should always classify it as important. (However, products in the ICP lists but not in the CPI may still be important.)
2. *Use expert judgment or common knowledge.* Statisticians can call on their own knowledge of what are widely available and commonly purchased brands of cigarettes, soap powder,

biscuits, toothpaste, and so forth. For example, cheddar cheese might be sold in almost all food shops, but Brie is available only in specialty shops. Cheddar, then, is important, and Brie is less important. Kleenex facial tissues are sold in every supermarket and pharmacy. A "100 piece box of Kleenex facial tissues" is thus an important product and other types of tissues are less important.

3. *Ask the experts.* Most often the experts are shopkeepers. The success of their business depends on knowing which products are best sellers and which are bought less often. For example, two kinds of breakfast cereal are specified in the product list: "Kellogg's Corn Flakes, family size" and "Kellogg's Country Store Muesli, 500 gram packet." The shopkeeper may say that both are best sellers and so both are important. However, it could be that only one is sold in large quantities, and so it becomes important and the other is less important.

An important product is one that has a large expenditure share within the basic heading to which it belongs. It may have a very small expenditure share within household consumption as a whole but still be important within its basic heading. For example, in many countries few people buy wine, but that does not mean that all the products specified within the wine basic heading are less important. In that heading, one or two types of wine may be best sellers, and the wine merchant can almost certainly identify them. These particular wines are important within the basic heading even though their expenditure share of total household consumption may be very small.

Several basic headings are rather heterogeneous—that is, they contain a range of products that serve different purposes. The products within heterogeneous basic headings should be split into homogeneous subgroups before deciding on importance. For example, the basic heading that includes newspapers, books, and stationery is heterogeneous and should be split into those groups before assigning importance to particular products. The garment basic heading is also heterogeneous because it includes clothing for men, women, and children. It also should be split into these three components before assigning importance.

Many of the heterogeneous basic headings are combinations of the more homogeneous and detailed ones in the Eurostat-OECD classification on which the ICP Expenditure Classification is based. The ICP Expenditure Classification shows which of these more homogeneous basic headings have been combined for the ICP regions. This guide is useful in splitting heterogeneous basic headings before allocating products to the important and less important categories.

The importance of products should be taken into account both while the product lists are being drawn up and while the prices are being validated. When the core list and the regional product lists are being drawn up, the statisticians involved must determine, by means of a presurvey, the important products for each basic heading and ensure that these products are included in the core and regional lists.

When both lists have been finalized, the country statisticians should then consider all the products within each basic heading. The lists will already include products identified as important in their countries, but now they will also include products identified as important by other countries in the region. Each of these products should be evaluated using the three basic rules just noted and be classified as either important or less important.

Being identified as less important does not mean that the product can be ignored. Countries will provide prices for all products they have identified as important. But they also are required to price products they have classified as less important in order to provide links with other countries.

Finally, the guidelines provided earlier in this chapter should be used to determine the number of products to include within a basic heading and the minimum number of products that countries should price.

Sample Design and Determining the Number of Outlets

This section provides the guidelines needed to determine the number of outlets, their type, and their location. As stated in chapter 4, the target price is the weighted average of the prices at which a product is sold during different times of the year and around the country using the quantities purchased by month and location. This definition implies that the sample must relate to the entire country and to the entire year. In some countries, auxiliary data can be used to calibrate capital city data to the country and a point in time price to the entire year.

The required sample size is not dependent on the size of the country but on the heterogeneity of prices across the retail markets. The greater the price variability across the markets, the larger will be the sample required for the same level of precision.

Although a national annual average price must emerge from the data collection, each country must work within the framework of information available to make up a sampling frame and select the desired sales outlets. Ideally, each country should have a frame or register of all sales outlets frequented by consumers, and the volume of sales should be known for each outlet. This register could be stratified by size, or samples of outlets could be selected using probabilities proportionate to their volume of sales. The problem is that even if the measures of size were available, they may not always reflect the sales of individual products. For example, a meat market may also sell fruits and vegetables, but its volume of sales is more reflective of the meat sales. Because of cost considerations, it is good practice to price what is available in an outlet once the price collector is there.

For these reasons, a purposive sample of outlets was used for the 2005 ICP price collection, as is usually the practice for the CPI price surveys. A starting point is the frame established for the CPI (United Nations Economic Commission for Europe et al. 2009, chap. 5). One problem, though, is that the CPI price surveys in many countries are urban-based. This approach is appropriate when the relative price changes over time are the same across the urban and rural sectors. Many countries, however, have distinctive rural and urban sectors that exhibit very different pricing patterns and levels. Even though they reflect the same changes in prices over time, they may have different price levels. In these cases, the sample size for both the rural and urban price collections should be large enough to provide reliable estimates for each sector. Countries should use information from the most recent household expenditure survey to determine the relative coverage of the urban and rural sectors. Table 7B.3 in annex B is an overview of the rural expenditures as a percentage of the total for selected countries and product categories. Rural expenditures make up a large portion of the total for food items. It is also quite likely that the products consumed in rural areas may not be the same as those consumed in urban areas. And yet it is also likely that some of the products to be surveyed such as motor cars are available only in urban areas.

The subject garnering the most questions about the 2005 ICP was probably the degree of urban and rural price coverage. Table 7B.4 in annex B, provided in response to those questions, shows the urban and rural coverage by country. It reveals a lack of consistency in the coverage of rural areas, which led to questions about the reliability of the data for some purposes. Therefore, a goal for the 2011 ICP is to improve the coverage of rural areas.

TABLE 7.4 Outlet Types and Location Indicators

Outlet type	Examples	Capital city, other urban, rural
Large shop	Supermarkets, hypermarkets, department stores	
Medium or small shop	Mini-markets, kiosks, neighborhood shops, grocery stores, convenience stores	
Market	Open markets, covered markets, wet markets	
Street outlet	Mobile shops, street vendors	
Bulk and discount store	Wholesale stores, discount stores	
Specialized store	Supply stores, hardware stores, furniture stores	
Private service provider	Taxi cabs, hotels, restaurants, private schools, private hospitals	
Public or semi-public service provider	Water suppliers, electric power companies, public schools, public hospitals	
Other kind of trade	Online (Internet) shopping sites, catalogue orders	

Source: ICP.

The selection of the outlets is especially important because different products have different distribution profiles (see table 7.4). Some products are sold mostly in supermarkets, but may also be available in a range of other outlets, from specialty shops to the local traditional markets. Prices for the same product can vary from outlet type to outlet type because of varying circumstances such as the services provided. For these reasons, the selection of outlets should take into account the different types of outlets and their relative share of the overall expenditures. This procedure will usually require expert judgment because of the lack of a sample frame with expenditures by outlet or outlet type. Some guidelines or considerations follow for the selection of outlets:

- The selection of outlets by type should be in proportion to the volume of their sales of the products to be surveyed.
- The variability of the prices within and between outlet types should be considered. The guidelines provided in annex B on the number of products to be priced apply here as well and should be used to determine the number of outlets to be included in the price collection. In other words, the expected standard deviation of product prices across outlets should be used as a guide. A useful guide if standard deviations are available is an approximation, or one-fourth (maximum price – minimum price).
- Location of the outlets, especially the urban and rural domains, should also be considered. Again, the number of outlets by location should be in proportion to each area's share of the volume of sales.
- The number of outlets or price observations that should be collected must be determined. Information is needed on the variability of the prices, and decisions must be made about the desired level of precision following the guidelines in annex A.

The advantage of selecting outlets by type and location and volume of sales is that it provides a self-weighting sample, thereby simplifying estimation of the national average prices.

In response to the questions of data users, countries are being asked to provide the following indicators for each observation of product prices for the 2011 price collection. This procedure will allow each country to break down the national average prices into urban and rural components in order to better understand the price distributions and to respond to questions about the national coverage of the product. This information will also give each country a better understanding of how the underlying rural and urban price levels affected their PPPs.

In an ICP context, the number of outlets or price observations will depend on the required precision and the relative importance of the product in the basic heading. The size of the sample may vary from country to country. The variability of the prices among outlets also will tend to vary among countries. The appropriate size of sample will depend on the net result of a set of interacting factors, and national coordinators may wish to consult with regional coordinators on this matter. It also must be remembered that a product PPP is the ratio of the estimated average prices in two different countries. It may not be optimal for one country to spend a lot of resources achieving a high degree of precision in its estimated price for some particular product if other countries do not, or cannot, do the same. This matter may call for some collective discussion and some general guidelines at the regional level. Such guidelines would have to be specific to a particular set of countries and a particular set of products.

The difficulty and costs of collecting outlet prices could vary significantly among different types of products. When it is difficult to collect prices for a particular type of product—because, for example, the product is not very common and found only in a very few widely dispersed outlets—it may be cost-effective to not try to collect any prices for that product and concentrate on collecting prices for products that are more important and readily available. Such a strategy may increase the total number of price observations for important products, but it does risk introducing bias by reducing the number of products priced.

Role of Data Validation in the Survey Framework

As explained at the outset of this chapter, determining the product specifications and the number of products to price, among other things, is an iterative process. It is essential that the product specifications be reviewed after the first data collection using the diagnostics from the Quaranta and Dikhanov tables described in chapter 9. In the rice example in table 7.2, the standard deviations range from 0.05 to 0.30. The medium grain product is possibly the culprit—perhaps the product specification is too "loose" or one or more countries misinterpreted the specifications. The specifications for any product resulting in relative prices with standard deviations of over 0.30 or different from those of the other countries should be examined thoroughly. It may turn out that a product is not comparable and should be removed from the list, or that it should be redefined for the next round of data collection.

The concept of importance will be used in the 2011 ICP; it will be determined by every country for every product priced. The important or less important coding should also be part of the data validation exercise to ensure it is applied consistently across countries. If important products reflect those with large expenditure shares in the basic heading, relative prices could be expected to be nearer the mean than less important products.

Because the importance coding will be finalized during data validation, countries should also be asked to price items they consider to be less important. One simple guideline: price less important items available in the outlets being surveyed for the important products. Countries should not go to great expense to add outlets specifically to price less important products.

Regional coordinators were given guidelines based on the statistical variability of the relative prices of products in each basic heading to use in determining the number of products to be priced. These guidelines, along with the relative share of the basic heading of the total expenditures, contribute to the decision about the number of products to price. Similar principles also apply to determining the number outlets and the number of individual price observations to obtain.

The final significant requirement is that each price observation be coded to indicate the outlet type and the urban or rural dimension. This information will be helpful in determining whether a product is comparable across countries.

Summary and Conclusions

The survey framework provides the foundation for collection of the prices that underlie the estimation of PPPs. The concept of comparability is met by very carefully describing the characteristics and attributes of each product. Because it is not possible to price every possible product available to consumers, decisions have to be made about the number to be priced in each basic heading and the strategy to use to ensure that national annual average prices are obtained. Countries differ widely in what they consume. Therefore, the relative importance of each product also needs to be considered. This chapter provides a review of these issues using data from the 2005 ICP round and how the outcome can be used to improve the results of the 2011 ICP.

ANNEX A

Structured Product Descriptions

Structure product definitions (SPDs) provide a structured method for systematically describing all price-determining characteristics for every possible product consumers can purchase. These characteristics are used to define the different kinds of milk, for example, that can be purchased. Tables 7A.1 and 7A.2 list the SPDs for milk and women's clothing.

TABLE 7A.1 Milk SPD

International Comparison of Prices Program - Structured Product Description

ICP heading	11.01.14.1	Fresh milk	
ICP cluster	01	Fresh milk	FJ011-01A, 02A

Quantity and packaging

Package type

Code	Package type		Code	Package type	
	Aseptic package			Carton	
	Bag			Cardboard carton	
	Boil-in bag		C1	**Carton, type not specified,**	
	Cooking bag			Other	T
	Plastic (polyethylene) bag			Crock	
	Vacum-packed bricks (bags)			Cylinder	
	Bag, type not specified,			Envelop or packet	
	Other	T		Filter rings	
	Bake 'n' serve			Recycling package	
	Bottle or Jar			Tin	
	Aluminum			Airtight tin	
	Aluminum bottle			Metal tin	
	Glass			Tin, type not specified,	
C3	**Glass bottle**			Other	T
C3	**Glass jar**			Tray	
	Plastic			Flat tray	
C2	**Plastic bottle**			Microwave safe tray or dish	
	Squeeze bottle			Plastic tray	
C2	**Plastic jar**			Serving tray or dish	
	Plastic jug			Tray, type not specified,	
	Bottle or Jar, type not specified,			Other	T
	Other	T		Tub	
	Bottle in box			Plastic tub	
	Box			Tub, type not specified,	
	Paperboard box			Other	T
	Single unit box			Tube	
	Box, type not specified,			Tumbler	
	Other	T		Wax coated	
	Bulk or Loose			Wrapping	
	Bulk			Paper wrapping	
	Loose, not pre-packaged			Plastic (foil) wrapping	
	Unpackaged (out of bin or bulk)			Wrapping, type not specified	
	Cut to order from slab			Other	T
	Handpacked			Container	
	Can			Cardboard container	
	Aerosol/pressurized can			Glass container	
	Metal can (including aluminum)			Plastic container	
	Can, type not specified,			Container, type not specified,	
	Other	T		Other	T
			C99	**Other**	T

Serving

Designed for serving from package

Number of units in package — N

Size of unit — N

Unit of measure

Code	Unit of measure	
	Weight	
	Grams	
	Kilograms	
	Ounces	
	Pounds	
	Other	T
	Volume	
D99	Milliliters	
D99	Deciliters	
D99	Liters	
D99	Fluid ounces	
D4	Pints	
D3	Quarts	
D1, D2	Gallons	
D99	Other	T
	Count	
	Packages	
	Pieces	

Labeling

- Contents
  - Count
  - Volume
  - Weight
- Nutrition
- Ingredients

Unit package type

- Box
- Packet/envelope
- Contains individually wrapped portion

TABLE 7A.1 Milk SPD *(continued)*

Source/Destination

- Domestic ☐
- Import ☐

Country (if import) ☐ T

Seasonal availability

- All year ☐
- Jan ☐ / Feb ☐ / Mar ☐
- Apr ☐ / May ☐ / June ☐
- July ☐ / August ☐ / September ☐
- October ☐ / November ☐ / December ☐

Representativity

- Representative ☐
- Available, but not representative ☐
- Not available ☐

Product characteristics
(Ideally, information should be read from a label or other product documentation. If unlabeled, then value entered by collector based on respondent's assessment, or as a last resort, collector's assessment. Please note for which characteristics collector assessment had to be made in the 'Other item identifiers' section.)

Where sold

- A1 Sold at store ☐
- A2 Dairy delivered to home ☐

Organic certification

- Government-certified organic ☐ (B2)
- B3 Other organic claim ☐
- TB tested ☐

Variety

- Whole milk ☐
- C2 Skim/nonfat milk ☐
- C1 Buttermilk ☐
- C3 Low fat milk ☐
- Fat content of low fat milk (%) ☐ T
- C4D2 Other milk-Lactose reduced
- C4D3 Other milk-Acidophilus milk

Type

- Cow ☐
- Buffalo ☐
- C4D4 Goat ☐
- Camel ☐
- Sheep ☐
- Other ☐

Features

- F1 Fortified (Vitamins added) ☐
- F2 Not fortified ☐
- Reconstituted ☐
- Not reconstituted ☐
- Pasteurised ☐
- Not pasteurised ☐
- Flavoured ☐
- Unflavoured ☐
- C5 Ultra High Temperature (UHT) ☐

Flavor

- Chocolate ☐
- Strawberry ☐
- Other flavor ☐ T

Fat content

- Natural (3-4%) ☐
- 1.5% - 2.5% ☐
- Less than 1.5% ☐
- Other ☐ T

Brand

E99 ☐ L

Other Features

G99 ☐ L
H99 ☐ L
I99 ☐ L

Comments

J99 ☐ L
K99 ☐ L
L99 ☐ L

Source: ICP.

TABLE 7A.2 Women's Garment SPD

International Comparison of Prices Program - Structured Product Description

ICP heading	11.03.12.2	Women's clothing	
ICP cluster	04	Women's shirts, blouses, other tops	AC031 - 02

Quantity and packaging

- Count
- Pieces

Source/Destination

Domestic		Country (if import)
Import	A199	T

Seasonal availability

All year			
January	April	July	October
February	May	August	November
March	June	September	December

Representativity

- Representative
- Available, but not representative
- Not available

Product characteristics

(Ideally, information should be read from a label or other product documentation. If unlabeled, then value entered by collector based on respondent's assessment, or as a last resort, collector's assessment. Please note for which characteristics collector assessment had to be made in the 'Comments' section.)

	STYLE		BRAND/LABEL CATEGORY		SLEEVE LENGTH		FABRIC DESIGN
A1	Blouse/shirt	C1	International	D1	Long	E1	No design/solid, single color
A2	Open-front shirt	C2	National/regional	D2	Short	E2	Printed
A3	Pullover	C3, C4, C5	Brandless	D3	Sleeveless	E3	Multicolor, fiber or yarn dyed
A4	Sweatshirt		Brand imitation	D99	Other sleeve length, T	E4	Jacquard or dobby design
A5	One-piece leotard					F99	Other design, T
A6	Vest						
	Salwar/Hameez						
	Salwar/Dupatta						
A99	Other top, T						

TABLE 7A.2 Women's Garment SPD (*continued*)

	CLOSURE			DETAILS/ FEATURES			FABRIC			NECK STYLE	
R1	No closure		U1	Pleated front		AD1	Knit		AC1	Turtleneck	
R2	Single button (front or back)		V1	Embroidery		AD2	Woven		AC2	Collar	
R3	Partial button front		W1	Ruffles		AD99	Other fabric,	T	AC3	Crew neck	
R4	Full button front		X1	Lace					AC4	V-neck	
R99	Other closure,	T	Y1	Rib knit cuffs and/or bottom					AC5	Round neck	
			AA99	Other details/features,	T				AC99	Other neck style,	T
			AB1	No details/features							

	SPECIFIC FIBER CONTENT			CLEANING METHOD			OTHER PRICE FACTORS			SIZE RANGE	
H99	Silk (%)	N	S1	Dry clean only					T1	Juniors	
			S2	Machine wash		AE99		T	T2	Petites	
I99	Rayon (%)	N		Hand wash					T3	Misses	
			S99	Other cleaning method	T	AF99		T	T4	Women's plus sizes	
J99	Linen (%)	N								Small	
				Not labeled,	T					Medium	
K99	Cotton (%)	N								Large	
									T99	Other size range,	T
L99	Polyester (%)	N									
M99	Acetate (%)	N									
N99	Acrylic (%)	N									
P99	Spandex (%)	N									
O99	Other fiber (%)	T									
	Content not labeled (Assessed by collector)	T									

	Brand/Product Name	
G99		L
	Other Item Features	
		L
		L
		L
	Comments	
AJ99		L
AK99		L
		L

Source: ICP.

ANNEX B

Determining the Number of Products to Price and the Number of Price Observations

This annex provides the framework for determining the number of product specifications to be prepared by basic heading, the number of products that countries should price, and the number of price observations to be made for each product. The number of price observations will translate into the number of outlets to be selected for the price survey.

What follows examines the relationship between the size of the sample, whether it be the number of products to be priced or the number of price observations, and the probable margin of error, or precision, attached to the national annual average price or the basic heading PPP. The same points about margin of error also apply to the desired level of precision for the estimated basic heading PPPs. This analysis draws on classic sampling theory. The central limit theorem states that if a population has an arithmetic mean μ and a finite variance σ^2, then the distribution of the sample mean in repeated random samples drawn from that population approaches the normal distribution with a mean μ and a variance σ/n as the sample size n increases.

The sample mean provides an unbiased estimate of the population mean. The probability of the sample mean not deviating from the population mean by more than a certain amount can then be derived from the area under the normal curve. In this way, probable margins of error can be attached to sample means. An explanation of sampling errors and confidence intervals can be found in any textbook on probability and statistical theory.

In practice, the population standard deviation σ will not be known, but it can be estimated from the sample itself, from other samples drawn from the same population, or from previous surveys. It is convenient to replace the estimated value s of the standard deviation by its value relative to the estimated mean m—that is, s/m. This is the relative standard error as measured during price collection to determine the national average price. It also applies to the relative standard deviations of the relative prices as evaluated in the Quaranta and Dikhanov tables.

It is then possible to construct tables showing, for example, the minimum size of sample needed to ensure that the probability of the sample mean deviating from the population mean will not exceed some specified amount (see table 7B.1). The table is constructed on the assumption that a 10 percent level of significance is required. Its use may be illustrated by the following example.

TABLE 7B.1 Sample Sizes by Target Precision and Relative Standard Deviation, with 10 Percent Significance Level

	Estimated relative standard deviation: *s/m*				
	0.05	0.1	0.2	0.3	0.4
Target precision (%)	Number of products or number of price observations				
5	3	10	45	100	176
10	1	3	10	25	100
15		1	5	10	20

Source: ICP.

Suppose that the estimated relative standard deviation, s/m, is 0.2 or 20 percent (third column) and also that the required precision level is 5 percent (first row). The entry in the first row, third column, is 45. Thus a sample of 45 is needed to ensure that there is 90 percent probability that the sample mean does not deviate from the population mean by more than 5 percent.

The greater the variance in the population, the lower is the level of precision in the estimated mean for any given size of sample. Conversely, the larger the size of the sample, the greater is the level of precision in the estimated mean achieved for any given variance in the population. The size of sample needed to achieve a given level of precision, say 5 percent, may increase sharply with the relative standard deviation—for example, when s/m increases for 0.2–0.3, the minimum sample size needed more than doubles, from 45 to 100.

Table 7B.2 shows the relative standard deviations and sampling errors for selected countries and products. The main point is that the variability in prices across basic headings differs considerably. Rice, for example, is more homogeneous than garments. Variability must be considered when determining the number of products to be priced. Tables 7B.3 and 7B.4 are described in the text.

TABLE 7B.2 Basic Heading PPPs, Relative Standard Deviations of Product PPPs, Number of Products Priced, Relative Standard Deviations, and Sampling Errors

	Country					
	A	B	C	D	E	F
Aggregated basic heading PPPs	2.933	634.5	676.9	4.052	285.6	7.879
Relative standard deviation of basic heading PPPs	0.245	0.234	0.2856	0.2981	0.298	0.303
	Basic headings					
Rice (6 products)						
PPP	1.794	853.146	1,046.6	4.801	19.975	319.551
Number of products priced	2	5	2	6	3	3
Relative standard deviation	0.050	0.172	0.236	0.285	0.298	0.303
Relative sampling error	0.035	0.077	0.169	0.117	0.172	0.175
Fresh or chilled fruit (12 products)						
PPP	1.770	384.203	327.819	1.900	15.649	276.714
Number of products priced	7	6	11	9	11	9
Relative standard deviation	0.374	0.252	0.194	0.32	0.188	0.202306
Relative sampling error	0.141	0.103	0.058	0.109	0.057	0.067
Garments (68 products)						
PPP	2.863	689.751	925.769	4.898	22.222	393.127
Number of products priced	38	46	47	58	54	41
Relative standard deviation	0.252	0.261	0.243	0.300	0.243	0.239
Relative sampling error	0.041	0.039	0.035	0.039	0.033	0.037
Electricity (5 products)						
PPP	5.674	853.378	828.622	1.2855	14.729	349.603
Number of products priced	5	5	5	5	5	3
Relative standard deviation	0.039	0.039	0.039	0.169	0.094	0.081
Relative sampling error	0.018	0.018	0.017	0.076	0.042	0.081

(continued)

TABLE 7B.2 Basic Heading PPPs, Relative Standard Deviations of Product PPPs, Number of Products Priced, Relative Standard Deviations, and Sampling Errors (*continued*)

	Country					
	A	B	C	D	E	F
Pharmaceutical products (43 products)						
PPP	4.398	955.445	1212.91	7.88	18.289	310.953
Number of products priced	12	19	8	12	13	12
Relative standard deviation	0.384	0.268	0.271	0.262	0.277	0.329
Relative sampling error	0.111	0.062	0.096	0.076	0.077	0.095

Source: ICP.

TABLE 7B.3 Rural Expenditures as a Percentage of Total, Selected Countries and Products

Basc heading items	Senegal	S. Africa	India	Indonesia	Brazil	Kazakhstan	Yemen, Rep.
Rice	51.28	43.71	67.31	57.24	24.76	45.88	36.30
Other cereals, flour, and other products	63.44	54.06	63.18	69.92	34.06	66.33	60.84
Bread	25.54	32.37	36.36	30.88	9.61	33.44	3.53
Other bakery products	68.66	15.58	51.80	40.30	16.61	37.75	34.16
Pasta products	23.30	18.61	34.65	37.91	20.29	51.18	23.97
Beef and veal	13.25	29.50	60.05	24.00	19.94	33.90	23.29
Pork	8.48	18.81	65.26	55.76	32.08	35.12	0.00
Lamb, mutton, and goat	31.39	17.01	53.20	46.05	29.41	79.06	33.72
Poultry	14.40	34.59	57.49	32.04	21.36	31.09	31.61
Other meats and meat preparations	46.37	19.34	68.68	16.35	20.99	24.11	20.61
Fresh, chilled, or frozen fish and seafood	27.42	16.31	68.68	44.34	30.50	34.62	22.85
Preserved or processed fish and seafood	46.07	41.22	59.20	50.66	15.83	20.67	31.03
Fresh milk	50.35	22.82	55.59	24.68	22.91	47.41	90.13
Preserved milk and other milk products	17.38	30.88	49.99	22.85	13.13	40.41	50.10
Cheese	1.23	13.41	0.00	3.79	13.08	19.77	17.69
Eggs and egg-based products	5.34	33.41	56.37	41.30	23.90	34.67	29.43
Butter and margarine	7.05	24.41	46.47	11.04	13.62	40.19	51.42
Other edible oils and fats	41.80	37.28	57.76	51.48	24.20	43.78	34.01
Fresh or chilled fruits	42.81	26.59	48.22	39.20	15.10	27.22	28.27
Frozen, preserved, or processed fruit and fruit-based products	71.07	18.19	45.98	44.43	28.67	27.89	35.03
Fresh or chilled vegetables other than potatoes	31.33	29.96	57.24	48.99	26.41	34.49	30.46
Fresh or chilled potatoes	26.79	38.46	66.31	50.71	23.77	42.08	30.91
Frozen, preserved, or processed vegetables and vegetable-based products	19.85	31.57	59.37	45.20	18.16	42.07	31.41
Sugar	48.32	47.72	61.93	53.15	29.83	44.48	44.66

TABLE 7B.3 Rural Expenditures as a Percentage of Total, Selected Countries and Products (*continued*)

Basic heading items	Senegal	S. Africa	India	Indonesia	Brazil	Kazakhstan	Yemen, Rep.
Jams, marmalades, and honey	32.00	21.23	27.76	20.95	19.40	45.15	36.16
Confectionery, chocolate, and ice cream	20.27	14.41	48.26	19.30	11.76	38.17	45.14
Food products not elsewhere classified	41.94	27.50	56.42	35.98	18.72	37.95	39.13
Coffee, tea, and cocoa	50.33	31.18	48.59	45.55	22.88	44.24	45.78
Mineral waters, soft drinks, fruit and vegetable juices	16.93	22.58	29.32	13.76	11.01	29.76	20.22
Spirits	27.10	20.02	60.25	80.09	13.07	45.77	0.00
Wine	23.04	26.13	79.00	47.24	16.60	34.52	0.00
Beer	22.35	34.65	38.20	28.95	13.37	25.03	0.00
Tobacco	48.75	23.65	62.12	48.87	13.68	34.53	27.31
Clothing material, other articles of clothing, and clothing accessories	31.57	27.61	63.07	43.78	12.92	28.91	33.56
Garments	40.00	26.02	55.92	42.74	12.75	34.11	29.89
Cleaning, repair, and hire of clothing	28.58	10.77	58.69	36.92	9.16	13.55	33.84
Shoes and other footwear	29.79	27.41	50.99	40.29	12.69	36.71	31.85
Repair and hire of footwear	31.25	0.00	0.00	0.00	0.00	0.00	30.28
Actual and imputed rentals for housing	25.95	18.57	1.99	25.29	8.52	0.00	9.41
Maintenance and repair of the dwelling	59.64	14.70	63.09	37.73	13.69	0.00	21.49
Water supply	15.80	8.71	18.71	8.66	3.50	18.45	18.26
Miscellaneous services relating to the dwelling	0.00	7.09	0.00	0.00	12.01	2.23	61.10
Electricity	6.30	16.99	36.61	29.57	8.55	32.82	10.88
Gas	6.08	54.03	35.12	25.25	17.19	40.62	39.78

Source: ICP.

TABLE 7B.4 Sales Outlet Information by Location

Country/Economy	Outlet information by location	
	Region or state or province	Urban or rural
Bangladesh	23 districts (out of 64)	urban (37 markets) and rural (20 markets), mostly included in CPI
Bhutan	20 districts + 2 big cities	2 cities, 21 urban towns, all major rural areas
Brunei Darussalam	3 districts	small country
Cambodia	capital + 5 provincial cities	urban
China	11 large cities	primarily urban
Hong Kong SAR, China		urban and rural
Macao SAR, China	entire area	
Taiwan, China	16 survey areas	urban and rural (8 cities and 34 towns/townships)

(*continued*)

TABLE 7B.4 Sales Outlet Information by Location (*continued*)

Country	Outlet information by location	
	Region or state or province	Urban or rural
Fiji	2 cities + 4 towns	small country
India	22 states	31 urban centers (collect data on everything) and 201 rural villages (collect data only on food, clothing, and footwear and education)
Indonesia	28 provinces to represent urban-rural, West-East Indonesia, Java–outer islands, and large-medium cities	
Iran, Islamic Rep.	30 provinces	urban in 30 provinces (30 capitals + 50 other cities) and rural in 28 provinces (62 villages)
Lao PDR	capital + 7 provinces	urban in capital and 4 provinces and rural in 3 provinces
Malaysia	14 states	urban (36 capitals and urban centers) and rural (15 rural centers)
Maldives	capital + 4 other islands	small country
Mongolia	capital + 21 provinces	urban (capital + 2 cities) and rural (19 provinces)
Nepal	4 domains (mountain, hill, terai, Kathmandu)	urban (14 centers) and rural (17 centers)
Pakistan	4 provinces	urban (35 cities and 71 markets)
Philippines	17 regions	urban for capital and urban or rural for other regions
Singapore	throughout economy	small country
Sri Lanka	24 districts	urban and rural (17 districts are both, 3 are only urban, and 4 are only rural)
Thailand	16 provinces and capital	urban
Vietnam	20 provinces	urban and rural
Argentina	Grand Buenos Aires	urban
Bolivia	capital + 3 cities	urban
Brazil	6 major cities	urban
Chile	capital + 12 cities	urban
Colombia	capital + 3 major cities	urban
Ecuador	2 major cities	urban
Paraguay	Gran Asunción	urban
Peru	capital + 4 cities	urban
Uruguay	capital + 4 cities	urban
Venezuela, RB	Grand Caracas	urban
Austria	capital city	urban
Belgium	capital city	urban
Germany	capital city	urban
Luxembourg	capital city	urban

TABLE 7B.4 Sales Outlet Information by Location (*continued*)

Country	Outlet information by location	
	Region or state or province	Urban or rural
Netherlands	capital city with main urban areas	urban
Czech Republic	capital city	urban
Hungary	capital city	urban
Poland	capital city	urban
Slovak Republic	capital city	urban
Slovenia	capital city	urban
Switzerland	capital city	urban
Denmark	capital city	urban
Finland	capital city	urban
Ireland	capital city	urban
Sweden	capital city	urban
United Kingdom	capital city	urban
Estonia	capital city	urban
Latvia	capital city	urban
Lithuania	capital city	urban
Iceland	capital city	urban
Norway	capital city	urban
France	capital city	urban
Greece	capital city	urban
Italy	capital city	urban
Portugal	capital city	urban
Spain	capital city	urban
Cyprus	capital city	urban
Malta	capital city	urban
Bulgaria	capital city	urban
Romania	capital city with main urban areas	urban
Turkey	capital city	urban
Australia	capital city with main urban areas	urban
Canada	capital city with main urban areas	urban
Japan	capital city with main urban areas	urban
Korea, Rep.	capital city with main urban areas	urban
Mexico	capital city with main urban areas	urban
New Zealand	capital city with main urban areas	urban
United States	capital city with main urban areas	urban
Israel	capital city with main urban areas	urban
Albania	capital city	urban
Bosnia and Herzegovina	capital city	urban
Croatia	capital city	urban
Macedonia, FYR	capital city	urban

(*continued*)

TABLE 7B.4 Sales Outlet Information by Location (*continued*)

Country	Outlet information by location	
	Region or state or province	**Urban or rural**
Montenegro	capital city	urban
Serbia	capital city	urban
Armenia	throughout country	
Belarus	throughout country	
Kazakhstan	throughout country	
Kyrgyz Republic	throughout country	
Moldova	throughout country	
Azerbaijan	capital city	urban
Ukraine	capital city	urban
Georgia	capital city	urban
Russian Federation		
Tajikistan	food throughout country, but others in Dushanbe	
Angola	9 provinces	urban (provincial capital) + 2–3 rural areas accessible from the provincial capital
Benin	all 12 departments	urban (urban centers) and rural (villages closest to urban centers)
Botswana	every census district: at least one collection center (32, 52% population and 69% consumption)	urban (all towns or cities, 100%, and some urban villages, 63%) and rural (villages, 4%)
Burkina Faso	10 regions	regional center and adjacent rural area with largest population within a radius of about 20 km
Burundi	7 zones	urban (urban centers)
Cameroon	all 10 regions	urban (10 urban centers) and rural (10 rural areas)
Cape Verde	3 islands	urban and rural on all three islands
Central African Republic	7 administrative regions/10 prefectures	urban (urban centers) and rural (rural locality closest to urban centers)
Chad	8 regions	urban and additional rural markets
Comoros	all 3 islands	urban and rural (331 towns or villages)
Congo, Dem. Rep.	11 provinces	urban (10 centers) and rural (10 centers)
Congo, Rep.	11 departments	urban (6 centers) and rural (20 locations)
Côte d'Ivoire	capital + all 9 other regions	urban (10 regional centers) and rural (9 largest prefectures near regional centers)
Equatorial Guinea	6 provinces/8 municipalities	urban or rural
Egypt, Arab Rep.	11 governorates (66 collection centers)	urban (2 governorates) and urban and rural (9 governorates)
Ethiopia	13 regions	Addis + 12 urban areas + new rural areas
Gabon	5 zones + 2 largest cities	urban (123 outlets) and rural (only weekly markets, 7)
Gambia, The	all 8 regions/8 local government areas	

TABLE 7B.4 Sales Outlet Information by Location (*continued*)

Country	Outlet information by location	
	Region or state or province	**Urban or rural**
Ghana	10 regions	41 urban + 19 rural markets
Guinea	capital + 4 zones	urban and rural (1 regional capital and 1 rural weekly market nearby for each zone)
Guinea-Bissau	capital + 7 regions	urban and rural (except for capital, all regions have both)
Kenya	all regions	Nairobi (10 areas) + 15 urban centers + 10 new rural centers
Lesotho	all 10 regions	urban + additional 1–2 villages for each region
Liberia	all 5 regions	urban (5 largest towns in regions) and rural (rural area surrounding largest town)
Madagascar	6 provinces	urban (7 large urban centers, 8 other urban centers) and rural (25 rural locations)
Malawi	all 27 districts (except Island of Likoma)	urban and rural: 4 cities and 29 rural centers (6 total for districts: 4 cities + 1 each for other districts)
Mali	capital + 8 regions	urban and rural
Mauritania	13 regions	urban (13 regional centers) and rural (5 rural centers in 3 regions)
Mauritius	all 10 districts	urban and rural
Morocco	8 regions	urban (8 regional centers) and rural (14 rural markets)
Mozambique	4 provinces	urban (4 cities) and rural (2 villages in each province)
Namibia	3 zones (9 out of 13 regions)	urban (capital) and surrounding rural areas
Niger	capital + 7 administrative regions	urban (capital + 7 regional centers) and rural (7 largest rural weekly markets nearby)
Nigeria	6 zones	46 rural centers and 23 urban centers sampled within 6 zones and by urban/rural (to achieve 5 price observations per center per item)
Rwanda	capital + all 12 provinces	urban (capital + 12 provincial centers + 3 other cities) and rural (1 location in each province)
São Tomé and Príncipe	2 islands/8 districts	urban (29 centers) and rural (14 centers)
Senegal	5 regions	urban (8 centers) and rural (5 centers)
Sierra Leone	4 provinces/regions	urban (5) and rural (3) collection centers
South Africa	9 provinces	urban (50 collection centers)
Sudan	16 states (northern Sudan)	urban (28 largest markets in state capital cities + 1 additional market in other town for each state) and rural (additional 2 rural village markets for each state)
Swaziland	10 towns	urban (10 centers) and rural (9 centers)

(*continued*)

TABLE 7B.4 Sales Outlet Information by Location (*continued*)

Country	Outlet information by location	
	Region or state or province	Urban or rural
Tanzania	7 zones (11 regions)	urban (11 out of 20 CPI centers) and rural (1 center each for the same 10 regions, each with 4 villages having weekly markets)
Togo	capital + 5 regions	urban and rural
Tunisia	7 regions/24 governorates	urban and rural
Uganda	capital + 4 zones	urban (6 urban centers + 1 more in northern zone) and rural (8 centers)
Zambia	all 9 provinces (41 districts)	urban (10 centers) and rural (38 centers)
Zimbabwe	all 10 provinces	urban (88 centers) and rural (32 centers)
Bahrain		urban
Egypt, Arab Rep.	3 regions	urban/rural
Iraq	capital + several large cities	urban
Jordan	3 regions/all kingdom governors (12)	urban/rural
Kuwait		urban
Lebanon	5 regions	mostly urban with some coverage of rural towns
Oman	6 regions	urban
Qatar	3 regions	urban
Saudi Arabia	most regions	mostly urban with some rural coverage (Bedouin villages) for some groups
Syrian Arab Republic	Damascus metropolitan area	mostly urban with relatively low coverage of rural areas
Yemen, Rep.	most regions	mostly urban with some rural coverage for some groups

Source: ICP.
Note: CPI = consumer price index.

REFERENCES

United Nations Economic Commission for Europe, International Labour Organization, International Monetary Fund, Organisation for Economic Co-operation and Development, Statistical Office of the European Communities, World Bank, and Office for National Statistics, United Kingdom. 2009. *Practical Guide to Producing Consumer Price Indices.* New York and Geneva: United Nations.

World Bank. 2007. *ICP 2005 Methodological Handbook.* http://web.worldbank.org/WBSITE/EXTERNAL/DATASTATISTICS/ICPEXT/0,,contentMDK:20126612~pagePK:60002244~piPK:62002388~theSitePK:270065,00.html.

CHAPTER 8

The Ring Comparison: Linking the Regions

Frederic A. Vogel

Chapters 4, 5, and 6 provide the theoretical basis for the methods used to estimate basic heading purchasing price parities (PPPs), and then aggregate them to the gross domestic product (GDP), first at the regional level (chapter 5) and then at the global level (chapter 6). The method of choice is to first estimate basic heading PPPs at the regional level.[1] It is for comparability purposes that the International Comparison Program (ICP) divides the world into major regions. When each region develops a basket of goods and services that are representative of the expenditures of its countries, it is likely that many of these products will be important to a large number of countries. This approach improves the quality of the price comparisons between countries within regions, but it is also important that countries be compared across regions. For example, the PPPs for China and India can be computed between countries within Asia, but not between those countries and, say, Brazil or the United States.

This situation presents a major dilemma for the ICP. For comparability purposes, each region not only chooses what to price independently of other regions, but also can adopt the PPP estimation methodologies that are best suited for the economic structure and statistical capacity of its countries. The other chapters in this book describe the different methodologies and provide reasons for the choices made. Chapter 1 describes the concepts (e.g., transitivity and base country invariance) and the properties of multilateral comparisons. Although these properties apply to the estimation of PPPs between countries in the same region, it is also essential that they be met for the comparisons of countries in different regions for the global comparison. The estimation process for computing PPPs between countries in different regions must also take into account the fixity concept—that is, the ranking and relative volumes of countries within a region must be preserved. To illustrate, the results for the Asia-Pacific region in the 2005 ICP indicated that the real GDP for China was 2.28 times larger than India's real GDP. The fixity concept means that after the countries are linked to the rest of the world, China's real GDP is still 2.28 times larger than India's.

Chapter 4 describes the theory and methods for the computation of basic heading PPPs within and between regions. It also explains the requirement that two sets of basic heading PPPs be used to link countries across regions. The first set is the *within-region* basic heading PPPs based on region-specific product lists and the estimation methodology specific to each region. The second set is the *multilateral between-region* PPPs based on the national average prices for a global set of products called the Ring list. A subset of countries within each region priced the Ring list in addition to providing prices for their regional basket. Chapter 6 sets out the methodology to aggregate the linked PPPs to the GDP.

This chapter describes the concepts underlying the linking methods used in the 2005 ICP. It outlines the steps taken to create a global list of products out of the regional baskets and the choice of countries to price it. It also reviews the price collection and validation procedures and provides the results. The chapter concludes with lessons learned and recommendations for the 2011 ICP.

Linking Methods

The bridge method shown in equation (8.1) is a simple way to link two regions and relies on one country pricing both sets of regional baskets (World Bank 2007). If country k provides the average prices for products in both regions A and B, then the PPP between any country t in region B and any country s in region A can be derived as

$$PPP^{s,t} = PPP^{s,k} \cdot PPP^{k,t} \tag{8.1}$$

where $PPP^{s,k}$ is the PPP between countries s and k based on the prices both countries collected for region A, and $PPP^{k,t}$ is the PPP between countries k and t based on region B prices.

The problem is that the PPP between countries s and t is dependent on the choice of country k to provide the linkage and will differ depending on the country chosen to price both regional baskets. The number of alternative PPPs between countries in different regions is the number of countries in the two regions. In the previous ICP round, Japan was used to link the Eurostat–OECD (Organisation for Economic Co-operation and Development) comparison with Asia and Mexico with Latin America. However, this method is arbitrary, depending on the country chosen to price both baskets. Therefore, the goal for the 2005 ICP was to provide a method to link countries across regions that was not dependent on the choice of a single country to conduct the additional price surveys.

For the 2005 ICP, a between-region PPP (Diewert 2004) was defined as a PPP that compares the prices in two regions after the prices in each region have been converted into a common regional currency. As described in chapter 13 of the *ICP 2005 Methodological Handbook* (World Bank 2007) and chapters 4 and 6 of this volume, the basic heading PPP between two countries in different regions can be obtained using a between-region PPP to obtain PPPs between countries in different regions. The PPP between country t in region B and country s in region A was described in chapter 13 of the *ICP 2005 Methodological Handbook* as

$$PPP^{s,t} = PPP^{s,A1} \cdot PPP^{A1,B1} \cdot PPP^{B1,t}. \tag{8.2}$$

$PPP^{s,A1}$ is the *within-region* basic heading PPP between the regional reference country $A1$, whose currency is used as the regional numeraire, and country s as calculated by region A. $PPP^{A1,B1}$ is the basic heading PPP between regions A and B expressed in terms of the two regional numeraire currencies—that is, those of the regional reference countries *A1* and *B1*. This *between-region* PPP in the 2005 ICP was calculated by the Global Office using prices collected in the Ring program. $PPP^{B1,t}$ is the *within-region* PPP between country *t* and the reference country *B1* as calculated by region *B*.

The goal for the 2005 ICP was to determine a multilateral set of between-region PPPs such as $PPP^{A1,B1}$ that was not dependent on the choice of a single country to determine the linking and that was invariant to the choice of reference country and numeraire currency in both regions.

The bridge method described in equation (8.1) was used in the 2005 ICP to link countries in the Commonwealth of Independent States (CIS) region because the countries, lacking resources, were unable to furnish the Ring prices. It was also recognized that the price structures of the CIS countries were similar, and so they could be linked using the Russian Federation as the linking country. Equation (8.2) shows the linking method used to link the other regions. The between-region PPPs were based on a subset of countries (the so-called Ring countries) within each region pricing a global set of products in each basic heading. As noted earlier, this global product list was called the Ring list for which Ring prices were obtained. The Ring list was a composite of items priced in each region. The Ring countries first priced their regional list and then the Ring list. Chapters 4 and 6 describe the statistical methods used to link countries across regions. However, for the purposes of this chapter a simple example is shown in figure 8.1 to illustrate the process, which is central to the remainder of this chapter.

Box 1 in figure 8.1 shows the Ring prices for 10 products in a basic heading for countries A–D in region I, E–G in region II, and so forth. The prices shown are in the currency of each country.

The bottom row (box 2) shows the within-region basic heading PPP for each country to its regional base country. Country A is the base for region I, and country E is the base for region II. The purpose of the Ring comparison is to compute the between-region PPPs—that is, for each basic heading the PPP between regions I and II and between regions I and III. Therefore, the next step is to convert the Ring prices in each region into a common regional currency. This is done by dividing the Ring prices for each country by the *respective within-region PPPs*. These "deflated prices" are shown in box 3. The prices for the base countries remain the same.

The matrix in box 3 now contains in effect prices for three regions expressed in three regional currencies. The same Country Product Dummy (CPD) method used to compute within-region basic heading PPPs and described in previous chapters is used to compute the between-region PPPs from the matrix of deflated Ring prices. Box 4 shows the PPP between regions I and II to be 10.56. Region I is the base, and so its PPP equals 1.0.

The between-region PPPs for each basic heading are called linking factors because they are used as scalars to calibrate the within-region PPPs to the base region. Box 5 shows that the global PPP for this basic heading for each country in region II is simply the product of the within-region PPP and 10.56. The global PPP for the regional base country is equal to the linking factor.

The use of a single scalar for each basic heading in each region ensures that the within-region relative volumes and so forth remain the same. Therefore, the fixity property is preserved. Just as important, this method is base country–invariant, and transitivity is ensured. However, these properties are conditional on the choice of countries to price the Ring list.

The use of multiple countries to compute the regional linking factors is a vast improvement over the bridge method, which relies on a single country. However, the Ring concept is still dependent on the choice of countries to price the Ring list—a different set of countries could produce different linking factors. The next section describes how the Ring countries were selected.

FIGURE 8.1 Linking Factors: A Numerical Example

1

Ring prices—BH	Region I				Region II			Region III
Product	A	B	C	D	E	F	G	H
1	2	100		25	20	600		etc.
2	5		12			900	450	
3	6	270	15			1,000	400	
4		320	70		180	5,000		
5	8	280		120	120	2,000	500	
6		210	60		100		350	
7			50	140				
8		120	12	100	80	800		
9	2			10	25	1,500	150	
10					40		260	
2 PPPs (within region)	1	30	5	13	1	20	6	

3

Deflated prices	Region I				Region II			Region III
Product	A	B	C	D	E	F	G	H
1	2	3		2	20	20		etc.
2	5		2			30	75	
3	6	9	3			33	67	
4		11	14		180	167		
5	8	9		9	120	67	83	
6		7	12		100		58	
7			10	11				
8		4	2	8	80	27		
9	2			1	25	50	25	
10					40		43	

4

Regional coefficients (PPPs)			
Method	I	II	III
CPD	1	10.56	etc.

Country	Region	PPPs (within region)	5 Linking factors	6 Global PPP
A	I	1	1	1
B	I	30	1	30
C	I	5	1	5
D	I	13	1	13
E	II	1	10.56	10.56
F	II	30	10.56	316.80
G	II	6	10.56	63.36
H	III	etc.	etc.	etc.

Base country for region I for the ICP: United States

Base country for the ICP: OECD

Source: ICP 2005.

Selecting the Ring Countries

Ideally, all countries would have priced the Ring list, but because of resources a sample of 18 countries was chosen to do the additional pricing. The selection of the 18 countries to price the Ring list was purposive rather than random; each country had to meet the following requirements:

- Availability of a wide range of products and services comparable to those in at least two other regions
- Capability of providing prices and expenditure weights for all of the GDP aggregates
- Willing to take on the extra work of pricing the Ring list.

Table 8.1 lists the Ring countries by region. The number of countries in a region differed because Africa has nearly 50 countries, whereas South America and Western Asia each has only 10 countries. Because none of the countries in the CIS region priced the Ring list, that region was linked to the OECD by Russia, which priced both the OECD and CIS lists. This was the bridge method shown in equation (8.1).

The Ring countries were chosen before the regional results became available. Therefore, information about the relative price levels and structures from the regional comparison was not available when making the final selection of countries. The results of the Ring survey are used later in this chapter to evaluate that selection. The next section describes the steps taken to develop the Ring list.

Developing the Ring List

The Ring list covered only basic headings in the household consumption aggregate of the GDP; it excluded those for health, education, and housing rentals. The Global Office developed global lists and specifications for the health, education, and housing basic headings, as well as those for general government, equipment, and construction. Therefore, it was not necessary to develop a separate Ring list for those basic headings. The same data were used for both the regional and Ring comparisons. The nature of these basic headings made it difficult to prepare the pricing specifications; they required expertise and time not available in every region. Because of the complexity of these basic headings, separate chapters are devoted in this volume to each.

The starting point for developing the Ring list was to merge the product lists from the five ICP regions and the Eurostat-OECD comparison. For simplicity purposes, all are referred to as

TABLE 8.1 Ring Countries/Economy by 2005 ICP Region

Africa	Asia-Pacific	Eurostat-OECD	South America	Western Asia
Cameroon	Hong Kong SAR, China	Estonia	Brazil	Jordan
Egypt, Arab Rep.	Malaysia	Japan	Chile	Oman
Kenya	Philippines	Slovenia		
Senegal	Sri Lanka	United Kingdom		
South Africa				
Zambia				

Source: World Bank 2008.

regions in the remainder of this chapter. Annex A lists the number of products in each major category by region.

A first review revealed very few exact matches between the regional lists. Even when the same type of product was found in different regions, the price-determining characteristics such as package type and size were defined differently. There were also differences in quality and terminology—for example, some rice was sold loose instead of packaged, and an item called a biscuit in one region was called a cookie in another. Two different approaches, depending on the type of product, were adopted to construct the Ring list. First, the products purchased by households were split into two groups. Group (a) consisted of consumption goods usually purchased in retail outlets such as shops, market stalls, supermarkets, and department stores. Group (b) consisted mostly of services such as transport, communications, health, education, restaurants, and hotels.

The regional product lists for group (a) were then consolidated, resulting in over 5,500 products grouped by cluster within basic headings. The starting point for the group (b) services was the specifications from the Eurostat-OECD comparison. These products were much more difficult to define, and therefore the specifications used in the ongoing Eurostat-OECD region were used as a starting point instead of trying to consolidate those lists from the other regions. The group (b) list contained about 1,000 items and services. Both lists were sent to the regional coordinators and Ring countries, and they simply identified those products and services "as defined" that were available in their respective markets.

Products and services that could only be priced by Ring countries within the same region were eliminated. This review reduced the combined lists from the two groups to about 1,200 items. The next step was to establish targets for the number of Ring products to be priced within each basic heading. The methods described in chapter 7 using the expenditure share, homogeneity of products, and expected relative price variation of products within each basic heading were used to establish target numbers. These targets ranged from 2 for eggs to over 90 for pharmaceutical products.

The next step was to harmonize the product descriptions for the remaining items. This step was a challenge, and the Global Office staff became experts in how the same product was defined across the world. A draft catalog containing the harmonized descriptions and pictures (where available) was sent to the regional coordinators and Ring countries. The regional coordinators brought representatives from the Ring countries together to provide detailed comments about each description, propose changes to the descriptions, add new products, or delete others. They also were asked to identify products that were representative of the patterns of consumption in their country (R), or were available but not representative (A). The purpose of this classification was to identify those products that might be available to be priced but were not usually purchased by the average consumer in his or her country. These products generally have higher prices, and so the classification was to be used in the estimation process. More is said about this process in the section presenting the data analysis results.

The Global Office incorporated the comments, additions, and deletions from the regional coordinators and Ring countries to create an updated Ring list. The distribution of the number of products by basic heading was also reviewed to determine the final number to remain on the list. The draft catalog was updated and sent to the regions and Ring countries for a final review. The Global Office then organized a workshop that included the regional coordinators and selected national experts to finalize the list. This effort resulted in revisions, including the addition of some products and the deletion of others. The end result was a global list of 1,095 household consumption goods and services and the accompanying product specifications. The distribution of the products in this final list is shown in the Ring column in annex A. The number of items in the global lists for general government, construction, and equipment is also shown.

Collecting the Ring Prices

The process to develop the Ring list did not begin until all regions had finalized their regional specifications. Thus the regional data collection was under way while the Ring list was being developed. However, the main factor affecting the timing of the Ring data collection was the size of the Ring list, which, except for the Eurostat-OECD, exceeded the size of the regional lists. As a result, none of the Ring countries had the capacity to collect the Ring prices until they had completed the regional data collection, which meant that the Ring price collection did not begin until 2006. In addition, resources were not available to support a Ring price collection that covered each country for a full year. The data for the Ring prices were therefore collected only at one point in time and only in the capital city.

The Eurostat-OECD countries typically only collect prices in the capital city and at one point in time for their comparison. These countries use their consumer price index (CPI) and other data to backcast the point-in-time data to an annual average and also to calibrate the capital city prices to the national level. Annex B provides an example of the worksheet that Ring countries were required to submit. The ratio of the capital city average prices to the national level was derived from the regional PPP data collection or other sources. The data for backcasting to 2005 were taken from each country's consumer price index.

Validating the Ring Prices

The prices collected for the Ring products were subjected to the same stringent diagnostic tests and validation procedures used by each country and region for the regional price data described in detail in chapter 9. This process began with each Ring country validating those prices in the same way in which they validated the prices for the regional comparison. Each country did have the benefit of the information on price levels from their regional data collection, but they had to validate prices for products that were not in that collection and for which they may not have had much prior knowledge.

The data validation for the regional comparisons was conducted independently by each region, whereas the group of 18 Ring countries was treated as a separate region administered by the Global Office. When each country had completed its validation of the Ring prices, it was submitted to the ICP Global Office for the remaining steps of the validation.

The most intensive validation focused on the between-country review of the relative prices of individual products within a basic heading, treating the set of 18 countries as a single region. The first step was to convert each country's prices for each product within a basic heading into a common currency using both the exchange rate and the Ring country basic heading PPPs based on the Ring prices. Because this was the first time product prices from countries representing all regions of the world were compared, this first review was conducted without the benefit of having the within-region results.

Similar to what was found in the regional data validation, the Ring prices validation revealed two kinds of outliers. One was a country price (in the common currency) that differed significantly from the common currency prices for the other countries. For example, short grain rice prices in the common currency were about the same for all of the Ring countries except one whose price was less than the average. The question was whether this price should be included even after country verification. In many cases, after reviews with the regional coordinator such prices were deleted. The other type of outlier was a product outlier. The standard deviation of the deviations of the national prices from the international average prices for each product within a basic heading was used to identify products for which there was a lack of consistency in the price levels reported by countries. This lack of consistency was generally caused by the product being poorly or loosely defined (see chapter 7) in such a way that comparable products were not being priced. Because there was not sufficient time to redefine these products, they were simply dropped after extensive review.

A main concern arising from this first review was that the basic dilemma of comparability and representativity became a greater problem for the Ring list because of the diversity in the economic size and structure of countries in different regions. The dilemma is that one wants to measure the same goods and services across countries. Ideally, these same goods and services should also be representative of the consumption in each country. The basic concern was whether the Ring list contained too many products common to rich countries but rare and expensive in poor countries. Two questions then evolved: Did each country price the same product? And if a price was submitted, was it representative of the consumption patterns in the region? The reason for classifying products as representative or nonrepresentative was that one would expect representative products to be sold in greater quantities with lower prices than would be observed for nonrepresentative products.

This data validation indicated that the concept of representativity was not consistently applied across the Ring countries. The national price statisticians were not able to agree on a workable definition of representativity that was consistent across countries and regions. Where one would expect representative products to be those with lower prices, the opposite was often true. Because the representativity variable added another source of variability to the results, it was not used to compute the between-region PPPs. As discussed in chapter 7, the representativity concept was used only by the Eurostat-OECD comparison and the CIS region.

Although the analysis just described was useful in determining the prices and products that needed additional review, it was also necessary to compare the price levels between regions because that comparison would be the basis for the between-region PPPs. For example, one would expect price levels to be lower in Africa than what was observed in the Eurostat-OECD countries. Again, the diagnostics just described were used to identify problem prices and products. An additional step was to compare the consistency between regional and Ring results once information from the regional comparisons became available.

The Ring list differed from the regional lists because its products were defined to be comparable between countries in different regions. The question was whether the relative prices at the product level based on the regional and Ring prices should be similar for countries in the same region.

The next stage of the data validation was to evaluate whether relative price levels from the regional comparisons were similar to price levels from the Ring comparison for countries in the same region.

Table 8.2 shows the within-region rankings of Ring countries based on aggregated price level indexes (PLIs) from the regional comparison, then based on the Ring comparison before and after prices were deflated. (These aggregations came from the Dikhanov table as part of the validation, and so were not weighted.) The computations treated the 18 countries as a region with base UK = 1.0 for columns (2)–(5). The main points follow:

- Column (1) shows the within-region rankings of the aggregated PLIs by country from the respective *regional comparisons.* For example, in Africa's regional comparison price levels among the six Ring countries were the highest in South Africa followed by Zambia and the lowest in the Arab Republic of Egypt. In the Eurostat-OECD region, Japan had

TABLE 8.2 Regional and Ring Price Level Indexes and Their Rankings, ICP 2005

	Regional rank[a] (1)	PLI, Ring (2)	Ring rank (3)	PLI, deflated (4)	Deflated rank (5)
Brazil	2	0.664	1	0.664	1
Chile	1	0.664	2	0.645	2
Jordan	2	0.570	1	0.568	1
Oman	1	0.560	2	0.560	2
Cameroon	4	0.686	1	0.686	2
Senegal	3	0.615	3	0.630	4
Egypt, Arab Rep.	6	0.384	6	0.642	3
Kenya	5	0.550	4	0.730	1
South Africa	1	0.680	2	0.593	5
Zambia	2	0.536	5	0.522	6
United Kingdom	2	1.000	2	1.000	2
Estonia	4	0.700	4	1.022	4
Japan	1	1.165	1	0.975	1
Slovenia	3	0.815	3	1.016	3
Malaysia	2	0.541	2	0.770	2
Hong Kong SAR, China	1	0.672	1	0.672	4
Philippines	3	0.437	4	0.729	3
Sri Lanka	4	0.530	3	0.890	1

Source: The Ring analysis for the 2005 ICP was provided by Imededdine Jerbi, ICP Global Office.
a. The global ranking is the same because of the fixity requirement.

the highest PLI, and Hong Kong SAR, China, had the highest in Asia among the respective Ring countries in those regions. Recall that the principle of fixity requires that these within-region rankings be preserved after each region has been linked.

- Column (2) shows the aggregated PLI for each country based on the Ring prices. The Ring countries were treated as one region, with the United Kingdom as the base. The PLI for Cameroon is exceeded only by those for the Eurostat-OECD countries; it is the largest in the Africa region. The price levels for Africa excluding Egypt were larger than expected, especially compared with those for Asia, which had lower than expected price levels. This finding raised two questions: Did the Ring list adequately represent the products widely consumed in the Africa and Asia-Pacific regions? Or should some countries not have been included in the Ring comparison?
- Column (3) shows the within-region rankings of the PLIs in column (2). Cameroon went from having the fourth-highest PLI among the six African countries in the regional comparison to a first-place ranking based on the Ring prices. Zambia went from having the second-highest PLI in the regional comparison to the fifth highest based on Ring prices. The question is whether the PLIs within the Ring countries were consistent with those from the regional comparisons. Because the product lists were different, some inconsistencies would be expected. In addition, the within-region multilateral PPPs and price level indexes were based on countries not in the 18-country multilateral

Ring computations. However, one would expect the rankings to be somewhat consistent. Although the respective rankings of the PLIs from the regional and Ring prices were not exactly the same in the South America, Western Asia, and Eurostat-OECD regions, they were similar.

- Column (4) shows the aggregated Ring PLIs after the Ring prices for each country were deflated using the basic heading PPPs from the regional comparisons. For example, Hong Kong SAR, China and the United Kingdom were the base countries for the Asia-Pacific and Eurostat-OECD regions, respectively. The Eurostat-OECD region was also the base region as indicated by the PLI = 1 in both columns (2) and (3) for the United Kingdom. The Ring prices in each Asia-Pacific country were transformed into Hong Kong SAR, China prices using the within-region PPPs of each country to Hong Kong SAR, China and so on for the rest of the regions. In theory, the resulting PLIs for each group of countries should be about the same, and they are similar in the South America, Western Asia, and the Eurostat-OECD regions. However, there is considerable variability in the deflated PLIs for the Africa and Asia-Pacific regions.
- Column (5) shows the within-region ranking of the PLIs. Egypt went from the significantly lowest in price level to the third most expensive country among the six African countries. South Africa moved from having the highest PLI to having the fifth highest. In the Asia-Pacific region, Sri Lanka became the most expensive country and Hong Kong SAR, China the cheapest. These are two examples in which the classification of "representative" may have made a considerable difference.

The conclusion of this analysis was that the Ring results for the Eurostat-OECD, Western Asia, and South American countries were consistent with the respective regional comparisons. However, the lack of consistency between the regional and Ring results in Africa and the Asia-Pacific raised the question of whether some countries should be considered outliers. For example, a Ring country should represent the average regional price structure—that is, shares of expenditures by basic heading are similar, as are the price levels. Sergeev (2007) offered another approach to determining whether some countries were possible outliers using coefficients of similarity of price structures. An analysis using this approach revealed that possible outliers were Cameroon, Zambia, and Egypt in Africa, Sri Lanka in the Asia-Pacific, and Japan in the Eurostat-OECD comparison.

As a result of these two sets of analysis, another in-depth review of the product specifications and prices was undertaken to determine whether there was a developed country bias in the product choices and descriptions. In addition, the prices of about 200 products showing the greatest price variability were observed by a team of ICP experts in markets in the United Kingdom, Slovenia, Hong Kong SAR, China, and Malaysia. These market visits generally confirmed that the price collections were consistent across countries and regions.

The final stage of analysis was to compute the linking factors by excluding countries that were possible outliers. This computation provided an evaluation of the effect of the Ring data on the linking factors, but it was not possible to carry out a similar analysis on the regional basic heading PPPs; they had to be used as provided by each region. Recall that a subjective process was used to choose the initial set of Ring countries. Rather than add more subjectivity to the process, all 18 countries were included in the estimation of the final linking factors.

The overall validation of the Ring prices went through four iterations that included the regional coordinators and representatives of some of the Ring countries. Over 11,600 average prices (about seven average product prices per country per basic heading) were submitted for the 1,000-plus Ring products. At the end of the validation, over 2,000 individual product prices were deleted, or about 20 percent. In addition, about 60 products were deleted when it was not possible to determine whether any of the country prices were plausible.

Although the Ring prices were subjected to detailed scrutiny, the basic heading PPPs from the regional comparisons were taken "as is" because the regional results had already been published. Therefore, it was not possible to review the regional results that were not consistent with those from the Ring countries.

The following analysis provides a look at the basic heading–level PPPs from the Ring comparison first based on the original Ring prices and then based on the Ring prices after they were deflated by the respective within-region PPPs. This analysis will reveal the consistency of the within-region PPPs and Ring PPPs. It takes into account the fact that PPP levels vary considerably across basic headings.

Table 8.3 presents results for three countries and some selected basic headings. The columns labeled "Ring prices" contain the ratios of the basic heading PPP to the aggregated PPP using the Ring prices. The columns labeled "deflated Ring prices" contain the ratios of the Ring basic heading PPPs to the aggregated PPPs after they were deflated, again across the 18 Ring countries treated as a region. In Sri Lanka, for example, the Ring PPP for electricity was 0.15 of the aggregated PPP, but after being deflated using its regional PPPs, electricity moved to 1.27 of the aggregated level. The differences for gas were even larger. Similar or larger differences were shown by the other countries in which a PPP from the Ring prices was considerably below the average PPP, but after deflation by the within-region PPP it became much larger than the average. There were differences in the opposite direction as well.

These diagnostics point out inconsistencies between the Ring and regional data by basic heading and should lead to another review of those data. Thus the within-region PPPs should have been subjected to review as part of the Ring analysis.

The outcome of this analysis was that the variability and lack of consistency were attributed to three factors. First, so that the Ring list would contain products comparable across regions, it contained many products that would not have been widely purchased by consumers in every country. The representativity classification gives more weight to items sold in greater quantities, which are assumed to have lower prices. But as pointed out earlier in this chapter, this classification process was not used. Therefore, if the Ring list contained a large number of nonrepresentative items so that comparable products could be priced, the result would be higher price levels for those countries in which, even though they could price the items, it was likely that those items would be

TABLE 8.3 Ratio of Basic Heading Ring and Deflated Ring PPPs to Aggregated PPPs, Selected Countries

	Egypt, Arab Rep.		Sri Lanka		Japan	
	Basic heading PPP/aggregated PPP		Basic heading PPP/aggregated PPP		Basic heading PPP/aggregated PPP	
	Ring prices	Deflated Ring prices	Ring prices	Deflated Ring prices	Ring prices	Deflated Ring prices
Bread	0.83	3.76	0.07	0.91	1.45	0.44
Electricity	0.65	0.93	0.15	1.27	0.04	0.04
Gas	0.85	0.97	1.89	5.46	2.10	0.35
Therapeutic appliances	0.50	5.00	0.34	0.03	0.56	1.51

Sources: ICP 2011 and data analysis by Imededdine Jerbi, ICP Global Office.

available only in specialty shops and as a result more expensive. This outcome would lower the real expenditures of those countries compared with those in the Eurostat-OECD comparison. Second, even though the Ring comparison was a vast improvement over the bridge method, the results were still dependent on the choice of countries to price the Ring products. A different set of Ring countries may have provided different results. Third, estimation of the linking factors is dependent on a set of Ring prices that are then deflated by the within-region basic heading PPPs. However, the regions were allowed to publish their results before validation of the Ring prices was complete. There was therefore no opportunity to seek a review of the within-region basic heading PPPs not consistent with the relative prices from the Ring countries.

Linking Basic Headings Not Included in the Ring Comparison

This section is an overview of how the basic headings not included in the Ring comparison were linked.

Actual and Imputed Rentals for Housing

Chapters 3, 12, and 17 describe the three methods used in the 2005 ICP to estimate housing PPPs: rental prices, quantity indicators, and relative volumes. PPPs based on rental prices are computed by means of the same methods used for prices in other basic headings. These rental prices are also used to represent owner-occupied housing. Some countries have limited rental markets. Therefore, a method based on the quantity and quality of housing (the quantity method) was used to impute PPPs in the Asia-Pacific and Africa regions. Both of these regions have limited rental markets, pointing to the use of quantity indicators. However, because countries in those regions had difficulties providing housing quantities, the relative volume of household consumption expenditures was used as the reference volume for actual and imputed rentals and to impute PPPs. Rental PPPs were thus neutral because being neutral did not affect the per capita volumes for private household consumption. All other regions were able to use either rental prices or the quantity method or a combination.

All countries, including those in the Africa and Asia-Pacific regions, were requested to submit quantity and quality data to the Global Office. From this set, data on housing quantities for 106 countries were used in a CPD regression to estimate between-region PPPs. This matrix of quantity and quality indicators was too sparse to estimate PPPs at the individual country level. However, it was sufficient to compute the between-region PPPs for the five groups of countries. Chapter 12 on dwelling services contains considerable detail on these different methods. The dilemma is that the use of relative volumes to impute PPPs in Africa and the Asia-Pacific may have overstated the rental PPPs in those countries in which there is considerable informal housing. If so, this overstatement would have lowered the real expenditures in those countries compared with those in the rest of the world.

Health, Education, and Government Compensation

Chapters 11, 15, and 16 provide background on how government expenditures enter into the estimation of PPPs for health and education. Chapter 16 summarizes the issues on the use of productivity adjustments for the government compensation basic headings. There was no separate

Ring list for government compensation because all countries submitted salary results for the same set of occupations. There was also considerable overlap between the ICP global occupations and those used by the Eurostat-OECD and CIS countries. The main difference was that the regional PPPs for government compensation were adjusted for productivity in the Africa, Asia-Pacific, and Western Asia regions. The adjustments increased the spread of the real expenditures for compensation in countries in those regions. Without those adjustments, the very low salaries in many countries would have resulted in real expenditures at implausibly high levels.

The dilemma was how to link countries in these regions with the rest of the world where no adjustments for productivity were made. One consideration was that there was no need for productivity adjustments in the other regions. However, within each region were countries similar to those in Africa, the Asia-Pacific, and Western Asia where adjustments were made. Compensation data not adjusted for productivity for 75 countries representing all regions were used to compute between-region PPPs. If the linking factors were adjusted for productivity, then the spread between ICP countries and those in the Eurostat-OECD would be increased. Thus care should be taken in making comparisons between, say, India (productivity adjustment) and Tajikistan (no adjustment).

Equipment and Construction

Global specifications were priced by all countries in the ICP regions and the Ring countries in the Eurostat-OECD region. The same prices were used for both the regional results and the estimation of linking factors.

Results

This section provides some basic heading regional linking factors from the 2005 ICP and explains how they are related to the global-level PPPs—that is, all countries linked to US = 1.0.

Table 8.4 shows the between-region PPPs or linking factors for a selected set of basic headings and for the GDP. The between-region PPP for the rice basic heading for the Asia-Pacific region was 5.81. The rice basic heading PPP linked to US = 1.0 for each country in the Asia-Pacific region was its within-region PPP multiplied by 5.81. The rice PPPs for China and India (from the Asia-Pacific region with Hong Kong SAR, China = 1.00) were 0.53 and 2.64, respectively. When each was multiplied by 5.81, the global PPPs (US = 1.0) for China and India were 3.08 and 15.34, respectively. Each basic heading linking factor is a regional scalar that, when multiplied by each country's within-region basic heading PPP, becomes the global PPP. Because the linking factor is a scalar, the PPPs between countries within the region remain the same whether they are compared at the global level or the regional level. The PPP for China/India is 0.200 using the regional PPPs (0.53/2.64) or the global PPPs (3.08/15.34).

Equation (8.2) and the example in figure 8.1 both show that the linking factor for each basic heading is also the global PPP for the regional base countries. Hong Kong SAR, China; Brazil; the United Kingdom; South Africa; and Oman were the regional base countries for the estimation of the between-region PPPs for the Asia-Pacific, South America, Eurostat-OECD, Africa, and Western Asia regions. The rice basic heading PPP for Hong Kong SAR, China linked to the United States is 5.81. This relationship holds for every level of aggregation. In other words, the linking factor for the GDP level of aggregation for Africa is the PPP for South Africa linked to US = 1.0. The regional linking factors can be observed for every region and level of aggregation by simply looking at the PPP of the regional base country.

TABLE 8.4 Linking Factors for Selected Basic Headings: Between-Region Basic Heading PPPs, ICP 2005 (US = 1.0)

Basic heading	Asia-Pacific	South America	Eurostat-OECD	CIS	Africa	Western Asia
1101111 Rice	5.81	1.26	0.65	15.52	4.84	0.23
1101121 Beef and veal	8.12	0.76	0.68	12.13	4.33	0.24
1101131 Fresh or frozen fish and seafood	4.45	1.30	0.46	13.19	3.22	0.14
1103121 Garments	5.84	2.42	0.68	27.62	5.47	0.28
1104111 Actual and imputed rentals for housing	7.96	1.03	0.49	4.57	2.40	0.70
110451 Electricity	9.92	4.29	0.81	9.33	5.65	0.22
110611 Pharmaceutical products	6.83	2.35	0.39	14.75	10.82	0.37
110612 Other medical products	8.29	3.89	0.69	11.81	10.27	0.56
110613 Therapeutic appliances and equipment	6.46	1.89	0.77	30.99	5.61	0.44
110621 Medical Services	3.47	1.39	0.48	4.08	2.60	0.09
110622 Dental services	1.55	0.35	0.39	4.86	0.85	0.10
110623 Paramedical services	2.96	0.77	0.79	4.18	2.24	0.12
110630 Hospital services	2.29	0.51	0.39	2.74	2.03	0.12
110711 Motor cars	11.69	3.16	0.70	27.96	7.76	0.31
110712 Motorcycles	12.18	3.29	0.66	34.14	8.09	0.33
111000 Education	4.39	1.45	0.40	1.53	2.79	0.17
130221 Compensation of employees—health services	1.46	0.19	0.23	0.71	0.72	0.08
130421 Compensation of employees—education services	1.75	0.36	0.45	1.53	1.06	0.11
140111 Compensation of employees—collective services	1.92	0.50	0.50	3.50	1.15	0.10
150110 Metal products and equipment	8.26	3.38	0.68	29.76	6.26	0.39
150120 Transport equipment	5.89	1.94	0.55	21.45	5.45	0.19
150210 Residential buildings	3.60	0.93	0.70	13.67	3.47	0.11
150220 Nonresidential buildings	3.85	0.95	0.85	14.81	3.67	0.12
150230 Civil engineering works	4.95	1.27	0.73	14.59	5.14	0.16
GDP	5.69	1.36	0.65	12.74	3.87	0.23
Coefficient of variation, all basic headings	0.54	0.47	0.36	0.54	0.87	0.60

Source: ICP 2005.

The linking factors for the CIS column are the PPPs of Russia to US = 1.0, with Russia included in the Eurostat-OECD computations. Thus the relative levels of the linking factors for each basic heading in the CIS region are based on Russia.

Table 8.4 also shows the variability in the linking factors across the basic headings compared with the GDP linking factors. The lowest level for all regions is the compensation of employees for health services. Recall that the within-region PPPs for the Africa, Asia-Pacific, and Western Asia regions were adjusted for productivity, but the linking factors were not adjusted. These linking factors would likely have been larger had they also been adjusted for productivity. Also note that the linking factors are generally lower for services than they are for goods.

The final line in table 8.4 is the coefficient of variation, which measures the average dispersion of the basic heading linking factors around the GDP linking factors. The dispersion of the linking factors was generally greater than those observed for the respective regional comparisons. Perhaps this is to be expected because countries within regions are more alike in price structures, and the linking factors have to bring together every region of the world. On the other hand, it could mean that the variability in the linking factors was the result of the countries selected to price the Ring products—in other words, the selected countries may not have been representative of their respective regions.

The variability in the linking factors was likely also caused by the different methods used across regions. For example, PPPs for dwelling services were computed three different ways. Productivity adjustments were applied to government compensation in three regions, but were not used when estimating linking factors. The Eurostat-OECD and CIS regions applied the representativity concept, but it was not used in the other regions or in the estimation of linking factors.

Lessons Learned

The following lessons were learned from the Ring comparison in the 2005 ICP. First, the list of Ring products had to contain products comparable across countries in different regions. Not all of these products were representative of purchases in every country. Therefore, unless some way is found to classify products by importance, they all receive equal weight in the estimation of linking factors. A lesson learned, then, was that the process to determine representativity should be simplified. The concept of importance described in chapter 7 will be implemented and also made a part of the data validation exercise.

Second, because Ring countries should represent the regional price and economic structures, they should be selected using the within-region PPP results. In addition, the variability across countries suggests that more countries should submit prices for a global list.

Third, the two-stage estimation of between-region linking factors depends on the within-region PPPs to deflate Ring prices to regional currencies. The data validation of the within-region basic heading PPPs should not be completed until the linking factors have also been finalized. An outlier linking factor may be the cause of the within-region PPP, not the Ring data.

Fourth, Dikhanov (2009) showed that a core list that contained only about 30 percent of the original list of Ring products still provided consistent results. From this finding emerged the method used to link regions in the 2011 ICP. A set of global core products has been developed that will be a subset of every region's regional list. Every country will provide prices for the global core list, thereby fully satisfying the transitivity and invariance properties directly. In addition, data from all countries will be used to estimate the between-region linking factors, which means the linking is not conditional on the choice of countries.

Fifth, although it is important that regions have choices of methodology, too many different methods were used, making the linking process even more difficult. The next section summarizes the actions to be taken for the 2011 ICP to minimize the regional differences.

The Way Forward

The linking methodology used for the 2005 ICP was a huge improvement over what was used for previous rounds. Much was learned from the Ring exercise, and it is guiding the choice of methods for the 2011 round.

A set of global products was prepared for household consumption items—the so-called core list. Each region decided which elements of the core list would be part of its regional data collection. Thus every country will be pricing a set of global products, and so every country's data will be used to estimate the between-region linking factors. The ICP Global Office developed global specifications for health, education, quantities of housing, government compensation, equipment, and construction; the regional and global lists are the same.

The definition of *representativity* was simplified (it is now called "importance") to mainly describe products widely consumed. Chapter 7 provides details on the use of the importance concept for the regional and core products.

The validation of the regional and core product prices will proceed in parallel so that inconsistencies across the two lists can be identified and removed.

Finally, regions will be allowed flexibility in how they estimate the within-region PPPs for dwellings (price or quantity methods) and government compensation (with or without productivity adjustments). However, the linking method for dwellings will require that all countries submit the data on housing quantities as described in chapter 12. The global aggregation used for government compensation will incorporate productivity adjustments for all countries in all regions (even if a region's results were not adjusted).

ANNEX A

Number of Products in Major Categories, by Region and Ring, ICP 2005

Category	Africa	Asia-Pacific	CIS	Eurostat-OECD	South America	Western Asia	Ring
Food and nonalcoholic beverages	356	223	198	422	147	353	281
Alcoholic beverages and tobacco	41	19	20	72	8	21	30
Clothing and footwear	128	78	104	319	136	162	132
Housing and utilities	21	17	22	64	18	12	35
Furnishings and household equipment	95	85	91	460	77	83	124
Health	144	112	75	244	51	69	162
Transportation	55	65	47	365	33	29	96
Communication	19	19	16	81	8	12	28
Recreation and culture	49	70	79	336	54	59	96
Education	7	7	7	5	10	11	7
Restaurants and hotels	51	25	45	117	14	20	60
Miscellaneous goods and services	34	56	36	136	22	31	44
Total consumption	*1,000*	*776*	*740*	*2,621*	*578*	*862*	*1,095*
General government	*50*	*50*	*50*	*50*	*50*	*50*	*50*
Construction	*34*	*34*	*34*	*34*	*34*	*34*	*34*
Equipment	*108*	*108*	*108*	*108*	*108*	*108*	*108*

Source: ICP 2005.

ANNEX B

Worksheet to Provide Indexes to Backcast Ring Prices to 2005 and from Capital City to National Level

ICP 2005—Instruction for Submitting Indexes for Ring Country Prices

Please fill out the lowest available level.

Country Name		XXXXXX	Ring Survey Date (Month, 2006)	Reference CPI for the Ring Survey Date (Month, 2006)	Reference CPI (Annual, 2005)	Ratio of Capital to National Prices
Nº	Code	Description				
1	100000	**GROSS DOMESTIC PRODUCT**				
2	110000	**FINAL CONSUMPTION EXPENDITURE BY HOUSEHOLDS**				
3	110100	**FOOD AND NONALCOHOLIC BEVERAGES**				
4	110110	**Food**				
5	110111	*Bread and cereals*				
6	110111.1	Rice				
7	110111.2	Other cereals, flour, and other cereal products				
8	110111.3	Bread				
9	110111.4	Other bakery products				
10	110111.5	Pasta products				
11	110112	*Meat*				
12	110112.1	Beef and veal				
13	110112.2	Pork				
14	110112.3	Lamb, mutton, and goat				
15	110112.4	Poultry				
16	110112.5*	Other meats and meat preparations				
17	110113	*Fish*				
18	110113.1	Fresh, chilled, or frozen fish and seafood				
19	110113.2	Preserved or processed fish and seafood				
20	110114	*Milk, cheese, and eggs*				
21	110114.1	Fresh milk				
22	110114.2	Preserved milk and other milk products				
23	110114.3	Cheese				

Source: ICP 2005.

NOTE

1. The five geographic regions were Africa, Asia-Pacific, Commonwealth of Independent States, South America, and Western Asia. The Eurostat-OECD comparison constituted the sixth region.

REFERENCES

Diewert, W. E. 2004. "On the Stochastic Approach to Linking the Regions in the ICP." Discussion Paper 04-16, Department of Economics, University of British Columbia, Vancouver.

Dikhanov, Yuri. 2009. "Efficiency of the Core Product List in International Comparisons." Report prepared for Technical Advisory Group meeting, World Bank, Washington, DC, October 1–2.

Sergeev, Sergey. 2007. "Use of Coefficients of Similarity of Price Structures in the Ring Comparison." Paper prepared for the Technical Advisory Group, International Comparison Program, World Bank, Washington, DC.

Vogel, Frederic A. 2009. "Lessons Learned from ICP 2005." Report prepared for Technical Advisory Group meeting, World Bank, Washington, DC, October 1–2.

World Bank. 2007. *ICP 2005 Methodological Handbook*. http://web.worldbank.org/WBSITE/EXTERNAL/DATASTATISTICS/ICPEXT/0,,contentMDK:20126612~pagePK:60002244~piPK:62002388~theSitePK:270065,00.html.

———. 2008. *Global Purchasing Power Parities and Real Expenditures: 2005 International Comparison Program*. http://siteresources.worldbank.org/ICPINT/Resources/icp-final.pdf.

CHAPTER 9

Validation of ICP Regional Prices and Basic Heading PPPs

David Roberts

The national coordinating agencies (NCAs) of countries participating in regional comparisons of the International Comparison Program (ICP) provide the regional coordinating agency (RCA) with a set of national annual purchasers' prices for a selection of items chosen from a common list of precisely defined products. The prices refer to the year of the comparison and cover the whole range of final goods and services included in the gross domestic product (GDP). They are used to calculate purchasing power parities (PPPs) for basic headings, and the basic heading PPPs are used to derive intraregional measures of price and volume relatives for the countries participating in the comparison. The measures are subsequently published by the RCA, thereby reaching a variety of users, including policy makers, economic analysts, researchers, politicians, and journalists, as well as the general public. If the measures are to contribute accurately to informed debate, it is essential that the prices on which the PPPs are based are rigorously checked and corrected for error—that is, validated—before the PPPs are calculated. The validation of price data is thus a priority for ICP regional comparisons. This chapter describes how the ICP validates regional price data. The same procedures are employed to validate price data collected across regions in order to combine them in a global comparison.

Two types of error are considered here: sampling error and nonsampling error. Sampling error occurs because the prices on which the PPPs are based are collected from a sample of outlets rather than from all outlets. Nonsampling error occurs for reasons such as pricing the wrong product or incorrectly recording the product's price or unit of measure. An important distinction between the two types of error is that sampling error would disappear if prices were collected by an enumeration of all outlets, but nonsampling error would not; it would continue to occur. Sampling error is controlled before price collection through sample design; nonsampling error is handled both before and during price collection through good survey design and management and after price collection through validation. ICP validation is directed at nonsampling error and not sampling error. The objective is to minimize, if not eliminate, the incidence of nonsampling error among regional price data after collection. This goal is achieved by editing and verification. Editing consists of checking prices for possible errors. Verification consists of either confirming that the prices identified as possible errors are correct or correcting them if they are not.

Validation is an iterative process requiring a number of rounds of editing and verification. Possible errors are found by identifying prices that have a measure of divergence that is greater than a given critical value or a value that falls outside a given range of acceptable values. The divergence measures are generally defined by the parameters of the series being edited—parameters such as the average and the standard deviation. Hence if some of the possible errors identified in the initial edit are found to be actual errors and are corrected, the parameters of the price series will change and so will the divergence measures of each price remaining in the series. A second edit will find new possible errors that must be verified. Again, when the actual errors are corrected, the parameters of the price series will change, which may lead to more possible errors being detected if a third edit is made. Usually the number of new possible errors falls as the validation progresses, until the return on further rounds is considered marginal and not worth pursuing. Time is also a consideration: first, because of the need to release data on a timely basis and, second, because the longer the delay between price collection and verification, the more difficult it becomes to correct the prices that are wrong.

ICP validation comprises two separate processes: one to edit and verify the prices collected by a single country, referred to as *intra*country validation; the other to edit and verify the prices collected by all countries participating in the regional comparison, referred to as *inter*country validation. Intracountry validation is directed at a country's individual price observations and the average prices to which they give rise. The objective is to verify that price collectors *within a country* have priced comparable products and have priced them correctly. It is carried out by the country's NCA, with or without input from the RCA, depending on the region. Intercountry validation is directed at the average prices reported by participating countries and the price ratios that the average prices generate between the countries. The objective is to verify that price collectors *in different countries* have priced products that are comparable across the countries and have priced them correctly. Intercountry validation takes place after intracountry validation and is carried out jointly by the RCA and the NCAs. Both processes are explained in this chapter.

Before considering the validation processes, it is important to emphasize that prevention is preferable to correction. The incidence of nonsampling error can be significantly reduced through good survey design and management. Price collections should be carefully planned, efficiently carried out, and properly supervised; product specifications should be sufficiently detailed to enable price collectors to identify products unambiguously in the outlets they visit; price collectors should be well trained, given clear instructions, and provided with price reporting forms that are user-friendly; fieldwork should be closely monitored to ensure that price collectors record the prices, quantities, and other data required; and the staff engaged in processing and validating the prices should be properly trained and supervised. Validation complements good survey practice. Failure to observe good survey practice will not be rectified through editing and verification, however thorough.

Possible Errors, Errors, and Outliers

For a price comparison to be valid, the products whose prices are being compared must be comparable—that is, the same or equivalent—and the prices themselves have to be free from error and bias. Failure to meet either one of these requirements negates the comparison. To avoid this happening, the editing and verification procedures employed for the ICP regional comparisons focus on the main types of nonsampling error: product error and price error.

A *product error* occurs when price collectors price products that do not match the product specification and then neglect to report having done so. Perhaps they are not aware of the mismatch, such as when the product specification is too loose,[1] or perhaps they price a substitute product as required by the pricing guidelines but do not mention this on the price reporting form. Price collectors are usually instructed to collect the price of a substitute product if they are unable to find the product specified. They are further instructed to flag the substitution and to note the differences between the substitute product and the specified product. Flagging brings the substitution to the attention of the NCA, which, together with the RCA, can then decide what to do with the price collected. It may be possible to adjust the price for quality differences between the product priced and the product specified. Or, if other countries report prices for the same substitute product,[2] price comparisons can be made for the substitute product, as well as for the product originally specified. If neither of these options is available, the price will have to be discarded. Substitution does not in itself introduce error. It is the failure of price collectors to flag and document the substitution that gives rise to a product error.[3]

A *price error* occurs when price collectors price products that do match the product specification but record the price incorrectly, or they record the price correctly and error is introduced afterward in the process of reporting and transmitting the price. Associated with each price is a quantity: the specified quantity (the quantity to be priced) and the reference quantity (the quantity to which the price collected is to be adjusted). Price error can also arise because, even though the price is correctly recorded, the quantity priced is recorded incorrectly (or it is recorded correctly and error is introduced later during processing), so that the adjusted price for the reference quantity, which is the price that is validated, will be wrong as well.[4]

Editing for product errors and price errors involves identifying prices that have extreme values—that is, prices whose values are determined to be either too high or too low vis-à-vis the average according to the criteria used. The price may score a value for a given test that exceeds a predetermined critical value, or its value may fall outside some prespecified range of acceptable values. Both are standard ways of detecting errors in survey data, and both are employed by the ICP. Prices with extreme values are not necessarily wrong. But the fact that their values are considered extreme suggests that they could be wrong—that is, they are possible errors and need to be investigated. It is not ICP practice to reject prices with extreme values outright; rather, the ICP first establishes whether they are genuine observations. Then it can decide how to deal with them. Prices with extreme values that are found to be wrong are errors and should be corrected or dropped. Prices with extreme values that are shown to be accurate observations are "outliers"[5] and should be retained if they are part of the population defined by the rest of the price observations. In practice, it is not unusual for outliers that meet this criterion to be "corrected"—that is, discarded or replaced by an imputed value—in order to remove the "noise" they introduce into the data set.

Inliers and Bias

Just as all prices that have a test score above a critical value or a value that falls outside a range of acceptable values are not necessarily errors, all prices that have a test score below the critical value or within the range of acceptable values are not necessarily free from product error or price error. These prices—sometimes referred to as "inliers"—are not picked up during the editing for extreme values, at least not initially. However, because validation is an iterative process, they may be detected at a later stage. Another and perhaps surer way of finding inliers during intracountry validation is, in addition to editing all the prices together, to group them by type of outlet and location and to edit each group separately. In this way, extreme values, and possible inliers, which were not considered extreme when all the prices were being edited together, will emerge.

Editing by type of outlet and location is not an option for intercountry validation because there are no internationally agreed definitions of outlet types or of urban and rural. Moreover, not all countries collect prices in rural areas; instead, they use spatial coefficients to adjust urban prices to national prices. Even so, editing prices by type of outlet and location during intracountry validation can aid intercountry validation by allowing the mix of outlets and locations at which individual products were priced to be analyzed. This analysis is of particular relevance to those products found to have extreme average prices during intercountry validation. These average prices may be extreme not because of outliers or undetected inliers in the underlying price observations, but because they are biased—a bias caused by their prices being observed at a selection of outlets and locations that do not fit their distribution profile.[6]

The selection of outlets for a price survey is supposed to mirror consumer purchasing patterns at various outlet types for the products being priced. For example, if consumers purchase 60 percent of their clothing and footwear from supermarkets, 20 percent from department stores, and 20 percent from specialty shops, a sample of 10 outlets for the clothing and footwear survey would include six supermarkets, two department stores, and two specialty shops. And if 70 percent of these purchases were made in urban areas and 30 percent in rural areas, seven of the selected outlets would be in urban areas and three in rural areas. Selecting outlets in this way introduces implicit weights to accommodate the varying service elements of outlets and their impacts on price.[7] Unbiased average prices are the result.[8]

In general, the NCAs try to select outlets in line with the distribution profiles of the products being surveyed as far as they are known. The selection will not be specific to each type of product being surveyed, but to the group of products overall. Hence, although the selection will be representative of the distribution profile of the group, it will not necessarily be representative of the distribution profiles of all products within the group, and the average price of those products for which the outlet location mix is wrong will be either too high or too low. For example, if the distribution of underwear purchases is 80 percent supermarkets, 10 percent department stores, and 10 percent specialty shops, the 60/20/20 selection described earlier for clothing and footwear would systematically overstate the average prices for underwear because the service element of department stores and specialty shops is normally greater than that of supermarkets, and their prices are correspondingly higher.

This problem is insoluble because the resources for price collection are limited. An outlet selection that is appropriate for a broad group of products will inevitably be unsuitable for some of the types of products included in the broad group. It is simply not feasible to design a sample of outlets that is appropriate for each and every item to be priced. The problem has to be addressed after price collection. Intracountry validation of average prices by outlet type and location can help to identify products for which the output location mix is not representative. In particular, it can be used to identify products whose average prices are biased by the dominance of one specific outlet type. The average prices of such products can be corrected by suppressing price observations from outlet types that are overrepresented or by duplicating the price observations from outlet types that are underrepresented.

The selection of outlets, whether randomized or purposive, can result in choosing outlets that are themselves outliers and not representative of the purchasing patterns of the average consumer. If the selection of outlets has been randomized, the outlier outlets must be retained because dropping them would undermine the theoretical justification for random selection. But if the selection was purposive, the answer is not so clear. The objective behind purposive sampling is to select a set of outlets that are representative of those used by households most of the time. If the prices at a selected outlet do not conform to the price levels of other outlets of the same type, being consistently higher or consistently lower, the outlet is an outlier and should be replaced by one whose prices are closer to the average. Intracountry validation of average prices by outlet type and location helps to identify outlier outlets.

Validation Process

Validation consists of two distinct processes: intracountry validation and intercountry validation. Intracountry validation precedes intercountry validation. It is designed to establish that price collectors within the same country have priced products that match the product specifications and that the prices they have reported are correct. Those conducting intracountry editing search for extreme values first among the individual prices that a country has collected for each product it has chosen to survey and then among the average prices for these products. The editing and subsequent verification are the responsibility of the country's NCA. It is carried out without reference to the price data of other countries.[9] When the NCA has completed intracountry validation, it provides the RCA with validated average prices for the products it priced plus the coefficient of variation, the maximum-minimum ratio, and the number of price observations for each of the average prices reported. These are reviewed by the RCA before starting intercountry validation.

Intercountry validation is designed to establish that price collectors in different countries have priced products that are comparable between countries—in other words, that they have all interpreted the product specifications in the same way—and that the prices they have reported are correct. Those conducting intercountry editing look for extreme values among the average prices that the region's NCAs have reported to the RCA for the same products within a basic heading. In undertaking this task, they convert the average prices, which are expressed in national currencies, to a common currency. Both exchange rates and PPPs are used to carry out this process, as explained later. After being converted, the average prices of each NCA are checked against the average prices of the other NCAs in the region. This task cannot be carried out effectively without the lead and active participation of the RCA and the NCAs agreeing to share their average prices with each other.

Intracountry editing usually consists of two rounds of editing and verification and takes about two or more months to complete. Intercountry validation requires on average four rounds of editing and verification and some four months to complete. Intercountry validation takes longer because of the interactions that arise during validation between the data sets of different countries. Revisions introduced by one NCA can alter the outcome of the edits made on the prices of other NCAs. Dealing with such revisions can be time-consuming because not all countries participating in the comparison are covered in the early rounds of validation; they are introduced in later rounds as their average prices become available. For this reason, intercountry validation can take longer than four months.[10] The process is not complete until all countries in the region have been included in the intercountry diagnostic tables and their NCAs have signed off on the validation and formally approved their revised price data.

An important feature of intercountry validation is the iterative nature of the process, with the intercountry diagnostic tables going back and forth between the RCA and the region's NCAs. The process begins with the NCAs sending their average prices to the RCA. The RCA then compiles the diagnostic tables, examines them, identifies prices that seem implausible, and sends the tables with its queries to the NCAs. Once the NCAs have investigated the RCA's queries, the NCAs revise the incorrect prices and send them back to the RCA. After entering the corrections into the database, the RCA recalculates the diagnostic tables, reviews them, and sends them to the NCAs with further questions about the reliability of specific prices. The process continues until both the RCA and the NCAs consider the revised price data to be final.

The intercountry diagnostic tables referred to are called Quaranta tables and Dikhanov tables in the rest of this chapter. They are explained and compared in the annex.

Intracountry Validation

Central to intracountry validation is the validation and averaging module. The module generates two diagnostic tables for use by the NCAs as they edit the individual prices they have observed and the average prices to which the individual prices give rise. These diagnostic tables are the price observation table and the average price table (see tables 9.1a and 9.2a). A price observation table is created for each product priced within a basic heading. The columns list the individual prices observed, other characteristics of the product, and the results of diagnostic tests designed to identify possible errors. The average price table contains the prices and diagnostics for every product in the basic heading. Although the NCA reviews both tables, the RCA sees only the average price table. The price observation table identifies extreme values among the *individual prices* collected for a specific product, whereas the average price table flags extreme values among the *average prices* of the products priced. Common to both tables are fields 01–04, which identify the product and specify the reference quantity (the quantity to which the price observations are to be adjusted when a product specification gives a range for the quantity to be priced). It is the individual prices and the average price for the reference quantity that are validated.[11]

The first step in the validation process is to enter the individual prices and related information into the module (fields 05–15 of table 9.1a). Data entry should be done as soon as possible after price collection, so that price collectors and outlet personnel still have a clear recollection of the circumstances prevailing when the prices were collected. Ideally, the individual prices would be entered and screened the day after they are collected, which will allow field supervisors to catch and correct the mistakes of price collectors from the outset of the process.

The second step, after the details of each price observation have been entered, is to check the entries to ensure that the product codes are correct and that the codes and the corresponding price observations have been entered in sequence. There should be numeric entries only for reference quantity, quantity observed, and price observed. The quantity observed should be in the same unit as the reference quantity. The importance indicator[12] should be entered for all price observations of products that are important.

Intracountry editing has two stages. The first involves identifying extreme values among the individual prices listed in the price observation table. The second involves identifying extreme values among the average prices of the products listed in the average price table. An extreme value is defined as an individual price or average price that for a given test scores a value that falls outside a predetermined critical value.

The diagnostic tests, which are based on statistical theory, all involve measures of variability. If prices are normally distributed, they are centered on the mean, and the standard deviation provides a measure of the average departure from it. Ninety-five percent of the observations will be in the range of the mean plus or minus two standard deviations, and 99 percent plus or minus three standard deviations. In many cases, however, the prices will follow a distribution shaped like a right triangle (mostly low prices with a declining number of higher prices). The mean and standard deviation are both functions of the minimum and maximum values. The diagnostics used to validate prices take into account both kinds of distributions:

- Extreme values among price observations in the price observation table are identified by means of two tests: the ratio to average price test and the T-value test.

  Ratio to average price test. The ratio to average price is the ratio of the reference quantity price for a price observation to the average reference quantity price for the product. To pass the test, the ratio has to be within the range of 0.5–1.5. In other words, an individual price is expected to be no less than half of the mean or no more than double the mean price. A price observation with a ratio that falls outside this range fails the test and will be flagged in the price observation table as having an extreme value that needs to be checked. This is a simple first test because it does not rely on the standard deviation, which is also affected by an extreme value.

  The choice of the range 0.5–1.5 as the critical value is based on statistical theory and practical experience from previous data collections. Product specifications, which are as precise as possible, are expected to provide price observations that are less than plus or minus half the average price if the product specification has been priced correctly.

  T-value test. The T-value is the ratio of the deviation of the reference quantity price for a price observation from the average reference quantity price for the product to the standard deviation of the product. To pass the test, the ratio must be 2.0 or less (any value greater than 2.0 is suspect because it falls outside the 95 percent confidence interval). A price observation with a ratio greater than 2.0 fails the test and will be flagged in the price observation table as having an extreme value requiring investigation.
- Extreme values among average prices shown in the average price table are also identified by two tests: the max-min ratio test and the coefficient of variation test.

  Max-min ratio test. The max-min ratio is the ratio of the maximum reference quantity price observed for the product to the minimum reference quantity price observed for the product. An average price with a ratio greater than 2.0 fails the test and will be flagged in the average price table as having an extreme value that needs to be verified. The ratio of 2.0 implies a coefficient of variation (standard deviation/mean) of 10–15 percent or a 95 percent confidence interval of 20–30 percent.

  Coefficient of variation test. The coefficient of variation is the standard deviation for the product expressed as a percentage of the average price for the product. To pass the test, the coefficient of variation should be 20 percent or below. An average price with a coefficient of variation greater than 20 percent fails the test and will be flagged in the average price table as having an extreme value that requires verification.

  As with the ratio to average price test, the critical values are based on expectations arising from the precision of the product specifications. These two tests produce similar results. The max-min ratio test is most useful when a price observation differs considerably from the rest of the observations. When the coefficient of variation test shows a large value, it may indicate that the product was too loosely specified.

The validation and averaging module is programmed to flag price observations and average prices that have test values that fall outside the critical values. It is the reliability of the individual prices of the flagged price observations and of the flagged average prices that has to be established. Or, more precisely, it is the reliability of the flagged price observations and of the price observations underlying the flagged average prices that the NCA must investigate.[13]

The NCA should first check that flagged price observations have been entered correctly into the module. In other words, it should verify that the prices in the price observation table are the same as those on the price reporting forms. If they are not the same, the price in the table should be corrected and the modification noted in field 20. If they are the same, the prices have been entered correctly. The NCA will have to revisit the outlets where the prices were collected to ascertain whether the products priced match the product specifications and whether the prices reported are correct. If the product matches the product specification and the correct price has been reported, verification is complete. The extreme value is established as an accurate observation and an outlier—a finding that should be noted in field 19 of the table. If the product priced does not match the product specification or if the price has been reported incorrectly, the situation must be rectified by finding a product in the outlet that does match the product specification and pricing it or establishing the correct price for the product originally priced if it is still available.

The following courses of action are open to the NCA:

- Price observations that are flagged and found to be incorrect are either suppressed or replaced by the correct observation.
- Price observations that are flagged as failing the ratio to average price test—but not the T-value test—and found to be correct are outliers. An outlier should be retained if it is a valid observation and part of the population as defined by the rest of the price observations. This can be established by recalculating the average price and the standard deviation without including the outlier and using them to derive a T-value for the outlier. If the T-value is now greater than 2.0, the outlier, though accurate, is not valid and should be suppressed. If the T-value still does not fall outside the critical value, then the observation is valid and should be retained at least initially. Later, during intercountry validation, it can be decided whether it should be suppressed or replaced by an imputation.
- Price observations that are flagged as failing the T-value test and found to be correct are also outliers. Even so, they should be suppressed because they clearly are not part of the same population as the other price observations, even when included in the calculation of the average price and standard deviation.

In all cases, the suppression or correction of a price observation should be noted in field 20 of the price observation table.

Table 9.1a illustrates how the price observation table looks when first generated and after the first review by the NCA: extreme values are in boldface, the NCA comments are in field 19. All the price observations for rice A are shown as having failed the ratio to average price test, though only one, in field 16, column 8, is flagged as having failed the T-value test. All the observations for rice A appear to need verification, but do they? A closer examination reveals that only one observation needs investigating initially, and that is the 499.00 price with the high T-value. It is 10 times larger than the other observations and dominates the average price and the standard deviation, all of which explain the poor showing of the other observations in the ratio to average price test.

Table 9.1b shows the price observation table after verification. On investigation, the 499.00 was found to be a price error. The price had been recorded incorrectly during data entry. It has been replaced by the correct price as noted in field 20. As a result, the observation no longer fails the T-value test, and all the remaining observations pass the ratio to average price test.

In Table 9.1b, the two observations with shaded columns did not match the product specification. In the corner shop (outlet 19), the rice priced was sold loose and not in a packet as

TABLE 9.1a Validation Process: Price Observation Table after First Review by National Coordinating Agency and before Verification

	Field	After first review and before verification								
01	Product code	1101111.0111								
02	Abbreviated product description	rice A, packet 400–600 grams								
03	Reference quantity	500								
04	Unit of reference quantity	grams								
05	Date of observation	dd/mm/yy	dd/mm/yy	dd/mm/yy	dd/mm/yy	dd/mm/yy	dd/mm/yy	dd/mm/yy	dd/mm/yy	dd/mm/yy
06	Price collector identifier	A	A	B	B	C	C	C	D	D
07	Outlet identifier	001	009	015	019	025	036	037	048	051
08	Location of outlet	rural	rural	rural	rural	urban	urban	urban	urban	urban
09	Type of outlet	market	market	market	corner shop	supermarket	market	corner shop	kiosk	supermarket
10	Quantity observed	400	400	400	500	1,000	400	600	450	400
11	Unit of observed quantity	grams	grams	grams	grams	grams	grams	grams	grams	grams
12	Price observed	28.72	31.92	31.92	50.00	80.00	34.32	59.88	449.10	44.00
13	Importance indicator	*	*	*	*				*	*
14	Price type	bargained	bargained	bargained	regular	discounted	bargained	regular	regular	regular
15	Additional information				sold loose	only packet size available				
16	Reference quantity price	35.90	39.90	39.90	50.00	40.00	42.90	49.90	499.00	55.00
17	Ratio to average price	**0.38**	**0.42**	**0.42**	**0.53**	**0.42**	**0.45**	**0.53**	**5.27**	**0.58**
18	T-value	−0.39	−0.36	−0.36	−0.29	−0.36	−0.34	−0.30	**2.66**	−0.26
19	NCA comments				mismatch	mismatch			verify	
20.	Status of price observation	original	original	original	original	original	original	original	original	original
	Column number	*1*	*2*	*3*	*4*	*5*	*6*	*7*	*8*	*9*

Note: A product is important if it is a volume seller. Important products are identified by an asterisk (*) and are often referred to as "asterisk products."

TABLE 9.1b Validation Process: Price Observation Table after Verification

	Field	After verification								
01	Product code	1101111.0111								
02	Abbreviated product description	rice A, packet 400–600 grams								
03	Reference quantity	500								
04	Unit of reference quantity	grams								
05	Date of observation	dd/mm/yy	dd/mm/yy	dd/mm/yy	dd/mm/yy	dd/mm/yy	dd/mm/yy	dd/mm/yy	dd/mm/yy	dd/mm/yy
06	Price collector identifier	A	A	B	B	C	C	C	D	D
07	Outlet identifier	001	009	015	019	025	036	037	048	051
08	Location of outlet	rural	rural	rural	rural	urban	urban	urban	urban	urban
09	Type of outlet	market	market	market	corner shop	supermarket	market	corner shop	kiosk	supermarket
10	Quantity observed	400	400	400	500	1000	400	600	450	400
11	Unit of observed quantity	grams	grams	grams	grams	grams	grams	grams	grams	grams
12	Price observed	28.72	31.92	31.92	50.00	80.00	34.32	59.88	44.91	44.00
13	Importance indicator	*	*	*	*		*	*	*	*
14	Price type	regular	regular	regular	bargained	discounted	regular	regular	regular	regular
15	Additional information				sold loose	only packet size available	asterisk added	asterisk added		
16	Reference quantity price	35.90	39.90	39.90	50.00	40.00	42.90	49.90	49.90	55.00
17	Ratio to average price	0.82	0.91	0.91			0.98	1.14	1.14	1.25
18	T-value	−1.12	−0.56	−0.56			−0.14	0.84	0.84	1.55
19	NCA comments				mismatch	mismatch			price error	
20	Status of price observation	original	original	original	suppressed	suppressed	original	original	corrected 49.90	original
	Column number	*1*	*2*	*3*	*4*	*5*	*6*	*7*	*8*	*9*

specified, while in the supermarket (outlet 25) the size of the packet priced was well outside the size range specified. The price collectors had priced these substitute products because rice A was not sold in packets in the corner shop or in smaller packets in the supermarket. Because the prices of the substitute products could not be used, they have been suppressed as recorded in field 20. Note that these observations are mismatches and not product errors, because the price collectors flagged the substitutions (see field 15). They would have been product errors if they had not been flagged. They would have been inliers as well because their values would not have been detected as extreme. This demonstrates the importance of reviewing the additional information provided by price collectors, as well as the individual prices themselves, and not just relying on the mechanical identification of extreme values.

As seen in the example that follows, the suppression or correction of extreme values among price observations will introduce changes that will affect the possible error status of the average price, especially those with high max-min ratios. A high coefficient of variation, on the other hand, can be due to reasons other than a straightforward product error or price error. The price of the product may vary greatly among different types of outlets, or the product may not have been priced consistently across outlets because either the product specification was too broad or it was interpreted differently by different price collectors.

Providing the price observations are correct and a comparable product has been priced across outlets, price variation arising from different outlet types is an economic fact of life. The average price should be kept and the reason for the variation explained to the RCA. It is possible that the mix of outlet types selected for the survey does not reflect the distribution profile of the product in question. If so, it should be investigated and, if necessary, the mix adjusted as appropriate by suppressing prices from those types of outlets that are overrepresented or by duplicating the prices from those types of outlets that are underrepresented.

Products with average prices whose variation is caused by too broad a specification or inconsistent pricing across outlets should be deleted unless they are important *and* the basic heading does not have a sufficient number of products. In this case, they and their average prices should be retained provisionally, and this should be noted in field 30 of the average price table. Later, it can be decided with the RCA whether the products should be dropped, retained, or split on the basis of what other NCAs in the region have reported.

Table 9.2a illustrates how the average price table looks when first generated before any corrections are made to the underlying price observation table (table 9.1a). The average price for rice A is shown as failing both the max-min ratio test and the coefficient of variation test. To find the reason, it is necessary to return to the price observation table and the price error in column 8. Table 9.2b shows the average price table after verification or, more correctly, after verification of its price observation table and correction of column 8. As a result of this correction, the average price passes both the max-min ratio test and the coefficient of variation test.

The validation of individual prices and average prices proceeds product by product across the basic headings. After the second round of validation, most if not all extreme values identified will have been investigated. There may still be extreme values among the price observations and the average prices, but these will have been documented and they can be removed later, during the intercountry validation, if necessary. On completion of the intracountry validation, the NCA sends the average price table to the RCA, which reviews it before entering the average prices into the average price diagnostic module for intercountry validation. The review may give the RCA cause to send the table back to the NCA after it highlights the anomalies among the average prices that need further explanation. The NCA then returns the table to the RCA after it addresses the questions posed by the RCA and corrects the average prices as required.

TABLE 9.2a Average Price Table after First Edit by National Coordinating Agency (NCA) and before Verification

Field		After first edit and before verification		
01	Product code	1101111.0111	1101111.0112	1101111.0113
02	Abbreviated product description	rice A, packet 400–600 grams	rice B, packet 250–500 grams	rice C, sold loose
03	Reference quantity	500	500	1000
04	Unit of reference quantity	grams	grams	grams
21	Reference period	mm/yy	mm/yy	mm/yy
22	Number of observations	9	5	10
23	No. with importance indicator	5	5	10
24	Average price of product	94.72	46.75	45.46
25	Maximum price for product	499.00	69.00	59.90
26	Minimum price for product	35.90	39.90	32.90
27	Max-min ratio	**13.9**	1.7	1.8
28	Standard deviation	151.7	12.63	8.8
29	Coefficient of variation	**160.2**	**27.0**	19.4
30	NCA comments	verify	verify	accept
31	Status of average price	original	original	original

TABLE 9.2b Average Price Table after Verification

Field		After verification		
01	Product code	1101111.0111	1101111.0112	1101111.0113
02	Abbreviated product description	rice A, packet 400–600 grams	rice B, packet 250–500 grams	rice C, sold loose
03	Reference quantity	500	500	1,000
04	Unit of reference quantity	grams	grams	grams
21	Reference period	mm/yy	mm/yy	mm/yy
22	Number of observations	7	4	10
23	No. with importance indicator	7	4	10
24	Average price of product	43.92	41.19	45.46
25	Maximum price for product	55.00	45.00	59.90
26	Minimum price for product	35.90	39.90	32.90
27	Max-min ratio	1.5	1.1	1.8
28	Standard deviation	7.2	2.5	8.8
29	Coefficient of variation	16.3	6.2	19.4
30	NCA comments	verified	verified	accept
31	Status of average price	corrected	corrected	original

Intercountry Validation

Intercountry validation is designed to screen the average prices reported by the region's NCAs for possible errors and to assess the reliability of the PPPs they provide. The objective is to verify that the average prices are for comparable products across countries and that the products have been correctly priced—in other words, to ascertain that the NCAs have interpreted the product specifications in the same way and that they have also priced them accurately. This is done by comparing the average prices for the same product across countries and by analyzing the dispersion of the price ratios that the average prices generate between countries across products and across countries. In short, intercountry editing involves detecting extreme values among the average prices through the corresponding price ratios. It is during this process that the final selection of products to be included in the final computation is made.

Because the NCAs report prices in national currencies, the average prices can be compared only if they are expressed in a common currency. Once converted to a common currency, the average prices of different countries for the same product can be compared with each other and the extreme values identified according to predetermined criteria. But prices, even when expressed in the same currency, cannot be compared across products directly. On the other hand, the price ratios of countries pricing a product can be compared with the equivalent price ratios for other products, providing that they have first been "standardized." Standardized price ratios for a product are the ratios between the individual average prices of the countries pricing the product and the geometric mean of the average prices of all the countries pricing the product when the average prices are expressed in a common currency.[14] Together, tables 9.3a and 9.3b provide a numerical example how these ratios are computed and interpreted. The annex to this chapter shows these data as they are examined using Quaranta and Dikhanov tables. The data in these tables reflect the outcome of several data validations; the purpose is to explain the data validation concepts.

Both exchange rates and PPPs are used in intercountry validation to convert the average prices to a common currency, and both the exchange rate–converted average prices and the PPP-converted average prices are used to derive standardized price ratios. The standardized price ratios based on

TABLE 9.3a Example of Data Validation Using Exchange Rates for Four Countries and Three Products

		Rice basic heading, country details—exchange rate review				
		Country A	**Country B**	**Country C**	**Country D**	**Geometric mean**
1	NC-price 1	5,770	2.11	1.82	1.98	
2	NC-price 2	21,757	7.87	4.66	7.60	
3	NC-price 3	7,075	3.10	2.59	3.09	
4	XR	3,830	1.84	0.759	1.00	
5	XR P 1	1.51	1.15	2.40	1.98	1.69
6	XR P 2	5.68	4.27	6.14	7.60	5.80
7	XR P 3	1.85	1.68	3.40	3.09	2.39
8	XR-ratio 1	89	68	142	117	
9	XR-ratio 2	98	74	106	131	
10	XR-ratio 3	77	70	142	129	

Note: NC = national currency; XR = exchange rate.

TABLE 9.3b Example of Data Validation Using PPPs for Four Countries and Three Products

		Rice basic heading, country details					
		Country A	Country B	Country C	Country D	Geometric mean	Variation coefficient
1	NC-rice 1	5,770	2.11	1.82	1.98		
2	NC-rice 2	21,757	7.87	4.66	7.60		
3	NC-rice 3	7,075	3.10	2.59	3.09		
4	PPP-rice 1	2,914	1.07	0.92	1.00		
5	PPP-rice 2	2,662	1.04	0.61	1.00		
6	PPP-rice 3	2,230	1.00	0.84	1.00		
7	PPP-rice	2,673	1.04	0.779	1.00		
8	PPP-price 1	2.16	2.04	2.34	1.98	2.13	
9	PPP-price 2	8.14	7.60	5.98	7.60	7.28	
10	PPP-price 3	2.65	3.00	3.32	3.09	3.00	
11	PPP-ratio 1	102	96	110	93		7.5
12	PPP-ratio 2	112	104	82	104		12.7
13	PPP-ratio 3	88	100	111	103		9.3
14							
15	Variation coefficient	11.8	4.2	16.1	6.1		9.75

Note: NC = national currency.

exchange rate–converted prices are called XR-ratios, and the standardized price ratios based on PPP-converted prices are called PPP-ratios.[15] Both XR-ratios and PPP-ratios are edited and verified. But only PPP-ratios are used to generate the measures of dispersion referred to shortly.

The PPPs used to convert the average prices to a common currency are calculated from the average prices being validated across countries. This means that editing starts with PPPs based on prices that still have to be verified. These opening PPPs are likely to be unreliable, and the flagging of extreme values among the PPP-ratios is likely to be unreliable as well. Exchange rates, on the other hand, are not determined by the average prices and remain unaffected by them. For this reason, XR-ratios are used in the initial stages of validation. It may appear paradoxical to use XR-ratios to edit the prices from which PPPs are to be derived in view of the fact that PPPs are calculated because exchange rate–converted prices do not reflect the price levels of countries. But experience shows that XR-ratios provide a better "feel" for the reliability of the average prices reported at the beginning of the validation process. Experience also shows that many of the ratios initially identified as extreme values among the XR-ratios are found to be incorrect.

Table 9.3a provides an example of using exchange rates to validate prices across countries. The example is for the rice basic heading with four countries and three products. Rows 1–3 show the national annual average price in the currency of each country for each product, and row 4 each country's exchange rate to country D, whose exchange rate is 1.00 because it is the base. The questions are, did each country price the same or a similar product, and are the prices recorded in the same units? Should the product have been included? Therefore, the next step is to convert each product price to the currency of country D, using the respective exchange rates, to obtain an average product price across countries. These product prices—exchange rate prices or XR-prices—and the respective geometric means are shown in rows 5–7. Even though the prices are now in a common currency, it is readily seen that the price levels differ by product and across countries. Product 2 is several times more expensive than the other products, and all product prices in country B are relatively cheap. In order to examine the country-product relationship in more detail, the standardized exchange rate ratios or XR-ratios are shown in rows 8–10. These are simply each country's XR-price for a product divided by the geometric mean of the product price. Country C shows the most variability, suggesting a review of its average prices for products 1 and 3. Product 3 is the most variable, suggesting that the specifications used to define its characteristics be reviewed across all countries.

The next data validation step is to repeat the steps just shown but using PPPs to convert the national product prices to a common currency. The first step is to compute the product PPPs and aggregate them to country PPPs as shown in table 9.3b. For simplicity purposes, the prices in national currency are repeated in rows 1–3. Rows 4–6 show the product PPPs, which are simply each country's price in its currency divided by country D's price in its currency. The result is a product PPP with country D as the base. As discussed in previous chapters, any country could be chosen as the base. Row 7 shows the aggregated or average PPP for rice for each country—this can be determined using any of the methods described in previous chapters. When the average product prices for each country are divided by the respective PPPs, they are converted to each product's PPP price and its mean as shown in rows 4–6. Because PPPs remove price level differences between countries, one would expect the PPP product prices for each product to be similar, with little variation from the geometric mean.

The PPP ratios in rows 11–13 (PPP price divided by the mean product price) show the variability between countries and between products. The variation coefficients in row 15 are a measure of the variability of the product PPPs for each country (country variation coefficient). Again, country C shows the most variability—twice that of countries B and D. In practice, this may indicate that country C did not price enough items, or that there may be a problem with the price for product 2, which is at a different level than the other products in that country.

The product variation coefficients shown in rows 11–13 measure dispersion among the PPP ratios for each product. In theory, these standardized PPP prices should be the same. Product 2 in country C should be examined again. The variation coefficient representing variability across products and across countries is shown in row 15. This coefficient is most useful when comparing PPPs across basic headings and will be discussed in more detail shortly.

Intercountry validation is an iterative process that can involve several iterations or rounds before being completed. After each round, as incorrect prices are removed or corrected, the PPPs will become more reliable, and so, too, will the flagging of extreme values among the PPP-ratios. Hence as validation progresses, the focus on extreme values shifts from those among the XR-ratios to those among the PPP-ratios. The aim of the exercise is to remove, or at least reduce, the extreme values among the PPP-ratios. If this is achieved, the extreme values remaining among the XR-ratios can be ignored. XR-ratios and PPP-ratios that fall outside the 80–125 range are flagged as having an extreme value requiring verification.

Variation coefficients with values above 33 percent are extreme, requiring the NCAs to investigate the PPP-ratios that are flagged among the PPP-ratios covered by the coefficient. Besides being editing tools, the coefficients provide the means to monitor progress during validation and, at its conclusion, to assess how effective the whole process of editing and verification has been in reducing the incidence of nonsampling error among the price data. Coefficients should be significantly smaller at the end of validation than they were at the beginning.

Outliers

Editing a basic heading with a Quaranta table or an aggregate with a Dikhanov table entails identifying average prices with extreme values or, more precisely, the PPP-ratios with extreme values. The average prices underlying the PPP-ratios flagged as extreme values are the only possible errors. They are not errors by definition, no matter how well established are the criteria used to identify them. They cannot be removed automatically. They have to be referred back to the NCAs reporting them for verification. The NCAs are required to investigate the average prices returned to them as possible errors and to confirm whether they are correct or incorrect. When prices are found to be incorrect, the NCAs are expected to correct them; otherwise, they are suppressed. But if they are found to be correct, they are outliers, and the decision has to be made whether to keep them, to replace them with an imputed value, or to drop them—not necessarily an easy decision. One compromise would be to review the importance classification to ensure important products are classified correctly. Some of the deviations, even larger ones, can be legitimate. Individual economies may have particular pricing policies, such as low fuel prices in some of the oil-producing countries. Such prices may be flagged as extreme values, but they would not be incorrect, and it would be wrong to remove them despite the "noise" they may introduce into the data set.

If, however, there are no extenuating circumstances, the disturbance created by an outlier can have an impact, not only on the PPP for the country reporting the outlier but also on the PPPs for other countries in the regional comparison. In such cases, replacing the outlier with an imputed value or suppressing it are options to be considered. If, within the context of a basic heading, the outlying average price refers to a product that is particularly important for the reporting country, deleting it may not be justified, though imputing a value may be. But if the average price refers to a product that is less important or not important, removing it is probably warranted. Whatever action is taken, it has to be decided jointly by the country's NCA and the RCA on a case-by-case basis.

The annex to this chapter provides a more detailed review of the validation process through use of the Quaranta and Dikhanov tables, which are designed specifically for data validation. The next section is an overview of the process to review PPPs across basic headings. Those readers not familiar with Quaranta and Dikhanov tables may want to review the annex before continuing to the next section.

Validation of Basic Heading PPPs

Dikhanov tables are generally compiled for a group of basic headings constituting an aggregate. Validation at the aggregate level puts the editing and verification of average prices into a broader context. In other words, are the average prices consistent not just within the basic heading, but also within a larger set of products in different basic headings? Editing at the aggregate level enables inconsistencies to be identified that would not be found by editing solely at the basic heading level. For example, suppose that for alcoholic beverages a country priced all the products in quarts instead of liters as specified. The price ratios would be consistent within the basic heading, but they would not be consistent with the country's price ratios in other basic headings. Such errors are identified by editing across basic headings. In this respect, it is useful to compile Dikhanov tables at different levels of aggregation. For example, basic headings covering food items could first be checked in a Dikhanov table covering food and nonalcoholic beverages and subsequently in a Dikhanov table covering all household final consumption expenditure (HFCE).

An example of a Dikhanov table for an aggregate, in this case household final consumption expenditure, is given in Table 9.4a. A modified version—with CPD residuals converted to PPP-ratios and standard deviations shown as variation coefficients—appears in table 9.4b. Neither table is complete. CPD residuals (PPP-ratios) are shown for only 22 of the 864 products priced and for only 9 of the 18 countries included in the comparison. Note also that the PPPs for the aggregate, HFCE, are not weighted. They have been calculated by a CPD that uses the whole set of products and their prices without taking basic heading expenditures into account.

Table 9.4a has two parts. The first part provides summary information (PPPs, standard deviations, and price levels) by country for the aggregate. The second part covers the basic headings constituting the aggregate. For each basic heading there are two sections: one with the same summary information by country but for the basic heading; the other with CPD residuals and product variation coefficients for the products priced for the basic heading. Table 9.4a shows the residuals in log form. To assist in the identification of extreme values among the CPD residuals, the residuals are coded as follows:

CPD residuals with values	Font	PPP-ratio equivalence
Between −0.25 and 0.25	No emphasis	Between 78 and 128
Between −0.75 and −0.25 or 0.25 and 0.75	Italics	Between 47 and 78 or 128 and 212
Between −2.0 and −0.75 or 0.75 and 2.0	Boldface	Between 14 and 47 or 212 and 739
Less than −2.0 or greater than 2.0	Boldface italics	Less than 14 or greater than 739

All residuals distinguished by font should be investigated. All should be checked rigorously, but those in boldface and boldface italics particularly so. Table 9.4b shows the residuals in percentage terms, making it easier to interpret directly.

The first part of table 9.4a facilitates the comparison of PPPs (or price level indexes) across the basic headings. It is to be expected that PPPs will vary from basic heading to basic heading, even in homogeneous regions. And yet it is important that the variability between basic heading PPPs be reviewed and validated to ensure that the PPPs are plausible. For example, the PPPs for fruit for countries D, G, and I are about 40 percent higher than their PPPs for vegetables, while for the other countries the two sets of PPPs are of a similar order of magnitude. This situation may reflect reality, or it may be that the fruit selected for the product list are not representative for these countries, but that possibility needs to be verified. In the case of country I, the average prices of green sweet bell pepper and eggplant would seem to be the problem. If the average prices are verified as correct, a case could be made for dropping the two of them because both the product standard deviation for the pepper and the country standard deviation for the basic heading are over the 0.30 critical value. A similar argument could be developed for garlic in country F if the average price reported is shown to be accurate.

It can also be seen from the tables that the distinguishing fonts help to identify those products having average prices that need verification. But, more important, they make identification of possible problem countries easier—see, for example, countries A, C, and D in the table.

It is at this stage that the classification of importance should be validated. In other words, one would not expect the price for an important product to be an outlier. This could also indicate a possible product selection error.

TABLE 9.4a Dikhanov Table for an Aggregate (Household Final Consumption Expenditure, HFCE), Countries A–I

Item code	Item name	A 2005	B 2005	C 2005	D 2005	E 2005	F 2005	G 2005	H 2005	I 2005	STD 1 STD 3	Items/countries
1100000	**HFCE**											
	PPP	4.052	16.02	0.739	75.69	43.7	7.879	96.76	1.000	5,227		
	STD 2	0.291	0.221	0.297	0.258	0.240	0.279	0.249	0.271	0.276	0.510	
	No. of items priced	567	608	450	566	525	420	481	611	457		864
	XR (LCU/US$)	5.779	13.01	0.709	75.55	51.88	6.359	102.3	0.571	4,464		
	Rebased XR	10.12	22.78	1.242	132.3	90.87	11.14	179.2	1.000	7,817		
	PLI	0.400	0.703	0.595	0.572	0.481	0.707	0.540	1.000	0.669		
1101161	**Fresh or chilled fruit**											
	PPP	1.900	15.65	0.423	57.09	48.31	6.580	99.68	1.000	6,074		
	STD	0.326	0.189	0.353	0.395	0.260	0.164	0.364	0.204	0.126		
	PLI	0.188	0.687	0.341	0.431	0.532	0.591	0.556	1.000	0.777		
1101161.01	Apple: golden delicious		−0.080	0.177		−0.050	0.002	0.105	*−0.290*	0.092	0.145	12
1101161.02	Apple: red delicious		−0.140	0.189		−0.180	0.039	*0.273*	*−0.300*	0.079	0.194	13
1101161.03	Apple: local variety	−0.050	*−0.320*	*0.258*			*0.271*		−0.030		0.248	9
1101161.04	Banana	*0.285*	*0.457*	*0.581*	−0.330	−0.390	0.050	−0.150	0.184	0.223	0.287	18
1101161.05	Red grapes	*−0.510*	−0.010	*−0.250*	*0.482*	0.174	0.055		0.038	−0.140	0.265	15
1101161.06	Green grapes	*−0.610*	−0.120	*−0.300*	*0.414*	*0.292*	−0.100	*0.484*	−0.130	−0.070	0.285	16
1101161.07	Grapefruit	0.184	0.099	*−0.550*	*0.501*		−0.120	−0.160	−0.020		0.246	14
1101161.08	Lemon	*0.363*	0.030	−0.120	*−0.420*		0.027	*−0.640*	*0.447*		0.361	14
1101161.09	Mandarin		0.157	*−0.380*	−0.200	*0.345*	−0.000	−0.090	0.234		0.243	13
1101161.10	Orange	0.024	−0.060	*0.397*	*−0.510*	0.187	−0.110	*0.451*	−0.050	−0.040	0.234	16
1101161.11	Pear	*0.260*	−0.010			*−0.390*	*−0.380*	*0.245*	−0.120	−0.190	0.268	14
1101161.12	Watermelon	0.051			0.072	0.012	*0.258*	*−0.530*	0.036	0.040	0.228	13

1101171	**Fresh or chilled vegetables**											
	PPP	1.557	14.29	0.370	32.00	44.66	5.708	63.49	1.000	3,425		
	STD	0.292	0.503	0.321	0.254	0.239	0.383	0.255	0.337	0.608		
	PLI	0.154	0.627	0.298	0.242	0.492	0.513	0.354	1.000	0.438		
1101171.01	Cucumber	0.066		0.124	−0.170	−0.230	0.009	*−0.290*		0.220	0.272	13
1101171.02	Garlic	0.227	*0.354*	−0.090	*0.290*	*−0.300*	**−0.930**	0.137	0.027		0.448	17
1101171.03	Round tomato	*−0.390*	*0.391*	*−0.400*	−0.120	0.045	*0.408*	−0.130	0.221	0.145	0.250	16
1101171.04	Green sweet bell pepper	*−0.410*	*0.479*	*0.256*	−0.000	−0.140	0.226		*0.587*	**−1.100**	0.400	16
1101171.05	Green cabbage	*0.444*	*−0.480*	*0.475*	*−0.310*	*0.515*	*0.256*	0.105		−0.700	0.325	17
1101171.06	Carrots	−0.030	*−0.640*	*0.367*	−0.000	−0.140	0.138	*0.525*	*−0.440*		0.295	17
1101171.07	Cauliflower	*0.286*	*0.503*	*−0.440*	*0.351*	−0.060	−0.070		−0.110		0.272	16
1101171.08	Onion	0.118	*−0.610*	0.059	*0.394*	*0.302*	−0.030	0.049	*−0.280*	*0.266*	0.295	18
1101171.09	Maize			*−0.340*	−0.050	0.122		−0.070		*0.424*	0.203	10
1101171.10	Eggplant	*−0.300*			*−0.370*	−0.120		*−0.320*		*0.748*	0.317	13

TABLE 9.4b Modified Dikhanov Table for an Aggregate (Household Final Consumption Expenditure, HFCE), Countries A–I

Item code	Item name	A	B	C	D	E	F	G	H	I	Var. co. 1	Items/countries
		2005	2005	2005	2005	2005	2005	2005	2005	2005	Var. co. 3	
1100000	**HFCE**											
	PPP	4.052	16.02	0.739	75.69	43.7	7.879	96.76	1.000	5,227		
	Var. co. 2	29.1	22.1	29.7	25.8	24.0	27.9	24.9	27.1	27.6	51.0	
	No. of items priced	567	608	450	566	525	420	481	611	457		864
	XR (LCU/US$)	5.779	13.01	0.709	75.55	51.88	6.359	102.3	0.571	4,464		
	Rebased XR	10.12	22.78	1.242	132.3	90.87	11.14	179.2	1.000	7,817		
	PLI	40.0	70.3	59.5	57.2	48.1	70.7	54.0	100.0	66.9		
1101161	**Fresh or chilled fruit**											
	PPP	1.900	15.65	0.423	57.09	48.31	6.580	99.68	1.000	6,074		
	Var. co. 2	32.6	18.9	35.3	39.5	26.0	16.4	36.4	20.4	12.6		
	PLI	18.8	68.7	34.1	43.1	53.2	59.1	55.6	100.0	77.7		
1101161.01	Apple: golden delicious		92.3	119.4		95.1	100.2	111.1	*74.8*	109.6	14.5	12
1101161.02	Apple: red delicious		86.9	120.8		83.5	104.0	*131.4*	*74.1*	108.2	19.4	13
1101161.03	Apple: local variety	95.1	*72.6*	*129.4*			*131.1*		97.0		24.8	9
1101161.04	Banana	*133.0*	*157.9*	*178.8*	*71.9*	*67.7*	105.1	86.1	120.2	125.0	28.7	18
1101161.05	Red grapes	*60.0*	99.0	*77.9*	*161.9*	119.0	105.7		103.9	86.9	26.5	15
1101161.06	Green grapes	*54.3*	88.7	*74.1*	*151.3*	*133.9*	90.5	*162.3*	87.8	93.2	28.5	16
1101161.07	Grapefruit	120.2	110.4	*57.7*	*165.0*		88.7	85.2	98.0		24.6	14
1101161.08	Lemon	*143.8*	103.0	88.7	*65.7*		102.7	*52.7*	*156.4*		36.1	14
1101161.09	Mandarin		117.0	*68.4*	81.9	*141.2*	100.0	91.4	126.4		24.3	13
1101161.10	Orange	102.4	94.2	*148.7*	*60.0*	120.6	89.6	*157.0*	95.1	96.1	23.4	16
1101161.11	Pear	*126.7*	99.0			*67.7*	*68.4*	127.8	88.7	82.7	26.8	14
1101161.12	Watermelon	105.2			107.5	101.2	*129.4*	*58.9*	103.7	104.1	22.8	13

1101171	**Fresh or chilled vegetables**											
	PPP	1.557	14.29	0.370	32.00	44.66	5.708	63.49	1.000	3,425		
	Var. co. 2	29.2	50.3	32.1	25.4	23.9	38.3	25.5	33.7	60.8		
	PLI	15.4	62.7	29.8	24.2	49.2	51.3	35.4	100.0	43.8		
1101171.01	Cucumber	106.8		113.2	84.4	79.5	100.9	*74.8*		124.6	27.2	13
1101171.02	Garlic	125.5	*142.5*	91.4	*133.6*	*74.1*	**39.5**	114.7	102.7		44.8	17
1101171.03	Round tomato	*67.7*	*147.8*	*67.0*	88.7	104.6	*150.4*	87.8	124.7	115.6	25.0	16
1101171.04	Green sweet bell pepper	*66.4*	*161.4*	*129.2*	100.0	86.9	125.4		*179.9*	**33.3**	40.0	16
1101171.05	Green cabbage	*155.9*	*61.9*	*160.8*	*73.3*	*167.4*	*129.2*	111.1		49.7	32.5	17
1101171.06	Carrots	97.0	*52.7*	*144.3*	100.0	86.9	114.8	*169.0*	*64.4*		29.5	17
1101171.07	Cauliflower	*133.1*	*165.4*	*64.4*	*142.0*	94.2	93.2		89.6		27.2	16
1101171.08	Onion	112.5	*54.3*	106.1	*148.3*	*135.3*	97.0	105.0	*75.6*	*130.5*	29.5	18
1101171.09	Maize			*71.2*	95.1	113.0		93.2		*153.8*	20.3	10
1101171.10	Eggplant	*74.1*			*69.1*	88.7		*72.6*		*211.3*	31.7	13

Source (both tables): 2005 ICP.
Note: STD = standard deviation; XR = exchange rate; LCU = local currency unit; PLI = price level index; var. co. = variation coefficient.

Conclusion

Intercountry validation is an iterative process. It can commence before all countries participating in the regional comparison have supplied their average prices. After each iteration or verification round, the RCA will change the region's price database in line with the findings reported by the NCAs of countries covered in the round, add the prices of countries joining the validation process to the database, and rerun the average price diagnostic module to produce new Quaranta and Dikhanov tables. These tables will identify new extreme values as a result of the changes introduced by the RCA, and these will need to be investigated by the NCAs. Gradually, after a number of rounds of verification and after the prices of all countries participating in the comparison have been included in the database, there will be convergence, and the return on further rounds of verification will be deemed marginal by the NCAs and the RCA and not worth pursuing. The intercountry validation is now complete. *In signing off from the validation process, NCAs are accepting responsibility for their average prices*. The process is concluded when the NCAs formally approve the validated price data.

ANNEX

Quaranta and Dikhanov Tables

Both the Quaranta and Dikhanov tables provide similar measures of price variation for products and countries employing either basic heading PPPs for editing basic headings individually or PPPs for an aggregate[16] for editing across the basic headings constituting the aggregate. The Dikhanov table is specific to the Country Product Dummy (CPD) or Country Product Representative Dummy (CPRD) method of calculating PPPs, whereas the Quaranta table has a broader application that includes the Gini-Éltetö-Köves-Szulc (GEKS) and GEKS* methods as well as the CPD and CPRD methods.[17] ICP regions used the CPD method in the 2005 comparison.

Quaranta tables are employed to edit prices within basic headings, and Dikhanov tables are used to edit prices within aggregates of several basic headings. Editing prices within a basic heading is the purpose for which the Quaranta table was originally intended. It provides a large amount of information about product prices, but the presentation is outdated, which makes it cumbersome when applied to a large number of products such as that priced for an aggregate.[18] A Dikhanov table contains much of the same information as a Quaranta table,[19] but it is programmed to hide certain items, which can be called up if required so that only key series are displayed. The more compact format of the Dikhanov table plus the color scheme used to identify different levels of extreme values make it better-suited to editing prices across the basic headings and products comprising an aggregate.

The average price diagnostic module produces a multiple of Quaranta tables, one for each basic heading being validated, and one Dikhanov table for the corresponding aggregate. The RCA makes the Quaranta tables and the Dikhanov table available to the NCAs at the same time. This leaves open the question of whether intercountry validation should begin with the Quaranta tables or with the Dikhanov table. Some analysts prefer to start with Quaranta tables and consult the Dikhanov table after there have been a number of rounds of verification in which the PPPs are more reliable. Others prefer to begin with the Dikhanov table, using it to identify countries and products that need investigating and subsequently organizing the investigation around the Quaranta tables. One argument in favor of the first approach is that most, if not all, operations relating to a comparison are organized around the basic headings. In particular, PPPs are first calculated and averaged at the level of the basic heading, and it is basic heading PPPs that are weighted during aggregation. It therefore seems logical and consistent to start validation at the basic heading level with the Quaranta tables. Another argument is that the Dikhanov table does not give the same prominence as Quaranta tables to the XR-ratios, which are required in the early stages of intercountry validation. In the Dikhanov table, they are a pull-up item, and extreme values are not flagged. Quaranta tables give equal weight to the XR-ratios and the PPP-ratios, and extreme values among both are flagged.

Table 9A.1 is an example of a Quaranta table. The numbers in italics have been added for ease of reference, and the explanatory notes follow the table. The table has three sections. The first section gives general details about the table of which the more important are the calculation method *[6]*, the range of acceptable values for XR-ratios and PPP-ratios *[7]*, and the numeraire *[8]*. The second section gives summary information for the basic heading that relates either

TABLE 9A.1 A Quaranta Table

QUARANTA TABLE DETAILS				
[1] **Region:** Asia	*[2]* **Survey:** Food and beverages	*[3]* **Time period:** 1st quarter 2011	*[4]* **Version:** Final	*[5]* **Date:** 30.06.11
[6] **Calculation method:** CPD	*[7]* **Limits of XR- and PPP-ratios:** 80%, 125%	*[8]* **Numeraire:** LCU of country D		*[9]* **Page:** 1

BASIC HEADING AND COUNTRY DETAILS

[10] **1101111 Rice** | *[11]* **Av. weight:** 45.1 | *[12]* **No. of items:** 3 | *[13]* **Var. co. 1:** 9.5

[14] Country	*[15]* XR	*[16]* PPP	*[17]* PLI (%)	*[18]* Weight	*[19]* No. of items	*[20]* Var. co. 2
A	3,830.9492	2,673.8500	69.8	23.8	3: *1	11.8
B	1.8439	1.0353	56.1	34.6	3: *3	4.2
C	0.7594	0.7791	102.6	58.3	3: *1	16.1
D	1.0000	1.0000	100.0	63.9	3: *2	6.1

PRODUCT DETAILS BY COUNTRY

1 *[21]* **1101111.0111 Rice, long grain, 500–1,000 g packet** *[22]* **Var. co. 3:** 7.5

[23] Country	*[24]* NC-price	*[25]* Asterisks	*[26]* Quotations	*[27]* Var. co. 4	*[28]* XR-price	*[30]* XR-ratio	*[31]* PPP-price	*[33]* PPP-ratio
A	5,770.58	*	15	5.1	1.51	89	2.16	102
B	2.11	*	13	4.4	1.15	68	2.04	96
C	1.82		9	21.2	2.40	142	2.34	110
D	1.98		5	16.8	1.98	117	1.98	93
				[29] GM = 1.69		*[32]* GM = 2.13		

2 *[21]* **1101111.0112 Rice, short grain, 500–1,000 g packet** *[22]* **Var. co. 3:** 12.7

[23] Country	*[24]* NC-price	*[25]* Asterisks	*[26]* Quotations	*[27]* Var. co. 4	*[28]* XR-price	*[30]* XR-ratio	*[31]* PPP-price	*[33]* PPP-ratio
A	21,757.60		9	14.2	5.68	98	8.14	112
B	7.87	*	10	7.7	4.27	74	7.60	104
C	4.66	*	15	9.1	6.14	106	5.98	82
D	7.60	*	8	8.9	7.60	131	7.60	104
				[29] GM = 5.80		*[32]* GM = 7.28		

3 *[21]* **1101111.0113 Rice, basmati, 500–1,000 g packet** *[22]* **Var. co. 3:** 9.3

[23] Country	*[24]* NC-price	*[25]* Asterisks	*[26]* Quotations	*[27]* Var. co. 4	*[28]* XR-price	*[30]* XR-ratio	*[31]* PPP-price	*[33]* PPP-ratio
A	7,075.88		6	15.3	1.85	77	2.65	88
B	3.10	*	14	10.4	1.68	70	3.00	100
C	2.59		7	24.7	3.40	142	3.32	111
D	3.09	*	10	10.2	3.09	129	3.09	103
				[29] GM = 2.39		*[32]* GM = 3.00		

Notes to table 9A.1

QUARANTA TABLE DETAILS		
[1]	**Region**	Region covered by the table.
[2]	**Survey**	Type of product covered by the table.
[3]	**Time period**	Period during which the prices for the products covered by the table were collected.
[4]	**Version**	Version of the table: first, second, third, . . . , final.
[5]	**Date**	Date the table was computed.
[6]	**Calculation method**	Method used to calculate the basic heading PPPs in column *[16]*. Currently, the CPD, but it could also be the CPRD, the GEKS, or the GEKS*.
[7]	**Limits of XR- and PPP-ratios**	The range in which the XR-ratios in column *[30]* and the PPP-ratios in column *[33]* should lie if they are not to be flagged as extreme values. Currently, 80–125, but 65–155 is also used. The intervals of the ranges are not equal because it is the relative deviations from a geometric mean that are being measured.
[8]	**Numeraire**	Currency selected as numeraire. RCAs may choose the currency of any of their countries as numeraire.
[9]	**Page**	Page number. Depending on the number of products priced and the number of countries pricing them, a Quaranta table for a basic heading can cover a large number of pages.
BASIC HEADING AND COUNTRY DETAILS		
[10]		Code and name of the basic heading covered by the table.
[11]	**Av. weight**	Average expenditure weight for the group of countries covered by the basic heading. The unweighted arithmetic mean of the national weights in column *[18]*. Like the national weights, it is scaled to 100,000.
[12]	**No. of items**	Number of products specified and priced for the basic heading.
[13]	**Var. co. 1**	Overall variation coefficient or, more precisely, the average product variation coefficient for the products priced for the basic heading. It is calculated as the unweighted arithmetic mean of the product variation coefficients at *[22]*. It measures the average variation of the PPP-ratios in column *[33]* of all products priced for the basic heading. It is flagged when greater than 33 percent.
[14]	**Country**	Abbreviated names of countries covered by the table.
[15]	**XR**	Market exchange rates of the countries expressed as the number of units of national currency per unit of the numeraire currency specified in *[8]*.
[16]	**PPP**	Purchasing power parities for the basic heading calculated as specified in *[6]* and expressed as the number of units of national currency per unit of the selected numeraire currency specified in *[8]*. The prices used to calculate the PPPs are the average prices in national currencies that countries report for the products they priced for the basic heading—that is, the NC-prices in column *[24]*.
[17]	**PLI**	Price level indexes. The PPPs in column *[16]* expressed as a percentage of the corresponding exchange rate in column *[15]*.
[18]	**Weight**	National expenditure weights scaled to 100,000. That part of a country's GDP that is spent on the basic heading when both expenditures are expressed in national currency and valued at national price levels.
[19]	**No. of items**	Number of products priced by each country for the basis heading and the number of products priced by each country that are important—that is, the number of products assigned an asterisk (*).
[20]	**Var. co. 2**	Country variation coefficient. The standard deviation of the country's PPP-ratios in column *[33]* for all products priced by the country for the basic heading expressed as a percentage of the arithmetic mean of the country's PPP-ratios in column *[33]* for all products priced by the country for the basic heading. It is flagged when greater than 33 percent.
PRODUCT DETAILS BY COUNTRY		
[21]		Code, name, and summary definition of the product covered in the subsequent product section.
[22]	**Var. co. 3**	Product variation coefficient. The standard deviation of the product's PPP-ratios in column *[33]* expressed as a percentage of the arithmetic mean of the product's PPP-ratios in column *[33]*. It is flagged when greater than 33 percent.

(*continued*)

Notes to table 9A.1 (*continued*)

PRODUCT DETAILS BY COUNTRY		
[23]	**Country**	Abbreviated names of countries covered by the table.
[24]	**NC-price**	Average price in national currency (NC).
[25]	**Asterisks**	Importance indicator. Generally, important products are indicated by an asterisk (*).
[26]	**Quotations**	Number of price observations on which the average prices in national currency in column *[24]* are based.
[27]	**Var. co. 4**	Price observation variation coefficient. The standard deviation of the price observations underlying the product's average price in column *[24]* expressed as a percentage of the arithmetic mean of the price observations underlying the product's average price in column *[24]*. It is flagged when greater than 20 percent.
[28]	**XR-price**	The average prices in national currency in column *[24]* converted to the numeraire currency with the exchange rates in column *[15]*.
[29]	**GM**	Geometric mean of the exchange rate–converted prices in column *[28]*. The use of a geometric mean here and in *[32]* ensures invariance with respect to choice of numeraire.
[30]	**XR-ratio**	Standardized price ratios based on the exchange rate–converted prices in column *[28]*. The XR-prices expressed as a percentage of their geometric mean at *[29]*.
[31]	**PPP-price**	The average prices in national currency in column *[24]* converted to the numeraire currency with the PPPs in column *[16]*.
[32]	**GM**	Geometric mean of the PPP-converted prices in column *[31]*.
[33]	**PPP-ratio**	Standardized price ratios based on the PPP-converted prices in column *[31]*. The PPP-prices expressed as a percentage of their geometric mean at *[32]*.

to the basic heading as a whole or to each country covered by the basic heading. It is this section that contains the overall variation coefficient *[13]*, the PPPs *[16]*, the expenditure weights *[18]*, and the country variation coefficients *[20]* for the basic heading. The third section covers the products priced for the basic heading. Each product has its own subsection that shows the product variation coefficient *[22]*; the average prices reported by countries in national currencies *[24]*—these are the prices being validated and the prices with which the PPPs shown in the table are calculated; the average prices converted to a common currency with exchange rates *[28]*, their geometric mean *[29]*, and their XR-ratios *[30]*; and the average prices converted to a common currency with the PPPs for the basic heading *[31]*, their geometric mean *[32]*, and their PPP-ratios *[33]*.

Examples of a Dikhanov table appear in tables 9A.2, 9A.3, and 9A.4. Reference numbers in italics have been added, and explanations are given in the notes that follow the tables. For illustrative purposes, the tables cover the same basic heading as the Quaranta table, even though Dikhanov tables are usually produced for aggregates. Comparing a Quaranta table with a Dikhanov table for the same basic heading is good way of understanding their similarities and differences, providing the PPPs for both tables are calculated with a CPD. Table 9A.2 is the extended version of a Dikhanov table with the pull-up series (the series that is usually hidden) exposed. This series is the average price in national currency *[16]*, the number of price observations on which the average price is based *[17]*, the price observation variation coefficient *[18]*, and the XR-ratio *[19]*. Table 9A.3 shows what the Dikhanov table looks like when the pull-up items are hidden, which is how the Dikhanov table is usually presented. The table has two sections. One gives summary information on the basic heading and countries, including the PPPs *[4]*, the country standard deviations *[5]*, and the overall standard deviation *[6]*. The other

TABLE 9A.2 A Dikhanov Table for a Basic Heading (Extended Version)

Code	Name	*[1]* A *[2]* Q1 2011	*[1]* B *[2]* Q1 2011	*[1]* C *[2]* Q1 2011	*[1]* D *[2]* Q1 2011	STD 1 STD 3	Items/ countries
[3] 1101111	*[3]* Rice						
	[4] PPP	2,673.85	1.0353	0.7791	1.0000		
	[5] STD 2	0.0974	0.0341	0.1391	0.0505	*[6]* 0.0902	
	[7] No. of items priced	3	3	3	3		*[8]* 3
	[9] XR (LCU/US$)	1,473	0.709	0.292	0.3845		
	[10] Rebased XR	3,830.94	1.8439	0.7594	1.000		
	[11] PLI	0.698	0.561	1.026	1.000		
[12] 1101111.0111	*[12]* Rice, long grain	*[13]* 0.01505	*[13]* −0.04068	*[13]* 0.09660	*[13]* −0.07097	*[14]* 0.0637	*[15]* 4
	[16] Average price	*5,770.58*	*2.11*	*1.82*	*1.98*		
	[17] No. of observations	*15*	*13*	*9*	*5*		
	[18] Variation coefficient	*5.1*	*4.4*	*21.2*	*16.8*		
	[19] XR-ratio	*89.0*	*67.7*	*141.9*	*117.0*		
[12] 1101111.0112	*[12]* Rice, short grain	*[13]* 0.11105	*[13]* 0.04284	*[13]* −0.19665	*[13]* 0.04277	*[14]* 0.1169	*[15]* 4
	[16] Average price	*21,757.60*	*7.87*	*4.66*	*7.60*		
	[17] No. of observations	*9*	*10*	*15*	*8*		
	[18] Variation coefficient	*14.2*	*7.7*	*9.1*	*8.9*		
	[19] XR-ratio	*97.9*	*73.6*	*105.8*	*131.1*		
[12] 1101111.0113	*[12]* Rice, basmati	*[13]* −0.12610	*[13]* −0.00216	*[13]* 0.10005	*[13]* 0.02820	*[14]* 0.0817	*[15]* 4
	[16] Average price	*7,075.88*	*3.10*	*2.59*	*3.09*		
	[17] No. of observations	*6*	*14*	*7*	*10*		
	[18] Variation coefficient	*15.3*	*10.4*	*24.7*	*10.2*		
	[19] XR-ratio	*77.3*	*70.4*	*142.4*	*129.2*		

contains the CPD residuals *[13]* and their standard deviations *[14]* for the products priced by countries. CPD residuals and their derivation are explained in the notes to tables 9A.2, 9A.3, and 9A.4. An examination of the Quaranta and Dikhanov tables shows that the CPD residuals in the Dikhanov table are equal to the logarithms of the PPP-ratios in the Quaranta table. The CPD residual of 0.01505 for long grain rice for country A in tables 9A.2 and 9A.3 is equal to the log of 1.015, where 101.5 is the corresponding PPP-ratio in table 9A.1. Note that this identity holds only if the PPPs in both tables are calculated with a CPD and if the products are included in the calculation as a single group—that is, either as a basic heading or as an aggregate. It will not hold if the CPD is used for the Dikhanov table and the GEKS for the Quaranta table.

TABLE 9A.3 A Dikhanov Table for a Basic Heading (Collapsed Version)

Code	Name	*[1]* A *[2]* Q1 2011	*[1]* B *[2]* Q1 2011	*[1]* C *[2]* Q1 2011	*[1]* D *[2]* Q1 2011	STD 1 STD 2	Items/ countries
[3] 1101111	*[3]* Rice						
	[4] PPP	2,673.85	1.0353	0.7791	1.0000		
	[5] STD 2	0.0974	0.0341	0.1391	0.0505	*[6]* 0.0902	
	[7] No. of items priced	3	3	3	3		*[8]* 3
	[9] XR (LCU/US$)	1,473	0.709	0.292	0.3845		
	[10] Rebased XR	3,830.94	1.8439	0.7594	1.000		
	[11] PLI	0.698	0.561	1.026	1.000		
[12] 1101111.0111	*[12]* Rice, long grain	*[13]* 0.01505	*[13]* −0.04068	*[13]* 0.09660	*[13]* −0.07097	*[14]* 0.0637	*[15]* 4
[12] 1101111.0112	*[12]* Rice, short grain	*[13]* 0.11105	*[13]* 0.04284	*[13]* −0.19665	*[13]* 0.04277	*[14]* 0.1169	*[15]* 4
[12] 1101111.0113	*[12]* Rice, basmati	*[13]* −0.12610	*[13]* −0.00216	*[13]* 0.10005	*[13]* 0.02820	*[14]* 0.0817	*[15]* 4

Nor will it hold if the CPD residuals for products in the basic heading in the Dikhanov table are based on PPPs for an aggregate and the PPP-ratios in the Quaranta table are derived with PPPs for the basic heading. Table 9A.4 shows the CPD residuals of tables 9A.2 and 9A.3 expressed as PPP-ratios.

The standard deviations for the CPD residuals in the Dikhanov table are actually variation coefficients because the mean of the residuals is 1. They have been expressed as variation coefficients (i.e., multiplied by100) in table 9A.4 to facilitate comparison with the variation coefficients in the Quaranta table in table 9A.1. The two sets of coefficients are not the same because of differences in

TABLE 9A.4 A Modified Dikhanov Table for a Basic Heading (Collapsed Version)

Code	Name	A 2011	B 2011	C 2011	D 2011	Var. co. 1 Var. co. 3	Items/ countries
1101111	Rice						
	PPP	2,673.85	1.0353	0.7791	1.0000		
	Var. co. 2	9.7	3.4	13.9	5.1	9.0	
	No. of items priced	3	3	3	3		3
	XR (LCU/US$)	1,473	0.709	0.292	0.3845		
	Rebased XR	3,830.94	1.8439	0.7594	1.000		
	PLI	69.8	56.1	102.6	100.0		
1101111.0111	Rice, long grain	101.5	96.0	110.1	93.1	6.4	4
1101111.0112	Rice, short grain	111.7	104.4	82.1	104.4	11.7	4
1101111.0113	Rice, basmati	88.2	99.8	110.6	102.9	8.2	4

Source (all tables): 2005 ICP.

Notes to tables 9A.2, 9A.3, and 9A.4

[1]	Abbreviated names of countries covered by the table.
[2]	Period during which the prices for the products covered by the table were collected.
[3]	Code and name of the basic heading or aggregate covered by the table.
[4]	Purchasing power parities for the basic heading or aggregate covered by the table. They are expressed as the number of local currency units per unit of the selected numeraire currency. The prices used to calculate the PPPs are the average prices in local currencies that countries report for the products they priced for the basic heading or aggregate—that is, the average prices in row *[16]*.
[5]	STD 2: standard deviation of each country's CPD or CPRD residuals for the basic heading or aggregate. It can be converted to a country variation coefficient by multiplying by 100. The mean of each country's residuals is 1.
[6]	STD 1: standard deviation of the CPD or CPRD residuals of all products priced for the basic heading or aggregate. It can be converted to an overall variation coefficient for products by multiplying by 100. The mean of all product residuals is 1.
[7]	Number of products priced by each country.
[8]	Number of products specified for the basic heading or aggregate.
[9]	Market exchange rates of countries expressed as the number of local currency units per U.S. dollar.
[10]	Exchange rates *[9]* rebased to the numeraire currency. Number of local currency units per unit of numeraire currency.
[11]	Price level indexes. The PPPs in row *[4]* expressed as a ratio of the corresponding rebased exchange rates in row *[10]*.
[12]	Code and name of the product covered.
[13]	CPD or CPRD residuals by product and country.
[14]	STD 3: standard deviation of the product's CPD or CPRD residuals. It can be converted to a product variation coefficient by multiplying by 100. The mean of a product's residuals is 1.
[15]	Number of countries pricing the product.
[16]	Average price in local currency units.
[17]	Number of price observations on which the average prices at *[16]* are based.
[18]	Price observation variation coefficient.
[19]	Price ratios based on exchange rate–converted prices. The converted prices expressed as a percentage of their geometric mean.

computation. The overall variation coefficient in the Quaranta table is an average of the variations coefficients of the products priced for the basic heading, whereas the overall variation coefficient in the Dikhanov table is computed with all the CPD residuals in the table's product section, thereby ensuring consistency between the overall variation coefficient, the product variation coefficients, and the country variation coefficients. In addition, the product variation coefficients in the Quaranta table should in theory be calculated using logarithms because the PPP-ratios are based on the geometric mean of the PPP-prices, but for practical reasons they are calculated using the arithmetic mean and standard deviation of the PPP-ratios. This is not the case with the product variation coefficients in the Dikhanov table. These are based on CPD residuals that, as just mentioned, are logarithms of the PPP-ratios. Despite the computation differences, the two sets of variation coefficients are of similar orders of magnitude and reliability in terms of identifying extreme values.

The version of the Dikhanov table presented in table 9A.4 is more user-friendly than the version in table 9A.3 because it uses the same terminology and concepts in the Quaranta table. It is therefore easier to move back and forth between the two tables during validation. The option of having a Dikhanov table showing CPD residuals expressed as PPP-ratios and their standard deviations as variation coefficients still has to be added to the average price diagnostic module.

A comparison of the Quaranta table and its Dikhanov counterpart shows that they have the following indicators of extreme values in common:

- The *overall variation coefficient* measures dispersion among all the PPP-ratios for a basic heading. In doing so, it measures the homogeneity of the price structures of the countries covered by the basic heading and the reliability of the PPPs calculated for the basic heading. The higher the value of the coefficient, the less homogeneous are the price structures and the less reliable are the PPPs. A value that exceeds 33 percent is extreme.

  During verification of extreme values, priority should be given to basic headings with a coefficient value greater than 33 percent, particularly if they have a large expenditure weight. Basic headings with large expenditure weights will have greater influence on the overall PPPs than basic headings with small expenditure weights. Only Quaranta tables give expenditure weights.

  The value of the coefficient should fall as validation progresses, thereby providing a means of assessing the overall effectiveness of the validation process.
- The *country variation coefficient* measures dispersion among a country's PPP-ratios for a basic heading. In other words, it measures the variation in a country's price levels among the products it priced for the basic heading and the reliability of its PPP for the basic heading. The higher the value of the coefficient, the less uniform are the country's price levels and the less reliable are its PPPs. A value that exceeds 33 percent is extreme.

  During verification, NCAs should give priority to basic headings for which the value of the country variation coefficient is greater than 33 percent, particularly if the expenditure weight for the basic heading is large.

  The coefficient should decline in value as validation progresses. This allows NCAs to assess the effectiveness of their validation.

  The country variation coefficient complements the product variation coefficient (next item) by bringing a different perspective to the same set of data. Focusing on countries rather than products can help to detect countries that have suspect data. In this respect, it is better to use the Dikhanov table with its wider coverage of products to detect errant countries.
- The *product variation coefficient*, the most important of the variation coefficients for validation purposes, measures dispersion among the PPP-ratios for a product. It is an indicator of comparability and accuracy and addresses the questions of whether the NCAs pricing the product priced the same product or an equivalent product and whether they priced it correctly. The higher the value of the coefficient, the less uniform are the product's price levels and the more suspect are the product's comparability and the accuracy of its pricing across countries. Such products are candidates for splitting or deletion, and the RCA should ensure that they are thoroughly investigated by the NCAs. During validation, priority should be given to products with a variation coefficient greater than 33 percent.
- *XR-ratios* are standardized price ratios based on exchange rate–converted average prices. This proxy measure allows the average prices for a product to be compared across countries. It facilitates the identification of extreme values among price ratios for a product at the beginning of the intercountry validation when PPPs and PPP-ratios are likely to be unreliable because they are based on the average prices that are being validated. Initially, XR-ratios outside the range of 80–125 should be investigated during the first and second round of validation. In later rounds, when the PPP-ratios become more reliable, extreme

values among the XR-ratios can be ignored. For this indicator, it is better to consult the Quaranta table because the series is clearly displayed with extreme values flagged.

- *PPP-ratios* are standardized price ratios based on PPP-converted average-prices. It is the correct measure with which to compare the average prices for a product across countries and the average prices of a country across products. It is the extreme values among these price ratios for a product that intercountry validation seeks to identify and verify. Ratios outside the range of 80–125 should be investigated.
- The *price observation variation coefficient* measures variation in the price observations on which the average price reported for a product by a country is based. It is taken straight from the average price table. It is used to identify extreme values among average prices during intracountry validation when average prices with a variation coefficient over 20 percent are considered extreme. Should the variation coefficient remain over 20 percent after intracountry validation, the NCA may need to reedit the underlying price observations if there are extreme values among the product's PPP-ratios or if the product variation coefficient is over 33 percent.
- *Price level indexes* measure the differences in price levels between countries for the basic heading. They are useful for comparing the consistency of relative price levels across basic headings.

NOTES

1. When a product specification is too loose, the problem is not so much that the product priced does not match the product specified (because it probably does), but that it is not comparable with the products that other price collectors, both within the country and in other countries, have matched and priced for the same specification. Within a country, the problem can be ameliorated by the NCA and price collectors agreeing on how generic specifications are to be interpreted and what products are to be priced before starting price collection. This will not avoid differences in interpretation between countries that will only become apparent during validation.
2. This can happen when the product specification refers to a specific model that is in the process of being replaced in some countries by a later model—not an infrequent occurrence in the case of household durables.
3. This situation amplifies the earlier observation that price collectors should be well trained and given clear instructions, as well as price reporting forms that are user-friendly. Also, fieldwork should be closely monitored to ensure that price collectors record the prices, quantities, and other data required. Training and field supervision do not eliminate product errors, but they do reduce the incidence.
4. Even if the price and specified quantity are recorded correctly, a price error can be introduced if the price is not adjusted correctly to the reference quantity.
5. The terms *extreme value* and *outlier* are often used synonymously. In this text, *outlier* is reserved for extreme values that have been verified as being correct. On identification, an *extreme value* is a possible error; after verification it is either an error or an outlier.
6. Different products have different distribution profiles. Some products are sold mostly in supermarkets; other products are sold mainly in specialty shops.
7. Prices for the same product can vary from one outlet type to another because it is being sold under varying conditions or circumstances. The conditions or circumstances of sale constitute a service element. If the service element changes from one outlet type to another, the

product being purchased is not the same at both outlets even if it is identical physically. What is actually being bought is a composite product—that is, the product itself plus the service element. The difference in the service element is a quality difference and contributes to the price difference. When those averaging the prices collected for the product take no account of the different service elements of the outlets at which they were observed, the average price is likely to be too high or too low

8. Whether these average prices lead to unbiased price relatives depends on whether the products surveyed have similar distribution profiles in the other countries participating in the comparison and on whether the outlets selected have equivalent service elements in all countries.
9. Originally, it was intended that the RCA would participate in intracountry validation to ensure that a common standard of rigor was maintained across the region. In some regions, the RCA is involved, but in others it is not because of the strict interpretation of confidentiality by countries in the region. In regions in which the RCA is involved in intracountry validation, a country's price observations are reviewed only by its NCA and the RCA; they are not made available to anyone else either inside or outside the region. Experience suggests that RCA participation in intracountry validation may be counterproductive. When the RCA is involved, the NCAs have a tendency to halt being proactive, as required; instead, they become reactive, expecting the RCA to take the initiative.
10. The importance of completing validation on time cannot be overstated. Prices for consumer products are usually collected monthly, with editing and verification carried out quarterly. Thus large numbers of price observations must be processed. Every effort should be made to avoid a backlog, which could delay the regional comparison (and possibly the global comparison). It could also be detrimental to quality. The longer it takes to validate the price data, the harder it becomes to rectify the errors identified during validation. Moreover, to reduce the backlog and catch up on lost time, the RCA and the NCAs may be tempted to cut corners by editing and verifying the prices less rigorously.
11. For example, in table 9.1a the reference quantity is 500 grams (fields 03 and 04), but price collectors may price any quantity in the range of 400–600 grams (field 02). The prices of the quantities priced (fields 10, 11, and 12) are subsequently adjusted to price per 500 grams (field 16). It is the adjusted prices in field 16 that are validated and averaged to give the average price (field 24) in table 9.3a.
12. A distinction is made between products that are important and products that are not when calculating PPPs for a basic heading. Countries are therefore required to indicate which of the products they have priced for a basic heading are important for them. A product is important if it is a volume seller. Important products are identified by an asterisk (*) and are often referred to as "asterisk products."
13. The price observation table and the average price table are linked. The average prices in the average price table are derived from the individual prices in the price observation table. Modifying an individual price will automatically change the corresponding average price. Each average price can be "opened up" to display the individual prices on which it is based. Thus if an average price is flagged as an extreme value, the underlying price observations can be called up to see whether any of them are flagged as extreme values and the cause of the average price being flagged. It follows from this that the two stages of intracountry validation can be done in reverse—that is, starting with average prices rather than price observations. The disadvantage of the approach is that there is a danger that the additional information provided by price collectors will be overlooked.

14. A standardized price ratio equals $\left(\frac{\text{CC-Price}_{1A}}{[\text{CC-Price}_{1A} * \text{CC-Price}_{1B} * \ldots \text{CC-Price}_{1N}]^{\frac{1}{N}}}\right)100$, where CC-Price_{1A} is the average price for product 1 in country A in the common currency. CC-Price_{1A} is itself equal to $\frac{\text{NC-Price}_{1A}}{\text{CC}_{1A}}$, where NC-Price_{1A} is the average price for product 1 in country A in national currency, and CC_{1A} is the currency conversion rate between the national currency of country A and the common currency. The currency conversion rate is either the exchange rate or the PPP: $\text{CC}_{1A} = \text{XR}_{1A}$ or PPP_{1A}.
15. Also known as CUP-ratios. CUP stands for conventional unit for expressing parities. It is usually an artificial currency unit such as the purchasing power standard (PPS) employed by Eurostat.
16. That is, an aggregate from the aggregation hierarchy of the expenditure classification such as food and beverages, clothing and footwear, household final consumption, or GDP.
17. The CPRD should be employed to calculate PPPs for Quaranta and Dikhanov tables only if the information on the importance of products is reliable. Experience suggests that this is not usually the case. For this reason, it is recommended that Quaranta and Dikhanov tables be first derived with the CPD, and that the CPRD be reserved for the final iterations and the validation of product importance. Large differences between CPD and CPRD residuals and standard deviations would indicate data problems, particularly with the selection of important products. The same holds for the EKS*. PPPs should not be calculated for Quaranta tables with this method if the allocation of importance indicators is suspect. Instead, the GEKS method should be employed, at least during the early stages of validation.
18. The format of the Quaranta table, which dates from the early 1990s, was designed so that the table could be printed on A4 paper.
19. This was not always so. For example, earlier versions of the Dikhanov tables did not contain the XR-ratios on which intercountry validation focuses at the beginning.

CHAPTER 10

Validation of Basic Heading and Aggregated PPPs: When Does Validation End and Estimation Begin?

FREDERIC A. VOGEL

The previous chapter described the huge, complicated effort by the International Comparison Program (ICP) that goes into validation of the prices collected for over a thousand products, first at the country level and then between countries, to ensure not only that comparable products were priced but also that they were national annual averages. Although much has been written about the subsequent steps taken to aggregate basic heading purchasing power parities (PPPs) to the gross domestic product (GDP), little has been said about data validation for these steps. Therefore, this chapter adds a new dimension to data validation by examining the aggregation steps and the validation of the PPP and expenditure data used for each.[1]

The chapter begins with a review of these steps to set the stage for the data validation to be introduced at each level. It is followed by a review of different data validation tools using results from the 2005 ICP. These validation tools range from simple data plots to cluster analysis to models that account for the inherent variability in the bilateral PPPs. The chapter concludes with a discussion of when data validation should end and estimation should begin. The data analysis has two purposes: first, to point out where more validation is needed, and, second, to point out that some countries have patterns of prices and expenditures that give them the appearance of outliers in the data analysis, even using quality data. Thus arises the dilemma of when validation ends and estimation begins.

From Basic Heading PPPs to GDP: Overview of the Steps

The data validation and estimation processes described here begin with the matrix of 129 basic heading PPPs for 146 countries after all countries across the six ICP regions[2] have been linked to a common global currency. The estimation process to obtain these basic heading PPPs is described in chapter 4; the PPPs are transitive and base country–invariant. Chapter 9 describes the considerable effort made to validate the prices underlying the basic heading PPPs. The within-country PPPs will vary across the basic headings. However, one would expect some internal consistency. Price levels in poor countries are generally lower than those in richer countries and should show a similar pattern across basic headings. The following section discusses how to examine the basic heading PPPs within countries, and then by country within each basic heading. This analysis will point out basic headings and countries in which the underlying prices should be again reviewed.

An additional matrix, 129 × 146, contains the basic heading expenditures expressed in the currency of each country. Chapter 6 describes the multistage process used to estimate global PPPs that begins with estimation of the within-region basic heading PPPs. These are then calibrated to a global currency using between-region linking factors. The final step is to average the basic heading PPPs to the GDP. The analysis presented here is based on a direct aggregation of the 129 basic heading PPPs to the GDP level, which is also described in chapter 6. The global aggregation is being used in this chapter mainly to illustrate the data validation steps to be considered.

The first step in the global aggregation process is to compute the weighted average of the basic heading PPPs using expenditure weights to obtain the PPP at the GDP for each pair of countries. Because the distribution of the expenditure shares will differ for each country, the issue is how the weights should be used in the aggregation. Chapter 5 describes how the PPPs are first averaged to the GDP using the expenditure weights for country *j*, then again for country *k*. These are the Laspeyres and Paasche indexes, respectively.

The Laspeyres index is

$$PPP_L^{j,k} = \sum_{n=1}^{N} w_n^j PPP_n^{j,k} \tag{10.1}$$

which is a weighted average of the PPPs of country *j* to country *k* across the *N* basic headings using country *j* weights. The Paasche index between the same two countries is

$$PPP_P^{j,k} = \frac{1}{\sum_{n=1}^{N} \frac{w_n^k}{PPP_n^{j,k}}} \tag{10.2}$$

using country *K* weights.

The Laspeyres and Paasche indexes result in different estimates of the PPP for the GDP of each country. As described in chapter 1, one of the fundamental principles underlying the ICP is that countries be treated symmetrically or equally. This principle is incorporated by taking the geometric average of the Laspeyres and Paasche indexes, which is the Fisher index—$PPP_F^{j,k}$—for each pair of countries. The result is a matrix of 146 × 146 Fisher indexes for every combination of two countries. Because these indexes are not transitive, the Gini-Éltetö-Köves-Szulc (GEKS) method is applied to provide transitivity. Chapters 1 and 5 describe this process. As shown in the discussion of tables 10.4 and 10.5 in this chapter, the Fisher matrix can be used to derive for each country row a set of two direct and 144 indirect PPPs. The geometric mean of the direct and indirect parities for countries *j* and *k* is the GEKS PPPs, which are then transitive and base country–invariant. Again, the respective direct and indirect PPPs are treated equally with the computation of the geometric average.

The next section reviews the basic heading PPPs and expenditure weights in order to point out the additional data validation steps that should be taken. This review is followed by a look at the Laspeyres and Paasche indexes and how they depart from the Fisher index. The penultimate section reviews the direct and indirect PPPs using the GEKS method to achieve transitivity. The chapter concludes by considering this question: when does validation end and estimation begin?

Validating Basic Heading PPPs

The first validation is to review the variability of the basic heading PPPs within each country for the presence of outliers. The data set is the matrix of 129 basic headings times 146 countries. The analysis is based on the assumption that the within-country price levels across the basic headings are consistent—a poor country usually has lower price levels than a richer country. Recall that no expenditure or quantity weights enter into the estimation of basic heading PPPs.

For the analysis to follow, the basic heading PPPs to the U.S. dollar are standardized to the price level index (PLI)[3] for world = 100 so that the relative price levels across countries can be directly compared. The distributions of the basic heading PLIs by country are shown in figure 10.1 using box and whisker plots introduced by Tukey (1977). Box plots are nonparametric and indicate the degree of dispersion and skewness of the data and identify outliers. Construction of the box plots starts by simply sorting the basic heading PLIs from the smallest to the largest within each country. For this example, each box contains 80 percent of the basic heading PLIs for each country. Ten percent of the basic headings have PLIs larger than the top boundary of the box, and 10 percent have PLIs smaller than the bottom boundary. Each box contains a whisker, which indicates the maximum and minimum basic heading PLIs. The line shown inside each box is the PPP of the median point—half of the basic heading PLIs in each country are larger and half are smaller. Note that the median value is not always in the center of the box; the distance above or below the midpoint is an indication of skewness.

Figure 10.1 shows the countries grouped by region and then within region in order from the country with the largest median value to the smallest median value. The PLIs are shown in log scale with world = 100 (ln 100 = 4.6). Figure 10.2 shows the box plots for each of the 129 basic headings sorted by basic heading from the largest to the smallest median PLI values. Although the box plots in both figures generally show considerable consistency in the size of the boxes across basic headings and countries, there are outliers that need to be examined.

In figure 10.1, the ranking of the countries by region by median value shows, as expected, that the Eurostat–Organisation for Economic Co-operation and Development (OECD) countries have the highest price levels. However, Angola and Equatorial Guinea, which are relatively poor, have the 19th and 21st largest median values, respectively, suggesting they be examined in more detail. In both cases, the basic heading with the maximum value is "passenger transport by air." Figure 10.2 shows that this basic heading has the highest median value and also one of the largest maximum values, which is attributable to Equatorial Guinea followed closely by Angola. A closer examination of the data reveals that the PLIs for passenger transport by air provide the maximum value for more countries than for any other basic heading. This is an indication that the specifications for the pricing of this basic heading should be examined.

A similar review of the minimum values shows that they depart more from the median than do the maximum values. Several countries have minimum values that warrant additional review. Many of the minimum values are from the basic headings for compensation and medical services. These PPPs are difficult to compare across regions because not all made adjustments for productivity.

The purpose of these figures is to illustrate that even though there was an intensive data validation of the product prices, the distribution of the resulting PPPs by country and by basic heading should be examined for PLIs that do not seem plausible. For example, six countries have maximum and minimum basic heading PLIs that differ by a factor of over 100.

FIGURE 10.1 Box and Whisker Plots of Price Level Indexes by Region and Country/Economy (world = 100)

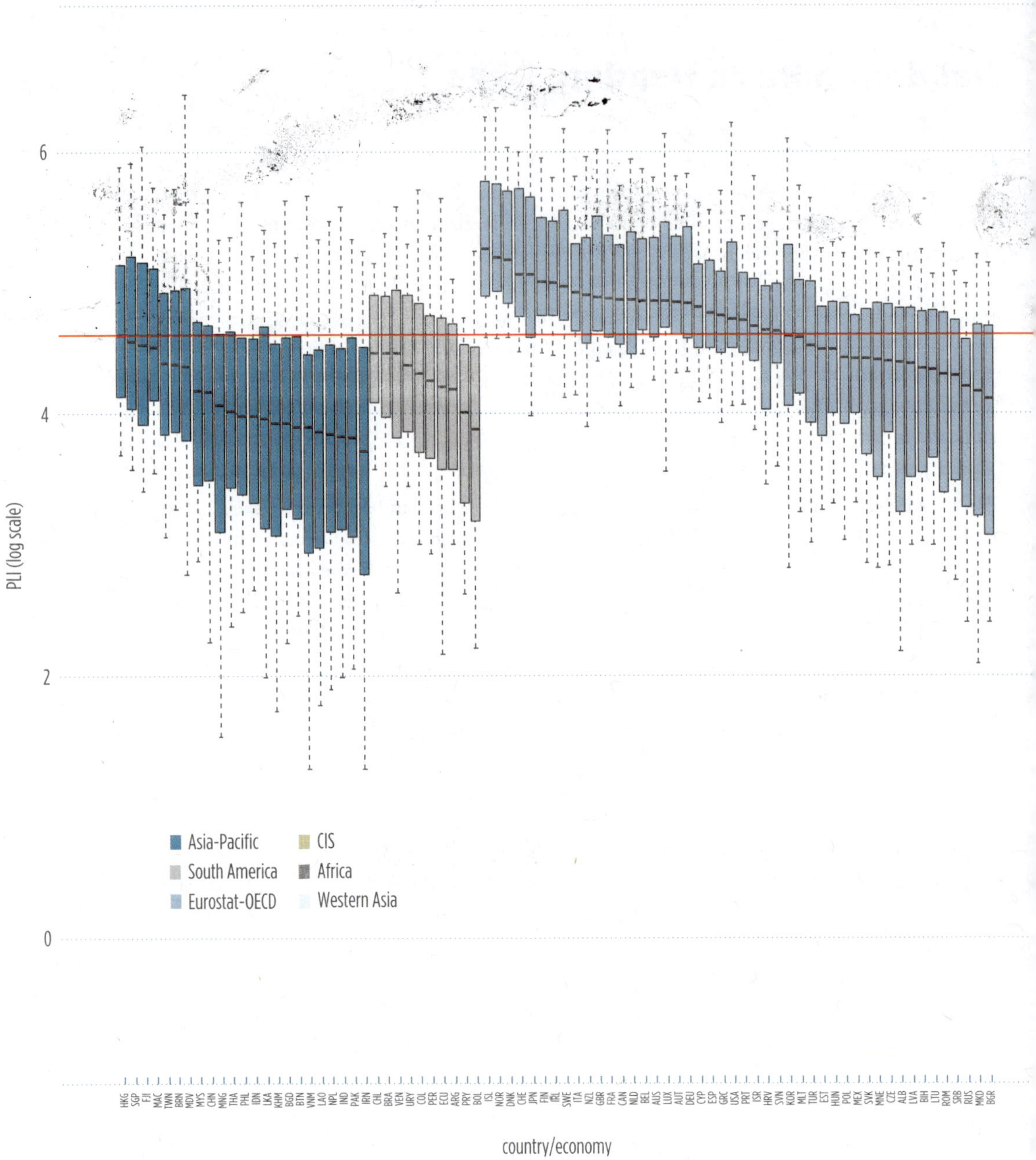

Sources: ICP 2005 and computations by Min Ji Lee, ICP Global Office.
Note: See annex to this chapter for country/economy codes.

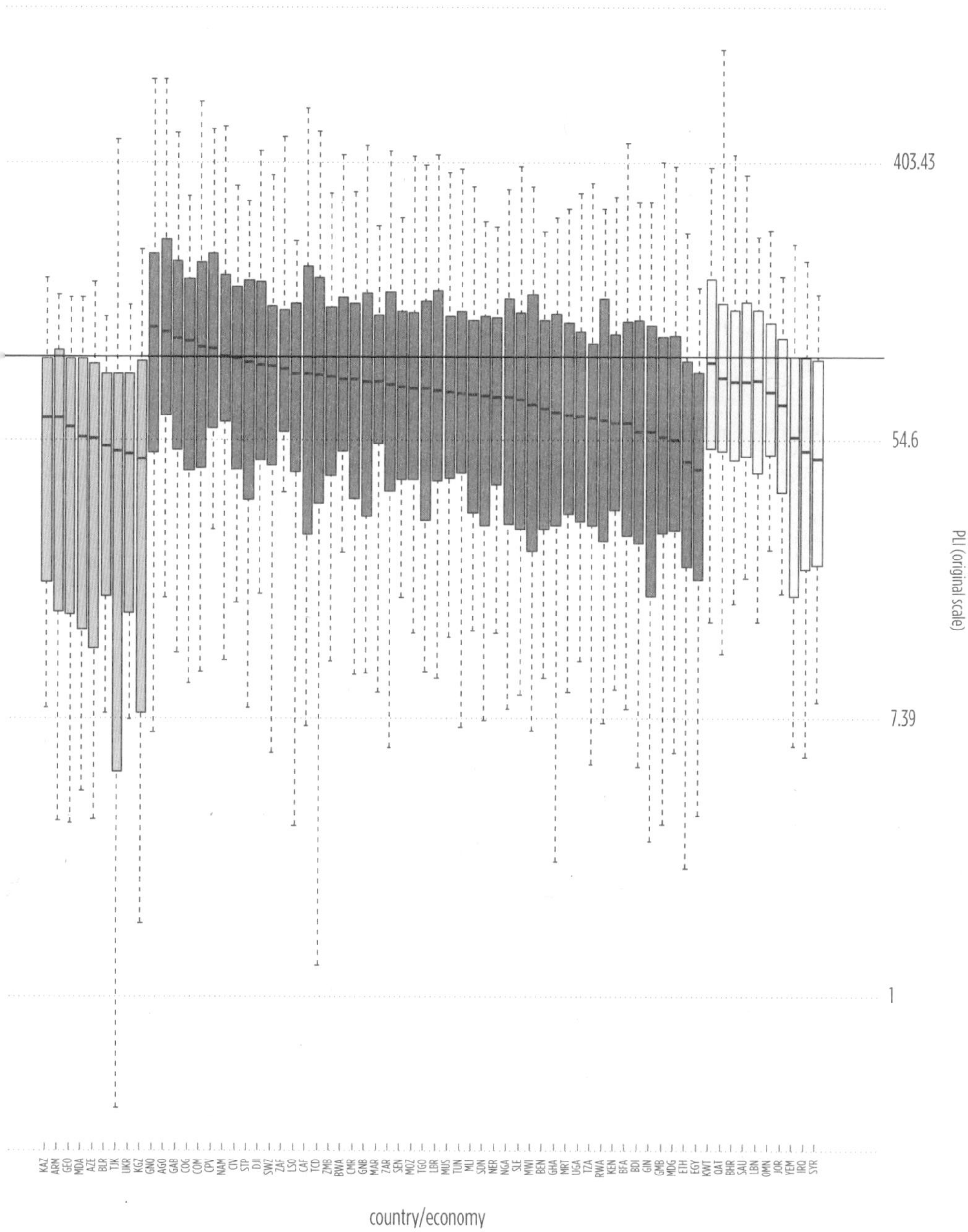
403.43
54.6
7.39
1
PLI (original scale)
KAZ ARM GEO MDA AZE BLR TJK UKR KGZ GNQ AGO GAB COG COM CPV NAM CIV STP DJI SWZ ZAF LSO CAF TCD ZMB BWA CMR GNB MAR ZAR SEN MOZ TGO LBR MUS TUN MLI SDN NER NGA SLE MWI BEN GHA MRT UGA TZA RWA KEN BFA BDI GIN GMB MDG ETH EGY KWT QAT BHR SAU LBN OMN JOR YEM IRQ SYR
country/economy

FIGURE 10.2 Box and Whisker Plots of Price Level Indexes by Basic Heading (world = 100)

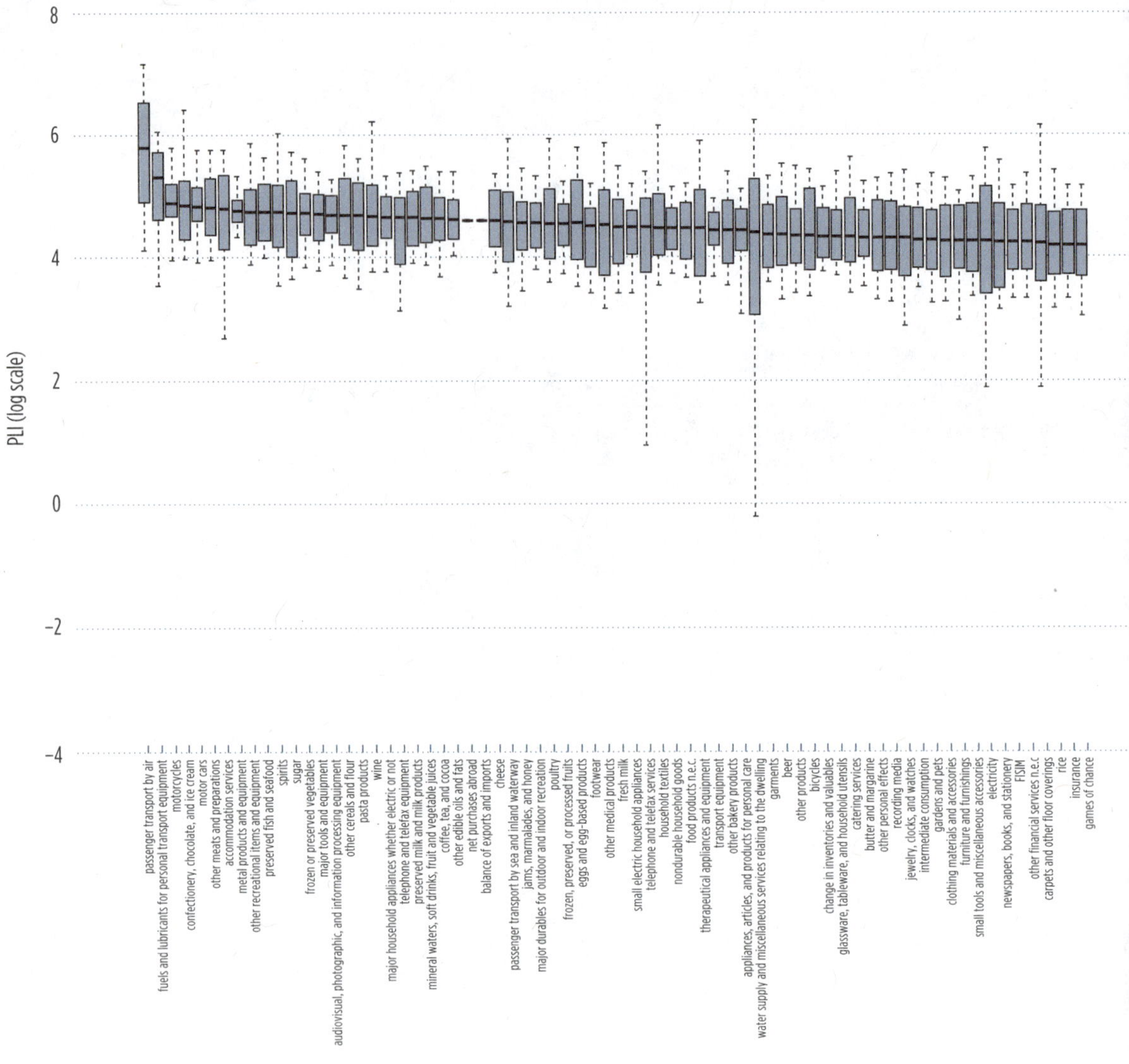

Sources: ICP 2005 and computations by Min Ji Lee, ICP Global Office.

Validating Basic Heading Expenditure Weights

Neither the Quaranta nor Dikhanov tables in the previous chapter are used to validate the basic heading expenditure weights, which points to a weakness in the data validation methodology. The starting point for the proposed validation is the matrix of national expenditures by basic heading by country. The "ICP Operational Guidelines" (World Bank 2011) describe a series of validation steps, first within each country, then across countries within regions, and finally across all countries.

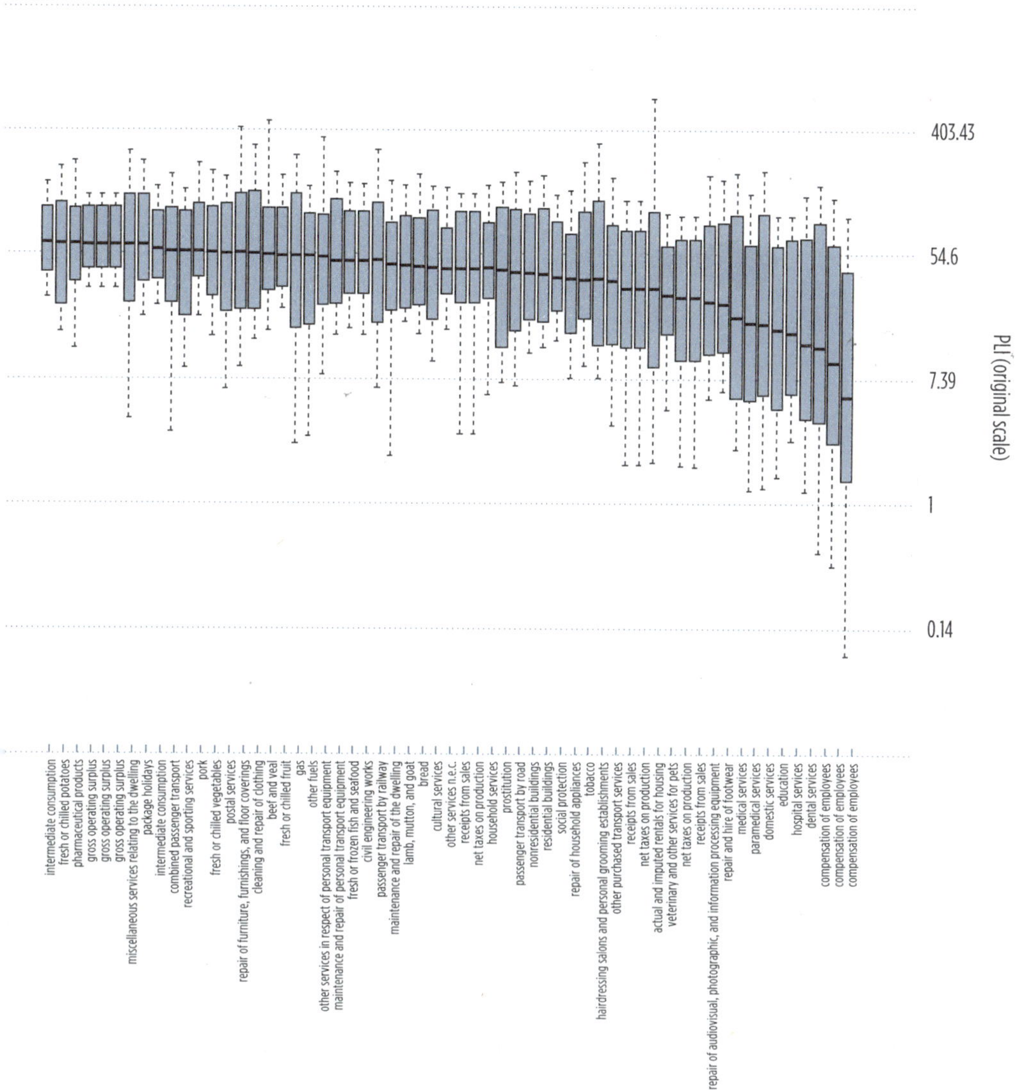

The within-country basic heading expenditures and shares are reviewed for

- Completeness, simply meaning that, with few exceptions, expenditures should be recorded for every basic heading
- Plausibility when comparing per capita values and expenditure shares across basic headings
- Temporal consistency with breakdowns for other years.

In each case, outliers are flagged for additional review.

The within-region and then between-region reviews compare expenditure shares, per capita nominal expenditures, and per capita indexes between countries having similar economic structures, with outliers flagged. Once the preliminary PPPs are available, per capita real expenditure values can be compared between same-cluster countries. Also, the deflated basic heading expenditures can be used to validate the respective price and quantity relationships, as discussed in the next section.

The purpose of this section is to review diagnostic procedures to identify potential basic heading expenditure values and shares that are outliers. A simple validation step begins by converting the basic heading expenditure values to expenditure shares and then reviewing the maximum and minimum shares across countries by basic heading and comparing them to the median value. The same approach can be applied to vectors of per capita real expenditure values for household consumption expenditure.

Table 10.1 provides the maximum, median, and minimum shares for basic headings for which a country reported expenditure shares greater than 10 percent of GDP. The maximum and minimum cells each represent different countries, but for the same basic heading shown in the first column. The largest expenditure share for any basic heading (21 percent) is shown by Moldova for residential buildings. The minimum share for residential buildings is 0.04 percent, shown by

TABLE 10.1 National Maximum, Median, and Minimum Expenditure Shares for Basic Headings with Maximum Values Greater than 10 Percent of GDP, and Maximum to Median and Median to Minimum Ratios

Basic heading	Maximum % share	Median % share	Minimum % share	Maximum to median ratio	Median to minimum ratio
Residential buildings	21.0	4.19	0.04	5.0	**105**
Other cereals and flour	19.6	0.63	0.01	**30.8**	**63**
Metal products and equipment	19.1	5.92	0.52	3.2	11
Rice	17.4	0.48	0.003	**36.3**	**160**
Actual and imputed rentals for housing	17.0	6.10	0.066	2.78	**92**
Nonresidential buildings	15.5	3.32	0	4.67	—
Education	15.1	1.65	0.10	9.16	16.5
Compensation of employees	14.7	4.40	1.17	3.34	3.8
Civil engineering works	14.6	3.01	0	4.86	—
Fresh milk	**11.6**	0.40	0	**29.2**	—
Transport equipment	11.4	2.27	0.08	5.0	**28**
Fresh or chilled potatoes	**11.4**	0.44	0.004	**25.8**	**110**
Catering services	10.0	1.94	0	5.14	—
Beer	**10.0**	0.34	0	**29.6**	—

Source: 2005 ICP.
Note: The numbers in boldface indicate that the basic heading expenditures for the countries with those numbers should be reviewed.

Kuwait. For other cereals and flour, the maximum (19.6 percent) and minimum (0.01 percent) shares are shown by Ethiopia and Japan, respectively. Although some basic heading expenditure shares, such as the maximum values for actual and imputed rentals for housing and civil engineering works, are plausible, questions should be raised about the values for items such as fresh milk, potatoes, and beer for countries with expenditure shares equal to or greater than 10 percent of GDP. Some of the minimum expenditure shares are also implausible, especially where countries reported zero values.

Another useful validation tool is to examine the ratios of the maximum and minimum values to the median. The median is the midpoint of the distribution, and thus its value is not affected by the maximum or minimum values. However, extreme differences of the maximum and minimum values to the median should be examined. The maximum expenditure exceeds the median by over 25 times for five basic headings in this group, indicating that expenditures for the countries reporting those values be reviewed. Table 10.1 only shows maximum to median ratios for countries with the largest maximum share values. The data validation should include a review of all basic headings with maximum to median ratios exceeding 25.

The median to minimum ratios far exceed the maximum to median ratios. The minimum values for over 78 of the basic headings are zero in at least one country. The zero values more likely indicate a failure of measurement rather than no consumption for the basic heading. From a data validation point of view, the main problem with expenditure shares is basic headings with small values. The basic heading expenditures for the countries with boldface numbers should be reviewed.

In summary, basic heading expenditures must be validated following an examination of the maximum and minimum values by basic heading and by country. The max/med and med/min ratios should also be reviewed to determine where there may be potential problems with basic heading expenditures in some countries.

The methods discussed so far to validate basic heading PPPs and expenditures treat each separately. The next section examines the results obtained when the basic heading PPPs are averaged to the GDP using expenditure values as the weights. At this and subsequent stages, the validation becomes more difficult because the PPPs and weights need to be considered together.

Evaluating the Fisher Matrix

Global aggregation of the 129 basic heading PPPs to the GDP begins with estimation of the Laspeyres and Paasche indexes as shown in equations (10.1) and (10.2) for each pair of countries. The Fisher index,

$$PPP_F^{j,k} \equiv \left(PPP_L^{j,k} PPP_P^{j,k}\right)^{\frac{1}{2}}, \quad (10.3)$$

for each pair of countries results in a matrix of 146 × 146 countries with PPPs at the GDP level. The robustness of each bilateral PPP is dependent on the similarity of the price and expenditure structures between the two countries. If they are similar, the Laspeyres and Paasche results for each bilateral PPP will be similar as well. The degree of this similarity can be measured by simply using the difference between them based on the Paasche-Laspeyres spread (PLS) shown by Hill (2011) as

$$PLS_{jk}^{s} = \frac{MAX\left(P_{jk}^{P}, P_{jk}^{L}\right)}{MIN\left(P_{jk}^{P}, P_{jk}^{L}\right)}. \quad (10.4)$$

FIGURE 10.3 Box and Whisker Plots of Paasche-Laspeyres Spreads by Region and Country/Economy

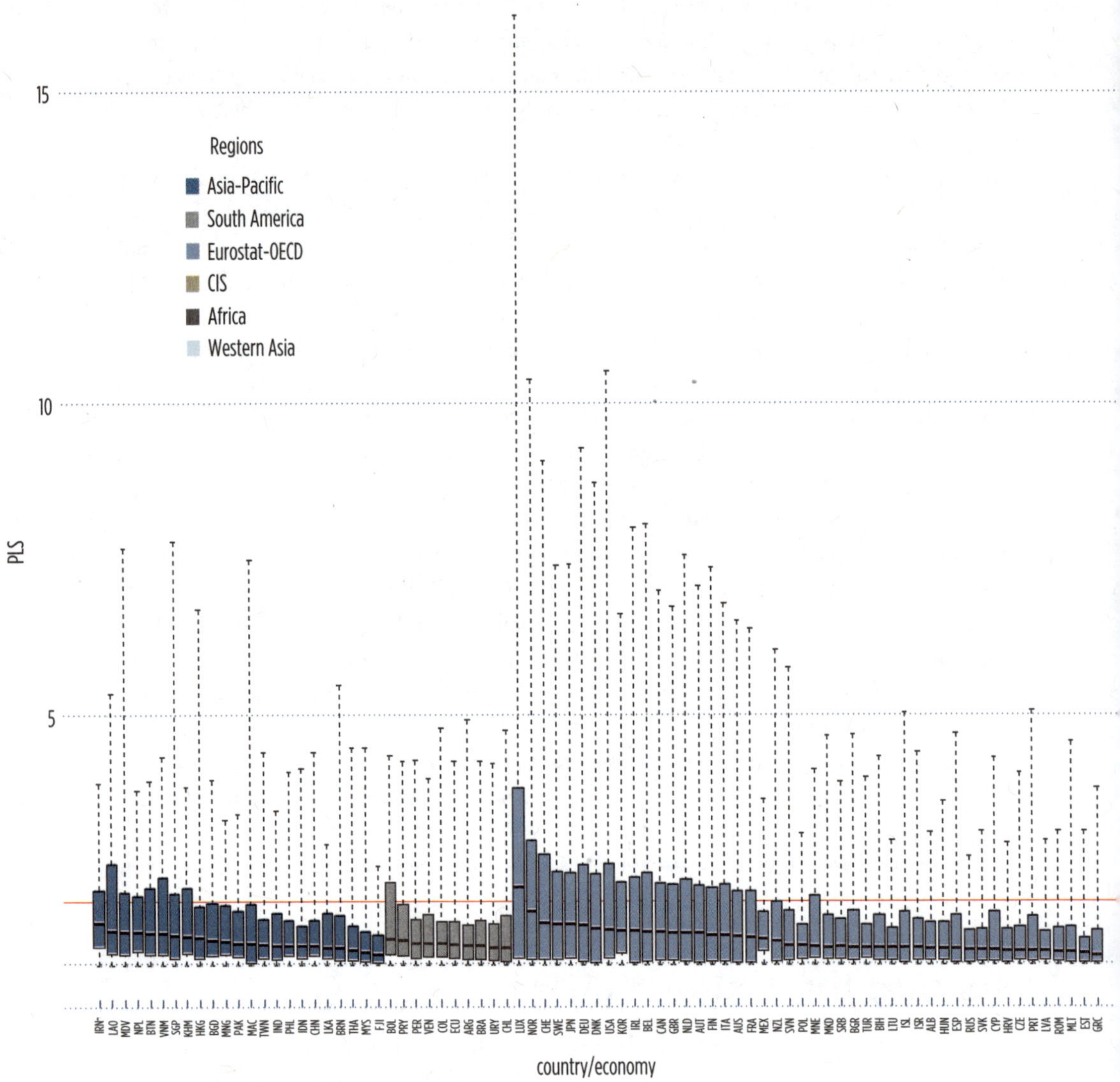

Sources: ICP 2005 and computations by Min Ji Lee, ICP Global Office.
Note: See annex to this chapter for country/economy codes.

It is not unreasonable that these spreads become large for some of the bilateral comparisons because of the extreme differences in price and expenditure structures. This matter has been addressed by Diewert (2001, 2009), Aten and Heston (2009), and Hill (1999, 2011), who mainly seek ways of overcoming these differences when moving from bilateral to multilateral estimates by taking the structural differences into account in the estimation. A later section provides more about their approaches. Here, the PLS is examined first as another step in data validation.

In the box and whisker plots in figure 10.3, the countries are grouped first by region and then by the median value of the PLS. The plot for each country shows the distribution of its PLS in relation to that of the 145 other countries. The box contains 80 percent of the values and the whiskers the maximum and minimum values. The minimum value is 1.00. Therefore, the analysis focuses on the

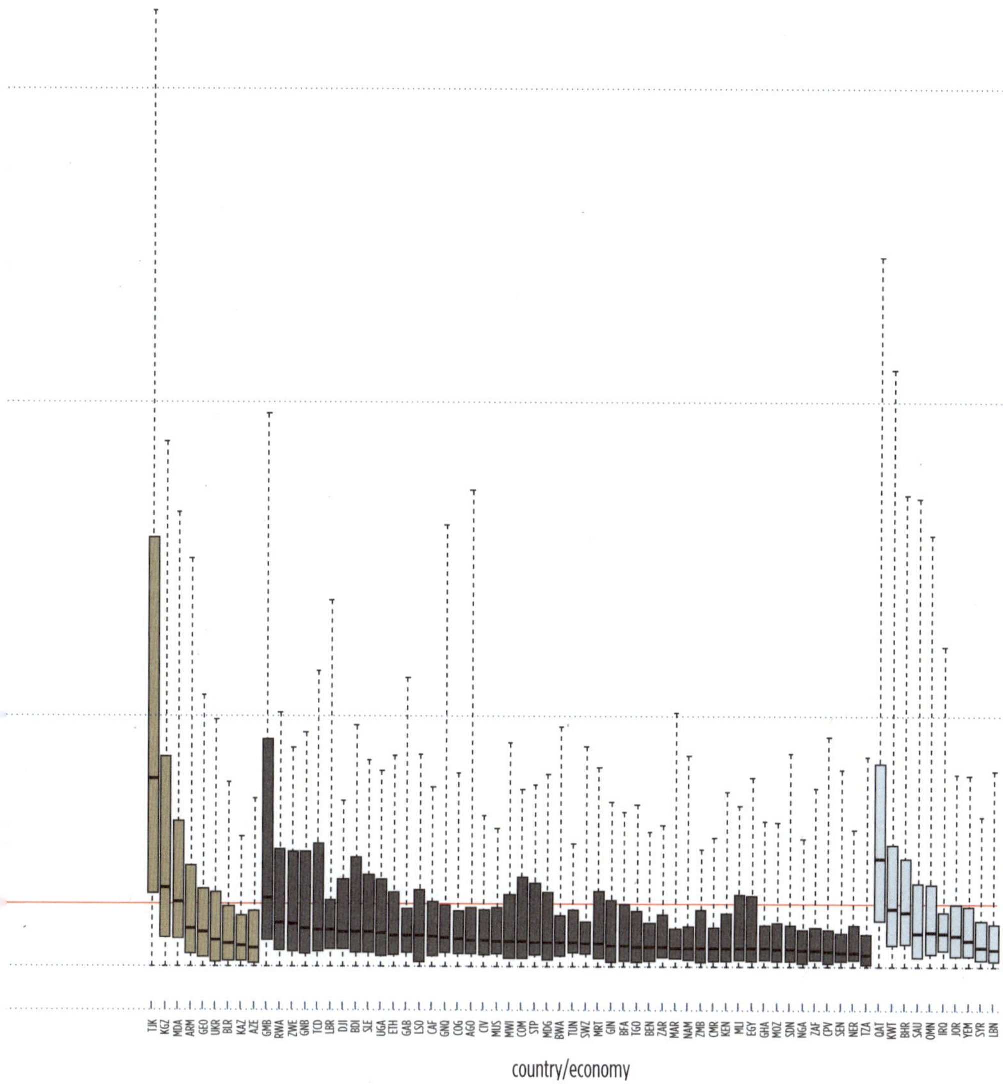

maximum values. Luxembourg and Tajikistan have the largest maximum value (PLS = 16.23), and in this case it is the maximum bilateral PLS of the 146 countries. The maximum values across the 146 countries are represented by only three countries: Tajikistan, with the maximum value for 104 of the 146 countries, and Qatar and Luxembourg, with the maximum values of 31 and 11 countries, respectively. There are regional relationships as well. For example, a closer look at the maximum PLS for the CIS countries reveals it is always the spread with Qatar that has the largest value.

Examination of the data reveals that four countries—Tajikistan, Qatar, Kyrgyz Republic, and Luxembourg—have a bilateral PLS greater than 2.00 with 135, 112, 89, and 84 other countries, respectively. Table 10.2 shows the 10 countries with the largest number of bilateral PLSs greater than 2.00. The United States is also shown because it is the base country for the comparison.

The analysis so far points out that the price (PPPs) and quantity data for the countries in table 10.2 across the basic headings are not consistent with each other, as well as with a large number of other countries. At this stage, it is not clear whether there is a problem with the PPPs and expenditures, which would require more data validation, or whether the data are valid, which then poses an estimation issue. The following discussion provides some additional validation steps that can be used when evaluating the Fisher PPPs.

Chapter 12 in the *ICP 2005 Methodological Handbook* (World Bank 2007) defines the Laspeyres quantity index as

$$Q_L^{j,k} = \frac{\sum_{i=1}^{n} p_i^j q_i^k}{\sum_{i=1}^{n} p_i^j q_i^j} \qquad (10.5)$$

which is the ratio of the real expenditures at GDP between the two countries when the quantities in both countries are valued at country *j*'s prices, and the Paasche quantity index as

$$Q_P^{jk} = \frac{\sum_{i=1}^{n} p_i^k q_i^k}{\sum_{i=1}^{n} p_i^k q_i^j} \qquad (10.6)$$

which is the ratio of the real expenditures at GDP in the two countries when the quantities in both are valued at country *k*'s prices.

As with the PPPs, the Fisher quantity index is the geometric mean of the Laspeyres and Paasche quantity indexes. Hill (2011) proposes computing upper and lower price and quantity

TABLE 10.2 Paasche-Laspeyres Spreads for Countries with Largest Number of Bilateral PLSs Greater than 2.0

	No. of PLSs > 2.0	No. times max.	LUX	NOR	CHE	KGZ	MDA	TJK	BHR	KWT	QAT	GMB	USA
LUX	84	11	1.00	1.10	1.00	8.53	5.44	16.23	1.64	1.42	1.74	9.80	1.12
NOR	67		—	1.00	1.04	5.80	3.94	10.48	1.55	1.55	2.07	6.29	1.23
CHE	54		—	—	1.00	5.30	3.94	9.09	1.46	1.46	1.98	5.81	1.11
KGZ	89		—	—	—	1.00	1.08	1.18	5.71	6.39	9.36	1.87	5.54
MDA	77		—	—	—	—	1.00	1.69	4.88	5.27	8.24	1.86	3.65
TJK	135	104	—	—	—	—	—	1.00	8.51	10.50	12.30	2.75	10.53
BHR	58		—	—	—	—	—	—	1.00	1.04	1.30	5.03	1.49
KWT	66		—	—	—	—	—	—	—	1.00	1.04	5.97	1.42
QAT	112	31	—	—	—	—	—	—	—	—	1.00	7.21	1.98
GMB	79		—	—	—	—	—	—	—	—	—	1.00	7.21
USA	41												1.00

Source: ICP 2005.
Note: See annex to this chapter for country codes.

relatives to determine whether the large values of the PLS are caused by PPP or expenditure outliers. Basic headings with large upper or lower quantity or price relatives should be further examined. Hill's analysis of the 2005 ICP data for Africa shows that the extensive validation of prices led to fewer large PPP relatives than were found for quantity relatives. His other finding is that the upper quantity relatives were considerably smaller than the lower quantity relatives. Analysis of the 2005 ICP data for Asia produces similar results, which are summarized in table 10.3.

TABLE 10.3 Twenty-five Largest Upper and Lower Quantity Relatives: Asia-Pacific Region, ICP 2005

Upper quantity relatives			Lower quantity relatives		
96.7	MNG	Lamb, mutton, and goat	2,556.9	BTN	Catering services
64.8	LKA	Other purchased transport services	1,200.9	THA	Butter and margarine
52.7	FJI	Household services	1,056.3	LKA	Maintenance and repair of personal transport equipment
35.5	BTN	Cheese	731.5	KHM	Telephone and telefax services
33.3	BTN	Therapeutical appliances and equipment	681.1	LAO	Frozen, preserved, or processed fruits
32.0	PAK	Cleaning and repair of clothing	525.4	MAC	Household services
27.8	BTN	Butter and margarine	402.9	FJI	Motorcycles
25.9	IRN	Telephone and telefax services	277.1	LKA	Repair of household appliances
25.7	NPL	Fresh milk	233.5	BTN	Confectionery, chocolate, and ice cream
25.1	IRN	Gas	225.6	BRN	Other fuels
22.6	NPL	Other cereals and flour	216.5	BTN	Other recreational items and equipment
22.6	NPL	Butter and margarine	186.7	KHM	Insurance
22.5	PAK	Postal services	168.3	BTN	Lamb, mutton, and goat
21.6	LKA	Veterinary and other services for pets	142.6	THA	Lamb, mutton, and goat
20.9	LKA	Major tools and equipment	139.0	NPL	Other services in respect of personal transport equipment
20.8	PAK	Repair and hire of footwear	132.8	HKG	Other fuels
20.7	BTN	Major tools and equipment	117.2	SGP	Other fuels
20.1	PAK	Veterinary and other services for pets	90.3	HKG	Repair of furniture, furnishings, and floor coverings
19.1	PAK	Fresh milk	84.7	KHM	Telephone and telefax equipment
18.4	HKG	Telephone and telefax equipment	77.0	LAO	Therapeutical appliances and equipment
18.2	NPL	Lamb, mutton, and goat	73.2	BGD	Frozen, preserved, or processed fruits
17.8	BGD	Fresh or chilled potatoes	68.3	MNG	Fresh or frozen fish and seafood
17.7	IRN	Other fuels	67.0	TWN	Other fuels
17.3	IND	Fresh milk	65.9	MDV	Maintenance and repair of personal transport equipment
16.5	LKA	Frozen, preserved, or processed fruits	64.7	BTN	Bicycles

Sources: ICP 2005 and computations by Min Ji Lee, ICP Global Office.
Note: See annex to this chapter for country/economy codes.

TABLE 10.4 Dendrogram Showing Clustering of 146 ICP 2005 Countries/Economies Based on Quantity Relatives

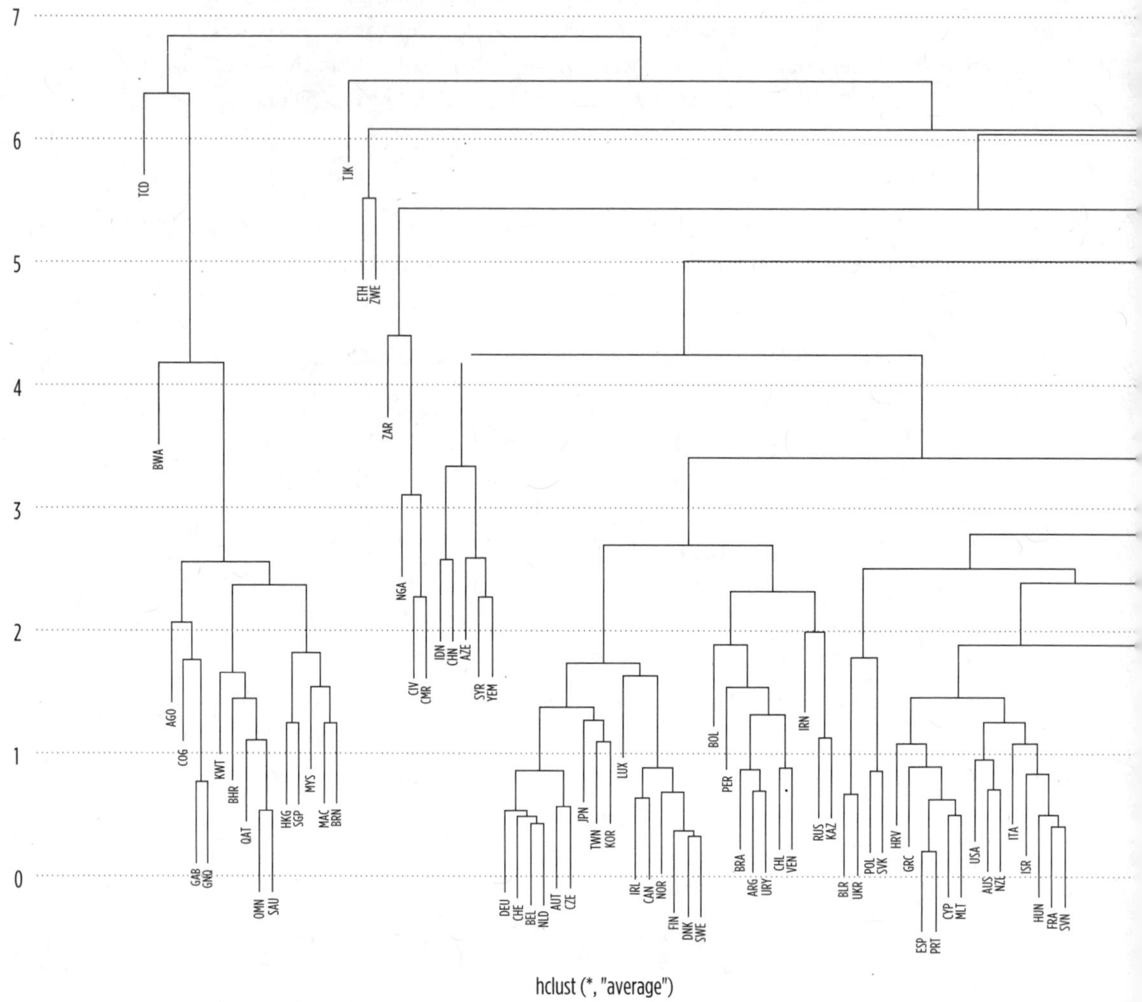

Sources: ICP 2005 and computations by Min Ji Lee, ICP Global Office.

The upper quantity relative shows the relative size of a basic heading in a country compared with the average of that of all countries when taking the size of the economy into account. The upper quantity relative of 96.7 for Mongolia means that its spending on lamb, mutton, and goat is 96 times larger than the average across countries in the Asia-Pacific region. Conversely, the lower quantity relative of 2,556.9 for Bhutan means its expenditures for catering services are $\frac{1}{2{,}556.9}$ of the average. The data for these basic headings may be correct, but they should be reviewed because they are so different. A final point is that the upper quantity relatives are considerably less than the lower quantity relatives. The conclusion reached is that basic heading expenditures that are very small should be further validated.

The PLSs and price and quantity relatives just described can be placed in a dissimilarity matrix of 146 × 146. Hill (2011) suggests using cluster analysis that seeks observation pairs with the smallest measures of dissimilarity, groups them, and then seeks the next set of

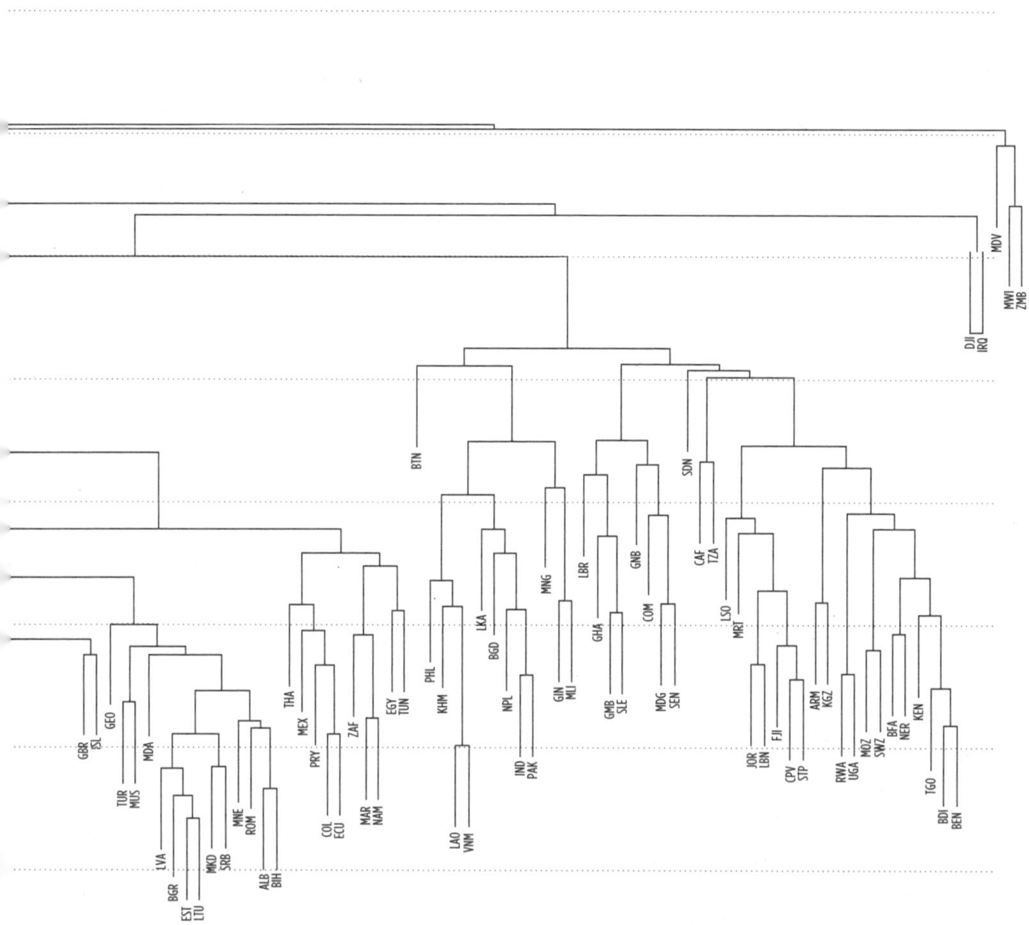

hclust (*, "average")

similar measures. This method groups country pairs that are similar in structure of prices and quantities. Those exceeding a desired value of similarity are not included, suggesting they be reviewed again.

Figure 10.4, a dendogram based on quantity relatives, shows how the countries are clustered; it is over the full set of basic headings and includes all 146 countries. Although a dozen countries are different from the rest, they are generally the same ones appearing in the diagnostics just described. The dendogram still does not answer the question of whether there is a problem with the data for some basic headings, or whether they are simply different in economic structure from the remaining countries. The basic analysis of the PPPs, expenditure weights, and PLSs as described in earlier sections of this chapter should be repeated for countries appearing as outliers.

At this stage, the issue is likely no longer a data validation one, but simply that some countries have significantly different price and expenditure structures. The issue, then, is their effect on the final estimation step, which is the GEKS procedure to achieve transitivity.

From Bilateral PPPs to Multilateral PPPs

The starting point for the GEKS method is the 146 × 146 matrix of Fisher PPPs. This matrix contains the PPPs between every pair of countries in the comparison. Table 10.4 is a partial matrix of nine countries. Each country is represented in a row and a column; the Macao SAR, China, row, for example, shows the PPP of it to each of the other countries shown in the respective columns. These PPPs are not transitive. For example, the direct PPP of Hong Kong SAR, China, to Macao SAR, China is 1.03. The indirect PPP of Hong Kong SAR, China to Macao SAR, China through India (1.141) is the PPP of Hong Kong SAR, China to India (0.38) divided by the PPP of Macao SAR, China to India (0.33) and is different from the direct PPP. Therefore, the PPPs are not transitive.

The purpose of the GEKS method as described in chapters 1, 4, and 5 is to ensure that the PPPs between any two countries can be obtained either directly or indirectly with any other country with the same results. This is achieved by first computing all of the direct and indirect PPPs for the countries in each row with US = 1 by dividing each row in table 10.4 by the USA row. There will be two direct PPPs in each row—each country to itself and with the US = 1—and (n - 2) or 144 indirect PPPs. The GEKS PPP is then the geometric mean of these direct and indirect PPPs. These PPPs are transitive, which means the PPP between any two countries will equal the PPP when it is obtained through a third country. The direct and indirect PPPs are treated equally to satisfy the symmetric requirement. The consequences are discussed in the next section.

Table 10.5 shows the direct and indirect PPPs with US = 1.00 for the same countries shown in table 10.4. For example, the PPPs in the Hong Kong SAR, China row are the direct and indirect PPPs relative to the United States. HGK/HGK and HGK/USA are the direct PPPs, and the others are indirect PPPs through the country in the column heading. The final multilateral PPP for each country to US = 1.00 is obtained by taking the geometric mean of each row, which in effect gives equal weight to every country. Table 10.5 shows that the direct and indirect PPPs differ—for example, the PPP for Brunei to the United States is 1.08 when linked through Singapore and 0.76 when linked through Bhutan, a 1.44 times difference.

A final step in the data validation effort is to review the variability of the direct and indirect PPPs for each country. Table 10.6 lists countries with the largest ratios of the maximum to

TABLE 10.4 Partial Matrix of Fisher PPPs, Selected Countries/Economies

Country/ Economy	HKG	MAC	SGP	TWN	BRN	BGD	BTN	IND	USA
HKG	1.00	1.03	4.97	0.31	5.77	0.26	0.36	0.38	5.87
MAC	0.97	1.00	4.91	0.29	5.70	0.23	0.34	0.33	5.61
SGP	0.20	0.20	1.00	0.06	1.14	0.05	0.07	0.07	1.23
TWN	3.25	3.50	16.57	1.00	20.07	0.92	1.26	1.32	17.62
BRN	0.17	0.18	0.88	0.05	1.00	0.04	0.06	0.06	0.92
BGD	3.91	4.35	20.52	1.09	25.78	1.00	1.46	1.59	20.52
BTN	2.79	2.90	15.36	0.79	17.57	0.68	1.00	1.05	13.34
IND	2.62	2.99	14.32	0.76	17.03	0.63	0.95	1.00	14.01
USA	0.17	0.18	0.81	0.06	1.08	0.05	0.07	0.07	1.00

Source: ICP 2005.
Note: See annex to this chapter for country/economy codes.

TABLE 10.5 Direct and Indirect PPPs, Selected Countries/Economies (US = 1.00)

Country/ Economy	HKG	MAC	SGP	TWN	BRN	BGD	BTN	IND	USA
HKG	*5.87*	5.79	6.13	5.41	5.32	5.25	4.77	5.34	*5.87*
MAC	5.70	*5.61*	6.06	5.04	5.26	4.72	4.59	4.69	*5.61*
SGP	1.18	1.14	*1.23*	1.06	1.05	1.00	0.87	0.98	*1.23*
TWN	19.11	19.63	20.46	*17.62*	18.51	18.82	16.81	18.43	*17.62*
BRN	1.02	0.98	1.08	0.88	*0.92*	0.80	0.76	0.82	*0.92*
BGD	22.97	24.42	25.33	19.21	23.77	*20.52*	19.53	22.29	*20.52*
BTN	16.41	16.30	18.95	13.98	16.21	14.02	*13.34*	14.69	*13.34*
IND	15.41	16.79	17.67	13.40	15.70	12.90	12.72	*14.01*	*14.01*
USA	1.00	1.00	1.00	1.00	1.00	1.00	1.00	1.00	*1.00*

Source: ICP 2005.
Note: See annex to this chapter for country/economy codes.

TABLE 10.6 Measures of Variability of Direct and Indirect PPPs (US = 1.00) for Countries with Largest Maximum to Minimum Ratios

Country	Max/min indirect PPPs (1)	Relative standard deviation of direct and indirect PPPs (2)	Direct PPP/GEKS (3)	GEKS PLI-weighted PLS/GEKS (4)
TZA	3.59	0.18	1.19	1.01
QAT	2.78	0.15	1.18	1.05
TJK	2.76	0.15	0.83	1.09
LAO	2.63	0.14	0.93	1.00
VNM	2.56	0.14	0.99	1.04
KHM	2.56	0.13	0.94	1.00
GNQ	2.50	0.15	1.16	0.99
KGZ	2.41	0.14	0.88	1.00
GMB	2.28	0.16	0.72	0.98
MDA	2.11	0.13	0.98	1.00
BHR	1.72	0.11	1.11	0.96
LUX	1.66	0.09	1.10	1.00
KWT	1.63	0.11	1.13	1.00
NOR	1.50	0.08	1.12	1.02
CHE	1.36	0.06	1.09	0.97

Source: 2005 ICP and Aten-Heston weighted PLS/GEKS.
Note: See annex to this chapter for country codes. PLI = price level index; PLS = Paasche-Laspeyres spread; GEKS = Gini-Éltetö-Köves-Szulc.

minimum values of the indirect PPPs. Tanzania shows the largest differences, followed by Qatar and Tajikistan. Note, however, that the variability here is considerably less than that shown by the PLS spreads; the largest PLS is over 16, while the largest maximum to minimum ratio of direct and indirect PPPs is 3.59. Generally, many of the same countries appear as outliers in both cases.

Column (2) of table 10.6 lists the relative standard deviations of the direct and indirect PPPs as expressed by the median divided by the standard deviation. The values decline rapidly, indicating that there are only a small number of outlier values for these countries.

Column (3) shows the relative difference between the direct PPP for each country to the United States and the GEKS PPP, which is the geometric mean of the direct and all indirect PPPs. The real GDP for Tanzania is 1.19 times larger than if the direct PPP had been used. Ratios greater than 1.00 show the amount by which the real GDP is increased by the GEKS process; ratios less than 1.00 the amount it was reduced by the GEKS process.

Column (4), taken from Aten and Heston (2009), is discussed in the next section.

Recall that the variability measures for each country include indirect PPPs through every other country in the comparison—in this case, 146 countries. Although the data for those countries with the greatest variability should receive another review, the reality is that at this stage the differences are more likely to be caused by the extreme differences in the economic structures of the economies. The following section considers the question of whether all indirect PPPs should be given equal weight in the GEKS process.

When Does Validation End and Estimation Begin?

Countries that appear as outliers in the analysis steps described in this chapter may have quality data and are simply different in structure from the other countries. From a statistical point of view, they contribute more to measurement error than do the other countries, suggesting that they should be treated differently in the estimation process. Hill (1999, 2011), Aten and Heston (2009), Diewert (2009), and others have considered this dimension of the GEKS. Hill proposes the minimum spanning tree approach, which is a method to first compute PPPs for the countries most similar and then bring in countries less similar in a way that preserves fixity of the first set. The problem is determining the criteria for grouping the countries; the final results are very sensitive to the methods used to choose countries for each step. There is also a problem of circularity, because the final results are needed to set up the spanning tree paths.

Aten and Heston (2009) raise the question whether all Fisher indexes are equal. This question translates into whether the direct and indirect PPPs in the GEKS process should receive equal weights. Aten and Heston provide an example in which the PLS becomes a variable in estimation of the final PPPs. This is done by expressing the GEKS process as a least squares estimate and adding the PLS as a variable. Column (4) in table 10.6 is the ratio of GEKS/PLS to GEKS. Note that considerable adjustments are made for countries such as Qatar and Tajikistan that also have the largest PLS. Aten and Heston show results based on this and other methods for all countries using the variability present in the estimation process. They conclude that consideration should be given to using additional variables or weights to deal with the wide differences in economic structure across countries.

Conclusion

Several validation steps have been analyzed in this chapter, starting with those for the basic heading PPPs and expenditure weights. The outcome of this analysis is that considerable attention should be given to the validation of expenditure weights using the methods suggested by Hill (2011). The analysis also suggests that the matrix of Fisher PPPs be reviewed and validated. Analysis of the 2005 and 2011 benchmark data should continue to reveal estimation methods that better deal with the variability arising from countries of different economic structures.

A final conclusion is that there are large differences in economic structures across countries. Countries with high price levels will have different economic structures than those with low price levels. Developing countries generally have larger shares in food consumption and smaller shares in services. Over 180 countries and economies will participate in the 2011 ICP compared with the 146 that took part in the 2005 ICP. The additional countries will contribute to the variability. In response, Aten and Heston (2009) raise the question of whether there should be a departure from use of the democratic or equal weighting inherent in the GEKS process.

ANNEX

Three-Letter Country/Economy Codes, International Organization for Standardization

ABW	Aruba	CHL	Chile	GIB	Gibraltar
AFG	Afghanistan	CHN	China	GIN	Guinea
AGO	Angola	CIV	Côte d'Ivoire	GLP	Guadeloupe
ALB	Albania	CMR	Cameroon	GMB	Gambia, The
AND	Andorra	COD	Congo, Dem. Rep.	GNB	Guinea-Bissau
ARE	United Arab Emirates	COG	Congo, Rep.	GNQ	Equatorial Guinea
ARG	Argentina	COL	Colombia	GRC	Greece
ARM	Armenia	COM	Comoros	GRD	Grenada
ATA	Antarctica	CPV	Cape Verde	GRL	Greenland
ATG	Antigua and Barbuda	CRI	Costa Rica	GTM	Guatemala
AUS	Australia	CUB	Cuba	GUF	French Guiana
AUT	Austria	CYM	Cayman Islands	GUM	Guam
AZE	Azerbaijan	CYP	Cyprus	GUY	Guyana
BDI	Burundi	CZE	Czech Republic	HKG	Hong Kong SAR, China
BEL	Belgium	DEU	Germany	HND	Honduras
BEN	Benin	DJI	Djibouti	HRV	Croatia
BFA	Burkina Faso	DMA	Dominica	HTI	Haiti
BGD	Bangladesh	DNK	Denmark	HUN	Hungary
BGR	Bulgaria	DOM	Dominican Republic	IDN	Indonesia
BHR	Bahrain	DZA	Algeria	IND	India
BHS	Bahamas, The	ECU	Ecuador	IRL	Ireland
BIH	Bosnia and Herzegovina	EGY	Egypt, Arab Rep.	IRN	Iran, Islamic Rep.
BLR	Belarus	ERI	Eritrea	IRQ	Iraq
BLZ	Belize	ESP	Spain	ISL	Iceland
BMU	Bermuda	EST	Estonia	ISR	Israel
BOL	Bolivia	ETH	Ethiopia	ITA	Italy
BRA	Brazil	FIN	Finland	JAM	Jamaica
BRB	Barbados	FJI	Fiji	JOR	Jordan
BRN	Brunei Darussalam	FRA	France	JPN	Japan
BTN	Bhutan	FSM	Micronesia, Fed. Sts.	KAZ	Kazakhstan
BWA	Botswana	GAB	Gabon	KEN	Kenya
CAF	Central African Republic	GBR	United Kingdom	KGZ	Kyrgyz Republic
CAN	Canada	GEO	Georgia	KHM	Cambodia
CHE	Switzerland	GHA	Ghana	KIR	Kiribati

KNA	Saint Kitts and Nevis	NGA	Nigeria	SUR	Suriname
KOR	Korea, Rep.	NIC	Nicaragua	SVK	Slovak Republic
KWT	Kuwait	NLD	Netherlands	SVN	Slovenia
LAO	Lao PDR	NOR	Norway	SWE	Sweden
LBN	Lebanon	NPL	Nepal	SWZ	Swaziland
LBR	Liberia	NRU	Nauru	SYC	Seychelles
LBY	Libya	NZL	New Zealand	SYR	Syrian Arab Republic
LIE	Liechtenstein	OMN	Oman	TCD	Chad
LKA	Sri Lanka	PAK	Pakistan	TGO	Togo
LSO	Lesotho	PAN	Panama	THA	Thailand
LTU	Lithuania	PCN	Pitcairn	TJK	Tajikistan
LUX	Luxembourg	PER	Peru	TKM	Turkmenistan
LVA	Latvia	PHL	Philippines	TLS	Timor-Leste
MAC	Macao SAR, China	PLW	Palau	TON	Tonga
MAR	Morocco	PNG	Papua New Guinea	TTO	Trinidad and Tobago
MCO	Monaco	POL	Poland	TUN	Tunisia
MDA	Moldova	PRI	Puerto Rico	TUR	Turkey
MDG	Madagascar	PRK	Korea, Dem. People's Rep.	TUV	Tuvalu
MDV	Maldives	PRT	Portugal	TWN	Taiwan, China
MEX	Mexico	PRY	Paraguay	TZA	Tanzania
MHL	Marshall Islands	PYF	French Polynesia	UGA	Uganda
MKD	Macedonia, FYR	QAT	Qatar	UKR	Ukraine
MLI	Mali	ROU	Romania	URY	Uruguay
MLT	Malta	RUS	Russian Federation	USA	United States
MMR	Myanmar	RWA	Rwanda	UZB	Uzbekistan
MNE	Montenegro	SAU	Saudi Arabia	VEN	Venezuela, RB
MNG	Mongolia	SDN	Sudan	VGB	Virgin Islands, British
MOZ	Mozambique	SEN	Senegal	VIR	Virgin Islands, U.S.
MRT	Mauritania	SGP	Singapore	VNM	Vietnam
MSR	Montserrat	SLB	Solomon Islands	VUT	Vanuatu
MTQ	Martinique	SLE	Sierra Leone	WSM	Samoa
MUS	Mauritius	SLV	El Salvador	YEM	Yemen, Rep.
MWI	Malawi	SMR	San Marino	ZAF	South Africa
MYS	Malaysia	SOM	Somalia	ZMB	Zambia
NAM	Namibia	SRB	Serbia	ZWE	Zimbabwe
NCL	New Caledonia	SSD	Republic of South Sudan		
NER	Niger	STP	São Tomé and Príncipe		

NOTES

1. The author is grateful for the computations and data plots provided by Min Ji Lee, ICP Global Office, World Bank.
2. The five geographic ICP regions in 2005 were Africa, Asia-Pacific, Commonwealth of Independent States (CIS), South America, and Western Asia. The Eurostat-OECD members constitute a sixth region for purposes of the analysis provided in this chapter.
3. Zimbabwe was omitted from the analysis shown in figures 10.1 and 10.2 based on price level indexes because an official exchange rate was not determined due to extreme volatility during 2005.

REFERENCES

Aten, Bettina, and Alan Heston. 2009. "Are All Fishers Equal?" http://pwt.econ.upenn.edu/papers/paperev.html.

Diewert, W. Erwin. 2001. "Similarity and Dissimilarity Indexes: An Axiomatic Approach." Discussion Paper No. 02-10, revised March 2006. Department of Economics, University of British Columbia.

———. 2009. "Similarity Indexes and Criteria for Spatial Linking." In *Purchasing Power of Currencies: Recent Advances in Methods and Applications*, ed. D. D. Rao. Cheltenham, U.K.: Edward Elgar.

Hill, R. J. 1999. "Comparing Price Levels across Countries using Minimum Spanning Trees." *Review of Economics and Statistics* 81: 135–42.

———. 2011. "Cluster Formation, Data Validation and Outlier Detection in the International Comparison Program—An Application to the African Region." Paper prepared for African Development Bank, Statistics Department, Statistical Capacity Building Department. http://siteresources.worldbank.org/ICPINT/resources/270056-1255977007108/6483550-1257349667891/6544465-1316197687477/03.02_110926_ICP-TAG06_Validation-Hill.pdf.

Tukey, John W. 1977. *Exploratory Data Analysis*. Boston: Addison-Wesley.

World Bank. 2007. *ICP 2005 Methodological Handbook*. http://web.worldbank.org/WBSITE/EXTERNAL/DATASTATISTICS/ICPEXT/0,,contentMDK:20126612~pagePK:60002244~piPK:62002388~theSitePK:270065,00.html.

———. 2011. "ICP Operational Guidelines—National Account Validation." International Comparison Program, World Bank. http://www.worldbank.org/data/icp.

CHAPTER 11

Health and Education

Derek Blades

This chapter describes the kinds of data needed to calculate purchasing power parities (PPPs) for health and education. Data are required on prices to calculate basic heading PPPs and on government and household expenditures to weight the basic heading PPPs to obtain PPPs for higher levels of aggregation.

Most of the chapter describes how the 2005 round of the International Comparison Program (ICP) was conducted. The final section describes the changes that, building on earlier experience, will be introduced in the 2011 round.

In this volume, chapter 15 on government services (compensation) explains the general treatment of government services in the ICP, and much of what is written there also applies to government expenditures on health and education. However, this chapter is both narrower than chapter 15 because it deals only with government expenditures on health and education, and yet broader than chapter 15 because it also deals with household expenditures on health and education.

Special Features of Health and Education

Countries have different arrangements for providing their citizens with health and education goods and services. In a few countries, households are left to their own devices and must purchase these from private schools, clinics, hospitals, and so on. At the other extreme, a few governments supply all their citizens with health and education goods and services without charge. In the vast majority of countries, however, health and education are provided through a mixture of government-run and private schools, clinics, hospitals, and other institutions. Because of the different ways in which health and education services are provided, the ICP tries to measure the total volumes actually *consumed* by households regardless of whether they are paid for by households themselves or by government. This chapter explains how this measurement is made. Related to this explanation, in the remainder of this chapter the term *services* is generally inclusive of goods and benefits.

This chapter also describes how to compare the real output of health and education services produced by governments in different countries. The services that governments produce are not sold at market prices, and national accountants have assumed that the value of the outputs of such services is equal to the cost of their inputs. Traditionally, that is how the gross output and value added of government (and, where relevant, nonprofit institutions serving households, NPISH) have been measured in the national accounts, and the same procedure has been used for international comparisons.

Recently, however, many developments in the areas of both health and education have suggested that, over a period of years, the value of outputs is not equal to the value of the inputs used to produce them. In health services, for example, notable improvements have been made in diagnostic equipment, new treatments have been devised for cancer and AIDS patients, and microsurgery has drastically reduced recovery times so that patients are discharged much sooner than before. Meanwhile, anyone who looks only at the costs of providing education and health services is ignoring the fact that some countries are using their inputs more efficiently than other countries because they are making better use of new technical developments in providing these services. The changes that will be introduced in the 2011 ICP to capture these productivity differences in the provision of health and education services are explained in the last section of this chapter.

Organization of This Chapter

In the sections that follow, the first, health goods and services, explains the concept of "actual consumption" as the sum of individual household expenditures and government expenditures on health services. Because actual consumption covers both the household and government sectors, the estimation of PPPs requires information on both the prices of medical products and services *purchased* by households and the production costs of health services *produced* by government. In the second section, education services receive the same treatment.

Compensation of employees is the main cost component of the government's production of health and education services. For the 2005 ICP, countries were required to provide information on the compensation of employees for 50 standard government occupations using the *System of National Accounts* (SNA) definition of employee compensation (Commission of the European Communities et al. 1993). The third section explains how this requirement was implemented.

For three ICP regions—Africa, Asia-Pacific, and Western Asia—PPPs calculated by comparing the compensation of employees produced results that were judged to be implausible because of the great differences in the levels of government salaries among countries in these regions. Some poor countries in which government salaries were usually very low were shown as having larger government services in real terms than the richer countries in which government salaries were much higher. An adjustment was therefore made for all government services, including health and education. This adjustment, which was based on the estimated ratios of capital assets per employee, is described in the fourth section of this chapter. However, the description there is brief because full details are given in chapter 16 on government services (productivity adjustments).

The final section of this chapter describes the changes planned for the 2011 ICP round based on the lessons learned in the 2005 and earlier rounds.

As noted earlier, chapter 15 on government services (compensation) explains the data requirements and methods used to calculate PPPs for all government services, both collective and individual. Thus to the extent possible, this chapter tries to avoid repeating chapter 15, and instead refers the reader to that chapter.

Health Goods and Services

This section illustrates how the household and government expenditures for health are combined in order to make comparisons across countries with different levels of government input to what is actually consumed by households.

Actual Consumption of Health Care

In some countries, the government provides households with most of the health goods and services they need. In other countries, households must buy most health goods and services in the market. Thus the only way to make useful comparisons among all countries is to compare the *actual consumption* of health goods and services regardless of whether government or private households actually incur the *expenditure*. Actual consumption is obtained by combining purchases of health goods and services by both households and government with the value of the health goods and services produced by government.

Basic Headings for Health Goods and Services

Box 11.1 shows the basic headings for final expenditures on health goods and services. These basic headings fall into two categories: *goods and services* and *production costs*. The basic headings for *goods and services* (110611.1 to 130212.4) refer to purchases by households and government of health goods and services from market producers. Examples are medicines, bandages, dental treatments, and therapeutic massage. The same specifications are used for collecting the prices of pharmaceutical products, other medical products, therapeutic appliances, and medical services whether purchased by households or by government.

The basic headings for *production costs* (130221.1 to 130225.1) refer to health services produced by the doctors and other health workers, clinics, hospitals, convalescence homes, and so forth funded by government. Because these services are not sold on the market, there is no market price at which they can be valued. Instead, the value of these services is taken as equal to the costs of production. Compensation of employees and intermediate consumption are the main production costs. Gross operating surplus

BOX 11.1 Basic Headings: Expenditures on Health Goods and Services

The total of the expenditure on the following basic headings by both households and government make up the *actual consumption* of households of health goods and services.

Individual consumption expenditure by households

Medical products, appliances, and equipment

110611.1 Pharmaceutical products
110612.1 Other medical products
110613.1 Therapeutic appliances and equipment

Outpatient services

110621.1 Outpatient medical services
110622.1 Outpatient dental services
110623.1 Outpatient paramedical services

Hospital services

110631.1 Hospital services

Individual consumption expenditure by government

Health benefits and reimbursements

130211.1 Pharmaceutical products
130211.2 Other medical products
130211.3 Therapeutic appliances and equipment
130212.1 Outpatient medical services
130212.2 Outpatient dental services
130212.3 Outpatient paramedical services
130212.4 Hospital services

Production of health services

130221.1 Compensation of employees
130222.1 Intermediate consumption
130223.1 Gross operating surplus
130224.1 Net taxes on production
130225.1 Receipts from sales *(minus)*

usually consists only of consumption of fixed capital, and there is no net operating surplus. However, certain types of health services provided by government may be sold at market prices in some countries, and in this case there will also be a net operating surplus. Net taxes on production (taxes *minus* subsidies) are small or zero in many countries. Receipts from sales (if any) are then deducted to obtain the net cost of producing health services. This deduction is carried out to avoid double counting, because payments made by households for government health services are already included as household expenditures in the basic headings under "health" (group 1106 in the ICP expenditure classification).

Health Basic Heading Expenditures

Countries are required to supply expenditures in their national currency for all the basic headings shown in box 11.1.

For *individual consumption expenditure by households*, the expenditures should be the amounts *actually* paid by households to purchase health goods and services. In some countries, households pay only part of the cost of health goods and services and the government pays the rest. The government may pay its share of the costs directly to the provider—such as the pharmacy, doctor, or hospital. In this case, the expenditure shown for households is only the part they pay. Or people may pay the full cost directly to the provider and are then reimbursed by the government. In this case, the expenditures shown are the amounts paid by the purchaser *minus* the reimbursement.

Reimbursements are deducted only if they come from the government. If a household is reimbursed by a private health insurance company, no deduction is made, and the expenditures recorded for households are the full costs without deducting any reimbursements received from insurance companies. (Premiums paid to private health insurance companies *minus* reimbursements are recorded under the basic heading 111251.1, insurance. They are regarded as purchases of insurance services and not health services.)

For the *individual consumption expenditure by government*, the expenditures for the basic headings listed under health benefits and reimbursements are again the amounts *actually* paid:

- The total costs paid by the government for health goods and services provided free to households
- The government's share of the total costs in cases in which the government pays part of the cost directly to the providers
- The amounts paid to households in cases in which households initially pay the full cost but are then reimbursed by government for part or all of the costs.

Expenditures for the basic headings listed under "production of health services" are the amounts recorded in government accounts for compensation of health workers, purchases of goods and services as intermediate consumption in operating hospitals and other health facilities, net taxes on production, and the gross operating surplus, *minus* any receipts from sales.

All or most of the gross operating surplus consists of consumption of fixed capital (CFC). The 1993 SNA explains that the CFC should be calculated using the current replacement costs of the assets concerned—hospital buildings, medical equipment, ambulances, and so on (Commission of the European Communities et al. 1993, paras. 6.179–6.200). Some countries have not yet calculated estimates of consumption of fixed capital according to the SNA rules. These countries will have to use estimates of depreciation as shown in the government accounts. Because these estimates are usually based on historic costs, "depreciation" is almost always lower than the CFC—and by substantial amounts in countries that have had high rates of inflation. This factor affects not only the comparability of the expenditure weights but also that of total GDP. Countries participating in the 2011 ICP should therefore attempt to estimate CFC on government assets according to the SNA recommendations.

As noted earlier, net operating surplus and net taxes on production are usually zero. Receipts from sales consist mainly of fees for medical services paid by households to government hospitals and clinics. Because these expenditures are already included in the household expenditure, they must be deducted here to avoid double counting.

Prices for Health Goods and Services

In addition to providing expenditure weights, basic headings are the starting point for countries to select the specific goods and services they will price in order to calculate PPPs. Table 11.1 lists examples of products selected for the household expenditure on pharmaceuticals, other medical products, therapeutic appliances, and medical services.

TABLE 11.1 Examples of Health-Related Products, Appliances, and Services Selected for Household Expenditure

Type of product, appliance, or services	Description
Pharmaceutical products	
Acetaminophen/Paracetamol (international brand)	Dose: 500 mg; size of quantity: 10; form: tablet; medicine category: anti-inflammatory; purpose: maintenance; trade name: Tylenol; laboratory: McNeil
Co-trimoxazole (national brand)	Dose: (8 + 40) mg/ml; size of quantity: 100 ml; form: pediatric suspension; medicine category: antibacterial; purpose: otitis media (ear infection); trade name: Septrin; laboratory: GlaxoSmithKline
Ranitidine (generic brand)	Dose: 150 mg; size of quantity: 10; form: tablet; medicine category: antacid; purpose: maintenance; trade name: Zantac; laboratory: Glaxo Wellcome
Salbutamol (international brand)	Dose: 0.1 mg per dose; size of quantity: 1; form: inhaler; medicine category: anti-asthmatic; purpose: maintenance; trade name: Ventolin; laboratory: GlaxoSmithKline
Other medical products	
Adhesive bactericidal plaster	Price for: 1 piece; type: bactericidal; brand: well known; intended use: for wounds; dimensions: 1.9 × 7.2 cm; packaging: 10 pieces; comments: specify brand
Pregnancy test set	Price for: 1 set; brand: well known; type: midstream test; intended use: urine test for early detection of pregnancy; packaging: plastic package; comments: specify brand
Therapeutic appliances and equipment	
Mineral spectacle lenses	Price for: 2 pieces; type: corrected curve; brand: well known; material: ordinary mineral lens; features: orbicular, not tinted, no astigmatism; focus: point focal; spherical power: ± 2 diopters; price excludes: additional accessories and special processing mounting; comments: specify brand and price for 2 lenses
Complete set for measuring arterial pressure	Price for: 1 piece; brand: well known; complete set: phonendoscope, aerotonometer membranous, supercharger, compression blood pressure cuff; comments: specify brand and price for a set
Medical services	
Consultation with a general medical practitioner (public)	Price for: 1 service; duration: ± 15–20 minutes; timing: normal working hours; standard examination: yes; issuance: prescription; service type: public health service
Consultation with a general medical practitioner (private)	Price for: 1 service; duration: ± 15–20 minutes; timing: normal working hours; standard examination: yes; issuance: prescription; service type: private health service

Source: ICP.

As noted earlier, the same specifications are used for pharmaceutical products, other medical products, therapeutic appliances, and medical services whether they are purchased by households or by government. In addition, the same set of national average prices is used to estimate the PPPs for both household and government expenditures because no separate price collection is carried out for health goods and services purchased by households as opposed to those purchased by government. For the goods and services selected for all basic headings for the household expenditure and for basic headings for government under "health benefits and reimbursements," the prices must refer to *full market prices*. This is an important point: even though costs may be shared between government and households so that purchasers pay less than the full price when they buy medicines or visit a doctor, the prices reported must always be the full prices. Thus the price collectors will often be reporting prices that no one is actually paying, but the prices reflect the overall value of the products.

In practice, this situation usually does not present a problem for the price collectors. Generally, the pharmacist, doctor, and dentist are all able to report the full market prices for the goods and services they provide. When that is not the case, in some countries the full prices of the goods and services can be obtained only by consulting the accounting records for the government department responsible for the provision and supervision of health care.

"Hospital services" (basic headings 110631.1 and 130212.4) covers the medical services, pharmaceuticals, food, and accommodation provided to patients who stay overnight in a hospital during the course of their treatment. The quality of and the ways in which these services are provided differ greatly from country to country. Indeed, in the past it has proved very difficult to collect internationally comparable prices for hospital services. For that reason, a reference PPP is used for these two basic headings.

For the production of health services by government, countries report costs for compensation of employees as explained later in this chapter. For all other basic headings within this heading, no prices are required because reference PPPs are used. Table 11.2 shows the reference PPPs used for health services.

Figure 11.1 summarizes this section on health goods and services by showing the expenditures and prices required for the health basic headings.

TABLE 11.2 Reference PPPs, Health Services

Basic heading		Reference PPP
Individual consumption expenditure by households		
110631.1	Hospital services	PPPs for production of health services by government (before deducting receipts from sales)
Individual consumption expenditure by government		
130212.4	Hospital services	PPPs for production of health services by government (before deducting receipts from sales)
130322.1	Intermediate consumption	PPPs for individual consumption expenditure by households on the domestic market (excluding all basic headings with reference PPPs)
130223.1	Gross operating surplus	PPPs for gross fixed capital formation
130224.1	Net taxes on production	PPPs for production of health services by government (excluding net taxes on production and before deducting receipts from sales)
130225.1	Receipts from sales	PPPs for production of health services by government (before deducting receipts from sales)

Source: ICP.

FIGURE 11.1 Expenditures and Prices Required for Health Basic Headings

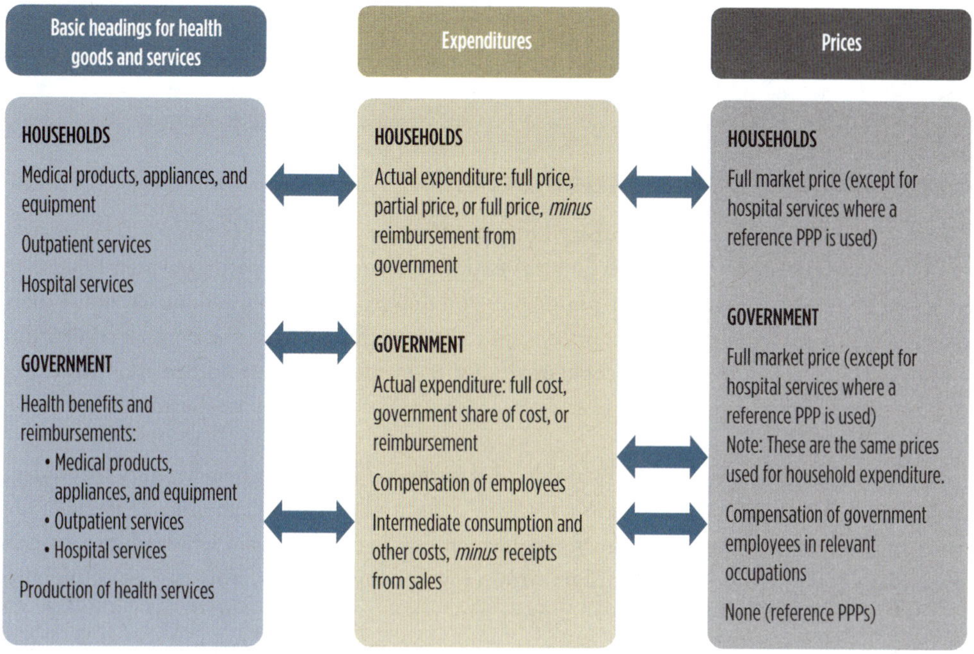

Source: ICP.

Education Services

Many of the issues surrounding the estimation of education PPPs are similar to those described earlier for health, and therefore many of the same concepts apply.

Actual Consumption of Education Services

Like health services, education services are both provided to households by government and purchased directly by households. The actual household consumption of education is defined as the sum of individual consumption expenditures by households and by government.

Education services include adult education courses, language schools, and pre-primary nursery schools, as well as primary, secondary, and tertiary education. However, driving lessons and recreational courses such as bridge and painting lessons are excluded. Education services may be provided through radio, television, and the Internet, as well as through conventional classroom teaching.

Basic Headings for Education

Box 11.2 shows the basic headings relevant to expenditures on education services.

Like those for health, the education basic headings fall into two categories: purchases by households and government of services from schools and universities (111011.1 and 130411.1) and the costs of production of education services provided directly by government (130421.1 to 130425.1). However, unlike for health, basic headings for education purchases refer only to services; no goods are involved. Purchases by households of school uniforms, textbooks, exercise books, and other goods are not included in expenditures on education.

These cost components of the production of education services provided directly by government—such as compensation of employees, intermediate consumption, and gross operating surplus—are identical to those described earlier for health services.

Expenditures on Education Services

Countries are required to estimate expenditures on all the basic headings in box 11.2. For households, the expenditures will cover fees for private education and also any partial payments that may be levied by public and government-run schools and universities. In some countries, households may be reimbursed for all or part of their education expenses through bursaries or other scholarship awards from the government. Household expenditures on education are recorded after deducting these receipts; as it is for health services, the expenditures recorded here are the amounts actually paid by households.

For government, expenditures are divided between "education benefits and reimbursements" and "production of education services." The first of these expenditures is generally quite small in most countries. It consists of payments such as bursaries or scholarships awarded to specially gifted children or to children from low-income families. This basic heading also covers payments made to meet the education requirements of children with special needs. By contrast, production of education services is a very large item in many countries; it is the costs of operating government-run schools, colleges, and universities. These costs consist mainly of employee compensation and intermediate consumption. Gross operating surplus is usually only the consumption of fixed capital; there is no net operating surplus. As noted in the discussion of health services, consumption of fixed capital should be calculated using current replacement costs. Depreciation as recorded in the government accounts will almost always be based on historic costs and may substantially underestimate CFC as defined according to SNA recommendations.

In many countries, the fees paid to government-run schools are quite significant. These fees are already included in the household expenditure on education services (111011.1), and so must be deducted to obtain the net expenditure by government on running schools and universities.

BOX 11.2 Basic Headings: Expenditures on Education Services

The total of the expenditure on the following basic headings by both households and government make up the *actual consumption* of households of education and services.

Individual consumption expenditure by households

111011.1 Education

Individual consumption expenditure by government

Education benefits and reimbursements

130411.1 Education benefits and reimbursements

Production of education services

130421.1 Compensation of employees
130422.1 Intermediate consumption
130423.1 Gross operating surplus
130424.1 Net taxes on production
130425.1 Receipts from sales *(minus)*

Prices for Education Services

Prices are required only for household purchases of education services (111011.1)—that is, education services from private (nongovernment) schools and universities. Here are two examples of the kinds of services for which prices are required:

- *Upper secondary education.* Specifications: (1) pupil is age 15 at beginning of school year; (2) pupil can receive a general school leaving certificate giving access to university-level education; (3) pupil attends day school (not boarding school); (4) pupil is a national of the country concerned; (5) pupil pays annual fee for education only, excluding payments for meals and collateral services.
- *Other education programs (foreign language course or lessons).* Specifications: (1) group study; (2) English or French language; (3) intermediate level; (4) one-hour lessons; (5) fee per lesson.

Countries must report the full prices for the education services purchased. If households pay only part of the cost and the remainder is paid by government, the price reported is the sum of the two components. In general, private (nongovernment) schools and universities can provide information on the full prices of the courses they offer—both the part paid by the student and the subsidy, if any, provided by the government.

For the production of education services by government, countries report the costs of employee compensation as explained later in this chapter. For all other basic headings within this heading, no prices are required because reference PPPs are used. Table 11.3 lists the reference PPPs used for the other cost components, as well as for the basic heading education benefits and reimbursements (130411.1).

Figure 11.2 summarizes this section on education services and shows the expenditures and prices required for the education basic headings.

TABLE 11.3 Reference PPPs: Education Services

Basic heading		Reference PPP
Individual consumption expenditure by government		
Education benefits and reimbursements		
130411.1	Education benefits and reimbursements	PPPs for production of education services by government (before deducting receipts from sales)
Production of education services		
130422.1	Intermediate consumption	PPPs for individual consumption expenditure by households on the domestic market (excluding all basic headings with reference PPPs)
130423.1	Gross operating surplus	PPPs for gross fixed capital formation
130424.1	Net taxes on production	PPPs for production of education services by government (without net taxes on production and before deducting receipts from sales)
130425.1	Receipts from sales	PPPs for production of education services by government (before deducting receipts from sales)

Source: ICP.

FIGURE 11.2 Expenditures and Prices Required for Education Basic Headings

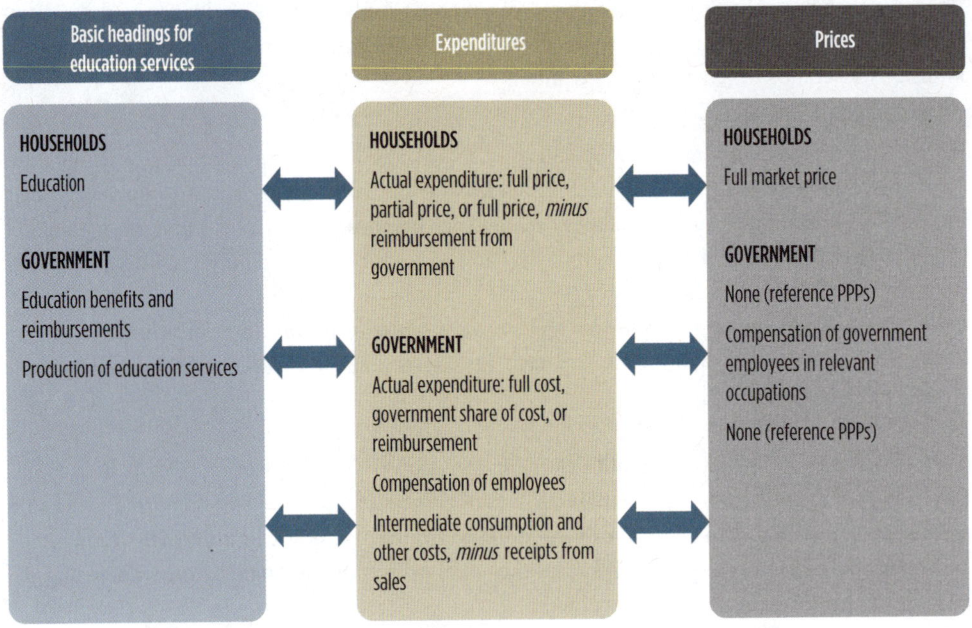

Source: ICP.

Compensation of Employees

Employee compensation is the most important basic heading within the production of both health and education services. The basic headings for the production of other government services also include employee compensation, and the collection of comparable statistics on compensation of government employees is an important part of the ICP. For the 2005 ICP, countries were required to collect information on the compensation paid to persons working in 50 different government occupations. They included 13 health occupations and 5 occupations in education.

Table 11.4 lists these and the other occupations for which the compensation of employees was required for the 2005 ICP. Several of the occupations listed in table 11.4 are relevant to more than one type of service. For example, nurses are primarily relevant to health services, but they also may be employed in schools. Likewise, secretaries, cleaners, and drivers are employed in the production of education, health, and collective services. Thus the information on compensation of employees for these and other occupations could be used to calculate PPPs for more than one basic heading.

PPPs are calculated for each basic heading by taking the unweighted geometric averages of the price relatives (strictly speaking, the "compensation relatives") for all the relevant occupations. For example, the PPP for basic heading 130221.1 (compensation of employees for the production of health services) is obtained by calculating the price relatives for occupations 101 to 113 in table 11.4 and finding their geometric average. For basic heading 130421.1 (compensation of employees for the production of education services), the PPP will be based on occupations 301 to 305 as well as occupations 106, 201 to 212, and 216, because persons with these occupations are also employed in schools and universities.

Occupations 102 and 103—doctor with 20 years of seniority and doctor with 10 years of seniority—specify the length of time the person has served in the post. For all other occupations, compensation is required for persons with five years of seniority.

TABLE 11.4 Government Occupations, ICP 2005

Health services	**Collective services (continued)**
101 Doctor, head of department	213 Policeman/woman
102 Doctor (20 years of seniority)	214 Prison guard
103 Doctor (10 years of seniority)	215 Firefighter
104 Nurse, head of department	216 Social worker
105 Nurse, operating theatre	217 Town planner
106 Nurse	218 Civil engineer
107 Nursing auxiliary	219 Draftsman/draftswoman
108 Physiotherapist	220 Construction laborer
109 Laboratory assistant	221 Chauffeur
110 Hospital chief executive	222 Agricultural scientist
111 Secretary (hospital)	223 Librarian
112 Cook (not head cook)	224 Database administrator
113 Community health worker	225 Web administrator
Collective services	226 Bodyguard (protecting senior officials)
201 Finance department manager	**Education services**
202 Executive official (skill level III)	301 Kindergarten teacher
203 Executive official (skill level IV)	302 Primary teacher
204 Computer operator	303 Secondary teacher
205 Bookkeeping clerk	304 University lecturer
206 Data entry clerk	305 Head teacher
207 Secretary (not hospital)	**Defense services**
208 Telephone switchboard operator	401 Army: private of infantry
209 Messenger	402 Army: commander of infantry regiment
210 Maintenance electrician	403 Navy: able seaman
211 Building caretaker	404 Navy: commander of frigate
212 Cleaner	405 Air force: airman (ground crew)
	406 Air force: fighter pilot/wing commander

Source: ICP.

The employee compensation that participating countries are to report for the selected occupations is described in chapter 15 on government services (compensation) and so is not repeated here. Compensation of government employees is calculated from the basic salaries and wages that are laid down in government salary scales. The procedure to be followed is also described in chapter 15.

The main points from chapter 15 on compensation of employees can be summarized as follows:

- Compensation of employees is consistent with the definition in the 1993 SNA. It includes basic wages and salaries, allowances in cash, income in kind in the form of food and accommodation, and employers' actual or imputed social security contributions.

- The *annual* compensation of employees must be reported for each selected occupation—not a particularly difficult requirement. Salary scales usually show annual amounts, and any revisions of the salary scales during the reference year are relatively straightforward to accommodate.
- Compensation of employees should also be the national average, taking into account the differences in compensation in different parts of the country. Quite often, health and education workers employed in the capital city or main commercial center may receive a cost-of-living allowance because prices are usually higher in those centers than in the rest of the country. These allowances must be weighted by the percentages of health and education workers that receive them in order to obtain average compensation for the country as a whole.
- For international comparisons, the employee compensation reported for the selected occupations should be adjusted for differences in the *numbers of hours worked* in the different countries. In addition to employee compensation, countries are required to report the number of hours regularly worked per week and the number of weeks worked per year after deducting annual leave and public holidays.

Productivity Adjustment for Health and Education Services

A review of the information on compensation of government workers in the Asia-Pacific region for the 2005 ICP revealed that the initial results, even after extensive validation of the data, did not appear to yield plausible volume measures. In particular, the quantities of government services in poor countries such as the Lao People's Democratic Republic greatly exceeded those in Hong Kong SAR, China, or Singapore. Similarly, in Western Asia the initial results produced volumes of comparison-resistant services for the Republic of Yemen that were much larger than those of its oil-rich neighbors. In Africa, too, implausibly large differences were found for several countries.

For the 2005 ICP, a productivity adjustment was therefore made for compensation of employees for all government services—health, education, and collective services—in the Asia-Pacific, Western Asia, and Africa regions. The adjustment was based on estimates of the value of fixed capital assets per employee, the assumption being that government employees in poor countries are less productive than those in the richer countries because they work with a smaller and less efficient stock of capital equipment. The adjustment method, which uses a Cobb-Douglas production function, is described in chapter 16 on government services (productivity adjustments) and is not repeated here. The same adjustment was made for health, education, and collective government services.

New Developments for ICP 2011

This section describes the changes planned for the 2011 ICP round based on the lessons learned in the 2005 and earlier rounds of the ICP.

Use of Output Measures

Member countries of the Organisation for Economic Co-operation and Development (OECD) and the European Union have for some years been looking for ways to replace input measures of government services by true output measures. This issue is becoming increasingly important as expenditures on both health and education services absorb a rising share of national budgets. Input measures cannot capture productivity increases, which are particularly striking in the health field.

A 2009 study by OECD deals with the estimation of output measures of education and health services produced by governments (Schreyer 2009).[1] It considers the measures that can be used both over time within a country and for international comparisons.

For education, chapter 3 of the OECD study explains the procedure for international comparisons as follows:

> The following steps describe the basic procedure to estimate output-based PPPs or their equivalent in form of a direct volume index:
>
> - Stratification of expenditure on education services into homogeneous groups;
> - For each stratum, identification of the quantity measure of education services;
> - For each stratum, identification of the quality measure of education services. By combining it with the quantity indicator, a quality-adjusted volume or a spatial price index (PPP) can be derived.

The "homogeneous groups" used are five International Standard Classification of Education (ISCED)[2] levels of education: (1) ISCED 0, pre-primary education; (2) ISCED 1, primary education or first stage of basic education; (3) ISCED 2, lower secondary or second stage of basic education; (4) ISCED 3 + 4, upper secondary and postsecondary nontertiary education; and (5) ISCED 5 + 6, tertiary education (including category "unknown").

The "quantity measure" is the number of pupils at each level. Use of the number of pupil-hours is preferable, but comparable information is not available for many countries.

The "quality measure" is based on country scores from the OECD's Programme for International Student Assessment (PISA).[3] PISA tests 15-year-olds in science, literacy, mathematics, and general knowledge and now covers 62 countries. Two other international studies organized by the International Association for the Evaluation of Educational Achievement (IEA) are the Trends in International Mathematics and Science Study (TIMSS) and Progress in International Reading Literacy Survey (PIRL). The OECD study explains that "an important advantage of PISA is that it provides results that are corrected for the economic, social and cultural status of students (the so-called ESCS adjustment)" (Schreyer 2009). By eliminating the effects of economic and social status on country scores, the corrected PISA results are better indicators of the quality of teaching. However, for those countries not covered by PISA, data from TIMSS and PIRL have been used.

Using 2005 data, the OECD study compares output measures, with and without quality adjustment, with input measures for the 30 OECD member countries plus Israel and the Russian Federation—see table 11.5. The comparison reveals that the use of output measures makes a substantial difference for most countries: in more than half, the output measure (with quality adjustment) differs by more than 20 percent from the input measure. The output measure also sharply reduces the variability between countries. According to the OECD study:

> In the input method, the index ranges from 43 (Turkey) to 189 (Iceland) whereas it varies between 70 (Russian Federation) and 130 (Iceland) under the output approach. For countries such as Iceland, Australia and Sweden, extremely high volumes in the input approach reduce to a more plausible level when an output method is applied. The introduction of the quality adjustment with PISA seems to [have a] rather limited influence on results. The adjustment is biggest for Poland where the index goes up by 8% (from 101 to 110). (Schreyer 2009)

TABLE 11.5 Indexes of Real Final Expenditure per Head on Education (OECD = 100)

	Output method						
	With quality adjustment	Rank	Without quality adjustment	Rank	Input method	Rank	% change between input and output with quality adjustment
Iceland	130	−1	133	−2	189	−1	45.5
Israel	125	−2	134	−1	159	−3	−27.0
Mexico	124	−3	128	−3	92	−24	25.4
New Zealand	123	−4	119	−4	103	−17	16.4
Korea, Rep.	120	−5	116	−5	99	−21	17.7
United Kingdom	116	−6	111	−7	91	−25	21.6
Belgium	112	−7	112	−6	128	−8	13.7
Poland	110	−8	101	−16	87	−27	21.2
Australia	109	−9	106	−11	159	−2	−45.8
Denmark	107	−10	108	−9	133	−5	−24.1
Finland	106	−11	101	−17	105	−16	1.1
United States	106	−12	108	−10	127	−9	−20.4
Slovak Republic	105	−13	103	−15	85	−28	18.6
France	104	−14	104	−12	115	−13	−10.2
Norway	102	−15	109	−8	129	−6	−26.3
Netherlands	102	−16	98	−19	117	−12	−15.4
Sweden	101	−17	103	−13	148	−4	−46.7
OECD	100	−18	100	−18	100	−20	0.0
Czech Republic	97	−19	95	−20	98	−22	−1.3
Turkey	96	−20	103	−14	43	−33	55.3
Hungary	95	−21	90	−21	95	−23	−0.1
Canada	91	−22	85	−27	128	−7	−41.6
Ireland	90	−23	87	−23	118	−11	−31.5
Portugal	88	−24	88	−22	77	−31	12.5
Austria	87	−25	87	−24	114	−14	−30.3
Spain	87	−26	86	−26	100	−19	−15.9
Greece	86	−27	86	−25	101	−18	−17.0
Luxembourg	86	−28	83	−29	124	−10	−45.5
Switzerland	81	−29	82	−30	106	−15	−30.0
Italy	81	−30	83	−28	87	−26	−8.1
Germany	80	−31	78	−31	58	−32	27.4
Japan	79	−32	77	−32	83	−29	−5.1
Russian Federation	70	−33	69	−33	80	−30	−14.1

Source: Schreyer 2009.

For health, output measures are being recommended so far only for hospital services. The output PPPs will be based on the relative costs of about 20 surgical procedures and about 10 nonsurgical treatments. Various options have been considered for quality adjustments, but it has proved difficult to find comparable data, and no adjustments are planned for the 2011 ICP. Presently, experiments are under way with about a dozen countries, and the exact procedure that will be used for the 2011 ICP has not yet been determined.

Whether similar output measures will be used for other regions has also not been decided. It is possible that because of data limitations the input approach as applied in the 2005 round will have to be used again, with or without a productivity adjustment.

Government Occupations

The list of the 50 government occupations used for the 2005 ICP appears in table 11.4. For 2011, an updated list of 38 occupations will be used, of which 18 are relevant for health services and 16 for education—see table 11.6, which lists both the ICP and International Standard Classification of Occupations (ISCO) codes and job titles. The list was drawn up in consultation with the regional coordinators and representatives of a small sample of countries from the Africa, Western Asia, and Asia-Pacific regions. Other than the Eurostat-OECD countries, all countries will use this list.

Except for the Eurostat-OECD countries, government pay scales will continue to be used to calculate the compensation of employees, but countries will supply data for employees in each occupation at four career points: entry-level and after 5, 10, and 20 years of service. Unweighted averages of the four will be used to calculate PPPs.

The Eurostat-OECD group will use a list of only 26 occupations, but most of these will be comparable with the occupations in table 11.6. In addition, government pay scales will no longer be used to calculate employee compensation because in many of the Eurostat-OECD countries government employees now negotiate their salaries based on past performance. Countries will calculate average compensation using data on total wage bills and numbers employed. Some Eurostat-OECD countries will be asked to calculate as well the compensation of employees for the four career points to provide a link with countries in other regions.

Actual Versus Official Number of Hours of Work

In countries in which government salaries are very low, it may be the accepted practice that government workers are actually on the job for fewer hours than the official number, which is usually about 40 hours per week. In this way, employees can take a second job to supplement their government salaries. The salary comparisons are based on compensation per hour, and the denominator should be the actual rather than the official number of hours of work. If the official number of hours is greater than the actual number of hours worked, using the official number of hours as the denominator will mean that the compensation per hour is understated and thus the volume of government services will be overstated. Special efforts will be made in the 2011 ICP to ensure that countries report realistic estimates of the number of hours actually worked by government employees. The reporting form for compensation of employees to be used for the 2011 ICP appears in chapter 15. It asks countries to report both the official and actual number of hours worked in cases in which some government employees systematically work fewer than the official number of hours.

TABLE 11.6 Occupations by Function, ICP 2011

ICP code and job title	ISCO code and job title	Health	Education	Other
1 Member of parliament	1111 Legislator			X
2 Senior government official	1112 Senior government officials	X	X	X
3 Hospital manager	1120 Managing directors and chief executives	X		
4 Data processing manager	1330 Information and communications technology service managers			X
5 Secondary school principal	1345 Education managers		X	
6 Government statistician	2120 Mathematicians, actuaries, and statisticians			X
7 Hospital doctor	2211 Generalist medical practitioner	X		
8 Specialist doctor	2212 Specialist medical practitioner	X		
9 Hospital nurse	2221 Nursing professionals	X		
10 University teacher	2310 University and higher education teachers		X	
11 Vocational education teacher	2320 Vocational education teachers		X	
12 Primary school teacher	2341 Primary education teachers		X	
13 Secondary school teacher	2330 Secondary education teachers		X	
14 Government accountant	2411 Accountants			X
15 Human resources professional	2423 Personnel and careers professionals			X
16 Database administrator	2522 Systems administrators			X
17 Judge	2612 Judge			X
18 Government economist	2631 Economist			X
19 Laboratory assistant	3212 Medical and pathology laboratory technicians	X		
20 Auxiliary nurse	3221 Nursing associate professionals	X		
21 Medical records clerk	3252 Medical records and health information technicians	X		
22 Office supervisor	3341 Office supervisors			X
23 Medical secretary (hospital)	3344 Medical secretaries	X		
24 Customs inspector	3351 Customs and border inspectors			X
25 Computer operator	3513 Computer network and systems technicians			X
26 Secretary (not medical)	4120 Secretaries	X	X	X
27 Accounting and bookkeeping clerks	4311 Accounting and bookkeeping clerks	X	X	X
28 Payroll clerk	4313 Payroll clerks	X	X	X
29 Cook	5120 Cooks	X	X	X
30 Building caretaker	5153 Building caretakers	X	X	X
31 Teacher's aide	5312 Teacher's aides		X	
32 Firefighter	5411 Firefighters			X
33 Policeman/woman	5412 Police officers			X
34 Prison guard	5413 Prison guards			X
35 Driver (general duty)	8322 Car, taxi, and van drivers	X	X	X
36 Office cleaner	9112 Cleaners and helpers in offices, hotels, and other establishments	X	X	X
37 Kitchen helper	9412 Kitchen helpers	X	X	X
38 Messenger	9621 Messengers	X	X	X
Total		18	16	24

Sources: ICP and International Standard Classification of Occupations (ISCO).

Nonprofit Institutions Serving Households (NPISH)

In the 2005 ICP, the Eurostat-OECD countries were required to break down expenditures by NPISH into six functional groups: housing, health, recreation and culture, education, social protection, and other services. In the other regions, no breakdown of NPISH was requested because it was assumed that many countries had very little information on NPISH and that their expenditures were relatively unimportant. However, this assumption turned out to be unfounded—in several countries a significant number of schools, hospitals, and clinics are operated by NPISH. In South America, for example, many schools and health facilities are operated by the Catholic Church, and thus an ad hoc survey had to be conducted to estimate NPISH expenditures on providing health and education services in this region. Only expenditure data were collected, and PPPs were obtained using reference PPPs based essentially on compensation of government health and education workers.

For the 2011 ICP, the ICP expenditure classification will be revised by creating three new basic headings for NPISH:

- 120111.1 health
- 120211.1 education
- 120311.1 other services.

All regions will be required to provide expenditure data for these three basic headings. The expenditures of NPISH will be calculated, as for government, by summing their costs and deducting receipts from sales of services. Also in the 2011 round, reference PPPs drawn from government health and education services will likely be used again as PPPs.

Conclusion

In most countries, health and education services are provided by both market and nonmarket producers. In the ICP, expenditures on services from both sources are combined in order to compare the "actual consumption" of health and education services across countries. Consumption of health and education services has important implications for both welfare and future economic growth. The intercountry comparison of the total volume of these services consumed by households is therefore an important output of the ICP.

In the national accounts, market health and education services are measured in the same way as any other market services, whereas nonmarket services have traditionally been measured by adding up the costs of providing them. The same approach has been used in previous rounds of the ICP, but in the 2011 round the OECD-Eurostat group will use better methods for comparing some nonmarket health and education services. These countries will try to measure the output of these government services rather than the costs of the inputs used to produce them. A few countries in other regions may also be able to use an output rather than input approach, but it is most likely that PPPs for other regions will continue to be based on inputs rather than outputs. A more realistic measurement of government-produced health and education services remains a goal for future rounds of the ICP.

NOTES

1. Paul Schreyer is the main author of this report, with contributions by Alain Gallais, Sandra Hopkins, Francette Koechlin, and Seppo Varjonen.
2. UNESCO, Paris, 1997.
3. For details, see http://www.pisa.oecd.org.

REFERENCES

Commission of the European Communities, International Monetary Fund, Organisation for Economic Co-operation and Development, United Nations, and World Bank. 1993. *System of National Accounts 1993.* http://unstats.un.org/unsd/sna1993/toctop.asp?L1=5.

Schreyer, Paul. 2009. "Towards Measuring the Volume of Output of Education and Health Services." STD/CSTAT/WPNA/(2009)1, Organisation for Economic Co-operation and Development, Paris, July.

CHAPTER 12

Dwelling Services

Alan Heston

Household dwelling service expenditures consist of market-rented housing and imputations for nonmarket rents and owner-occupied housing. Estimation of these expenditures is treated in chapter 3 on the framework of expenditures on the gross domestic product (GDP). As will become clear in this chapter and in chapter 3, it is essential that dwelling expenditures embody the average rents of the dwellings/floor area of specified types of dwellings common in a country.

Comparison of housing across countries is difficult because of the varying mix of owner-occupied versus rented dwellings, which can also be affected by various forms of subsidies. As explained in chapter 3, there are different ways to estimate the overall expenditures on housing for the national accounts. The methods used to estimate purchasing power parities (PPPs) are dependent on how the underlying national account expenditures are computed. Table 12.1 is an overview of the methods used to estimate expenditures and PPPs for rental and owner-occupied housing.

The first section of this chapter briefly describes the rental survey and the quantity or direct volume methods used in estimating the PPPs and volumes of dwelling services and their relationship to the expenditure estimates. The second section discusses these methods, as well as the consumption equivalent method used to develop the dwelling service estimates actually used in the 2005 round of the International Comparison Program (ICP) in the six ICP regions. This variety of methods posed a major problem of linking the regions, a subject treated in the third section of this chapter. The chapter concludes with the lessons learned from the 2005 experience and a discussion of plans for the 2011 round.

A very large set of literature is associated with the issues discussed in this chapter. The papers related to the February 2010 meeting of the ICP's 2011 Technical Advisory Group (TAG) deal with the estimation of housing rents in both temporal and spatial comparisons by some of the leading experts in the field.[1]

TABLE 12.1 Overview of Data Sources for Expenditures and PPPs for Rental and Owner-Occupied Housing

Housing classification	Expenditures	PPPs
Rental	Rentals	Rental surveys by size and type of housing
Owner-occupied	Rental equivalents	Rental surveys
	User cost	Quantity or direct volume method
All housing	Rental equivalent and user cost	Consumption equivalent method (CEM)

Source: Adapted from http://siteresources.worldbank.org/ICPINT/Resources/270056-1255977007108/6483550-1257349667891/6544465-1272763721734/03.01_ICP-TAG03_DwellingServices-N.pdf.

Methods of Estimating Dwelling PPPs

The Technical Advisory Group recommended that the regions use one or both of the methods utilized by the European Union (EU) and the Organisation for Economic Co-operation and Development (OECD) in their comparisons (hereafter referred to as the Eurostat-OECD comparison). The method originally employed by Eurostat-OECD required rents from surveys of different housing types of varying sizes, age, and amenities. PPPs were obtained by averaging price relatives (in this case rent relatives) for identical, or very similar, dwellings in each country. This method is called here the *direct rent* method (see next section). Table 12.2 illustrates the stratification used for flats (the terms *flat* and *apartment* are used interchangeably in this chapter). A similar stratification was used for single-dwelling housing. Rental surveys can be analyzed in more than one way, including estimation of PPPs using hedonic regressions, which is discussed as well in the following section on direct rents. Also discussed in that section is the application of user cost, as described in chapter 3, to obtain expenditures for particular types of dwellings.

TABLE 12.2 Criteria Used in the 2002 Eurostat-OECD Round of Comparisons

Type of housing	Age in years	Number of rooms	Total size of dwelling (m^2)	Reference size (m^2)	Central heating
Flat	> 49	1–2	25–75	50	No
Flat	> 49	1–2	25–75	50	Yes
Flat	> 49	3	70–150	110	No
Flat	> 49	≥ 3	70–150	110	Yes
Flat	24–49	1–2	25–75	50	No
Flat	24–49	1–2	25–75	50	Yes
Flat	24–49	≥ 3	70–150	110	No
Flat	24–49	≥ 3	70–150	110	Yes
Flat	< 24	1–2	25–75	50	No
Flat	< 24	1–2	25–75	50	Yes
Flat	< 24	≥ 3	70–150	110	No
Flat	< 24	≥ 3	70–150	110	Yes

Source: Eurostat and OECD 2006, 82.

As the EU expanded, it was found that in several of the new member countries rental markets were either limited to capital cities or the rents were highly subsidized, or both. In these cases, Eurostat-OECD introduced a *direct volume* method that indirectly estimated PPPs by dividing expenditures by the number of dwellings adjusted for size and some amenities, including central heating. A continuing theme of this chapter is that the *direct rent* method is the other way of saying the *indirect volume* method. Conversely, the *direct volume* method can also be termed the *indirect rent* method. Each of these methods is discussed in more detail later in this overall section.

Direct Rent Approach

This section is an overview of the direct rent approach, first using stratified samples by dwelling type and then using random rental surveys to estimate rental cells.

Direct Rent Approach Using Stratified Samples by Dwelling Type

Dwelling rents are unlike many services because location is such a key price-determining feature. Location is less important for actual renters because they can change their location more easily than owners. Homeownership has some benefits not enjoyed by renters, but the value of the dwelling services that owners receive is not so easily measured. The *System of National Accounts* calls for statistical agencies to include in their estimates of expenditures the explicit dwelling services of renters and the implicit dwelling services of owners, including both the site rent and the rent of the structure (Commission of the European Communities et al. 2008). Statistical agencies in OECD countries have used different approaches for imputing the dwelling expenditures associated with owner-occupied housing, the most common being equivalent rent. This method assumes that the rental rates for rented dwellings by age, size, and amenities can be applied to similar types of owner-occupied housing. Diewert (2009) has provided a thorough discussion of a number of OECD methods of imputation, including some important measurement issues that arise in implementation.[2]

Eurostat-OECD estimates rental PPPs using a sample of rental housing stratified by location within countries and by character of dwelling (apartment or house, size, central heating).[3] Rents per square meter by strata are then compared across countries. The rental parities are aggregated, using as weights the number of owner-occupied units by strata to obtain the PPPs for nonrenters. This was the method recommended for the 2005 ICP for countries with national housing surveys in which a substantial number of units were rented at market rates.

Use of Random Rental Surveys to Estimate Rental Cells

The Eurostat-OECD practice of building up rent comparisons for different strata of dwellings can be achieved by purposeful sampling of the average rents of each rental cell. Or from a national survey, average rents can be calculated for those cells, given enough observations. An alternative for countries such as the United States, where there is a regular national sample of rental units, is to use the coefficients from a hedonic rent regression to fill in the cells. In the 1975 ICP, there were 61 rental cells or a potential of 2,074 (34 * 61) average rents, of which 615 were important enough in the housing censuses of the 34 countries to warrant a rental estimate. As for the framework for estimation of these rents, 21 (10 EU) of the 34 countries provided estimates of average rent for those cells that were important in their housing censuses. The other 13 countries provided rent samples permitting estimation of coefficients on the various characteristics that determine rent such as number of rooms or an area measure, electricity, and flush toilet.[4] These coefficients were used to estimate rents for the relevant cells for these 13 countries.

The general framework in the 2005 ICP for the direct price approach is to produce estimates of average rent for cells that are important in the housing stock of each country. As noted, this is similar to the approach used in earlier rounds of the ICP. However, in the Eurostat-OECD approach, the matrix of rent cell information is aggregated using the Gini-Éltető-Köves-Szulc (GEKS) method, whereas it is also possible to use a Country Product Dummy (CPD) weighted by housing quantities in aggregation, as was done in the 1975 ICP. The weighted CPD aggregation permits estimation of the quality of the housing stock of each country, a feature that is discussed in the section on direct volume measures.

Alternative Direct Rent Estimates Applying User Cost

Economists generally regard user cost as the preferred model of the flow of services from any durable asset, including housing. Diewert (2009) has been an advocate, but also has set out some of the problems of implementing user cost estimation of the services of owner-occupied housing, especially as a basis for consumer price indexes (CPIs). Some countries are unable to use rental equivalence to estimate expenditures on owner-occupied housing because of inadequate rental surveys—generally there is a lack of a rental market other than for high-income households in the capital or other large cities. In such cases, countries were advised for the 2005 and 2011 ICPs to implement the user cost method to estimate total expenditures on owner-occupied housing. If user cost is the recommended basis for estimating dwelling service expenditures, can it also be the basis for estimating PPPs for dwelling services, at least for owner-occupied housing?

User cost was used as a basis for estimating rental cells in the 1975 ICP for certain types of rural specifications—for example, a 400-square-meter dwelling with no piped water, electricity, or toilet, with a mud brick or wattle type exterior, and with a weight-bearing roof of local materials. The key variables would be current cost of construction, expected service life, annual maintenance costs, and opportunity cost of investment capital. The last was typically taken as a rate that could be earned on postal savings and the like, not the borrowing cost, and is assumed to be 5 percent in the example. To illustrate, suppose a minimal rural structure cost \$1,000, including the imputed wages of the family labor used in construction, and was expected to last five years. Suppose the structure was put up on January 1, 2010. On December 31, 2010, the remaining value of the structure would be \$800. User cost would be \$1,000 - 800/1.05 = \$238. In other words, the owner used up the depreciation of the structure and the lost income (the opportunity cost) to obtain the flow of dwelling services from the structure.[5]

To move from the user cost of a specified structure in current prices to the average rental cost of all such structures in a country, it is necessary to make some adjustment for the average age of the stock of this specification. However, if straight-line depreciation is used in my example, then the user cost will be independent of the age of the structure, and, like the one-horse shay, the walls will come crumbling down at the end of the fifth year. The main point is that user cost can serve as a useful check on specific rent cells that may not be available from rental surveys. It also can serve as a check on indirect rent for types of dwellings from the direct volume method, the next subject for discussion.

Direct Volume Method

This section provides an overview of the quantity or direct volume method of estimating PPPs for housing.

Number of Structures by Type and Location

In the 2005 ICP, it was anticipated that in some regions there would not be adequate rental markets or not enough rental survey information available to pursue the direct rent approach. Because their organizations accommodated the diverse economic structures of some of their new and associate members, the experience of the EU and OECD has served as a guide to the alternative direct volume approach. The *Eurostat-OECD Methodological Manual on Purchasing Power Parities* (Eurostat and OECD 2006, 83–84) provides a short exposition, and Sergeev (2004) presented a paper to TAG describing the approach in more detail, including the experience in the 2000 Eurostat-OECD comparisons. However, many of these countries had very different climates and building practices compared with the new EU-OECD countries, and so it was necessary for the 2005 ICP to develop the special questionnaire shown in the annex to this chapter for the direct volume approach.

The direct volume approach requires census-type information on number, location, and type of structure. Definitions of urban and rural areas differ across countries, but typically structures are enumerated by rural and urban areas and by political division in larger countries. Distinctions between building type may include significant details such as high-rise, walk-up, or garden apartment; attached or single-family house; traditional or modern structure; temporary building, trailer home, or the like. Sometimes, the type of exterior wall and type of floor or roof are part of the stratification. In India, for example, there are groupings for *pucca* (good) and *kutcha* (less durable) housing.

Quality Indicators for Dwellings

Eurostat-OECD used the number of structures adjusted for the availability of water, electricity, and flush toilets in a structure, as well as the availability of central heating. In the 2005 ICP questionnaire for other regions, these items were not included because it was felt that central heating and air-conditioning were not generally available in housing census information.

Table 12.3 illustrates the quantity method using the 2005 data for the South America region. This region was chosen for several reasons, but mainly because it actually applied the method to all of its countries. Rows 1–3 provide the data using the recommended method for 2005. The geometric mean of the percentage of dwellings with electricity, water, and indoor plumbing is given in row 4; it is the quality measure used to adjust the quantities. In the third section of this chapter, the discussion covers the merits of equal weighting of the three components as opposed to giving more weight to the presence of indoor toilets, which is likely to also be a proxy for many other indicators of quality.

Chile has the highest quality indicator at almost 93 percent, while Bolivia has the lowest, less than 44 percent, so the range is fairly large. Information on number of dwellings, number of rooms, and total area was requested, but countries in South America generally only had available the number of bedrooms as a size measure of dwellings. Rows 5–7 provide information on number of bedrooms per dwelling, persons per dwelling, and persons per bedroom, which are measures of living density. (Living density will be included with other quality indicators in the 2011 ICP round.) Row 8 gives the per capita expenditures (at exchange rate) of households for rented and owner-occupied housing from the national accounts. These expenditures are put on a base of Argentina equal to 100 in row 9.

There are two ways to use this quantity and expenditure information to obtain the same results. One can begin with either a direct volume index or a unit value index, both deriving from the basic identity $\text{EXPD}_A = \text{PD}_A * \text{QD}_A$, where EXPD is expenditure on dwelling rents, and PD and QD are the price and quantity of dwelling services in country A. Comparing country B with A, one gets $\frac{\text{EXPD}_B}{\text{EXPD}_A} = \frac{\text{PD}_B}{\text{PD}_A} * \frac{\text{QD}_B}{\text{QD}_A}$. Now observe the expenditure and quantity ratios. Dividing the expenditure ratios by the quantity ratios yields the price ratios. And if one divides the expenditures by the individual quantities, one gets unit values that form the numerator and denominator of the price ratio. This simple identity underlies most ICP calculations and also reinforces the desirability of having independent observations on both prices and quantities as mutual checks.

TABLE 12.3 Direct Volume Method of Estimating Rental Services: South America, 2005

		Argentina	Bolivia	Brazil	Chile	Colombia	Ecuador	Paraguay	Peru	Uruguay	Venezuela, RB
1	% electricity	95.4	64.4	94.5	97.1	95.4	73.4	89.2	72.0	95.9	96.8
2	% piped water	84.1	33.5	73.0	91.0	86.1	56.7	52.6	60.0	87.8	85.5
3	% private bath	71.5	38.9	62.7	90.4	87.2	55.3	58.8	56.1	78.7	78.0
4	Quality, 0–100%	83.1	43.8	75.6	92.8	89.5	61.3	65.1	62.3	87.2	86.4
5	Bedrooms per dwelling	2.3	1.7	2.0	2.4	2.3	1.6	1.9	1.9	2.2	2.2
6	Persons per dwelling	3.7	4.2	3.8	4.0	4.3	4.4	4.7	4.6	3.4	4.7
7	Persons per bedroom	1.6	2.5	1.9	1.7	1.9	2.7	2.5	2.4	1.5	2.1
8	Housing exp., PC$ @ XR	341.4	49.8	360.0	445.7	204.1	169.9	108.0	50.5	489.8	244.2
9	Index of per capita exp.	100.0	14.5	105.4	130.6	59.8	49.8	31.6	14.8	143.5	71.5
10	PC bedrooms, adjusted	0.512	0.176	0.396	0.561	0.480	0.224	0.263	0.259	0.573	0.404
11	Volume index, Argentina = 100	100.0	34.3	77.4	109.5	93.7	43.7	51.3	50.5	111.9	78.9
12	PL = PPP/XR of housing	100.0	42.5	136.3	119.2	63.8	113.8	61.7	29.3	128.2	90.7
13	Exp. per adj. BR, $XR	666.4	283.4	908.3	794.2	425.0	758.1	411.4	195.5	854.1	604.2

Source: Derived from data processed by Statistics Canada for the 2005 ICP.
Note: PC = per capita; XR = exchange rate; BR = bedroom.

These two ways are illustrated in the remaining rows of table 12.3. First, row 10 provides the per capita bedrooms, quality-adjusted; Argentina has 0.512 persons per bedroom. This number is obtained by taking the reciprocal of persons per bedroom in row 7 times the quality factor as a fraction—that is, $0.512 = \frac{1}{1.622} * 0.8309$. The volume index in row 11 puts the per capita–adjusted bedrooms in an index with Argentina equal to 100. The price level for housing in row 12 (Argentina = 100) is then derived by dividing the index of per capita expenditures in row 9 by the volume index in row 11.

The second method begins by asking: what are the real housing expenditures per quality-adjusted bedroom? These are given in row 13, and are obtained by dividing row 8 (nominal expenditures for total housing) by row 10 (the implied PPP based on the direct volume comparison using persons per bedroom, adjusted for quality). Again, dividing each element in row 13 by the value in Argentina as a percentage, one obtains an alternative way of deriving row 12, the price level of housing. And from the price level one can easily derive the volume index given in row 11 (row 9 divided by row 12 as an index), again using the basic ICP identity.

Having reviewed the mechanics of the direct volume method, what can one say about the results in table 12.3? In general, the direct volume method produces plausible results for South

America, though one could raise several questions. Are housing services in Colombia really more than in República Bolivariana de Venezuela? And are those in Uruguay more than in Chile? Again, if there are errors they could be due to expenditure data being too low in Chile and República Bolivariana de Venezuela, for example, or quality measures being overstated in Colombia. I will return to this when the procedures used in other regions are discussed later in this chapter.

Heterogeneity of Quantity Indicators across Countries and Regions

The South America case illustrates several of the problem areas in making comparisons of dwelling expenditures, including the nonuniformity of housing data across countries. South America chose as its quantity indicator number of bedrooms, which was not originally requested from countries. Rather, the ICP manual and other documents of the 2005 ICP sought square meters of internal living space as the preferred indicator. But even this indicator is difficult to define because of the flexible use that can be made of balconies, verandas, noncovered courtyards, and the like in countries with mild temperatures much of the year. Some affluent countries such as the United States use only the number of rooms, not area, as their principal measure. As described later in this chapter in the section on linking the regions, the only quantity indicator available in all countries where data were available to the ICP Global Office in 2005 was number of dwellings. Number of rooms was next in frequency, and area in square meters was the last of the items initially requested. The number of bedrooms was the only indicator provided by South America, a situation brought about in part because that region was completing its comparison while other regions were processing their responses to the questionnaire. For purposes of linking the regions, it was necessary to collect some additional data on numbers of bedrooms from some countries outside the South America region and to add some data on total rooms for several countries.

Not only did lack of uniformity of housing censuses introduce problems of linking regions, but there was also the uneven availability and quality of dwelling quantity measures within regions. For example, how should outliers be treated if these were the official figures that countries used in their publications?[6] And how should the indicators be combined when there are many missing values? The usual approach in the ICP is to use a multilateral method such as the CPD or GEKS, which in fact is what was done to link the regions. But before turning to linking, a discussion of the methods used in the 2005 ICP is in order.

Comparisons of Dwelling Services: The 2005 Experience

The quantity method used in the South America region has already been set out in table 12.3. This table will be considered again after discussing the Asia-Pacific region, where the decision was made to use neither the direct quantity nor the direct rent method. Instead, it used the consumption equivalent method (CEM). The Africa region elected to follow the Asia-Pacific region and use CEM as well, which is compared with the quantity method used in South America. That comparison is followed by a discussion of the regions that used some combination of the direct quantity and the direct rent methods: Western Asia and Eurostat-OECD.

The Experience in the Asia-Pacific and Africa

All regions face the problem that expenditures on dwelling services are estimated by different methods yielding totals that often are not comparable across countries. Furthermore, there are reasons to believe there is a tendency for the expenditures on dwelling services to be systematically understated in lower-income countries with a low percentage of rental dwellings and a high percentage of traditional dwellings. These problems are discussed more fully in chapter 3. The result affects the estimation of indirect volumes where the direct rent approach is used and of indirect PPPs where the direct quantity approach is used, assuming that both of the direct approaches are close to the truth.

However, if the direct rent or quantity estimates are themselves also in doubt, then one is at sea without a rudder unless other independent data can be used as a check. This is the situation faced by the Asia-Pacific region. Its validation of the national accounts led to some questions about the expenditures on dwelling services of some countries in the region. And, as mentioned, the quantity information in some countries was in doubt, part of which was probably due to the lack of clarity in the survey questions or the lack of time for countries to provide the data and for the regional office validation. In contrast to regions that chose to use different methods for different countries, the Asia-Pacific region wished to apply one method to all countries—CEM.

How does CEM work? The fundamental assumption is that the volume of rental services in an economy rises with the volume of private individual consumption (PIC) less rents. Thus the share of rents to private individual consumption will be the same across all countries in a region. CEM can also be thought of as a method that chooses to use a reference volume to measure rental services. The PPP for housing was the PPP for individual consumption expenditures by households (excluding expenditures for housing). This neutral approach meant that housing had no effect on the overall PPP for individual consumption. One obvious problem of using the method is that it tells the user nothing about the true volume of housing services in a country, and so it is not comparable across regions. Furthermore, if the expenditures on housing services are doubtful in some countries, the indirect PPPs for housing may strain credibility. This proved to be the case in Africa, which, as Deaton (2010) has pointed out, had unfortunate consequences when the results were not correctly applied in the estimation of world poverty.[7]

For the South American countries, it is simple enough to compare the CEM approach with the quantity results in table 12.3. This exercise is set out in table 12.4. Row 1 of table 12.4 expresses the basic volume comparison in row 11 of table 12.3 as an index, with the average of all the South American countries as 100. An index of private individual consumption from the 2005 ICP with South America as 100 is given in row 2. The assumption of the CEM approach is that the index of the volume of rents per capita in row 1 would be the same as PIC in row 2. The index of rent volumes divided by PIC, normalized to SA = 100, is given in row 3. Examination of the indexes in row 3 reveals that in only three of the 10 countries is the direct volume approach within 15 percent of the CEM result, while another three are in the 15–25 percent range. The departures of direct quantity and CEM results for the remaining four countries are above 25 percent—not an encouraging finding. However, there does not appear to be any pattern of differences associated with per capita GDP, and so, at least for volumes, there does not appear to be any bias in the CEM approach. However, the departures from 100 in row 3 are large enough to question the reliability of comparisons of housing volumes of countries in Africa and the Asia-Pacific with countries in different regions.

Expenditures on dwelling services as a percentage of consumption of the South American countries are given in row 4 of table 12.4. The range is from under 5 percent to over 13 percent in a moderately homogeneous region. This same range across all countries in the 2005 ICP went from under 2 percent to over 20 percent, and so actual and imputed rents are a very important expenditure heading, with greater reported variance than actual variance because there is a pattern of low-income countries tending to underestimate dwelling services.

Meanwhile, table 12.4 provides yet another check on the results in table 12.3. This illustration compares indirect price levels with some available direct price levels that were examined but not used in the South American comparison. The indirect and direct price levels are given in rows 5

TABLE 12.4 Comparisons of the Direct Quantity Approach with CEM and Direct Rents: South America, 2005

		Argentina	Bolivia	Brazil	Chile	Colombia	Ecuador	Paraguay	Peru	Uruguay	Venezuela, RB
1	Direct volume index, SA = 100	133.2	45.7	103.0	145.8	124.8	58.2	68.3	67.2	149.0	105.1
2	Real PIC per capita, SA = 100	94.5	59.8	120.5	128.8	100.8	91.4	97.5	70.2	117.3	119.3
3	Direct volume/ PIC, SA = 100[a]	143.2	77.6	86.8	115.1	125.8	64.8	71.1	97.3	129.1	89.5
4	Housing as % of consumption	11.5	7.4	12.4	10.5	11.3	9.3	6.1	4.9	13.3	9.5
5	Indirect PL rents, SA = 100	113.0	48.0	154.0	134.7	72.1	128.5	69.7	33.1	144.8	102.4
6	Direct PL rents, SA = 100	96.2	75.3	124.3	128.9	92.1	61.8	163.2	61.6	82.7	114.5
7	Direct/indirect rents, SA = 100[a]	72.0	132.5	68.2	80.9	108.1	40.7	197.8	157.1	48.3	94.5
8	Indirect volume index, SA = 100	111.2	60.4	117.3	98.9	74.0	196.8	40.5	51.0	165.7	84.7
9	Indirect/direct volume, SA = 100[a]	75.1	118.9	102.4	61.0	53.3	303.8	53.3	68.2	100.0	72.5

Source: Derived from data processed by Statistics Canada for the 2005 ICP.
Note: SA = South America; PIC = private individual consumption; PL = price level.
a. Because the average of ratios is not the ratio of the averages, the indexes are based on the ratios divided by the average ratio.

and 6, respectively, and their ratio as an index appears in row 7. Even if the direct quantity ratios are reliable, the indirect price ratios may be too high or too low if the expenditures are too large or too small, as is the case for Brazil, Peru, and Uruguay.

Another way to use the direct rent comparisons is to derive indirect volumes, which are shown in row 8. An index of the indirect to direct volumes is given in row 9. The index in row 9 reveals quite large differences for Ecuador, Peru, Paraguay, and Uruguay, which again may be partly due to inaccurate expenditures. Certainly if one had only to choose between the direct volume method and the direct rent method for South America, the direct volume method is the appropriate choice. But what about applying a combination of the two approaches? As noted, Uruguay appears high using direct volumes, but it is even higher using the direct rent approach, so nothing is gained there. But certainly Colombia looks more plausible using the indirect rather than the direct volume method. This is not the place to recommend any particular combination of the methods, but only to suggest that more regions consider this approach for the 2011 ICP round.

The Experience in the Eurostat-OECD and Western Asia Regions

Eurostat-OECD

There is ample documentation of the use of both the direct and indirect volume approaches in manuals on Eurostat-OECD practice (see Eurostat and OECD 2006 and Sergeev 2004), and it will not be repeated here. The main point is that as the number of associate and full members of Eurostat-OECD increased, some countries did not have an adequate rental market to survey rental housing at market rates in order to provide comparable inputs to the original rental classification shown in table 12.2. A direct quantity approach was used in countries in which it did not seem appropriate to launch a rental survey. The linking was carried out through countries that carried out both approaches.

Table 12.5 does not take up the linking, but it does illustrate the country groups within the EU by whether they had rental surveys or used the direct quantity approach. Of more interest, table 12.5 makes the same comparison of the PPPs based on the CEM imputation for 33 countries in the EU that was made for the 10 countries in South America.[8] The first 22 countries used rental surveys to indirectly measure volumes, and the remaining 11 countries used the direct volume approach. Column (1) of table 12.5 provides the CEM volume index and column (2) the indirect and direct rent volume indexes, both based on EU33 = 100. Column (3) expresses the difference of (1) - (2) as a percentage of column (2).

The standard deviation of the direct rent differences is 27.1, with an average of 8.3. For the direct volume countries, the corresponding numbers are 18.8 and –19.4. Clearly, the large standard deviations suggest the high variability across countries on how well CEM proxies the volume of rental services. But of more interest is the average direction of the differences. The relative volume of rental services is less than the remainder of household consumption for many EU countries using the rental survey. And the opposite is true for those countries using the direct volume approach. This result is counterintuitive because most of the direct rent countries have substantially higher incomes than those using direct volumes. Normally, lower-income-per-capita countries will have a lower share of consumption devoted to dwelling services, whereas the opposite appears to emerge from table 12.5. An explanation of this finding is that the direct quantity approach tends to overstate dwelling services compared with direct rent surveys for countries at the same level of income. The reason for this is that direct rent surveys are better at holding housing quality constant compared with the direct quantity method. Further support for this conjecture is provided in the concluding section.

Western Asia

Several countries in Western Asia had limited quantity and quality information about their housing stock, several had doubtful expenditures, and several had both problems. All the countries in Western Asia obtained consumer price information on rents from their CPIs, and so they chose three types of rentals and also conducted a direct rent comparison for all, except Lebanon. Estimated rent levels were developed using both weighted and unweighted CPD equations. These two CPD estimates were very similar, and the geometric mean appears in column (2) of table 12.6, where the countries are ordered by their per capita domestic absorption (PCDA) in column (1).[9]

Two indirect rent indexes were also estimated, one of which used the same approach that table 12.3 illustrated for South America. The second quality measure assigned amenities two-thirds of the weight and average size of dwelling one-third of the weight. This adjustment is further discussed in the next section. Other than Jordan, in all countries these two measures were within 10 percent of each other; their geometric mean is given in column (3). The final estimated price level of market and owner-occupied dwellings for each country was the geometric mean of the direct and indirect estimates. The price level for Lebanon clearly looks out of line, most likely because expenditures on dwelling services have been underestimated. Availability of direct rent observations would have yielded more reasonable rent estimates for Lebanon, but perhaps at the expense of reasonable volume estimates. Because of the possible errors in expenditures, and both direct and indirect rents, the final choice in Western Asia to use the estimates in column (4) appeared less subjective than making judgments about the data submissions of each country. And it probably reduced errors on average over all of the countries.

TABLE 12.5 Comparisons of the Direct Quantity Approach with CEM: European Union, 2005

	Countries, direct rents	Real PIC per capita, EU = 100 (1)	Indirect volume (2)	Percent difference (3)
1	Germany	126.0	130.6	−3.5
2	Belgium	121.9	107.7	13.2
3	Denmark	112.6	125.8	−10.4
4	Greece	119.9	84.8	41.3
5	Spain	127.1	71.7	77.3
6	France	125.7	120.2	4.5
7	Ireland	116.0	107.1	8.3
8	Italy	123.3	104.0	18.6
9	Luxembourg	251.3	191.9	31.0
10	Netherlands	126.7	105.0	20.7
11	Austria	146.7	135.0	8.7
12	Portugal	98.6	65.8	49.9
13	Finland	101.1	122.0	−17.1
14	Sweden	100.9	150.4	−32.9
15	United Kingdom	143.8	145.4	−1.1
16	Cyprus	136.4	130.4	4.6
17	Czech Republic	70.4	96.9	−27.3
18	Hungary	63.7	81.6	−22.0
19	Malta	105.3	82.0	28.5
20	Iceland	135.0	128.5	5.0
21	Norway	120.3	170.7	−29.5
22	Switzerland	148.5	129.8	14.4
23	Estonia	58.7	64.5	−8.9
24	Latvia	50.0	59.8	−16.4
25	Lithuania	62.8	60.0	4.6
26	Poland	54.6	65.1	−16.1
27	Slovak Republici	60.7	77.3	−21.5
28	Slovenia	90.3	82.8	9.0
29	Bulgaria	39.8	63.9	−37.8
30	Romania	38.6	43.9	−12.1
31	Turkey	31.3	65.9	−52.5
32	Croatia	60.3	74.7	−19.3
33	Macedonia, FYR	31.6	54.9	−42.4
		2,838.7	3,019.9	
		86.0	91.5	

Note: PIC = private individual consumption.

TABLE 12.6 Direct Quantity and Direct Rent Indexes: Western Asia, 2005 (Western Asia = 100)

Country	PCDA (1)	Direct rent price level (2)	Indirect price level (3)	Combined (4)
Yemen, Rep.	11.4	35.2	22.3	28.0
Iraq	15.9	29.3	27.7	28.5
Syria	20.1	46.6	26.5	35.1
Jordan	21.3	53.1	84.9	67.1
Egypt, Arab Rep.	25.0	8.5	11.5	9.9
Oman	101.0	74.1	115.3	92.4
Saudi Arabia	105.4	65.1	87.6	75.5
Bahrain	135.4	163.1	162.5	162.8
Kuwait	223.3	171.6	123.3	145.5
Qatar	341.1	349.7	337.8	343.7
Lebanon			8.5	

Note: PCDA = per capita domestic absorption.

Linking the Regions: The 2005 Experience

Unlike for many consumption basic headings, it was agreed that the ICP Global Office would receive quantity information on housing from all countries, as well as the Ring countries (see chapter 8). This recommendation was made after the regional protocols were in place, so initially only three regions—Africa, South America, and Western Asia—provided data on all countries to the Global Office. No quantity information was available for the Commonwealth of Independent States (CIS) and only for Ring countries in Asia. Subsequently, Eurostat-OECD supplied quantity information for all countries for which it was available. The problem was how to put the regional results in a form in which they could be linked to other regions.

In the work reported here, there are 106 countries, of which 103 responded to the questionnaire in the annex to this chapter. Mexico and the United States were added; the data were obtained from national sources that also included number of bedrooms in order to overlap with South America. China was added as well because of its size, the sparseness of the Asian data, and the ready availability of published data on rural and urban housing stock. Responses by the countries to the housing questionnaire facilitated adjusting measures of housing volume for quality based on shares of water, electricity, and indoor toilets in country dwelling stocks. However, the data submissions had many gaps, including the basic quantity measures themselves. Although all countries provided the total number of residential units, the other volume measures were often sparse. The situation in South America has been discussed. For other regions, the number of rooms and floor area were requested, but were supplied only by about half the countries.

Clearly, gaps in the data must be addressed if comparisons are to be made. The approach used is multilateral in nature because it appeared to be an objective way to deal with the gaps in the quantity data. In this approximation, the Ring countries were treated like any other country, in part because the data gaps in the Ring countries were also significant. And as mentioned earlier, the available data from national sources were also used to improve the overlap of the country and volume coverage.[10]

Columns (1)–(3) in table 12.7a provide the numbers submitted by the first 10 countries, with three of them reproducing the South American entries in table 12.3. Column (4) is the quality

TABLE 12.7a Illustration of Quality Measure Estimates in Estimation of Regional Linking Factors: Selected Countries, 2005

	Water share (1)	Electric share (2)	Toilet share (3)	Quality 1 (4)	Quality 2 (5)
Argentina	0.841	0.954	0.715	0.831	0.887
Bahrain	1.000	1.000	1.000	1.000	1.000
Bangladesh	0.311	0.068	0.143	0.145	0.430
Benin	0.226	0.100	0.028	0.086	0.391
Bhutan	0.411	0.586	0.143	0.325	0.550
Bolivia	0.340	0.640	0.389	0.439	0.626
Botswana	0.226	0.210	0.384	0.263	0.509
Brazil	0.730	0.950	0.627	0.758	0.838
Brunei Darussalam	0.935	0.982	0.914	0.943	0.962
Central African Republic	0.060	0.603	0.133	0.169	0.446

Source: Derived from data provided by countries to the ICP Global Office.

measure introduced in table 12.3—namely, the geometric mean of columns (1)–(3) to obtain quality measure 1 (Q1). If a country reported a 0 share for any amenity, then the geometric mean would be 0.0 and the quality-adjusted quantity would be 0.0. Although an unlikely occurrence, it is not a conceptually clean measure. Further studies suggest that amenities add at least double the value to a dwelling compared with its size in rooms or floor area. To roughly allow for this effect, quality measure 2 (Q2) gives space a weight of one-third and amenities a weight of two-thirds; this measure is given in column (5).[11] It can be seen that the two quality measures approach each other, moving from lower to higher measures of Q1.

As noted, only a few countries provided number of rooms or area in square meters. Another 10-country illustration of the dwelling data is presented in table 12.7b, which provides a sense of the gaps in response. Column (1) is the number of dwelling units, and columns (2) and (3) are persons per dwelling and dwellings per person, respectively. Unfortunately, the persons per dwelling differences do not tell one whether houses are bigger in some countries or there is simply less space per person. For example, Oman has almost double the number of persons per dwelling as Singapore, 7.395 versus 4.109. Is this because housing is more crowded in Oman or because its dwellings are larger? Unfortunately, this cannot be determined on the basis of amenities and dwelling numbers alone. Columns (4)–(6) indicate by an "x" whether a volume measure is available for a country in addition to the total number of dwellings. Nigeria and Saudi Arabia, for example, only provided the number of dwellings. As noted, it was possible to obtain total rooms for a few South American countries such as Peru, giving them three space measures. Most countries in table 12.7b and in the whole sample have just two space measures.

To deal with the incomplete data, a form of the CPD approach is estimated as

$$\ln \text{(indicating log)} \left(\frac{\text{Exp}}{Q_{ij}}\right) = \alpha + \beta_i R_i + \delta_j VT_j + \lambda(M_k) \tag{12.1}$$

where $\frac{\text{Exp}}{Q_{ij}}$ is the quality-adjusted volume of housing of a country in region i per unit of volume measure type j. There are 106 countries and four types of housing measures: number of units, number of rooms, number of bedrooms, and floor area. The total number of observations

TABLE 12.7b Density per Dwelling and Availability of Space Measures: Selected Countries, 2005

	Number of dwellings	Persons per dwelling	Dwellings per capita	Rooms	Bedrooms	Area
Nepal	4,161,000	6.521	0.153	X		X
Nigeria	28,000,000	4.693	0.213			
Oman	347,134	7.395	0.135	X		X
Pakistan	23,000,000	6.842	0.146	X		
Paraguay	1,098,005	5.609	0.178		X	
Peru	5,926,821	4.719	0.212	X	X	
Philippines	17,000,000	5.002	0.200			X
Qatar	126,203	6.441	0.155	X		
Saudi Arabia	3,991,783	6.156	0.162			
Singapore	1,059,000	4.109	0.243	X		

Source: Derived from data provided by countries to the ICP Global Office.

in the estimation was 230, which is slightly more than half the possible 424 (4 * 106) observations.

Equation (12.1) is semi-log with three dummy or class variables on the right-hand side: R for each of the five regions, VT for volume type, and M_k, where the subscript k indexes countries into one of three groups based on the modernity of the stock of dwelling in each country derived from a combination of survey responses. The equation parameters and statistics are given in table 12.8.

TABLE 12.8 Log Unit Values on Region and Quality

Measure	Variable	Parameter estimate	Standard error	t-value
Quality-adjusted unit value measure	Intercept	7.374	0.184	40.02
	Area	−4.334	0.171	−25.34
	Room	−1.081	0.162	−6.68
	Bedroom	−0.445	0.339	−1.31
	Dwelling	0.000		
Modernity measure	High	1.075	0.166	6.48
	Medium	0.000		
	Low	−1.115	0.185	−6.04
Region	AFR	−1.579	0.237	−6.67
	ASIA	−0.852	0.205	−4.17
	LAC	−1.080	0.272	−3.96
	WASIA	−0.392	0.240	−1.63
	Eurostat-OECD	0.000		

Source: Estimated from country submissions for the 2005 ICP.
Note: RMSE = root mean square error; AFR = Africa; LAC = Latin America and the Caribbean; WASIA = Western Asia; Eurostat-OECD = European Union–Organisation for Economic Co-operation and Development. RMSE = 0.977.

When there is an intercept, one of each class is assigned the value 0.0 because the equation is not otherwise defined. Most of the variation in the dependent variable is explained by differences in unit values (expenditure per), with dwelling type the highest, followed by per bedroom, per room, and lowest per square meter, in that order. For this reason, the *VT* class variable gives rise to the relatively high value of R^2.

The modernity classification attempts to capture survey responses to several questions. Countries were asked for the shares of dwellings that were modern or traditional, the shares in urban and rural areas, the share rented, and the like. The large number of gaps meant that using these variables individually would substantially reduce the number of observations for any regression equation. It was decided to group countries into low, medium, and high, based on partial responses that would measure features of housing stocks that would not be captured in the three amenity variables: water, electricity, and toilet. The coefficients on the modernity measure are significant, and the signs are sensible. The coefficients on the unit value types are also in the expected direction, being highest per dwelling and least per square meter. The coefficient on bedrooms is not statistically significant, which is probably explained by the fact that there were so few observations.

The significance of the equation as a whole is weak as measured by the high root mean square error (RMSE) of 0.977. An identical equation was estimated using country in place of region, and the RMSE was 0.290 and R^2 was 0.991, a seemingly preferable equation. However, the primary concern in linking the regions is to obtain low standard errors of the regional coefficients. It turns out that if a regional effect is identified in an equation also including countries, the standard errors of the regional coefficients are much higher than those in table 12.8. So for the purpose of linking, the choice was made to use linking factors similar to those in table 12.8.[12] With Eurostat-OECD equal to 100, these were 20.6 for Africa, 42.7 for Asia-Pacific, 34.0 for South America, and 67.6 for Western Asia as shown by the anti-log (e^x) of the respective parameter estimates. It seems likely that the Asia-Pacific number is high relative to the South American index. This is probably the result of the small overlap of the volume measure of the South American countries with those of other regions, and with the relatively small number of countries from the Asia-Pacific region represented in table 12.8.

To summarize, the linking of the regions just described will be much improved if all the countries provide more complete responses to the form in the annex to this chapter. It is hoped this will be a learning experience that will improve the quantity and quality of information received from the 2005 ICP countries and the newly participating countries in 2011. However, comparisons across regions will only be as good as the country comparisons within regions, and as good as the comparability of the direct rent and direct volume methods.

Moving On to 2011 Based on the ICP Experience

Making good comparisons of dwelling services is difficult for individual countries over time and even harder for different cities in or regions of the same country. So it is not surprising that the ICP has also faced problems in comparing this single most important expenditure heading within household consumption. Two messages seem to be flowing from the experience in previous ICP rounds. First, there are the efforts carried out by Eurostat-OECD to link their new associate and older member countries when the new countries are not able to carry out rental surveys. Second, a case is made for supplementing surveys using the direct volume approach with as much direct rent information as may be available from other sources.

Using the Direct Volume Approach for All Countries

Plans have already been made to ask all countries to respond to a direct volume questionnaire as part of the 2011 ICP data collection process. In addition, these responses should be made available to the Global Office for all countries. Because Eurostat-OECD operates on a schedule that is at least one year in advance of the global comparison, whatever estimates they make using the direct volume linking for some of their countries will have been completed before those of the other regions. For the other regions, the Global Office should receive the responses from all the regions by the end of 2011—that is, at the same time the other consumer heading prices are being collected. Furthermore, it is proposed that the Global Office begin processing at the start of the validation procedure, not after it is carried out in the regions.

Because this is a departure from previous practice, a justification is appropriate. In the 2005 round, the questionnaires were received after regional validation. The Global Office raised a number of questions about country responses with the regions, but the regional coordinators were not able to elicit country responses to the queries. Because many of the questions arise from anomalies that emerge from comparisons across regions, it is important that these questions be raised while countries are still receptive to queries about validation. This proposal also puts pressure on the Global Office to process the direct volume questionnaires in a prompt fashion so that, if necessary, other options can be considered.

The previous section described the attempt to link the regions for 2005. It is proposed that some version of this approach be implemented as part of the 2011 ICP. With direct volume data from all the countries, it would be possible to straightforwardly estimate a transitive set of basic heading parities across the countries. This approach would offer two choices. First, it would directly provide regional linking factors, because the link would be the same whether a country or a country average served as the numeraire for a region. Eurostat-OECD will want to preserve their regional results, and this is easily done.

For regions that have not yet completed their own regional comparison, there is a second choice: they could simply use some or all of the multilateral indirect rental parities for their own countries. For example, this would remain an option for regions such as Western Asia that used some direct rent and some indirect rent parities. And if regions had already completed their own comparisons for dwelling services, they could choose to use these results in the manner of Eurostat-OECD. Finally, regions could examine the multilateral results and then decide whether to carry out and use their comparison of dwelling services. In short, there are a number of advantages for the regions as well as for the Global Office if it undertakes a multilateral comparison of direct volumes in any event and does so as early as possible.

The Advantages of Also Collecting Direct Rent Data

The experience in the 2005 ICP made clear the desirability of improving estimates of expenditures on the dwelling services of owner-occupied units. Even if direct volume estimates are accurate, indirect PPPs will be too small if the expenditures are underestimated. Conversely, even accurate direct rent estimates will lead to indirect volumes that are too low if expenditures are underestimated. This is one reason that in the 2011 ICP round great emphasis is being placed on improving the expenditure estimates for dwelling services and several other difficult basic headings.

Even if the ICP plans to go with the direct volume approach, one advantage of having both direct and indirect rent information is as a further check on expenditures. But there is another more important consideration: direct volume measures do not capture enough important quality features of housing. To illustrate this point, consider first a study of rents for Germany reported by Claudia

Kurz and Johannes Hoffmann of the Deutsche Bundesbank (2004) that is also instructive about rental equivalence. The data are collected annually from about 2,500 renters and 1,600 owners as part of the German Socio-Economic Panel (GSOEP). The characteristics of the dwellings are fairly detailed as to location by region, size of city, as well as four neighborhood groups.

Table 12.9 presents some summary statistics for renters and owners based on the 1998 survey. Rents of owner-occupied units are estimated by the owner, a survey practice that is fairly common though often questioned. In many respects, owners live in different places and in better accommodation than renters, as can be seen by the share of each group in different neighborhoods and different-sized cities (rows 5–10 in table 12.9).

Rows 2–3 provide the basic rent statistics for renters and owners, and one surprising feature is that the rent per square meter is higher for owners than for renters. This is surprising on several counts. First, renters are more concentrated in large cities and in the central areas of cities (49 versus 19 percent), where rents are typically higher. Second, rents per square meter typically decline with size of dwelling for a number of reasons. However, this is not the case in table 12.9, where the average rent is rising slightly more than average size. One quality characteristic appears in table 12.9—see row 4 on the share of units with a garden—and here owners are more than twice as likely to have a garden. For other survey indicators of quality, renters are similar to owners. The conclusion drawn is that there are dimensions of quality that are not captured in the measures collected in the direct volume approach, but that are present in more complete rental surveys.

Kurz and Hoffmann also estimate a hedonic regression showing the systematic decline in rents by size of city, dwelling type, size, age and availability of gallery/garden, plumbing, and heating. The coefficient on the log of rent rises less proportionately than size of dwelling and declines with age of dwelling. In the first ICP report (Kravis et al. 1975, 122), a similar hedonic equation was estimated for the United States using a sample of 39,100 renters from urban locations compiled by the Bureau for Labor Statistics (BLS) for 1967. Although the U.S. sample is from many years ago, the relationships of the German and U.S. hedonic regressions are similar—that is, the log of rent rises with size of urban center, number of rooms, and number of bathrooms (or baths), and declines with the age and condition of the structure.

TABLE 12.9 Rent Sample: Germany, 1998

	Germany	Renters	Owners
1	Average rent	793	1,362
2	Size (m^2)	70.6	116.2
3	Rent per m^2	11.2	11.7211704
	Share of sample		
4	With garden	0.28	0.88
5	Residential area	0.68	0.80
6	Mixed area	0.29	0.18
	By city size		
7	> 500,000	0.57	0.34
8	100,000–500,000	0.13	0.08
9	50,000–100,000	0.03	0.04
10	50,000–20,000	0.10	0.18

Source: Adapted from Kurz and Hoffmann 2004.

A feature of the BLS sample deserves special mention: it provides number of baths, and in 1967, 5 percent of the sampled units had no bath or a shared bath. Increments are half-bath, full bath, one and a half baths, and two or more. The coefficients are, respectively, 0.065, 0.227, 0.406, and 0.665, and all are different from zero at the 1 percent level. These coefficients indicate that, given other features of a unit, rents rise by roughly 6 percent for a half-bath to 66 percent for two or more baths. Why such a large effect for number of baths? I suggest it is because they represent other rent-determining qualities of a dwelling that are not otherwise measured. However, such quality effects are not captured in the adjustments made in the direct volume approach. In the example just given, the presence of a full bath added 23 percent to rents, or roughly one-third of the rental increment of two or more baths. Similar studies are done annually using U.S. data in which there is a single bathroom coefficient. For 2008 and 2009, the coefficient is 0.18 in separate regressions for renters and homeowners, all estimated with over 27,000 observations. This implies that two bathrooms add 36 percent to rent and two and a half bathrooms add 45 percent.[13] These effects are still large, though somewhat less than 40 years earlier.

The general point is that most housing censuses in lower-income countries provide data on a limited number of rent-determining characteristics of housing. With limited information available, the direct volume approach can measure only a small part of the quality differences of the housing stock between low- and high-income countries. For most countries using the direct rent approach, the level of detail on their housing stock is also greater, but that does not help in comparisons with countries for which there is less detail. In short, linking via the direct volume approach reduces the comparison to a very small number of rent-determining characteristics.

Another window on this problem from a previous ICP round is provided in table 12.10. Some partial hedonic regression results are reported for selected 1975 ICP countries ranging in

TABLE 12.10 Rent Equations Based on National Relationships: Selected Countries, 1975

		Colombia	India[a]	Japan	Korea, Rep.	Malaysia[b]	Thailand	United States[c]	Uruguay
1	Base rent	13.17103984	2.409307876	13.50067385	18.79545455	8.604166667	14.66045142		3.552173913
2	Water, elec., toilet	30.78072012	5.616096659	23.53167453	32.76047727	19.29054167	19.79160942	52.17	10.86254783
3	(Water, elec., toilet)/base	2.337	2.331	1.743	1.743	2.242	1.35		3.058
4	Average rent, $ @ XR	49.8218335	3.332935561	47.36859838		27.27916667	22.2767419	174.7	37.77826087
5	Average/ (water, elec., toilet)	1.618605195	0.593461218	2.012971849		1.414121342	1.125564952	3.348667817	3.477845297
6	Sample size	2,707	17,326	4,048	1,970	3,061	1,814	9,995	1,161
7	RMSE	0.555	0.71	0.422	0.363	0.591	0.438	0.311	0.218
8	R^2	0.62	0.441	0.624	0.606	0.693	0.443	0.585	0.814
9	Per capita GDP PPPs	1,609	470	4,907	1,484	1,541	936	7,176	2,844

Source: Kravis, Heston, and Summers 1982, table 2-9, 56.
Note: Base rent refers to a unit built in 1945–59, 35 square meters in size, with water and electricity. XR = exchange rate; RMSE = root mean square error.
a. Row 4 is approximated for India.
b. The numerator was approximated for Malaysia.
c. The base rent could not be estimated for the United States because there were too few observations.

income from India to the United States as given in row 9. Row 1 provides the base rent in U.S. dollars at exchange rates of a dwelling that is 35 square meters, with water and electricity, and built in the 1945–59 period. Row 2 is the rent with water, electricity, and flush toilet—the quality adjustment factors for the direct volume approach. Row 3 is the ratio of a dwelling with water, electricity, and flush toilet to the base rent, except for the United States for which the base rent could not be estimated for lack of relevant rental units. For the remaining countries except Thailand, the addition of a flush toilet adds much more to the rent than would be called for if these three quality indicators were of equal importance, a point made earlier in this chapter and in this section.

Row 4 gives the average rent of all dwellings in the samples except for the Republic of Korea, the consequence of the simpler and time-consuming computing capacity of the period. Row 5, which gives the ratio of the average to row 2, reinforces the point of this section. The average dwellings in the higher-income countries have more unmeasured elements of quality and much higher rents compared with the quality-adjusted volume as usually estimated using the direct volume approach.

Figure 12.1 illustrates two plots of points with the per capita GDP of each country (US = 100) on the horizontal axis and the rent per month on the vertical axis. The upper line of squares (series 2) shows how the plot of average rents of dwellings with water, electricity, and flush toilet of a given size (square meters) rises with the per capita income of the countries, not controlling for other amenities. The set of diamonds (series 1) shows how rent rises per dwelling of a given size in the same countries for a dwelling identified using the quantity method—that is, a dwelling with water, electricity, and a flush toilet but no other amenities.

FIGURE 12.1 Plot of Rents against Per Capita GDP (United States = 100)

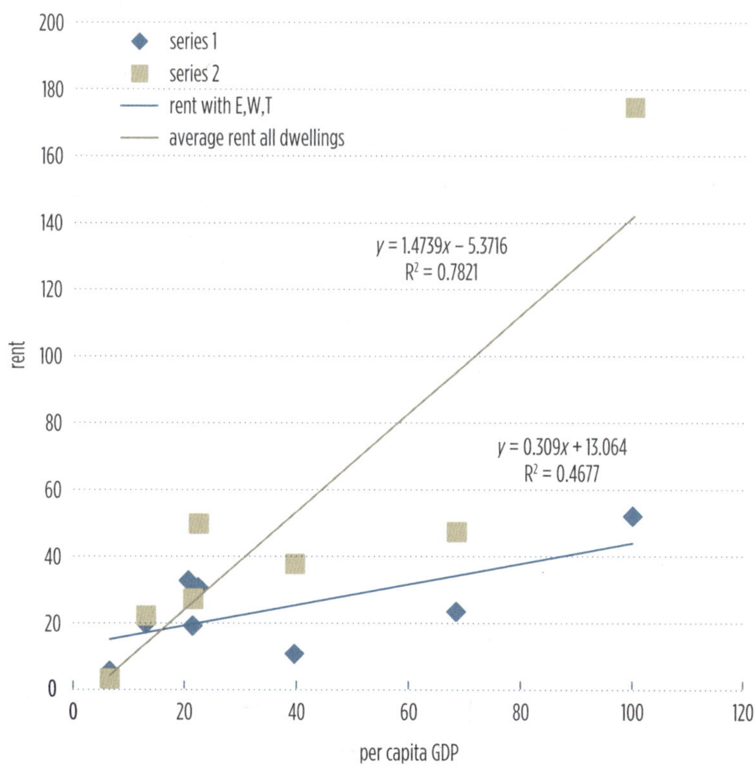

Source: Estimated from table 12.10.

Why do the two plots of points have such different slopes yielding much higher rent differentials at higher levels of GDP per capita? The reason is that many quality features of dwellings are associated with number of bathrooms and other features of dwellings in higher-income countries that are not captured in direct quantity comparisons. For example, in the hedonic rent studies with which the author is familiar, the coefficient on additional half or full bathrooms appears to add much more to estimated rents than one might expect given the extra capital cost involved. The interpretation is that as one moves from the availability of an inside flush toilet to more than one bathroom, there will also be many other less measurable quality features of the dwelling yielding higher rents.

The consequence is that the PPPs for rental dwellings estimated indirectly via direct quantity comparisons are likely too low and the volumes too high compared with estimation from market rents. The effect will be systematic across income levels because rental surveys are available in higher-income countries. In the past, this may have been offset in practice by a systematic understatement of dwelling expenditures in lower-income countries. If rent expenditures are improved in the 2011 ICP, then the problem will become even more apparent.

Figure 12.2 plots the ratio of average rent to rent with just electricity, water, and toilet against per capita GDP. Because the intercept in figure 12.2 is essentially 1.0, the relationship says that moving from a country with 5 percent to a country with 80 percent of the per capita GDP of the

FIGURE 12.2 Ratio of Average Rent to Electricity, Water, Toilet (E, W, T) Rent on Per Capita GDP (United States = 100)

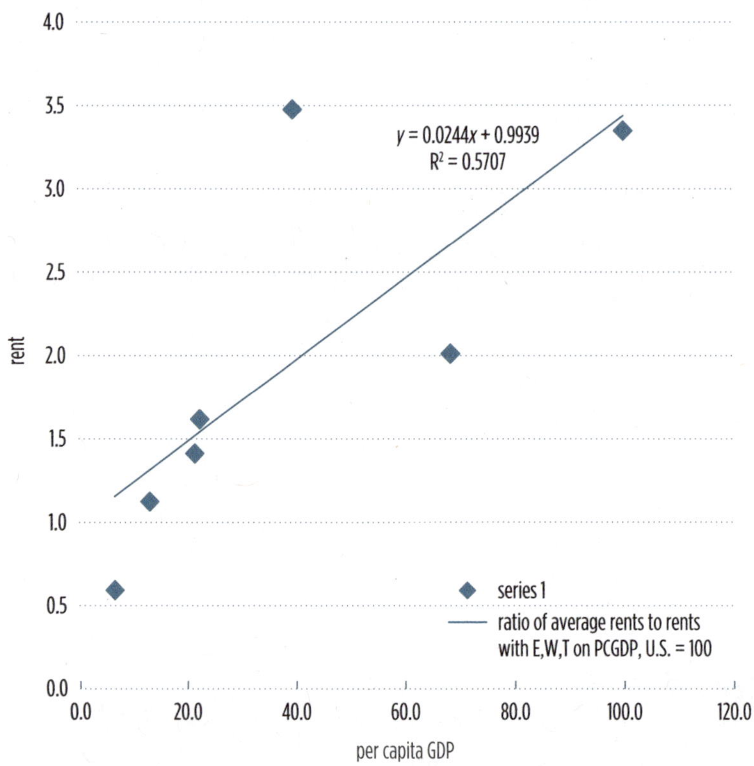

Source: Estimated from table 12.10.

United States would lead to a difference of 83 percent in the estimated price level of rents, the direct volume method being lower—that is, [0.0244 * (80 – 5)] –1 as a percent. This implies a large effect on total rents and could make a difference in consumption of 3 or 4 percent, even for countries reporting rents of only 5 percent of individual consumption.

There is no reason to believe that the 1975 relationship is not present today, but that does not make the earlier quantitative illustration necessarily a guide to exactly what should be done in the 2011 ICP round. However, serious consideration needs to be given to the issue raised here. It should be possible to analyze more recent data for more countries to consider whether some systematic adjustment is required when linking groups of countries using the two different methods.

ANNEX

Worksheet for Quantity of Housing and Amenities

Reference year for benchmark

Country

Provide these breakdowns or others available for your country:

	1. Total of all dwellings	2. Type of construction of dwellings			3. Location of dwellings		
		a. Modern construction		b. Traditional	a. Size of urban area		b. Rural
		(1) Houses	(2) Flats		(1) Large	(2) Other	
Number of dwelling units							
Number of rooms							
Total area in m^2 of the unit							
Percentage of dwelling units with							
1–2 rooms							
3–4 rooms							
5+ rooms							
Percentage of dwelling units with							
Electricity							
Inside water							
Private toilet							
Central heating							
Air-conditioning							
Percentage of dwelling units							
Rented							
Owner-occupied							
Assumed growth rate from benchmark period to 2005							

Source: Described on p. 147 of World Bank 2008.

NOTES

1. These papers are posted on the World Bank's ICP website under Technical Advisory Group: http://web.worldbank.org/WBSITE/EXTERNAL/DATASTATISTICS/ICPEXT/0,,contentMDK:22388553~pagePK:60002244~piPK:62002388~theSitePK:270065,00.html.
2. Some countries use the increase in the replacement value of quality-adjusted housing as a measure of the services of owner-occupied housing, and some use a form of user cost. In rental equivalence, the concept of dwelling services is gross rent on the expenditure side, while the landlord must deduct costs such as maintenance, insurance, and depreciation in arriving at rental income on the income side of the accounts.
3. Both the direct rent and direct volume methods are described more fully in the *Eurostat-OECD Methodological Manual on Purchasing Power Parities,* including the 48 strata of rental housing (Eurostat and OECD 2006, 80–84). The rental equivalence approach has been subjected to criticism in the United States because it is thought that rented units tend to be of lower quality, and therefore the approach underestimates the dwelling services of higher-value, owner-occupied units. In particular, the substantial decline in the ratio of rent to the price of houses, from low- to high-priced dwellings, is not adequately taken into account.
4. This discussion is based on Kravis, Heston, and Summers (1982, 54–59). The rent samples varied in size from a few hundred to over 10,000. It is important to note that even a nonrandom sample may produce unbiased regression coefficients on the most important rent-determining features such as floor area and baths, though not necessarily an unbiased estimate of the average rent level. However, so long as one has a reasonable estimate of the difference between, say, capital city and other city rents, one can use a rental sample from a capital city to approximate all cities.
5. Here it is assumed that the structure required no maintenance and that, contrary to fact, the land value is not to be included in the illustration. Diewert (2009, sec. 8.4) provides a detailed discussion of how maintenance versus renovation should be treated. Typically, recurring maintenance is a current consumption item, and so it is not part of the user cost of a structure, whereas a renovation with a life of over a year would be capitalized and a user cost estimated. The alternative, which in many ways is conceptually clearer, is to treat the annual maintenance as a necessary rate of expenditure associated with the normal depreciation of a structure. However, for illustrative purposes it is simpler to treat maintenance as a current expenditure. With respect to land value, it should be included in the calculation of user cost, even if the service life of the land is infinite because the owner could have received the opportunity cost of the land value.
6. An important illustration is China, which publishes an average floor area per person for the population that appears very high by international standards.
7. Deaton (2010, 14–15) shows that the problem arose because several of the poorest countries were used, appropriately enough, to establish a world poverty line for 2005. But several of these countries, such as Ghana, Chad, and Tajikistan, had estimates of expenditures on housing services that were unrealistically low. The per capita volume of housing of these countries under CEM would be much higher than justified by the expenditures on housing. Therefore, the indirect rent indexes were too low. Because this lowered the PPPs of consumption for these countries, it converted their poverty lines to a higher international value than appropriate. As a consequence, for large countries such as China and India that had reasonable estimates of dwelling expenditures, the poverty line was raised, thereby placing over 100 million more people in poverty in these two countries alone.
8. I would like to thank Sergey Sergeev for the calculations underlying table 12.5 and especially for the suggestion that they would be as interesting for the EU as for South America.

9. See Heston and Hamadeh (2010) for more details. Domestic absorption is referred to as in the *System of National Accounts.* It is the sum of domestic expenditures, excluding the net foreign balance, and therefore differs from GDP.
10. As noted, national sources were used for Mexico and the United States in order to overlap number of bedrooms with the South American countries. Further supplementary household survey data were used for Bangladesh, Benin, Bhutan, Bolivia, Niger, and Peru to fill the gaps in questionnaire responses on number of rooms, share of traditional and rural housing, and related information. This was particularly important for South America, where information on number of bedrooms was available from the regional comparison.
11. The calculation of the second quality measure is $Q2 = \frac{(1 + 2 \cdot Q1)}{3}$. For example, Benin is $\frac{(1 + 2 \cdot 0.086)}{3} = \frac{1.172}{3}$ or 0.391.
12. Because data for additional countries became available after the linking was completed, the equation reported in table 12.8 contains more observations than were actually used for the report.
13. These coefficient estimates are based on experimental work being done jointly by the BLS and Bureau of Economic Analysis to estimate regional PPPs to convert personal incomes.

REFERENCES

Commission of the European Communities, International Monetary Fund, Organisation for Economic Co-operation and Development, United Nations, and World Bank. 2008. *System of National Accounts 2008.* http://unstats.un.org/unsd/nationalaccount/SNA2008.pdf.

Deaton, Angus. 2010. "Price Indexes, Inequality, and the Measurement of Poverty." *American Economic Review* 100 (March): 5–34.

Diewert, W. Erwin. 2009. "Durables and Owner-Occupied Housing in a Consumer Price Index." In *Price Index Concepts and Measurement,* ed. W. Erwin Diewert, John Greenlees, and Charles R. Hulten. Chicago: University of Chicago Press.

Eurostat and OECD (Organisation for Economic Co-operation and Development). 2006. *Eurostat-OECD Methodological Manual on Purchasing Power Parities.* Paris: OECD.

Heston, Alan, and Nada Hamadeh. 2010. "Owner Occupied Housing in Western Asia." Paper 01.02. Meeting, Technical Advisory Group, International Comparison Program, World Bank, February 17–19.

Kravis, Irving, Alan Heston, and Robert Summers. 1982. *World Product and Income.* Washington, DC, and Baltimore: World Bank and Johns Hopkins University Press.

Kravis, Irving, Zoltan Kennessey, Alan Heston, and Robert Summers. 1975. *A System of International Comparisons of Gross Product and Purchasing Power.* Washington, DC, and Baltimore: World Bank and Johns Hopkins University Press.

Kurz, Claudia, and Johannes Hoffmann. 2004. "A Rental-Equivalence Index for Owner-Occupied Housing in West Germany 1985 to 1998." Discussion Paper Series 1: Economic Studies from Deutsche Bundesbank.

Sergeev, Sergey. 2004. "International Comparisons of Housing (Experience from the European Comparison Program)." Meeting, Technical Advisory Group, International Comparison Program, Washington, DC, January 21–23.

World Bank. 2008. *Global Purchasing Power Parities and Real Expenditures, 2005 International Comparison Program.* http://siteresources.worldbank.org/ICPINT/Resources/icp-final.pdf.

CHAPTER 13

Construction

PAUL McCARTHY

Gross fixed capital formation on construction (hereafter simply construction) is a major component of the expenditure on gross domestic product (GDP). The 2005 International Comparison Program (ICP) revealed that about two-thirds of the 146 participating economies had a construction share of GDP of between 9 and 18 percent. The average share of construction within GDP was 11.9 percent, but there were major variations around this average, ranging from a low of 1.6 percent in Nigeria to a high of 38.7 percent in Bhutan.

The purpose of this chapter is to provide the conceptual framework underlying the estimation of construction purchasing power parities (PPPs), explain the different pricing methods, and describe the methodology used in the 2005 ICP by the Eurostat–Organisation for Economic Co-operation and Development (OECD) and ICP regions. It concludes with a brief evaluation of the basket of construction components (BOCC) method used in the ICP regions, with some lessons learned for the 2011 ICP round.

The 1993 *System of National Accounts* (Commission of the European Communities et al., 1993) divides construction into three major components, which were used as basic headings in the 2005 ICP:

- *Dwellings* (residential buildings) are buildings used entirely or primarily as residences. Examples are detached and semidetached houses, apartments, houseboats, barges, mobile homes, and caravans used as principal residences of households. They include any associated structures, such as garages, and all permanent fixtures customarily installed in residences.
- *Nonresidential buildings* are buildings other than dwellings, including fixtures, facilities, and equipment that are integral parts of the structures and the costs of site clearance and preparation. They include stables, barns, warehouses, industrial buildings, commercial buildings, buildings for public entertainment, hotels, restaurants, schools, hospitals, churches, and stadiums.

- *Other structures* (civil engineering works) consist of structures other than buildings. They include highways, suburban roads, railways, airfield runways, bridges, tunnels, subways, waterways, harbors, dams, sewer systems, mines, pipelines, communication cables, transmission lines, power lines, and sports fields.

Conceptual Framework Underlying the Estimation of Construction PPPs

Many factors can affect comparisons of goods and services between countries, particularly when one must ensure that the products specified are comparable. Construction poses special problems because most construction outputs are unique, despite some superficial similarities. For example, no two office buildings are identical, nor are civil engineering projects such as bridges or dams because they have design features that cater to factors such as location or span. One example is China's Three Gorges Dam. Its construction made up a significant portion of the construction expenditures in China in 2005. However, no similar activity is under way in the world for comparison purposes. In addition, large projects such as these are rarely completed within a single accounting period, which makes pricing them even more difficult. Special techniques are thus needed to determine what is priced for comparison purposes for construction.

Any method of producing PPPs for construction is necessarily based on a series of compromises and approximations. For example, the type of dwelling specified has to take into account any variations in structure or components to accommodate local conditions such as the weather conditions in different parts of a region, perhaps requiring heating systems in colder areas and cooling systems in warmer areas. More than one specification could be used to overcome this problem in a region that is geographically diverse, but multiple specifications would require some countries to price more than one type of dwelling, which adds to the overall cost of data collection.

Two alternative pricing methods are available for comparing construction prices between countries. The first is so-called input pricing, and the second is output pricing, which is generally based on pricing models (such as of a bridge) that are comparable across countries.

Input pricing is based on recording the prices of all major material and labor inputs for a range of different types of construction projects and combining them using weights that reflect the relative importance of each input in each type of project. Project inputs are analyzed using the concept of an "average" or "typical" project of each type. For example, the inputs for an average office building may be based on a quantity surveyor's analysis of the inputs for different office buildings, ranging in height from only a few floors to many floors. The inputs include labor (such as concreters, electricians, and carpenters), as well as materials (such as cement, steel, and timber) and other inputs (such as hiring equipment). The main problem with comparing prices across countries by pricing inputs is that productivity differences are not measured because the amounts of labor required to assemble the various materials are assumed to be the same across countries. It could be assumed that productivity is some non-zero amount, but there is little point in doing so unless some means is available to impute different productivity levels for the countries being compared. In practice, it is not possible to systematically measure productivity using input pricing. The productivity issue can be partly overcome by obtaining contractors' rates rather than wage rates for particular parts of a project (such as the price for pouring a concrete slab of 100 square meters), but such an approach still does not solve the problem for those parts of construction projects that generally use salaried employees rather than contractors. Another problem is that overhead costs are not included. Overhead includes, for example, the costs of maintaining an office with the staff and resources needed to manage the construction activities. Without including overhead costs, it is assumed they are the same relative size across countries. Profit margins, an element of overhead, are also assumed to be the same across countries, but that is rarely an accurate assumption for the construction industry.

Applying the input pricing approach to the ICP involves collecting the prices of a range of inputs (materials, labor, and equipment) that are common to the countries being compared. Materials would include products such as cement, steel, and timber, but the detailed specifications would have to be meaningful in all the countries in the comparison. Labor would relate to the occupations engaged in building, and the basis of the comparison would be the compensation (wages plus other related costs) of those workers. The prices required for equipment relate to the cost of using the equipment, and so the usual approach is to collect details of the prices paid to hire the types of equipment commonly used in construction.

As stated earlier, the main disadvantage of using input prices for a comparison is that an assumption is made that labor productivity is identical across the countries being compared. This assumption is probably unlikely, however, especially in a region composed of countries at very different stages of economic development.

Output pricing involves specifying some typical kinds of projects within a country and then asking construction professionals to quote a price for building the whole project, much like they would tender for a project. In this way, the quoted prices relate to the construction outputs rather than the inputs, and so the effects of changes in productivity and profit margins are taken into account. However, it is a costly exercise to specify and then price the various models required to cover adequately the range of projects in the construction industry. Also, construction techniques tend to change fairly rapidly, and so it becomes necessary to respecify the models periodically to ensure they remain relevant.

The output approach in the ICP is based on pricing models of complete construction projects. In practice, the models do not reflect a particular project in any country; rather, they are designed to embody a broad range of features typically found in buildings in the region, with the purpose of defining models that are comparable across countries. The objective is to obtain purchasers' prices that are consistent with the values in the national accounts. In practice, though, it is difficult to include the overhead, such as contractors' margins, because a subjective judgment is required, and it is difficult to ensure that the methods to estimate margins are consistently applied from one country to another. However, the overhead must be included to meet the requirements of an output price. The next section is an overview of the bills of quantities approach as used in the Eurostat-OECD comparison program. It is a form of output pricing.

Bills of Quantities

Historically, the ICP construction PPPs were based on a model-based technique known as the bills of quantities (BOQ) approach. It involved specifying in detail the components of various standard construction projects that covered the typical kinds of dwellings and a broad range of nonresidential buildings and civil engineering works (see box 13.1). The specifications were not based on actual projects; rather, in each case they were designed to reflect a hypothetical structure containing components representing the types of construction methods that were relatively common in the countries being compared and whose characteristics were roughly an average of those in the countries. The goal was for the models to be as representative as possible within each country and also to achieve comparability between countries. For example, the components underlying

BOX 13.1 Projects Specified for the BOQ Approach

The BOQ approach involved pricing detailed bills of quantities for a number of construction projects that were designed to be representative of such projects in the countries being compared. The projects were artificial in the sense that they did not necessarily exist in any country in the exact form specified—see chapter 6 of the *Eurostat-OECD Methodological Manual on Purchasing Power Parities* (Eurostat and OECD 2006) for more details.

The projects specified in the 2005 Eurostat–OECD PPP Programme were as follows (note that projects 5, 6, 7, and 12 were priced, where relevant, only by non-European OECD countries):

Residential buildings

01. European single-family house
02. Portuguese single-family house
03. Nordic single-family house
04. Apartment in a multi-apartment building
05. North American single-family house
06. Japanese single-family house
07. Australasian house

Nonresidential buildings

08. Agricultural shed
09. European factory building
10. Office building
11. Primary school
12. Japanese factory building

Civil engineering works

13. Asphalt road
14. Concrete road
15. Bridge
16. Concrete main sewer

excavating the site, pouring foundations, building walls, and other such activities were all specified in detail, taking into account the construction techniques used. In practice, though, the BOQ approach was based on obtaining costs for a large number of detailed components. Some included both materials and labor (such as a price for installed components rather than just the materials involved), but specific allowances were required for some overhead items such as project management and profits. The total price of each project was obtained by summing the costs of all the components—that is, the sum of the unit price times the number of units for each component. The PPPs were computed at the project level.

The BOQ is an output pricing approach when project overhead is included. The prices for a contractor to provide an individual finished component are the output prices for that component. For example, the price for supplying and installing a specific amount of a product (such as a brick wall that is 3 meters high and 300 square meters in total size) represents an output price for that particular element of a complete building project. However, when the (output) prices for all the components of a construction project are combined to provide a total price for the project, the outcome is a price somewhere between an input price and an output price because it excludes the overall project management costs and profits. Specifically adding allowances for this overhead to the aggregated prices for the components would result in an output price for the whole project.

The main problem with the BOQ approach is that it is very resource-intensive. Because the expertise required is not generally available in national statistical offices, the work must be contracted out. Pricing all the components in each project is costly because professional building analysts, such as quantity surveyors, must be employed, and the models themselves have to be respecified periodically, which is also an expensive exercise because of the expert resources required. In addition, although the BOQ approach may result in comparable prices for each model, the models themselves are not necessarily representative of construction projects in many of the countries being compared because of the compromises required to ensure they are comparable across countries.

After an extensive analysis of data covering several years, Eurostat found that about 40 percent of the number of items in the specifications for construction components accounted for 85–95 percent of the value of projects (Stapel 2002). Based on an analysis of the effects of using a "reduced list" of items in the bills of quantities, the study concluded that there was little difference in the average construction price level indexes for virtually all of the European Union countries when the pricing was based on a reduced list that contained about half the number of items in the full list. The study also concluded that "an appreciable amount of pricing effort contributes very little to the assessment of comparative levels. The number of items [priced] could be roughly halved and still one would catch about 90 percent of the project values." As a result, in 2001 Eurostat moved to a reduced list for pricing construction projects.

Alternative Pricing Methods

The ICP's Global Office investigated the possibility of using the "reduced product list" BOQ approach in the 2005 ICP, but it concluded that the cost would still be too high because of the number of models that would have to be specified in each region. Some alternatives were then examined. The countries in the Commonwealth of Independent States (CIS) collect input prices for a wide variety of construction components and then impute project prices using models specific to construction practices in the region. These countries use similar construction practices, which simplifies the modeling approach. This method contains many elements of an output pricing approach. However, because of the diversity of production practices many additional and more complex models would be required for this method to be used in the Africa, Asia-Pacific, South America, and Western Asia regions.

For these reasons, a completely new approach was adopted. It embodied some input pricing features, but was designed to approximate output prices as closely as possible. The method was based on pricing a relatively limited number of construction components designed to be as comparable as possible across countries. It became known as the basket of construction components approach.

Basket of Construction Components Approach

The BOCC approach, used in the 2005 ICP, involved collecting prices for a range of major construction components and basic inputs that were common across countries. The term *construction components* was used to describe specific physical outputs that are produced as intermediate steps in construction projects. A key element of this process was that the overall price estimated for each component was related to an installed component, including the costs of materials, labor, and equipment—that is, the price was closely related to an output price rather than to an input price.

The objective of the BOCC approach was to provide simpler and less costly price comparisons for construction than was possible using the BOQ method. An important goal was to develop a technique that would enable construction to be priced in major locations within each country and that would result in comparable prices for similar components across countries that had different labor and equipment mixes because of their different levels of economic development.

Aggregation Levels: Definitions

The BOCC process was based on pricing two kinds of components: composite components and basic inputs. Annex A lists both for each construction basic heading (note that many of the composite components and basic inputs appear in more than one construction basic heading). For PPP estimation purposes, composite components and basic inputs were grouped into the systems shown in the tables in annex B. Most detailed was the *component* or *basic input*, followed by the *system* and, finally, the *basic heading*. These aggregation levels were defined by the developers of the BOCC system (see Walsh and Sawhney 2004b). Paraphrased, they are as follows:

- *Basic input item.* A construction material or form of labor that can be described in such a way that "like with like" can be priced across countries. The prices collected for basic inputs were, in effect, input prices.
- *Composite component.* A combination of materials assembled in their final intended location and clearly identifiable as having a simple purpose within a project—that is, it is one of the building blocks of a system. An example is a structural column. In the 2005 ICP, a composite component consisted of a combination of materials, labor, and equipment appropriate to the means and methods employed in a given country.
- *System.* A set of related components within a project that satisfy a given function. For example, the substructure system within a building is intended to denote that set of components that serve the purpose of supporting the building. It would not include the heating and ventilation equipment or nonstructural exterior covering. In the 2005 ICP, some of the basic and composite components appeared in more than one system. For example, concrete appeared in three systems for residential buildings, and sand appeared in five systems (see annex B). These multiple appearances provided an implied weighting of the different components as determined by the frequency with which they appeared in different systems.
- *Basic heading.* The entirety of the construction enterprise for each residential or nonresidential building and other construction.

Components and Basic Inputs

The BOCC method consisted of 22 composite components (such as a column footing or earthworks) and 12 basic input components, consisting of rent for four types of equipment (such as a backhoe or a centrifugal pump), six types of basic building materials (such as Portland cement or reinforcing steel), and both skilled and unskilled labor.

The price for each basic component was a price for a construction input. The collection form for Portland cement, a basic component, appears in annex C. The form provides detailed specifications and indicates that prices are collected for three different quantities. The collection form for skilled labor also appears in annex C. Again, it provides the specifications and captures compensation data for six different kinds of skilled labor. The prices of the basic components neither reflected any measure of productivity nor contained any margins for profit and overhead. Therefore, they were input prices.

The price for each composite component reflected both the cost of the materials and the cost of the labor and equipment used in assembling those materials to produce a particular output such as a column footing or a structural column. As a result, this price partially met the requirements of an output price because it reflected the effect of productivity differences between countries by providing the total cost of materials, labor, and equipment combined in the appropriate proportions in each country. However, it did not reflect profits and overhead.

The starting point for calculating the price for a composite *component* was to obtain the total cost of the materials, labor, and equipment relevant to that component. For example, the collection form for the component "interior painting" (see annex C) described the paintwork as covering 100 square meters, including a typical level of surface preparation for a new surface free from defects. Three coats were required—one mist coat and two full coats of emulsion paint on an interior surface—and they were to be applied in a new building without flooring so that no drip or spill protection was necessary, but window and door masking were needed. The price required was the total cost of the completed output, including the cost of the paint, the labor involved (both skilled and unskilled), and the hire of any equipment that may have been used. From the ICP viewpoint, the advantage of such a specification was that each country could include the types and amounts of labor and equipment typically used in the country, allowing productivity differences between countries to be taken into account. By recording the "price" as the total cost of a well-defined output, the process was similar to the "like with like" process adopted for pricing products in the ICP in which the price required is for a single product whose specifications are defined in detail. In each case, though, the prices entering into the total cost are required to be expressed in terms of the purchasers' prices—that is, the applicable taxes (minus subsidies), including any nondeductible value added taxes (VAT), are part of the price, as are the relevant trade and transport margins.

In theory, the BOCC approach enabled countries at different levels of economic development to combine labor and equipment in proportions that reflected their use within each country rather than use a one-size-fits-all approach. In practice, at the component level the proportions were taken into account by collecting details on the cost of each labor, material, and equipment (hire) input (i.e., the price times quantity of each) and summing them to obtain a total cost for the component (see the example in the preceding paragraph). As a result, the proportions of labor to materials would differ between countries, depending on the quantities of each that a country included in the total cost of each component.

Pricing Basis

The basis of the national accounts valuation of expenditures on GDP is the purchasers' prices, which are the amounts paid by the purchasers, excluding any deductible VAT, in order to take delivery of a unit of a good or service at the time and place required by the purchasers. The prices estimated for components using the BOCC approach were based on the direct costs to the construction company of materials, labor, and the hire of equipment, including product taxes such as nondeductible VAT, but excluding profit margins, project management costs, and fees for construction specialists such as architects and quantity surveyors. As a result, the component prices were not completely consistent with the national accounts expenditures on gross fixed capital formation, which were valued at the purchaser's price. In the BOQ approach, the contractors' margins were added to the prices estimated for each model. However, determining contractors' margins is difficult, even for construction industry professionals, because so many factors can influence them such as the state of the economy, level of activity in the construction industry, length of the project, and region in which a project is located. The uncertainties involved led to a decision that no specific allowance would be made for these margins in the BOCC approach, which is equivalent to assuming that the margins are proportional to the measured prices for each project in each country.

When price levels are compared in different countries, the errors introduced by assuming margins are proportional to the measured prices may be significant. The project management overhead will always be an extra amount that should be added to the other construction costs actually priced. However, profit margins may be negative in some extreme circumstances, such as when demand for construction has fallen markedly because of the economic situation (e.g., following the collapse of a property price bubble). An extreme case could be two countries with their economies at opposite ends of the economic cycle in the ICP benchmark year. For example, in a country that has suffered a collapse in property prices it is likely that profit margins in the construction industry would be low, perhaps even negative (i.e., construction companies would be operating at a loss) if businesses wanted to keep skilled workers on their payroll in the expectation of a forthcoming turnaround in construction activity. Companies operating in another country that is experiencing buoyant conditions in the construction industry would be making a profit, perhaps even a higher level than usual if demand were sufficiently strong. Clearly, assuming that profit margins are a fixed share of other construction costs would not provide an accurate price comparison between these two countries. However, because of the difficulty in objectively measuring the profitability of construction businesses in different countries, it was not possible to obtain the data needed to adjust the price levels for overhead. The lack of data precluded even a subjective assessment of the likely impacts of such differences on the 2005 ICP price levels for construction.

In addition to the requirements just noted, the prices for construction were required to be the national average prices, which meant that they should be the prices observed in various regions in a country and weighted together, using the relative quantities of construction activity in each region as weights. Ideally, the annual average prices for 2005 were required, but to minimize collection costs each national statistical office was allowed to provide prices as of mid-2005, provided that inflation was low in the country concerned.

Estimating Construction PPPs

Eight systems were identified for each of residential and nonresidential buildings: site work, substructure, superstructure, exterior shell, interior partitions, interior/exterior finishes, mechanical and plumbing, and electrical (see annex B for details of the components allocated to each system). Civil engineering works consisted of six systems: site work, substructure, electrical equipment, superstructure, underground utility, and mechanical equipment. Various components were "reused" in different combinations within each system in each type of project. For example, the basic component, Portland cement, was used in six of the eight systems for residential buildings. Another basic component, aggregate base, was part of the site work system in residential and nonresidential buildings and in civil engineering works, and was also a component of the substructure system in all three types of projects.

The first step in estimating PPPs took place at the system level within a basic heading. As noted, the three tables in annex B show the systems used for each basic heading and the mixture of composite and basic components making up each system. Each composite and basic component was treated as a product, and the first estimation of PPPs was at the system level. The site work system for residential and nonresidential buildings contained 10 prices/costs that formed the first stage of estimation of the PPPs. The PPP for site work for each country was based on aggregation of the relative prices of the 10 items in the site work system. Thus the basic heading PPP emerged from the aggregation of the system PPPs.

No weights were applied to the different composite or basic components making up each system. However, some of the composite and basic components appeared in more than one system.

Their frequency of appearance was an implied form of weighting. As one could see, sand and labor were used more frequently than other components. The problem was that the estimation of PPPs included combining complex components that reflected output prices with basic components that were essentially input prices.

The Country Product Dummy (CPD) regression method was used to obtain a PPP at the system level. The outcome of the BOCC approach was that the costs of each construction component could be compared directly between countries.

Weights

The original goal of the BOCC approach was to use different weights in each country for aggregating the basic and composite components to systems to reflect the relative importance of each within each construction system in each country. Annex B shows that the components of the systems for residential and nonresidential construction are essentially the same except for a single item of equipment hire. However, each component and system within the basic heading was to receive different weights relevant to residential and nonresidential construction, respectively.

The BOCC approach was designed to use weights at three separate levels known as the W1, W2, and W3 weights. The W1 weights were the expenditure aggregates for the three basic headings making up construction—that is, gross fixed capital formation on residential buildings, nonresidential buildings, and civil engineering works. The W2 weights were intended to be used in aggregating the system PPPs to the basic heading. The W3 weights were intended to weight together the component PPPs in order to obtain the system PPPs underlying each of the three basic headings.

In practice, the W1 weights were provided by all countries. However, their quality varied because some countries did not compile estimates of expenditures on GDP (including construction) as a regular part of their national accounts. In such cases, special procedures were adopted to estimate values for these basic headings (see chapter 3 for details).

The process intended to obtain W2 weights was to employ a construction expert to advise on the shares that each of the systems would have within each of the three basic headings within gross fixed capital formation on construction. The idea was to use bills of quantity from past investigations into construction projects (e.g., for estimating the weights for time series price indexes of construction). However, an insufficient number of countries had access to these types of data to make the approach viable, and so regional average weights were used for all countries within each region other than Western Asia. There, subregional weights were used, one set for Gulf countries and another set for the remaining countries within the region.

The original purpose of the W3 weights was to aggregate relative prices for the basic and composite components up to the system level. They were designed to take into account the potentially diverse shares of the components of construction in different countries (even within a single region). But as occurred for the W2 weights, it proved impossible to derive the W3 weights, and so component PPPs were aggregated to those for systems without weights using the CPD method.

The inability of countries to provide the data required to apply the W2 and W3 weights was the major shortcoming of the BOCC approach. Other significant shortcomings were as follows:

- Expert consultants were required for the data collection and validation, which increased the data collection costs and moved the work out of the national statistical office.

- The BOCC comparison was essentially a comparison of basic components. The extra cost of obtaining the composite component costs was not justified because they were weighted equally with basic components in the PPP estimation process.
- Because of the mixture of input and output prices, the goal of including productivity in the measurement was not met.
- Because profit and overhead margins were not included for either the composite or basic components, the PPPs were not consistent with the price structures in the national accounts expenditures for construction.

Data Validation

The procedures adopted for validating construction prices were similar to those used for other parts of the ICP. The first step was to check the consistency of prices collected for similar products in different localities within a country. The next step was to compare similar products in different countries, an exercise undertaken by the ICP's regional offices. Countries were grouped in two ways for this part of the exercise, first by subregion and second by the similarity of construction techniques. Countries were consulted on any apparent inconsistencies, and any revisions to prices as a result of this stage were incorporated into the process. In some regions, a final stage was to convene a small group of construction experts who examined the relative prices within each country and compared prices across countries. Based on their experience in the construction industry, they flagged any prices that appeared to be implausible, and the regional office then followed up these queries with the countries involved if time permitted.

Linking Regions

The 2005 ICP was conducted in six regions: five geographic regions—Africa, Asia-Pacific, CIS, South America, and Western Asia—plus the Eurostat-OECD "region." The results for each of these regions were obtained independently of those for each of the other regions. The final step in the 2005 ICP was to amalgamate the results for the countries in each region into a set of worldwide results that would enable any pair of countries to be compared, no matter in which region their initial results were compiled.

Chapter 8 in this volume is an overview of the process followed to calibrate the regional PPPs to a global level and enable the comparison of countries in different regions. As described in that chapter, a global list of products was established for household consumption. Two to four countries—so-called Ring countries—from each region priced this global list in addition to the products in their regional comparison. The PPPs from the global list were used to estimate regional linking factors to combine the regional PPPs. This process was followed for the household consumption basic headings. The BOCC methodology described earlier was followed by the Africa, Asia-Pacific, Western Asia, and South America regions. Therefore, the same data were used to compute the linking factors. The four Ring countries from the Eurostat-OECD region provided the BOCC data as well as the BOQ data. The Russian Federation priced both the BOQ and its regional specifications, and thus was used as the linking country to bring the CIS region into the global set of PPPs.

Some Interesting Comparisons

The ICP provides several ways in which to compare the effects of construction in different countries. The real expenditure on construction, expressed in international dollars with the United States as the base, indicates which countries contribute the most to construction activity worldwide. The GDPs of the world's 10 largest economies are shown in table 13.1, together with their real expenditures on construction. It is no surprise to see that the world's three largest economies—the United States, China, and Japan—also have the largest real expenditures on construction for the 2005 reference year. However, construction activity in China, the world's second-largest economy, is almost double that in the world's largest economy (United States), with real expenditures in international dollars of $2,623,761 million and $1,341,500 million, respectively. Japan is a distant third with $497,295 million, followed closely by India with $496,908 million.

Four countries outside the 10 largest economies have real expenditures on construction that are higher than some of those included in the latter group. They are the Republic of Korea ($254,042 million), Indonesia ($203,274 million), Spain ($191,726 million), and Canada ($157,426 million). Together, they contribute an additional 9.1 percent of the world's construction activity.

The most prominent aspect of table 13.1 is the extremely large share of worldwide construction activity contributed by China (29.8 percent of the total, compared with a 9.7 percent share of world GDP). When measured by adjusting to a common currency using exchange rates, China's share of worldwide construction activity is only 11.7 percent, while that of the United States is 25.3 percent (the corresponding shares of world GDP are 5.1 percent and 27.9 percent). The reason for the large difference is that these shares are not adjusted for the effect of the differences in price levels between China and the United States. It emphasizes the importance of compiling PPPs, which adjust for both differences in exchange rates and price levels between countries.

TABLE 13.1 GDPs and Real Expenditures on Construction, World's 10 Largest Economies

Country	GDP (international $ millions)	GDP, share of world (%)	Construction expenditure (international $ millions)	Construction expenditure, share of world (%)
United States	12,376,100	22.5	1,341,500	15.2
China	5,333,230	9.7	2,623,761	29.8
Japan	3,870,282	7.0	497,295	5.6
Germany	2,514,783	4.6	212,933	2.4
India	2,340,997	4.3	496,908	5.6
United Kingdom	1,901,710	3.5	141,765	1.6
France	1,862,193	3.4	216,964	2.5
Russian Federation	1,697,541	3.1	146,408	1.7
Italy	1,626,326	3.0	188,984	2.1
Brazil	1,583,162	2.9	144,515	1.6
Total, top 10	35,106,324	63.9	6,011,033	68.2
World	54,975,662	100.0	8,818,601	100.0

Source: ICP 2005.

TABLE 13.2 Per Capita Real Expenditures on Construction and GDPs: 10 Countries/Economy

Country/ Economies	GDP (international $)	GDP index (world = 100.0)	Construction (international $)	Construction index (world = 100.0)
Qatar	68,696	765.8	18,850	1,309.9
Kuwait	44,947	501.0	11,692	812.5
Luxembourg	70,014	780.4	9,153	636.1
Macao SAR, China	37,256	415.3	9,138	635.0
Iceland	35,630	397.2	7,894	548.6
Bahrain	27,236	303.6	6,922	481.0
Singapore	41,479	462.4	6,815	473.6
Ireland	38,058	424.2	6,696	465.3
Korea, Rep.	21,342	237.9	5,277	366.7
Brunei Darussalam	47,465	529.1	4,910	341.2
World	8,971	100.0	1,439	100.0

Source: ICP 2005.

A very different picture is observed when per capita real expenditures on construction are compared. Table 13.2 shows these expenditures for the 10 countries with the largest per capita real construction expenditures worldwide, together with their real expenditures on GDP.

Table 13.2 presents a completely different perspective on construction activity. The top 10 countries classified on the basis of their per capita real expenditures on construction do not include any of the world's 10 largest economies. In each case, their per capita real expenditures are several times as large as the world average, and the largest (Qatar, index = 1,309.9) is more than 12 times the world average.

Lessons Learned from Using the BOCC in ICP 2005

The underlying principle of the BOCC was that the construction costs of residential and nonresidential buildings and civil engineering works could be compared by pricing the major components of the construction of each. The set of 34 components identified for pricing included 12 that were basic input items such as building materials, labor, and the rental costs for four types of equipment. The data collection form for each basic item captured the average purchaser's cost for different quantities, such as three different quantities of Portland cement (annex C). The costs of skilled labor were obtained for six different occupations, ranging from bricklayers to machine operators, and aggregated into a single "skilled labor" category (annex C).

The 22 composite components included parts of the construction process such as earthworks, a column footing, or an interior wall. The data to be collected for each composite component included materials, labor, and equipment. However, the main objective was to obtain the total cost of each component, which was the comparison variable—that is, the equivalent of the price for a single product. Meanwhile, there was considerable overlap between the composite components and basic items. For example, a column footing is a composite component, but the total cost included concrete (which is also a composite component), reinforcing steel, and different kinds of skilled and unskilled labor, which were basic components that were also priced separately. The difference was that the concrete etc. in the composite component was included as a total cost, whereas an average price was captured for each basic item.

The idea of pricing composite components was based on the premise that it would be easier to calculate the cost of components than the cost of an entire project. In addition, it was assumed that the components were fundamental parts of construction projects that were comparable across countries. The total cost of a component would then capture the relative trade-offs between countries of labor versus capital. In other words, the component costs reflected the relative contributions of labor, equipment, and materials in each country. Although the costs of the composite components were assumed to be more easily obtained than the data on the bills of quantities, in practice the input of experts was still required for data collection.

The component costs were based on the purchasers' prices of the material, labor, and rental of equipment. These costs did not include any profit margin or overhead expenses for architects and other construction experts. The comparison based on costs assumes that the profit margins and overhead costs are proportional to the overall costs across countries.

The basic and composite components were combined into different sets of systems for residential and nonresidential dwellings and civil engineering works. Four composite components (aggregate base, earthwork, exterior sidewalk, and concrete) and six basic items (aggregate, Portland cement, sand, backhoe (hire), unskilled labor, and skilled labor) were combined in the site work system. The comparison variable for each composite item was the total cost, and the average price was used for basic components. The composite component costs included the combined total cost of materials, labor, and equipment. For example, the total cost of labor in the composite component would be correlated with the average input costs of the different types of workers. Some additional points follow:

- Each system for PPP estimation was to be treated like a basic heading, which meant there would be no weights applied to the composite component costs and basic item prices within each system.
- The basic input items were not independent—for example, concrete includes cement, sand, and aggregates, all of which were also included as basic components.
- The sidewalk composite component also includes concrete (which is made up of cement, sand, and aggregate).
- If the total cost were provided for every composite component and average prices for every basic item, 24 variables would be priced for the site work system.
- Even though there were no explicit quantity weights within any system, the components were implicitly weighted because the "price" was the total cost of each of the separate elements. For example, the composite components made up only four of the 24 items. Sand was priced for three different components (two composite components and in its own right as a basic component), and so it effectively was three of the 24 items. Concrete, which reflects the prices of sand, cement, and aggregates, could be said to make up almost half of the variables being compared. Skilled labor, with its six different types, had twice the weight of the other composite components.
- A review of the other systems in annex B shows a similar pattern. The basic component—sand—appears in six of the eight systems, and skilled and unskilled labor are in seven of the eight systems. One could say, then, that the most important things to price for residential housing were sand and labor.

Once the PPPs for each system were computed, the next step was to weight these to the residential PPP. These system weights, or W2 weights, were to be determined for each country individually. Regions and countries were advised to use construction experts to obtain the system weights for each country as a whole, taking into account differences in the construction inputs in different areas in the country. In practice, it was difficult for most countries to furnish the system weights. As a result, system weights were determined for each region for the residential and non-residential and civil engineering basic headings. In effect, all countries within a region received the same weights for aggregation at this level.

Summary

The introduction of the BOCC approach in the 2005 ICP round was an attempt to produce robust comparisons of construction prices for all participating countries at an affordable cost. The data collection worked well. The regional linking was considered to be a much better process than that used in previous ICP rounds. However, the main problem with the BOCC approach was the inability of countries to provide the information required to produce the W2 and W3 weights, which were a critical part of the overall approach. In addition, the BOCC approach was intended to be sufficiently straightforward that pricing could be undertaken by staff in national statistical offices. However, in practice it proved necessary to use construction experts to collect the price data required for the BOCC approach.

Last but not least, the method called for pricing both the composite and basic components of construction. Although the composite components provided an output price reflecting productivity differences between countries, the prices still did not reflect profit and margin differences between countries. The basic component prices were, in effect, input prices, which did not capture productivity differences or profits and overhead. Mixing input with output prices reduced the attempt to partially measure output prices.

On the positive side, detailed specifications were developed for the basic and composite components that could be used as building blocks for future data collection for the ICP or for producer price indexes at the national level.

Possible alternative approaches are being investigated in the early stages of the 2011 ICP round to determine whether a potentially better method is available for comparing gross fixed capital formation on construction that could be introduced in that round.

ANNEX A

Construction Components Included in Basic Headings for Residential and Nonresidential Buildings and Civil Engineering Works, ICP 2005

Construction components	Residential buildings	Nonresidential buildings	Civil engineering works
Composite components			
Column footing	X	X	
Culvert			X
Drilled shaft			X
Earthwork	X	X	X
Electrical service point	X	X	
Exterior painting	X	X	
Exterior wall cement plaster	X	X	
Interior ceiling plaster	X	X	
Interior painting	X	X	
Interior wall ceiling plaster	X	X	
Roadway lane			X
Round bridge pier			X
Structural column (round)	X	X	
Structural column (square)	X	X	
Round bridge pier			X
Aluminum frame (window)	X	X	
Bridge T-beam			X
Bridge spread footing			X
Concrete airfield pavement			X
Exterior sidewalk	X	X	
Masonry interior wall	X	X	
Concrete	X	X	X
Basic inputs			
Equipment hire			
Backhoe	X	X	X
Vibratory plate compactor		X	X
Centrifugal pump			X
Sand filter			X

(*continued*)

Construction components	Residential buildings	Nonresidential buildings	Civil engineering works
Materials			
Portland cement	x	x	x
Aggregate	x	x	x
Sand	x	x	x
Reinforcing steel	x	x	x
Structural steel	x	x	x
Plywood	x	x	x
Labor			
Unskilled	x	x	x
Skilled	x	x	x

Source: World Bank 2007.

ANNEX B

Components of Systems: Residential and Nonresidential Buildings and Civil Engineering Works, ICP 2005

1. Components of systems for residential buildings

System	Component	System	Component
Site work	Aggregate base	Exterior shell	Aluminum frame window
	Earthwork		*Sand*
	Exterior sidewalk		*Portland cement*
	Concrete		*Unskilled labor*
	Aggregate		*Skilled labor*
	Portland cement	Interior partitions	Masonry interior wall
	Sand		*Portland cement*
	Backhoe		*Sand*
	Unskilled labor		*Plywood*
	Skilled labor		*Unskilled labor*
Substructure	Aggregate base		*Skilled labor*
	Column footing	Interior/exterior finishes	Exterior wall cement plaster
	Concrete		Interior ceiling plaster
	Aggregate		Interior wall plaster
	Portland cement		*Exterior paint*
	Reinforcing steel		*Interior paint*
	Sand		*Portland cement*
	Backhoe		*Sand*
	Plywood		*Plywood*
Superstructure	Structural column round		*Unskilled labor*
	Structural column square		*Skilled labor*
	Concrete	Mechanical and plumbing	*Unskilled labor*
	Aggregate		*Skilled labor*
	Portland cement	Electrical	Electrical service point
	Reinforcing steel		*Unskilled labor*
	Sand		*Skilled labor*
	Structural steel		
	Plywood		
	Unskilled labor		
	Skilled labor		

(continued)

2. Components of systems for nonresidential buildings

System	Component	System	Component
Site work	Aggregate base	Exterior shell	Aluminum frame window
	Earthwork		*Sand*
	Exterior sidewalk		*Portland cement*
	Concrete		*Unskilled labor*
	Aggregate		*Skilled labor*
	Portland cement	Interior partitions	Masonry interior wall
	Sand		*Portland cement*
	Backhoe		*Sand*
	Unskilled labor		*Plywood*
	Skilled labor		*Unskilled labor*
Substructure	Aggregate base		*Skilled labor*
	Column footing	Interior/exterior finishes	Exterior wall cement plaster
	Concrete		Interior ceiling plaster
	Aggregate		Interior wall plaster
	Portland cement		*Exterior paint*
	Reinforcing steel		*Interior paint*
	Sand		*Portland cement*
	Backhoe		*Sand*
	Plywood		*Plywood*
Superstructure	Structural column round		*Unskilled labor*
	Structural column square		*Skilled labor*
	Concrete	Mechanical and plumbing	*Vibratory plate compactor*
	Aggregate		*Unskilled labor*
	Portland cement		*Skilled labor*
	Reinforcing steel	Electrical	Electrical service point
	Sand		*Unskilled labor*
	Structural steel		*Skilled labor*
	Plywood		
	Unskilled labor		
	Skilled labor		

3. Components of systems for civil engineering works

System	Component	System	Component
Site work	Concrete	Superstructure	Roadway lane
	Aggregate base		Bridge T beam
	Earthwork		Concrete airfield pavement
	Portland cement		Concrete
	Aggregate		*Aggregate*
	Backhoe		*Plywood*
	Sand		*Portland cement*
	Unskilled labor		*Reinforcing steel*
	Skilled labor		*Sand*
Substructure	Round bridge pier		*Structural steel*
	Bridge spread footings		*Unskilled labor*
	Aggregate base		*Skilled labor*
	Concrete	Underground utility	Culvert
	Aggregate		Drilled shaft
	Portland cement		Concrete
	Reinforcing steel		*Backhoe*
	Sand		*Portland cement*
	Backhoe		*Sand*
	Plywood		*Sand filter*
	Unskilled labor		*Unskilled labor*
	Skilled labor		*Skilled labor*
Electrical equipment	Electrical service point	Mechanical equipment	*Vibratory plate compactor*
	Unskilled labor		*Centrifugal pump*
	Skilled labor		*Portland cement*
			Unskilled labor
			Skilled labor

Source: World Bank 2007.
Note: Basic inputs are shown in italics.

ANNEX C

Collection Forms: Portland Cement, Skilled Labor, and Interior Painting, ICP 2005

1. Portland cement

150200.0.23 Portland Cement

Observation [ ]
☐ (Auto Calc)

Source Information:

- Date of price collection (dd/mm/yyyy): [ ]
- Country: [ ]
- Describe source of price:
  - ☐ Material supply
  - ☐ Informal or temporary sales location
  - ☐ Average, Price Index data collection
  - ☐ General contractor
  - ☐ Specialty contractor
  - ☐ Other: ( )
- Price is for year:
  - ☐ 2005
  - ☐ 2006

Details:

Cement to be priced shall be ordinary Portland cement that is used for typical concrete work in a variety of residential, nonresidential, and civil works projects. Cement used for these purposes is generally categorized into the following categories:

- Type I – for use when the special properties specified for any other type are not required
- Type IA – air-entraining cement for the same uses as Type I, where air-entrapment is desired
- Type II – for general use, more especially when moderate sulfate resistance or moderate heat of hydration is desired
- Type IIA – air-entraining cement for the same uses as Type II, where air-entrapment is desired
- Type III – for use when high early strength is desired
- Type IIIA – air-entraining cement for the same uses as Type III, where air-entrapment is desired
- Type IV – for use when a low heat of hydration is desired
- Type V – for use when high sulfate resistance is desired

Even though the roman numerals-based designation of the types may be prevalent in only certain regions of the world, the general categorization is applicable worldwide. Whichever type of cement is most commonly used in the country should be priced.

Quality and Packaging:

- Package size (kg): [ ]
- Package type (paper sack, cloth sack, etc.): [ ]
- Volume effects:
  - Price for single package: [ ]
  - Discount for larger quantities: [ ]

Source:

- Domestic:
  Manufacturer: [ ]
- Imported:
  Country of origin: [ ]
  Manufacturer: [ ]

Product Characteristics:

Percent volcanic ash: [ ]
Fineness: [ ]
Compressive strength (MPa): [ ]
Type (I, II, III, IV, V, IA, IIA, IIIA): [ ]
Soundness: [ ]
Specific gravity: [ ]

Pricing Information:

Material costs *(in national currency)*

Type	Quantity (column 1)	Units of measure	Unit cost (column 2)	Extended material costs (column 1 × column 2)
Ordinary Portland cement	10.000	Cubic meters		0.00
Ordinary Portland cement	100.000	Cubic meters		0.00
Ordinary Portland cement	200.000	Cubic meters		0.00

Comments (*if any*):

2. Skilled labor

150200.0.29 Skilled Labor

Observation

☐ (Auto Calc)

Source Information:

- Date of price collection (dd/mm/yyyy):
- Country:
- Describe source of price:
  - ☐ General contractor
  - ☐ Specialty contractor
  - ☐ Average, Price Index data collection
  - ☐ Other: ( )
- Price is for year:
  - ☐ 2005 ☐ 2006

Details:

Provide details of the compensation of employees for the following six kinds of skilled workers:

- Bricklayer
- Plumber
- Carpenter
- Structural steel worker
- Electrician
- Machine operator

A **skilled worker** is one that has had training in one of these trades. The training may consist of an apprenticeship, on-the-job training, or training in a technical college or similar institution.

Compensation of employees includes wages and salaries (before deductions for social contributions such as health or retirement benefits, income taxes, or trade union dues) *plus* social contributions made by the employers, *plus* in-kind benefits such as meals or housing.

You may report one of the following:

- Rates per hour for regular hours (i.e., excluding overtime)
- Rates per day (specify the regular number, excluding overtime, of hours worked per day)
- Rates per week (specify the regular number, excluding overtime, of hours worked per week).

Depending on the choice to report rates per hour or per day or per week, you will need to impute rates for social security contributions and income in kind and record them in the table below.

The rates should refer to skilled labor employed on a construction project near a major urban center.

(*continued*)

Pricing Information:

Compensation of employees *(in national currency)*

		Complete one of these columns numbered 1 to 3				
	Compensation of employees	**Rate per hour (1)**	**Rate per day (2)**	**Regular hours worked per day**	**Rate per week (3)**	**Regular hours worked per week**
Bricklayer	Wages					
	Social security contributions paid by employers					
	Income in kind					
	Total	0.00	0.00		0.00	
Plumber	Wages					
	Social security contributions paid by employers					
	Income in kind					
	Total	0.00	0.00		0.00	
Carpenter	Wages					
	Social security contributions paid by employers					
	Income in kind					
	Total	0.00	0.00		0.00	
Structural steel worker	Wages					
	Social security contributions paid by employers					
	Income in kind					
	Total	0.00	0.00		0.00	
Electrician	Wages					
	Social security contributions paid by employers					
	Income in kind					
	Total	0.00	0.00		0.00	
Machine operator	Wages					
	Social security contributions paid by employers					
	Income in kind					
	Total	0.00	0.00		0.00	

Comments (*if any*):

3. Interior painting

150200.0.17 Interior Painting

Observation ☐ (Auto Calc)

Source Information:

- Date of price collection (dd/mm/yyyy):
- Country:
- Describe source of price:
  - ☐ Architect
  - ☐ Engineer
  - ☐ Average, Price Index data collection
  - ☐ General contractor
  - ☐ Specialty contractor
  - ☐ Other: ( )
- Price is for year:
  - ☐ 2005
  - ☐ 2006

Quantity and Details:

This component is intended for collection of pricing data for one mist coat and two full coats of emulsion paint on interior surface in a residential building or nonresidential building. The SPD (structured production description) is for painting as a finishing/decoration item. Assume that the surface to be painted is a plastered or rendered surface. For purposes of this pricing, assume that the painting is being provided on the first floor of a residential or nonresidential building (e.g., office building). The price is to be provided for 100 square meters of painting, including an allowance for a typical level of surface preparation (filling, patching, etc.). The plastered surfaces are to be perfectly smooth, free from defect, and ready for decorations. Assume new construction, without flooring installed, so drip/spill protection is not needed. Assume that window/door masking is required.

Product Characteristics:

- Paint Type:

Pricing Information:

Material costs *(in national currency)*

Type	Quantity (column 1)	Units of measure	Unit cost (column 2)	Extended material costs (column 1 × column 2)
Interior emulsion paint				0.00
				0.00
				0.00
				0.00
				0.00
				0.00
				0.00
TOTAL COST OF MATERIALS *(in national currency)*				**0.00 (a)**

Labor costs *(in national currency)*

Type	Number of hours required (column 1)	Rate per hour (column 2)	Extended labor costs (column 1 × column 2)
Unskilled labor			0.00
Skilled labor (list by type):			
			0.00
			0.00
			0.00
			0.00
TOTAL COST OF LABOR *(in national currency)*			**0.00 (b)**

(continued)

Equipment costs *(in national currency)*

Type	Number of hours required (column 1)	Rate per hour (column 2)	Extended labor costs (column 1 × column 2)
			0.00
			0.00
			0.00
			0.00
			0.00
			0.00
TOTAL COST OF EQUIPMENT *(in national currency)*			**0.00 (c)**
Total price for interior painting *(in national currency—sum of a, b, and c)*:			

Comments (*if any*):

REFERENCES

Commission of the European Communities, International Monetary Fund, Organisation for Economic Co-operation and Development, United Nations, and World Bank. 1993. *System of National Accounts 1993*. http://unstats.un.org/unsd/sna1993/toctop.asp?L1=5.

———. 2008. *System of National Accounts 2008*. http://unstats.un.org/unsd/nationalaccount/SNA2008.pdf.

Eurostat. 1999. *Handbook on Quarterly National Accounts*. http://epp.eurostat.ec.europa.eu/cache/ITY_OFFPUB/CA-22-99-781/EN/CA-22-99-781-EN.PDF.

Eurostat and OECD (Organisation for Economic Co-operation and Development). 2006. *Eurostat-OECD Methodological Manual on Purchasing Power Parities*. Paris: OECD.

Stapel, Silke (Eurostat). 2002. "The Eurostat Construction Price Surveys: History, Current Methodology and New Ways for the Future." Paper presented to the International Conference on ICP, World Bank, Washington, DC, March 11–13. http://siteresources.worldbank.org/ICPINT/Resources/Stapel-constructionF.doc.

Walsh, Kenneth, and Anil Sawhney. 2004a. *International Comparison of Cost for the Construction Sector: An Implementation Framework for the Basket of Construction Components Approach*. Report submitted to African Development Bank and World Bank Group. http://siteresources.worldbank.org/ICPINT/Resources/Implementation_Framework_for_BOCC_05.doc.

———. 2004b. *International Comparison of Cost for the Construction Sector: Process for Implementation of the Basket of Construction Components Approach*. Report submitted to African Development Bank and World Bank Group. http://siteresources.worldbank.org/ICPINT/Resources/Implementation_Process_for_BOCC_Approach_05.doc.

———. 2005. *International Comparison of Cost for the Construction Sector: Identification of Construction Systems and Components for the BOCC Approach*. Report submitted to World Bank Group. http://siteresources.worldbank.org/ICPINT/Resources/Identification_of_Construction_Systems_05.doc.

World Bank. 2007. *ICP 2005 Methodological Handbook*. http://web.worldbank.org/WBSITE/EXTERNAL/DATASTATISTICS/ICPEXT/0,,contentMDK:20962711~menuPK:2666036~pagePK:60002244~piPK:62002388~theSitePK:270065,00.html.

CHAPTER 14

Machinery and Equipment

Derek Blades

This chapter explains how products were defined and prices were collected for the expenditure classification "machinery and equipment" in the 2005 round of the International Comparison Program (ICP).

Several items of machinery and equipment—such as computers, motor vehicles, and furniture for restaurants and hotels—are purchased by households. It is not just the nature of the good that determines whether it falls within the classification machinery and equipment, but also who buys it. Identical passenger vehicles are classified as a household final consumption expenditure if households buy them, but as machinery and equipment if car rental companies buy them.

The procedure adopted for collecting prices for machinery and equipment in the 2005 ICP was similar to that used for household goods and services. Structured product descriptions (SPDs) were developed for different kinds of equipment and then converted to product specifications (PSs) so that comparable products could be priced in all countries. There were, however, some differences in that procedure and the one used for household goods and services.

- Because machinery and equipment are used in production, the technical characteristics that determine the performance of a machine or piece of equipment are very important. Examples of such characteristics are torque, power, speed, reach, and lifting capacity. However, for the 2005 ICP round many statistical offices may not have had the in-house expertise needed to appraise technical parameters of this kind. As a result, they may have needed to hire outside experts to decide whether particular kinds of equipment available in their countries were equivalent to those specified in the SPDs/PSs.
- A relatively small number of enterprises in some countries produce most of the machinery and equipment priced for the ICP. Thus countries were buying very similar products from a small number of manufacturers, and an SPD/PS for machinery and equipment typically referred to a specific model made by a particular producer.

- Machinery and equipment are purchased by producers—private enterprises, government, and nonprofit institutions. Because, as noted, the staff of statistical offices tend to be less familiar with machinery and equipment than with the goods and services purchased by households, the Global Office took the lead in drawing up the SPDs/PSs for the 2005 ICP round.
- Purchases of equipment tend to be made sporadically. Individual enterprises do not buy the same or similar types of equipment each year because that equipment is expected to last for several years. Thus in small countries there may be no purchases in some years of several types of equipment specified in the SPDs/PSs. It was therefore difficult in the 2005 ICP for countries to decide which products were sufficiently important to price.
- Some equipment goods are unique. Each one is designed for a specific location or purpose, and only one of its kind is produced. Examples are sea vessels, oil platforms, and nuclear power plants. No attempt was made in the ICP to price unique items of machinery and equipment. Pricing was confined to standard, generally mass-produced items.

In the ICP classification, the category machinery and equipment is broken down into two groups, metal products and equipment and transport equipment, and these are further disaggregated into eight basic headings (see boxes 14.1 and 14.2 for examples of the items included in the basic headings of these two groups). Countries are required to collect the prices of several specified items within most of these basic headings.

The first section of this chapter explains the standard method used by all countries taking part in the 2005 ICP (except for the 46 countries whose participation in the ICP was coordinated by Eurostat and the Organisation for Economic Co-operation and Development, OECD) to price machinery and equipment (also called equipment goods in the rest of this chapter). The method used by the Eurostat-OECD countries is described in the second section of this chapter. Both groups relied on very similar methods, thereby allowing a high degree of comparability between the resulting purchasing power parities (PPPs).

BOX 14.1 Coverage: Metal Products and Equipment Group

Fabricated metal products, except machinery and equipment. Prefabricated buildings of metal; bridges, bridge sections, towers, and lattice masts of iron or steel; reservoirs, tanks, vats, and similar containers of iron, steel, or aluminum for all materials; central heating radiators and boilers; steam generators; nuclear reactors; hand tools; casks, drums, cans, boxes, and similar containers of iron, steel, or aluminum for all materials except gas.

General-purpose machinery. Engines and turbines except aircraft, vehicle, and cycle engines; pumps and compressors; ovens other than bakery ovens; furnaces, furnace burners, and incinerators; lifting and handling equipment such as jacks and hoists for raising vehicles, derricks, cranes, forklift trucks, skip hoists, lifts, escalators, and moving walkways; nondomestic cooling and ventilation equipment.

Special-purpose machinery. Agricultural and forestry machinery; machine tools; machinery for metallurgy, mining, quarrying, and construction; machinery for food, beverage, and tobacco processing; machinery for textile, apparel, and leather production; other special-purpose machinery.

Electrical and optical equipment. Typewriters and word processing machines; cash registers; photocopying apparatus and printing machinery; automatic banknote dispensers and coin-sorting machines; computers and related equipment; electric motors, generators, and transformers; electricity distribution and control apparatus; accumulators and batteries; lighting equipment; radio and television equipment; electric apparatus for line telephony; sound or video recording apparatus; medical, dental, and veterinary equipment, instruments, and appliances; instruments and appliances for measuring, checking, testing, navigating, and other purposes; industrial process control equipment.

Other manufactured goods n.e.c. (not elsewhere classified). Office, shop, and hotel furniture, etc.

Software. Computer software that a producer expects to use in production for more than one year; includes purchases of off-the-shelf software and expenditure on development of software within the enterprise.

BOX 14.2 Coverage: Transport Equipment Group

Motor vehicles, trailers, and semitrailers. Passenger cars, taxi cabs, vans, buses, coaches, trolley buses, lorries, trucks, tankers, tractor units for semitrailers, trailers, semitrailers, caravans, and special-purpose motor vehicles such as dumpers for off-highway use, breakdown lorries, crane lorries, ambulances, fire trucks, concrete mixer lorries, road sweeper lorries, mobile radiological units, and motorized sleighs, including their bodies (coachwork), specialized parts, and engines.

Other transport equipment. Cruise ships, excursion boats, ferry boats, hovercraft, cargo ships, barges, lighters, tankers, refrigerated vessels, fishing vessels, factory ships; tugboats and pusher craft, ice-breakers, dredgers, cable ships, light vessels, research vessels, and other nontrading ships (except naval ships); floating docks, floating dredges, oil rigs, and other floating or submersible drilling or production platforms; specialized ship parts other than engines; all vessels that have undergone extensive reconstruction and conversion; all railway and tramway locomotives, maintenance and service vehicles and rolling stock (such as passenger coaches, luggage vans, post office coaches, goods wagons, tank wagons, and refrigerated vans) intended for railway service or for service in mining and industrial operations; their specialized parts other than engines; airplanes, helicopters, balloons, gliders, spacecraft, and satellites, including their specialized parts and engines.

Experience from the 2005 ICP suggests that for the 2011 ICP some countries will not be able to follow the standard method for pricing machinery and equipment. Thus the third section of this chapter describes an alternative method that may be used—the price factor method (PFM). Suitable only for countries that import most of their machinery and equipment, it involves tracking the various costs or "price factors" that intervene between the ex-factory price of machinery and equipment and its price when installed by the purchaser.

The final section of this chapter draws lessons from the 2005 ICP for possible improvements in the 2011 ICP.

Standard Method for Pricing Equipment Goods

The standard method for pricing equipment goods is similar to that followed for consumer goods and services; countries collect prices for identical or very similar products—sometimes referred to as "specification pricing."

Pricing Rules

To be consistent with the national accounts, countries are required to provide prices for equipment goods that are consistent with the valuation of those goods as fixed capital assets in the national accounts. Thus the prices must include import duties and other product taxes actually paid by the purchaser, the costs of transporting the asset to the place where it will be used, and any charges for installing the asset so that it ready for use in production. Deducted from the price are any of the discounts generally available to most producers.

The following rules should be observed in reporting prices for equipment goods:

- *Transport costs.* When the prices of equipment goods do not include transport costs, these costs should be estimated by countries. They would determine the average distance over which the items are transported from the factory where they are made or, for imports, the port of entry.
- *Installation costs.* Costs are usually associated with the installation of fixed equipment, and these costs are included in the gross fixed capital formation (GFCF) in the national accounts. Installation charges include not only those paid by the purchaser for physical installation of an item at a factory or other site but also any charges for testing or calibrating the equipment. In the case of transport equipment, there are usually no installation costs.

- *Product taxes.* The price should only include nondeductible product taxes. Countries that levy a value added tax (VAT) normally allow purchasers to deduct the full amount of the tax on capital goods. Sales and other product taxes, and sometimes import duties, may also be fully or partly deductible on capital goods.
- *Discounts.* The price should refer to the purchase of a single item so that it is not affected by discounts that may be available for large orders. The price of the single item should be reported after deducting any discount that is customarily available to most purchasers and that is available for most of the year.

The national average prices are required. Country experts follow two guidelines in deciding how these prices are to be collected. First, in some small countries it may be sufficient to collect prices in only a single location such as the capital city or the largest industrial or commercial town. Second, in larger countries that have several centers of significant industrial and commercial activity, prices will have to be collected in several of these centers in order to calculate a national average price.

In many countries, a single dealer has the rights to sell the specified type of equipment. In this case, a single price observation will be sufficient. In other countries, however, there may be several distributors of the specified type of equipment, and in this case several price observations will be required to establish the average national price. The decision as to whether one or more price observations are necessary is left to the national experts.

The prices reported should be the average prices for the reference year—that is, they should be the average of the prices collected at regular intervals throughout the year. However, experience shows that if all countries price equipment goods during the same period, there is no need to collect prices throughout the year. Price collection at midyear was recommended for the 2005 ICP.

A significant proportion of the GFCF in equipment goods in some countries consists of imports of second-hand goods, some of which may have been reconditioned. Second-hand goods that are comparable for pricing purposes are difficult to find. Substantial quality adjustments may be necessary to make the prices comparable, and such quality adjustments are presently not feasible. Thus in the 2005 ICP price collection was confined to new equipment goods. The prices of second-hand equipment goods were not used even when those goods were actually more representative than new goods. Second-hand goods will also be omitted from pricing in the 2011 ICP.

Structured Product Descriptions for Equipment Goods

In the 2005 ICP, the SPDs were drawn up by the Global Office in much the same way as those for household consumer goods and services. However, for consumer goods and services each region converted the SPDs to product specifications after the participating countries agreed on which consumer goods and services are commonly purchased by households in their countries. For equipment goods, the Global Office converted the SPDs to PSs for 108 "core" items, and these PSs served as the starting point for the regional coordinators in drawing up their own regional lists. Regional lists included not only a minimum of 80 equipment goods drawn from the core list but also other equipment goods that were important for particular regions.

The SPDs/PSs drawn up by the Global Office were used in the following manner for the 2005 ICP:

- For each type of equipment good, the Global Office identified the manufacturers and model numbers of the equipment to be priced. At least two manufacturers and model numbers were specified for each SPD/PS.

- Countries were asked to provide prices for the models in the order of preference in which they were listed—specifically, the first model listed was to be priced by countries if it was available and in common use; if not, the next model in the list was to be priced, and so on.
- If two or more of the listed models were available and in common use, countries were asked to provide prices for all of them.
- If none of the models listed was available and in common use, countries were asked to price an equivalent model commonly used. An equivalent model was one that met the same needs with equal efficiency. The country entered the name of the manufacturer and the model number in the "other model" space on the SPD/PS reporting form (see box 14.3).

If countries decided to price a model other than one of those specified in the SPD/PS, they also had to provide information on the product characteristics. This part of the SPD/PS did not have to be completed if prices were reported for one of the specified items of equipment.

Format of an SPD/PS

Box 14.3 is an example of an SPD/PS for equipment goods. The air compressor depicted is commonly used to power construction equipment such as pneumatic drills and ground compactors. The form begins with a short description of an air compressor together with a picture of a typical model. The manufacturer's name and model number are then listed for the "preferred model," followed by two alternatives. If a country decided to price one or more of these three models, it provided the price information called for in the next part of the SPD/PS.

If a country decided to price none of the three specified models because they were not available or were only rarely purchased in the country, it selected an equivalent model and gave the manufacturer's name and model number in the space provided. It then supplied the price as well as the "product characteristics." Both the "main characteristics" and "other features" were required.

The product characteristics of "other models" were used by the regional coordinator to determine whether those models really were equivalent to one of the three specified models. If the coordinator decided that the other model was indeed equivalent, its price was used to calculate price relatives with whichever of the three specified models was considered most similar to the other model. If the other model was found to be not equivalent to any of the three specified models, the price information was discarded, or the regional coordinator found the other model to be equivalent to another model priced by another country. In this case, a new product was created for this type of air compressor, and the price information was used to calculate a PPP for the two counties concerned (new products created this way are referred to as "splittings.")

Core Items and Regional Lists

Table 14.1 shows how the 108 core items identified by the Global Office for the 2005 ICP were distributed among the basic headings for equipment goods. The full list of the core items used in the 2005 ICP appears in annex A.

When regions drew up their own lists for the equipment goods to be priced, they looked first at these 108 items and included at least 80 of them in their own regional lists. They also included items not on the core list if those items were important in their countries.

Sources of Price Information

The prices of equipment goods can be obtained directly from producers, importers, or distributors, or from their catalogues. For the 2005 ICP, the prices were collected by the method or combination of methods that countries found the most convenient such as personal visit, telephone, letter, or Internet.

BOX 14.3 Example of SPD/PS for Equipment Goods

Basic Heading: General-Purpose Machinery Basic Heading Code: 150112.1
Product Name: COMPRESSOR **Code: 01**

DESCRIPTION
These are air compressors. They may be electrically driven or powered by a diesel or gasoline engine. They are most often used to power construction and drilling equipment.

MANUFACTURER AND MODEL NUMBER

Preference order	Manufacturer	Model number
Preferred model	Atlas-Copco	XM 659P
Alternative 1	Mitsubishi	400098
Alternative 2	Rand	L-M 51
Other model	Specify ________	Specify ________

PRICE (in local currency units)

A	**Price of equipment**	
B	Installation cost if not included in A	
C	Transportation cost if not included in A	
D	Nondeductible tax if not included in A	
E	Deductible tax if included in A	
F	Discount if not included in A	
G	**Total cost [A + B + C + D − E − F]**	

PRODUCT CHARACTERISTICS
This part is to be completed only if *other model* has been priced.
Main Characteristics

Power required (kW)	
Max. pressure (bars)	
Rated operating pressure (bars)	
Rated delivery volume (liters/min.)	
Shipping weight (kg)	
Max. speed (rpm)	
Sound level	
Maximum pressure (dBA)	
Operating pressure and volume (dBA)	

BOX 14.3 Example of SPD/PS for Equipment Goods (*continued*)

Other Features

Rotary
☐ Rotary screw
☐ Reciprocating piston
Integral storage (liters): __________
Number of stages: __________
Outlet size: __________
Number of outlets: __________
☐ Sump drain
☐ Storage drain
Cooling: ☐ Air
☐ Liquid
☐ Closed system
☐ Open system

Controls: ☐ Mechanical ☐ Electrical
☐ Hydraulic ☐ Electronic

☐ Integral discharge dryer
☐ Portable
☐ Stationary

Height (mm): __________
Length (mm): __________
Width (mm): __________

Drive: ☐ Belt
☐ Shaft/disconnect
☐ Direct/coupled

TABLE 14.1 Core List of Equipment Goods, ICP 2005

Basic heading	Description	Number of products
150111.1	FABRICATED METAL PRODUCTS	5
150112.1	GENERAL-PURPOSE MACHINERY	15
	A. Engines and turbines, pumps, and compressors	10
	B. Other general-purpose machinery	5
150113.1	SPECIAL-PURPOSE MACHINERY	39
	A. Agricultural and forestry machinery	2
	B. Machine tools	6
	C. Machinery for metallurgy, mining, quarrying, and construction	22
	D. Machinery for food, beverage, and tobacco processing	4
	E. Machinery for textile, apparel, and leather production	0
	F. Other special-purpose machinery	5
150114.1	ELECTRICAL AND OPTICAL EQUIPMENT	29
	A. Office machinery	5
	B. Computers and other information processing equipment	9
	C. Electrical machinery and apparatus	2
	D. Radio, television, and communications equipment and apparatus	3
	E. Medical, precision, and optical instruments, watches, and clocks	10
150115.1	OTHER MANUFACTURED GOODS n.e.c.	0
150121.1	MOTOR VEHICLES, TRAILERS, AND SEMITRAILERS	11
150121.2	OTHER ROAD TRANSPORT	0
150122.1	OTHER TRANSPORT	0
150311.1	SOFTWARE	9
TOTAL		108

Source: ICP.

However, the prices had to be adjusted to conform to the valuation principles that, as just described, called for taking into account transport charges, installation costs, product taxes, and discounts.

The sources most often used for collecting the price information were the following:

- *Within a national statistical office.* Those who compile a producer price or an import price index are likely to have the most familiarity with the types of goods being compared for these basic headings. For some items such as automobiles and computers, the comparisons used for household consumption are also relevant to equipment, although the prices collected for the household consumption expenditure had to be adjusted by subtracting the value added taxes and other product taxes that are payable by households but usually can be deducted by enterprises.
- *Within the country.* Equipment distributors and dealers know which models are available, their detailed characteristics, and prices. When prices were obtained from dealers, countries had to ensure that all product taxes and installation charges were included.

  Government departments purchase transport and other equipment on a regular basis. Such purchases are often centralized under a "public works" or "central supply" department. They may buy directly from manufacturers, but often they will also use local dealers and distributors.
- *Outside the country.* A list of websites of equipment goods manufacturers was provided to countries for the 2005 ICP. Websites, which are often available in more than one language and may be tailored to a particular region, usually give all the technical information needed for the SPDs/PSs. They often also provide the names and contact information for dealers and distributors. However, in the 2005 ICP round the price information obtained from websites had to be adjusted to conform to the valuation principles just outlined for taking into account transport charges, installation costs, product taxes, and discounts.

Editing Prices

In the 2005 ICP, the main responsibility for editing the technical characteristics of the goods that countries priced for the equipment goods survey rested with the regional coordinator. Countries, however, had to ensure that the regional coordinator was able to identify matches and mismatches among the goods priced. Before sending their prices to the regional coordinator, countries were required to verify that the reporting forms were complete—that is, they contained the name and number of the make and model priced and the product characteristics. It is in the interest of countries to provide this information from the beginning because it reduces the subsequent response burden that editing imposes.

Editing the prices of equipment goods by simply examining and comparing their prices alone is not sufficient because of the complexity of the items priced. The prices for some specifications may appear plausible and consistent across countries, but the goods priced are not necessarily comparable. The technical characteristics of the items that are not outliers still must be checked against each other, and any mismatches discovered must be treated in the same manner as outliers identified by the editing procedure.

In the 2005 ICP round, the technical characteristics of outliers identified by regional coordinators using the Dikhanov or Quaranta editing procedure were checked against the technical characteristics of the items priced by other countries. As a result, either the technical characteristics of the outlier matched the technical characteristics of the items priced by at least some of the other countries, or the technical characteristics did not match the technical characteristics of any of the items priced by the other countries. In the first case, the outlier was referred back to the reporting country, which was asked to confirm the price. In the second case, the country was asked to provide a price for an equipment good whose technical characteristics matched the technical characteristics of the goods priced by some of the other countries. Depending on the country's response, the price of the outlier was retained, replaced, or dropped.

Eurostat-OECD Methodology

The general approach used for the Eurostat-OECD countries was very similar to the standard method used by other regions, although there were some differences in detail.[1] The sample Eurostat-OECD product specification and reporting form shown in box 14.4 is for a tractor unit—that is, the power unit of a heavy-goods vehicle consisting of the engine, driver's cab, and power train. Countries were asked to price a particular model of a Mercedes-Benz tractor unit. One difference between this form and the SPD/PS described earlier is that the product characteristics of the proposed model are listed, and even if a country prices precisely this model it is still required to report the product characteristics because a model may have different technical characteristics in other countries. The standard method followed by other regions and described in previous section assumes that a model number guarantees that it will be identical no matter where it is sold.

In the example shown in box 14.4, the reporting country (Austria) had priced a different make and model because, as explained in the notes section, "The model specified is not available. Expected on the market early next year." The Scania tractor unit differs from the proposed model in a number of ways—for example, it is heavier, has fewer gears, and has a higher power output. The Austrian pricing experts, nevertheless, concluded that the Scania is equivalent to the Mercedes-Benz, and Eurostat-OECD agreed with them.

The SPDs/PSs used in the standard method for the 2005 ICP listed all the alternative models on the same reporting form. By contrast, each Eurostat-OECD form referred to a single make and model, but there were usually several alternatives for each product. In the case of a tractor unit, for example, three different models were proposed, and three separate forms were provided. Unlike the SPD/PS, the Eurostat-OECD form did not specifically ask countries to propose their own models if none of the proposed models was considered suitable. However, countries were allowed to report the prices of models that were judged to be technically different from the proposed models, which could lead to the creation of new products ("splittings") in the same way described earlier for the standard method.

Table 14.2 shows the number of products, the number of alternative specifications, and the minimum number of products that the Eurostat-OECD countries were required to price for each type of equipment for the 2005 ICP round. For most types, countries were required to price between three and five items.

Another difference between the Eurostat-OECD reporting form and the SPD/PS described in the previous section is that the Eurostat-OECD countries were required to specify whether the products they had priced were "representative." According to the Eurostat-OECD PPP manual, "the product priced is representative [if] its price level is representative of the price level in the country for that type of product. Representative products are usually those most frequently sold. As representative products generally have lower price levels than unrepresentative products, it is important to know about the representativity of products when validating their prices and calculating their PPPs" (Eurostat and OECD 2006). In explanation, the equipment goods that a country has identified as representative are given more weight in calculating its PPPs, and it is widely accepted that this method produces a more accurate set of PPPs.

BOX 14.4 Product Specification and Price Reporting Form Used by Eurostat-OECD: An Example

EQUIPMENT GOODS SURVEY 200X				**Country**
16.11: Tractor unit				***Austria***
Product		**Proposed**		**Priced**
Make (and nationality):		Mercedes Benz (German)		***Scania (Swedish)***
Model:		ABC–18-4x2		***XYZ-19-4x2***
Specifications		**Metric**	**Imperial**	**National**
01	GVW	18,000 kg	17.7 tons	***19,000 kg***
02	Wheelbase	5,700 mm	224 in.	***5,500 mm***
03	Engine capacity	11,946 L	729 cu. in.	***12.0 L***
04	Engine power output	292 kW	394 bhp	***338 kW***
05	Gearbox: number of forward speeds	16	16	***14***
06	Type of suspension: front	spring	spring	***spring***
07	Type of suspension: rear	air	air	***air***
08	Type of braking	ABS	ABS	***ABS***
09	Type of cab	1,845 mm	73 in.	***1,900 mm***
10	With standard roof	yes	yes	***yes***
11	Fixed fifth wheel coupling	included	included	***included***
12				
Terms and conditions				
a	Order quantity	one	one	***one***
b	Unit price	one	one	***10,500***
c	Currency	specify	specify	***euros***
d	Delivery costs to be included	yes	yes	***yes***
e	Installation costs to be included	no	no	***no***
f	Discount to be included	yes (%)	yes (%)	***−525 (i.e., 5% of the unit price of €10,500)***
Total unit price without VAT				9,975
Representativity and comparability				
Is the product priced representative (yes) or unrepresentative (no)?				***yes***
Is the product priced identical (1), equivalent (2), or not comparable (3) to the one specified?				***2***
Options				
Price of standard model. No options available.				
Notes				
The model specified is not available. Expected on the market early next year.				
Delivery costs not invoiced separately. Included in unit price.				
Website address				
www.mercedesbenz.com				

Note: This example merely illustrates the basic format and content of the reporting form; the technical details and reported price are fictitious.

TABLE 14.2 Pricing Schedule: Eurostat-OECD Countries, 2003

Expenditure classification code	Price collecting code	Basic heading	Number of products	Number of alternative specifications	Minimum number of *products* to be priced
150111.1	01	Fabricated metal products, except machinery and equipment	5	13	3
150112.1	02	Engines and turbines, pumps, and compressors	4	6	3
150112.2	03	Other general-purpose machinery	6	17	4
150113.1	04	Agricultural and forestry machinery	10	28	5
150113.2	05	Machine tools	7	11	5
150113.3	06	Machinery for metallurgy, mining, quarrying, and construction	5	9	3
150113.4	07	Machinery for food, beverage, and tobacco processing	5	15	3
150113.5	08	Machinery for textile, apparel, and leather production	7	12	5
150113.6	09	Other special-purpose machinery	6	17	5
150114.1	10	Office machinery	4	9	3
150114.2	11	Computers and other information processing equipment	7	13	6
150114.3	12	Electrical machinery and apparatus	6	15	4
150114.4	13	Radio, television, and communications equipment and apparatus	5	5	4
150114.5	14	Medical, precision, and optical instruments, watches, and clocks	11	22	7
15a0115.1	15	Other manufactured goods n.e.c.	3	6	3
150121.1	16	Motor vehicles, trailers, and semitrailers	18	30	12
150312.1	17	Software	7	7	5
Total			116	235	80

Source: ICP.
Note: The pricing schedule is not fixed. It evolves from one price survey to the next.

Overall, it is clear that the Eurostat-OECD methodology and the standard method described in the preceding section were very similar. However, there were some differences:

- The Eurostat-OECD countries were required to conduct "presurveys" to determine the availability of different types of equipment and whether new products had been introduced or old products phased out. They then used the presurvey results when they jointly drew up the product list.
- The Eurostat-OECD reporting form allowed for the possibility that a given model number may have different technical characteristics when sold in different markets.
- The Eurostat-OECD countries were required to identify representative products.

For these reasons, the Eurostat-OECD approach is likely to produce more accurate PPPs, but the two methods are sufficiently similar to ensure good comparability between the Eurostat-OECD countries and those in other regions.

Calculating Approximate PPPs Using the Price Factor Method (PFM)

The standard method, which requires countries to price specified products, is generally accepted as the most accurate way to calculate PPPs for equipment goods. The alternative, the price factor method, is certainly inferior, but it is described here because the standard method proved difficult for many countries in the 2005 ICP. The SPDs/PSs referred to items that were not commonly used in their countries, or purchases of specific types of equipment goods were sporadic, making it difficult to identify a realistic price for a piece of equipment that may not have been purchased in a recent year. Another problem was expense; national statistical offices usually do not have the in-house expertise needed to collect prices for equipment goods. Some had to hire equipment experts to identify the products specified in the SPD/PS or find close substitutes if what was specified in the SPD/PS was not available in their countries. In some cases, outside experts also had to be consulted to determine the price.

The method described here is a fallback solution for countries that do not have the financial resources or expertise to use the standard method. It is called the price factor method because it involves decomposing the price of machinery and equipment into its component "price factors." The countries that would use the PFM would import almost all of their equipment goods, and so the PFM starts with the ex-factory price of an equipment good in the exporting country and follows it through to its final price when it is installed and ready to use in the importing country.

Pros and Cons of the Price Factor Method

One advantage of the PFM is that (approximate) PPPs are obtained using information that is already available in many national statistical offices. Countries that have an input-output or supply and use table—even if it not very recent—will have estimates of the margins and other costs required by the PFM. Countries that use a commodity flow method for estimating gross fixed capital formation will have the estimates as well. For these reasons, the PFM is an attractive alternative for countries with limited resources.

By means of the standard method, PPPs are obtained from the ratios of the prices of particular types of equipment goods *installed and ready for use* at the purchasers' establishments in each country. For an imported equipment good, this price can be broken down into the ex-factory price of the good and a series of costs, or "margins," that the purchaser incurs to bring it from where it was produced to where it will be used in production. These margins are shown in box 14.5. They consist essentially of transport and trade margins, customs duties and other taxes, and, except for transport equipment, installation costs.

Consider two countries, A and B, that import a particular kind of equipment good from the same producer. If all the margins incurred by countries A and B are expressed in a common currency—say U.S. dollars—then

$$\frac{P_A}{P_B} = \frac{XR_{\frac{A}{US}}(F + a_1 + a_2 + \cdots + a_n)}{XR_{\frac{B}{US}}(F + n_1 + b_2 + \cdots + b_n)} \tag{14.1}$$

where P_A and P_B are the installed, ready-to-use prices of the machine in countries A and B, both expressed in their national currencies; $XR_{\frac{A}{US}}$ and $XR_{\frac{B}{US}}$ are the number of units of A's and B's currency that can be purchased for US$1.00; F is the ex-factory price of the machine in U.S. dollars; $a_1 \ldots$ are the n margins in U.S. dollars incurred by the importer in country A, both in the exporting

BOX 14.5 Components of the Price of an Imported Equipment Good Installed and Ready for Use in the Importing Country

Ex-factory price in exporting country

plus	surcharge minus discount for country or region
plus	product taxes minus subsidies in exporting country
plus	trade margin in exporting country
plus	transport within exporting country
plus	wharfage (fee for using the wharf) in exporting country
plus	fee for customs documentation in exporting country
equals	*f.o.b. (free on board) price in exporting country*
plus	international freight
plus	insurance costs
equals	*c.i.f. (cost, insurance, freight) price in importing country*
plus	fee for customs documentation in importing country
plus	customs duty in importing country
plus	wharfage (fee for using the wharf) in importing country
plus	product taxes minus subsidies in importing country
plus	trade margins in importing country
plus	transport within importing country
plus	installation costs at the purchaser's establishment
equals	*installed, ready-to-use price in importing country*

country and in country A itself; and $b_1 \ldots$ are the n margins in U.S. dollars incurred by the importer in country B, both in the exporting country and in country B itself.

Because $\frac{P_A}{P_B}$ is the bilateral *purchasing power parity* for the machine in question with B as the base country, and because $\frac{XR_{\frac{A}{US}}}{XR_{\frac{B}{US}}}$ is the exchange rate between countries A and B, equation (14.1) can be rewritten as

$$PPP_{\frac{A}{B}} = \frac{XR_{\frac{A}{B}}(F + a_1 + a_2 + \cdots + a_n)}{(F + b_1 + b_2 + \cdots b_n)} \tag{14.2}$$

where $PPP_{\frac{A}{B}}$ is the bilateral PPP using B as the base country, and $XR_{\frac{A}{B}}$ is the exchange rate between countries A and B—specifically, the number of units of currency A that can be purchased by one unit of currency B.

If the a's and b's are converted to ratios of the ex-factory price and are denoted by α's and β's, equation (14.2) can be rewritten as

$$PPP_{\frac{A}{B}} = \frac{XR_{\frac{A}{B}}\left(F + F\sum_{i=1}^{n}\alpha_i\right)}{F + F\sum_{i=1}^{n}\beta_i} \tag{14.3}$$

or

$$PPP_{\frac{A}{B}} = XR_{\frac{A}{B}}\left(\frac{1 + \sum_{i=1}^{n}\alpha_i}{1 + \sum_{i=1}^{n}\beta_i}\right). \tag{14.4}$$

The term in brackets in (14.4) is an *adjustment factor*, required so that the exchange rate between countries A and B equals the PPP. It is one plus the sum of the margins paid in one country divided by one plus the sum of the margins paid in the other. These margins are the various items listed in box 14.5, expressed as ratios of the ex-factory price.

Practical Application

Data limitations require three modifications of the formulation of the "ideal" PFM given in equation (14.4).

When Ex-factory Prices Are Not Available

The adjustment factor in equation (14.4) requires knowledge of the ex-factory price of the piece of equipment in the exporting country. In practice, however, statistical offices in importing countries do not have information on ex-factory prices, nor do they usually have any information on the costs or margins incurred in the exporting country from the point at which the goods are being delivered to the point from which they are being exported.

Therefore, the costs or margins must be converted to the ratios of some other price that is likely to be similar in the countries concerned even if it is not identical. The best choice would be the f.o.b. price in the exporting country, but most countries record their imports at c.i.f. values—that is, they include the freight and insurance costs incurred to bring the goods to the port of entry. *It is therefore suggested here that the c.i.f. values of imported machinery and equipment be converted to an approximate f.o.b. basis using the ratio of total international insurance and freight charges to total merchandise imports.*

Moving from PPPs for Specific Types of Equipment Goods to Averages for All Equipment Goods

The earlier discussion dealt with a specific equipment good imported from a specific producer in an exporting country. However, it is proposed here that exchange rates be adjusted to approximate PPPs for two broad groups of equipment goods imported from all sources: metal products and equipment (150110.0) and transport equipment (150120.0). This adjustment means that the various margins used for the adjustment factor in equation (14.4) will not be the costs incurred for importing a specific type of equipment and machinery from a particular country, but rather averages for all of the two types of equipment goods from whatever country they are imported. For example, the transport margins must be the average margins charged on transporting metal products and equipment as a whole and transport equipment as a whole from the port of arrival to the place where they are to be used. The customs margin must be the average rate charged on imported metal products and equipment as a whole and on imported transport equipment as a whole.

Ignoring Some Margins

Several of the margins listed in box 14.5 may be zero or small relative to the initial ex-factory price and can be ignored. In addition, statisticians in the importing countries will not be able to estimate the costs incurred in the exporting country. The costs and margins that are likely to be relatively large and that countries could reasonably be expected to report are as follows:

- Customs duties
- Nondeductible VAT and other taxes on products

- Transport costs in the importing country
- Wholesale and retail trade margins in the importing country
- Installation costs.

Countries are also required to provide the c.i.f. values of imports of the two groups of equipment goods, the c.i.f. value of total merchandise imports, and the insurance and freight costs of total merchandise imports. The reporting form for collecting these eight items for the two groups of equipment goods, metal products and equipment and transport equipment, appears in annex B.

Calculating the Adjustment Factor

The information collected on the reporting form in annex B can be used by the regional coordinators to calculate an approximate version of the adjustment factor $\left(\frac{1 + \sum_{i=1}^{n}\alpha_i}{1 + \sum_{i=1}^{n}\beta_i}\right)$ and multiply it by the exchange rate to obtain an approximate PPP. The four steps are as follows:

1. The reported c.i.f. value of imports of each of the two groups of equipment goods—metal products and machinery and transport equipment—is converted to an approximate f.o.b. value using the ratio of total international insurance and freight to the c.i.f. value of total merchandise imports. This f.o.b. value is used as the closest practical approximation of the ex-factory values, which should, in principle, be used as the basis for calculating the ratios in the adjustment factor.
2. Each of the following items is calculated as a ratio of the (approximate) f.o.b. value of imported equipment goods: customs duties, nondeductible value added taxes and other taxes on products, transport costs in the importing country, retail and wholesale trade margins in the importing country, and installation costs. The calculations are made separately for the two groups, metal products and machinery and transport equipment. These ratios are summed for each country to obtain $1 + \sum_{i=1}^{n}\alpha_i$ for country A, $1 + \sum_{i=1}^{n}\beta_i$ for country B, and so on for all the countries in the region for which the PFM is being used.
3. The exchange rates between each pair of countries are then multiplied by the relevant adjustment factor to obtain pairs of bilateral PPPs for the two groups.
4. These bilateral PPPs are made transitive by the Gini-Éltetö-Köves-Szulc (GEKS) procedure.

Box 14.6 is a worked example showing the calculations for steps 1, 2, and 3 of the adjustment procedure for two countries. Because only two countries are used in this example, step 4 is not required. But when the PFM is used by more than two countries, the PPPs obtained for the two countries will have to be made transitive by the GEKS procedure.

In the worked example in box 14.6, the margins shown in the first part of the worksheet are generally higher in country A than in country B. As a result, the PPP for country A is higher than its exchange rate, and the PPP for country B is lower than its exchange rate. If the exchange rates had been used instead of the PPPs, the volume of equipment goods in country A would have been overestimated and the volume of equipment goods in country B underestimated.

BOX 14.6 Worked Example for Imported Metal Products and Machinery

The following shows how the first three steps just listed are carried out for metal products and machinery imported by two countries, A and B. The first part of the box lists the basic information required.

	Country A (national currency)	Country B (national currency)
C.i.f. value of imports of metal products and machinery	3,000	16,000
Customs duties	250	800
Nondeductible value added taxes and other taxes on products	300	1,000
Transport costs	80	300
Retail and wholesale trade margins	160	800
Installation costs	120	580
C.i.f. value of all merchandise imports	75,000	340,000
Insurance and freight on all merchandise imports	800	3,000
Units of local currency per U.S. dollar	35	75

At step 1, c.i.f. values are converted to approximate f.o.b. values. (These f.o.b. values are the closest practical approximation to the ex-factory values.)

Step 1:
Convert c.i.f. value of imports of metal products and machinery to approximate f.o.b. values

$$\text{Country A: } 3{,}000 \times \left[1 - \left(\frac{800}{75{,}000}\right)\right] = 2{,}968$$

$$\text{Country B: } 16{,}000 \times \left[1 - \left(\frac{3{,}000}{340{,}000}\right)\right] = 15{,}859$$

At step 2, the sums of each country's customs duties, nondeductible value added taxes, and other products on taxes, transport costs, retail and wholesale trade margins, and installation costs are converted to ratios of the approximate f.o.b. values of the goods imported by each country.

Step 2:

$$\text{Country A: } \frac{(250 + 300 + 160 + 80 + 120)}{2{,}968} = 0.307$$

$$\text{Country B: } \frac{(800 + 1{,}000 + 800 + 300 + 580)}{15{,}859} = 0.219$$

At step 3, the currency exchange rates between countries A and B are converted to approximate PPPs between A and B by multiplying them by the ratios of the margin ratios calculated in step 2.

Step 3:
Adjust exchange rates to approximate bilateral PPPs

$$\text{Country A: exchange rate } \frac{A}{B} = \frac{35}{75} = 0.467. \text{ Therefore PPP: } \frac{A}{B} = 0.467 \times \frac{(1 + 0.307)}{(1 + 0.219)} = 0.500$$

$$\text{Country B: exchange rate } \frac{B}{A} = \frac{75}{35} = 2.143. \text{ Therefore PPP: } \frac{B}{A} = 2.143 \times \frac{(1 + 0.219)}{(1 + 0.307)} = 2.000$$

Lessons from ICP 2005

There are three ways in which the calculation of PPPs for equipment goods could be improved in the 2011 ICP round:

1. The price reporting forms for the standard method should require countries to report the technical characteristics for all items that a country has priced even if countries have provided prices for just one of the specified models. At present, countries are required to

do this only if they have priced an "other model." Eurostat-OECD countries are required to report the technical characteristics of all the items priced because it has been found that an item with the same model number is not necessarily identical in every country. For example, manufacturers may adapt models to meet the legal safety standards, which differ from country to country. A safety feature mandatory in one country may not be incorporated in the model sold in a country with lower safety standards.

2. Each country should identify "important" items in the core and regional lists of equipment goods. An "important" product is one that accounts for a relatively large share of expenditure within each basic heading. In the 2011 ICP round, countries will be asked to do make such an identification for the goods and services included in the household final consumption expenditure, and it should not be too difficult to do the same for equipment goods.

   As noted earlier, Eurostat-OECD countries are asked to identify items that are "representative" of the price level of all the products included in each basic heading. The term *important* is used in the 2011 ICP instead of *representative*, but this change is not just one in terminology. *Representative* refers to price levels, whereas *important* refers only to the expenditure share of each product in the basic heading. Although this expenditure share cannot be known exactly, countries should be able to rank the various models of, say, forklift trucks by their likely shares in expenditures on items in the basic heading general-purpose machinery. The one or two that are "best-sellers" would be rated "important" and the others as "less important." Important products can be given more weight in calculating a country's PPP, which will lead to an improvement in accuracy.

3. The Global Office prepares the core list of equipment goods. In the ICP 2005 round, this task was carried out with relatively little input from the national statistical offices and regional coordinators because neither had much experience with the market for equipment goods in their countries. The experience gained in the 2005 round suggests that the regional coordinators and national statistical offices should have more say in the selection of products, brands, and models. In particular, countries should *suggest* that the equipment goods they have identified as important be included in the core list and *insist* that they be included in the regional list.

ANNEX A

Core List of Equipment Goods, ICP 2005

Basic heading code	Basic heading title	Product name	Product code	No. of products
150111.1	**FABRICATED METAL PRODUCTS**			
		Horizontal cylindrical storage tank (5,000 liters)	1	
		Horizontal cylindrical storage tank (10,000 liters)	2	
		Tank for storing liquid food and beverage products (1,000 liters)	3	
		Tank for storing liquid food and beverage products (5,000 liters)	4	
		Pressurized gas storage tank	5	**5**
150112.1	**GENERAL-PURPOSE MACHINERY**			
	A. Engines and turbines, pumps and compressors			
		Air compressor—small	1	
		Air Compressor—towed	2	
		Industrial diesel engine (heavy-duty)—tier 2, stage 2	3	
		Industrial diesel engine (heavy-duty)—tier 3, stage 3A	4	
		Light industrial diesel engine	5	
		Marine diesel engine (commercial)	6	
		Marine diesel engine (pleasure)	7	
		On-highway commercial diesel engine (heavy-duty)	8	
		Water pump—centrifugal	9	
		Water pump—jet	10	**10**
	B. Other general-purpose machinery			
		Air conditioner—residential	11	
		Air conditioner—room	12	
		Rough terrain forklift—extendable boom	13	
		Rough terrain crane	14	
		Telescopic boom truck crane	15	**5**
150113.1	**SPECIAL-PURPOSE MACHINERY**			
	A. Agricultural and forestry machinery			
		Compact tractor	1	
		Utility tractor	2	**2**
	B. Machine tools			
		MIG welder (arc welder)	3	
		Power circular saw	4	
		Power hand drill	5	
		Grinder power handheld	6	

Basic heading code	Basic heading title	Product name	Product code	No. of products
		Router	7	
		Sander	8	**6**
	C. Machinery for metallurgy, mining, quarrying, and construction			
		Backhoe loader	9	
		Crawler dozer—large	10	
		Crawler dozer—medium	11	
		Crawler dozer—small	12	
		Crawler loader—large	13	
		Crawler loader—medium	14	
		Crawler loader—small	15	
		Dumper1—rigid frame	16	
		Dumper2—over 30 tonnes	17	
		Dumper3—under 30 tonnes	18	
		Hydraulic excavator1—large	19	
		Hydraulic excavator2—compact	20	
		Hydraulic excavator3—mini	21	
		Motor grader	22	
		Skid steer loader	23	
		Skid steer loader—rubber track	24	
		Trenchless	25	
		Wheel dozer	26	
		Wheel loader1—large	27	
		Wheel loader2—midsize	28	
		Wheel loader3—compact	29	
		Wheel loader4—small	30	**22**
	D. Machinery for food, beverage, and tobacco processing			
		Mincing machine (0.5 kW power)	31	
		Mincing machine (1 kW power)	32	
		Spiral dough mixer (for 50 kg)	33	
		Spiral dough mixer (for 100 kg)	34	**4**
	E. Machinery for textile, apparel, and leather production			**0**
	F. Other special-purpose machinery			
		Blow molding machine for 50 liters	35	
		Blow molding machine for 100 liters	36	
		Injection molding machine for 50 tonnes (low-end)	37	
		Injection molding machine for 1,000 tonnes (high-end)	38	
		Extruder	39	**5**

(continued)

Basic heading code	Basic heading title	Product name	Product code	No. of products
150114.1	**ELECTRICAL AND OPTICAL EQUIPMENT**			
	A. Office machinery			
		Copier	1	
		Fax machine	2	
		Digital projector	3	
		Overhead projector	4	
		Paper shredder	5	**5**
	B. Computers and other information processing equipment			
		Desktop computer—Compaq	6	
		Desktop computer—Dell	7	
		Laptop computer	8	
		Inkjet printer	9	
		Laser printer	10	
		Multifunction printer	11	
		PDA	12	
		Scanner	13	
		Server	14	**9**
	C. Electrical machinery and apparatus			
		Electric motor	15	
		Generator	16	**2**
	D. Radio, television, and communications equipment and apparatus			
		2-way radio	17	
		DVD player	18	
		Security camera	19	**3**
	E. Medical, precision, and optical instruments, watches, and clocks			
		Anesthesia unit	20	
		Chemistry analyzer	21	
		CT scanner	22	
		Infant incubator	23	
		Infusion pump	24	
		Mammography unit	25	
		MRI	26	
		Patient monitor	27	
		Ultrasound	28	
		X-ray machine	29	**10**

Basic heading code	Basic heading title	Product name	Product code	No. of products
150115.1	**OTHER MANUFACTURED GOODS n.e.c.**			**0**
150121.1	**MOTOR VEHICLES, TRAILERS, AND SEMITRAILERS**			
		Commercial vehicle—28 passengers	1	
		Diesel minibus—8 passengers	2	
		Diesel minibus—15 passengers	3	
		Diesel minibus—21 passengers	4	
		Intracity bus—26–44 passengers	5	
		Intercity bus—45 passengers	6	
		Lorry cab chassis—5 tonnes	7	
		Lorry cab chassis—10 tonnes	8	
		Lorry cab chassis—15 tonnes	9	
		Pickup truck	10	
		Van truck	11	**11**
150311.1	**SOFTWARE**			
		Adobe Photoshop (10)	1	
		Adobe Photoshop (100)	2	
		MS Office 2003 Standard (10)	3	
		MS Office 2003 Standard (100)	4	
		MS Windows XP Professional (10)	5	
		MS Windows XP Professional (100)	6	
		Norton Antivirus (10)	7	
		Norton Antivirus (100)	8	
		SPSS V10	9	**9**
	TOTAL			**108**

Source: ICP.

ANNEX B

Reporting Form, Price Factor Method (PFM)

The reporting form that countries use to implement the PFM asks only for the costs and margins likely to be relatively large and that countries could reasonably be expected to report.

Reporting form for price factor method (PFM)

Country ______________ Currency unit ______________ Year ______________

Line no.	Description	Metal products and equipment (group 150110.0)	Transport equipment (group 150120.0)
1	C.i.f. value of imports of equipment goods		
2	Customs duties		
3	Nondeductible VAT and other taxes on products: *either* amount *or* percentage of line 1	 __________ ________%	 __________ ________%
4	Transport costs in the importing country *either* amount *or* percentage of line 1	 __________ ________%	 __________ ________%
5	Wholesale and retail trade margins in the importing country *either* amount *or* percentage of line 1	 __________ ________%	 __________ ________%
6	Installation costs *either* amount *or* percentage of line 1	 __________ ________%	 __________ ________%
7	Memorandum items Total imports of goods in c.i.f. values Total insurance and freight on all imports of goods, including those provided by residents as well as nonresidents.	 __________ __________	 __________ __________

Reporting form completed by: ______________

Position: ______________

E-mail address: ______________

Telephone: ______________

Postal address: ______________

____

Explanatory notes

Line 1. C.i.f. Value of Imports of Equipment Goods

The c.i.f. price (i.e., cost, insurance, and freight) is the price of a good delivered at the frontier of the importing country, including any insurance and freight charges incurred to that point but before the payment of any customs duties or other taxes on imports or trade and transport margins within the importing country. C.i.f. is the standard method for valuing merchandise imports, and thus the c.i.f. value of imported equipment goods can be obtained directly from the regular statistics on international merchandise trade.

The imports to be included here are those that form part of gross fixed capital formation (GFCF). Goods that form part of GFCF in equipment goods can be identified using either the SITC (Standard International Trade Classification) or the HS (Harmonized System) classifications of merchandise trade. A few goods, such as motor vehicles and personal computers, are imported both for capital formation and for final consumption by government or households. Imports for final consumption should be excluded. Countries that use some version of the commodity flow method for estimating GFCF will already have a key for assigning codes to GFCF or final consumption.

Note that no breakdown is called for beyond the group level of the ICP expenditure classification. This reporting form asks only for figures for total "metal products and machinery" and total "transport equipment."

Line 2. Customs Duties
The amount shown here should be the customs duties *due* on imports, although the amounts *actually paid* will usually be a good approximation and can be reported here. There are two ways in which this item can be estimated—either from records of customs duties collected or by applying the rates of customs duties to the c.i.f. values of imports:

- Most customs authorities classify their receipts according to the Harmonized System. The amounts collected on equipment goods can therefore be obtained by identifying the relevant HS codes. As noted above, it is necessary to distinguish duties collected on goods for GFCF from those collected on goods for the final consumption expenditure. The main problem here will affect motor vehicles, computers, hand tools, and metal furniture. This needs to be considered for these and similar products also purchased by households.
- If a single rate of customs duty is charged for all imports of investment goods, this item can be easily estimated by applying that rate to the value of imports shown in line 1. If different rates apply to different types of equipment goods or to imports from different countries, it will be necessary to calculate a weighted average of these rates using the c.i.f. values of the relevant imports as weights.

Line 3. Nondeductible Value Added Taxes and Other Taxes on Products
The amount shown here is the total amount of value added taxes, sales taxes, or other product taxes paid by the final purchaser of the imported item of equipment goods. In some countries, VAT and other product taxes are reimbursed or not charged on goods for GFCF. In such cases, there will be no entry for this item.

Line 4. Transport Costs in the Importing Country
These are the costs of transporting equipment goods from where they enter the country to the establishment of the purchaser. Many countries may have information on transport costs from an input-output or supply and use table. Other countries use some form of the commodity flow method to estimate GFCF in equipment goods. Use of this approach requires estimates of transport costs for equipment goods. Other countries will have to estimate the average distance over which imported equipment goods are carried from their point of arrival to the main industrial centers. They will also need estimates of freight rates per ton-kilometer and the tonnage of equipment goods transported.

Line 5. Retail and Wholesale Trade Margins in the Importing Country
No distinction is made between wholesale and retail margins.

Trade margins are the gross output of retail and wholesale enterprises. Imported goods are usually traded by large corporate enterprises that will keep standard accounting records. Input-output and supply and use tables are another possible source for some countries.

Line 6. Installation Costs
There are usually no installation costs for transport equipment.

For metal products and machinery, the costs of installation should include all costs of putting the item in place, connecting it to the power source, and calibrating and testing the equipment good so that it is functioning correctly. Countries that use some form of the commodity flow method to estimate GFCF in equipment goods will already have estimates of these costs.

Line 7. C.i.f. Value of Imports of Goods and International Insurance and Freight on All Imports of Goods
This memorandum item asks for the c.i.f. value of the *total* imports of goods and the *total* costs of international freight and insurance. The first item should be readily available from merchandise trade statistics.

The balance of payments will give the value of insurance and transport services provided by nonresident insurance and transport companies. In many countries, all, or mostly all, international freight and insurance are provided by nonresident companies. In some countries, however, it will be necessary to estimate insurance and freight services provided by resident companies. In the *Standard National Accounts* supply and use table, total international insurance and freight are one of the adjustment items in the supply matrix.

NOTE

1. For a full description of the methodology for equipment goods, see Eurostat and OECD (2006).

REFERENCE

Eurostat and OECD (Organisation for Economic Co-operation and Development). 2006. *Eurostat-OECD Methodological Manual on Purchasing Power Parities*. Paris: OECD.

CHAPTER 15

Government Services

DEREK BLADES

This chapter describes the information on government services required for the International Comparison Program (ICP). Because chapter 3 covers the expenditure weights needed for government consumption expenditures, that material is not repeated here. The chapter focuses mainly on the price information needed for government and, in particular, the data needed on compensation of government employees.

The chapter is broken down into two major sections—the 2005 ICP round and the 2011 round. It includes an overview of how government is treated in the ICP, covering both the collective and individual expenditures of government. However, some of government's individual expenditures on health and education services are covered in more detail in chapter 11.

ICP 2005

This section describes the procedures followed for the 2005 round of the ICP.

Definition of General Government

"General government" is the term used in the 1993 *System of National Accounts* (SNA)[1] to describe the "Institutional Sector" consisting of central, federal, regional, state, and local government units, and any social security funds controlled by these units. The armed forces and nonprofit institutions controlled and mainly financed by government are also included in the general government sector. These institutions vary from country to country, but they often are hospitals, clinics, schools, and universities. The nonprofit institutions included in "general government" should not be confused with the nonprofit institutions serving households (NPISH), which are financed by households and which form a separate institutional sector in the SNA. The kinds of bodies classified as NPISH typically include trade unions, religious organizations, and political parties.

The 1993 SNA provides for subsectors of general government—central, federal, state, and local governments, and social security funds, depending on the constitutional arrangements in each country. For the ICP, however, no subsectoring is required, and PPPs are calculated for general government as a whole. It is assumed that the prices of goods and services acquired by government are the same no matter which the level of government acquired them. Similarly, the data on compensation of employees are averages of compensation paid to government employees in a given occupation at each level of government for which that occupation is relevant. For simplicity's sake, the term *government* is used in this chapter to refer to the SNA institutional sector "general government."

Individual and Collective Services

Government final consumption expenditures are divided between two main aggregates in the ICP expenditure classification: individual services and collective services. They are distinguished because the individual consumption expenditure by government is one of three components of *actual individual consumption*, the other components being individual consumption expenditure by households and individual consumption expenditure by NPISH. Actual individual consumption measures what households consume rather than what they purchase (see chapter 3 on national accounts and chapter 11 on health and education expenditures). In the ICP, comparisons of household consumption are made using actual individual *consumption* rather than individual consumption *expenditure*. Countries differ widely in the extent to which government provides households with education, health, and other individual services. Actual household consumption is therefore more comparable between countries than household expenditure.

Individual Services

Expenditures on individual services constitute the *individual consumption expenditure by government*. Individual services are those that governments provide to households on an individual basis such as health and education. Some households benefit from these services while others do not. Collective services are provided to everyone on an equal basis; examples are defense, law and order, and research and development. No one household can consume more of these services than another household. The distinction between individual services and collective services is made by reference to the Classification of the Functions of Government (COFOG) 1998 classification (United Nations 2000). Table 15.1 lists individual and collective services by COFOG group. The functions of government defined as individual are denoted by "IS."

Individual consumption expenditure by government takes two forms:

1. The production of services by government for the benefit of individual households. Examples are running schools and hospitals. Here the government is itself organizing and financing the production of services for consumption by individual households.
2. The purchase of goods and services by government from other producers that are then passed on to households, either free or at prices below the costs of production, without any further processing by the government. Examples are medicines and medical services for outpatients. Some households receive these goods and services free or at very low prices at the point of delivery; other households pay the full price at the point of delivery and are later reimbursed, in part or in full, by the government. For the ICP, the purchase by government of goods and services for delivery to households is relevant for two functions: health and education. In the expenditure classification, they are described as *health benefits and reimbursements* and as *education benefits and reimbursements*.

TABLE 15.1 Collective Services (CS) and Individual Services (IS), COFOG Groups

COFOG group	COFOG group
01. GENERAL PUBLIC SERVICES	**05. ENVIRONMENT PROTECTION**
01.1 Executive and legislative organs, financial and fiscal affairs, external affairs (CS)	05.1 Waste management (CS)
	05.2 Waste water management (CS)
01.2 Foreign economic aid (CS)	05.3 Pollution abatement (CS)
01.3 General services (CS)	05.4 Protection of biodiversity and landscape (CS)
01.4 Basic research (CS)	05.5 R&D environment protection (CS)
01.5 R&D general public services (CS)	05.6 Environment protection n.e.c. (CS)
01.6 General public services n.e.c. (CS)	**06. HOUSING AND COMMUNITY AMENITIES**
01.7 Public debt transactions (CS)	06.1 Housing development (CS)
01.8 Transfers of a general character between different levels of government (CS)	06.2 Community development (CS)
	06.3 Water supply (CS)
02. DEFENSE	06.4 Street lighting (CS)
02.1 Military defense (CS)	06.5 R&D housing and community amenities (CS)
02.2 Civil defense (CS)	06.6 Housing and community amenities n.e.c. (CS)
02.3 Foreign military aid (CS)	**07. HEALTH**
02.4 R&D defense (CS)	07.1 Medical products, appliances, and equipment (IS)
02.5 Defense n.e.c. (CS)	07.2 Outpatient services (IS)
03. PUBLIC ORDER AND SAFETY	07.3 Hospital services (IS)
03.1 Police services (CS)	07.4 Public health services (IS)
03.2 Fire protection services (CS)	07.5 R&D health (CS)
03.3 Law courts (CS)	07.6 Health n.e.c. (CS)
03.4 Prisons (CS)	**08. RECREATION, CULTURE, AND RELIGION**
03.5 R&D public order and safety (CS)	08.1 Recreational and sporting services (IS)
03.6 Public order and safety n.e.c. (CS)	08.2 Cultural services (IS)
04. ECONOMIC AFFAIRS	08.3 Broadcasting and publishing services (CS)
04.1 General economic, commercial, and labor affairs (CS)	08.4 Religious and other community services (CS)
04.2 Agriculture, forestry, fishing, and hunting (CS)	08.5 R&D recreation, culture, and religion (CS)
04.3 Fuel and energy (CS)	08.6 Recreation, culture, and religion n.e.c. (CS)
04.4 Mining, manufacturing, and construction (CS)	**09. EDUCATION**
04.5 Transport (CS)	09.1 Preprimary and primary education (IS)
04.6 Communication (CS)	09.2 Secondary education (IS)
04.7 Other industries (CS)	09.3 Postsecondary nontertiary education (IS)
04.8 R&D economic affairs (CS)	09.4 Tertiary education (IS)
04.9 Economic affairs n.e.c. (CS)	09.5 Education not definable by level (IS)
	09.6 Subsidiary services to education (IS)
	09.7 R&D education (CS)
	09.8 Education n.e.c. (CS)

(continued)

TABLE 15.1 Collective Services (CS) and Individual Services (IS), COFOG Groups (*continued*)

COFOG group	COFOG group
10. SOCIAL PROTECTION	10.5 Unemployment (IS)
10.1 Sickness and disability (IS)	10.6 Housing (IS)
10.2 Old age (IS)	10.7 Social exclusion n.e.c. (IS)
10.3 Survivors (IS)	10.8 R&D social protection (CS)
10.4 Family and children (IS)	10.9 Social protection n.e.c. (CS)

Source: Classification of the Functions of Government (COFOG), United Nations Statistical Division.
Note: R&D = research and development; n.e.c. = not elsewhere classified.

Collective Services

Government consumption expenditure that is not individual is termed collective. As shown in table 15.1 (highlighted in gray and denoted by "CS"), collective government expenditures mainly fall under the broad headings of general public services, defense, public order and safety, economic affairs, and environmental protection, but they also include certain expenditures under housing, health, recreation and culture, education, and social protection that are considered to benefit the community at large. These expenditures are directed at formulating and administering government policy at the national level, at research and development, and at setting up and enforcing safety, environmental, or other standards.

By contrast with individual consumption expenditures, collective consumption expenditures take one form only: the production of services by the government. Collective consumption expenditures do not involve the purchase of goods and services for delivery to households.

ICP Basic Headings for Government

Table 15.2 shows government expenditure broken down into 26 basic headings: 21 cover expenditures on individual services; five cover expenditures on collective services. Three kinds of basic headings are shown:

1. *Health benefits and reimbursements.* This basic heading consists of goods and services, just like the other basic headings in the ICP expenditure classification.
2. *Production of health, education, and collective services.* These basic headings consist of the costs of producing these services.
3. Other groups: *housing, recreation and culture, education benefits* and *reimbursements*, and *social protection*. These basic headings consist of the total costs of providing these services: compensation of employees, intermediate consumption, gross operating surplus, net taxes on production, and receipts from sales.

For most of the basic headings in table 15.2—that is, those indicated with an asterisk (*)—no price data were required because purchasing power parities (PPPs) were obtained using reference PPPs. Reference PPPS are PPPs that were calculated for similar basic headings in other parts of the ICP expenditure classification (see chapter 17 for more details on reference PPPs).

TABLE 15.2 ICP Basic Headings for Individual Services and Collective Services

INDIVIDUAL SERVICES	
Housing	***Recreation and culture***
130111.1 Housing*	130311.1 Recreation and culture*
Health benefits and reimbursements	***Education benefits and reimbursements***
130211.1 Pharmaceutical products	130411.1 Education benefits and reimbursements*
130211.2 Other medical products	***Production of education services***
130211.3 Therapeutic appliances and equipment	130421.1 Compensation of employees
130212.1 Outpatient medical services	130422.1 Intermediate consumption*
130212.2 Outpatient dental services	130423.1 Gross operating surplus*
130212.3 Outpatient paramedical services	130424.1 Net taxes on production*
130212.4 Hospital services*	130425.1 Receipts from sales*
Production of health services	***Social protection***
130221.1 Compensation of employees	130511.1 Social protection*
130222.1 Intermediate consumption*	
130223.1 Gross operating surplus*	
130224.1 Net taxes on production*	
130225.1 Receipts from sales*	
COLLECTIVE SERVICES	
140111.1 Compensation of employees	140114.1 Net taxes on production*
140112.1 Intermediate consumption*	140115.1 Receipts from sales*
140113.1 Gross operating surplus*	

Source: ICP.
Note: Asterisk (*) indicates that no price data were required because PPPs were obtained using reference PPPs.

Price Data

This section provides an overview of the data collected and used for the estimation of PPPs for the government sector.

Health Benefits and Reimbursements

Governments in many countries purchase health services, pharmaceuticals, and other medical goods from market producers, and then pass them on to particular groups of households either free or at much reduced prices. This activity is financed differently from country to country. Some governments buy the goods or services directly from the producers and provide them without charge to households; other governments reimburse households, in full or in part, after the households themselves have made the purchase.

In the ICP, the prices paid for these goods and services are collected and used to calculate PPPs in the same way as PPPs for other goods and services. In all cases, the prices to be collected are the "total price." In countries in which households pay the whole purchaser's price to the market producer prior to being either completely or partially reimbursed by the government, the total price is the price that households pay before reimbursement (see chapter 11 on health and education).

In countries in which households pay only a portion of the purchaser's price to the market producer and the remainder is paid to the market producer by the government, the total price is the sum of the nonreimbursable part paid by households and the part paid by government. Suppose, for example, that households purchased 1,000 units of a pharmaceutical product and that the price per unit was €10, of which households paid €2 and the government €8. In the national accounts, €2,000 would be recorded as a household expenditure and €8,000 as a government expenditure. If the prices actually paid—that is, €2 by households and €8 by government—were used to deflate these expenditures, it would seem that both households and government each purchased 1,000 units or 2,000 units in total. But if the total amount paid—€10—was used, households would be shown, correctly, as having purchased 200 units and the government 800 units, for a total of 1,000 units.

In table 15.2, the last item shown under health benefits and reimbursements is hospital services. This item covers the provision of the medical services, pharmaceuticals, and such that patients who stay overnight in hospitals receive over the course of their treatment. The quality of and the ways in which these services are provided differ greatly from country to country, and in the past it has proved very difficult to collect internationally comparable prices for hospital services. For that reason, a reference PPP was used for this item in the 2005 ICP.

To summarize, prices are required only for the following basic headings: 130211.1, pharmaceutical products; 130211.2, other medical products; 130211.3, therapeutic appliances and equipment; 130212.1, outpatient medical services; 130212.2, outpatient dental services; and 130212.3, outpatient paramedical services. These goods and services are also basic headings under the household final consumption expenditure (basic headings 110611.0 to 110623.1), so that the same prices were used to calculate PPPs for both household and government expenditures.

Production of Health, Education, and Collective Services

In the national accounts, government services are valued at their costs of production, and the same approach is used in calculating PPPs for the ICP. In other words, the PPPs for production of government services were obtained by comparing the costs of producing them.

The costs of producing government services are (1) compensation of employees, (2) intermediate consumption, (3) net taxes on production, (4) gross operating surplus, and (5) (as a negative figure) receipts from sales.

Intermediate consumption covers a wide range of goods and services such as printing supplies, office rent, computer services, office cleaning, electricity, and so on. Intermediate consumption of defense services includes the purchase of weapons such as artillery pieces, rockets, warships, tanks, and war planes. Reference PPPs were used for this basic heading.

Net taxes on production consist of value added and sales taxes; duties on imports; taxes on the ownership of land, buildings, or other assets used in production; and taxes on the numbers of employees. Subsidies on production are considered to be negative taxes and so are deducted. In most countries, net taxes on the production of government services are insignificant or zero; they are included in table 15.2 mainly for completeness. Reference PPPs were used for this basic heading.

Gross operating surplus consists of net operating surplus plus consumption of fixed capital. In most countries, the net operating surplus is insignificant or zero, and so this item consists only of consumption of fixed capital. Consumption of fixed capital is the decline in value through wear and tear and obsolescence of government-owned buildings, roads, bridges and other structures, and of machinery and equipment such as computers, motor vehicles, and diagnostic equipment used in government hospitals. Reference PPPs were used for this basic heading.

Receipts from sales cover items such as partial charges for education and health services, passport fees, and entrance charges for museums. These expenditures are recorded under the household final consumption expenditure or the intermediate consumption of enterprises and so must be deducted from the government consumption expenditure. Receipts from sales are shown as a basic heading in table 15.1 for both individual and collective services, although in practice most receipts from sales will come under individual services. Reference PPPs were used for this basic heading.

Compensation of employees is the largest component of the costs of producing government services, and it is the only cost component for which "prices" were collected. Compensation of employees was reported for a selection of occupations in government, public education, and public health services. The ICP's Global Office, situated at the World Bank, selected the occupations, and countries in all regions used the same list. The intention was to represent the various education and skill levels commonly found among employees working in these government services.

Table 15.3 lists the 50 occupations used for the 2005 ICP round. They are based on the 1988 International Standard Classification of Occupations (ISCO-88), issued by the International

TABLE 15.3 Standard Government Occupations, ICP

Health services		213	Policeman/woman
101	Doctor, head of department	214	Prison guard
102	Doctor (20 years of seniority)	215	Fire fighter
103	Doctor (10 years of seniority)	216	Social worker
104	Nurse, head of department	217	Town planner
105	Nurse, operating theatre	218	Civil engineer
106	Nurse	219	Draftsman/draftswoman
107	Nursing auxiliary	220	Construction laborer
108	Physiotherapist	221	Chauffeur
109	Laboratory assistant	222	Agricultural scientist
110	Hospital chief executive	223	Librarian
111	Secretary (hospital)	224	Database administrator
112	Cook (not head cook)	225	Web administrator
113	Community health worker	226	Bodyguard (protecting senior officials)
Collective services		**Education services**	
201	Finance department manager	301	Kindergarten teacher
202	Executive official (skill level III)	302	Primary teacher
203	Executive official (skill level IV)	303	Secondary teacher
204	Computer operator	304	University lecturer
205	Bookkeeping clerk	305	Head teacher
206	Data entry clerk	**Defense services**	
207	Secretary (not hospital)	401	Army: private of infantry
208	Telephone switchboard operator	402	Army: commander of infantry regiment
209	Messenger	403	Navy: able seaman
210	Maintenance electrician	404	Navy: commander of frigate
211	Building caretaker	405	Air force: airman (ground crew)
212	Cleaner	406	Air force: fighter pilot/wing commander

Source: ICP.

Labour Organization (ILO) in 1990. Occupations are described in terms of the kind of work done. For two occupations, the length of time that the person has served in the post was specified: 102 (doctor with 20 years of seniority) and 103 (doctor with 10 years of seniority). For all other occupations, five years of seniority was used.

Several of the occupations in table 15.3 are relevant to more than one type of service. For example, nurses are primarily relevant to health services, but they also may be employed in schools. And secretaries, cleaners, and drivers are employed in the production of education, health, and collective services. Thus the information on compensation of employees for these and other occupations was used to calculate PPPs for more than one basic heading.

PPPs were calculated for each basic heading by taking the unweighted geometric averages of the price relatives for all the relevant occupations. Thus, for example, the PPP for basic heading 130421.1 (compensation of employees for the production of education services) was based on the six occupations 301–305 and on occupations 106, 201–212, and 216 because persons with these occupations are also employed in schools and universities.

The compensation of employees that participating countries were to report for the selected occupations is defined in box 15.1. It is consistent with the compensation of employees as defined in the 1993 SNA except in two respects. First, overtime payments were excluded from gross salaries and wages. Experience has shown that it is very difficult to obtain data on overtime that are comparable across countries. Although this omission resulted in volume measures that were marginally too high, their comparability was judged to be improved by ignoring overtime. Second, the only benefits in kind taken into account were the provision of free or subsidized housing and food or meals. Other forms of income in kind were both difficult to evaluate in ways that were internationally comparable and insignificant in the majority of countries.

BOX 15.1 Compensation of Government Employees

Compensation of government employees includes all payments in cash and in kind made by government in a year. These payments comprise the following:

- *Gross salaries and wages in cash* are recorded before deduction of taxes and social contributions payable by employees. They cover:
  - Basic salaries and wages as laid down in government salary scales (the note to table 15.4 explains how salary scales are used for this purpose).
  - Other payments over and above the basic salary or wage such as housing or residence allowance, passage or leave allowance, family allowance, special duty allowance or acting allowance, and 13th month pay and other cash payments except overtime payments (as noted earlier, it is very difficult to obtain data on overtime that are comparable across countries, and so overtime payments were excluded in the 2005 ICP).
- *Income in kind* covers things such as free or subsidized housing, meals, transport allowance, uniforms, and other items of clothing. Many of these benefits are difficult to evaluate because they can vary from one government institution to another. As a practical matter, only two kinds of income in kind were included in compensation of employees for the 2005 ICP: the provision of free or subsidized *housing* and free or subsidized *food or meals*. These items were valued at the cost to the employer of providing them. This was the cost of production when the items concerned were produced by the employer and the purchaser's price when they were bought by the employer and passed on to the employee.
- *Employers' actual social contributions* are payments made by governments to benefit their employees; they cover contributions for old-age pensions and for insurance against illness, accident, and disability. Contributions are calculated on the basis of the schemes in operation in each country. The governments of many countries, however, do not make any actual social contributions on behalf of their employees, and so this item was zero for those countries.
- *Imputed social contributions* are required in countries in which government employees receive social benefits such as pensions and health insurance, but the government does not make any payments into a social security fund to provide these benefits. Imputed social contributions are estimates of how much the government would have had to pay into a fund to provide the social benefits being provided to government employees. These estimates, or "imputations," were made in the same way as the corresponding imputations were made in the national account.

The compensation of employees reported for the selected occupations was calculated as follows. Underlying the compensation of employees paid by government were the basic salaries and wages laid down in government salary scales. Once the basic salary or wage was established for an occupation, it was relatively straightforward to compute the government's compensation of employees because most of the other components of compensation of employees (such as housing or residence allowance, family allowance, special duty allowance, and so forth) were normally related to the salary scale by being defined as percentage additions to the basic salary or wage. To determine the compensation of employees for the selected occupations, countries first located the basic salary or wage for each selected occupation in the government salary scales. The procedure applied is described in table 15.4.

The compensation of employees reported for each selected occupation must be *annual*—not a particularly difficult requirement. Salary scales usually show annual amounts, and any revisions of the salary scales during the reference year are relatively straightforward to accommodate. When there are revisions, a weighted average is calculated, with the weights being the number of months when the old rate applied and the number of months at the higher rate.

TABLE 15.4 Determining the Basic Salary for a Selected Occupation Using a Salary Scale

national currency

Grade and category	Step						
	1	2	3	4	5	6	7
P4	88,900	91,400	93,900	96,400	98,900	101,400	103,900
P3	76,800	78,800	80,800	82,800	84,800	86,800	89,000
P2	66,100	67,900	69,700	71,500	73,300	75,100	76,900
P1	53,600	55,000	56,400	57,800	59,200	60,600	62,000
T4	47,900	49,500	51,100	52,700	54,300	55,900	57,500
T3	41,200	42,600	44,000	45,400	46,800	48,200	49,600
T2	35,500	36,700	37,900	39,100	40,300	41,500	42,700
T1	31,100	32,100	33,100	34,100	35,100	36,100	37,100
W4	34,700	35,700	36,700	36,800	36,900	37,000	37,100
W3	31,300	32,300	33,300	34,300	35,300	36,300	37,300
W2	28,400	29,200	30,000	30,800	31,600	32,400	33,200
W1	25,700	26,500	27,300	28,100	28,900	29,700	30,050

Source: ICP.
Note: About the salary scale:

- Employees in public administrations are usually paid on the basis of a salary scale similar to the one shown in the table. The scale is divided into *grades*: P, T, and W. Grades generally correspond to levels of education or skills. Within grades are *categories* (four in this example), and each category divided into *steps*: 1–7 in this example. Each step is usually composed of 12 months, although steps of 18 or 24 months are not uncommon.
- The personnel recruitment office will know the usual entry level for each occupation. Suppose, for example, the entry level is step 1 of category T2 for the ICP occupation 34, prison guard. The base pay for an entry-level prison guard will then be 35,500. For a prison guard with five years of seniority, the base pay will be 40,300 (equivalent to five steps). But if each step were 18 months or 24 months, five years of seniority would be equivalent to four steps and a salary of 39,100 for 18-month steps and to three steps and a salary of 37,900 for 24-month steps.
- The base pay obtained from the salary scales is converted to *compensation of employees* by adding in any cash allowances, income in kind, and employers' actual or imputed contributions relevant for a prison guard at this level of the pay scale.

The compensation of employees should also be the *national average*, taking into account the differences in compensation that may arise both between various levels of government—that is, between central, regional, state, and local governments—and within the same level of government—that is, between different ministries and departments of central government or between different regional governments, state governments, or local governments. Unless there are national salary scales, it will be difficult to obtain national averages because the information on the various salary scales that must be consulted may not be readily available. Even if it is available, there is still the question of how to combine them. In principle, some form of weighted average should be used.

One solution in the absence of national salary scales is to only use the salary scales of the central government. The validity of this approach depends on the extent to which the wages and salaries paid by the central government are representative of those paid by the general government. Some adjustments may be necessary to make them more representative, such as excluding the allowance paid to compensate for the higher costs associated with working in the capital city. But it is not a complete solution, because in some countries people in some occupations—such as teachers or doctors—are employed only by regional, state, or local governments and not by the central government. For the selected occupations that fall into this group, the need to refer to the salary scales of the appropriate level of government remains.

For international comparisons, the compensation of employees reported for the selected occupations must be adjusted for differences in the numbers of hours worked in different countries. In addition to compensation of employees, countries were therefore required to report in the 2005 ICP the number of hours regularly worked per week—excluding overtime—and the number of weeks worked per year. The latter was obtained by deducting annual leave and public holidays. In the 2005 ICP round, this information was supplied on the reporting form shown in table 15.5.

TABLE 15.5 Information to Be Reported for Compensation of Employees in Government, ICP 2005

Occupation code number	e.g., 106
Occupation description	e.g., Nurse
Annual compensation of employees *of which:*	
Gross wages and salaries	
Employers' actual contributions to social security funds	
Employers' imputed contributions to social security funds	
Income in kind	
Housing	
Food and meals	
Number of regular hours worked per week	
Number of days worked per week	
Number of days of annual leave per year	
Number of public holidays per year	
Year for which data are reported (2005 or nearest year available)	
Currency unit	

Source: ICP.

Reference PPPs

In the 2005 ICP, of the 26 basic headings for government (see table 15.2), prices were collected for six health goods and services and information on the compensation of three types of employees. No price data were collected for the remaining 17 basic headings. The PPPs for these basic headings were calculated from price data collected for other basic headings. These so-called reference PPPs are listed in table 15.6.

The choice of reference PPP is self-explanatory in most cases. For example, the reference PPPs for housing were the PPPs for actual rentals, and the reference PPPs for gross operating surplus—which, in practice is equal to consumption of fixed capital because net operating surplus is likely to be insignificant—were the PPPs for gross fixed capital formation.

When there was no obvious choice of a reference PPP, a *neutral average* was chosen instead. For example, the reference PPPs for intermediate consumption in collective services were the PPPs for individual consumption expenditures by households on the domestic market (excluding all basic headings with reference PPPs) and the reference PPPs for recreation and culture and for social protection were the PPPs for individual consumption expenditures by government (excluding social protection and recreation and culture, and before deducting receipts from sales).

A certain amount of duplication was associated with the derivation of some reference PPPs. For example, the reference PPPs for hospital services were the PPPs for the production of health services by government before deducting receipts from sales. These reference PPPs were therefore weighted averages of the PPPs for compensation of employees, intermediate consumption, gross operating surplus, and net taxes on production. Of these four items, only the PPPs for compensation of employees were based directly on price data. The PPPs for intermediate consumption, gross operating surplus, and net taxes on production were themselves reference PPPs.

Reporting Prices

Prices were required for six types of medical goods and services: pharmaceutical products, other medical goods, therapeutic appliances and equipment, and medical, dental, and paramedical outpatient services. However, no separate price collection was required for purchases by government. Prices for all six types of medical goods and services were collected for the relevant basic headings under individual household consumption expenditures. These same prices were used for the relevant government basic headings. For government, the only additional price collection was related to compensation of employees. Table 15.5 shows the information required for each of the selected occupations.

Validation of Prices

Before reporting compensation of employees on the form shown in table 15.5, participating countries had to look at the internal coherency of the data set. For example, doctors usually earn more than nurses; head teachers earn more than other teachers; officers in the armed forces earn more than privates, able seamen, and airmen; executive officials earn more than drivers; and drivers earn more than messengers. Income differentials between occupations that are contrary to expectations had to be verified and errors identified in this way had to be corrected.

TABLE 15.6 Reference PPPs for Government Services

Basic heading	Reference PPPs
INDIVIDUAL SERVICES	
Housing	
130111.1 Housing	PPPs for actual rentals
Health benefits and reimbursements	
130212.4 Hospital services	PPPs for production of health services by government (before deducting receipts from sales)
Production of health services	
130322.1 Intermediate consumption	PPPs for individual consumption expenditure by households on the domestic market (excluding all basic headings with reference PPPs)
130223.1 Gross operating surplus	PPPs for gross fixed capital formation
130224.1 Net taxes on production	PPPs for production of health services by government (without net taxes on production and before deducting receipts from sales)
130225.1 Receipts from sales	PPPs for production of health services by government (before deducting receipts from sales)
Recreation and culture	
130311.1 Recreation and culture	PPPs for individual consumption expenditure by government (excluding social protection and recreation and culture, and before deducting receipts from sales)
Education benefits and reimbursements	
130411.1 Education benefits and reimbursements	PPPs for production of education services by government (before deducting receipts from sales)
Production of education services	
130422.1 Intermediate consumption	PPPs for individual consumption expenditure by households on the domestic market (excluding all basic headings with reference PPPs)
130423.1 Gross operating surplus	PPPs for gross fixed capital formation
130424.1 Net taxes on production	PPPs for production of education services by government (without net taxes on production and before deducting receipts from sales)
130425.1 Receipts from sales	PPPs for production of education services by government (before deducting receipts from sales)
Social protection	
130511.1 Social protection	PPPs for individual consumption expenditure by government (excluding social protection and recreation and culture, and before deducting receipts from sales)
COLLECTIVE SERVICES	
140112.1 Intermediate consumption	PPPs for individual consumption expenditure by households on the domestic market (excluding all basic headings with reference PPPs)
140113.1 Gross operating surplus	PPPs for gross fixed capital formation
140114.1 Net taxes on production	PPPs for production of collective services by government (without net taxes on production and before deducting receipts from sales)
140115.1 Receipts from sales	PPPs for production of collective services by government (before deducting receipts from sales)

Source: ICP.

ICP 2011

This section explains the changes that will be made for the 2011 ICP round.

Extent of the Changes

Most of the procedures used for the 2005 ICP and described in the previous section will be retained for the 2011 ICP. In particular, the number and definitions of the basic headings for government will not be changed; the only special "price" information required for government refers to the compensation of employees. The prices of health goods and services collected for basic headings under household expenditure will continue to be used for the relevant basic headings under government expenditure. And government pay scales will be used to calculate employee compensation.

The changes planned for the 2011 ICP are as follows:

- The list of government occupations has been updated and reduced from 50 to 38 and is now aligned with the latest version of the International Standard Classification of Occupations (ISCO-08), issued by the ILO in 2010.[2]
- Countries will be asked to provide compensation for employees at four different stages of their careers: on first appointment and after 5, 10, and 20 years of experience in the same occupation.
- The types of income in kind included in compensation of employees have been expanded to cover, in addition to accommodation and clothing, free and subsidized transportation and other forms of income in kind.
- Countries will be asked to report the number of hours *actually worked*, in addition to the official hours, because in several countries in which government salaries are very low, it is the accepted practice that government employees may take time off to earn money in a secondary occupation.
- A new reporting form asks for information on government current and capital expenditures broken down by two levels of government: *central or federal* and all *other levels*.
- For government individual expenditures on education and health services, attempts will be made to find output measures to replace the input approach used in all earlier rounds of the ICP.

As for the last point, the use of output measures is experimental, and in the 2011 ICP the data on compensation of employees required for the input approach will still be required for health and education occupations. These experimental output measures are described in chapter 11 on health and education services and so are not explained here, but the other changes for the 2011 ICP are described in the rest of this section.

Revised List of Government Occupations

The list of government occupations for the 2011 ICP has been aligned with the 2008 version of the ISCO and now covers 38 occupations typical of government collective services and government health and education services (see table 15.7). It covers only civilian occupations because information sought in the 2005 ICP on military occupations was found to be unreliable and noncomparable.

TABLE 15.7 List of Occupations, ICP 2011

ICP code and job title	Description	ISCO-08 code and job title
1 Member of parliament	Members of parliament debate, make, ratify, amend, or repeal laws, public rules, and regulations. Members of parliament may be elected or appointed.	1111: Legislators
2 Senior government official	This senior government official is a permanent civil servant who is one level below a minister and may be described as "permanent secretary," "deputy minister," "director general," etc. This senior government official reports directly to the minister. These senior government officials may be working in any central or federal government ministry or department.	1112: Senior government officials
3 Hospital manager	Hospital managers formulate and review the policies and plan, direct, coordinate, and evaluate the overall activities of government-funded hospitals, clinics, and similar establishments.	1120: Managing directors and chief executives
4 Data processing manager	Data processing managers plan, direct, and coordinate the acquisition, development, maintenance, and use of computer and telecommunication systems.	1330: Information and communications technology service managers
5 Secondary school principal	Secondary school principals plan, direct, coordinate, and evaluate the educational and administrative aspects of secondary schools. "Principals" are also referred to as "head masters," "head mistresses," and "head teachers."	1345: Education managers
6 Government statistician	Government statisticians collect, edit, tabulate, and publish economic, demographic, and social statistics. Government statisticians will have a professional, tertiary-level qualification in statistics or in a related field such as mathematics or demography. In many statistical offices, there is a hierarchy of professional statistician grades such as assistant statistician, statistician, principal statistician, and senior statistician. Details of compensation should be provided for the grade that includes the largest number of statisticians.	2120: Mathematicians, actuaries, and statisticians
7 Hospital doctor	Medical doctors study, diagnose, treat, and prevent illness, disease, injury, and other physical and mental impairments in humans through the application of the principles and procedures of modern medicine.	2211: Generalist medical practitioners
8 Specialist doctor	Specialist doctors study, diagnose, treat, and prevent illness, disease, injury, and other physical and mental impairments in humans. They specialize in certain disease categories, types of patient, or methods of treatment, and may conduct medical education and research in their chosen areas of specialization. Examples of specialist doctors are pediatricians; dermatologists; gynecologists; orthopedic specialists; rheumatologists; cancer specialists; ear, nose, and throat specialists; cardiologists; gerontologists; ophthalmologists; and urologists.	2212: Specialist medical practitioners
9 Hospital nurse	Hospital nurses provide treatment, support, and care services for people who are in need of nursing care because of the effects of aging, injury, illness, or other physical or mental impairment, or potential risks to health. They carry out their tasks under the supervision of doctors or senior nurses. Hospital nurses will have had formal training of at least one year and will have a nationally recognized nursing qualification. The level and length of the training will depend on the standards applied in each country.	2221: Nursing professionals
10 University teacher	University and higher education teachers prepare and deliver lectures and conduct tutorials in one or more subjects within a prescribed course of study at a university or other higher education institution. They conduct research and prepare scholarly papers for publication in peer-reviewed journals.	2310: University and higher education teachers

TABLE 15.7 List of Occupations, ICP 2011 (*continued*)

ICP code and job title	Description	ISCO-08 code and job title
11 Vocational education teacher	Vocational education teachers teach or instruct vocational or occupational subjects in adult and further education institutions and to senior students in secondary schools and colleges. They prepare students for employment in specific occupations.	2320: Vocational education teachers
12 Primary school teacher	Primary school teachers teach a range of subjects at the primary education level.	2341: Primary education teachers
13 Secondary school teacher	Secondary education teachers teach one or more subjects at the secondary education level, excluding subjects intended to prepare students for employment in specific occupations.	2330: Secondary education teachers
14 Government accountants	Government accountants plan, organize, and administer accounting systems for government ministries, departments, and other agencies. They verify that the revenue and expenditure records maintained by government agencies are accurate and in compliance with current legislation. Government accountants will have a recognized qualification in accounting, which is usually acquired at a tertiary or post-tertiary education level.	2411: Accountants
15 Human resources professional	Human resources professionals work in "personnel" or "human resources" departments either in government ministries or in a department or ministry dedicated to recruitment and personnel management.	2423: Personnel and careers professionals
16 Database administrator	Database administrators develop, control, and maintain one or more databases in a government ministry or department.	2522: Systems administrators
17 Judge	Judges preside over civil and criminal proceedings in courts of law. The judge will have qualifications in the practice of law at the tertiary level or higher and will be entitled to try both civil and criminal cases.	2612: Judges
18 Government economist	Government economists conduct research, monitor data, analyze information, and prepare reports and plans to resolve economic and financial problems of government. The government economist for which compensation details are required should be working in a ministry of finance or ministry of economy.	2631: Economists
19 Laboratory assistant	Laboratory assistants perform technical tasks in hospital laboratories to help medical staff determine the causes of diseases and monitor the effectiveness of treatments.	3212: Medical and pathology laboratory technicians
20 Auxiliary nurse	Auxiliary nurses assist medical, nursing, and midwifery professionals in their duties. Nursing auxiliaries may or may not have a recognized medical qualification.	3221: Nursing associate professionals
21 Medical records clerk	Medical records clerks maintain the health records of patients. They are responsible for the storage and retrieval of these records in government medical facilities and other health care facilities	3252: Medical records and health information technicians
22 Office supervisors	Office supervisors supervise and coordinate the activities of clerical support workers.	3341: Office supervisors
23 Medical secretary (hospital)	Medical secretaries (hospital), using specialized knowledge of medical terminology and health care delivery procedures, assist health professionals and other workers by performing a variety of communication, documentation, administrative, and internal coordination functions.	3344: Medical secretaries
24 Customs inspector	Customs inspectors examine goods crossing international land, sea, or air borders to determine whether they are allowed to be imported or exported and to assess customs duties payable.	3351: Customs and border inspectors
25 Computer operator	Computer operators maintain networks and other data communications systems.	3513: Computer network and systems technicians

(*continued*)

TABLE 15.7 List of Occupations, ICP 2011 (*continued*)

ICP code and job title	Description	ISCO-08 code and job title
26 Secretaries (not medical)	Secretaries (not medical) use word-processing equipment to transcribe correspondence and other documents, check and format documents prepared by other staff, deal with incoming and outgoing mail, and screen requests for meetings with senior staff.	4120: Secretaries
27 Accounting and bookkeeping clerks	Accounting and bookkeeping clerks compute, classify, and record numerical data to keep financial records complete. They perform any combination of routine calculating, posting, and verifying duties to obtain primary financial data for use in maintaining records on receipts and expenditures.	4311: Accounting and bookkeeping clerks
28 Payroll clerks	Payroll clerks collect, verify, and process payroll information and compute pay and benefit entitlements for government employees working in one or more government ministries.	4313: Payroll clerks
29 Cooks	Cooks plan, organize, prepare, and cook meals in canteens and other eating places in schools, universities, hospitals, and government offices.	5120: Cooks
30 Building caretaker	Building caretakers take care of schools, hospitals, university buildings, and government offices, and maintain them and associated grounds in a clean and orderly condition. Other terms used for "building caretaker" are "concierge" and "janitor."	5153: Building caretakers
31 Teachers' aides	Teachers' aides perform nonteaching duties to assist teaching staff, and provide care and supervision for children in schools and preschools.	5312: Teachers' aides
32 Firefighter	Firefighters respond to calls to extinguish fires and to deal with other civil emergencies.	5411: Firefighters
33 Policeman or policewoman	Policemen and policewomen maintain law and order and enforce laws and regulations. Work typically involves gaining familiarity with an area and the persons living in it, noting suspicious activities, patrolling assigned areas, rendering first aid, making investigations, maintaining logs of their activities, and giving evidence in legal proceedings. They generally work under the supervision of police inspectors or detectives. Examples of the occupations classified here include constable, patrolman/patrolwoman, police officer, river or harbor policeman/policewoman.	5412: Police officers
34 Prison guard	Prison guards watch over and maintain discipline among inmates of prisons, reformatories, or penitentiaries.	5413: Prison guards
35 Driver (general duty)	Drivers drive motor cars and vans to transport passengers, mail, or goods. They maintain their vehicles in a clean and roadworthy condition.	8322: Car, taxi, and van drivers
36 Office cleaners	Office cleaners perform various cleaning tasks in order to keep clean and tidy the interiors and fixtures of government offices.	9112: Cleaners and helpers in offices, hotels, and other establishments
37 Kitchen helpers	Kitchen helpers clear tables, clean kitchen areas, wash dishes, prepare ingredients, and perform other duties to assist workers who prepare or serve food and beverages. Kitchen helpers work in canteens and restaurants in schools, universities, hospitals, and government ministries and departments.	9412: Kitchen helpers
38 Messengers	Messengers carry and deliver messages, packages, and other items within an establishment or between establishments. They deliver messages either on foot or using vehicles such as bicycles and motor scooters.	9621: Messengers

Source: ICP.

Reporting Form for Compensation of Employees

The questionnaire for compensation of employees appears in table 15.8. A separate form will be completed for each of the four career points from entry level to 20 years of experience. The list of types of income in kind has been expanded to include transportation and other forms of income in kind. In addition, cash allowances for housing, food, meals, and so forth are now shown separately. In the 2005 reporting form (see table 15.5), these cash allowances were to be included in the basic salary but were not itemized separately. Another important change is that countries are asked to

TABLE 15.8 Questionnaire for Compensation of Employees, ICP 2011

Item no.	Information to be supplied on compensation of employees in selected occupations	Example
1	**Year for which data are reported**	2011 (yyyy)
2	**ICP occupation code and name**	9 Hospital nurse
3	**ISCO code and name**	2221 Nursing professionals
4	**Currency unit**	Hundred pesos/dollars/ thousand rupees . . .
5	**Level (tick)** Entry level ☐ 5 years ☐ 10 years ☐ 20 years ☐	
6	***Cash remuneration***	
7	**Base pay**	40,000
8	**Allowances and other additions to pay in cash:**	
9	Housing	6,000
10	Transportation	3,000
11	Food and meals	1,000
12	Other allowances	2,000
13	**Employers' social security contributions:**	
14	Actual contributions	Not applicable
15	Imputed contributions	3,000
16	***In-kind remuneration:***	
17	Housing	3,000
18	Transportation	1,000
19	Food and meals	1,400
20	Other in-kind remuneration	1,000
21	***Total remuneration***	61,400
22	**Number of *regular (official)* work-hours per week**	36 hours
23	**Number of *actual* hours worked per week**	24 hours
24	**Number of days of annual leave per year**	20 days
25	**Number of work-days per week**	5 days
26	**Number of public holidays per year**	10 days

Source: ICP.

TABLE 15.9 Explanatory Notes to Table 15.8, Reporting Form for Compensation of Employees

Item no.	Explanatory note
5	Complete a separate questionnaire for each level of experience: entry level, 5 years, 10 years, and 20 years.
7	Base pay is the annual salary according to the government pay scale.
9–12	These are cash payments received by employees in addition to their base pay. "Other allowances" include housing allowances, electricity and water allowances, expatriation allowances, home leave allowances, bonus payments if these are made to all employees regardless of their performance, payments for travel to their home town for annual leave, "hard living" allowances for staff posted to distant or dangerous areas, and any other similar types of payments in cash.
14 and 15	In most countries, government employees are affiliated with some kind of social security scheme that provides retirement pensions, health insurance, and similar benefits. A government may make regular payments into a social security fund for its employees and thus enter the amount paid each year in line 14. In many countries, governments provide social security benefits to their employees but do not make payments into a social security fund. In this case, an "imputed" contribution is entered in line 15. It should be calculated in the same way as imputed social security contributions are calculated for national accounts.
17–20	In-kind remuneration is the value of goods and services provided to government employees free of charge. In some countries, school teachers and hospital staff are provided with free or subsidized accommodations. Raw foodstuffs and cooked meals may also be provided, as well as free or subsidized transport by bus or train. In-kind remuneration should be valued at the cost to the government of supplying these goods or services.
22	Report here the number of hours per week that the employee is expected to work according to government regulations.
23	In many countries, it is accepted practice that government employees work less than the regular (official) hours per week. They may have second jobs as teachers, accountants, or similar occupations. The best estimates of the hours per week actually worked by employees in this occupation should be reported here.

report hours actually worked when the hours are systematically less than the official hours. The explanatory notes are given in table 15.9.

Total Government Expenditures

Table 15.10 is the reporting form for total government expenditures. It covers both collective and individual government expenditures and gross fixed capital formation, as well as current outlays.

The changes planned for the 2011 ICP build on the experience of the 2005 ICP, which in turn built on the experience gained in earlier ICP rounds. Proper measurement of the services produced by governments is both important and difficult. It is important because in many countries governments are large and growing and the general public would like to know how efficiently their taxes are being used to provide collective and individual services. Measurement is difficult because there are no market prices to value government services, and so output usually has to be valued at the cost of the inputs used to produce them. If these costs go up, the output of government services goes up by the same amount, but there is no certain guarantee that this extra output is wanted by, or useful for, the taxpayers who finance it. It is for this reason that attempts will be made in the 2011 ICP to compare the real output of government health and education services in participating countries. Even if these attempts prove unsuccessful, the experience gained will be available for those who will design future rounds of the ICP.

TABLE 15.10 Questionnaire on Government Expenditures, ICP 2011

Item no.	Item	Level of government		
		General	Central or federal	Other levels
Enter amounts in national currency. Specify units ______				
1	Wages and salaries in cash			
2	Employer's contribution to social security funds			
3	Actual			
4	Imputed			
5	Benefits in kind			
6	Housing			
7	Transportation			
8	Food and meals			
9	Other in-kind benefits			
10	Intermediate consumption expenditure			
11	Other taxes less subsidies on production			
11	Consumption of fixed capital			
13	Net operating surplus			
14	Sales and fees (minus)			
15	Gross fixed capital formation			
16	Year 20_____			

Source: ICP.
Note: Explanation of items:

General government includes all levels of government such as federal, central, provincial, state, municipal, and local government agencies. Report expenditures separately for the central or federal government and for all other levels of government combined.

Item 1. Wages and salaries in cash. This item covers all cash payments to government workers and includes overtime payments, performance bonuses, leave allowances, family allowances, cost of living allowances, and similar payments in addition to regular wages and salaries.

Item 2. Employer's contribution to social security funds. If the government contributes to a social security fund on behalf of its employees, enter the total amount of these contributions under item 3, "Actual." Many governments do not contribute to a fund, but nevertheless provide pensions and health and other benefits to their employees. In this case, the SNA requires countries to estimate what the contribution would have been if these benefits were being paid for out of a social security fund. In item 4, enter the estimate shown in the national accounts.

Item 5. Benefits in kind cover all benefits such as provision of free or subsidized food or meals, free or subsidized accommodations, free or subsidized transport, and so forth. All benefits in kind should be valued at the cost to government of providing them to its employees.

Item 10. Intermediate consumption expenditure consists of the goods and services purchased by government to provide health, education, defense, and all other services. This expenditure may include rent, electricity, office supplies, teaching materials, and medical goods. It excludes any of the goods and services included above as benefits in kind under item 5.

Item 11. Other taxes less subsidies on production. These include employment taxes and taxes on property. Governments rarely impose taxes on themselves, and this item will be zero in most countries.

Item 12. Consumption of fixed capital should be based on capital stock estimates valued at current market prices. In practice, not many countries have these estimates and can only report depreciation based on historic (or "acquisition") values.

Item 13. Net operating surplus. "Net" means that the operating surplus is calculated after deducting consumption of fixed capital. It is very rare that government agencies have a net operating surplus, but it can happen that local authorities may earn a net operating surplus from a local bus or tram service, for example. For most countries, this item will be zero.

Item 14. Sales and fees are "negative" consumption and have to be deducted. They may include items such as museum entrance charges, passport fees, and licenses to own pets or firearms.

Item 15. Gross fixed capital formation by government consists mainly of expenditures on plant and machinery, buildings, roads, bridges, and other structures. Expenditures on mineral exploration, development of orchards, timber tracts, land improvement, and computer software and databases are also included.

Item 16. Data should be supplied for the most recent year for which final estimates of government expenditures are available.

NOTES

1. See Commission of the European Communities et al. (1993). The detailed definition of *government* is given in paragraphs 4.101–4.131.
2. See http://www.ilo.org/public/english/bureau/stat/isco/index.htm.

REFERENCES

Commission of the European Communities, International Monetary Fund, Organisation for Economic Co-operation and Development, United Nations, and World Bank. 1993. *System of National Accounts 1993*. http://unstats.un.org/unsd/sna1993/toctop.asp?L1=5.

United Nations. 2000. "Classification of the Functions of Government (COFOG)." In *Classification of Expenditure According to Purpose*. New York: United Nations.

CHAPTER 16

Government Services: Productivity Adjustments

ALAN HESTON

This chapter addresses questions about how the International Comparison Program (ICP) measures the output flowing from expenditures that are not directly purchased by final users. These are often referred to as nonpriced or comparison-resistant services. In the ICP literature, the main headings are "individual government expenditures for education and health" and "collective expenditures provided by governments or nongovernmental organizations" (NGOs). Annex A to this chapter sets out the way in which these basic headings were priced in the 2005 round of the ICP in the context of all basic headings under government. Chapter 11 in this volume discusses the government basic headings in more detail, especially the distinction between individual and collective government expenditures.

Individual government expenditures for health and education fall into two categories: (1) benefits and reimbursements and (2) production of services. Purchasing power parities (PPPs) for benefits and services are based on prices, as described in chapter 11. PPPs for the production of health and education services are based on input costs as measured by compensation of employees, intermediate consumption, and other categories shown in the table in annex A. The comparison-resistant services include collective government expenditures and actual household expenditures on education and health by both households and government. The purpose of this chapter is (1) to explain how some of the PPPs for three basic headings for compensation of employees were in some cases adjusted for productivity, (2) to describe the pros and cons of such adjustments and their effects, and (3) to offer suggestions for improvement.

The first section of this chapter summarizes how the estimation was carried out in the 2005 ICP round within each region. Where output is not market-priced, PPPs can be derived for the labor inputs in these expenditure headings by comparing salaries for different skill and occupational employment categories based on international standard definitions. Using these salary comparisons as the equivalent of PPPs and then dividing expenditures by the PPP provides indirect quantity comparisons of these services. However, the method can produce improbable volumes for low-salary countries such as Tajikistan, Republic of Yemen, and Cambodia. The reason in part is that salaries are lower in lower-income countries because personnel are accompanied by less capital and are therefore producing less output than in higher-income countries. Lower productivity also results because supervisors are under little pressure to use staff efficiently when their salaries are so low and the value of their output is so hard to measure, which is true of government and education especially. This problem was recognized early on in the ICP's work when there were fewer countries, but it was even more evident in the 2005 ICP round when the range of salaries across the 146 countries was much larger.

In the report on the 1975 ICP, Kravis, Heston, and Summers (1982) devote chapter 5 to these comparison-resistant services. Two points from this chapter are noted here. The first point, covered in the second section of this chapter, deals with evidence on whether the PPPs for priced services can be used to approximate the PPPs for comparison-resistant services. The third section of this chapter discusses some of the methods considered to deal with this problem in the early ICP rounds. The fourth section then deals with how the regions were linked in the 2005 ICP round and considers whether the linking could have taken into account the different methods used in the regions. The chapter concludes with a discussion of an alternative for improving comparability across regions that might be considered for the 2011 ICP.

Treatment of Comparison-Resistant Services in the 2005 ICP Round

In preparation for the 2005 ICP, countries in the European Union (represented by its national statistical office, Eurostat) and the Organisation for Economic Co-operation and Development (OECD) had lengthy discussions on how to compare nonpriced services. They decided on compensation of employees. These discussions were informed by earlier experience in linking associated countries to the Eurostat-OECD comparison.[1] In the end, the Eurostat-OECD countries agreed to base PPPs for comparison-resistant services in 2005 on salary comparisons, stratified by type of occupation and skill. Because the Commonwealth of Independent States (CIS) was linked to the Eurostat-OECD region through the Russian Federation, 50 countries were already committed to basing PPPs on salary comparisons. In view of this constraint on the global comparison, it was decided initially to follow the same procedure in the other regions. Chapter 15 of this volume describes the occupations for which salaries were obtained and the overall framework for data collection.

The Final 2005 Approach

In the 2005 round, the publication schedule for the South America region was ahead of that for other regions; it followed the method used by the Eurostat-OECD comparison. However, the review of the salary information for the Asia-Pacific region revealed that the initial results, even after extensive validation of the data, did not appear to yield plausible value measures. In particular, the indirect quantities for poor countries such as the Lao People's Democratic Republic for headings such as collective government services greatly exceeded those for Hong Kong SAR, China, or Singapore. Similarly, in Western Asia the initial results produced volumes of comparison-resistant services for the Republic of Yemen that were much larger than those for its oil-rich neighbors.

The Asia-Pacific region was the first to introduce productivity adjustments for the headings of publicly provided education, health, and collective government services. This method is described in appendix D of the final report of the 2005 ICP (World Bank 2008).[2] A Cobb-Douglas production function was used to adjust for productivity differences across countries in a manner similar to that used in 1975 ICP round for education, health, and collective government services, as described in the next section.[3] Following the notation in the final report (World Bank 2008, appendix D), output Y is a function of labor L and capital K. The labor and capital coefficients are α and $(1 - \alpha)$. The constant returns to scale production function is given as

$$Y = cL^{\alpha}K^{1-\alpha}. \tag{16.1}$$

The productivity adjustment involves estimation of the relationship of output per worker to accompanying inputs, in this case labor. Equation (16.1) may then be rewritten as

$$\frac{Y}{L} = c\left(\frac{K}{L}\right)^{1-\alpha}. \tag{16.2}$$

The value of α is unknown, but, according to appendix D of the 2005 ICP report, "similarly empirical studies have found values of α to be in the range of 0.5 to 0.7 for low- to high-income economies, respectively" (World Bank 2008, 180).

Assuming these values hold across the 2005 ICP countries, then grouping countries into low, medium, and high income, combined with their capital output levels, allows estimation of their labor productivity.

Because data were not initially requested from countries, there was no information on capital stock or labor specific to education, health, or collective government services on which to fall back. It was heroically assumed that L was the population aged 15–64, which implied that labor force participation rates for that age cohort were the same across the wide range of 2005 countries. The next data problem was K, the capital stock information; it was available for some countries in Asia, but only a few in Africa and Western Asia. Again, a very strong assumption had to be made: for the few countries available, the range of capital output ratios, from 2.5 to 3.5, applied to all countries. Because these values rose from low- to medium- to high-income countries, the values of 2.5, 3.0, and 3.5 were assigned to those countries, respectively.

The next problem was to group countries in the Asia-Pacific, Western Asia, and Africa regions into the three income groups. The initial groupings were proposed in regional meetings, and typically agreement was reached without change. Thus each country had an assumed capital output ratio and value of $(1 - \alpha)$, the inputs necessary to estimate equation (16.2). In application of the assumed values, the country-specific value of c, obtained from an initial Gini-Éltetö-Köves-Szulc (GEKS) gross domestic product (GDP) aggregation, was substituted into (16.2) for each country in the regional comparison.[4] This method provided an adjusted estimate of output per worker that might lead to moving countries into a different income group and performing another iteration—see table 16.1 for a noniterative illustration that includes seven countries (or economies) in Africa, the Asia-Pacific, and Western Asia where a productivity adjustment was implemented. It also includes four countries that made no adjustment of salaries when estimating the PPP for staff in converting health, education, and collective government expenditures to volumes of output. These countries are Russia, which took part in both the Eurostat-OECD and CIS regional comparisons, and the Kyrgyz Republic, which took part only in the CIS comparison, along with Bolivia and Chile.

In table 16.1, the selected countries are assigned per capita GDP (PCGDP) groups in column (1). The per worker GDP from 2005 is given in column (2), which uses the International Labour Organization (ILO) labor force measure (L) as the denominator. Column (3) uses the proportion of population aged 15–64. The ILO measure is a census, not employment, number, but it does illustrate differences in reported participation rates among countries. The difference between columns (2) and (3) is low in the Lao PDR and very high in the Republic of Yemen, where reportedly few women are said to be in the labor force. Applying the "aged 15–64" labor definition

TABLE 16.1 Simplified Illustration of 2005 ICP Productivity Adjustment

international dollars as determined by PPPs

Selected country or economy	PCGDP group (1)	GDP/*L*, ILO (2)	GDP/*L*, 15–64 (3)	GDP/*L*, HK = 100 (4)	Adj. for *K*/*L*, HK = 100 (5)	PCGDP, HK = 100 (6)	PA, all countries (7)
No productivity adjustment							
Bolivia	Low	7,990	6,063	12.5	13.6	10.2	9.3
Chile	Medium	29,494	18,369	37.8	40.3	34.3	32.3
Kyrgyz Republic	Low	3,908	2,743	5.7	6.1	4.8	4.3
Russian Federation	Medium	22,823	16,658	34.3	36.6	33.3	31.2
Productivity adjustment							
China	Low	6,892	5,752	11.9	12.9	11.4	11.4
Hong Kong SAR, China	High	68,785	48,535	100.0	100.0	100.0	100.0
India	Low	5,393	3,326	6.9	7.4	6.0	6.0
Lao PDR	Low	3,744	3,246	6.7	7.3	5.0	5.0
Nepal	Low	2,661	1,891	3.9	4.2	3.0	3.0
South Africa	Medium	23,425	13,116	27.0	28.8	23.7	23.7
Yemen, Rep.	Low	9,647	4,512	9.3	10.1	6.4	6.4

Source: ICP 2005.
Note: PCGDP = per capita gross domestic product; ILO = International Labour Organization; *L* = labor; HK = Hong Kong SAR, China; *K* = capital; PA = productivity adjustment.

used in the 2005 ICP for productivity adjustments, GDP per worker level, with HK (Hong Kong SAR) equal to 100, appears in column (4). Hong Kong SAR, China was taken as the high-income economy in the Asia-Pacific for which no productivity adjustment was made.

The GDP per worker figure in column (4), when adjusted for the capital per worker group of each country, yields column (5) with HK = 100. Column (6) provides the per capita GDP of each country, with HK = 100, based on the 2005 ICP. Column (7) shows the per capita GDP adjusted for productivity (PA) for the first four countries for which no adjustment was done. For the last seven countries, the 2005 ICP numbers from column (6) are repeated. For the group of four countries, the adjustment for capital ranges from 6.6 to 8.8 percent in terms of GDP per capita. Applying a productivity adjustment to all countries would have the effect of changing the relative positions of poor and middle-income countries with respect to each other, but would have little effect on the range from poor to rich countries. The larger effect for low- and medium-income countries is between countries with and without a productivity adjustment. This effect is also clear in column (5). For Nepal, the Republic of Yemen, the Kyrgyz Republic, India, and Lao PDR, the volume of the three compensation headings would be under 10 percent of what they would have been with no adjustment; for Bolivia and China between 10 and 15 percent; and for Chile, Russia, and South Africa between 25 and 40 percent.

Effects of Productivity Adjustments on the Global Comparison

These adjustments are clearly large. One cannot infer from column (5) the effect on GDP per capita of the countries. This depends on their actual salary PPPs and expenditure shares of the compensation headings. In gauging the impact on global comparisons, the exact aggregation procedure makes a difference within and between regions.[5] However, some insight may be gained from looking at the 2005 ICP report, in particular tables 3–6, which provide 19 subaggregates of exchange rate and PPP converted per capita and total expenditures (World Bank 2008). From these subaggregates, three aggregates of PPP-converted and one aggregate of exchange rate–converted expenditures were calculated:

1. HECG1 = education, health, and collective government expenditures
2. HECG2 = 1 above from national accounts (the same as exchange rate–converted) expenditures
3. Domestic absorption (DA) = GDP minus the balance of exports and imports and changes in inventories. This is used to avoid problems with negative expenditures and can be derived two ways, as shown in 4 and 5.
4. PPP-converted domestic absorption (DA1) = GDP – exports + imports – changes in inventories = actual consumption + gross domestic fixed capital formation + collective government
5. DA2 = sum of 13 headings of actual consumption + collective government + gross fixed capital formation (sum of four components).

The table in annex B makes clear that the groupings HECG1 and HECG2 combine both private and public expenditures on health and education. HECG1 and HECG2 are shares of comparison-resistant services to domestic absorption using PPP conversions from the 2005 ICP round and shares at national prices. Table 16.2 compares the ratios of PPP-converted shares to shares at national prices. Countries are grouped by size of the ratio and region. The average ratio is quite large; the share at PPPs is 2.46 times larger than national shares, which are in turn 19.2 percent of GDP across the 146 countries. As discussed later in this chapter, this somewhat overstates the effect of the PPPs used to convert comparison-resistant services. But first, the striking differences across the regions in table 16.2 must be noted. The CIS and Asia-Pacific regions have average ratios well over 3.0; Africa is also high. Western Asia and South America are similar and still near 2.0, whereas half of the Eurostat-OECD countries, largely high-income, are below 1.5, with many less than 1.1. A noticeable split is apparent in Western Asia, with four of the Gulf countries comparable to their well-off Eurostat-OECD counterparts.

TABLE 16.2 Distribution by Region of Ratios of PPP-Converted Shares of Domestic Absorption of Public Expenditures on Education, Health, and Collective Government Wages and Salaries to Exchange Rate–Converted Shares

Ratio	Africa	Asia-Pacific	CIS (over domestic absorption)	Eurostat-OECD	South America	Western Asia	Total countries
1.0–1.5	4			25	1	4	34
1.5–2.0	9	3		8	7		27
2.0–3.0	18	8	2	11	2	5	46
3.0–4.0	12	7	6	1		1	27
> 4.0	5	5	2				12
Total countries	48	23	10	45	10	10	146
Average ratio	2.77	3.25	3.60	1.69	1.85	2.10	2.46

Source: ICP 2005.

TABLE 16.3 Distribution by Region of Ratios of Sum of GEKS Components (C + I + G) to GEKS

Ratio	Africa	Asia-Pacific	CIS (over domestic absorption)	Eurostat-OECD	South America	Western Asia	Total countries
0.95–1.05				14			14
1.05–1.10				13		4	17
1.10–1.15	7	9		6	7	1	30
1.15–1.20	9	8	4	9	2	3	35
1.20–1.25	14	3	4	2	1	1	25
>1.25	18	3	2	1		1	25
Total countries	48	23	10	45	10	10	146
Average ratio	0.997	1.144	1.092	1.010	1.019	1.061	1.043

Source: ICP 2005.
Note: GEKS = Gini-Éltetö-Köves-Szulc; C = actual final consumption; I = investment or capital formation; G = government.

These ratios can be misleadingly high because the denominator shares in national currencies must sum to 1.0, but not the numerator shares. The ratio of DA2 to DA1 in table 16.3 illustrates the nonadditive character of indexes such as the GEKS. As can be seen, the average of these ratios tended to be greater than 1.0 in the 2005 ICP, with the CIS and Asia-Pacific regions greater than 1.2, the Eurostat-OECD region less than 1.1, and the remaining regions between 1.1 and 1.2. But 25 countries have ratios greater than 1.25, and the ratio can approach 2.0 such as for The Gambia, with five countries exceeding 1.5. The country information underlying tables 16.2 and 16.3 is provided in the annex B table. The ratios greater than 1.0 in table 16.3 are the effect of the comparison-resistant services shown in table 16.2.

The main conclusion from tables 16.2 and 16.3 is that the estimates for comparison-resistant services in 2005 produced large increases in PPP-converted shares for low-income countries, even in regions in which productivity adjustments were made such as the Asia-Pacific. In regions with lower-income countries but in which no productivity adjustments were made, such as the CIS, it appears that there were even larger increases in shares of PPP-converted comparison-resistant services compared with shares at national prices. For these reasons, efforts are under way to improve the methods that will be used in the 2011 ICP, and the general outline of an improved approach to treatment of education has been recommended for all regions, although the final form of this method is not yet available. This chapter now turns to the question of whether guidance for the 2011 ICP round can be gained from experiences in rounds of the ICP before 2005.

Experiments with Priced and Nonpriced Services

The report by Kravis, Heston, and Summers (1982) on the third round of the ICP in 1975 compared the PPPs of priced services such as shoe repair, haircuts, and dry cleaning with nonpriced services, based on the 16 countries in the 1970 ICP, Phase II. Of the 151 basic expenditure headings, 10 were comparison-resistant services and 21 were priced services comprising, respectively, 11 and 16 percent of total expenditures on GDP. The definition of *priced services* includes all services in individual household consumption for which prices were collected for given specifications. The concept of service items usually involves the final purchaser consuming the service at the point of sale, either an establishment such as a restaurant or an automobile repair shop, a medical facility, or, in their place of residence, say, furnace repair. The service price includes the cost of labor, equipment, and parts. The distinction between services and commodities is not clear in many instances, but the broad split has shown up in predictable PPP differences in countries moving across the per capita GDP spectrum.

The relationships between the price level of priced services (P_P) and market-priced commodities (P_C) and per capita GDP (all indexed to US = 100) in logs from Kravis, Heston, and Summers (1982, 137), with standard errors of the coefficients in parentheses, are

$$\ln P_P = 2.351\ (.321) + .414\ (.090)\ \ln \text{PCGDP}; \quad R^2 = .57; \text{RMSE} = .322; n = 16 \tag{16.3}$$

and

$$\ln P_C = 3.317\ (.128) + .266\ (.036)\ \ln \text{PCGDP}; \quad R^2 = .78; \text{RMSE} = .129; n = 16. \tag{16.4}$$

To illustrate the meaning of equations (16.3) and (16.4), consider country A with a per capita GDP that is 90 percent of the U.S. GDP and country B with a per capita GDP that is 5 percent of the U.S. GDP. The price level of priced services for country A will be 3.3 times that of country B, whereas for commodities the multiple between country A and B is only 2.2. It follows that the ratio of PPPs of priced services to PPPs of commodities rises with per capita GDP. One explanation for this relationship is the Balassa-Samuelson effect (Balassa 1964; Samuelson 1964). It is based on the nontradability of most priced and nonpriced services and the assumption that productivity in services grows more slowly than commodities.[6] Labor is usually mobile within countries so that wage rates for similar skills will be comparable, whether in the production of traded commodities or nontraded services.[7]

But it also turns out that the PPP for nonpriced services rises more rapidly with per capita GDP than for priced services, so that the ratio of price levels for comparison-resistant to priced services also rises with GDP. The average ratio of prices for comparison-resistant services to market services for Kenya and India, the lowest of the 16 countries in 1970, was 32.5, and for France and Germany, the countries just below the United States (at 100 by definition), 86.5. As will be discussed shortly, the 2005 ICP results for 146 countries display a similar relationship.

How does one explain this relationship? Is there less physical capital per worker in the education, health, and collective services than in other services? Does physical capital per worker rise more rapidly in these nonpriced services than in priced services? Or, as is more likely, are both effects evident? And is labor monitoring less in low-wage countries compared with high-wage countries? If so, it would lead to larger productivity differences between priced and nonpriced services in low-wage countries. The data needed to answer these questions are not available. However, because the 2005 ICP exhibited a similar relationship, it is worth noting the adjustments considered for the 1975 ICP.

Kravis, Heston, and Summers (1982) made some illustrative and informative calculations that took into account the relative importance of the comparison-resistant services in expenditures. Equal productivity PPPs based on salary comparisons were replaced by the PPPs for priced services, and the PPPs for all other basic headings were used in separate Geary-Khamis (GK) aggregations. The effects on per capita income for the averages of the first and second quartiles of the 16 countries for 1970 are as follows. If the published GDP per capita of the first quartile average (Kenya, India, the Philippines, and Republic of Korea) is 100, then, using the PPPs of priced services, the index is 87—that is, if staff in education, health, and collective government services were only as productive as labor in priced services in their countries, the per capita GDP of the lowest quartile would be only 87 percent compared with using the equal productivity assumption. For the next poorest quartile (Colombia, Malaysia, Islamic Republic of Iran, and Hungary), the comparable result is 95 percent, or a 5 percent reduction in per capita GDP.

Labor mobility is subject to some constraints, including premiums in larger organizations, but, in general, workers can move between commodity and service sectors so that similar skills tend to receive similar pay. It is then plausible to believe that market-priced service PPPs might be a reasonable approximation of the PPP for nonpriced services. Kravis, Heston, and Summers (1982, 140) conclude that the "results for middle and high-income countries are insensitive to the treatment of comparison resistant services. More is at stake for the low-income countries."

As a result of these findings, several modifications of the equal productivity assumption were introduced in the 1975 ICP round for the different headings of comparison-resistant services, which are discussed in the next section.[8]

How did these results hold up for the 2005 ICP? First, these results cannot be compared directly with those in the 2005 ICP because researchers had access only to a set of 129 basic headings of expenditures and PPPs—a data set with less detail than that in the 2005 ICP report. Furthermore, these PPPs already embodied the productivity adjustment used for the Africa, Asia-Pacific, and Western Asia regions, so the comparison was not as clear as that for the 1970 ICP. The comparisons reported in table 16.4 use only two EKS aggregations over the 128 basic headings of domestic absorption, which is GDP less the net foreign balance and net expenditures of residents abroad. Domestic absorption was used because the net foreign balance and net expenditures of residents abroad have never been handled satisfactorily in the history of the ICP, and because DA is a meaningful measure of the bundle of goods and services that countries distribute among various basic headings of expenditures.[9]

Table 16.4 is based on two EKS aggregations of the 2005 ICP basic headings. The first is similar to that in the final report except that the aggregation is over all countries and fixity is not observed.[10] The second uses the same aggregation, but substitutes the PPPs for priced services for each country for compensation payments for collective government and publicly provided education and health care. This table summarizes the results by region. The table in annex C provides the basic headings used for priced and nonpriced services.

Table 16.4 presents the distribution of countries within each region by the ratio of the PPP or the DA of the second aggregation (using priced services) to the first aggregation. If the ratio for

TABLE 16.4 Distribution by Region of Ratio of PPP for Domestic Absorption Using PPP for Priced Services to PPP for Domestic Absorption in ICP 2005, Both Aggregated by EKS over All Countries

Ratio	Africa	Asia-Pacific	CIS	Eurostat-OECD	South America	Western Asia	Total
0.95–1.05				14			14
1.05–1.15	6	9		19	5	5	44
1.15–1.25	23	11	8	11	5	5	63
1.25–1.35	17	3	1	1			22
> 1.35	2		1				3
Total	48	23	10	45	10	10	146
Average ratio	1.24	1.18	1.23	1.10	1.15	1.13	1.17

Source: ICP 2005.
Note: EKS = Éltetö, Köves, and Szulc.

a country is greater than 1.0, the corresponding estimate of DA per capita relative to the United States will be smaller using the PPP for priced services. The use of priced services PPPs would produce smaller estimates of per capita DA for most countries; the average is 17 percent for all 146 countries. The pattern by region is plausible. The difference is smallest in the Eurostat-OECD countries and highest in the CIS countries in which no productivity adjustment was made and in Africa where the base comparison already includes a productivity adjustment. In general, the pattern in table 16.4 is consistent with the Kravis, Heston, and Summers results of a generation earlier, when the biggest effect of this substitution was on lower-income countries and regions.

One conclusion of this chapter is that the use of the PPP for priced services is a possible fallback should problems arise with other methods, or as a useful validation tool. It has the advantage of being simple and transparent to implement. It assumes that the relationship between productivity in collective government services and in publicly provided education and health services is similar across countries. However, because some such assumption is involved in most approaches, perhaps it is not a major limitation. This approach also depends on good estimates of the PPPs for priced services, which are difficult to specify, leading to less than robust results. In fact, the inability of countries to collect enough priced service items led Kravis, Heston, and Summers (1982) to use alternative methods in the 1975 ICP round. When the OECD considered using priced services in the late 1980s, the proposal was abandoned because of data limitations.

Was the coverage of priced services adequate enough in the 2005 ICP to justify a recommendation for use of the PPP for priced services as an alternative treatment of comparison-resistant services? More research is required to answer this question. Such research might include looking into (1) the sensitivity of the results to alternative bundles of priced services; (2) the implicit volume comparisons for these services relative to alternative estimates; and (3) whether the use of priced services might be combined with other methods.

Other Methods for Dealing with Nonpriced Services Up to the 1975 Round

The previous section examined the approach used in the 2005 ICP for comparison-resistant services and the possible use of the PPPs of priced services. This section considers some other approaches from previous ICPs. This discussion is not exhaustive because of space constraints and because Sergeev (1998) has provided an excellent summary of methods used in the early rounds of the ICP and especially those developed from 1975 to 1998 for comparing nonpriced expenditure basic headings for the Eurostat-OECD comparisons. Some of these methods were used only to link countries in Eastern and Western Europe for which Sergeev provides interesting illustrations. Here the focus is on some of the methods considered in Kravis, Heston, and Summers (1982).

Health Personnel

Because there had been criticism of the treatment of services in the 1970 ICP, more data were requested for the 1975 ICP in the health field, including numbers of medical personnel by type, stock of health capital, and directly priced physician services. Various studies were consulted, and the passing rates of medical students on a standard test were compiled for the 32 of the 34 ICP countries in 1975 that had medical schools (Kravis, Heston, and Summers 1982, 152). Many checks were carried out on the method eventually adopted, but here three main points on the treatment of health are especially relevant for future ICP considerations.

First, it is extremely useful to collect as much quantity, quality, and direct price and wage information as possible for health services. To illustrate, the 1970 ICP used only direct quantity comparisons for medical personnel, which is analogous to 2005 in that equal productivity of personnel was assumed. Initially, the 2005 ICP was going to assume equal productivity as well, but the quantities were to be derived indirectly by dividing expenditures on personnel by PPPs estimated from salary comparisons. Certainly, one would like to obtain comparable results by these two approaches because both make the same assumptions about productivity. However, this is possible only when both salary and direct quantity information are collected. The same principle would apply to other expenditure groupings, including education, collective government services, construction, and dwelling services.

Second, in the health field many directly priced medical services purchased by households are used in the ICP, such as physician visits, X-rays, and lab tests. These can be directly compared with the PPPs derived from salary comparisons of hospital personnel or the PPPs derived from expenditures and quantities of medical personnel. Furthermore, the 1975 ICP also used direct quantities consumed by households such as hospital bed-days and measures such as number of physicians or nurses per person, which are slightly closer to output. Measures of output of medical services would be ideal, but the results of the research under way are unlikely to be operational for the 2011 ICP comparisons.

Third, the use of crude production functions to better approximate medical output requires some heroic assumptions, but even Cobb-Douglas functions provide a useful framework for comparisons. In the 1975 ICP, the attempt to collect information on the stock of medical capital was not a great success in that only 8 of the 34 countries could provide estimates. However, the range of countries included low-, middle-, and high-income. Health capital was broken into hospitals and all the rest. These observations were stylized into adjustment factors for health personnel to approximate equivalence in the productivity of dentists, nurses, and physicians in the 1975 ICP. For countries with less than 30 percent of U.S. per capita GDP, the divisor for personnel was 1.30, and for countries between 30 and 50 percent, it was 1.15 (Kravis, Heston, and Summers 1982, 143).

The 1975 approach was similar to that used for some regions in the 2005 ICP except that the latter used capital per worker for the whole economy across all publicly provided comparison-resistant services, including hospitals. Kravis, Heston, and Summers (1982) used hospital capital and hospital bed-days in a production function that produced adjustment factors similar to those for personnel, and so the same adjustment was made for hospital bed-days as just described. In addition, the adjustments covered all medical personnel whether or not they were employed in hospitals or were providing market-priced services. One important conclusion of the 1975 ICP treatment of health was that the direct price measures of the PPPs of health services, such as doctor visits, rise with per capita income much faster than the PPPs measured indirectly by dividing expenditures by labor input, about which more follows.

Education

Capital stock measures for education were harder to obtain in the 1975 ICP because only three countries supplied data. Furthermore, the role of physical capital in producing educational services was more ambiguous than in health services. For these reasons, no adjustment was attempted for capital by Kravis, Heston, and Summers (1982). Cross-country studies based on common tests in local languages conducted around 1970 revealed that "the home variables were relatively less important and the school inputs (relating to inputs such as teachers and library facilities) more important in explaining school performance in developing countries than in developed countries"

(Kravis, Heston, and Summers 1982, 156). However, the state of the art of cross-country testing methodology did not appear robust enough in 1975 to be used as a tool in making volume comparisons across countries.

As with health, both direct quantity and price data were collected for education, including the number of students and teachers at the primary and secondary levels. Salary data for teachers for five levels of teacher education were collected as well; a Country Product Dummy (CPD) was run to provide estimates of relative salaries across ICP countries adjusted for the relative education level of teachers. These direct PPPs based on salaries were then compared with indirect measures derived from dividing expenditures by teacher quantities. As for medical personnel, there is a systematic relationship between direct and indirect PPPs and per capita income. Because the latter rises faster than the former, the ratio of direct to indirect PPPs declines as per capita GDPs rise. Based on this relationship, a downward adjustment was made to the direct quantity estimates, which decreased from 80 percent for the lowest of four per capita income groups, 32 percent for the second, and 12 percent for the third, all relative to the top group of per capita income (Kravis, Heston, and Summers 1982, 159).

These adjusted teacher quantities represent the inputs to education and for want of any other measure would also represent the output. Another output measure is the number of students taught, but many problems are associated with the pupil measure as well. What is the relationship of class size to educational output? The number of pupils registered, the most typical figure available, is not necessarily the number who are attending and eventually graduating. In the end, the square root of the product of the adjusted quantity of teachers and the number of pupils was taken as the output of primary and secondary education. No adjustment was made for third-level education. Also, in the 1975 ICP, administrative expenses on education were excluded from the total education expenditures when dividing by the above quantity of numbers of teachers and pupils to derive indirect PPPs. Finally, the method to be adopted by the Eurostat-OECD countries in their 2011 comparisons uses test information to make an adjustment (in fact, small) to the measure of output, the number of primary and secondary students.

The method used for the Eurostat-OECD countries for 2011 may prove more difficult when extended to 180 countries in 2011. Although this approach is along the lines of the ICP approach before 2005, Kravis, Heston, and Summers (1982) found, based on their experience, that information on the salaries of teachers and their average years of training would also be useful. There is every reason to believe that quantity measures of students in primary and secondary education may overstate the output of the education sector for low-income countries, with the degree of overstatement declining with per capita income.

Collective Government Expenditures on Personnel

As for the 1970 ICP, a questionnaire was distributed in 1975 to countries to obtain information on capital in government. However, the response was not sufficient to form a basis for any adjustment. Eventually, it was decided to use the same adjustment factors used for health personnel—that is, a 30 percent adjustment for the lowest group of countries and 15 percent for the next group, with per capita GDPs of between 30 and 50 percent that of the United States.

The principal conclusion to emerge from the review in this section is summarized in figure 16.1 (figure 5-1 in Kravis, Heston, and Summers 1982). The horizontal axis, r, is the per capita GDP of a country relative to that of the United States, and the vertical axis is the price level of comparison-resistant services. The direct price level measure at lower incomes begins at a higher point than the price level indirectly measured by dividing expenditures by quantities or a

FIGURE 16.1 Relationship of Direct and Indirect PPP Estimates to Per Capita GDP

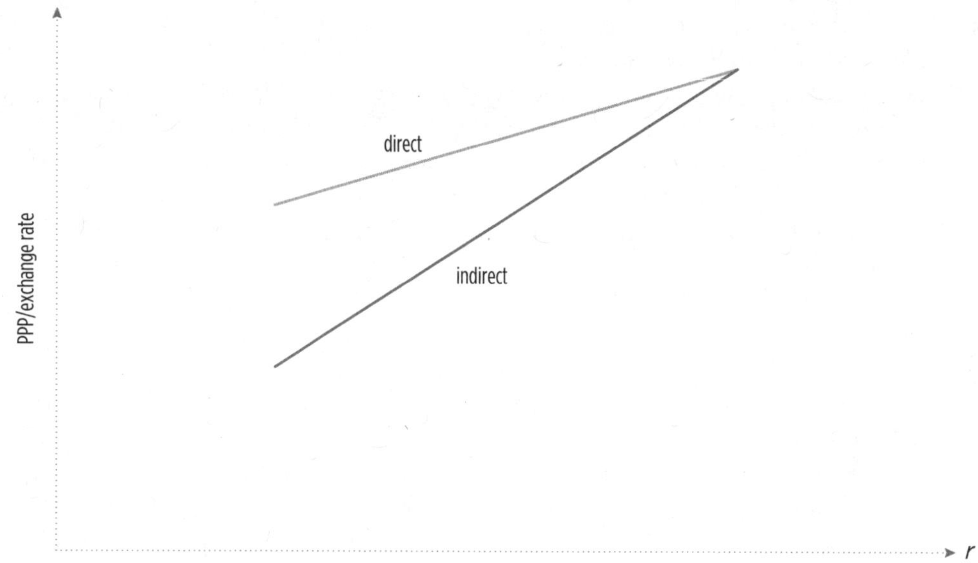

Source: Kravis, Heston, and Summers 1982.

price level estimated from salary comparisons. However, the direct measure rises more slowly with incomes, so that at moderately high incomes both measures yield comparable estimates of the price level. This pattern also appears in other difficult-to-measure sectors such as imputed rents for homeowners. When rents are measured directly, holding constant amenities of housing, they are higher than when measured by the quantity approach in which only a few elements of quality are captured. If, as Kravis, Heston, and Summers (1982) conclude, figure 16.1 captures a general phenomenon, then it provides strong support for collecting as much information as available for hard-to-compare expenditure headings.

Linking Issues for Regions in 2005

This chapter has covered the 2005 ICP procedures within each region, but not the linking of regions. The problem of linking regions first arose in the context of whether all expenditure groups should be linked through the 18 Ring countries that had agreed to undertake pricing of a large number of shop items (see chapters 1 and 8 for an explanation of the Ring and linking concepts). However, common questionnaires were used for areas such as housing and government salaries. Would it then be more appropriate to use data from all countries for linking or just the Ring countries? Because Ring countries did not appear likely to supply better-quality data for housing or salaries in some regions, an agreement was reached in the Global Office to use data for all countries. The Eurostat-OECD region was one exception to this pattern because the decision to use data from all countries instead of just the Ring was made after the Ring country protocol was adopted. South America was another exception because for budgetary reasons it was the first region to complete its work, and its salary classification was not comparable, so only the Ring countries, Brazil and Chile, were used for linking.

TABLE 16.5 Estimated Salary Differences across Regions in Education, Health, and Collective Government Services

	Coefficient	Anti-log	Standard error	*t*-value
Intercept	10.65	42,183.00	0.0905	117.72
Africa	−2.65	7.04	0.0972	−27.31
Asia-Pacific	−2.28	10.18	0.1029	−22.31
South America	−1.57	20.78	0.1208	−13
Western Asia	−1.71	18.14	0.1149	−14.86
Eurostat-OECD	0	100		
$n = 75$	$R^2 = .400$	Coeff. var. = 12.697	RMSE = 1.081	ln_wage mean = 8.514

Source: ICP 2005.
Note: RMSE = root mean square error. No CIS countries were in the data set.

The data available to the Global Office included wage data for 75 countries. For each country, there were data on the job and the occupational grouping (administration, defense, education, and health). In addition, a simple grouping by skill designation was assigned to each job, and, of course, countries were assigned to their region. Early estimates suggested that because of the spotty, variable character of the salary observations, it was best to omit defense from the estimation, thereby reducing the number of salary observations from 1,876 to 1,730. Several of these variables were collinear so that, for example, a CPD could not be estimated for a region and individual countries and for a job and occupational grouping or skill level. Table 16.5 provides the results of a CPD regression in which only regional and sectoral coefficients are estimated, but the latter are not shown.[11] Because country variation is not taken into account in table 16.5, the explained variance is fairly low. All of the coefficients are significant, and the rank of the regions is plausible. The second column of table 16.5 shows the anti-log of the regional coefficients in the table as a percentage of the Eurostat-OECD countries. Roughly speaking, salaries for comparable occupations are 14 times higher in the Eurostat-OECD countries than in Africa, and at least five times higher in the other regions. If expenditures were converted by these PPPs, they would greatly raise the estimated quantities of these comparison-resistant services. Again, no CIS countries were in the data set, although wages in several of these countries were quite low compared with those of the Eurostat-OECD countries (the salary data were not adjusted for calculation of the regional parameters used for linking, or, put another way, the between-region PPPs were not adjusted for productivity).

When the equation allows for individual country coefficients instead of regions, the explained variance is, of course, much higher ($R^2 = .97$). With the United Kingdom as the base (the nine Eurostat-OECD countries in the regression average 98 percent of the United Kingdom), Bolivia is only 5 percent of the United Kingdom, and many countries in Africa are even lower. Table 16.5 reinforces the need to follow up the initial steps taken in the 2005 ICP to make some adjustment for productivity.

A Proposal for Linking in 2011 and Conclusions

The linking issue was important for comparison-resistant services in the 2005 ICP because the productivity adjustment was made in three of the six regions, leading to likely noncomparability. For a country like Bolivia or Tajikistan where no productivity adjustment was made, per capita incomes would be less comparable with similar countries in Africa, the Asia-Pacific, or Western Asia. The issue is further complicated because the actual aggregation to the global level in 2005 was not carried out using the 146 countries individually; rather, it was carried out using five regional aggregates, the CIS included with the Eurostat-OECD. It was not possible in the end to obtain satisfactory regional adjustment factors to improve on a simple Ring country comparison.[12] As a consequence, a lack of comparability of low- and middle-income countries across different regions remains in the final 2005 ICP report. A somewhat different approach is explored here that uses as much salary information as is available to the Global Office and makes a rough allowance for productivity differentials across the regions based on the human and physical capital stock.

Estimates of Productivity by Country

Using the 2005 data, this section illustrates an alternative method of linking based on individual country productivity adjustments relying on a Cobb-Douglas production function across all the regions. Physical capital K_p and labor force estimates L are from the Penn World Table (PWT), and human capital estimates K_h are from the Barro-Lee data set.[13] The education measure is the average number of years of primary and secondary school completed. In equations (16.5) and (16.6), the dependent variable is the log of $\frac{GDP}{L}$, and in the first equation only $\frac{K_p}{L}$ is on the right side, whereas K_h is also included in the second equation:

$$\ln \frac{GDP}{L} = 4.56 + .704 \ln \frac{K_p}{L}; \quad R^2 = .799; n = 106 \tag{16.5}$$

$$\ln \frac{GDP}{L} = 4.87 + .552 \ln \frac{K_p}{L} + .455 * \ln K_h; \quad R^2 = .786; n = 87. \tag{16.6}$$

All the coefficients are significant, but for K_h only at the 5 percent level. The first equation covers more countries, which makes it preferable for the illustration that follows. In addition, when the ratio of the estimated to actual value is taken, the standard deviation is significantly larger for the equation including K_h (.0827 versus .065). Thus the specification or data problems associated with including human capital in the productivity equation require more research to justify inclusion.

A Productivity Adjustment

The direction of productivity adjustment across countries is clear. The method adopted in the Asia-Pacific region is one that certainly moves in the right direction in that most agree that output per government, health, or education worker is likely to increase with more capital per worker. The approach suggested here is illustrated for the 2005 ICP research data set. The following estimates were made.

First, output per worker estimates were based on estimating equation (16.5) for the 106 countries in the PWT data set. These estimates were extended to the remaining countries based on the relationship of the estimated log of output per worker for the 106 countries to per capita GDP from an initial GEKS estimate. This estimating equation had an R^2 of .465 with sensible coefficients, although if this method were adopted in the future one would want a tighter estimating equation. Applying the equation coefficients to the per capita GDPs of the remaining 40 countries yielded estimates of the log of output per worker. Another limitation on this illustration is that these estimates refer to the whole economy, not labor in comparison-resistant services.

Second, these output per worker estimates were used to obtain adjustment factors that ranged from 1 to 4, going from high- to low-income countries. The admittedly very rough groupings were as follows: output per worker greater than US$40,000 was assigned 1.0; $30,000–40,000, 1.2; $20,000–30,000, 1.5; $15,000–20,000, 2.0; $10,000–15,000, 2.5; $5,000–10,000, 3.3; and under $5,000, 4.0. These factors were used to adjust the parities obtained from wage comparisons to obtain new input parities for the compensation headings of comparison resistant-services.[14]

Third, aggregations were run using unadjusted and adjusted compensation figures to gauge the impact on the results. Although this step might eventually prove to be an effective adjustment for individual countries, that is not the purpose of the present exercise. It is already agreed that the Eurostat-OECD and CIS countries will not make any adjustment within their regions for the 2011 ICP round. One reason is that these regions are already moving toward quantity comparisons for education services and exploring possibilities for the health sector.

The purpose of this exercise is to propose a method that would allow regions to retain whatever method they choose for the regional exercise while at the same time linking the regions in a way that would permit the adjustment across regions to improve comparability. The results of this exercise are reported in table 16.6. Two aggregation methods have been used, both producing similar results. One is the GEKS method and the other a weighted CPD, labeled CPDW. The share of each region of global domestic absorption is calculated with and without adjustment for each of the two methods. These shares are simply obtained by adding up the total GDP of each country in a region and dividing by the global total. The total DA (world) is also provided for each method. As can be seen, without the productivity adjustment the world total is larger than with the adjustment because less output of these services is attributed to many of the lower-income countries.[15]

But more important, the shares of each region are also substantially affected. The Eurostat-OECD share goes up because few of its countries are affected by the adjustment, while the shares of all the other regions go down—Africa by more than 5 percent. The effect is larger for GEKS than for CPDW. These effects are similar to what would result if one used the PPP for nonpriced services for the compensation headings of comparison-resistant services—that is, the regional pattern of table 16.6 is similar to that of the priced service exercise summarized in table 16.4 where the effect would be strongest for Africa and less so for South America and Western Asia. However, it is clear that the variation in the PPP for nonpriced services is subject to more error than even the rough productivity adjustment of table 16.6.

TABLE 16.6 Estimated Effect of Productivity across 146 ICP 2005 Countries by Region—Share of Global Domestic Absorption

Region	GEKS, no adjustment	GEKS, adjustment	CPDW, no adjustment	CPDW, adjustment
Africa	0.0313	0.028	0.0309	0.0288
Asia-Pacific	0.2384	0.2196	0.2371	0.2250
CIS	0.0421	0.0390	0.0400	0.0380
Eurostat-OECD	0.6236	0.6529	0.6271	0.6471
South America	0.0509	0.0468	0.0510	0.0476
Western Asia	0.0138	0.0133	0.0139	0.0136
World (US$ billions)	60,071	55,202	60,085	55,249

Source: Penn World Tables.
Note: GEKS = Gini-Éltetö-Köves-Szulc; CPDW = Country Product Dummy-Weighted.

How would this proposal improve the global comparisons? The adjusted shares provide a regional total that can be distributed among the countries in a region in the same way as the regional comparison. But this approach has a cost in that comparability across basic heading parities is reduced. However, because greater interest centers on aggregate comparisons across countries, the type of adjustment in table 16.6, which provides a more complete picture, has a major advantage. The effects of the productivity adjustment are systematic across regions, and therefore attributing adjusted shares to each region will improve the comparability of total DA and GDP per capita across the regions more than carrying out an adjustment in some regions but not others.

In summary, this general method is likely to be useful for improving the comparability of comparison-resistant service volumes across countries when regions adopt different methods as appears likely in 2011 for collective government, health, and perhaps education and dwelling services. Dwelling services are explored in more detail in chapter 12. The other principal conclusion of this chapter relevant to the 2011 ICP is implicit in figure 16.1: indirectly estimated price levels tend to be systematically lower compared with direct price comparisons for low-income countries. In view of the heterogeneity of available national statistical bases, there is no simple solution to this problem, but there is a simple message. In much the same way that expenditure surveys and commodity flow tables are used as checks on each other in national accounts, collecting more information on the headache headings in the ICP can provide similarly useful checks on PPP and volume estimates.

The major suggestions for moving forward to the 2011 ICP are to (1) carry out productivity adjustments where needed, depending on the methods used in each region; (2) adjust estimated regional PPPs for linking for productivity; (3) determine labor and capital data requirements for regional and national adjustments; and (4) collect as much auxiliary data as possible about health, government, and education. Such data would include numbers of employees stratified by skill and occupation, pupils, and hospital bed-days.

ANNEX A

Summary of the Components of Individual Consumption by Households and Government for Health and Education: Their Role in the Estimation of PPPs

This annex illustrates the context in which productivity adjustments were made in the 2005 ICP for the basic headings for compensation of employees. The accompanying table shows the detailed headings of concern in this chapter and makes clear that some health and education expenditures are part of the individual consumption of households, including partial or full payment for visits to doctors and dentists, some lab services, and some tuition payments to private and public educational institutions. Many education, health, and collective government expenditures are for purchases of supplies and maintenance and depreciation of buildings and equipment. For these basic headings, reference PPPs—PPPs usually based on direct prices collected for other basic headings—are used. In the 2005 ICP, the PPPs for the three compensation lines shown in the following table were based on direct comparisons of salaries and benefits in cash and in kind for selected occupations, some specific and a few common to education, health, and collective government services. Compensation of government employees appears in the actual consumption of households and in collective services.

As the following table shows, a category such as health is made up of a combination of household and government individual expenditures for which PPPs are computed using prices for some aggregates and compensation of employees for other aggregates. All enter into the overall PPP for health. The same is true to a lesser extent for education. As noted in the table, the reference PPP for hospitals is based on the PPP for government purchases of health services and as such is heavily based on compensation-derived PPPs.

Finally, it should be noted that the term *comparison-resistant* services has usually referred to all the headings in the table, both private and collective expenditures.

A. Health goods and services

Individual consumption by households for health (1)	Basis for PPPs (2)	Individual consumption by government for health (3)	Basis for PPPs (4)
Health		Health benefits and reimbursements	
Medical products, appliances, and equipment	Prices	*Medical products, appliances, and equipment*	Col. (2) prices
Outpatient services	Prices	*Outpatient services*	Col. (2) prices
Hospital services	Reference	*Hospital services*	Reference
		Production of health services by government	
		Compensation of employees	Salaries of health-related occupations
		Intermediate consumption	Reference
		Operating surplus	Reference
		Net taxes	Reference
		Receipts from sales	Reference

B. Education

Individual consumption by households for education	Basis for PPPs	Individual consumption by government for education	Basis for PPPs
Education	PPPs from private education	**Education benefits and reimbursement**	Col. (2) prices
		Production of education services	
		Compensation of employees	Salaries of education-related occupations
		Intermediate consumption	Reference
		Operating surplus	Reference
		Net taxes	Reference
		Receipts from sales	Reference

C. Collective consumption expenditure by government

		Production of collective services for general government	Basis for PPPs
		Compensation of employees	Compensation of employees by occupation for general government
		Intermediate consumption	Reference
		Operating surplus	Reference
		Net taxes	Reference
		Receipts from sales	Reference

Source: ICP 2005.

ANNEX B

Effects of Productivity Adjustments on the Global Comparison in International Dollars (PPP or Exchange Rate)

	PCDA (1)	PCSumDA (2)	Ratio of PCsumDA to PCDA (3)	EKS (%) HECG/DA (5)	% Nat cur HECG/DA (6)	Col. (5)/ col. (6) (7)	Real health + Ed + C gov exp (8)
Bangladesh	1,295	1,414	1.09	36.4	10.5	3.49	472
Bhutan	3,901	5,159	1.32	57.1	17.2	3.33	2,229
Brunei Darussalam	35,733	35,145	0.98	63.0	37.2	1.69	22,497
Cambodia	1,459	2,053	1.41	85.1	15.2	5.60	1,242
China	3,986	4,657	1.17	49.1	16.7	2.93	1,956
Hong Kong SAR, China	32,338	32,627	1.01	29.8	17.3	1.72	9,647
Macao SAR, China	28,200	22,786	0.81	25.1	16.4	1.53	7,079
Taiwan, China	25,360	30,261	1.19	54.6	22.1	2.47	13,854
Fiji	4,822	5,848	1.21	49.7	15.9	3.14	2;398
India	2,141	2,489	1.16	51.7	14.8	3.50	1,106
Indonesia	3,170	3,244	1.02	33.4	11.2	2.98	1,059
Iran, Islamic Rep.	10,496	11,228	1.07	46.7	16.2	2.89	4,901
Lao PDR	1,856	2,572	1.39	76.4	16.3	4.69	1,418
Malaysia	10,259	10,212	1.00	39.7	17.0	2.34	4,073
Maldives	4,531	7,624	1.68	100.4	21.5	4.67	4,549
Mongolia	2,672	3,583	1.34	73.6	14.2	5.17	1,967
Nepal	1,135	1,372	1.21	55.2	14.7	3.76	626
Pakistan	2,437	2,943	1.21	52.8	14.4	3.65	1,286
Philippines	2,972	3,089	1.04	43.2	14.6	2.95	1,284
Singapore	33,543	33,033	0.98	35.0	20.5	1.71	11,732
Sri Lanka	3,583	3,699	1.03	34.4	9.9	3.48	1,233
Thailand	6,887	7,750	1.13	46.3	17.7	2.61	3,187
Vietnam	2,163	3,180	1.47	85.3	16.3	5.23	1,844
Asia-Pacific	11,781,385	13,481,449	1.14	48.3	16.3	2.96	5,691,615
Argentina	10,749	10,648	0.99	33.7	19.6	1.72	3,625
Bolivia	3,575	4,115	1.15	60.3	22.2	2.71	2,154
Brazil	8,401	8,875	1.06	45.9	27.8	1.65	3,857
Chile	11,607	10,846	0.93	29.4	20.3	1.45	3,411
Colombia	6,314	6,767	1.07	44.2	24.3	1.82	2,792
Ecuador	6,559	6,398	0.98	34.1	17.3	1.96	2,234

(continued)

	PCDA (1)	PCSumDA (2)	Ratio of PCsumDA to PCDA (3)	EKS (%) HECG/DA (5)	% Nat cur HECG/DA (6)	Col. (5)/ col. (6) (7)	Real health + Ed + C gov exp (8)
Paraguay	3,952	4,018	1.02	30.6	14.1	2.17	1,209
Peru	6,294	5,969	0.95	30.2	19.3	1.56	1,903
Uruguay	9,112	9,107	1.00	34.7	20.4	1.70	3,159
Venezuela, RB	8,779	7,748	0.88	32.8	19.5	1.68	2,883
South America	2,985,901	3,042,959	1.02	40.7	24.5	1.66	1,215,767
Albania	5,949	6,599	1.11	36.8	11.2	3.28	2,188
Australia	33,442	33,790	1.01	30.3	23.1	1.31	10,130
Austria	32,291	32,058	0.99	26.3	20.3	1.29	8,492
Belgium	30,745	31,211	1.02	29.8	24.0	1.24	9,147
Bosnia and Herzegovina	7,657	8,971	1.17	39.4	18.2	2.17	3,016
Bulgaria	9,924	11,191	1.13	47.4	18.1	2.62	4,704
Canada	33,745	33,901	1.00	25.8	21.4	1.20	8,710
Croatia	13,963	15,138	1.08	37.5	21.1	1.78	5,240
Cyprus	25,046	24,778	0.99	26.9	20.8	1.29	6,744
Czech Republic	19,890	21,167	1.06	39.2	23.1	1.70	7,798
Denmark	31,367	32204	1.03	29.1	23.2	1.26	9,133
Estonia	17,313	17886	1.03	36.6	16.9	2.16	6,335
Finland	28,388	28555	1.01	28.8	21.9	1.31	8,183
France	29,954	30356	1.01	28.7	22.0	1.30	8,611
Germany	28,787	29349	1.02	27.4	21.6	1.27	7,884
Greece	27,131	26766	0.99	29.7	20.2	1.47	8,056
Hungary	17,133	18417	1.07	39.4	22.4	1.76	6,752
Iceland	42,464	43262	1.02	27.8	21.7	1.28	11,787
Ireland	32,107	32417	1.01	26.1	19.1	1.37	8,377
Israel	23,790	25204	1.06	40.9	28.8	1.42	9,733
Japan	29,796	30567	1.03	30.3	20.0	1.51	9,034
Korea, Rep.	20,954	21510	1.03	30.7	19.6	1.57	6,431
Latvia	14,230	15434	1.08	42.0	17.5	2.39	5,970
Lithuania	14,637	15747	1.08	40.8	17.9	2.28	5,973
Luxembourg	51,504	52155	1.01	21.2	20.1	1.05	10,899
Macedonia, FYR	7,886	8,773	1.11	41.5	18.0	2.30	3,274
Malta	21,194	21,805	1.03	33.5	21.0	1.60	7,101
Mexico	11,436	11,543	1.01	32.3	16.3	1.97	3,688
Montenegro	8,468	10,071	1.19	57.7	26.5	2.17	4,883
Netherlands	31,638	32,414	1.02	30.5	23.6	1.29	9,665
New Zealand	25,105	24,828	0.99	28.1	19.4	1.45	7,048
Norway	36,837	37,611	1.02	29.0	22.3	1.30	10,695

	PCDA (1)	PCSumDA (2)	Ratio of PCsumDA to PCDA (3)	EKS (%) HECG/DA (5)	% Nat cur HECG/DA (6)	Col. (5)/ col. (6) (7)	Real health + Ed + C gov exp (8)
Poland	13,600	15,154	1.11	39.3	20.1	1.96	5,348
Portugal	21,527	21,515	1.00	29.7	23.2	1.28	6,399
Romania	9,847	10,761	1.09	43.4	18.5	2.35	4,273
Serbia	9,379	9,745	1.04	35.9	15.1	2.38	3,368
Slovak Republic	16,328	17,834	1.09	39.6	19.6	2.02	6,468
Slovenia	23,115	23,144	1.00	29.4	21.0	1.40	6,794
Spain	28,649	28,254	0.99	26.9	18.6	1.45	7,701
Sweden	28,972	30,530	1.05	33.5	24.4	1.38	9,720
Switzerland	32,286	33,022	1.02	26.1	20.6	1.27	8,418
Turkey	8,119	8,284	1.02	28.5	14.0	2.04	2,316
United Kingdom	32,915	32,760	1.00	25.7	19.8	1.30	8,462
United States	44,081	43,957	1.00	28.4	28.4	1.00	12,521
Eurostat-OECD	35,269,786	35,625,954	1.01	29.0	23.4	1.24	10,227,966
Armenia	4,104	5,282	1.29	49.6	12.6	3.93	2,035
Azerbaijan	4,487	4,746	1.06	41.7	12.0	3.47	1,872
Belarus	8,519	10,937	1.28	55.4	20.9	2.65	4,716
Georgia	3,767	4,925	1.31	55.0	17.4	3.17	2,073
Kazakhstan	8,367	10,900	1.30	63.4	18.0	3.52	5,307
Kyrgyz Republic	1,816	2,930	1.61	75.7	15.5	4.89	1,374
Moldova	2,700	4,753	1.76	77.7	14.3	5.42	2,099
Tajikistan	1,476	2,734	1.85	104.0	12.9	8.05	1,535
Ukraine	5,568	7,570	1.36	63.1	20.0	3.16	3,516
CIS	2,162,344	2,360,383	1.09	45.6	19.0	2.40	985,287
Angola	3,019	2,333	0.77	30.7	22.2	1.39	928
Benin	1,423	1,496	1.05	37.2	13.5	2.76	530
Botswana	11,244	8,195	0.73	36.6	29.2	1.25	4,111
Burkina Faso	1,194	1,232	1.03	41.9	20.7	2.03	500
Burundi	418	529	1.26	69.8	17.2	4.06	292
Cameroon	1,994	1,782	0.89	29.0	11.6	2.51	578
Cape Verde	3,401	4,254	1.25	44.1	15.8	2.80	1,501
Central African Republic	700	698	1.00	30.6	10.9	2.82	214
Chad	1,680	1988	1.18	77.7	9.1	8.56	1306
Comoros	1,138	1266	1.11	52.8	13.8	3.83	601
Congo, Dem. Rep.	262	258	0.98	41.9	13.9	3.02	110
Congo, Rep.	2,817	2,161	0.77	44.1	20.9	2.12	1,243
Côte d'Ivoire	1,515	1,332	0.88	31.1	17.7	1.76	471
Djibouti	1,959	2,063	1.05	46.8	26.5	1.77	918

(continued)

	PCDA (1)	PCSumDA (2)	Ratio of PCsumDA to PCDA (3)	EKS (%) HECG/DA (5)	% Nat cur HECG/DA (6)	Col. (5)/ col. (6) (7)	Real health + Ed + C gov exp (8)
Egypt, Arab Rep.	5,003	5,690	1.14	55.5	16.6	3.34	2,774
Equatorial Guinea	9,553	6,048	0.63	22.5	8.2	2.74	2,147
Ethiopia	611	561	0.92	25.3	14.4	1.76	155
Gabon	10,565	8,482	0.80	39.5	19.1	2.07	4,176
Gambia, The	811	1,598	1.97	152.6	37.4	4.08	1,237
Ghana	1,300	1,430	1.10	40.3	14.1	2.85	524
Guinea	948	1,023	1.08	48.0	15.8	3.03	455
Guinea-Bissau	622	771	1.24	64.4	20.5	3.15	400
Kenya	1,418	1,709	1.20	58.1	23.2	2.50	825
Lesotho	1,795	2,802	1.56	83.0	20.0	4.15	1,490
Liberia	407	552	1.36	82.0	22.8	3.60	334
Madagascar	1,034	1,360	1.32	73.5	19.1	3.85	760
Malawi	725	935	1.29	62.0	22.8	2.72	449
Mauritania	2,040	2,330	1.14	45.5	13.8	3.30	929
Mauritius	10,429	11,618	1.11	43.1	17.7	2.43	4,497
Morocco	3,669	3,586	0.98	31.1	21.3	1.46	1,142
Mozambique	780	778	1.00	37.4	16.2	2.31	291
Namibia	4,646	5,546	1.19	61.4	29.4	2.09	2,853
Niger	644	667	1.04	41.6	16.9	2.46	268
Nigeria	1,773	1,368	0.77	18.4	10.6	1.74	326
Rwanda	851	1,023	1.20	61.2	17.7	3.46	521
São Tomé and Príncipe	1,681	1,997	1.19	53.6	14.9	3.61	901
Senegal	1,783	1,790	1.00	34.9	15.1	2.31	622
Sierra Leone	858	1,328	1.55	97.5	30.2	3.23	836
South Africa	8,476	8,859	1.05	45.3	26.0	1.74	3,842
Sudan	2,342	1,947	0.83	17.0	8.0	2.12	399
Swaziland	4,455	4,867	1.09	54.6	19.7	2.77	2,431
Tanzania	1,048	816	0.78	17.0	7.7	2.22	178
Togo	995	1,141	1.15	45.3	13.9	3.25	451
Tunisia	6,456	6,279	0.97	30.8	17.5	1.77	1,991
Uganda	1,033	982	0.95	29.1	19.6	1.49	301
Zambia	1,244	1,435	1.15	40.6	21.4	1.90	505
Zimbabwe	552	683	1.24	64.2	11.0	5.85	354
Africa	1,821,701	1,816,152	1.00	39.8	18.9	2.11	725,704
Bahrain	23,095	23,008	1.00	31.4	22.8	1.38	7,249
Iraq	3,175	4,385	1.38	95.8	41.5	2.31	3,043

	PCDA (1)	PCSumDA (2)	Ratio of PCsumDA to PCDA (3)	EKS (%) HECG/DA (5)	% Nat cur HECG/DA (6)	Col. (5)/ col. (6) (7)	Real health + Ed + C gov exp (8)
Jordan	5,219	6,778	1.30	52.9	20.1	2.63	2,762
Kuwait	33,031	29,994	0.91	28.1	26.1	1.08	9,297
Lebanon	11,431	14,861	1.30	59.3	27.2	2.18	6,783
Oman	168,94	16,935	1.00	38.3	28.5	1.34	6,475
Qatar	50,248	52,753	1.05	26.7	20.5	1.30	13,438
Saudi Arabia	16,573	15,716	0.95	39.1	32.8	1.19	6,479
Syrian Arab Republic	4,013	4,849	1.21	53.0	17.9	2.96	2,127
Yemen, Rep.	2,226	2,538	1.14	47.9	15.3	3.13	1,066
Western Asia	844,324	896,140	1.06	46.4	26.8	1.73	391,800
World	548,65,442	57,223,036	1.04	35.1			19,238,139

Note: PCDA = per capita domestic absorption; PCSumDA = per capita domestic absorption from sum of 13 basic headings of actual consumption plus collective government plus gross fixed capital formation; HECG = health, education, collective government; EKS (%) HECG/DA = ratio of HECG PPP expenditures to domestic absorption; column (6) is same as column (5) except DA based on exchange rates; full caption of column (8) is real health, education, and collective government expenditures.

ANNEX C

Priced and Nonpriced Services, ICP 2005

Priced commodities		Priced services	
110111.1	Rice	110314.1	Cleaning and repair of clothing
110111.2	Other cereals and flour	110322.1	Repair and hire of footwear
110111.3	Bread	110410	Actual and imputed rentals for housing
110111.4	Other bakery products	110430	Maintenance and repair of the dwelling
110111.5	Pasta products	110440	Water supply and miscellaneous services relating to the dwelling
110112.1	Beef and veal	110442	Miscellaneous services relating to the dwelling
110112.2	Pork	110451	Electricity
110112.3	Lamb, mutton, and goat	110452	Gas
110112.4	Poultry	110453	Other fuels
110112.5	Other meats and preparations	110513	Repair of furniture, furnishings, and floor coverings
110113.1	Fresh or frozen fish and seafood	110533	Repair of household appliances
110113.2	Preserved fish and seafood	110562.1	Domestic services
110114.1	Fresh milk	110562.2	Household services
110114.2	Preserved milk and milk products	110621	Medical services
110114.3	Cheese	110622	Dental services
110114.4	Eggs and egg-based products	110623	Paramedical services
110115.1	Butter and margarine	110630	Hospital services
110115.3	Other edible oils and fats	110723	Maintenance and repair of personal transport equipment
110116.1	Fresh or chilled fruit	110724	Other services in respect of personal transport equipment
110116.2	Frozen, preserved, or processed fruits	110731	Passenger transport by railway
110117.1	Fresh or chilled vegetables	110732	Passenger transport by road
110117.2	Fresh or chilled potatoes	110733	Passenger transport by air
110117.3	Frozen or preserved vegetables	110734	Passenger transport by sea and inland waterway
110118.1	Sugar	110735	Combined passenger transport
110118.2	Jams, marmalades, and honey	110736	Other purchased transport services
110118.3	Confectionery, chocolate, and ice cream	110810	Postal services
110119	Food products n.e.c.	110830	Telephone and telefax services
110121	Coffee, tea, and cocoa	110915	Repair of audiovisual, photographic, and information-processing equipment
110122	Mineral waters, soft drinks, fruit and vegetable juices	110935	Veterinary and other services for pets
110211.1	Spirits	110941	Recreational and sporting services

Priced commodities		Priced services	
110212.1	Wine	110942	Cultural services
110213.1	Beer	110943	Games of chance
110220	Tobacco	110960	Package holidays
110311.1	Clothing materials and accessories	111000	Education
110312.1	Garments	111110	Catering services
110321.1	Footwear	111120	Accommodation services
110511	Furniture and furnishings	111211	Hairdressing salons and personal grooming establishments
110512	Carpets and other floor coverings	111220	Prostitution
110520	Household textiles	111240	Social protection
110531	Major household appliances whether electric or not	111250	Insurance
110532	Small electric household appliances	111261	FISIM
110540	Glassware, tableware, and household utensils	111262	Other financial services n.e.c
110551	Major tools and equipment	111270	Other services n.e.c.
110552	Small tools and miscellaneous accessories	*Nonpriced services as in the first two sections of annex A on education and health services*	
110561	Nondurable household goods	130221	Compensation of employees
110611	Pharmaceutical products	130222	Intermediate consumption
110612	Other medical products	130223	Gross operating surplus
110711	Motor cars	130421	Compensation of employees
110712	Motorcycles	130422	Intermediate consumption
110713	Bicycles	130423	Gross operating surplus
110722	Fuels and lubricants for personal transport equipment	130424	Net taxes on production
110820	Telephone and telefax equipment	140111	Compensation of employees
110911	Audiovisual, photographic, and information processing equipment	140112	Intermediate consumption
110914	Recording media	140113	Gross operating surplus
110921	Major durables for outdoor and indoor recreation	140114	Net taxes on production
110931	Other recreational items and equipment	140115	Receipts from sales
110933	Gardens and pets		
110950	Newspapers, books, and stationery		
111212	Appliances, articles, and products for personal care		
111231	Jewelry, clocks, and watches		
111232	Other personal effects		

Source: ICP.
Note: n.e.c. = not elsewhere classified.

NOTES

1. This experience is summarized in Sergeev (1998) and so is not covered here.
2. The preliminary report of the Asian Development Bank (2007, appendix D) describes this method and provides some quantitative illustrations of the effects of the adjustments. The final report on the ADB website provides an abbreviated description.
3. The 1975 ICP used a small sample of countries with estimates of health capital to obtain adjustment factors, and the 2005 ICP used estimates of capital per worker for the whole economy. Another difference between the two rounds is that the 2005 ICP applied the adjustment factor to salaries and then used the salaries to obtain indirect quantities. The 1975 ICP adjusted quantities to obtain indirect PPPs.
4. In this chapter, EKS, the aggregation method found in the 2005 ICP report, is used interchangeably with GEKS, an increasingly popular abbreviation that acknowledges that the method originated with statistician Corrado Gini.
5. For example, the effect within a region would depend on whether the GEKS or Iklé-Dikhanov-Balk (IDB) method—the harmonically share-weighted Gheary-Kharmis (GK) method—was used. In the global comparison, it would depend on whether EKS was performed on the regions or on individual countries.
6. The Balassa-Samuelson effect is based on the fact that commodities are largely tradable, whereas services, especially comparison-resistant services, are largely nontradable. See Heston, Summers, and Nuxoll (1994), where this effect is tested and where alternative explanations are also cited.
7. The tradable-nontradable distinction is not as tidy as it is made to appear. Consumers are tourists, but they also travel to seek health care in other countries. Likewise, construction companies seek projects outside their home countries. Both are some examples of how loose the distinction can be.
8. In the 1990s, when Eurostat-OECD began to make comparisons for nonmember countries, especially in Eastern Europe and the former Soviet Union, some experiments were made using priced services PPPs for comparison-resistant services. However, as in many rounds of the ICP, the number of observations on priced services was not considered adequate.
9. Foreign trade can be handled properly by estimating export and import PPPs separately. Because this estimation involves additional price comparisons, typically the ICP has converted the net foreign balance by a common conversion factor. The exchange rate was used in the 2005 ICP, and the PPP for domestic absorption was used in some earlier ICPs. Use of the exchange rate is not base country–invariant and has an asymmetric effect for countries with price levels below the exchange rate as to whether they are running a trade deficit or surplus.
10. According to OECD, *fixity* refers to "the practice of fixing the results of an International Comparison Programme (ICP) aggregation for a country group when the country group is compared with a larger group. For example, the relation of France and Italy as given by Geary-Khamis or EKS for the 15 EU countries would be fixed so that within OECD, the France-Italy relationship would be preserved" (http://stats.oecd.org/glossary/detail.asp?ID=5527). Even when fixity is observed, an aggregation across the five ICP regions (CIS is included with the Eurostat-OECD comparison) produces results different from an aggregation of the 146 individual countries.
11. The ranking of types of employment is not particularly meaningful because administration, for example, may have been mainly lower-level employees, whereas education has mainly higher levels in the particular mix of occupations sampled within the broad groupings of administration, health, and education.

12. It was possible to estimate from a CPD equation coefficients for the regions. However, these estimates were based on wage comparisons for different occupations, much like the regional comparisons, and simply reproduced what had been found within regions—that is, based on wage and salary comparisons, indirect quantity estimates for low-income regions would be implausibly large.
13. The labor force data are available at http://pwt.econ.upenn.edu. The physical capital series is preliminary and not yet posted on the web. Country studies of China, India, and Indonesia were used to supplement the PWT estimates. For the Barro-Lee data set, see http://www.cid.harvard.edu/ciddata/ciddata.html. This chapter was being written as the Barro-Lee data set was being updated, and so it was not yet clear whether the new data would have broader coverage and more explanatory power. The India and Indonesia estimates are based on Eng (2008), and the China estimate is based on Wu (2009).
14. For the Eurostat-OECD, CIS, and South America regions, the basic heading compensation parities were from the research input of the 2005 ICP. For the Africa, Asia-Pacific, and Western Asia regions, where the research input compensation parities have already been adjusted, the wage-estimating equations discussed in the text were used to derive parities based on the United Kingdom. These could in turn be put on a U.S. base. Some countries in these three regions were not in the wage equation and so had to be estimated by a short-cut equation based on per capita income—a method that should be improved.
15. This exercise used only the three compensation headings in the table in annex A for collective consumption and government purchases of individual health and education services. Because the PPP for public purchases of health services was partially used for household purchases of hospital services, table 16.6 provides a more complete comparison than if only household purchases of hospital services had also been included.

REFERENCES

Asian Development Bank. 2007. *2005 International Comparison Program in Asia and the Pacific: Purchasing Power Parity Preliminary Report.* Manila: ADB.

Balassa, Bela. 1964. "The Purchasing Power Parity Doctrine: A Reappraisal." *Journal of Political Economy* 72 (6): 584–96.

Eng, Pierre van der. 2008. "Capital Formation and Capital Stock in Indonesia, 1950–2007." Working paper, Australian National University, December.

Heston, Alan, Robert Summers, and Daniel Nuxoll. 1994. "The Differential Productivity Hypothesis and Purchasing Power Parities: Some New Evidence." *Review of International Economics* (October).

Kravis, Irving, Alan Heston, and Robert Summers. 1982. *World Product and Income: International Comparisons of Real Gross Product.* Baltimore: Johns Hopkins University Press.

Samuelson, Paul. 1964. "Theoretical Notes on Trade Problems." *Review of Economics and Statistics* 46 (2): 145–54.

Sergeev, Sergey. 1998. "Comparison of Non-Market Services at Cross Roads (Experience, Considerations, Proposals)." Item 8, Statistical Commission and Economic Commission for Europe Conference of European Statisticians, Consultation, Vienna, June 3–5, 1998.

World Bank. 2008. *Global Purchasing Power Parities and Real Expenditures: 2005 International Comparison Program.* http://siteresources.worldbank.org/ICPINT/Resources/icp-final.pdf.

Wu, Yanrui. 2009. "China's Capital Stock by Sector and by Region." Discussion Paper 09.02, Business School, University of Western Australia.

CHAPTER 17

Reference PPPs

DEREK BLADES AND YURI DIKHANOV

In the 2005 International Comparison Program (ICP), the gross domestic product (GDP) was broken down into 155 basic beadings covering all final expenditures on GDP: consumption expenditures, capital formation, and the trade balance. The standard procedure was to calculate purchasing power parities (PPPs) by comparing the prices of a selection of the goods and services. However, just as in all previous rounds of the ICP, prices were not collected in the 2005 ICP for goods and services representing all 155 basic headings, mainly because it would have been too expensive and even impossible. In addition, for some basic headings no prices were available—the gross operating surplus of government is one example. For basic headings for which no price data were collected, purchasing power parities were calculated by using reference PPPs[1]—that is, PPPs based on one or more other basic headings that had already been calculated.

It would, of course, be possible to calculate overall PPPs without taking into account the basic headings for which no prices were collected. The expenditure shares of these PPPs would be dropped and PPPs calculated only for the remaining basic headings for which prices were actually collected. But this was not done because users want the results to reflect the full GDP. Reference PPPs have been used in all previous rounds of the ICP and will be used again in the 2011 round.

The countries agreed on which basic headings would be covered by reference PPPs, but the regional coordinators made the decisions on which PPPs to use as reference PPPs. Reference PPPs were introduced into the calculations when the regional coordinators were calculating PPPs for their region. Reference PPPs are more of an issue for the regional offices and the ICP Global Office than for the participating countries.

The purpose of this chapter is to explain which reference PPPs were used in 2005 ICP, how much of GDP was covered by reference PPPs, and what the difference would have been had PPPs been calculated using only the price data actually collected. A final section considers whether any changes should be made in the use of reference PPPs for the 2011 ICP.

Different Kinds of Reference PPPs

Reference PPPs can be categorized as follows:

- Price-based reference PPPs
  - Specific
  - Neutral
- Volume-based reference PPPs
- Exchange rate reference PPPs.

The sections that follow describe these reference PPPs.

Price-Based Reference PPPs

Virtually all the reference PPPs used for the ICP are price-based rather than volume-based. They are price relatives (PPPs) that have already been calculated by comparing the prices of goods and services classified under other basic headings. Some are PPPs of basic headings that are thought to be similar to those for which no prices have been collected. "Similar" means here that if the missing prices were available, it is likely that their price relatives vis-à-vis other countries would be close to the PPPs of the basic heading selected as the reference PPP. These PPPs are referred to here as *specific* reference PPPs. They may be the PPPs for a single basic heading or an average of the PPPs for several basic headings. In latter case, they will be geometric averages of the selected PPPs weighted by expenditure shares.

In other cases, reference PPPs are the PPPs of a large group of basic headings such as all the basic headings under gross fixed capital formation for which prices have been collected. In this case, the purpose is to ensure that the use of a reference PPP will not change the PPP for that larger group. These are referred to here as *neutral* reference PPPs because the intention is that they have no impact on the PPPs of the larger group of basic headings.

Here are some examples of specific and neutral price-based reference PPPs used in the 2005 round of the ICP:

- Specific price-based reference PPPs
  - PPP for the basic heading actual and imputed rentals for housing used as the reference PPP for the basic heading miscellaneous services relating to the dwelling
  - PPP for the basic heading recreational and sporting services used as the reference PPP for the basic heading games of chance
  - Geometric, weighted averages of all basic headings under transport and restaurants and hotels used as the reference PPP for the basic heading package holidays.
- Neutral price-based reference PPPs:
  - PPP for household final consumption expenditure on the domestic market (excluding health and education basic headings and reference PPP basic headings) used as the reference PPP for the basic heading narcotics
  - PPPs for gross fixed capital formation used as reference PPPs for the basic heading other products (part of gross fixed capital formation)
  - PPP for household consumption expenditure (excluding reference PPP basic headings) used as the reference PPP for the basic heading social protection (part of household consumption expenditure).

Volume-Based Reference PPPs

In previous rounds of the ICP, reference PPPs were always based on other PPPs—that is, on price relatives. For the 2005 ICP, the Asia-Pacific and Africa regions[2] used reference volume relatives for the basic heading actual and imputed rentals for housing (dwelling services for short). This was the first time this procedure was used for the ICP.

The standard procedure for calculating PPPs for dwelling services is to compare the rents paid in different countries for similar types of dwellings as described in chapter 12 on dwelling services. In many countries, this procedure is not feasible because almost all dwellings are occupied by their owners, and so there is only a small and unrepresentative rental market. To deal with this situation, an alternative method was recommended for the 2005 ICP in which PPPs for dwelling services were obtained by first calculating volume relatives based on the quality-adjusted quantities of dwellings in each country. These volume relatives were then divided into expenditure relatives to obtain PPPs. In both Asia-Pacific and Africa, it was found that neither of these methods could be used; the data on actual rents, housing expenditures, and the quantity and quality of dwellings were judged to be too unreliable. In this situation, the only solution was to use some kind of reference PPP.

A first suggestion was to use the overall PPP for household final consumption expenditure (HFCE, calculated with expenditure on dwelling services omitted) as the reference PPP for dwelling services. The overall PPP for household consumption expenditure would not be affected by using a neutral PPP of this kind. The problem, however, was that country estimates of expenditures on dwelling services were thought to be very unreliable in both the Asia-Pacific and Africa regions. Dividing badly estimated expenditure relatives by neutral price relatives would necessarily produce unreliable volume relatives, thereby distorting the HFCE aggregate in real terms. But this was not desirable because the main objective of the ICP is to produce good volume comparisons between countries. The problem can be explained as follows:

$$\frac{\text{expenditure on } DS \text{ in country } A}{\text{expenditure on } DS \text{ in country } B} - \frac{\text{price of } DS \text{ in country } A}{\text{price of } DS \text{ in country } B} = \frac{\text{volume of } DS \text{ in country } A}{\text{volume of } DS \text{ in country } B}$$

DS refers to dwelling services. The first term in the equation is an expenditure relative known from the national accounts of countries *A* and *B*. The second term is the price relative (or PPP)—that is, the price of dwelling services in country *A* divided by the price of dwelling services in country *B*. Dividing the expenditure relative by the price relative gives the volume relative shown on the right-hand side. If the expenditure relative is unreliable, dividing it by a neutral price relative will transfer that unreliability to the volume relative. The alternative is to use a neutral volume relative on the right-hand side so that the unreliability inherent in the expenditure relative is transferred to the price relative (or PPP).[3] Because of the higher priority attached to the volume comparisons than to the PPP, this alternative was accepted as the lesser of two evils. The relative volume of household consumption expenditures was used as the reference volume relative for dwelling services, and an (unreliable) PPP was obtained by dividing this volume relative into the expenditure relative.

Exchange Rate Reference PPPs

Exchange rates were used for the two basic headings exports of goods and services and imports of goods and services and for the two basic headings final consumption expenditure of resident households in the rest of the world and final consumption expenditure of nonresident households in the economic territory.[4] Although exchange rates are described here as reference PPPs, many observers would dispute this. They would argue that, by definition, the exchange rate is the PPP for all imports and exports, including those that are purchased directly by households when they travel abroad.

An alternative view is possible for PPPs for foreign trade, however. If exports and imports are treated in exactly the same way as other products, the PPPs so obtained would not necessarily be the same as exchange rates. To take a simple example, suppose two countries export an identical type of banana and use the same currency such as the CFA (Central African franc). If trade were entirely free, the f.o.b. (free on board) export prices of a ton of bananas would necessarily be the same in the two countries—if not, the country with the higher f.o.b. price would never export any bananas. And in this situation, the exchange rates would indeed equal the PPPs calculated as their price relatives: both would be unity in this case. But, in practice, markets are not free, and those for many internationally traded goods are regulated by special trade agreements—bananas being a particular case in point. In addition, the c.i.f. (cost, insurance, and freight) prices of a ton of these bananas would not be the same in the importing countries because, apart from differences in the f.o.b. prices, the international freight and insurance costs may also differ. In short, if PPPs were calculated for banana exports and imports by comparing, respectively, f.o.b. and c.i.f. prices, it is certain that they would not equal exchange rates in all cases.

Purchases by residents abroad and purchases by nonresidents in the domestic territory can also be treated with PPPs different from exchange rates. These are basically tourist expenditures on things such as transport, hotels, and restaurant meals. The bilateral PPP for hotel rooms or train tickets purchased by nonresidents in country *A* is the ratio of the prices in country *A* divided by the prices of a similar hotel room or train journey purchased by nonresidents in country *B*. There is no reason to expect that this PPP would be the same as exchange rates.

For exports and imports, it would be very expensive to collect prices in order to calculate PPPs in the same way as for other items of final expenditure, and the use of exchange rates can be justified on practical grounds. For net purchases by residents abroad, however, the alternative just provided may be preferable to the use of exchange rates. In any event, it appears to be correct to regard exchange rates as reference PPPs rather than as true, measured PPPs.

Basic Headings for Which Reference PPPs Were Used in ICP 2005

Table 17.1 shows the basic headings for which each of the six regions used reference PPPs in the 2005 ICP. The kinds of reference PPPs used are indicated: volume-based (V), price-based specific (S), price-based neutral (N), and exchange rates (X).

Reference PPPs were the least used in South America (32 basic headings) and the most used in Western Asia (39 basic headings). They were used for most of the basic headings under government and for a substantial number of basic headings under household expenditure. In all regions except Western Asia, neutral reference PPPs were used more often than specific reference PPPs. Western Asia used reference PPPs for more basic headings than the other regions, but tried to find specific rather than neutral reference PPPs for most of them.

TABLE 17.1 Basic Headings for Which Reference PPPs Were Used in ICP 2005 by Region

Code	Basic heading	Eurostat—OECD	CIS	Asia-Pacific	Africa	Western Asia	South America
HOUSEHOLDS							
110231.1	Narcotics	N	N				
110411.1	Actual and imputed rentals for housing			V	V		
110441.1	Water supply					N	
110442.1	Miscellaneous dwelling services	S	S	S	S	N	S
110513.1	Repair of furniture			S	S	S	S
110533.1	Repair of household appliances			S	S	S	S
110562.1	Domestic services			S	S		
110562.2	Household services			S	S	S	S
110631.1	Hospital services	S	S				
110712.1	Motorcycles			S	S	S	S
110714.1	Animal-drawn vehicles	N	N			S	
110731.1	Passenger transport by railway					S	
110734.1	Passenger transport by sea			S	S	S	S
110735.1	Combined passenger transport			S	S	S	S
110736.1	Other transport services			S	S		S
110921.1	Major durables for recreation			S	S		S
110923.1	Maintenance of other major durables					S	
110933.1	Garden and pets			N	N		N
110935.1	Veterinary and pet services			N	N	S	N
110943.1	Games of chance	N	N	N	N	S	N
110961.1	Package holidays	S	S				
111011.1	Education	S	S				
111221.1	Prostitution	N	N				
111241.1	Social protection	N	N	N	N	N	N
111251.1	Insurance	N	N	N	N	N	N
111261.1	FISIM	N	N	N	N	N	N
111262.1	Other financial services			N	N	N	N

(continued)

TABLE 17.1 Basic Headings for Which Reference PPPs Were Used in ICP 2005 by Region (*continued*)

Code	Basic heading	Eurostat—OECD	CIS	Asia-Pacific	Africa	Western Asia	South America
111271.1	Other services			N	N	N	N
111311.1/2	Net purchases by residents in the rest of the world	X	X	X	X	X	X
NONPROFIT INSTITUTIONS SERVING HOUSEHOLDS (NPISH)							
120111.1	NPISH consumption	N	N				
GOVERNMENT							
130111.1	Housing	S	S				
130212.4	Hospital services	S	S				
130222.1	Intermediate consumption: health	N	N	N	N	N	N
130223.1	Gross operating surplus: health	S	S	S	S	S	S
130224.1	Net taxes on production: health	S	S	N	N	N	N
130225.1	Receipts from sales: health	S	S	N	N	N	N
130311.1	Recreation and culture	N	N	S			
130411.1	Education benefits and reimbursements	S	S				
130422.1	Intermediate consumption: education	N	N	N	N	N	N
130423.1	Gross operating surplus: education	S	S	S	S	S	S
130424.1	Net taxes on production: education	S	S	N	N	S	N
130425.1	Receipt from sales: education	S	S	N	N	S	N
130511.1	Social protection	N	N				
140112.1	Intermediate consumption: collective services	N	N	N	N	N	N
140113.1	Gross operating surplus: collective services	S	S	S	S	S	S
140114.1	Net taxes on production: collective services	S	S	N	N	S	N
140115.1	Receipts from sales: collective services	S	S	N	N	S	N

TABLE 17.1 Basic Headings for Which Reference PPPs Were Used in ICP 2005 by Region (*continued*)

Code	Basic heading	Eurostat–OECD	CIS	Asia-Pacific	Africa	Western Asia	South America
GROSS FIXED CAPITAL FORMATION							
150111.1	Fabricated metal products					S	
150115.1	Other manufactured goods					S	
150121.2	Other road transport					S	
150122.1	Other transport equipment	N	N			S	
150311.1	Other products	N	N	N	N		N
INVENTORIES AND VALUABLES							
160111.1/2	Change in inventories	S	S	S	S	S	S
160211.1/2	Net acquisitions of valuables	S	S				
BALANCE OF EXPORTS AND IMPORTS							
170111.1/2	Net exports of goods and services	X	X	X	X	X	X
Total number of reference PPPs		***34***	***34***	***35***	***34***	***39***	***32***
Of which __ are reference volume relative				***1***	***1***		
Reference PPPs: specific		***14***	***14***	***14***	***13***	***25***	***12***
Reference PPPs: neutral		***20***	***20***	***18***	***18***	***12***	***18***
Exchange rates		***2***	***2***	***2***	***2***	***2***	***2***

Source: ICP 2005.
Note: V = reference volume relative; S = specific reference PPP; N = neutral reference PPP; X = market exchange rate; FISIM = financial intermediation services indirectly measured.

What Were the Reference PPPs?

The 2005 "ICP Operational Manual" (World Bank 2005) provides guidelines on the basic headings for which reference PPPs could be used and suggests the reference PPPs to be used in each case. Table 17.2 shows the PPPs recommended in the *ICP 2005 Methodological Handbook* (World Bank 2007).

Specific reference PPPs are highlighted in the table. The distinction between specific and neutral reference PPPs is usually obvious, but there are some borderline cases. For example, gross fixed capital formation is shown as a *neutral* reference PPP in table 17.2 when it is used for the basic heading other products (capital formation,) but when it is used as a reference PPP for government gross operating surplus it is shown as a *specific* reference PPP. In the first case, the intention was most likely to avoid affecting the PPP for gross fixed capital formation (hence it is a neutral reference PPP), whereas in the second case it is used because the price relatives of gross fixed capital formation are assumed to be similar to those of consumption of fixed capital, which is by far the

TABLE 17.2 Reference PPPs Recommended by the Global Office for ICP 2005

Code	Basic heading	Reference PPPs
110231.1	Narcotics	PPPs for individual consumption expenditure by households (excluding health and education basic headings and reference PPP basic headings)
110442.1	Miscellaneous dwelling services	PPPs for actual and imputed rents
110631.1	Hospital services	PPPs for production of health services by government (without net taxes on production and receipts from sales)
110714.1	Animal-drawn vehicles	PPPs for individual consumption expenditure by households (excluding health and education basic headings and reference PPP basic headings)
110943.1	Games of chance	PPPs for individual consumption expenditure by households (excluding health and education basic headings and Eurostat-OECD reference PPP basic headings)
110961.1	Package holidays	Weighted average of PPPs for transport services and restaurants and hotels
111011.1	Education	PPPs for production of education services by government (without net taxes on production and receipts from sales)
111221.1	Prostitution	PPPs for individual consumption expenditure by households (excluding health and education basic headings and reference PPP basic headings)
111241.1	Social protection	PPPs for government final consumption expenditure (excluding social protection, recreation and culture, and housing)
111251.1	Insurance	PPPs for individual consumption expenditure by households (excluding health and education basic headings and reference PPP basic headings)
111261.1	FISIM	PPPs for individual consumption expenditure by households (excluding health and education basic headings and reference PPP basic headings)
111311.1	Expenditures by residents in the rest of the world	Exchange rates
111311.2	Expenditures by nonresidents in the economic territory	Exchange rates
120111.1	NPISH consumption	PPPs for government final consumption expenditure (excluding social protection, recreation and culture, and housing)
130111.1	Housing (government)	PPPs for actual and imputed rents
130212.4	Hospital services (government)	PPPs for production of health services by government (without net taxes on production and receipts from sales)
130222.1	Intermediate consumption: health services	PPPs for individual consumption expenditure by households (excluding health and education basic headings and reference PPP basic headings)
130223.1	Gross operating surplus: health services	PPPs for gross fixed capital formation
130224.1	Net taxes on production: health services	PPPs for production of health services by government (without net taxes on production and receipts from sales)
130225.1	Receipts from sales: health services	PPPs for production of health services by government (without net taxes on production and receipts from sales)

TABLE 17.2 Reference PPPs Recommended by the Global Office for ICP 2005 (*continued*)

Code	Basic heading	Reference PPPs
1303111	Recreation and culture	PPPs for government final consumption expenditure (excluding social protection, recreation and culture, and housing)
1304111	Education benefits and reimbursements	PPPs for production of education services by government (without net taxes on production and receipts from sales)
1304221	Intermediate consumption: education	PPPs for individual consumption expenditure by households (excluding health and education basic headings and reference PPP basic headings)
1304231	Gross operating surplus: education	PPPs for gross fixed capital formation
1304241	Net taxes on production: education	PPPs for production of education services by government (without net taxes on production and receipts from sales)
1304251	Receipt from sales: education	PPPs for production of education services by government (without net taxes on production and receipts from sales)
1305111	Social protection	PPPs for government final consumption expenditure (excluding social protection, recreation and culture, and housing)
1401121	Intermediate consumption: collective services	PPPs for individual consumption expenditure by households (excluding health and education basic headings and reference PPP basic headings)
1401131	Gross operating surplus: collective services	PPPs for gross fixed capital formation
1401141	Net taxes on production: collective services	PPPs for production of collective services by government (without net taxes on production and receipts from sales)
1401151	Receipts from sales: collective services	PPPs for production of collective services by government (without net taxes on production and receipts from sales)
1501221	Other transport equipment	PPPs for gross fixed capital formation
1503111	Other products (GFCF)	PPPs for gross fixed capital formation
1601111	Opening value of inventories	Weighted average of PPPs for consumer goods and equipment goods
1601112	Closing value of inventories	Weighted average of PPPs for consumer goods and equipment goods
1602111	Acquisitions of valuables	PPPs for jewelry, clocks, and watches
1602112	Disposals of valuables	PPPs for jewelry, clocks, and watches
1701111	Exports of goods and services	Exchange rates
1701112	Imports of goods and services	Exchange rates

Source: ICP 2005.
Note: FISIM = financial intermediation services indirectly measured; NPISH = nonprofit institutions serving households; GFCF = gross fixed capital formation.

largest item in the gross operating surplus of government. Another example is provided by PPPs for production of education services by government; they are used as reference PPPs for net taxes on production: education. Here they are shown as *specific* PPPs on the assumption that they have been selected because their price relatives are assumed to be similar to those for the production of education services. However, it could equally well be that PPPs for production of education services by government were selected as reference PPPs because that would have a neutral effect on the overall PPP for government education services.

This list of basic headings and the recommended reference PPPs were based on the experience of the Eurostat-OECD group. The CIS region followed these guidelines strictly, but, as can be seen in table 17.1, other regions did not. The reference PPPs used by each region are shown in annex A. The main departures from table 17.2 can be summarized as follows:

- Most regions used more reference PPPs than recommended for the household consumption expenditure. These were mostly basic headings for services rather than goods—domestic, household, repair, financial, and insurance services were covered by reference PPPs in all regions except the Eurostat-OECD and CIS. In general, they were also basic headings with rather low expenditure weights, and so the regions concerned decided it was not a good use of scarce resources to price items under these basic headings.
- For the government consumption expenditure, the Asia-Pacific, Africa, Western Asia, and South America regions are shown as using fewer reference PPPs than the Eurostat-OECD and CIS regions, mainly because the missing basic headings such as housing, social protection, and recreation and culture carried zero or near zero expenditure weights and so were ignored.

The neutral PPP most commonly recommended in the ICP manual was PPPs for the individual consumption expenditure by households (excluding the health and education basic headings and reference PPP basic headings).

Table 17.3 shows the percentages of GDP covered by reference PPPs in each region and the relative importance of the basic headings for which reference PPPs were used. As an indication of their relative importance, basic headings accounting for more than 0.5 percent of GDP are highlighted. According to the table, the following basic headings accounted for more than 0.5 percent of GDP in at least half of the regions:

- Maintenance and repair of the dwelling
- Social protection (under household consumption)
- Insurance
- Intermediate consumption: health services
- Intermediate consumption: education services
- Intermediate consumption: collective services
- Gross operating surplus: collective services
- Receipts from sales: collective services
- Other products (under gross fixed capital formation)
- Changes in inventories

In addition, the two foreign balances for which exchange rate reference PPPs were used also accounted for large shares of GDP, as did the basic heading for actual and imputed rentals for housing. Reference volume relatives were used for this basic heading in the Asia-Pacific and Africa regions.

TABLE 17.3 Percentage of GDP Accounted for by Reference PPPS in ICP 2005

	Eurostat-OECD	CIS	Asia-Pacific	Africa	Western Asia	South America	All regions[a]
Household final consumption expenditure							
110410 Actual and imputed rentals for housing			6.37	4.54			5.46
110430 Maintenance and repair of the dwelling	0.61	1.73	0.53	0.54	0.41	0.53	0.72
110440 Water supply and misc. services relating to the dwelling					0.45		0.45
110442 Miscellaneous services relating to the dwelling	0.38	0.14	0.18	0.25	0.25	0.13	0.22
110513 Repair of furniture, furnishings, and floor coverings			0.02	0.12	0.08	0.04	0.06
110533 Repair of household appliances			0.03	0.07	0.07	0.07	0.06
110562.1 Domestic services			0.30	0.42			0.36
110562.2 Household services			0.08	0.16	0.12	0.02	0.10
110630 Hospital services	1.14	0.68					0.91
110712 Motorcycles			0.49	0.12	0.02	0.13	0.19
110731 Passenger transport by railway					0.00		0.00
110734 Passenger transport by sea and inland waterway			0.08	0.09	0.00	0.03	0.05
110735 Combined passenger transport			0.00	0.16	0.08	0.02	0.06
110736 Other purchased transport services			0.11	0.34		0.05	0.17
110921 Major durables for outdoor and indoor recreation			0.05	0.13		0.02	0.07
110933 Gardens and pets			0.06	0.08		0.12	0.09
110935 Veterinary and other services for pets			0.02	0.07	0.01	0.02	0.03
110943 Games of chance	0.56	0.08	0.36	0.17	0.00	0.15	0.22
110960 Package holidays	0.41	0.14					0.27
111000 Education	1.58	1.77					1.68
111220 Prostitution	0.03	0.00		0.01		0.00	0.01
111240 Social protection	1.72	0.85	0.73	0.39	0.34	0.21	0.71
111250 Insurance	1.10	0.16	0.52	0.24	0.17	0.67	0.48
111261 FISIM	0.64	0.00	0.48	0.25	0.49	0.26	0.35
111262 Other financial services n.e.c.			0.17	0.32	0.13	0.45	0.35
111270 Other services n.e.c.			0.62	0.32	0.22	1.03	0.52
111300 Net purchases abroad	−1.38	0.61	0.00	−0.75	0.21	0.00	−0.22
Government final consumption expenditure							
130222 Intermediate consumption: health services	0.94	0.97	0.47	0.31	0.97	0.90	0.76
130223 Gross operating surplus: health services	0.13	0.20	0.02	0.14	0.05	0.11	0.11
130224 Net taxes on production: health services	0.02	0.14	0.00	0.05	0.00	0.01	0.04
130225 Receipts from sales: health services	−0.26	−0.06	0.00	−0.05	−0.16	−0.07	−0.10

(continued)

TABLE 17.3 Percentage of GDP Accounted for by Reference PPPS in ICP 2005 (*continued*)

	Eurostat-OECD	CIS	Asia-Pacific	Africa	Western Asia	South America	All regions[a]
130422 Intermediate consumption: education services	0.88	1.28	0.62	0.51	0.56	0.43	0.72
130423 Gross operating surplus: education services	0.28	0.27	0.06	0.28	0.15	0.12	0.19
130424 Net taxes on production: education services	0.02	0.01	0.00	0.04	0.07	0.01	0.03
130425 Receipts from sales: education services	−0.38	−0.30	0.00	−0.09	−0.45	−0.14	−0.23
140112 Intermediate consumption: collective services	3.85	3.61	3.01	3.97	5.19	2.72	3.72
140113 Gross operating surplus: collective services	1.23	0.79	0.27	1.49	0.49	0.46	0.79
140114 Net taxes on production: collective services	0.03	0.02	0.09	0.31	0.00	0.04	0.08
140115 Receipts from sales: collective services	−1.20	−0.36	0.00	−0.57	−0.86	−0.52	−0.58
Gross fixed capital formation							
150300 Other products	1.65	1.81	2.28	0.93		0.76	1.50
Changes in inventories and valuables							
160000 Change in inventories and valuables	1.29	2.29	2.22	2.00	0.84	0.76	1.57
Balance of exports and imports							
180000 Balance of exports and imports	−3.18	−7.53	1.89	−8.10	9.92	4.17	−0.47
Total of above	**13.57**	**10.20**	**22.42**	**9.58**	**21.60**	**14.14**	**15.25**
Reference PPPs without changes in inventories and valuables, the balance of exports and imports, and net purchases abroad	**16.85**	**14.83**	**18.30**	**16.42**	**10.63**	**9.21**	**14.37**

Source: ICP 2005.
Note: FISIM = financial intermediation services indirectly measured; n.e.c. = not elsewhere classified.
a. Averages for the regions using reference PPPs.

The last two lines of table 17.3 summarize the importance of reference PPPs in each region and for all regions together. Shown on the first line, "total of above," are the sums of the percentages in each column. Those sums include the three balance items: the changes in inventories and valuables, the net exports of goods and services, and the net purchases abroad by residents. This means that a region that made extensive use of reference PPPs for the nonbalance basic headings will seem to have made little use of them if these balance items were negative. For example, Africa, as a region, reported a larger negative trade balance, which gives the false impression that Africa made little use of reference PPPs. Western Asia, by contrast, had a large positive trade balance, which exaggerates the use made of reference PPPs in that region.

The last line omits these balance items and gives a better picture of the extent to which reference PPPs were used in the different regions. Overall, just over 14 percent of GDP was covered by reference PPPs, with South America having the lowest coverage at 9 percent and Asia-Pacific twice that at 18 percent.

Table 17.4 lists the countries that participated in the 2005 ICP ranked by the percentage of GDP covered by reference PPPs. The percentages omit the two trade balances and the

TABLE 17.4 Percentage of GDP for Which Reference PPPS Were Used in ICP 2005

Country/Economy	% of GDP	Country/Economy	% of GDP	Country/Economy	% of GDP	Country/Economy	% of GDP
Paraguay	3.5	Yemen, Rep.	10.9	Sri Lanka	14.2	Czech Republic	17.5
Qatar	3.6	Bosnia and Herzegovina	11.0	Senegal	14.2	Slovak Republic	17.7
Venezuela, RB	4.6	Cameroon	11.2	Cyprus	14.2	Liberia	18.1
Ecuador	5.0	Thailand	11.3	Indonesia	14.2	China	18.1
Kuwait	5.4	Angola	11.4	Benin	14.3	Israel	18.2
Bolivia	5.9	Russian Federation	11.5	Poland	14.4	Mauritius	18.4
Syrian Arab Republic	6.1	Latvia	11.5	New Zealand	14.4	Vietnam	18.4
Mozambique	6.4	Romania	11.6	Hungary	14.5	United Kingdom	18.5
Mexico	6.8	Luxembourg	11.6	Jordan	14.5	Ethiopia	18.7
Tanzania	6.8	Ireland	11.8	Kazakhstan	14.5	Denmark	18.9
Turkey	6.9	Zimbabwe	11.8	France	14.6	Iran, Islamic Rep.	18.9
Saudi Arabia	7.1	Ukraine	11.8	Philippines	14.6	Nepal	19.0
Ghana	7.4	Estonia	11.9	Austria	14.9	Mongolia	19.2
Argentina	7.4	Bulgaria	12.2	Uganda	14.9	Lao PDR	19.2
Chile	7.4	Comoros	12.2	Brunei Darussalam	15.1	Namibia	19.4
Oman	7.7	Bahrain	12.3	Kenya	15.2	Djibouti	19.5
Nigeria	7.8	Mali	12.4	Germany	15.4	Australia	19.6
Congo, Rep.	7.8	Tunisia	12.5	Norway	15.6	Malawi	19.6
Uruguay	8.1	Iraq	12.5	Japan	15.7	Chad	19.7
Armenia	8.3	Canada	12.5	Rwanda	15.7	Hong Kong SAR, China	19.8
Lithuania	9.2	Azerbaijan	12.7	Sierra Leone	15.8	Malaysia	19.9
Peru	9.2	Slovenia	12.8	Singapore	15.8	Sweden	20.1
Sudan	9.2	Croatia	12.9	São Tomé and Príncipe	15.9	Niger	22.2
Equatorial Guinea	9.4	Egypt, Arab Rep.	12.9	Burundi	15.9	Burkina Faso	22.4
Lebanon	9.4	Bangladesh	12.9	Korea, Rep.	16.0	Gambia, The	22.5
Guinea	9.4	Montenegro	13.2	Brazil	16.0	United States	22.5
Botswana	9.5	Kyrgyz Republic	13.2	Lesotho	16.1	Netherlands	22.6
Belarus	9.6	Italy	13.5	Mauritania	16.1	Madagascar	22.6
Macao SAR, China	9.6	Pakistan	13.5	Finland	16.4	Taiwan, China	22.7
Macedonia, FYR	9.7	Gabon	13.5	Congo, Dem. Rep.	16.4	South Africa	23.0
Greece	9.8	Iceland	13.5	Togo	16.4	Guinea-Bissau	23.1
Albania	10.1	Portugal	13.6	Switzerland	16.5	Cape Verde	24.2
Central African Republic	10.2	Morocco	13.7	Belgium	16.8	Fiji	30.2
Serbia	10.2	Malta	13.8	Swaziland	16.9	Zambia	30.4
Georgia	10.6	Moldova	13.8	Bhutan	17.2	Maldives	37.4
Tajikistan	10.7	Cambodia	13.9	Spain	17.4		
Colombia	10.8	India	14.0	Côte d'Ivoire	17.4		

Source: ICP 2005.

FIGURE 17.1 Number of Countries by Share of Basic Headings Estimated with Reference PPPs

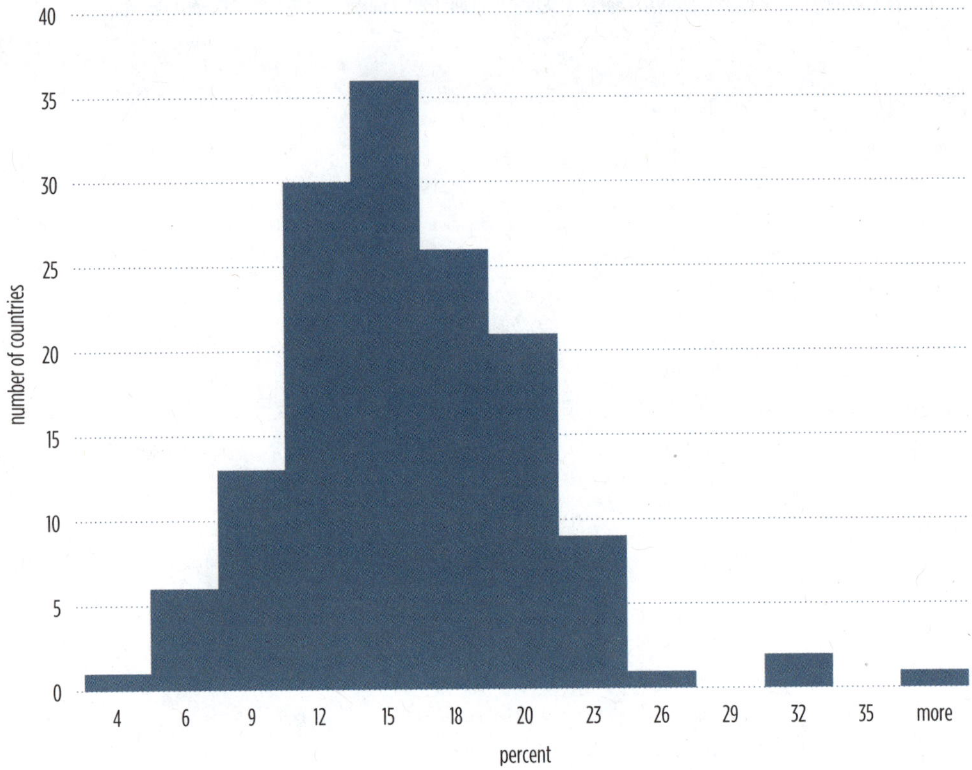

Source: ICP 2005.

changes in inventories and valuables and correspond to those shown in the bottom line of table 17.3.

The countries in table 17.4 with lower percentages mostly reported low government expenditures, while those with the higher percentages usually had much higher government expenditures (both collective and individual) and, in the African and Asian countries, large shares of actual and imputed rentals for housing. Figure 17.1 shows that the country percentages are fairly evenly distributed around the global mean of 14 percent.

How Did the Use of Reference PPPs Affect the Results of the Comparison?

The figures and tables in this section compare the 2005 published PPP for GDP with what the PPP for GDP would have been had it been calculated, first, without using price-based reference PPPs and, second, without using exchange rate reference PPPs.

Table 17.5 shows the percentage differences between GDP PPPs calculated without price-based reference PPPs. A negative figure means that the use of price-based reference PPPs reduced

TABLE 17.5 Differences between GDP PPP without Price-Based Reference PPPs and Published GDP PPP

percentage of published GDP PPP

Country/Economy	%	Country/Economy	%	Country/Economy	%	Country/Economy	%
Bosnia and Herzegovina	−0.0	Iran, Islamic Rep.	−0.6	Slovenia	1.3	Belgium	2.0
Swaziland	0.0	South Africa	0.6	Taiwan, China	1.3	Australia	2.1
Montenegro	−0.0	Argentina	0.6	Cape Verde	1.3	Burkina Faso	−2.4
Mauritius	0.0	Benin	−0.6	Ireland	1.3	Vietnam	−2.4
Maldives	0.1	Congo, Dem. Rep.	−0.6	Malaysia	1.3	Sierra Leone	−2.5
Venezuela, RB	0.1	Uruguay	0.6	Singapore	1.3	Lebanon	2.5
Zambia	−0.1	Denmark	0.6	Congo, Rep.	−1.3	Cyprus	2.6
Paraguay	−0.1	Romania	0.6	Japan	1.3	Portugal	2.6
Poland	0.1	Cambodia	−0.6	Croatia	1.3	Spain	2.6
Colombia	−0.2	Gabon	−0.7	Côte d'Ivoire	−1.4	Qatar	2.6
Senegal	−0.2	Ecuador	0.7	Jordan	1.5	Korea, Rep.	2.6
Namibia	0.2	Philippines	−0.8	Bulgaria	−1.5	Iceland	2.9
Tanzania	−0.2	Kenya	−0.8	Netherlands	1.5	Fiji	2.9
Lithuania	−0.2	Brunei Darussalam	0.8	Guinea	−1.5	Lao PDR	−3.0
Thailand	0.2	Nigeria	−0.8	Israel	1.5	Kazakhstan	−3.1
Latvia	−0.3	Yemen, Rep.	0.8	Hong Kong SAR, China	1.5	Serbia	−3.1
Slovak Republic	−0.3	Morocco	0.8	Togo	−1.6	Madagascar	−3.1
Cameroon	−0.3	Finland	0.9	Sri Lanka	−1.6	Malawi	−3.2
Macao SAR, China	0.3	Uganda	−0.9	Mali	−1.6	Iraq	3.2
Comoros	−0.3	Albania	0.9	Austria	1.6	Mauritania	−3.2
Lesotho	−0.3	Chile	0.9	Syrian Arab Republic	1.6	Kuwait	3.3
Sweden	0.3	Bhutan	−0.9	Botswana	−1.7	Russian Federation	−3.3
Rwanda	−0.3	Indonesia	1.0	Malta	1.7	Saudi Arabia	3.4
Mozambique	−0.4	Hungary	1.0	Germany	1.7	United States	3.4
Bolivia	−0.4	Ghana	−1.0	United Kingdom	1.7	Belarus	−3.4
India	−0.4	Pakistan	−1.0	Italy	1.7	Bahrain	3.7
Bangladesh	0.4	Sudan	−1.0	Niger	−1.8	Oman	3.9
Turkey	0.4	Czech Republic	1.1	Luxembourg	1.8	Armenia	−3.9
Zimbabwe	−0.4	Angola	−1.1	Macedonia, FYR	−1.8	Georgia	−3.9
China	−0.5	Central African Republic	−1.1	France	1.9	Azerbaijan	−4.5
Norway	−0.5	Egypt, Arab Rep.	−1.2	New Zealand	1.9	Ukraine	−4.7
Estonia	0.5	Mexico	1.2	São Tomé and Príncipe	−1.9	Guinea-Bissau	−4.7
Peru	0.5	Ethiopia	−1.2	Burundi	−1.9	Chad	−6.3
Djibouti	−0.5	Equatorial Guinea	−1.2	Switzerland	2.0	Kyrgyz Republic	−7.2
Brazil	0.5	Nepal	−1.2	Canada	2.0	Gambia, The	−8.6
Tunisia	0.6	Mongolia	−1.3	Liberia	−2.0	Moldova	−9.5
						Tajikistan	−11.2

Source: ICP 2005.
Note: Countries/economies are ranked in ascending order of the absolute value of the difference.

FIGURE 17.2 Effect of Price-Based Reference PPPs: Difference between Published PPP for GDP and PPP for GDP without Price-Based Reference Basic Headings, by Country within ICP Region

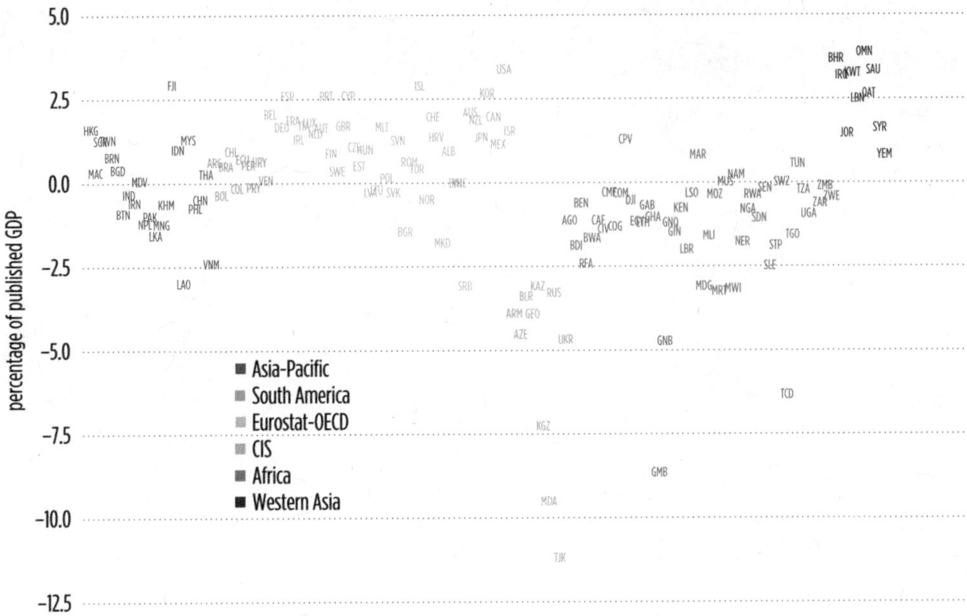

Source: ICP 2005.
Note: See annex B for country/economy codes.

the GDP PPP actually published compared with what the GDP PPP would have been had no reference PPPs been used. Most of the differences are positive, indicating that the use of price-based reference PPPs had an upward impact on the calculation of PPPs for GDP.

Figure 17.2 shows the distribution of the 146 participating countries, ordered by region. In four regions—Asia-Pacific, South America, Eurostat-OECD, and Africa—the differences are mostly quite small; the differences for countries in the CIS and Western Asia groups are somewhat larger.

The histogram in figure 17.3 shows that the differences are less than ±1.5 percent for 60 percent of the countries and less than 2.5 percent for three-quarters of them. Several countries from the CIS and Africa regions, however, display significant negative differences of more than 6 percent. Many of the price-based reference PPPs were selected because they would have a neutral effect on the calculation of the overall PPPs, so this result is not unexpected. Even though reference PPPs were used for quite high shares of GDP in many countries, the reference PPPs selected did not much influence the overall results. The Western Asia region preferred specific to neutral reference PPPs, which may explain why the differences are somewhat larger for countries in this region.

Table 17.6 and figures 17.4 and 17.5 show the effects of using exchange-rate based PPPs. The differences are substantially larger than for price-based reference PPPs—they go from nearly –7 percent for Iceland to over +11 percent for Moldova and The Gambia.

In interpreting these differences, it is important to remember that they depend on both the size of the balances (of trade and direct purchases abroad) and on the extent to which exchange rates differ from PPPs. If the total balance of the two items is zero or small, the differences shown in

FIGURE 17.3 Number of Countries by Size of Differences between GDP PPP without Price-Based Reference PPPs and Published GDP PPP

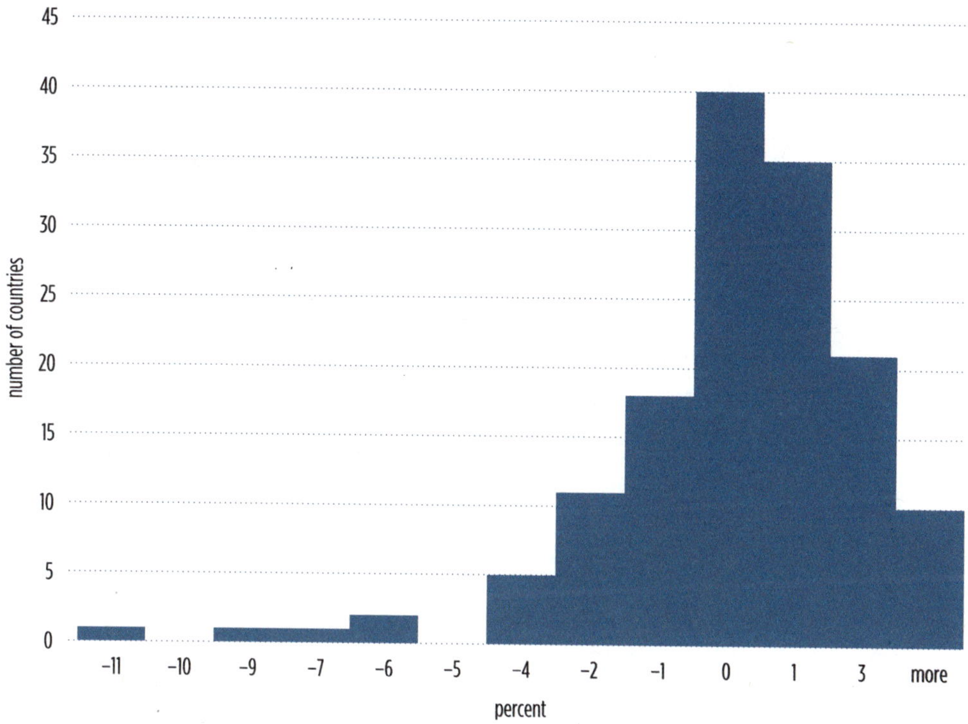

Source: ICP 2005.

table 17.6 will also be zero or small. If the total balance is larger, the difference shown in table 17.6 will depend on how far the exchange rate diverges from the GDP PPP.

Lessons for ICP 2011

The decision about when to use reference PPPs rather than collect prices for a basic heading must be made by the countries in each region in consultation with the regional coordinators. That decision will depend on the resources available for price collection and on the importance of the basic headings. The choice of reference PPPs is similarly a matter for consultation between the countries and their regional coordinators. The Global Office can nevertheless offer some guidance based on the experience in previous rounds of the ICP. Seven suggestions emerge from the discussion in this chapter:

1. Four basic headings for which reference PPPs were used were identified as particularly important in terms of their GDP shares. These are maintenance and repair of the dwelling; social protection (under household consumption); insurance;[5] and other products (under gross fixed capital formation). It should be possible to find prices for representative items in at least some of these basic headings for the 2011 ICP so that their PPPs are measured directly from actual prices.

TABLE 17.6 Difference between GDP PPP without Exchange Rate–Based Reference PPPs and Published GDP PPP

percentage of published GDP PPP

Country/ Economy	%	Country/ Economy	%	Country/ Economy	%	Country/ Economy	%
Ecuador	0.0	Azerbaijan	−0.5	Ukraine	1.2	Malta	−2.5
Cameroon	0.0	Indonesia	−0.5	Benin	1.2	Croatia	−2.6
Korea, Rep.	−0.1	Belarus	0.5	Botswana	−1.3	Equatorial Guinea	2.6
Czech Republic	−0.1	Kuwait	0.5	Niger	1.3	Denmark	2.7
Poland	−0.1	Senegal	0.6	Chad	−1.3	Malaysia	−2.7
Côte d'Ivoire	0.1	Peru	−0.6	São Tomé and Príncipe	1.3	Uganda	2.9
Colombia	−0.1	Argentina	−0.6	India	1.4	Spain	−3.0
Zambia	0.1	Turkey	−0.7	United Kingdom	−1.4	Macao SAR, China	3.0
Slovak Republic	0.1	Montenegro	0.7	Qatar	−1.4	Zimbabwe	−3.1
Swaziland	−0.1	Mali	0.7	Egypt, Arab Rep.	1.6	Malawi	3.1
Djibouti	−0.1	Mozambique	0.7	Paraguay	1.6	Bulgaria	3.1
Bolivia	−0.1	Italy	−0.8	Belgium	1.7	Netherlands	3.2
Venezuela, RB	−0.1	Sudan	0.8	Russian Federation	−1.7	Portugal	−3.3
Mauritius	0.1	Liberia	0.8	Angola	1.7	Switzerland	3.3
Congo, Dem. Rep.	−0.1	Central Africa Republic	0.8	Gabon	−1.7	Guinea-Bissau	3.4
Chile	0.2	Estonia	−0.8	Tanzania	1.7	Sweden	3.4
Comoros	−0.2	China	−0.8	Bosnia Herzegovina	1.8	Rwanda	3.5
Latvia	0.2	Kazakhstan	−0.9	Bangladesh	2.0	Armenia	3.5
Iraq	−0.2	Congo, Rep.	0.9	Oman	−2.0	Lao PDR	3.6
Brazil	−0.2	Canada	0.9	New Zealand	−2.0	Bhutan	3.9
Uruguay	−0.2	Guinea	0.9	Lesotho	2.0	Fiji	−4.0
Hungary	−0.3	Slovenia	−0.9	Vietnam	2.0	Cape Verde	−4.0
Maldives	−0.3	Hong Kong SAR, China	0.9	Germany	2.1	Madagascar	4.1
Lithuania	0.3	Philippines	0.9	Ghana	2.1	Georgia	4.1
Mexico	−0.3	France	−1.0	United States	−2.1	Sierra Leone	4.1
Israel	−0.3	Bahrain	−1.0	Kenya	2.2	Cyprus	−4.4
Tunisia	0.3	Saudi Arabia	−1.0	Brunei Darussalam	−2.2	Ethiopia	4.5
Syrian Arab Republic	−0.3	Yemen, Rep.	−1.0	Pakistan	2.2	Nepal	4.6
Taiwan, China	−0.4	Albania	1.0	Serbia	2.3	Tajikistan	6.3
Thailand	0.4	Singapore	1.1	Jordan	2.3	Iceland	−6.7
South Africa	−0.4	Iran, Islamic Rep.	−1.1	Burkina Faso	2.3	Mauritania	6.8
Morocco	−0.4	Namibia	−1.1	Burundi	2.3	Ireland	7.1
Lebanon	0.4	Cambodia	1.1	Sri Lanka	2.4	Kyrgyz Republic	7.7
Japan	0.4	Australia	−1.2	Togo	2.4	Norway	10.4
Austria	0.5	Mongolia	1.2	Finland	2.5	Luxembourg	10.5
Romania	0.5	Nigeria	−1.2	Macedonia, FYR	2.5	Moldova	11.2
						Gambia, The	11.7

Source: ICP 2005.

FIGURE 17.4 Effect of Exchange Rate Reference PPPs: Difference between Published PPP for GDP and PPP for GDP without Exchange Rate Reference PPPs, by Country within ICP Region

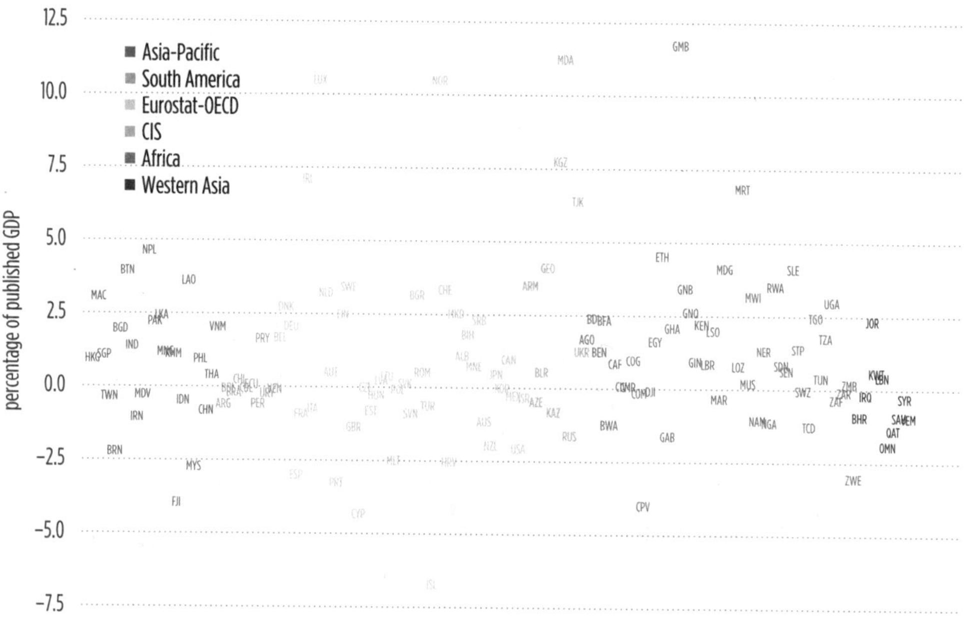

Source: ICP 2005.
Note: See annex B for country/economy codes.

2. Some regions should consider collecting prices for goods and services that have significant weights in their own regions. Motorcycles in Asia-Pacific, domestic services in Africa, and nongovernmental education in the Eurostat-OECD and CIS regions are some examples.
3. As a general rule, it is probably best to not mix goods and services. If a reference PPP is to be used for a goods basic heading, the reference PPP should also be based on a goods basic heading. And, of course, the same applies to services. The reason for this rule is that we know from past rounds that the relative prices of goods and services are usually very different between countries. In the 2005 round, the PPPs for major household appliances, small electric household appliances, and small tools and miscellaneous accessories were used as reference PPPs for domestic services in both the Asia-Pacific and Africa regions. It probably would have been better to use service basic headings as the reference.
4. The weighted geometric averages of PPPs for tourist-type expenditures—on hotels, restaurants, and transport, for example—would probably be better reference PPPs for net resident expenditures abroad than exchange rates.
5. Where feasible, specific reference PPPs are to be preferred to neutral ones. In the 2005 ICP round, the Western Asia region used averages of the PPPs for gardens and pets, medical services, and paramedical services as a reference PPP for veterinary and pet services and PPPs for recreational and sporting services as reference PPPs for games of chance. Other regions used neutral reference PPPs in both cases.

FIGURE 17.5 Number of Countries by Size of Differences between GDP PPP without Exchange Rate PPPs and Published GDP PPP

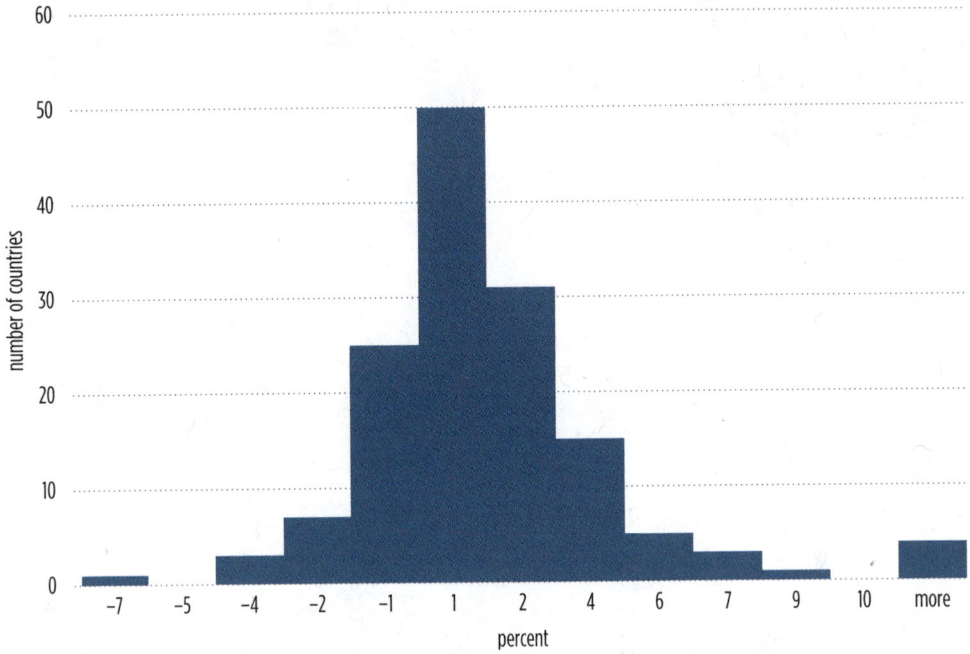

Source: ICP 2005.

6. The use of reference PPPs for actual and imputed rentals for housing should be avoided in the 2011 round. The Asia-Pacific and Africa regions may need more help in providing rental data and data on the quantity and quality of dwellings, so that one or other of the preferred methods can be used to calculate PPPs for this important basic heading. The use of the volume-based reference PPP in the 2005 round undoubtedly affected the reliability of the PPPs for these regions, although the size and direction of the errors cannot be known.
7. Finally, it would be useful to review the reference PPPs at the data validation stage. In the 2005 ICP round, great care was taken with the price validation, but the reference PPPs were not evaluated with the same care.

ANNEX A

Reference PPP Basic Headings (BHs)

BH: Spirits	**BH code: 110211.1**
Western Asia	Nonalcoholic beverages (Kuwait, Qatar, Saudi Arabia, Yemen, Rep.)
BH: Wine	**BH code: 110212.1**
Western Asia	Nonalcoholic beverages (Kuwait, Qatar, Saudi Arabia, Yemen, Rep.)
BH: Beer	**BH code: 110213.1**
Western Asia	Nonalcoholic beverages (Kuwait, Qatar, Saudi Arabia, Yemen, Rep.)
BH: Narcotics	**BH code: 110231.1**
Eurostat-OECD	Individual consumption expenditure by households, excluding health BHs, education BHs, reference PPP BHs
BH: Water supply	**BH code: 110441.1**
Western Asia	Individual consumption expenditure by households, excluding reference PPP BHs
BH: Miscellaneous dwelling services	**BH code: 110442.1**
Eurostat-OECD	Actual and imputed rents
Asia-Pacific	Maintenance of the dwelling; water supply
Africa	Maintenance of the dwelling; water supply
Western Asia	Individual consumption expenditure by households, excluding reference PPP BHs
South America	Maintenance of the dwelling; water supply
BH: Repair of furniture	**BH code: 110513.1**
Asia-Pacific	Maintenance of the dwelling
Africa	Maintenance of the dwelling
Western Asia	Geometric mean of PPPs for cleaning; repair and hire of clothing; repair and hire of footwear; maintenance and repair of the dwelling
South America	Maintenance of the dwelling
BH: Repair of household appliances	**BH code: 110533.1**
Asia-Pacific	Maintenance of the dwelling
Africa	Maintenance of the dwelling
Western Asia	Geometric mean of PPPs for cleaning; repair and hire of clothing; repair and hire of footwear; maintenance and repair of the dwelling
South America	Maintenance of the dwelling
BH: Domestic services	**BH code: 110562.1**
Asia-Pacific	Major household appliances; small electric household appliances; small tools and misc. accessories
Africa	Major household appliances; small electric household appliances; small tools and misc. accessories
BH: Household services	**BH code: 110562.2**
Asia-Pacific	Maintenance of the dwelling

(*continued*)

Africa	Maintenance of the dwelling
Western Asia	Domestic services
South America	Maintenance of the dwelling
BH: Hospital services	**BH code: 110631.1**
Eurostat-OECD	Production of health services by government without net taxes on production and receipts from sales
BH: Motorcycles	**BH code: 110712.1**
Asia-Pacific	Motor cars
Africa	Motor cars
Western Asia	Motor cars
South America	Motor cars
BH: Animal-drawn vehicles	**BH code: 110714.1**
Eurostat-OECD	Individual consumption expenditure by households, excluding health BHs, education BHs, reference PPP BHs
Western Asia	Bicycles
BH: Passenger transport by railway	**BH code: 110731.1**
Western Asia	Passenger transport by road
BH: Passenger transport by sea	**BH code: 110734.1**
Asia-Pacific	Transport BHs, excluding motor cars; bicycles, reference PPP BHs
Africa	Transport BHs, excluding motor cars; bicycles, reference PPP BHs
Western Asia	Geometric mean of PPPs for passenger transport by road and passenger transport by air
South America	Transport BHs, excluding motor cars, bicycles, reference PPP BHs
BH: Combined passenger transport	**BH code: 110735.1**
Asia-Pacific	Transport BHs, excluding motor cars, bicycles, reference PPP BHs
Africa	Transport BHs, excluding motor cars, bicycles, reference PPP BHs
Western Asia	Passenger transport by road
South America	Transport BHs, excluding motor cars, bicycles, reference PPP BHs
BH: Other transport services	**BH code: 110736.1**
Asia-Pacific	Transport BHs, excluding, motor cars, bicycles, reference PPP BHs
Africa	Transport BHs, excluding motor cars, bicycles, reference PPP BHs
South America	Transport BHs, excluding motor cars, bicycles, reference PPP BHs
BH: Major durables for recreation	**BH code: 110921.1**
Asia-Pacific	Bicycles; audiovisual, photographic, and computer equipment
Africa	Bicycles; audiovisual, photographic, and computer equipment
South America	Bicycles; audiovisual, photographic, and computer equipment
BH: Maintenance of other major durables	**BH code: 110923.1**
Western Asia	Repair of audiovisual, photographic, and information processing equipment
BH: Garden and pets	**BH code: 110933.1**
Asia-Pacific	Individual consumption expenditure by households, excluding net final consumption expenditure of resident households in the rest of the world, major tools and equipment, hospital services, reference PPP BHs

Africa	Individual consumption expenditure by households, excluding net final consumption expenditure of resident households in the rest of the world, major tools and equipment, reference PPP BHs
South America	Individual consumption expenditure by households, excluding domestic services, reference PPP BHs
BH: Veterinary and pet services	**BH code: 110935.1**
Asia-Pacific	Individual consumption expenditure by households, excluding net final consumption expenditure of resident households in the rest of the world, major tools and equipment, hospital services, reference PPP BHs
Africa	Individual consumption expenditure by households, excluding net final consumption expenditure of resident households in the rest of the world, major tools and equipment, reference PPP BHs
Western Asia	Geometric mean of the PPPs for gardens and pets; medical services; paramedical services
South America	Individual consumption expenditure by households, excluding domestic services, reference PPP BHs
BH: Games of chance	**BH code: 110943.1**
Eurostat-OECD	Individual consumption expenditure by households, excluding health BHs, education BHs, reference PPP BHs
Asia-Pacific	Individual consumption expenditure by households, excluding net final consumption expenditure of resident households in the rest of the world, major tools and equipment, hospital services, reference PPP BHs
Africa	Individual consumption expenditure by households, excluding net final consumption expenditure of resident households in the rest of the world, major tools and equipment, reference PPP BHs
Western Asia	Recreational and sporting services
South America	Individual consumption expenditure by households, excluding domestic services, reference PPP BHs
BH: Package holidays	**BH code: 110961.1**
Eurostat-OECD	Weighted average of PPPs for transport services; restaurants and hotels
BH: Education	**BH code: 111011.1**
Eurostat-OECD	Production of education services by government without net taxes on production and receipts from sales
BH: Prostitution	**BH code: 111221.1**
Eurostat-OECD	Individual consumption expenditure by households, excluding health BHs, education BHs, reference PPP BHs
BH: Social protection	**BH code: 111241.1**
Eurostat-OECD	Government final consumption expenditure, excluding social protection, recreation and culture, housing
Asia-Pacific	Individual consumption expenditure by households, excluding health, education, net final consumption expenditure of resident households in the rest of the world, major tools and equipment, hospital services, reference PPP BHs
Africa	Compensation of employees; machinery and equipment BHs; construction BHs; individual consumption expenditure by households, excluding net final consumption expenditure of resident households in the rest of the world, major tools and equipment, reference PPP BHs
Western Asia	Individual consumption expenditure by households
South America	Compensation of employees; machinery and equipment BHs; construction BHs; individual consumption expenditure by households, excluding domestic services, reference PPP BHs

(*continued*)

BH: Insurance	**BH code: 111251.1**
Eurostat-OECD	Individual consumption expenditure by households, excluding health BHs, education BHs, reference PPP BHs
Asia-Pacific	Individual consumption expenditure by households, excluding health, education, net final consumption expenditure of resident households in the rest of the world, major tools and equipment, hospital services, reference PPP BHs
Africa	Individual consumption expenditure by households, excluding net final consumption expenditure of resident households in the rest of the world, major tools and equipment, reference PPP BHs
Western Asia	Individual consumption expenditure by households, excluding reference PPP BHs
South America	Individual consumption expenditure by households, excluding domestic services, reference PPP BHs
BH: FISIM	**BH code: 111261.1**
Eurostat-OECD	Individual consumption expenditure by households, excluding health BHs, education BHs, reference PPP BHs
Asia-Pacific	Individual consumption expenditure by households, excluding health, education, net final consumption expenditure of resident households in the rest of the world, major tools and equipment, hospital services, reference PPP BHs
Africa	Individual consumption expenditure by households, excluding net final consumption expenditure of resident households in the rest of the world, major tools and equipment, reference PPP BHs
Western Asia	Individual consumption expenditure by households, excluding reference PPP BHs
South America	Individual consumption expenditure by households, excluding domestic services, reference PPP BHs
BH: Other financial services	**BH code: 111262.1**
Asia-Pacific	Individual consumption expenditure by households, excluding health, education, net final consumption expenditure of resident households in the rest of the world, major tools and equipment, hospital services, reference PPP BHs
Africa	Individual consumption expenditure by households, excluding net final consumption expenditure of resident households in the rest of the world, major tools and equipment, reference PPP BHs
Western Asia	Individual consumption expenditure by households, excluding reference PPP BHs
South America	Individual consumption expenditure by households, excluding domestic services, reference PPP BHs
BH: Other services	**BH code: 111271.1**
Asia-Pacific	Individual consumption expenditure by households, excluding health, education, net final consumption expenditure of resident households in the rest of the world, major tools and equipment, hospital services, reference PPP BHs
Africa	Individual consumption expenditure by households, excluding net final consumption expenditure of resident households in the rest of the world, major tools and equipment, reference PPP BHs
Western Asia	Individual consumption expenditure by households, excluding reference PPP BHs
South America	Individual consumption expenditure by households, excluding domestic services, reference PPP BHs
BH: Purchases by residents in the rest of the world	**BH code: 111311.1**
Eurostat-OECD	Exchange rates
West Asia	Exchange rates

BH: Purchases by nonresidents in the country	BH code: 111311.2
Eurostat-OECD	Exchange rates
BH: NPISH consumption	**BH code: 120111.1**
Eurostat-OECD	Government final consumption expenditure, excluding social protection, recreation and culture, housing
BH: Housing	**BH code: 130111.1**
Eurostat-OECD	Actual and imputed rents
BH: Hospital services	**BH code: 130212.4**
Eurostat-OECD	Production of health services by government without net taxes on production and receipts from sales
BH: Intermediate consumption	**BH code: 130222.1**
Eurostat-OECD	Individual consumption expenditure by households, excluding health BHs, education BHs, reference PPP BHs
Asia-Pacific	Individual consumption expenditure by households, excluding net final consumption expenditure of resident households in the rest of the world, major tools and equipment, hospital services, reference PPP BHs
Africa	Individual consumption expenditure by households, excluding net final consumption expenditure of resident households in the rest of the world, major tools and equipment, reference PPP BHs
Western Asia	Individual consumption expenditure by households, excluding reference PPP BHs
South America	Individual consumption expenditure by households, excluding domestic services, reference PPP BHs
BH: Gross operating surplus	**BH code: 130223.1**
Eurostat-OECD	Gross fixed capital formation
Asia-Pacific	Machinery and equipment BHs; construction BHs
Africa	Machinery and equipment BHs; construction BHs
Western Asia	Gross fixed capital formation, excluding reference PPP BHs
South America	Machinery and equipment BHs; construction BHs
BH: Net taxes on production	**BH code: 130224.1**
Eurostat-OECD	Production of health services by government without net taxes on production and receipts from sales
Asia-Pacific	Compensation of employees; machinery and equipment BHs; construction BHs; individual consumption expenditure by households, excluding net final consumption expenditure of resident households in the rest of the world, major tools and equipment, hospital services, reference PPP BH
Africa	Compensation of employees; machinery and equipment BHs; construction BHs; individual consumption expenditure by households, excluding net final consumption expenditure of resident households in the rest of the world, major tools and equipment, and reference PPP BHs
Western Asia	Production of health services, excluding reference PPP BHs
South America	Compensation of employees; machinery and equipment BHs; construction BHs; individual consumption expenditure by households, excluding domestic services, reference PPP BHs
BH: Receipts from sales	**BH code: 130225.1**
Eurostat-OECD	Production of health services by government without net taxes on production and receipts from sales

(*continued*)

Asia-Pacific	Compensation of employees; machinery and equipment BHs; construction BHs; individual consumption expenditure by households, excluding net final consumption expenditure of resident households in the rest of the world, major tools and equipment, hospital services, reference PPP BHs
Africa	Compensation of employees; machinery and equipment BHs; construction BHs; individual consumption expenditure by households, excluding net final consumption expenditure of resident households in the rest of the world, major tools and equipment, reference PPP BHs
Western Asia	Production of health services, excluding reference PPP BHs
South America	Compensation of employees; machinery and equipment BHs; construction BHs; individual consumption expenditure by households, excluding domestic services, reference PPP BHs
BH: Recreation and culture	**BH code: 130311.1**
Eurostat-OECD	Government final consumption expenditure, excluding social protection, recreation and culture, housing
Asia-Pacific	Recreational and sporting services; cultural services
BH: Education benefits and reimbursements	**BH code: 130411.1**
Eurostat-OECD	Production of education services by government without net taxes on production and receipts from sales
BH: Intermediate consumption	**BH code: 130422.1**
Eurostat-OECD	Individual consumption expenditure by households, excluding health BHs, education BHs, reference PPP BHs
Asia-Pacific	Individual consumption expenditure by households, excluding net final consumption expenditure of resident households in the rest of the world, major tools and equipment, hospital services, reference PPP BHs
Africa	Individual consumption expenditure by households, excluding net final consumption expenditure of resident households in the rest of the world, major tools and equipment, reference PPP BHs.
Western Asia	Individual consumption expenditure by households, excluding reference PPP BHs
South America	Individual consumption expenditure by households, excluding domestic services, reference PPP BHs
BH: Gross operating surplus	**BH code: 130423.1**
Eurostat-OECD	Gross fixed capital formation
Asia-Pacific	Machinery and equipment BHs; construction BHs
Africa	Machinery and equipment BHs; construction BHs
Western Asia	Gross fixed capital formation, excluding reference PPPs BHs
South America	Machinery and equipment BHs; construction BHs
BH: Net taxes on production	**BH code: 130424.1**
Eurostat-OECD	Production of education services by government without net taxes on production and receipts from sales
Asia-Pacific	Compensation of employees; machinery and equipment BHs; construction BHs; individual consumption expenditure by households, excluding net final consumption expenditure of resident households in the rest of the world, major tools and equipment, hospital services, reference PPP BHs
Africa	Compensation of employees; machinery and equipment BHs; construction BHs; individual consumption expenditure by households, excluding net final consumption expenditure of resident households in the rest of the world, major tools and equipment, reference PPP BHs
Western Asia	Production of education services, excluding reference PPP BHs
South America	Compensation of employees; machinery and equipment BHs; construction BHs; individual consumption expenditure by households, excluding domestic services, reference PPP BHs

BH: Receipt from sales	**BH code: 130425.1**
Eurostat-OECD	Production of education services by government without net taxes on production and receipts from sales
Asia-Pacific	Compensation of employees; machinery and equipment BHs; construction BHs; individual consumption expenditure by households, excluding net final consumption expenditure of resident households in the rest of the world, major tools and equipment, hospital services, reference PPP BHs
Africa	Compensation of employees; machinery and equipment BHs; construction BHs; individual consumption expenditure by households, excluding net final consumption expenditure of resident households in the rest of the world, major tools and equipment, reference PPP BHs
Western Asia	Production of education services, excluding reference PPP BHs
South America	Compensation of employees; machinery and equipment BHs; construction BHs; individual consumption expenditure by households, excluding domestic services, reference PPP BHs
BH: Social protection	**BH code: 130511.1**
Eurostat-OECD	Government final consumption expenditure, excluding social protection, recreation and culture, housing
BH: Intermediate consumption	**BH code: 140112.1**
Eurostat-OECD	Individual consumption expenditure by households, excluding health BHs, education BHs, reference PPP BHs
Asia-Pacific	Machinery and equipment BHs; construction BHs; individual consumption expenditure by households, excluding net final consumption expenditure of resident households in the rest of the world, major tools and equipment, hospital services, reference PPP BHs
Africa	Machinery and equipment BHs; construction BHs; individual consumption expenditure by households, excluding net final consumption expenditure of resident households in the rest of the world, major tools and equipment, reference PPP BHs
Western Asia	Individual consumption expenditure by households, excluding reference PPP BHs
South America	Machinery and equipment BHs; construction BHs; individual consumption expenditure by households, excluding domestic services, reference PPP BHs
BH: Gross operating surplus	**BH code: 140113.1**
Eurostat-OECD	Gross fixed capital formation
Asia-Pacific	Machinery and equipment BHs; construction BHs
Africa	Machinery and equipment BHs; construction BHs
Western Asia	Gross fixed capital formation, excluding reference PPPs BHs
South America	Machinery and equipment BHs; construction BHs
BH: Net taxes on production	**BH code: 140114.1**
Eurostat-OECD	Production of collective services by government without net taxes on production and receipts from sales
Asia-Pacific	Compensation of employees; machinery and equipment BHs; construction BHs; individual consumption expenditure by households, excluding net final consumption expenditure of resident households in the rest of the world, major tools and equipment, hospital services, reference PPP BHs
Africa	Compensation of employees; machinery and equipment BHs; construction BHs; individual consumption expenditure by households, excluding net final consumption expenditure of resident households in the rest of the world, major tools and equipment, reference PPP BHs
Western Asia	Collective services, excluding reference PPP BHs
South America	Compensation of employees; machinery and equipment BHs; construction BHs; individual consumption expenditure by households, excluding domestic services, reference PPP BHs

(*continued*)

BH: Receipts from sales	**BH code: 140115.1**
Eurostat-OECD	Production of collective services by government without net taxes on production and receipts from sales
Asia/Pacific	Compensation of employees; machinery and equipment BHs; construction BHs; individual consumption expenditure by households, excluding net final consumption expenditure of resident households in the rest of the world, major tools and equipment, hospital services, reference PPP BHs
Africa	Compensation of employees; machinery and equipment BHs; construction BHs; individual consumption expenditure by households, excluding net final consumption expenditure of resident households in the rest of the world, major tools and equipment, reference PPP BHs
West Asia	Collective services, excluding reference PPP BHs
South America	Compensation of employees; machinery and equipment BHs; construction BHs; individual consumption expenditure by households, excluding domestic services, reference PPP BHs
BH: Fabricated metal products	**BH code: 150111.1**
Western Asia	Metal products and equipment, excluding reference PPP BHs
BH: Other manufactured goods	**BH code: 150115.1**
Western Asia	Metal products and equipment, excluding reference PPP BHs
BH: Other road transport	**BH code: 150121.2**
Western Asia	Motor vehicles, trailers, and semitrailers
BH: Other transport equipment	**BH code: 150122.1**
Eurostat-OECD	Gross fixed capital formation
Western Asia	Motor vehicles, trailers, and semitrailers
BH: Other products	**BH code: 150311.1**
Eurostat-OECD	Gross fixed capital formation
Asia-Pacific	Machinery and equipment BHs; construction BHs
Africa	Machinery and equipment BHs; construction BHs
South America	Machinery and equipment BHs; construction BHs
BH: Opening value of inventories	**BH code: 1601111**
Eurostat-OECD	Weighted average of PPPs for consumer goods and equipment goods
Western Asia	Geometric mean of PPPs for durable goods BHs
BH: Closing value of inventories	**BH code: 160111.2**
Eurostat-OECD	Weighted average of PPPs for consumer goods and equipment goods
BH: Acquisitions of valuables	**BH code: 160211.1**
Eurostat-OECD	Jewelry, clocks, and watches
BH: Disposals of valuables	**BH code: 160211.2**
Eurostat-OECD	Jewelry, clocks, and watches
BH: Exports of goods and services	**BH code: 170111.1**
Eurostat-OECD	Exchange rates
West Asia	Exchange rates
BH: Imports of goods and services	**BH code: 170111.2**
Eurostat-OECD	Exchange rates

Source: ICP.

ANNEX B

Country/Economy Codes

Country	Code	Country	Code	Country	Code
Albania	ALB	Denmark	DNK	Lao PDR	LAO
Angola	AGO	Djibouti	DJI	Latvia	LVA
Argentina	ARG	Ecuador	ECU	Lebanon	LBN
Armenia	ARM	Egypt, Arab Rep.	EGY	Lesotho	LSO
Australia	AUS	Equatorial Guinea	GNQ	Liberia	LBR
Austria	AUT	Estonia	EST	Lithuania	LTU
Azerbaijan	AZE	Ethiopia	ETH	Luxembourg	LUX
Bahrain	BHR	Fiji	FJI	Macao SAR, China	MAC
Bangladesh	BGD	Finland	FIN	Macedonia, FYR	MKD
Belgium	BEL	France	FRA	Madagascar	MDG
Benin	BEN	Gabon	GAB	Malawi	MWI
Bhutan	BTN	Gambia, The	GMB	Malaysia	MYS
Bolivia	BOL	Georgia	GEO	Maldives	MDV
Bosnia and Herzegovina	BIH	Germany	DEU	Mali	MLI
Botswana	BWA	Ghana	GHA	Malta	MLT
Brazil	BRA	Greece	GRC	Mauritania	MRT
Brunei Darussalam	BRN	Guinea	GIN	Mauritius	MUS
Bulgaria	BGR	Guinea-Bissau	GNB	Mexico	MEX
Burkina Faso	BFA	Hong Kong SAR, China	HKG	Moldova	MDA
Burundi	BDI	Hungary	HUN	Mongolia	MNG
Cambodia	KHM	Iceland	ISL	Montenegro	MNE
Cameroon	CMR	India	IND	Morocco	MAR
Canada	CAN	Indonesia	IDN	Mozambique	MOZ
Cape Verde	CPV	Iran, Islamic Rep.	IRN	Namibia	NAM
Central African Republic	CAF	Iraq	IRQ	Nepal	NPL
Chad	TCD	Ireland	IRL	Netherlands	NLD
Chile	CHL	Israel	ISR	New Zealand	NZL
China	CHN	Italy	ITA	Niger	NER
Colombia	COL	Japan	JPN	Nigeria	NGA
Comoros	COM	Jordan	JOR	Norway	NOR
Congo, Dem. Rep.	COG	Kazakhstan	KAZ	Oman	OMN
Côte d'Ivoire	CIV	Kenya	KEN	Pakistan	PAK
Croatia	HRV	Korea, Rep.	KOR	Paraguay	PRY
Cyprus	CYP	Kuwait	KWT	Peru	PER
Czech Republic	CZE	Kyrgyz Republic	KGZ	Philippines	PHL

(continued)

Country	Code	Country	Code	Country	Code
Poland	POL	Slovenia	SVN	Togo	TGO
Portugal	PRT	South Africa	ZAF	Tunisia	TUN
Qatar	QAT	Spain	ESP	Turkey	TUR
Romania	ROM	Sri Lanka	LKA	Uganda	UGA
Russian Federation	RUS	Sudan	SDN	Ukraine	UKR
Rwanda	RWA	Swaziland	SWZ	United Kingdom	GBR
São Tomé and Príncipe	STP	Sweden	SWE	United States	USA
Saudi Arabia	SAU	Switzerland	CHE	Uruguay	URY
Senegal	SEN	Syrian Arab Republic	SYR	Venezuela, RB	VEN
Serbia	SRB	Taiwan, China	TWN	Vietnam	VNM
Sierra Leone	SLE	Tajikistan	TJK	Yemen, Rep.	YEM
Singapore	SGP	Tanzania	TZA	Zambia	ZMB
Slovak Republic	SVK	Thailand	THA	Zimbabwe	ZWE

NOTES

1. The qualifier *reference* raises the question "Referring to what?" Terms such as *surrogate PPPs* or *proxy PPPs* might be easier to understand. However, the term *reference PPPs* is firmly embedded in the literature on international comparisons and so is used throughout this chapter.
2. The five geographic ICP regions in 2005 were Africa, Asia-Pacific, Commonwealth of Independent States (CIS), South America, and Western Asia. The Eurostat–Organisation for Economic Co-operation and Development (OECD) members constituted a sixth region.
3. A calculation was made based on earlier comparisons, in which for large groups of countries the dwelling services in real terms were found to be approximately proportionate to the overall real HFCE. That supported the reference volume neutrality argument.
4. In practice, all regions except the Eurostat–Organisation for Economic Co-operation and Development (OECD) collapsed these pairs of basic headings to single "balance" basic headings: exports minus imports and purchases abroad by residents minus purchases in the domestic territory by nonresidents. Note that the basic headings final consumption expenditure of resident households in the rest of the world and final consumption expenditure of nonresident households in the economic territory are adjustment items that are not usually required if estimates of household consumption expenditure are based on a household expenditure survey. This is, in practice, how many countries outside the Eurostat-OECD and CIS groups estimate the household consumption expenditure, and these countries did not therefore need to estimate these basic headings.
5. The basic heading insurance covers only the service charge and not the whole of the insurance premium. The insurance service charge cannot be measured directly, but it is reasonable to assume that PPPs for service charges will be close to PPPs calculated from premiums.

REFERENCES

World Bank. 2005. "ICP Operational Manual." http://siteresources.worldbank.org/ICPINT/Resources/ICPOperationalManual2005.pdf.

———. 2007. *ICP 2005 Methodological Handbook.* http://web.worldbank.org/WBSITE/EXTERNAL/DATASTATISTICS/ICPEXT/0,,contentMDK:20126612~pagePK:60002244~piPK:62002388~theSitePK:270065,00.html.

CHAPTER 18

Extrapolating PPPs and Comparing ICP Benchmark Results

PAUL MCCARTHY

The International Comparison Program (ICP) provides estimates of the gross domestic product (GDP) and its main expenditure components for most countries in the world expressed in a common currency and at consistent price levels for a specific reference year (2005 for the estimates in this book). In this respect, the estimates are different from those more commonly available in a country's national accounts, in which the evolution of an economy over time can be analyzed through the annual (or quarterly) time series data that are available. The output of the ICP is often referred to as a "snapshot" of the relationships between the economies of participating countries because the data relate to the level of economic activity in each country in a single reference year.

The 2005 ICP provided detailed purchasing power parity (PPP) data for 146 countries. Because of the cost of conducting a worldwide project such as the ICP, the PPPs for most countries are produced infrequently. For example, the 2011 ICP round is taking place six years after the 2005 ICP. But PPPs and related data (real expenditures and price level indexes, PLIs) for some countries are available more frequently. For example, Eurostat, the European Union's statistical office, produces annual PPPs for its member and candidate countries using a "rolling benchmark" approach,[1] and the Organisation for Economic Co-operation and Development (OECD) currently produces PPPs, real expenditures, and PLIs for its non-European member countries every three years.

The availability of firm PPP-based expenditure data for 2005 for so many countries has resulted in increased interest in PPPs by analysts engaged in worldwide comparisons of economic activity. One outcome has been that analysts want to obtain PPPs and real expenditures for countries that did not participate in the 2005 ICP. In past ICP rounds, PPPs and real expenditures for nonparticipating countries have been estimated using regression models. The number of countries for which these imputed estimates were required in the 2005 ICP was lower than in previous rounds but, even so, PPPs were estimated for 42 countries in addition to the 146 countries that participated in the 2005 ICP. In practice, though, the accuracy of the results from this imputation procedure depends on a number of assumptions, and so the results are not as accurate as the estimates for the countries that participated in the ICP. The demand for these data has been met by imputing PPPs for these 42 countries using a regression model. Another outcome has been the need for PPPs that are more up-to-date than those from the 2005 ICP. As a consequence, the 2005 PPPs have been extrapolated to later years for countries not included in the annual Eurostat PPP Programme. One result is that the PPPs extrapolated for each out-year are being used as though they form a time series that can be applied directly to the annual values of national accounts aggregates such as GDP. Despite the shortcomings involved, many research studies are based on this type of procedure because the only alternative is to use exchange rates, which, for obvious reasons, is not a viable method for most international comparisons.

Various organizations provide estimates of PPPs for years other than benchmark years. The OECD extrapolates PPPs for GDP from its latest benchmark for each successive year because of the demand by users for annual PPPs. It also interpolates between past benchmarks to form a time series of annual PPPs and real expenditures. The University of Pennsylvania's Center for International Comparisons of Production, Income and Prices compiles the Penn World Table (PWT), which provides an annual series of PPP-based real expenditures and PLIs to meet the demand for this type of data. However, problems arise in using PPPs as though they are times series because PPPs are designed for comparing economic activity between countries (i.e., a spatial comparison) rather than comparing changes across time, which is the more common method of analyzing national accounts. Conceptually, it is impossible to maintain consistency simultaneously across both space and time except under very restrictive assumptions. A time series of PPPs may provide plausible results provided that the economic structures of the countries involved in the comparison do not change rapidly. However, distorted results are likely to be obtained if the economies of the countries are dissimilar or the economic structures of the countries are changing at very different rates (e.g., the United States and China in recent years).

This chapter covers in some detail the issues involved in using PPPs in a time series mode. The goal is to alert users of PPP-related data to the types of assumptions that underlie extrapolated and backcast PPPs and real expenditures so that they can make informed decisions about the data they are using. It is clear that, despite their shortcomings when used as a time series, PPPs still provide much more firmly based international comparisons for most purposes than the oft-used alternative of market exchange rates.

Before readers venture further into a chapter that introduces some fairly complex concepts, it may be helpful to clarify some of the terms used in the context of this chapter. The tables in a time series of national accounts are generally expressed in terms of values, but these values may be expressed in terms of "current prices" or "constant prices." Values expressed in terms of current prices may be referred to as "current values" or "current price values" or even just "values," with "current prices" being understood from the context. A value can be thought of as being obtained by multiplying the quantity of a particular product by its unit price. For example, the value of 100 tons of wheat at a price of $250 per ton would be $25,000. As prices change over time, the current value will change even if the underlying quantity remains the same, and so a time series of annual current values includes the combined effects of quantity changes and price changes from year to year. For many types of analysis, it is useful to identify the underlying quantity of activity. However, once a value includes more than one product, it is impossible to obtain meaningful quantities (the old problem of being unable to add apples and oranges). Therefore, a time series of "constant price values" is estimated by removing the effects on the current values of price changes over time. The mechanics of this process may vary significantly but can be thought of as dividing a price index of relevant products into the corresponding current values. These price indexes are generally called "deflators." In algebraic terms: constant price value = current value/deflator.

It is necessary to specify a particular "base year" in estimating a series of constant price values. The level of the constant price value for each component of GDP in the base year will be equal to its current value, but the constant price values in other years will be different from the current values (unless there is no change in prices from the base year to the year being considered). Constant price values are often referred to in the national accounts as "volumes." Changes in constant price values from year to year may be linked together to form a "chained volume." Volumes are estimated for many components of GDP and then summed to obtain the volume of GDP. In the ICP, the current values of GDP and its components are generally described as values expressed in "local currency units" or "national currency units" to stress the fact that they are in units not comparable from one country to another. These values are divided by PPPs to express them in terms of a common currency, with the resultant values called "real expenditures" (sometimes also referred to as "volumes") because the effects of price level differences across countries have been removed. In the ICP, values in local currency units that have been converted to a common currency by dividing them by exchange rates are called "nominal values" because they still include the effects of price level differences between the countries as well as the volume differences.

Estimating PPPs for Nonbenchmark Years

The statistical framework for national accounts is provided in the *System of National Accounts 2008* (Commission of the European Communities et al. 2008). Chapter 15 on price and volume measures describes the techniques most commonly used in estimating volumes. The chapter also describes some of the issues involved in obtaining PPPs and real expenditures for international comparisons, and paragraphs 15.232 and 15.233 describe how PPPs are usually estimated for nonbenchmark years:

> 15.232 The method commonly used to extrapolate PPPs from their benchmark year to another year is to use the ratio of the national accounts deflators from each country compared with a numeraire country (generally the United States of America) to move each country's PPPs forward from the benchmark. The PPPs derived are then applied to the relevant national accounts component to obtain volumes [real expenditures] expressed in a common currency for the year in question.
>
> 15.233 Theoretically, the best means of extrapolating PPPs from a benchmark year would be to use time series of prices at the individual product level from each country in the ICP to extrapolate the prices of the individual products included in the ICP benchmark. In practice, it is not possible to use this type of procedure in extrapolating PPP benchmarks because the detailed price data needed are not available in all the countries. Therefore, an approach based on extrapolating at a macro level (for GDP or for a handful of components of GDP) is generally adopted. Leaving aside the data problems involved in collecting consistent data from all the countries involved, a major conceptual question arises with this process because it can be demonstrated mathematically that it is impossible to maintain consistency across both time and space. In other words, extrapolating PPPs using time series of prices at a broad level such as GDP will not result in a match with the benchmark PPP-based estimates even if all the data are perfectly consistent.

Consistency between Time and Space

The nature of the differences between GDP volume growth rates, as measured by the time series national accounts and as implied by PPP benchmarks, has been investigated intermittently since the initial phases of the ICP. Examples of such investigations are found in Khamis (1977) and chapter 8 of the official report of the 1975 ICP (Statistical Office of the United Nations and World Bank 1982). This issue was very important then because ICP rounds were run only once every five years in the 1970s, and the differences between "actual results" (i.e., PPP benchmark estimates) and "extrapolated results" (i.e., extrapolating from the latest benchmark using time series) were significant in many cases. The broad reasons for these differences are well known and include issues such as the different product baskets used in the time series national accounts deflators and in estimating the PPPs, different computational methods, different weighting patterns, and so forth.

More recently, these issues have been investigated further because of the growing interest in international comparisons over time. An interesting analysis of the problems in maintaining consistency in PPPs simultaneously across time and space has been presented by Dalgaard and Sørensen (2002). They demonstrate that, conceptually, it is impossible to maintain such consistency (except under the completely unrealistic condition of having a common fixed price vector in all periods, which implies that the price structure in every country is identical in each period). This conclusion holds no matter which index number formulas are chosen for estimating both the time series price indexes and the PPPs in the selected years. Briefly, the reason is that index number formulas are designed either to measure price changes over time (e.g., a consumer price index, CPI) or to measure prices levels between countries (i.e., PPPs), but they are not designed to measure both of these aspects simultaneously.

In practice, annual PPPs are produced to meet user demand for the annual real expenditures that can be obtained using these PPPs to "deflate" the national accounts values. A method commonly used to produce annual PPPs is based on a macro approach (as outlined in paragraphs 15.232 and 15.233 of the 2008 *System of National Accounts*, SNA) mainly because of the lack of data to adopt a more detailed method. It involves interpolating between benchmark years or extrapolating from the latest benchmark year using the implicit price deflators (IPDs) for GDP for each country involved. The process is to divide the IPD for GDP for each country in turn by the IPD for GDP in a reference country (usually the United States) and apply that ratio to the PPP for GDP in the relevant country in the benchmark year (the IPDs for all countries must be re–referenced to 100 in the benchmark year before calculating the ratio). The formula underlying this approach is

$$PPP_{t+1}^{A} = PPP_{t}^{A} \times \left(\frac{IPD_{t+1}^{A}}{IPD_{t+1}^{R}} \right)$$

where PPP_{t+1}^{A} equals the PPP for country A in year $t + 1$; PPP_{t}^{A} equals the PPP for country A in year t; IPD_{t+1}^{A} equals the IPD for GDP in country A in year $t + 1$ (base =100 in year t); and IPD_{t+1}^{R} equals the IPD for GDP in the reference country (R) in year $t + 1$ (base = 100 in year t).

This procedure can be extended to lower-level aggregates. For example, the PPPs in year $t + 1$ for household final consumption expenditure, government final consumption expenditure, gross fixed capital formation, and net exports of goods and services may be estimated in this way, and then weighted together in the usual way to obtain an estimate of the PPP for GDP in year $t + 1$. However, the results obtained in this way will not be identical to those derived from a full ICP round in which value data for more than 150 basic headings are available. There is no single reason; the various factors potentially affecting the outcome for individual countries depend on the structure of their economies and changes in the structure since year t compared with those in other countries.

The PPPs and real expenditures extrapolated for each year using this methodology may appear to produce an annual time series of PPPs and real expenditures consistent with those that will ultimately be estimated in the next ICP round. However, this is not so, even in the unlikely event that all the underlying national accounts data are completely consistent for all countries and the prices used in estimating PPPs are consistent with the national accounts values (i.e., prices for all products are annual national average prices). In practice, there are many possible reasons why the extrapolated series do not match with the next benchmark, and these are described in some detail later in this chapter. Time series index number theory and spatial (cross-country) index number theory are each very complex in its own right. In effect, the procedures involved in extrapolating PPPs across time combine some of the elements of these two complex theoretical topics. It is impossible to completely merge the time series and spatial concepts, and so inevitably assumptions have to be made that may be more realistic in some circumstances than in others. In particular, extrapolating the PPP or real expenditure for total GDP can yield some quite misleading results at times.

Dalgaard and Sørensen (2002) provide a simple example that shows how inconsistent results can be obtained for PPPs if they are extrapolated at the level of total GDP. The example shows how an implausible outcome arises when PPPs for GDP are extrapolated from a benchmark year even when prices for similar products are moving identically in each of two the countries being compared. It could be extended to cover the situation in which PPPs are extrapolated for only a handful of broad aggregates, such as those for household final consumption expenditure, government final consumption expenditure, gross fixed capital formation, and net exports of goods and services.

The example provided by Dalgaard and Sørensen (2002) assumes that the two countries involved (country A and country B) have the same GDP and price level in year *t*. Expenditure on GDP consists of two products, "goods" and "services." Goods comprise 80 percent of GDP in country A but only 20 percent in country B. Conversely, services are 20 percent of GDP in country A and 80 percent in country B. The prices (in local currency units) for goods in year *t* are 1.00 in each of countries A and B, and they remain the same in both cases in the next benchmark year (referred to as year *t* + 1). The prices for services are 1.00 in year *t* in both countries, but they double to 2.00 in year *t* + 1 in both countries, whereas there is no change in the quantities of goods and services produced between years *t* and *t* + 1. The details are summarized in table 18.1.

The PPPs for both products are 1.00 in year *t* (1.00/1.00 for goods and for services), which means that the PPP for GDP is also 1.00 in that year. The PPPs for both products are 1.00 in year *t* + 1 (1.00/1.00 for goods and 2.00/2.00 for services), and so the PPP for GDP remains equal to 1.00 in year *t* + 1. The PPPs between countries A and B are 1.00 for both goods and services in year *t* and year *t* + 1. Therefore, the PPPs for GDP in both years must also be 1.00. Table 18.2 summarizes the PPPs.

TABLE 18.1 Values and Prices of Goods and Services

	Country A				Country B			
Product	GDP, year *t*	Price, year *t*	Price, year *t* + 1	GDP, year *t* + 1	GDP, year *t*	Price, year *t*	Price, year *t* + 1	GDP, year *t* + 1
Goods	80	1.00	1.00	80	20	1.00	1.00	20
Services	20	1.00	2.00	40	80	1.00	2.00	160
GDP	100			120	100			180

TABLE 18.2 PPPs of Goods and Services

Product	$PPP\left(\frac{A}{B}\right)$, year t	$PPP\left(\frac{A}{B}\right)$, year $t+1$
Goods	$1.00\left(=\frac{1.00}{1.00}\right)$	$1.00\left(=\frac{1.00}{1.00}\right)$
Services	$1.00\left(=\frac{1.00}{1.00}\right)$	$1.00\left(=\frac{2.00}{2.00}\right)$
GDP	1.00	1.00

The volume of GDP in year $t + 1$ with year t as the base year can be calculated by deriving the price deflators for goods and for services in both countries and then dividing these deflators into the corresponding values and summing the results to obtain the volume of GDP. The price deflators in year t are equal to 100.0 because that is the base year. In year $t + 1$, they are obtained by dividing the year $t + 1$ price for goods and for services by the corresponding price in year t (i.e., 1.00/1.00 * 100 = 100.0 for goods and 2.00/1.00 * 100 = 200.0 for services in both countries). Table 18.3 provides details of the steps involved in obtaining the volumes of goods and services and of GDP in year $t + 1$.

The implicit price deflator for GDP is obtained by taking the value of GDP at current prices (from table 18.1) and dividing it by the volume of GDP from table 18.3. The IPD for GDP in year $t + 1$ in country A is 120.0 (= 120/100 * 100) and in country B it is 180 (= 180/100 * 100). Tables 18.1 and 18.3 can now be combined to summarize the details underlying these deflators (table 18.4).

The common method used to extrapolate the PPPs from year t to year $t + 1$ is to apply the ratio of the GDP deflators (both based on year $t = 100$) in year $t + 1$ to move forward the year t PPP for GDP. Based on the deflators from table 18.1, the ratio of the GDP deflators between country B and country A in year $t + 1$ is 1.50 (= 180.0/120.0). Therefore, the PPP for GDP between country B and country A would be estimated as 1.50 (= 1.00 × 1.5) rather than 1.00, which is the PPP estimated when the full set of data is available (see table 18.2).

Likewise, the estimated PPP for GDP between country A and country B is not 1.00. The ratio of the GDP deflators in year $t + 1$ for country A to country B is 0.67 (= 1.20/1.80), and so the extrapolated PPP between country A and country B would be 0.67 (= 1.00 × 0.67).

TABLE 18.3 Volumes of Goods and Services

	Country A				Country B			
Product	GDP, year t	Price deflator, year t	Price deflator, year $t+1$	Volume, year $t+1$	GDP, year t	Price deflator, year t	Price deflator, year $t+1$	GDP, year $t+1$
Goods	80	100.0	100.0	80	20	100.0	100.0	20
Services	20	100.0	200.0	$20\left(=\frac{40}{200.0}*100.0\right)$	80	100.0	200.0	$80\left(=\frac{160}{200.0}*100.0\right)$
GDP volume	100			100	100			100

TABLE 18.4 Summary of Current Prices, Volumes, and Price Deflators for Goods, Services, and GDP

Product		Country A		Country B	
		Year t	Year $t+1$	Year t	Year $t+1$
Current prices	Goods	80	80	20	20
	Services	20	40	80	160
	GDP	*100*	*120*	*100*	*180*
Volumes	Goods	80	80	20	20
	Services	20	20	80	80
	GDP	*100*	*100*	*100*	*100*
Price deflators	Goods	100.0	100.0	100.0	100.0
	Services	100.0	200.0	100.0	200.0
	GDP	*100.0*	*120.0*	*100.0*	*180.0*

The reason for these anomalous results is that the economic structure of the two countries is so different—goods dominate the economic activity in country A, whereas services are far more important than goods in country B, and the prices of services have changed markedly compared with those for goods.

It is important to note that a different set of results would be obtained if the PPPs for individual components of GDP (i.e., each basic heading) were extrapolated using the relevant price changes. The basic heading PPPs could then be weighted together to obtain PPPs for higher-level expenditure aggregates using the same types of processes as in a full ICP round. In the example just given, the price changes for goods and for services are identical in both countries. Therefore, extrapolating the year t prices for each of the two components of GDP and producing PPPs for both in year t + 1 would result in PPPs of 1.00 for goods and for services. As a result, aggregating them to a PPP for GDP would produce the same results for GDP as those shown in table 18.2 (i.e., the PPP for GDP would be 1.00 in both year t and year t + 1). In practice, the best results from an extrapolation procedure would be obtained if the PPPs for each of the 155 ICP basic headings were extrapolated individually using the relationship between the price relatives for each basic heading in each country and those in a reference country (see Biggeri and Laureti 2011).

A technique that is used in practice as a compromise between the extremes of extrapolating at the basic heading level or for GDP in total is to extrapolate PPPs at some intermediate level between the basic heading and GDP (e.g., for major aggregates such as household final consumption expenditure, government final consumption expenditure, gross fixed capital formation, and net exports of goods and services). In such a case, the PPPs extrapolated at this intermediate level are then weighted together to estimate a PPP for GDP. The time series in the PWT are based on this type of technique, which overcomes some of the significant differences in economic structure between countries. However, it is important to note that extrapolating at the level of total household final consumption expenditure using either the national accounts deflator for this aggregate or the CPI will produce different results from those obtained by extrapolating PPPs for each basic heading within this aggregate and then weighting them together to provide a PPP for total household final consumption expenditure.

Extrapolating at levels of aggregation above the basic heading, such as total GDP, yields results that are reference country–invariant. In other words, the choice of reference country should not affect the results obtained using extrapolation methods based on applying price indicators to national accounts values above the basic heading level. However, the process of extrapolating at the level of GDP depends on a number of assumptions about the conceptual and practical features of the data. For example, it is assumed that the reference country and the other country in the extrapolation have similar economic structures and that their economies are evolving in a similar manner. On a practical level, in compiling their national accounts countries follow the standards set out in the *System of National Accounts* (SNA) to varying degrees. Even in countries that closely follow the SNA standards, the national accounts will potentially differ in some ways that may be significant when deflators are used to extrapolate PPPs. For example, the source data available may lead to inconsistencies in the ways in which some estimates are calculated, or the statistical techniques used in some countries may differ in others, with an impact on the consistency of the respective GDP deflators. A common difference is that some countries use hedonic techniques to varying degrees to adjust prices for quality change in products such as computers, motor vehicles, or houses, and the use of "output indicators" to estimate volumes (such as for surgical procedures) varies significantly across countries. In such cases, extrapolating PPPs using changes in GDP deflators can produce distorted results because of the effects of these different statistical treatments on these deflators in different countries.

Eurostat Rolling Benchmark Approach

As noted, Biggeri and Laureti (2011) have concluded that the best means of extrapolating PPPs is to individually extrapolate the PPPs for each basic heading using time series price indexes. Eurostat uses this type of procedure in its "rolling benchmark approach." The rolling benchmark is based on pricing part of the product lists each half-year within a three-year cycle and extrapolating them to subsequent years using time series price indexes that are specific to each basic heading.

Eurostat describes the process in its methodological manual (Eurostat and OECD 2005):

> 2.24 The rolling benchmark approach facilitates annual comparisons as follows. The starting point is the matrix of basic heading PPPs by participating country for the reference year, t. In the subsequent year, $t + 1$, some of the basic heading PPPs are replaced by new PPPs calculated using prices collected during $t + 1$, while the basic heading PPPs that have not been replaced are advanced to $t + 1$ using temporal adjustment factors specific to these basic headings. All the basic heading PPPs in the matrix now refer to $t + 1$. Aggregating the matrix with expenditure weights for $t + 1$ gives PPPs and real final expenditures for each level of aggregation up to the level of GDP with which a comparison can be made for the new reference year, $t + 1$. By continuing the cycle of replacement, extrapolation and aggregation through $t + 2$, $t + 3$, $t + 4$, etc., comparisons can be made for the reference years $t + 2$, $t + 3$, $t + 4$, etc. As over a third of all basic heading PPPs are recalculated each year, all the basic heading PPPs in the matrix for any given reference year have been replaced, at least once, during the 36 months prior to its close.

Most basic headings within household final consumption expenditure are managed in this way, although prices for rents (actual and imputed) are collected every year because of the difficulties in obtaining consistent time series of prices to extrapolate the PPPs for rents. Likewise, price data for compensation of employees are collected annually. Initially, prices were collected for gross fixed capital formation (equipment goods and construction projects) every year. However, this changed after 2005 to a biannual price collection to reduce costs. National accounts expenditures at the basic heading level are collected annually, as are annual average exchange rates and data on average annual resident population. Spatial adjustment factors are estimated in those countries in which the PPP surveys cover only part of the country (e.g., the capital city).

Household final consumption expenditure is split into six surveys, and prices are collected for the basic headings in each group during a half-year. The six groups and the period for which prices were collected for the 2005 round are:

01. Food, drink, and tobacco	first half of 2003
02. Personal appearance	second half of 2003
03. House and garden	first half of 2004
04. Transport, restaurants, and hotels	second half of 2004
05. Services	first half of 2005
06. Furniture and health	second half of 2005.

The main advantages of the rolling benchmark are that reliable annual PPPs can be produced, costs are reduced, and national statistics offices can plan on a regular work cycle for their staff collecting prices.

Penn World Table

The Penn World Table (PWT) is maintained by the Center for International Comparisons of Production, Income and Prices at the University of Pennsylvania. It provides a time series of PPP-based national accounts data for more than 180 countries from 1950. The PPPs and real expenditures in the PWT are estimated by extrapolating and backcasting PPP-based estimates from the ICP (the "benchmark"). They are calculated at an intermediate stage between the detailed rolling benchmark approach adopted by Eurostat and the broad-based approach of using either GDP volume growth to extrapolate real expenditures on GDP or relative changes in GDP deflators to extrapolate the PPPs for GDP. In this way, they provide a compromise between the problems caused by extrapolating at the level of GDP (see the earlier discussion of the consistency between time and space) and the detailed data required to extrapolate PPPs for every basic heading and then weighting them together to obtain a PPP for GDP.

The starting point for the latest PWT time series (PWT 7.1) is the global set of basic heading PPPs and expenditures from the 2005 ICP. PPPs are estimated for actual consumption (C), collective government consumption (G), gross fixed capital formation (I), and net exports of goods and services. In earlier versions of the PWT, the Geary-Khamis (GK) method was used so that the results were additive. Therefore, GDP could be estimated as the sum of these four major components. PWT 7.1 integrates the 2005 ICP into the estimates and produces its preferred series using a variant of the Gini-Éltetö-Köves-Szulc (GEKS) aggregation method for the initial shares in 2005 and its current price series in earlier years. The reference PPPs for C, G, and I for 2005 are moved backward and forward from 2005 by the changes in the prices of each of these major components for each country and aggregated to an estimate of "domestic absorption" (also referred to at times in national accounting as "domestic final demand"). The international trade balance is treated separately and then combined with domestic absorption to provide the estimate for GDP. As in previous versions, the PWT provides current and constant price estimates of the shares of consumption, investment, and government to GDP.

International Comparisons in *World Development Indicators*

International comparisons are published regularly by the World Bank in its annual publication *World Development Indicators* (WDI). Three different methodologies are used in converting some major national accounts aggregates—gross national income[2] (GNI) or gross domestic product—into a common currency (U.S. dollars) to compare them across countries. In the 2010 issue of the WDI, in table 1.1, size of the economy, and table 1.6, GNI is expressed in U.S. dollars using the World Bank's Atlas method (an adjusted exchange rate method that is described in the next paragraph) and also by using PPPs extrapolated to the reference year (2008 in the 2010 edition of the WDI). In table 4.2, structure of output, in the 2010 edition of the WDI, the levels of GDP for countries are expressed in U.S. dollars using exchange rates to convert them from each country's national currency into U.S. dollars (World Bank 2010).

In effect, the Atlas method produces smoothed exchange rates with some additional adjustments for relative differences in inflation rates. The goal is "to reduce the impact of exchange rate fluctuations in the cross-country comparison of national incomes" (World Bank 2010). Briefly, the first step is to take a three-year moving average of the country's exchange rate (based on the current year plus the two preceding years) and adjust it for differences in the GDP deflator between the country and those in Japan, the United Kingdom, the United States, and the Euro Area. Clearly, it is essentially an exchange rate method of adjusting values into a common currency, albeit one that removes the effects of short-term volatility in the exchange rates. As a result, it suffers from the problem that, like regular exchange rates, it does not remove the effects of differences in price levels between countries. Despite this shortcoming, exchange rate methods are more appropriate than PPPs for some international comparisons in limited circumstances. The WDI Atlas method is described in detail in annex A of this chapter.

The estimates of GNI adjusted to a common currency by PPPs are based on the PPPs from the 2005 ICP extrapolated to the latest reference year using the macro approach (described in the earlier section on consistency between time and space) of applying to the 2005 PPP the ratio of the GDP deflators for each country in turn to the GDP deflator for the United States in the reference year.

Two features of the ICP since its inception almost a half-century ago have been the gradual increase in the number of countries participating in each round and the methodological developments over time, particularly in the 2005 ICP when new methods of specifying products and linking regions were introduced. In addition, some countries have dropped out of the program between one round and the next and then participated again in a subsequent round. As a result, for many countries outside the Eurostat-OECD region, it has been difficult to interpolate PPPs between adjoining rounds. Some analysts have used the imputed PPPs for nonparticipating countries as a benchmark (or benchmarks) for interpolation, while others have simply backcast from the latest ICP round and ignored the PPPs available from earlier rounds. The 2011 ICP will build on the 2005 round by providing a new benchmark for almost all the countries that participated in 2005, using very similar methods so that the effects of methodological change will be less pronounced than was the case previously. Therefore, it will be possible to assess the impact of simple backcasting the 2011 PPPs (e.g., using the volume changes in a country's national accounts) against the benchmarks provided by the 2005 ICP.

Constant PPPs

One way suggested to maintain consistency in real expenditures simultaneously across countries and across time is to use a single year as a benchmark for a time series. The national accounts values for the base year are adjusted to a common currency using PPPs, and then the growth rates in GDP volumes are applied to these base year values to obtain a series of real expenditures for years before or after the base year. By definition, the percentage changes in these real expenditures on GDP for any individual country are identical to those published by that country in its time series of GDP volumes. This type of comparison is generally referred to as being estimated using "constant PPPs." In fact, the real expenditures series generated by this type of process are broadly equivalent to a fixed-base time series of volumes, and they suffer from the same kinds of shortcomings as these types of volumes.

An assumption underlying this estimation is that the relative levels of the real expenditures in the chosen base year are relevant to all the other years in the series. However, in practice economic structures (both prices and volumes) change at different rates in different countries. As a result, comparing the relative levels of real expenditures in different countries using this type of data will yield results that are potentially very different, depending on which year is chosen as the base year. There is no way to select an ideal base year because the relationships between countries are changing so rapidly. For example, over the last few years the economic growth in most European countries has been much lower than that in most Asian countries. Therefore, using 2011 as a base year would result in Asian countries being closer to the European countries for every year in the series than would be the case if 2005 were used as the base year. In other words, the relativities between countries for all years in the series are highly dependent on the base year chosen. In this respect, a time series at constant PPPs is similar to a set of volumes by industry within a country when they have been estimated using a fixed-base year. In such a case, the relationships within each year between the volumes of gross product in each industry will depend on the base year chosen because the economic structure of a country changes over time.

One use of these series based on "constant PPPs" is to estimate regional totals (and therefore growth rates in regional real expenditures). However, the percentage changes in a regional total will vary depending on the base year chosen for the constant PPPs in the same way that the percentage changes in GDP volumes will vary for an individual country when a base year is changed in a fixed-base volume series.

Why Extrapolations Differ from a Subsequent Benchmark in Practice

PPPs can be extrapolated at any level, ranging from the basic heading up to GDP, with the more detailed methods likely to produce better results. However, the broader levels are more likely to be used in practice because of the lack of time series price data at the basic heading level that are consistent across countries. The first part of this chapter showed that extrapolation methods based on GDP or its high-level aggregates such as household final consumption expenditure should not be expected to produce PPPs that match those from a new benchmark year. However, the fact remains that there is a demonstrated user need for PPPs to be produced frequently (preferably annually), and so it is essential to use extrapolation techniques, even though experience over the last decade or so has shown that one needs to understand how the PPPs extrapolated from one benchmark year will differ from the following benchmark.

In practice, some reasonable results have been obtained using broadly based extrapolation procedures, but it is more common that, for at least some of the countries involved, the extrapolated PPPs will differ significantly from a subsequent benchmark round for a number of reasons. In some cases, it may be possible to identify a single underlying reason that is largely responsible for such differences, but usually several factors are involved, and they may change over time or for different pairs (or groups) of countries. The following list is a summary of the potential issues affecting the reliability of the outcomes. Some of these issues are discussed in more detail in other sections in this chapter. They have been classified under two headings, "general" and "extrapolation above the basic heading level." The "general" heading has been applied to those issues that have an impact on PPP and real expenditure estimation and extrapolation no matter whether they are at the basic heading level or at a more aggregated level (i.e., GDP in total or for major components of GDP such as household final consumption expenditure and so forth, which are then aggregated to GDP). The heading "extrapolation above the basic heading level" covers those issues that would not affect the results obtained by extrapolating PPPs at the basic heading level and then weighting them to higher-level aggregates, but that do have an impact on the outcomes obtained from extrapolating PPPs for GDP or its major aggregates.

General

- The products to be priced in the ICP are carefully defined to ensure comparability between countries, but the products priced in the time series used in estimating the volumes in a country's national accounts are selected on the basis that they are the most representative products available in a country. In addition, the set of prices used in a country's time series price indexes is much broader than those that can be included in the ICP.
- The prices in a country's time series price indexes (e.g., the CPI) are adjusted for quality changes over time, and countries do not use common methods to adjust for these changes. For example, hedonic methods are used to a different extent across countries (or not at all in many countries), with the result that the quality-adjusted time series are not consistent across countries. In particular, the U.S. Bureau of Economic Analysis uses hedonic methods more extensively in estimating the national accounts deflators than virtually all other countries. Therefore, if the price changes over time in the U.S. GDP deflator are lower than those in other countries because of using hedonics, then their price levels extrapolated forward from a benchmark year would be too high compared with those of the United States, which is commonly used as the reference country.
- In the national accounts, very few countries adjust their volumes of nonmarket services for productivity changes. Therefore, differences in productivity over time in different countries will be reflected in the GDP deflators as part of the price changes, leading to an inconsistency between countries in the deflators used as extrapolators.
- The methods used to estimate price indexes and national accounts volumes are evolving, and these will affect the comparability of ICP results over time. In addition, the methods used in the 2005 ICP differed significantly from those used in the 1993 round. For example, structured product descriptions (SPDs) were used to describe each product's characteristics; different aggregation methods were used; adjustments were made

for productivity differences between countries in some regions; and a new procedure, the Ring list approach, was introduced to link the regions. The differences in methodology between the 2005 and 2011 ICP rounds are less pronounced, but could still have an impact on the comparability of these two rounds. For example, the methods used to estimate construction prices have been changed; productivity adjustments are likely to be used more widely in 2011; housing services (i.e., actual and imputed rents) will be estimated differently; and the methods used to link regions will change.

- Countries revise their GDP estimates as firmer data become available. Significant revisions occur when a country undertakes a "major revision" of its GDP estimates, which generally involves a complete reassessment of the data in the national accounts and the assumptions involved in combining various data sets. As a result, inconsistencies arise between the GDP estimates in a time series compared with those provided for the ICP. For example, comparing the GDP estimates supplied for the 2005 ICP with the 2005 GDP estimates available in the United Nations Statistics Division's national accounts database for 2010 reveals that 15 of the 146 countries have revised their 2005 GDP level by more than 10 percent, 19 countries have revised it by between 5 and 10 percent, and 16 have revised it by between 2 and 5 percent. In other words, over one-third of the countries participating in the 2005 ICP have revised their 2005 GDP level by more than 2 percent between providing their national accounts data for the 2005 ICP and releasing their 2010 national accounts. Only 19 countries did not revise their 2005 GDP at all during that time. One way of overcoming this problem would be to recompute the real expenditures on GDP, applying the 2005 PPPs to the revised national GDP estimates for 2005 so that they are consistent with the GDP estimates provided by countries for the 2011 ICP.

Extrapolation above the Basic Heading Level

- The weighting patterns used in a country's time series price indexes are specific to that country, whereas those underlying the ICP results are an amalgam of those for the countries participating in the ICP. (The example in the section on consistency between time and space illustrates the type of impact that can arise from this source.)
- An assumption underlying the technique of extrapolating PPPs at the level of GDP is that the structure of each country's economy is similar to that of the numeraire country and is changing in the same way over time. In practice, the structures of different countries' economies differ significantly, particularly when developing economies are being compared with a developed economy (e.g., the Chinese economy has been developing rapidly in recent years, and its structure has changed in a significantly different way from that of the United States).
- Many countries use chain-linked volumes in their time series because of the distortions introduced by using a fixed-base year for any length of time. As a result, the GDP deflators for such countries behave differently than those for countries that use the more traditional fixed-base methods to estimate their GDP volumes. In addition, a long-observed characteristic of volume measures is that the growth rates in fixed-base GDP volumes have an upward bias for years after the base year, and so comparing volumes based on different base years for countries involves matching series that are not strictly comparable.
- In the ICP, a reference PPP (exchange rate) is used for the net balance of international trade in goods and services. Changes in the terms of trade are treated as a volume effect

in the ICP because they directly affect the value of exports or imports, but they do not generally cause an equivalent change in the exchange rate, at least in the short term. For example, a large rise in oil prices will translate into a large increase in the oil-producing country's value of exports (assuming the volume of exports does not decline significantly) and so in the value of its GDP. Applying the exchange rate to the value of exports will result in a large increase in the real expenditure on exports and therefore in the real expenditure on GDP. However, changes in the terms of trade are included in the GDP deflators (i.e., as a price effect) used to extrapolate PPPs. For example, an increase in the value of exports because of an increase in oil prices but with the same volume exported is reflected as a price effect in the time series of export deflators and so in the time series of GDP deflators. This factor often has a large effect, particularly for those countries whose exports can significantly affect their terms of trade, such as commodity exporters.

Chapter 15 of the 2008 SNA describes a number of the issues involved in extrapolating/interpolating PPPs from and between benchmarks (Commission of the European Communities et al. 2008).

An important characteristic of the PPPs extrapolated from 2005 (or any other benchmark year) to other (nonbenchmark) years is that the PPPs are transitive in each year to which they have been extrapolated, provided they were transitive in the benchmark year (which was the case with the PPPs from the 2005 ICP). Annex B of this chapter, devoted to the transitivity of PPPs extrapolated using the GDP deflator method, demonstrates that this property is preserved in the extrapolated PPPs. Preserving transitivity when GDP is extrapolated by aggregating a number of extrapolated components is a more difficult proposition. It is true that the extrapolated PPPs for each individual component of GDP are transitive, whether they are at the basic heading level or for a higher-level aggregate such as household final consumption expenditure. However, aggregating these (transitive) extrapolated PPPs to any higher-level aggregate, including GDP, will generate PPPs that are not transitive. A separate step, such as the GEKS procedure (see chapter 5), is required to ensure that the PPPs for the higher-level aggregates are transitive.

One of the problems in assessing how well an extrapolated series matches a subsequent benchmark is that, outside the Eurostat-OECD PPP Programme, the PPPs produced for many countries in earlier years are not based on a PPP price survey. For example, China participated for the first time in the ICP in the 2005 round, although PPPs and real expenditures had been estimated for China for many years based on a variety of methods, including partial sets of price data and national accounts and more mechanical approaches such as regression techniques. As a result, extrapolating the 1993 PPP for such countries to 2005 and checking how well the extrapolated PPP matches the 2005 benchmark incurs not only the error arising in the extrapolation process but also the effects of any errors in the 1993 starting point itself.

Assumptions about Countries with Similar Economic Structures

Two critical assumptions underlying an extrapolated series of PPPs and real expenditures are that the reference country has an economic structure similar to that of the country being compared, and that their economies are evolving in a similar way over time. If these assumptions are not satisfied, the extrapolated series will potentially be different from the PPPs that would have been estimated using a complete price survey and detailed national accounts. The extent of the differences would depend on the degree to which the structure of the economies *and* their price levels differ. In this regard, the situation is similar to that in a time series of prices where it does not matter what weights are applied in a situation in which the prices of all products are changing at the same rate. However, it is clear from the prices collected in the 2005 ICP that the price structures of countries are significantly different, even for neighboring countries with broadly similar economies. In particular, the price structures of high-income and low-income countries are rarely similar, and so any differences in economic structure assume greater importance. In this context, it is interesting to compare the economic structures of China and the United States over the last few decades. Table 18.5 shows the percentage of GDP contributed by each major expenditure aggregate for each fifth year from 1985 to 2010.

Some of the more interesting points of table 18.5 are the following:

- The relatively high share of household final consumption expenditure in the United States compared with that in China
- The very high share of gross fixed capital formation in China (construction is a very high share of this component in China) compared with that in the United States
- The marked decline in the share of GDP contributed by household final consumption expenditure in China, particularly between 2000 and 2010, compared with the slow but steady increase in its share in the United States
- The positive share of the net balance of exports and imports of goods and services in China in each year shown since 1990 compared with the negative share of GDP contributed by this component in the United States.

TABLE 18.5 Evolving Economic Structures of China and the United States, 1985–2010

percentage of GDP

Country	Year	HFCE	GGFCE	GFCF	Inventories	Exports	Imports	Net trade	GDP
China	1985	51.6	14.3	29.4	8.7	9.2	13.2	−4.0	100.0
United States	1985	64.9	17.5	19.7	0.6	7.2	10.0	−2.8	100.0
China	1990	48.8	13.6	25.0	9.9	15.5	12.9	2.6	100.0
United States	1990	66.6	17.0	17.4	0.2	9.6	10.9	−1.3	100.0
China	1995	44.9	13.3	33.0	7.3	19.4	17.9	1.6	100.0
United States	1995	67.8	15.4	17.7	0.4	11.0	12.3	−1.2	100.0
China	2000	46.4	15.9	34.3	1.0	23.4	21.0	2.4	100.0
United States	2000	69.0	14.3	20.0	0.6	11.0	14.9	−3.9	100.0
China	2005	38.8	14.1	39.7	1.9	36.6	31.2	5.5	100.0
United States	2005	70.1	15.8	19.5	0.4	10.4	16.1	−5.8	100.0
China	2010	35.0	13.1	46.9	2.4	27.0	23.0	4.0	100.0
United States	2010	70.9	17.5	14.7	0.5	12.7	16.3	−3.6	100.0

Source: United Nations Statistics Division.
Note: HFCE = household final consumption expenditure; GGFCE = general government final consumption expenditure; GFCF = gross fixed capital formation; inventories = change in inventories; exports = exports of goods and services; imports = imports of goods and services; net trade = net balance of exports and imports of goods and services. The data in this table were taken from the 2010 national accounts database maintained by the United Nations Statistics Division, and so they incorporate any revisions made to the 2005 data since they were provided to the ICP Global Office for use in the 2005 ICP.

The more fundamental issues, though, are that the structure of expenditure on GDP in China is in no way similar to that of the United States in the periods shown, and the changes in shares over time are in opposite directions in the major aggregates of household final consumption expenditure and gross fixed capital formation. An important implication is that extrapolating (or backcasting) the 2005 Chinese PPP for GDP, which is the only one based on an actual data collection, is problematic when the underlying assumptions of similarity in the structure and evolution between GDP in China and the United States are taken into account.

One method used to backcast the real expenditures on GDP in China has been to take the real expenditure on GDP from the 2005 ICP and then use the growth rates in China's GDP volumes from the time series national accounts to backcast that level, expressed in U.S. dollars for each year involved (e.g., see Bhalla 2008). It is instructive to consider the unrealistic assumptions underlying this process. Most critically, the relationship between the price level of GDP in China and in the United States is assumed to be identical in every backcast year to that observed in the 2005 ICP. The huge relative changes in the composition of GDP in the two countries shown in table 18.5 would indicate that this critical assumption is unlikely to hold, particularly in view of the different PPPs observed for individual components of GDP in China in 2005—see table 1, purchasing power parities, local currency units per $US, in the report of the 2005 ICP (World Bank 2008).

Effects of Changes in the Terms of Trade

The ratio of the price of exports of goods and services to the price of imports of goods and services is referred to as the terms of trade. The economies of many countries are often affected by large changes in the terms of trade, particularly those countries that are major resource exporters, such as the oil-producing countries, or commodity exporters, such as many countries in Sub-Saharan Africa. The effects of any such changes are recorded, correctly, as part of GDP whether measured using the expenditure, income, or production approach. For example, if a country's entire oil production is exported and the price of oil doubles from 300 to 600 currency units from one year to the next while oil volumes and every other aspect of the country's economy remain the same, then the value of oil exports doubles (an increase of 300), and so the value of expenditure on GDP increases by 300. The value of mining production also increases by 300, and so the production-based GDP increases by 300. On the income side of the national accounts, the operating surplus of the oil businesses increases by 300, and so income-based GDP also increases by 300, thereby preserving the equality between the three separate measures of GDP.

The expenditure-based estimates of GDP provide the values in the ICP, but a reference PPP (exchange rates) is applied to exports and imports of goods and services. A sudden change in the terms of trade does not affect a country's exchange rate commensurately, and so the increase of 300 in this example will be recorded largely as an increase in the real expenditure on GDP. On the other hand, if the GDP deflator method is used to extrapolate a PPP and real expenditure benchmark, then this increase in the value of exports is recorded as a price increase because there is no increase in the volume of oil produced, leading to a mismatch between the extrapolated PPPs and those from a benchmark.

The following method could be used to take account of this effect: extrapolate the net exports of goods and services separately from the components of domestic final demand and adjust the rise in export prices due to the oil price increase so that they will be more consistent with those obtained from a benchmark comparison. Testing this process has shown that some significant gains can be made in the accuracy of the extrapolated PPPs for some countries. However, it does not eliminate the problem because the countries participating in the ICP have very diverse economies. In practice, many different factors affect a country's exports (and imports), and so the effects of changes in the terms of trade are rarely sufficiently clear-cut to be attributable to a single cause such as an increase in oil prices.

The Balassa-Samuelson Effect

In the early 1960s, Balassa (1964) and Samuelson (1964) independently hypothesized that price levels in high-income countries are systematically higher than those in poorer ones. Decades later, Rogoff (1996) found substantial empirical support for the Balassa-Samuelson effect, but in limited circumstances. He found that the effect is most marked when very poor and very rich countries are being compared, but it is generally less apparent when the comparison is between a group of relatively rich countries. The development of the PWT provided new data that confirmed that the Balassa-Samuelson effect did exist in practice. It also led to a related theory called the Penn effect.[3] This effect is based on the finding that expenditures on GDP adjusted to a common currency using market exchange rates systematically understate PPP-based real expenditures on GDP for low-income countries compared with high-income countries. In other words, the gap between GDP (and thus per capita GDP) for high-income countries and low-income countries is exaggerated when market exchange rates are used to adjust each country's GDP into a common currency. Data from all the ICP rounds to date have confirmed the Penn effect.

Ravallion (2010) describes the rationale for the Penn effect as follows:

> In using the Balassa-Samuelson model to explain why PPPs tend to be lower (relative to market exchange rates) in poorer countries, it is assumed that the more developed the country the higher its labor productivity in traded goods, but that productivity for non-traded goods does not vary systematically with level of development. A higher marginal product of labor in traded goods production comes with a higher wage rate, which is also binding on the non-traded goods sector (given that labor is freely mobile), implying a higher price of non-traded goods in more developed countries and thus a higher overall price level. By the same reasoning, low real wages in poor countries entail that non-traded goods tend to be cheaper. The ratio of the purchasing power parity rate to the market exchange rate will thus be an increasing function of income.

Using data from the 2005 ICP, Ravallion further developed the Penn effect by introducing what he termed the dynamic Penn effect (DPE). The DPE describes the tendency for the gap between exchange rate–based and PPP-based comparisons of GDP to narrow as the per capita real GDP for low-income countries increases relative to that of high-income countries. The importance of the DPE is that it may provide a means of adjusting extrapolated data so that they better match the next ICP benchmark.

The data from the 2011 ICP will be important in terms of providing a firm benchmark to assess whether taking account of the DPE in the extrapolated series leads to more accurate estimates than those obtained using the current methods.

Differences between the 2005 and 2011 Benchmarks Caused by Changes in Methodology

Extrapolating between benchmarks is also affected by changes in methodology between the two years involved. The major methodological changes from the 2005 ICP to the 2011 ICP are the following:

- Estimates of dwelling rents will be based on the quantity method instead of reference volumes in the Asia-Pacific and Africa regions. However, the PPPs using the reference volume method could be computed for 2011 so that the effect on the 2011 results of the change to the quantity method can be computed.
- The products priced in the global core list will have an impact on regional PPPs. Regional PPPs can be computed with and without core items to determine their impact in 2011.
- Using the important/less important classification (see chapter 7) will affect the 2011 PPPs. In 2011 the PPPs, real expenditures, and price level indexes could be computed without those classifications (as in the 2005 round) to determine the effect of using this classification.
- The global aggregation method proposed in 2011 will produce results that differ from those obtained from the two-stage method used in 2005. The PPPs based on the method used in 2005 should be computed to determine the effect of this change in methodology.
- In 2005 productivity adjustments were made in three of the six ICP regions (Africa, Asia-Pacific, Western Asia), but the regional linking factors were computed without any productivity adjustments. In the 2011 ICP round, it is likely that some regions will use productivity adjustments, but others will not. However, linking factors across all regions will be computed with productivity adjustments included for all regions.
- The construction methodology is changing in the 2011 round, but it is so different from that used in the 2005 round that it will be difficult to compare the effects of the change.

Once the 2011 results have been finalized, it will be possible to estimate the effects of most of the methodological changes. However, it is important to emphasize that the differences estimated in this way will provide indications of the effects of these changes rather than precise amounts.

Improving Extrapolation Methods

It is in the interests of all users of PPPs to have PPPs for nonbenchmark years that are as accurate as possible. It is clear that different methods will almost certainly lead to different results, and so it is incumbent upon users to assess the implications of the underlying assumptions for their analysis. The 2005 ICP has provided an impetus to improve extrapolation methods, and a number of researchers are investigating some promising alternative methods. The results of the 2011 ICP, which will be a firm benchmark for virtually all the 146 countries that participated in the 2005 ICP, will provide researchers with a much better data set than has been available to assess the reliability of the various methods.

Possible means of improving methods for extrapolating PPPs include:

- Extrapolating at the most detailed level possible rather than just for GDP. However, experience has shown that lack of consistent, detailed price data will limit the possibilities.

- Adjusting the price extrapolators for any terms of trade effect (e.g., by treating net trade separately from the rest of GDP and using a domestic final demand deflator for this latter component)
- Systematically taking the dynamic Penn effect into account in the extrapolated PPPs, using regression techniques to estimate the size of the effect.

In addition, several researchers (e.g., Hill 2004; Feenstra, Ma, and Rao 2009) are working on completely new methods, such as econometric-based techniques, to provide more reliable time series of PPPs and real expenditures.

Estimating PPPs for Nonparticipating Countries

Even though a record number of countries (146 in six regions) participated in the 2005 ICP, more than 50 countries did not take part. Many of these countries were in the lower-income group, which is the main interest of many of those using the ICP results for poverty analysis. As a result, PPPs were imputed for GDP for many of these countries using regression techniques, as done in earlier ICP rounds. In the 2005 ICP, PPPs were imputed for 42 countries that had not participated in the program. The method used was based on two explanatory variables in a logarithmic model to estimate GDP per capita. The explanatory variables were (1) GNI per capita, expressed in U.S. dollars estimated using the World Bank Atlas method; and (2) the secondary (school) gross enrollment rate.

A detailed description of the model used was provided in the global report for the 2005 ICP (World Bank 2007), and the relevant parts are in annex C to this chapter.

Comparing ICP Benchmark Results

The results of the successive ICP rounds are independent of each other because they are expressed in terms of the price levels prevailing in participating countries in each of the years involved. As for comparing the results of two ICP rounds, it is useful to consider real expenditures and PLIs separately, despite the close links between them.

Earlier, this chapter described the problems involved in maintaining consistency simultaneously across time and space. Although these problems were in the context of extrapolating PPPs and real expenditures from one ICP round to the next, they also have implications for comparisons of results from successive ICP benchmarks. Directly comparing the ICP estimates of real expenditures for 2011 with those for 2005 should be carried out with the understanding that price levels not only changed between 2005 and 2011 but also changed to a different extent across countries. Comparing the index of per capita real expenditure on GDP for a country in two different years relative to a world (or regional) average should be undertaken with the understanding that the structure of this average is likely to have changed between ICP rounds and to varying extents, depending on the countries involved. For example, a country with a large GDP and a higher than average growth rate in its volumes will affect the world average real expenditure on GDP to a different extent in two successive ICP rounds. The impact of such a country on a regional average will be even more pronounced. For example, the total real expenditure in the Asia-Pacific region is dominated by China and, to a lesser extent, India. Therefore, the economic behavior of these two countries will have a significant impact on the average real expenditure for that region in each ICP round.

TABLE 18.6 Estimated Real Expenditures on GDP (2011), Big 5 Region

Country	2005 ICP, real expenditure	2005 PPP	% change 2005 to 2011, GDP IPD	2011 PPP	2011 PPP (US = 1.00)	2011 GDP, current prices	2011 real expenditures on GDP
United States	*12,376,100*	1.00	13.4	1.134	1.00	15,064,816	*15,064,816*
China	*5,333,230*	3.45	33.2	4.594	4.05	45,821,758	*11,308,355*
Japan	*3,870,282*	129.55	−6.5	121.105	106.82	469,545,267	*4,395,654*
Germany	*2,514,783*	0.89	5.6	0.940	0.83	2,568,196	*3,098,360*
India	*2,340,997*	14.67	51.2	22.185	19.57	87,454,896	*4,469,339*
Regional total	*26,435,392*						*38,336,523*

Source: IMF 2011.
Note: IPD = implicit price deflator.

As an example of the type of issues that might arise, this section examines the implications of the very different growth rates for the five countries that had the world's highest real GDP in the 2005 ICP: the United States, China, Japan, Germany, and India (the "Big 5" region). Table 18.6 provides the 2005 ICP estimates of real expenditure on GDP for each of these countries, as well as the corresponding PPP for GDP. The 2005 PPP for each country is extrapolated to 2011 using the percentage changes in the GDP deflators between 2005 and 2011. These PPPs are based on national accounts data for 2005 and estimates for 2011 from the September quarter of the 2011 World Economic Outlook database maintained by the International Monetary Fund (IMF 2011). The 2011 PPPs are then re-referenced to a base of US = 1.00. The 2011 GDP in current price terms are IMF estimates for 2011, and the 2011 real expenditures on GDP are obtained for each country by dividing the 2011 GDP by the extrapolated 2011 PPP (US = 1.00).

A key point that comes out of this table is that the 2011 real expenditures on GDP cannot be directly compared with those from 2005 because they are expressed in terms of the different price levels in each of those two years. Table 18.7 extends table 18.6 by including details of growth rates between 2005 and 2011.

In table 18.7, the United States has an index of real expenditure on GDP of 234 (compared with the Big 5 regional average of 100) in 2005, but this drops to 196 in 2011. The apparent implication is that the U.S. economy contracted over this period, whereas in fact it grew by just over 5 percent. The decline observed indicates that the U.S. economy grew significantly less than the regional average—indeed, 16 percent less as shown in column (5) of table 18.7. Column (5) also shows that China and India grew significantly more than the regional average (46 percent and 32 percent, respectively), and that the United States, Japan, and Germany all grew less than the regional average. However, the *level* of GDP was higher in the United States in both years than it was in China, although clearly the gap between them narrowed. Column (9) of table 18.7 shows the GDP volume growth, *relative to the regional average,* from the time series national accounts. The figures align very closely with the relative changes in real expenditures on GDP in column (5). However, this alignment is a function of the extrapolation methods used, and in practice the differences are likely to be much larger once the 2011 ICP results can be substituted for the extrapolated estimates in column (2) of this table. It is important to note that the relative growth rates in real expenditures in columns (5) and (9) are not proper temporal volume changes because they combine elements of both volume and price changes.

TABLE 18.7 Comparing Changes in Volumes and in Real Expenditures on GDP, Big 5 Region

Country	2005 ICP, real expenditure on GDP (1)	2011 real expenditure on GDP (2)	2005 ICP, index of real expenditure on GDP (3)	Index of 2011 real expenditure on GDP (4)	PPP-implied relative growth rate of real expenditure (%) (5)	2005 GDP volume (national estimates, local currency) (6)	2011 GDP volume (national estimates, local currency) (7)	% change 2005 to 2011 (GDP volume) (8)	National accounts relative volume growth rate (%) (9)
United States	12,376,100	15,064,816	234	196	−16	12,622.95	13,287.89	5.3	−17
China	5,333,230	11,308,355	101	147	46	8,307.14	15,457.37	86.1	47
Japan	3,870,282	4,395,654	73	57	−22	536,762.20	537,356.11	0.1	−21
Germany	2,514,783	3,098,360	48	40	−15	2,220.95	2,428.52	9.3	−13
India	2,340,997	4,469,339	44	58	32	34,489.09	55,929.10	62.2	28
Sum	26,435,392	38,336,524							
Average	5,287,078	7,667,305	100	100					

Source: IMF 2011.

TABLE 18.8 Real Expenditures on GDP (Regional Average = 100), Big 5 Region

Country	2005 ICP, real expenditure on GDP (1)	2011 real expenditure on GDP (2)	2005 ICP, index of real expenditure on GDP (3)	Index of 2011 real expenditure on GDP (4)	2005 real expenditure on GDP, share of regional total (%) (5)	2011 real expenditure on GDP, share of regional total (%) (6)
United States	12,376,100	15,064,816	234	196	46.8	39.3
China	5,333,230	11,308,355	101	147	20.2	29.5
Japan	3,870,282	4,395,654	73	57	14.6	11.5
Germany	2,514,783	3,098,360	48	40	9.5	8.1
India	2,340,997	4,469,339	44	58	8.9	11.7
Regional average	*5,287,078*	*7,667,305*	*100*	*100*	*100.0*	*100.0*

Source: IMF 2011.

This example can be taken a step further by comparing each country's share of the region's total real expenditure. The data in columns (1)–(4) of table 18.8 have been taken from the corresponding columns in table 18.7. Columns (5) and (6) show each country's share of the regional total in 2005 and 2011.

In table 18.8, the index numbers for the United States, Japan, and Germany are all lower in 2011 (compared with the regional average) than they are in 2005, even though the GDP volumes in all three countries rose between 2005 and 2011, albeit by only 0.1 percent in Japan—see column (8) of table 18.7. The reason for this is that the growth in GDP volumes in China (86.1 percent) and India (62.2 percent) between 2005 and 2011 resulted in a much higher share for each of these two countries in the 2011 regional total than that in 2005. Columns (5) and (6) of table 18.8 show the country shares of real expenditure on GDP in 2005 and 2011, respectively. It is clear from these two columns that the shares of China and India in the Big 5 region have increased significantly at the expense of the United States, Japan, and Germany. As a result, to make sense of the changes in the indexes of real expenditure on GDP between 2005 and 2011, it must be understood that the base (i.e., the regional average) is different in each year, even though the indexes within each individual year provide useful information. Comparing the changes in the shares of the regional totals between the two years helps explain the changes in the indexes of real expenditure on GDP between 2005 and 2011.

One solution to this problem of the real expenditures being expressed in terms of different price levels would be to adjust the values to take account of price changes between 2005 and 2011. However, the results depend on the country chosen as the base country for the price level adjustments. In other words, one set of results would be obtained if the price changes in the United States were used to adjust the 2011 real expenditures to a 2005 price level. A different set of results would be obtained if, for example, price changes in China were used to adjust the changes in real expenditures between the two years.

Similar issues are encountered in attempting to interpret the PLIs between two successive ICP rounds. PLIs are expressed in terms of a base—a country or, more commonly, a regional or world average. The size of countries' economies changes over time, as does the price level, and so the effect that any individual country's PLI has on the regional or world average changes between ICP rounds. Therefore, the fact that a country's PLI is higher (or lower) in one ICP round than in another does not provide useful information in isolation. It needs to be interpreted in conjunction with other information on the composition of the regional or world average on which it is based.

In summary, the ICP is designed to compare the real expenditures for countries within a year rather than across years. However, it is possible to analyze the changes in real expenditure for a country compared with the changes in real expenditure of a base country, or group of countries (i.e., the relative changes). For example, assessing the relationship between pairs of countries is possible, such as "the real expenditure on GDP for country A was x percent higher than that for country B in 2011 compared with y percent higher in 2005." The key point is that comparisons of the levels recorded in 2005 and 2011 between groups of countries (such as regional or world comparisons) will be more problematic because of the different composition of the regional (world) average in the two years. Rather than directly comparing the levels, it is necessary to take the extra step of estimating the relative changes between the two years to explain the observed differences.

Conclusion

Collecting the data required to estimate PPPs and real expenditures is a time-consuming and costly exercise. The first ICP, in 1967, produced data for a small number of countries, and the 2011 ICP (with more than 180 participating countries) will be the eighth round overall. Therefore, an average of more than six years separates each round. Because of increasing interest in international comparisons, PPPs and real expenditures are required more frequently than once every six years, and so various methods have been developed to produce annual estimates for the nonbenchmark years. The different methods do not produce the same results, nor will they necessarily match well with subsequent benchmarks. In assessing the usefulness of the extrapolated PPPs and real expenditures, it is necessary to understand the assumptions underlying the extrapolation procedures. This chapter is designed to provide details about the various assumptions involved so that users can determine the method(s) that best suit their circumstances. However, one critical point for users to consider is that experience has shown that extrapolating PPPs and real expenditures will result in much more realistic data than the alternative of using market exchange rates to convert values into a common currency.

Comparing the results from two ICP rounds is not a straightforward exercise because the real expenditures for each year are expressed in terms of the (different) price levels for each of those years. In interpreting the results from successive ICP rounds, it is necessary to note that the real expenditures and price levels are expressed in relation to another country or to a regional average. As a result, a decline in the relative position of one country within a region (or the world as a whole) does not necessarily mean that the economic activity (or the price level) in the country concerned has declined. Rather, it means that the economic activity (or the price level) in that country has increased less rapidly than those in the other countries being compared.

Some of the improvements made for the ICP 2011 offer methods to more effectively extrapolate PPPs in the future. For example, the set of core products used to link the regions could be used to obtain some prices between benchmarks to estimate PPPs for aggregates below the GDP. Efforts to harmonize CPIs across countries will also contribute to improved extrapolations.

This chapter closes with a note in annex D that provides an empirical analysis of the extrapolation compared with a new benchmark. The analysis is based on Eurostat data for the household final consumption expenditure (HFCE) aggregate in 17 European countries to show the divergence for a number of six yearly extrapolations compared with the benchmark estimates. Note that the results would be different if a more diverse range of countries were included or if the analysis were based on GDP instead of on HFCE.

ANNEX A

World Bank Atlas Method

The following is an extract from World Development Indicators 2010 *(World Bank 2010, 435).*

In calculating GNI (gross national income) and GNI per capita in U.S. dollars for certain operational purposes, the World Bank uses the *Atlas* conversion factor. The purpose of the *Atlas* conversion factor is to reduce the impact of exchange rate fluctuations in the cross-country comparison of national incomes.

The *Atlas* conversion factor for any year is the average of a country's exchange rate (or alternative conversion factor) for that year and its exchange rates for the two preceding years, adjusted for the difference between the rate of inflation in the country and that in Japan, the United Kingdom, the United States, and the euro area. A country's inflation rate is measured by the change in its GDP deflator.

The inflation rate for Japan, the United Kingdom, the United States, and the euro area, representing international inflation, is measured by the change in the "SDR deflator." (Special drawing rights, or SDRs, are the International Monetary Fund's unit of account.) The SDR deflator is calculated as a weighted average of these countries' GDP deflators in SDR terms, the weights being the amount of each country's currency in one SDR unit. Weights vary over time because both the composition of the SDR and the relative exchange rates for each currency change. The SDR deflator is calculated in SDR terms first and then converted to U.S. dollars using the SDR to dollar *Atlas* conversion factor. The *Atlas* conversion factor is then applied to a country's GNI. The resulting GNI in U.S. dollars is divided by the midyear population to derive GNI per capita.

When official exchange rates are deemed to be unreliable or unrepresentative of the effective exchange rate during a period, an alternative estimate of the exchange rate is used in the *Atlas* formula (see below).

The following formulas describe the calculation of the *Atlas* conversion factor for year t:

$$e_t^* = \frac{1}{3}\left[e_{t-2}\left(\frac{p_t}{p_{t-2}} \Big/ \frac{p_t^{S\$}}{p_{t-2}^{S\$}} \right) + e_{t-1}\left(\frac{p_t}{p_{t-1}} \Big/ \frac{p_t^{S\$}}{p_{t-1}^{S\$}} \right) + e_t \right]$$

and the calculation of GNI per capita in U.S. dollars for year t:

$$y_t^{\$} = \frac{\left(\dfrac{Y_t}{N_t} \right)}{e_t^*}$$

Where

e_t^* is the *Atlas* conversion factor (national currency to the U.S. dollar) for year t

e_t is the average annual exchange rate (national currency to the U.S. dollar) for year t

p_t is the GDP deflator for year t

$p_t^{S\$}$ is the SDR deflator in U.S. dollar terms for year t
$y_t^{\$}$ is the *Atlas* GNI per capita in U.S. dollars in year t
Y_t is current GNI (local currency) for year t
N_t is the midyear population for year t.

Alternative conversion factors

The World Bank systematically assesses the appropriateness of official exchange rates as conversion factors. An alternative conversion factor is used when the official exchange rate is judged to diverge by an exceptionally large margin from the rate effectively applied to domestic transactions of foreign currencies and traded products. This applies to only a small number of countries, as shown in *Primary data documentation.* Alternative conversion factors are used in the *Atlas* methodology and elsewhere in *World Development Indicators* as single-year conversion factors.

ANNEX B

Transitivity of PPPs Extrapolated Using the GDP Deflator Method

In the 2005 ICP, the PPPs for all countries were transitive. Transitivity is an important condition in the ICP because it ensures consistency in the results between any pair of countries, no matter whether they are calculated directly between the two countries concerned or indirectly via a third country. For example, in the 2005 ICP the transitivity condition for countries A, B, and C requires that

$$PPP^{2005}_{A/C} = PPP^{2005}_{A/B} \times PPP^{2005}_{B/C} \tag{18B.1}$$

where $PPP^{2005}_{A/C}$ is the PPP for country A compared with country C in 2005.

The GDP deflator method used to extrapolate PPPs from a benchmark year to other years is described in the section in this chapter that discusses the consistency between time and space. A useful characteristic of this method is that the extrapolated PPPs are also transitive, and so no special adjustments are required.

Extrapolating PPPs to year t using the GDP deflator method for countries A, B, and C results in the following:

$$PPP^{t}_{A} = PPP^{2005}_{A} \times \frac{IPD^{t}_{A}}{IPD^{t}_{US}} \tag{18B.2}$$

$$PPP^{t}_{B} = PPP^{2005}_{B} \times \frac{IPD^{t}_{B}}{IPD^{t}_{US}} \tag{18B.3}$$

$$PPP^{t}_{C} = PPP^{2005}_{C} \times \frac{IPD^{t}_{C}}{IPD^{t}_{US}} \tag{18B.4}$$

where PPP^{t}_{A} is the PPP for country A in year t; IPD^{t}_{A} is the implicit price deflator for GDP in country A in year t (base 2005 = 100); and IPD^{t}_{US} is the implicit price deflator for GDP in the United States in year t (base 2005 = 100).

Using the relationships in (18B.2) and (18B.3), the PPP between countries A and B in year t is

$$\begin{aligned} PPP^{t}_{A/B} &= \left(PPP^{2005}_{A} \times \frac{IPD^{t}_{A}}{IPD^{t}_{US}} \right) \div \left(PPP^{2005}_{B} \times \frac{IPD^{t}_{B}}{IPD^{t}_{US}} \right) \\ &= \left(\frac{PPP^{2005}_{A}}{PPP^{2005}_{B}} \right) \times \left(\frac{IPD^{t}_{A}}{IPD^{t}_{B}} \right). \end{aligned} \tag{18B.5}$$

Similarly, from (18B.3) and (18B.4) the PPP between countries B and C in year t is

$$PPP^t_{B/C} = \left(\frac{PPP^{2005}_B}{PPP^{2005}_C}\right) \times \left(\frac{IPD^t_B}{IPD^t_C}\right) \tag{18B.6}$$

and from (18B.2) and (18B.4) the PPP between countries A and C in year t is

$$PPP^t_{A/C} = \left(\frac{PPP^{2005}_A}{PPP^{2005}_C}\right) \times \left(\frac{IPD^t_A}{IPD^t_C}\right). \tag{18B.7}$$

For transitivity to hold in the extrapolated series, one needs to show that $PPP^t_{A/C} = PPP^t_{A/B} \times PPP^t_{B/C}$. Based on (18B.7), this can be re-expressed in terms of the extrapolated series as

$$PPP^t_{A/C} = \left(\frac{PPP^{2005}_A}{PPP^{2005}_C}\right) \times \left(\frac{IPD^t_A}{IPD^t_C}\right). \tag{18B.8}$$

Using the relationships in (18B.5) and (18B.6),

$$\begin{aligned} PPP^t_{A/B} \times PPP^t_{B/C} &= \left[\left(\frac{PPP^{2005}_A}{PPP^{2005}_B}\right) \times \left(\frac{IPD^t_A}{IPD^t_B}\right)\right] \times \left[\left(\frac{PPP^{2005}_B}{PPP^{2005}_C}\right) \times \left(\frac{IPD^t_B}{IPD^t_C}\right)\right] \\ &= \left[\left(\frac{PPP^{2005}_A}{PPP^{2005}_B}\right) \times \left(\frac{PPP^{2005}_B}{PPP^{2005}_C}\right)\right] \times \left[\left(\frac{IPD^t_A}{IPD^t_B} \times \frac{IPD^t_B}{IPD^t_C}\right)\right] \\ &= \left(\frac{PPP^{2005}_A}{PPP^{2005}_C}\right) \times \left(\frac{IPD^t_A}{IPD^t_C}\right), \end{aligned}$$

as required in (18B.8).

Therefore, the conclusion is that the PPPs in year t extrapolated from 2005 using the GDP deflator method will be transitive in year t provided they were transitive in 2005.

ANNEX C

Estimation of PPPs for Nonbenchmark Economies

The following is an extract from Global Purchasing Power Parities and Real Expenditures: 2005 International Comparison Program *(World Bank 2008, 164).*

Each year, the World Bank includes estimates of PPPs for nonbenchmark economies in its *World Development Indicators* publication and database, relying on an estimating equation using information from the benchmark economies. The following estimating equation (5) was used to impute values for missing economies from the previous round (1993–96) of the ICP:

$$\text{Ln}\left(\frac{\text{GDP}}{\text{cap}}\right) = 0.3402 + 0.5851^*\text{Ln}\left(\frac{\text{GNI}}{\text{cap}}\right) + 0.2941^*\text{Ln(SGER)} \qquad (5)$$

where:

$\frac{\text{GDP}}{\text{cap}}$ is the ICP benchmark estimate of GDP per capita (PPP)

$\frac{\text{GNI}}{\text{cap}}$ is gross national income (GNI) per capita in US$ estimated by the World Bank Atlas method and

SGER is the secondary (school) gross enrollment rate.

All three variables are indexed to the corresponding values for the United States (United States = 100). This model was first estimated using the benchmark results from earlier rounds and reestimated when the 1993–96 results became available.

Using the preliminary results from ICP 2005, the model or equation (5) was reestimated to be model or equation (6):

$$\text{Ln}\left(\frac{\text{GDP}}{\text{cap}}\right) = 0.3553 + 0.6994^*\text{Ln}\left(\frac{\text{GNI}}{\text{cap}}\right) + 0.2292^*\text{Ln(SGER)} \qquad (6)$$

The fit of the model might be improved by including additional independent variables correlated with factor productivity and wage differentials because of imperfect labor mobility between economies and between trading sectors and nontrading sectors. However, full exploration of various model specifications is beyond the scope of this preliminary exercise, which is intended to replicate the existing method so that other methods can be compared with it.

The above model is used to impute for nonbenchmark economies (the results are shown in table 8). For a small number of economies whose Atlas GNI per capita of 2005 are not available, the model or equation (6) is adjusted to replace $\frac{\text{GNI}}{\text{cap}}$ with GDP per capita in US$ and is reestimated with all available data in model or equation (7):

$$\text{Ln}\left(\frac{\text{GDP}}{\text{cap}}\text{ PPP}\right) = 0.1987 + 0.7147^*\text{Ln}\left(\frac{\text{GDP}}{\text{cap}}\text{ US\$}\right) + 0.2422^*\text{Ln(SGER)} \qquad (7)$$

The input data and the reference GDP per capita in US$ are mainly taken from the *World Development Indicators* database (April 2008).

The 42 countries for which 2005 PPPs were imputed were:

- Afghanistan
- Algeria
- Antigua and Barbuda
- Bahamas, The
- Barbados
- Belize
- Costa Rica
- Dominica
- Dominican Republic
- El Salvador
- Eritrea
- Grenada
- Guatemala
- Guyana
- Haiti
- Honduras
- Jamaica
- Kiribati
- Libya
- Marshall Islands
- Micronesia, Federated States
- Myanmar
- Nicaragua
- Palau
- Panama
- Papua New Guinea
- Samoa
- San Marino
- Seychelles
- Solomon Islands
- St. Kitts and Nevis
- St. Lucia
- St. Vincent
- Suriname
- Timor-Leste
- Tonga
- Trinidad and Tobago
- Turkmenistan
- United Arab Emirates
- Uzbekistan
- Vanuatu
- West Bank and Gaza

ANNEX D

A Note on Extrapolating PPPs

Robert Inklaar and Marcel P. Timmer
(University of Groningen)

Price level comparisons across countries are carried out infrequently, but there is a strong demand for more frequent estimates. A common approach is to extrapolate the benchmark PPP using data on price changes from the CPI or GDP implicit deflator. However, as this chapter makes clear, there are conceptual and practical reasons why there will often be a mismatch between PPPs extrapolated from a benchmark and the actual subsequent benchmark. To summarize, if the economic structure differs between countries at either point in time, then extrapolating GDP PPPs using GDP deflators will lead to a mismatch between the actual GDP PPPs and the extrapolated version, even if the price trends at the detailed level are identical. In addition, there are many practical reasons why extrapolation leads to different results than a subsequent benchmark. These include differences in price sampling, weighting, and the omission of terms of trade in comparing GDP across countries.

In this note, we aim to provide some quantitative insight into this issue and distinguish between the systematic and nonsystematic reasons extrapolation differs from actual benchmarks. This chapter lists a range of systematic reasons: differences due to weighting (an index number problem), omitted prices (e.g., terms of trade), revisions to time series but not to level comparisons, quality adjustment of prices in some countries, and productivity adjustment of nonmarket services. In all these cases, better data or measurement can remove these sources of differences. Nonsystematic differences are harder to deal with—in particular, differences in the sampling frame (comparability over time or across countries) and weighting below the basic heading level. At the basic heading level, these differences will seem more like random error because solving them is highly problematic. Only if a common data set of individual price quotes is used to estimate price changes over time and across countries would we be able to eliminate these as a source of differences between extrapolated and benchmark PPPs. However, even having such data sets would not completely eliminate such differences in practice, although the data sets should reduce them significantly.

To quantify the importance of nonsystematic differences, we analyze a data set that does not suffer from most of the systematic differences identified in this chapter, and then proceed to eliminate the remaining systematic differences. For this purpose, we use Eurostat's household final consumption expenditure PPP and harmonized inflation data for 17 European countries (the old EU-15 plus Iceland and Norway) for the period 1996–2010. By analyzing only HFCE, we find there are fewer systematic differences because prices for exports, imports, and nonmarket services are not needed. By focusing on these 17 countries, we presumably also minimize many nonsystematic differences because these are all wealthy countries, and the recent period will also lessen any mismatch between methods used for computing time series and cross-country relative prices.

Under Eurostat's rolling benchmark approach, relative prices for one-third of the HFC products are measured in a given year, and these are extrapolated using a detailed CPI series in the subsequent two years. This way, there are annual observations for 146 HFC basic headings, and the HFC categories can be matched to the detailed inflation series from Eurostat's harmonized index of consumer prices (HICP) data set.

To gauge the importance of systematic and nonsystematic differences in this data set, we use four methods to compute the relative prices for the total HFC expenditure:

1. A GEKS aggregate of the 146 basic headings as given by Eurostat
2. A GEKS aggregate of the 146 basic headings, where the basic headings are extrapolated using the most detailed inflation data available
3. A GEKS aggregate of the 146 basic headings, where the basic headings are extrapolated using the aggregate inflation rate
4. An extrapolation of the overall HFC price level using the aggregate inflation rate (i.e., global extrapolation).

To mimic the ICP situation, we extrapolated six years, using the 1996 price levels in combination with inflation rates for the period 1996–2002. After six years, a new ICP benchmark would be available to replace the last extrapolation. This means there are nine sets of extrapolated HFC price levels to compare (1996–2002, 1997–2003, and so forth).

Method 1 is the same as that used by Eurostat, and the results correspond closely to the published HFC price levels.[4] Method 2 extrapolates basic heading prices in the same way as Eurostat, but introduces no new benchmark information. The difference between results based on methods 1 and 2 is thus an indication of the importance of differences in sampling, methods of price collection, definition of goods, and weighting below the basic heading level—that is, nonsystematic differences. Method 3 omits price trends at the detailed level, but uses the same multilateral index number method to compute relative prices. Comparing results based on this method to global extrapolation (method 4) is the real-life counterpart to the stylized example of common price trends but different weights. The difference in results between methods 2 and 4 can be seen as an upper bound to the index number problem: both methods use the same price trends (HICP), but employ different weighting.

Table 18D.1 summarizes the comparison of the four methods.[5] Columns (1), (2), and (3) compare HFC price levels calculated using methods 2–4 to method 1, the official approach. Columns (4) and (5) compare method 4 (global extrapolation) to methods 2 and 3. The results show that method 2 (extrapolating using detailed inflation rates and then aggregating) comes closer to the official results than either of the other two methods. However, the differences are still notable at around 3 percent. The results also show that methods 2, 3, and 4 are much closer to each other than to method 1. This finding suggests that even in this data set, nonsystematic differences are

TABLE 18D.1 Absolute Difference between HFC Price Levels, Methods 1 (PL1) to 4 (PL4)

percent

	PL2/PL1 (1)	PL3/PL1 (2)	PL4/PL1 (3)	PL4/PL2 (4)	PL4/PL3 (5)
Mean	3.6	4.1	4.1	1.5	0.6
Median	2.6	3.1	3.3	1.4	0.5
25th percentile	1.3	1.4	1.8	0.7	0.2
75th percentile	5.2	5.7	6.0	2.1	0.8
Min	0.0	0.0	0.0	0.0	0.0
Max	12.0	16.2	14.3	5.4	2.9

Note: Summary statistics calculated across 144 observations: nine sets of price levels (1996–2002 to 2004–10) and 16 countries vis-à-vis Germany.

the major source of differences. It also shows that the index number problem—see column (4)—is modest in this context, with a median difference of 1.4 percent. However, despite the nonsystematic differences being quantitatively more important than systematic differences, table 18D.1 also shows that extrapolating at a detailed level and then aggregating (method 2) leads to smaller differences with the eventual benchmark than with global extrapolation (method 4). Evaluated at the median, the difference decreases by about 20 percent (2.6 versus 3.3 percent).

Conclusion

From this analysis, we have learned the following:

- Extrapolated PPPs will in general not match a subsequent benchmark, even when accounting for all systematic differences such as using the same weighting above the basic heading level.
- Nonsystematic differences are more important for explaining the differences between extrapolated PPPs and subsequent benchmarks. This finding may well be specific to the data set of household final consumption expenditure in 17 European countries since 1996.
- Removing systematic differences by extrapolating PPPs using prices at a detailed level and aggregating using the same multilateral index number method as the original benchmark brings the extrapolated PPPs closer to a subsequent benchmark than using global extrapolation. In the current setting, the gain is comparatively modest (±20 percent), but in the ICP setting all systematic differences are larger, so the gain should be larger as well.
- Probably the only way to reduce nonsystematic differences would be to more extensively draw on the same prices for international comparisons used for price indexes over time, such as the CPI.
- Fewer systematic differences arise in analyzing HFC than in analyzing GDP. The prices for the other components of GDP are less firmly based than those for HFC, and so the likelihood of inconsistencies between the prices provided by participating countries is higher. As a result, conducting a similar analysis on GDP would almost certainly result in larger differences than those observed for HFC.

NOTES

1. The rolling benchmark approach involves collecting prices for household final consumption expenditure within a three-year cycle; about one-sixth of the prices are collected each half-year, and PPPs at the basic heading level are extrapolated by price indexes that are specific to each basic heading. Prices for products in the government final consumption expenditure and in gross fixed capital formation are collected more frequently.
2. Gross national income (GNI) is defined in the 2008 SNA as GDP plus compensation of employees receivable from abroad plus property income receivable from abroad plus taxes less subsidies on production receivable from abroad less compensation of employees payable abroad less property income payable abroad and less taxes plus subsidies on production payable abroad.
3. This term was first used by Kravis et al. (1975) in referring to results in the 1970 ICP publication. The term was coined because of the heavy involvement in that ICP round of Irving Kravis, Alan Heston, and Robert Summers from the University of Pennsylvania.

4. There are some weighting differences because in later years more countries are included, but this has a comparatively minor effect.
5. The detailed results confirm that the results from table 18D.1 are similar across countries and over the years.

REFERENCES

Balassa, Bela. 1964. "The Purchasing Power Parity Doctrine: A Reappraisal." *Journal of Political Economy* 72.

Bhalla, Surjit S. 2008. "World Bank—Most Asians Dead in 1950." *Business Standard* (India), August 23. http://www.business-standard.com/india/.

Biggeri, Luigi, and Tiziana Laureti. 2011. "Understanding Changes in PPPs over Time: A Proposal for the Extrapolation for Household Consumption Using CPI Data." Paper prepared for the 6th ICP Technical Advisory Group Meeting, Washington DC, October.

Commission of the European Communities, International Monetary Fund, Organisation for Economic Co-operation and Development, United Nations, and World Bank. 2008. *System of National Accounts 2008*. http://unstats.un.org/unsd/nationalaccount/docs/SNA2008.pdf.

Dalgaard, Esben, and Henrik Sejerbo Sørensen (Statistics Denmark). 2002. "Consistency between PPP Benchmarks and National Price and Volume Indices." Paper prepared for the 27th General Conference of the International Association for Research in Income and Wealth, Stockholm, August.

Eurostat and OECD (Organisation for Economic Co-operation and Development). 2006. *Eurostat-OECD Methodological Manual on Purchasing Power Parities.* Paris: OECD.

Feenstra, Robert C., Hong Ma, and D. S. Prasada Rao. 2009. "Consistent Comparisons of Real Incomes across Time and Space." *Macroeconomic Dynamics* 13 (Supplement 2): 169–93.

Hill, Robert J. 2004. "Constructing Price Indexes across Space and Time: The Case of the European Union." *American Economic Review* 94 (5):1379–1410.

IMF (International Monetary Fund). 2011. World Economic Outlook Database. http://www.imf.org/external/pubs/ft/weo/2011/02/weodata/index.aspx.

Khamis, S. H. 1977. "Spatio-temporal Index Numbers." *Bulletin of the International Statistical Institute* 47 (4): 272–75.

Kravis, I. B., Z. Kenessey, A. W. Heston, and R. Summers. 1975. *A System of International Comparisons of Gross Product and Purchasing Power.* Baltimore: Johns Hopkins University Press.

Ravallion, Martin. 2010. "Price Levels and Economic Growth: Making Sense of the PPP Changes between ICP Rounds." Policy Research Working Paper 5229, World Bank, Washington, DC.

Rogoff, Kenneth. 1996. "The Purchasing Power Parity Puzzle." *Journal of Economic Literature* 34 (June): 647–68.

Samuelson, Paul. 1964. "Theoretical Notes on Trade Problems." *Review of Economics and Statistics* 46.

———. 1994. "Facets of Balassa Samuelson Thirty Years Later." *Review of International Economics* 2 (3).

Statistical Office of the United Nations and World Bank. 1982. *World Product and Income: International Comparisons of Real Gross Product.* Washington, DC: World Bank.

World Bank. 2008. *Global Purchasing Power Parities and Real Expenditures: 2005 International Comparison Program.* http://siteresources.worldbank.org/ICPINT/Resources/icp-final.pdf.

———. 2010. *World Bank Indicators 2010.* http://data.worldbank.org/data-catalog/world-development-indicators/wdi-2010.

Results and Empirical Analysis, ICP 2005

Yuri Dikhanov and Frederic A. Vogel

The 2005 results of the International Comparison Program (ICP) brought with them a new understanding of the size and composition of the world economy. The values of the gross domestic product (GDP) and its aggregates were estimated on a common currency basis, corrected for differences in price levels and unaffected by transitory movements in exchange rates.

This chapter provides a bird's-eye view of the global economy based on the 2005 ICP results. In addition, it presents an empirical analysis of the impact of the concepts and methods used on the final results. For example, earlier chapters reviewed extensively the basic concepts such as fixity and additivity. This chapter examines the impact of these concepts on the final results. It also presents different aggregation methodologies, their strengths and weaknesses, and the choices made for the 2005 and 2011 comparisons.

Bird's-Eye View of the Global Economy

The four figures in this section provide an overview of the world economy using purchasing power parity (PPP) measures of GDP, as described in *Global Purchasing Power Parities and Real Expenditures: 2005 International Comparison Program* (World Bank 2008).

Figure 19.1 shows the distribution of the world GDP among low-, middle-, and high-income countries when using PPPs and exchange rates.[1] The world share of GDP for middle-income economies increases from 19 to 32 percent of the world economy when using PPPs to convert the national GDPs to a common currency instead of exchange rates. The share of the world economy held by low-income economies more than doubles using PPPs, but the striking disparity is that 35 percent of the world population produces 7 percent of the global GDP. Only 17 percent of the world population produces 61 percent of the global GDP.

FIGURE 19.1 World Shares: GDP at PPP versus GDP at U.S. Dollars

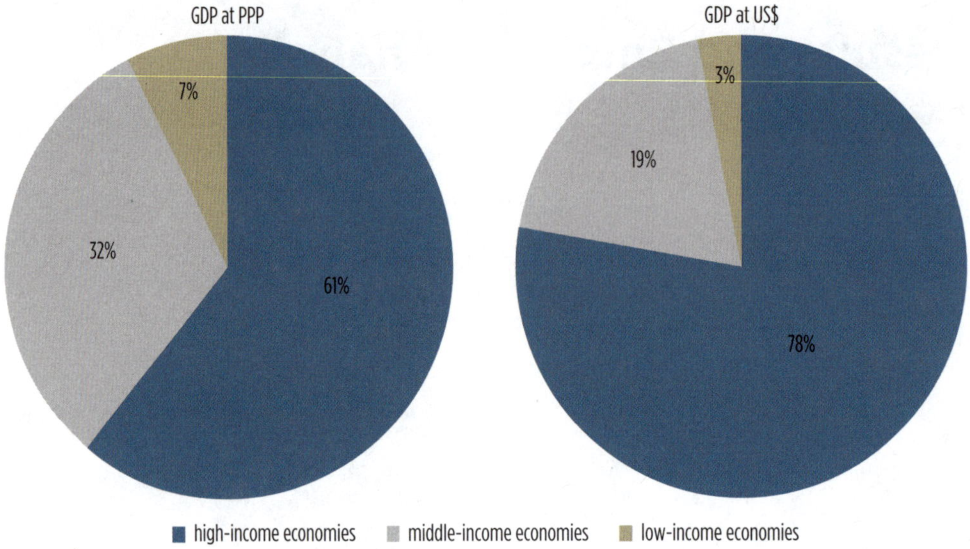

Source: World Bank 2008.

According to the 2005 ICP PPP estimates of GDP, the United States remains the largest economy, with 22.5 percent of the total, followed by China and Japan, with 9.7 and 7.0 percent, respectively. The 12 largest economies together account for two-thirds of the global GDP and include Brazil, China, India, Mexico, and the Russian Federation. These five low- or middle-income countries collectively account for almost 22 percent of the global economy.

There are also interesting results by region. The African economy is dominated by the Arab Republic of Egypt, Morocco, Nigeria, South Africa, and Sudan, which account for two-thirds of the region's GDP.[2] Brazil accounts for one-half of the South American economy. Russia accounts for three-fourths of the GDP of the Commonwealth of Independent States (CIS), China and India account for two-thirds of the Asia-Pacific's GDP, and Saudi Arabia is the largest country in Western Asia.

Figure 19.2 shows the distribution of global GDP by country or economy. The economies are arranged in the order of GDP per capita along the horizontal axis and presented as rectangles whose length along the horizontal scale corresponds to share of the world population. The vertical scale shows the PPP-based index of GDP per capita, which is each economy's GDP per capita as a percentage of the world average (world = 100). Each economy's GDP is thus represented by the rectangular area or the product of population and GDP per capita for direct comparison across economies.

In figure 19.2, the economies are arranged in increasing order of GDP per capita. The intersection of the 100 percent line with the rectangles illustrates that about three-fourths of the world population is in economies below the world average for per capita GDP. Both China and India have GDP per capita below the world average; however, they have the second- and fifth-largest economies because, combined, they account for 40 percent of the world population. The United States, with the sixth-largest GDP per capita, is at the right. The remaining countries are indicated by the dark lines because of their small populations.

FIGURE 19.2 Distribution of Global GDP by Country

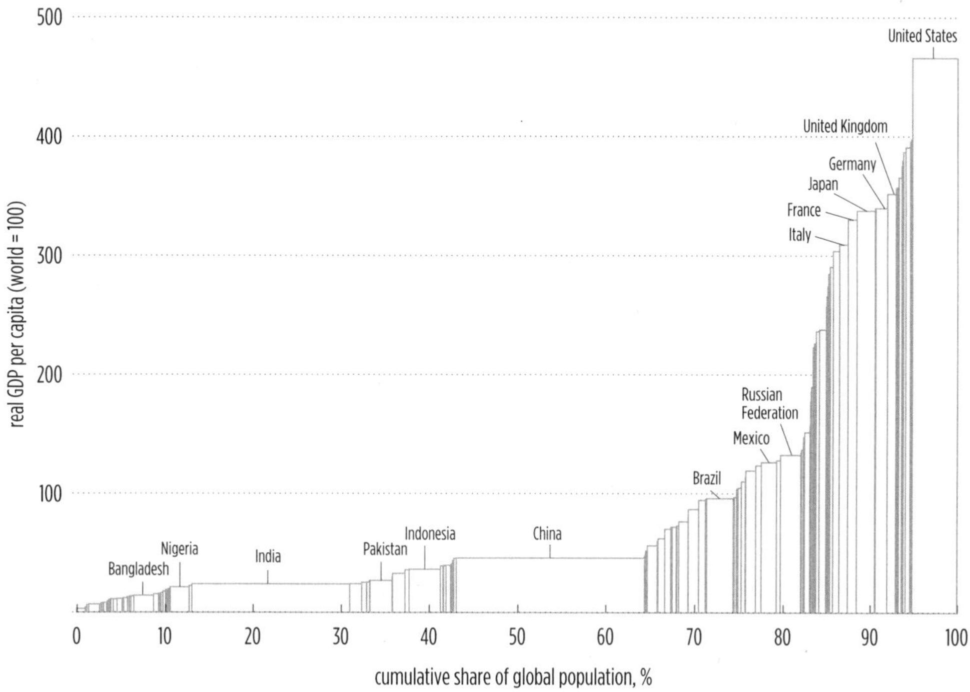

Source: World Bank 2008.
Note: Countries are in the order of increasing real GDP per capita. The area of each rectangle corresponds to the share in global GDP of the corresponding country. The economies with the highest GDP per capita—Luxembourg, Qatar, Norway, Brunei Darussalam, and Kuwait—are not visible in this figure because together they account for less than 1 percent of the world economy in total and a much smaller share of the world population. The United States is the sixth-largest economy in GDP per capita.

Figure 19.3 provides another view of GDP per capita across countries, this time plotted against the price level indexes (US = 100). Recall that the price level index (PLI) is the ratio of the PPP to a corresponding exchange rate and is used to compare price levels between economies. Figure 19.3 is a multidimensional comparison of the PLI with per capita GDP scaled to the size of the economy. The country spheres are color-coded by ICP region.[3] The PPPs and exchange rates are expressed through the PLI; the per capita expenditures reflect each country's affluence and the size of the sphere its GDP. An important observation is that, in general, price levels increase as countries become more developed. Another observation is that the relationship between price levels and GDP per capita is not uniform for individual countries, especially at the higher income levels. For example, the PLI for Iceland is about 60 percent higher than that for the United States, whereas Iceland's GDP per capita is below the U.S. level.

Regressing the log PLIs on log per capita GDP in nominal terms, we can estimate the static Balassa-Samuelson effect (or the static Penn effect)[4] for the 2005 ICP comparison:

$$\ln(PLI_i) = \underset{(0.0359)}{-0.0774} + \underset{(0.0115)}{0.2131} \ln(Y_i) + \hat{\varepsilon}_i$$

$R^2 = 0.7045$; standard error of regression (MSE) = 0.2341.

FIGURE 19.3 Price Level Index versus GDP Per Capita (US = 100)

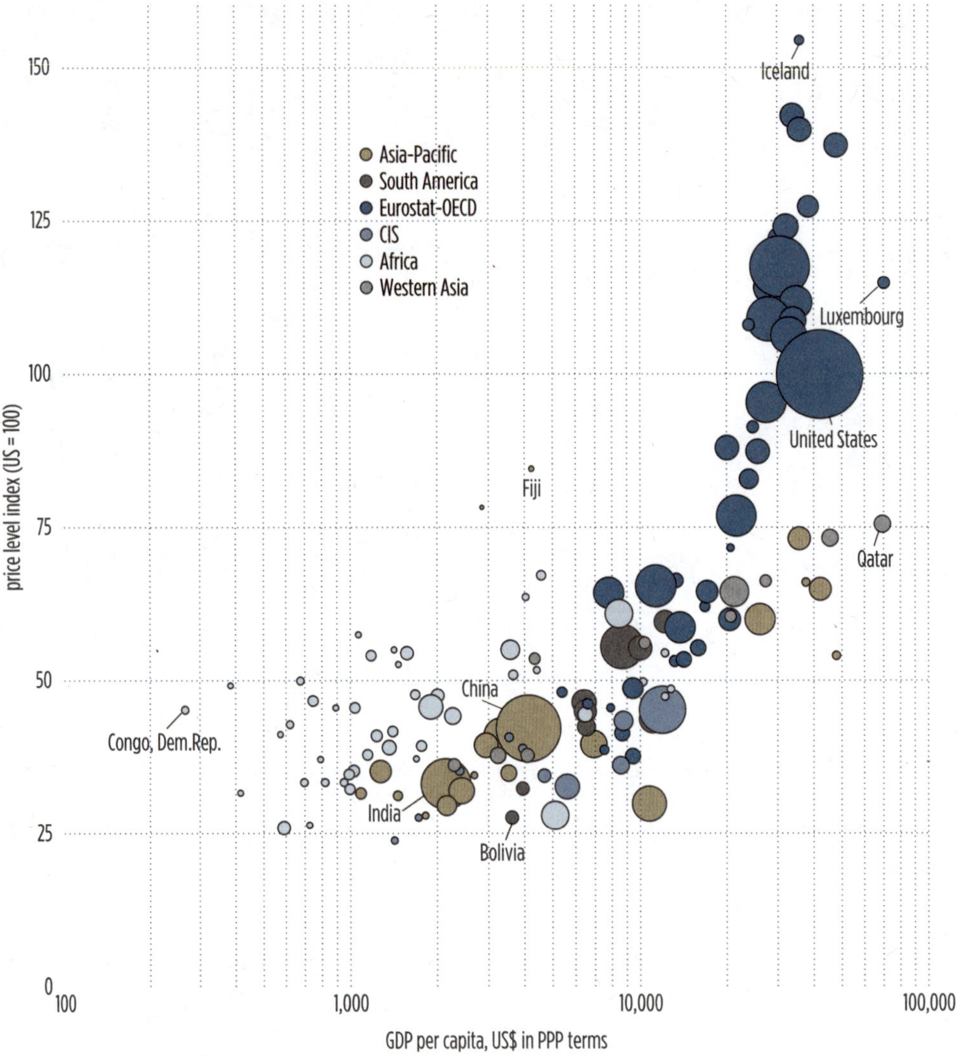

Source: World Bank 2008.
Note: Economies are represented by spheres, the size of which is proportional to GDP in PPP terms. Country spheres and labels are color-coded by ICP region. See annex to chapter 10 for country codes.

This means that with each percent of increase in the nominal per capita GDP, the price level (PLI) increases by 0.2131 percent (in relative terms, versus the United States). As mentioned earlier, this relationship is not very strong. But using this formulation, we can predict the PLI or real GDP for a country with the standard error of estimate of 23.4 percent.[5]

It is possible to get a better fit when using a nonparametric regression. In particular, in figure 19.4 the LOESS (locally weighted polynomial regression) with Epanechnikov kernel was used (Cleveland and Devlin 1988). The LOESS fit (the thick line in beige) is contrasted with the cubic fit presented for comparison. It is clear from figure 19.4 that the relationship of log price level versus log income per capita at exchange rate is strongly nonlinear. The standard error for the LOESS regression is 0.18, still high, but significantly lower than for the linear formulation.

FIGURE 19.4 Log Price Level Index (PLI) versus Log GDP Per Capita, at Exchange Rate

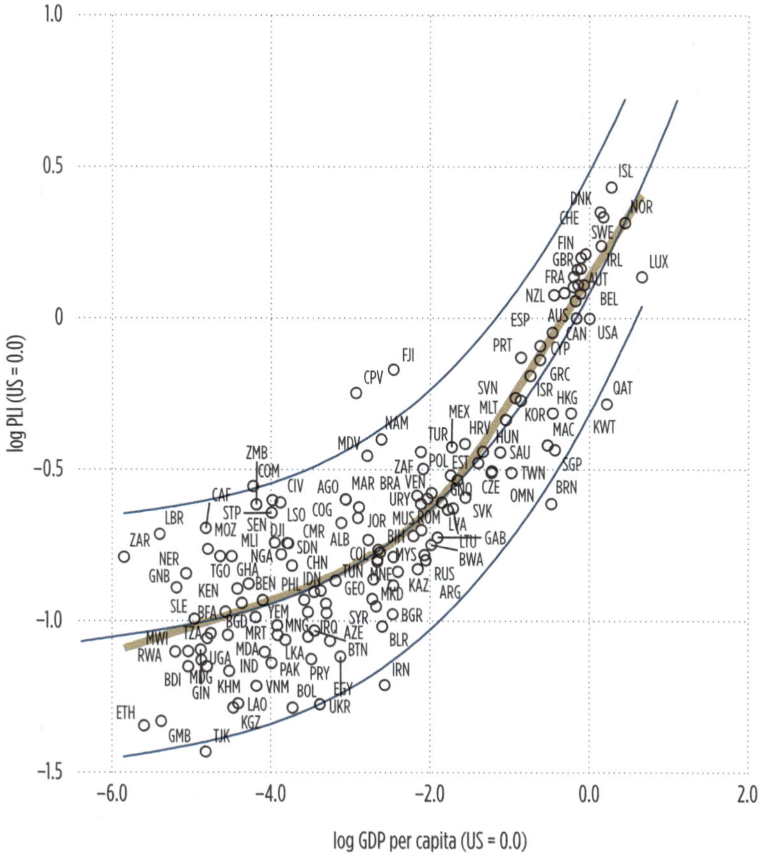

Note: See annex to chapter 10 for country/economy abbreviations.

Impact of Methods Used to Apply Regional Fixity

Earlier chapters described in great detail the different methods and concepts involved in estimating PPPs. They pointed out that any properly defined multilateral process to estimate the PPPs between any two countries will be affected by the other countries in the comparison. The PPP between Mexico and Germany, for example, will depend on the other countries in the comparison. Chapter 10 described these sources of variability in considerable detail.

To eliminate influences from nonregional countries, the ICP follows this principle: first estimate PPPs at the regional level and then carry out the global aggregation in such a way that intraregional relativities for prices and real expenditures are retained. This is called *fixity.* The rationale for the fixity requirement is the following: because the countries within each region would utilize a common item list and are likely have more similar price and economic structures, it would make more sense to make comparisons among them than comparisons with out-of-region countries. Chapters 4–6 showed how these regional PPPs were estimated in the 2005 ICP, and then linked to other regions for the global comparison. This linking was done in a way that ensured the fixity concept was met. The fixity concept thus defined ensures that the relative position (ratio of PLI or real expenditures) between any pair of countries in a region remains the same in both the regional and global comparisons. This concept also allows for different timing of preparation and publication of the regional results.

However, the composition of the ICP regions has moved from a mostly geographic base to a more organization-based distribution. In particular, the Eurostat-OECD region includes the Republic of Korea, Japan, Mexico, and Russia.[6] In addition, composition of the regions changes from one comparison to another: in 1993 China and India did not take part in the ICP, whereas in 2005 both countries were part of the Asia-Pacific region. At the same time, Japan and Korea were part of the Asia-Pacific region in 1993 but not in 2005.

This section compares the results derived by imposing fixity using the two-stage approach applied by the 2005 ICP with the results based on a one-stage global aggregation in which fixity is not imposed on the global GDP or aggregates. Regional fixity can be restored by distributing the sum of regional totals from the one-stage global aggregation to the respective countries in each region based on the regional aggregation.

The results are shown in table 19.1 for the six ICP regions and selected countries. Columns (1) and (4) show GDP per capita as a percentage of the world average and world shares, respectively,

TABLE 19.1 GDP Per Capita Indexes and World Shares with Two-Stage and One-Stage Aggregations

	GDP per capita indexes (world = 100)			GDP world shares		
	GEKS			GEKS		
	Two-stage (1)	One-stage (2)	Ratio (3)	Two-stage (4)	One-stage (5)	Ratio (6)
Asia-Pacific	40.0	43.8	1.10	21.9	23.2	1.06
South America	93.8	91.9	0.98	5.6	5.3	0.95
Eurostat-OECD	295.3	299.3	1.01	66.3	65.2	0.98
CIS	102.5	116.6	1.14	4.1	4.5	1.10
Africa	24.8	26.8	1.08	3.3	3.2	0.96
Western Asia	86.0	89.6	1.04	2.5	2.5	1.01
World	8,971	9,210		54,976	58,329	
China	45.6	50.4	1.11	9.70	10.42	1.07
India	23.7	25.9	1.09	4.26	4.51	1.06
Brazil	95.8	93.4	0.98	2.88	2.72	0.95
Russian Federation	132.2	147.6	1.12	3.09	3.34	1.08
Tajikistan	15.8	23.2	1.47	0.24	0.27	1.12
South Africa	94.5	93.1	0.99	0.72	0.69	0.96
Egypt, Arab Rep.	56.3	56.9	1.01	0.64	0.64	0.99
United States	464.5	452.5	0.97	22.51	21.2	0.94

Source: Estimated on the basis of ICP 2005 detailed inputs.
Note: GEKS = Gini-Éltetö-Köves-Szulc. Summation of shares across regions greater than 100 because Russia and Egypt are included in two regions.

as published in World Bank (2008). They are based on the Gini-Éltető-Köves-Szulc (GEKS) aggregation method. The table also shows world GDP per capita and world GDP for the one-stage and two-stage cases.

The GEKS aggregation with fixity as implemented in 2005 is a two-stage process, as shown in chapter 10. As a preliminary step, the regional aggregation is carried out according to the regional methodology—that is, with the GEKS indexes, or, in the case of Africa, with the Iklé-Dikhanov-Balk (IDB) method. Sometimes, the regional aggregation is a multistage process itself, as in the Eurostat-OECD region.

The inputs for both the one-stage and two-stage global aggregations is the within-region basic heading PPPs and the between-region linking factors that convert the within-region PPPs to a set of transitive global basic heading PPPs. The two-stage method of aggregation to the GDP and each subcomponent is as follows:

- *Stage one.* Use the regional basic heading real expenditures as calculated by the regions to assemble the regional totals (super countries) at regional prices.
- *Stage two.* Use the GEKS method to conduct the global aggregation using the regional totals by basic heading and interregional linking factors at the level of GDP and its components.

After that process, the regional totals at the level of GDP and its components will be redistributed according to the regional results to ensure fixity.

An alternative (one-stage) global aggregation process is to compute the GEKS results directly at each level of aggregation using the full matrix of 129 basic heading PPPs for the 146 countries after they have been linked to a common global currency, without assembling the regional totals. After the global aggregation is computed, the GEKS results are normalized to have the same intra-regional relativities as in the regional comparison (i.e., fixity is applied in the same fashion as in the two-stage case).

The PPPs between any two countries in the one-stage aggregation are affected by countries from every region. All countries are treated equally in every stage of aggregation regardless of their economic size. Thus the PPP between, say, Brazil and India is computed directly rather than via the interregional linking factors. In addition, the PPPs between any two countries are affected by the indirect PPPs based on each of the remaining 144 countries as shown in chapter 10.

In this chapter, fixity has not been applied in the one-stage process—that is, the difference between the one- and two-stage processes under consideration here includes both effects of fixity and an extra stage in aggregation.

The one-stage global aggregation with no fixity imposed increases the per capita expenditures as a percentage of the global measure in the Asia-Pacific, CIS, and Africa regions, and more specifically in China, India, Russia, and Tajikistan.

Columns (4) and (5) show the world shares by region and country for the one- and two-stage cases. The U.S. real GDP share in the world decreases with the one-stage aggregation. However, as shown in column (6) the distribution of GDP across regions and countries changes considerably, clearly indicating that the choice of method has a significant effect.

The country shares of world GDP for China, India, and Russia become larger when the one-stage global GEKS aggregation without fixity is used, and, correspondingly, the relative price levels become lower. At the same time, the price levels for Brazil, South Africa, and Egypt become higher when the one-stage aggregation is used. Figure 19.5 plots the differences between the two methods for all the countries in the comparison. The regression line is based on the nonparametric

FIGURE 19.5 Ratio of Two-Stage GEKS with Fixity to One-Stage GEKS without Fixity versus GEKS GDP Per Capita

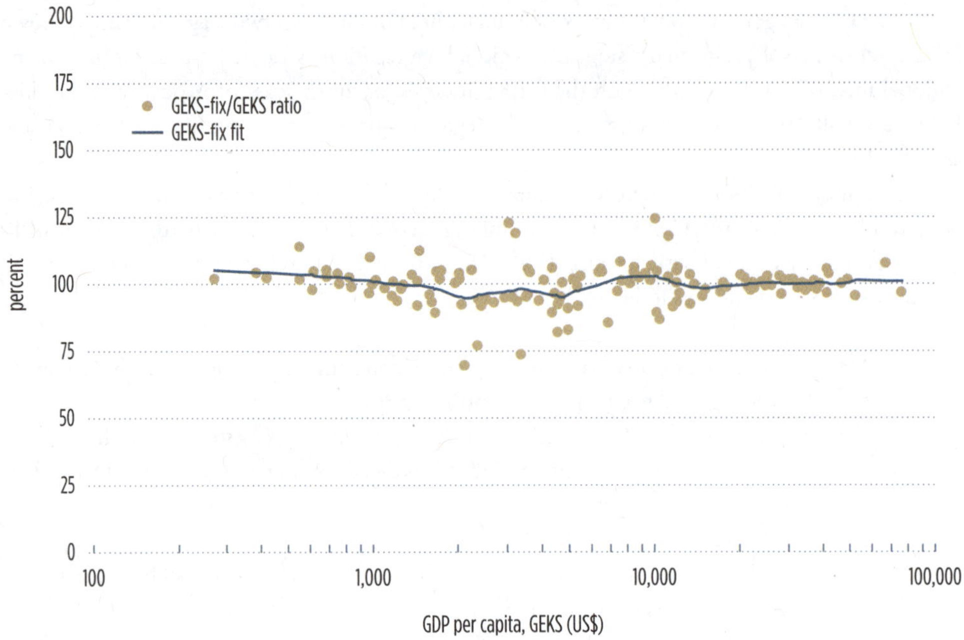

Source: Estimated on the basis of ICP 2005 detailed inputs.
Note: GEKS = Gini-Éltető-Köves-Szulc.

LOESS procedure. Some countries (in particular, Tajikistan and the Kyrgyz Republic) exhibit very high deviations, which probably indicate the limitations of the methodology.

This effect should be taken into account when comparing the 2011 and 2005 ICP rounds, because the 2011 methodology of linking the regions will generate results for regions in their entirety closer to the one-stage calculation as presented here. For example, in the one-stage calculation the GDP level of the Asia-Pacific region is estimated as 10 percent higher than the official results, and at the same time the relative positions of India, China, and other Asian countries *within* the region would not change when fixity is applied. This means the positions of countries in Asia vis-à-vis the world move in accordance with the level change in that region.

The GEKS Method and Additivity

Additivity is a desired statistical property for international comparisons. For example, the expenditures in national currency for each basic heading divided by the respective PPPs should add to the sum of the basic heading expenditures (in national currency) divided by the aggregated food PPP. The addition of major aggregate expenditures in PPP terms to GDP should equal the real expenditures obtained by dividing GDP expenditures in national currencies by the aggregated PPP for GDP.

Different methods can be used to average basic heading PPPs to aggregates of GDP and to GDP. In chapter 5 of this volume, Diewert describes the properties of the three primary methods—GEKS, IDB, and Geary-Khamis (GK)—used to aggregate basic heading PPPs to the higher levels, including GDP. There, he examines the additive property and the economic approach to making multilateral comparisons.

The GEKS method does not provide results that are additive, whereas both the GK and IDB methods do satisfy that property. Diewert shows that GEKS satisfies the economic approach to index number theory, that it is one of the superlative multilateral methods, and that it satisfies some important axiomatic properties.

He also explains that additive methods are not consistent with economic utility across countries. Countries whose price vectors diverge widely from the "international or world" prices used in additive methods will produce quantity shares that are biased upward. In other words, the GDP shares in countries whose price vectors are out of line with the "international price" will be biased upward using additive methods.[7]

For these reasons, the method of choice for the global aggregation for the 2005 ICP and also for the 2011 ICP is the GEKS method, even though its results are not additive. The rest of this section briefly reviews the main aggregates and the impact of the lack of additivity.

The data in tables 19.2 and 19.3 are derived from table 4, real expenditures by aggregate and the GDP, in World Bank (2008). This table provides real expenditures separately for machinery and equipment, construction, and other products. Then, the respective PPPs for these aggregates are averaged to provide real expenditures for gross fixed capital formation (GFCF). The sum of the real expenditures for machinery and equipment, construction, and other products is not the same as the real expenditures for GFCF after the respective PPPs are aggregated, and therefore is not additive. A similar comparison can be made by adding real expenditures for aggregates making up actual individual consumption (AIC) and comparing that with AIC real expenditures and also at the level of GDP.

Table 19.2 shows the sum of the real expenditures for the aggregates making up GDP, AIC, and GFCF as the ratio of the real expenditures from the aggregated PPPs for the six regions and the world. The first column shows that the largest difference for GDP is 4 percent in the Asia-Pacific region; all others are essentially the same considering the statistical variability inherent in the methods. However, the differences become considerably larger for subaggregates of GDP. The sum of real expenditures for machinery and equipment, construction, and other products is 32 percent larger in the Asia-Pacific region than the aggregated value of gross fixed capital formation.

TABLE 19.2 Effect of GEKS on Additivity Shown by Sum of Individual Aggregates as a Ratio to Overall Aggregate for GDP, AIC, and GFCF, by Region

Region	Sum GDP/GDP	Sum AIC/AIC	Sum GFCF/GFCF
Asia-Pacific	1.04	1.21	1.32
South America	1.00	1.03	1.04
Eurostat-OECD	1.00	1.02	1.01
CIS	0.99	1.16	1.07
Africa	1.02	1.03	1.08
Western Asia	1.01	1.14	1.08
World	1.01	1.06	1.11

Source: ICP 2005.
Note: AIC = actual individual consumption; GFCF = gross fixed capital formation.

TABLE 19.3 Effect of GEKS on Additivity as Shown by Sum of Individual Aggregates as a Ratio to Overall GDP, AIC, and GFCF, Asia-Pacific Region

	Sum GDP/GDP	Sum AIC/AIC	Sum GFCF/GFCF
Bangladesh	1.06	1.04	1.59
Bhutan	1.17	1.33	1.71
Brunei Darussalam	0.93	1.22	1.23
Cambodia	1.07	1.41	1.28
China	1.05	1.28	1.44
Hong Kong SAR, China	0.96	1.08	0.92
Macao SAR, China	0.83	1.10	1.26
Taiwan, China	1.04	1.22	0.93
Fiji	1.17	1.09	0.93
India	1.05	1.20	1.14
Indonesia	1.01	1.01	1.60
Iran, Islamic Rep.	1.01	1.21	0.98
Lao PDR	1.24	1.27	1.29
Malaysia	0.94	1.11	0.96
Maldives	1.28	1.88	0.96
Mongolia	1.06	1.52	1.08
Nepal	1.11	1.18	1.50
Pakistan	1.10	1.14	1.22
Philippines	1.04	1.09	1.17
Singapore	0.92	1.10	0.97
Sri Lanka	1.11	0.93	1.28
Thailand	1.04	1.15	0.90
Vietnam	1.08	1.66	1.52

Source: ICP 2005.
Note: AIC = actual individual consumption; GFCF = gross fixed capital formation.

Table 19.3 shows the same comparisons shown in table 19.2, but for countries in the Asia-Pacific region. It is obvious that the differences between the respective sums and the PPP aggregate are considerably larger at the country level. The main contributor to the differences for the capital formation aggregate is the construction category, in which real expenditures for some countries exceed the aggregated capital formation amount. Large differences are also shown for the actual individual consumption category. The differences become much smaller at the GDP level.

What are the consequences of the lack of additivity? First, the main purpose of the ICP is to obtain comparisons that are consistent with economic utility across countries. In addition, the GEKS treats countries symmetrically and equally in the aggregation, as shown in the examples in chapter 10. Therefore, the main consequence of the lack of additivity is that the PLIs and real expenditures for each component and aggregate of GDP must be considered separately and used to understand the comparisons across countries. They should not be used for within-country comparisons. Second, the most appropriate comparison for gross fixed capital formation is use of the real expenditures for that aggregate and not the summation of the individual components. Therefore, the primary consequence of the lack of additivity is that analysis of the economic structure within countries is difficult. In other words, it is difficult to contrast the contribution of each GDP component and aggregates to GDP by country when, for example, answering the question what is the distribution of expenditures on health and education when viewed as a percentage of the GDP, in real terms?

The next section reviews the real GDP and main aggregates when different aggregation methods are used.

GDP by Method of Aggregation

This section compares four methods used to estimate PPPs and thus the global real value of GDP. Chapters 4, 5, and 6 provide a complete review of these methods. However, a brief summary is presented here to provide context for the discussion of the methods.

The *GEKS method* was described earlier in this chapter in the discussion on fixity. The *GK method* is a global aggregation using the 129 basic heading expenditures and PPPs for the 146 countries. The real expenditures for each country based on the sum of the country's individual basic heading expenditures are weighted by an international price held constant across countries. The result is a set of real expenditures that are additive to the ICP. However, large countries will make larger contributions to determination of the international prices, which therefore will be more representative of the larger countries in the comparison.

The *IDB method* is a global aggregation using the 129 × 146 matrices of basic heading PPPs and expenditures. Chapter 5 provides a detailed discussion of the properties of the IDB method, which also produces additive results. The method is very similar to the GK method except that international prices are determined in a way that reduces the effect of large countries, and, as a result, reduces the Gerschenkron effect.[8] The IDB method treats all countries equally, as does the GEKS.

Either or both methods will be of interest to those seeking a method that is additive across countries and commodity groups. Therefore, what follows reviews the results by method, beginning with table 19.4, which shows the real GDP by method of aggregation by ICP region and world.

TABLE 19.4 Real GDP by Method of Aggregation by ICP Region and World

US$ millions

Region	GEKS, two-stage	GEKS, one-stage	GK	IDB
Asia-Pacific	12,020.7	13,529.6	13,463	12,599
South America	3,078.1	3,103.4	2,975	2,771
Eurostat-OECD	36,469.0	38,033.5	37,134	36,788
CIS	2,269.2	2,648.3	2,509	2,281
Africa	1,835.6	1,877.0	1,998	1,702
Western Asia	1,354.1	1,454.9	1,516	1,420
World	54,975.6	58,329.0	57,457	55,579

Source: ICP 2005.
Note: GEKS = Gini-Éltető-Köves-Szulc; GK = Geary-Khamis: IDB = Iklé-Dikhanov-Balk.
World Total after adjusting duplication of Russia in the Eurostat, OECD and CIS regions and Egypt in the Africa and Western Asia regions.

The numbers in table 19.4 are expressed in U.S. dollars, and thus the changes in world totals reflect the relative changes in the U.S. GDP share in the world. In other words, using the GK method the U.S. dollar is valued 4.5 percent less than when using the two-stage GEKS, and so forth.

The two GEKS aggregations are interesting because they simply show the effect of directly aggregating country PPPs across regions and the respective larger differences in price levels encountered. Also interesting is that the GEKS two-stage, GEKS one-stage, and IDB values are very similar, suggesting they are not statistically different.

The effect of the four methods on the size of the regional and country economies is now shown using their shares of the world economies. Table 19.5 shows the percentage of each region's real GDP of the world total for each aggregation method.

The GK versus GEKS (two-stage) method shows larger shares of the world for the Asia-Pacific, CIS, Africa, and Western Asia regions. The world shares are reduced for the South America and Eurostat-OECD regions. The effect of the large country weights on the international price for the GK was to raise the shares of the poorer regions and lower them in the higher-income countries.

It can be concluded, then, that the differences between methods at the regional level are not large because of the smoothing effect of having countries at various levels of development in each region—for example, Asia has some of the richest and the poorest countries in the world, and the Gerschenkron effect in the GK case would not be so distinct at the regional level. The general relationship between the GEKS and the additive methods shows that the IDB maintains additivity with little impact on the country shares for most regions.

At the individual country level, the picture is quite different; the differences are much more pronounced. Figure 19.6 compares the different methods at the country level using GDP per capita. The GEKS one-stage GDP per capita for each country is in the denominator. The graph shows a scatter plot of the ratios of the GK and IDB measures of GDP to the GEKS one-stage estimates. Because the GK and IDB are one-stage methods, they are compared with the GEKS one-stage values. That comparison explicitly shows the greater bias inherent in the GK for countries with the lower GDP per capita and decreases as the per capita measure increases. It also has a larger number of outliers. The IDB/GEKS ratio is greater than 25 percent for only one country; otherwise, the ratios are evenly distributed around the regression line (nonparametric LOESS fit). The result is that the IDB method produces results similar to those produced by the GEKS method, and it gives additive results. The Gerschenkron effect is clearly visible in the GK case.

TABLE 19.5 Real Gross Domestic Product by Method of Aggregation by ICP Region and World (shares, world = 100)

Region	GEKS, two-stage	GEKS, one-stage	GK	IDB
Asia-Pacific	21.87	23.20	23.43	22.67
South America	5.60	5.32	5.18	4.99
Eurostat-OECD	66.34	65.21	64.63	66.19
CIS	4.13	4.54	4.37	4.10
Africa	3.34	3.22	3.48	3.06
Western Asia	2.46	2.49	2.64	2.55
World	100.00	100.00	100.00	100.00

Source: ICP 2005.
Summation across regions greater than 100 because Russia and Egypt are included in two regions.

FIGURE 19.6 GK/GEKS Ratio and IDB/GEKS Ratio versus GEKS GDP Per Capita by Country

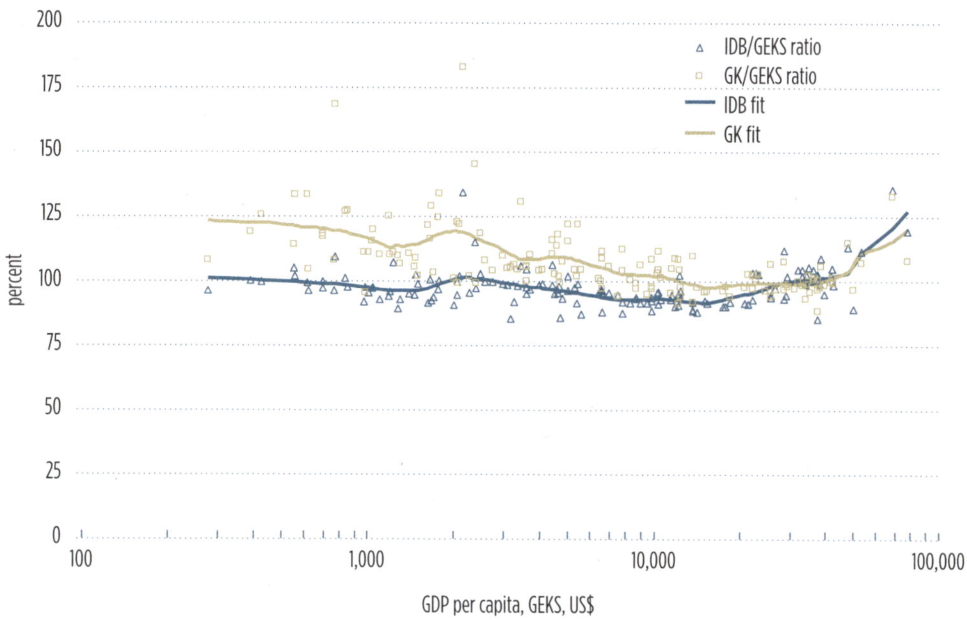

Note: GEKS = Gini-Éltető-Köves-Szulc; GK = Geary-Khamis; IDB = Iklé-Dikhanov-Balk.

The next section is an overview of the structural information that can be gleaned using an additive method—in this case the IDB.

Structure of the World GDP and Its Aggregates

The annex to this chapter presents the item shares resulting from the IDB aggregation, which are additive to the GDP for each country. Using this table, one can examine the distribution of the aggregates of the real GDP expenditures. Some examples follow.

Twelve percent of the world's GDP is for food and nonalcoholic beverages. Africa spends over a fourth of its GDP on these products, but the Eurostat-OECD spends only 10 percent. Many of the poorer countries spend over a third to a half of their GDP on food. The table shows that the expenditures on food decline as the size of the economy increases.

Health expenditures account for 6 percent of the world GDP, but with a smaller range: 3.8 percent in Western Asia and 6.4 percent in the Eurostat-OECD region. In only six countries are health expenditures 10 percent or more of GDP. A similar picture emerges for education expenditures, where the range is from 2.8 percent for the Eurostat-OECD countries to 6.6 percent for the CIS countries.

Government expenditures (individual and collective) account for 12 percent of the world GDP. Shares by region range from 29 percent for Africa to 12 percent for the Asia-Pacific. Eleven countries spend one-fourth or more of their GDP on government.

Construction accounts for 13 percent of the world GDP. The Asia-Pacific region leads the way, spending nearly a fourth of its GDP on construction. Only about 9 percent of the Eurostat-OECD region's GDP is spent on construction. However, this region has the largest share of machinery and equipment expenditures (11 percent), compared with 8 percent for the Asia-Pacific region. This implies that there is a labor productivity factor in which more labor is used in Asia and more equipment is used in the Eurostat-OECD region to achieve a given level of construction.

It is left to the reader to review the distributions at the country level, especially by economic size, where it is clear that countries with rapid growth have large shares for investment.

Conclusion

This chapter provides an overview of the results of the 2005 ICP, as well as an analysis to clarify the concepts of fixity and additivity. It then compares the different methods of estimating PPPs that incorporate these concepts.

A conclusion from this analysis is that the ICP results are very robust. Although different methods of estimation provide somewhat different answers, the results are within the range of statistical variability. And although the IDB method does have a residual Gerschenkron effect, its results are close to those produced by the GEKS method, but it provides additivity, which is important for structural analysis. It is also shown that regional fixity may have a significant effect on the results.

ANNEX

Real Expenditure Item Shares at World Average Prices

percent

Economy	Gross domestic product	Actual individual consumption	Food and nonalcoholic beverages	Alcoholic beverages, tobacco, and narcotics	Clothing and footwear	Housing, water, electricity, gas, and other fuels	Furnishings, household equipment, and maintenance	Health	Transport	Communication	Recreation and culture
Bangladesh	100.0	71.8	41.1	1.8	4.2	7.8	2.7	3.0	2.2	0.3	0.5
Bhutan	100.0	42.9	16.6	1.0	2.9	5.1	2.1	6.4	0.7	0.2	1.4
Brunei Darussalam	100.0	28.9	6.1	0.1	1.4	2.2	1.1	1.4	5.8	1.7	2.4
Cambodia	100.0	82.6	38.6	2.7	1.5	6.0	1.3	10.4	4.6	0.2	2.0
China	100.0	40.0	10.6	0.5	1.8	4.2	1.4	4.5	1.6	2.7	2.2
Hong Kong SAR, China	100.0	56.3	6.0	0.3	8.5	5.0	3.4	3.5	3.1	2.8	9.1
Macao SAR, China	100.0	28.4	4.5	0.3	2.0	2.6	0.5	2.1	2.5	2.0	5.1
Taiwan, China	100.0	65.1	8.8	1.4	3.3	5.5	3.3	8.1	6.5	3.8	7.2
Fiji	100.0	90.8	30.9	2.2	3.5	9.8	11.0	5.9	8.8	0.8	5.0
India	100.0	66.3	23.6	0.7	4.3	6.2	1.4	9.0	7.8	1.2	1.2
Indonesia	100.0	68.8	32.1	0.8	3.5	8.9	2.0	1.8	4.0	0.9	1.3
Iran, Islamic Rep.	100.0	65.8	9.7	0.4	3.8	12.5	2.7	6.7	6.3	14.9	1.6
Lao PDR	100.0	57.0	25.7	2.0	0.9	9.5	1.4	3.0	3.0	0.2	1.6
Malaysia	100.0	51.2	10.3	0.4	1.4	4.8	2.7	2.6	8.2	3.2	2.5
Maldives	100.0	53.0	14.4	1.2	2.3	4.5	2.2	7.4	1.5	2.8	2.1
Mongolia	100.0	59.8	22.2	1.1	6.2	5.3	1.9	5.5	3.3	1.2	1.8
Nepal	100.0	77.9	43.2	1.2	5.2	6.4	1.7	9.2	1.8	0.2	0.8
Pakistan	100.0	81.1	34.7	0.5	7.1	11.8	1.8	8.2	4.0	2.4	2.2
Philippines	100.0	73.1	35.8	2.2	1.7	6.8	1.4	2.3	4.0	2.4	0.8
Singapore	100.0	38.1	3.9	0.3	1.6	3.2	2.5	3.0	5.4	1.9	6.2
Sri Lanka	100.0	75.3	26.9	1.4	9.6	6.5	4.1	2.9	13.1	0.6	2.2
Thailand	100.0	63.6	11.0	1.9	4.8	5.2	3.4	5.5	9.3	0.9	3.7
Vietnam	100.0	57.3	18.2	0.9	2.0	5.3	2.1	8.0	2.7	0.6	2.6
Asia-Pacific	**100.0**	**54.1**	**16.1**	**0.7**	**3.1**	**5.9**	**1.8**	**5.6**	**4.2**	**3.0**	**2.4**
Argentina	100.0	70.2	20.8	3.0	3.0	9.6	2.8	5.9	6.5	3.8	3.6
Bolivia	100.0	80.5	23.0	1.0	1.9	9.6	3.6	6.1	15.7	1.3	0.7
Brazil	100.0	68.6	15.6	2.8	2.6	8.3	3.5	7.1	7.6	3.0	2.5
Chile	100.0	60.2	13.5	1.9	4.6	8.9	3.9	4.7	8.6	1.4	2.7
Colombia	100.0	70.2	18.2	3.2	2.9	12.4	3.4	6.5	6.6	2.0	2.0
Ecuador	100.0	68.6	20.6	1.7	4.4	6.9	5.0	4.7	10.8	3.3	3.0
Paraguay	100.0	84.2	35.9	2.1	4.9	11.4	3.5	3.4	6.6	2.3	3.4
Peru	100.0	69.5	22.6	1.3	4.8	6.8	3.1	3.2	6.6	1.7	2.8
Uruguay	100.0	77.7	20.6	3.1	4.0	11.7	4.7	6.6	9.7	2.9	3.4
Venezuela, RB	100.0	57.7	16.1	2.9	1.7	8.0	2.4	3.7	7.2	3.2	1.8

Education	Restaurants and hotels	Miscellaneous goods and services	Net purchases abroad	Private individual consumption	Individual consumption by government	General government	Gross fixed capital formation	Machinery and equipment	Construction	Other products	Stocks	Net exports
4.6	1.2	2.2	0.0	70.4	1.3	2.7	29.8	3.6	25.9	0.3	0	-4
2.5	0.0	3.9	0.0	32.8	10.3	8.7	58.2	5.9	51.5	0.8	0	-10
3.4	1.5	1.8	0.0	24.4	4.3	16.0	13.8	3.6	9.3	0.9	0	41
9.4	2.9	3.0	0.0	74.5	9.4	6.5	11.6	3.1	8.4	0.1	0	-1
3.3	1.6	5.6	0.0	34.7	6.5	8.6	46.9	8.0	36.6	2.4	1	3
1.7	5.4	7.6	0.0	54.1	2.1	3.7	26.7	15.1	10.4	1.3	0	14
1.4	3.4	2.0	0.0	25.5	2.5	3.4	29.6	7.6	21.5	0.5	1	38
4.1	5.6	7.4	0.0	61.2	3.5	8.0	22.8	11.8	9.0	2.0	0	4
5.8	2.3	4.8	0.0	84.0	6.6	8.4	32.7	16.4	11.7	4.6	2	-34
4.1	0.9	6.1	0.0	62.4	3.4	4.9	26.4	9.8	16.0	0.6	4	-2
4.9	4.7	4.0	0.0	66.1	2.6	3.6	24.8	2.6	21.5	0.6	0	3
2.5	0.5	4.2	0.0	61.2	3.7	5.5	15.5	7.3	7.7	0.5	11	2
7.0	1.3	1.3	0.0	51.0	6.4	16.1	30.4	5.5	19.5	5.5	2	-5
4.2	3.8	7.4	0.0	44.9	6.3	7.0	25.3	12.2	12.4	0.7	0	17
11.9	0.5	2.3	0.0	42.8	10.5	16.1	56.6	21.8	20.6	14.2	0	-26
9.8	0.2	1.3	0.0	48.4	13.0	6.6	29.8	8.4	15.2	6.3	6	-3
3.8	1.3	3.0	0.0	75.5	2.3	3.6	21.7	1.7	16.2	3.8	6	-9
4.8	0.3	3.4	0.0	77.5	3.3	5.0	16.3	4.8	10.3	1.1	1	-4
6.2	2.3	7.3	0.0	70.5	2.5	4.2	14.8	4.3	9.3	1.2	11	-3
2.0	3.4	4.7	0.0	35.5	2.4	7.0	29.2	14.5	14.1	0.7	-4	30
2.6	0.9	4.4	0.0	68.2	7.6	6.0	21.9	5.8	15.6	0.5	3	-6
4.8	9.7	3.2	0.0	58.1	5.4	5.0	29.7	16.2	13.4	0.2	3	-1
10.0	3.3	1.7	0.0	50.6	8.1	6.9	35.6	5.3	27.9	2.5	2	-2
3.8	**2.2**	**5.4**	**0.0**	**49.5**	**4.9**	**6.7**	**34.4**	**8.4**	**24.4**	**1.5**	**3**	**2**
2.2	3.8	5.2	0.0	67.3	2.9	5.5	20.7	7.0	13.1	0.6	-1	4
10.3	5.3	1.9	0.0	68.0	12.5	7.2	9.6	2.6	6.6	0.5	1	2
3.6	3.4	8.5	0.0	62.4	6.2	10.9	17.4	7.6	8.4	1.4	0	3
2.6	2.0	5.2	0.0	56.9	3.2	5.0	24.1	9.0	14.9	0.2	2	9
3.4	5.8	3.7	0.0	64.3	5.8	9.0	20.9	5.5	14.5	0.9	1	-1
3.5	2.0	2.7	0.0	64.0	4.6	5.1	25.1	6.8	17.8	0.5	3	-1
3.7	3.1	3.6	0.0	80.5	3.6	4.1	14.8	5.0	9.6	0.2	0	-3
3.1	5.5	8.0	0.0	67.1	2.5	4.9	22.0	3.8	16.4	1.8	0	4
2.5	3.3	5.2	0.0	74.4	3.3	5.1	14.8	6.3	8.0	0.5	0	2
3.1	4.7	3.2	0.0	53.8	3.9	4.9	16.4	7.0	8.6	0.8	3	18

(continued)

Economy	Gross domestic product	Actual individual consumption	Food and nonalcoholic beverages	Alcoholic beverages, tobacco, and narcotics	Clothing and footwear	Housing, water, electricity, gas, and other fuels	Furnishings, household equipment, and maintenance	Health	Transport	Communication	Recreation and culture
South America	**100.0**	**67.9**	**17.3**	**2.7**	**3.0**	**8.8**	**3.3**	**6.1**	**7.5**	**2.8**	**2.6**
Albania	100.0	87.4	22.9	4.3	3.1	15.5	4.7	8.4	8.8	2.5	4.8
Australia	100.0	64.3	7.8	1.8	3.2	8.6	4.3	5.0	9.9	1.6	7.4
Austria	100.0	64.4	8.5	2.0	4.7	9.3	5.5	4.7	8.7	1.9	7.4
Belgium	100.0	63.1	9.3	2.3	3.4	7.6	3.3	5.6	9.4	1.3	5.4
Bosnia and Herzegovina	100.0	109.5	33.9	7.1	3.9	19.6	7.7	7.5	6.3	3.2	4.5
Bulgaria	100.0	81.3	17.6	2.6	1.9	16.4	2.7	6.8	10.5	2.3	4.3
Canada	100.0	64.9	6.7	1.6	2.8	10.3	3.8	4.4	11.9	1.4	6.8
Croatia	100.0	71.2	20.1	2.9	3.5	16.2	6.6	7.5	6.8	2.6	6.4
Cyprus	100.0	74.7	15.3	4.8	5.8	11.9	5.2	3.8	13.2	3.8	6.8
Czech Republic	100.0	63.6	11.0	4.3	2.0	11.6	2.6	6.5	5.7	1.2	7.5
Denmark	100.0	58.5	7.2	2.2	3.2	8.2	3.6	4.5	6.6	1.9	6.2
Estonia	100.0	69.0	13.9	5.6	3.6	9.8	3.9	5.1	7.6	1.7	6.3
Finland	100.0	60.6	8.8	2.4	2.9	8.3	3.5	5.5	7.1	2.4	6.4
France	100.0	74.3	11.8	2.1	4.3	9.9	4.4	7.1	11.1	1.9	7.1
Germany	100.0	68.3	9.4	2.4	3.6	8.6	4.8	6.6	9.7	1.7	5.7
Greece	100.0	72.8	8.5	3.3	5.3	12.4	3.6	10.0	4.3	1.4	3.6
Hungary	100.0	72.5	12.6	5.1	1.8	11.9	4.3	7.4	8.0	2.1	5.7
Iceland	100.0	90.9	9.9	2.1	3.3	10.0	5.3	7.1	16.5	2.5	8.7
Ireland	100.0	51.2	3.5	1.6	3.3	5.5	3.8	3.9	7.1	1.7	4.1
Israel	100.0	66.4	12.7	1.3	2.6	10.9	4.1	4.6	7.3	3.0	5.2
Italy	100.0	68.5	11.4	1.5	6.1	9.0	5.1	5.8	9.9	2.0	4.5
Japan	100.0	65.1	7.4	2.3	2.0	9.0	3.1	8.4	8.6	2.0	6.9
Korea, Rep.	100.0	54.1	6.4	1.2	2.0	6.2	2.6	6.2	6.2	4.2	3.5
Latvia	100.0	76.6	17.3	5.2	3.3	13.1	2.4	5.8	6.7	1.7	6.3
Lithuania	100.0	82.0	22.7	5.0	3.9	11.5	3.9	7.0	8.6	1.8	5.3
Luxembourg	100.0	43.5	3.3	3.2	1.2	3.4	2.3	3.5	6.9	0.5	2.7
Macedonia, FYR	100.0	86.4	27.4	3.0	3.8	19.7	3.1	6.0	5.7	3.5	1.7
Malta	100.0	80.2	16.4	1.8	4.4	11.5	6.2	6.0	10.0	3.3	8.6
Mexico	100.0	79.2	23.2	2.6	2.5	7.9	6.4	3.2	14.8	1.0	2.2
Montenegro	100.0	82.3	26.0	3.8	2.7	17.3	2.9	6.2	4.0	4.7	2.2
Netherlands	100.0	60.3	8.8	1.6	3.4	6.7	3.8	4.5	5.9	2.6	6.1
New Zealand	100.0	73.0	11.3	2.8	3.4	10.0	4.5	4.4	13.8	2.0	9.5
Norway	100.0	44.3	5.5	1.0	2.2	6.4	2.8	3.9	5.2	1.5	5.0
Poland	100.0	75.7	17.6	4.3	2.0	16.7	2.8	6.4	4.4	1.5	4.8
Portugal	100.0	82.5	16.1	2.8	6.5	8.4	5.5	7.7	10.8	2.1	6.4
Romania	100.0	81.5	22.5	3.9	2.2	14.0	4.0	7.4	10.3	1.0	4.4
Russian Federation	100.0	67.2	18.0	4.6	3.8	8.8	2.1	5.5	6.6	1.9	3.6
Serbia	100.0	81.5	20.5	4.6	2.2	18.6	2.9	6.5	4.9	4.7	3.4
Slovak Republic	100.0	71.0	13.4	3.4	2.2	15.6	3.2	6.5	4.4	1.4	6.1
Slovenia	100.0	63.7	10.6	3.1	3.2	9.4	3.9	5.7	10.0	2.5	6.0
Spain	100.0	73.5	13.2	2.3	4.5	7.2	3.7	6.9	9.3	1.8	6.6
Sweden	100.0	61.0	7.8	1.6	3.0	9.5	3.0	5.4	7.1	2.6	6.1

Education	Restaurants and hotels	Miscellaneous goods and services	Net purchases abroad	Private individual consumption	Individual consumption by government	General government	Gross fixed capital formation	Machinery and equipment	Construction	Other products	Stocks	Net exports
3.3	**3.8**	**6.7**	**0.0**	**62.8**	**5.1**	**8.4**	**18.9**	**7.0**	**10.7**	**1.1**	**0**	**5**
4.6	4.9	6.0	-3.1	79.8	8.3	7.1	35.5	16.9	17.0	1.6	-4	-26
3.6	5.2	7.5	-0.9	57.9	4.6	9.4	29.8	16.4	11.1	2.4	0	-4
2.4	7.6	7.1	-4.6	54.1	5.0	4.6	22.6	13.8	7.5	1.3	1	8
2.5	2.6	9.1	1.7	51.3	6.0	4.9	25.2	15.6	7.4	2.3	1	6
5.7	6.8	6.8	-3.4	100.4	8.3	8.8	25.5	10.7	14.1	0.6	0	-44
6.4	8.8	3.6	-2.6	70.9	11.0	9.4	19.8	9.7	9.6	0.4	3	-14
2.5	3.8	9.1	0.5	55.6	5.9	5.6	23.0	10.8	10.7	1.5	1	6
4.2	4.9	6.0	-16.3	61.5	8.0	7.6	31.8	13.5	17.1	1.2	2	-13
3.4	9.4	9.8	-18.3	67.5	4.8	7.7	22.1	7.6	14.0	0.5	1	-5
3.6	4.3	5.6	-2.3	52.2	8.7	9.5	23.0	11.1	10.8	1.1	1	3
3.0	2.1	10.2	-0.2	45.9	9.1	5.9	25.6	14.9	6.4	4.2	1	9
5.1	4.4	6.4	-4.2	57.7	9.5	7.2	28.7	13.5	14.6	0.6	4	-9
2.8	3.0	8.3	-0.3	47.9	8.2	5.8	21.5	9.4	9.4	2.7	2	10
2.6	3.7	9.8	-0.9	60.3	8.1	5.4	21.9	10.4	9.4	2.2	1	-2
1.5	3.3	9.1	2.1	57.6	4.3	5.1	19.2	11.6	6.2	1.4	0	8
8.5	8.9	4.6	-4.2	60.8	9.6	13.0	21.7	6.4	14.4	1.3	0	-6
4.0	3.1	8.3	-1.5	59.0	10.1	7.3	20.7	10.6	9.0	1.1	1	-2
4.5	4.2	7.8	9.8	74.5	10.3	7.1	48.7	23.9	21.8	3.1	0	-47
2.6	6.4	7.2	0.6	42.1	5.3	3.7	22.9	9.1	12.7	1.1	0	22
5.1	2.6	7.9	-0.5	55.2	8.8	11.1	21.0	10.2	9.1	1.6	1	0
1.9	6.3	7.0	-1.7	60.0	5.4	6.0	25.6	14.6	8.3	2.6	0	0
1.9	4.3	8.4	0.8	55.3	5.5	6.1	26.1	12.5	9.9	3.7	0	2
2.9	3.2	8.7	0.9	48.8	3.0	6.2	35.2	12.0	20.9	2.3	2	3
6.1	3.4	4.2	1.2	66.4	9.1	9.2	27.9	16.2	11.0	0.7	4	-18
5.3	2.1	5.7	-0.9	71.3	10.2	6.0	18.2	9.0	8.5	0.7	2	-9
1.4	2.1	5.2	8.1	35.1	3.6	3.8	18.7	7.8	8.6	2.3	2	32
4.3	3.2	4.5	0.7	77.8	8.2	9.8	15.6	4.9	10.3	0.4	3	-15
3.3	11.7	9.5	-12.4	70.1	7.4	7.0	21.6	8.6	11.1	2.0	0	-9
4.8	5.5	5.9	-0.6	74.0	4.3	2.8	17.0	8.8	8.0	0.2	3	-2
3.9	0.9	6.4	1.3	73.2	9.3	23.1	17.4	6.9	9.3	1.2	-2	-20
2.4	2.6	12.2	0.3	48.0	7.2	7.6	19.2	9.7	6.7	2.8	0	13
3.0	6.5	6.6	-4.1	62.8	6.8	6.0	24.8	14.1	9.0	1.7	1	-5
1.7	1.7	5.6	2.1	35.3	5.2	4.8	19.2	9.6	6.1	3.5	3	29
4.3	1.6	9.6	-0.3	65.6	8.4	6.5	17.1	7.7	8.1	1.3	1	0
2.6	8.8	9.5	-3.7	71.4	5.8	6.0	27.9	9.9	13.8	4.2	1	-18
4.8	4.0	3.2	-0.2	70.3	10.0	9.3	21.4	10.4	10.4	0.7	0	-12
4.9	1.5	4.7	1.1	56.3	10.8	6.1	14.4	5.8	7.5	1.1	3	9
4.1	1.7	7.9	-0.3	70.1	10.4	6.3	17.7	8.2	8.7	0.9	15	-20
4.0	4.6	6.2	-0.1	61.7	8.1	9.7	23.1	12.5	9.2	1.4	2	-6
3.0	4.4	6.4	-4.0	54.6	6.7	5.9	29.3	13.5	14.6	1.3	2	-1
2.4	12.6	8.1	-5.0	64.1	6.3	5.9	31.8	12.0	13.9	5.9	0	-11
3.6	2.2	9.5	-0.1	45.1	10.6	6.0	20.2	13.5	3.9	2.7	0	13

(continued)

Economy	Gross domestic product	Actual individual consumption	Food and nonalcoholic beverages	Alcoholic beverages, tobacco, and narcotics	Clothing and footwear	Housing, water, electricity, gas, and other fuels	Furnishings, household equipment, and maintenance	Health	Transport	Communication	Recreation and culture
Switzerland	100.0	56.7	7.9	3.0	3.2	7.0	3.2	4.4	6.3	1.8	5.9
Turkey	100.0	77.0	19.8	2.6	4.6	20.9	5.7	2.0	6.7	2.3	1.7
United Kingdom	100.0	82.0	8.2	1.7	5.0	9.7	4.5	6.5	12.1	2.0	9.7
United States	100.0	80.8	8.0	1.7	4.6	8.3	4.9	6.7	16.9	1.3	8.1
Eurostat-OECD	**100.0**	**72.8**	**10.0**	**2.2**	**3.9**	**9.0**	**4.3**	**6.4**	**11.8**	**1.7**	**6.6**
Armenia	100.0	88.6	42.9	2.4	1.4	19.8	0.9	5.6	2.6	0.6	1.0
Azerbaijan	100.0	67.1	32.8	1.1	1.8	9.2	2.1	5.3	4.4	0.5	1.2
Belarus	100.0	77.1	24.2	3.0	2.7	13.8	1.7	7.9	3.7	4.9	2.3
Georgia	100.0	84.1	23.5	3.6	1.2	15.6	1.6	8.3	10.3	2.0	3.8
Kazakhstan	100.0	66.4	13.7	2.7	3.6	9.3	1.5	7.6	6.8	0.7	2.9
Kyrgyz Republic	100.0	93.5	27.2	5.9	2.8	20.6	1.4	7.1	6.5	1.0	1.4
Moldova	100.0	101.2	18.7	7.5	1.9	32.9	3.8	3.8	7.1	2.6	3.7
Russian Federation	100.0	67.1	17.8	4.6	3.8	8.8	2.1	5.5	6.7	1.9	3.7
Tajikistan	100.0	91.0	21.3	0.3	1.2	30.3	0.9	10.4	3.4	0.5	1.2
Ukraine	100.0	80.7	24.0	4.3	1.9	14.5	1.6	6.9	7.1	1.8	3.2
CIS	**100.0**	**70.1**	**19.1**	**4.3**	**3.4**	**10.3**	**1.9**	**5.9**	**6.5**	**1.9**	**3.4**
Angola	100.0	23.5	8.5	1.2	1.1	3.7	1.3	1.2	1.0	0.1	0.4
Benin	100.0	77.7	29.3	1.7	7.8	15.0	2.4	3.0	4.8	0.5	1.5
Botswana	100.0	26.9	5.6	2.3	1.8	3.1	1.6	1.5	3.4	0.9	0.5
Burkina Faso	100.0	73.0	30.1	5.8	3.5	10.5	5.2	2.2	3.6	0.3	1.1
Burundi	100.0	68.4	24.9	2.6	3.4	9.9	2.5	4.9	3.2	1.4	1.5
Cameroon	100.0	76.8	33.1	1.8	7.3	9.1	7.3	1.7	4.7	0.4	1.0
Cape Verde	100.0	91.7	33.9	1.7	2.9	16.9	4.2	3.4	5.9	2.6	3.1
Central African Republic	100.0	93.9	47.6	8.5	8.1	13.4	5.5	1.5	2.2	0.5	1.9
Chad	100.0	51.7	18.1	0.5	0.9	4.2	2.5	2.6	7.4	0.2	2.2
Comoros	100.0	79.0	53.9	0.8	4.7	10.8	0.2	1.9	0.5	0.6	0.5
Congo, Dem. Rep.	100.0	55.9	31.5	1.1	3.8	8.3	1.6	2.6	1.4	0.2	0.5
Congo, Rep.	100.0	35.3	10.9	1.3	0.7	5.7	1.0	2.4	1.9	0.8	0.6
Côte d'Ivoire	100.0	77.7	34.1	2.6	3.0	11.5	6.7	2.3	6.2	1.1	2.3
Djibouti	100.0	61.5	18.0	13.3	1.4	9.3	3.2	2.3	3.3	0.2	0.3
Egypt, Arab Rep.	100.0	72.9	28.8	1.8	5.3	7.1	2.8	5.7	3.5	1.0	1.6
Equatorial Guinea	100.0	30.1	10.5	1.1	1.1	4.7	1.0	3.2	2.1	0.5	0.4
Ethiopia	100.0	80.5	45.6	0.5	3.8	13.5	6.1	1.8	1.6	0.2	0.3
Gabon	100.0	30.7	9.2	0.7	1.4	4.6	0.7	2.5	1.6	0.6	0.7
Gambia, The	100.0	78.2	18.3	0.6	7.5	7.4	2.3	7.3	1.2	1.1	4.2
Ghana	100.0	80.1	30.1	1.4	8.6	12.2	4.5	5.8	3.8	0.2	2.2
Guinea	100.0	72.1	23.2	3.2	5.8	7.7	6.7	7.6	4.0	0.1	1.3
Guinea-Bissau	100.0	71.4	36.2	1.3	4.8	13.2	4.1	2.4	3.2	0.1	2.4
Kenya	100.0	89.8	29.5	2.3	3.5	11.8	4.6	8.8	7.5	1.0	4.8
Lesotho	100.0	120.9	37.6	3.6	14.0	12.4	6.4	19.1	5.0	1.0	1.3

Education	Restaurants and hotels	Miscellaneous goods and services	Net purchases abroad	Private individual consumption	Individual consumption by government	General government	Gross fixed capital formation	Machinery and equipment	Construction	Other products	Stocks	Net exports
2.1	4.8	8.7	-0.6	51.4	2.8	3.5	27.0	18.8	6.0	2.3	1	12
3.5	2.7	4.5	0.0	72.6	4.0	7.2	20.0	11.4	8.6	0.0	5	-10
2.2	7.2	12.5	1.7	68.9	8.4	6.5	19.6	11.0	5.5	3.1	1	-9
2.8	6.2	11.3	0.0	77.0	3.3	7.8	22.9	10.9	8.5	3.5	0	-12
2.8	**5.2**	**9.3**	**0.0**	**64.9**	**5.3**	**6.6**	**22.9**	**11.2**	**8.9**	**2.7**	**1**	**-3**
9.5	0.3	1.4	0.2	80.3	8.6	5.2	16.6	1.9	14.5	0.1	-2	-9
8.6	0.9	1.1	-1.7	53.6	13.9	4.4	26.8	14.2	7.9	4.7	-3	5
8.6	1.4	2.6	0.6	59.8	16.1	5.2	17.2	7.5	9.6	0.1	0	0
8.9	3.6	0.9	0.6	76.1	9.0	5.3	18.9	7.7	10.6	0.6	5	-13
12.9	1.7	2.7	-0.6	57.2	7.9	4.6	21.0	6.7	11.3	3.0	2	6
12.5	1.6	3.5	-0.2	75.5	19.6	7.1	6.2	1.8	4.1	0.3	0	-7
13.6	1.1	3.2	0.4	87.8	13.2	3.8	11.3	1.8	8.9	0.6	4	-20
4.9	1.5	4.7	1.1	56.3	10.8	6.1	14.4	5.9	7.5	1.1	3	10
19.3	0.1	0.7	1.1	60.7	33.1	6.7	2.8	1.4	1.1	0.3	4	-5
10.4	1.4	4.1	-0.2	65.8	13.9	4.8	13.5	5.7	7.2	0.6	1	0
6.6	**1.5**	**4.3**	**0.8**	**58.3**	**11.5**	**5.8**	**14.9**	**6.0**	**7.8**	**1.2**	**2**	**7**
1.4	0.6	3.1	0.0	21.6	1.9	12.4	38.2	13.4	24.8	0.0	0	26
4.1	5.3	3.8	-1.5	74.1	3.6	10.1	19.8	4.1	15.4	0.3	-1	-6
4.8	0.0	1.4	0.0	23.6	3.4	19.2	24.4	12.6	11.2	0.5	18	11
4.2	3.5	3.0	0.0	69.4	3.6	20.1	17.5	5.1	10.6	1.8	1	-11
10.1	1.6	2.8	-0.4	62.0	6.4	17.0	18.2	5.0	12.5	0.7	2	-5
3.7	4.2	1.8	0.8	73.8	3.0	7.9	14.4	6.3	8.0	0.2	2	-1
9.2	2.7	5.1	0.0	87.2	4.5	8.1	48.3	21.0	26.5	0.9	-1	-47
4.4	1.9	3.3	-5.1	91.8	2.1	7.6	7.2	1.3	4.7	1.1	0	-9
11.4	0.2	1.7	-0.1	39.4	12.3	25.0	14.2	4.8	6.3	3.1	4	5
4.7	0.0	0.0	0.5	78.6	0.4	23.6	11.5	4.4	6.5	0.6	2	-16
2.3	0.7	2.0	0.0	55.3	0.6	15.8	26.6	0.8	20.1	5.7	1	0
6.1	2.7	1.4	-0.3	28.6	6.6	11.1	11.7	2.2	9.4	0.1	0	42
2.3	1.1	3.6	1.0	75.6	2.1	9.1	5.5	3.0	2.2	0.2	2	5
6.3	1.4	2.8	-0.4	54.7	6.8	21.9	17.1	4.4	11.9	0.8	0	-1
9.8	1.7	4.4	-0.7	62.5	10.4	14.6	12.8	3.8	8.7	0.3	1	-1
2.3	1.1	2.1	0.0	29.1	1.0	5.8	26.3	16.0	6.4	3.9	-1	38
2.2	1.9	3.4	-0.4	78.3	2.2	11.3	17.0	3.1	13.6	0.3	0	-9
4.3	0.7	2.2	1.5	26.0	4.8	11.5	26.8	11.5	10.8	4.5	0	31
24.9	0.3	3.2	0.0	67.7	10.5	31.4	10.6	4.8	4.8	1.0	4	-24
6.8	0.0	4.6	0.0	78.0	2.1	6.3	28.4	18.7	8.6	1.2	0	-15
7.6	1.5	2.8	0.6	68.9	3.1	5.5	22.8	8.2	13.4	1.2	2	-2
3.1	0.3	0.3	0.0	69.7	1.7	29.5	15.1	5.5	9.0	0.6	4	-21
9.0	5.2	4.7	-2.9	83.7	6.1	7.0	14.5	6.6	7.8	0.1	-2	-9
15.6	0.2	4.6	0.1	112.6	8.3	7.4	25.6	4.5	21.1	0.0	0	-54

(*continued*)

Economy	Gross domestic product	Actual individual consumption	Food and nonalcoholic beverages	Alcoholic beverages, tobacco, and narcotics	Clothing and footwear	Housing, water, electricity, gas, and other fuels	Furnishings, household equipment, and maintenance	Health	Transport	Communication	Recreation and culture
Liberia	100.0	71.1	15.7	3.0	8.9	8.8	3.3	4.6	0.9	1.1	1.1
Madagascar	100.0	78.6	38.2	1.6	3.5	13.2	3.1	3.0	1.5	0.3	0.5
Malawi	100.0	74.0	14.4	1.2	2.3	13.9	1.6	10.1	6.4	0.6	6.8
Mali	100.0	71.8	31.8	2.0	4.2	9.1	4.3	3.1	5.8	0.4	2.1
Mauritania	100.0	68.2	36.5	0.8	4.9	8.0	2.7	3.9	2.7	0.4	0.7
Mauritius	100.0	74.1	20.6	4.0	4.3	14.4	4.8	4.4	5.9	2.6	3.7
Morocco	100.0	63.7	26.3	1.3	3.5	11.6	3.6	2.3	5.8	2.7	2.5
Mozambique	100.0	81.0	47.3	2.0	4.3	10.6	1.8	3.2	2.0	0.1	1.5
Namibia	100.0	61.4	19.1	2.3	3.8	6.9	3.6	7.1	6.4	0.4	1.8
Niger	100.0	77.7	32.6	2.0	7.8	10.7	3.7	2.7	4.6	0.3	3.4
Nigeria	100.0	71.0	30.0	0.7	4.9	12.7	5.8	2.7	3.5	0.1	1.0
Rwanda	100.0	74.0	34.9	7.9	1.9	8.6	2.8	3.6	2.4	0.2	0.7
São Tomé and Príncipe	100.0	96.9	49.7	3.9	2.9	11.7	3.2	6.1	7.4	0.7	1.3
Senegal	100.0	80.7	37.0	3.1	4.7	11.4	5.4	4.0	2.6	3.7	2.9
Sierra Leone	100.0	89.8	28.6	2.8	7.9	14.4	1.9	14.3	1.8	0.8	2.7
South Africa	100.0	70.4	16.8	3.7	4.1	8.3	4.0	6.5	11.2	1.3	3.1
Sudan	100.0	83.8	42.6	0.7	5.5	12.6	6.0	2.1	6.3	0.1	3.1
Swaziland	100.0	74.6	30.7	0.5	3.2	7.7	4.3	14.1	4.3	0.6	1.9
Tanzania	100.0	81.3	54.6	2.2	6.2	7.2	3.1	1.7	2.6	0.0	0.8
Togo	100.0	102.1	44.2	4.6	4.9	16.1	2.5	2.8	12.4	0.8	1.9
Tunisia	100.0	66.9	19.2	2.5	3.9	10.5	5.7	3.8	5.0	0.7	1.5
Uganda	100.0	82.1	31.1	3.6	2.4	16.5	3.9	5.0	3.2	0.5	1.7
Zambia	100.0	76.0	9.5	0.1	4.7	20.1	4.8	8.6	6.9	0.1	9.6
Zimbabwe	100.0	80.0	32.4	3.0	10.1	11.2	5.0	1.0	2.6	0.4	1.8
Africa	**100.0**	**70.5**	**26.6**	**2.1**	**4.5**	**9.6**	**4.1**	**4.5**	**5.5**	**0.9**	**2.0**
Bahrain	100.0	48.7	12.0	0.3	3.7	5.1	5.4	3.2	7.9	0.8	1.4
Egypt, Arab Rep.	100.0	77.5	30.7	1.3	6.2	10.5	2.5	5.1	7.7	0.7	3.7
Iraq	100.0	55.3	17.9	0.3	3.2	4.0	6.8	9.6	6.1	0.8	0.6
Jordan	100.0	91.0	31.3	2.6	6.0	7.5	3.3	6.1	14.3	3.3	1.3
Kuwait	100.0	33.8	7.5	0.1	2.3	3.8	5.4	1.3	7.3	0.7	1.1
Lebanon	100.0	81.5	31.3	1.7	3.5	8.3	5.5	5.3	9.7	0.7	2.6
Oman	100.0	39.2	11.3	0.2	2.8	2.9	2.4	1.4	7.7	1.1	0.9
Qatar	100.0	19.9	3.7	0.1	1.3	1.2	1.5	1.2	6.7	0.8	0.6
Saudi Arabia	100.0	35.0	7.9	0.2	2.8	3.0	4.1	2.6	6.2	0.5	0.9
Syrian Arab Republic	100.0	75.1	35.2	0.2	6.1	11.6	2.6	6.5	3.3	0.3	1.1
Yemen, Rep.	100.0	65.1	25.9	1.6	6.0	8.4	2.2	3.6	5.3	0.2	0.9
Western Asia	**100.0**	**51.5**	**17.1**	**0.6**	**3.9**	**5.7**	**3.7**	**3.8**	**6.8**	**0.7**	**1.6**
WORLD	**100**	**68**	**12**	**2**	**4**	**8**	**4**	**6**	**9**	**2**	**5**

Source: ICP 2005.

Education	Restaurants and hotels	Miscellaneous goods and services	Net purchases abroad	Private individual consumption	Individual consumption by government	General government	Gross fixed capital formation	Machinery and equipment	Construction	Other products	Stocks	Net exports
17.9	0.4	5.4	0.0	69.0	2.1	8.3	20.4	17.9	2.4	0.0	15	-15
12.7	1.1	0.8	-0.9	74.7	3.9	13.2	17.1	6.0	10.7	0.5	2	-11
7.9	1.4	7.2	0.2	73.6	0.4	10.2	26.0	5.8	20.1	0.0	2	-12
5.4	1.5	2.1	0.0	67.7	4.1	16.9	12.2	8.5	3.7	0.0	7	-8
4.4	0.5	2.2	0.5	63.2	5.0	18.0	53.0	17.5	34.1	1.5	6	-46
6.5	2.6	2.9	-2.5	65.0	9.1	10.6	20.6	8.1	12.5	0.0	1	-7
3.7	3.4	3.3	-6.4	59.9	3.8	9.2	32.6	17.0	13.4	2.1	2	-8
5.7	0.3	1.7	0.4	75.7	5.3	9.8	19.6	7.7	11.9	0.0	2	-12
7.5	1.6	5.7	-4.7	53.1	8.2	14.2	27.9	15.2	11.4	1.3	2	-5
2.9	3.7	3.4	-0.1	75.4	2.3	13.5	18.9	5.3	13.1	0.5	2	-12
5.5	0.4	3.5	0.0	67.0	4.0	8.2	11.4	9.9	1.5	0.0	0	9
8.1	1.2	1.7	-0.1	68.2	5.8	18.0	18.3	5.9	12.4	0.0	1	-11
6.6	1.1	2.0	0.5	92.8	4.1	17.0	18.1	7.8	9.0	1.3	2	-34
3.5	0.7	3.2	-1.6	76.7	3.9	8.2	23.9	4.7	18.3	0.8	3	-16
9.8	0.7	4.0	0.0	83.3	6.5	18.4	10.7	5.3	5.2	0.2	0	-19
4.8	1.5	6.4	-1.4	64.4	6.0	9.8	19.5	13.4	6.1	0.0	2	-1
1.2	0.1	3.2	0.4	83.4	0.4	5.9	16.4	9.2	7.2	0.0	4	-10
4.7	0.4	2.4	0.0	71.3	3.3	8.1	20.7	6.8	12.7	1.2	1	-5
1.4	0.0	1.4	0.0	80.4	0.9	6.6	20.1	7.1	12.5	0.4	0	-8
7.3	2.2	3.1	-0.8	97.6	4.5	11.2	13.4	4.6	8.1	0.6	1	-27
2.8	11.8	3.6	-3.9	62.4	4.5	9.2	24.8	7.6	16.6	0.7	0	-1
10.7	2.1	1.5	0.0	75.5	6.7	10.4	17.3	3.4	13.8	0.0	0	-10
7.6	0.0	4.0	0.0	67.9	8.1	12.4	24.6	12.4	12.2	0.0	1	-14
11.6	0.2	0.9	0.0	68.2	11.8	18.1	11.8	6.7	5.1	0.0	1	-11
5.9	**1.9**	**4.1**	**-1.0**	**64.9**	**5.6**	**10.9**	**18.2**	**8.9**	**8.8**	**0.5**	**1**	**-1**
2.5	0.8	2.7	2.9	45.6	3.1	3.5	26.3	7.2	19.0	0.1	1	20
3.9	1.4	4.5	-0.7	73.8	3.7	6.4	16.5	4.7	11.2	0.6	1	-1
4.7	0.1	1.2	0.0	45.7	9.6	29.0	8.5	4.9	2.3	1.2	7	1
6.8	3.6	4.7	0.3	83.1	7.9	8.9	38.2	14.2	20.0	4.0	4	-43
1.8	0.7	1.8	0.0	31.3	2.5	6.6	22.3	3.5	18.8	0.0	3	35
6.0	4.7	4.9	-3.0	78.0	3.5	8.4	35.8	6.2	23.5	6.1	0	-26
2.3	0.6	4.9	0.6	36.2	3.1	11.3	25.9	13.5	8.5	3.9	0	23
1.5	0.3	1.0	0.0	17.8	2.1	5.1	40.7	21.1	18.3	1.3	3	31
3.0	1.1	1.7	1.3	30.3	4.8	8.7	23.7	10.4	11.2	2.0	2	31
6.5	1.4	0.3	0.0	68.2	6.9	6.4	25.9	9.5	16.4	0.0	-8	1
4.9	1.2	5.0	-0.1	59.5	5.6	7.7	25.1	5.4	19.1	0.5	0	3
3.5	**1.2**	**2.6**	**0.3**	**47.0**	**4.6**	**9.1**	**22.5**	**8.4**	**12.7**	**1.4**	**1**	**16**
3	**4**	**8**	**0**	**61**	**5**	**7**	**25**	**10**	**13**	**2**	**1**	**-1**

NOTES

1. The World Bank classification is as follows: low-income countries: per capita income (using exchange rates) below \$905; middle-income countries: per capita income between \$905 and \$11,115; high-income countries: per capita income greater than \$11,115.
2. Algeria did not participate in the 2005 ICP.
3. The five geographic ICP regions in 2005 were Africa, Asia-Pacific, Commonwealth of Independent States (CIS), South America, and Western Asia. The Eurostat–Organisation for Economic Co-operation and Development (OECD) members constituted a sixth region.
4. The Balassa-Samuelson model (Balassa 1964; Samuelson 1964) explains higher price levels in more developed countries by their higher relative productivity in traded goods (versus nontraded). Bhagwati (1984) explains it with cheaper services (which are essentially wages) in poorer countries.
5. Reformulating the regression in log per capita GDP in PPP terms $[\ln(Y^{PPP}_i) = \ln(Y_i) - \ln(PLI_i)]$, we obtain an equivalent presentation:

$$\ln(Y^{PPP}_i) = \underset{(0.0359)}{-0.0774} + \underset{(0.0115)}{0.7869} \ln(Y_i) + \hat{\varepsilon}_i$$

   $R^2 = 0.9702$; standard error of regression (MSE) = 0.2341.

   Note that the standard errors of the coefficients and MSE remained the same, and thus the predictive power of the regression. The formulation says that for each percent of increase in nominal per capita GDP, the real per capita GDP increases by 0.7869 percent and the PLI increases by 0.2131 percent (in relative terms, versus the United States).
6. Russia took part in two regional comparisons, Eurostat-OECD and CIS.
7. In the past, using the GK method, for example, would lead to increases in poorer countries' GDP. See the discussion about the IDB method in the next section.
8. The Gerschenkron effect in international comparisons is an upward bias in the GDP of countries with price structures dissimilar to the "international" price vector. Because the OECD countries greatly influence the international price structure in the GK formula, using the GK leads to an increase in the poorer countries' GDP. The IDB minimizes this bias by allowing all countries to have the same effect on the "international" price structure.

REFERENCES

Balassa, Bela. 1964. "The Purchasing Power Parity Doctrine: A Reappraisal." *Journal of Political Economy* 72 (6): 584–96.

Bhagwati, J. 1984. "Why Are Services Cheaper in Poor Countries?" *Economic Journal* 94: 279–86.

Cleveland, William S., and Susan J. Devlin. 1988. "Locally Weighted Regression: An Approach to Regression Analysis by Local Fitting." *Journal of the American Statistical Association* 83 (403): 596–610.

Samuelson, Paul. 1964. "Theoretical Notes on Trade Problems." *Review of Economics and Statistics* 46 (2): 145–54.

World Bank. 2008. *Global Purchasing Power Parities and Real Expenditures: 2005 International Comparison Program.* http://siteresources.worldbank.org/ICPINT/Resources/icp-final.pdf.

CHAPTER 20

Absolute Poverty Measures for the Developing World, 1981–2008

Shaohua Chen and Martin Ravallion

For the purposes of measuring poverty in the world as a whole, the World Bank's "$1 a day" measures have aimed to apply a common standard, anchored to what "poverty" means in the world's poorest countries.[1] By this view, two people with the same purchasing power over commodities should be treated the same way—both are either poor or not poor—even if they live in different countries.[2] And by focusing on how poverty is defined in the poorest countries, the $1 a day line gives the global poverty measures a salience in focusing on the world's poorest in absolute terms.

Implementing this approach requires data on prices to permit comparisons between countries. International comparisons of economic aggregates have long recognized that market exchange rates—which tend to equate purchasing power in terms of internationally traded goods—are deceptive, given that some commodities are not traded; this includes services but also many goods, including some food staples. Furthermore, there is likely to be a systematic effect, stemming from the fact that low real wages in developing countries entail that labor-intensive, nontraded goods tend to be relatively cheap. In the literature, this is known as the "Balassa-Samuelson effect" (see Balassa 1964; Samuelson 1964). And it is the now widely accepted explanation for an empirical finding known as the "Penn effect," which is that comparisons of gross domestic product (GDP) based on market exchange rates tend to understate the real incomes of developing countries.[3] Similarly, market exchange rates overstate the extent of poverty in the world. For this reason, global economic measurement, including poverty measurement, has used purchasing power parity (PPP) rates rather than market exchange rates. A PPP is the conversion rate for a given currency into a reference currency (invariably the U.S. dollar) with the aim of assuring parity in terms of purchasing power over commodities, both internationally traded and nontraded.

This chapter reports on a major update of the World Bank's global poverty estimates. It draws on three main data sources. The first source is the 2005 International Comparison Program (ICP). The main data source for estimating PPPs has been the price surveys carried out within countries for the ICP. This started in 1968 with PPP estimates for just 10 countries, based on rather crude price surveys.[4] A better-funded round of the ICP in 2005, managed globally by the World Bank's Development Data Group, introduced a number of improvements in the data and estimation methods for PPPs (World Bank 2008). The new ICP data imply some dramatic revisions to past estimates, consistent with the view that the old ICP data had underestimated the cost of living in poor countries. The Penn effect is still evident, but it was overstated in the past.

The 2005 ICP also greatly expanded country coverage. Particularly notable is the fact that China participated officially for the first time, and the results have naturally attracted much attention, given that they suggest that China's economy in 2005 was 40 percent smaller than thought.[5] The new PPP for China is about half the market exchange rate; prior estimates for 1993 had suggested it was about one-quarter of the market rate.[6]

While the 2005 ICP round was clearly a significant advance over previous rounds, one problem was that (like prior rounds) there was a degree of "urban bias" in the ICP price surveys in that the sampling of outlets for collecting prices did not always properly represent rural areas, where, in most developing countries, prices tend to be lower. This clearly matters to poverty measurement. Based on the information provided by the ICP team at the World Bank (drawing on information from regional ICP offices), we identify a number of countries where such a bias is likely (including China), and we implement a correction, drawing on supplementary data on the differentials in national poverty lines between urban and rural areas.

The second data source is a new compilation of poverty lines for developing countries provided by Ravallion, Chen, and Sangraula (2008). Using these data, we implement an updated international poverty line and test robustness to that choice. Recognizing that the new PPPs also change the U.S. dollar value of national poverty lines in the poorest countries, our international poverty line of $1.25 per day in 2005 is deliberately lower than the 2005 value in the United States of our old international line. The new line is the mean of the national poverty lines for the poorest 15 countries in terms of consumption per capita. To test the robustness of our main qualitative results to the choice of poverty line, we also give results for $1.00 and $2.00 per day in 2005 prices. The lower bound (not to be confused with the old "$1 a day" line, which was not in 2005 prices) corresponds fairly closely to the national poverty line used by India (prior to an upward revision in 2010 to India's official poverty lines), while the $2.00 line is the median poverty line found among developing countries as a whole (Ravallion, Chen, and Sangraula 2008).

The third data source is our update of the coverage of the household survey database. As far as possible, we rely on household surveys for measuring poverty, following past practice. In this chapter, we draw on 850 surveys spanning 1979–2011 and 125 countries. Our methods of analyzing these data follow Chen and Ravallion (2010). The international poverty line is converted to local currencies in the ICP benchmark year and is then converted to the prices prevailing at the time of the relevant household survey using the best available consumer price index (CPI) for that country. (Equivalently, the survey data on household consumption or income for the survey year are expressed in the prices of the ICP base year and then converted to PPP dollars.) The poverty rate is then calculated from that survey. All intertemporal comparisons are real, as assessed using the country-specific CPI. We make estimates at three-year intervals over 1981–2008. Interpolation/extrapolation methods are used to line up the survey-based estimates with these reference years, including 2008.

The 2005 ICP Round and Its Implications for Global Poverty Measures

The 2005 ICP round was the most complete and thorough assessment to date of how the cost of living varies across countries. The world was divided into six regions with different product lists for each.[7] Even though all regions participated in the 2005 ICP, the participation rate was lower for South America. The ICP collected primary data on the prices for 600–1,000 (depending on the region) goods and services grouped under 155 "basic headings" deemed to be comparable across countries. The prices were typically obtained from a large sample of outlets in each country. The price surveys were conducted by the national statistics offices in each country, under the supervision of the regional authorities.[8]

The 2005 ICP was a clear improvement over earlier rounds. First, the number of countries participating was larger (146, as compared with 117 in 1993). This is also the first time that a number of countries—including China, to which we return—participated in the ICP. Second, the surveys were implemented on a more scientific basis. The 2005 ICP used stricter standards in defining internationally comparable qualities for the goods identified in the ICP price surveys. Third, new methods were used for measuring government compensation and housing. Adjustments were also made for the lower average productivity of public sector workers in developing countries (lowering the imputed value of the services derived from public administration, education, and health). Fourth, Ring comparisons (linking regional PPP estimates through global prices) were carried out for more countries (18 in all—a marked improvement over past ICP rounds). Otherwise, the PPPs calculated from the ICP data (and reported in World Bank 2008) followed standard methods—as in the past, the Bank uses a multilateral extension of the bilateral Fisher price index known as the Gini-Éltetö-Köves-Szulc (GEKS) method.[9]

Although these are clear improvements, the 2005 PPPs still have some limitations.[10] For example, there is a problem of urban bias in the ICP price surveys for a number of countries (the next section describes our methods of addressing this problem). As argued in Ravallion, Datt, and van de Walle (1991), a further concern is that the weights attached to different commodities in the conventional PPP rate may not be appropriate for the poor. Deaton and Dupriez (2008) have estimated "PPPs for the poor" for a subset of countries with the required data, but the results do not suggest that the implied reweighting has much impact on the consumption PPP, as we show in Chen and Ravallion (2010).[11] Another limitation is that the PPP is a national average. Just as the cost of living tends to be lower in poorer countries, one expects it to be lower in poorer regions within one country, especially in rural areas. In Ravallion, Chen, and Sangraula (2007), we allowed for the urban-rural cost of living differences facing the poor, and provided an urban-rural breakdown of our prior global poverty measures using the 1993 PPP. We plan to update these estimates in future work.

Some dramatic revisions of past PPPs were implied by the 2005 ICP round, not least for the two most populous developing countries, China and India (neither of which actually participated in the 1993 ICP). For example, the 1993 consumption PPP used for China was ¥ 1.42 to the U.S. dollar (updating an earlier estimate by Ruoen and Chen 1995), while the new estimate based on the 2005 ICP is ¥ 3.46 (¥ 4.09 if one excludes government consumption). The corresponding "price level index" (PPP divided by the market exchange rate, US = 100) went from 25 percent in 1993 to 52 percent in 2005. So the Penn effect is still evident, but the size of this effect has declined markedly, with a new PPP at about half the market exchange rate rather than one-quarter. Adjusting solely for the inflation rates in the United States and China, one would have expected the 2005 PPP to be ¥ 1.80, not ¥ 3.46. Similarly, India's 1993 consumption PPP was Rs 7.0, while the 2005 PPP is Rs 16, and the price level index rose from 23 percent to 35 percent. If one updated the 1993 PPP for inflation, the result would be a 2005 PPP of Rs 11 rather than Rs 16.

These PPP revisions have important implications for our global poverty measures. At any given poverty line in $PPP, the poverty count will tend to rise, given that the bulk of PPPs have risen for developing countries. However, the same changes in the PPPs also alter the international poverty line because it is anchored to the national poverty lines in the poorest countries. Next, we turn to the international poverty line.

International Poverty Line

In setting an international poverty line using the 2005 ICP, we follow the same approach used in our past work—namely, that the line should be representative of the national lines found in the poorest countries—in the spirit of the original "$1 a day" line (Ravallion, Datt, and van de Walle 1991; World Bank 1990). For this purpose, Ravallion, Chen, and Sangraula (2008) compiled a new set of national poverty lines for developing countries drawn from the World Bank's country-specific *Poverty Assessments* and the Poverty Reduction Strategy Papers prepared by the governments of the countries concerned. While the Ravallion, Datt, and van de Walle (1991) data set on national poverty lines was drawn from sources for the 1980s, the new and larger compilation produced by Ravallion, Chen, and Sangraula (2008) are all post-1990, such that in no case do the proximate sources overlap. These national poverty lines were converted to a common currency using the new set of household consumption PPPs based on the 2005 round of the ICP.

Figure 20.1 plots the poverty lines compiled by Ravallion, Chen, and Sangraula (2008) converted to $PPPs per day against log private consumption per capita also at 2005 purchasing power parity. Complete data are available for the 74 developing countries shown in figure 20.1. The figure also includes a nonparametric regression of the national poverty lines against log mean consumption. Above a certain point, the poverty line rises with mean consumption. The overall elasticity of the poverty line to mean consumption is about 0.7. However, the slope (and hence elasticity) is essentially zero among the poorest 20 or so countries, where absolute poverty clearly dominates.

On the basis of the pattern evident in figure 20.1, Ravallion, Chen, and Sangraula (2008) proposed an international poverty line of $1.25 per day for 2005, which is the mean of the lines found in the poorest 15 countries in terms of consumption per capita: Chad, Ethiopia, The Gambia, Ghana, Guinea-Bissau, Malawi, Mali, Mozambique, Nepal, Niger, Rwanda, Sierra Leone, Tanzania, Tajikistan, and Uganda. (Their median poverty line is very similar, at $1.27 per day.) Consumption per capita for this group ranges from $1.03 to $1.87 per day with a mean of $1.40 per day. The level of this poverty line is quite robust to the choice of the poorest 15 countries (taking plus or minus five countries ranked by consumption per capita). However, it makes sense to focus on the poorest 15, since the econometric tests reported by Ravallion, Chen, and Sangraula imply that national poverty lines tend to rise with consumption per person when it exceeds about $2.00 per day, which is near the upper bound of the consumption levels found among these 15 countries. Of course, there is still a variance in the national poverty lines at any given level of mean consumption, including among the poorest countries. The poverty lines found among the poorest 15 countries vary from $0.70 to $1.90 per day, and Ravallion, Chen, and Sangraula estimate the robust standard error of the $1.25 line to be $0.10 per day.

We use the same PPPs to convert the international lines to local currency. As noted at the outset of this chapter, the main source of sampling bias in the 2005 ICP appears to be that the surveys were largely confined to urban areas in some countries. For example, the ICP survey for China was confined to 11 cities. Although the survey included some surrounding rural areas of these cities, it cannot be considered representative of rural China—evidence on this point

FIGURE 20.1 National Poverty Lines Plotted against Mean Consumption

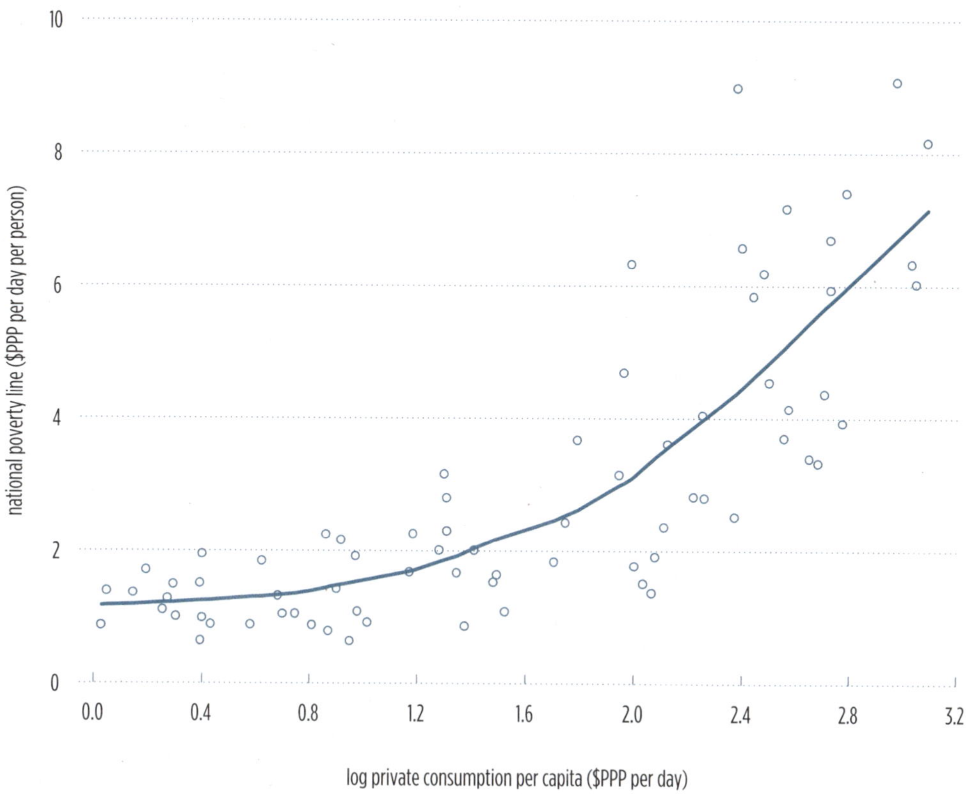

is provided by Chen and Ravallion (2008a). Based on ICP sampling information, we treat the 2005 consumption PPPs as urban PPPs for Argentina, Bolivia, Brazil, Cambodia, Chile, China, Colombia, Ecuador, Pakistan, Peru, Thailand, and Uruguay. We then use existing differentials in urban-rural poverty lines at the country level for these countries (from Ravallion, Chen, and Sangraula 2007) to correct the national PPP for the purpose of measuring poverty. For India, the ICP included rural areas, but they were underrepresented. We derived urban and rural poverty lines consistent with both the urban-rural differential in the national poverty lines and the relevant features of the design of the ICP samples for India.[12]

Household Survey Data

We have estimated all poverty measures ourselves from the primary (unit record or tabulated) sample survey data rather than relying on preexisting poverty measures. And all of our previous estimates have been updated to assure internal consistency. Households are ranked by either consumption or income per person. The distributions are weighted by household size and sample expansion factors. Thus our poverty counts give the number of people living in households with per capita consumption or income below the international poverty line. The primary data come in various forms, ranging from microdata (the most common) to specially designed grouped tabulations from the raw data, constructed following our guidelines.

Our reliance on survey data merits comment in the light of a debate in the literature about the implications for global poverty measures of the discrepancies found between aggregate household consumption as estimated from surveys and the private consumption component of domestic absorption in the national accounts, which tends to be higher than the survey mean. Some researchers have argued that the survey mean should be ignored and replaced by consumption per capita from the national accounts, though still using the surveys for measuring inequality.[13] This will yield lower poverty measures for most countries; for some countries (including India) it will also yield a higher rate of poverty reduction over time. However, other researchers (including us) have argued that there is no basis for assuming that the gap between the survey mean and national accounts consumption is entirely due to errors in the surveys. The national accounts numbers are no less questionable in many developing countries, and the discrepancy between the two data sources reflects a number of real factors, including differences in what is being included in the two measures (Deaton 2005; Ravallion 2000, 2003).[14] Nor is it plausible that the discrepancy is distribution-neutral in that the surveys get inequality right and the mean wrong. There is likely to be some underreporting or selective compliance in a household survey, but it would seem unlikely that these sources of error would only affect the mean and not the measure of inequality.[15]

We draw on 850 surveys for 125 countries. The most recent survey for each country is used for our 2008 estimate; in those surveys about 2.1 million households were interviewed. Overall, the surveys were conducted mostly by national statistics offices as part of their routine operations. Not all the available surveys are included. A survey was dropped if there were known to be serious comparability problems with the rest of the data set. Also, we do not use surveys for 2006 or 2007 when we already have a survey for 2008—the latest reference year for which we provide estimates in this chapter. As in past work, we have tried to eliminate obvious comparability problems, either by re-estimating the consumption/income aggregates or the more radical step of dropping a survey. However, there are problems with which we cannot deal. For example, it is known that differences in survey methods (such as questionnaire design) can create non-negligible differences in the estimates obtained for consumption or income.

Following past practice, poverty is assessed using household per capita expenditure on consumption or household income per capita as measured from the national sample surveys.[16] When there is a choice, we use consumption in preference to income on the basis that consumption is likely to be the better measure of current welfare on both theoretical and practical grounds.[17] Of the 850 surveys, 521 allow us to estimate the distribution of consumption expenditures. This is true of all the surveys used in the Middle East and North Africa, South Asia, and Sub-Saharan Africa, though income surveys are more common in Latin America.[18] Given that savings and credit can be used to smooth consumption from income shocks, one expects higher inequality for income than for consumption for the same place and data.

The measures of consumption (or income when consumption is unavailable) in our survey data set are reasonably comprehensive, including both cash spending and imputed values for consumption from own production. But we acknowledge that even the best consumption data may not adequately reflect certain "nonmarket" dimensions of welfare, such as access to certain public services, or intrahousehold inequalities. For these reasons, our poverty measures need to be supplemented by other data, such as on infant and child mortality, in order to obtain a more complete picture of how living standards are evolving.

We use standard poverty measures for which the aggregate measure is the (population-weighted) sum of individual measures. In this chapter, we report three such poverty measures.[19] The first measure is the *headcount index*, given by the percentage of the population living in households with consumption or income per person below the poverty line. We also give estimates of the *number of poor*, as obtained by applying the estimated headcount index to the population of each region under the assumption that the countries without surveys are a random subsample of the region. Our third measure is the *poverty gap index*, which is the mean distance below the poverty line as a proportion of the line where the mean is taken over the whole population, counting the nonpoor as having zero poverty gaps.

Having converted the international poverty line at purchasing power parity to the local currency in 2005 prices, we convert it to the prices prevailing at each survey date using the best available country-specific consumer price index.[20] The weights in this index may or may not accord well with consumer budget shares at the poverty line. In periods of relative price shifts, this will bias our comparisons of the incidence of poverty over time, depending on the extent of utility-compensated substitution possibilities for people at the poverty line.

Given the steep rise in food prices around 2008, we made an extra effort to ensure that the price indexes we were using adequately reflected those increases at the country level. This step was carried out in consultation with the World Bank's poverty experts for each country. In some cases, such as India, we were already using CPIs that were anchored reasonably well to the consumption behavior of the poor, so nothing needed to be done. However, for about 15 countries (including China) for which food prices increased faster than other prices, we determined that the currently available CPI attached too low a weight to food, and we reweighted the index to assure that its food share accorded reasonably well with food spending patterns in a neighborhood of the poverty line. For another 22 countries, we used CPIs provided by the Bank's country offices that were deemed to adequately reflect the rise in food prices. Most of these showed higher inflation than the CPI from the World Bank's Development Data Platform (DDP).

In the remaining 75 countries in our database, the CPI is from the DDP. As a check, we compared the implied rates of inflation with the food price index produced by the International Labour Organization (ILO). For 65 of these countries, the rate of inflation between 2005 and 2008 was over 90 percent of the rate implied by the ILO's food price index. (In 15 countries, the inflation rate was actually higher than the ILO food price index, and for 39 it was over 95 percent.) In the remaining 10 countries, the CPI increased by less than 90 percent of the ILO index. We cannot rule out the possibility that the price indexes we have used for these 10 countries are understating price increases for the poor over the period 2005–08, although the countries concerned represent only 3 percent of total population in the developing world, and so the problem is minor.

The population weights for urban and rural poverty measures, as well as across countries, are also from the World Bank's DDP.

We started the series in 1981 and made estimates at three-year intervals, up to 2008. Of the 125 countries, 20 have only one survey, 15 have two surveys, 12 have three surveys, while 78 have four or more surveys over the period, of which 31 have 10 or more surveys. If there is only one survey for a country, then we estimate measures for each reference year by applying the growth rate in real private consumption per person from the national accounts to the survey mean—assuming that the Lorenz curve for that country does not change.[21] This seems to be the best option for dealing with this problem, though there can be no guarantee that the Lorenz curve would not have shifted or that a survey-based measure of consumption would have grown at the same rate as private consumption in the national accounts. For example, growth in the latter might reflect growth in spending by nonprofit organizations (which are not separated from households in the national accounts for most developing countries) rather than household spending (Ravallion 2003).

For those countries with multiple surveys, we use the annual national accounts data for interpolation purposes given the irregular spacing of the surveys. We first estimate mean consumption at the reference year using the national accounts growth rate between the survey year and the reference year. Suppose the reference year is 1993 and we have two surveys for, say, 1989 and 1995. We have two means at the reference year based on two surveys, M93(89) and M93(95), where M93(*t*) is the estimated mean for 1993 using the survey for year *t*. Based on the 1989 distribution and M93(89), we get H93(89), the headcount index obtained using the 1993 mean and the 1989 distribution. Similarly, based on the 1995 distribution and M93, we get H93(95). The poverty headcount for 1993 is then estimated by the weighted average of H93(89) and H93(95).[22]

In the aggregate, 90 percent of the population of the developing world is represented by surveys within two years of 2008.[23] Survey coverage by region varies from 47 percent of the population of the Middle East and North Africa to 98 percent of the population of South Asia. Naturally, the further back we go, the fewer the number of surveys, reflecting the expansion in household survey data collection for developing countries since the 1980s. And coverage deteriorates in the last year or two of the series because of the lags in survey processing.

Most regions are quite well covered from the latter half of the 1980s (East and South Asia being well covered from 1981 on).[24] Not surprisingly, the coverage is weak in Eastern Europe and Central Asia for the 1980s; many of these countries did not officially exist then. More worrying is the weak coverage for Sub-Saharan Africa in the 1980s; indeed, our estimates for the early 1980s rely heavily on projections based on distributions around 1990. Table 20.1 gives the average survey year by region for each reference year.

Comparing table 20.1 with the corresponding table in Chen and Ravallion (2008b) reveals how much improvement there has been in reducing the lags in survey data availability. In 2004 and 2008, we reported results (see Chen and Ravallion 2004, 2008b) for reference years (2001 and 2005) that were three years prior to the time of writing (namely, 2001, 2005, versus 2008). Table 20.2 gives the average lag in survey data availability by region (where zero means no lag for the latest reference year). The overall mean lag fell between 2001 and 2005 from 1.6 to 0.6 years, but only fell slightly (to 0.5 years) between 2005 and 2008. For the region with the lowest mean lag for 2001, East Asia and Pacific, the average lag is down to zero. For the region with the highest lag in 2001, Sub-Saharan Africa, the lag has also fallen appreciably, from 4.0 to 1.4 years. The Middle East and North Africa is now the region with the highest mean lag in survey data availability, 2.9 years, and the lag has actually increased in that region—the only one in which this has happened.

TABLE 20.1 Average Date of Surveys Used for Each Reference Year by Region

	Average date of surveys used for each reference year									
Region	**1981**	**1984**	**1987**	**1990**	**1993**	**1996**	**1999**	**2002**	**2005**	**2008**
East Asia and Pacific	1982.2	1984.5	1987.1	1990.1	1993.0	1995.9	1999.1	2001.9	2004.9	2008.0
Eastern Europe and Central Asia	1988.5	1988.5	1988.7	1990.9	1993.0	1996.5	1998.8	2001.7	2004.8	2007.5
Latin America and the Caribbean	1983.9	1985.0	1987.0	1990.3	1993.0	1996.0	1999.0	2001.9	2004.9	2007.6
Middle East and North Africa	1990.8	1990.8	1990.6	1992.2	1994.0	1996.9	1999.9	2002.0	2003.8	2005.1
South Asia	1981.3	1985.3	1987.5	1990.2	1993.4	1998.5	1999.0	1999.5	2004.7	2007.9
Sub-Saharan Africa	1991.9	1992.2	1992.3	1992.4	1994.9	1997.7	1999.9	2001.9	2005.0	2006.6
Total	**1984.3**	**1986.2**	**1988.2**	**1990.6**	**1993.4**	**1997.2**	**1999.2**	**2001.0**	**2004.8**	**2007.5**

TABLE 20.2 Average Lag in Survey Data Availability for Latest Reference Year by Region

Region	2001	2005	2008
East Asia and Pacific	0.6	0.1	0.0
Eastern Europe and Central Asia	1.3	0.7	0.5
Latin America and the Caribbean	0.9	0.4	0.4
Middle East and North Africa	2.2	1.6	2.9
South Asia	1.6	0.5	0.1
Sub-Saharan Africa	4.0	1.5	1.4
Total	**1.6**	**0.6**	**0.5**

Sources: 2001: Chen and Ravallion 2004; 2005: Chen and Ravallion 2008b; 2008.

The lags in table 20.2 reflect both the frequency of surveys and our access to the data. Based on our observations in assembling the database for this study, we would conjecture that the large lag for the Middle East and North Africa is due more to access to existing surveys than to the frequency of those surveys, while for Sub-Saharan Africa it is due more to the infrequent production of adequate surveys.

The second indicator is the percentage of the population covered by household surveys. Table 20.3 gives the coverage rate by region for each reference year. A country is defined as being covered if there is a survey (in our database) within two years of the reference date (a five-year window). Note that our method only requires one survey per country, although we have almost six surveys per country on average. But naturally, *ceteris paribus*, the more surveys we have for a given country the more confident we are about the estimates.

The weak coverage for Eastern Europe and Central Asia, the Middle East and North Africa, and Sub-Saharan Africa in the 1980s is evident in table 20.3. Our estimates for these regions in the 1980s are heavily dependent on the extrapolations from the national accounts data. We will discuss the likely biases.

Note that there is a "hole" in coverage for South Asia in 1999. This gap reflects the well-known comparability problem due to India's National Sample Survey (NSS) for 1999/2000.[25]

TABLE 20.3 Percentage of Population Represented by Household Surveys, 1981–2008

	Survey-covered population (%) two years away from reference year									
Region	1981	1984	1987	1990	1993	1996	1999	2002	2005	2008
East Asia and Pacific	73.4	85.1	88.5	92.4	93.3	93.7	93.4	93.5	93.2	93.6
Eastern Europe and Central Asia	0.0	8.4	93.6	81.5	87.3	97.1	93.9	96.3	94.7	89.9
Latin America and the Caribbean	55.9	71.5	92.3	94.9	91.8	95.9	97.7	97.5	95.9	94.5
Middle East and North Africa	0.0	40.3	40.7	76.8	65.3	81.7	70.0	21.5	85.7	46.7
South Asia	87.6	89.0	96.6	96.6	98.2	98.2	19.6	98.1	98.0	97.9
Sub-Saharan Africa	11.3	23.6	32.8	46.0	68.8	68.0	53.1	65.7	82.7	77.9
Total	**56.7**	**67.3**	**82.9**	**86.4**	**89.5**	**91.6**	**67.7**	**87.9**	**93.1**	**89.7**

We decided to drop that NSS survey round, given that we now have a new survey for 2004/05 that we consider to be reasonably comparable to the previous survey round of 1993/94. We also decided to only use the five-year rounds of the NSS, which have larger samples and more detailed and more comparable consumption modules (aside from the 1999/2000 round). Unfortunately, this leaves a 10-year gap in our survey coverage for India; the estimates for India over the intervening period use our interpolation method, as described earlier. Including all available survey rounds for India adds to the variability in the series but does not change the trend.[26]

Measures of Global Poverty

We report aggregate results over 1981–2008 for the regions of the developing world and (given their populations) China and India. Jointly with this chapter, we have updated the World Bank's

TABLE 20.4 Poverty Measures for $1.00 per Day by Region, 1981–2008

	Percentage of population below $1.00 per day in 2005 PPP									
Region	**1981**	**1984**	**1987**	**1990**	**1993**	**1996**	**1999**	**2002**	**2005**	**2008**
East Asia and Pacific	66.1	49.4	38.7	40.6	35.4	23.3	23.6	17.8	9.5	7.8
China	73.5	52.9	38.0	44.0	37.7	23.7	24.1	19.1	9.2	7.4
Eastern Europe and Central Asia	1.0	0.8	0.8	1.1	1.5	2.1	2.1	1.2	0.8	0.3
Latin America and the Caribbean	7.9	9.2	8.5	8.8	8.1	8.1	8.8	8.9	6.5	5.0
Middle East and North Africa	4.0	3.2	2.6	2.2	1.7	1.8	2.0	1.6	1.4	1.2
South Asia	43.6	39.7	37.6	36.1	33.7	30.7	27.9	26.9	22.9	19.9
Sub-Saharan Africa	40.4	44.2	43.6	45.6	48.7	47.2	47.0	44.7	41.1	37.3
Total	**41.6**	**34.7**	**30.1**	**30.8**	**28.7**	**23.5**	**23.1**	**20.6**	**16.0**	**14.0**
Total, excl. China	29.9	28.2	27.3	26.2	25.6	23.4	22.8	21.0	18.1	16.0
	Number of persons (millions) below $1.00 per day in 2005 PPP									
Region	**1981**	**1984**	**1987**	**1990**	**1993**	**1996**	**1999**	**2002**	**2005**	**2008**
East Asia and Pacific	939.5	736.1	606.8	669.0	607.4	415.2	434.3	336.9	185.2	154.7
China	730.4	548.6	412.4	499.1	444.4	288.7	302.2	244.7	119.7	97.4
Eastern Europe and Central Asia	4.1	3.4	3.5	4.9	6.9	9.8	9.7	5.6	3.6	1.3
Latin America and the Caribbean	28.9	35.8	34.9	38.5	37.5	39.0	44.3	47.0	35.8	28.2
Middle East and North Africa	6.8	6.0	5.3	4.8	4.2	4.7	5.3	4.5	4.3	3.8
South Asia	405.1	396.5	403.0	413.6	411.6	397.7	382.7	389.1	346.8	315.1
Sub-Saharan Africa	160.8	191.4	205.5	233.9	270.5	283.6	305.5	313.4	310.4	302.8
Total	**1,545.3**	**1,369.3**	**1,258.9**	**1,364.7**	**1,338.1**	**1,150.0**	**1,181.9**	**1,096.5**	**886.1**	**805.9**
Total, excl. China	814.9	820.7	846.6	865.6	893.7	861.3	879.7	851.8	766.4	708.6

Note: Regions with survey coverage less than 50 percent are highlighted.

PovcalNet website to provide public access to the underlying country-level data set, so that users can replicate these results and try different assumptions, including different poverty measures, poverty lines, and country groupings.[27]

Tables 20.4–20.6 give the estimated poverty rates—the percentage of the population living below the poverty line—for \$1.00, \$1.25, and \$2.00 per day, at three-year intervals from 1981 to 2008. Over the 28-year period, the percentage of the population of the developing world living below \$1.25 per day was halved, falling from 52 percent to 22 percent. The number of poor fell by 600 million, from 1.9 billion to 1.3 billion over 1981–2008 (table 20.5). The trend rate of decline in the \$1.25 per day poverty rate over 1981–2008 was 1 percentage point per year. (Regressing the poverty rate on time, the estimated trend is –1.03 percent per year with a standard error of 0.06 percent, $R^2 = 0.97$). Projecting this trend forward to 2015, the estimated headcount index for that year is 16.1 percent (standard error of 1.4 percent). Given that the 1990 poverty rate was 43.1 percent, this calculation implies that the developing world as a whole is on track to

TABLE 20.5 Poverty Measures for \$1.25 per Day by Region, 1981–2008

	Percentage of population below \$1.25 per day in 2005 PPP									
Region	**1981**	**1984**	**1987**	**1990**	**1993**	**1996**	**1999**	**2002**	**2005**	**2008**
East Asia and Pacific	77.2	65.0	54.1	56.2	50.7	35.9	35.6	27.6	17.1	14.3
China	84.0	69.4	54.0	60.2	53.7	36.4	35.6	28.4	16.3	13.1
Eastern Europe and Central Asia	1.9	1.6	1.5	1.9	2.9	3.9	3.8	2.3	1.3	0.5
Latin America and the Caribbean	11.9	13.6	12.0	12.2	11.4	11.1	11.9	11.9	8.7	6.5
Middle East and North Africa	9.6	8.0	7.1	5.8	4.8	4.8	5.0	4.2	3.5	2.7
South Asia	61.1	57.4	55.3	53.8	51.7	48.6	45.1	44.3	39.4	36.0
Sub-Saharan Africa	51.5	55.2	54.4	56.5	59.4	58.1	58.0	55.7	52.3	47.5
Total	**52.2**	**47.1**	**42.3**	**43.1**	**40.9**	**34.8**	**34.1**	**30.8**	**25.1**	**22.4**
Total, excl. China	40.5	39.1	38.1	37.2	36.6	34.3	33.6	31.5	27.8	25.2
	Number of persons (millions) below \$1.25 per day in 2005 PPP									
Region	**1981**	**1984**	**1987**	**1990**	**1993**	**1996**	**1999**	**2002**	**2005**	**2008**
East Asia and Pacific	1,096.5	970.0	847.6	926.4	870.8	639.7	655.6	523.1	332.1	284.4
China	835.1	719.9	585.7	683.2	632.7	442.8	446.3	363.1	211.9	173.0
Eastern Europe and Central Asia	8.2	6.9	6.8	8.9	13.7	18.2	17.8	10.6	6.3	2.2
Latin America and the Caribbean	43.3	52.9	49.3	53.4	52.5	53.6	60.1	62.7	47.6	36.8
Middle East and North Africa	16.5	15.1	14.6	13.0	11.5	12.3	13.6	12.0	10.5	8.6
South Asia	568.4	573.8	593.0	617.3	631.9	630.8	619.5	640.5	598.3	570.9
Sub-Saharan Africa	204.9	239.1	256.8	289.7	330.0	349.4	376.8	390.4	394.9	386.0
Total	**1,937.8**	**1,857.7**	**1,768.2**	**1,908.6**	**1,910.3**	**1,704.0**	**1,743.4**	**1,639.3**	**1,389.6**	**1,289.0**
Total, excl. China	1,102.8	1,137.8	1,182.5	1,225.5	1,277.6	1,261.2	1,297.0	1,276.2	1,177.7	1,116.0

Note: Regions with survey coverage less than 50 percent are highlighted.

TABLE 20.6 Poverty Measures for $2.00 per Day by Region, 1981–2008

	Percentage of population below $2.00 per day in 2005 PPP									
Region	**1981**	**1984**	**1987**	**1990**	**1993**	**1996**	**1999**	**2002**	**2005**	**2008**
East Asia and Pacific	92.4	88.3	81.6	81.0	75.8	64.0	61.7	51.9	39.0	33.2
China	97.8	92.9	83.7	84.6	78.6	65.1	61.4	51.2	36.9	29.8
Eastern Europe and Central Asia	8.3	6.7	6.3	6.9	9.2	11.2	12.1	7.9	4.6	2.2
Latin America and the Caribbean	23.8	26.8	22.4	22.4	21.7	21.0	22.0	22.2	16.7	12.4
Middle East and North Africa	30.1	27.1	26.1	23.5	22.1	22.2	22.0	19.7	17.4	13.9
South Asia	87.2	85.6	84.5	83.6	82.7	80.7	77.8	77.4	73.4	70.9
Sub-Saharan Africa	72.2	74.7	74.3	76.0	78.1	77.5	77.5	76.1	74.1	69.2
Total	**69.6**	**68.0**	**64.8**	**64.6**	**63.1**	**58.6**	**57.4**	**53.5**	**46.9**	**43.0**
Total, excl. China	59.3	59.1	58.2	57.7	57.8	56.4	56.1	54.2	49.9	47.0
	Number of persons (millions) below $2.00 per day in 2005 PPP									
Region	**1981**	**1984**	**1987**	**1990**	**1993**	**1996**	**1999**	**2002**	**2005**	**2008**
East Asia and Pacific	1,312.9	1,316.3	1,279.0	1,333.8	1,300.7	1,139.9	1,137.6	983.9	757.5	659.2
China	972.1	963.3	907.1	960.8	926.3	792.1	769.7	654.9	481.6	394.6
Eastern Europe and Central Asia	35.7	29.5	28.8	31.9	43.1	52.8	57.0	37.2	21.7	10.4
Latin America and the Caribbean	86.6	104.2	92.2	97.6	99.9	101.7	111.4	117.6	91.7	70.5
Middle East and North Africa	51.8	51.2	53.9	52.9	53.5	57.1	59.8	56.8	52.7	44.4
South Asia	810.6	854.8	905.9	958.8	1,010.4	1,047.3	1,068.8	1,119.7	1,113.1	1,124.6
Sub-Saharan Africa	287.6	323.8	350.4	389.2	434.0	466.0	503.3	533.3	559.1	562.3
Total	**2,585.3**	**2,680.0**	**2,710.2**	**2,864.1**	**2,941.5**	**2,864.8**	**2,937.9**	**2,848.4**	**2,595.8**	**2,471.4**
Total, excl. China	1,613.2	1,716.7	1,803.1	1,903.3	2,015.2	2,072.7	2,168.2	2,193.5	2,114.2	2,076.8

Note: Regions with survey coverage less than 50 percent are highlighted.

achieve well before 2015 the first Millennium Development Goal (MDG) of halving the 1990 poverty rate.[28]

The 1 percentage point per year rate of decline in the poverty rate also holds if one focuses on the period since 1990 (not just because this is the base year for the MDG but also recalling that the data for the 1980s are weaker). The $1.25 poverty rate fell 9 percentage points in the 10 years of the 1980s (from 52 percent to 43 percent), and a further 20 points in the 18 years from 1990 to 2008.

Comparing tables 20.4, 20.5, and 20.6, the qualitative comparisons over time are generally robust to the choice of poverty line. Indeed, for any given pair of reference years in tables 20.4–20.6 the direction of change in the aggregate headcount index is the same across all poverty lines.

China's success against absolute poverty has clearly played a major role in this overall progress. Tables 20.4–20.6 repeat the calculations excluding China. Strikingly, the number of people

FIGURE 20.2 Headcount Indexes for Developing World, 1981–2008

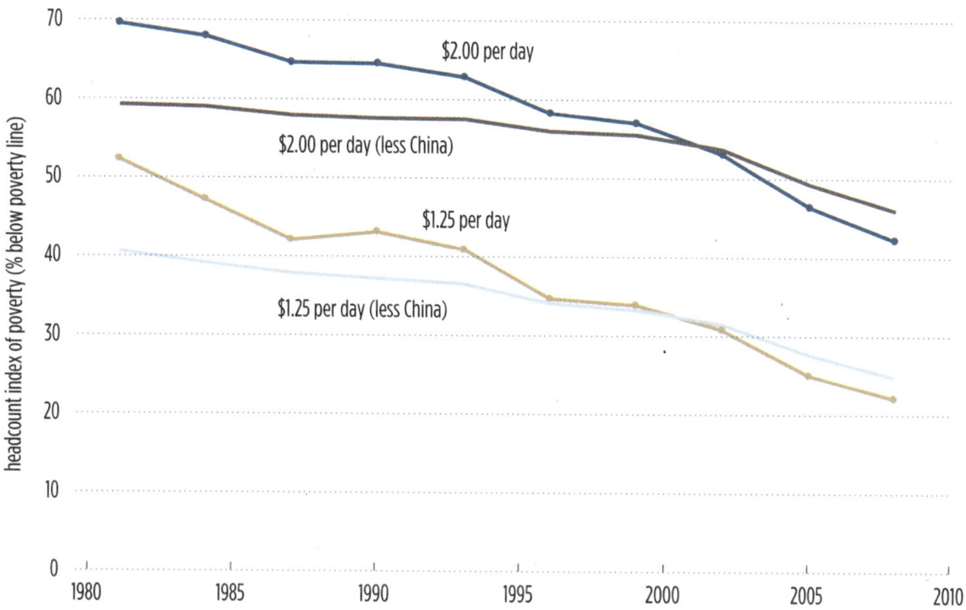

Notes: Poverty lines in 2005 prices.

outside China living below $1.25 per day is no lower in 2008 than in 1981, although it rose, then fell, with a marked decline since 1999, from 1.3 to 1.1 billion.

Figure 20.2 plots the poverty rates over time with and without China. Excluding China, the $1.25 per day poverty rate falls from 40 percent to 25 percent over 1981–2008, with a rate of decline that is half the trend including China. The regression estimate of the trend falls to –0.53 percent per year (standard error of 0.05 percent, $R^2 = 0.94$). Based on our new estimates, the projected value for 2015 is 23.5 percent (standard error of 1.05 percent), which is well over half the 1990 value of 37 percent (table 20.4). So past trends do not suggest that the developing world as a whole outside China is on track to reach the MDG for poverty reduction.

Our new estimates suggest only slightly less progress in absolute terms in climbing above the $2.00 per day poverty line than the $1.25 line (though less in proportionate terms). The poverty rate by this higher standard fell from 70 percent in 1981 to 43 percent in 2008 (table 20.6). The trend is also about 1 percent per year (a regression coefficient on time of –0.97, standard error of 0.09). Excluding China, the trend is only 0.4 percent per year (a regression coefficient of -0.44, standard error of 0.07 percent). In proportionate terms, however, the rate of progress has clearly been lower for the higher poverty line.

The number of people living below $2.00 per day has fallen over the period as a whole, but only because of the progress since 1999 (table 20.6). The number of people living *between* $1.25 and $2.00 per day almost doubled from 648 million to 1.18 billion between 1981 and 2008. This marked "bunching up" of people just above the $1.25 line suggests that the poverty rate according to that line could rise sharply with aggregate economic contraction.

To test whether the claim that poverty has fallen is robust to the choice of the international poverty line, figure 20.3 plots the cumulative distribution function (CDF) up to a maximum

FIGURE 20.3 Cumulative Distribution Functions Up to U.S. Poverty Line

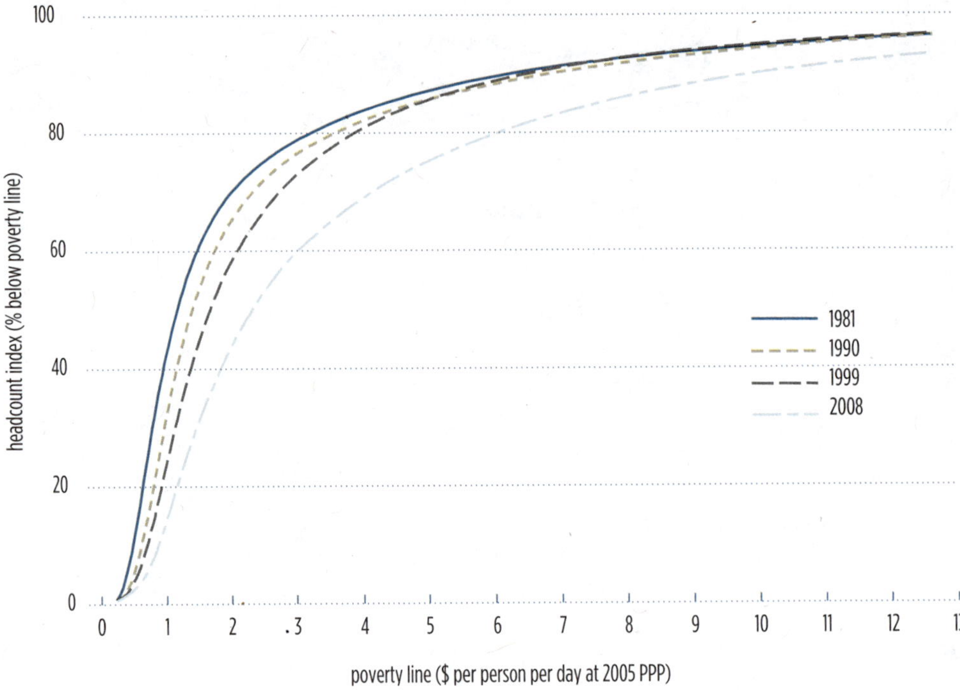

poverty line of $13.00 per person per day, which is the official line for the United States in 2005 (for a family of four). As can be seen from figure 20.1, this is higher than the highest poverty line found in any developing country (though still lower than national poverty lines in a number of other developed countries; see Ravallion 2012). To avoid cluttering, in figure 20.3 we give four CDFs at nine-year intervals. The claim that poverty fell between in either 1981, 1990, or 1999 and 2008 is robust. This also holds for a broad class of additive poverty measures, including those that penalize inequality among the poor (Atkinson 1987). The claim that poverty fell over time from 1981 to 1990 to 1999 is only robust up to about $5.00 per day.

Regional Differences

Tables 20.4–20.6 also provide regional breakdowns. The regional rankings are not robust to the choice of the poverty line. Two changes are notable. First, at the lower lines (under $2.00 per day) Sub-Saharan Africa has the highest incidence of poverty, but this switches to South Asia at the $2.00 per day line. Second, the Middle East and North Africa's poverty rate exceeds Latin America and the Caribbean's at the $2.00 line, but the ranking reverses at the lower lines.

The notable changes in regional poverty rankings over time are evident in tables 20.4–20.6. Figure 20.4 plots the $1.25 per day poverty rate for the three regions that account for the bulk of the poor—East Asia, South Asia, and Sub-Saharan Africa. There, we see a marked reversal of fortunes. Looking back to 1981, East Asia was the region with the highest incidence of poverty, with 77 percent of the population living below $1.25 per day. South Asia had the next highest poverty rate, followed by

FIGURE 20.4 Differing Fortunes for Poor People in Three Regions, 1981–2008

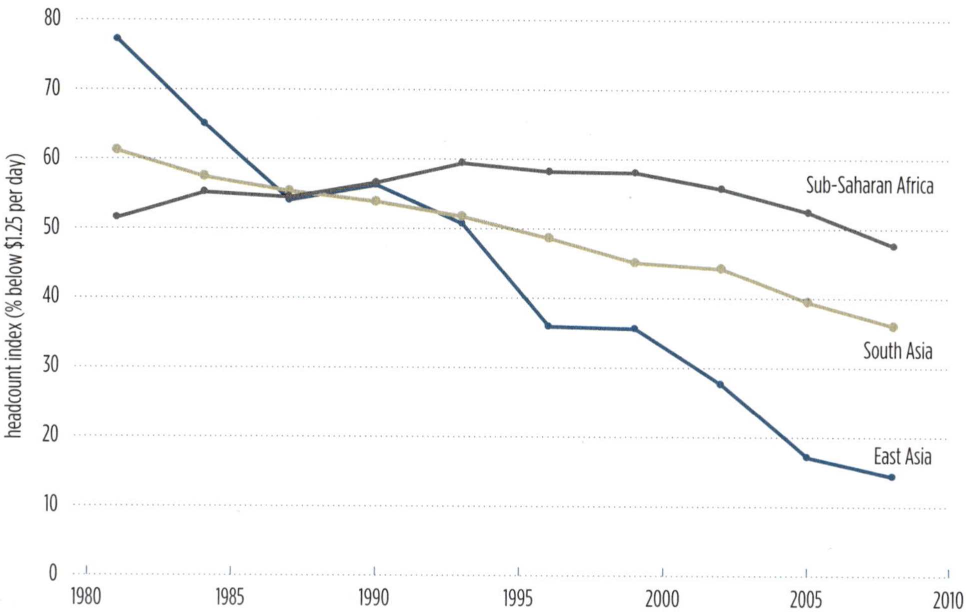

Sub-Saharan Africa, Latin America and the Caribbean, the Middle East and North Africa, and Eastern Europe and Central Asia. By the early 1990s, Sub-Saharan Africa had swapped places with East Asia, and by 2008 East Asia's poverty rate had fallen to 14 percent, while Sub-Saharan Africa's was 48 percent.

Thus the composition of world poverty has changed noticeably over time. The number of poor has fallen sharply in East Asia, but risen elsewhere. For East Asia, the first MDG of halving the 1990 poverty rate by 2015 was already reached by 2002. Again, China's progress against absolute poverty was a key factor. Looking back to 1981, China's incidence of poverty (measured by the percentage below $1.25 per day) was roughly twice that for the rest of the developing world. By about 2000, China's poverty rate had fallen below average, and over 600 million fewer people were living under $1.25 per day in 2008 than in 1981. Progress was uneven over time, with setbacks in some periods (the late 1980s) and more rapid progress in others (the early 1980s and mid-1990s). In a 2007 article, Ravallion and Chen (2007) identify a number of factors (including policies) that account for this uneven progress against poverty over time (and space) in China.

Over 1981–2008, the $1.25 poverty rate in South Asia fell from 61 percent to 36 percent. This was not sufficient to bring down the number of poor over the period as a whole, but the poverty count in South Asia has been falling since 1999 (table 20.5). If the trend over the period as a whole in South Asia were to continue until 2015, the poverty rate would fall to 31.2 percent (standard error of 0.84 percent), which is more than half its 1990 value. So South Asia is not on track to attain the poverty MDG without a higher trend rate of poverty reduction. (This is also true if one focuses on the period since 1990.)

The extent of the "bunching up" that has occurred between the $1.25 and $2.00 per day poverty lines is particularly striking in both East and South Asia, where a total of about 900 million people are living *between* these two lines, roughly equally split between the two sides of Asia.

We find a declining poverty rate in Latin America and the Caribbean by both lines, but not sufficient to reduce the count of the number of poor over the 1981–2008 period as a whole, though with more encouraging signs of progress since 1999.

The Middle East and North Africa region has experienced a fairly steady decline in the poverty rate, though (again) not sufficient to avoid a rising count in the number of poor in that region. However, our estimates for this region are affected by weak coverage in the 1980s and also recently, given the previously noted lags in the public availability of survey data.

We find a generally rising incidence and number of poor in Eastern Europe and Central Asia until 1999, but falling poverty measures since then. The paucity of survey data for this region in the 1980s should be noted. Thus our estimates are heavily based on extrapolations, which do not allow for any changes in distribution. One would expect that distribution was better from the point of view of the poor in Eastern Europe and Central Asia in the 1980s, in which case poverty would have been even lower than we estimate—and the increase over time even larger.

The incidence of poverty by the $1.25 line in Sub-Saharan Africa in 2008 is the lowest it has been over the whole period—2008 is the first time the $1.25 poverty rate fell below 50 percent (table 20.5). The rate increased until the mid-1990s, but there has been an encouraging downward trend since then. The number of poor by our $1.25 per day standard almost doubled in Sub-Saharan Africa over 1981–2008, from 205 million to almost 390 million. The share of the world's poor by this measure living in Africa rose from 11 percent in 1981 to 30 percent in 2008.

Poverty Gaps

The poverty gap (PG) indexes for $1.25 per day appear in table 20.7. The aggregate PG index for 2008 is 7 percent of the poverty line, representing about 0.3 percent of global GDP.[29]

Comparing tables 20.5 and 20.7, it can be seen that the regional rankings in terms of the poverty gap index are similar to those for the headcount index, and the changes over time follow similar patterns. The PG measures magnify the interregional differences in the headcount indexes.

TABLE 20.7 Poverty Gap Index for $1.25 Per Day, 1981–2008

	Poverty gap below $1.25 per day in 2005 PPP									
Region	**1981**	**1984**	**1987**	**1990**	**1993**	**1996**	**1999**	**2002**	**2005**	**2008**
East Asia and Pacific	34.9	23.8	18.7	19.1	16.4	10.5	10.7	8.0	4.2	3.4
China	39.3	25.6	18.5	20.7	17.7	10.7	11.1	8.7	4.0	3.2
Eastern Europe and Central Asia	0.5	0.4	0.4	0.6	0.8	1.1	1.0	0.6	0.4	0.2
Latin America and the Caribbean	4.4	5.0	5.0	5.4	5.1	5.1	5.6	5.7	4.3	3.3
Middle East and North Africa	1.9	1.5	1.3	1.1	0.9	0.9	1.0	0.8	0.7	0.6
South Asia	20.5	18.3	16.9	16.1	14.9	13.4	12.2	11.7	9.9	8.6
Sub-Saharan Africa	21.8	24.1	24.1	25.4	27.3	26.0	26.0	24.7	22.5	20.6
Total	**21.4**	**16.9**	**14.6**	**14.8**	**13.8**	**11.2**	**11.1**	**9.9**	**7.7**	**6.9**
Total, excl. China	14.8	13.8	13.3	12.8	12.5	11.4	11.1	10.3	8.9	7.9

Note: Regions with survey coverage less than 50 percent are highlighted.

The most striking feature of the results in table 20.7 is the depth of poverty in Africa, with a \$1.25 per day poverty gap index of almost 21 percent—more than twice that of the next poorest region by this measure, South Asia. This is because the mean consumption or income of the poor is lower in Sub-Saharan Africa (as shown in Chen and Ravallion 2010).

Conclusions

Thanks to the efforts and support of national statistics offices and international agencies, and to improved technologies, the available data on the key ingredients in poverty measurement—representative samples of household consumption expenditures (or incomes) and data on prices—have improved greatly since global poverty monitoring began. The country coverage of credible household survey data suitable for measuring poverty has improved markedly, the frequency of data has increased, public access to these data has improved, and the lags in data availability have been reduced appreciably. And with the substantial global effort that went into the 2005 International Comparison Program, we are also in a better position to assure that the poverty lines used in different countries have similar purchasing power, so that two people living in different countries but with the same real standard of living are treated the same way. The results of the 2005 ICP imply a higher cost of living in developing countries than past ICP data have indicated; the "Penn effect," then, is still evident, but it has been overstated.

There are still many data issues that cloud knowledge about poverty in the world. While there are many more household surveys, their quality is uneven, and their comparability is sometimes questionable. Forming regional aggregates helps average out the errors, but may not eliminate them. Access to survey data has been uneven, with some countries and regions (notably the Middle East and North Africa) lagging appreciably in this respect. And while the 2005 ICP was an improvement, there are still a number of problems, of which the likely urban bias in the price surveys for some countries stands out, in our view.

In this chapter, we have combined the new data on prices from the 2005 ICP and 850 household surveys spanning 125 countries to update our previous estimates of global absolute poverty measures. This chapter has described our methods and presented the main results. Along with this chapter, a substantially revised and updated version of the Bank's website PovcalNet has been released. It provides public access to the primary data in order to replicate these estimates and to make estimates for selected countries and alternative poverty lines.

We find that the overall percentage of the population of the developing world living below \$1.25 per day in 2008 was 22 percent, as compared with 52 percent in 1981. That means that 1.3 billion people in 2008 lived below \$1.25 per day, as compared with 1.9 billion in 1981. There was less progress in reducing the number living below \$2.00 per day. We estimate that 2.5 billion people in 2008 consumed less than \$2.00 per day, as compared with 2.6 billion in 1981.

For the first time since this monitoring task began, the new estimates presented here indicate a decline in both the poverty rate and the number of poor in all six regions of the developing world. Even so, progress has been quite uneven across these regions. We have seen dramatic progress in East Asia. In the early 1980s, East Asia was the region with the *highest* incidence of poverty in the world, with 77 percent living below \$1.25 per day in 1981. By 2008 this had fallen to 14 percent. In China alone, 662 million fewer people were living in poverty by the \$1.25 standard in 2008 than in 1981.

However, in the developing world *outside* China, the \$1.25 poverty rate fell from 41 percent to 25 percent over 1981–2008. However, this was not enough to bring down the total number of poor, which was about 1.1 billion in both 1981 and 2008, although rising in the 1980s and 1990s and then falling appreciably since 1999. In South Asia, the $1.25 per day poverty rate fell between 1981 and 2008, from 61 percent to 36 percent. The proportion of poor is lower now in South Asia than any time since 1981. The number of poor had been generally rising in Latin America and the Caribbean until 2002. But we have seen sharply falling poverty counts (and percentage poor) in that region since then. The rising incidence and number of poor in Eastern Europe and Central Asia have also been reversed since 2000. In the Middle East and North Africa, 8.6 million people—or 2.7 percent of the population—were living on less than $1.25 per day in 2008, down from 16.5 million in 1981. However, the poor survey coverage for that region creates uncertainty about the estimated poverty rates. For the first time since 1981, we have seen less than half the population of Sub-Saharan Africa living below $1.25 per day. Forty-seven percent lived below this poverty line in 2008, as compared with 51 percent in 1981. The $1.25 per day poverty rate in that region has fallen almost 10 percentage points since 1999.

Although there is clearly some good news here, a great many people remain poor and vulnerable in all regions. At the current rate of progress, there will still be about 1 billion people living below $1.25 per day in 2015. Most of the 649 million fewer poor by the $1.25 per day standard over 1981–2008 are still poor by the standards of middle-income developing countries, and certainly by the standards of what poverty means in rich countries. There has been less long-run progress in getting over the $2.00 per day hurdle. The number of people living *between* $1.25 and $2.00 per day almost doubled between 1981 and 2008, from 648 million to 1.18 billion. The marked bunching up just above the $1.25 per day line points to the fact that a great many people remain vulnerable.

NOTES

1. A great many colleagues at the World Bank have helped us obtain the necessary data for this chapter and answered our many questions. An important acknowledgment goes to the staff of over 100 national statistics offices who collected the primary household and price survey data. Our thanks go to Prem Sangraula and Qinghua Zhao for their invaluable help in setting up the data sets we have used here. We have also benefited from the comments of numerous colleagues throughout the Bank. These are our views and should not be attributed to the World Bank or any affiliated organization.
2. Ravallion (2008) provides a theoretical justification for this view and discusses the validity of the welfare assumptions on which it is based. Ravallion and Chen (2011) propose a set of "weakly relative" poverty lines that can allow for relative deprivation and costs of social inclusion and provide estimates for developing countries.
3. The term *Penn effect* stems from the Penn World Table (PWT—see Summers and Heston 1991), which provided the price level indexes across countries that were used to establish this effect empirically.
4. The ICP started as a joint project of the United Nations and University of Pennsylvania, with support from the Ford Foundation and World Bank. Prior to 2000, the Penn World Table was the main source of the PPPs for consumption used in the World Bank's global poverty measures. In 2000 we switched to the PPPs estimated by the Bank's Development Data Group. There are methodological differences between the PWT and the Bank's PPPs, as discussed in Ackland, Dowrick, and Freyens (2006) and World Bank (2008, appendix G).

5. With the PPP revisions implied by the 2005 ICP round, China's GDP per capita at purchasing power parity for 2005 falls from $6,760 to $4,091 (World Bank 2008). This downward revision reflects the method used to update the PPP over time between ICP rounds, as well as the changes between rounds. Ravallion (forthcoming) argues that the updating method used by the World Bank's annual *World Development Indicators* has not properly allowed for changes in the structure of the economy in rapidly growing developing counties; in effect, the method has not allowed for the Balassa-Samuelson effect over time. This has led to unnecessarily large data revisions when the new ICP data become available.
6. The old estimate was based a bilateral comparison of 1986 prices between the United States and China as documented in Ruoen and Chen (1995).
7. The five geographic ICP regions in 2005 were Africa, Asia-Pacific, Commonwealth of Independent States (CIS), South America, and Western Asia. The Eurostat–Organisation for Economic Co-operation and Development (OECD) members constituted a sixth region.
8. The PPPs were based on a price survey of 98 of 116 countries. For the other 18 countries, the PPPs were estimated by ICP staff from a regression model. Those countries were Algeria, Costa Rica, Dominican Republic, El Salvador, Guatemala, Guyana, Haiti, Honduras, Jamaica, Nicaragua, Panama, Papua New Guinea, St. Lucia, Suriname, Timor-Leste, Trinidad and Tobago, Turkmenistan, and Uzbekistan.
9. On the advantages of this method over the alternative (Geary-Khamis) method, see Ackland, Dowrick, and Freyens (2006). In the 2005 ICP, the Africa region chose a different aggregation method (African Development Bank 2007). World Bank (2008) describes this method as having only minor differences with the GEKS method.
10. For a fuller discussion of these issues, see Deaton and Heston (2010) and Ravallion (2010).
11. The Asian Development Bank (2008) has taken a further step of implementing special price surveys for Asian countries to collect prices on explicitly lower qualities of selected items than those identified in the standard ICP. The use of lower-quality goods essentially lowers the poverty line. In terms of the impact on the poverty counts for Asia in 2005, the ADB's method is equivalent to using a poverty line of about $1.20 per day by our methods. This calculation is based on a log linear interpolation between the relevant poverty lines.
12. For food, clothing, and footwear, 72 percent of the 717 sampled price outlets in India were in urban areas and only 28 percent in rural areas. For other goods, the outlets were solely urban. The ICP took simple averages of these prices. It was assumed that goods other than food, clothing, and footwear had the same prices in rural and urban areas. Then the implicit urban and rural international poverty lines for India consistent with the 2005 ICP have weights of 0.72 and 0.28, respectively. The ratio of the urban official poverty line for India in 2004/05 to the rural line is 1.51. Because the 2005 consumption PPP for India is Rs 15.60 (World Bank 2008), the rupee values of the international line of $1.25 per day for urban and rural areas in 2005 can then be backed out, and are Rs 21.53 and Rs 14.24 a day, respectively.
13. See Bhalla (2002) and Karshenas (2003), though their methods differ. Others have used a similar method based on GDP rather than consumption (including Sala-i-Martin 2006 and Bourguignon and Morrisson 2002), though this appears to have been done more for computational convenience as it did not require estimation from microdata.
14. For example, national accounts private consumption includes imputed rents for owner-occupied housing, imputed services from financial intermediaries, and the expenditures of nonprofit organizations, but none of these are included in consumption aggregates from

standard household surveys. Surveys, on the other hand, are undoubtedly better at picking up consumption from activities in the informal sector.

15. Korinek, Mistiaen, and Ravallion (2006) examine the implications of selective compliance for measures of poverty and inequality. They find that correcting for selective compliance in the Current Population Survey for the United States leads to a higher inequality measure but has little effect on measures of poverty.
16. The use of a "per capita" normalization is standard in the literature on developing countries. This stems from the general presumption that there is rather little scope for economies of size in consumption for poor people. However, that assumption can be questioned—see Lanjouw and Ravallion (1995).
17. Consumption requires fewer imputations and assumptions, is likely to be reported more accurately, and is arguably a better measure of current economic welfare than income. For further discussion, see Ravallion (1994, 2003) and Deaton and Zaidi (2002). It has also been argued that consumption is a better welfare indicator in developed countries—see Slesnick (1998).
18. For a few cases, we do not have consumption distributions, but we still have survey-based estimates of mean consumption. Then we replace the income mean by the consumption mean, leaving the Lorenz curve the same (i.e., all incomes are scaled up by the ratio of the consumption mean to the income mean). There is, however, no obvious basis for adjusting the Lorenz curve.
19. PovcalNet provides a wider range of measures drawn from the literature on poverty measurement. See http://econ.worldbank.org/povcalnet.
20. Note that the same poverty line is generally used for urban and rural areas. There are three exceptions—China, India, and Indonesia—where we estimate poverty measures separately for urban and rural areas and use sector-specific CPIs.
21. For a few countries in Sub-Saharan Africa for which private consumption per capita is missing from the DDP, we use GDP instead.
22. Thus $H93 = \left[\frac{(1995 - 1993)}{(1995 - 1989)}\right] \cdot H93(89) + \left[\frac{(1993 - 1989)}{(1995 - 1989)}\right] \cdot H93(95)$. In a small number of cases, this method did not give sensible results in that either M93(89) or M93(95) was outside the interval [M(89), M(95)], even though the national accounts growth rates were positive for both 1989–93 and 1993–95. In these cases, we scaled down the growth rates according to the survey means for 1989 and 1995.
23. Some countries have graduated from the set of developing countries; we apply the same definition over time to avoid selection bias. In this chapter, our definition is anchored to 2005.
24. China's survey data for the early 1980s are probably less reliable than those for later years, as discussed in Chen and Ravallion (2004), where we also describe our methods of adjusting for certain comparability problems in the Chinese data, including changes in valuation methods.
25. Further discussion and references can be found in Datt and Ravallion (2002).
26. If one uses the 1999/2000 survey for India, one obtains a sharp fall in that year and a subsequent rise in poverty incidence to 2005. However, this is clearly spurious, being driven by the fact that the 1999/2000 survey overestimates the level of consumption relative to other survey rounds.
27. See http://econ.worldbank.org/povcalnet.
28. Our preliminary estimate for 2010 using survey data representing about 80 percent of the population of the developing world indicates that the first MDG was in fact achieved that year.

29. This assumes that no one lives below our international poverty line in the member countries of the OECD. Under this assumption, the aggregate poverty gap as a percentage of global GDP is $PG \cdot \left(\frac{Z}{\overline{Y}}\right) \cdot \frac{N}{NW}$ where PG is the poverty gap index (in percent), Z is the poverty line, $\overline{Y}$ is global GDP per capita, N is the population of the developing world, and NW is world population.

REFERENCES

Ackland, Robert, Steve Dowrick, and Benoit Freyens. 2006. "Measuring Global Poverty: Why PPP Methods Matter." Australian National University, Canberra.

African Development Bank. 2007. *Comparative Consumption and Price Levels in African Countries.* Tunis: African Development Bank.

Asian Development Bank. 2008. *Comparing Poverty across Countries: The Role of Purchasing Power Parities.* Manila: Asian Development Bank.

Atkinson, Anthony B. 1987. "On the Measurement of Poverty." *Econometrica* 55: 749–64.

Balassa, Bela. 1964. "The Purchasing Power Parity Doctrine: A Reappraisal." *Journal of Political Economy* 72 (6): 584–96.

Bhalla, Surjit. 2002. *Imagine There's No Country: Poverty, Inequality and Growth in the Era of Globalization.* Washington, DC: Institute for International Economics.

Bourguignon, François, and Christian Morrisson. 2002. "Inequality among World Citizens: 1820–1992." *American Economic Review* 92 (4): 727–44.

Chen, Shaohua, and Martin Ravallion. 2001. "How Did the World's Poor Fare in the 1990s?" *Review of Income and Wealth* 47 (3): 283–300.

———. 2004. "How Have the World's Poorest Fared since the Early 1980s?" *World Bank Research Observer* 19/2: 141–70.

———. 2008a. "China Is Poorer than We Thought, but No Less Successful in the Fight against Poverty." In *Debates on the Measurement of Poverty*, ed. Sudhir Anand, Paul Segal, and Joseph Stiglitz. New York: Oxford University Press.

———. 2008b. "The Developing World Is Poorer than We Thought, but No Less Successful in the Fight against Poverty." Policy Research Working Paper 4703, World Bank, Washington, DC.

———. 2010. "The Developing World Is Poorer than We Thought, but No Less Successful in the Fight against Poverty." *Quarterly Journal of Economics* 125 (4): 1577–1625.

Datt, Gaurav, and Martin Ravallion. 2002. "Has India's Post-Reform Economic Growth Left the Poor Behind." *Journal of Economic Perspectives* 16 (3): 89–108.

Deaton, Angus. 2005. "Measuring Poverty in a Growing World (or Measuring Growth in a Poor World)." *Review of Economics and Statistics* 87: 353–78.

Deaton, Angus, and Olivier Dupriez. 2008. "Poverty PPPs around the World: An Update and Progress Report." Development Data Group, World Bank, Washington, DC.

Deaton, Angus, and Alan Heston. 2010. "Understanding PPPs and PPP-Based National Accounts." *American Economic Journal: Macroeconomics* 2 (4): 1–35.

Deaton, Angus, and Salman Zaidi. 2002. "Guidelines for Constructing Consumption Aggregates for Welfare Analysis." Living Standards Measurement Study Working Paper 135, World Bank, Washington, DC.

Karshenas, Massoud. 2003. "Global Poverty: National Accounts Based versus Survey Based Estimates." *Development and Change* 34 (4): 683–712.

Korinek, Anton, Johan Mistiaen, and Martin Ravallion. 2006. "Survey Nonresponse and the Distribution of Income." *Journal of Economic Inequality* 4 (2): 33–55.

Lanjouw, Peter, and Martin Ravallion. 1995. "Poverty and Household Size." *Economic Journal* 105: 1415–35.

Ravallion, Martin. 1994. *Poverty Comparisons*. Chur, Switzerland: Harwood Academic Press.

———. 2000. "Should Poverty Measures Be Anchored to the National Accounts?" *Economic and Political Weekly* 34 (August 26): 3245–52.

———. 2003. "Measuring Aggregate Economic Welfare in Developing Countries: How Well Do National Accounts and Surveys Agree?" *Review of Economics and Statistics* 85: 645–52.

———. 2008. "On the Welfarist Rationale for Relative Poverty Lines." In *The Oxford Handbook of Arguments for a Better World: Essays in Honor of Amartya Sen,* Vol. 1, *Ethics, Welfare and Measurement*, ed. Kaushik Basu and Ravi Kanbur. New York: Oxford University Press.

———. 2010. "Understanding PPPs and PPP-Based National Accounts: A Comment." *American Economic Journal: Macroeconomics* 2 (4): 46–52.

———. 2012. "Poverty Lines across the World." In *Oxford Handbook of the Economics of Poverty*, ed. Philip N. Jefferson. New York: Oxford University Press.

———. Forthcoming. "Price Levels and Economic Growth: Making Sense of Revisions to Data on Real Incomes." *Review of Income and Wealth*.

Ravallion, Martin, and Shaohua Chen. 2007. "China's (Uneven) Progress against Poverty." *Journal of Development Economics* 82 (1): 1–42.

———. 2011. "Weakly Relative Poverty." *Review of Economics and Statistics* 93 (4): 1251–61.

Ravallion, Martin, Shaohua Chen, and Prem Sangraula. 2007. "New Evidence on the Urbanization of Global Poverty." *Population and Development Review* 33 (4): 667–702.

———. 2008. "Dollar a Day Revisited." Policy Research Working Paper 4620, World Bank, Washington, DC.

Ravallion, Martin, Gaurav Datt, and Dominique van de Walle. 1991. "Quantifying Absolute Poverty in the Developing World." *Review of Income and Wealth* 37: 345–61.

Ruoen, Ren, and Kai Chen. 1995. "China's GDP in US Dollars Based on Purchasing Power Parity." Policy Research Working Paper 1415, World Bank, Washington, DC.

Sala-i-Martin, Xavier. 2006. "The World Distribution of Income: Falling Poverty and … Convergence. Period." *Quarterly Journal of Economics* 121 (2): 351–97.

Samuelson, Paul. 1964. "Theoretical Notes on Trade Problems." *Review of Economics and Statistics* 46 (2): 145–54.

Slesnick, Daniel. 1998. "Empirical Approaches to Measuring Welfare." *Journal of Economic Literature* 36: 2108–65.

Summers, Robert, and Alan Heston. 1991. "The Penn World Table (Mark 5): An Extended Set of International Comparisons, 1950–1988." *Quarterly Journal of Economics* 106: 327–68.

World Bank. 1990. *World Development Report 1990–1991: Poverty*. New York: Oxford University Press.

———. 2008. *Global Purchasing Power Parities and Real Expenditures: 2005 International Comparison Program*. http://siteresources.worldbank.org/ICPINT/Resources/icp-final.pdf.

CHAPTER 21

PPP Exchange Rates for the Global Poor

Angus S. Deaton and Olivier Dupriez

The first of the Millennium Development Goals targets global poverty.[1] The global poverty number is estimated by the World Bank as a worldwide count of people who live below a common international poverty line. This line, loosely referred to as the dollar-a-day line, is calculated as an average over the world's poorest countries of their national poverty lines expressed in international dollars; the average is then converted back to local currency to calculate each country's counts of those living below the line. The counts come from household surveys, the number and coverage of which have steadily increased over the years. The conversion of national poverty lines to international currency and the conversion of the global line back to local currency are both done using purchasing power parity (PPP) exchange rates from the various rounds of the International Comparison Program (ICP). These PPPs, unlike market exchange rates, are constructed as multilateral price indexes using directly observed consumer prices in many countries. This chapter is about the construction of the PPPs and their effect on the poverty estimates.

In the first dollar-a-day poverty calculations, the World Bank (1990) used price indexes for gross domestic product (GDP), but this practice was later improved by the use of price indexes for household consumption. Yet even this may be misleading if the price indexes for national aggregate consumption are different from those relevant for people who live at or around the global poverty line. Price indexes are weighted averages of prices, and both weights and prices could be wrong. The prices collected by the ICP, which are average national prices, may be different from the prices faced by those at the poverty line, and the expenditure patterns at the poverty line are certainly different from the aggregate expenditure patterns in the national accounts that provide the weights for the consumption PPPs published by the ICP. This chapter is concerned with the second of these issues, the recalculation of purchasing power parity exchange rates using the expenditure patterns

---

This chapter was originally published in the *American Economic Journal: Applied Economics* 3 (April 2011): 137–166, and is reprinted with permission of the authors and the American Economic Association.

of those at the global poverty line, as well as the effect such rates have on estimates of global poverty. We shall refer to the poverty-weighted purchasing power parities as PPPPs or P4s, as opposed to the aggregate-weighted PPPs or P3s. We recognize the possible importance of the first issue, but our procedures and calculations use the national prices of goods and services collected by the ICP so that our P4 indexes differ from the P3s published by the ICP only in the methods that we use to turn these prices into national price indexes.

Although our objectives are relatively modest, there are substantial technical issues to be faced. First, in order to calculate the appropriate weights in each country, we need to identify those who are close to the local currency equivalent of the global poverty line. But to convert the global line to local currency, we need the P4s, so that the P4s and their weights need to be simultaneously calculated. Second, the global poverty line is itself calculated from the local lines converted to international units using the P4s, so that our calculations need to solve simultaneously for weights, price indexes, and the global poverty line. Third, the current standard procedure uses *aggregate* data from the *national accounts* to calculate the PPPs and the global poverty line in international dollars, but then takes the global poverty line to *household survey* data to calculate the numbers of poor people in each country. In the calculations in this chapter, we examine what happens when we use household survey data throughout. We use (1) local currency prices (or more accurately "parities" or commodity-specific PPPs) for 102 basic headings of household consumption from the 2005 round of the ICP, (2) nationally representative household surveys from 62 poor countries, and (3) national poverty lines in local currency for 50 countries, and combine (1), (2), and (3) to calculate a set of poverty-weighted purchasing power parity exchange rates for consumption, a global poverty line, and a set of global poverty counts for each country and the world as a whole. The 62 countries for which we have survey data represent 83 percent of the population of the countries included in the global poverty counts; the 50 poverty lines cover 79 percent of the population of poor countries. Fourth, when calculating P4s, we cannot follow the usual practice with P3s of taking the United States as base because there are no households in the United States at a poverty line in the vicinity of a dollar a day whose expenditure patterns can be used to calculate the price indexes. Our calculations use only information from the much poorer countries included in the global poverty count, and we calculate a set of P4s for those countries alone. This has the great advantage that neither prices nor expenditure patterns in rich countries have any effect on either P4s or the global poverty count, and that we are not using a "global" poverty line at which much of the (rich) world could not survive.

Perhaps surprisingly, our main result is that, for the poor countries of the world, their P4s are very similar to the P3s. What differences exist come less from using expenditure patterns of the poor to reweight the price indexes and more from data inconsistencies between data from household surveys and data from national accounts. Our poverty counts, however, are considerably lower than the World Bank counts, not on account of differences between P3s and P4s, but because of the way we average the national poverty lines to derive the global line. Our counts are close to those published by the World Bank before the revision that was done subsequent to the 2005 ICP.

This chapter is laid out as follows. In section 1 we review the theory of the P4 indexes and the differences between P3s and P4s. We work with three different types of multilateral indexes: the Fisher and Törnqvist versions of the Éltetö-Köves-Szulc (EKS) index, and the weighted Country Product Dummy index. We show that the P3 and P4 indexes for any pair of countries will differ according to the cross-commodity correlation between relative prices and income elasticities. If food is relatively expensive in poor countries, this will raise the P4 relative to the P3 for a poor country relative to a rich country, but these differences will be muted within poor countries as a group. We also explain how we handle the simultaneous determination of the P4s and the global poverty line, as well as a number of alternative procedures for setting the line. Finally, we discuss the construction of standard errors for our price indexes. One concern is with the sample size of some of our household surveys, so that we need to ensure that using samples, as opposed to populations, does not compromise the precision of the estimates. Another concern is related to the fact that, in a world where relative prices are different in different countries, different index number formulas give different answers, and we develop a standard error concept that captures the degree of uncertainty from this cause.

Section 2 discusses practical issues. We discuss how the ICP constructs the prices for the basic headings of consumption, and how we need to modify those procedures. We discuss the matching of consumption categories in the household surveys to the basic headings of consumption in the ICP and note that there are several categories—rent and health being perhaps the most important—that are not adequately represented in the surveys. Beyond that, some surveys contain imputations for the use value of durables, as opposed to expenditures on those items in the national accounts and the ICP. As a result, even when we calculate P3s as opposed to P4s, our estimates will not coincide with those in the ICP. A final practical issue is that, for some countries, the ICP collected only urban prices, and we have good evidence from many countries that urban prices are higher than rural prices, so that an adjustment is necessary.

Section 3 presents our results. One major conclusion is that, provided we use household survey data in both calculations, the reweighting to a poverty basis makes little difference, so that our P3s are close to our P4s. However, our P3s are somewhat further away from the P3s in the ICP, in part because of our different aggregation procedures (definitions of the indexes) and in part because the survey-based estimates of aggregate expenditure patterns differ from those presented in the national accounts. As is often the case, data discrepancies are more important than conceptual issues. We use our P4s to calculate poverty counts, by region and for the world as a whole; our poverty count is a good deal lower than the official count because of the way that we construct our global poverty line.

1. Poverty-Weighted Purchasing Power Parity Exchange Rates: Theory

Purchasing power parity exchange rates are multilateral price indexes designed to summarize price levels in each of a group of countries relative to an arbitrarily selected base country. Here, we are interested in price indexes for household consumption, and wish to depart from the standard practice of calculating indexes for aggregate national consumption. Instead, our aim is to calculate indexes using weights for people that are at, or at least close to, the global poverty line.

1.1 Definition of the Multilateral Price Indexes

We have M countries, labeled using the index c. In each, there is a vector of prices for N items of consumption, labeled using the index n, so that p_n^c is the price of good n in country c. Associated with those prices is a pattern of consumption, which we shall typically measure in terms of the shares of the budget devoted to each good, denoted s_n^c. The sum of these non-negative budget shares over n is unity for each country c, so that they can be thought of as weights. They are defined as the expenditure on each good divided by the total expenditure on all goods; we shall separate aggregate from poverty line budget shares below.

There are two different types of PPP indexes that we shall compute, the Gini-Éltetö-Köves-Szulc (GEKS) type, and the weighted Country Product Dummy (CPDW) type. GEKS indexes begin from a set of superlative price indexes (Diewert 1976) calculated for each pair of countries. We work with two standard superlative indexes, the first of which is the Törnqvist index, defined as

$$\ln P_T^{cd} = \frac{1}{2}\sum_{n=1}^{N}(s_n^c + s_n^d)\ln\frac{p_n^c}{p_n^d}. \tag{21.1}$$

We adopt the convention that the reference country, here c, comes first in the superscript on the index, followed by the comparison country, here d. The Törnqvist index is a weighted geometric average of the price relatives of each good, with the weights the average of the two budget shares in c and d. The second index is the Fisher ideal index, defined as the geometric mean of the Paasche index and the Laspeyres index so that, in logarithms,

$$\ln P_F^{cd} = 0.5*\ln\left[\sum_{n=1}^{N} s_n^c \frac{p_n^d}{p_n^c}\right] - 0.5*\ln\left[\sum_{n=1}^{N} s_n^d \frac{p_n^c}{p_n^d}\right]. \tag{21.2}$$

The first term in brackets on the right-hand side is the Laspeyres index for d relative to c, while the second term in brackets is the Laspeyres for c relative to d, which is identical to the reciprocal of the Paasche for d relative to c. The log Fisher and Törnqvist indexes in (21.1) and (21.2) give a skew-symmetric M by M matrix of index numbers comparing each country with each other country. In practice, a matrix of price indexes is less useful than a vector of price levels, or multilateral indexes, one for each country relative to a numeraire country, with each representing a purchasing power version of exchange rates. In order to compress the information in (21.2) into this form, the matrix is converted into a set of international PPP exchange rates by applying an (essentially atheoretical but convenient) adjustment first proposed by Gini (1924) and later rediscovered, so that it is here referred to as the GEKS procedure. The GEKS PPP price index for c in country 1's units is

$$P_F^c = \left(\prod_{j=1}^{M} P_F^{1j} P_F^{jc}\right)^{\frac{1}{M}} \tag{21.3}$$

for the GEKS-Fisher, with an identical formula, with T replacing F, for the GEKS-Törnqvist. Country 1 is the arbitrarily selected base country whose currency is taken as the numeraire; the choice simply defines the scale, leaving the ratios of indexes between countries unchanged. Each index inside the brackets in (21.3) is the price level of c relative to 1 computed via country j, so that the GEKS index comes from taking a geometric average of these indexes over all possible intermediate countries, and this adjustment converts the matrix of country by country indexes into a single vector of price levels, one for each country.

We also work with PPP indexes using the weighted Country Product Dummy method; an unweighted version of this traces back to Summers (1973), with the weighted version developed by Prasada Rao—see, for example, Selvanathan and Rao (1994), and Rao (1990, 2005). The CPDW method projects prices onto a set of country and product dummies by running a weighted regression of the form

$$\ln p_n^c = \alpha^c + \beta_n + \varepsilon_n^c \tag{21.4}$$

where the weights are the budget shares of each good in each country s_n^c. The estimated α^c (with the base country omitted from the regression and $\alpha^1 = 0$) are the logarithms of the estimated PPPs. The argument for the budget shares weights is the same as for other price index calculations: goods with large (small) budget shares should count more (less) in the calculations. Equation (21.4) *defines* the projection and should not be taken as a model of prices.

We make no use of the Geary-Khamis (GK) system of PPPs as used, for example, in the Penn World Table. The GK method prices all goods at a set of world prices that are quantity-weighted averages of individual country prices, so that countries with the largest physical volume of consumption of a good get greatest weight in the construction of the composite world prices. The use of such prices has the effect of overstating the level of consumption—and underestimating poverty—in the poorest countries. The official PPPs from the 2005 ICP that are published in World Bank (2008a) are hybrid indexes; all but the Africa region used GEKS indexes for their internal PPPs, but the regions are assembled into a global system using specially developed formulas, so that the ICP's global numbers differ from what would come out from a single global calculation like those we use in this chapter—see World Bank (2008a) and Deaton and Heston (2010) for explanations and discussion.

1.2 Budget Shares and How They Matter

The GEKS and CPDW formulas allow us to calculate a set of PPPs given prices and budget shares; the difference between P3s and P4s comes from the choice of the latter. In the calculations for poverty-weighted PPPs, we use the budget shares for households at or near the global poverty line, measured from household surveys. The ICP, by contrast, uses budget shares that are the shares of aggregate consumers' expenditure on each good in the aggregate of consumers' expenditure in total. If s_n^{ch} is the budget share on good n by household h in country c, the aggregate budget shares that go into the ICP indexes, which are the ratio of *aggregate* expenditure on n to *aggregate* expenditure on all goods, can be written in terms of household expenditures as the expenditure weighted average

$$\bar{s}_n^c = \frac{\sum_{h=1}^{H} x^{ch} s_n^{ch}}{\sum_{h=1}^{H} x^{ch}} \tag{21.5}$$

where x^{ch} is the total expenditure of household h. Price indexes using weights such as (21.5) are referred to as plutocratic indexes (Prais 1959), because the budget share of each household is weighted by total expenditure and those who spend more are weighted more heavily. Note that (21.5) can be estimated either from household survey data by aggregating across households or, because it is a ratio of aggregates, from national accounts data. In principle but not in practice, these are identical.

The weights that we shall use for the poverty PPPs are not (21.5), but

$$\bar{s}_n^c(z^c) = E\left[s_n^{ch} \,\middle|\, \left(\frac{x^{ch}}{n^{ch}}\right) = z^c \right] \tag{21.6}$$

where n^{ch} is household size and z^c is the poverty line in local currency, so that according to (21.6), the budget shares for poverty weighting are the average budget shares of households at the poverty line z^c, which is indexed by the country c because it is the common global poverty line expressed in local currency of c.

A main concern of this chapter is the difference between plutocratic multilateral indexes, which use (21.5), and poverty-weighted indexes, which use (21.6). Useful insights can be obtained from the two-country case, and from a simple specification of the way that budget shares differ with total expenditure. Suppose that the budget shares in each country are linear functions of the logarithm of total expenditures, a functional form that often fits the data well and that is consistent with choice theory—see, for example, Deaton and Muellbauer (1980, chap. 3.)

$$s_{nh}^{c} = \xi_{0n}^{c} + \xi_{1n}^{c} \ln \tilde{x}_{h} + v_{nh}^{c} \tag{21.7}$$

where c is the country, v_{nh} is a disturbance term, and ξ_{0n}^{c} and ξ_{1n}^{c} are commodity- and country-specific parameters. For each country, the ξ_{1n}^{c} parameters add to zero over all the goods in the budget, while the ξ_{0n}^{c} parameters add to one. If we use (21.7) to calculate the Törnqvist indexes for two countries, the poverty-weighted price index can be calculated explicitly, and the difference between it, P_{T}^{12}, and the plutocratic Törnqvist index, $\tilde{P}_{T}^{12}$, can be written as

$$\ln P_{T}^{12} - \ln \tilde{P}_{T}^{12} = 0.5\sum_{n=1}^{N}[\xi_{1n}^{1} (\ln z^{1} - \ln y^{1}) + \xi_{1n}^{2} (\ln z^{2} - \ln y^{2})] \ln \frac{p_{n}^{2}}{p_{n}^{1}} \tag{21.8}$$

where z^1 and z^2 are the two local currency poverty lines, and y^c is an (entropy) inequality-adjusted measure of mean expenditure

$$\ln y^{c} = \sum_{h} \left[\frac{x_{h}^{c} \ln x_{h}^{c}}{\sum_{h} x_{h}^{c}} \right] \tag{21.9}$$

and where y^c is measured in local prices. These equations tell us that if the effects of income on the budget shares, as measured by the ξ_{1n}^{c} parameters, are orthogonal, for each country, to the logarithms of the price relatives, the plutocratic and poverty-weighted indexes will be the same. When these orthogonality conditions fail, the plutocratic and poverty-weighted indexes will differ by an amount that depends on the correlation between the ξ_{1n}^{c}'s and the relative prices, on the inequality-adjusted levels of living in the two countries, and on the poverty line.

To illustrate with an important case, if we are comparing a rich(er) country with a poor(er) country, and if food in both is mostly traded, then food will be relatively expensive in the poor country, as is typically the case. Suppose that there are only two goods, food f and nonfood n, and that the Engel curve parameters $\xi_{1f} = -\xi_{1n}$ are the same in both countries (ξ_{1f} is typically estimated to be around –0.15.) Then (21.8) becomes

$$\ln \frac{P_{T}^{12}}{\tilde{P}_{T}^{12}} = \xi_{1f} \ln \sqrt{\frac{z^{1}z^{2}}{y^{1}y^{2}}} \ln \left(\frac{p_{f}^{2}}{p_{n}^{2}} \bigg/ \frac{p_{f}^{1}}{p_{n}^{1}} \right) \tag{21.10}$$

which is positive if food is relatively more expensive in the poor country, and if the poverty lines are less than inequality-adjusted mean expenditure in both countries. In this example, the P4 index for the poor country relative to the rich country will be *higher* than the corresponding P3 index, essentially because the food share is declining in income and the relatively higher food price gets more weight in the P4 index than in the P3 index. The size of the effect will be larger the larger the Engel effect and the larger the distance between the poverty lines and inequality-adjusted mean expenditures in both countries. It is a good deal harder to think of any such systematic effects between countries at similar levels of development, which, as we shall see, is the relevant case here where we calculate P3s and P4s for a set of relatively poor countries.

The above argument is specific to the Törnqvist and to the two country cases. But the argument about the correlation between Engel patterns and the structure of relative prices is clearly a general one, and should serve as a rough guide to the way in which we would expect P4 indexes to differ from P3 indexes. The extension to multiple countries is harder to derive formally, but practical experience (at least where relative prices are not too dissimilar) has been that the GEKS adjustment of the matrices of Fisher and Törnqvist indexes is typically not very large, so that the final index is likely to be dominated by the pairwise indexes, not by the final GEKS adjustment.

1.3 Defining the Poverty Lines and Dealing with Simultaneity

The global poverty line is an average of national poverty lines each converted to a common currency using P3s or P4s, which are also used to convert the global line back to its local equivalents. The budget shares used in the P4s, (21.6), depend on these local equivalents of the global line, so that the global line, the budget shares, and the P4s must be calculated simultaneously. If the global poverty line were known in the base international currency—we use Indian rupees—and if the Engel curves satisfy (21.7), there is a closed-form solution for the Törnqvist P4s. This is derived in Deaton and Dupriez (2009), and we use this, together with the Indian national poverty line, as the starting point for a set of iterative calculations. From the closed-form solution, we calculate a new global line and its local currency equivalents, which are then used to define new budget shares by (21.6), and new P4s, and so on. The budget shares, (21.6), are themselves a local (kernel) weighted average of budget shares for households near the local poverty line, and a bandwidth parameter allows us to trade off sample size, on the one hand, against focus on households near the poverty line, on the other.

In general, it is not possible to guarantee that there exists a unique solution for the set of poverty-weighted PPP indexes. However, we know that uniqueness is guaranteed for the GEKS–Törnqvist when the Engel curves satisfy (21.7). It is also straightforward to show that in the case where all countries have the same tastes, and the price indexes are cost-of-living indexes, there is a unique solution.

We consider three different choices of global poverty line. The first variant, and our baseline case, calculates a global poverty line from 50 countries that are included both in our set of household surveys and in the compilation of local poverty lines in Ravallion, Chen, and Sangraula (2009), henceforth RCS. At each iteration of the P4 calculations, we convert these 50 lines to world rupees (our international numeraire currency) and take a weighted average using as weights the numbers of people below the line in each of the countries. The second variant is the same as the first, but with the 50 local poverty lines multiplied by two before we start; this is similar in spirit to looking at one and two dollars a day. Our third variant follows RCS and calculates the international line as the simple average of the world rupee value of the local poverty lines of Chad, Ethiopia, The Gambia, Ghana, Malawi, Mali, Mozambique, Nepal, Niger, Rwanda, Sierra Leone, Tajikistan, Tanzania, and Uganda. (RCS also include Guinea-Bissau, for which we lack survey data.) Deaton (2010) discusses further the advantages and disadvantages of focusing on these specific countries.

1.4 Standard Errors for the Estimated Purchasing Power Parity Indexes

Our calculations of P4s use household surveys whose sample sizes vary from country to country, and sample sizes are further restricted when we focus on households close to the poverty line. To assess the effects of these finite samples, we calculate standard errors for our estimated price indexes. All of the P4s (and survey-based P3s) are functions of sample means from the surveys, whose designs—sample sizes, weighting, stratification—we know. The formulas are derived in detail in Deaton and Dupriez (2009) and can be implemented using any software that handles complex survey design.

We also provide a second kind of standard errors, which we refer to as the "failure of arbitrage" standard errors ("failure of the law of one price" would be an alternative). These come from the following conceptual experiment. Suppose that we write the price of good n in country c in the form (21.4) in which the logarithm of price is the sum of a country effect, a commodity effect, and an error. In a world of perfect arbitrage, where relative prices were the same in all countries and absolute prices differed only according to the currency unit, the error terms in (21.4) would be zero, and the α^c would be the logarithms of the PPPs, of the exchange rates, or of any reasonable index of prices in the country. Because perfect arbitrage does not hold, the ε_n^c are not zero, and different index number formulas will give different answers. It is this variability across indexes that is captured by the "failure of arbitrage" standard errors. This measure of model uncertainty is similar in concept to the use of the Paasche and Laspeyres Spread, another measure of the extent to which different price formulas give different answers when relative prices differ across countries.

In calculating our "failure of arbitrage" standard errors, the conceptual experiment is one in which we think of ε_n^c as drawn repeatedly, which generates stochastic prices according to (21.4), which are then combined with nonstochastic expenditure weights to generate stochastic P3s and P4s whose standard errors are calculated. Note that these standard errors are conditional on the budget shares which we take as fixed. It is easy to imagine an alternative set of standard errors which models the dependence of the weights on the prices—for example, through a cross-country model of consumer behavior. We do not consider that extension here, in large part because we do not want to commit to any such model, instead regarding the failure of arbitrage standard errors as descriptive measures of the dispersion of the ε_n^c—not directly but through the PPP indexes. Once again, the formulas are developed in Deaton and Dupriez (2009).

2. Practical Issues: Linking ICP Prices to Household Survey Data

In this section, we discuss how to bring together the prices of goods and services from the ICP and the budget weights from the household surveys. There are some immediate differences between the two projects. First, the ICP covers all of the countries in the world, at least in principle, while our interest is confined to the countries that are included in the global poverty count. As we shall see, this necessitates some prior screening and processing of the ICP price data. Second, not all of the relevant countries in the ICP have household surveys, and some do not allow them to be used for poverty-related analysis. Third, the surveys that we use were not collected for the purpose of calculating international price indexes. In particular, the categories of consumption for which we have data are not uniform across countries, and none match exactly the list of consumption goods that is used for the ICP itself, some of which are not covered in the surveys at all. We discuss each of these issues.

At its heart, the ICP is a large-scale price collection effort in which a list of commodities is priced in many countries. In practice, it is impossible to use a single list for all countries of the world, and for this and for management reasons, the 146 countries that were included in the 2005 round were broken up into six geographic regions. At a first stage, each region carried out its own regional calculations in which PPP indexes were calculated for all of the countries in each region, with a separate numeraire currency in each region. At a second stage, these regional estimates were linked to give a global set of PPPs with the (international) U.S. dollar as the unit of account. At the first stage in each region, the prices for the detailed regional list in each country are combined to give prices for 155 "basic headings" of GDP, 110 of which are items of "individual consumption expenditures by households." These are then linked through a set of "Ring" countries, strategically placed in each region, to give a global list of basic heading parities in a single numeraire currency—the process was developed by Diewert (2008), which contains a full account; see also Hill (2007a, 2007b). Deaton and Heston (2010) explain the procedure in more detail and discuss some of its strengths and weaknesses.

For the calculations here, we recalculate the global list of parities for basic headings but excluding the Organisation for Economic Co-operation and Development (OECD) region because we want our calculations to exclude price data from the rich countries. Our global P4s are developed entirely from information from the countries whose poverty is being measured, and neither the total number of global poor nor of the globally poor in any poor country should depend on commodity prices or expenditure patterns in rich countries. In practice, this change makes very little difference, and the prices we use for each basic heading in each country are almost identical to those used by the ICP. Given those prices, and the 62 ICP non-OECD countries for which we have survey data, we calculate our P3 and P4 indexes, treating all countries simultaneously irrespective of their region.

When the survey categories are finer than the basic headings for consumption in the ICP, they can be aggregated up to match. The harder case is when the categories are larger in the survey than in the ICP, or are neither larger nor smaller but different. For example, one basic head in the ICP consumption is "butter and margarine"; a survey might have these two separate, or part of a larger group, "butter, margarine, and edible oils," or have two categories, one of which contains butter together with other items, and one of which contains margarine together with other items. In the two last cases, our procedure is to aggregate the survey categories until we have a category that contains multiple whole basic headings, and then to split the aggregate according to the proportions in the national accounts on a household by household basis. Following the same example, if we have a survey category "butter, margarine, and edible oils" and if the country's national accounts show that, in aggregate, two-thirds of the category is edible oils, we then go through the survey data, household by household, and allocate two-thirds of each household's recorded expenditure to edible oils and one-third to butter and margarine. There are clearly other and potentially more sophisticated ways of synchronizing the two lists, some of which might be worth experimental calculations. However, the example of butter and margarine was chosen to illustrate a typical case. All of the surveys used here have many categories of consumption, and there is no case in which we were forced to allocate large groupings, such as cereals, let alone all food.

In all cases, we used the latest national household survey that was available to us. In the worst cases (Argentina and Djibouti from 1996 and Burundi from 1998), weights calculated from the survey were almost a decade older than the ICP prices (2005). All of the other surveys used here are post-2000, with 2003 the modal year; the countries, survey names, and year of data collection are listed in appendix A4 of Deaton and Dupriez (2009). While it would be ideal to be able to match expenditure weights to the year of survey prices, we would expect the expenditure patterns—especially those of the poor—to change slowly enough that even a lag as long as a decade is unlikely to invalidate the procedure. Indeed, most statistical offices around the world construct their domestic consumer price indexes with weights that are several years (in extreme cases several decades) older than the prices themselves.

There are a number of cases where consumption items that are basic headings in the ICP do not appear in the survey. Indeed, there is considerable diversity in survey questionnaires and methodology. The number of consumption items covered in questionnaires varies from 39 in Djibouti (recall method, with 64 out of the 105 basic headings omitted) to 6,927 in Brazil (diary method, with only 7 basic headings not covered). On average, 23 of the 105 basic headings are "missing" in survey questionnaires. In most cases, these are basic headings that represent very limited consumption shares (e.g., animal-drawn vehicles). It is clear that there is an urgent need to improve and harmonize practices of household consumption measurement in surveys.

It is useful to separate items that are indeed consumed, but are not collected in the survey, from items that are not consumed but still appear in the ICP lists. The most important example of the former is owner-occupier rents. Such imputed flows are rarely collected directly (though in places where there is an active rental market, it is sometimes possible to ask owners how much their home could be rented for), but are imputed ex post from housing characteristics weighted up according to the coefficients in a hedonic regression estimated on the (selected) subset of rented houses. This method is probably good enough to give an average for the national income accounts, but we doubt that it gives adequate answers at the individual level, and we were not successful in calculating satisfactory estimates to add back into our surveys. One major concern with any attempt to do so is that rental markets are mostly urban, so that a hedonic regression will primarily reflect the value of housing amenities in towns and cities. To take those coefficients and use them to impute rents to rural housing runs the risk of attributing consumption to the poor that bears little relationship to the real rental value of their homes. The situation is further compromised by the fact that, in many of our surveys, we do not have adequate documentation of how the rental category was constructed. Given this, and some unsatisfactory early experiments, we eventually dropped the rental category from all the surveys, so that our P3s and P4s exclude this category; note that "dropping" a category is equivalent to assuming that its P3 or P4 is the same as the overall P3 or P4 for the country. This is clearly unsatisfactory but is probably the best that can be done, especially once we recognize that the ICP parities for this category are also problematic—see Deaton and Heston (2010) and Deaton (2010) for discussion.

An even more extreme case is financial intermediation services indirectly measured (FISIM). According to current national accounting practice, the profits of banks and insurance companies, which in competitive markets would be equal to the value of financial intermediation and risk-bearing services to their customers, are added into the estimates of consumption by households. Once again, these items do not show up in the surveys. While we can imagine imputing FISIM to survey households according to some formula, we have chosen not to do so, in part reflecting our skepticism about the extent to which households around the global poverty line receive much benefit from these services.

There are also a number of items that (almost) never appear in surveys, and which in some cases do not appear in the ICP price surveys, including purchases of narcotics and prostitution, as well as "purchases by non-residential households in the economic territory of the country." Together with rent and FISIM, we drop these items from the lists. A number of other expenditure items are also excluded—namely purchases of animal-drawn vehicles, the maintenance and repair of major durables used for recreation and culture, and purchases by residential households in the rest of the world (though some of these items are probably included in other basic headings). After all of these exclusions, our calculations are based on 102 out of the 110 consumption basic headings in the ICP.

There are also items that are included in the ICP but are not purchased in some countries, and where the ICP has no prices. Two notable examples are pork and alcohol in Muslim countries. We do not want to drop these items, however, because there are valid observations on both prices and expenditures for the majority of the countries in the groups, and we do not want to discard that information. For such cases, our procedure is to impute the missing price using the CPD regressions (21.4) so that, for example, we impute a price for pork in Bangladesh using the country effect for Bangladesh (which essentially gives us the exchange rate for Bangladesh) and the "pork effects" from the other countries, which give us a typical relative price for pork. We then leave the item in the survey expenditure files, but assign zero expenditure to all households.

One aspect of the surveys that cannot be defended is measurement error. There are good studies for a number of countries that compare national accounts and survey estimates of comparably defined items, and they frequently find large differences. For example, Triplett (1997) has found such differences for the United States, even for items that are almost certainly well measured in the national accounts. Studies in India tend to favor the accuracy of the survey estimates over those from the national accounts, at least for food and apart from some special cases, such as Kulshesthra and Kar (2005). Note that we are not concerned here with the increasing divergence in many countries between total expenditures in the surveys and the national accounts, documented, for example, in Deaton (2005). That discrepancy is important for the measurement of poverty (and of GDP), but price indexes are invariant to the scale of consumption and depend only on its distribution. Unfortunately, the plausible accounts of the survey error—selective nonresponse by the richest or poorest households, or item-based nonresponse—will also affect the distribution over commodities. In consequence, differences in indexes—even aggregate plutocratic indexes—according to whether they are constructed with national accounts or survey weights, will reflect both deliberate choices about the definition of goods and accidental choices that come from poorly understood measurement errors.

Another important issue is the treatment of China. China collects household survey data from both rural and urban households and publishes summary tables annually in the *Statistical Abstract of China*. However, the household-level data were not made available to us for this work. Adding China to the list of countries without data is unattractive given its importance in the poverty calculations, and to avoid this we use the published data in a way that allows us to estimate the pattern of expenditures for Chinese households at various levels of household per capita expenditure, essentially by creating a synthetic survey that is consistent with the Engel curve and other information in the published tables. An account of our procedures is given in appendix A2 of Deaton and Dupriez (2009).

A final issue in matching ICP prices to the surveys is the treatment of rural and urban sectors. All of our surveys are nationally representative and cover both rural and urban households. In contrast, the ICP collected only urban prices in a number of countries, including most of Latin America, but also in China, while in India urban outlets were overrepresented in the price surveys. For the urban-only countries, we need a measure of the price of consumption in rural relative to urban, and for this we follow Chen and Ravallion (2010) and use the ratio of rural to urban poverty lines in those countries. While it is a big assumption that the ratio of the poverty lines correctly measures the relative price levels, there is no other obvious source of such information, and some correction is necessary. For countries where the adjustment is made, we adjust our surveys prior to the calculations by converting all household expenditures to urban prices by scaling up per capita household expenditure for each rural household by the ratio of the urban to rural poverty line. Once this adjustment is made, the sectors are ignored, and the survey treated as a single national sample to which the global poverty line, converted at the urban PPP, can be applied to calculate expenditure weights and counts of the numbers in poverty. India is treated somewhat differently: first, to take account of the fact that, although the ICP collected both urban and rural prices, the former were overrepresented, and, second, to recognize that the ratio of official urban to rural poverty lines is implausibly high, and has long been suspected to be the result of a computational error (Deaton 2003). Deaton and Dupriez (2009, appendix A1) detail the Indian calculations.

3. Results: PPPs, PPPPs, and Global Poverty Estimates

In this section, we present the various PPPs based on different data sources, and different weighting schemes, as well as their standard errors. We focus on measures of the differences between them. We then turn to the implications for the measurement of global poverty. The detailed country results are contained in the annex to this chapter; in the text, we show summary tables of differences between indexes, as well as global results. Annex table 21A.3 (column 3) contains the country by country PPPPs that can be used in other applications.

3.1 PPP (P3) Price Indexes from Surveys and National Accounts

We start with the standard PPPs (P3s) using aggregate expenditure shares taken either directly from the national accounts or aggregated up from the surveys. Annex table 21A.1 shows our country by country calculations of the aggregate (plutocratic) purchasing power parity exchange rates for household consumption together with those from the ICP. There are 62 countries, and they are listed regionally, Asia first, then South America, Western Asia, and Africa. The ICP numbers in the first column come from the ICP final report (World Bank 2008a) and relate to "individual consumption expenditures by households." Our own calculations in this table, with two calculations each for GEKS-Fisher, GEKS-Törnqvist, and CPDW, use both surveys and national accounts, so that both sets of weights relate to aggregate national purchases, with one estimated from aggregating up the surveys and one estimated directly from the national accounts. If the survey and national accounts consumption data were consistent, and had the same coverage of goods and services, the two calculations would give the same results. The ICP estimates in the first column are a subset of the global estimates that come from the global parities for each basic heading, which were constructed differently from our numbers (see the discussion in section 2). Our calculations, for both national accounts and survey-based aggregate weights, treat all 62 countries symmetrically in a single calculation. We are also using parities for the basic headings that were recalculated without data from the rich countries (see section 2), though this makes almost no difference in practice.

In table 21A.1, all of the P3 exchange rates are divided by the market exchange rates listed in World Bank (2008a) so that the numbers listed can be interpreted as the "price of consumption" in each country. This measure allows us to express all of the indexes in the same units, unobscured by differences in the "size" of currencies, which leads to PPP rates that can range from 1,000 to 0.001 and eases formal comparison between the indexes. The base country is India, so that all Indian figures are unity. For other countries, if the price of consumption is less than one, the P3 exchange in terms of rupees is lower than the market exchange rate in rupees, so that a rupee converted at the market exchange rate will buy more consumption than it will in India. According to the ICP numbers in table 21A.1, column 1, Fiji (2.59), Cape Verde (2.49), Gabon (2.38), and the Maldives (2.15) have the highest consumption price levels among these countries—for comparison, the figure for the United States is 2.83—and only Tajikistan (0.84), Kyrgyz Republic (0.89), Bolivia (0.90), Ethiopia (0.90), Paraguay (0.97), Pakistan (0.98), and the Lao People's Democratic Republic (0.99) have price levels lower than India's. In spite of many of the African countries being poorer than India, only one of those listed here has a lower consumption price level.

The final six paired columns of table 21A.1 show the aggregate prices of consumption according to the three aggregation formulas and the two sources of weights. The immediate impression is that, in spite of the different weighting schemes and different procedures, our indexes are close to the official ones. The correlation with the ICP price of consumption across the 62 countries is

0.9275 and 0.9337 for the survey and national accounts versions of the GEKS-Fisher, 0.9307 and 0.9360 for the GEKS-Törnqvist, and 0.9256 and 0.9346 for the CPDW; note that these are not correlations for the raw P3s, which would be artificially inflated by the variation in currency units from country to country, but the correlations of the price of consumption, whose magnitude is comparable across countries.

Table 21.1 summarizes the similarities and differences in the indexes. The top panel presents distances between pairs of indexes using the root mean squared difference over countries for each pair of indexes. The first important finding is that the distances in the first row are larger than any of the others, showing that the official ICP number is further away from *all* of our indexes (RMSEs of around 0.15–0.16) than any of our indexes are from one another. The ICP index and our national accounts–based indexes use the same information, but differ for two reasons. One is that our indexes are calculated in one step using a single aggregation formula rather than different aggregation formulas by region. The second is that our indexes use only 102 of the

TABLE 21.1 Survey-Based (S) and NAS-Based Estimates (N) of the Price of Aggregate Consumption

	ICP	Fisher (N)	Fisher (S)	Törnqvist (N)	Törnqvist (S)	CPDW (N)	CPDW (S)
				Root mean square distance			
ICP	0	0.156	0.150	0.147	0.146	0.149	0.148
Fisher (N)		0	0.065	0.033	0.068	0.050	0.088
Fisher (S)			0	0.054	0.023	0.078	0.047
Törnqvist (N)				0	0.048	0.042	0.067
Törnqvist (S)					0	0.066	0.070
CPDW (N)						0	0.078
CPDW (S)							0
				Summary statistics			
Mean	1.402	1.463	1.44	1.453	1.437	1.445	1.421
Standard deviation	0.389	0.404	0.377	0.39	0.372	0.404	0.373
				Regressions of log of ratio of survey to national accounts basis			
		Estimate	***t*-value**	**Estimate**	***t*-value**	**Estimate**	***t*-value**
ln *y*		-0.0170	(2.1)	-0.0107	(2.1)	−0.0200	(2.3)
Asia		0.0055	(0.1)	0.0077	(0.3)	0.0143	(0.3)
Africa		-0.0334	(0.7)	-0.0221	(0.7)	−0.0345	(0.7)
Latin America		0.0086	(0.2)	0.0041	(0.1)	0.0019	(0.0)
Central Asia		0.0283	(0.6)	0.0020	(0.0)	0.0011	(0.2)
constant		0.1313	(1.5)	0.0825	(1.7)	0.1542	(1.7)
F-regions (*p*)		2.69	0.041	2.53	0.051	2.97	0.056

Note: NAS = national accounts. The top panel shows the root mean squared difference between pairs of consumption price indexes over the 62 countries. The country price indexes are those shown in table 21A.1. Means and standard deviations in the second panel refer to the same indexes. The final panel shows regressions of the log of the ratio of the survey-based to national accounts–based estimates on the log of per capita GDP in PPP$ (from the 2008 World Development Indicators) and dummies for the ICP regions. For these regressions, India is treated as a region, and is the base country, so that Asia refers to non-Indian Asia.

105 consumption basic headings in the ICP; we exclude housing rental (actual and imputed), FISIM, and prostitution in order to match our national accounts–based (NAS) and survey results. As we shall see in section 3.3, these differences have substantial effects on the calculated P3s. In terms of table 21.1, recalculating the NAS-based PPPs using 105 basic headings, instead of 102, reduces the mean squared error (MSE) with the Fisher NAS index, 0.156 in table 21.1, to 0.099 (not shown), with the remainder of the discrepancy coming from the different methods of calculation.

The distances between the survey- and national accounts–based (102 basic headings) versions of our consumption price indexes are only 0.065 (Fisher), 0.048 (Törnqvist), and 0.078 (CPDW), less than half the size of the difference between our survey-based indexes and the ICP national accounts–based indexes. These differences are important, but smaller than the differences induced by the combination of dropping some basic headings and using the ICP method of calculation. The top panel of table 21.1 also shows that the GEKS-Fisher and GEKS-Törnqvist indexes are typically close to one another—whether the weights come from surveys or from national accounts—and that both are somewhat further away from either of the CPDW indexes. Within a weighting scheme—national accounts or surveys—different indexes tend to be closer to one another than are the same indexes across weighting schemes. The overall conclusion is that the most important difference comes from the procedures used in the ICP versus those adopted here, as well as the exclusion of three basic headings. The second most important difference is between whether the aggregate expenditure weights come from the surveys or from the national accounts. Least important is the choice of formula, with Fisher and Törnqvist closer to one another than either is to the CPDW.

The second panel shows the means and standard deviations of the indexes. The standard deviations are very similar, but the ICP mean is about 3 percent lower than the others. Put differently, and in comparison with the direct calculations, the regional structure of the ICP, and other differences in calculation, results in the Indian consumption price level being higher relative to the other countries listed here. The dropping of the three basic headings turns out not to be important; replacing them and recalculating the NAS-based PPPs with 105 basic headings give the same estimates as with 102 basic headings.

The final panel of table 21.1 shows a series of regressions that test for systematic differences between the national accounts and survey versions of our indexes. These help understand why the indexes differ, but will also help impute indexes for countries where we have national accounts but no survey estimates of household consumption patterns. The estimates show that survey estimates are lower in better-off countries, with the ratio falling by between 1 and 2 percent for every doubling of per capita income. Even so, the effects are barely significant. The *F*-statistics for the regional effects are typically close to significance at the 5 percent level, but tend to be inconsistent across indexes and quite small. It is not clear whether it would be worthwhile using these results to estimate survey-based indexes in countries without surveys, rather than simply using the national accounts–based indexes themselves.

We have looked in more detail at the reasons for the differences between the national accounts and the survey-based indexes. Since both indexes use the same parities for the 102 basic headings, differences are driven entirely by the pattern of expenditures over the parities. We have calculated, for each survey, the correlation between the (processed) survey-based estimates of the aggregate budget shares and those from the national accounts for all categories of consumption and for the subgroup of food, drinks, tobacco, and narcotics. It is not obvious what to expect of these numbers, nor how low a correlation would have to be to be a source for concern. There are a few very low numbers, even for the somewhat easier to measure food category. In an extreme case, the budget shares from the 2003 survey of Chad correlate with the national accounts numbers at only 0.090 over all goods, and only 0.023 for food. There are a number of other correlations under 0.5. We have done some cross-checking of these numbers, and as is usually the case in comparing surveys and national accounts, the problems are not easily attributable to one side or the other.

Table 21A.2 presents the standard errors associated with the plutocratic survey-based PPPs. We show only the GEKS-Fisher and the CPDW; the results for the GEKS-Törnqvist are similar to those for the GEKS-Fisher, and indeed the estimates of the sampling standard errors are identical. We present the PPPs themselves here rather than price of consumption; the former is the latter multiplied by the market rate of exchange of local currency to rupees. The standard errors are the standard errors of the logarithms of the PPPs, and so can be thought of as relative standard errors. They are also the standard errors for the logarithms of the prices of consumption in table 21A.1. There are two main points. First, the sampling errors are very small. Although some of the surveys have small sample sizes, the sampling standard errors for the PPP indexes are negligible. Second, the same is not true for the standard errors associated with failure of arbitrage or failure of the law of one price. Akin to the Paasche and Laspeyres Spread, these standard errors measure the uncertainty associated with picking one particular index number when relative prices are not the same in different countries. These standard errors are typically in the vicinity of from 8 to 10 percent, as opposed to a half to a tenth of 1 percent for the sampling standard errors. This finding of negligible standard errors from sampling, but substantial uncertainty from variations in relative prices, characterizes all of our results.

3.2 Poverty-Weighted Purchasing Power Parities, P4s

Table 21A.3 shows the first set of poverty-weighted PPPs or P4s; these are calculated using all 50 poverty lines that we have available according to the first variant described in section 1.3, in which the global poverty line is the poverty-weighted average of the individual lines converted to world rupees. Column 1 shows the closed-form approximation to the Törnqvist P4 that serves as the starting point for the further calculation, followed by the iteratively calculated Törnqvist indexes at bandwidths of 1, 0.5, and 0.1 standard deviations of the log per capita total expenditure; we use a bi-weight kernel

$$K(t) = \frac{15}{16}(1-t^2)^2 \quad if\,|\,t\,| \leq 1$$

$$K(t) = 0 \quad if\,|\,t\,| > 1 \qquad (21.11)$$

where t is the difference between the household's per capita total expenditure and the local currency version of the international poverty line divided by the bandwidth. The final two columns show the Fisher and CPDW P4s, both calculated using the smallest (0.1 standard deviation) bandwidth. The Törnqvist closed-form starting value is something of an outlier relative to the other indexes which are once again very similar to one another. Choosing a good bandwidth is a question of trading off bias against variance; a small bandwidth means we only use households near the poverty line, but the result is a larger sampling variance in our estimates. Tables 21A.4 and 21A.5 show how this works; table 21A.5 lists the numbers of households at each bandwidth for the indexes in table 21A.3, while table 21A.4 lists the corresponding standard errors of the log PPPPs. For example, in a country with a large survey such as Indonesia, there are 22,760 households in the band around the poverty line when the bandwidth is 1 standard deviation, which falls to 10,415 with a bandwidth of a half, and only 1,916 with a bandwidth of 0.1. The corresponding sampling standard errors rise from 0.06 to 0.08 to 0.15 of 1 percent so that even with the smallest bandwidth, the sampling errors are negligible. Even for countries with much smaller sample sizes in the surveys, where the standard errors are correspondingly larger—for example, Paraguay—the sampling standard errors at the smallest bandwidth are not much more than 1 percent.

Table 21.2 extends table 21.1 and shows the root mean square differences of the distances between the various indexes expressed, as before, as the price of consumption. In this table, F, T, and C stand for Fisher, Törnqvist, and CPDW, respectively, while N and S stand for national accounts and surveys so that, for example, F(S) and T(N) are the plutocratic Fisher index using survey weights and the plutocratic Törnqvist index using expenditure weights from the national accounts. The indexes with numbers refer to the bandwidth, so that F1.0, F0.5, and F0.1 are the Fisher P4 prices of consumption calculated at bandwidths of 1.0, 0.5, and 0.1 of a standard deviation of the logarithm of per capita household expenditure. The first row shows, as expected, that the ICP price levels of consumption are relatively far away from the other indexes, with distances of from around 0.15 to 0.18. Our recalculated national accounts indexes are closer to the P4 indexes, and their survey-based counterparts are closer still. The three national accounts P3 indexes are between 0.09 and 0.11 away from the Fisher and Törnqvist P4s, and from 0.14 to 0.17 from the CPDW version of the P4. The survey-based P3 indexes, which use the same data as the P4s, are closer, from about 0.05 to 0.07 away from the Fisher and Törnqvist and from 0.09 to 0.12 for the CPDW. The closed-form Törnqvist approximation that we use to start the iterations for the

TABLE 21.2 Comparing Distances between Pairs of Alternative Indexes (root mean square differences over 62 countries of price of consumption)

	T0	F1.0	F0.5	F0.1	T1.0	T0.5	T0.1	C1.0	C0.5	C0.1
ICP	0.179	0.154	0.155	0.158	0.153	0.156	0.157	0.171	0.176	0.178
F(N)	0.105	0.101	0.104	0.104	0.102	0.106	106.000	0.158	0.164	0.167
T(N)	0.093	0.090	0.093	0.093	0.086	0.089	0.090	0.144	0.150	0.153
C(N)	0.107	0.103	0.105	0.105	0.099	0.102	0.102	0.144	0.149	0.152
F(S)	0.073	0.054	0.057	0.057	0.056	0.060	0.060	0.114	0.120	0.123
T(S)	0.073	0.058	0.061	0.062	0.052	0.056	0.057	0.112	0.119	0.121
C(S)	0.084	0.062	0.064	0.065	0.055	0.057	0.057	0.092	0.098	0.102
T0	0	0.062	0.064	0.064	0.058	0.061	0.062	0.121	0.126	0.127
F1.0	—	0	0.006	0.011	0.023	0.024	0.026	0.075	0.081	0.084
F0.5		—	0	0.010	0.023	0.022	0.024	0.072	0.077	0.080
F0.1			—	0	0.027	0.026	0.026	0.074	0.079	0.081
T1.0				—	0	0.006	0.012	0.073	0.079	0.082
T0.5					—	0	0.008	0.069	0.075	0.078
T0.1						—	0	0.069	0.074	0.077
C1.0							—	0	0.011	0.023
C0.5								—	0	0.019
C0.1									—	0

Note: F = Fisher; T = Törnqvist; C = CPDW; N = national accounts; S = survey. ICP stands for the price of consumption expenditures by individual households—that is, the PPP divided by the exchange rate. F(p), T(p), and C(p) are the aggregate (plutocratic) indexes computed from the surveys, Fisher, Törnqvist, and CPDW, respectively, again divided by the foreign exchange rate. The other indexes are indicated by their first letter, and by the bandwidths in terms of standard deviations of log PCE, 1.0, 0.5, or 0.1.

P4s is about as far away from the final P4s as the plutocratic survey-based indexes, so these latter could just as well have been used for starting values. Once we look within the P4 indexes alone, changing the bandwidth does not move the indexes apart by much, especially within a specific index, though, as is to be expected, the adjacent bandwidths are closer than are the two extremes. Even here, the CPDW P4 is not only further away from the other two indexes than they are from one another, but it also shows the largest internal changes as the bandwidth is reduced.

Table 21.3 examines the effects of different global poverty line procedures on the poverty-based purchasing power parity indexes. We consider two alternatives corresponding to the variants discussed in section 1.3: multiplying the 50 poverty lines by two, and the RCS procedure using only the local poverty line of 15 (here 14) very poor countries.

Table 21.3 shows that the different methods of calculating the global line do not have much effect on the poverty-weighted P4 indexes. Replacing (*a*) the 50 lines with poverty weighting by (*b*) 14 of the 15 poorest country lines used by RCS (we have no survey data for one country) with no weighting makes very little difference, with distances from the original consumption prices of 0.014 and 0.013 for the Fisher and Törnqvist and of 0.036 for the CPDW. Doubling the poverty lines moves the indexes somewhat further, though the distances are only 0.050 for the Fisher, 0.048 for the Törnqvist, and 0.084 for the CPDW, comparable to the distance moved by shifting from the survey-based P3s to P4s. The means of the original and RCS consumption prices are close, with some increase when we double the underlying poverty lines; this presumably reflects the changing balance of global poverty between India and the rest of the world as the poverty lines

TABLE 21.3 Comparing Distances between P4s under Different Poverty Lines (means, s.d.'s, and root mean square differences over 62 countries of price of consumption)

	Mean	Standard deviation	Distance from P4 with PL × 2	Distance from P4 with RCS PL
Fisher				
Original	1.404	0.379	0.057	0.014
PL × 2	1.455	0.384	0	0.050
RCS PL	1.410	0.376	—	0
Törnqvist				
Original	1.402	0.372	0.053	0.013
PL × 2	1.448	0.378	0	0.048
RCS PL	1.406	0.372	—	0
CPDW				
Original	1.347	0.373	0.101	0.036
PL × 2	1.437	0.381	0	0.084
RCS PL	1.362	0.364	—	0

Note: RCS = Ravallion, Chen, and Sangraula; PL = poverty line. Original indexes are the prices of consumption based on the P4 index with bandwidth of 0.1 standard deviations; the global poverty line is calculated by weighting by the number of poor people in each of the 50 countries. The PL x 2 uses the same 50 country poverty lines as in the original calculation, but multiplied by two; again, the global line is weighted by the number of people below the line in each country. This alternative is intended to mimic the comparison between dollar-a-day poverty and two-dollar-a-day poverty. The consumption price indexes with RCS PL are intended to mimic Ravallion, Chen, and Sangraula's (2009) global poverty line. They are calculated using the poverty lines for 14 of their 15 countries—we do not have data for Guinea-Bissau, which is excluded—and without weighting, so that the global poverty line is the unweighted average of the P4 converted value of the 14 lines.

are moved up, though the exact mechanism is not obvious. Once again the CPDW indexes are not only further away from the Fisher and Törnqvist than they are from one another, but the CPDW indexes are less internally stable, moving further when we vary the underlying poverty lines.

Table 21.4 looks for systematic patterns by income and region between the P4 and P3 indexes. In these regressions, the dependent variable is the logarithm of the ratio of the P4—using bandwidths of 0.1 standard deviations—to our calculated P3s using the national accounts weights. The reason for this choice is that these P3s are available for countries where there are no survey data, and are therefore the starting point for imputing P4s in the absence of survey data. None of the estimated regression coefficients are significant at conventional levels, so an argument could be made for simply using the P3 indexes. Even so, comparison with the results in table 21.1, which compared the survey- and national accounts–based P3s, shows that the income effects here are similar, so that most of the difference between the P4s and P3s can be traced to differences between the surveys and the national accounts expenditure patterns, consistently with other evidence on the indexes.

Table 21A.3, the table of country P4s, is one of the main results of the research program summarized here, and we hope these numbers will be used by others who wish to make international comparisons of the living standards of the global poor. In our own work, we have used column 3, the Törnqvist index with a bandwidth of 0.5, and we would recommend against using the CPDW, but other choices are possible. We also recognize that these numbers are more immediately comprehensible in U.S. dollars, for which we would recommend using a rate of 16.11 rupees to the dollar, the derivation of which is discussed in connection with table 21.5. Finally, it should be noted that all of the calculations in this chapter are for the calendar year 2005. For other years—at least until the results of the 2011 ICP become available—a rough updating procedure is to use the country consumer price indexes (available in the World Development Indicators); the (obvious) formula is

$$P_r^{ij} = P_t^{ij} \frac{\pi_j^{rt}}{\pi_i^{rt}} \tag{21.12}$$

where i is the base country, j is the comparison, t is the base year (2005), r is the year desired, and π_i^{rt} is the ratio of country i's consumer price index (CPI) in year r to year t. For countries that we do not cover, either because they do not appear in ICP 2005 or because there are no surveys, the results in table 21.4 support the use of the PPPs from the ICP itself.

TABLE 21.4 Income and Regional Effects in Poverty PPPs versus PPPs and the ICP Consumption PPP

	Fisher		Törnqvist		CPDW	
	Log of ratio of P4 with bandwidth 0.1 to P3 with NAS weights					
ln y	−0.0166	(1.6)	−0.0140	(1.7)	−0.0241	(1.8)
Asia	−0.0202	(0.3)	−0.0206	(0.4)	−0.0366	(0.5)
Africa	−0.0556	(1.0)	−0.0459	(1.0)	−0.0943	(1.2)
Latin America	−0.0275	(0.4)	−0.0218	(0.4)	−0.0351	(0.4)
Western Asia	−0.0353	(0.6)	−0.0429	(0.9)	−0.0826	(1.0)
Constant	0.1280	(1.3)	0.1079	(1.4)	0.1858	(1.1)
F regions (p)	0.99	0.42	0.89	0.48	1.75	0.15

Note: CPDW = Country Product Dummy-Weighted. India is the omitted "region." The last row shows the F-statistic for the omission of the regions, together with the associated p-value.

3.3 Global Poverty Estimates

We conclude with the main use of our poverty-weighted PPPs, which is the re-estimation of global poverty. As is already clear, our P4s are relatively close to the P3s from the ICP, so that the substitution of poverty weights for plutocratic national accounts weights will not, in and of itself, make a large difference to global poverty counts. However, this is far from being true of the choice of procedure for calculating the global poverty line. When we compute the global poverty line using the weighted average of the 50 national poverty lines, with numbers of people in poverty as weights, we get sharply lower global counts than when we use the lines from the 15 poorest countries, which is how the World Bank calculates its numbers. The main reason for this difference is the fact that India is included in the 50, but not in the 15. India has a large number of poor people and, by international standards, a low national poverty line. The global poverty line, and the associated global poverty count, is much lower when India is included than when it is excluded—see Deaton (2010) for further discussion and arguments for India's inclusion, the most important of which is the discontinuity with previous poverty counts that comes from its exclusion.

Table 21.5 presents poverty estimates for the world and for its main regions, with different PPPs and different procedures for calculating the global line. The first set of numbers reproduces the Bank's poverty counts for 2005 (World Bank 2008b). The Bank's poverty line is $38 per person per month (first row), calculated as the unweighted average of the PPP value of the local lines of 15 of the world's poorest countries (second row) with the conversion done using the P3s (third row) from the ICP (fourth row.) These parameters give a global poverty total of 1.32 billion, with the distribution over regions as shown. In the next three columns, we use P4s, and show the three different aggregation formulas: CPDW, Fisher, and Törnqvist. Because we lack household survey data for Guinea-Bissau, which is one of the 15 countries, we work with the remaining 14. This exclusion makes almost no difference, and we can reproduce the first column very closely using the 14 countries and the PPPs from the ICP (calculations not shown here).

Using P4s and 14 countries for the global line, the global poverty count varies from 1.13 billion using the Törnqvist to 1.21 using the CPDW. (For the GEKS indexes the range is only 1.13–1.16.) The reduction in global poverty from the Bank numbers, from 1.32 billion, comes primarily from our treatment of housing rental in the 14 index countries for several of whom the ICP parity estimates of housing are incorrect, essentially because the national accounts make little or no allowance for imputed rents. The ICP treatment of housing is entirely appropriate for its main purpose, which is the estimation of GDP, but is not appropriate for poverty calculations—see Deaton and Heston (2010) and Deaton (2010) for further discussion. Our treatment of rentals, which assumes that the parity for rentals is the same as for consumption as a whole, raises the P3s and P4s for several of the index countries, which lowers their poverty lines in international currency, so that our poverty lines—shown here in international rupees given that we cannot include the United States in our P4s—are lower than the Bank's, and a lower line gives a lower poverty count.

The final three columns in table 21.5 show our preferred poverty estimates, preferred because they take all poverty lines into account, with appropriate weights. Here we use poverty lines, not just from the 14 poorest countries, but from the 50 countries whose poverty lines are included in RCS. Because these countries differ in levels of development and poverty rates, we use our P4s to convert their poverty lines, and then take a weighted average using as weights the numbers of poor people in each country. These calculations are done simultaneously with the calculation of the P4s, so that the international rupee value of the local poverty lines, the local poverty counts, and the P4s are all mutually consistent once the calculations are completed.

These global poverty lines are sharply lower, not only than the Bank's line, but also than our own P4 lines using only 14 countries. The largest contributor to this difference is the inclusion of

TABLE 21.5 Number of Poor People in 2005 by Region Using Different Poverty Lines and Purchasing Power Parity Exchange Rates

millions

Global poverty line (international $ or rupees)		$38	Rs 576.86	Rs 557.00	Rs 547.83	Rs 495.06	Rs 487.94	Rs 484.96
No. of national poverty lines used		15	14	14	14	50	50	50
PPP type		P3	P4	P4	P4	P4	P4	P4
Aggregation formula		ICP	CPDW	Fisher	Törnqvist	CPDW	Fisher	Törnqvist
Rupees per US$		15.60	13.58	17.21	16.05	13.68	17.40	16.11
Line in US$ per day		$1.25	$1.40	$1.06	$1.12	$1.19	$0.92	$0.99
	Population	**Number of poor**						
World	5,202	1,319	1,209	1,164	1,129	867	874	865
East Asia and Pacific	1,811	308	243	234	231	149	155	159
South Asia	1,451	585	550	516	493	380	370	361
Latin America and Caribbean	535	44	42	40	38	31	31	30
East and Central Europe	465	17	14	11	12	9	9	9
Sub-Saharan Africa	698	355	353	356	349	294	306	303
Middle East and North Africa	242	9	6	5	5	3	3	3

Note: CPDW = Country Product Dummy-Weighted. The global poverty line is in terms of monthly per capita expenditure in international dollars (first column) or international rupees (other columns). The poverty lines for all the P4 versions are calculated simultaneously with the P4s and the poverty counts. For comparison, the PPP for individual consumption by households from the 2005 ICP for India in international dollars is 15.60, so that $38 converts to 592.8 rupees; this PPP is not used in our own calculations.

India in the 50 countries. India has a very low poverty line relative to its level of GDP per capita, and makes a large contribution to global poverty, so its inclusion in the 50-country calculation brings down the global line and the global count. After the 2005 round of the ICP, the Bank recalculated its global line with the new P3s and chose a new index group, which excluded India. As was the case with the 14-country-based P4s, there is little difference in counts according to the aggregation formula used for the P4s, and for all three cases we estimate the global poverty count to be between 865 and 874 million people. Compared with the Bank's estimate of 1.32 billion, more than 100 million comes from our better treatment of housing, and the rest from the inclusion of more countries—particularly India—in the global poverty line.

How can we think about the poverty lines in table 21.5 in terms of dollars? While we recognize that it is inevitable that people will want such numbers, a good reason for *not* calculating them is that the structure of the United States—or of other advanced economies—is quite different from the structures of the economies where the global poor live, so that index numbers that compare the two are subject to a great deal of uncertainty and vary greatly across aggregation formulas. It is to avoid this unnecessary uncertainty that we have computed both P3s and P4s using only information from the countries included in the global poverty count. Even so, in recognition of the demand, we present PPPs from international rupees to dollars; these are strictly "below-the-line" calculations that do not feed back into any of the poverty calculations in the table.

The calculations are done as follows. We first convert the basic heading prices for the 62 countries into international rupees using the P4s for local currency to international rupees. We then compute 62 pair-wise price indexes (rupees per dollar) comparing the prices in each country with U.S. prices using the poverty line weights from the 62 countries and national accounts consumption weights from the United States. Note that there are no poverty line weights for the United States because no one lives at that level, and, in any case, there is an argument for making the comparison using the weights of an above-middle-class American—a member of the audience for international poverty statistics. The resulting rupee to dollar exchange rates vary across aggregation methods, but are virtually independent of the country used for the comparison (e.g., the Fisher index varies only from 17.3 to 17.5 across the 62 countries), so we take simple averages over the group of countries used in the poverty line calculations, either 14 or 50 in table 21.5. The results are shown in the fifth (PPP) and sixth (poverty line in dollars per day) rows of table 21.5; in the first column we use the consumption PPP from the ICP, as is done in the Bank's calculations.

We tend to disfavor the CPDW on theoretical grounds, so we are left with daily per person global poverty lines of \$0.99 (Törnqvist) and \$0.92 (Fisher). Not much weight should be attached to the fact that these numbers are so close to the original dollar a day—which is around \$1.45 at 2005 prices. Moreover, the full range from \$0.92 to \$1.19 reflects not the uncertainty in the global line itself, which varies only from 485 to 495 international rupees a month, but the difficulty of making purchasing power comparisons between the United States and poor countries, comparisons which need not (and in our view should not) play any part in calculating the global line.

6. Summary and Conclusions

Our aim in this chapter is to show how to calculate purchasing power parity exchange rates that reflect the consumption patterns of poor people around the world, poverty-based PPPs, or P4s, rather than the familiar P3s. P4s, unlike P3s, require household survey information, but there are currently enough household surveys to cover the vast majority of the world's poor population. P4s, unlike P3s, need to be calculated simultaneously with the global poverty line, because the price indexes depend on the line and the line depends on the price indexes. The fixed point can be calculated explicitly in a special case, though here we use an iterative procedure that works more generally. We have developed formulas for standard errors of our estimates in order to address the concern that some of the household surveys have small samples, so that the estimates might be too noisy for use. In practice, the standard errors from sampling are small, negligibly so relative to the more general uncertainty associated with the choice of index number formula. The design and detail of household surveys vary widely across the world, and many compromises and assumptions have to be made to adapt the survey data to match the prices from the International Comparison Program. We believe our procedures are unlikely to be a source of much error in our final estimates.

In the end, poverty-weighted purchasing power parity exchange rates look very much like the regular purchasing power parity exchange rates that use weights from the national accounts, certainly when we confine ourselves to comparisons that do not involve the rich countries of the world. Although it is true that poor people have different consumption patterns from the aggregate patterns in the national accounts, the reweighting is similar in different countries, so that the price indexes between each pair do not usually change by much. There are, of course, exceptions, but the weighting differences between P4s and P3s are probably not of great importance for estimating global poverty.

A larger source of difference between the P3s and P4s is data inconsistency between household surveys and national accounts, so that the consumption pattern in one is often different from the consumption pattern in the other, even when we use both to estimate aggregate consumption. Some of this comes from difference in definition and coverage—FISIM and owner-occupied rental equivalence are not collected in surveys, nor (usually) are expenditures on narcotics or prostitution. Perhaps more important are measurement errors in either the surveys or the national accounts or both. Yet even the differences in these weights do not generate large differences between P3s and P4s.

When we use our preferred P4s to calculate global poverty, we find global poverty counts that are close to the World Bank's estimates *prior* to the revisions that accompanied the revision of the ICP, somewhat less than 900 million people, as opposed to the Bank's new estimates of 1.3 billion. This difference comes, not from our use of P4s as opposed to P3s, but from our inclusion of India's national poverty line in the calculation of the global line, and, to a lesser extent, from our discarding the faulty housing parities from the 2005 ICP. The Bank's new global poverty line does not include India's line, and is therefore much higher than our line, or indeed the Bank's earlier line.

There are a number of important issues that we do not address. First among these is that we make no attempt to use separate *prices* for the poor. Instead, we confine ourselves to reweighting the same prices to match the expenditure patterns of households near the global poverty line. The Asian Development Bank (ADB 2008) has undertaken experimental work to identify the prices paid by the poor, by collecting prices in shops and markets thought to be patronized by the poor and by specifying varieties of goods that are typically purchased by the poor. One potential weakness of these procedures is that it is unclear exactly what and where the poor buy, and the ADB's specifications were set by groups of experts. Perhaps a better source of such information is to use the unit values in household surveys, which have the advantage of relating to actual purchases by poor people. The corresponding disadvantage is that there is no obvious way of specifying quality, or of controlling for quality variation across poor and nonpoor. A useful project would be to compare unit values with the prices collected for the 2005 ICP.

Our work also raises a number of issues that are relevant for future work on the ICP and on household surveys. For the former, it is clear that, in some respects, the demands of national accounting and of poverty work are different. For example, for poverty work we need prices paid by consumers, not prices paid by governments on behalf of consumers—a distinction that is particularly troubling in the case of health-related goods such as pharmaceuticals. It is also the case that when direct measurements break down or are difficult, the supplementary imputations that are suitable for estimating national accounts are sometimes different than those that would make the most sense for estimating poverty.

On household surveys, our plea is mostly for greater harmonization across countries. We realize that surveys are used for different purposes in different countries, and that a survey that works in one country may be useless in another. Nevertheless, greater standardization is certainly possible in some cases, not only in data collection, but in the reporting and documentation of survey design.

ANNEX

Country Tables

TABLE 21A.1 Consumption Prices Using National Aggregate Expenditures as Weights

	Pc ICP	Pc Fisher		Pc Törnqvist		Pc CPDW	
		NAS	Survey	NAS	Survey	NAS	Survey
India	1	1	1	1	1	1	1
Bangladesh	1.120	1.091	1.077	1.079	1.063	1.098	1.073
Bhutan	1.183	1.158	1.139	1.135	1.128	1.126	1.142
Cambodia	1.116	1.111	1.175	1.092	1.147	1.057	1.135
China	1.411	1.404	1.354	1.410	1.389	1.399	1.361
Fiji	2.589	2.222	2.124	2.162	2.106	2.184	2.079
Indonesia	1.221	1.185	1.184	1.163	1.169	1.143	1.168
Lao PDR	0.993	1.043	1.090	1.048	1.076	1.033	1.123
Malaysia	1.577	1.497	1.440	1.471	1.439	1.416	1.379
Maldives	2.150	1.716	1.721	1.708	1.702	1.668	1.613
Mongolia	1.225	1.217	1.234	1.204	1.216	1.166	1.172
Nepal	1.048	0.989	1.003	0.976	0.999	0.950	0.999
Pakistan	0.984	1.038	1.071	1.029	1.055	1.005	1.052
Philippines	1.241	1.238	1.249	1.221	1.238	1.194	1.199
Sri Lanka	1.126	1.178	1.150	1.157	1.142	1.128	1.106
Thailand	1.227	1.306	1.299	1.268	1.273	1.219	1.232
Vietnam	1.055	1.031	1.058	1.044	1.069	1.028	1.048
Argentina	1.318	1.383	1.347	1.374	1.359	1.363	1.326
Bolivia	0.900	1.020	1.056	1.007	1.043	0.955	1.013
Brazil	1.828	1.992	1.951	1.912	1.888	1.956	1.917
Colombia	1.452	1.676	1.693	1.642	1.644	1.619	1.595
Paraguay	0.974	1.094	1.074	1.083	1.074	1.051	1.030
Peru	1.416	1.670	1.621	1.642	1.571	1.677	1.540
Armenia	1.212	1.146	1.164	1.142	1.143	1.140	1.124
Azerbaijan	1.039	0.961	0.883	0.968	0.933	0.987	0.918
Kazakhstan	1.382	1.070	1.060	1.100	1.068	1.122	1.068
Kyrgyz Republic	0.896	0.789	0.807	0.823	0.837	0.822	0.856
Tajikistan	0.840	0.613	0.775	0.783	0.821	0.755	0.844
Yemen, Rep.	1.345	1.201	1.150	1.166	1.156	1.139	1.150
Benin	1.475	1.545	1.448	1.544	1.490	1.576	1.499
Burkina Faso	1.299	1.417	1.382	1.389	1.379	1.388	1.376
Burundi	1.168	1.283	1.214	1.298	1.212	1.301	1.163

TABLE 21A.1 Consumption Prices Using National Aggregate Expenditures as Weights (*continued*)

	Pc ICP	Pc Fisher		Pc Törnqvist		Pc CPDW	
		NAS	Survey	NAS	Survey	NAS	Survey
Cameroon	1.578	1.690	1.681	1.674	1.686	1.665	1.655
Cape Verde	2.493	2.402	2.295	2.383	2.286	2.382	2.264
Chad	1.755	1.995	1.882	1.944	1.847	2.082	1.849
Congo, Dem. Rep.	1.886	1.975	1.989	1.934	1.961	1.976	2.010
Congo, Rep.	2.013	2.122	2.072	2.111	2.072	2.122	2.083
Côte d'Ivoire	1.746	1.850	1.828	1.837	1.846	1.859	1.850
Djibouti	1.715	1.950	2.051	1.935	2.025	1.796	1.985
Ethiopia	0.897	1.068	1.039	1.035	1.016	0.982	0.978
Gabon	2.378	2.505	2.469	2.507	2.483	2.565	2.525
Gambia, The	1.023	1.224	1.314	1.232	1.296	1.147	1.247
Ghana	1.394	1.593	1.540	1.577	1.540	1.572	1.516
Guinea	1.148	1.260	1.254	1.272	1.270	1.310	1.328
Kenya	1.223	1.380	1.340	1.370	1.335	1.377	1.326
Lesotho	1.523	1.671	1.726	1.712	1.721	1.650	1.677
Madagascar	1.066	1.111	1.153	1.132	1.159	1.171	1.211
Malawi	1.359	1.572	1.462	1.577	1.501	1.559	1.482
Mali	1.552	1.663	1.585	1.641	1.590	1.654	1.601
Mauritania	1.341	1.569	1.530	1.534	1.507	1.521	1.469
Morocco	1.756	1.929	1.777	1.897	1.800	1.901	1.772
Mozambique	1.409	1.658	1.471	1.616	1.477	1.578	1.395
Niger	1.433	1.602	1.575	1.579	1.570	1.567	1.575
Nigeria	1.692	1.836	1.826	1.827	1.824	1.874	1.848
Rwanda	1.200	1.287	1.352	1.284	1.375	1.211	1.331
Senegal	1.598	1.768	1.742	1.751	1.727	1.758	1.696
Sierra Leone	1.361	1.597	1.571	1.593	1.576	1.539	1.510
South Africa	2.032	2.172	2.034	2.129	2.013	2.168	2.016
Swaziland	1.657	1.815	1.709	1.816	1.726	1.761	1.590
Tanzania	1.218	1.304	1.267	1.269	1.248	1.284	1.257
Togo	1.513	1.644	1.595	1.631	1.605	1.681	1.618
Uganda	1.182	1.240	1.172	1.257	1.205	1.230	1.154

Note: Pc = price of consumption; NAS = national accounts-based; CPDW = Country Product Dummy-Weighted. The first column is from the ICP final report (World Bank 2008a), and is the PPP for individual consumption expenditures by households divided by the foreign exchange rate, the "price of consumption" with India as base. The second, third, and fourth columns are prices of consumption using the parities for 102 basic heads, but using estimates of aggregate weights first from the national accounts, then from the household surveys. The first column and the first column of each pair differ only in the aggregation formulas, the Ring structure, and the merging of regional parities for the basic headings of consumption.

TABLE 21A.2 PPPs (P3s) for Consumption Using National Aggregates from Surveys and the Standard Errors (se) of Their Logarithms

	Pc Fisher			Pc CPDW		
	PPP	se(1)	se(2)	PPP	se(1)	se(2)
India	1.000	—	—	1.000	—	—
Bangladesh	1.571	0.0010	0.0836	1.565	0.0040	0.1048
Bhutan	1.139	0.0012	0.0693	1.142	0.0025	0.0828
Cambodia	109.1	0.0007	0.1040	105.4	0.0027	0.1308
China	0.251	0.0004	0.0975	0.253	0.0029	0.1293
Fiji	0.081	0.0011	0.0815	0.080	0.0038	0.0967
Indonesia	260.6	0.0004	0.0757	257.0	0.0026	0.0940
Lao PDR	263.2	0.0040	0.1000	271.4	0.0027	0.1370
Malaysia	0.124	0.0052	0.0862	0.118	0.0035	0.1128
Maldives	0.499	0.0062	0.0954	0.468	0.0038	0.1219
Mongolia	33.73	0.0007	0.0851	32.02	0.0031	0.1039
Nepal	1.622	0.0014	0.0848	1.616	0.0090	0.1046
Pakistan	1.446	0.0005	0.0799	1.420	0.0039	0.0941
Philippines	1.560	0.0005	0.0858	1.498	0.0040	0.1040
Sri Lanka	2.621	0.0006	0.0861	2.521	0.0032	0.1051
Thailand	1.185	0.0005	0.0765	1.124	0.0028	0.0877
Vietnam	380.6	0.0010	0.0860	376.9	0.0033	0.1104
Argentina	0.089	0.0008	0.0813	0.087	0.0045	0.0982
Bolivia	0.193	0.0015	0.0790	0.185	0.0048	0.0946
Brazil	0.107	0.0012	0.0986	0.106	0.0035	0.1196
Colombia	89.07	0.0011	0.0795	83.93	0.0034	0.0938
Paraguay	150.5	0.0017	0.0830	144.3	0.0034	0.1026
Peru	0.121	0.0010	0.0798	0.115	0.0038	0.0906
Armenia	12.08	0.0025	0.0791	11.66	0.0039	0.0894
Azerbaijan	94.62	0.0043	0.0950	98.37	0.0039	0.1164
Kazakhstan	3.195	0.0006	0.0809	3.219	0.0106	0.0921
Kyrgyz Republic	0.751	0.0041	0.0969	0.796	0.0049	0.1076
Tajikistan	0.055	0.0026	0.0974	0.060	0.0052	0.1061
Yemen, Rep.	4.993	0.0017	0.0868	4.991	0.0033	0.1035
Benin	17.32	0.0014	0.0966	17.93	0.0057	0.1323
Burkina Faso	16.53	0.0011	0.0746	16.45	0.0032	0.0906
Burundi	29.78	0.0022	0.1077	28.52	0.0047	0.1544
Cameroon	20.11	0.0014	0.0715	19.79	0.0028	0.0855
Cape Verde	4.613	0.0022	0.0893	4.551	0.0031	0.1051
Chad	22.52	0.0012	0.0742	22.12	0.0023	0.0884
Congo, Dem. Rep.	21.37	0.0008	0.0706	21.60	0.0033	0.0867
Congo, Rep.	24.78	0.0012	0.0755	24.92	0.0027	0.0883

TABLE 21A.2 PPPs (P3s) for Consumption Using National Aggregates from Surveys and the Standard Errors (se) of Their Logarithms (*continued*)

	Pc Fisher			Pc CPDW		
	PPP	se(1)	se(2)	PPP	se(1)	se(2)
Côte d'Ivoire	21.86	0.0018	0.0741	22.12	0.0034	0.0906
Djibouti	8.267	0.0010	0.0774	7.999	0.0041	0.0970
Ethiopia	0.204	0.0013	0.0846	0.192	0.0055	0.0970
Gabon	29.54	0.0009	0.0805	30.20	0.0030	0.0942
Gambia, The	0.852	0.0025	0.0800	0.808	0.0030	0.0935
Ghana	316.8	0.0009	0.0751	312.0	0.0069	0.0866
Guinea	103.7	0.0019	0.0975	109.8	0.0028	0.1237
Kenya	2.295	0.0010	0.0703	2.272	0.0026	0.0847
Lesotho	0.249	0.0019	0.0752	0.242	0.0032	0.0900
Madagascar	52.44	0.0023	0.0817	55.06	0.0039	0.0984
Malawi	3.927	0.0031	0.1121	3.980	0.0037	0.1549
Mali	18.96	0.0008	0.0710	19.15	0.0036	0.0859
Mauritania	9.190	0.0009	0.0751	8.823	0.0047	0.0900
Morocco	0.357	0.0008	0.0923	0.356	0.0033	0.1095
Mozambique	777.9	0.0030	0.0989	737.5	0.0031	0.1317
Niger	18.84	0.0011	0.0723	18.83	0.0024	0.0883
Nigeria	5.435	0.0011	0.0861	5.500	0.0029	0.1009
Rwanda	17.10	0.0021	0.0971	16.83	0.0031	0.1273
Senegal	20.83	0.0006	0.0700	20.28	0.0031	0.0843
Sierra Leone	103.3	0.0025	0.0848	99.26	0.0077	0.0989
South Africa	0.293	0.0014	0.0832	0.291	0.0030	0.1004
Swaziland	0.246	0.0040	0.0831	0.229	0.0027	0.1068
Tanzania	32.15	0.0013	0.0743	31.91	0.0046	0.0887
Togo	19.08	0.0009	0.0775	19.35	0.0029	0.0912
Uganda	47.33	0.0019	0.1105	46.58	0.0033	0.1536

Note: CPDW = Country Product Dummy-Weighted. Pc is the aggregate (plutocratic) consumption PPP expressed in local currency per Indian rupee. The Törnqvist index is not shown because the results are similar to those for the Fisher index. The second and third columns of each set show the standard errors associated with sampling from the household surveys and the standard errors associated with the failure of arbitrage. Standard errors are standard errors of the logarithms of the PPPs shown in the first column. Standard errors for India and China are not shown; the former is the base country, while for China we are using synthetic data that match the published tables.

TABLE 21A.3 Poverty-Weighted PPPs at Various Bandwidths

	Törnqvist indexes				Fisher	CPDW
	Approx.	1.0	0.5	0.1	0.1	0.1
India	1.000	1.000	1.000	1.000	1.000	1.000
Bangladesh	1.479	1.501	1.496	1.494	1.517	1.510
Bhutan	1.114	1.089	1.086	1.086	1.098	1.081
Cambodia	102.9	103.0	102.5	102.3	104.0	100.2
China	0.252	0.253	0.252	0.252	0.246	0.241
Fiji	0.082	0.080	0.080	0.080	0.081	0.077
Indonesia	259.3	252.5	251.5	251.0	255.3	245.5
Lao PDR	260.6	251.8	251.3	252.7	256.1	260.3
Malaysia	0.128	0.124	0.124	0.123	0.125	0.117
Maldives	0.532	0.506	0.501	0.491	0.505	0.484
Mongolia	33.84	32.92	32.83	32.74	33.23	30.65
Nepal	1.487	1.535	1.532	1.531	1.539	1.514
Pakistan	1.490	1.438	1.440	1.439	1.457	1.396
Philippines	1.522	1.482	1.476	1.473	1.486	1.382
Sri Lanka	2.554	2.521	2.514	2.509	2.526	2.346
Thailand	1.183	1.121	1.113	1.120	1.156	0.963
Vietnam	359.0	357.8	355.4	354.3	354.7	336.3
Argentina	0.083	0.081	0.081	0.081	0.080	0.073
Bolivia	0.192	0.183	0.183	0.183	0.186	0.175
Brazil	0.100	0.101	0.101	0.102	0.103	0.106
Colombia	93.99	87.81	87.78	88.47	89.99	86.33
Paraguay	147.8	144.9	144.1	145.2	145.4	138.0
Peru	0.122	0.117	0.117	0.118	0.120	0.114
Armenia	12.29	11.56	11.51	11.51	11.68	10.97
Azerbaijan	96.61	95.28	95.34	96.47	89.41	90.59
Kazakhstan	2.999	2.998	2.998	2.998	3.006	2.890
Kyrgyz Republic	0.799	0.755	0.744	0.741	0.740	0.715
Republic Tajikistan	0.060	0.055	0.056	0.056	0.048	0.054
Yemen, Rep.	4.885	4.781	4.750	4.795	4.631	4.494
Benin	18.26	17.70	17.68	17.64	17.14	16.87
Burkina Faso	16.12	15.97	15.93	15.91	15.90	15.40
Burundi	30.07	29.19	29.17	29.10	29.20	26.63
Cameroon	20.08	19.69	19.68	19.65	19.59	18.62
Cape Verde	4.308	4.297	4.273	4.303	4.354	4.067
Chad	23.17	22.12	22.11	22.10	22.48	21.46
Congo, Dem. Rep.	21.30	20.93	20.91	20.88	21.10	20.81
Congo, Rep.	26.19	24.68	24.66	24.67	24.52	23.89

TABLE 21A.3 Poverty-Weighted PPPs at Various Bandwidths (*continued*)

	Törnqvist indexes				Fisher	CPDW
	Approx.	**1.0**	**0.5**	**0.1**	**0.1**	**0.1**
Côte d'Ivoire	22.20	21.62	21.58	21.52	21.47	21.16
Djibouti	8.169	7.999	7.974	8.024	8.122	7.913
Ethiopia	0.200	0.194	0.194	0.193	0.197	0.178
Gabon	29.91	29.47	29.56	29.77	29.57	30.67
Gambia, The	0.912	0.855	0.855	0.853	0.859	0.785
Ghana	350.4	322.8	323.0	322.2	321.8	302.3
Guinea	111.3	105.8	105.8	105.8	104.2	109.0
Kenya	2.287	2.242	2.239	2.237	2.256	2.141
Lesotho	0.253	0.242	0.242	0.241	0.241	0.226
Madagascar	54.38	53.06	52.98	52.97	52.33	56.57
Malawi	3.993	3.909	3.903	3.887	3.782	3.622
Mali	19.29	18.73	18.70	18.71	18.60	18.38
Mauritania	9.466	8.942	8.919	8.875	9.066	8.415
Morocco	0.351	0.336	0.330	0.326	0.324	0.292
Mozambique	707.9	718.9	715.7	714.7	709.6	637.6
Niger	19.02	18.51	18.49	18.48	18.56	17.99
Nigeria	6.217	5.604	5.610	5.621	5.604	5.352
Rwanda	17.32	16.93	17.00	16.99	16.64	15.73
Senegal	21.13	20.28	20.24	20.24	20.45	19.45
Sierra Leone	107.8	103.5	103.5	103.2	102.9	96.47
South Africa	0.265	0.265	0.264	0.262	0.266	0.246
Swaziland	0.257	0.247	0.247	0.249	0.248	0.225
Tanzania	32.00	31.22	31.17	31.15	31.39	30.46
Togo	19.89	19.16	19.14	19.15	19.04	18.70
Uganda	46.74	46.15	46.04	45.76	44.34	40.90

Note: CPDW = Country Product Dummy-Weighted. Calculations using formulas described in the text. These are based on 50 local poverty lines and use 102 basic heads. The global poverty line is calculated by weighting each country's poverty line in international rupees by the estimated number of people below the line in that country.

TABLE 21A.4 Estimates of Standard Errors of Log P4s from Sampling

percent

	T(1.0)	T(0.5)	T(0.1)	F(0.1)	CPD(0.1)
India	—	0.00	0.00	0.00	0.00
Bangladesh	0.07	0.09	0.15	0.18	0.32
Bhutan	0.15	0.17	0.33	0.54	0.69
Cambodia	0.15	0.18	0.30	0.28	0.61
China	*0.05*	*0.06*	*0.13*	*0.13*	*0.30*
Indonesia	0.06	0.08	0.15	0.13	0.29
Fiji	0.16	0.24	0.58	0.87	1.25
Lao PDR	0.17	0.19	0.32	0.27	0.65
Malaysia	0.25	0.62	0.64	0.87	2.76
Maldives	0.52	0.83	1.59	1.49	3.24
Mongolia	0.18	0.21	0.38	0.30	0.79
Nepal	0.14	0.16	0.25	0.23	0.51
Pakistan	0.10	0.13	0.22	0.19	0.49
Philippines	0.09	0.12	0.20	0.20	0.37
Sri Lanka	0.10	0.13	0.26	0.25	0.62
Thailand	0.65	1.02	2.10	0.54	0.78
Vietnam	0.11	0.15	0.29	0.27	0.61
Argentina	0.19	0.32	1.09	1.13	1.06
Bolivia	0.24	0.29	0.76	0.74	1.27
Brazil	0.24	0.36	0.83	0.66	1.18
Colombia	0.19	0.31	0.65	0.61	1.25
Paraguay	0.36	0.48	1.28	1.06	2.01
Peru	0.20	0.29	0.63	0.45	1.33
Armenia	0.16	0.23	0.47	0.62	0.92
Azerbaijan	0.33	0.52	0.92	3.11	2.95
Kazakhstan	0.37	0.66	0.45	0.34	1.27
Kyrgyz Republic	0.57	0.83	1.56	1.39	2.28
Tajikistan	0.28	0.46	1.42	0.65	2.28
Yemen, Rep.	0.52	0.76	2.05	0.90	2.24
Benin	0.16	0.18	0.33	0.36	0.55
Burkina Faso	0.09	0.11	0.22	0.24	0.46
Burundi	0.24	0.27	0.46	0.44	1.04
Cameroon	0.25	0.28	0.41	0.53	0.74
Cape Verde	0.31	0.40	0.56	0.62	1.18
Chad	0.10	0.12	0.24	0.27	0.46
Congo, Dem. Rep.	0.12	0.16	0.30	0.21	0.51
Congo, Rep.	0.13	0.18	0.30	0.32	0.61

TABLE 21A.4 Estimates of Standard Errors of Log P4s from Sampling *(continued)*

percent

	T(1.0)	T(0.5)	T(0.1)	F(0.1)	CPD(0.1)
Côte d'Ivoire	0.12	0.15	0.28	0.34	0.53
Djibouti	0.19	0.29	0.53	0.68	1.02
Ethiopia	0.13	0.15	0.26	0.26	0.55
Gabon	0.20	0.30	0.68	0.70	1.15
Gambia, The	0.32	0.37	0.62	0.63	1.38
Ghana	0.08	0.11	0.23	0.26	0.47
Guinea	0.21	0.26	0.47	0.51	0.86
Kenya	0.08	0.09	0.17	0.22	0.34
Lesotho	0.14	0.18	0.33	0.41	0.62
Madagascar	0.20	0.26	0.54	0.57	1.12
Malawi	0.14	0.17	0.34	0.41	0.59
Mali	0.09	0.12	0.25	0.29	0.47
Mauritania	0.15	0.19	0.35	0.35	0.68
Morocco	0.13	0.26	0.79	0.87	1.68
Mozambique	0.20	0.22	0.34	0.43	0.69
Niger	0.08	0.10	0.18	0.21	0.36
Nigeria	0.09	0.11	0.21	0.22	0.40
Rwanda	0.19	0.23	0.39	0.47	0.88
Senegal	0.08	0.10	0.16	0.17	0.31
Sierra Leone	0.20	0.22	0.34	0.44	0.68
South Africa	0.09	0.12	0.23	0.21	0.44
Swaziland	0.21	0.28	0.60	0.79	1.03
Tanzania	0.15	0.19	0.31	0.36	0.62
Togo	0.09	0.11	0.19	0.25	0.37
Uganda	0.17	0.21	0.41	0.41	0.70

Note: The figures shown have been multiplied by 100, and are already standard errors of logs. Hence, for example, the estimated standard error of the log of the Törnqvist P4 for the Maldives with bandwidth 1 is 0.0052, or a little over half of 1 percent. For Armenia, Azerbaijan, Fiji, Ghana, Kazakhstan, Tajikistan, Kyrgyz Republic, and Morocco, we do not have information on the survey design and have assumed that the surveys are unstratified simple random samples, so that the standard errors shown are almost certainly too small. A synthetic data set was used for China.

TABLE 21A.5 Number of Observations within the Bandwidth around the Poverty Lines

	Sample size	T(1.0)	T(0.5)	T(0.1)	F(0.1)	CPD(0.1)
India	124,644	78,724	45,623	9,670	9,761	10,003
Bangladesh	7,448	5,595	3,049	616	631	638
Bhutan	4,007	1,047	469	84	82	81
Cambodia	14,984	7,014	3,392	641	683	650
China[a]	*2,000*	*721*	*363*	*74*	*71*	*71*
Indonesia	64,422	22,760	10,415	1,916	2,098	1,918
Fiji	5,244	1,761	807	158	158	149
Lao PDR	8,071	5,589	3,197	658	678	686
Malaysia	14,084	363	76	11	14	8
Maldives	2,728	157	42	11	11	7
Mongolia	11,162	4,112	1,913	339	371	334
Nepal	3,912	2,329	1,349	301	305	305
Pakistan	15,839	6,993	3,198	573	613	547
Philippines	42,094	17,839	8,998	1,814	1,882	1,673
Sri Lanka	16,924	4,484	1,785	342	360	258
Thailand	34,785	414	80	8	13	5
Vietnam	9,189	4,224	1,938	345	353	340
Argentina	27,245	2,304	798	135	136	109
Bolivia	5,732	1,125	415	77	77	72
Brazil	48,466	8,446	3,138	568	593	635
Colombia	22,949	2,357	880	166	169	163
Paraguay	2,682	580	260	51	47	52
Peru	18,911	3,464	1,227	219	217	214
Armenia	6,816	873	322	62	63	60
Azerbaijan	7,820	1,038	338	64	43	51
Kazakhstan	11,986	128	44	6	6	6
Kyrgyz Republic	1,081	210	81	14	16	14
Tajikistan	4,160	768	290	51	23	52
Yemen, Rep.	13,136	1,327	460	67	71	73
Benin	5,350	3,552	2,008	422	427	430
Burkina Faso	8,494	5,795	3,330	674	677	685
Burundi	6,668	3,807	2,124	444	436	463
Cameroon	10,992	5,111	2,603	522	524	482
Cape Verde	4,584	1,967	965	186	197	173
Chad	6,697	4,279	2,318	445	469	448
Congo, Dem. Rep.	11,959	6,626	3,508	713	709	714
Congo, Rep.	5,002	2,742	1,389	284	284	276
Côte d'Ivoire	10,800	5,473	2,769	562	564	567

TABLE 21A.5 Number of Observations within the Bandwidth around the Poverty Lines (*continued*)

	Sample size	T(1.0)	T(0.5)	T(0.1)	F(0.1)	CPD(0.1)
Djibouti	2,380	794	344	45	49	49
Ethiopia	16,672	7,966	4,206	898	956	697
Gabon	6,379	1,070	424	74	74	93
Gambia, The	2,238	1,326	737	167	171	137
Ghana	8,687	4,513	2,335	443	442	442
Guinea	7,095	4,901	2,755	571	568	569
Kenya	13,154	8,055	4,534	942	966	932
Lesotho	5,992	3,532	1,876	404	404	418
Madagascar	5,078	996	391	56	60	82
Malawi	11,280	7,428	4,048	838	855	889
Mali	4,494	3,065	1,843	401	400	406
Mauritania	9,385	2,991	1,335	245	279	219
Morocco	14,243	5,508	1,085	96	93	70
Mozambique	8,700	5,931	3,400	679	668	698
Niger	6,689	4,419	2,438	528	521	532
Nigeria	19,158	13,019	7,350	1,572	1,565	1,574
Rwanda	6,900	3,326	1,496	266	268	297
Senegal	6,594	4,095	2,266	483	490	464
Sierra Leone	3,719	2,717	1,574	352	353	353
South Africa	26,215	10,039	4,772	948	959	913
Swaziland	3,794	2,907	1,739	343	344	385
Tanzania	22,178	13,996	7,670	1,601	1,587	1,604
Togo	7,500	5,218	3,011	616	616	616
Uganda	9,711	6,295	3,641	755	755	737

Note: T = Törnqvist; F = Fisher; CPD = Country Product Dummy. The first column is total number of households in the survey.

a. A synthetic data set was used for China (see text and appendix A2 of Deaton and Dupriez 2009).

NOTE

1. We acknowledge invaluable assistance and advice from Bettina Aten, Shaida Badiee, Misha Belkindas, Yonas Biru, Shaohua Chen, Tefera Bekele Degefu, Yuri Dikhanov, Erwin Diewert, Alan Heston, D. S. Prasada Rao, Martin Ravallion, Sam Schulhofer-Wohl, Eric Swanson, Changqing Sun, and Fred Vogel, as well as from the referees and editors of this journal.

REFERENCES

ADB (Asian Development Bank). 2008. "Research Study on Poverty-Specific Purchasing Power Parities for Selected Countries in Asia and the Pacific." Manila, March.

Chen, Shaohua, and Martin Ravallion. 2010. "The Developing World Is Poorer than We Thought, but No Less Successful in the Fight against Poverty." *Quarterly Journal of Economics* 125 (4): 1577–1625.

Deaton, Angus. 2003. "Prices and Poverty in India, 1987–2000." *Economic and Political Weekly,* January 25, 362–68.

———. 2005. "Measuring Poverty in a Growing World (or Measuring Growth in a Poor World." *Review of Economics and Statistics* 87: 1, 1–19.

———. 2010. "Price Indexes, Inequality, and the Measurement of World Poverty." *American Economic Review* 100: 1, 5–31.

Deaton, Angus, and Olivier Dupriez. 2009. "Global Poverty and Global Price Indexes." World Bank, Washington, DC, and Princeton University, Princeton, NJ. http://www.princeton.edu/~deaton/downloads/Global_Poverty_and_Global_Price_Indexes.pdf.

Deaton, Angus, and Alan Heston. 2010. "Understanding PPPs and PPP-Based National Accounts." *American Economic Journal: Macroeconomics* 2 (4): 1–35.

Deaton, Angus, and John Muellbauer. 1980. *Economics and Consumer Behavior.* New York: Cambridge University Press.

Diewert, W. Erwin. 1976. "Exact and Superlative Indexes." *Journal of Econometrics* 4 (2): 115–45.

———. 2008. "New Methodology for Linking the Regions." DP 08-07, Department of Economics, University of British Columbia, July.

Gini, Corrado. 1924. "Quelques considérations au sujet de la construction des nombres indices des prix et des questions analogues." *Metron* 4 (1): 3–162.

Hill, Peter. 2007a. "The Ring Program: Linking the Regions." In *ICP 2005 Methodological Handbook.* http://siteresources.worldbank.org/ICPINT/Resources/Ch13_Ring_Feb07.doc.

———. 2007b. "Ring Comparison—Linking Within-Region PPPs Using Between-Region PPPs." In *ICP 2005 Methodological Handbook.* http://siteresources.worldbank.org/ICPINT/Resources/ch14_Linking_Apr_06.doc.

Kulshesthra, A. C., and Aloke Kar. 2005. "Estimates of Food Consumption Expenditure from Household Surveys and National Accounts." In *The Great Indian Poverty Debate,* ed. Angus Deaton and Valerie Kozel. Delhi: Macmillan, 102–18.

Prais, Sigbert J. 1959. "Whose Cost of Living?" *Review of Economic Studies* 26: 126–34.

Rao, D. S. Prasada. 1990. "A System of Log-Change Index Numbers for Multilateral Comparisons." *Comparisons of Prices and Real Products in Latin America,* ed. J. Salazar-Carillo and D. S. Prasada Rao, 127–39. New York: Elsevier Science Publishers.

———. 2005. "On the Equivalence of the Generalized Country-Product-Dummy (CPD) Method and the Rao System for Multilateral Comparisons." *Review of Income and Wealth* 51 (4): 571–80.

Ravallion, Martin, Shaohua Chen, and Prem Sangraula. 2009. "Dollar a Day Revisited." *World Bank Economic Review* 23 (2): 163–84.

Selvanathan, E. A., and D. S. Prasada Rao. 1994. *Index Numbers: A Stochastic Approach.* Ann Arbor: University of Michigan Press.

Summers, Robert. 1973. "International Comparisons with Incomplete Data." *Review of Income and Wealth* 29 (1): 1–16.

Triplett, Jack E. 1997. "Measuring Consumption: The Post-1973 Slowdown and the Research Issues." *Federal Reserve Bank of St Louis Review* (May/June): 9–42.

World Bank. 1990. *World Development Report 1990: Poverty.* New York: Oxford University Press.

———. 2008a. *Global Purchasing Power Parities and Real Expenditures: 2005 International Comparison Program.* Washington, DC: World Bank.

———. 2008b. *Poverty Data: A Supplement to the World Development Indicators 2008.* Washington, DC: World Bank.

CHAPTER 22

International Relative Price Levels: An Empirical Analysis

CHARLES THOMAS, JAIME MARQUEZ, SEAN FAHLE, AND JAMES COONAN

This chapter characterizes the structure of international relative price levels using cross-sectional and time series data.[1] The cross-sectional data consist of the 2005 benchmark purchasing power parities (PPPs) of the International Comparison Program (ICP) for 146 countries and 155 basic headings for products and services. These benchmarks embody methodological improvements enhancing product comparability and are the first to include actual price observations for China. The time series data consist of the PPPs reported by the 2008 World Development Indicators (WDI), which is the first set of indicators to use the new PPPs to revise the time series data. We use these data to measure bilateral relative price levels for 34 countries from 1980 to 2007. We then aggregate these bilateral relative prices with time-varying trade weights to obtain the evolution of a country's international relative price level.

In this chapter, we also use these data to answer questions of interest to international economists: Are the prices of a given product equalized across countries as one might expect based on the purchasing power parity hypothesis?[2] If not, is the resulting dispersion of relative prices across countries related to whether the product is internationally tradable? Furthermore, is there a systematic relation between the cross-country dispersion of relative price levels and that of income levels? If so, is that relation sensitive to whether the product is tradable? How comparable are our WDI-based measures of international relative prices with those based on the widely used Penn World Table (PWT), specifically Version 6.2? This comparison allows a quantitative assessment of the importance of the 2005 benchmarks.[3] Finally, how large are the differences between our measure of international relative prices and the widely used indexes of real effective exchange rates (REERs)? Such a comparison is relevant because existing REERs cannot, by design, capture the level effects from changes in the country composition of world trade.

Our analysis leads to several findings. First, the cross-country dispersion of prices at the level of basic headings depends importantly on whether the basic heading is tradable. Differences in the level of development across countries are relevant to explain the dispersion of prices. Previous research reached similar conclusions, but these findings confirm that the results hold up with more comparable and complete price data. Second, countries' aggregates of international relative prices based on the 2008 WDI data differ substantially from those based on the PWT 6.2 data. Finally, depictions of price movements based on our international relative prices are fundamentally different from those based on existing REERs.

Cross-Sectional Evidence

Data

The ICP provided the 2005 benchmark PPPs for 146 countries and 155 basic headings.[4] It also provided the 2005 values for gross domestic product (GDP), expenditures on each basic heading, population, and market exchange rates.[5]

The 2005 ICP benchmarks have two advantages over previous benchmarks. First, they are the first to include actual price observations for China and the first since 1985 to include actual price observations for India (the 1993 results for both countries were imputed). Indeed, as Deaton and Heston (2008) note, previous price data for these countries have been based on partial information and indirect methods. Second, the price collection for the 2005 benchmarks relied on the ICP's structured product descriptions, which is a list of standardized attributes used to identify a product as narrowly as possible (World Bank 2008, 142). This identification enhances the comparability of prices.[6]

Empirical Results

Using this information, we measure the 2005 bilateral relative price level of the United States with respect to country j in basic heading i as

$$(22.1) \qquad q^i_{j,us} = \frac{E_{j/\$}}{PPP^i_j}; \qquad i = 1, \dots, 92; j = 1, \dots, 144$$

where $E_{j/\$}$ is the 2005 market exchange rate for country j with respect to the U.S. dollar, and PPP^i_j is the PPP exchange rate of the i-th basic heading in the j-th country. A value of two for $q^i_{j,us}$ means that the price level in the United States for the i-th basic heading is twice the price level of the same basic heading in country j.

Figure 22.1 shows the percentiles of the distribution of $\ln q^i_{j,us}$ across countries. To facilitate the presentation, we first split these distributions in two groups, tradable and nontradable, and then rank each group using its median.[7] The figure shows that the median of the distributions for nontradable products is generally higher than that for tradable products.[8] Also, the dispersion of relative prices for tradables is considerably smaller than the one for nontradables.

We now examine the extent to which the cross-country dispersion of relative prices is related to the cross-country dispersion of income levels.[9] To that end, we assume that

$$(22.2) \qquad \ln q^i = \alpha_i + \beta_i \cdot \ln y + u_i; \qquad i = 1, \dots, 92; u_i \sim N(0, \sigma^2_i)$$

where $q^i = q^i_{1,us}, \dots, q^i_{j,us}, \dots, q^i_{144,us}$; y is a 144×1 vector of relative per capita GDPs, measured as $q^i_{144,us}$, the international dollar value of the j-th country's per capita GDP relative to that of the United States; and u_i is a 144×1 vector of disturbances assumed to be white noise.

Figure 22.2 shows the estimates of β_i and their 95 percent confidence bands. We arranged these estimates using the ordering of figure 22.1 as the template. The results indicate that these estimates are generally negative and significant. In other words, an *increase* in the per capita income of the j-th country relative to U.S. per capita income tends to lower the q^i for that country, which corresponds to an *increase* in the price of the i-th good in the j-th country relative to the corresponding U.S. price. Note also that nontradables have the largest estimate of β_i (in absolute value). This pattern has an economic explanation: an increase in income of the j-th country raises the demand for tradable and nontradable products, but the latter are supplied locally only. Hence an increase in the prices of these nontradable products drives them higher relative to U.S. prices. For tradable products, the existing forces to arbitrage prices are already reducing price differences with respect to the United States, and hence differences in the level of development are quantitatively less important.

Overall, the evidence from figures 22.1 and 22.2 suggests that differences in both the level of development and tradability are relevant considerations in explaining the cross-country dispersion of relative prices for the basic headings used here.

Time Series Evidence

We now turn to the evolution of relative prices over time. To this end, we use the 2008 WDI data for purchasing power parities at the GDP level and market exchange rates for 1980–2007 for 29 countries.[10] An important advantage of these PPPs is that they rest on the ICP benchmarks, meaning that the comparisons across time and space rest on the same (high-quality) price data.

We begin by measuring the U.S. bilateral relative price with respect to the k-th country as

$$q_{us,k,t} = \frac{E_{k/\$,t}}{PPP_{k/us,t}} \tag{22.3}$$

where $E_{k/\$,t}$ is the market exchange rate between the k-th currency and the U.S. dollar, and $PPP_{k/us,t}$ is the corresponding PPP exchange rate reported by the WDI. Note that a value of two for $q_{us,k}$ means that the *basket* of products produced in country k is twice as expensive in the United States as in country k.

To measure relative prices for other countries, we exploit the transitivity of PPPs. Thus we estimate q_{jk} as

$$q_{jk} = \frac{q_{us,k}}{q_{us,j}}. \tag{22.4}$$

From these bilateral relative prices we obtain a multilateral measure using a geometric mean,

$$Q^g_{jt} = \prod_{\substack{k=1 \\ k\neq j}}^{29} (q_{jk,t})^{w_{jk,t}}, \tag{22.5}$$

where Q^g_{jt} is the international relative price of the j-th country, and $w_{jk,t}$ is the time-varying trade weight associated with the k-th country. For weights, we follow the method adopted by the

FIGURE 22.1 Distribution of Relative Prices: Selected Basic Headings, 2005

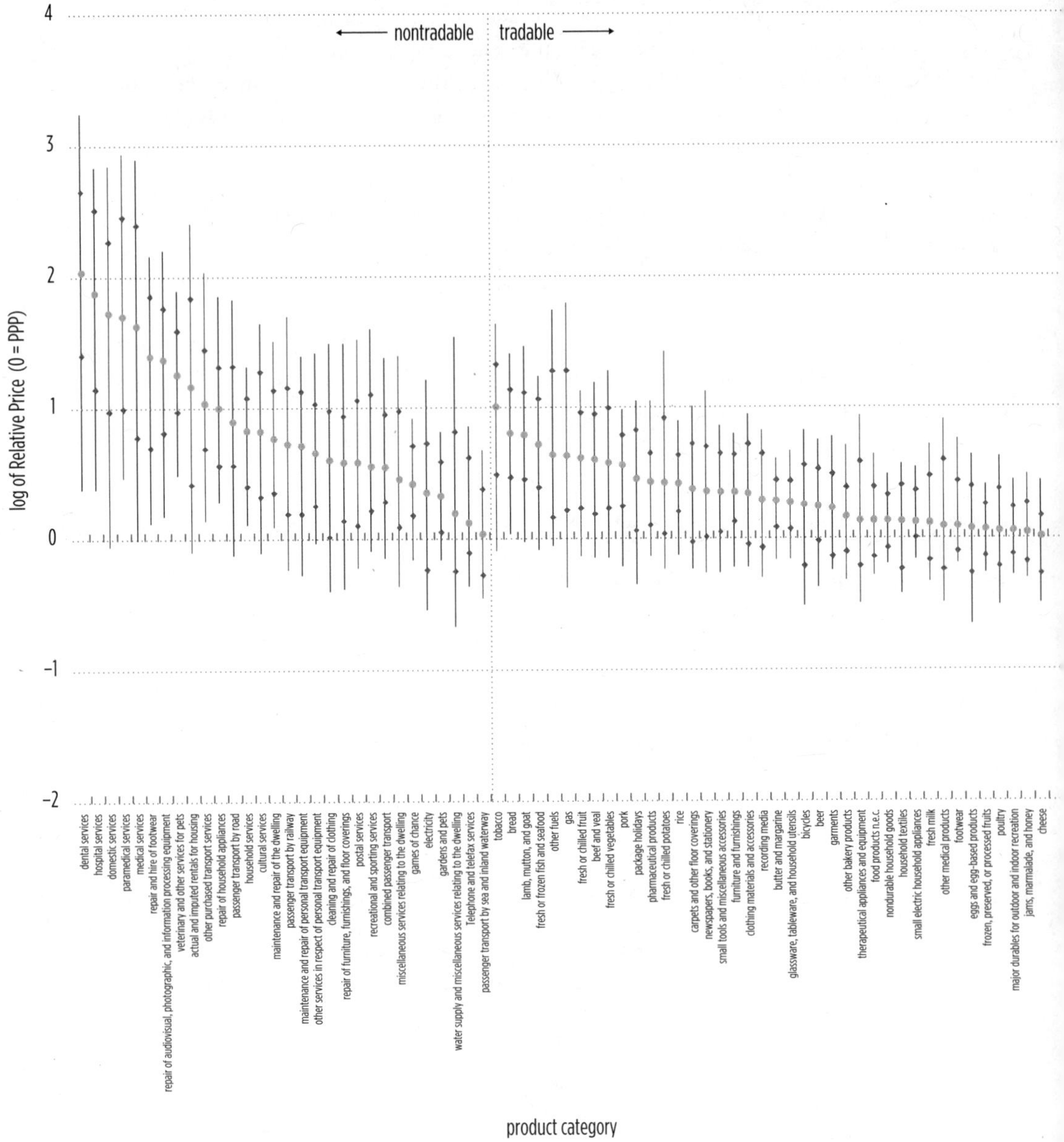

Federal Reserve for its broad dollar index (Leahy 1998). These weights are designed to reflect the composition of world trade from the standpoint of the j-th country.[11] Equation (22.5) has two important properties. First, a value of two means that prices in the j-th country are twice as high as the average of its trading partners. Second, even if prices levels were fixed, the Q^g for each country changes as the composition of world trade changes.[12]

The next section discusses how this measure of relative prices differs across countries. It is followed by a section that compares the evolution of this measure to the more familiar chained indexes of real effective exchange rates.

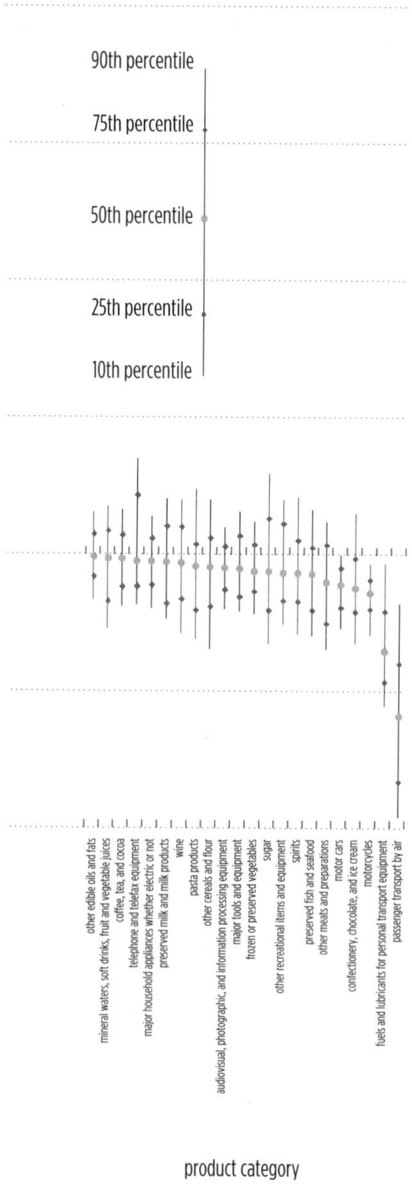

International Relative Prices

Our calculations for Q^g (table 22.1) show that the WDI-based measures of international relative prices differ markedly across countries. For example, the prices in 2007 (column [6]) for China and India are less than half those of their trading partners, whereas Japan's prices are about 50 percent higher than those of its trading partners. The U.S. international relative prices, which are among the highest, were the highest during the mid-1980s. Moreover, price measures based on the 2008 WDI differ significantly from those based on PWT 6.2. For example, the 2007 international

FIGURE 22.2 Confidence Intervals (95 Percent Level) for Estimate of β_i in Equation (22.2)

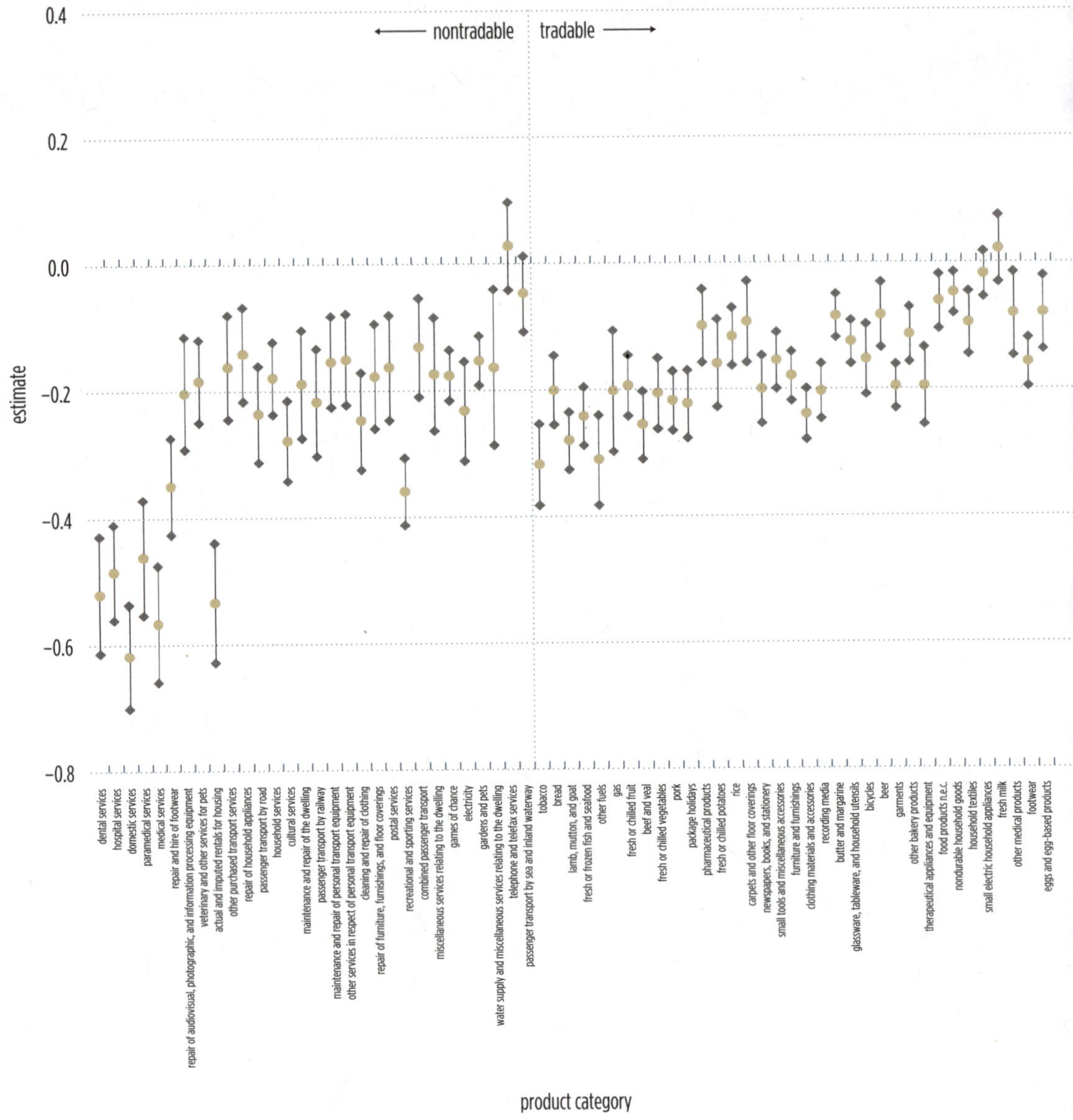

relative price for China is 0.50 using WDI data and 0.33 using PWT data, a gap of 52 percent. Thirteen countries have an average price revision of at least 20 percent (column [13]). The revisions are also noticeable for countries with significant trade with China: 18 percent for Japan and 13 percent for Korea. A few countries have relatively small revisions: Mexico, the United Kingdom, and the United States.

Finally, international relative prices have increased since 1995 for most countries. Many factors are responsible for this pattern, but two of them are of interest. First, the development of emerging market countries, with the accompanying increase in the demand for nontradables, raises those countries' general price levels, everything else unchanged. Second, the rapid expansion of

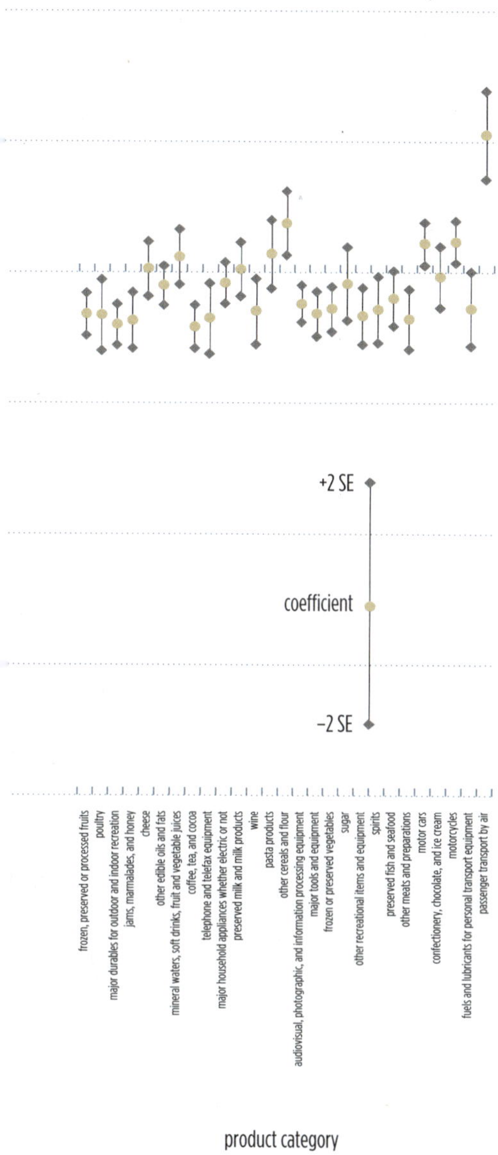

exports of low-priced products from emerging market economies lowers the average world price of tradables, and, because these exports are a large share of industrial countries' imports, raises their prices relative to world prices.

Real Effective Exchange Rate Indexes

We now compare our WDI-based international relative prices with existing measures of real effective exchange rate indexes. This comparison is of interest because most analyses of the role of international competitiveness in external imbalances use chained indexes of real effective exchange rates.

TABLE 22.1 International Relative Prices for WDI and PWT, Quarter 1 of Selected Years

	WDI						PWT						
Country	1980q1 (1)	1985q1 (2)	1990q1 (3)	1995q1 (4)	2000q1 (5)	2007q1 (6)	1980q1 (7)	1985q1 (8)	1990q1 (9)	1995q1 (10)	2000q1 (11)	2007q1[a] (12)	Average revision, 1995–2007[b] (13)
Argentina	0.56	0.80	0.58	1.11	1.12	0.62	1.53	0.76	0.49	0.86	0.94	*0.51*	23.3
Australia	1.18	1.30	1.05	1.01	1.08	1.37	1.26	1.30	1.18	1.07	1.12	*1.57*	−7.3
Austria	0.92	0.90	0.98	1.05	1.01	1.07	0.95	0.83	1.05	1.32	1.10	*1.43*	−17.9
Belgium	1.17	0.87	0.96	1.06	1.04	1.13	1.33	0.91	1.17	1.41	1.17	*1.55*	−21.0
Brazil	0.51	0.53	0.69	0.62	0.71	0.72	0.43	0.44	0.69	0.71	0.58	*0.78*	0.7
Canada	1.07	1.08	1.10	0.95	0.90	1.15	1.03	1.16	1.17	0.97	0.99	*1.25*	−6.4
Chile	0.92	0.77	0.52	0.61	0.69	0.81	0.70	0.59	0.47	0.54	0.58	*0.64*	19.5
China	0.84	0.74	0.40	0.35	0.45	0.50	0.70	0.45	0.27	0.22	0.27	*0.33*	59.1
Finland	1.03	1.13	1.35	1.12	1.23	1.36	1.04	1.12	1.41	1.58	1.46	*1.76*	−22.5
France	1.21	1.06	1.15	1.17	1.12	1.16	1.31	0.99	1.23	1.34	1.12	*1.42*	−10.3
Germany	1.17	0.97	1.09	1.23	1.18	1.18	1.27	0.93	1.21	1.48	1.22	*1.54*	−14.5
India	0.62	0.64	0.46	0.33	0.38	0.41	0.39	0.39	0.26	0.21	0.23	*0.27*	58.1
Indonesia	0.79	0.77	0.44	0.43	0.33	0.60	0.43	0.42	0.27	0.27	0.24	*0.38*	51.6
Ireland	0.90	0.92	0.98	0.98	1.05	1.23	1.02	0.98	1.13	1.24	1.16	*1.59*	−17.7
Italy	0.74	0.84	0.98	0.90	0.97	1.15	0.92	0.84	1.18	1.09	1.14	*1.58*	−19.9
Japan	1.19	1.12	1.70	2.11	1.86	1.55	1.17	1.29	1.65	2.54	2.45	*1.79*	−18.1
Korea, Rep.	0.69	0.67	0.71	0.82	0.71	1.04	0.69	0.69	0.72	0.84	0.88	*1.24*	−12.6
Malaysia	0.86	0.84	0.58	0.56	0.50	0.65	0.71	0.74	0.52	0.51	0.45	*0.58*	11.0
Mexico	0.63	0.56	0.46	0.50	0.61	0.75	0.71	0.66	0.54	0.44	0.77	*0.91*	−8.2

Netherlands	1.23	1.04	1.06	1.09	1.04	1.22	1.33	0.95	1.18	1.38	1.21	*1.76*	−21.9
Philippines	0.56	0.54	0.46	0.50	0.51	0.54	0.38	0.38	0.31	0.34	0.33	*0.38*	47.9
Portugal	0.55	0.53	0.60	0.77	0.80	0.89	0.57	0.47	0.61	0.76	0.71	*1.05*	−0.4
Singapore	0.75	0.86	0.74	0.94	0.97	0.93	0.82	1.00	0.91	1.13	1.12	*1.24*	−18.4
Spain	0.86	0.70	0.85	0.85	0.83	0.93	1.00	0.73	1.04	1.04	0.94	*1.38*	−20.9
Sweden	1.38	1.16	1.31	1.18	1.22	1.25	1.40	1.22	1.39	1.23	1.32	*1.41*	−7.7
Switzerland	1.27	1.18	1.27	1.40	1.35	1.40	1.27	1.20	1.36	1.62	1.45	*1.53*	−9.7
Thailand	0.68	0.67	0.55	0.57	0.51	0.55	0.46	0.45	0.39	0.40	0.39	*0.51*	27.0
United Kingdom	0.85	0.88	0.96	0.97	1.17	1.31	1.00	0.83	0.97	0.96	1.24	*1.38*	−3.2
United States	1.02	1.48	1.08	1.10	1.31	1.31	1.06	1.48	1.09	1.12	1.31	*1.37*	−2.1

Source: Data from World Development Indicators and Penn World Table.
Note: WDI = World Development Indicators; PWT = Penn World Table.
a. Based on extrapolations of PWT 6.2 through 2007.
b. For the years shown in the table.

However, as shown shortly, these chained indexes cannot capture the direct effects that changes in the country composition of world trade have on international relative price levels.

To see this, note that the most widely used alternative to $Q^g_{j,t}$ is the chained aggregate, which is a weighted average of the growth rates of bilateral relative prices:

$$\frac{Q^c_{jt}}{Q^c_{j,t-1}} = \prod_{\substack{k=1 \\ k \neq j}}^{34} \left(\frac{\frac{P_{k,t}}{P_{k,t-1}} \cdot \frac{E_{j/k,t}}{E_{j/k,t-1}}}{\frac{P_{j,t}}{P_{j,t-1}}} \right)^{w_{jk,t}} \tag{22.6}$$

where $P_{k,t}$ is an "arbitrary" measure of prices in the k-th country, $P_{j,t}$ is an "arbitrary" measure of prices in the j-th country, and $E_{j/k,t}$ is the price of the currency of the k-th country in terms of the currency of the j-th country. This formulation is appealing because it relies on growth rates without having to measure price levels as such. For example, the term $\frac{P_{k,t}}{P_{k,t0}}$ could be the consumer price index (CPI) for the k-th country with t_0 as the base period. Indeed, the Bank for International Settlements (BIS) REER, which we use as a comparator, is based on CPIs (see Klau and Fung 2006). We use the BIS measure, which we denote as $Q^{bis}_{j,t}$, because it is well known and available for many emerging market economies.[13]

To facilitate our comparison with the BIS REER, we note that price series analogous to the CPIs, but based on GDP baskets, are implicit in the $q_{jk,t}$'s used in constructing $Q^g_{j,t}$. A suitable rearrangement of terms in equation (22.6) yields

$$\frac{Q^c_{jt}}{Q^c_{j,t-1}} = \prod_{\substack{k=1 \\ k \neq j}}^{29} \left(\frac{\frac{P_{k,t}}{P_{j,t}} \cdot E_{j/k,t}}{\frac{P_{k,t-1}}{P_{j,t-1}} \cdot E_{j/k,t-1}} \right)^{w_{jk,t}} = \prod_{\substack{k=1 \\ k \neq j}}^{29} \left(\frac{q_{jk,t}}{q_{jk,t-1}} \right)^{w_{jk,t}}. \tag{22.7}$$

Because this $Q^c_{j,t}$ is based on the same underlying price data as $Q^g_{j,t}$, we can more easily identify those differences attributable to the aggregation method as opposed to those attributable to the use of different underlying price data.

Specifically, logarithmic differentiation of $Q^c_{j,t}$ and $Q^g_{j,t}$ yields

$$\hat{Q}^g_{jt} = \sum_k w_{jk,t} \cdot dlnq_{jk,t} + \sum_k dw_{jk,t} \cdot lnq_{jk,t} \tag{22.8}$$

and

$$\hat{Q}^c_{jt} = \sum_k w_{jk,t} \cdot dlnq_{jk,t} \tag{22.9}$$

where ˆ denotes a growth rate. Thus if prices are constant, then $\hat{Q}^c_{jt} = 0$ necessarily, whereas $\hat{Q}^g_{jt}$ could differ from zero. Furthermore, the difference in growth rates between the geometric and the chained aggregate is

$$\hat{Q}^g_{jt} - \hat{Q}^c_{jt} = \sum_k dw_{jk,t} \cdot lnq_{jk,t}, \tag{22.10}$$

that is, if the weights are constant, then the two growth rates are identical. But if the weights are not constant, then the difference in growth rates reflects the interaction between each period's distribution of the level of bilateral relative prices and the evolution of the weights.

Table 22.2 compares the cumulative growth rates of Q_t^g and Q_t^{bis} from 1995 to 2007 (note that the subscript j has been dropped). Our calculations indicate that China's international relative price increases by 42 percent if one uses Q_t^g (column [1]) and 18 percent if one uses Q_t^{bis} (column [2]).

TABLE 22.2 Growth Rates of International Relative Prices, 1995–2007

	Growth rates			Growth rate differentials		
Country	Q^g (1)	Q^{bis} (2)	Q^c (3)	Q^g - Q^{bis} (4)	Q^g - Q^c (5)	Q^c - Q^{bis} (6)
Argentina	−44	−49	−52	5	8	−3
Australia	36	21	16	15	20	−5
Austria	2	−6	−4	8	6	2
Belgium	7	−5	0	11	6	5
Brazil	15	−14	3	30	13	17
Canada	21	16	11	5	10	−5
Chile	33	−2	20	35	13	22
China	42	18	32	24	10	14
Finland	21	−9	8	31	13	17
France	−1	−5	−7	4	6	−2
Germany	−4	−12	−12	7	8	0
India	24	3	8	21	17	5
Indonesia	39	−8	15	47	24	23
Ireland	26	20	23	6	3	3
Italy	28	15	16	13	12	1
Japan	−26	−37	−35	11	8	3
Korea, Rep.	27	9	6	18	21	−3
Malaysia	17	−13	0	30	17	13
Mexico	50	63	35	−13	15	−28
Netherlands	12	0	−1	11	13	−1
Philippines	7	−8	−7	15	14	1
Portugal	16	7	8	9	8	1
Singapore	−1	−9	−15	8	14	−5
Spain	9	12	3	−3	6	−9
Sweden	6	−9	−1	15	7	7
Switzerland	0	−15	−7	15	7	8
Thailand	−3	−6	−18	4	15	−11
United Kingdom	35	20	27	16	9	7
United States	19	7	3	12	16	−4

Note: Calculations based on the dates used in table 22.1.

Seven additional countries have gaps of at least 20 percent (column [4]). Furthermore, Q^g and Q^{bis} move in opposite directions, in our sample, for 10 countries: the differences in measures are not solely about magnitudes. These two findings suggest, then, that our characterization of international relative prices is fundamentally different from the one implied by the BIS measure.

Several reasons could be given for the difference in growth rates between Q_t^g and Q_t^{bis}: aggregation methods, price measures, and country weights. A simple decomposition shows that most of the difference in growth rates can be attributed to differences in aggregation methods. In doing so, we express the gap in growth rates between Q_t^g and Q_t^{bis} as

$$\hat{Q}_t^g - \hat{Q}_t^{bis} = \left(\hat{Q}_t^g - \hat{Q}_t^c\right) + \left(\hat{Q}_t^c - \hat{Q}_t^{bis}\right). \tag{22.11}$$

The Q_t^c used here is based on the same relative prices and weights as $\hat{Q}_t^g$. The only difference between these two measures can be attributed to the choice of aggregation method—that is, the difference between a geometric aggregate and a chain-weighted aggregate. Thus $(\hat{Q}_t^g - \hat{Q}_t^c)$ captures the effects of aggregation methods alone. The term $(\hat{Q}^c - \hat{Q}^{bis})$ captures the importance of the remaining factors: price measures and weighing schemes. Column (5) in table 22.2 shows that the difference between $\hat{Q}^g$ and $\hat{Q}^c$ explains most of the gap between $\hat{Q}^g$ and $\hat{Q}^{bis}$.[14] In other words, we find that the interactions between price levels and the structure of trade are sufficiently important to induce divergences between Q_t^{bis} and Q_t^g.

Conclusion

This chapter characterizes the distributions of relative price levels across countries, products, and time. We begin by studying the cross-country distributions of 2005 relative price levels across 144 countries for 92 detailed product categories. We find that the cross-country dispersion of relative price levels depends importantly on whether the basic heading is tradable. Differences in the level of development are also relevant for explaining the dispersion of prices.

We continue our analysis with a study of time series PPP data from the World Development Indicators and exchange rate data for 34 countries spanning 1980–2007. The WDI data have the benefit of being derived from the ICP benchmarks. We use these components to construct bilateral relative price levels, which are then aggregated using a geometric mean and weighted using time-varying trade weights. We find that countries' aggregates of international relative prices based on the 2008 WDI data differ substantially from those based on data from Version 6.2 of the Penn World Table. Finally, depictions of price movements based on our international relative prices are fundamentally different from those based on existing REERs. We do not interpret these divergences as a call to abandon existing effective exchange rate indexes. Rather, we interpret these divergences as an opportunity for Q_t^g to complement the information in those indexes, a role that is likely to be present so long as changes in the pattern of trade continue. In this case, the ongoing efforts by the International Comparison Program are central to understanding international relative prices.

NOTES

1. The views in this chapter are solely the responsibility of the authors and should not be interpreted as reflecting the views of the Board of Governors of the Federal Reserve System or of any other person associated with the Federal Reserve System. Preliminary versions of this

paper were presented at George Washington University, the meetings of the fall 2009 Midwest International Economics Group (Penn State), and the fall 2009 Workshop of the Federal Reserve Board. We are grateful to Nada Hamadeh for providing the ICP data and to both Frederic A. Vogel and D. S. Prasada Rao for numerous comments on an earlier draft of this chapter.

2. This hypothesis indicates that, in the absence of transportation costs and government regulations, arbitrage equalizes the price for a given product across all countries when expressed in a common currency. For reviews, see Froot and Rogoff (1995), Taylor (2003), Chinn (2005), and Klau and Fung (2006). Other relevant papers include those by Lipsey, Molinari, and Kravis (1990); Hooper and Richardson (1991); and Turner and Van't dack (1993).
3. For details on the PWT, see Heston, Summers, and Aten (2006). For an introduction, see Summers and Heston (1991) and Gulde and Schulze-Ghattas (1993). Our comparison focuses on PWT 6.2 for two reasons. First, it allows us to compare results described in this chapter to previous work such as that by Thomas, Marquez, and Fahle (2008). Second, PWT 6.3 does not incorporate price data for China, and so little is lost by focusing on PWT 6.2.
4. A *basic heading* is the lowest level of disaggregation for which PPPs are computed (World Bank 2008, 14). An example of a basic heading is "confectionery, chocolate, and ice cream." These PPPs are constructed to equalize the dollar price of the associated basic heading across countries. Chapters 6 and 7 of the World Bank's *Global Purchasing Power Parities and Real Expenditures: 2005 International Comparison Program* describe the methodology used in the computation of PPPs at the basic heading level (World Bank 2008).
5. The data file received had incomplete data for Zambia and Zimbabwe, and so they are excluded from our analysis. Also, in response to suggestions from ICP staff, we excluded those items associated with government activities such as government production of health services, collective services, and social protection, because the cross-country comparability of these items is not sufficient for the purposes of this chapter.
6. See Chen and Ravallion (2008), appendix G of World Bank (2008), and Deaton and Heston (2008).
7. The tradable and nontradable split is, admittedly, ad hoc and based on the authors' *a priori* views. Thus further work is needed to assess the robustness of these results.
8. Tobacco and gas are, however, important exceptions because they are tradable products but have the largest relative prices—indeed, higher than many of the relative prices for nontradable products. One possible explanation for this seemingly odd result is that tobacco and gas are taxed at lower rates in the United States than in other countries.
9. See Obstfeld and Rogoff (1996) for a review.
10. Specifically, we use the 29 countries (or economies) included in the broad measure of the Federal Reserve's real effective value of the dollar (Leahy 1998): Argentina, Australia, Austria, Belgium, Brazil, Canada, Chile, China, Finland, France, Germany, India, Indonesia, Ireland, Italy, Japan, Republic of Korea, Malaysia, Mexico, the Netherlands, the Philippines, Portugal, Singapore, Spain, Sweden, Switzerland, Thailand, United Kingdom, and United States.
11. Specifically, the un-normalized broad weight for a given country is $\omega_{jk,t} = 0.5 \cdot \mu_{jk,t} + 0.25 \cdot \xi_{jk,t} + 0.25 \cdot \varsigma_{jk,t}$, where $\mu_{jk,t}$ is the share of imports from the k-th country, $\xi_{jk,t}$ is the export share to the k-th country, and $\varsigma_{jk,t}$ is the extent to which exports to the k-th country compete with exports from other countries. The normalized broad weight of the j-th country relative to the k-th country is $w_{jk,t} = \frac{\omega_{jk,t}}{\sum_i \omega_{jk,t}}$. We use data from the International Monetary Fund's Direction of Trade Statistics.

12. The exception is the case in which all relative prices are fixed at the value of one.
13. Q_t^{bis} uses time-varying weights reflecting world trade shares in manufactures.
14. In 16 countries, the gap between $\hat{Q}^g$ and $\hat{Q}^c$ is more than twice the absolute value of the gap between $\hat{Q}^{bis}$ and $\hat{Q}^c$.

REFERENCES

Chen, S., and M. Ravallion. 2008. "China Is Poorer than We Thought, but No Less Successful in the Fight against Poverty." Policy Research Working Paper 4621, World Bank, Washington, DC.

Chinn, M. 2005. "A Primer on Real Effective Exchange Rates: Determinants, Overvaluation, Trade Flows and Competitive Devaluation." NBER Working Paper No. 11521, National Bureau of Economic Research, Cambridge, MA.

Deaton, A., and A. Heston. 2008. "Understanding PPPs and PPP-based National Accounts." NBER Working Paper No. 14499, National Bureau of Economic Research, Cambridge, MA.

Froot, K., and K. Rogoff. 1995. "Perspectives on PPP and Long-run Real Exchange Rates." In *Handbook of International Economics,* Vol. 3, ed. G. Grossman and K. Rogoff. Amsterdam: North-Holland.

Gulde, A. M., and M. Schulze-Ghattas. 1993. "Purchasing Power Parity Based Weights for the World Economic Outlook." *World Economic Outlook.* Washington, DC: International Monetary Fund, December.

Heston, A., R. Summers, and B. Aten. 2006. "Penn World Table Version 6.2." Center for International Comparisons of Production, Income and Prices, University of Pennsylvania.

Hooper, P., and J. Richardson, eds. 1991. *International Economic Transactions: Issues in Measurement and Empirical Research.* Chicago: University of Chicago Press.

Klau, M., and S. Fung. 2006. "The New BIS Effective Exchange Rate Indices." *BIS Quarterly Review* (March): 51–65.

Leahy, M. 1998. "New Summary Measures of the Foreign Exchange Value of the Dollar." *Federal Reserve Bulletin* 811–18.

Lipsey, R., L. Molinary, and I. Kravis. 1990. "Measures of Prices and Price Competitiveness in International Trade in Manufactured Goods." NBER Working Paper No. 3442, National Bureau of Economic Research, Cambridge, MA.

Obstfeld, M., and K. Rogoff. 1996. *Foundations of International Macroeconomics.* Cambridge, MA: MIT Press.

Summers, R., and A. Heston. 1991. "The Penn World Table (Mark 5): An Expanded Set of International Comparisons, 1950–1988." *Quarterly Journal of Economics* (106): 327–68.

Taylor, M. 2003. "Purchasing Power Parity." *Review of International Economics* 11: 436–52.

Thomas, C., J. Marquez, and S. Fahle. 2008. "Measuring U.S. International Relative Prices." International Finance Discussion Paper No. 917, Federal Reserve Board, Washington, DC.

Turner, P., and J. Van't dack. 1993. "Measuring International Price and Cost Competitiveness." BIS Economic Papers, No. 39, Bank for International Settlements, Basel, Switzerland.

World Bank. 2008. *Global Purchasing Power Parities and Real Expenditures: 2005 International Comparison Program.* http://siteresources.worldbank.org/ICPINT/Resources/icp-final.pdf.

CHAPTER 23

PPP Estimates: Applications by the International Monetary Fund

Mick Silver[1]

The International Monetary Fund (IMF) is an international organization of 187 countries that works to foster global monetary cooperation, secure financial stability, facilitate international trade, promote high employment and sustainable economic growth, and reduce poverty. Through its economic surveillance, the IMF tracks the economic health of its member countries, alerting them to risks on the horizon and providing policy advice. It also lends to countries in difficulty and provides technical assistance and training to help countries improve economic management. This work is backed by IMF research and statistics available in publications that include the *World Economic Outlook* (WEO).[2] The WEO focuses on major economic policy issues, as well as on analysis of economic developments and prospects. It presents IMF staff analysis and projections of economic developments at the global level and for major country groups and many individual countries.

The IMF's resources are drawn mainly from member countries' quota subscriptions. Quotas broadly reflect the relative size of each member's economy—for example, the larger a country's economy in terms of output, the larger its quota tends to be. The largest member of the IMF is the United States, with a quota of SDR 37.1 billion (about US$56.7 billion), and the smallest member is Tuvalu, with a quota of SDR 1.8 million (about US$2.8 million).[3] A member country's voting power in IMF decisions is largely determined by its quota subscription, which is the maximum amount of financial resources the member is obliged to provide to the IMF. Quotas also have a bearing on the amount of financing a member can obtain from the IMF (its access limit). When a country joins the IMF, it is assigned an initial quota in the same range as the quotas of existing members that are broadly comparable in economic size and characteristics. The IMF uses a quota formula to guide the assessment of a member's relative position. The IMF has used purchasing power parity (PPP)–adjusted gross domestic product (GDP) measures in its *World Economic*

This chapter was originally published as IMF WP/10/253, *IMF Applications of Purchasing Power Parity Estimates,* by Mick Silver. Reprinted with permission. It reflects quota arrangements at end of 2010. See http://www.imf.org/external/np/exr/facts/quotas.htm for more recent developments.

Outlook since 1993 and, more recently, as an element of the formula used to help guide decisions on the distribution of its members' quotas.[4]

This chapter begins by briefly outlining the IMF's use of the International Comparison Program's (ICP) PPP estimates.[5] The focus then moves to PPP measurement issues that are particularly salient to the IMF's usage. The measurement issues considered include country coverage and the imputation of PPP estimates for member countries not participating in the ICP, PPP estimates for nonbenchmark years, the timeliness and periodicity of PPP estimates and updating mechanisms, country groupings, and transparency. This focus is not to detract from the importance of minimizing measurement errors and biases in weights and price surveys, including issues relating to sampling, data collection, validation, and aggregation methods for the estimates. These matters are adequately covered in preceding chapters. This chapter ends with a brief summary.

Use of PPPs by the IMF

An important use of GDP volume at purchasing power parity (PPP GDP) is as an element of the formula used to help guide decisions on the distribution of the quotas of IMF members. IMF use of PPPs is also naturally pervasive in the research and analytical work of the IMF staff given their concern with monitoring and analyzing levels and changes of macroeconomic indicators across economies and over time for country groups. Their research output can be found in the *IMF G-20 Surveillance Notes, Global Financial Stability Report, Regional Economic Outlook Reports, Staff Position Notes, Working Paper Series,* and *World Economic Outlook,*[6] as well as in external (to the IMF) publications. The account here is limited to the IMF's use of PPP adjustments for the WEO, although the issues raised are indicative of the general use of PPP adjustments, not least because many IMF researchers use the WEO database.[7]

Determining Quotas

The quota subscription of a member country of the IMF not only determines the amount of financial resources the member is obliged to provide to the IMF, the amount of financing it can obtain from the IMF (its access limit), and its share in a general allocation of special drawing rights (SDRs),[8] but also largely determines its voting power in IMF decisions. On April 28, 2008, a large-scale quota and voice reform was adopted by the Board of Governors of the IMF. Its aim was to make quotas more responsive to economic realities by increasing the representation of members, many of which are emerging market economies whose weight and role in the global economy have increased, and, at the same time, giving low-income countries more say in the IMF's decision making. This reform marked the first time GDP calculated with PPP "exchange rates" has appeared as an argument in the debate over the IMF quota formula.[9]

The current quota formula is the weighted average of GDP (weight of 50 percent), openness (30 percent), variability (15 percent), and international reserves (5 percent). For the formula, GDP is measured as a blend of GDP based on a market exchange rate (weight of 60 percent) and on PPPs (40 percent). Both the market exchange and PPP GDP weights are an average of the data of the last three years. The 2008 data set therefore requires GDP data for 2006–08. A compression factor of 0.95 is applied to the linear combination of the four variables to reduce the dispersion of calculated quotas. The previous formula included GDP but measured only at market prices. The new formula is outlined in box 23.1 and the previous one in box 23.2.[10]

The process leading to the adoption of the new quota formula and the rationale for the IMF's inclusion of PPP-based GDP estimates is well documented.[11] The amalgam of market exchange

BOX 23.1 The New Quota Formula

The new quota formula includes four quota variables—GDP, openness, variability, and reserves—expressed in shares of global totals, with the variables assigned weights totaling 1.0. The formula also includes a compression factor that reduces dispersion in calculated quota shares.

The new formula is

$$CQS = (0.5 \times Y + 0.3 \times O + 0.15 \times V + 0.05 \times R)^k$$

where

CQS = calculated quota share;

Y = blend of GDP converted at market rates and PPPs averaged over a three-year period (the weights of market-based and PPP GDP are 0.60 and 0.4, respectively);

O = annual average of the sum of current payments and current receipts (goods, services, income, and transfers) over a five-year period;

V = variability of current receipts and net capital flows (measured as a standard deviation from the centered 3-year trend over a 13-year period);

R = 12-month average over a year of official reserves (foreign exchange, SDR holdings, reserve position in the IMF, and monetary gold); and

k = compression factor of 0.95. The compression factor is applied to the uncompressed calculated quota shares, which are then rescaled to sum to 100.

and PPP GDP weights was justified as capturing the central role of quotas in the IMF's financial operations, for which nominal GDP at market exchange rates is the most relevant, as well as the IMF's nonfinancial activities, for which PPP GDP can be viewed as a relevant way to capture the relative volume of goods and services produced by economies. Yet the inclusion of the PPP GDP and the compression factor was recognized as one of the most difficult aspects of the deliberations (IMF 2008, para. 7). As a result, the Executive Board of the IMF decided to include them in the formula for a period of 20 years, after which their inclusion will be reviewed.

At the IMF's annual meetings in Singapore in September 2006, the membership endorsed a program to modernize and reform quotas and voice. Members agreed to a package of reforms that included a new quota formula, an initial ad hoc increase in quotas for the most underrepresented members, and a second round of ad hoc quota increases based on the new formula. The new formula was the basis for guiding a comprehensive "second round" of quota reform that was agreed on in April 2008.[12]

BOX 23.2 The Previous Five Quota Formulas

Bretton Woods: $Q1 = (0.01Y + 0.025R + 0.05P + 0.2276VC)(1 + C/Y)$

Scheme III: $Q2 = (0.0065Y + 0.0205125R + 0.078P + 0.4052VC)(1 + C/Y)$

Scheme IV: $Q3 = (0.0045Y + 0.03896768R + 0.07P + 0.76976VC)(1 + C/Y)$

Scheme M4: $Q4 = 0.005Y + 0.042280464R + 0.044(P + C) + 0.8352VC$

Scheme M7: $Q5 = 0.0045Y + 0.05281008R + 0.039(P + C) + 1.0432VC$

where

Q1, Q2, Q3, Q4, and Q5 = calculated quotas for each formula;

Y = GDP at current market prices for a recent year;

R = 12-month average of gold, foreign exchange reserves, SDR holdings, and reserve positions in the IMF for a recent year;

P = annual average of current payments (goods, services, income, and private transfers) for a recent five-year period;

C = annual average of current receipts (goods, services, income, and private transfers) for a recent five-year period; and

VC = variability of current receipts, defined as one standard deviation from the centered 5-year moving average, for a recent 13-year period.

For each of the four non-Bretton Woods formulas, quota calculations are multiplied by an adjustment factor so that the sum of the calculations across members equals that derived from the Bretton Woods formula. The calculated quota of a member is the higher of the Bretton Woods calculation and the average of the lowest two of the remaining four calculations (after adjustment).

Of note is that including PPP GDP in the formula was facilitated by the updated PPP GDP data, which incorporated the new parity rates published by the International Comparison Program in December 2007. These data reflect substantial improvements in the methodology and consistency of the PPP estimates. Earlier, data quality issues and the coverage of the world's economies had impeded consideration of using the PPP GDP (IMF 2007, 5). The use of the PPP GDP variable in the formula had a significant impact on the distribution of calculated quota shares by increasing those of emerging and developing countries. Table 23.1 presents the *calculated* quota shares under the old and new formulas for the major economies, responsible in total for about 80 percent of the world's PPP GDP. Not all of the differences in shares were the result of the adoption of the PPP GDP. Boxes 23.1 and 23.2 reveal that other factors also influenced the outcomes for calculated

TABLE 23.1 IMF Quota Shares under Different Formulas

	Quota shares		
	Previous five formulas	New formula	Percentage difference: new to previous
United States	16.284	18.991	16.62
Japan	7.011	8.032	14.56
Germany	6.850	6.227	−9.09
China	6.137	6.390	4.12
United Kingdom	5.240	4.429	−15.48
France	4.129	4.016	−2.74
Italy	3.317	3.336	0.57
Canada	3.065	2.569	−16.18
Netherlands	2.897	1.930	−33.38
Korea, Rep.	2.512	2.245	−10.63
Belgium	2.270	1.504	−33.74
Spain	2.237	2.304	3.00
Singapore	1.929	1.031	−46.55
Mexico	1.841	1.970	7.01
Russian Federation	1.702	2.053	20.62
Ireland	1.660	1.173	−29.34
Switzerland	1.485	1.211	−18.45
Malaysia	1.374	0.859	−37.48
Luxembourg	1.369	0.624	−54.42
India	1.287	1.997	55.17
Australia	1.205	1.321	9.63
Sweden	1.172	0.993	−15.27
Austria	1.129	0.913	−19.13
Brazil	1.069	1.725	61.37
Denmark	1.040	0.853	−17.98
Saudi Arabia	1.030	0.835	−18.93

Source: IMF 2008, table 1.
Note: The quota shares here are derived from the calculated formulas only.

quota shares such as raising the effective weight for the GDP and reducing that for openness. However, the substantive nature of the changes is noteworthy: increases of over 50 percent for India and Brazil and decreases of a similar magnitude for Luxembourg and Singapore. Major economies saw their calculated quota shares change considerably—for example, the United States, 16.6 percent; Japan, 14.6 percent; Germany, –9.1 percent; and the United Kingdom, –15.5 percent.

The PPP GDP was also used as a criterion to identify dynamism by bringing forward expected future growth for those countries most out of line in their PPP GDP. Specifically, emerging market and developing economies whose shares in the global PPP GDP were substantially larger (by more than 75 percent) than their actual pre-Singapore quota shares received a minimum nominal quota increase ("boost") of 40 percent. Among the countries that benefited from the boost were Brazil, India, and Vietnam.

The PPP-based GDP data used for the quota calculations based on the new formula are taken from the WEO database. The WEO PPP-based GDP is derived by dividing a country's nominal GDP in its own currency by its PPP relative to the United States.[13] The WEO PPP-based data are converted into SDR units using the SDR-US$ period average exchange rate. The WEO PPPs are based on ICP data for 2003–05 that were published in December 2007. These data were then extended in the WEO database by using the growth in relative GDP deflators (the deflator of a country divided by the deflator of the United States).

Uses of PPPs in the *World Economic Outlook*

The WEO reports for composite groups of economies a wide range of world, regional, and analytic aggregates of economic indicators. These aggregates are either sums or weighted averages of the individual country indicators. Composites for data relating to the domestic economy, whether growth rates or ratios, are generally weighted by GDP country shares valued at PPP—that is, the nominal GDP divided by the PPP exchange rate.[14] The PPP GDP weights used in the WEO are expressed in international dollars. Exceptions are the results for groups of economies for exchange rates, interest rates, growth rates of monetary aggregates, the external economy, unemployment rates and employment, and the domestic economy for the Euro Area (IMF 2009, 181).[15]

Estimates of regional and world output and their growth, and forecasts thereof, are key macroeconomic indicators reported in the WEO. Because the appropriate weighting scheme may depend on the issue being considered, the WEO reports (in table A.1 of its statistical appendix) alternative measures of world output using both PPP and market exchange rates. The value of world output in 2009 increased from an estimated US$54,864 billion to $68,651 billion when valued at PPP as opposed to market exchange rates. The projected growth in world GDP volume between 2009 and 2014 also differed: 28.7 percent compared with 30.2 percent for GDP at market exchange rates as opposed to PPPs (IMF 2009, 189). Naturally, GDP growth for each country is the same whether exchange rates or PPPs are used. However, the country shares in world GDP used as weights to derive world output growth differ, depending on whether the GDP shares are valued at PPP or market exchange rates.

The weights used in the WEO between rounds are updated by the growth in the relative GDP (the country's GDP deflator divided by the U.S. GDP deflator).[16] However, this approach is not equivalent to the data-rich country price comparisons that constitute an ICP round (see the next section of this chapter).

The weighting system for economies used in the WEO can change over time. For example, table A16 of the April 2009 WEO provides a summary of sources and uses of world savings as a percentage of GDP (IMF 2009). Composites for groups of economies are calculated as the sum of the U.S. dollar values for the relevant individual economy. This differs from the calculations in the April 2005 and earlier issues of the WEO, where the composites were weighted by estimates of GDP valued at PPP as a share of total world GDP (see the next section).

The IMF's *International Financial Statistics* (IFS) also uses PPP-based weights for some of its regional and global aggregates: global consumer price indexes (CPIs), producer and wholesale price indexes (PPIs/WPIs), GDP volume, GDP deflator, gross capital formation as a percentage of GDP, and final consumption expenditure as a percentage of GDP. The IFS PPP weights are updated and revised from the WEO about every five years for the base years 1953, 1958, 1963, 1970, 1975, 1980, 1984–86, 1990, 1995, 2000, and 2005. The values of the PPP weights of the base years are used for the subsequent intervening subperiod. The updates do not take effect immediately, not least because of the time lag between collecting the survey data for the PPP and their compilation and publication. The most recent update referring to the 2005 PPP weights was updated in the October 2008 WEO, taking effect in the IFS from May 2009 onward. Countries whose weights are not available from the WEO are excluded from the IFS aggregation process.

PPP Measurement Issues of Concern to the IMF

Earlier chapters of this volume have covered a range of technical issues, all of which affect the reliability of the ICP results and all of which are of concern to the IMF. These issues include the reliability of the data used for price comparisons and the GDP expenditure components for the weights, an area in which the IMF actively helps countries.[17] Some more specific issues relevant to the IMF's use of PPPs are described in this section.

Country Coverage

The IMF's use of PPPs relies on estimates provided by the ICP.[18] The last round of survey-based estimates was conducted in 2005, and the next is planned for 2011.[19] Over the history of ICP rounds, the number of participating countries has noticeably increased—from 10 countries in 1970, to 16 in 1973, 34 in 1975, 60 in 1980, and 64 in 1985. After a partial program in 1990, the 1993 participation level reached a new high—118 countries covering all regions of the world for the first time. Although 118 countries participated in the 1993 comparisons, many countries used reduced information surveys that proved to be relatively unreliable, notably China (Deaton and Heston 2008). The 2005 ICP round, on which the IMF bases its PPP GDP variable, covered 146 economies.[20] Indeed, it marked a turning point for many countries because of the significant changes shown in the size of many economies.[21] And yet the IMF, an organization of 187 countries, had to rely in part on an estimation routine for the PPP variable for 36 countries.[22] Particularly serious was the exclusion from the 2005 ICP of all the countries of Central America and the Caribbean and the participation of only 10 countries in South America, mainly because of a lack of resources.[23]

In country coverage, two key issues emerge. The first is to ensure that in subsequent rounds the number of participating countries increases. At this stage, it is too early to comment on the number of countries participating in the 2011 round, although the World Bank expects over 170 countries (World Bank 2010, 23–26, para. 16).

The second issue is to ensure the reliability and integrity of the methods for estimating PPPs for the nonparticipating countries.[24] The World Bank's methodology for estimating PPPs for non-benchmark countries is documented in Changqing and Swanson (2009).[25] Using data for all benchmark countries, researchers estimated regression equation price level indexes (PLIs), defined as the ratio of PPP GDP (also for PPP private consumption) to a corresponding market exchange rate, normalized with the United States equal to 100. The explanatory variables include GDP per capita in U.S. dollars; imports and exports as shares of GDP (for GDP but not private consumption); ratio of dependents to working-age population; dummy variables for countries in Sub-Saharan Africa, member states of the Organisation for Economic Co-operation and Development (OECD), island economies, and landlocked developing economies; and interaction terms for GDP per capita with the previously mentioned dummy variables.

The value added of these country PPP estimates to the IMF lies not only in their ready availability, but also in their independent derivation as part of the ICP. As with most econometric work, alternative estimates could be generated with different specifications and estimators. However, the availability of these "official" and independently derived estimates allows the IMF to sidestep such issues. What is important to IMF usage is that the estimates, along with an account of their methodology, are available on a timely basis and that some indication is available as to which countries may have very wide prediction intervals.[26] Indeed, for IMF usage one consideration in devising the specification for the model might be ensuring that it is robust to extreme prediction intervals, especially for the larger of the nonbenchmark countries.

PPP Estimates for Nonbenchmark Years

PPP GDP estimates based on ICP benchmark price surveys are available only periodically—the last benchmark rounds were in 1993 and 2005.[27]

PPP benchmark survey-based weights are normally updated at about five-year intervals. Index number theory and international guidelines would advise that the weights be updated more frequently, especially if consumption/GDP component shares are subject to change. If the weights are highly volatile for some groups, a case could perhaps be made for a rolling update. And yet despite these concerns, the infrequency of ICP updates results in a concomitant infrequency of PPP GDP weight updates, unless the PPP GDP figures are based on extrapolated annual figures using benchmark data from the ICP rounds. Extrapolations to provide annual PPPs for a country, as used in the IMF's work, are based on multiplying the country's last round's PPP GDP estimates, relative to the United States, by the country's volume growth in GDP between the last round and the year in question. The resulting volume-inflated measure is then multiplied by the U.S. inflation rate to provide an estimate in U.S. dollars.[28] Countries whose volume estimates are based on weights that change rapidly—say, annually—are less likely to have their PPP GDP estimates drift above the PPP GDP estimate from the next ICP round. Many advanced economies, which constitute much of the quota allocation, compile annually chain-weighted volume GDP estimates.[29] But many other countries fall short of this requirement.

New PPP estimates from new ICP rounds act as benchmarks for these extrapolated estimates. The PPP estimates for the 2005 benchmark year replaced benchmark PPP estimates that dated back to the benchmark figures for 1993 or earlier for most emerging market and developing countries.[30] The revisions to PPP rates as a result of the 2005 round led to a substantial reduction in the PPP-based GDP of some large, fast-growing economies and consequently reduced their estimated contribution to global growth. In the October 2007 issue of *World Economic Outlook*, the IMF's estimate for global growth in 2007 was revised down to 4.7 percent from 5.2 percent, based on the 2005 PPP results. Downward revisions of the PPP-based GDP of two of the world's fastest-growing economies, China and India, were mainly responsible for the overall reduction in global growth estimates. For 2007, China's share of global output was revised to an estimated 10.9 percent (down from 15.8 percent), and India's share declined to 4.6 percent, from 6.4 percent

(Elekdag and Lall 2008). The 2005 ICP round benefited from some significant methodological advances, as outlined in Deaton and Heston (2008), Diewert (2008) and World Bank (2008). The extent of these advances may not be repeated in future rounds.

PPP GDP estimates for nonbenchmark years are available, using different methodologies, in versions of the Penn World Table (PWT), *World Development Indicators* (WDI), and *World Economic Outlook*. Recent research on such estimates, mainly relating to the PWT but also applying to WDI and WEO estimates, have highlighted serious inconsistencies in the results across versions of the PWT[31] (Johnson et al. 2009) and country inconsistencies between growth rates and per capita PPP GDP estimates (Bhalla 2008). A major concern is that the growth rates used to derive estimates for the nonbenchmark years are based on domestic, not international, (PPP) prices and that the share weights of the growth rates are based on some hybrid of international and domestic prices (see also Deaton and Heston 2008). Johnson et al. (2009) demonstrate that economic studies using annual data are generally not "safe" in terms of their robustness to data revisions, except for countries with high-quality data (generally OECD countries). PPP GDP–level data also are not considered "safe" when looking at cross-country comparisons in nonbenchmark years. Johnson et al. find that estimates for smaller countries are more inconsistent and the variability increases as the distance of the data from the benchmark round increases. While there may be deficiencies in the extrapolated estimates, there remains a case for using such estimates on the basis that a weighting system that relies on estimates of annual figures is better than an assumption of no change. The implication for IMF use of these estimates is the need for more frequent rounds and updates of PPP estimates. One possibility in view of their high resource cost is better integration of the ICP methodology with CPI and PPI programs so that price data that could perhaps be used for PPP programs are collected regularly as part of the routine compilation of national statistics. A second possibility is that a "mini" ICP exercise be held between rounds, as is currently under way for the Asia region. But neither of these proposals negates the need to improve the estimation procedures for nonbenchmark years. Proposals for doing so can be found in Deaton and Heston (2008) and Johnson et al. (2009).

Timeliness

PPP estimates are based on intercountry price comparisons for the basic headings of economic activities that comprise GDP—155 for the 2005 ICP round—and their counterpart expenditure weights. Arising from this process are some key aspects of timeliness that are important to the IMF.

First and foremost, it is important to minimize the time lag between the completion of the price surveys and validation of the source data and the compilation of the (regional and global) PPPs. There is a natural time lag between the survey results and publication of the final global results and a trade-off between the reliability and the timeliness of the results. For the 2005 ICP round, the final global results were published in December 2007. The expectation for the 2011 round is that the results will be published during February–June 2014 (World Bank 2010, 23–26, para. 27). For logistical reasons, not all countries, and expenditure components within countries, collect prices over the same period. For the 2011 round, the plan is that the price surveys for household expenditures on goods and services will be conducted in 2011. However, in some small countries in the Caribbean, price surveys for these goods and services will take place in 2012. Price surveys for nonhousehold goods and services (education, health, compensation of government employees, equipment, and construction) will be carried out concomitantly with the compilation of the relevant expenditures data, from early 2011 to the end of 2012 (World Bank 2010, 23–26, para. 26). A "mini" ICP round for Asian countries will be undertaken to update their PPP estimates to a reference year of 2009.

A second aspect of timeliness is the time lag between the period(s) to which the component GDP expenditure data for the basic headings relate and the period(s) to which the price surveys relate. For example, the 2005 ICP round was based on price surveys principally conducted in 2005, although at the time the PPP estimates were compiled, not all countries had 2005 expenditure estimates available for all components of the GDP. Related to this problem is the procedure used to "update" the GDP estimates to 2005 if timely ones are not available.[32]

Finally, another aspect of timeliness is the need to issue estimates for nonparticipating countries and detailed information on their estimation procedures shortly after those of participating countries.

Groupings of Economies

The ICP is organized and executed on a regional basis. In the 2005 round, the regions were Africa, Asia-Pacific, Commonwealth of Independent States (CIS), South America, Western Asia, and the Eurostat-OECD countries, with regional aggregates published for countries in these groups. Membership of the ICP regional groups is related to the ICP sample design, which does not necessarily correspond to the standard regional aggregates maintained by the United Nations,[33] the member state groupings for the UN Regional Commissions,[34] or those used by the various international organizations, including the IMF. For example, countries such as Georgia and the Islamic Republic of Iran do not belong to any of the regional coordinating agencies. Countries such as Chile, the Arab Republic of Egypt, Mexico, and Sudan belong to more than one regional group. However, because PPP estimates for basic headings and GDP are provided for individual economies, it is not essential that the IMF and ICP groupings be the same; using the core data, the IMF can aggregate country PPP GDP in whatever manner it deems appropriate.

Large Economies

For large economies such as China and India, country-specific methodological issues may draw attention. For example, Deaton and Heston (2008) point out that price collection for China is limited to 11 cities and their mainly urban surrounding areas. Although the figures were adjusted to make them more geographically representative, it has been argued that the failure to include lower rural prices led to an overstatement of the PPP GDP deflator, suggested by Deaton and Heston to be by a little less than 10 percent. India, by contrast, has a long tradition of collecting urban and rural prices, and other large developed economies have smaller rural populations that to a large extent shop at urban outlets or chains.

Transparency

Because PPP estimates are used to help guide decisions on the distribution of members' quotas, which in turn help determine members' financial obligations, the allocation of a general increase in SDRs, and voting power in IMF decisions, there has to be transparency as to how the results are derived and disseminated. For the 2005 ICP round, a detailed operational manual and methodology handbook were usefully published on the ICP website (World Bank 2005, 2007), and similar publications are planned for the 2011 round. These publications do not incorporate and benefit from the many methodological innovations and twists and turns in the detail of the work as it proceeds. However, methodological papers are published as the round proceeds, mainly driven by members of the Technical Advisory Group and authors commissioned by the World Bank to examine particular issues. For the 2005 round, a quarterly ICP e-newsletter was published to inform users about new developments and regional issues. Meanwhile, each region produced a separate publication that contained not only its results, but also details about region-specific methodological issues. The final results of the ICP round were then published, along with technical details (World Bank 2008). In a very real sense, the IMF relies on the professionalism of the ICP program for the GDP PPP estimates. The integrity of such figures lies in the care and attention given to collection of source data and compilation methods, and openness about the methods employed ensures that the integrity of the results can be defended.

Summary

The PPP GDP estimates produced by the ICP are important to the IMF; they are an element of the formula that helps to guide decisions on the distribution of members' quotas, as described in this chapter. Furthermore, much of the analysis and monitoring of output and other key macroeconomic indicators across countries, and for regional, global, and analytic groups over time, require PPP estimates. The account in this chapter of the use of PPP-adjusted estimates in the WEO is indicative of such work. Because the IMF naturally seeks minimization of errors and bias in the source data for the PPP estimates and aggregation techniques,[35] the rigor of the discussion of such issues in the preceding chapters is welcome. The issues of particular concern to the IMF's usage are raised in this chapter and include country coverage and PPP estimates for member countries not participating in the ICP; PPP estimates for nonbenchmark years; the timeliness and periodicity of PPP estimates; groupings of economies; and transparency.

NOTES

1. The views expressed herein are those of the author and should not be attributed to the IMF, its Executive Board, or its management. Acknowledgments are extended to Yuri Dikhanov (World Bank), Yutong Li (IMF), D.S. Prasada Rao (University of Queensland), Frederic A. Vogel (World Bank), Kim Zieschang (IMF), and members of the IMF Finance and Research Departments (notably Sheila Bassett and Toh Kuan, respectively) who reviewed the paper.
2. Information on IMF research, statistics, and the WEO is available on the IMF's website, http://www.imf.org/external/index.htm, under the tabs "Research," "Data and Statistics," and "Publications." Copies of the WEO can be downloaded from the IMF website under "Publications." See also http://www.imf.org/external/ns/cs.aspx?id=29.
3. SDRs are special drawing rights.
4. Members' calculated quota shares using the quota formula are distinct from their actual quota shares.
5. Earlier accounts of the IMF's use of PPP estimates include Gulde and Schulze-Ghattas (1993) and Wagner (1995).
6. These are all available at http://www.imf.org/external/research/index.aspx.
7. Available for the October 2009 *World Economic Outlook* at http://www.imf.org/external/pubs/ft/weo/2009/02/weodata/index.aspx.
8. The SDR is an international reserve asset created by the IMF in 1969 to supplement its member countries' official reserves. Its value is based on a basket of four key international currencies: the euro, Japanese yen, pound sterling, and U.S. dollar. SDRs can be exchanged for freely usable currencies.

9. PPP GDP for a given economy is the volume of goods and services produced for final uses by that economy relative to other economies. It is calculated by deflating GDP at market prices by the PPP price level index, allowing comparisons across countries for a given period. Although the term *PPP exchange rate* is used in IMF publications and this chapter in describing such use, PPPs are not exchange rates (the prices of currencies in terms of one another). They are spatial price indexes for GDP by expenditure, and the deflated GDPs using PPPs are volumes expressed in a numeraire currency, not nominal amounts converted into another currency. It is more precise to refer to them without the "exchange rate" modifier.
10. The oldest, the Bretton Woods formula, originally contained five variables: national income, official reserves, imports, export variability, and the ratio of exports to national income. A multiformula approach was introduced in the 1960s, when the Bretton Woods formula was supplemented with four other formulas. National income was replaced by gross domestic product, and the trade variables were expanded to include services and transfers. Current account transactions and variability were given larger weights. The quota formulas were last modified in 1982–83 by reducing the weight of the variability variable and reintroducing reserves as a variable while retaining the basic structure of the formulas.
11. IMF documents, data, and simulations over the period June 2006–April 2008 are available at http://www.imf.org/external/np/fin/quotas/pubs/index.htm.
12. For details on the second round of quota reform, see IMF (2008, para. 9).
13. The choice of numeraire country is arbitrary and does not affect the calculations, because PPPs are adjusted to be transitive across countries.
14. For a discussion of the use of PPP weights against market exchange rates, see IMF (2003, box 1.2) and Zieschang (2008).
15. Composites for exchange rates, interest rates, and the growth rates of monetary aggregates are weighted by GDP converted to U.S. dollars at market exchange rates. Composites for the Euro Area use GDP weights. For unemployment rates and employment growth, the weights are country labor force as a share of the group labor force. Composites relating to the external economy are sums of individual country data after conversion to U.S. dollars at market exchange rates. Composites of changes in foreign trade volumes and prices are weighted by the U.S. dollar value of exports or imports as a share of total world or group trade in exports or imports.
16. The PPP-based GDP *share weights* used in the WEO for composite groups of economies are based on a vintage of data that differs from that of the PPP-based GDP estimates used in the WEO for international comparisons. The share weights are calculated using the previous version of the WEO database, and PPP-based GDP estimates are calculated using the most recent estimates of nominal GDP and the PPP exchange rate. For example, each country's share weight in October 2007 is based on nominal GDP and the PPP exchange rate as of the April 2007 WEO. The PPP-based GDP estimates in the October 2007 WEO were calculated from the October 2007 estimates of nominal GDP and the PPP exchange rate.
17. The IMF's Statistics Department (STA) has an extensive program of technical assistance (TA) in the form of missions to individual countries and regional and international training courses. In the financial year 2010, the Real Sector Division of STA was responsible for nine training courses or seminars and 223 TA missions on price statistics and national accounts. Such missions promulgate international standards, including those given in the *Consumer Price Index Manual* (ILO et al. 2004a), *Producer Price Index Manual* (ILO et al. 2004b), *Export and Import Price Index Manual* (ILO et al. 2009), and *System of National Accounts 2008* (Commission of the European Communities et al. 2008). Improved national accounts expenditure estimates

naturally lead to improved PPP weights. There is also a synergy between the improved consumer price index methodology and the ICP price surveys, especially for sampling issues, variety specification, and price collection and validation—issues considered in this volume.

18. Details are available at http://siteresources.worldbank.org/ICPEXT/Resources/ICP_2011.html.
19. At its 39th session, the United Nations Statistical Commission (UNSC) asked the World Bank to host the Global Office and take on global program coordination of the 2011 ICP round, which the Bank accepted. After the Friends of Chair evaluation of the ICP, the UNSC at its 40th session in February 2009 gave the final go-ahead for the 2011 round. Since that session of the UNSC, significant progress has been made in preparing for the 2011 round. During this period, the ICP governance structure was put in place: the hiring of the global manager was completed in April 2009, and the new Global Office was established. Meanwhile, the Executive Board, the Technical Advisory Group, and the regional coordinating bodies were set up, and they held their first meetings in September–October 2009.
20. The Eurostat-OECD PPP Programme continued to include some economies that were not members of the Organisation for Economic Co-operation and Development (OECD) and the European Union in its 1996, 1999, and 2002 rounds. The number of economies participating in each of those rounds was 32, 43, and 42, respectively. The Eurostat-OECD PPP Programme is responsible for 46 of the 146 countries included in the 2005 ICP round. OECD, in collaboration with the European Commission, spearheads the program in member countries, and the World Bank coordinates activities for the rest of the world.
21. For a history of the ICP, see http://web.worldbank.org/WBSITE/EXTERNAL/DATASTATISTICS/ICPEXT/0,,contentMDK:20118245~menuPK:62002075~pagePK:60002244~piPK:62002388~theSitePK:270065~isCURL:Y,00.html, and World Bank (2008, appendix A).
22. The World Bank/ICP provided the IMF with the PPP exchange rate estimates for these countries based on regression analysis.
23. As outlined by Barcena (2009). The excluded countries are relatively small. The largest, as measured by percentage contribution to global PPP GDP, including their estimates, were Algeria and the United Arab Emirates at 0.34 percent and 0.27 percent, respectively (source: IMF's WEO database).
24. Wagner (1995) discusses the possibility of countries choosing to not participate if they believe the formula used for nonparticipating countries will provide a more beneficial outcome.
25. An account of an estimation procedure that differs from that given in Changqing and Swanson (2009) appears in World Bank (2008, 164–5), but the database for the World Bank's *World Development Indicators*, from which the IMF estimates are drawn, uses the methodology in Changqing and Swanson (2009).
26. Country estimates may have relatively large prediction intervals in spite of the high $\bar{R}^2$ often found for the regressions. Prediction intervals depend on the sum of squared residuals, sample size, and (sum of squared) distances of the explanatory variables from the mean of the variables.
27. References to the ICP 1993/96 round are heard on occasion. The results of the 1993 round were presented in "1996 terms"—that is, the 1993 basic heading PPPs were re-referenced to 1996 with (usually) one deflator.
28. This is equivalent to taking the country's PPP, relative to that of the United States, in the benchmark year and extrapolating it by the growth rate in the country's GDP deflator relative to the growth rate in the United States' GDP deflator. Weights are calculated each year as nominal GDP in the national currency divided by the extrapolated PPP. The method is akin to that described by Rao et al. (2010, S68) and is invariant to the choice of the numeraire country—the United States in this instance.

29. These countries are following the recommendations of the 2008 *System of National Accounts* (see chapter 3), adopted by the 39th session of the United Nations Statistical Commission, February 26–29, 2008, http://unstats.un.org/unsd/nationalaccount/sna.asp.
30. Rao et al. (2010) advocate a new approach that uses a state-space formulation designed to generate predictions of PPPs, along with their standard errors, over time and across countries that are broadly consistent with benchmark data on PPPs and observed country-specific price movements. The method uses PPP data from all the benchmark rounds. It derives a weighted average of the extrapolations from different benchmarks, which is superior to the current practice of basing extrapolations on data from a single benchmark round. PPP estimates for nonbenchmark years by Rao et al. (2010) differed considerably from the extrapolated Penn World Table Version 6.2 (PWT 6.2) estimates.
31. However, the current PWT 6.3 does not yet use the 2005 survey results. The period to which the weights pertain, the weight reference period—say, 2000—is used to weight series for the surrounding five years: 1998, 1999, 2000, 2001, and 2002. There is also a two-year implementation period, so the 2000 weights are applied to the 1998–2002 five-year series in 2004, and similarly for other five-year intervals. This approach implies that a weight update for the 2005 weights will be applied to 2003–07 inclusive and will take place in 2009.
32. GDP figures are not revised just to update them to 2005. The data for nominal GDP at market prices underlying the 2005 PPP data for some of the 48 countries covered by the African Development Bank (AfDB) may be higher than similar data submitted to the IMF's *International Financial Statistics.* This difference reflects a massive effort by the AfDB to improve these data (e.g., to add informal sector estimates). However, it is not clear whether the authorities in some of these countries have adopted these data as official estimates.
33. http://unpan1.un.org/intradoc/groups/public/documents/un/unpan008092.pdf.
34. http://www.un.org/Depts/otherprgs.htm.
35. IMF staff serve on the ICP Executive Board and Technical Advisory Group. Research on PPP methodological issues is also conducted by IMF staff (e.g., see Silver 2009).

REFERENCES

Barcena, Alicia. 2009. "Interview with the Executive Secretary of ECLAC." *ICP Bulletin* 6 (March): 1, 4–15.

Bhalla, Surjit S. 2008. "World Bank—Most Asians Dead in 1950." *Business Standard,* August 23.

Changqing, Sun, and Eric Swanson. 2009. "Estimation of PPPs for Non-Benchmark Economies for the 2005 ICP Round." *ICP Bulletin* 6 (March): 1, 20–23.

Commission of the European Communities, International Monetary Fund, Organisation for Economic Co-operation and Development, United Nations, and World Bank. 2008. *System of National Accounts 2008.* UN: pre-edit version of Volume 1, approved by the Bureau of the UN Statistical Commission, August 2008. http://unstats.un.org/unsd/nationalaccount/sna.asp.

Deaton, Angus, and Alan Heston. 2008. "Understanding PPPs and PPP-Based National Accounts." Preliminary version presented at Conference on Research in Income and Wealth (CRIW)–National Bureau of Economic Research (NBER) Summer Workshop, July 14–15.

Diewert, W. Erwin. 2008. "New Methodology for Linking Regional PPPS." *ICP Bulletin* 5 (August): 1, 10–21.

Elekdag, Selim, and Subir Lall. 2008. "Global Growth Estimates Trimmed after PPP Revisions." *IMF Survey Magazine,* January 8. http://www.imf.org/external/pubs/ft/survey/so/2008/RES018A.htm.

Gulde, Anne Marie, and Marianne Schulze-Ghattas. 1993. "Purchasing Power Parity Based Weights for the *World Economic Outlook.*" *World Economic and Financial Surveys, Staff Studies for the World Economic Outlook 1993,* Part IV. http://www.imf.org/external/pubs/ft/wefs/1993/eng/studies/index.htm.

ILO (International Labour Office), International Monetary Fund, Organisation for Economic Co-operation and Development, Eurostat, United Nations Economic Commission for Europe, and World Bank. 2004a. *Consumer Price Index Manual: Theory and Practice.* Geneva: ILO. http://www.ilo.org/public/english/bureau/stat/guides/cpi/index.htm.

———. 2004b. *Producer Price Index Manual: Theory and Practice.* Geneva: ILO. http://www.ilo.org/public/english/bureau/stat/guides/cpi/index.htm.

———. 2009. *Export and Import Price Index Manual: Theory and Practice.* Geneva: ILO. http://www.ilo.org/public/english/bureau/stat/guides/cpi/index.htm.

IMF (International Monetary Fund). 2003. *World Economic Outlook.* Washington, DC: IMF, September. Various editions available at http://www.imf.org/external/ns/cs.aspx?id=29.

———. 2007. "A New Quota Formula—Additional Considerations, Statistical Appendix." March 14. http://www.imf.org/external/np/fin/quotas/pubs/.

———. 2008. "Reform of Quota and Voice in the International Monetary Fund—Report of the Executive Board to the Board of Governors." Washington DC, April 7. http://www.imf.org/external/pp/longres.aspx?id=4242.

Johnson, Simon, William Larson, Chris Papageorgiou, and Arvind Subramanian. 2009. "Is Newer Better? Penn World Table Revisions and Their Impact on Growth Estimates." NBER Working Paper Series, Number 15455, National Bureau of Economic Research, Cambridge, MA, October. http://www.nber.org/papers/w15455.

Rao, D.S. Prasada, Alicia Rambaldi, and Howard Doran. 2010. "Extrapolation of Purchasing Power Parities Using Multiple Benchmarks and Auxiliary Information: A New Approach." *Review of Income and Wealth* 56 (S1): S59–98.

Silver, Mick. 2009. "The Hedonic Country Product Dummy Method and Quality Adjustments for Purchasing Power Parity Calculations." Working Paper WP/09/271, International Monetary Fund, Washington, DC, December.

Wagner, Nancy. 1995. "A Review of PPP-Adjusted GDP Estimation and Its Potential Use for the Fund's Operational Purposes." Working Paper WP/95/18, International Monetary Fund, Washington, DC.

World Bank. 2005. "ICP Operational Manual." http://siteresources.worldbank.org/ICPINT/Resources/ICPOperationalManual2005.pdf.

———. 2007. *ICP 2005 Methodological Handbook.* http://web.worldbank.org/WBSITE/EXTERNAL/DATASTATISTICS/ICPEXT/0,,contentMDK:20126612~pagePK:60002244~piPK:62002388~theSitePK:270065,00.html.

———. 2008. *Global Purchasing Power Parities and Real Expenditures: 2005 International Comparison Program.* http://siteresources.worldbank.org/ICPINT/Resources/icp-final.pdf.

———. 2010. "Report of the World Bank on the International Comparison Programme to the United Nations Statistical Commission." 41st session, February.

Zieschang, Kim. 2008. "Integrating Regional GDP Aggregates Based on Exchange Rates and Inter-Country Comparisons Based on Purchasing Power Parity." *ICP Bulletin* (December).

CHAPTER 24

Using Expenditure PPPs for Sectoral Output and Productivity Comparisons

Robert Inklaar and Marcel P. Timmer

Purchasing power parities (PPPs) have a wide range of analytical and policy applications.[1] Traditionally, PPPs have been used for international comparisons of income, expenditure, and output. Most well known are the comparisons of levels of gross domestic product (GDP) per capita as published by the World Bank (e.g., World Bank 2008). Differences in GDP per capita across countries are mainly determined by levels of labor productivity at the aggregate economy level. Today, comparative series of output per worker and per hour worked are being produced routinely by various statistical organizations and in academia, such as the Penn World Table and the series produced by the Organisation for Economic Co-operation and Development (OECD), Conference Board, and Groningen Growth and Development Centre (GGDC) at the University of Groningen.

Various useful analytical applications of productivity levels, however, are also found at the more detailed level of individual industries. Because of the large differences in economic structure across countries, international comparisons of output and productivity at the sector level (agriculture, manufacturing, and services) provide useful complements to comparisons of GDP by expenditure categories. Previous research has shown that a low overall level of productivity is not necessarily indicative of large gaps in all sectors. Generally, it is assumed that productivity gaps in manufacturing can be large, and that gaps in services productivity across countries are much smaller. This well-known finding is at the heart of the Harrod-Balassa-Samuelson effect and often invoked to explain the lower relative prices of services in low-income countries compared with high-income countries. Also, studies of convergence and divergence in the world economy are increasingly being made at the industry level. Tests of international trade theories and endogenous growth models require measures relative to the world productivity frontier by sector.

By definition, a major part of the research in these areas requires PPPs from the production side rather than from the expenditure side—that is, PPPs should reflect the differences in the output prices of goods and services rather than the expenditure prices. In the remainder of this chapter, we call these production PPPs. Comparisons of productivity, loosely defined as output per unit of inputs, also require the relative prices of capital inputs, labor inputs, and intermediate inputs. This so-called industry of origin approach was pioneered by Paige and Bombach (1959) in a comparison of the United Kingdom and the United States. The earlier work was then conveniently summarized by Kravis (1976). Over the last two decades, this method was further developed and used in the International Comparisons of Output and Productivity (ICOP) project at the University of Groningen and at the National Institute of Economic and Social Research in London (O'Mahony 1999). Van Ark and Maddison (1994) and Maddison and van Ark (2002) provide an overview of the progress made in the early phase of this project through the research input of a dozen scholars and work on about 30 countries. More recently, sectoral output and productivity trends for a large set of countries were provided by the EU KLEMS database (available at http://www.euklems.net and discussed by Timmer et al. 2010). However, it appears that production PPPs were scarce and empirically difficult to obtain, which mainly related to the lack of readily available producer price surveys.

An alternative to the industry of origin approach is to use data from internationally coordinated surveys on expenditure prices such as those collected for the International Comparison Program (ICP) under the auspices of the United Nations and the World Bank (Kravis, Heston, and Summers 1982; Summers and Heston 1991). Since the early 1980s, OECD has regularly published estimates of expenditure PPPs derived from its joint program with Eurostat. Expenditure-based PPP comparisons are based on purchasers' prices of final goods and services with a detailed product specification. Hence, to apply them to output and productivity comparisons by industry, the PPPs have to be mapped from expenditure categories to industry groups.

The expenditure approach to sectoral PPPs was pioneered by Jorgenson, Kuroda, and Nishimizu (1987) and most recently applied by Sørensen and Schjerning (2008) and van Biesebroeck (2009). In general, PPPs based on expenditure price surveys suffer less from quality problems than unit values because product comparisons are based on detailed specifications. However, the approach also has some drawbacks for comparisons of output and productivity at the industry level because it requires detailed adjustments for margins, taxes, and international trade. Furthermore, by definition these PPPs only cover prices for final expenditure and do not reflect the relative prices of intermediate goods. Following Pilat (1996), van Ark and Timmer (2009) argue that a mixture of PPPs derived from the expenditure and industry of origin approaches should be used for productivity comparisons at the industry level. Building on this idea, Inklaar and Timmer (2009) have constructed the GGDC Productivity Level database. This database provides comparisons of output, inputs, and productivity at a detailed industry level for a set of 30 OECD countries for 1997, and it is publicly available at http://www.ggdc.net/databases/levels.htm. The PPPs used for this database are a combination of production- and expenditure-side PPPs. This study also provides price comparisons of capital, labor, and intermediate inputs, alongside output price comparisons, so that large-scale comparisons of multifactor productivity at the sector level became feasible.

This chapter begins by outlining what types of PPPs are needed for sectoral, single-, and multifactor productivity comparisons by industry. We argue in the first section that, given the limited availability of production PPPs, expenditure PPPs from the ICP are indispensable in facilitating these comparisons. However, until now the literature has not clearly described what adjustments are needed to convert PPPs by expenditure category into output PPPs by industry and under which conditions expenditure PPPs would provide a good proxy for production PPPs. The main contribution of this chapter is to derive these adjustments and conditions based on a system of supply-use tables (SUTs). SUTs are a major building block of the national accounts in many countries. They provide a systematic framework of the flows of goods and services from production and imports to final expenditure.

The second section of this chapter shows the usefulness of the derivation and confrontation of various types of prices (basic and purchasers' prices) in a SUT system. For example, this system provides clear guidance on how the prices of consumption goods and intermediate inputs are related to the output prices of industries. These relationships can be used to generate cross-checks in case different data sources (from the production and expenditure sides) exist or to illustrate the adjustments to be made to the expenditure PPPs to be used in sectoral productivity comparisons. Using a supply-use framework, we show that final expenditure prices need to be adjusted for trade and transportation margins, for taxes and subsidies, for the prices of exports and imports, and finally for the prices of intermediate use in order to provide a good proxy for output prices.

Because of these adjustments, the usefulness of expenditure PPPs in sectoral productivity comparisons differs across sectors. This difference is illustrated with some results from the GGDC Productivity Level database for OECD countries in the third section of this chapter. The fourth section presents some productivity comparisons, and the final section some concluding remarks. In those remarks, we stress the mutual dependence and potential spillovers from sectoral productivity comparisons and expenditure results from the ICP.

Methodology for Productivity Comparisons

In this section, we present the methodology for comparing levels of output, input, and productivity across countries that we used in constructing the GGDC Productivity Level database (Inklaar and Timmer 2009). Because we were trying to construct a comparable set of productivity measures for a large number of countries and industries at the same time, various choices had to be made, not only about the use of particular index number formulas, but also about their actual implementation. This section lays out the basic methodology (for a more detailed discussion of methodology and empirics, see Inklaar and Timmer 2009).

The main aim of the GGDC Productivity Level database is to compare productivity between countries. The accounts provide so-called binary comparisons—that is, comparisons between a country c and a base country that is the same in all comparisons. Because the greatest interest lies in comparing the performance of countries to the world productivity and technology leader, it is natural that we choose the United States as our base country in the productivity comparisons.[2] The most commonly used single productivity measure for international comparisons of levels is *labor productivity*. This term is generally defined as an output measure divided by a labor input measure. The labor input measure can be the number of persons employed, number of employees, or number of hours worked. The output measure can be either the volume of gross output or the volume of value added. If Q^{VA} is value added and H is hours worked, then value added–based labor productivity (LP_VA) is given by

$$LP\_VA_c = \frac{\dfrac{Q_c^{VA}}{H_c}}{\dfrac{Q_{US}^{VA}}{H_{US}}}. \quad (24.1)$$

Alternatively, more than one input can be accounted for—the so-called multifactor productivity (MFP) measures. MFP measures are well rooted in economic theory, but because of their heavy data requirements they are used much less than single productivity measures such as labor productivity. MFP and labor productivity measures are not independent of each other. Multifactor productivity measures can be used to explain single-factor productivity differences. For example, differences in labor productivity levels can be explained by differences in the ratio of capital to labor and differences in multifactor productivity. These and other links have been established with the help of the economic theory of production.

The GGDC Productivity Level accounts provide estimates for both value added–based MFP, taking into account both labor and capital services, and gross output–based MFP, taking into account labor, capital, and intermediate inputs. In this chapter, we outline only the methodology for value added–based measures. Following Jorgenson and Nishimizu (1978), we define the translog quantity index of difference in multifactor productivity based on value added (*MFP_VA*). This index is defined as

$$\ln MFP\_VA_c = \ln \frac{Q_c^{VA}}{Q_{US}^{VA}} - \hat{w}_K \ln \frac{Q_c^K}{Q_{US}^K} - \hat{w}_L \ln \frac{Q_c^L}{Q_{US}^L} \tag{24.2}$$

where Q^K is the quantity of capital services, Q^L is the quantity of labor services, and $\hat{w}_K$ is the share of capital services in value added averaged over the two countries—that is, $\hat{w}_K = \frac{1}{2}(w_c^K + w_{US}^K)$, where $w_c^K = \frac{V_c^K}{(V_c^K + V_c^L)}$, with V_c^K the nominal value of capital services compensation in country c in national currency and similarly for labor, so that $\hat{w}_K + \hat{w}_L = 1$. Under the standard neoclassical assumptions, this measure indicates the difference in the level of technology between the two countries (see Jorgenson and Nishimizu 1978).

Formulas (24.1) and (24.2) indicate that comparable volume measures of output and input for the two countries are needed. When a single output is being compared, physical measures such as numbers of cars are possible. However, when comparisons are made at the industry or aggregate level where output is not represented by a single product, output is given in terms of real values. In that case, a correction for differences in relative price levels between countries is needed. This is usually done with a purchasing power parity (*PPP*) that indicates the ratio of the price of output in one country relative to that in another country, each given in local currencies.

Volume indexes are calculated implicitly by the ratio of the nominal values and the relevant price indexes. For example, the aggregate value added quantity in country c is given by

$$Q_c^{VA} = \frac{V_c^{VA}}{PPP_c^{VA}}. \tag{24.3}$$

For labor input, one can use number of workers or total hours worked as a volume measure. However, for multifactor productivity comparisons one would also like to include the composition of labor in terms of various labor types with different productivities—for example, low- and high-skilled labor. This can be done by choosing an appropriate PPP based on relative wages so that

$$Q_c^L = \frac{V_c^L}{PPP_c^L} \tag{24.4}$$

where V_c^L is the nominal value of labor compensation in country c (in national currency), and PPP_c^L is the relative price of labor services in country c. Similarly, for aggregate capital input in country c

$$Q_c^K = \frac{\tilde{V}_c^K}{PPP_c^K} \tag{24.5}$$

where $\tilde{V}_c^K$ is the nominal value of ex ante capital compensation in country c, and PPP_c^K is the relative price of capital services in country c.[3]

One of the main applications in productivity comparisons is so-called level accounting. Level accounts provide a decomposition of differences in value added per hour worked into differences in capital per hour worked (capital intensity), in labor composition (skill intensity), and in MFP. This decomposition is carried out as

$$\text{(24.6)} \qquad \ln \frac{\dfrac{VA_c}{H_c}}{\dfrac{VA_{US}}{H_{US}}} = \hat{w}_L \ln \frac{\dfrac{Q_c^L}{H_c}}{\dfrac{Q_{US}^L}{H_{US}}} + \hat{w}_K \ln \frac{\dfrac{Q_c^K}{H_c}}{\dfrac{Q_{US}^K}{H_{US}}} + \ln MFP\_VA_c$$

where $\hat{w}_L$ and $\hat{w}_K$ are defined as in equation (24.2).

The PPPs for outputs and inputs required in (24.3)–(24.5) are derived on the basis of detailed sets of output and input prices.[4] Prices are aggregated using the multilateral translog price indexes (CCD index) introduced by Caves, Christensen, and Diewert (1982). Basically, in this methodology an artificial country is created by averaging over all countries in the data set. This constructed country is then used as a bridge when making binary comparisons between two countries. This method creates so-called transitive PPPs that are base country–independent (see chapters 1, 4, and 5 in this volume for further discussion). As with our MFP indexes, the PPPs are normalized with the United States equal to one. Labor and capital volume indexes grounded in production theory should take into account the composition of each factor input such as different levels of skills or types of capital goods, in particular information and communication technology (ICT) assets versus non-ICT assets. For labor, this can be achieved by deflation with an appropriate PPP (PPP_c^L) based on the relative wages of each labor type l as follows:

$$\text{(24.7)} \qquad \ln PPP_c^L = \sum_l \overline{w}_l^L \left[\ln PPP_{l,c}^L - \overline{\ln PPP_l^L}\right]$$

where the bar in the last term indicates a geometric average over all countries indexed by c running from 1 to N, and N is the number of countries. It follows that $\overline{\ln PPP_l^L} = 1/N \sum_c \ln PPP_{l,c}^L$ and $\overline{w}_l^L$ is the average weight of labor type l defined as $\overline{w}_l^L = \frac{1}{2}[w_{l,c}^L + \sum_c (w_{l,c}^L / N)]$ with $w_{l,c}^L$ the share of labor type l in total labor compensation in country c: $w_{l,c}^L = V_{l,c}^L / V_c^L$. The PPP for each labor type is derived on the basis of relative wages. A similar procedure is applied for the derivation of PPPs for capital PPP_c^K, output PPP_c^Y, and intermediate inputs PPP_c^X.

For the deflation of value added, a double deflation procedure is used based on separate PPPs for gross output and intermediate inputs as required (Jorgenson, Kuroda, and Nishimizu 1987). We follow a CCD-like approach by taking a geometric mean of all possible binary Törnqvist indexes for a particular country c. First, we calculate the binary value added PPP for each country pair (c,d) as follows:

$$\text{(24.8)} \qquad \left[\ln PPP_c^Z - \ln PPP_d^Z\right] = \frac{1}{1 - \overline{w}_X^Y}\left[(\ln PPP_C^Y - \ln PPP_d^Y) - \overline{w}_X^Y (\ln PPP_c^X - \ln PPP_d^X)\right].$$

The weight $\overline{w}_X^Y$ is the share of intermediate inputs in gross output, averaged over the two countries.

Second, a GEKS (Gini-Éltetö-Köves-Szulc) procedure is applied to multilateralize the set of value added PPP binaries given in (24.8), as in Caves, Christensen, and Diewert (1982). Together, these equations provide the system used to derive MFP measures consistent with neoclassical production theory.

Output and Expenditure Prices within a Supply-Use Table Framework

The theoretically most appropriate approach for international comparisons of output and productivity levels is to apply PPPs that are based on the industry of origin approach. Various alternative ways can be used to obtain PPPs for gross output, partly depending on the data availability for individual industries. One way is to make use of producer prices for specified products, but these are scarce because large-scale international surveys of production prices are not conducted. The most widely used approach to obtain production PPPs is the unit value ratio (UVR) method. This method makes use of production statistics such as censuses or business statistics surveys that record the output values and quantities for product items. By dividing the output value by the corresponding quantities, one obtains unit values, which can then be used for calculating unit value ratios for matched items between countries. Because of lack of data, this approach can be used only for a limited set of industries and countries. In addition, unit value ratios can suffer from quality adjustment problems in international comparisons. Detailed product characteristics are difficult to observe directly from production statistics because those statistics report quantity and values for product groups rather than for specified products, and product descriptions are often brief.[5]

An alternative to the industry of origin approach is to use data from internationally coordinated surveys on expenditure prices such as in the International Comparison Program (ICP). Expenditure-based PPP comparisons are based on the purchasers' prices of final goods and services with a detailed product specification. Hence, to apply them to output and productivity comparisons by industry, basic heading PPPs need to be mapped from expenditure categories to industry groups. However, so far no one has clearly outlined under which conditions expenditure PPPs provide a good proxy for the PPPs of gross output and what kind of adjustments are needed. In this section, we use the basic balance equation between supply and use of goods in the supply-use table framework to derive an exact relationship between expenditure and industry output prices. This relationship is used to indicate which adjustments need to be made to expenditure prices so they are a reasonable proxy for basic output prices. Alternatively, the adjustments can be used to assess the usefulness of expenditure PPPs in output comparisons.

Supply-use tables provide a convenient way of summarizing and presenting a coherent set of economic transactions within a country. Whereas a supply table indicates for each product where it comes from (domestically produced or imported), the use table provides information on product use as intermediate or final consumption. In the SUT framework, the valuation of domestic output is at basic prices, while the use of products is recorded at purchasers' prices.[6] This distinction is crucial in the link between expenditure and production PPPs (Commission of the European Communities et al. 1993, sec. VI.J):

> purchaser's price = basic price of the product received by the producer + taxes on the product[7] – subsidies on the product + trade and transport margins in delivering the product to the purchaser.

This section provides an exposition of the full structure of the SUT framework. The following notation is used, which includes commodities i ($i = 1, \ldots, m$) and industries j ($j = 1, \ldots, n$); quantities are indicated with capitals:

S_i = quantity of total supply of product i
U_i = quantity of total use of product i

M_i = imported quantity of product i
F_i = quantity of product i for final domestic demand
E_i = quantity of product i exported
Y_{ij} = quantity of commodity i produced by industry j
X_{ij} = quantity of commodity i used as intermediate input by industry j
L_j = value of labor services used in industry j
K_j = value of capital services used in industry j.

Lowercase p's are used for the corresponding prices:

p_{ij}^{Y} = basic price received by industry j for selling commodity i
p_{ij}^{X} = purchaser's price paid by industry j for intermediate consumption of commodity i
p_{i}^{M} = basic (c.i.f.) price of imported commodity i
p_{i}^{F} = purchaser's price for final domestic demand of commodity i
p_{i}^{E} = purchaser's (f.o.b.) price of exported commodity i.

Margins and taxes are defined as follows:

T = total taxes net of subsidies on products
R = total trade and transport margins
r_{i}^{S} = trade and transport margin rate on supplied product i
t_{i}^{S} = net tax rate on supplied product i.

Finally, a capital V in front of a quantity symbol is used to indicate its value through multiplication by the corresponding price.

Table 24.1 is a simplified outline of a supply-use table.[8] In both the supply and use tables, commodities are in the rows and industries in the columns. The use table indicates the usage for each product i: intermediate, final domestic demand, or export. The last column indicates total use. The entries are at the purchasers' prices. In addition, the use table contains a so-called value added block. For each industry j, total intermediate input at purchasers' prices plus value added at the basic price adds up to gross output at basic prices (last row). The supply table indicates the origin of each product, whether domestic production or import. The fourth column records total supply at basic prices. The other columns provide information on taxes and subsidies on products and trade and transport margins. These are needed to arrive at the total supply at purchasers' prices, which can be set against total use at purchasers' prices from the use table. The output of all products produced in industry j valued at basic prices sums to gross output at basic prices in this industry (last row in the supply table).

The supply and use tables are linked by two basic identities: row and column. The column identity requires identity for each industry between the sum of gross output over all products produced in an industry, on the one hand, and value added plus intermediate consumption, on the other:

$$VX_j + VK_j + VL_j = VY_j. \tag{24.9}$$

The row identity requires balance between use and supply for each product and links the expenditure and production approaches at the product level. The identity should hold in terms of both quantities and values. In quantity terms,

$$X_i + F_i + E_i = S_i. \tag{24.10}$$

TABLE 24.1 Outline of a Supply-Use Table

USE table at purchasers' prices								
		Industries **1.... *j* .... *n***	**Total intermediate use**	**Final domestic demand**	**Exports f.o.b.**	**Total use at purchasers' prices**		
Commodities	1 : i : *m*	.... $P_{Xij} X_{ij}$	VX_i	$P_{Fi} F_i$	$P_{Ei} E_i$	$VX_i + VF_i + VE_i$		
Total intermediate input at purchasers' prices		.... VX_j	VX	VF	VE	$VX + VF + VE$		
Gross value added at basic prices		.... $Kj + Lj$						
Gross output at basic prices		.... VY_j						
SUPPLY table at basic prices								
		Industries **1.... *j* .... *n***	**Total domestic supply**	**Import c.i.f.**	**Total supply at basic prices**	**Taxes minus subsidies**	**Trade and transport margins**	**Total supply at purchasers' prices**
Commodities	1 : i : *m*	.... $P_{Yij} Y_{ij}$	VY_i	$P_{Mi} M_i$	$VS_i = VY_i + VM_i$	$t_i VS_i$	$r_i VS_i$	$(1 + t_i + r_i) VS_i$
Total at basic prices	....	VY_j	VY	VM	$VS = VY + VM$	T	R	$VS + R + T$

This identity states that the quantity of supply of product i must be equal to its use, consisting of intermediate use, final domestic demand, and exports. In value terms, at purchasers' prices the identity is

$$VX_i + VF_i + VE_i = VS_i + T_i + R_i. \tag{24.11}$$

The value of total intermediate use of i (VX_i) is equal to the sum of values of intermediate use of i by all producers, and the total value of supply (VS_i) is equal to the value of supply by all producers and imports. By rewriting values as the product of prices and quantities, (24.11) can be stated as

$$\sum_j p_{ij}^X X_{ij} + p_i^F F_i + p_i^E E_i = (1 + t_i^S + r_i^S)\left(\sum_j p_{ij}^Y Y_{ij} + p_i^M M_i\right). \tag{24.12}$$

By rewriting equation (24.12), the relationship between purchasers' prices (p_{ij}^X, p_i^F, p_i^E), on the one hand, and basic output prices (p_{ij}^Y), on the other, can be derived. This identity provides the basic relationship between the final domestic demand price and the output price at the product level, which we are seeking. To bring out this relationship more clearly, we assume, without loss of generality, that there is only one basic price in the system for an individual product i—that is, the basic output price of a product is independent from its industry of origin:

$$p_{ij}^Y = p_i^Y. \tag{24.13}$$

By rearranging equation (24.12), substituting (24.13), and using identity (24.10), the following basic result can be derived (omitting index i for clarity). Under the assumption given in (24.13), the general relationship between basic output prices and final domestic demand prices can be written as

$$p^Y = \frac{1}{(1 + t^S + r^S)} p^F + A^{E,M} + A^X. \tag{24.14}$$

This is a key result for our purpose. It indicates that three types of adjustments are needed to derive an output price from a final domestic demand price: an adjustment for margins and taxes, an adjustment for international trade ($A^{E,M}$), and an adjustment for intermediate consumption (A^X). The latter two are given by

$$\mathrm{A}^{E,M} = \frac{1}{(1 + t^S + r^S)}\left[(P^E - P^F)\frac{E}{Y} - \left((1 + t^S + r^S)P^M - P^F\right)\frac{M}{Y}\right] \tag{24.15a}$$

and

$$A^X = \frac{1}{(1 + t^S + r^S)} \sum_j (P_j^X - P^F)\frac{X_j}{Y}. \tag{24.15b}$$

The first term on the right-hand side of (24.14) is the final expenditure price,[9] adjusted for average net taxes and margins on total supply of the product. The second adjustment is for international trade, given in (24.15a). This is especially important for comparisons involving small, open economies. The size of the adjustment depends on the differences between the final expenditure prices and the export and import prices, and on the ratios of export and import quantities to total domestic output. The third adjustment in (24.15b) depends on the size of the differences between the final expenditure price and the intermediate consumption price for a particular item, and on the ratio of intermediate consumption to total domestic output for that item. This basic result suggests that if export, import, and domestic prices differ, for products that are characterized by larger shares of imports and exports or intermediate consumption in total output, expenditure prices will be poorer proxies for output prices. But for industries that are mainly producing for final consumption and whose products are hardly internationally traded, an adjusted final expenditure price might be a reasonable proxy for the industry output price. This type of information can be derived from input-output tables.

Using this result, we can also state the adjustments needed for expenditure PPPs to properly reflect output PPPs:

$$(24.16) \qquad PPP_c^Y = \frac{\dfrac{1}{(1+t_c^S+r_c^S)}\,p_c^F + A_c^{E,M} + A_c^X}{\dfrac{1}{(1+t_{US}^S+r_{US}^S)}\,p_{US}^F + A_{US}^{E,M} + A_{US}^X}.$$

If the adjustments for international trade and intermediate consumption are assumed to be zero in both countries, (12.16) is simplified to

$$(24.17) \qquad PPP_c^Y = \frac{(1+t_{US}^S+r_{US}^S)}{(1+t_c^S+r_c^S)}\,PPP_c^F.$$

In this case, the expenditure PPP, adjusted for average net taxes and margins on total supply of the product, equals the output PPP. In fact, this adjusted expenditure PPP has been used as a proxy for output prices by, for example, Jorgenson, Kuroda, and Nishimizu (1987), Lee and Tang (2000), and most recently Sørensen and Schjerning (2008) and van Biesebroeck (2009). However, (24.17) shows that two further adjustments may be needed. In a pioneering attempt, Hooper (1996) tried to adjust expenditure PPPs for international trade prices, but his methodology was ad hoc, and the adjustments were based on very aggregate data. As a result, this approach was not pursued. Also, adjustments for intermediate consumption have not yet been tried, and there is little hope in view of the paucity of data on prices for intermediate consumption. The conclusion is that only the first adjustment for margins and taxes is feasible in practice. The expected size of the other adjustments that need to be made but cannot provides information about the possible bias associated with the use of expenditure PPPs as a proxy for output PPPs.

Based on information from input-output tables (see van Ark and Timmer 2009), it is possible to make some general statements about the possible biases, in particular in comparisons involving small, open economies with large export and import shares. This bias will differ for each sector. For industries that mainly produce goods for intermediate demand such as agriculture, mining, transport, basic goods manufacturing, and business services, expenditure PPPs (E-PPPs) are not useful as proxies for output PPPs (O-PPPs).[10] On the other hand, E-PPPs appear acceptable for relative price differences in food manufacturing, utilities, and communications after adjusting for taxes and margins. E-PPPs are also useful for construction, hotels, and real estate activities because final expenditure shares are very high for these sectors and imports are negligible.

PPPs in the GGDC Productivity Level Database

This section discusses the sources and methodology of the PPPs for output, intermediate input, labor, and capital used in the GGDC Productivity Level database. This set of PPPs is based on a combination of expenditure and production PPPs.

Output and Value Added PPPs

The output PPPs used in the GGDC Productivity Level database rely heavily on a study by Timmer, Ypma, and van Ark (2007). They presented a new and comprehensive data set of bilateral output PPPs for a set of 30 OECD countries, with the United States as the base country at the industry level for the year 1997. This data set is based on a combination of several data sources, both from the expenditure and industry of origin approaches. Expenditure PPPs by expenditure category were taken from the OECD comparison allocated to industries. For example, the expenditure prices of bread and sugar were allocated to food manufacturing. In a second step, the expenditure PPPs were adjusted to a basic price concept by "peeling off" trade and transport margins and taxes net of subsidies as outlined in the previous section. Production PPPs were based mainly on unit value ratios. The choice for PPPs derived from either the expenditure or industry of origin approach was in part dictated by the availability of price data for a particular (three-digit) industry and a careful assessment of the usefulness of each in case both alternatives were available. This approach is outlined in Timmer, Ypma, and van Ark (2007) and van Ark and Timmer (2009).

Table 24.2 gives the type of PPP used for output for major sectors. In addition, its quality is assessed. PPPs are ranked from 1 (very poor) to 5 (very good) on the basis of the following criteria. The quality of E-PPPs at the industry level depends on the share of final expenditure in total use and the share of import in total supply, as described in the previous section. This quality can be evaluated on the bases of input-output tables, also as described earlier. The criteria for assessing the quality of O-PPPs are different from those for E-PPPs. Conceptually, O-PPPs refer to the prices of domestically produced products. But as discussed earlier, the main weaknesses of O-PPPs are the product mix and quality problems. Especially for high-tech goods, or heterogeneous services, O-PPPs can be affected. In addition, for many services no data are available on unit values because of a lack of appropriate value data and the difficulty in defining quantities. O-PPPs are therefore particularly useful for industries for which products are relatively homogeneous and for which differences in product quality problems are small.

Agricultural output consists almost exclusively of the products used for intermediate input by other firms, not for final consumption. Therefore, expenditure PPPs cannot be used as a proxy for agricultural output PPPs. Instead, the agricultural PPPs for this study are developed along the same lines as earlier ICOP work on agriculture (Rao 1993). We rely exclusively on production PPPs based on producer prices from the FAOSTAT database of the Food and Agriculture Organization (FAO). This database contains a very extensive set of quantities and farm price values of up to 146 agricultural products. Similarly, for mining and most manufacturing industries unit value ratios are used. Unit values for European countries are derived from PRODCOM, which has a harmonized set of product data for European Union member states. The PRODCOM database includes quantities and sales values by product, linked to the NACE classification, for up to 7,000 product items.[11] This database is essentially based on the original national production censuses and industry surveys, but uses a harmonized product coding system. PRODCOM greatly enhances the number of product matches on the basis of which unit value ratios were constructed. For non-European countries, it uses comparable data from national production surveys. In addition, it applies hedonic

TABLE 24.2 Source and Grading for Industry PPPs in GGDC Productivity Level Database

Industry	ISIC rev. 3 code	Grade	PPP type used	Remark
A. Output PPPs				
Agriculture	01–05	5	O-PPP	Homogeneous goods
Mining and quarrying	10–14	4	O-PPP	Homogeneous goods
Manufacturing	15–37	4	E-PPP/O-PPP	
Food, drink, and tobacco	15, 16	4	Mainly O-PPP	Homogeneous goods
Basic goods	17, 20, 21, 23–28	4	Mainly O-PPP	Homogeneous goods
Nondurable	18, 19, 22, 36, 37	4	Mainly O-PPP	Homogeneous goods
Durable	29–35	2	Mainly E-PPP	Quality, import, and coverage problem
Electricity, gas, and water supply	40, 41	4	E-PPP/O-PPP	Homogeneous goods
Construction	45	4	E-PPP	High expenditure share
Trade	50–52	2	O-PPP/E-PPP	Quality problem
Hotels and catering	55	4	E-PPP	High expenditure share
Transport	60–63	3	O-PPP	Quality problem
Communications	64	3	O-PPP	Quality problem
Finance	65–67	0	E-PPP	Reference PPP
Real estate activities	70	4	E-PPP	High expenditure share
Business services	71–74	1	E-PPP	Small expenditure share
Public administration and defense	75	1	Mainly wages	Based on input PPPs
Education and health	80, 85	1	Mainly wages	Based on input PPPs
Other services	90–95	2	E-PPP	Different product mix
B. Intermediate input PPPs				
All industries		1–4	E-PPP/O-PPP	Based on output PPPs, so grade depends on mix of input products
C. Capital input PPPs, all industries				
Construction		3	E-PPP	PPP for investments
Machinery and equipment		4	E-PPP	PPP for investments
D. Labor input, all industries		4	Wages	Relative wages for various labor types

Note: Ranking: 0 = not available; 1 = very poor; 2 = poor; 3 = acceptable; 4 = useful; 5 = very useful. E-PPP refers to expenditure PPPs for the OECD from the 1999 round, and O-PP.P refers to production PPPs for 1997 from Timmer, Ypma, and van Ark (2007); ISIC = International Standard Industrial Classification.

UVRs for cars. Much of the output in manufacturing industries such as textiles, pulp and paper, basic metals, nonmetallic minerals, and chemicals consists of relatively homogeneous basic goods, and hence the quality of the O-PPPs is relatively high. This is not true for industries producing more sophisticated specialized goods such as in electrical and nonelectrical equipment, transport equipment, and instrument manufacturing. For these industries, the data set mainly makes use of adjusted component expenditure PPPs from the ICP. Although their quality is higher than that of unit value ratios, quality problems also plague purchaser's price comparisons of high-tech goods.

E-PPPs cannot be directly used for the distribution sector, because the output in this sector is measured as the margin of sales over purchases and separate deflation of intermediate purchases is necessary. But with an adjustment for the margin to sales ratio for each item, E-PPPs can be used for the retail sector. For retail trade, expenditure PPPs for individual expenditure categories were directly applied to sales output. The PPP at the margin level is derived as a weighted average of the sales PPPs of all goods, corrected for differences in the margin to sales ratios between two countries. In the case of wholesale trade, only the unit values of goods purchased by the wholesale sector are observable. Margin PPPs are derived by adjusting for differences in margin to cost ratios between two countries. Information on retail and wholesale sales, purchases, and margins were obtained from national trade census and survey data. Although this approach is superior to using unadjusted E-PPPs, it only partially corrects for differences in the quality of the trade service provided—see Timmer and Ypma (2006) for additional discussion on this approach.

For transport and communication services, UVRs were used, based on value and quantity data from a wide variety of international sources. Because of the high level of intermediate use, E-PPPs are only poor proxies. But given the relatively broad descriptions of the products used (up to nine product groups are distinguished), the quality of the UVRs is lower than that for manufacturing industries.

For other sectors (e.g., construction), production PPPs are very poor or nonexistent, and adjusted expenditure PPPs are used extensively. Conceptually, expenditure PPPs are a very good proxy for the PPPs for the gross output of construction, hotel and restaurant, and real estate activities[12] because almost all the output of these industries is for final expenditure, with very little export and import activity, so that adjustments need only be minimal. However, the quality of the ICP expenditure PPPs themselves is not always particularly high (e.g., for construction).

For other industries, expenditure PPPs are poor proxies because a sizable share of these services is used for intermediate, not final, consumption. And the mix of services used by producers will differ considerably from the services used by final consumers, such as for business and other services. Because we lack alternatives, we use adjusted expenditure PPPs, but note in table 24.2 that they are a poor proxy for an output PPP.

The expenditure PPP for finance is a reference PPP that is based on the overall expenditure PPP rather than on the relative prices of financial services. Because of the way in which financial output is currently deflated in most national accounts, this practice is perhaps defendable, but it is clearly unsatisfactory, and more research is needed to measure both financial output and prices.

For public administration, education and health expenditure PPPs have not been used. In almost all countries, the output in these sectors is measured by means of inputs. There is a recent tendency in some countries to come up with genuine output measures. However, by and large our assumption that output is measured by inputs holds true, in particular for our benchmark year, 1997. By implication, productivity levels should be the same across all countries. Put otherwise, output PPPs should be a weighted sum of the input PPPs, with weights indicating the share of each input in total output. However, when we compared our input PPPs with the expenditure PPPs given by the OECD for these industries, large differences were found. In particular, the labor PPPs used by the OECD are rather different from our labor PPPs. Further scrutiny of the ICP PPPs for this sector is warranted (see chapter 11 of this book). Therefore, we decided to define the output PPPs for nonmarket services (industries L, M, N, and P) as a weighted sum of our input PPPs. Consequently, the comparative multifactor productivity levels in these industries are all equal to one by definition.

Intermediate input PPPs should reflect the costs of acquiring intermediate deliveries and match the price concept used in the input-output tables, hence at basic prices plus net taxes. The data problems associated with obtaining input PPPs for individual industries are larger than those associated with output. There is often no input price parallel to the output PPPs. Business statistics surveys and production censuses provide little or no information on quantities and values of inputs in manufacturing, and for nonmanufacturing industries the information is largely absent. Moreover, by definition, PPPs from the expenditure side do not reflect the prices of intermediate inputs because they cover only the final expenditure categories. In this study, we use output PPPs as a proxy for relative intermediate input prices under the assumption that the basic price of a good is independent of its use—that is, we use the same gross output PPP of an industry to deflate all intermediate deliveries from this industry to other industries. The aggregate intermediate input PPP for a particular industry can be derived by weighting intermediate inputs at the output PPP from the delivering industries. Imported goods are identified separately, and exchange rates are used as conversion factors for imports. Ideally, one would like to have separate estimates of import PPPs based on trade data because there is little evidence that the law of one price holds for all goods even when internationally traded. However, so far these data are not readily available.

PPPs for output and intermediate input can be combined to calculate PPPs for value added as described earlier. Table 24.3 presents value added PPPs for the market economy and three main sectors

TABLE 24.3 Various Alternative Value Added PPP Measures: Selected Countries, 1997

national currency per U.S. dollar

		Value added PPPs				
	GDP (OECD)	Market economy	Manufacturing	Other goods	Market services	Exchange rate
Australia	1.32	1.44	1.88	0.99	1.48	1.35
Austria	0.92	1.26	1.36	1.19	1.22	0.89
Belgium	0.91	1.06	0.94	1.26	1.06	0.89
Czech Republic	12.70	16.00	15.20	15.40	18.10	31.70
Denmark	8.43	9.07	11.16	11.22	7.81	6.60
Finland	1.00	1.02	1.01	0.85	1.08	0.87
France	0.97	1.18	1.07	1.48	1.13	0.89
Germany	0.99	1.08	1.05	1.52	1.01	0.89
Hungary	85.00	96.50	89.90	132.10	90.90	186.80
Ireland	0.85	0.99	1.13	1.17	0.94	0.84
Italy	0.82	0.96	0.70	1.02	1.07	0.88
Japan	168.00	229.00	166.00	366.00	230.00	121.00
Luxembourg	0.96	0.94	1.13	1.77	0.75	0.89
Netherlands	0.91	0.99	1.09	1.44	0.88	0.89
Portugal	0.67	0.75	0.91	0.82	0.68	0.87
Slovenia	0.46	0.59	0.53	0.69	0.62	0.67
Spain	0.72	0.86	0.87	0.93	0.84	0.88
Sweden	9.30	10.30	10.40	10.00	10.20	7.63
United Kingdom	0.63	0.75	0.74	0.85	0.71	0.61
United States	1.00	1.00	1.00	1.00	1.00	1.00

Sources: Value added PPPs are based on the GGDC Productivity Level database (Inklaar and Timmer 2009); GDP PPPs and exchange rates are from OECD (2002). The GDP PPP is extrapolated from 1999; see OECD (2002).

Note: All entries are in national currency per U.S. dollar. For countries that adopted the euro in 1999, the 1999 conversion rate was used on the pre-euro currencies.

of the economy—manufacturing, other goods, and market services—for 1997. In addition, it provides PPPs for aggregate GDP and exchange rates as available from the OECD; both have been used as alternatives in previous studies. As noted in the literature, this approach ignores the differences in prices across various industries, as well as the differences in the prices of intermediate inputs and outputs—generally seen as a major weakness (Sørensen 2001). Instead, the value added PPPs have been derived by separate deflation of output and intermediate inputs as in equation (24.9). As shown in table 24.3, the ratio of sectoral value added to GDP PPPs can vary between 75 percent and more than 200 percent. The PPPs for the market economy are generally higher than the GDP PPPs, mainly because the latter includes nonmarket services, which, according to the OECD PPP results, are expensive in the United States compared with other countries. Importantly, the table shows large differences in relative prices across sectors, confirming the findings by Sørenson and Schjerning (2008) and van Biesebroeck (2009). For example, the PPP for other goods in Japan is much higher than the PPP for manufacturing goods. This difference is mainly due to the high output prices in the agriculture sector, which is famous for its weak competitiveness and strong import protection (van Ark and Pilat 1993). The use of an overall GDP PPP would greatly overestimate productivity levels in this sector. On balance, the value added PPPs for manufacturing differ by about 16 percent from the GDP PPP across our set of countries (absolute log differences). This directly translates into a 16 percent difference in measures of productivity levels. For market services, the difference is comparable (15 percent), while for other goods it is even bigger (32 percent).

Labor and Capital PPPs

Comparisons that use a homogeneous (or "raw") labor concept in the denominator of the productivity equation, such as number of workers or total hours worked, do not need currency converters for labor input because the comparison is already given in terms of volume. In the case of a heterogeneous labor concept—for example, workers of different skill types—labor input PPPs are needed to correct total labor compensation for differences in the relative prices of different categories of workers. Ideally, this labor input PPP should be based on labor costs, including all costs incurred by the producers in the employment of labor such as taxes levied, health cost payments, other types of insurance and contributions to retirement paid by the employer, financial benefits such as stock options, and the value of payments in kind and allowances (such as housing and rent).

The PPP for labor represents the relative price of one unit of labor between two countries. For each type of labor, relative wages can be calculated. The EU KLEMS Growth Accounts distinguish between 18 different labor types: two gender categories, three age categories, and three educational attainment categories. The educational attainment categories are low skilled (preprimary, primary, and lower secondary education—International Standard Classification of Education [ISCED] 0–2), medium skilled (upper secondary education, ISCED 3), and high skilled (total tertiary education, ISCED 5–7). However, in particular for level comparisons this classification is rough and might be misleading because educational systems in Europe and the United States are very different. In particular, the different roles of vocational schooling systems cause problems of comparability across countries. For example, in Germany vocational training is important to entering many occupations, but this is less prevalent in the United States. Based on the work by the Britain' s National Institute of Economic and Social Research (see Mason, O'Leary, and Vecchi 2009), we made a more detailed comparison and further decomposed the medium-skill level into three categories for a total of five. Further research on the comparability of schooling qualifications across countries is needed, however.

To convert capital input measured in national prices into common prices, capital input PPPs must be developed. Capital PPPs give the relative price of the use of a unit of capital in two countries from the purchaser's perspective. The calculation of the capital input PPP is less straightforward than for output, intermediate input, or labor input PPPs because of the conceptualization of capital input as capital services rather than capital stocks. To obtain the relative prices for capital input, we follow Jorgenson and Nishimizu (1978). Under the assumption that the relative efficiency of new capital goods is the same in both countries, PPP^K_k, the relative rental price of asset k between country C and the base country, the United States, is calculated as

$$PPP^K_k = PPP^I_k \frac{\dfrac{p^K_{k,C}}{p^I_{k,C}}}{\dfrac{p^K_{k,US}}{p^I_{k,US}}}. \tag{24.18}$$

This definition indicates that the relative rental price of a unit of capital between two countries depends on the relative purchaser's price of a new capital good of asset k between country C and the United States ($PPP^I_{k,t}$) and the relative cost of capital input, with p^K_k the user cost and p^I_k the investment price. One can think of the user cost ratio p^K_k/p^I_k as the relative price of hiring a similar capital good for one year in both countries. In the absence of taxation, the familiar cost of capital equation for asset type k can be written as (Jorgenson and Griliches 1967)[13]

$$\frac{p^K_k}{p^I_{k.}} \approx r + \delta_k + \hat{p}^I_k. \tag{24.19}$$

This formula shows that the user cost is determined by the nominal rate of return (r), the rate of economic depreciation (δ), and the asset-specific capital gains measured as the change in investment price ($\hat{p}^I_k$).

Investment PPPs are collected in the OECD ICP program and are available for 35 capital assets from the OECD (2002) for 1999. Because they are already at purchasers' prices, no adjustment is needed to arrive at the input price concept. The PPPs for the 35 assets are aggregated to the eight assets in this study using a CCD aggregation procedure. Investment deflators by asset and industry from the EU KLEMS database are used to move these PPPs to the benchmark year, 1997. The rates of depreciation are geometric rates that vary across assets, but are assumed to be identical across countries as in the EU KLEMS growth accounts (originally based on Fraumeni 1997). Because we use the ex ante approach to capital measurement, the nominal rate of return is the 10-year government bond yield for 1997 taken from the International Monetary Fund's database International Financial Statistics. It indicates the opportunity cost of using the investment fund in a risk-free alternative. The asset revaluation term can be derived from investment price indexes. To minimize the impact of sometimes volatile changes, annual averages over the period 1992–97 are used. Finally, we multiply the asset- and industry-specific rental prices with the capital stock taken from the capital input files from the EU KLEMS database (March 2008 release) to derive the ex ante capital compensation. This will typically differ from the (ex post) capital compensation as given in the national accounts. We normalize the compensation by asset to the national accounts figure by proportionality.[14]

Table 24.4 is an overview of the labor and capital PPPs for the market economy in 1997. For reference, we also include the value added PPP for each country. It appears that capital services are relatively expensive in most countries compared with the United States—the capital input PPP is often much higher than the value added or the labor PPP. Especially in Eastern Europe and Ireland, the use of capital in production is expensive. Labor-input PPPs, on the other hand, vary widely across the set of countries. In countries such as Belgium, Denmark, Germany, and the Netherlands, wages are relatively high, whereas in the lower-income countries such as Portugal, Spain, and those in Eastern Europe, the labor input is

TABLE 24.4 Labor and Capital PPPs: Selected Countries, 1997

national currency per U.S. dollar

	Value added PPP	Labor input PPP	Capital input PPP
Australia	1.44	1.23	1.68
Austria	1.26	0.95	0.98
Belgium	1.06	1.22	1.07
Czech Republic	16.05	5.37	37.81
Denmark	9.07	9.86	9.50
Finland	1.02	0.95	1.09
France	1.18	1.04	1.31
Germany	1.08	1.13	1.17
Hungary	96.52	31.40	218.60
Ireland	0.99	0.72	1.24
Italy	0.96	0.85	0.88
Japan	229.30	120.36	128.14
Luxembourg	0.94	1.15	1.13
Netherlands	0.99	1.00	1.07
Portugal	0.75	0.48	0.93
Slovenia	0.59	0.32	0.99
Spain	0.86	0.66	0.82
Sweden	10.31	9.20	11.64
United Kingdom	0.75	0.60	0.82
United States	1.00	1.00	1.00

Sources: GGDC Productivity Level database (Inklaar and Timmer 2009).
Note: All entries are in national currency per U.S. dollar. For countries that adopted the euro in 1999, the 1999 conversion rate was used on the pre-euro currencies.

cheap. But that is not because the share of low-skilled workers is higher in the latter set of countries; we compare the wages of groups of workers with equivalent levels of educational attainment in all countries.[15]

Productivity Level Comparisons for the OECD

The GGDC Productivity Level database provides a wide range of results on comparative prices, input and output quantities, and productivity at the industry level. In this section, we provide only a selection of the data available in the GGDC Productivity Level database; detailed results can be found at http://www.ggdc.net/databases/levels.htm. We also discuss the sensitivity of the results.

Productivity Levels

Basically, our productivity level comparisons are based on deflating nominal inputs and output as given in national input-output tables by a set of relative prices. The nominal values of inputs and outputs are based on national industry by industry input-output tables (IOTs), with separate information on domestic and imported supplies of commodities. IOTs are not available for all countries in a common benchmark year, and so we used supply-use tables to construct comparable IOTs. The starting point of our analysis is the national supply-use table for each country, valued in national currency for 1997. For Canada, the United States, and Australia, these tables were obtained from the national statistical offices. Eurostat makes these tables available for the European countries based on a common industry classification and at a sufficient level of industry detail for the purposes of this study. For Canada, the United States, and Australia, the classification for these tables had to be adjusted to the European industry classification. The value added block of the use table distinguishes only two primary factors—capital and labor—and so further disaggregation of these factor inputs is required. We use the labor and capital compensation given in the EU KLEMS database in which a correction is made for the labor income of the self-employed. Total hours worked and wages for each of the 18 labor types is taken from the EU KLEMS database (O'Mahony and Timmer 2009) and extended to 30 types by incorporating more detailed educational attainment data. Capital compensation is split into three ICT assets (computers, communication equipment, and software) and five non-ICT assets (residential structures, nonresidential structures, transport equipment, other non-ICT equipment, and other assets). The share of each asset in total compensation is based on capital rental prices using the ex ante approach. We multiply the asset- and industry-specific rental prices with the capital stock taken from the capital input files from the EU KLEMS database to derive the ex ante capital compensation. This will typically differ from the (ex post) capital compensation given in the national accounts. We normalize the compensation by asset to the national accounts figure by proportionality.

It is useful at this stage to present an example of the level accounting method for a flavor of the type of results that can be derived. We use the comparison of output, inputs, and productivity in transport equipment manufacturing in Germany with those in the United States in 1997. Table 24.5 is an overview of the nominal output and inputs in each country and the corresponding

TABLE 24.5 Example of Input-Output Comparison, Transport Equipment Manufacturing: Germany and United States, 1997

	Nominal values			Relative volume (Germany/ United States)
	Germany (billion euros)	United States (billion US$)	PPP (euro/US$)	
Sectoral output	141.8	454.8	1.25	0.25
Sectoral intermediate inputs	87.2	291.5	0.96	0.31
Energy	2.7	3.7	1.32	0.55
Materials	63.0	180.1	0.94	0.37
Services	21.5	107.8	1.02	0.20
Gross value added	54.7	163.2	2.04	0.16
Labor	43.1	122.6	1.36	0.26
High-skilled	10.4	34.9	1.32	0.23
Non-high-skilled	32.8	87.7	1.37	0.27
Capital	11.6	40.6	1.13	0.42
ICT capital	1.3	10.5	0.94	0.22
Non-ICT capital	10.2	30.1	1.16	0.48

Note: ICT = information and communication technology. Relative volumes are derived as the nominal value of Germany divided by the corresponding PPP over the nominal value of the United States, except for capital. Relative volumes for capital are determined based on the ex ante approach to capital measurement (see text).

PPPs. The values in the first two columns are at national prices: euros for Germany and U.S. dollars for the United States. The PPPs in the third column are given in euros per U.S. dollar. These PPPs are based on industry-specific prices of outputs and detailed inputs. They show that energy inputs and particularly labor are more expensive in Germany than in the United States, whereas materials and ICT capital are relatively cheap. In the final column, we give relative volumes derived as nominal value for Germany divided by the corresponding PPP over the nominal value for the United States, except for capital. The relative volumes for capital are determined based on the ex ante approach to capital measurement. The final column shows that the U.S. transport equipment output is four times as big as that of Germany. Production in the United States uses relatively less energy and non-ICT capital, but more services inputs and ICT capital than in Germany.

The GGDC Productivity Level database contains data only for the benchmark year, 1997. An attractive feature of the database is that it complements the EU KLEMS growth and productivity accounts by providing comparative levels and follows it in terms of country and industry coverage, variable definition, and basic data (O'Mahony and Timmer 2009). As such, the level and growth accounts for the benchmark year, 1997, can be used together in comparative analyses of long-run productivity trends. Tables 24.6 and 24.7 provide labor and multifactor productivity levels for the year 2005. These results are based on our preferred set of estimates for 1997 (using a mix of PPPs), extrapolated to 2005, which is the latest year for which data are available in the EU KLEMS database (March 2008 release). To update a volume comparison to 2005, we simply apply the relative volume growth rates between the two countries for the period 1997–2005.[16] Our comparisons of the market economy exclude public administration, health, education, and real estate because we consider these sectors to be more meaningful than comparisons for the total economy. Output in these sectors is measured mostly through inputs, and relative productivity levels should be one by definition.

Table 24.6 shows large differences in value added per hour worked within the OECD area. Belgian labor productivity levels are equal to those of the United States, but all other countries are lagging behind. Relative levels in France, Germany, and the United Kingdom are 70–80 percent, and less than 60 percent in Italy and Spain. Levels in Greece and Portugal are even below 40 percent of the U.S. level. In almost all European countries, comparative levels are highest in (nonelectrical) manufacturing, while gaps are typically much bigger for market services.

Table 24.7 provides measures of multifactor productivity. Assuming a common technology across countries, MFPs are an indication of the relative levels of the efficiency of input use between countries. They are measured as the difference in output between countries when differences in all inputs have been accounted for. Under the set of neoclassical assumptions, differences in MFP levels can be interpreted as differences in the level of disembodied technology. In table 24.7, we provide levels for the year 2005 for a set of 20 countries for which capital data are available. Estimates are given for six major sectors and higher aggregates with United States equal to one. It appears that European MFP gaps are smaller than labor productivity gaps because of the higher inputs in the United States compared with those in most European countries. In terms of both capital and skills, inputs in the United States are generally higher than in other countries. In most countries, the MFP gap is smallest in manufacturing and biggest in market services. Within market services, MFP levels are generally high in trade and financial services, but low in transport and business services.

Sensitivity of PPPs and Productivity Levels

A particular issue in level accounts is the double deflation of value added. In theory, the price of value added should be based on the prices of output and the prices of intermediate inputs. As such, the data requirements for a value added–based MFP measure are exactly the same as for

TABLE 24.6 Value Added per Hour Worked: OECD Countries, 2005 (US = 1)

	MARKT	ELECOM	MexElec	OtherG	MSERV	DISTR	FINBU	PERS
AUS	0.69	0.38	0.53	1.41	0.67	0.64	0.69	0.75
AUT	0.61	0.37	0.71	0.80	0.58	0.60	0.47	0.93
BEL	1.00	0.53	1.37	1.16	0.91	0.97	0.84	0.82
CYP	0.48	0.59	0.28	0.60	0.59	0.58	1.13	0.57
CZE	0.36	0.10	0.39	0.42	0.36	0.48	0.26	0.55
DNK	0.80	0.36	0.65	0.87	0.93	1.10	0.78	0.97
ESP	0.57	0.35	0.60	0.57	0.61	0.62	0.70	0.75
EST	0.24	0.04	0.10	0.38	0.30	0.24	0.86	0.52
FIN	0.83	0.92	1.09	0.70	0.69	1.10	0.41	0.59
FRA	0.74	0.69	0.95	0.59	0.76	0.89	0.57	1.01
GER	0.80	0.58	0.93	0.63	0.82	0.88	0.71	1.01
GRE	0.39	0.35	0.37	0.37	0.44	0.37	0.49	0.79
HUN	0.40	0.27	0.37	0.35	0.42	0.28	0.57	1.04
IRL	0.84	0.42	1.74	0.43	0.75	0.65	1.06	0.67
ITA	0.58	0.49	0.81	0.66	0.51	0.46	0.69	0.45
JAP	0.50	0.66	0.69	0.30	0.49	0.47	0.63	0.48
KOR	0.41	0.59	0.73	0.37	0.25	0.21	0.45	0.23
LTU	0.24	0.05	0.17	0.29	0.30	0.34	0.29	0.56
LUX	1.23	2.33	0.99	0.58	1.56	1.42	1.59	0.76
LVA	0.31	0.14	0.12	0.51	0.40	0.39	0.63	0.50
MLT	0.38	0.15	0.25	0.47	0.41	0.43	0.37	0.86
NLD	0.88	0.52	1.04	0.76	0.96	1.54	0.65	0.91
POL	0.38	0.09	0.35	0.26	0.56	0.66	0.61	0.63
PRT	0.34	0.31	0.27	0.24	0.49	0.50	0.90	0.40
SVK	0.31	0.11	0.20	0.43	0.42	0.32	0.50	0.96
SVN	0.07	0.04	0.02	0.05	0.20	0.13	0.27	0.40
SWE	0.90	2.49	0.92	0.87	0.82	0.80	0.74	0.52
UK	0.67	0.75	0.80	0.67	0.66	0.58	0.64	0.57
USA	1.00	1.00	1.00	1.00	1.00	1.00	1.00	1.00

Source: GGDC Productivity Level database (Inklaar and Timmer 2009).
Note: See note to annex table for country codes. MARKT = market economy; ELECOM = electrical machinery, post, and communication services; MexElec = total manufacturing, excluding electrical; OtherG = other production; MSERV = market services, excluding post and telecommunications; DISTR = distribution; FINBU = finance and business, except real estate; PERS = personal services.

a gross output–based MFP measure. However, in practice, for the reasons discussed shortly, the prices of intermediate inputs are often ignored, and the PPP for gross output is used instead. This approach is called single deflation, as opposed to double deflation in which the prices of intermediate inputs are taken into account as in equation (24.8). Single deflation has some significant problems: as long as relative intermediate input prices do not move in tandem with relative output prices across countries, measures of single-deflated value added will be biased. However, in practice

TABLE 24.7 Multifactor Productivity: Selected Countries, 2005 (US = 1)

	MARKT	ELECOM	MexElec	OtherG	MSERV	DISTR	FINBU	PERS
AUS	0.76	0.50	0.59	1.38	0.76	0.68	0.88	0.63
AUT	0.69	0.48	0.77	0.98	0.64	0.62	0.57	0.82
BEL	0.89	0.51	1.18	1.06	0.82	0.74	0.91	0.84
CZE	0.46	0.19	0.56	0.59	0.43	0.47	0.37	0.55
DNK	0.85	0.52	0.72	0.86	1.02	1.12	0.99	0.78
ESP	0.73	0.42	0.67	0.91	0.78	0.61	0.95	0.88
FIN	0.92	1.27	1.11	0.87	0.79	1.07	0.64	0.49
FRA	0.82	0.94	1.00	0.76	0.81	0.91	0.61	0.95
GER	0.86	0.81	0.99	0.75	0.85	0.98	0.68	0.86
HUN	0.49	0.48	0.55	0.55	0.46	0.32	0.81	0.43
IRL	0.97	0.56	1.61	0.58	0.90	0.70	1.55	0.53
ITA	0.66	0.62	0.84	0.79	0.60	0.45	0.76	0.61
JAP	0.47	0.66	0.60	0.33	0.46	0.43	0.52	0.34
LUX	1.13	1.37	0.95	0.71	1.35	1.18	1.81	0.70
NLD	0.94	0.55	1.02	0.83	1.04	1.55	0.79	0.79
PRT	0.63	0.44	0.57	0.57	0.78	0.70	1.07	0.64
SVN	0.08	0.06	0.03	0.05	0.23	0.13	0.35	0.34
SWE	0.86	2.65	0.87	0.95	0.77	0.70	0.73	0.45
UK	0.79	0.92	0.93	0.79	0.77	0.67	0.82	0.55
USA	1.00	1.00	1.00	1.00	1.00	1.00	1.00	1.00

Source: GGDC Productivity Level database (Inklaar and Timmer 2009).
Note: See note to annex table for country codes. MARKT = market economy; ELECOM = electrical machinery, post, and communication services; MexElec = total manufacturing, excluding electrical; OtherG = other production; MSERV = market services, excluding post and telecommunications; DISTR = distribution; FINBU = finance and business, except real estate; PERS = personal services. MFP is value added–based (double-deflated).

double deflation also has a number of well-known problems. For one thing, double deflation puts larger requirements on the data because intermediate input PPPs are needed in addition to the PPPs for gross output. However, the intermediate input PPPs are not directly available and must be constructed on the basis of output prices (see the third section of this chapter). Hill (1971) suggests that the use of single deflation may be less misleading than the use of double deflation when material input prices are measured with error. This problem is aggravated by the fact that double-deflated value added is defined as the output volume minus the intermediate input volume. A small percentage measurement error in the volume of gross output appears as a much larger percentage error in the volume of double-deflated value added than is the case for the volume of single-deflated value added (see Hill 1971, 19). This may be one of the reasons the International Comparison Program opted in the 1950s and 1960s for the expenditure approach to GDP rather than the industry of origin approach.

Inklaar and Timmer (2008) have shown that the sensitivity of productivity level comparisons to the choice of single or double deflation techniques increases with the level of industry detail. At the market economy level, differences are large only for countries with exchange rates that are much higher than the GDP PPP in 1997 (e.g., Eastern European countries, but also Denmark). Also at the major sector levels, differences are generally small and can go either way. Differences are smallest for market services, which is to be expected because of the low share of intermediates in output. As such, measurement errors in intermediate input prices have only a minor impact. Differences can be larger for the goods-producing sectors because the intermediate input share is much larger; typically these shares are 60 percent, but only 30 percent for services.

As discussed earlier, our preferred choice of PPPs is based on a mix of the industry of origin UVRs and expenditure PPPs provided by Timmer, Ypma, and van Ark (2007). As an alternative, the GGDC Productivity Level database provides a set of results based on expenditure prices only. This illustrates the empirical differences between our mixed approach and the pure expenditure approach as followed, for example, by Sørenson and Schjerning (2008) and van Biesebroeck (2009). The alternative set is based only on expenditure PPPs, except for agriculture and mining for which no expenditure PPPs exist, as discussed earlier. For these industries, UVR estimates are used. Similarly, for distributive trade no expenditure PPP is available. The overall GDP expenditure PPP is used instead. Figure 24.1 shows the sensitivity of the comparisons to the choice of PPP set. It gives the log ratio of value added using a mix of PPPs (our preferred choice) and using PPPs from the expenditure side only.

Figure 24.1 reveals that differences can go either way because mixed PPPs are sometimes higher or lower than expenditure PPPs. For goods production, differences are relatively minor and often within 5 percent bounds. The differences for market services can be much larger, however. For example, real value added in Italy, the Republic of Korea, and Japan is more than 15 percent higher than that in the United States when using expenditure PPPs only. A more detailed analysis at the industry level reveals that this difference stems from differences for the trade and transportation sectors. The annex to this chapter provides detailed results by sector. For the other market

FIGURE 24.1 Difference in Value Added Based on Alternative PPP Sets: Selected Countries, 1997

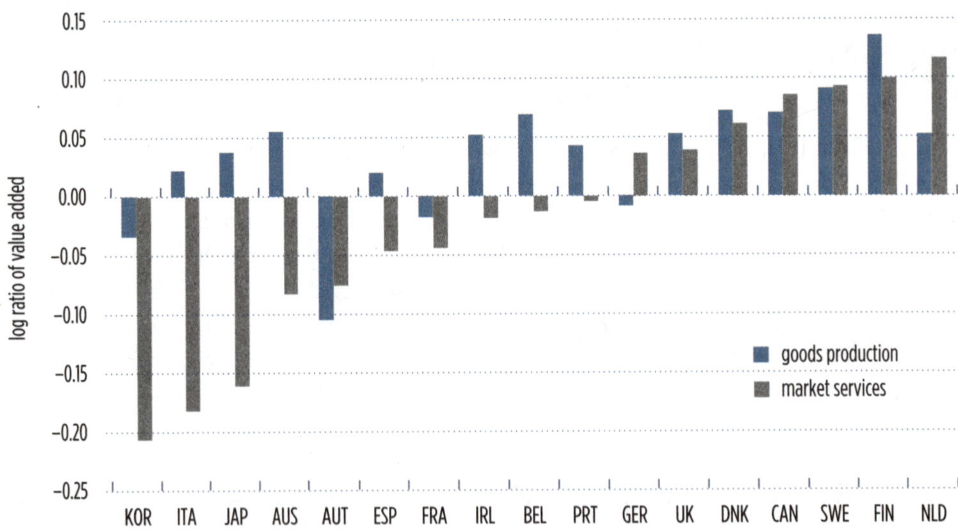

Source: Annex table.
Note: See note to annex table for country codes. Graph shows the log ratio of value added using mix of PPPs (our preferred choice) and using PPPs from the expenditure side only. Value added is single-deflated.

service industries, only expenditure PPPs are available, and hence PPPs in the two sets are the same. Expenditure PPPs for these services are extremely low in various Asian and Eastern European countries. Arguably, these expenditure PPPs refer to highly subsidized prices for public transportation that have little relevance to the transport prices facing firms. It seems nearly impossible to correct for the huge amounts of direct and indirect subsidies from published national account statistics. By contrast, estimates of distribution PPPs based on expenditure prices appear to be too high for Nordic countries. The annex further shows that the lower the level of aggregation, the bigger differences can become. For some individual industry by country cells, the two estimates diverge markedly.

Conclusion

In this chapter, we have outlined a method for productivity level comparisons at the industry level and presented some results for a set of 30 OECD countries from the GGDC Productivity Level database. Productivity level comparisons by sector require not only PPPs for output, but also for intermediate input, capital, and labor inputs. This type of data is not only of interest to academics and international organizations, but also to the business community in, for example, deriving unit labor costs (O'Connor 2008). We discussed the importance of PPPs collected by the ICP for these types of studies. Comparisons of output prices from the production side are scarce and need to be complemented by expenditure PPPs, in particular for durable manufacturing goods, construction, and various services sectors (hotels, real estate, business, and personal services). In addition, expenditure PPPs for investment goods are crucial for the construction of capital input PPPs.

We also have outlined the types of adjustments needed to transform expenditure PPPs based on the purchaser's price concept to industry output PPPs based on the basic price concept. Using the supply-use table framework, we were able to indicate under what conditions expenditure PPPs adjusted for net taxes and margins provide a reasonable proxy for output PPPs. In general, the higher the degree of intermediate use and international trade of a product, the lower is the usefulness of an expenditure PPP. The confrontation of expenditure and output PPPs in the SUT framework is also useful for providing cross-checks on the plausibility of various sets of PPPs. For example, we found that expenditure PPPs for public administration, education, and health deviated strongly from the relative wage data on the production side. This finding raises new questions about the validity of the PPPs, and further scrutiny is warranted. It also illustrates the important synergies between international comparisons from the expenditure and the production sides.

Because of the limited availability of output PPPs, expenditure PPPs are crucial for productivity level comparisons within the OECD as analyzed in this chapter. Given the greater scarcity of production PPPs outside the OECD, the need for expenditure PPPs is even more so for comparisons of non-OECD member countries. New work is now being undertaken to provide new productivity level comparisons for a larger set of countries, including Brazil, China, India, Indonesia, Mexico, and the Russian Federation. Global comparisons of productivity will rely heavily on the results of the latest ICP benchmark (World Bank 2008).

ANNEX

Sensitivity to Choice of PPPs, 1997

	TOT	MARKT	ELECOM	GOODS	MexElec	OtherG	MSERV	DISTR	G	60t63	FINBU	J	71t74	PERS	NONMAR
AUS	**0.99**	**0.98**	**0.80**	**1.06**	1.05	1.06	**0.92**	0.87	*0.82*	*0.98*	1.00	*1.00*	*1.00*	1.00	**1.00**
AUT	**0.93**	**0.91**	**0.92**	**0.90**	0.86	0.99	**0.93**	0.83	*0.87*	*0.75*	1.00	*1.00*	*1.00*	1.00	**1.00**
BEL	**1.02**	**1.03**	**1.20**	**1.07**	1.09	1.03	**0.99**	0.92	*1.11*	*0.60*	1.00	*1.00*	*1.00*	1.00	**1.00**
CAN	**1.06**	**1.08**	**1.24**	**1.07**	1.04	1.11	**1.09**	1.14	*0.97*	*1.63*	1.00	*1.00*	*1.00*	1.00	**1.00**
CYP	**0.94**	**0.93**	**0.51**	**0.97**	0.98	0.96	**0.90**	0.89	*0.92*	*0.81*	1.00	*1.00*	*1.00*	1.00	**1.00**
CZE	**0.91**	**0.89**	**0.86**	**0.97**	0.94	1.02	**0.80**	0.65	*0.82*	*0.40*	1.00	*1.00*	*1.00*	1.00	**1.00**
DNK	**1.04**	**1.06**	**0.88**	**1.08**	1.11	1.04	**1.06**	1.12	*1.28*	*0.82*	1.00	*1.00*	*1.00*	1.00	**1.00**
ESP	**0.99**	**0.99**	**0.91**	**1.02**	1.01	1.04	**0.95**	0.92	*1.03*	*0.70*	1.00	*1.00*	*1.00*	1.00	**0.99**
EST	**0.86**	**0.82**	**0.71**	**0.97**	0.93	1.05	**0.69**	0.51	*0.74*	*0.28*	1.00	*1.00*	*1.00*	1.00	**1.00**
FIN	**1.08**	**1.11**	**1.04**	**1.15**	1.21	1.03	**1.11**	1.18	*1.27*	*0.98*	1.00	*1.00*	*1.00*	1.00	**1.00**
FRA	**0.98**	**0.97**	**0.89**	**0.98**	0.96	1.02	**0.96**	0.94	*1.04*	*0.73*	1.00	*1.00*	*1.00*	1.00	**1.00**
GER	**1.01**	**1.01**	**0.97**	**0.99**	0.98	1.02	**1.04**	1.08	*1.20*	*0.84*	1.00	*1.00*	*1.00*	1.00	**1.00**
GRC	**0.89**	**0.85**	**0.67**	**0.99**	0.98	0.97	**0.73**	0.55	*0.64*	*0.37*	1.00	*1.00*	*1.00*	1.00	**1.00**
HUN	**0.96**	**0.94**	**1.08**	**1.01**	1.02	1.00	**0.89**	0.72	*0.70*	*0.76*	1.00	*1.00*	*1.00*	1.00	**1.00**
IRL	**1.00**	**1.00**	**0.82**	**1.05**	1.11	1.00	**0.98**	0.97	*1.14*	*0.70*	1.00	*1.00*	*1.00*	1.00	**0.99**
ITA	**0.94**	**0.92**	**1.00**	**1.02**	1.01	1.04	**0.83**	0.68	*0.77*	*0.48*	1.00	*1.00*	*1.00*	1.00	**1.00**
JAP	**0.96**	**0.94**	**0.87**	**1.04**	1.04	1.01	**0.85**	0.75	*0.70*	*0.85*	1.00	*1.00*	*1.00*	1.00	**1.00**
KOR	**0.92**	**0.89**	**0.69**	**0.97**	0.92	1.02	**0.81**	0.71	*0.70*	*0.70*	1.00	*1.00*	*1.00*	1.00	**1.00**

LTU	**0.84**	**0.80**	**0.53**	**0.94**	0.91	0.97	**0.66**	0.54	*0.62*	*0.38*	1.00	*1.00*	*1.00*	1.00	**1.00**
LUX	**1.02**	**1.03**	**0.98**	**1.03**	1.05	0.99	**1.02**	1.10	*1.24*	*0.85*	1.00	*1.00*	*1.00*	1.00	**1.00**
LVA	**0.92**	**0.90**	**1.45**	**0.93**	0.88	1.01	**0.87**	0.69	*0.69*	*0.65*	1.00	*1.00*	*1.00*	1.00	**1.00**
MLT	**0.96**	**0.94**	**0.69**	**0.96**	0.99	0.94	**0.92**	0.94	*0.74*	*1.31*	1.00	*1.00*	*1.00*	1.00	**1.00**
NLD	**1.06**	**1.08**	**0.98**	**1.05**	1.03	1.09	**1.12**	1.28	*1.18*	*1.51*	1.00	*1.00*	*1.00*	1.00	**1.00**
POL	**1.01**	**1.01**	**0.82**	**1.06**	1.05	1.05	**0.97**	0.96	*0.95*	*1.00*	1.00	*1.00*	*1.00*	1.00	**1.00**
PRT	**1.01**	**1.01**	**0.82**	**1.04**	1.07	0.99	**1.00**	1.03	*1.04*	*1.00*	1.00	*1.00*	*1.00*	1.00	**1.00**
SVK	**0.85**	**0.81**	**0.90**	**0.89**	0.89	0.93	**0.72**	0.53	*0.67*	*0.32*	1.00	*1.00*	*1.00*	1.00	**1.00**
SVN	**0.97**	**0.90**	**0.77**	**1.00**	0.99	1.04	**0.80**	0.65	*0.73*	*0.50*	1.00	*1.00*	*1.00*	1.00	**1.30**
SWE	**1.06**	**1.08**	**1.45**	**1.10**	1.13	1.04	**1.10**	1.03	*1.00*	*1.02*	1.00	*1.00*	*1.00*	1.00	**1.00**
UK	**1.03**	**1.04**	**1.37**	**1.05**	1.08	1.01	**1.04**	0.97	*0.90*	*1.08*	1.00	*1.00*	*1.00*	1.00	**1.00**
USA	**1.00**	**1.00**	**1.00**	**1.00**	1.00	1.00	**1.00**	1.00	*1.00*	*1.00*	1.00	*1.00*	*1.00*	1.00	**1.00**

Source: Calculations based on the GGDC Productivity Level database.
Note: Column headings indicate industry groupings. Headings at higher levels (boldface) indicate aggregations of industries at lower level. MARKT = market economy; ELECOM = electrical machinery, post, and communication services; MexElec = total manufacturing, excluding electrical; OtherG = other production; MSERV = market services, excluding post and telecommunications; DISTR = distribution; G = trade; 60t63 = transport services; FINBU = finance and business, except real estate; J = finance; 71t74 = business services; PERS = personal services. Table shows log ratio of value added using mix of PPPs (our preferred choice) and using PPPs from expenditure side only. Value added is single-deflated. AUS = Australia; AUT = Austria; BEL = Belgium; CAN = Canada; CYP = Cyprus; CZE = Czech Republic; DNK = Denmark; ESP = Spain; EST = Estonia; FIN = Finland; FRA = France; GER = Germany; GRC = Greece; HUN = Hungary; IRL = Ireland; ITA = Italy; JAP = Japan; KOR = Korea, Rep.; LTU = Lithuania; LUX = Luxembourg; LVA = Latvia; MLT = Malta; NLD = Netherlands; POL = Poland; PRT = Portugal; SVK = Slovak Republic; SVN = Slovenia; SWE = Sweden; UK = United Kingdom; USA = United States.

NOTES

1. The authors would like to thank Bart van Ark and D. S. Prasada Rao for useful comments and suggestions on an earlier draft of this chapter. The research for this chapter was part of the EU KLEMS project on Growth and Productivity in the European Union. This project was supported by the Research Directorate General of the European Commission, as part of the 6th Framework Programme, Priority 8, "Policy Support and Anticipating Scientific and Technological Needs."
2. Using the United States as our base country does not imply the use of a star system of comparisons. As discussed later, we will use base-invariant productivity measures.
3. Note that because of our approach to capital measurement, capital compensation in this formula is based on ex ante measures of rates of return and will differ from the ex post measure of capital compensation used as the weight in equation (24.2).
4. We aggregate over prices rather than over quantities because variation in prices across countries is much less than variation in quantities (also see Allen and Diewert 1981).
5. See van Ark and Timmer (2009) for a recent survey.
6. Exports are valued at free on board (f.o.b.) prices and the imports at cost, insurance, and freight (c.i.f.) prices. The export f.o.b. price is essentially a purchaser's price, including net taxes and trade and transport margins up to the border of the exporting country. The import c.i.f. price is essentially a basic price, excluding net taxes levied after crossing the border and trade and transport margins within the country.
7. Taxes include any taxes on products at the sales point such as a sales or a value added tax.
8. See the Eurostat manual on supply-use tables for more information (Eurostat 2008).
9. We use the terms *final expenditure price* and *final domestic demand* interchangeably.
10. In addition, subsidies on certain transport service categories are very difficult to peel off from the final expenditure price (e.g., bus, subway, and rail transport prices).
11. NACE is the acronym used for the General Industrial Classification of Economic Activities within the European Communities.
12. This PPP can be based on the expenditure PPP for rents.
13. This formula is an approximation because we exclude second-order effects. Country subscripts are dropped to avoid cluttering.
14. See Oulton (2007) for this hybrid approach to capital measurement.
15. See the caveats in the previous section.
16. At the lowest level of aggregation, this procedure delivers the same numbers as the alternative of extrapolating the PPPs based on national deflators. At higher levels of aggregation, differences become large, with the size of the difference related to the changing output shares.

REFERENCES

Allen, R. C., and W. E. Diewert. 1981. "Direct versus Implicit Superlative Index Number Formulae." *Review of Economics and Statistics* 63: 430–35.

Caves, D. W., L. R. Christensen, and W. E. Diewert. 1982. "Multilateral Comparisons of Output, Input and Productivity Using Superlative Index Numbers." *Economic Journal* 92: 73–86.

Commission of the European Communities, International Monetary Fund, Organisation for Economic Co-operation and Development, United Nations, and World Bank. 1993. *System of National Accounts 1993.* http://unstats.un.org/unsd/nationalaccount/sna.asp.

Eurostat. 2008. *Eurostat Manual of Supply, Use and Input-Output Tables.* Brussels: European Communities.

Fraumeni, B. M. 1997. "The Measurement of Depreciation in the U.S. National Income and Product Accounts." *Survey of Current Business* (July): 7–23.

Hill, T. P. 1971. *The Measurement of Real Product: A Theoretical and Empirical Analysis of the Growth Rates for Different Industries and Countries.* Paris: Organisation for Economic Co-operation and Development.

Hooper, P. 1996. "Comparing Manufacturing Output Levels among the Major Industrial Countries." In *Productivity, International Comparison and Measurement Issues,* OECD Proceedings. Paris: Organisation for Economic Co-operation and Development.

Inklaar, R., and M. P. Timmer. 2008. "GGDC Productivity Level Database: International Comparisons of Output, Inputs and Productivity at the Industry Level." GGDC Research Memorandum GD-104, Groningen Growth and Development Centre, University of Groningen.

———. 2009. "Productivity Convergence across Industries and Countries: The Importance of Theory-Based Measurement." *Macroeconomic Dynamics* 13 (Supplement 2): 218–40.

Jorgenson, D. W., and Z. Griliches. 1967. "The Explanation of Productivity Change." *Review of Economic Studies* 34 (3): 249–83.

Jorgenson, D. W., and M. Nishimizu. 1978. "U.S. and Japanese Economic Growth, 1952–1974: An International Comparison." *Economic Journal* 88: 707–26.

Jorgenson, D. W., M. Kuroda, and M. Nishimizu. 1987. "Japan-U.S. Industry-Level Productivity Comparisons, 1960–1979." *Journal of the Japanese and International Economies* 1: 1–30.

Kravis, I. B. 1976. "A Survey of International Comparisons of Productivity." *Economic Journal* 86 (March): 1–44.

Kravis, I. B., A. Heston, and R. Summers. 1982. *World Product and Income.* Baltimore: Johns Hopkins University Press.

Lee, F., and J. Tang. 2000. "Productivity Levels and International Competitiveness between Canadian and U.S. Industries." *American Economic Review* 90 (2): 176–79.

Maddison, A., and B. van Ark. 2002. "The International Comparison of Real Product and Productivity." In *The Asian Economies in the Twentieth Century,* ed. A. Maddison, D. S. Prasada Rao, and W. F. Shepherd, 5–26. Cheltenham, U.K.: Edward Elgar.

Mason, G., B. O'Leary, and M. Vecchi. 2009. "Cross-country Analysis of Productivity and Skills at Sector Level." Report to Sector Skills Development Agency, National Institute of Economic and Social Research, London.

O'Connor, J. 2008. "Business Uses of PPPs: Challenges and Opportunities." *ICP Bulletin* (August).

OECD (Organisation for Economic Co-operation and Development). 2002. *Purchasing Power Parities and Real Expenditures, 1999 Benchmark Year.* Paris: OECD.

O'Mahony, M. 1999. *Britain's Productivity Performance 1950–1996—An International Perspective.* London: National Institute of Economic and Social Research.

O'Mahony, M., and M. P. Timmer. 2009. "Output, Input and Productivity Measures at the Industry Level: The EU KLEMS Database." *Economic Journal* 119 (538): F374–F403.

Oulton, Nicholas. 2007. "Ex Post versus Ex Ante Measures of the User Cost of Capital." *Review of Income and Wealth* 53 (2): 295–317.

Paige, D., and G. Bombach. 1959. *A Comparison of National Output and Productivity.* Paris: Organisation for European Economic Co-operation.

Pilat, D. 1996. "Labour Productivity Levels in OECD Countries: Estimates for Manufacturing and Selected Service Sectors." Economics Department Working Paper No. 169, Organisation for European Economic Co-operation, Paris.

Prasada Rao, D. S. 1993. *Inter-Country Comparisons of Agricultural Output and Productivity.* Rome: Food and Agriculture Organization.

Sørensen, A. 2001. "Comparing Apples to Oranges: Productivity Convergence and Measurement across Industries and Countries: Comment." *American Economic Review* 91 (4): 1160–67.

Sørensen, A., and B. Schjerning. 2008. "Productivity Measurement in Manufacturing and the Expenditure Approach." *Review of International Economics* 16 (2): 327–40.

Summers, R., and A. Heston. 1991. "The Penn World Table (Mark 5): An Expanded Set of International Comparisons, 1950–1988." *Quarterly Journal of Economics* 106: 327–68.

Timmer, M. P., M. O'Mahony, B. van Ark, and R. Inklaar. 2010. *Economic Growth in Europe.* Cambridge, U.K.: Cambridge University Press.

Timmer, M. P., and G. Ypma. 2006. "Productivity Levels in Distributive Trades: A New ICOP Dataset for OECD Countries." Working Paper GD-83, Groningen Growth and Development Centre, University of Groningen.

Timmer, M. P., G. Ypma, and B. van Ark. 2007. "PPPs for Industry Output: A New Dataset for International Comparisons." Working Paper GD-82, Groningen Growth and Development Centre, University of Groningen.

van Ark, B., and A. Maddison. 1994. "The International Comparison of Real Product and Productivity." Research Memorandum No. 567 (GD-6), Groningen Growth and Development Centre, University of Groningen.

van Ark, B., and M. P. Timmer. 2009. "Purchasing Power Parity Adjustments for Productivity Level Comparisons." In *Purchasing Power Parities: Methods and Applications,* ed. D. S. Prasada Rao, chap. 14. Cheltenham, U.K.: Edward Elgar.

van Biesebroeck, J. 2009. "Cross-Country Conversion Factors for Sectoral Productivity Comparisons." *Journal of Productivity Analysis* 32 (2): 63–79.

World Bank. 2008. *Global Purchasing Power Parities and Real Expenditures: 2005 International Comparison Program.* http://siteresources.worldbank.org/ICPINT/Resources/icp-final.pdf.

Abbreviations

BH	basic heading
BOCC	basket of construction components
BOQ	bills of quantities approach
CEM	consumption equivalent method
CFC	consumption of fixed capital
CIS	Commonwealth of Independent States
CISSTAT	Interstate Statistical Committee of the Commonwealth of Independent States
CPD	Country Product Dummy
CPDW	Country Product Dummy-Weighted
CPI	consumer price index
CPRD	Country Product Representative Dummy
DECDG	Development Data Group (World Bank)
DHS	Demographic and Health Surveys
ECLAC	Economic Commission for Latin America and the Caribbean
EKS	Éltetö-Köves-Szulc
ESCWA	Economic and Social Commission for Western Asia
FISIM	financial intermediation services indirectly measured
GDP	gross domestic product
GEKS	Gini-Éltetö-Köves-Szulc
GFCF	gross fixed capital formation
GK	Geary-Khamis
HFCE	household final consumption expenditure
ICP	International Comparison Program
IDB	Iklé-Dikhanov-Balk

ISCED	International Standard Classification of Education
ISCO	International Standard Classification of Occupations
NCA	national coordinating agency
NPISH	nonprofit institutions serving households
OECD	Organisation for Economic Co-operation and Development
PFM	price factor method
PLI	price level index
PPP	purchasing power parity
PWT	Penn World Table
RCA	regional coordinating agency
REER	real effective exchange rate
RMSE	root mean square error
SAR	special administrative region
SNA	*System of National Accounts*
SPD	structured product description
SUT	supply-use table
TAG	Technical Advisory Group (ICP)
UNSC	United Nations Statistical Commission

Country/Economy: The use of *country* in this book is inclusive of *economies*, such as Hong Kong SAR, China; Macao SAR, China; and Taiwan, China.

Glossary

actual final individual consumption. A measure of the individual goods and services that households actually consume. It includes what households purchase, plus the value of services such as education and health that households receive from the government and nonprofit institutions serving households (NPISH).

additivity. A property of aggregation methods in which the values of the national accounts aggregates of countries participating in a comparison are equal to the sum of the values of their components when both aggregates and components are valued at current national prices. Additivity requires that this identity be preserved when the aggregates and their components are valued at international prices. An aggregation method is additive if, for each country being compared, it provides real values for basic headings that sum to the real values of the aggregates of which they are components. An additive aggregation method provides volumes that satisfy the average test for volumes, but are subject to the Gerschenkron effect.

aggregate. The sum of a set of transactions relating to a specified flow of goods and services in a given period, such as the total purchases made by resident households on consumer goods and services, the total expenditure by government on collective services, or the total value of gross fixed capital formation. The term *aggregate* is also used to refer to the value of the specified set of transactions.

aggregation. The procedure of computing PPPs above the basic heading level. The term also refers to the process of weighting, summing, and averaging basic heading PPPs to obtain PPPs for each level of aggregation up to and including GDP.

base country invariance. The resulting property when the relative PPPs, price level indexes, and volume indexes of countries are not affected by the choice of currency or the choice of country as the reference or base country.

basic heading. The lowest level of aggregation of items in the GDP breakdown for which PPPs are calculated. In theory, a basic heading is a group of similar well-defined goods or services. In practice, it is the lowest level of final expenditure for which explicit expenditure weights can be estimated. Thus an actual basic heading can cover a broader range of products than is theoretically desirable. Basic headings are the building blocks of a comparison. It is at the level of the basic heading that expenditures are defined, products selected, prices collected, prices edited, and PPPs first calculated and averaged.

basket. The common list of well-defined goods and services from which countries participating in a comparison make a selection of products to price for the purpose of compiling PPPs. Also referred to as product list or item list.

basket of construction components (BOCC) approach. An approach to estimating construction PPPs used in the 2005 ICP. It involves collecting prices for a range of major construction components and basic inputs common across countries. The term *construction components* is used to describe specific physical outputs produced as intermediate steps in construction projects. A key element of this process is that the overall price estimated for each component is related to an installed component, including the costs of materials, labor, and equipment—that is, the price is closely related to an output price rather than to an input price.

bias. A systematic error in a PPP or volume index. Bias can arise for a number of reasons, including failure to respect representativity, comparability, or consistency; the price collection and measurement procedures followed; or the calculation and aggregation formula employed.

Big Mac index. An index developed and used by the *Economist* to illustrate the use of PPPs. It is based on the price of a McDonald's Big Mac hamburger compared across countries.

bilateral comparison. See **binary comparison**.

bilateral PPPs. PPPs based on a binary comparison between two countries.

bills of quantities (BOQ) method. An approach used in the Eurostat-OECD comparison to estimate construction PPPs. Product specifications detail the costs of labor, materials, and equipment required to build a standard construction project. They include profit or loss, architect's or engineer's fees, and overhead expenses. The BOQ approach involves pricing detailed bills of quantities for a number of construction projects that are designed to be representative of such projects in the countries being compared.

binary comparison. A price or volume comparison between two countries that draws on data only for those two countries. It is also known as a bilateral comparison—that is, a PPP between two countries calculated using only the prices and weights for those two countries.

bridge country. A country that provides the link or bridge between two separate comparisons or regions involving different groups of countries. The bridge country participates in both comparisons and, by doing so, enables comparison of the countries in one comparison with the countries in the other comparison and vice versa.

characteristicity. The property that requires transitive multilateral comparisons between members of a group of countries to deviate as little as possible from their binary PPP. A transitive multilateral comparison between a pair of countries is influenced by the price and quantity data of all other participating countries. Therefore, a requirement is that these influences be kept to a minimum.

characteristics. The physical and economic attributes of a product that serve to identify it and enable it to be located under some heading of a product classification. The term also refers to the technical parameters and price-determining properties of a product listed in a product specification.

Classification of the Functions of Government (COFOG). A classification used mainly to determine which final consumption expenditures of general government benefit households individually and which benefit households collectively. For example, education is individual; police protection is collective.

Classification of Individual Consumption According to Purpose (COICOP). A classification of the individual consumption expenditures of three institutional sectors—households, nonprofit institutions serving households (NPISH), and general government—by the ends they wish to achieve through these expenditures. Individual consumption expenditures are made for the benefit of individual households. All final consumption expenditures by households and NPISH are defined as individual; only the final consumption expenditures by general government on individual services are treated as individual.

collective consumption expenditure by government. Expenditures incurred by general and local governments for collective consumption services such as defense, justice, general administration, and protection of the environment.

comparability. A characteristic achieved by requiring countries participating in a comparison to price products that are identical or, if not identical, equivalent. Pricing comparable products ensures that differences in prices between countries for a product reflect actual price differences and are not influenced by differences in quality. Two or more products are said to be comparable if either their physical and economic characteristics are identical, or they are sufficiently similar that consumers are generally indifferent about the choice of product.

comparison-resistant. A term used to describe nonmarket services that are difficult to compare across countries. Examples are equivalent rents for owner-occupied housing, certain government services, and many construction activities.

compensation of employees. All payments in cash and in kind made by employers to employees in return for work carried out by the employees during the accounting period. These payments comprise gross wages and salaries in cash and in kind, employers' actual social contributions, and imputed social contributions. Compensation of employees is the largest component of the costs of producing government services, and it is the only cost component for which prices were collected in the 2005 ICP round. Compensation of employees was reported for a selection of occupations in government, public education, and public health services.

consistency. A characteristic achieved by requiring that the prices collected by countries are consistent with the prices underlying their estimates of final expenditure on GDP. In most cases, this means that the prices collected should be national annual average purchasers' prices. At the basis of a comparison is the identity—expenditure = price × volume—and volumes are obtained by dividing expenditures by prices.

consumer price index (CPI). An index of price changes within a country across time.

consumption of fixed capital. The reduction in the value of the fixed assets used in production during the accounting period resulting from physical deterioration, normal obsolescence, or normal accidental damage.

country. The use of country in this book is inclusive of World Bank member countries as well as economies, such as Hong Kong SAR, China; Macao SAR, China; and Taiwan, China.

Country Product Dummy (CPD) method. The multilateral method used by the ICP to obtain transitive and base country–invariant PPPs at the basic heading level through regression analysis. It treats the calculation of PPPs as a matter of statistical inference—an estimation problem rather than an index number problem. The underlying hypothesis is that, apart from random disturbance, the PPPs for individual products within a basic heading are all constant between any given pair of countries. In other words, it is assumed that the pattern of relative prices of the different products within a given basic heading is the same in all countries. It is also assumed that each country has its own overall price level for the basic heading, and that level fixes the levels of absolute prices of the products in the basic heading for the country.

Country Product Dummy-Weighted (CPDW) method. A modified CPD model in which specific weights are used for "important" or representative products. The results are transitive and base-invariant.

Country Product Representative Dummy (CPRD) method. A modified CPD model in which implied weights are used for representative products. The results are transitive and base-invariant.

country variation coefficient. A measure of dispersion among a country's PPP ratios for a basic heading. In other words, it measures the variation in a country's price levels among the products it priced for the basic heading and the reliability of its PPP for the basic heading.

data validation. The statistical process used to review prices and PPPs and expenditure weights at the different levels of aggregation.

deflation. The division of the current value of some aggregate by a price index—described as a deflator—to value its quantities at the prices of the price reference period.

Dikhanov table. A tool for price diagnostics and data validation that is specific to the Country Product Dummy (CPD) methods of calculating PPPs. The Dikhanov table is also used to edit prices within aggregates of several basic headings. It contains much of the same information as a Quaranta table, but it is better-suited to editing prices across the basic headings and products comprising an aggregate.

direct rent approach. An approach to estimating PPPs for owner-occupied housing based on the equivalent rental rates for rented dwellings. This method assumes that the rental rates for rented dwellings by age, size, and amenities can be applied to similar types of owner-occupied housing. The *System of National Accounts* calls for statistical agencies to include in their estimates of expenditures the explicit dwelling services of renters and the implicit dwelling services of owners, including both the site rent and the rent of the structure.

direct volume method. A method for estimating PPPs for owner-occupied housing (also known as the **quantity method**). A volume comparison between two or more countries consists of comparing the quantities of housing. The direct volume approach requires census-type information on number, location, and type of structure. The volume of dwelling services is obtained in two stages. First, a simple measure of the quantity of dwelling services is calculated using either the floor space or the number of rooms in all dwellings. Quality indicators referring to amenities such as electricity and running water are then used to convert these quantity measures into volume measures.

economy. Economies include administrative areas such as Hong Kong SAR, China; Macao SAR, China; and Taiwan, China.

European Comparison Program. The ICP regional program for Europe, carried out under the auspices of the United Nations Economic Commission for Europe. It is organized by Eurostat, the Organisation for Economic Co-operation and Development (OECD), the Interstate Statistical Committee of the Commonwealth of Independent States (CISSTAT), and the Federal State Statistics Service of the Russian Federation (Rosstat).

Eurostat-OECD PPP Programme. A program that provides PPPs on a three-year cycle for the European Union and OECD countries under the coordination of Eurostat (the statistical office of the EU) and OECD. The program is closely coordinated with the ICP, which includes the rest of the world, to ensure results are comparable. While separate, the Eurostat-OECD comparison is considered to be a sixth ICP region for discussion purposes in this volume.

exchange rate reference PPP. The type of PPP produced when exchange rates are used as the PPPs for these basic headings: exports of goods and services, imports of goods and services, final consumption expenditure of resident households in the rest of the world, and final consumption expenditure of nonresident households in the economic territory.

Executive Board, ICP. The body that provides strategic leadership and decisions about ICP's priorities, standards, overall work program, and budget (see annex A of chapter 2 for the list of members for the 2005 ICP round). Representation on the Executive Board is agency-based (either an international organization or a national statistics office), with the proviso that representatives be very senior staff.

exhaustiveness. A term that describes the process to ensure the completeness of GDP expenditures by including, for example, expenditures for illicit purchases, home or own production, and animal-drawn vehicles.

expenditure measure of GDP. The expenditure measure of GDP (also known as expenditures in national accounts) derived as the sum of expenditures on final consumption by households and by government added to gross capital formation and exports (minus imports). This measure is based on the principle that all of the final products are either purchased by someone or put into inventories. The breakdown of GDP into aggregates and basic headings for the ICP is based on the expenditure method because it is easier to obtain the underlying prices for these components. The values of final expenditures recorded in the national accounts are closely associated with the data and prices used for the national consumer and producer price indexes for household consumption and equipment purchases by businesses, respectively.

expenditure weight. The share of expenditure components in current-price GDP.

extrapolation. The method used to estimate PPPs for the years between benchmark surveys.

financial intermediation services indirectly measured (FISIM). An indirect measure of the value of the financial intermediation services that financial institutions provide clients but for which they do not charge explicitly. FISIM is paid by everyone (households, unincorporated enterprises, corporations, and government) who use the services of banks and other types of financial institutions.

Fisher-type PPP. The PPP for a basic heading or an aggregate between two countries that is defined as the geometric mean of the Laspeyres-type PPP and the Paasche-type PPP for the basic heading or the aggregate. The formulation depends on whether they are being used to calculate basic heading PPPs or to aggregate basic heading PPPs.

fixity. The convention whereby the price and volume relativities between a group of countries that were established in a comparison covering just that group of countries remain unchanged, or fixed, when the countries of the group are included in comparisons with a wider group of countries. For example, the price and volume relativities of the ICP regions and Eurostat-OECD comparison remain unchanged in the global comparison. If fixity were not imposed, the PPP between any two countries would differ for the regional and global comparisons.

Geary-Khamis (GK) method. An average-price method to compute PPPs and real final expenditures above the basic heading level that are additive across the aggregates. It entails valuing a matrix of quantities using a vector of international prices. The vector is obtained by averaging national prices across participating countries after they have been converted to a common currency with PPPs and weighted by quantities. The PPPs are obtained by averaging within participating countries the ratios of national and international prices weighted by expenditure. The international prices and the PPPs are defined by a system of interrelated linear equations that must be solved simultaneously. The GK method produces PPPs that are transitive and real final expenditures that are additive. Among its disadvantages, a change in the composition of the group can change significantly the international prices, as well as the relationships between countries, and the real final expenditures are subject to the Gerschenkron effect, which can be large. The result is that the price structures of poor countries are raised because the larger richer countries receive a greater weight. GK results are considered better-suited to the analysis of price and volume structures across countries.

general government. The institutional sector that consists of central, regional, state, and local government units, together with the social security funds imposed and controlled by those units. It includes nonprofit institutions engaged in nonmarket production that are controlled and mainly financed by government units or social security funds. Also referred to as government.

Gerschenkron effect. An effect applicable only to aggregation methods that use either a reference price structure (i.e., each country's quantities are valued by a uniform set of prices) or a reference volume structure (i.e., each country's prices are used to value a uniform set of quantities) to compare countries. For methods employing a reference price structure, a country's share of total GDP (i.e., the total for the group of countries being compared) will rise as the reference price structure becomes less characteristic of its own price structure. For methods employing a reference volume structure, a country's share of total GDP will fall as the reference volume structure becomes less characteristic of its own volume structure. The Gerschenkron effect arises because of the negative correlation between prices and volumes. Per capita expenditures in poor countries become larger because the higher prices from the larger countries receive more weight. The Geary-Khamis and Iklé-Dikhanov-Balk methods are subject to this effect.

Gini-Éltetö-Köves-Szulc (GEKS) method. Formerly known as the Èltetö-Köves-Szulc (EKS) method, a procedure whereby any set of intransitive binary index numbers are made transitive. The GEKS method is based on averaging the direct PPPs between any two countries with the PPPs that can be obtained indirectly. The resulting GEKS PPPs provide real final expenditures that are not additive but, more important, are not subject to the Gerschenkron effect. All countries are treated equally at each stage of aggregation regardless of the size of their GDP. The GEKS* method is the same as the GEKS method but with the addition of implied weights for importance or representativity.

global core list. The set of 601 items added to the regional lists of goods and services to be priced for the main price survey on household consumption. This common list will provide the basis to link the within-region PPPs across regions for the 2011 ICP.

Global Office, ICP. The office established in 2002 in the World Bank to carry out the day-to-day work required to implement the ICP worldwide. The global manager is responsible for its operations, supported by a team of professional statisticians and administrative staff. The Global Office reports regularly to the Executive Board on work programs and budgets. It is subject to the World Bank's administrative and fiduciary rules and regulations, including all requirements related to the confidentiality of data. On day-to-day activities, the Global Office reports to the director of the World Bank's Development Data Group.

government final consumption expenditure. Expenditure, including imputed expenditure, incurred by general government on both individual consumption goods and services and collective consumption services.

gross domestic product (GDP). A measure that can be estimated using three approaches that, in theory, yield the same result. The expenditure approach used for the ICP is the summation of all the final expenditures incurred by the country's resident institutional sectors during the accounting period. The main aggregates of GDP are individual consumption expenditure by households, individual consumption expenditure by government, collective consumption expenditure by government, and gross fixed capital formation.

gross fixed capital formation. An aggregate that includes the basic headings for construction, machinery and equipment, and other products such as software.

gross operating surplus. A term that refers to net operating surplus plus consumption of fixed capital. In most countries, the net operating surplus is insignificant or zero, and so this item consists only of consumption of fixed capital. Consumption of fixed capital is the decline in value through wear and tear and obsolescence of government-owned buildings, roads, bridges, and other structures and of machinery and equipment such as computers, motor vehicles, and diagnostic equipment used in government hospitals. Reference PPPs are used for this basic heading.

health. The aggregate that includes expenditures by households on medical products, appliances and equipment, outpatient services, and hospital services. It also includes expenditures by government on health benefits and reimbursements and on production of health services.

household. A small group of persons who share the same living accommodation, who pool some or all of their income and wealth, and who consume certain types of goods and services collectively, mainly food and housing. A household can consist of only one person.

household final consumption expenditure. The expenditure, including imputed expenditure, incurred by resident households on individual consumption goods and services, including those sold at prices that are not economically significant.

Iklé-Dikhanov-Balk (IDB) method. A method of computing weighted averages of PPPs that produces additive results. However, the results are not consistent with economic comparisons of utility across countries. In addition, large countries have a greater impact on the final results. If large countries have higher prices, then the impact is to raise the price levels of the poorer, smaller countries. The IDB method has a smaller large-country effect (Gerschenkron effect) than the GK method, which is also additive.

importance. A characteristic applied to products. An important product is one that has a large expenditure share within the basic heading to which it belongs. An important product may have a very small expenditure share within household consumption as a whole but still be important within its basic heading.

imputation. A statistical method applied when data values are missing. In the 2005 ICP, PPPs at the level of GDP were imputed for countries that did not participate. When participating countries were not able to provide data for some basic headings, the basic heading PPPs were imputed.

income in kind. Free or subsidized housing, meals, transport allowance, uniforms, and other items of clothing. These items are valued at the cost to the employer of providing them—that is, the cost of production when the items were produced by the employer and the purchaser's price when they were bought by the employer and passed on to the employee.

indirect comparison. A price or volume comparison between two countries made through a third country. For example, for countries A, B, and C the PPP between A and C is obtained by dividing the PPP between A and B by the PPP between C and B: PPP(A/C) = PPP(A/B) ÷ PPP(C/B).

individual consumption expenditure by government. The actual and imputed final consumption expenditure incurred by general government on individual goods and services.

individual consumption expenditure by households. The actual and imputed final consumption expenditure incurred by households on individual goods and services. It also includes expenditure on individual goods and services sold at prices that are not economically significant. By definition, all final consumption expenditures of households are for the benefit of individual households and are individual. Also referred to as the final consumption expenditure of households and household final consumption expenditure.

individual consumption expenditure by NPISH. The actual and imputed final consumption expenditure incurred by nonprofit institutions serving households (NPISH) on individual goods and services. In practice, most final consumption expenditures of NPISH are individual in nature, and so for simplicity's sake all final consumption expenditures of NPISH are treated by convention as individual. Also referred to as the final consumption expenditure of NPISH and social transfers in kind.

input pricing. The approach used to obtain PPPs for nonmarket services. For government, the input price is compensation of employees. The basket of construction components (BOCC) method for estimating construction PPPs is based on prices of all major material and labor inputs for a range of different types of construction projects.

intermediate consumption. The value of the goods and services, other than fixed assets, that are used or consumed as inputs by a process of production.

International Comparison Program (ICP). A research project launched in the 1960s with the ultimate goal of establishing a regular program providing worldwide PPP comparisons of GDP. Comparisons were organized for 1970 (10 countries), 1973 (16), 1975 (34), 1980 (60), 1985 (64), and 1993 (83). The responsibility for these comparisons was shared by the United Nations Statistics Division and the University of Pennsylvania. The World Bank coordinated the 2005 ICP round and continues with the 2011 round.

international dollars. A term used to describe the currency unit based on PPP exchange rates to the U.S. dollar. The purchasing power parities at the global level for each economy are computed at United States = 1.00, making the U.S. dollar the numeraire currency. These PPP conversion factors transform GDP and aggregates in national currency into a common world currency referred to as real expenditures in international dollars.

item. A good or service precisely defined for use in price collection, or a good or service defined by an item specification and included in an item list.

Jevons index. The geometric average of individual product PPPs between two countries that becomes the basic heading PPP. If the matrix is full (no missing prices), the basic heading PPP is transitive.

Jevons-GEKS index. The Jevons index made transitive by the Gini-Éltetö-Köves-Szulc (GEKS) method with less than a full price table. Jevons-GEKS* is the Jevons index made transitive when implied weights are used for representative or important products.

Laspeyres price index. Weighted averages of the elementary basic heading PPPs using the expenditure shares of the base country as the weights.

linking methods. The methods used when PPPs are first computed between countries within the same region and then calibrated to the rest of the world. The linking method provides PPPs between countries in different regions. The Ring and bridge methods were used for the 2005 ICP.

machinery and equipment. The aggregate that includes fabricated metal products, general-purpose machinery, special-purpose machinery, electrical and optical equipment, transport equipment, and other manufactured goods.

max-min ratio test. Method used to identify values that are outliers based on comparing the maximum to the minimum value.

multilateral comparison. A price or volume comparison of more than two countries simultaneously that produces consistent relations among all pairs of countries (i.e., one that satisfies the transitivity requirement). The PPPs between any two countries are influenced by their respective PPPs to all of the other countries.

national coordinating agencies. In most countries or economies, several different agencies provide the national accounts and price data for the ICP. In such cases, one agency is nominated as the national coordinating office, and within that agency a national ICP coordinator is appointed.

nominal expenditures. National GDP values converted to a common currency using exchange rates. These values reflect both volume and price differences between countries.

nonprofit institutions serving households (NPISH). Nonprofit institutions that are not predominantly financed and controlled by government and that provide goods or services to households free or at prices that are not economically significant. Their main resources are voluntary contributions by households.

nonresidential buildings. Buildings other than dwellings, including fixtures, facilities, and equipment that are integral parts of the structures.

numeraire currency. The term used for the currency unit selected to be the common currency in which PPPs and final expenditures on GDP (nominal and volumes) are expressed. The numeraire is usually an actual currency (such as the U.S. dollar), but it can be an artificial currency unit developed for the purposes of PPP comparisons.

other products. The basic heading that includes products of agriculture, forestry, fisheries, and aquaculture, as well as software products.

overall variation coefficient. A measure of dispersion among all the PPP ratios for a basic heading. In measuring dispersion, the coefficient also measures the homogeneity of the price structures of the countries covered by the basic heading and the reliability of the PPPs calculated for the basic heading. The higher the value of the coefficient, the less homogeneous are the price structures and the less reliable are the PPPs.

Paasche-Laspeyres spread (PLS). The ratio of the Paasche price index to the Laspeyres price index.

Paasche price index. Weighted averages of the elementary basic heading PPPs using the expenditure shares of the nonbase country as the weights. It can be viewed as the harmonic average of the individual PPPs using the expenditure shares of the nonbase country as the weights.

poverty line. An income level that is based on the cost of a quantity of food for a minimum diet of the poor that provides adequate nutrition plus an allowance for nonfood spending. Purchasing power parities are used to adjust national poverty lines to the international dollar.

price level index (PLI). The ratio of the basic heading PPP to the exchange rate. It is expressed as an index on a base of 100.

productivity adjustment. An adjustment made to the prices paid by nonmarket producers for labor, capital, and intermediate inputs, so that the prices correspond to a common level of multifactor productivity. In practice, it is an adjustment made to the prices (compensation of government employees) paid by nonmarket producers (government entities) for labor, so that they represent the same level of labor productivity.

product specification. A description or list of characteristics derived from the structured product definitions that can be used to identify a product selected for pricing. It ensures that countries price comparable items. A product specification can be either brand- and model-specific (i.e., a specification in which a particular brand and model or a cluster of comparable brands, and possibly models, is stipulated) or generic (i.e., a specification in which only the relevant price-determining and technical characteristics are given and no brand or cluster of brands is designated).

purchaser's price. Amount paid at market prices by the purchaser, excluding any deductible value added taxes or similar deductible tax, to take delivery of a unit of a good or service at the time and place required by the purchaser. The purchaser's price of a good includes any transport charges paid separately by the purchaser to take delivery at the required time and place.

purchasing power parity (PPP). A price ratio that measures the number of units of country A's currency needed to purchase in country A the same quantity of an individual good or service that can be purchased by one unit of country B's currency in country B. PPPs are currency converters that eliminate the effects of the differences in price levels between countries.

quantity method. A method used to indirectly estimate PPPs for dwellings where there is no rental market. Relative measures of quantities of housing between countries and the relationship of expenditures equal to price times quantities in the national accounts are used to indirectly estimate PPPs.

Quaranta table. A tool that provides measures of price variation for products and countries in order to validate prices within a basic heading.

real final expenditures. National final expenditures on GDP that have been converted to a common currency and valued at a uniform price level with PPPs. Expenditures so converted reflect only volume differences between countries. Also referred to as real values.

reference PPPs. PPPs used for basic headings for which no prices are collected. These PPPs are based on prices collected for other basic headings. Reference PPPs can be categorized as (1) price-based reference PPPs (including specific and neutral), (2) volume-based reference PPPs, and (3) exchange rate reference PPPs.

reference volume method. Method used to estimate PPPs for housing in the Africa and Asia regions. The relative volumes for housing are made equal to the relative volumes of household consumption, excluding housing.

representative product. Product that accounts for a large expenditure share in the basic heading and also reflects the overall price levels of all products in the basic heading.

Ring product. A product in the Ring list, which is a composite of items priced in each region for the 2005 ICP. The Ring countries first priced their regional list and then the Ring list. The Ring prices were used to compute the between-region PPPs used to calibrate within-region PPPs to a global currency.

services. Outputs produced to order that cannot be traded separately from their production. Ownership rights cannot be established over services, and, by the time their production is completed, they must have been provided to the consumers. An exception to this rule is a group of industries generally classified as service industries. Some of outputs of these industries have the characteristics of goods. These industries are concerned with the provision, storage, communication, and dissemination of information, advice, and entertainment in the broadest sense of those terms. The products of these industries, where ownership rights can be established, may be classified as either goods or services, depending on the medium by which these outputs are supplied.

standard error. A statistical measure that shows the inherent variability of prices resulting from different marketing, packaging, and location attributes. Also used to estimate the sampling error, which is the variability resulting when a sample of prices is observed rather than based on a complete census. Errors may be random or systematic. Random errors are generally referred to as standard errors. Systematic errors are called biases.

structured product description (SPD) method. A new method introduced for the 2005 ICP that provides a systematic, consistent way to describe the price-determining characteristics of products. SPDs provide all possible combinations of characteristics such as package type, package size, various qualities, and brands. The specifications of the products actually priced are derived from the SPDs.

supply and use tables. Tables that provide a convenient way of summarizing and presenting a coherent set of economic transactions within a country. A supply table indicates for each product where it comes from (domestically produced or imported); a use table provides information on product use as intermediate or final consumption.

survey framework. A framework that includes the processes used (1) to describe the price-determining characteristics of each product to ensure that like products are priced across countries, (2) to determine the number of products to be priced, and (3) to select the sample of outlets where the prices will be obtained.

System of National Accounts. A coherent, consistent, and integrated set of macroeconomic accounts, balance sheets, and tables based on a set of internationally agreed-on concepts, definitions, classifications, and accounting rules.

taxes on production. Taxes on the goods and services produced as outputs by resident enterprises that become payable as a result of the production of these goods or services (i.e., taxes payable per unit of good or service produced, such as excise duties and nondeductible value added taxes), plus taxes that resident enterprises may pay as a consequence of engaging in production (e.g., payroll taxes and taxes on motor vehicles). The former are called taxes on products, and the latter are called other taxes on production.

Technical Advisory Group (TAG), ICP. The group responsible for providing advice on technical issues related to the International Comparison Program. It resolves conceptual and methodological matters (see annex B of chapter 2 for the membership list for the 2005 ICP round). TAG members, appointed by the Executive Board, are all internationally known experts in the fields of prices or national accounts.

transitivity. The property whereby the direct PPP between any two countries (or regions) yields the same result as an indirect comparison via a third country (or region). It is sometimes referred to as circularity.

transport. An aggregate that includes expenditures on the purchase of vehicles, operation of personal transport equipment, and transport services.

user cost method. A method to estimate the costs that owners of dwellings would have to take into account in fixing a market rent if they decided to rent their dwellings to other people.

valuables. Produced assets that are not used primarily for production or consumption, that are expected to appreciate (or at least not decline in real value), that do not deteriorate over time under normal conditions, and that are acquired and held primarily as stores of values.

value added tax (VAT). A tax on products collected in stages by enterprises. This wide-ranging tax is usually designed to cover most or all goods and services. Producers are obliged to pay to government only the difference between the VAT on their sales and the VAT on their purchases for intermediate consumption or capital formation. The VAT is not usually levied on exports.